THE OFFICIAL PRICE GUIDE TO®
Antique & Modern Firearms

BY
DAVID BYRON

EDITOR
THOMAS E. HUDGEONS III

THIRD EDITION
THE HOUSE OF COLLECTIBLES, INC., ORLANDO, FLORIDA 32809

IMPORTANT NOTICE. All of the information, including valuations, in this book has been compiled from the most reliable sources, and every effort has been made to eliminate errors and questionable data. Nevertheless the possibility of error, in a work of such immense scope, always exists. The publisher will not be held responsible for losses which may occur, in the purchase, sale, or other transaction of items, because of information contained herein. Readers who feel they have discovered errors are invited to WRITE and inform us, so they may be corrected in subsequent editions. Those seeking further information on the topics covered in this book, each of which, because of the nature of the publication, must be treated briefly, are advised to use the specialized House of Collectibles OFFICIAL GUIDES.

© MCMLXXXIII The House of Collectibles, Inc.

All rights reserved. No part of this book may be reproduced or utilized in any form or by any means, electronic or mechanical, including photocopying, recording, or by any information storage and retrieval system, without permission in writing from the publisher.

Published by: The House of Collectibles, Inc.
              Orlando Central Park
              1900 Premier Row
              Orlando, FL 32809
              Phone: (305) 857-9095

Printed in the United States of America

Library of Congress Catalog Card Number: 81-81803

ISBN: 0-87637-363-5 / Paperback

TABLE OF CONTENTS

Introduction	1
Factors That Determine Value	1
Historic Relics	4
Trends	4
Legal Classification of Firearms	5
How to Buy and Sell Firearms	6
The National Rifle Association of America	9
Glossary	14
Shotgun Gauges	22
Ammunition Interchangeability	23
How to Use This Guide	24
Alphabetical Listing of Manufacturers, Importers and Brand Names	25
A & R Sales — Azul	25
Babcock — Bustindiu, Juan Esteban	50
C.A.C. — Czechoslavakian Military	90
Daisy — DWM	138
E.A. — Express	151
Fabrique D'Armes De Guerre — FTL	161
Galand, Charles Francois — Gyrojet	181
Hackett, Edwin and George — Hy Score Arms	194
IAB — Izarra	229
J & R — Jupiter	243
Kaba Spezial — Kynoch Gun Factory	247
Lahti — Lyman Gun Sight Corp	256
Maadi — Mutti, Giesu	273
Napoleon — Nunnemacher, Abraham	312
Oak Leaf — Oxford Arms Co.	323
P.A.F. — Purdey, Jas & Sons	325
Qual — Queen City	342
Radium — Ryan, Thomas	343
Sable — Swiss Military	380
T.A.C. — Tyrol	437
Uhlinger, W.L. & Co. — U.S. Revolver Co.	449
Valiant — Vulcan Arms Co.	464
Waffenfabrik Bern-Wuethrich	469
Yato — Young, John	504
Z — Zulaica	505
Collector Cartridges	508
Index	521

ACKNOWLEDGMENTS

The prices listed in this guide were gathered from dealers, collectors, auctions, and ads in collectors' publications. They were then computer sorted and double-checked to ensure maximum reliability.

I wish to extend to the following people, companies, organizations, and especially the many unnamed people who helped, my sincere gratitude for the assistance they freely gave.

Sherry Rich of Browning
Bill Mrock of the B.A.T.F.
Tim Pancurak of Thompson-Center
Nadine Ljutic of Ljutic Industries
Jim Casillo and Fred Paddock of Navy Arms
Vicky Barton of Universal
Fred Karp of Sears, Roebuck & Co.
Brian Herrick of Hi Standard
Charley Gara of Charter Arms
Nolen Jackson of Wichita Engineering & Supply
Sharon Cunningham of Dixie Gun Works
Sandy Reardon of Colt
Chris Graziano of Ruger
Judy Schroepfer of Kreighoff
Jinny Sundius of Marlin
Earl Harrington of Savage
Fred Hill of Dan Wesson
Bob Magee of Interarms
Ron Vogel of F.I.E.
Roger Simonet of W. Glaser Waffen
Dick Williams

Charles Meyers, Florida Regional Crime Lab
Linda Lassotta of Heckler & Koch
Dot Ferreira of Remington
James R. Steffey of Detonics
Tol Cherry
Nancy Damone of Mossberg
Deanna McDermott of U.S. Repeating Arms
Bruce Hacker of Ventura Imports
Debbie Dean of Weatherby's
I.W. Walentiny of Tradewinds
Marian Partridge of Ithaca
Syd Rachwal
Robert Simpson
Sam Constanzo
Don Valenti
David Rachwal
Peter Potter
Alvin Snaper
Col. Mel Pfankuche
Bill Drollinger
Dick Sherk
O.L. Sonny Peacock

FACTORS THAT DETERMINE VALUE / 1

INTRODUCTION

For years, first as a retail gun dealer and gunsmith and later as an exporter and dealer of collector guns, I used to bemoan the fact that there was no easy to use reference to help identify and price both the common and, more importantly, the uncommon guns. Another problem that I encountered as a dealer was determining the legal classification of a particular firearm and again there was no handy reference to rely on. And so, almost as a matter of business survival, I began recording prices and classifications for my own use. This process, developing over the years from a large card file to a computer data base, has led to the compiling of this book. This book should be considered a working tool for dealers and collectors. It delivers the hard facts that dealers and collectors have asked for in a easy to use format. This edition contains over 20,000 prices, with the legal (B.A.T.F.) classification and description of every gun listed.

The prices for this edition have been gathered from auction results, advertisements in collectors' periodicals, dealer newsletters and collectors. The prices are then computer sorted and averaged. Research is done continuously, constantly updating both prices and company information, providing the reader with the most current and accurate information available.

FACTORS THAT DETERMINE VALUE

CONDITION
With the passage of time everything deteriorates and guns are no exception. Use, abuse, wear and aging all adversely affect the price of guns to a varying degree, and in the case of collectable guns the difference in price can be very significant. Because of the importance of describing the condition of a gun the N.R.A. devised a set of guidelines to standardize firearms grading. The prices listed in this guide are for guns in N.R.A. Very Good and N.R.A. Excellent condition (*Antiques are N.R.A. Antique Very Good to Antique Fine*), and you can easily adjust those prices to determine the value of your gun if it does not fall into either of those categories. But strict grading of condition following N.R.A. guidelines is essential.

There are two sets of standards, one for modern guns and one for antique guns. The price adjustments for each are different.

Antique firearms in excellent to new condition add 25% to 100% to the "excellent" price depending on scarcity and demand. For antiques in good condition, deduct 30% to 35% from "very good."

Modern firearms in good condition deduct 20% to 25% from "very good"; fair condition, deduct 45% to 55%. Arms in "perfect" to "new" add 30% to 75% depending on collectability.

Any collectable firearm, no matter how poor the condition (so long as it hasn't been crushed or melted), should fetch 20% to 30% of the "very good" price. As the saying goes, "Old guns never die, they just get reblued."

N.R.A. CONDITION GUIDELINES
NEW: Not previously sold at retail, in same condition as current factory production.
NEW-DISCONTINUED: Same as New, but discontinued model.

2 / FACTORS THAT DETERMINE VALUE

The following definitions will apply to all secondhand articles:
PERFECT: In new condition in every respect.
EXCELLENT: New condition, used but little, no noticeable marring of wood or metal, bluing perfect (except at muzzle or sharp edges).
VERY GOOD: In perfect working condition, no appreciable wear on working surfaces, no corrosion or pitting, only minor surface dents or scratches.
GOOD: In safe working condition, minor wear on working surfaces, no broken parts, no corrosion or pitting that will interfere with proper functioning.
FAIR: In safe working condition, but well worn, perhaps requiring replacement of minor parts or adjustments, which should be indicated in advertisement, no rust, but may have corrosion pits which do not render article unsafe or inoperable.

Another set of standards applies to "antique" arms as follows:
FACTORY NEW: 100% original finish and parts, everything perfect.
EXCELLENT: All parts and 80%-100% finish original; all letters, numerals, designs sharp; unmarred wood, fine bore.
FINE: All parts and over 30% finish original; all letters, numerals, designs sharp; only minor wood marks, good bore.
VERY GOOD: Up to 30% original finish, all original parts; metal surfaces smooth, with all edges sharp; clear letters, numerals, designs, wood slightly scratched or bruised; bore on collector items disregarded.
GOOD: Only minor replacement parts; metal smoothly rusted or lightly pitted in places; cleaned or reblued; principal letters, numerals, designs legible; wood refinished, scratched, bruised, or with minor cracks repaired; mechanism in good working order.
FAIR: Some major parts replaced; minor replacements; metal may be lightly pitted all over, vigorously cleaned or reblued, edges partly rounded; wood scratched, bruised, cracked or repaired; mechanism in working order. ‡

ORNAMENTATION
Engraving
It's hard to generalize about art, and that is what engraving is. You must examine a number of examples to learn to judge the quality of the work.

Crude engraving: sparse, add about 25%; medium coverage, add 50% to 75%; full coverage add 100% to 125%.

High quality engraving: sparse, add 50% to 100%; medium coverage, add 150% to 200%; full coverage, add 300% up.

Ornate, high quality work with gold inlays, etc., add 400% up.

Wood carving and marquetry (stock inlays)
This is also in the realm of art, and you should try to look at as many specimens as possible to compare craftsmanship.

Carvings: simple, add $10 to $40 each depending on the quality of execution; complex, add $60 to $150. Full coverage, good quality, add $125 up. Remember that a poor carving (such as crude initials) will detract from the value.

Inlays: simple, add $10 to $25 each; ornate, add $50 up. Exotic materials, such as ivory or mother-of-pearl, can double the value of the inlay. The value of wire inlays depends as much on the coverage as the execution.

Note: N.R.A. Grading Standards reprinted with the permission of the N.R.A.

FACTORS THAT DETERMINE VALUE / 3

Simple wire inlays using brass or German silver should start at $35 each, tripling if silver is used, and multiplying by 10 if gold is used. Initial shields that are unmarked and not standard equipment on the gun add $10; $20 for sterling silver; $75 for 14k gold.

Heat carving, stampings, and woodburnings are becoming increasingly common and should not be confused with real carving. These should add about $20 if done well.

Custom checkering
As with carving, craftsmanship is paramount. A poorly done checkering job will lower the value of a gun. Nicely executed patterns on a long gun, add $25 to $40. Fine, complex patterns with wide coverage, add $50 up.

Gold damascening:
The is the art of applying gold leaf or gold plate in a fancy pattern, usually in conjunction with engraving, and should not be confused with gold inlay. Simple patterns, add $50 to $75; fancy patterns, add $250 to $375.

LOCATION OF SALE
As this guide lists average national prices, several regional factors must be considered.

Antiques: If a particular arm was made in your area, or saw wide service there, there should be more interest in it. This increased market demand will run prices 10% to 15% higher than listed. The converse is also true.

Modern: Much depends on the type of area you live in. In wide-open places where long-range shooting is possible, high-powered rifles may bring 10% over value listed, whereas shotguns will be 15% less. In wooded areas the reverse will occur. In high crime areas, handguns for home protection will bring premiums. Trap and skeet generally stay constant. Wherever you are, judge the type of hobby shooting most prevalent, and the types of guns used for it will follow the above pattern.

SPECIAL MARKINGS AND COMMEMORATIVES
Standard firearms of most all companies have at some time been ordered or issued with special markings, special features, or as commemoratives. The important consideration in this section is that all deviations from the norm be factory original.

Special markings
Governments, law enforcement agencies, and stores have ordered the factory to put special marks on guns, and the main requirement in adding value to a gun with these marks is that the gun itself be collectable. The percentage additions shown reflect "common" variations. Rare marks on already very scarce guns may run five to ten times that percentage; however, caution is advisable since this particular market is limited and highly specialized, and as always with rare items, when you get out of your field it's best to consult an expert.

Police or agency markings in lieu of regular marks (not overstamps or extra stamps), add 25% to 50%; trade marks of stores in exotic locales (Rhodesia, etc.), add 50% to 75%; foreign military marks, add 50% to 75%.

Mismarked guns: No stamps, upside-down stamps, wrong markings, etc., add 100% up depending on the collectability of the gun itself.

Special features: This section applies to custom modifications done by the factory and not listed under a particular manufacturer elsewhere in this guide.

Special sights, add 10% to 15%; special metal finish (nickel, etc.), add 10% to 15%; extra-fancy wood on long guns, add 15% to 25%; special barrel lengths, add 20% to 30%.

Commemoratives

One very important question to ask yourself: Is this gun a standard mass-produced item with just an extra stamp or applied token, or is it actually from a limited production and different from standard in style and embellishment? If your gun falls into the first category, appreciation will be quite slow; if the latter, than the value will rise sharply for the first two or three years, thereafter leveling off to a little better than the inflation rate. For the value to be maintained, commemoratives should be kept in new condition in original packaging with all papers and accessories. Shooting, and subsequent wear, drastically affect the price. Current values are listed under the manufacturer of the individual item.

HISTORIC RELICS

Documentation is the key word in connecting an old gun with a historic event or famous person. Saying "it used to belong to grandpa and he was so and so" just isn't enough. To be absolutely certain of a weapon's ownership or use, records contemporary with its use must be available. They can be factory records showing the gun's disposition, wills, diaries, etc. Lacking that, if there is strong evidence of ownership such as a name engraved and some documentation showing that the person could have owned it, then it should be labeled "probably." "Grandpa" testimony without supporting evidence can be labeled "possibly." The value of a historic relic transcends the worth of the gun, and depends on the fame (or infamy) of the owner, the artistic value, the location of the sale, and the intangible "mood" of the public as to what period of history is "in."

A plain Colt Single Action Army revolver belonging to Bat Masterson brought $36,000 at auction. A very ornate flintlock fowler made for Louis XIII fetched $300,000 as a work of art several years ago. Although these prices are the exception rather than the rule, if you have an authentic relic it would be worth your while to contact an expert for an appraisal.

An arm with the label "probably" would bring anywhere between 25% and 75% of the "definite's" price depending on buyer belief in its authenticity. "Possibly" may bring only double the value of the gun alone.

TRENDS

Prices for obsolete military arms are still rising steadily, with the obscure variations being extremely volatile. Adding fuel to this upward pressure is a recent ruling from the B.A.T.F. reclassifying military arms used in World War II and before as curios. Excellent buys are still available on common variations of bolt action rifles used by the major powers, and occasionally importers find a cache of antique arms or former police issue weapons. These usually hit the market at a good price for investors. The best bets will be high quality European police handguns.

Guns with Damascus steel barrels are starting to catch on, but they can still be had at reasonable prices. Look for high quality unusual twist designs to rise the fastest.

Continental European weapons made prior to World War II have been leap-frogging in price due to a very heavy buying pressure from Europe, but the market is not neccessarily firm and there have been wide price swings. This is the area for the speculator, with the best bets being pre-1898 military revolvers, and high quality, low production, pistols. As the availability of guns diminishes, also look for the myriad Spanish pocket pistols of the World War I era to climb, as well as high-grade American shotguns from the lesser known makers, and obsolete .22 rifles.

Prices for para-military arms should continue to be firm, though not rising as quickly as the general run of collectables. The exception will be machine guns and silenced arms, a new and growing field of interest for most collectors. Items that will not hold their price will be some of the newer machine guns of low quality that are now appearing.

The market has been virtually flooded with commemorative arms of every description, and many collectors have paused to catch their breaths. The prices of the "standard" commemoratives have stabilized, while the very limited high grade guns have enjoyed a reasonable increase.

Prices of collectable guns, in general, should rise 15% to 25% per year. As always, seasonal adjustments should be made on the common guns, checking the type of sport shooting in your area and deducting 10% to 15% for arms "out of season."

LEGAL CLASSIFICATIONS OF FIREARMS

There are four classifications of firearms used by the Bureau of Alcohol, Tobacco, and Firearms of the Treasury Department.

Antique: Any firearm manufactured in or before 1898, and replicas that do not fire rim-fire or center-fire cartridges readily available in commercial trade. Antiques are exempt from federal regulation.

Modern: Firearms manufactured after 1898, excluding Replica Antiques, and with special regulations for Class III arms.

Curios and Relics: Certain modern firearms that can be sent interstate to licensed collectors.

Class III Arms: This includes machine guns, silencers, short (under 18") shotguns, short (under 16") rifles, modern smoothbore handguns, and modern arms with a rifled bore diameter greater than .50".

All of the above may be legally owned, notwithstanding federal regulations and local restrictions in a few areas. For further information, contact your local office of the Bureau of Alcohol, Tobacco, and Firearms.

A SPECIAL NOTE ABOUT LEGAL CLASSIFICATIONS

Curios: This is a subdivision of "modern" and pertains to arms that may be sent interstate to licensed collectors. However, there is a great deal of confusion as to what constitutes a "curio". The B.A.T.F. issues a yearly list of arms so classified, which is constantly changing and, by virtue of time and space limitations, is incomplete.

Since this guide followed the curio list in force at the time of writing, far more arms are "curios" than are described as such.

The following is the federal guideline to use to determine if a specific firearm or cartridge is a "curio". It must:

1. have been manufactured at least 50 years prior to the current date, but not including replicas therof; or

2. be certified by the curator of a municipal, state, or federal museum that exhibits firearms to be curios or relics of museum interest; or

3. derive a substantial part of its monetary value from the fact that it is novel, rare, or bizarre, or from the fact of its association with some historical figure, period, or event.

Collectors wishing to obtain a curio or relic determination from ATF on a specific firearm or round of ammunition should submit a letter to the Chief of the Firearms Technology Branch, Bureau of Alcohol, Tobacco, and Firearms, Washington, D.C. 20226. The letter should include a complete physical description of the firearm or ammunition, stating the reasons that the collector believes that the firearm or ammunition in question merits such classification, and supporting data concerning the history of the firearm or ammunition, including production figures, if available, and market value.

Antiques: Many arms listed in this guide were produced between dates overlapping the "antique" determination date. In cases where experts have given a recognized serial number cutoff for "antiques" I have tried to include it. In other instances where arms have no numbers, or where no number is generally recognized as the magic one, I have classified them as modern and leave it to a specialist to make an individual determination.

HOW TO BUY AND SELL FIREARMS

BUYING COLLECTORS GUNS
Where to buy

Reliable estimates place the number of guns in private hands in the U.S. at over 100 million! Quite a lot, but if you've picked out the special items you wish to collect and started looking you've probably noticed that you can generally find everything but what you need. So where do you go to find them? There are several sources.

Mail Order. Even though the Gun Control Act of 1968 prohibited the mailing of firearms to individuals, the mail order gun business is alive and well. However, the method is a little different because of the laws and the nature of the business. According to U.S. law only federally licensed gun dealers may ship and receive modern firearms, but many dealers for a small fee will be happy to receive the gun you've ordered and transfer it to you. Another alternative for the collector is to apply for a collector's license from the Bureau of Alcohol, Tobacco and Firearms. This license allows the collector to receive and send interstate shipments of modern firearms that are classified as classified as curios to another licensee. For more information about licenses contact your local office of the B.A.T.F.

Mail order done properly is legal and fairly simple and, most importantly, an excellent way to build your collection and to take advantage of prices that may be more competitive than in your local area. Most specialist mail order dealers are very reputable, and many offer an inspection period so that you may return the gun in the same condition as it arrived if you're not satisfied. Almost all of the dealers of collectable guns advertise, and many have regular lists of guns offered for sale that you can subscribe to for a nominal rate. Many gun magazines and collector newsletters have classified sections that provide good leads, but an excellent starting point would be Shotgun News (P.O. Box 669, Hastings, Nebr. 68901).

Gun Shows. There are a great many gun shows held in all parts of the U.S. with good frequency. They provide an opportunity to examine a large number of collectable guns at one place, and a chance to bargain with the owners for a better price. Gun show listings can be found in magazines such as Gun Report (P.O. Box 111, Aledo, Ill. 61231)

Gun Shops. Gun stores and pawn shops offer an exciting chance to find a collector's item at a good price because they may not have a market to sell some of the more interesting items. As a result they sometimes buy low and sell low in order to turn their inventory.

Private Individuals. This category includes non-gun shops as well as individuals, and this is the area where real caution must be exercised. Although bargains may be found, many times people have an inflated idea of the value of their gun, and very often the article for sale is misidentified. Remember, knowledge is power!

Pitfalls

Refinished Guns. A refinished gun can be beautiful. Unfortunately it also drastically reduces the value of a collector's item, so it's valuable to know how to spot refinishing. Most of the time when a gun is reblued or replated it must be heavily polished to remove small pits. A good craftsman will keep all of the edges sharp, will preserve the lettering, and will avoid "ripple" (waves polished into the gun in places where the metal should be flat). Poor craftsmen will remove lettering, round edges, and in general remove too much metal. The finish on a good job will be even and bright, on a poor job it will look splotchy and uneven. If you suspect that a gun has been refinished look for these signs: the lettering will have "drag-out marks" (one edge of the letter will be furrowed from polishing); the quality of finish doesn't match the original factory job; parts have been finished to a different color than original. Remember, most factories did an excellent job of finishing.

Upgrades. Upgrading is taking a normal gun that is in decent condition and engraving or otherwise embellishing it so that it is more valuable. In many cases a good upgrade comes within 60% to 70% of the value of the factory original if the job is well done. But beware of guns that people try to pass off as original. The best defense is education. If you're interested in high grade guns try to examine as many known originals as you can to get a feel for that factory's style and quality, or enlist the aid of an expert to help you.

Fakes. Counterfeits, it seems, have always been with us, and as with any item of value, low cost reproductions have been made and passed along as the real thing. Thjere are all kinds of reproductions, from the crude kitchen table conversion with the uneven lettering stamps to the ultra-sophisticated copy made with some original parts. Fakes include complete reproductions of antique guns to ⅛" police stamps on World War II German pistols. Once again knowledge is everything. Learn all you can before buying, and on valuable items buy from someone you can trust. Most dealers of collectable guns are extremely honest, and it's very rare to hear of a dealer intentionally trying to sell a fake.

Condition Descriptions. The N.R.A. guidelines are not always used by dealers and collectors when describing their guns. Many times there will be descriptions such as "95% blue" or "near mint," which while they sound good sometimes mask a multitude of sins. Just because someone uses either vague descriptions or their own grading does not necessarily mean that they're trying to hide something. Sometimes people get entrenched in their ways and you have to learn their system. But it does pay to ask a few questions to make sure that everything is functioning as it should be, and that all of the parts are there. Accurate percentage descriptions are an acquired skill and when used in conjuction with a good description can give an accurate picture, but be sure that you have complete information.

SELLING COLLECTOR GUNS

As important as buying is the ability to sell what you have, and there are many ways to do this. The major things to consider when you sell is how fast do you want to sell your guns and how much do you want for them. The two are not necessarily mutually exclusive, but usually if you want top price you have to compete with the dealer and it takes time. Always remember that guns are cashable items and the choice of what you are willing to take for them is yours and will be based on your salesmanship.

Where to sell
Gun Stores. The local gun dealer generally cannot pay you a top price on a collectable gun unless he has a good market for it. Even then he must make a profit. But this is a good source to sell your guns quickly.
Specialist and Mail Order Dealers. Many times these dealers will pay somewhat higher prices and work on a slimmer margin because they have built up customer lists over the years and may have a guaranteed resale of your gun.
Your Own Ad. This may be the way to get the most for your guns, but it also takes the longest and requires the cooperation of a gun licensee for shipping. There is usually a four to eight week time lag between the time you place an ad and the time it is in print and the publication distributed. Additionally, you also have the cost of the ad to consider as well as the cost of packaging and shipping.
Gun Shows. This can provide not only a place to sell your guns but a great meeting ground for fellow collectors. Of course your salesmanship is of prime importance to get your best price, but you will meet people with similar interests who may be very interested in buying what you have.
Auctions. This can sometimes be a risky venture. In an unreserved auction the highest bid wins, and if there is a bad crowd your guns could go for very little, and to add insult to injury you will have to pay a commission. In a reserved auction you are allowed to set a reasonable bottom figure, and if the gun does not reach that amount you get it back. However, you will generally have to pay a small commission to have it returned on reserve. But the other side of the coin is that people sometimes get carried away at an auction, and many times guns fetch a much higher price than what is expected. With auctions you have to be lucky.

Recordkeeping
U.S. law is very specific about a firearms licensee's recordkeeping responsibilities, but although the private individual is not required to, he should also keep records. Suggested information to keep for your own use would include the name and address of the person you acquired the gun from and the date, the make, model, caliber, type, and serial number of your gun, and when you sell it the name and address of the buyer and the date you sold it. It would also be handy to keep a record of the price you paid.

THE NATIONAL RIFLE ASSOCIATION OF AMERICA

The right to private ownership of firearms, a right so obviously vital to gun collectors as well as sportsmen, has been one of the causes championed by the National Rifle Association of Washington, D.C. This historic organization, now more than a century old and numbering well over 2 million members, has also made vast contributions toward the study, technology, history, and safe use of firearms. Nearly all U.S. gun dealers, and a large proportion of collectors, are members of the NRA, and have derived numerous benefits from membership.

Most readers of this book are, undoubtedly, already familiar with the NRA. But a work on firearms collecting could hardly be complete without a few words on the organization, and (at the end of this brief article) information on becoming a member.

While the firearms hobbyist has his choice of many organizations to join, membership in the nationwide NRA seems almost basic for anyone interested in gun collecting. The NRA's strength, supplied by its ever-increasing roster of members, insures a strong voice for the hobby. Whether the collector cares to realize it or not, there are individuals — including some in government — who would strangle the hobby by outlawing the possession, sale, or trade of ALL firearms ... or who would support such stringent restrictions on firearms ownership that gun collection would, for all practical purposes, come to an end. This is a battle that is never officially over. The tide can be kept in the collector's favor ONLY by interested parties making themselves known and counted. And the fact that NRA membership has increased more dramatically, in recent years, than ever in the past is solid evidence that the future will be bright for gun enthusiasts.

The National Rifle Association has many goals and serves multitudes of purposes. The public hears, occasionally, of its activities in lobbying against gun control legislation. Seldom does the news media report the numerous other NRA functions. Among these is its continuing efforts to promote better understanding of the safe use and care of all types of firearms. In conjunction with this goal the NRA holds many seminars on gun-use instruction, as well as field meets and other training activity for firearms owners. It believes — and the belief is an historic one, a long tradition of the organization — that citizens well-trained in the use of firearms will be better citizens, and will be more capable of contributing to the defense of themselves, their community, and the nation. The NRA is also very active in conservation programs, to preserve endangered species and to encourage hunting only when and where the hunter presents no danger to the ecology.

THE HISTORY

The NRA is now more than 110 years old, having been chartered (originally by the State of New York) in 1871. It was born as an almost direct outgrowth of the Civil War. Of the many lessons that came from the war's battlefields, one was imprinted indelibly on the minds of officers: the majority of infantry soldiers were simply unskilled in the use of firearms. Even the most rudimentary rules of gun use were foreign to them. In part the military was to blame. It devoted more attention to parade marching

KEITH M. GAFFANEY
NRA President

HARLON B. CARTER
Executive Vice President

and drills than to firearms instruction. If Uncle Sam could not be counted on to do the job, it was then the responsibility of concerned citizens to promote firearms training. In 1871 the New York National Guard comprised a number of such concerned citizens. They were all ex-Union veterans and had seen, at first hand, the severity of the problem in combat. So in September of that year an ambitious group of 15 of them collected to establish an organization — the first of its kind in the country. It would strive to instill pride in proper gun handling and marksmanship, to increase the level of firearms knowledge among U.S. citizens, and, in this way, better prepare Americans for military service in the event of war. It was a lofty ideal, but history showed it was achievable. A hundred years earlier, the American colonists were highly skilled in firearms use, because the necessity to hunt and protect one's property left little choice in the matter. There was no doubt that proper education could once again hone the shooting skills of the average citizen.

It was decided to model the organization after Britain's National Rifle Association, so the name National Rifle Association of America was chosen. A leader with military background and national recognition was a necessity; one was found in the person of General Ambrose Burnside, who had served in the Civil War. On November 17, 1871, the charter was formally granted. But the new organization faced stiff challenges. The "media" of that time consisted almost wholly of newspapers, and newspaper accounts of the young NRA brought no groundswell of membership. There were the inevitable difficulties with funding, which limited the number of tournaments and other activities; and the hazards faced by changes in the government's administration, since some Presidents were more supportive of the NRA than others.

Though times occasionally looked bleak, the organization pushed forward, spread its message, and succeeded in surviving. Finally the country was awakened to the truth of the NRA's warnings about ill-prepared soldiers, when the Spanish-American War broke out in the late 1890's This conflict brought immediate attention to the NRA, and when the war ended things began changing. In 1903 the government established its National Board for the Promotion of Rifle Practice, and NRA training activities were greatly increased. Thanks to the NRA, which grew impressively in the years from 1903 to 1916, the country was far better prepared for entry into World War I than it could otherwise have been. Many of the enlisted men had received NRA training. This was doubly so, 25 years later, when America went into World War II. In the meantime, the NRA was also at work with law enforcement agencies, on federal and local levels, to promote more effective firearms use by police officers. The firearms collector, if he takes interest in memorabilia, has certainly seen and perhaps owned some of the NRA award medals. These handsome medals took the place of large-size trophies of earlier years, and were eagerly competed for in NRA-sanctioned events. A number of types exist, for competition among civilians and law enforcement agents.

After World War II, the NRA inaugurated the first hunter safety program, designed to eliminate hunting accidents arising from ignorance of firearms use and/or poor marksmanship. Then in 1975 came the epochal establishment of the NRA Institute for Legislative Action, to protect the right of law-abiding citizens to own firearms.

The two millionth member was added to the NRA membership rolls in 1981 — a striking record of growth for an organization that began with little more than guts, hope and 15 far-sighted members 110 years earlier.

THE NRA INSTITUTE FOR LEGISLATIVE ACTION

The NRA's Institute for Legislative Action performs many functions. It monitors all gun-related bills put before Congress, to study their fairness and seek change when necessary. It likewise keeps careful watch on court rulings in all parts of the country, in cases involving the right to own and bear arms or similar questions. When rulings are made contrary to the NRA's positions, it often assigns attorneys and allocates funds for the preparation of appeals, and to date has been very successful in this phase of its operations. Also, the NRA's Institute for Legislative Action publishes a number of informative booklets, which are distributed free of charge to law-makers, schools, and libraries. Information and literature is also distributed at gun shows, state fairs and other public gatherings. The Institute maintains a Speakers' Bureau, which lectures at schools and social organizations. Through tireless effort, and in numerous different ways, the Institute circulates the NRA's message on citizens' constitutional right to own firearms.

NRA FIELD SERVICES

The NRA Field Services are designed primarily for furthering the goals of the organization's founders: promoting a better understanding of firearms use among private citizens. Officers of the Field Services work closely with those of the Institute for Legislative Action in a number of interrelated areas. One of the primary arms of the NRA Field Services is its Volunteer Resources Department, which recruits and trains volunteer members. The Range Development Department, also a branch of Field Services, is active in inspecting target-shooting ranges at various firearms clubs. One of the goals of the NRA, through its Field Services, is to arrive at a level of standardization in rifle and pistol tournaments so that each tournament is held under similar conditions and with corresponding rules and regulations. This, of course, is an aid to the shooter and a springboard to developing increased skill, rather than having to adapt to different rules and conditions at each tournament. Shooting tournaments are growing at such a rapid rate that the NRA has had to greatly expand its staff to keep pace with the demand for skilled range and tournament supervision. The Field Services are also involved with selection of suitable sites for tournament and practice ranges; design of ranges for maximum efficiency and safety; and legal assistance on all aspects of range establishment and operation. This is vital because the laws of individual states sometimes differ and a range operator must be fully informed of the local applicable laws.

In 1981, the NRA reached an all-time high in the number of its affiliated range clubs, with 12,560. Also, in 1981, the Field Services appointed separate State Association Coordinators for the range clubs in each State, thereby providing an individual with local knowledge to work directly with the clubs in his state and act as a kind of liason between them and the NRA.

One of the chief aspects of Field Services is the NRA Range Loan Program, which has so far supplied more than $400,000 to local clubs for the establishment or renovation of their range shooting facilities.

NRA PUBLIC AFFAIRS

The NRA Public Affairs department is the link between the NRA and the general public — "general public" meaning persons who are not members of the NRA nor who are even gun owners or hunting enthusiasts. Its purpose is to explain the position of NRA members and sportsmen in general, on various affairs, to the public. This is of course of great significance because the general public elects the country's legislators and, in a roundabout way, makes its laws. Whenever an issue arises, involving the ownership of firearms or anything to concern hunters and gun hobbyists, the Public Affairs branch of the NRA prepares its view and disseminates it to the news media. Usually, the matters involved in legal questions or other complex subjects need to be put into plain language for the public to better understand. This is seldom done by the news media itself, which contains many elements opposed to the principles of the NRA. Unfortunately some segments of the public have formed very false conclusions about gun owners and hunters, and about the motives of the NRA. They assume that hunters are automatically bad for the ecology and that firearms ownership among private citizens breeds criminal activity. One project of the NRA Public Affairs department has been an advertising campaign in various national magazines, picturing the hunter and gun hobbyist as he really is: just an average citizen like the "general public" and not someone to be feared or shunned.

But the Public Affairs activities go deeper than this. They involve the development of such tools as the Library Starter Kit, designed to be placed into public and school libraries and containing various publications on the positive aspects of hunting, shooting, and gun ownership. The NRA strongly believes that gun education, like other forms of education, is most effective when begun early, and that the rudiments of gun knowledge should be taught to even very young children.

NRA GENERAL OPERATIONS

General Operations of the National Rifle Association comprise: Membership Services; Competitions; Hunter Services; Junior Programs; Education and Training; Police Activities. All of these interrelated activities bring the NRA's activities and purposes close to the public. Among the Membership Services is of course the well-known *American Rifleman* magazine, which is sent automatically to NRA members. The most widely read and authoritative publication of its kind, it carries articles on all aspects of hunting, shooting, gun care, and related topics, authored by experts in their fields; and also the latest reports on news of interest to hunters and gun hobbyists, in the way of pending legislation, improvements in gun design, inauguration of new clubs and so on.

One of the highlights of the NRA General Operations is its sponsorship of shooting tournaments, which has been a vital function of the organization since its earliest pioneer days. The number of events and the total of competitors has constantly increased over the years, reaching unprecedented heights in 1981 (the most recent year for which statistics are available). In 1981 the NRA's famous National Matches were participated in by 3,054 contestants, and attended by a total of 5,880 spectators. They were held at Camp Perry, Ohio. The NRA is likewise active in sponsoring collegiate shooting competitions, and in 1981 organized the first National Collegiate Pistol Championships at Massachusetts Institute of Technology.

The NRA's Youth Programs include National Junior Olympic Shooting Camps, State Junior Olympic Shooting Camps, National Junior Smallbore Camp, Junior Rifle and Pistol Clubs, Junior Gun Collecting Activities, 4-H State Shooting Sports Programs, and a variety of programs in partnership with the Boy Scouts of America. In addition to rifle and pistol shooting for youth, the NRA also sponsors air-gun shooting matches.

MEMBERSHIP

Membership in the NRA is both inexpensive and rewarding, for anyone interested in firearms. Membership places one in league with all the leading sportsmen and gun hobbyists of the country, and adds further weight to the NRA's ability to carry out its programs and objectives.

NRA
- ☐ 1 Year .... $ 15
- ☐ 3 Years ... $ 40
- ☐ 5 Years ... $ 60
- ☐ Life $300

NRA SENIOR
(65 and over)
- ☐ 1 Year .... $ 10
- ☐ Life $150

NRA ASSOCIATE
(spouse)
(without magazine)
- ☐ 1 Year .... $ 10
- ☐ Life $100

NRA JUNIOR
(under 20)
- ☐ 1 Year .... $ 12
- ☐ 1 Year .... $ 5
(without magazine)
- ☐ Life $150

Foreign: Canada add $2.00; other countries add $3.00 postage per year.

GLOSSARY

ACP. Abbreviation for Automatic Colt Pistol, applied to ammunition designed originally or adopted by Colt.

ACTION. That part of a firearm made up of the breech and the parts designed to fire and cycle cartridges.

ADJUSTABLE CHOKE. Device attached to the muzzle of a shotgun enabling a change of choke by a rotational adjustment or by changing tubes.

ANTIQUE. A legal classification that in the U.S. is applied to weapons manufactured in or before 1898, and replicas that don't fire fixed ammunition.

ARSENAL. Military installation that stores and usually upgrades and modifies military weapons, and sometimes also applies to governmental weapon manufacturing facilities.

AUTOMATIC. Action type that ejects a spent cartridge and brings a fresh cartridge into firing position without manual intervention and has the capability of firing more than one shot with each pull of the trigger.

AUTOMATIC EJECTOR. Cases are ejected from the firearm when the action is opened without any manual intervention.

AUTOMATIC REVOLVER. Firearm action which resembles a conventional revolver except that on firing the cylinder is rotated and the hammer recocked by the recoil energy of the firing cartridge.

AUTOMATIC SAFETY. A block that prevents firing which is applied by the gun every time the action is cycled.

AYDT ACTION. A singleshot action utilizing a curved breechblock and a hinged section below the forward part of the chamber. The breechblock moves downward in an arc when pressure is applied to the finger lever.

BACKSTRAP. Rearmost part of the grip portion of a handgun frame.

BACK LOCK. Self-contained hammer, sear, and spring mounted on a single plate with the exposed hammer on the forward part of the plate, set into the side of a gun.

BARREL. Tube through which the bullet or shot passes on firing.

BARREL BAND. Metal band that secures the barrel to the forend.

BARRELED ACTION. The assembled barrel and complete action.

BARREL LINER. Thin steel tube usually permanently inserted into the barrel to either change the caliber, restore the gun, or to make the gun more functional when the barrel is formed from softer material.

BAYONET LUG. Metal projection at the end of the barrel for attaching a bayonet.

BAYONET. A knife or spike designed to be attached to a firearm.

BEAD SIGHT. Usually a round bead on the forward top of the barrel to aid in aiming (pointing) without the aid of a rear sight.

BEAVERTAIL FOREND. A wide, hand-filling forestock on long guns.

BENCHREST RIFLE. A heavy rifle designed for accurate shooting supported on a bench.

BIPOD. A two legged support attached to the forend of a rifle.

GLOSSARY / 15

BLOWBACK ACTION. Automatic and semi-automatic action in which the breechblock is held forward only by spring pressure and cycles from the rearward gas thrust of the fired cartridge.

BLOW FORWARD ACTION. Automatic and semi-automatic action which has a fixed breechblock and in which spring pressure secures a barrel that reciprocates and cycles the action from the pressure of expanding gasses when a cartridge is fired.

BLUE. An artificial oxidation process that yeilds some rust protection and leaves steel surfaces with a blue-black color.

BLUNDERBUSS. A smoothbore weapon with a very flared muzzle.

BOLT ACTION. A manual action cycled by moving a reciprocating breechbolt.

BORE. The inside of a barrel; the diameter of a barrel.

BOX LOCK. Generally a break top action which contains the hammer, sear, springs and trigger in an integral unit directly behind the breech.

BREAK TOP. Action which exposes the breech by unlocking and the barrel(s) tipping downward, rotating on a point just forward of the breech.

BREECH. Rear end of the barrel; that part of the action that contacts the rear of the cartridge.

BREECHBOLT. The part of the action that secures the cartridge in the chamber.

BULL BARREL. A heavy barrel, usually with no taper.

BUTT. The rearmost portion of a stock.

BUTT PLATE. A plate fastened to the rear of the butt.

CALIBER. Bore diameter usually measured land to land in decimals of an inch or in millimeters.

CARBINE. A short, lightweight rifle.

CARTRIDGE. A self contained unit of ammunition.

CASE HARDENED. A surface hardening on that firearms is usually done so as to leave a broad spectrum of colors on the metal.

CENTER FIRE. Cartridge that contains a primer in the center of the base of the case.

CHAMBER. Portion of the gun in which the cartridge is placed.

CHECKERING. Geometric carving in the shape of parallel lines that cross to form diamonds, and used for both beauty and to provide a better hand grip.

CHEEKPIECE. A raised portion of the stock where the shooter's cheek touches the butt.

CHOKE. A muzzle constriction on shotguns which is used to control the pattern of shot.

CLIP. A detachable box that holds feeds ammunition into the gun by spring pressure.

COMBINATION GUN. A multi-barreled weapon that has a rifle barrel and a shotgun barrel.

CONDITION. The state of newness or wear of a gun. See the introduction for a complete description.

16 / GLOSSARY

CONVERSION. The rebuilding of a military arm into a sporting arm; converting the arm to use a different cartridge;changing the general configuration of a gun.

CURIO. Curios and Relics are a legal subclassification of modern arms. See the complete defination in the introduction.

CUT-OFF. A device that can stop the flow of ammunitionfrom the magazine.

CYLINDER. The rotating container with cartridge chambers in a revolver.

DAMASCENE. An overlay of metal, usually gold leaf, sometimes combined with light engraving and used for decoration.

DAMASCENING. Also called Engine Turning or Jeweling, this is an ornamental polishing consisting of repeated and overlapping circles.

DAMASCUS. A metal formed usually by twisting strands of iron and steel and repeatedly hammer-welding them.

DERINGER. A small percussion pistol developed by Henry Deringer.

DERRINGER. A copy of the Deringer, now meaning any very small manually operated pistol.

DOUBLE ACTION. The ability to both cock and fire a gun by the single pull of a trigger.

DOUBLE-BARREL. A gun having two barrels.

DOUBLE TRIGGER. A gun having two triggers, each usually firing a different trigger.

DRILLING. A three-barreled gun usually consisting of two shotgun barrels and one rifle barrel.

DUMMY SIDEPLATES. Metal plates usually used for decorative purposes and on the sides of boxlock actions to simulate sidelocks.

DUST COVER. Usually a sliding or turning piece of sheet metal used to keep foreign matter out of the action.

EJECTOR. Metal stud or rod that forcibly knocks cases out of the chamber.

ENGRAVING. Metal carving for decoration.

EXPRESS SIGHTS. The rear open rifle sight that has folding leafs for different elevations.

EXTRACTOR. The metal part that lifts the case out of the chamber.

FALLING BLOCK. Singleshot action type in which the breechblock moves vertically, propelled by a finger lever.

FIELD GRADE. Usually the standard grade of gun with little or no embellishment.

FINGER GROOVE. A groove cut into the forend of a long gun to aid in gripping.

FINISH. Materials used to coat the wood or the treatment of the metal parts.

FIXED SIGHTS. Non-adjustable sights.

FLASH HIDER. A device that reduces the amount of muzzle flash.

FLINTLOCK. Muzzle-loading action type that utilizes a hammer holding a flint that strikes a spring-loaded frizzen/pan cover to produce ignition.

FLOBERT. Singleshot action for low power cartridges employing a hammer and rotating breechblock.

FLUTED BARREL. A barrel with longitudinal grooves cut into it for decoration and for strength.

FOLDING GUN. Usually a break-top shotgun that pivots until folded in half.

FOREND. The forward part of a long gun's stock forward of the breech and under the barrel.

FRAME. The metal part of the gun that contains the action

FREE PISTOL. A handgun designed for certain types of target shooting.

FREE RIFLE. A rifle designed for certain types of target shooting.

FRIZZEN. The part of the flintlock or snaphaunce lock that is hit by the flint to produce sparks.

FURNITURE. Metal parts except for the action and barrel.

GALLERY GUN. A gun designed to fire .22 Shorts for use in shooting galleries.

GAS OPERATED. Automatic or semi-automatic action type using vented gasses from the fired cartridge to cycle the action.

GAUGE. A unit of shotgun bore measurement derived from the number of lead balls of that diameter to a pound.

GERMAN SILVER. Also known as nickel silver, consisting of copper, nickel and zinc, used for gun decorations.

GRIP. The portion of the gun to the rear of the trigger that is held by the firing hand.

GRIPFRAME. On handguns that portion of the frame that is held by the hand.

GRIPS. On handguns the stocks.

GRIP SAFETY. A mechanical block that is released when the gun is held by hand in the firing position.

GRIPSTRAP. The exposed metal portion of the gripframe to the front or rear of the grips.

HAMMER. The part of the mechanism that hits and imparts thrust to the firing pin.

HAMMERLESS. A term applied to both striker-actuated guns and guns with hammers hidden within the action.

HAMMER SHROUD. A device that covers the sides of a hammer, while leaving the top exposed.

HANDGUARD. On rifles the forestock above the barrel and forward of the breech.

HANDGUN. A firearm designed to be held and fired with one hand.

HEAT CARVING. Decorative patterns in wood formed either by heat or the combination of heat and pressure.

HOLSTER STOCK. A holster usually made of wood, or wood and leather, that attaches to a handgun for use as a shoulderstock.

HOODED SIGHT. A front sight with a protective cover over it.

INLAY. Decoration made by inlaying patterns on metal or wood.

IRON SIGHTS. Open sights, usually with a rear sight adjustable for elevation, and a front sight adjustable for windage by drifting it.

KENTUCKY RIFLE. A style of gun developed around 1770 in Pennslyvania, and produced first in flintlock and later in percussion varieties.

KNURLING. Checkering on metal.

LANYARD RING. A ring used to secure the gun by a lanyard to the shooter so it won't be lost if dropped.

LEVER ACTION. Usually a repeating type of action with a reciprocating breechblock powered by a finger lever.

LIP-FIRE. An early type of rimfire cartridge.

LOCK. The part of the action that carries the firing mechanism.

LONG GUN. A term used to describe rifles and shotguns.

MAGAZINE. In repeating arms a storage device that feeds cartridges into the breech.

MAGNUM. Usually refers to arms or cartridges that more powerful than normal, or of higher pressure.

MANNLICHER. In common usage does not refer to the man or his guns but to a type of rifle stock in which the forestock extends to the end of the muzzle.

MANUAL SAFETY. A block which prevents discharge that must be engaged and disengaged manually.

MARTINI ACTION. A singleshot action that utilizes a rear pivoting breechblock with a striker operated by finger lever.

MATCH RIFLE. A rifle specifically designed for target shooting.

MATCHLOCK. A muzzle loading arm that uses "Slow Match" to ignite a priming charge.

MATTE FINISH. A dull finish that does not reflect light.

MAUSER ACTION. A type of reciprocating turn-bolt action.

MIQUELET LOCK. A flintlock action that has an exposed sear on the outside of the lockplate.

MODERN. A legal term applied to cartridge firearms manufactured after 1898. Also see the introduction.

MONTE CARLO. A raised portion on the top of the buttstock that elevates the cheek over the level of the buttplate.

MUSKET. A long military style gun with a long forend.

MUZZLE. The most forward end of the barrel.

MUZZLE BRAKE. A device to capture powder gasses at the end of the muzzle to reduce recoil and barrel climb.

MUZZLE LOADER. A black powder arm that is loaded through the muzzle.

NIPPLE. The hollow projection that the percussion cap is fitted to.

OCTAGON BARREL. A barrel with the outside ground into an octagonal shape.

OFF-HAND RIFLE. A target rifle designed to be held, not rested.

OPEN SIGHTS. Iron Sights.

OVER-UNDER. Barrel mounting on double barreled guns with the barrels superposed over one another.

PALM REST. Hand support on the forend of an off-hand match rifle.

PAN. The place on flintlock and earlier arms in which the priming powder is placed.

PARKERIZED. A matte, phosphated finish that is highly rust resistant and usually placed on military arms.

PATCH BOX. A container inletted into the butt of a muzzle loading long gun.

PEEP SIGHT. A circular rear sight with a small hole in the center to aim through.

PEPPERBOX. A revolving pistol with multiple rotating barrels.

PERCUSSION ARM. A muzzle loader that uses a percussion cap placed over a nipple to ignite the powder charge.

PERCUSSION CAP. A small disc that contains a fulminating chemical to ignite a powder charge.

PINFIRE. A type of cartridge with an exposed side pin that detonates the primer when strick.

PISTOL. A non-revolving handgun.

PISTOL GRIP. The grip on a pistol.

PLAINS RIFLE. Percussion rifle design of the mid-1800's developed in St. Louis.

POCKET REVOLVER. A small revolver.

PORT. An opening into the action for ejected cases to pass through; an opening for gasses to flow through.

PROOF. The testing of a gun to see if it stands the stress of firing.

PUMP ACTION. Slide Action.

RAMP SIGHT. A front sight mounted on a ramp.

RAMROD. A rod used to push the charge down the barrel of a muzzle loader.

RECEIVER. The part of the frame that houses the bolt or breechblock

RECOIL. The rearward push of the gun when fired.

RECOIL OPERATED. An automatic or semi-automatic action that is cycled by the recoil from the fired cartridge.

RECOIL PAD. A rubber pad at the end of the butt to absorb recoil.

REPEATER. Capable of firing more that one round of ammunition; having a magazine.

REVOLVER. A firearm with a revolving cylinder containing multiple chambers.

RIFLE. A long gun with a rifled barrel,

RIFLING. Grooves cut into the bore to impart a spin to a bullet.

RIMFIRE. Cartridges containing the priming compound in the rim.

ROLLING BLOCK. Action with a pivoting breechblock that rotates ahead of the hammer, and which is locked by the hammer.

SADDLE RING. A ring on the side of rifles to attach a lanyard to.

SAFETY. A mechanical block that prevents the gun from firing.

SAWED-OFF SHOTGUN. A legal term describing a shotgun with barrels shorter than 16"; a Class 3 weapon.

SCHNABEL FOREND. A downcurving projection at the end of a forestock.

20 / GLOSSARY

SCHUETZEN RIFLE. A type of fancy singleshot target rifle used for off-hand matches.

SCOPE. Telescopic sights.

SCOPE BASES. The mounts that attaches scopes to guns.

SEAR. That part of the action that engages the striker or hammer, and allows them to fall when released by the trigger.

SEMI-AUTOMATIC. Action type that ejects the spent case and cycles a new round into the chamber with the energy of the fired round, and only fires one shot with each pull of the trigger.

SET TRIGGER. A trigger that can be "cocked" so that the final pull is very light.

SHOTGUN. A smoothbore gun designed to fire small shot pellets.

SIDE-BY-SIDE. A double barreled gun with the barrels mounted next to each other.

SIDEHAMMER. A gun having the hammer mounted on the side rather than in the center.

SIDE LEVER. A gun with the action operating lever on the side of the action.

SIDEPLATE. A plate that covers the action, or that the action is mounted on.

SIDELOCK. An action that is contained on the inside of a plate mounted directly behind the breech.

SIGHT. A device that allows precise aim.

SILENCER. A device that reduces the noise of firing.

SINGLE ACTION. An action type that requires manual cocking for each shot.

SINGLESHOT. A gun capable of firing only one shot; having no magazine.

SLIDE. The reciprocating part of a semi-automatic pistol containing the breechblock.

SLIDE ACTION. A repeating action with a reciprocating forestock connected to the breechbolt.

SLING. A carrying strap on a long gun.

SLUG GUN. A shotgun designed to shoot lead slugs rather than pellets.

SNAPHAUNCE. An early form of flintlock with a manual frizzen.

SOLID FRAME. A non-takedown gun; a revolver that does not have a hinged frame.

SOLID RIB. A raised sighting plane on a barrel.

SPLINTER FOREND. A small wood forend under the barrel.

SPORTERIZED. A conversion of military arms to sporting type.

SPUR TRIGGER. A trigger with no guard, but protected by a sheath.

STOCK. The non-metal portion of the gun which is actually held.

STRIKER. A spring activated firing pin held in place by a sear which when released has enough energy to fire a primer.

SWIVELS. The metal loop that the sling is attached to.

TAKEDOWN. Capable of coming apart easily.

TARGET. Designed for target shooting.

GLOSSARY / 21

TARGET STOCK. A stock designed for target shooting.

THUMBHOLE STOCK. A stock with a hole for the thumb to wrap around in the pistol grip.

THUMB REST. A ledge on the side of target grips for the thumb to rest on.

TIP-UP. A revolver with a frame hinged at the upper rear portion; a single shot pistol that has a break-top action.

TOGGLE ACTION. A semi-automatic action with a toggle joint that locks the breechblock.

TOP LEVER. An action actuated or opened with a lever on top.

TOP STRAP. The portion of a revolver above the cylinder.

TOUCH HOLE. The hole into the chamber area on muzzle loaders through which the priming flash ignites the charge.

TRIGGER. The exterior sear release.

TRIGGER GUARD. A band usually of metal that encircles the trigger preventing accidental discharge.

TUBE FEED. A magazine with cartridges loaded behind one another instead of stacked.

TWIST BARREL. A gun with superposed barrels that are manually turned to bring a fresh charge into play; damascus steel barrel.

UNDER LEVER. An action actuated or opened by a lever underneath the action.

UNDERHAMMER. An action with the hammer on the bottom of the frame.

VARMINT RIFLE. A heavy barreled small caliber hunting rifle designed for accuracy.

VENT RIB. A raised sighting plane on barrels with air vents between it and the barrel.

VIERLING. A combination weapon with four barrels.

WHEEL-LOCK. A muzzle loading action that used a spring operated spinning wheel to ignite sparks.

WILDCAT. A non-standard cartridge.

SHOTGUN GAUGES

The gauge of a shotgun or any smoothbore was standardized in the last half of the nineteenth century in England by the Gun Barrel Proof Act of 1868. Until that time the general rule of thumb among gunmakers was the formula that gauge was the number of round lead balls of a given bore diameter in a pound. This still holds true with the exception of the obsolete letter gauges, and .410 gauge which is the actual bore diameter.

Gauge	Diameter	Gauge	Diameter
A	2.000"	23	.587"
B	1.938"	24	.579"
C	1.875"	25	.571"
D	1.813"	26	.563"
E	1.750"	27	.556"
F	1.688"	28	.550"
1	1.669"	29	.543"
H	1.625"	30	.537"
J	1.563"	31	.531"
K	1.500"	32	.526"
L	1.438"	33	.520"
M	1.375"	34	.515"
2	1.325"	35	.510"
O	1.313"	36	.506"
P	1.250"	37	.501"
3	1.157"	38	.497"
4	1.052"	39	.492"
5	.976"	40	.488"
6	.919"	41	.484"
7	.873"	42	.480"
8	.835"	43	.476"
9	.803"	44	.473"
10	.775"	45	.469"
11	.751"	46	.466"
12	.729"	47	.463"
13	.710"	48	.459"
14	.693"	49	.456"
15	.677"	50	.453"
16	.662"		
17	.649"		
18	.637"	.410	.410"
19	.626"		
20	.615"		
21	.605"		
22	.596"		

AMMUNITION INTERCHANGEABILITY

Many calibers (or cartridges) are known by more than one name and there are some that, while having different case sizes, can fit in an arm chambered for another caliber. Other cartridges may have a one-way interchangeability because of power. Caution must always be used when interchanging ammunition for gaps as small as several thousandths of an inch between the cartridge case and the limits of the chamber can destroy a gun and injure the shooter.

.22 W.R.F.
.22 Remington Special
.22 Win. M-1890

.25 Stevens Short R.F. in
.25 Stevens, but not the reverse

.25-20 Marlin
.25-20 Remington
.25-20 W.C.F.
.25-20 Win.

.25 Automatic
.25 A.C.P.
6.35mm Browning
6.35mm Automatic Pistol

.30-30 Marlin
.30-30 Savage
.30-30 W.C.F.
.30-30 Win.

.32 Short R.F. in
.32 Long R.F., but not the reverse

.32 Short Colt in
.32 Long Colt, but not the reverse (not to be used in .32 S&W or .32 S&W Long)

.32 A.C.P.
.32 Colt Automatic
7.65mm Automatic Pistol
7.65mm Browning

.32 S&W in
.32 S&W Long, but not the reverse

.32 Colt New Police
.32 Colt Police Positive
.32 S&W Long

.32-20 Colt
.32-20 Marlin
.32-20 Win.
.32-20 W.C.F.
.32-20 Win. & Marlin
.32 Marlin
.32 Rem.
.32 Win.
.32 W.C.F.
(Hi Speed are for rifles only)

.38 S&W
.38 Colt New Police

.38 Short Colt in
.38 Long Colt, but not the reverse. Both can be used in .38 Special.

.38 Colt Special
.38 S&W Special
.38 Targetmaster
.38-44 Special
(Hi Speed or Plus P cartridges are not to be used in light frame guns. Check with the manufacturer.)

.38 Marlin
.38 Rem.
.38 W.C.F.
.38 Win.
.38-40 Win.

.38 Automatic (A.C.P.) in
.38 Super but not the reverse.

24 / HOW TO USE THIS GUIDE

.380 Automatic
.380 A.C.P.
9mm Browning Short
9mm Corto
9mm Kurz

9mm Luger
9mm Parabellum
(9x19mm is Plus P)

.44 S&W Russian in
.44 Special, but not the reverse

.44 S&W Special in
.44 Magnum, but not the reverse

.44 Marlin
.44 Rem.
.44 Win.
.44 W.C.F.
.44-40 Win.

.45-70 Government
.45-70 Marlin
.45-70 Win.
.45-70-405

HOW TO USE THIS GUIDE

The values listed in this guide are based on the national average retail price for modern firearms ranging from *N.R.A. Very Good* to *N.R.A. Excellent* for modern arms, and from *N.R.A. Very Good* to *N.R.A. Fine* for antiques. Unless otherwise noted the price quoted is for the most common variant of a particular gun.

For the sake of simplicity the following organization has been adopted for this book:
1. Manufacturer, importer, or brand name
2. Type of gun
3. Type of action
4. Model
5. Caliber or gauge

To find your gun in this guide first look under the name of the manufacturer, importer, or brand name, then look under the subdivision "type of gun" (i.e., rifle, handgun, etc.). For instance if you want to find a "General Hood Centennial" Colt Scout .22 l.r.r.f. single action revolver, look for:

COLT; Handgun; Revolver; General Hood Centennial, .22 l.r.r.f.

If nothing is known about the origin of a particular gun, an approximation of the value can be determined by checking the categories of: "type of action" (wheel lock, percussion, cartridge weapon, etc.), "Unknown Maker." To further aid in evaluating guns of unknown origin look under "Firearms, Custom Made," "Plains Rifles," "Scheutzen Rifles," and "Kentucky Rifles and Pistols."

In some cases there is a general listing for a manufacturer or a specific model of gun with the instructions "add" a given value. These additions should be made for all guns in the listed category that have the modification mentioned.

	V.G.	EXC.

A & R SALES
South El Monte, Calif. Current.
HANDGUN, SEMI-AUTOMATIC
☐ **Government**, .45 ACP, Lightweight, Clip Fed "Parts Gun" *Modern* 165.00 245.00
RIFLE, SEMI-AUTOMATIC
☐ **Mark IV Sporter**, .308 Win., Clip Fed, Version of M-14, Adjustable Sights, *Modern* 320.00 450.00

ABBEY, GEORGE T.
Chicago, Ill. 1858-1875.
RIFLE, PERCUSSION
☐ **.44**, Octagon Barrel, Brass Furniture, *Antique* 375.00 525.00
☐ **.44**, Double Barrel, Over-Under, Brass Furniture, *Antique* 700.00 950.00

ABBEY, J.F. & CO.
Chicago, Ill. 1871-1875. Also made by Abbey & Foster.
RIFLE, PERCUSSION
☐ **Various Calibers**, *Antique* 275.00 400.00
SHOTGUN, PERCUSSION
☐ **Various Gauges**, *Antique* 325.00 475.00

ABILENE
See Mossberg

ACHA
Domingo Acha y Cia., Ermua, Spain 1927-1937.
HANDGUN, SEMI-AUTOMATIC
☐ **Ruby M1916**, .32 ACP, Clip Fed, *Curio* 85.00 135.00

ACME
Made by Hopkins & Allen, Sold by Merwin & Hulbert, c. 1880.
HANDGUN, REVOLVER
☐ **.22 Short R.F.**, 7 Shot, Spur Trigger, Solid Frame, Single Action, *Antique* 95.00 165.00
☐ **.32 Short R.F.**, 5 Shot, Spur Trigger, Solid Frame, Single Action, *Antique* 95.00 175.00

ACME ARMS
Maker unknown, sold by J. Stevens Arms Co., c. 1880.
HANDGUN, REVOLVER
☐ **.22 Short R.F.**, 7 Shot, Spur Trigger, Solid Frame, Single Action, *Antique* 95.00 160.00
☐ **.32 Short R.F.**, 5 Shot, Spur Trigger, Solid Frame, Single Action, *Antique* 95.00 175.00
SHOTGUN, DOUBLE BARREL, SIDE-BY-SIDE
☐ **12 Gauge**, Damascus Barrel, *Antique* 95.00 185.00

ACME HAMMERLESS
Made by Hopkins & Allen for Hulbert Bros. 1893.
HANDGUN, REVOLVER
☐ **.32 S & W**, 5 Shot, Top Break, Hammerless, Double Action, 2½" Barrel, *Antique* 70.00 125.00

	V.G.	EXC.
☐ .38 S & W, 5 Shot, Top Break, Hammerless, Double Action, 3" Barrel, *Antique*	70.00	125.00

ACRA
Tradename used by Reinhard Fajen of Warsaw, Mo., c. 1970.

RIFLE, BOLT ACTION
☐ **RA**, Various Calibers, Santa Barbara Barrelled Action, Checkered Stock, *Modern*	135.00	215.00
☐ **S24**, Various Calibers, Santa Barbara Barrelled Action, Fancy Checkering, *Modern*	150.00	235.00
☐ **M18**, Various Calibers, Santa Barbara Barrelled Action, Mannlicher Checkered Stock, *Modern*	180.00	295.00

ACTION
Modesto Santos; Eibar, Spain.

HANDGUN, SEMI-AUTOMATIC
☐ **Model 1920**, .25 ACP, Clip Fed, *Curio*	85.00	160.00
☐ **#2**, .32 ACP, Clip Fed, *Curio*	145.00	225.00

ADAMS
Made by Deane, Adams, & Deane, London, England.

HANDGUN, PERCUSSION
☐ **.38 M1851**, Revolver, Double Action, 4½" Barrel, *Antique*	500.00	875.00
☐ **.38 M1851**, Revolver, Double Action, 4½" Barrel, Cased with Accessories, *Antique*	725.00	1,000.00
☐ **.44 M1851**, Revolver, Double Action, 6" Barrel, *Antique*	400.00	650.00
☐ **.44 M1851**, Revolver, Double Action, 6" Barrel, Cased with Accessories, *Antique*	400.00	675.00
☐ **.500 M1851**, Dragoon, Revolver, Double Action, 8" Barrel, *Antique*	375.00	700.00
☐ **.500 M1851 Dragoon**, Revolver, Double Action, 8" Barrel, Cased with Accessories, *Antique*	600.00	950.00
☐ **.54 Beaumont-Adams**, Revolver, Double Action, 5½" Barrel, *Antique*	475.00	750.00
☐ **.54 Beaumont-Adams**, Revolver, Double Action, 5½" Barrel, Cased with Accessories, *Antique*	700.00	1,200.00

RIFLE, PERCUSSION
☐ **.50 Sporting Rifle**, Revolver, Double Action, 20" Barrel, *Antique*	475.00	750.00

ADAMS, JOSEPH
Birmingham, England 1767-1813.

RIFLE, FLINTLOCK
☐ **.65 Officers Model Brown Bess**, Musket, Military, *Antique*	850.00	1,450.00

ADAMY GEBRUDER
Suhl, Germany 1921-1939.

SHOTGUN, DOUBLE BARREL, OVER-UNDER
☐ **16 Ga.**, Automatic Ejector, Double Trigger, Engraved, Cased, *Modern*	1,250.00	1,850.00

ADIRONDACK ARMS CO.
Plattsburg, N.Y. 1870-1874. Purchased by Winchester 1874.

	V.G.	EXC.

RIFLE, LEVER ACTION
- ☐ **Robinson 1875 Patent**, Various Rimfires, Octagon Barrel, Open Rear Sight, *Antique* 775.00 1,350.00
- ☐ **Robinson Patent**, Various Calibers, Octagon Barrel, *Antique* 725.00 1,275.00

ADLER
Engelbrecht & Wolff; Zella St. Blasii, Germany 1904-1906.

HANDGUN, SEMI-AUTOMATIC
- ☐ **7.25 Adler**, Clip Fed, *Curio* 1,650.00 2,650.00

AERTS, JAN
Maastricht, Holland, c. 1650.

HANDGUN, FLINTLOCK
- ☐ **Ornate Pair**, Very Long Ebony Full Stock, Silver Inlay, High Quality, *Antique* .... 67,500.00+

AETNA
Made by Harrington & Richardson, c. 1876.

HANDGUN, REVOLVER
- ☐ **.22 Short R.F.**, 7 Shot, Spur Trigger, Solid Frame, Single Action, *Antique* 85.00 150.00
- ☐ **Aetna**, .32 Short R.F., 5 Shot, Spur Trigger, Solid Frame, Single Action, *Antique* 90.00 165.00
- ☐ **Aetna 2**, .32 Short R.F., 5 Shot, Spur Trigger, Solid Frame, Single Action, *Antique* 90.00 165.00
- ☐ **Aetna 2½**, .32 Short R.F., 5 Shot, Spur Trigger, Solid Frame, Single Action, *Antique* 90.00 165.00

AETNA ARMS CO.
N.Y.C., c. 1880.

HANDGUN, REVOLVER
- ☐ **.22 Short R.F.**, 7 Shot, Spur Trigger, Tip-Up, *Antique* 220.00 350.00
- ☐ **.32 Short R.F.**, 5 Shot, Spur Trigger, Tip-Up, *Antique* 245.00 380.00

AFFERBACH, WILLIAM
Philadelphia, Pa. 1860-1866.

HANDGUN, PERCUSSION
- ☐ **.40 Derringer**, Full Stock, *Antique* 425.00 650.00

AGAWAM ARMS
Agawam, Mass., c. 1970.

RIFLE, SINGLESHOT
- ☐ **M-68**, .22 L.R.R.F., Lever Action, Open Sights, *Modern* 25.00 50.00
- ☐ **M-68M**, .22 W.M.R., Lever Action, Open Sights, *Modern* 35.00 65.00

AJAX ARMY
Maker Unknown, Sold By E.C. Meacham Co., c. 1880.

HANDGUN, REVOLVER
- ☐ **.44 Short R.F.**, 5 Shot, Spur Trigger, Solid Frame, Single Action, *Antique* 175.00 275.00

AKRILL, E.
Probably St. Etienne, France, c. 1810.
RIFLE, FLINTLOCK
☐ **.69**, Smoothbore, Octagon Barrel, Damascus Barrel, Breech Loader, Plain, *Antique* 950.00 1,975.00

ALAMO
Tradename used by Stoeger Arms, c. 1958.
HANDGUN, REVOLVER
☐ **Alamo**, .22 L.R.R.F., Double Action, Ribbed Barrel, *Modern* 20.00 35.00

ALASKA
Made by Hood Firearms, Sold by E.C. Meacham Co. 1880.
HANDGUN, REVOLVER
☐ **.22 Short R.F.**, 7 Shot, Spur Trigger, Solid Frame, Single Action, *Antique* 95.00 160.00

ALASKAN
Skinner's Sportman's Supply, Juneau, Alaska, c. 1970.
RIFLE, BOLT ACTION
☐ **Standard**, Various Calibers, Checkered Stock, Sling Swivels, *Modern* 175.00 275.00
☐ **Magnum**, Various Calibers, Checkered Stock, Recoil Pad, Sling Swivels, *Modern* 200.00 295.00
☐ **Carbine**, Various Calibers, Checkered Stock, Sling Swivels, *Modern* 200.00 290.00

ALBRECHT, ANDREW
Lancaster, Pa. 1779-1782. See Kentucky Rifles and Pistols.

ALBRIGHT, HENRY
Lancaster, Pa. 1740-1745. See Kentucky Rifles and Pistols.

ALDENDERFER, M.
Lancaster, Pa. 1763-1784. See Kentucky Rifles and Pistols.

ALERT
Made by Hood Firearms Co., c. 1874.
HANDGUN, REVOLVER
☐ **.22 Short R.F.**, 7 Shot, Spur Trigger, Solid Frame, Single Action, *Antique* 90.00 160.00

ALEXIA
Made by Hopkins & Allen, c. 1880.
HANDGUN, REVOLVER
☐ **.22 Short R.F.**, 7 Shot, Spur Trigger, Solid Frame, Single Action, *Antique* 90.00 160.00
☐ **.32 Short R.F.**, 5 Shot, Spur Trigger, Solid Frame, Single Action, *Antique* 95.00 170.00
☐ **.38 Short R.F.**, 5 Shot, Spur Trigger, Solid Frame, Single Action, *Antique* 95.00 180.00
☐ **.41 Short R.F.**, 5 Shot, Spur Trigger, Solid Frame, Single Action, *Antique* 140.00 250.00

ALEXIS
Made by Hood Firearms Co., Sold by Turner & Ross Co. Boston, Mass.

	V.G.	EXC.

HANDGUN, REVOLVER
- ☐ **.22 Short R.F.**, 7 Shot, Spur Trigger, Solid Frame, Single Action, *Antique* .... 90.00 ... 160.00

ALFA
Armero Especialistas Reunidas, Eibar, Spain, c. 1920.

HANDGUN, REVOLVER
- ☐ **Colt Police Positive Type**, .38, Double Action, Blue, *Curio* .... 60.00 ... 120.00
- ☐ **S. & W. M & P Type**, .38, Double Action, Blue, *Curio* .... 60.00 ... 120.00
- ☐ **S. & W. #2 Type**, Various Calibers, Double Action, Blue, Break-Top, *Curio* .... 85.00 ... 140.00

ALFA
Adolf Frank, Hamburg, Germany, c. 1900.

HANDGUN, MANUAL REPEATER
- ☐ **"Reform" Type**, .230 C.F., Four-barrelled Repeater, Engraved, *Curio* .... 115.00 ... 190.00

HANDGUN, SEMI-AUTOMATIC
- ☐ **Pocket**, .25 ACP, Clip Fed, Blue, *Curio* .... 85.00 ... 125.00

RIFLE, PERCUSSION
- ☐ **Back-lock**, Various Calibers, Imitation Damascus Barrel, *Antique* ... 50.00 ... 80.00
- ☐ **Back-lock**, Various Calibers, Carved with Inlays, Imitation Damascus Barrel, *Antique* .... 85.00 ... 140.00

SHOTGUN, PERCUSSION
- ☐ **Double Barrel**, Various Gauges, Back-lock, Double Triggers, Damascus Barrels, *Antique* .... 65.00 ... 110.00
- ☐ **Double Barrel**, Various Gauges, Back-lock, Double Triggers, Damascus Barrels, Carved Stock, Engraved, *Antique* .... 120.00 ... 190.00

SHOTGUN, DOUBLE BARREL, SIDE-BY-SIDE
- ☐ **Greener Boxlock**, Various Gauges, Checkered Stock, Double Triggers, *Curio* .... 110.00 ... 180.00
- ☐ **Greener Boxlock**, Various Gauges, Checkered Stock, Double Triggers, Engraved, *Curio* .... 160.00 ... 245.00

SHOTGUN, SINGLESHOT
- ☐ **Roux Underlever**, Various Gauges, Tip-Down Barrel, No Forestock, *Curio* .... 35.00 ... 55.00
- ☐ **Nuss Underlever**, Various Gauges, Tip-Down Barrel, No Forestock, *Curio* .... 35.00 ... 55.00
- ☐ **Sidebutton**, Various Gauges, Tip-Down Barrel, No Forestock, *Curio* .... 30.00 ... 50.00

ALKARTASUNA
Spain Made by Alkartasuna Fabrica De Armas 1910-1922.

HANDGUN, SEMI-AUTOMATIC
- ☐ **Alkar 1924**, .25 ACP, Cartridge Counter, Grips, Clip Fed, *Curio* .... 220.00 ... 375.00
- ☐ **Pocket**, .32 ACP, Clip Fed, Long Grip, *Curio* .... 95.00 ... 175.00
- ☐ **Pocket**, .32 ACP, Clip Fed, Short Grip, *Curio* .... 95.00 ... 150.00
- ☐ **Vest Pocket**, .25 ACP, Clip Fed, Cartridge Counter, *Modern* .... 95.00 ... 170.00
- ☐ **Vest Pocket**, .25 ACP, Clip Fed, *Modern* .... 85.00 ... 150.00

ALLEGHENY WORKS
Allegheny, Pa. 1836-1875. See Kentucky Rifles and Pistols.

ALLEN
Made by Hopkins & Allen, c. 1880.

	V.G.	EXC.

HANDGUN, REVOLVER
- ☐ **22 Short R.F.**, 7 Shot, Spur Trigger, Solid Frame, Single Action, Antique 90.00 160.00

ALLEN
Tradename used by McKeown's Guns of Pekin, Ill., c. 1970.

SHOTGUN, DOUBLE BARREL, OVER-UNDER
- ☐ **MCK 68**, 12 Ga., Vent Rib, Double Triggers, Plain, *Modern* 200.00 290.00
- ☐ **Olympic 68**, 12 Ga., Vent Rib, Single Selective Trigger, Automatic Ejectors, Checkered Stock, Engraved, *Modern* 300.00 445.00
- ☐ **S201**, Various Gauges, Vent Rib, Double Triggers, Checkered Stock, Light Engraving, *Modern* 250.00 385.00
- ☐ **S201 Deluxe**, Various Gauges, Vent Rib, Single Trigger, Automatic Ejectors, Checkered Stock, Engraved, *Modern* 325.00 470.00

ALLEN & THURBER
Grafton, Mass. 1837-1842, Norwich, Conn. 1842-1847.

HANDGUN, PERCUSSION
- ☐ **.28 (Grafton) Pepperbox**, 6 Shot, 3" Barrel, *Antique*............... 575.00 1,250.00
- ☐ **.28 (Norwich) Pepperbox**, 6 Shot, Bar Hammer, 3" Barrel, *Antique* 275.00 575.00
- ☐ **.28 (Norwich) Pepperbox**, 6 Shot, Hammerless, 3" Barrel, *Antique* 325.00 675.00
- ☐ **.28, Singleshot**, Bar Hammer, Various Barrel Lengths, Half-Octagon Barrel, *Antique*.. 120.00 265.00
- ☐ **.31 (Grafton) Pepperbox**, 6 Shot, 3" Barrel, *Antique*............... 475.00 950.00
- ☐ **.31 (Norwich) Pepperbox**, 6 Shot, Bar Hammer, 3" Barrel, *Antique* 275.00 600.00
- ☐ **.31 (Norwich) Pepperbox**, 6 Shot, Hammerless, 3" Barrel, *Antique* 350.00 700.00
- ☐ **.31, Singleshot**, Tube Hammer, Various Barrel Lengths, Half-Octagon Barrel, *Antique*.. 550.00 950.00
- ☐ **.31, Singleshot**, Under Hammer, Various Barrel Lengths, Half-Octagon Barrel, *Antique*.. 275.00 650.00
- ☐ **.31, Singleshot**, Under Hammer, Various Barrel Lengths, Saw-Handle Grip, Half-Octagon Barrel, *Antique* 250.00 475.00
- ☐ **.31, "In-Line" Singleshot**, Center Hammer, Various Barrel Lengths, Half-Octagon Barrel, *Antique* 150.00 290.00
- ☐ **.34, Singleshot**, Side Hammer, Various Barrel Lengths, Half-Octagon Barrel, *Antique*.. 175.00 475.00
- ☐ **.36 (Grafton) Pepperbox**, 6" Barrel, *Antique* 700.00 1,250.00
- ☐ **.36 (Norwich) Pepperbox**, 6 Shot, Bar Hammer, 6" Barrel, *Antique* 400.00 750.00
- ☐ **.36 (Norwich) Pepperbox**, 6 Shot, Ring Trigger, 6" Barrel, *Antique* 575.00 1,050.00
- ☐ **.36, Singleshot**, Bar Hammer, Various Barrel Lengths, Half-Octagon Barrel, *Antique*.. 125.00 290.00
- ☐ **.36, Singleshot**, Center Hammer, Various Barrel Lengths, Half-Octagon Barrel, *Antique*.. 150.00 290.00
- ☐ **.41, Singleshot**, Side Hammer, Various Barrel Lengths, Half-Octagon Barrel, *Antique*.. 175.00 450.00

ALLEN & THURBER
Worcester, Mass. 1855-1856.

COMBINATION WEAPON, PERCUSSION
- ☐ **Over-Under**, Various Calibers, Rifle and Shotgun Barrels, *Antique* 650.00 1,550.00

HANDGUN, PERCUSSION
- ☐ **.28, Pepperbox**, Bar Hammer, Various Barrel Lengths, 5 Shot, *Antique* 200.00 425.00

	V.G.	EXC.
☐ **.31, Pepperbox**, Bar Hammer, 5 Shot, Various Barrel Lengths, *Antique*	250.00	475.00
☐ **.31, Pepperbox**, Thumb Hammer, 5 Shot, Various Barrel Lengths, *Antique*	300.00	575.00
☐ **.34, Pepperbox**, Bar Hammer, Various Barrel Lengths, 4 Shot, *Antique*	250.00	525.00
☐ **.36, Pepperbox**, Bar Hammer, 6 Shot, Various Barrel Lengths, *Antique*	450.00	875.00
☐ **.36, Target Pistol**, 12" Octagon Barrel, Adjustable Sights, Detachable Shoulder Stock, *Antique*	925.00	2,150.00

RIFLE, PERCUSSION

☐ **.43, Singleshot**, Sporting Rifle, *Antique*	475.00	750.00

ALLEN & WHEELOCK
Worcester, Mass. 1856-1865.

HANDGUN, PERCUSSION

	V.G.	EXC.
☐ **.25, Pepperbox**, 4" Barrel, 5 Shot, *Antique*	225.00	425.00
☐ **.36, Pepperbox**, 6" Barrel, 6 Shot, *Antique*	425.00	850.00
☐ **.28, Revolver**, Side Hammer, Octagon Barrel, 3" Barrel, 5 Shot, *Antique*	150.00	375.00
☐ **.31, Revolver**, Bar Hammer, Octagon Barrel, 2¼" Barrel, 5 Shot, *Antique*	140.00	290.00
☐ **.34, Revolver**, Bar Hammer, Octagon Barrel, 4" Barrel, 5 Shot, *Antique*	200.00	395.00
☐ **.34, Revolver**, Bar Hammer, Octagon Barrel, 4" Barrel, 5 Shot, *Antique*	200.00	395.00
☐ **.31, Revolver**, Side Hammer, Octagon Barrel, 3" Barrel, 5 Shot, *Antique*	150.00	375.00
☐ **.36, Revolver**, Center Hammer, Octagon Barrel, 3" Barrel, 6 Shot, Spur Trigger, *Antique*	175.00	430.00
☐ **.36, Revolver**, Side Hammer, Octagon Barrel, 6" Barrel, 6 Shot, *Antique*	350.00	875.00
☐ **.36, Revolver**, Center Hammer, Octagon Barrel, 7½" Barrel, 6 Shot, *Antique*	450.00	950.00
☐ **.44, Revolver**, Center Hammer, Half-Octagon Barrel, 7½" Barrel, 6 Shot, *Antique*	400.00	900.00

HANDGUN, REVOLVER

	V.G.	EXC.
☐ **.22 Short R.F.**, 7 Shot, Side Hammer, Solid Frame, *Antique*	125.00	270.00
☐ **.25 L.F.**, 7 Shot, Side Hammer, Solid Frame, *Antique*	275.00	435.00
☐ **.32 L.F.**, 6 Shot, Side Hammer, Solid Frame, *Antique*	300.00	575.00
☐ **.32 Short R.F.**, 6 Shot, Side Hammer, Solid Frame, *Antique*	125.00	270.00
☐ **.36 L.F.**, 6 Shot, Side Hammer, Solid Frame, *Antique*	375.00	635.00
☐ **.38 Short R.F.**, 6 Shot, Side Hammer, Solid Frame, *Antique*	125.00	290.00
☐ **.44 L.F.**, 6 Shot, Side Hammer, Solid Frame, *Antique*	500.00	950.00
☐ **.44 Short R.F.**, 6 Shot, Side Hammer, Solid Frame, *Antique*	175.00	325.00

HANDGUN, SINGLESHOT

	V.G.	EXC.
☐ **.22 Short R.F.**, Derringer, Spur Trigger, *Antique*	150.00	280.00
☐ **.22 Short R.F.**, Large Frame, Spur Trigger, *Antique*	150.00	235.00
☐ **.32 Short R.F.**, Derringer, Spur Trigger, *Antique*	300.00	570.00
☐ **.32 Short R.F.**, Large Frame, Spur Trigger, *Antique*	125.00	235.00
☐ **.41 Short R.F.**, Derringer, Spur Trigger, *Antique*	250.00	470.00

RIFLE, PERCUSSION

	V.G.	EXC.
☐ **.36 Allen Patent**, Carbine, Tap Breech Loader, *Antique*	425.00	775.00
☐ **.36 Allen Patent**, Tap Breech Loader, Sporting Rifle, *Antique*	375.00	750.00
☐ **.38 Sidehammer**, Plains Rifle, Iron Mounted, Walnut Stock, *Antique*	275.00	475.00

	V.G.	EXC.
☐ **.44 Center Hammer**, Octagon Barrel, Iron Frame, *Antique*	275.00	575.00
☐ **.44 Revolver**, Carbine, 6 Shot, *Antique*	4,000.00	9,750.00

RIFLE, REVOLVING
- ☐ **.44 L.F.**, Walnut Stock, 6 Shot, *Antique* 3,750.00   6,750.00

RIFLE, SINGLESHOT
- ☐ **.22 R.F.**, Falling Block, Sporting Rifle, *Antique* 275.00   450.00
- ☐ **.38 R.F.**, Falling Block, Sporting Rifle, *Antique* 250.00   375.00
- ☐ **.62 Allen R.F.**, Falling Block, Sporting Rifle, *Antique* ... 250.00   395.00
- ☐ **.64 Allen R.F.**, Falling Block, Sporting Rifle, *Antique* ... 250.00   395.00

SHOTGUN, PERCUSSION
- ☐ **12 Ga. Double**, Hammers, Light Engraving, *Antique* 225.00   365.00

SHOTGUN, DOUBLE BARREL, SIDE-BY-SIDE
- ☐ **12 Ga.**, Checkered Stock, Hammers, Double Triggers, *Antique* 200.00   400.00

ALLEN, C.B.
Springfield, Mass. 1836-1841. Also See U.S. Military.

HANDGUN, PERCUSSION
- ☐ **.36 Cochran Turret**, 7 Shot, 4¾" Barrel, *Antique* 6,000.00   8,500.00
- ☐ **.40 Cochran Turret**, 7 Shot, 5" Barrel, *Antique* 7,250.00   9,500.00
- ☐ **.35 Elgin Cutlass**, Octagon Barrel, with Built-in Knife, Smoothbore, *Antique* 3,500.00   5,250.00
- ☐ **.54 Elgin Cutlass**, Octagon Barrel, with Built-in Knife, Smoothbore, *Antique* 5,750.00   9,750.00

RIFLE, PERCUSSION
- ☐ **.40 Cochran Turret**, 7 Shot, Octagon Barrel, *Antique* 5,500.00   8,250.00
- ☐ **.40 Cochran Turret**, 9 Shot, Octagon Barrel, *Antique* 5,500.00   8,250.00

ALLEN, ETHAN
Grafton, Mass. 1835-1837, E. Allen & Co. Worcester, Mass. 1865-1871.

HANDGUN, PERCUSSION
- ☐ **Various Calibers**, Various Barrel Lengths, Under Hammer, Singleshot, Saw Handle Grip, *Antique* 250.00   450.00
- ☐ **.31, Singleshot**, Under Hammer, Half-Octagon Barrel, *Antique* 275.00   600.00
- ☐ **.31, Pepperbox**, 6 Shot, 3" Barrel, *Antique* 475.00   900.00
- ☐ **.36, Pepperbox**, 6 Shot, 5" Barrel, *Antique* 650.00   1,150.00

HANDGUN, REVOLVER
- ☐ **.22 Short R.F.**, 7 Shot, Side Hammer, Sheath Trigger, *Antique* 125.00   250.00
- ☐ **.32 Short R.F.**, 6 Shot, Side Hammer, Sheath Trigger, *Antique* 125.00   250.00

HANDGUN, SINGLESHOT
- ☐ **Derringer**, .32 Short R.F., Side-Swing Barrel, Round Barrel, *Antique* 300.00   550.00
- ☐ **Derringer**, .32 Short R.F., Side-Swing Barrel, Half-Octagon Barrel, *Antique* 150.00   225.00
- ☐ **Derringer**, .41 Short R.F., Side-Swing Barrel, Half-Octagon Barrel, *Antique* 250.00   450.00
- ☐ **Derringer**, .41 Short R.F., Side-Swing Barrel, Round Barrel, *Antique* 150.00   275.00
- ☐ **Derringer**, .41 Short R.F., Side-Swing Barrel, Octagon Barrel, *Antique* 150.00   275.00

RIFLE, SINGLESHOT
- ☐ **Various Rimfires**, Sporting Rifle, *Antique* 350.00   475.00

AMERICAN ARMS CO. / 33

	V.G.	EXC.

ALLEN, SILAS
Shrewsbury, Mass. 1796-1843. See Kentucky Rifles and Pistols.

ALLIES
Berasaluze Areitio-Arutena y Cia., Eibar, Spain, c. 1920.
HANDGUN, SEMI-AUTOMATIC
☐ **Model 1924**, .25 ACP, Clip Fed, *Curio* 95.00   160.00
☐ **Pocket**, .32 ACP, Clip Fed, *Curio* 95.00   165.00
☐ **Vest Pocket**, .25 ACP, Clip Fed, *Curio* 85.00   140.00
☐ **Vest Pocket**, .32 ACP, Clip Fed, Short Grip, *Curio* 95.00   150.00

ALL RIGHT FIREARMS CO.
Lawrence, Mass., c. 1876.
HANDGUN, REVOLVER
☐ **Little All Right Palm Pistol**, .22 Short R.F., Squeeze Trigger, 5 Shot, *Antique* 475.00   725.00

ALPINE INDUSTRIES
Los Angeles, Calif. 1962-1965.
RIFLE, SEMI-AUTOMATIC
☐ **M-1 Carbine**, .30 Carbine, Clip Fed, Military Style, *Modern* 150.00   250.00

ALSOP, C.R.
Middleton, Conn. 1858-1866.
HANDGUN, PERCUSSION
☐ **.36 Navy**, 5 Shot, Octagon Barrel, Spur Trigger, Top Hammer, Safety, *Antique* 900.00   1,700.00
☐ **.36 Navy**, 5 Shot, Octagon Barrel, Spur Trigger, Top Hammer, No Safety, *Antique* 650.00   1,250.00
☐ **.36 Pocket**, 5 Shot, Octagon Barrel, Spur Trigger, *Antique* 350.00   650.00

AMERICA
Made by Bliss & Goodyear, c. 1878.
HANDGUN, REVOLVER
☐ **.22 Short R.F.**, 7 Shot, Spur Trigger, Solid Frame, Single Action, *Antique* 95.00   160.00

AMERICA
Made by Norwich Falls Pistol Co., c. 1880.
HANDGUN, REVOLVER
☐ **.32 Long R.F.**, Double Action, Solid Frame, *Modern* 65.00   115.00

AMERICAN ARMS CO.
Boston, Mass. 1861-1897, Milwaukee, Wisc. 1897-1901. Purchased by Marlin 1901.
HANDGUN, DOUBLE BARREL, OVER-UNDER
☐ **Wheeler Pat.**, .22 Short R.F., 32 Short R.F., Brass Frame, Spur Trigger, *Antique* 475.00   700.00
☐ **Wheeler Pat**, .32 Short R.F., Brass Frame, Spur Trigger, *Antique* .. 325.00   475.00
☐ **Wheeler Pat**, .41 Short R.F., Brass Frame, Spur Trigger, *Antique* .. 400.00   690.00

HANDGUN, REVOLVER
☐ **.32 S & W**, 5 Shot, Double Action, Top Break, *Antique* 75.00   125.00
☐ **.38 S & W**, 5 Shot, Double Action, Top Break, *Antique* 80.00   140.00
☐ **.38 S & W**, 5 Shot, Single Action, Top Break, Spur Trigger, *Antique* 95.00   150.00
☐ **.32 S & W**, 5 Shot, Double Action, Top Break, Hammerless, *Antique* 100.00   175.00

34 / AMERICAN ARMS AND AMMUNITION COMPANY

	V.G.	EXC.
SHOTGUN, DOUBLE BARREL, SIDE-BY-SIDE		
☐ **12 Ga.**, Semi-Hammerless, Checkered Stock, *Antique*	275.00	450.00
☐ **Whitmore Patent**, 10 Ga., 2⅞", Hammerless, Checkered Stock, *Antique*	275.00	450.00
☐ **Whitmore Patent**, 12 Ga., Hammerless, Checkered Stock, *Antique*	350.00	500.00
SHOTGUN, SINGLESHOT		
☐ **12 Ga.**, Semi-Hammerless, Checkered Stock, *Antique*	150.00	250.00

AMERICAN ARMS & AMMUNITION CO.
Miami, Florida, c. 1979. Successors to Norton Armament Corp. (Norarmco).

HANDGUN, SEMI-AUTOMATIC
☐ **TP-70**, .22 L.R.R.F., Double Action, Stainless, Clip Fed, *Modern* ... 140.00 225.00
☐ **TP-70**, .25 ACP, Double Action, Stainless, Clip Fed, *Modern* 125.00 200.00

AMERICAN ARMS INTERNATIONAL
Salt Lake City, Utah, Current.

AUTOMATIC WEAPON, SUBMACHINE GUN
☐ **American 180**, .22 L.R.R.F., 177 Round Drum Magazine, Peep Sights, *Class 3* 250.00 375.00

RIFLE, SEMI-AUTOMATIC
☐ **American 180**, .22 L.R.R.F., 177 Round Drum Magazine, Peep Sights, *Modern* 250.00 375.00
☐ **Laser-Lok** Sight System, *Add $350.00-$450.00*
☐ **Extra Magazine**, *Add $50.00-$75.00*

AMERICAN BARLOCK WONDER
Made by Crescent for Sears-Roebuck & Co.

SHOTGUN, DOUBLE BARREL, SIDE-BY-SIDE
☐ **Various Gauges**, Outside Hammers, Damascus Barrel, *Modern* 100.00 175.00
☐ **Various Gauges**, Hammerless, Steel Barrel, *Modern* 135.00 200.00
☐ **Various Gauges**, Hammerless, Damascus Barrel, *Modern* 100.00 175.00
☐ **Various Gauges**, Outside Hammers, Steel Barrel, *Modern* 125.00 190.00

SHOTGUN, SINGLESHOT
☐ **Various Gauges**, Hammer, Steel Barrel, *Modern* 55.00 85.00

AMERICAN BOY
Made by Bliss & Goodyear for Townley Hdw. Co.

HANDGUN, REVOLVER
☐ **.32 Short R.F.**, Single Action, Solid Frame, Spur Trigger, 7 Shot, *Antique* 85.00 150.00

AMERICAN BULLDOG
Made by Johnson, Bye & Co., Worcester, Mass. 1882-1900.

HANDGUN, REVOLVER
☐ **.22 Short R.F.**, 7 Shot, Spur Trigger, Solid Frame, Single Action, *Antique* 95.00 175.00
☐ **.32 S & W**, 5 Shot, Spur Trigger, Solid Frame, Single Action, *Modern* 90.00 150.00
☐ **.32 Short R.F.**, 5 Shot, Spur Trigger, Solid Frame, Single Action, *Antique* 95.00 175.00
☐ **.38 S & W**, 5 Shot, Spur Trigger, Solid Frame, Single Action, *Modern* 90.00 155.00

	V.G.	EXC.
☐ .38 Short R.F., 5 Shot, Spur Trigger, Solid Frame, Single Action, Antique	95.00	180.00
☐ .41 Short C.F., 5 Shot, Spur Trigger, Solid Frame, Single Action, Antique	100.00	195.00

AMERICAN CHAMPION
SHOTGUN, SINGLESHOT
☐ M1899, 12 Gauge, Plain, *Modern* 65.00 125.00

AMERICAN FIREARMS CO.
San Antonio, Texas 1966-1974.
HANDGUN, SEMI-AUTOMATIC
☐ .22 L.R.R.F., Clip Fed, Stainless Steel, *Modern* 75.00 125.00
☐ .25 ACP, Clip Fed, Blue, *Modern* 55.00   95.00
☐ .25 ACP, Clip Fed, Stainless Steel, *Modern* 70.00 115.00
☐ .32 ACP, Clip Fed, Stainless Steel, *Modern* 65.00 145.00
☐ .380 ACP, Clip Fed, Stainless Steel, *Modern* 120.00 195.00

AMERICAN EAGLE
Made by Hopkins & Allen 1870-1898.
HANDGUN, REVOLVER
☐ .22 Short R.F., 7 Shot, Spur Trigger, Solid Frame, Single Action, Antique 95.00 175.00
☐ .32 Short R.F., 5 Shot, Spur Trigger, Solid Frame, Single Action, Antique 95.00 195.00

AMERICAN GUN CO.
Made by Crescent Firearms Co. Sold by H. & D. Folsom Co.
HANDGUN, REVOLVER
☐ .32 S & W, 5 Shot, Double Action, Top Break, *Modern* 60.00 125.00
☐ .32 S & W, 5 Shot, Double Action, Top Break, *Modern* 60.00 125.00
SHOTGUN, DOUBLE BARREL, SIDE-BY-SIDE
☐ Various Gauges, Outside Hammers, Damascus Barrel, *Modern* 100.00 175.00
☐ Various Gauges, Hammerless, Steel Barrel, *Modern* 135.00 200.00
☐ Various Gauges, Hammerless, Damascus Barrel, *Modern* 100.00 175.00
☐ Various Gauges, Outside Hammers, Steel Barrel, *Modern* 125.00 190.00
SHOTGUN, SINGLESHOT
☐ Various Gauges, Hammer, Steel Barrel, *Modern* 55.00   85.00

AMERICAN STANDARD TOOL CO.
Newark, N.J. 1865-1870, Successor to Manhattan Firearms Co.
HANDGUN, PERCUSSION
☐ Hero, .34, Screw Barrel, Center Hammer, Spur Trigger, *Antique* ... 85.00 175.00
HANDGUN, REVOLVER
☐ .22 Short R.F., 7 Shot, Spur Trigger, Tip-Up, *Antique* 200.00 350.00

AMERICUS
Made by Hopkins & Allen 1870-1900.
HANDGUN, REVOLVER
☐ .22 Short R.F., 7 Shot, Spur Trigger, Solid Frame, Single Action, Antique 95.00 170.00

36 / AMSDEN, B.W.

	V.G.	EXC.
☐ **.32 Short R.F.**, 5 Shot, Spur Trigger, Solid Frame, Single Action, Antique	95.00	180.00

AMSDEN, B.W.
Saratoga Springs, N.Y. 1852.
COMBINATION WEAPON, PERCUSSION
☐ **.40-16 Ga.**, Double Barrel, Rifled, *Antique*	750.00	975.00

RIFLE, PERCUSSION
☐ **.40**, Octagon Barrel, Set Trigger, Rifled, *Antique*	450.00	675.00
☐ **.44**, 3 Shot, 2 Nipples, Single Barrel, Rifled, *Antique*	1,750.00	2,750.00

AMT Skipper .45

AMT Back-Up .380

AMT
Arcadia Machine & Tool, since 1976 in Arcadia, Calif.
HANDGUN, SEMI-AUTOMATIC
☐ **Back Up**, .22 L.R.R.F., Stainless Steel, Clip Fed, *Modern*	145.00	195.00
☐ **Back Up**, .380 ACP, Stainless Steel, Clip Fed, *Modern*	145.00	195.00
☐ **Combat Skipper**, .45 ACP, Stainless Steel, Clip Fed, Fixed Sights, *Modern*	225.00	350.00
☐ **Government**, .45 ACP, Stainless Steel, Clip Fed, Fixed Sights, *Modern*	215.00	300.00
☐ **Hardballer**, .45 ACP, Stainless Steel, Clip Fed, Adjustable Sights, *Modern*	275.00	400.00
☐ **Longslide**, .45 ACP, Stainless Steel, Clip Fed, Adjustable Sights, *Modern*	350.00	500.00
☐ **Parts Gun**, .45 ACP, made with Stainless Steel Frame, *Modern*	170.00	250.00
☐ **Skipper**, .45 ACP, Stainless Steel, Clip Fed, Adjustable Sights, *Modern*	250.00	375.00

ANDRUS & OSBORNE
Canton, Conn. 1847-1850, moved to Southbridge, Mass. 1850-1851.
HANDGUN, PERCUSSION
☐ **.36 Underhammer**, Boot Pistol, Half-Octagon Barrel, *Antique*	125.00	245.00

APACHE / 37

	V.G.	EXC.

ANGSTADT, A. & J.
Berks County, Pa. 1792-1808. See Kentucky Rifles and U.S. Military.

ANGSTADT, PETER
Lancaster County, Pa. 1770-1777. See Kentucky Rifles & Pistols.

ANGUSH, JAMES
Lancaster County, Pa. 1771. See Kentucky Rifles & Pistols.

ANNELY, L.
London, England 1650-1700.
HANDGUN, FLINTLOCK
☐ **.62**, Holster Pistol, Brass Mounting, *Antique* 475.00   950.00

ANSCHUTZ, J.G.
Zella Mehlis, Germany 1922-1938, 1945 to date in Ulm, West Germany. Also see Savage Arms Co. for rifle listings.
HANDGUN, REVOLVER
☐ **J.G.A.**, 7mm C.F., Folding Trigger, Pocket Revolver, *Curio* 100.00   175.00

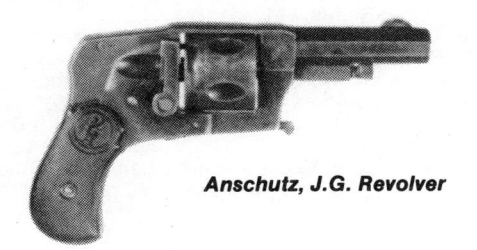

Anschutz, J.G. Revolver

ANSCHUTZ, E.
Philadelphia, Pa., c. 1860.
RIFLE, PERCUSSION
☐ **.36 Schutzen Rifle**, Octagon Barrel, Target, *Antique* 1,450.00   1,950.00

ANSCHUTZ, UDO
Zella Mehlis, Germany 1927-1939.
HANDGUN, SINGLESHOT
☐ **Record-Match M1933**, .22 L.R.R.F., Free Pistol, Martini Action,
   Fancy Stocks, Target Sights, *Modern* 350.00   650.00
☐ **Record-Match M210**, .22 L.R.R.F., Free Pistol, Martini Action,
   Fancy Stocks, Target Sights, Light Engraving, *Modern* 550.00   850.00

ANSTADT, JACOB
Kurztown, Pa. 1815-1817. See Kentucky Rifles and Pistols.

APACHE
Fab. de Armas Garantazadas, Spain, c. 1920.
HANDGUN, REVOLVER
☐ **Colt Police Positive Type**, .38, Double Action, 6 Shots, *Curio* 65.00   110.00

APACHE
Tempe, Ariz., c. 1970.

	V.G.	EXC.

RIFLE, SEMI-AUTOMATIC
☐ **Thompson Replica**, .45 ACP, Clip Fed, *Class 3* 90.00   150.00

APACHE
Made by Ojanguren y Vidosa; Eibar, Spain.
HANDGUN, SEMI-AUTOMATIC
☐ **.25 ACP**, Clip Fed, *Modern* 75.00   125.00

APAOLOZO HERMANOS
Zumorraga, Spain, c. 1925.
HANDGUN, REVOLVER
☐ **Colt Police Positive Type**, .38 Spec., Double Action, *Curio* 65.00   110.00

APEX RIFLE CO.
Sun Valley, Calif., c. 1952.
RIFLE, BOLT ACTION
☐ **Bantam Light Sporter**, Various Calibers, 7 Lbs., Monte Kennedy Stock, Standard Grade, No Sights, *Modern* 350.00   475.00
☐ **Apex Eight**, Various Calibers, 8 Lbs., Monte Kennedy Stock, Standard Grade, No Sights, *Modern* 300.00   425.00
☐ **Reliable Nine**, Various Calibers, 9 Lbs., Monte Kennedy Stock, Standard Grade, No Sights, *Modern* 300.00   425.00
☐ **Varmint & Target**, Various Calibers, Monte Kennedy Target Stock, Heavy Barrel, No Sights, *Modern* 350.00   500.00
☐ **Bench Rester**, Various Calibers, Monte Kennedy Laminated Stock with Rails, Bull Barrel, Canjar Trigger, *Modern* 450.00   650.00

ARAMBERRI
Spain
SHOTGUN, DOUBLE BARREL, SIDE-BY-SIDE
☐ **Boxlock**, 12 Gauge, Single Trigger, Checkered Stock, Vent Rib, *Modern* 135.00   190.00

ARGENTINE MILITARY
AUTOMATIC WEAPON, ASSAULT RIFLE
☐ **FN-FAL**, .308 Win., Clip Fed, *Class 3* 1,200.00 1,650.00

AUTOMATIC WEAPON, SUBMACHINE GUN
☐ **C-3**, .45 ACP, *Class 3* 250.00   375.00
☐ **C-4 Hafdasa**, .45 ACP, *Class 3* 200.00   350.00
☐ **M E M S**, 9mm Luger, *Class 3* 475.00   650.00
☐ **M1943**, .45 ACP, *Class 3* 225.00   350.00
☐ **M1946**, .45 ACP, *Class 3* 225.00   350.00
☐ **P A M**, 9mm Luger, *Class 3* 350.00   650.00
☐ **Star M D**, 9mm Luger, *Class 3* 475.00   750.00

HANDGUN, REVOLVER
☐ **Colt M 1985**, Double Trigger, Solid Frame, Swing-out Cylinder, Military, *Modern* 115.00   185.00

HANDGUN, SEMI-AUTOMATIC
☐ **Ballester-Molina**, .45 ACP, Clip Fed, *Modern* 175.00   275.00
☐ **Ballester-Rigaud**, .45 ACP, Clip Fed, *Modern* 180.00   300.00
☐ **Mannlicher M1905**, 7.63 Mannlicher, *Curio* 175.00   275.00

ARMALITE / 39

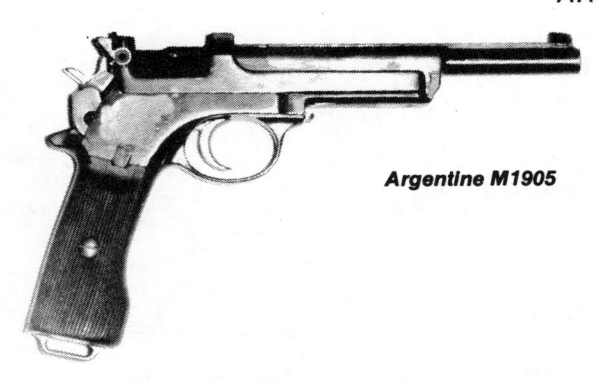

Argentine M1905

	V.G.	EXC.
☐ **Modelo 1916 (Colt 1911)**, .45 ACP, Clip Fed, *Modern*	275.00	425.00
☐ **Modelo 1927 (Colt 1911A1)**, .45 ACP, Clip Fed, *Modern*	325.00	475.00

RIFLE, BOLT ACTION
☐ **M 1908/09**, 7.65 Argentine, Carbine, Open Rear Sight, Full-Stocked Military, *Modern*	140.00	200.00
☐ **M 1891**, 7.65 Argentine, Rifle, Full Stocked Military, *Modern*	85.00	145.00
☐ **M 1891**, 7.65 Argentine, Carbine, Open Rear Sight, Full Stocked Military, *Modern*	95.00	155.00
☐ **M 1909**, 7.65 Argentine, Rifle, Full Stocked Military, *Modern*	85.00	135.00

RIFLE, SINGLESHOT
☐ **M1879**, .43 Mauser, Rolling Block, *Antique*	225.00	350.00

ARISTOCRAT
Made by Hopkins & Allen for Suplee Biddle Hardware 1870-1900.

HANDGUN, REVOLVER
☐ **.22 Short R.F.**, 7 Shot, Spur Trigger, Solid Frame, Single Action, *Antique*	95.00	160.00
☐ **.32 Short R.F.**, 5 Shot, Spur Trigger, Solid Frame, Single Action, *Antique*	90.00	175.00

ARISTOCRAT
Made by Stevens Arms.

SHOTGUN, DOUBLE BARREL, SIDE-BY-SIDE
☐ **M 315**, Various Gauges, Hammerless, Steel Barrel, *Modern*	95.00	165.00

ARIZAGA, GASPAR
Eibar, Spain.

HANDGUN, SEMI-AUTOMATIC
☐ **.32 ACP**, Clip Fed, *Modern*	95.00	145.00

ARMALITE
Costa Mesa, Calif.

AUTOMATIC WEAPON, ASSAULT RIFLE
☐ **AR-10**, .308 Win., Clip Fed, Commercial, *Class 3*	2,500.00	3,250.00
☐ **AR-18**, .223 Rem., Clip Fed, Commercial, *Class 3*	500.00	625.00
☐ **AR-18**, .223 Rem., Clip Fed, Folding Stock, *Class 3*	600.00	800.00

40 / ARMIJAGER

	V.G.	EXC.

RIFLE, SEMI-AUTOMATIC
- ☐ **AR-180** .223 Rem., Clip Fed, Folding Stock, *Modern* 275.00 475.00
- ☐ **AR-7 Explorer**, .22 L.R.R.F., Clip Fed, *Modern* 50.00 85.00
- ☐ **AR-7 Explorer Custom**, .22 L.R.R.F., Checkered Stock, Clip Fed, *Modern* 60.00 100.00

SHOTGUN, SEMI-AUTOMATIC
- ☐ **AR-17**, 12 Ga., Lightweight, *Modern* 400.00 600.00

ARMI JAGER
Turin, Italy.

HANDGUN, REVOLVER
- ☐ **Dakota**, Various Calibers, Single Action, Western Style, Various Barrel Lengths, *Modern* 75.00 135.00
- ☐ **Dakota**, Various Calibers, Single Action, Western Style, Engraved, Various Barrel Lengths, *Modern* 125.00 200.00
- ☐ **Dakota Sheriff**, Various Calibers, Single Action, Western Style, 3½" Barrel, *Modern* 90.00 150.00

RIFLE, SEMI-AUTOMATIC
- ☐ **AP-74 Standard**, .22 L.R.R.F., Military Style, Plastic Stock, *Modern* 60.00 90.00
- ☐ **AP-74 Standard**, .32 ACP, Military Style, Plastic Stock, *Modern* ... 65.00 100.00
- ☐ **AP-74**, .22 L.R.R.F., Military Style, Wood Stock, *Modern* 65.00 95.00
- ☐ **AP-74**, .32 ACP, Military Style, Wood Stock, *Modern* 70.00 110.00
- ☐ **AP-74 Commando**, .22 L.R.R.F., Military Style, Wood Stock, *Modern* 70.00 110.00

ARMINIUS
Herman Weihrauch Sportwaffenfabrik, Mellrichstadt/ Bayern, West Germany; for Current Models, See F.I.E.

HANDGUN, REVOLVER
- ☐ **HW-3**, .22 L.R.R.F., *Modern* 20.00 35.00
- ☐ **HW-3**, .32 S & W Long, *Modern* 25.00 45.00
- ☐ **HW-5**, .22 L.R.R.F., *Modern* 20.00 35.00
- ☐ **HW-5**, .32 S & W Long, *Modern* 25.00 40.00
- ☐ **HW-7**, .22 L.R.R.F., *Modern* 20.00 35.00
- ☐ **HW-9**, .22 L.R.R.F., Adjustable Sights, *Modern* 35.00 55.00

ARMINIUS
Friederich Pickert, Zella-Mehlis, Germany 1922-1939.

HANDGUN, REVOLVER
- ☐ **Model 1**, .22 L.R.R.F., Hammerless, *Modern* 85.00 130.00
- ☐ **Model 2**, .22 L.R.R.F., Hammer, *Modern* 85.00 130.00
- ☐ **Model 3**, .25 ACP, Hammerless, Folding Trigger, *Modern* 85.00 130.00
- ☐ **Model 4**, 5.5 Velo Dog, Hammerless, Folding Trigger, *Modern* 85.00 130.00
- ☐ **Model 5/1**, 7.5mm Swiss, Hammer, *Modern* 95.00 160.00
- ☐ **Model 5/2**, 7.62 Nagant, Hammer, *Modern* 85.00 150.00
- ☐ **Model 7**, .320 Revolver, Hammer, *Modern* 75.00 120.00
- ☐ **Model 8**, .320 Revolver, Hammerless, Folding Trigger, *Modern* 75.00 120.00
- ☐ **Model 9**, .32 ACP, Hammer, *Modern* 80.00 135.00
- ☐ **Model 10**, .32 ACP, Hammerless, Folding Trigger, *Modern* 85.00 130.00
- ☐ **Model 13**, .380 Revolver, Hammer, *Modern* 85.00 130.00
- ☐ **Model 14**, .380 Revolver, Hammerless, *Modern* 85.00 130.00

HANDGUN, SINGLESHOT
- ☐ **TP 1**, .22 L.R.R.F., Target Pistol, Hammer, *Modern* 195.00 350.00
- ☐ **TP 2**, .22 L.R.R.F., Hammerless, Set Triggers, *Modern* 195.00 350.00

ARMSPORT
Current Importers, Miami, Fla.

	V.G.	EXC.

HANDGUN, FLINTLOCK
- ☐ **Kentucky**, .45, Reproduction, *Antique* 45.00 75.00

HANDGUN, PERCUSSION
- ☐ **New Remington Army**, .44, Stainless Steel, Brass Trigger Guard, Reproduction, *Antique* 80.00 125.00
- ☐ **New Remington Army**, .44, Blue, Brass Trigger Guard, Reproduction, *Antique* 60.00 90.00
- ☐ **Whitney**, .36, Solid Frame, Brass Trigger Guard, Reproduction, *Antique* 60.00 90.00
- ☐ **Spiller & Burr**, .36, Solid Frame, Brass Frame, Reproduction, *Antique* 45.00 65.00
- ☐ **1851 Colt Navy**, .36, Brass Frame, Reproduction, *Antique* 45.00 70.00
- ☐ **1851 Colt Navy**, .44, Brass Frame, Reproduction, *Antique* 45.00 70.00
- ☐ **1851 Colt Navy**, .36, Steel Frame, Reproduction, *Antique* 55.00 85.00
- ☐ **1851 Colt Navy**, .44, Steel Frame, Reproduction, *Antique* 55.00 85.00
- ☐ **1860 Colt Army**, .44, Brass Frame, Reproduction, *Antique* 50.00 80.00
- ☐ **1860 Colt Army**, .44, Steel Frame, Reproduction, *Antique* 60.00 95.00
- ☐ **New Hartford Police**, .36, Reproduction, *Antique* 45.00 80.00
- ☐ **1847 Colt Walker**, .44, Reproduction, *Antique* 75.00 115.00
- ☐ **Corsair**, .44, Double Barrel, Reproduction, *Antique* 50.00 80.00
- ☐ **Kentucky**, .45 or .50, Reproduction, *Antique* 45.00 70.00
- ☐ **Patriot**, .45, Target Sights, Set Triggers, Reproduction, *Antique*.... 60.00 100.00

RIFLE, BOLT ACTION
- ☐ **Tikka**, Various Calibers, Open Sights, Checkered Stock, Clip Fed, *Modern* 275.00 375.00

RIFLE, LEVER ACTION
- ☐ **Premier 1873 Winchester**, Various Calibers, Rifle, Engraved, Reproduction, *Modern* 700.00 900.00
- ☐ **Premier 1873 Winchester**, Various Calibers, Carbine, Engraved, Reproduction, *Modern* 600.00 775.00

RIFLE, FLINTLOCK
- ☐ **Kentucky**, .45, Reproduction, *Antique* 100.00 145.00
- ☐ **Deluxe Kentucky**, .45, Reproduction, *Antique* 150.00 200.00
- ☐ **Hawkin**, .45, Reproduction, *Antique* 120.00 160.00
- ☐ **Deluxe Hawkin**, .50, Reproduction, *Antique* 130.00 170.00

RIFLE, PERCUSSION
- ☐ **Kentucky**, .45 or .50, Reproduction, *Antique* 95.00 140.00
- ☐ **Deluxe Kentucky**, .45, Reproduction, *Antique* 130.00 185.00
- ☐ **Hawkin**, Various Calibers, Reproduction, *Antique*................ 110.00 150.00
- ☐ **Deluxe Hawkin**, Various Calibers, Reproduction, *Antique* 120.00 160.00

COMBINATION WEAPON, OVER-UNDER
- ☐ **Tikka Turkey Gun**, 12 Ga. and .222 Rem., Vent Rib, Sling Swivels, Muzzle Break, Checkered Stock, *Modern* 425.00 575.00

RIFLE, DOUBLE BARREL, SIDE-BY-SIDE
- ☐ **Emperor**, Various Calibers, Holland and Holland Type Sidelock, Engraved, Checkered Stock, Extra Barrels, Cased, *Modern* 8,000.00 9,500.00
- ☐ **Emperor Deluxe**, Various Calibers, Holland and Holland Sidelock, Fancy Engraving, Checkered Stock, Extra Barrels, *Modern* 9,500.00 14,500.00

RIFLE, DOUBLE BARREL, OVER-UNDER
- ☐ **Emperor**, Various Calibers, Checkered Stock, Engraved, Extra Barrels, Cased, *Modern* 6,000.00 7,500.00
- ☐ **Express**, Various Calibers, Checkered Stock, Engraved, *Modern* ... 1,500.00 2,250.00

	V.G.	EXC.

SHOTGUN, PERCUSSION
- **Hook Breech**, Double Barrel, Side-by-Side, 10 and 12 Gauges, Reproduction, *Antique* 150.00   225.00

SHOTGUN, DOUBLE BARREL, SIDE-BY-SIDE
- **Goose Gun**, 10 Ga. 3½" Mag., Checkered Stock, *Modern* 350.00   450.00
- **Side-by-Side**, 12 and 20 Gauges, Checkered Stock, *Modern* 300.00   400.00
- **Express**, 12 and 20 Gauges, Holland and Holland Type Sidelock, Engraved, Checkered Stock, *Modern* 2,000.00   2,750.00
- **Western Double**, 12 Ga. Mag. 3", Outside Hammers Double Trigger, *Modern* 275.00   375.00

SHOTGUN, DOUBLE BARREL, OVER-UNDER
- **Premier**, 12 Ga., Skeet Grade, Checkered Stock, Engraved, *Modern* 1,000.00   1,350.00
- **Model 2500**, 12 and 20 Ga., Checkered Stock, Adjustable Choke, Single Selective Trigger, *Modern* 400.00   525.00
- **Special**, .410 Ga., Checkered Stock, Double Trigger, *Modern* 70.00   100.00

SHOTGUN, SINGLESHOT
- **Monotrap**, 12 Ga., Two Barrel Set, Checkered Stock, *Modern* 1,500.00   2,000.00
- **Monotrap**, 12 Ga., Checkered Stock, *Modern* 1,000.00   1,350.00

ARMSTRONG, JOHN
Gettysburg, Pa. 1813-1817. Also See Kentucky Rifles and Pistols.

ARRIOLA HERMANOS
Eibar, Spain, c. 1930.

HANDGUN, REVOLVER
- **Colt Police Positive Copy**, .38 Spec., Double Action, *Modern* 65.00   110.00

ARRIZABALAGA, HIJOS DE CALIXTO
Eibar, Spain, c. 1915.

HANDGUN, SEMI-AUTOMATIC
- **Ruby Type**, .32 ACP, Clip Fed, Blue, *Curio* 80.00   145.00

ASCASO, FRANCISCO
Tarassa, Spain, c. 1937.

HANDGUN, SEMI-AUTOMATIC
- **Astra 400 Copy**, 9mm, Clip Fed, Military Type, *Curio* 600.00   950.00

ASHEVILLE ARMORY
Asheville, N.C. 1861-1864.

RIFLE, PERCUSSION
- **.58 Enfield Type**, Rifled, Brass Furniture, Military, *Antique* 1,300.00   1,950.00

ASTRA
Founded in 1908 as Unceta y Esperanza in Eibar, Spain. In 1913 moved to Guernica, Spain and the name was reversed to Esperanza y Unceta; name changed again in 1926 to Unceta y Cia.; name changed again in 1953 to Astra-Unceta y Cia.

AUTOMATIC WEAPON, MACHINE-PISTOL
- **Model 901**, 7.63 Mauser, Holster Stock, *Class 3* 750.00   1,250.00
- **Model 902**, 7.63 Mauser, Holster Stock, *Class 3* 750.00   1,250.00
- **Model 903**, 7.63 Mauser, Holster Stock, *Class 3* 750.00   1,250.00
- **Model F**, 9mm Bayard Long, Holster Stock, *Class 3* 750.00   1,250.00

ASTRA / 43

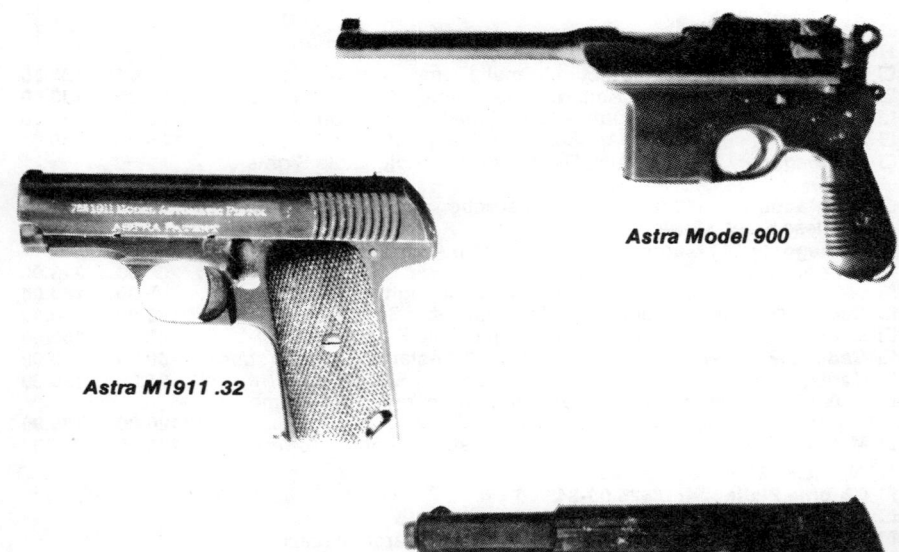

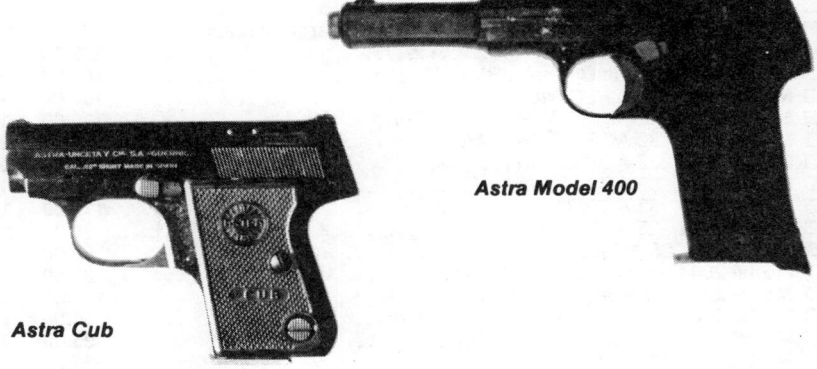

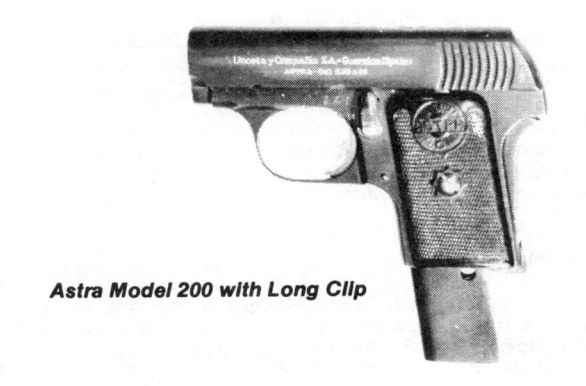

Astra Model 900

Astra M1911 .32

Astra Model 400

Astra Cub

Astra Model 200 with Long Clip

44 / ASTRA

	V.G.	EXC.

HANDGUN, REVOLVER
- ☐ **250**, .22 L.R.R.F., Double Action, Small Frame, *Modern* .... 80.00 — 135.00
- ☐ **250**, .22 W.M.R., Double Action, Small Frame, *Modern* .... 80.00 — 135.00
- ☐ **250**, .32 S & W Long, Double Action, Small Frame, *Modern* .... 70.00 — 130.00
- ☐ **250**, .38 Special, Double Action, Small Frame, *Modern* .... 85.00 — 140.00
- ☐ **357 Magnum**, .357 Magnum, Double Action, Adjustable Sights, *Modern* .... 150.00 — 235.00
- ☐ **357 Magnum**, .357 Magnum, Double Action, Adjustable Sights, Stainless Steel, *Modern* .... 185.00 — 275.00
- ☐ **44 Magnum**, .44 Magnum, Double Action, Adjustable Sights, *Modern* .... 200.00 — 325.00
- ☐ **960**, .38 Special, Double Action, Adjustable Sights, *Modern* .... 95.00 — 160.00
- ☐ **Cadix**, .22 L.R.R.F., Double Action, Adjustable Sights, *Modern* .... 80.00 — 140.00
- ☐ **Cadix**, .22 W.M.R., Double Action, Adjustable Sights, *Modern* ..... 90.00 — 150.00
- ☐ **Cadix**, .32 S & W Long, Double Action, Adjustable Sights, *Modern* 80.00 — 130.00
- ☐ **Cadix**, .38 Special, Double Action, Adjustable Sights, *Modern* ..... 95.00 — 155.00
- ☐ **Inox**, .38 Special, Stainless Steel, Double Action, Small Frame, *Modern* .... 120.00 — 185.00
- ☐ **Match**, .38 Special, Double Action, Adjustable Sights, *Modern* .... 100.00 — 165.00

HANDGUN, SEMI-AUTOMATIC
- ☐ **Chrome Plating**, *Add* $25.00-$45.00
- ☐ **Light Engraving**, *Add* $60.00-$110.00
- ☐ **A-80**, Various Calibers, Double Action, Blue, Large Magazine, *Modern* .... 225.00 — 375.00
- ☐ **Constable**, Various Calibers, Blue, *Modern* .... 165.00 — 240.00
- ☐ **Model 100**, .32 ACP, *Curio* .... 100.00 — 150.00
- ☐ **Model 100 Special**, .32 ACP, 9 Shot, *Curio* .... 120.00 — 175.00
- ☐ **Model 1000**, .32 ACP, 12 Shot, *Modern* .... 125.00 — 200.00
- ☐ **Model 1911**, .32 ACP, *Curio* .... 135.00 — 235.00
- ☐ **Model 1915**, .32 ACP, *Curio* .... 100.00 — 165.00
- ☐ **Model 1916**, .32 ACP, *Curio* .... 110.00 — 185.00
- ☐ **Model 1924**, .25 ACP, *Curio* .... 95.00 — 160.00
- ☐ **Model 200**, .25 ACP, *Modern* .... 85.00 — 145.00
- ☐ **Model 200 Firecat**, .25 ACP, *Modern* .... 90.00 — 135.00
- ☐ **Model 2000 Camper**, .22 Short R.F., *Modern* .... 100.00 — 160.00
- ☐ **Model 2000 Cub**, .22 Short R.F., *Modern* .... 95.00 — 150.00
- ☐ **Model 2000 Cub**, .25 ACP, *Modern* .... 95.00 — 150.00
- ☐ **Model 300**, .32 ACP, *Modern* .... 135.00 — 210.00
- ☐ **Model 300**, .32 ACP, Nazi-Proofed, *Curio* .... 325.00 — 450.00
- ☐ **Model 300**, .380 ACP, *Modern* .... 145.00 — 225.00
- ☐ **Model 300**, .380 ACP, Nazi-Proofed, *Curio* .... 325.00 — 450.00
- ☐ **Model 3000 (Late)**, .380 ACP, *Modern* .... 100.00 — 150.00
- ☐ **Model 400**, .32 ACP, *Modern* .... 450.00 — 650.00
- ☐ **Model 400**, 9mm Bayard Long, Nazi-Proofed, *Curio* .... 450.00 — 600.00
- ☐ **Model 400**, 9mm Bayard Long, *Modern* .... 175.00 — 300.00
- ☐ **Model 4000 Falcon**, Conversion Unit Only $65.00-$95.00
- ☐ **Model 4000 Falcon**, .22 L.R.R.F., *Modern* .... 140.00 — 200.00
- ☐ **Model 4000 Falcon**, .32 ACP, *Modern* .... 130.00 — 190.00
- ☐ **Model 4000 Falcon**, .380 ACP, *Modern* .... 130.00 — 190.00
- ☐ **Model 600**, .32 ACP, *Modern* .... 150.00 — 225.00
- ☐ **Model 600**, 9mm Luger, Nazi-Proofed, *Curio* .... 250.00 — 375.00
- ☐ **Model 600**, 9mm Luger, *Modern* .... 175.00 — 250.00
- ☐ **Model 700**, .32 ACP, *Curio* .... 450.00 — 650.00
- ☐ **Model 700 Special**, .32 ACP, 12 Shots, *Modern* .... 450.00 — 600.00
- ☐ **Model 7000**, .22 L.R.R.F., *Modern* .... 100.00 — 150.00
- ☐ **Model 800 Condor**, .380 ACP, *Modern* .... 120.00 — 175.00
- ☐ **Model 900**, 7.63 Mauser, Holster Stock, *Modern* .... 850.00 — 1,350.00

ATLAS ARMS / 45

	V.G.	EXC.
☐ **Model 900**, 9mm Luger, *Modern*	950.00	1,550.00
☐ **Model 902**, 9mm Bayard Long, Holster Stock, *Curio*	1,200.00	1,750.00
☐ **Model 903E**, .38 Super, *Modern*	1,100.00	1,750.00
☐ **Model 903E**, 7.63 Mauser, Holster Stock, *Modern*	850.00	1,250.00
☐ **Model 903E**, 9mm Bayard Long, *Modern*	800.00	1,250.00
☐ **Model 5000 Sport (Constable)**, .22 L.R.R.F. Target Pistol, *Modern*	175.00	275.00
☐ **Model TS-22**, .22 L.R.R.F. Target Pistol, Single Action, *Modern*	200.00	320.00

RIFLE, SEMI-AUTOMATIC
☐ **Model 1000**, .32 ACP, *Modern*	300.00	425.00
☐ **Model 3000 (Early)**, .32 ACP, *Modern*	100.00	165.00
☐ **Model 3000 (Late)**, .22 L.R.R.F., *Modern*	90.00	145.00
☐ **Model 3000 (Late)**, .32 ACP, *Modern*	95.00	150.00
☐ **Model 800 Condor**, 9mm Luger, *Curio*	450.00	595.00
☐ **Model 902**, 7.63 Mauser, *Modern*	1,000.00	1,500.00

SHOTGUN, DOUBLE BARREL, OVER-UNDER
☐ **Model 650**, 12 Gauge, Checkered Stock, Double Triggers, Vent Rib, *Modern*	175.00	275.00
☐ **Model 650E**, 12 Gauge, Checkered Stock, Double Triggers, Vent Rib, Selective Ejectors, *Modern*	225.00	375.00
☐ **Model 750**, 12 Gauge, Checkered Stock, Double Triggers, Vent Rib, *Modern*	225.00	375.00
☐ **Model 750E**, 12 Gauge, Checkered Stock, Single Trigger, Vent Rib, Selective Ejectors, *Modern*	325.00	475.00
☐ **Model 750 Skeet**, 12 Gauge, Checkered Stock, Single Trigger, Vent Rib, Selective Ejectors, *Modern*	345.00	500.00
☐ **Model 750 Trap**, 12 Gauge, Checkered Stock, Single Trigger, Vent Rib, Selective Ejectors, *Modern*	345.00	500.00
☐ **Model ID-13**, 12 Gauge, Checkered Stock, Single Trigger, Selective Ejectors, Vent Rib, *Modern*	300.00	450.00

SHOTGUN, DOUBLE BARREL, SIDE-BY-SIDE
☐ **Model 811**, 10 Gauge Magnum, Checkered Stock, Double Triggers, *Modern*	195.00	295.00
☐ **Model 805**, Various Gauges, Checkered Stock, Double Triggers, *Modern*	160.00	250.00

SHOTGUN, SINGLESHOT
☐ **Cyclops**, Various Gauges, Checkered Stock, *Modern*	55.00	85.00

ATIS
Ponte S. Marco, Italy.

SHOTGUN, SEMI-AUTOMATIC
☐ **12 Ga.**, Lightweight, Vent Rib, *Modern*	160.00	225.00
☐ **12 Ga.**, Lightweight, Vent Rib, Left-Hand, *Modern*	220.00	275.00

ATLAS
Domingo Acha y Cia., Ermua, Spain, c. 1920.

HANDGUN, SEMI-AUTOMATIC
☐ **Vest Pocket**, .25 ACP, Clip Fed, *Modern*	85.00	120.00

ATLAS ARMS
Chicago, Ill. from about 1962 to 1972.

HANDGUN, DOUBLE BARREL, OVER-UNDER
☐ **Derringer**, .22 L.R.R.F., Remington Style, *Modern*	30.00	50.00
☐ **Derringer**, .38 Spec., Remington Style, *Modern*	45.00	65.00

46 / ATKIN, HENRY E. AND COMPANY

	V.G.	EXC.

SHOTGUN, DOUBLE BARREL, SIDE-BY-SIDE
- ☐ **Model 145,** Various Gauges, Boxlock, Vent Rib, Engraved, Hammerless, Checkered Stock, *Modern* 320.00 425.00
- ☐ **Model 200,** Various Gauges, Boxlock, Double Triggers, Hammerless, Checkered Stock, *Modern* 160.00 245.00
- ☐ **Model 204,** Various Gauges, Boxlock, Single Trigger, Hammerless, Checkered Stock, *Modern* 220.00 295.00
- ☐ **Model 206,** Various Gauges, Boxlock, Single Trigger, Automatic Ejector, Hammerless, Checkered Stock, *Modern* 245.00 325.00
- ☐ **Model 208,** Various Gauges, Boxlock, Double Triggers, Vent Rib, Recoil Pad, *Modern* 220.00 295.00
- ☐ **Model 500,** Various Gauges, Boxlock, Double Triggers, Vent Rib, Recoil Pad, *Modern* 220.00 295.00

SHOTGUN, SINGLESHOT
- ☐ **Trap Gun,** 12 Gauge, Automatic Ejector, Engraved, Checkered Stock, *Modern* 365.00 475.00
- ☐ **Insuperable 101,** Various Gauges, Vent Rib, Engraved, Checkered Stock, *Modern* 55.00 85.00

SHOTGUN, DOUBLE BARREL, OVER-UNDER
- ☐ **Model 65,** Various Gauges, Boxlock, Double Triggers, Vent Rib, *Modern* 220.00 325.00
- ☐ **Model 65-ST,** Various Gauges, Boxlock, Single Trigger, Vent Rib, *Modern* 235.00 365.00
- ☐ **Model 87,** Various Gauges, Merkel Type Sidelock, Single Trigger, Vent Rib, Engraved, *Modern* 320.00 425.00
- ☐ **Model 150,** Various Gauges, Boxlock, Single Trigger, Vent Rib, *Modern* 235.00 365.00
- ☐ **Model 150,** Various Gauges, Boxlock, Single Trigger, Vent Rib, Automatic Ejectors, *Modern* 285.00 395.00
- ☐ **Model 160,** Various Gauges, Boxlock, Single Trigger, Vent Rib, Automatic Ejectors, *Modern* 320.00 425.00
- ☐ **Model 180,** Various Gauges, Boxlock, Single Trigger, Vent Rib, Automatic Ejectors, Light Engraving, *Modern* 365.00 475.00
- ☐ **Model 750,** Various Gauges, Merkel Type Sidelock, Single Trigger, Vent Rib, Engraved, *Modern* 320.00 425.00
- ☐ **Model 750,** Various Gauges, Merkel Type Sidelock, Single Trigger, Vent Rib, Engraved, Automatic Ejectors, *Modern* 365.00 495.00
- ☐ **Grand Prix,** 12 or 20 Gauge, Merkel Type Sidelock, Single Selective Trigger, Fancy Engraving, Automatic Ejectors, *Modern* ... 745.00 1,100.00

ATKIN, HENRY E. & CO.
London, England 1874-1900

SHOTGUN, DOUBLE BARREL, SIDE-BY-SIDE
- ☐ **Raleigh,** 12 Gauge, Sidelock, Double Triggers, Checkered Stock, Engraved, Automatic Ejectors, "Purdey" Barrels, *Modern* 5,000.00 8,000.00

AUBREY
Made by Meridan Arms Co., sold by Sears-Roebuck 1900-1930.

HANDGUN, REVOLVER
- ☐ **.32 S & W,** 5 Shot, Double Action, Top Break, *Modern* 55.00 95.00
- ☐ **.38 S & W,** 5 Shot, Double Action, Top Break, *Modern* 55.00 95.00

AUDAX
Trade name of Manufacture D'Armes Des Pyrenees, Hendaye, France, marketed by La Cartoucherie Francaise, Paris 1931-1939.

	V.G.	EXC.
HANDGUN, SEMI-AUTOMATIC		
☐ .25 ACP, Clip Fed, Magazine Disconnect, Grip Safety, *Modern*	75.00	135.00
☐ .32 ACP, Clip Fed, Magazine Disconnect, *Modern*	85.00	150.00

AUSTRALIAN MILITARY
RIFLE, BOLT ACTION
- ☐ **Mk. III**, .303 British, Clip Fed, WW I Issue, *Curio* 160.00 235.00
- ☐ **Mk. III**, .303 British, Clip Fed, WW II Issue, *Curio* 145.00 200.00

RIFLE, SINGLESHOT
- ☐ **Martini**, .32/40, Small Action, *Curio* 200.00 325.00

AUSTRIAN MILITARY
AUTOMATIC WEAPON, ASSAULT RIFLE
- ☐ **FN FAL**, .308 Win., *Class 3* 1,200.00 1,650.00

AUTOMATIC WEAPON, SUBMACHINE GUN
- ☐ **MP Solothurn 34**, 9mm Mauser, Clip Fed, *Class 3* 950.00 1,400.00
- ☐ **MP 34**, 9mm Luger, *Class 3* 600.00 850.00

HANDGUN, FLINTLOCK
- ☐ **.64 Dragoon**, with Shoulder Stock, Singleshot, *Antique* 500.00 775.00

HANDGUN, PERCUSSION
- ☐ **.64 Dragoon**, with Shoulder Stock, Singleshot, *Antique* 325.00 550.00

HANDGUN, REVOLVER
- ☐ **M1898 Rast Gasser**, 8mm Rast-Gasser, *Curio* 175.00 300.00

HANDGUN, SEMI-AUTOMATIC
- ☐ **M1907 Roth Steyr**, 8mm Roth-Steyr, *Curio* 175.00 325.00
- ☐ **M1908 Steyr**, 8mm Roth-Steyr, *Curio* 175.00 300.00
- ☐ **M1911 Steyr Hahn**, 9mm Steyr, *Curio* 225.00 375.00
- ☐ **M1912 Steyr Hahn**, 9mm Steyr, *Curio* 175.00 275.00
- ☐ **Mannlicher 1901**, 7.63 Mannlicher, *Curio* 200.00 375.00
- ☐ **Mannlicher 1905**, 7.63 Mannlicher, *Curio* 175.00 300.00

HANDGUN, SINGLESHOT
- ☐ **Werder Lightning**, 11mm, *Antique* 350.00 500.00

RIFLE, BOLT ACTION
- ☐ **M1883 Schulhof**, 11.15 x 58R Werndl, 8 Shot, *Antique*............ 350.00 500.00
- ☐ **M1885 Steyr**, 11.15 x 58R Werndl, Straight-Pull, *Antique* 275.00 400.00
- ☐ **M1886 Steyr**, 11.15 x 58R Werndl, Straight-Pull Bolt, *Antique* 80.00 150.00
- ☐ **M1888**, 8 x 50R Mannlicher, *Antique* 85.00 150.00
- ☐ **M1888/90**, 8 x 50R Mannlicher, *Antique* 75.00 125.00
- ☐ **M1890**, 8 x 50R Mannlicher, Carbine, *Antique* 80.00 125.00
- ☐ **M1895**, 8 x 50R Mannlicher, Carbine, *Modern* 80.00 125.00
- ☐ **M1895**, 8 x 50R Mannlicher, *Modern* 75.00 115.00
- ☐ **M1895 Stutzen**, 8 x 50R Mannlicher, *Modern* 90.00 175.00

AUTO MAG
Pasadena, Calif., Started about 1968. Made by T D E, Jurras Associates, and High Standard.

HANDGUN, SEMI-AUTOMATIC
- ☐ **Shoulder Stock Only**, *Class 3*, Add **$250.00-$350.00**
- ☐ **First Model (Calif.)**, .357 AMP, Clip Fed, Stainless Steel, Hammer, Adjustable Sights, Cased, *Modern* 850.00 1,450.00
- ☐ **First Model (Calif.)**, .44 AMP, Clip Fed, Stainless Steel, Hammer, Adjustable Sights, Cased, *Modern* 750.00 1,250.00

48 / AUTOMATIC

Austrian Military M1907 Roth Steyr

Auto Mag Model 180

	V.G.	EXC.
☐ **Model 160**, .357 AMP, Clip Fed, Stainless Steel, Hammer, Adjustable Sights, Cased, *Modern*	700.00	975.00
☐ **Model 170**, .41 JMP, Clip Fed, Stainless Steel, Hammer, Adjustable Sights, Cased, *Modern*	800.00	1,150.00
☐ **Model 260**, .357 AMP, Clip Fed, Stainless Steel, Hammer, Adjustable Sights, Cased, *Modern*	650.00	950.00
☐ **Model 280**, .44 AMP, Clip Fed, Stainless Steel, Hammer, Adjustable Sights, Cased, *Modern*	600.00	900.00

AUTOMATIC
Made by Hopkins & Allen, c. 1900.

HANDGUN, REVOLVER
☐ .32 S & W, 5 Shot, Top Break, Hammerless, Double Action, *Modern*	60.00	95.00
☐ .38 S & W, 5 Shot, Top Break, Hammerless, Double Action, *Modern*	60.00	95.00

AUTOMATIC HAMMERLESS
Made by Iver Johnson, c. 1900.

HANDGUN, REVOLVER
☐ .22 L.R.R.F., 7 Shot, Double Action, Top Break, Hammerless, *Modern*	55.00	95.00
☐ .32 S & W, 5 Shot, Top Break, Hammerless, Double Action, *Modern*	60.00	110.00
☐ .38 S & W, 5 Shot, Top Break, Hammerless, Double Action, *Modern*	60.00	110.00

AUTOMATIC PISTOL
Spain, Maker Unknown.

HANDGUN, SEMI-AUTOMATIC
☐ **Pocket**, .32 ACP, Clip Fed, *Modern*	60.00	95.00

	V.G.	EXC.

AUTOMATIC POLICE
See Forehand & Wadsworth.

AUTO-ORDINANCE CORP.
See Thompson.

AUTO-POINTER
Made by Yamamoto Mfg. Co., Imported by Sloans.
SHOTGUN, SEMI-AUTOMATIC
☐ **12 and 20 Gauges**, Tube Feed, Checkered Stock, *Modern* 180.00   280.00

AUTOSTAND
Made for ManuFrance by Mre. d'Armes des Pyrenees.
HANDGUN, SINGLESHOT
☐ **E-1 (Unique)**, .22 L.R.R.F., Target Pistol, Adjustable Sights,
Modern 65.00   90.00

AVENGER
HANDGUN, REVOLVER
☐ **.32 Long R.F.**, 5 Shot, Single Action, Spur Trigger, *Antique* 90.00   140.00

AVION
Azpiri y Cia., Eibar, Spain, c. 1915.
HANDGUN, SEMI-AUTOMATIC
☐ **Vest Pocket**, .25 ACP, Clip Fed, *Curio*........................... 65.00   110.00

A Y A
Aguirre y Aranzabal, Spain. Now Imported by Ventura.
SHOTGUN, DOUBLE BARREL, OVER-UNDER
☐ **Model 37 Super**, Various Gauges, Single Selective Trigger,
Automatic Ejector, Fancy Engraving, Sidelock, *Modern* 1,250.00   1,750.00
SHOTGUN, DOUBLE BARREL, SIDE-BY-SIDE
☐ **Bolero**, Various Gauges, Single Trigger, Checkered Stock, *Modern* 170.00   240.00
☐ **Matador**, Various Gauges, Single Selective Trigger, Checkered
Stock, Selective Ejector, *Modern*................................. 200.00   335.00
☐ **Matador II**, Various Gauges, Single Selective Trigger, Checkered
Stock, Selective Ejector, Vent Rib, *Modern*...................... 250.00   390.00
☐ **Model 1**, Various Gauges, Automatic Ejector, Sidelock, Fancy
Checkering, Engraved, Lightweight, *Modern*..................... 950.00   1,650.00
☐ **Model 117**, 12 Gauge, Sidelock, Single Selective Trigger,
Engraved, Checkered Stock, *Modern*............................. 475.00   700.00
☐ **Model 2**, Various Gauges, Automatic Ejector, Sidelock, Engraved,
Checkered Stock, Double Trigger, *Modern* 475.00   700.00
☐ **Model 53E**, 12 and 20 Gauges, Sidelock, Single Selective Trigger,
Fancy Checkering, Fancy Engraving, *Modern* 800.00   1,350.00
☐ **Model 56**, 12 and 20 Gauges, Sidelock, Raised Matted Rib, Fancy
Checkering, Fancy Engraving, *Modern* 950.00   1,850.00
☐ **Model 76**, 12 and 20 Gauges, Automatic Ejector, Single Selective
Trigger, Engraved, Checkered Stock, *Modern*..................... 275.00   425.00
☐ **Model XXV/SL**, 12 Ga., Sidelock, Automatic Ejector, Engraved
Checkered Stock, *Modern* 575.00   775.00

AZANZA Y ARRIZABALAGA
Eibar, Spain, c. 1916.

	V.G.	EXC.
HANDGUN, SEMI-AUTOMATIC		
☐ **M1916**, .32 ACP, Clip Fed, Long Grip, *Modern*	85.00	135.00

AZUL
Eulegio Aristegui, Eibar, Spain, c. 1930.

HANDGUN, SUBMACHINE GUN
☐ **Super Azul MM31**, 7.63mm Mauser, Selective Fire, Box Magazine, Class 3 .... 750.00 1,250.00

HANDGUN, SEMI-AUTOMATIC
☐ **Azul**, 7.63mm Mauser, Copy of Broomhandle Mauser, *Modern* 475.00 800.00
☐ **Azul**, .25 ACP, Clip Fed, Hammerless, *Modern* 75.00 115.00
☐ **Azul**, .32 ACP, Clip Fed, Hammerless, *Modern* 80.00 125.00
☐ **Azul**, .32 ACP, Clip Fed, Hammer, *Modern* 90.00 145.00

BABCOCK
Maker Unknown c. 1880

HANDGUN, REVOLVER
☐ **.32 Short R.F.**, 5 Shot, Spur Trigger, Solid Frame, Single Action, *Antique* 90.00 160.00

BABY BULLDOG
HANDGUN, REVOLVER
☐ **.22 L.R.R.F.**, Double Action, Hammerless, Folding Trigger, *Modern* 85.00 130.00
☐ **.32 Short R.F.**, Double Action, Hammerless, Folding Trigger, *Modern* 80.00 120.00

BABY RUSSIAN
Made by American Arms Co. c. 1890

☐ **.38 S & W**, 5 Shot, Single Action, Spur Trigger, Top Break, *Curio* 120.00 195.00

BACKHOUSE, RICHARD
Easton, Pa. 1774-1781. See Kentucky Rifles

BACKUP
See T D E and A M T

BACON ARMS CO.
Norwich, Conn. 1858-1891. Also known as Bacon & Co. and Bacon Mfg. Co.

HANDGUN, PERCUSSION
☐ **.34**, Boot Gun, Underhammer, Half-Octagon Barrel, *Antique* 175.00 295.00
☐ **6 Shot**, Fluted Barrel, Pepperbox, Under-Hammer, Pocket Pistol, *Antique* 550.00 750.00

HANDGUN, REVOLVER
☐ **.22 Short R.F.**, 7 Shot, Spur Trigger, Solid Frame, Single Action, *Antique* 95.00 185.00
☐ **.32 Short R.F.**, 5 Shot, Spur Trigger, Solid Frame, Single Action, *Antique* 95.00 170.00
☐ **.32 Short R.F.**, 6 Shot, Solid Frame, Spur Trigger, Single Action, *Antique* 155.00 285.00
☐ **.32 Short R.F.**, 6 Shot, Solid Frame, Single Action with Trigger Guard, *Antique* 130.00 260.00
☐ **"Navy"**, **.38 Long R.F.**, 6 Shot, 7½" Barrel, Solid Frame, Spur Trigger, Single Action, *Antique* 275.00 470.00

BAKER GUN AND FORGING COMPANY / 51

	V.G.	EXC.

HANDGUN, SINGLESHOT
☐ **Derringer**, .32 R.F., Spur Trigger, Side-Swing Barrel, *Antique* 160.00   320.00

BACHE
HANDGUN, FLINTLOCK
☐ **Belt Pistol**, Engraved, Gold Damascened, Silver Wire Stock Inlays,
Steel Furniture, Carved Stock, *Antique* 875.00 1,500.00

BAIKAL
Made in U.S.S.R., imported by Commercial Trading Imports.
SHOTGUN, DOUBLE BARREL, OVER-UNDER
☐ **MC-5-105**, 20 Gauge, Boxlock, Engraved, Checkered Stock,
Double Triggers, Solid Rib, Cased, *Modern* 550.00   800.00
☐ **MC-6-105**, 12 Gauge, Boxlock, Engraved, Checkered Stock,
Double Triggers, Solid Rib, Cased, *Modern* 750.00 1,250.00
☐ **MC-7-105**, 12 or 20 Gauge, Boxlock, Engraved, Checkered Stock,
Single Triggers, Selective Ejector, Solid Rib, Cased, *Modern* 1,400.00 2,150.00
☐ **MC-8-105**, 12 Gauge, Trap or Skeet, Boxlock, Engraved,
Checkered Stock, Single Trigger, Solid Rib, Cased, *Modern* 1,250.00 1,850.00
☐ **MC-109**, 12 Gauge, Sidelock, Engraved, Checkered Stock, Single
Selective Trigger, Selective Ejectors, Vent Rib, Cased, *Modern* 2,750.00 4,000.00
☐ **IJ-27E1C**, 12 or 20 Gauge, Boxlock, Engraved, Checkered Stock,
Single Selective Trigger, Selective Ejectors, Vent Rib, *Modern* 225.00   350.00
☐ **IJ-27E1C Silver**, 12 or 20 Gauge, Boxlock, Engraved, Checkered
Stock, Single Selective Trigger, Selective Ejectors, Vent Rib,
Modern 300.00   425.00
☐ **IJ-27E1C Super**, 12 or 20 Gauge, Boxlock, Engraved, Checkered
Stock, Single Selective Trigger, Selective Ejectors, Vent Rib,
Modern 390.00   575.00
☐ **TOZ-34E**, 12 or 28 Gauge, Boxlock, Engraved, Checkered Stock,
Double Triggers, Vent Rib, *Modern* 325.00   475.00
SHOTGUN, DOUBLE BARREL, SIDE-BY-SIDE
☐ **MC-110**, 12 or 20 Gauge, Boxlock, Engraved, Checkered Stock,
Double Triggers, Solid Rib, Cased, *Modern* 1,500.00 2,250.00
☐ **MC-111**, 12 Gauge, Sidelock, Engraved, Checkered Stock, Single
Selective Trigger, Selective Ejectors, Cased, *Modern* 2,750.00 4,000.00
☐ **IJ-58MAE**, 12 or 20 Gauge, Boxlock, Engraved, Checkered Stock,
Double Triggers, *Modern* 125.00   200.00
SHOTGUN, SINGLESHOT
☐ **IJ-18E**, 12 or 20 Gauges, Checkered Stock, *Modern* 35.00   55.00

BAKER GUN & FORGING CO.
Batavia, N.Y. 1886-1919, Purchased by Folsom in 1919.
RIFLE, SEMI-AUTOMATIC
☐ **Batavia**, .22 Short, Clip Fed, *Modern* 250.00   395.00
SHOTGUN, DOUBLE BARREL, SIDE-BY-SIDE
Single Trigger, Add **$85.00-150.00**
Deduct **50%** for Damascus Barrels
Automatic Ejectors, Add **$95.00-195.00**
☐ **Batavia Leader**, Various Gauges, Sidelock, Double Trigger,
Checkered Stock, *Modern* 275.00   425.00
☐ **Batavia Leader Special**, Various Gauges, Sidelock, Double Trigger,
Checkered Stock, Automatic Ejector, *Modern* 350.00   535.00

52 / BAKER GUN COMPANY

	V.G.	EXC.
☐ **Black Beauty**, Various Gauges, Sidelock, Double Trigger, Checkered Stock, *Modern*	375.00	595.00
☐ **Black Beauty Special**, Various Gauges, Sidelock, Double Trigger, Checkered Stock, Automatic Ejector, *Modern*	475.00	675.00
☐ **Deluxe ($1,000 Grade)**, Various Gauges, Sidelock, Fancy Wood, Fancy Engraving, Fancy Checkering, Automatic Ejector, *Modern*	8,900.00	13,250.00
☐ **Deluxe ($300 Grade)**, Various Gauges, Sidelock, Fancy Wood, Fancy Engraving, Fancy Checkering, Automatic Ejector, *Modern*	2,850.00	4,200.00
☐ **Expert**, Various Gauges, Sidelock, Fancy Wood, Fancy Engraving, Fancy Checkering, Automatic Ejector, *Modern*	2,000.00	2,950.00
☐ **Grade A**, Various Gauges, Sidelock, Hammerless, Engraved, Damascus Barrel, *Modern*	175.00	295.00
☐ **Grade B**, Various Gauges, Sidelock, Hammerless, Engraved, Damascus Barrels, *Modern*	175.00	280.00
☐ **Grade C Batavia**, Various Gauges, Boxlock, Hammerless, Engraved, Damascus Barrels, *Modern*	160.00	225.00
☐ **Grade H Deluxe**, Various Gauges, Sidelock, Fancy Engraving, *Modern*	2,500.00	3,450.00
☐ **Grade L Pigeon**, Various Gauges, Sidelock, Fancy Engraving, *Modern*	1,250.00	1,950.00
☐ **Grade N Krupp Trap**, 12 Ga., Sidelock, Engraved, *Modern*	800.00	1,250.00
☐ **Grade R**, Various Gauges, Sidelock, Light Engraving, *Modern*	375.00	625.00
☐ **Grade S**, Various Gauges, Sidelock, Light Engraving, *Modern*	350.00	525.00
Model 1896, 10 and 12 Gauges, Hammers, *Modern*	170.00	250.00
☐ **Model 1897**, Various Gauges, Hammers, *Modern*	170.00	250.00
☐ **New Baker Model**, 10 and 12 Gauges, Hammers, *Modern*	160.00	225.00
☐ **Paragon**, Various Gauges, Sidelock, Double Trigger, Engraved, Fancy Checkering, *Modern*	700.00	1,000.00
☐ **Paragon**, Various Gauges, Sidelock, Double Trigger, Engraved, Fancy Checkering, Automatic Ejector, *Modern*	800.00	1,350.00
☐ **Paragon Special**, 12 Ga., Sidelock, Fancy Wood, Fancy Engraving, *Modern*	950.00	1,600.00

SHOTGUN, SINGLESHOT
☐ **Elite**, 12 Ga., Vent Rib, Fancy Engraving, *Modern*	700.00	1,100.00
☐ **Sterling**, 12 Ga., Vent Rib, Light Engraving, *Modern*	500.00	700.00
☐ **Superba**, 12 Ga., Trap Grade, Fancy Wood, Fancy Engraving, Fancy Checkering, Automatic Ejector, *Antique*	1,850.00	2,600.00

BAKER GUN CO.
Made in Belgium for H & D Folsum Arms Co.

SHOTGUN, DOUBLE BARREL, SIDE-BY-SIDE
☐ **Various Gauges**, Outside Hammers, Damascus Barrel, *Antique*	80.00	150.00
☐ **Various Gauges**, Hammerless, Steel Barrel, *Antique*	95.00	175.00
☐ **Various Gauges**, Hammerless, Damascus Barrel, *Antique*	75.00	150.00
☐ **Various Gauges**, Outside Hammers, Steel Barrel, *Antique*	90.00	175.00

SHOTGUN, SINGLESHOT
☐ **Various Gauges**, Hammer, Steel Barrel, *Antique*	45.00	75.00

BAKER, EZEKIEL
London, England 1784-1825

HANDGUN, PERCUSSION
☐ **.58**, Holster Pistol, Round Barrel, Light Ornamentation, *Antique*	450.00	625.00

BAKER, JOHN
Providence, Pa. 1768-1775. See Kentucky Rifles.

BAKER, W.H. & CO.
Marathon, N.Y. 1870, Syracuse, N.Y. 1878-1886.

	V.G.	EXC.

COMBINATION WEAPON, DRILLING
- ☐ **Hammer Drilling**, Various Gauges, Damascus Barrels, Front Trigger Break, *Antique* 400.00   650.00

RIFLE, PERCUSSION
- ☐ **.60**, Brass Furniture, Scope Mounted, Target, Octagon Barrel, *Antique* 1,750.00   2,400.00

SHOTGUN, DOUBLE BARREL, SIDE-BY-SIDE
- ☐ **Hammer Double**, 10 and 12 Gauges, Damascus Barrels, Front Trigger Break, *Antique* 200.00   325.00

BALL & WILLIAMS
Worcester, Mass. 1861-1866.

RIFLE, SINGLESHOT
- ☐ **Ballard**, .44 Long R.F., Military, Carbine, Falling Block, *Antique* 550.00   725.00
- ☐ **Ballard**, .46 Long R.F., Kentucky Rifle, Falling Block, *Antique* 700.00   850.00
- ☐ **Ballard**, Various Rimfires, Falling Block, Sporting Rifle, *Antique* ... 350.00   500.00
- ☐ **Ballard**, Various Rimfires, Military, Falling Block, *Antique* 600.00   875.00
- ☐ **Merwin & Bray**, .54 Ballard R.F., Military, Carbine, Falling Block, *Antique* 550.00   825.00
- ☐ **Merwin & Bray**, Various Rimfires, Falling Block, Sporting Rifle, *Antique* 450.00   650.00

BALLARD RIFLE
Made by Ball & Williams 1861-1866, Merrimack Arms & Mfg. Co. 1866-1869, Brown Mfg. Co. 1869-1873, J.M. Marlin from 1875.

RIFLE, SINGLESHOT
- ☐ **#1½ Hunter (Marlin)**, .40-65 Ballard Everlasting, Falling Block, Sporting Rifle, Open Rear Sight, *Antique* 525.00   750.00
- ☐ **#1 Hunter (Marlin)**, .44 Long R F/C F, Falling Block, Sporting Rifle, Recoil Pad, *Antique* 525.00   750.00
- ☐ **#2 (Marlin)**, .44-40 WCF, Falling Block, Sporting Rifle, Open Rear Sight, *Antique* 575.00   825.00
- ☐ **#2 (Marlin)**, Various Calibers, Falling Block, Sporting Rifle, Recoil Pad, Early Model, *Antique* 525.00   750.00
- ☐ **#3½ (Marlin)**, .40-65 Ballard Everlasting, Falling Block, Target Rifle, Target Sights, Octagon Barrel, *Antique* 775.00   975.00
- ☐ **#3 Gallery (Marlin)**, .22 Short R.F., Falling Block, Target Rifle, Early Model, *Antique* 350.00   550.00
- ☐ **#4½ (Marlin)**, .40-65 Ballard Everlasting, Falling Block, Mid-Range Target Rifle, Checkered Stock, *Antique* 725.00   975.00
- ☐ **#4½ (Marlin)**, .45-70 Government, Falling Block, Sporting Rifle, *Antique* 700.00   925.00
- ☐ **#4½ (Marlin)**, Various Calibers, Falling Block, Sporting Rifle, *Antique* 645.00   850.00
- ☐ **#4½ (Marlin)**, Various Calibers, Falling Block, Mid-Range Target Rifle, Target Sights, Fancy Wood, *Antique* 850.00   1,450.00
- ☐ **#4 Perfection (Marlin)**, Various Calibers, Falling Block, Target Rifle, Target Sights, Set Trigger, Early Model, *Antique* 575.00   800.00
- ☐ **#5 Pacific (Marlin)**, .45-70 Government, Falling Block, Target Rifle, Open Rear Sight, Set Trigger, Octagon Barrel, *Antique* 575.00   925.00
- ☐ **#5 Pacific (Marlin)**, Various Calibers, Falling Block, Target Rifle, Open Rear Sight, Set Trigger, Octagon Barrel, *Antique* 475.00   775.00
- ☐ **#6½ (Marlin)**, .40-65 Ballard Everlasting, Falling Block, Off-Hand Target Rifle, Target Sights, Set Trigger, *Antique* 825.00   1,250.00

54 / BALLARD AND COMPANY

	V.G.	EXC.
☐ **#6½ (Marlin)**, Various Calibers, Falling Block, Mid-Range Target Rifle, *Antique*	875.00	1,350.00
☐ **#6 Pacific (Marlin)**, Various Calibers, Falling Block, Schutzen Rifle, Target Sights, Fancy Wood, Set Trigger, *Antique*	1,300.00	1,900.00
☐ **#7 A-1 (Marlin)**, .44-75 Ballard Everlasting, Falling Block, Creedmore Long Range, Target Sights, Fancy Wood, Set Trigger, *Antique*	1,900.00	2,600.00
☐ **#7 A (Marlin)**, .44-100 Ballard Everlasting, Falling Block, Long Range Target Rifle, Target Sights, Set Trigger, *Antique*	750.00	1,200.00
☐ **#7 A-1 (Marlin)**, .44-100 Ballard Everlasting, Falling Block, Long Range Target Rifle, Target Sights, Set Trigger, Fancy Wood, *Antique*	1,100.00	1,750.00
☐ **#7 A-1 Extra Deluxe**, .44-100 Ballard Everlasting, Falling Block, Long Range Target Rifle, Target Sights, Set Trigger, Fancy Wood, *Antique*	1,700.00	2,350.00
☐ **1½ Hunter (Marlin)**, .45-70 Government, Falling Block, Sporting Rifle, Open Rear Sight, *Antique*	575.00	825.00
☐ **1¾ Far West (Marlin)**, .40-65 Ballard Everlasting, Falling Block, Sporting Rifle, Open Rear Sight, Set Trigger, *Antique*	550.00	775.00
☐ **1¾ Far West (Marlin)**, .45-70 Government, Falling Block, Sporting Rifle, Open Rear Sight, Set Trigger, *Antique*	600.00	875.00
☐ **5½ Montana (Marlin)**, .45-100 Sharps, Falling Block, Sporting Rifle, Octagon Barrel, *Antique*	775.00	1,250.00
☐ **#8 (Marlin)**, .44-75 Ballard Everlasting, Falling Block, Creedmore Long Range, Target Sights, Pistol-Grip Stock, Set Trigger, *Antique*	425.00	750.00
☐ **#9 (Marlin)**, .44-75 Ballard Everlasting, Falling Block, Creedmore Long Range, Target Sights, Set Trigger, *Antique*	475.00	875.00
☐ **(Ball & Williams)**, .44 Long R.F., Military, Carbine, Falling Block, *Antique*	550.00	725.00
☐ **(Ball & Williams)**, .46 Long R.F., Kentucky Rifle, Falling Block, *Antique*	700.00	875.00
☐ **(Ball & Williams)**, .54 Ballard R.F., Military, Carbine, Falling Block, *Antique*	575.00	825.00
☐ **(Ball & Williams)**, Various Rimfires, Falling Block, Sporting Rifle, *Antique*	375.00	525.00
☐ **(Ball & Williams)**, Various Rimfires, Military, Falling Block, *Antique*	650.00	900.00
☐ **Brown Mfg. Co.**, .44 Long R.F., Falling Block, Mid-Range Target Rifle, *Antique*	725.00	975.00
☐ **Hunter**, .44 Long R F/C F, Falling Block, Sporting Rifle, Recoil Pad, *Antique*	475.00	625.00
☐ **Merrimack Arms**, .44 Long R.F., Falling Block, Carbine, *Antique*	550.00	775.00
☐ **Merrimack Arms**, .46 Long R.F., Falling Block, Military, *Antique*	650.00	850.00
☐ **Merrimack Arms**, .56-52 Spencer R.F., Falling Block, Carbine, *Antique*	550.00	775.00
☐ **Merrimack Arms**, Various Rimfires, Falling Block, Sporting Rifle, *Antique*	550.00	750.00
☐ **Merwin & Bray**, Various Rimfires, Falling Block, Sporting Rifle, *Antique*	450.00	650.00

BALLARD & CO.
Worcester, Mass 1861-1871. Also see U.S. Military.

RIFLE, SINGLESHOT

	V.G.	EXC.
☐ **#2 (Marlin)**, Various Calibers, Falling Block, Sporting Rifle, *Antique*	600.00	825.00
☐ **#3 Gallery (Marlin)**, Various Calibers, Falling Block, Target Rifle, *Antique*	575.00	725.00

BAUER FIREARMS / 55

	V.G.	EXC.
☐ **#3 Gallery (Marlin)**, Various Rimfires, Falling Block, Target Rifle, *Antique*	350.00	550.00
☐ **#3-F Gallery (Marlin)**, .22 Long R.F., Falling Block, Target Rifle, Fancy Wood, *Antique*	650.00	825.00
☐ **#4 Perfection (Marlin)**, Various Calibers, Falling Block, Target Rifle, Target Sights, Set Trigger, Octagon Barrel, *Antique*	550.00	800.00

BANG-UP
Made by Hopkins & Allen c. 1880.

HANDGUN, REVOLVER
☐ **.22 Short R.F.**, 7 Shot, Spur Trigger, Solid Frame, Single Action, *Antique*	90.00	160.00

BANISTER, T.
England, c. 1700.

HANDGUN, FLINTLOCK
☐ **Pocket Pistol**, Screw Barrel, Steel Mounts, Engraved, High Quality, *Antique*	975.00	1,650.00

BARKER, F.A.
Fayettesville, N.C. 1860-1864. See Confederate Military.

BARKER, T.
Made by Crescent; Also Made in Belgium.

SHOTGUN, DOUBLE BARREL, SIDE-BY-SIDE
☐ **Various Gauges**, Outside Hammers, Damascus Barrel, *Modern*	80.00	150.00
☐ **Various Gauges**, Hammerless, Steel Barrel, *Modern*	95.00	175.00
☐ **Various Gauges**, Hammerless, Damascus Barrel, *Modern*	75.00	150.00
☐ **Various Gauges**, Outside Hammers, Steel Barrel, *Modern*	90.00	175.00

SHOTGUN, SINGLESHOT
☐ **Various Gauges**, Hammer, Steel Barrel, *Modern*	45.00	75.00

BARLOW, J.
Moscow, Ind. 1836-1840. See Kentucky Rifles.

BARNETT & SON
London, England 1750-1832.

RIFLE, FLINTLOCK
☐ **.75, 3rd. Model Brown Bess**, Musket, Military, *Antique*	900.00	1,550.00

BARNETT, J. & SONS
London, England 1835-1875.

RIFLE, PERCUSSION
☐ **.577, C.W. Enfield**, Rifled, Musket, Military, *Antique*	425.00	675.00

BARRETT, J.
Wythesville, Va. 1857-1865. See Confederate Military.

BAUER FIREARMS
Fraser, Mich.

COMBINATION WEAPON, OVER-UNDER
☐ **Rabbit**, .22/.410, Metal Frame, Survival Gun, *Modern*	45.00	70.00

56 / BAUER, GEORGE

	V.G.	EXC.

HANDGUN, SEMI—AUTOMATIC
- ☐ **25-Bicentennial**, .25 ACP, Clip Fed, Pocket Pistol, Stainless Steel, Hammerless, Engraved, *Modern* 170.00 225.00
- ☐ **25-SS**, .25 ACP, Clip Fed, Pocket Pistol, Stainless Steel, Hammerless, *Modern* 65.00 95.00

BAUER, GEORGE
Lancaster, Pa. 1770-1781. See Kentucky Rifles.

BAY STATE ARMS CO.
Uxbridge & Worcester, Mass. 1873-1874.

RIFLE, SINGLESHOT
- ☐ **.32 Long R.F.**, Dropping Block, *Antique* 95.00 175.00
- ☐ **Various Calibers**, Target Rifle, *Antique* 575.00 825.00

SHOTGUN, SINGLESHOT
- ☐ **Davenport Patent**, 12 Ga., *Antique* 180.00 275.00

Bayard Model 1930

Bayard 1908 Pocket .32

BAYARD
Belgium. Made by Anciens Etablissments Pieper c. 1900.

HANDGUN, SEMI-AUTOMATIC
- ☐ **Bergmann/Bayard 1910**, 9mm Bayard, Clip Fed, Blue, Commercial, *Curio* 475.00 700.00
- ☐ **Bergmann/Bayard 1910**, 9mm Bayard, Clip Fed, Blue, Commercial, with Holster/Stock, *Curio* 550.00 875.00
- ☐ **Model 1908 Pocket**, .25 ACP, Blue, Clip Fed, *Modern* 95.00 175.00
- ☐ **Model 1910 Pocket**, .32 ACP, Blue, Clip Fed, *Modern* 135.00 225.00
- ☐ **Model 1911 Pocket**, .380 ACP, Blue, Clip Fed, *Modern* 165.00 275.00
- ☐ **Model 1912 Pocket**, .25 ACP, Blue, Clip Fed, *Modern* 95.00 175.00
- ☐ **Model 1923 Pocket**, .25 ACP, Blue, Clip Fed, *Modern* 115.00 185.00
- ☐ **Model 1923 Pocket**, .32 ACP, Blue, Clip Fed, *Modern* 135.00 225.00
- ☐ **Model 1923 Pocket**, .380 ACP, Blue, Clip Fed, *Modern* 165.00 265.00
- ☐ **Model 1930 Pocket**, .25 ACP, Blue, Clip Fed, *Modern* 115.00 185.00
- ☐ **Model 1930 Pocket**, .32 ACP, Blue, Clip Fed, *Modern* 145.00 215.00
- ☐ **Model 1930 Pocket**, .380 ACP, Blue, Clip Fed, *Modern* 165.00 275.00

HANDGUN, REVOLVER
- ☐ **S & W Style**, .32 S&W Long, Double Action, *Modern* 75.00 120.00
- ☐ **S & W Style**, .38 S&W, Double Action, *Modern* 75.00 125.00

	V.G.	EXC.

RIFLE, SINGLESHOT
- ☐ **Boy's Rifle**, .22 L.R.R.F., Plain, Takedown, *Modern* 30.00 50.00
- ☐ **Half-Auto Carbine**, .22 Short, Plain, *Curio* 35.00 65.00
- ☐ **Half-Auto Carbine**, .22 Short, Checkered Stock, *Curio* 50.00 85.00

SHOTGUN, DOUBLE BARREL, SIDE-BY-SIDE
- ☐ **Hammerless**, 12 Gauge, Double Triggers, Light Engraving, Boxlock, Steel Barrels, *Curio* 125.00 195.00
- ☐ **Hammer**, 12 Gauge, Double Triggers, Light Engraving, Boxlock, Damascus Barrels, *Curio* 80.00 145.00
- ☐ **Hammer**, 12 Gauge, Double Triggers, Light Engraving, Boxlock, Steel Barrels, *Curio* 95.00 165.00
- ☐ **Hammer**, 12 Gauge, Double Triggers, Fancy Engraving, Boxlock, Steel Barrels, *Curio* 170.00 275.00

BEATTIE, JAMES
London, England 1835-1865.

HANDGUN, PERCUSSION
- ☐ **.40 Six Shot**, Revolver, Octagon Barrel, Fancy Wood, Fancy Engraving, Cased with Accessories, *Antique* 2,900.00 3,750.00

BECK, GIDEON
Lancaster, Pa. 1780-1788. See Kentucky Rifles and Pistols.

BECK, JOHN
Lancaster, Pa. 1772-1777. See Kentucky Rifles and Pistols.

BECK, ISAAC
Miffinberg, Pa. 1830-1840.

RIFLE, PERCUSSION
- ☐ **.47**, Octagon Barrel, Brass Furniture, *Antique* 750.00 1,150.00

BEERSTECHER, FREDERICK
Lewisburg, Pa. 1849-1860.

HANDGUN, PERCUSSION
- ☐ **.40**, Double Shot, Superimposed Loading, Derringer Style, *Antique* 2,150.00 4,350.00

BEEMAN'S PRECISION
San Raphael, Calif., Importers.

RIFLE, BOLT ACTION
- ☐ **Weihrauch HW60**, .22 L.R.R.F., Singleshot Target Rifle, Target Sights, Target Stock, Heavy Barrel, *Modern* 250.00 375.00
- ☐ **FWB 2000**, .22 L.R.R.F., I.S.U. Singleshot Target Rifle, Target Sights, Target Stock, Heavy Barrel, *Modern* 400.00 575.00

BEHOLLA
Made by Becker & Hollander, Suhl, Germany c. 1910. Also made under this patent were the Stenda, Leonhardt, and Menta.

HANDGUN, SEMI-AUTOMATIC
- ☐ **.32 ACP**, Clip Fed, Commerical, *Modern* 125.00 225.00
- ☐ **.32 ACP**, Clip Fed, Gering, Commerical, *Modern* 125.00 225.00
- ☐ **.32 ACP**, Clip Fed, Military, *Modern* 145.00 250.00

BELGIAN MILITARY
Also see Browning, FN

	V.G.	EXC.
RIFLE, BOLT ACTION		
☐ **M 1924**, Various Calibers, Military, *Modern*	115.00	190.00
☐ **M 1930**, Various Calibers, Military, *Modern*	115.00	190.00
☐ **M 1934/30**, Various Calibers, Military, *Modern*	115.00	190.00
☐ **M 1950**, .30-06 Springfield, Military, *Modern*	165.00	250.00
☐ **M1889 Mauser**, Military, *Modern*	80.00	125.00
☐ **M1889 Mauser**, Carbine, Military, *Modern*	85.00	135.00
☐ **M1935 Mauser**, Military, *Modern*	95.00	165.00
☐ **M1936 Mauser**, Military, *Modern*	85.00	145.00
RIFLE, SEMI-AUTOMATIC		
☐ **M 1949**, .30-06 Springfield, Military, *Modern*	400.00	600.00
☐ **M 1949**, Various Calibers, Military, *Modern*	350.00	475.00

BELL, JOHN
Carlisle, Pa. c. 1800. See Kentucky Rifles and Pistols.

BELLMORE GUN CO.
Made by Crescent c. 1900.

	V.G.	EXC.
SHOTGUN, DOUBLE BARREL, SIDE-BY-SIDE		
☐ **Various Gauges**, Outside Hammers, Damascus Barrel, *Modern*	80.00	150.00
☐ **Various Gauges**, Hammerless, Steel Barrel, *Modern*	95.00	175.00
☐ **Various Gauges**, Hammerless, Damascus Barrel, *Modern*	75.00	150.00
☐ **Various Gauges**, Outside Hammers, Steel Barrel, *Modern*	90.00	175.00
SHOTGUN, SINGLESHOT		
☐ **Various Gauges**, Hammer, Steel Barrel, *Modern*	45.00	75.00

BENELLI
Made in Italy, imported by H & K Inc.

	V.G.	EXC.
HANDGUN, SEMI-AUTOMATIC		
☐ **B 76**, 9mm Luger, Clip Fed, Blue, *Modern*	175.00	265.00
SHOTGUN, SEMI-AUTOMATIC		
☐ **Model SL 121V**, 12 Gauge, Slug Gun, Open Sights, Checkered Stock, Recoil Pad, *Modern*	240.00	375.00
☐ **Model SL 121MI**, 12 Gauge, Police, Open Sights, Checkered Stock, Recoil Pad, *Modern*	250.00	380.00
☐ **Model SL 201**, 20 Gauge, Checkered Stock, Plain Barrel, *Modern*	225.00	345.00
☐ **Model 123V**, 12 Gauge, Standard Model, Checkered Stock, Vent Rib, *Modern*	225.00	345.00
☐ **Model 123V Deluxe**, 12 Gauge, Engraved Model, Checkered Stock, Vent Rib, *Modern*	300.00	450.00
☐ **Special Trap**, 12 Gauge, White Receiver, Checkered Stock, Vent Rib, *Modern*	375.00	550.00
☐ **Special Skeet**, 12 Gauge, White Receiver, Checkered Stock, Vent Rib, *Modern*	400.00	575.00

BENFER, AMOS
Beaverstown, Pa. c. 1810. See Kentucky Rifles and Pistols.

BERETTA
Pietro Beretta; Gardone V.T., Italy

	V.G.	EXC.

AUTOMATIC WEAPON, ASSAULT RIFLE
- ☐ **Model 70**, .223 Rem., Clip Fed, Plastic Stock, *Class 3* 600.00 950.00
- ☐ **Model BM59**, .308 Win., Clip Fed, Bipod, *Class 3* 650.00 975.00
- ☐ **BM59 Garand Conversion**, .308 Win., Clip Fed, Bipod, *Class 3* 950.00 1,450.00
- ☐ **Model SC70L**, .223 Rem., Clip Fed, Folding Stock, *Class 3* 575.00 800.00
- ☐ **Model SC70S**, .223 Rem., Clip Fed, Folding Stock, Short Barreled Rifle, *Class 3* 575.00 800.00

AUTOMATIC WEAPON, SUBMACHINE GUN
- ☐ **Model 12**, 9mm Luger, Clip Fed, Folding Stock, *Class 3* 350.00 500.00
- ☐ **Model 38/49**, 9mm Luger, Clip Fed, Wood Stock, *Class 3* 350.00 500.00
- ☐ **Model MP38/44**, 9mm Luger, Clip Fed, Military, *Class 3* 725.00 975.00
- ☐ **Model MP38A**, 9mm Luger, Clip Fed, Military, Wood Stock, *Class 3* 625.00 900.00
- ☐ **Model MP38A**, 9mm Luger, Clip Fed, Commercial, Wood Stock, *Class 3* 850.00 1,175.00

HANDGUN, SEMI-AUTOMATIC
- ☐ **1915**, .32 ACP, Clip Fed, Military, *Modern* 175.00 265.00
- ☐ **1915**, .380 ACP, Clip Fed, Military, *Modern* 265.00 350.00
- ☐ **1915/1919**, .32 ACP, Clip Fed, Military, *Modern* 200.00 275.00
- ☐ **1919 V P**, .25 ACP, Clip Fed, *Modern* 95.00 175.00
- ☐ **Cougar**, .380 ACP, Clip Fed, *Modern* 125.00 200.00
- ☐ **Jaguar**, .22 L.R.R.F., Clip Fed, *Modern* 95.00 175.00
- ☐ **Jetfire**, .25 ACP, Clip Fed, Blue, *Modern* 75.00 125.00
- ☐ **Jetfire**, .25 ACP, Clip Fed, Nickel, *Modern* 80.00 130.00
- ☐ **Minx**, .22 Short, Clip Fed, Blue, *Modern* 75.00 125.00
- ☐ **Minx**, .22 Short, Clip Fed, Nickel, *Modern* 80.00 130.00
- ☐ **Model 100**, .32 ACP, Clip Fed, *Modern* 95.00 160.00
- ☐ **Model 101**, .22 L.R.R.F., Clip Fed, Adjustable Sights, *Modern* 110.00 175.00
- ☐ **Model 1923**, 9mm Luger, Clip Fed, Military, *Modern* 225.00 350.00
- ☐ **Model 1923**, 9mm Luger, Clip Fed, Military, with Detachable Shoulder Stock, *Curio* 650.00 825.00
- ☐ **Model 1931 Navy**, .32 ACP, Clip Fed, Military, *Modern* 200.00 285.00
- ☐ **Model 1934**, .380 ACP, Clip Fed, Military, *Modern* 110.00 175.00
- ☐ **Model 1934**, .380 ACP, Clip Fed, Commercial, *Modern* 140.00 225.00
- ☐ **Model 1935**, .32 ACP, Clip Fed, Commercial, *Modern* 115.00 195.00
- ☐ **Model 1935**, .32 ACP, Clip Fed, Military, *Modern* 110.00 170.00
- ☐ **Model 318**, .25 ACP, Clip Fed, *Modern* 110.00 175.00
- ☐ **Model 418**, .25 ACP, Clip Fed, *Modern* 110.00 175.00
- ☐ **Model 420**, .25 ACP, Clip Fed, Chrome, Light Engraving, *Modern* ... 185.00 295.00
- ☐ **Model 421**, .25 ACP, Clip Fed, Gold Plated, Fancy Engraving, *Modern* 270.00 395.00
- ☐ **Model 70S**, .380 ACP, Clip Fed, *Modern* 125.00 210.00
- ☐ **Model 70T**, .32 ACP, Clip Fed, Adjustable Sights, *Modern* 115.00 195.00
- ☐ **Model 76**, .22 L.R.R.F., Clip Fed, Adjustable Sights, *Modern* 185.00 275.00
- ☐ **Model 81**, .32 ACP, Clip Fed, Double Action, *Modern* 200.00 315.00
- ☐ **Model 82**, .32 ACP, Clip Fed, Double Action, *Modern* 200.00 300.00
- ☐ **Model 84**, .380 ACP, Clip Fed, Double Action, *Modern* 200.00 300.00
- ☐ **Model 85**, .380 ACP, Clip Fed, Double Action, *Modern* 215.00 315.00
- ☐ **Model 84 Tercentennial**, .380 ACP, Clip Fed, Double Action, Engraved, Cased, *Modern* 750.00 1,250.00
- ☐ **Model 90**, .32 ACP, Clip Fed, Double Trigger, *Modern* 195.00 275.00
- ☐ **Model 92**, 9mm Luger, 13 Shot Clip Fed, Double Action, *Modern* ... 325.00 445.00
- ☐ **Model 92**, 9mm Luger, 15 Shot Clip Fed, Double Action, *Modern* ... 340.00 460.00
- ☐ **Model 948**, .22 L.R.R.F., Clip Fed, Lightweight, *Modern* 85.00 135.00
- ☐ **Model 949 Olympic**, .22 L.R.R.F., Clip Fed, Target Pistol, *Modern* 225.00 330.00
- ☐ **Model 949 Olympic**, .22 Short R.F., Clip Fed, Target Pistol, *Modern* 225.00 330.00

60 / BERETTA

Beretta Model 1935 .32 ACP

Beretta Bantan

Beretta 1915/19 .32

Beretta Model 1915

	V.G.	EXC.
☐ **Model 950 Minx**, .22 Short R.F., Clip Fed, 2" Barrel, *Modern*	90.00	135.00
☐ **Model 950B Minx**, .22 Short R.F., Clip Fed, 4" Barrel, *Modern*	90.00	140.00
☐ **Model 951 Brigadier**, 9mm Luger, Clip Fed, Commercial, *Modern*	225.00	325.00
☐ **Model 951 Egyptian**, 9mm Luger, Clip Fed, Military, *Curio*	450.00	675.00
☐ **Model 951 Israeli**, 9mm Luger, Clip Fed, Military, *Curio*	450.00	675.00
☐ **Puma**, .32 ACP, Clip Fed, *Modern*	115.00	195.00

RIFLE, SEMI-AUTOMATIC

	V.G.	EXC.
☐ **Olympia**, .22 L.R.R.F., Clip Fed, Tangent Sights, Checkered Stock, *Modern*	125.00	195.00
☐ **Silver Gyrfalcon**, .22 L.R.R.F., Checkered Stock, *Modern*	115.00	190.00
☐ **Super Sport**, .22 L.R.R.F., Fancy Checkering, Clip Fed, *Modern*	135.00	215.00

SHOTGUN, DOUBLE BARREL, OVER-UNDER

	V.G.	EXC.
☐ **Golden Snipe**, 12 and 20 Gauges, Single Trigger, Automatic Ejector, Engraved, Fancy Checkering, *Modern*	350.00	450.00
☐ **Golden Snipe**, 12 and 20 Gauges, Single Selective Trigger, Automatic Ejector, Engraved, Fancy Checkering, *Modern*	475.00	625.00
☐ **Golden Snipe Deluxe**, 12 and 20 Gauges, Single Selective Trigger, Automatic Ejector, Fancy Engraving, Fancy Checkering, *Modern*	490.00	700.00
☐ **Model ASEL**, 12 and 20 Gauges, Single Trigger, Checkered Stock, *Modern*	695.00	900.00
☐ **Model BL 1**, 12 Ga., Field Grade, Double Trigger, Checkered Stock, *Modern*	275.00	365.00

BERETTA / 61

	V.G.	EXC.
☐ **Model BL 2**, 12 Ga., Field Grade, Single Selective Trigger, Checkered Stock, *Modern*	325.00	445.00
☐ **Model BL 3**, 12 Ga., Trap Grade, Single Selective Trigger, Checkered Stock, Light Engraving, Vent Rib, *Modern*	400.00	515.00
☐ **Model BL 3**, Various Gauges, Skeet Grade, Single Selective Trigger, Checkered Stock, Light Engraving, Vent Rib, *Modern*	400.00	510.00
☐ **Model BL 3**, Various Gauges, Field Grade, Single Selective Trigger, Checkered Stock, Light Engraving, Vent Rib, *Modern*	400.00	510.00
☐ **Model BL 4**, 12 Ga., Trap Grade, Single Selective Trigger, Selective Ejector, Engraved, Vent Rib, *Modern*	550.00	700.00
☐ **Model BL 4**, Various Gauges, Skeet Grade, Single Selective Trigger, Selective Ejector, Engraved, Vent Rib, *Modern*	550.00	700.00
☐ **Model BL 4**, Various Gauges, Field Grade, Single Selective Trigger, Selective Ejector, Engraved, Vent Rib, *Modern*	475.00	650.00
☐ **Model BL 5**, 12 Ga., Trap Grade, Single Selective Trigger, Selective Ejector, Fancy Engraving, Vent Rib, *Modern*	745.00	975.00
☐ **Model BL 5**, Various Gauges, Skeet Grade, Single Selective Trigger, Selective Ejector, Fancy Engraving, Vent Rib, *Modern*	745.00	975.00
☐ **Model BL 5**, Various Gauges, Field Grade, Single Selective Trigger, Selective Ejector, Fancy Engraving, Vent Rib, *Modern*	675.00	900.00
☐ **Model BL 6**, 12 Ga., Trap Grade, Single Selective Trigger, Selective Ejector, Fancy Engraving, Vent Rib, *Modern*	995.00	1,375.00
☐ **Model BL 6**, Various Gauges, Field Grade, Single Selective Trigger, Selective Ejector, Fancy Engraving, Vent Rib, *Modern*	925.00	1,300.00
☐ **Model BL 6**, Various Gauges, Skeet Grade, Single Selective Trigger, Selective Ejector, Fancy Engraving, Vent Rib, *Modern*	995.00	1,350.00
☐ **Model S02**, 12 Ga., Sidelock, Selective Ejector, Single Trigger, Checkered Stock, Engraved, *Modern*	1,650.00	2,200.00
☐ **Model S03**, 12 Ga., Sidelock, Automatic Ejector, Single Selective Trigger, Fancy Engraving, Fancy Wood, *Modern*	2,550.00	3,400.00
☐ **Model S03 EELL**, 12 Ga., Sidelock, Automatic Ejector, Single Selective Trigger, Fancy Engraving, Fancy Wood, *Modern*	3,975.00	5,750.00
☐ **Model S03 EL**, 12 Ga. Sidelock, Automatic Ejector, Single Selective Trigger, Fancy Engraving, Fancy Wood, *Modern*	2,850.00	3,950.00
☐ **Model S04**, 12 Ga., Sidelock, Automatic Ejector, Single Trigger, Fancy Engraving, Fancy Wood, *Modern*	2,550.00	3,600.00
☐ **Model S05**, 12 Ga., Sidelock, Selective Ejector, Single Trigger, Fancy Engraving, Fancy Checkering, *Modern*	3,750.00	5,000.00
☐ **Model S55B**, 12 and 20 Gauges, Single Selective Trigger, Automatic Ejector, Vent Rib, Checkered Stock, *Modern*	415.00	550.00
☐ **Model S56E**, 12 and 20 Gauges, Single Selective Trigger, Automatic Ejector, Engraved, Checkered Stock, *Modern*	435.00	585.00
☐ **Model S58**, 12 Ga., Trap Grade, Automatic Ejector, Single Selective Trigger, Engraved, Checkered Stock, *Modern*	545.00	675.00
☐ **Model S58**, 12 and 20 Gauges, Skeet Grade, Automatic Ejector, Single Selective Trigger, Engraved, Checkered Stock, Light Engraving, *Modern*	565.00	700.00
☐ **Silver Snipe**, 12 and 20 Gauges, Single Trigger, Checkered Stock, Light Engraving, *Modern*	300.00	415.00
☐ **Silver Snipe**, 12 and 20 Gauges, Single Selective Trigger, Checkered Stock, Light Engraving, *Modern*	325.00	445.00
☐ **Silver Snipe**, 12 and 20 Gauges, Single Trigger, Checkered Stock, Light Engraving, Vent Rib, *Modern*	300.00	415.00
☐ **Silver Snipe**, 12 and 20 Gauges, Single Selective Trigger, Light Engraving, Vent Rib, *Modern*	545.00	725.00

62 / BERETTA

	V.G.	EXC.
☐ **Model 680**, 12 Gauge, Skeet Grade, Automatic Ejector, Single Selective Trigger, Engraved, Checkered Stock, Light Engraving, *Modern*	550.00	850.00
☐ **Model 680**, 12 Gauge, Trap Grade, Automatic Ejector, Single Selective Trigger, Checkered Stock, Light Engraving, *Modern*	550.00	850.00
☐ **Model 680**, 12 Gauge, Mono Trap Grade, Automatic Ejector, Single Trigger, Checkered Stock, Light Engraving, *Modern*	550.00	850.00
☐ **Model 686**, 12 Gauge, Field Grade, Automatic Ejector, Single Selective Trigger, Checkered Stock, Light Engraving, *Modern*	450.00	625.00
☐ **Model 687EL**, 12 Gauge, Skeet Grade, Automatic Ejector, Single Selective Trigger, Checkered Stock, Fancy Engraving, *Modern*	950.00	1,450.00

SHOTGUN, DOUBLE BARREL, SIDE-BY-SIDE

	V.G.	EXC.
☐ **Model 409PB**, Various Gauges, Double Trigger, Light Engraving, Checkered Stock, *Modern*	365.00	450.00
☐ **Model 410 Early**, 10 Ga. 3½", Double Trigger, Engraved, Checkered Stock, *Modern*	450.00	590.00
☐ **Model 410 Late**, 10 Ga. 3½", *Modern*	700.00	835.00
☐ **Model 410E**, Various Gauges, Double Trigger, Engraved, Checkered Stock, Automatic Ejector, *Modern*	465.00	625.00
☐ **Model 411E**, Various Gauges, Double Trigger, Engraved, Fancy Checkering, Automatic Ejector, *Modern*	645.00	925.00
☐ **Model 424**, 12 and 20 Gauges, Double Trigger, Light Engraving, Checkered Stock, *Modern*	400.00	550.00
☐ **Model 426E**, 12 and 20 Gauges, Single Selective Trigger, Automatic Ejector, Engraved, Checkered Stock, *Modern*	615.00	775.00
☐ **Model GR 2**, 12 and 20 Gauges, Double Trigger, Checkered Stock, Light Engraving, *Modern*	295.00	450.00
☐ **Model GR 3**, 12 and 20 Gauges, Single Selective Trigger, Checkered Stock, Light Engraving, *Modern*	350.00	515.00
☐ **Model GR 4**, 12 Ga., Single Selective Trigger, Selective Ejector, Checkered Stock, Engraved, *Modern*	425.00	595.00
☐ **Silver Hawk**, 10 Ga. 3½", Double Trigger, Magnum, *Modern*	410.00	565.00
☐ **Silver Hawk**, 12 Ga., Mag. 3", Double Trigger, Magnum, *Modern*	350.00	465.00
☐ **Silver Hawk**, 12 Ga. Mag. 3", Magnum, *Modern*	400.00	510.00
☐ **Silver Hawk**, Various Gauges, Double Trigger, Lightweight, *Modern*	300.00	415.00
☐ **Silver Hawk**, Various Gauges, Single Trigger, Lightweight, *Modern*	345.00	475.00

SHOTGUN, SEMI-AUTOMATIC

	V.G.	EXC.
☐ **Gold Lark**, 12 Ga., Vent Rib, Light Engraving, Checkered Stock, *Modern*	185.00	295.00
☐ **Model A301**, 12 Ga., Slug, Open Rear Sight, *Modern*	245.00	350.00
☐ **Model A301**, 12 Ga., Trap Grade, Vent Rib, *Modern*	265.00	385.00
☐ **Model A301**, 12 and 20 Gauges, Field Grade, Vent Rib, *Modern*	240.00	365.00
☐ **Model A301**, 12 and 20 Gauges, Skeet Grade, Vent Rib, *Modern*	240.00	365.00
☐ **Model A301**, 12 Ga., Mag. 3", Field Grade, Vent Rib, *Modern*	295.00	395.00
☐ **Model AL 1**, 12 and 20 Gauges, Checkered Stock, *Modern*	170.00	280.00
☐ **Model AL 2**, 12 Ga., Vent Rib, Trap Grade, Checkered Stock, *Modern*	225.00	295.00
☐ **Model AL 2**, 12 and 20 Gauges, Vent Rib, Checkered Stock, *Modern*	190.00	265.00
☐ **Model AL 2**, 12 and 20 Gauges, Vent Rib, Skeet Grade, Checkered Stock, *Modern*	220.00	295.00
☐ **Model AL 3**, 12 Ga., Vent Rib, Checkered Stock, Light Engraving, Trap Grade, *Modern*	270.00	365.00
☐ **Model AL 3**, 12 and 20 Gauges, Vent Rib, Checkered Stock, Light Engraving, *Modern*	240.00	345.00

	V.G.	EXC.
☐ **Model AL3**, 12 and 20 Gauges, Vent Rib, Checkered Stock, Light Engraving, Skeet Grade, *Modern*	245.00	335.00
☐ **Model AL 3**, 12 Ga. Mag. 3", Vent Rib, Checkered Stock, Light Engraving, *Modern*	270.00	375.00
☐ **Ruby Lark**, 12 Ga., Vent Rib, Fancy Engraving, Fancy Checkering, *Modern*	270.00	380.00
☐ **Silver Lark**, 12 Ga., Checkered Stock, *Modern*	135.00	210.00

SHOTGUN, SINGLESHOT

	V.G.	EXC.
☐ **Companion FS 1**, Various Gauges, Folding Gun, *Modern*	75.00	120.00
☐ **Model Mark II**, 12 Ga., Trap Grade, Vent Rib, Light Engraving, Checkered Stock, Monte Carlo Stock, *Modern*	265.00	395.00
☐ **Model TR 1**, 12 Ga., Trap Grade, Vent Rib, Light Engraving, Checkered Stock, Monte Carlo Stock, *Modern*	165.00	250.00

SHOTGUN, SLIDE ACTION

	V.G.	EXC.
☐ **Gold Pigeon**, 12 Ga., Vent Rib, Checkered Stock, Engraved, *Modern*	160.00	245.00
☐ **Gold Pigeon**, 12 Ga., Vent Rib, Fancy Engraving, Fancy Checkering, *Modern*	270.00	375.00
☐ **Model SL 2**, 12 Ga., Vent Rib, Checkered Stock, *Modern*	165.00	250.00
☐ **Ruby Pigeon**, 12 Ga., Vent Rib, Fancy Engraving, Fancy Checkering, *Modern*	385.00	525.00
☐ **Silver Pigeon**, 12 Ga., Light Engraving, Checkered Stock, *Modern*	125.00	200.00

BERETTA, GIOVANNI
Brescia, Italy c. 1700

HANDGUN, SNAPHAUNCE

	V.G.	EXC.
☐ **Belt Pistol**, Engraved, Carved, Light Ornamentation, *Antique*	2,750.00	3,750.00

BERGMANN
Gaggenau, Germany 1892-1944; Company Renamed Bergmann Erben 1931.

HANDGUN, SEMI-AUTOMATIC

	V.G.	EXC.
☐ **Model 1894**, 5mm, Blow Back, Clip Fed, Antique	9,750.00	17,000.00
☐ **Model 1894**, 8mm, Blow Back, Clip Fed, Antique	6,000.00	8,750.00
☐ **Model 1896 #2**, 5mm, Small Frame, Clip Fed, *Curio*	975.00	1,450.00
☐ **Model 1896 #3**, 6.5mm, Clip Fed, *Curio*	1,175.00	1,950.00
☐ **Model 1896 #4**, 8mm, Military, Clip Fed, *Curio*	1,350.00	2,350.00
☐ **Model 1897 #5**, 7.8mm, Clip Fed, *Curio*	1,675.00	2,650.00
☐ **Simplex**, 8mm, Clip Fed, *Curio*	575.00	975.00
☐ **Bergmann Mars**, 9mmB, Clip Fed, *Curio*	2,150.00	3,000.00
☐ **Bergmann/Bayard**, Model 1908, 9mmB, Clip Fed, *Curio*	600.00	900.00
☐ **Bergmann/Bayard**, Model 1910, 9mmB, Clip Fed, *Curio*	650.00	965.00
☐ **Bergmann/Bayard**, Model 1910/21, 9mmB, Clip Fed, *Curio*	475.00	700.00
☐ **Model 2**, .25 ACP, Clip Fed, *Modern*	175.00	295.00
☐ **Model 2A**, .25 ACP, Einhand, Clip Fed, *Modern*	225.00	335.00
☐ **Model 3**, .25 ACP, Long Grip, Clip Fed, *Modern*	175.00	275.00
☐ **Model 3A**, .25 ACP, Einhand, Long Grip, Clip Fed, *Modern*	250.00	365.00
☐ **Erben Special**, .32 ACP, Clip Fed, *Modern*	235.00	350.00
☐ **Erben Model I**, .25 ACP, Clip Fed, *Modern*	185.00	275.00
☐ **Erben Model II**, .25 ACP, Clip Fed, *Modern*	215.00	300.00

RIFLE, SEMI-AUTOMATIC

	V.G.	EXC.
☐ **Model 1897**, Karabiner, 7.8mm, Long Barrel, Detachable Stock, *Modern*	3,450.00	5,250.00

BERLIN, ABRAHAM
Caston, Pa. 1773-1786. See Kentucky Rifles and Pistols.

64 / BERNARDELLI

Bergmann Model 1896 #3

Bergmann Model 2

Bergmann Bayard 1910/21

Bergmann Bayard 1910

BERNARDELLI
Vincenzo Bernardelli, Gardon V.T., Italy

HANDGUN, SEMI—AUTOMATIC

	V.G.	EXC.
☐ **M1956**, 9mm Luger, Clip Fed, *Curio*	875.00	1,350.00
☐ **Model 100**, .22 L.R.R.F., Clip Fed, Blue, Target Pistol, *Modern*	195.00	265.00
☐ **Model 60**, .22 L.R.R.F., Clip Fed, Blue, *Modern*	95.00	150.00
☐ **Model 60**, .22 L.R.R.F., Clip Fed, Blue, 8" Barrel, Detachable Front Sight, Adjustable Sights, *Modern*	200.00	300.00
☐ **Model 60**, .32 ACP, Clip Fed, Blue, *Modern*	110.00	155.00
☐ **Model 60**, .380 ACP, Clip Fed, Blue, *Modern*	120.00	175.00
☐ **Model 80**, .22 L.R.R.F., Clip Fed, Blue, *Modern*	115.00	170.00
☐ **Model 80**, .22 L.R.R.F., Clip Fed, Blue, 6" Barrel, *Modern*	115.00	175.00
☐ **Model 80**, .32 ACP, Clip Fed, Blue, *Modern*	110.00	170.00
☐ **Model 80**, .380 ACP, Clip Fed, Blue, *Modern*	120.00	180.00
☐ **Model V P**, .22 L.R.R.F., Clip Fed, Blue, *Modern*	130.00	195.00
☐ **Model V P**, .25 ACP, Clip Fed, Blue, *Modern*	95.00	165.00
☐ **Standard**, .22 L.R.R.F., Clip Fed, Blue, *Modern*	95.00	165.00
☐ **Standard**, .22 L.R.R.F., Clip Fed, Blue, 6" Barrel, Detachable Front Sight, *Modern*	140.00	195.00
☐ **Standard**, .22 L.R.R.F., Clip Fed, Blue, 8" Barrel, Detachable Front Sight, *Modern*	160.00	250.00
☐ **Standard**, .22 L.R.R.F., Clip Fed, Blue, 10" Barrel, Detachable Front Sight, *Modern*	250.00	350.00
☐ **Standard**, .32 ACP, Original 17 Shot Clip only, Add **$30.00-$55.00**		

BERNARDELLI / 65

Bernardelli Standard .32, 8" Barrel

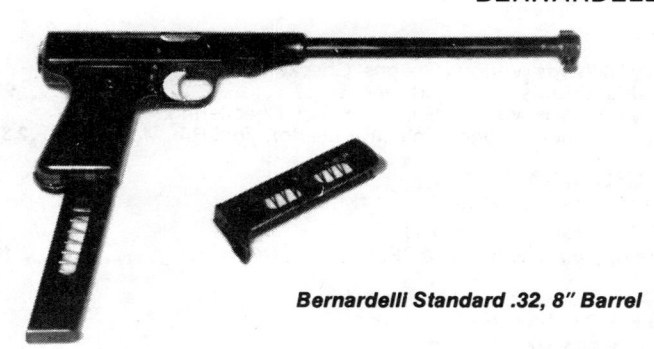

	V.G.	EXC.
☐ **Standard**, .32 ACP, Clip Fed, Blue, *Modern*	135.00	185.00
☐ **Standard**, .32 ACP, Clip Fed, Blue, 6" Barrel, Detachable Front Sight, *Modern*	185.00	265.00
☐ **Standard**, .32 ACP, Clip Fed, Blue, 8" Barrel, Detachable Front Sight, *Modern*	250.00	365.00
☐ **Standard**, .32 ACP, Clip Fed, Blue, 10" Barrel, Detachable Front Sight, *Modern*	295.00	395.00
☐ **Standard**, .380 ACP, Clip Fed, Blue, *Modern*	140.00	210.00
☐ **Standard**, 9mm Luger, Clip Fed, Blue, *Modern*	265.00	400.00

HANDGUN, REVOLVER

☐ **Standard**, .22 L.R.R.F. or .32 S&W Long, Double Action, Blue, *Modern*	160.00	260.00
☐ **Target**, .22 L.R.R.F., Double Action, Blue, Target Sights, *Modern*	175.00	280.00
☐ **Target**, .22 L.R.R.F., Double Action, Engraved, Chrome Plated, Target Sights, *Modern*	300.00	400.00

RIFLE, DOUBLE BARREL, OVER-UNDER

☐ **Various Calibers**, Checkered Stock, Engraved, *Modern*	725.00	995.00

SHOTGUN, DOUBLE BARREL, SIDE-BY-SIDE

☐ **Brescia**, 12 and 20 Gauges, Checkered Stock, Hammer, *Modern*	450.00	595.00
☐ **Elio**, 12 Ga., Checkered Stock, Light Engraving, Lightweight Selective Ejector, *Modern*	600.00	775.00
☐ **Game Cock**, 12 and 20 Gauges, Checkered Stock, Double Trigger, *Modern*	475.00	675.00
☐ **Game Cock Premier**, 12 and 20 Gauges, Checkered Stock, Single Trigger, Selective Ejector, *Modern*	600.00	825.00
☐ **Holland**, Various Gauges, Sidelock, Engraved, Checkered Stock, Automatic Ejector, *Modern*	1,600.00	2,875.00
☐ **Holland Deluxe**, Various Gauges, Sidelock, Fancy Engraving, Fancy Checkering, Automatic Ejector, *Modern*	1,950.00	3,500.00
☐ **Holland Presentation**, Various Gauges, Sidelock, Fancy Engraving, Fancy Checkering, Automatic Ejector, *Modern*	2,650.00	3,950.00
☐ **Italia**, 12 and 20 Gauges, Checkered Stock, Hammer, Light Engraving, *Modern*	485.00	700.00
☐ **Roma #3**, Various Gauges, Engraved, Checkered Stock, Automatic Ejector, *Modern*	425.00	650.00
☐ **Roma #4**, Various Gauges, Fancy Engraving, Fancy Checkering, Automatic Ejector, *Modern*	550.00	795.00
☐ **Roma #6**, Various Gauges, Fancy Engraving, Fancy Checkering, Automatic Ejector, *Modern*	700.00	900.00
☐ **St. Uberto F.S.**, 12 and 16 Gauges, Checkered Stock, Double Trigger, Automatic Ejector, *Modern*	475.00	675.00

66 / BERNARDON-MARTIN

	V.G.	EXC.
☐ **Wesley Richards**, Various Gauges, Checkered Stock, Light Engraving, Double Trigger, *Modern*	995.00	1,750.00
☐ **Wesley Richards**, Various Gauges, Fancy Checkering, Fancy Engraving, Single Trigger, Selective Ejector, Vent Rib, *Modern*	2,375.00	3,350.00

BERNARDON-MARTIN
St. Etienne, France 1906-1912.

HANDGUN, SEMI-AUTOMATIC
☐ **Automatique Francais**, .32 ACP, Clip Fed, *Curio* 195.00 275.00

BERSA
Baraldo S.A.C.I. Argentina.

HANDGUN, SEMI-AUTOMATIC
☐ **Model 62**, .22 L.R.R.F., Clip Fed, Blue, *Modern* 65.00 100.00
☐ **Model 97**, .380 A.C.P., Clip Fed, Blue, *Modern* 95.00 140.00
☐ **Model 622**, .22 L.R.R.F., Clip Fed, Blue, *Modern* 80.00 125.00
☐ **Model 644**, .22 L.R.R.F., Clip Fed, Blue, *Modern* 80.00 130.00

BERTUZZI
Gardone V.T., Italy; Imported by Ventura

SHOTGUN, DOUBLE BARREL, OVER—UNDER
☐ **Zeus**, 12 Ga., Sidelock, Automatic Ejector, Single Selective Trigger, Fancy Checkering, Fancy Engraving, *Modern* 2,150.00 2,750.00
☐ **Zeus Extra Lusso**, 12 Ga., Sidelock, Automatic Ejector, Single Selective Trigger, Fancy Checkering, Fancy Engraving, *Modern* ... 4,250.00 5,150.00

BICYCLE
Bicycle by Harrington & Richardson c. 1895.

HANDGUN, REVOLVER
☐ **.22 L.R.R.F.**, Top Break, Double Action, *Modern* 60.00 95.00
☐ **.32 S & W**, 5 Shot, Double Action, Top Break, *Modern* 60.00 95.00

BICYCLE
French, Maker Unknown.

HANDGUN, SINGLESHOT
☐ **.22 L.R.R.F.**, Auto Styling, *Modern* 225.00 345.00

BIG BONANZA
Made by Bacon Arms Co. c. 1880.

HANDGUN, REVOLVER
☐ **.22 Short R.F.**, 7 Shot, Spur Trigger, Solid Frame, Single Action, *Antique* 90.00 160.00

BIG HORN ARMS CO.
Watertown, S.D.

HANDGUN, SINGLESHOT
☐ **Target Pistol**, .22 Short, Plastic Stock, Vent Rib, *Modern* 75.00 135.00

SHOTGUN, SINGLESHOT
☐ **12 Ga. Short**, Plastic Stock, *Modern* 50.00 95.00

BILLINGHURST, WILLIAM
Rochester, N.Y. 1843-80

Big Horn .22 Pistol

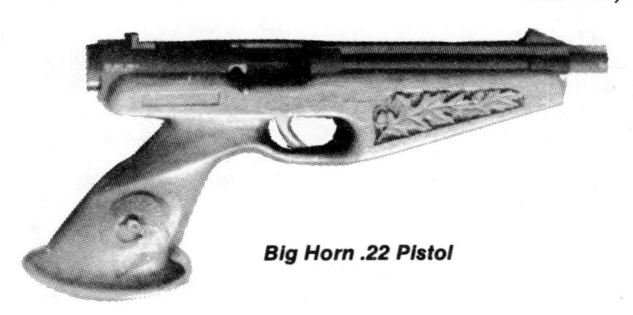

	V.G.	EXC.

HANDGUN, PERCUSSION
☐ **Buggy Pistol**, Various Calibers, Detachable Stock, Heavy Barrel, *Antique* 700.00 1,250.00

RIFLE, PERCUSSION
☐ .36, Revolver, 7 Shot, Octagon Barrel, *Antique* 1,950.00 2,550.00
☐ .40, Revolver, 7 Shot, Octagon Barrel, *Antique* 1,650.00 2,200.00

RIFLE, PILL LOCK
☐ .40, 7 Shot, Octagon Barrel, *Antique* 1,950.00 2,600.00
☐ .40, Carbine, 7 Shot, Octagon Barrel, *Antique* 1,950.00 2,600.00

BISBEE, D.H.
Norway, Me. 1835-1860.

RIFLE, PERCUSSION
☐ .44, Octagon Barrel, Silver Inlay, *Antique* 1,500.00 2,000.00

BISON
Imported from Germany by Jana International c. 1971.

HANDGUN, REVOLVER
☐ **.22 LR/.22 WMR Combo**, Adjustable Sights, Western Style, Single Action, *Modern* 25.00 45.00
☐ **.22 L.R.R.F.**, Adjustable Sights, Western Style, Single Action, *Modern* 25.00 40.00

BITTERLICH, FRANK J.
Nashville, Tenn. from about 1855 until about 1967.

HANDGUN, PERCUSSION
☐ **Derringer**, .40, Plain, *Antique* 500.00 925.00

BITTNER, GUSTAV
Vejprty, Bohemia, Austria-Hungary, c. 1893.

HANDGUN, MANUAL REPEATER
☐ **Model 1893**, 7.7mm Bittner, Box Magazine, Checkered Stocks, *Antique* 1,550.00 2,450.00

BLAKE, ANN
London, England c. 1812.

HANDGUN, FLINTLOCK
☐ **Holster Pistol**, .62, Walnut Stock, *Antique* 375.00 695.00

BLANCH, JOHN A.
London, England 1809-1835.

V.G.   EXC.

HANDGUN, PERCUSSION
- **.68 Pair**, Double Barrel, Side by Side, Officer's Belt Pistol, Engraved, Silver Inlay, Steel Furniture, Cased with Accessories, *Antique* 3,950.00   4,800.00
- **Pair**, Pocket Pistol, Converted from Flintlock, High Quality, Cased with Accessories, *Antique* 1,900.00   2,750.00

BLAND, T. & SONS
London & Birmingham, England from 1876.

SHOTGUN, DOUBLE BARREL, SIDE-BY-SIDE
- **12 Ga.**, Boxlock, Adjustable Choke, Color Case Hardened Frame, Engraved, *Modern* 1,350.00   1,900.00

BLANGLE, JOSEPH
Gratz, Styria, Austria, c. 1670.

RIFLE, WHEEL-LOCK
- **Brass Furniture**, Engraved, Silver Inlay, Light Ornamentation, Full-Stocked, *Antique* 4,750.00   6,800.00

BLEIBERG
London, England c. 1690.

HANDGUN, FLINTLOCK
- **Holster Pistol**, Engraved, Silver Inlay, High Quality, *Antique* 6,450.00   9,250.00

BLICKENSDOERFER & SCHILLING
St. Louis, Mo. 1871-1875.

RIFLE, PERCUSSION
- **.48**, Octagon Barrel, Fancy Wood, Brass Furniture, *Antique* 850.00   1,250.00

BLOODHOUND
Made by Hopkins & Allen, c. 1880.

HANDGUN, REVOLVER
- **.22 Short R.F.**, 7 Shot, Spur Trigger, Solid Frame, Single Action, *Antique* 85.00   150.00

BLUE JACKET
Made by Hopkins & Allen, c. 1880.

HANDGUN, REVOLVER
- **Model 1**, .22 Short R.F., 7 Shot, Spur Trigger, Solid Frame, Single Action, *Antique* 85.00   150.00
- **Model 2**, .32 Short R.F., 5 Shot, Spur Trigger, Solid Frame, Single Action, *Antique* 85.00   160.00

BLUE WHISTLER
Made by Hopkins & Allen, c. 1880.

HANDGUN, REVOLVER
- **.32 Short R.F.**, 5 Shot, Spur Trigger, Solid Frame, Single Action, *Antique* 85.00   160.00

BLUMENFELD
Memphis, Tenn. c. 1970

	V.G.	EXC.
SHOTGUN, SEMI-AUTOMATIC		
☐ **Volunteer Pointer**, 12 Gauge, Checkered Stock, *Modern*	120.00	195.00
SHOTGUN, DOUBLE BARREL, SIDE-BY-SIDE		
☐ **Arizaga**, 20 Gauge, Double Triggers, Checkered Stock, *Modern* ...	95.00	175.00

BLUNT, ORISON & SYMS
N.Y.C. 1837-1865.

HANDGUN, PERCUSSION
- ☐ **Boot Pistol**, Various Calibers, Bar Hammer, *Antique* .... 130.00 / 220.00
- ☐ **Boot Pistol**, Various Calibers, Side Hammer, *Antique* .... 165.00 / 270.00
- ☐ **Boot Pistol**, Various Calibers, Side Hammer, Ramrod, *Antique*..... 165.00 / 270.00
- ☐ **Boot Pistol**, Various Calibers, Ring Trigger, *Antique* .... 145.00 / 250.00
- ☐ **Boot Pistol**, Various Calibers, Underhammer, *Antique*............. 130.00 / 220.00
- ☐ **Pocket Pepperbox**, Various Calibers, Ring Trigger, *Antique* .... 185.00 / 320.00
- ☐ **Belt Pepperbox**, Various Calibers, Ring Trigger, *Antique* .... 195.00 / 320.00
- ☐ **Dragoon Pepperbox**, Various Calibers, Ring Trigger, *Antique* ..... 295.00 / 575.00

RIFLE, PERCUSSION
- ☐ **.37**, Octagon Barrel, Brass Furniture, *Antique* .... 495.00 / 650.00

BOITO
Brazil.

HANDGUN, SINGLESHOT
- ☐ **.44 C.F.**, Break-Open, Hammer, Blue, *Modern* .... 65.00 / 90.00

SHOTGUN, DOUBLE BARREL, OVER-UNDER
- ☐ **O/U**, 12 or 20 Gauge, Checkered Stock, *Modern*.................. 95.00 / 155.00

SHOTGUN, DOUBLE BARREL, SIDE-BY-SIDE
- ☐ **S/S**, 12 or 20 Gauge, Checkered Stock, *Modern* .... 85.00 / 130.00

SHOTGUN, SINGLESHOT
- ☐ **SS**, 12 or 20 Gauge, Checkered Stock, *Modern* .... 25.00 / 40.00

BONANZA
Made by Bacon Arms Co.

HANDGUN, REVOLVER
- ☐ **Model 1½**, .22 Short R.F., 7 Shot, Spur Trigger, Solid Frame, Single Action, *Antique* .... 85.00 / 160.00

BOND, EDWARD
London, England 1800-1830.

HANDGUN, FLINTLOCK
- ☐ **.68**, Pair Officers' Type, Holster Pistol, Brass Furniture, Plain, *Antique* .... 1,975.00 / 2,750.00

BOND, WM.
London, England 1798-1812.

HANDGUN, FLINTLOCK
- ☐ **Pair**, Folding Bayonet, Belt Pistol, Box Lock, Cannon Barrel, Brass Frame and Barrel, Cased with Accessories, *Antique* .... 4,250.00 / 5,750.00

BONEHILL, C.G.
Birmingham, England c. 1880.

	V.G.	EXC.

SHOTGUN, DOUBLE BARREL, OVER-UNDER
☐ **.450 N.E. 3¼"**, Under-Lever, Recoil Pad, Plain, *Modern* 750.00 1,250.00

BONIWITZ, JAMES
Lebanon, Pa. c. 1775. See Kentucky Rifles.

BOOWLES, R.
London, England c. 1690
HANDGUN, FLINTLOCK
☐ **Holster Pistol**, Engraved, Iron Mounts, Medium Quality, *Antique* ... 675.00 1,250.00

BOSS & CO. LTD.
London, England 1832 To Date
SHOTGUN, DOUBLE BARREL, OVER-UNDER
☐ **12. Ga.**, Single Selective Trigger, Straight Grip, Vent Rib, Trap Grade, Cased, *Modern* 14,000.00 18,000.00
☐ **16 Ga.**, Double Trigger, Plain, *Modern* 5,000.00 6,500.00
☐ **20 Ga.**, Single Selective Trigger, Vent Rib, High Quality, *Modern* 16,500.00 21,000.00

SHOTGUN, DOUBLE BARREL, SIDE-BY-SIDE
☐ **12 Ga.**, Vent Rib, Fancy Wood, Fancy Checkering, Fancy Engraving, *Modern* 4,500.00 6,000.00
☐ **Pair**, 12 Ga., Straight Grip, Plain, Cased, *Modern* 8,500.00 12,000.00

BOSTON BULLDOG
Made by Iver Johnson, sold by J.P. Lovell & Sons, Boston, Mass.
HANDGUN, REVOLVER
☐ **.22 Short R.F.**, 7 Shot, Double Action, Solid Frame, *Modern* 45.00 85.00
☐ **.32 S & W**, 5 Shot, Double Action, Solid Frame, *Modern* 45.00 80.00
☐ **.32 Short R.F.**, 5 Shot, Double Action, Solid Frame, *Modern* 45.00 75.00
☐ **.38 S & W**, 5 Shot, Double Action, Solid Frame, *Modern* 45.00 80.00
☐ **.38 Short R.F.**, 5 Shot, Double Action, Solid Frame, *Modern* 35.00 75.00

BOSWORTH
Lancaster, Pa. 1760-1775. See Kentucky Rifles.

BOYINGTON, JOHN
S. Coventry, Conn. 1841-1847.
RIFLE, PERCUSSION
☐ **.50**, Octagon Barrel, Brass Furniture, *Antique* 600.00 850.00

BOY'S CHOICE
Made by Hood Firearms Co. c. 1875.
HANDGUN, REVOLVER
☐ **.22 Short R.F.**, 7 Shot, Spur Trigger, Solid Frame, Single Action, *Antique* 90.00 160.00

BREDA
Brescia, Italy, Diana Import Co., Current
SHOTGUN, DOUBLE BARREL, OVER-UNDER
☐ **.410 Ga.**, Light Engraving, Checkered Stock, *Modern* 320.00 450.00

	V.G.	EXC.
SHOTGUN, SEMI-AUTOMATIC		
☐ **"Magnum"**, 12 Ga., Mag. 3", Checkered Stock, Vent Rib, Lightweight, *Modern*	300.00	395.00
☐ **Grade 1**, 12 Ga., Checkered Stock, Vent Rib, Lightweight, Engraved, *Modern*	350.00	450.00
☐ **Grade 2**, 12 Ga., Fancy Checkering, Vent Rib, Lightweight, Fancy Engraving, *Modern*	425.00	575.00
☐ **Grade 3**, 12 Ga., Fancy Checkering, Vent Rib, Lightweight, Fancy Engraving, *Modern*	500.00	650.00
☐ **Standard**, 12 Ga., Checkered Stock, Plain Barrel, Lightweight, *Modern*	175.00	250.00
☐ **Standard**, 12 Ga., Checkered Stock, Vent Rib, Lightweight *Modern*	185.00	265.00

BRF Junior Chrome

B.R.F.
Successor to Pretoria Arms Factory, South Africa, about 1957.

HANDGUN, SEMI-AUTOMATIC

☐ **"Junior"**, .25 ACP, Clip Fed, Blue, *Modern*	200.00	300.00
☐ **"Junior"**, .25 ACP, Clip Fed, Factory Chrome Plated, *Modern*	300.00	400.00
☐ **"Junior"**, for Cocking Indicator, Add $75-$125		

BRIGGS, WILLIAM
Norristown, Pa. 1848-1875.

SHOTGUN, PERCUSSION

☐ **12 Ga.**, Underhammer, *Antique*	240.00	325.00

BRITARMS
Aylesbury, England.

HANDGUN, SEMI-AUTOMATIC

☐ **M2000 Mk.II**, .22 L.R.R.F., Clip Fed, Target Pistol, *Modern*	575.00	850.00

BRITISH BULLDOG
Made by Forehand & Wadsworth.

HANDGUN, REVOLVER

☐ **.32 S & W**, 7 Shot, Double Action, Solid Frame, *Antique*	45.00	85.00
☐ **.38 S & W**, 6 Shot, Double Action, Solid Frame, *Antique*	45.00	85.00
☐ **.44 S & W**, 5 Shot, Double Action, Solid Frame, *Antique*	60.00	125.00

BRITISH BULLDOG
Made by Johnson, Bye, & Co., sold by J. P. Lovell 1881-1882.

72 / BRITISH MILITARY

| | V.G. | EXC. |

HANDGUN, REVOLVER
- ☐ **.32 S & W**, 5 Shot, Double Action, Solid Frame, *Modern* 45.00 85.00
- ☐ **.38 S & W**, 5 Shot, Double Action, Solid Frame, *Modern* 45.00 85.00
- ☐ **.44 S & W**, 5 Shot, Double Action, Solid Frame, *Modern* 60.00 125.00

BRITISH MILITARY
AUTOMATIC WEAPON, ASSAULT RIFLE
- ☐ **Sterling-AR18S**, .223 Rem., Clip Fed, Short Rifle, *Class 3* 750.00 1,250.00

AUTOMATIC WEAPON, HEAVY MACHINE GUN
- ☐ **M1906 Marlin**, .303 British, Belt Fed, Tripod, Potato Digger, Military, *Class 3* 1,450.00 2,100.00
- ☐ **Vickers Mk I**, .303 British, Belt Fed, Tripod, *Class 3* 4,800.00 6,000.00

AUTOMATIC WEAPON, LIGHT MACHINE GUN
- ☐ **Bren Mk II**, .303 British, Clip Fed, Bipod, *Class 3* 4,500.00 6,500.00
- ☐ **Hotchkiss Mk I***, .303 British, all Metal, Tripod, *Class 3* 995.00 1,800.00
- ☐ **Lewis Gun**, .303 British, Drum Magazine, Bipod, *Class 3* 1,450.00 2,000.00

AUTOMATIC WEAPON, SUBMACHINE GUN
- ☐ **Lanchester Mk I***, 9mm Luger, Wood Stock, Clip Fed, Military, *Class 3* 575.00 825.00
- ☐ **Lanchester Mk I***, 9mm Luger, Wood Stock, Dewat, Clip Fed, Military, *Class 3* 300.00 400.00
- ☐ **Sten Mk II**, 9mm Luger, all Metal, Clip Fed, Military, *Class 3* 445.00 695.00
- ☐ **Sten Mk II S**, 9mm Luger, Clip Fed, all Metal, Military, Silencer, *Class 3* 700.00 1,225.00
- ☐ **Sten Mk III**, 9mm Luger, Clip Fed, all Metal, Military, *Class 3* 550.00 775.00
- ☐ **Sterling L2A3**, 9mm, Clip Fed, all Metal, Military, *Class 3* 650.00 1,100.00
- ☐ **Sterling L3A1**, 9mm, Clip Fed, all Metal, Military, Silencer, *Class 3* 825.00 1,375.00
- ☐ **Thompson M1928**, .45 ACP, Clip Fed, with Compensator, Lyman Sights, Finned Barrel, *Class 3* 2,700.00 3,750.00

HANDGUN, FLINTLOCK
- ☐ **.58**, New Land M1796 Tower, Long Tapered Round Barrel, Belt Hook, Brass Furniture, *Antique* 1,200.00 1,800.00
- ☐ **.67**, George III Tower, Calvary Pistol, Military, Tapered Round Barrel, Brass Furniture, *Antique* 800.00 1,275.00
- ☐ **.80**, Modified M1796 Spooner, Holster Pistol, Plain Brass Furniture, *Antique* 995.00 1,550.00

HANDGUN, REVOLVER
- ☐ **#2 Mk I**, .38 S & W, Military, Top Break, *Curio* 85.00 150.00
- ☐ **#2 Mk I R.A.F.**, .38 S & W, Military, Top Break, *Curio* 95.00 165.00
- ☐ **S & W M38/200**, .38 S & W, Solid Frame, Swing-Out Cylinder, Double Action, Military, *Curio* 115.00 175.00
- ☐ **Webley Mk I**, .455 Revolver Mk I, Top Break, Round Butt, Military, *Antique* 175.00 275.00
- ☐ **Webley Mk I***, .455 Revolver Mk I, Top Break, Round Butt, Military, *Antique* 165.00 240.00
- ☐ **Webley Mk I****, .455 Revolver Mk I, Top Break, Round Butt, Military, *Curio* 125.00 195.00
- ☐ **Webley Mk II**, .455 Revolver Mk I, Top Break, Round Butt, Military, *Curio* 170.00 235.00
- ☐ **Webley Mk II***, .455 Revolver Mk I, Top Break, Round Butt, Military, *Curio* 135.00 200.00
- ☐ **Webley Mk II****, .455 Revolver Mk I, Top Break, Round Butt, Military, *Curio* 125.00 185.00
- ☐ **Webley Mk III**, .455 Revolver Mk I, Top Break, Round Butt, Military, *Curio* 165.00 250.00

BRITISH MILITARY / 73

British Military #1 MK III

British Military Webley MK VI, Buttstock

British Military Webley MK I No.2 .455

	V.G.	EXC.
☐ **Webley Mk IV**, .455 Revolver Mk I, Top Break, Round Butt, Military, *Curio*	150.00	220.00
☐ **Webley Mk V**, .455 Revolver Mk I, Top Break, Round Butt, Military, *Curio*	170.00	240.00
☐ **Webley Mk VI**, .455 Revolver Mk I, Top Break, Square Butt, Military, *Curio*	145.00	200.00
HANDGUN, SEMI-AUTOMATIC		
☐ **Webley Mk.I**, .455 Webley Auto, Clip Fed, *Curio*	190.00	300.00
☐ **Webley Mk.I No.2 R.A.F.**, .455 Webley Auto, Clip Fed, Cut for Shoulder Stock, *Curio*	550.00	900.00
☐ **Webley Mk.I No.2 R.A.F.**, .455 Webley Auto, Clip Fed, with Shoulder Stock, *Curio*	700.00	1,175.00
☐ **M1911A1 Colt**, .455 Webley Auto., Clip Fed, Military, *Curio*	350.00	500.00
HANDGUN, SINGLESHOT		
☐ **Welrod**, .32 ACP, Bolt Action, Silenced, *Class 3*	400.00	550.00
RIFLE, BOLT ACTION		
☐ **Lee Metford Mk I**, .303 British, Clip Fed, Carbine, *Curio*	145.00	225.00
☐ **Lee Metford Mk I**, .303 British, Clip Fed, *Curio*	130.00	195.00
☐ **Lee Metford MK 1 ***, .303 British, Clip Fed, Carbine, *Curio*	120.00	180.00
☐ **Lee Metford MK II**, .303 British, Clip Fed, *Curio*	115.00	185.00
☐ **Lee Metford MK II ***, .303 British, Clip Fed, *Curio*	140.00	225.00

74 / BRETTON

	V.G.	EXC.
☐ **M1896 Lee Metford**, .303 British, Clip Fed, Military, Carbine, *Curio*	95.00	170.00
☐ **Pattern 14 (U.S.)**, .303 British, *Curio*	125.00	195.00
☐ **SMLE #1 MK I**, .303 British, Military, *Curio*	125.00	200.00
☐ **SMLE #1 MK III**, .303 British, Military, *Curio*	95.00	175.00
☐ **SMLE #1 Mk III***, .303 British, Tangent Sights, Military, Ishapore, *Curio*	90.00	145.00
☐ **SMLE #1 MK III***, .303 British, Military, *Curio*	90.00	155.00
☐ **SMLE #2 MK IV**, .22 L.R.R.F., Singleshot, Training Rifle, *Curio*	115.00	180.00
☐ **SMLE #3 Mk I* (1914 Enfield)**, .303 British, Military, *Curio*	95.00	165.00
☐ **SMLE #4 MK I***, .303 British, Military, Lightweight, *Curio*	95.00	165.00
☐ **SMLE #4 Sniper**, .303 British, Military, Scope Mounted, *Curio*	375.00	500.00
☐ **SMLE #4 MK I***, .303 British, Military, Canadian, Lightweight, *Curio*	95.00	165.00
☐ **SMLE #4 MK I***, .303 British, Military, New Zealand, Lightweight, *Curio*	120.00	200.00
☐ **SMLE #4 MK I***, .303 British, Military, *Curio*	90.00	150.00
☐ **SMLE MK V Jungle Carbine**, .303 British, Peep Sights, Military, *Curio*	150.00	225.00
☐ **Santa Fe Jungle Carbine Mk.I MD12011**, .303 British, Peep Sights, No Flash Hider, Commercial, *Modern*	80.00	135.00
☐ **SMLE #7**, .22 L.R.R.F., Singleshot, Training Rifle, *Curio*	135.00	195.00
☐ **SMLE #8**, .22 L.R.R.F., Singleshot, Training Rifle, *Curio*	135.00	195.00
☐ **SMLE #9**, .22 L.R.R.F., Singleshot, Training Rifle, *Curio*	140.00	200.00
RIFLE, FLINTLOCK		
☐ **.75**, 1st Model Brown Bess, Musket, Brass Furniture, *Antique*	2,800.00	3,600.00
☐ **.75**, 2nd Model Brown Bess, Musket, Military, *Antique*	1,475.00	2,250.00
☐ **.75**, 3rd Model Brown Bess, Musket, Military, *Antique*	1,100.00	1,700.00
RIFLE, PERCUSSION		
☐ **.58 Snider-Enfield**, Military, Musket, *Antique*	375.00	550.00
☐ **.60 M1856 Tower**, Military, Musket, *Antique*	300.00	440.00
☐ **.60 M1869 Enfield**, Military, Musket, *Antique*	310.00	455.00
RIFLE, SINGLESHOT		
☐ **Martini-Henry**, .303 British, Carbine, *Antique*	130.00	225.00
☐ **Martini-Henry**, .303 British, *Antique*	150.00	245.00
☐ **Martini-Henry**, .577/.450 Martini-Henry, Carbine, *Antique*	125.00	215.00
☐ **Martini-Henry**, .577/.450 Martini-Henry, *Antique*	150.00	240.00
☐ **Martini-Henry**, .577/.450 Martini-Henry, Long Lever, *Antique*	110.00	195.00
SHOTGUN, SINGLESHOT		
☐ **Martini-Henry**, .12 Gauge Special, Long Lever, *Antique*	80.00	145.00

BRETTON
St. Etienne, France.

SHOTGUN, DOUBLE BARREL, OVER-UNDER

☐ **Standard**, 12 Gauge, Dural Frame, Double Triggers, Barrels Can Be Unscrewed, *Modern*	265.00	375.00
☐ **Deluxe**, 12 Gauge, Engraved, Dural Frame, Double Triggers, Barrels Can Be Unscrewed, *Modern*	350.00	485.00

BORCHARDT
Made by Ludwig Lowe, Berlin, Germany 1893-1897. In 1897 acquired by D.W.M., superseded by the Luger in 1900.

HANDGUN, SEMI-AUTOMATIC

☐ **Lowe**, 7.65mm Borchardt, Clip Fed, Blue, Cased with Accessories, *Antique*	4,900.00	8,750.00

	V.G.	EXC.
☐ **DWM**, 7.65mm Borchardt, Clip Fed, Blue, Cased with Accessories, Curio	4,200.00	7,500.00

BRNO
Ceska Zbrojovka, Brno, Czechoslovakia since 1922.

RIFLE, BOLT ACTION
	V.G.	EXC.
☐ **21 H**, Various Calibers, Sporting Rifle, Express Sights, Cheekpiece, Checkered Stock, Set Trigger, *Modern*	475.00	725.00
☐ **22 F**, Various Calibers, Sporting Rifle, Express Sights, Mannlicher, Checkered Stock, Set Trigger, *Modern*	500.00	750.00
☐ **Model I**, .22 L.R.R.F., Sporting Rifle, Express Sights, 5 Shot Clip, Checkered Stock, Set Trigger, *Modern*	220.00	375.00
☐ **Model II**, .22 L.R.R.F., Sporting Rifle, Express Sights, 5 Shot Clip, Fancy Wood, Set Trigger, *Modern*	240.00	395.00
☐ **Z-B Mauser**, .22 Hornet, Sporting Rifle, Express Sights, 5 Shot Clip, Checkered Stock, Set Trigger, *Modern*	500.00	750.00
☐ **ZKB 680 Fox**, .222 Rem., Clip Fed, Checkered Stock, Sling Swivels, *Modern*	220.00	350.00
☐ **ZKM 452**, .22 L.R.R.F., Clip Fed, Checkered Stock, Tangent Sights, *Modern*	75.00	130.00

RIFLE, DOUBLE BARREL, OVER-UNDER
	V.G.	EXC.
☐ **Super Express**, Various Calibers, Fancy Checkering, Sidelock, Engraved, Double Triggers, *Modern*	450.00	675.00
☐ **Super Express Grade III**, Various Calibers, Fancy Checkering, Sidelock, Fancy Engraving, Double Triggers, *Modern*	995.00	1,550.00
☐ **Super Express Grade IV**, Various Calibers, Fancy Checkering, Sidelock, Fancy Engraving, Double Triggers, *Modern*	635.00	1,200.00

RIFLE, SEMI-AUTOMATIC
	V.G.	EXC.
☐ **ZKM 581**, .22 L.R.R.F., Clip Fed, Checkered Stock, Tangent Sights, *Modern*	110.00	170.00

SHOTGUN, DOUBLE BARREL, OVER-UNDER
	V.G.	EXC.
☐ **Super**, 12 Gauge, Fancy Checkering, Sidelock, Plain, Ejectors, Double Triggers, *Modern*	325.00	675.00
☐ **Super Grade IV**, 12 Gauge, Fancy Checkering, Sidelock, Engraved, Ejectors, Double Triggers, *Modern*	465.00	850.00
☐ **Super Grade I**, 12 Gauge, Fancy Checkering, Sidelock, Fancy Engraving, Ejectors, Double Triggers, *Modern*	1,100.00	1,700.00
☐ **ZH 303 Field**, 12 Gauge, Boxlock, Checkered Stock, *Modern*	270.00	425.00

SHOTGUN, DOUBLE BARREL, SIDE-BY-SIDE
	V.G.	EXC.
☐ **ZP 47**, 12 Gauge, Sidelock, Double Triggers, Extractors, Checkered Stock, *Modern*	215.00	325.00
☐ **ZP 49**, 12 Gauge, Sidelock, Double Triggers, Ejectors, Checkered Stock, *Modern*	320.00	450.00

BROCKWAY, NORMAN S.
West Brookfield, Mass. 1861-1867, Bellows Falls, Vt. 1867-1900

RIFLE, PERCUSSION
	V.G.	EXC.
☐ **Various Calibers**, Target Rifle, *Antique*	1,275.00	2,200.00

BRONCO
Imported by Garcia, c. 1970

COMBINATION WEAPON, OVER-UNDER
	V.G.	EXC.
☐ **.22/.410**, Skeleton Stock, *Modern*	45.00	70.00

	V.G.	EXC.
RIFLE, SINGLESHOT		
☐ **Skeleton Stock**, *Modern*	30.00	55.00
SHOTGUN, SINGLESHOT		
☐ **.410 Ga.**, Skeleton Stock, *Modern*	45.00	60.00

BRONCO
Echave y Arizmendi, Eibar, Spain 1911-1974.

HANDGUN, SEMI—AUTOMATIC
☐ **1918 Vest Pocket**, .32 ACP, Clip Fed, *Curio*	85.00	145.00
☐ **Vest Pocket**, .25 ACP, Clip Fed, *Modern*	75.00	125.00
☐ **Vest Pocket**, .25 ACP, Clip Fed, Light Engraving, *Modern*	95.00	175.00

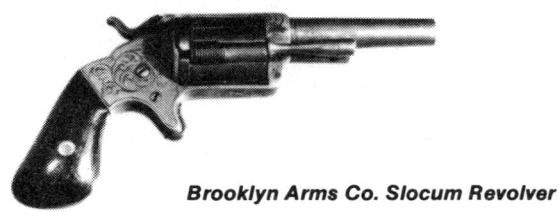

Brooklyn Arms Co. Slocum Revolver

BROOKLYN ARMS CO.
Brooklyn, N.Y. 1863-1867.

HANDGUN, REVOLVER
☐ **Slocum Patent**, .32 R.F., 5 Shot Cylinder with Sliding Chambers, Spur Trigger, Single Action, Engraved, *Antique*	225.00	375.00

BROWN, JOHN & SONS
Fremont, N.J. 1840-1871.

RIFLE, PERCUSSION
☐ **Various Calibers**, Sporting Rifle, *Antique*	675.00	1,200.00
☐ **.50**, Target Rifle, Scope Mounted, Set Trigger, *Antique*	1,300.00	1,950.00

BROWN MFG. CO.
Newburyport, Mass. 1869-73. Also see Ballard Rifles.

HANDGUN, SINGLESHOT
☐ **Southerner Derringer**, .41 R.F., Side-Swing Barrel, Spur Trigger, Brass Frame, *Antique*	165.00	275.00

RIFLE, BOLT ACTION
☐ **1853 Long Enfield**, .58 U.S. Musket, Converted from Percussion, Brass Furniture, *Antique*	435.00	595.00
☐ **U.S. M1861 Musket**, .58 U.S. Musket, Converted from Percussion, Brass Furniture, *Antique*	450.00	625.00

BROWN PRECISION CO.
San Jose, Calif. since 1975.

RIFLE, BOLT ACTION
☐ **Sporter**, Various Calibers, Fiberglass Stock, Rem. 700 Action, Sling Swivels, *Modern*	215.00	300.00

BROWNING
Established 1870 in St. Louis, Mo., now at Morgan, Utah. Also see F.N.

BROWNING / 77

Browning M1922

Browning Hi Power 9mm Military

Browning Model 1900

Browning 1903 9mm

	V.G.	EXC.

HANDGUN, SEMI-AUTOMATIC
- ☐ **Various Calibers**, Baby-.380-Hi Power Set, Renaissance, Nickel Plated, Engraved, *Modern* 3,250.00 4,750.00
- ☐ **380 Auto**, .380 ACP, Clip Fed, Renaissance, Nickel Plated, Engraved, *Modern* 975.00 1,450.00
- ☐ **380 Auto**, .380 ACP, Clip Fed, Adjustable Sights, *Modern* 185.00 325.00
- ☐ **380 Auto Standard**, .380 ACP, Clip Fed, *Modern* 175.00 250.00
- ☐ **Baby**, .25 ACP, Clip Fed, Lightweight, Nickel Plated, *Modern* 350.00 475.00
- ☐ **Baby**, .25 ACP, Clip Fed, Renaissance, Nickel Plated, Engraved, *Modern* 925.00 1,400.00
- ☐ **Baby Standard**, .25 ACP, Clip Fed, *Modern* 175.00 275.00
- ☐ **BDA 380**, .380 ACP, Clip Fed, Double Action, Fixed Sights, *Modern* 175.00 300.00
- ☐ **BDA 380**, .380 ACP, Clip Fed, Double Action, Fixed Sights, Nickel, *Modern* 200.00 335.00
- ☐ **BDA 38 Super**, .38 Super, Clip Fed, Double Action, Fixed Sights, *Modern* 525.00 775.00
- ☐ **BDA 45**, .45 ACP, Clip Fed, Double Action, 7 Shot, *Modern* 300.00 425.00
- ☐ **BDA 9**, 9mm Luger, Clip Fed, Double Action, 9 Shot, *Modern* 290.00 400.00

78 / BROWNING

	V.G.	EXC.
☐ **Challenger**, .22 L.R.R.F., Clip Fed, Checkered Wood Grips, Adjustable Sights, *Modern*	250.00	375.00
☐ **Challenger**, .22 L.R.R.F., Clip Fed, Renaissance, Checkered Wood Grips, Fancy Engraving, Nickel Plated, *Modern*	1,050.00	1,650.00
☐ **Challenger**, .22 L.R.R.F., Clip Fed, Checkered Wood Grips, Gold Inlays, Engraved, *Modern*	900.00	1,350.00
☐ **Challenger II**, .22 L.R.R.F., Clip Fed, Adjustable Sights, *Modern*	125.00	185.00
☐ **Challenger III**, .22 L.R.R.F., Clip Fed, Adjustable Sights, *Modern*	125.00	185.00
☐ **Hi Power**, 9mm, Clip Fed, Pre-War Military, Tangent Sights, *Curio*	700.00	1,100.00
☐ **Hi Power**, 9mm, Clip Fed, Pre-War Military, Tangent Sights, with Detachable Shoulder Stock, *Curio*	900.00	1,300.00
☐ **Hi Power**, 9mm, Clip Fed, Military, Tangent Sights, *Curio*	475.00	750.00
☐ **Hi Power**, 9mm, Clip Fed, Military, Tangent Sights, with Detachable Shoulder Stock, *Curio*	725.00	950.00
☐ **Hi Power**, 9mm, Clip Fed, Military, *Curio*	425.00	575.00
☐ **Hi Power**, 9mm, Clip Fed, Military, with Detachable Shoulder Stock, *Curio*	600.00	800.00
☐ **Hi Power**, 9mm, Clip Fed, Nazi-Marked Military, Tangent Sights, *Curio*	425.00	575.00
☐ **Hi Power**, 9mm, Clip Fed, Nazi-Marked Military, Tangent Sights, with Detachable Shoulder Stock, *Curio*	725.00	950.00
☐ **Hi Power**, 9mm, Clip Fed, Nazi-Marked Military, *Curio*	400.00	525.00
☐ **Hi Power**, 9mm, Clip Fed, Nazi-Marked Military, with Detachable Shoulder Stock, *Curio*	575.00	775.00
☐ **Hi Power Inglis #1 Mk I**, 9mm, Tangent Sights, Slotted for Shoulder Stock, Military, *Curio*	750.00	1,100.00
☐ **Hi Power Inglis #1 Mk I***, 9mm, Tangent Sights, Slotted for Shoulder Stock, Military, *Curio*	600.00	925.00
☐ **Hi Power Inglis #2 Mk I**, 9mm, Fixed Sights, Military, *Curio*	525.00	750.00
☐ **Hi Power Inglis #2 Mk I***, 9mm, Tangent Sights, Slotted for Shoulder Stock, Military, *Curio*	375.00	600.00
☐ **Hi Power "FM" Argentine**, 9mm, Clip Fed, Made Under License, Military, *Modern*	350.00	495.00
☐ **Hi Power Louis XVI**, Fancy Engraving, Nickel Plated, Fixed Sights, Cased, *Modern*	850.00	1,200.00
☐ **Hi Power Louis XVI**, Fancy Engraving, Nickel Plated, Adjustable Sights, Cased, *Modern*	900.00	1,225.00
☐ **Hi Power**, 9mm, Clip Fed, Renaissance, Nickel Plated, Engraved, *Modern*	900.00	1,450.00
☐ **Hi Power**, 9mm, Clip Fed, Renaissance, Nickel Plated, Engraved, Adjustable Sights, *Modern*	925.00	1,475.00
☐ **Hi Power**, 9mm, Clip Fed, with Lanyard Ring Hammer, Renaissance, Nickel Plated, Engraved, *Modern*	800.00	1,550.00
☐ **Hi Power**, 9mm, Clip Fed, with Lanyard Ring Hammer, Renaissance, Nickel Plated, Engraved, Tangent Sights, *Modern*	975.00	1,650.00
☐ **Hi Power Standard**, 9mm, Nickel Plating, *Add* **$30.00-$45.00**		
☐ **Hi Power Standard**, 9mm, Clip Fed, with Lanyard Ring Hammer, *Modern*	350.00	475.00
☐ **Hi Power Standard**, 9mm, Clip Fed, with Spur Hammer, *Modern*	280.00	375.00
☐ **Hi Power Standard**, 9mm, Clip Fed, with Spur Hammer, Adjustable Sights, *Modern*	275.00	425.00
☐ **Hi Power Standard**, 9mm, Clip Fed, with Spur Hammer, with Tangent Sights, *Modern*	525.00	750.00
☐ **Hi Power Standard**, 9mm, Clip Fed, with Spur Hammer, with Tangent Sights, Slotted for Shoulder Stock, *Modern*	790.00	1,100.00
☐ **Model 1900**, .32 ACP, Clip Fed, Early Type, No Lanyard Ring, *Curio*	250.00	375.00

	V.G.	EXC.
☐ **Model 1900**, .32 ACP, Clip Fed, *Curio*	145.00	245.00
☐ **Model 1900**, .32 ACP, Clip Fed, Nickel, *Curio*	155.00	275.00
☐ **Model 1900**, .32 ACP, Clip Fed, Military, *Curio*	175.00	300.00
☐ **Model 1903**, 9mm Browning Long, Clip Fed, *Curio*	300.00	425.00
☐ **Model 1903**, 9mm Browning Long, Clip Fed, Military, *Curio*	250.00	350.00
☐ **Model 1903**, 9mm Browning Long, Clip Fed, Cut for Shoulder Stock, Military, *Modern*	375.00	600.00
☐ **Model 1903**, 9mm Browning Long, Clip Fed, Cut for Shoulder Stock, With Holster Stock, Military, *Modern*	900.00	1,400.00
☐ **Model 1905**, .25 ACP, Clip Fed, Grip Safety, *Modern*	160.00	250.00
☐ **Model 1905**, .25 ACP, Clip Fed, Grip Safety, Nickel, *Modern*	300.00	400.00
☐ **Model 1906**, .25 ACP, Clip Fed, Grip Safety, Russian Contract, Nickel, *Modern*	400.00	600.00
☐ **Model 1910**, .32 ACP, Clip Fed, Japanese Military, *Curio*	350.00	500.00
☐ **Model 1910**, .32 ACP, Clip Fed, Peruvian Military, *Curio*	450.00	700.00
☐ **Model 1910**, .32 ACP, Clip Fed, Syrian Police, *Curio*	375.00	550.00
☐ **Model 1910**, .32 ACP, Clip Fed, Military, *Curio*	200.00	300.00
☐ **Model 1910**, .32 ACP, Clip Fed, *Modern*	145.00	200.00
☐ **Model 1910**, .380 ACP, Clip Fed, *Modern*	160.00	225.00
☐ **Model 1922**, .32 ACP, Clip Fed, *Modern*	135.00	200.00
☐ **Model 1922**, .32 ACP, Clip Fed, Nazi-Marked, Military, *Modern*	165.00	240.00
☐ **Model 1922**, .380 ACP, Clip Fed, Military, *Curio*	250.00	375.00
☐ **Model 1922**, .380 ACP, Clip Fed, Turkish Military, *Curio*	300.00	425.00
☐ **Model 1922**, .380 ACP, Clip Fed, Yugoslavian Military, *Curio*	300.00	425.00
☐ **Model 1922**, .380 ACP, Clip Fed, *Modern*	145.00	225.00
☐ **Medalist**, .22 L.R.R.F., Clip Fed, Checkered Wood Target Grips, Wood Forestock, Target Sights, *Modern*	450.00	600.00
☐ **Medalist**, .22 L.R.R.F., Clip Fed, Renaissance, Checkered Wood Target Grips, Fancy Engraving, Target Sights, *Modern*	2,350.00	3,000.00
☐ **Medalist**, .22 L.R.R.F., Clip Fed, Checkered Wood Target Grips, Wood Forestock, Gold Inlays, Engraved, *Modern*	1,775.00	2,400.00
☐ **Medalist International**, .22 L.R.R.F., Clip Fed, Checkered Wood Target Grips, Target Sights, *Modern*	400.00	550.00
☐ **Medalist International**, .22 L.R.R.F., Clip Fed, Checkered Wood Target Grips, Gold Inlays, Engraved, Target Sights, *Modern*	1,700.00	2,250.00
☐ **Medalist International**, .22 L.R.R.F., Clip Fed, Renaissance, Checkered Wood Target Grips, Fancy Engraving, Target Sights, *Modern*	2,200.00	2,850.00
☐ **Nomad**, .22 L.R.R.F., Clip Fed, Plastic Grips, Adjustable Sights, *Modern*	250.00	350.00

RIFLE, BOLT ACTION

	V.G.	EXC.
☐ **Model BBR**, Various Calibers, Checkered Stock, Modern	300.00	400.00
☐ **Exhibition Olympian Grade**, Various Calibers, Gold Inlays, Fancy Wood, Fancy Checkering, Engraved, *Modern*	6,800.00	8,700.00
☐ **Medallion Grade**, .458 Win. Mag., Long Action, Fancy Wood, Fancy Checkering, Engraved, Open Rear Sight, *Modern*	975.00	1,550.00
☐ **Medallion Grade**, Various Calibers, Short Action, Fancy Wood, Fancy Checkering, Engraved, *Modern*	975.00	1,450.00
☐ **Medallion Grade**, Various Calibers, Long Action, Fancy Wood, Fancy Checkering, Engraved, *Modern*	995.00	1,475.00
☐ **Medallion Grade**, Various Calibers, Long Action, Magnum, Fancy Wood, Fancy Checkering, Engraved, *Modern*	1,075.00	1,650.00
☐ **Olympian Grade**, .458 Win. Mag., Long Action, Fancy Wood, Fancy Checkering, Engraved, *Modern*	1,950.00	2,550.00
☐ **Olympian Grade**, Various Calibers, Short Action, Fancy Wood, Fancy Checkering, Fancy Engraving, *Modern*	1,975.00	2,700.00

80 / BROWNING

	V.G.	EXC.
☐ **Olympian Grade**, Various Calibers, Medium Action, Fancy Wood, Fancy Checkering, Fancy Engraving, *Modern*	1,700.00	2,300.00
☐ **Olympian Grade**, Various Calibers, Long Action, Fancy Wood, Fancy Checkering, Fancy Engraving, *Modern*	1,850.00	2,500.00
☐ **Olympian Grade**, Various Calibers, Long Action, Magnum, Fancy Wood, Fancy Checkering, Fancy Engraving, *Modern*	1,950.00	2,800.00
☐ **Safari Grade**, Various Calibers, Short Action, Checkered Stock, *Modern*	375.00	650.00
☐ **Safari Grade**, Various Calibers, Medium Action, Checkered Stock, *Modern*	475.00	700.00
☐ **Safari Grade**, Various Calibers, Long Action, Checkered Stock, *Modern*	525.00	800.00
☐ **Safari Grade**, Various Calibers, Long Action, Magnum, Checkered Stock, *Modern*	625.00	850.00
☐ **T-Bolt T-1**, .22 L.R.R.F., 5 Shot Clip, Plain, Open Rear Sight, *Modern*	85.00	150.00
☐ **T-Bolt T-1**, .22 L.R.R.F., 5 Shot Clip, Plain, Open Rear Sight, Left-Hand, *Modern*	110.00	185.00
☐ **T-Bolt T-2**, .22 L.R.R.F., 5 Shot Clip, Checkered Stock, Fancy Wood, Open Rear Sight, *Modern*	175.00	240.00

RIFLE, LEVER ACTION

	V.G.	EXC.
☐ **BL-22**, Belgian Manufacture, *Add* **15%-25%**		
☐ **BL-22 Grade 1**, .22 L.R.R.F., Tube Feed, Checkered Stock, *Modern*	150.00	195.00
☐ **BL-22 Grade 2**, .22 L.R.R.F., Tube Feed, Checkered Stock, Light Engraving, *Modern*	170.00	225.00
☐ **BLR**, Various Calibers, Center-Fire, Plain, Clip Fed, Belgian Manufacture, Checkered Stock, *Modern*	265.00	350.00
☐ **BLR**, Various Calibers, Center-Fire, Plain, Clip Fed, Checkered Stock, *Modern*	225.00	295.00
☐ **Model 92**, .44 Mag., Tube Feed, Open Sights, *Modern*	210.00	270.00
☐ **Model 92 Centennial**, Tube Feed, Open Sights, Commemorative, *Modern*	250.00	350.00

RIFLE, PERCUSSION

	V.G.	EXC.
☐ **J. Browning Mountain Rifle**, Various Calibers, Singleshot, Octagon Barrel, Open Rear Sight, Single Set Trigger, Brass Finish, Reproduction, *Antique*	220.00	325.00
☐ **J. Browning Mountain Rifle**, Various Calibers, Singleshot, Octagon Barrel, Open Rear Sight, Single Set Trigger, Browned Finish, Reproduction, *Antique*	220.00	325.00

RIFLE, SEMI-AUTOMATIC

	V.G.	EXC.
☐ **Auto-Rifle**, .22 L.R.R.F., Belgian Mfg., *Add* **20%-30%**		
☐ **Auto-Rifle Grade I**, .22 L.R.R.F., Tube Feed, Takedown, Open Rear Sight, Checkered Stock, *Modern*	140.00	200.00
☐ **Auto-Rifle Grade I**, .22 Short, Tube Feed, Takedown, Open Rear Sight, Checkered Stock, *Modern*	140.00	200.00
☐ **Auto-Rifle Grade II**, .22 L.R.R.F., Tube Feed, Takedown, Open Rear Sight, Satin Chrome Receiver, Engraved, *Modern*	220.00	300.00
☐ **Auto-Rifle Grade III**, .22 L.R.R.F., Takedown, Satin Chrome Receiver, Fancy Wood, Fancy Checkering, Fancy Engraving, Cased, *Modern*	525.00	650.00
☐ **BAR**, .22 L.R.R.F., Checkered Stock, *Modern*	125.00	185.00
☐ **BAR**, Various Calibers, Center-Fire, Belgian Mfg., *Add* **15%-25%**		
☐ **BAR**, Various Calibers, Center-Fire, Magnum Calibers *Add* **10%**		
☐ **BAR Grade 1**, Various Calibers, Center-Fire, Checkered Stock, Plain, *Modern*	325.00	425.00

BROWNING / 81

	V.G.	EXC.

- ☐ **BAR Grade 2**, Various Calibers, Center-Fire, Checkered Stock, Light Engraving, *Modern* 375.00   500.00
- ☐ **BAR Grade 3**, Various Calibers, Center-Fire, Fancy Wood, Fancy Checkering, Engraved, *Modern* 600.00   775.00
- ☐ **BAR Grade 4**, Various Calibers, Center-Fire, Fancy Wood, Fancy Checkering, Fancy Engraving, *Modern* 850.00 1,350.00
- ☐ **BAR Grade 5**, Various Calibers, Center-Fire, Fancy Wood, Fancy Checkering, Fancy Engraving, Gold Inlays, *Modern* 2,250.00 2,800.00

RIFLE, SINGLESHOT
- ☐ **Model 78**, Various Calibers, Various Barrel Styles, Checkered Stock, *Modern* 270.00   350.00
- ☐ **Model 78**, 45-70 Govt., Bicentennial Commemorative, Checkered Stock, *Modern* 1,250.00 1,950.00

RIFLE, DOUBLE BARREL, OVER-UNDER
- ☐ **Superposed Continental**, 20 Ga. and 30/06, Engraved, Fancy Wood, Fancy Checkering, *Modern* 2,750.00 3,500.00
- ☐ **Express Rifle**, 30/06 or .270 Win., Engraved, Fancy wood, Fancy Checkering, Cased, *Modern* 2,200.00 2,750.00
- ☐ **Centennial Superposed**, 20 Ga. and 30/06, Engraved, Fancy Checkering, Fancy Wood, Cased, Commemorative, *Modern* 5,000.00 7,250.00

RIFLE, SLIDE ACTION
- ☐ **BPR**, .22 L.R.R.F., Grade I, Checkered Stock, *Modern* 125.00   175.00
- ☐ **BPR**, .22 Mag., Grade I, Checkered Stock, *Modern* 135.00   190.00
- ☐ **BPR**, .22 Mag., Grade II, Checkered Stock, Engraved, *Modern* 175.00   250.00

SHOTGUN, DOUBLE BARREL, OVER—UNDER
- ☐ **Citori**, 12 Ga., Trap Grade, Vent Rib, Checkered Stock, *Modern* ... 425.00   550.00
- ☐ **Citori**, 12 and 20 Gauges, Standard Grade, Vent Rib, Checkered Stock, *Modern* 415.00   535.00
- ☐ **Citori**, 12 and 20 Gauges, Skeet Grade, Vent Rib, Checkered Stock, *Modern* 425.00   550.00
- ☐ **Citori International**, 12 Ga., Trap Grade, Vent Rib, Checkered Stock, *Modern* 475.00   600.00
- ☐ **Citori International**, 12 Ga., Skeet Grade, Vent Rib, Checkered Stock, *Modern* 475.00   600.00
- ☐ **Citori Grade II**, Various Gauges, Hunting Model, Engraved, Checkered Stock, Single Selective Trigger, *Modern* 650.00   850.00
- ☐ **Citori Grade II**, Trap and Skeet Models, *Add* **10%**
- ☐ **Citori Grade V**, Various Gauges, Fancy Engraving, Checkered Stock, Single Selective Trigger, *Modern* 900.00 1,350.00
- ☐ **Citori Grade V**, Trap and Skeet Models, *Add* **10%**
- ☐ **Superposed**, 12 Ga., Broadway Trap Model, Presentation Grade 4, Fancy Engraving, with Sideplates, Gold Inlays, Fancy Checkering, Fancy Wood, *Modern* 5,500.00 7,250.00
- ☐ **Superposed**, 12 Ga., Lightning Trap Model, Presentation Grade 4, Fancy Engraving, with Sideplates, Gold Inlays, Fancy Checkering, Fancy Wood, *Modern* 5,400.00 7,150.00
- ☐ **Superposed**, 12 Ga., Broadway Trap Model, Presentation Grade 4, Fancy Engraving, with Sideplates, Fancy Checkering, Fancy Wood, *Modern* 4,750.00 6,250.00
- ☐ **Superposed**, 12 Ga., Lightning Trap Model, Presentation Grade 4, Fancy Engraving, with Sideplates, Fancy Checkering, Fancy Wood, *Modern* 4,650.00 6,150.00
- ☐ **Superposed**, 12 Ga., Broadway Trap Model, Presentation Grade 3, Fancy Engraving, Gold Inlays, Fancy Checkering, Fancy Wood, *Modern* 4,250.00 5,500.00

82 / BROWNING

	V.G.	EXC.
☐ **Superposed**, 12 Ga., Lightning Trap Model, Presentation Grade 3, Fancy Engraving, Gold Inlays, Fancy Checkering, Fancy Wood, *Modern*	4,150.00	5,400.00
☐ **Superposed**, 12 Ga., Broadway Trap Model, Presentation Grade 2, Fancy Engraving, Fancy Checkering, Fancy Wood, *Modern*	2,750.00	3,400.00
☐ **Superposed**, 12 Ga., Lightning Trap Model, Presentation Grade 2, Fancy Engraving, Fancy Checkering, Fancy Wood, *Modern*	2,650.00	3,300.00
☐ **Superposed**, 12 Ga., Broadway Trap Model, Presentation Grade 2, Fancy Engraving, Gold Inlays, Fancy Checkering, Fancy Wood, *Modern*	3,000.00	4,000.00
☐ **Superposed**, 12 Ga., Lightning Trap Model, Presentation Grade 2, Fancy Engraving, Gold Inlays, Fancy Checkering, Fancy Wood, *Modern*	3,000.00	4,000.00
☐ **Superposed**, 12 Ga., Broadway Trap Model, Presentation Grade 1, Engraved, Gold Inlays, Fancy Checkering, Fancy Wood, *Modern*	2,250.00	3,000.00
☐ **Superposed**, 12 Ga., Lightning Trap Model, Presentation Grade 1, Engraved, Gold Inlays, Fancy Checkering, Fancy Wood, *Modern*	2,200.00	2,950.00
☐ **Superposed**, 12 Ga., Broadway Trap Model, Presentation Grade 1, Engraved, Fancy Checkering, Fancy Wood, *Modern*	2,000.00	2,750.00
☐ **Superposed**, 12 Ga., Lightning Trap Model, Presentation Grade 1, Engraved, Fancy Checkering, Fancy Wood, *Modern*	1,950.00	2,700.00
☐ **Superposed**, 12 and 20 Gauges, Lightning Skeet Model, Presentation Grade 4, Fancy Engraving, with Sideplates, Gold Inlays, Fancy Checkering, Fancy Wood, *Modern*	4,250.00	6,800.00
☐ **Superposed**, 12 and 20 Gauges, Super-Light Hunting Model, Presentation Grade 4, Extra Barrels, Fancy Engraving, with Sideplates, Gold Inlays, Fancy Checkering, Fancy Wood, *Modern*	6,000.00	7,500.00
☐ **Superposed**, 12 and 20 Gauges, Lightning Hunting Model, Presentation Grade 4, Fancy Engraving, with Sideplates, Gold Inlays, Fancy Checkering, Fancy Wood, Extra Barrels, *Modern*	6,000.00	7,500.00
☐ **Superposed**, 12 and 20 Gauges, Lightning Skeet Model, Presentation Grade 4, Fancy Engraving, with Sideplates, Fancy Checkering, Fancy Wood, Extra Barrels, *Modern*	5,000.00	7,000.00
☐ **Superposed**, 12 and 20 Gauges, Super-Light Hunting Model, Presentation Grade 4, Fancy Engraving, with Sideplates, Fancy Checkering, Fancy Wood, Extra Barrels, *Modern*	5,000.00	7,000.00
☐ **Superposed**, 12 and 20 Gauges, Lightning Hunting Model, Presentation Grade 4, Fancy Engraving, with Sideplates, Fancy Checkering, Fancy Wood, Extra Barrels, *Modern*	5,000.00	7,000.00
☐ **Superposed**, 12 and 20 Gauges, Lightning Skeet Model, Presentation Grade 3, Fancy Engraving, Gold Inlays, Fancy Checkering, Fancy Wood, *Modern*	3,400.00	4,750.00
☐ **Superposed**, 12 and 20 Gauges, Super-Light Hunting Model, Presentation Grade 2, Fancy Engraving, Fancy Checkering, Fancy Wood, Extra Barrels, *Modern*	2,900.00	4,400.00
☐ **Superposed**, 12 and 20 Gauges, Lightning Hunting Model, Presentation Grade 2, Fancy Engraving, Fancy Checkering, Fancy Wood, Extra Barrels, *Modern*	2,900.00	4,400.00
☐ **Superposed**, 12 and 20 Gauges, Lightning Skeet Model, Presentation Grade 2, Fancy Engraving, Gold Inlays, Fancy Checkering, Fancy Wood, *Modern*	3,000.00	4,000.00
☐ **Superposed**, 12 and 20 Gauges, Super-Light Hunting Model, Presentation Grade 2, Fancy Engraving, Gold Inlays, Fancy Checkering, Fancy Wood, Extra Barrels, *Modern*	3,850.00	5,350.00
☐ **Superposed**, 12 and 20 Gauges, Lightning Hunting Model, Presentation Grade 2, Fancy Engraving, Gold Inlays, Fancy Checkering, Fancy Wood, Extra Barrels, *Modern*	3,850.00	5,350.00

	V.G.	EXC.
☐ **Superposed**, 12 and 20 Gauges, Lightning Skeet Model, Presentation Grade 1, Engraved, Gold Inlays, Fancy Checkering, Fancy Wood, *Modern*	2,300.00	3,150.00
☐ **Superposed**, 12 and 20 Gauges, Super-Light Hunting Model, Presentation Grade 1, Engraved, Gold Inlays, Fancy Checkering, Fancy Wood, *Modern*	2,250.00	3,100.00
☐ **Superposed**, 12 and 20 Gauges, Lightning Hunting Model, Presentation Grade 1, Engraved, Gold Inlays, Fancy Checkering, Fancy Wood, *Modern*	2,200.00	3,100.00
☐ **Superposed**, 12 and 20 Gauges, Lightning Skeet Model, Presentation Grade 1, Engraved, Fancy Checkering, Fancy Wood, *Modern*	2,100.00	2,800.00
☐ **Superposed**, 12 and 20 Gauges, Super-Light Hunting Model, Presentation Grade 1, Engraved, Fancy Checkering, Fancy Wood, *Modern*	2,100.00	2,800.00
☐ **Superposed**, 12 and 20 Gauges, Lightning Hunting Model, Presentation Grade 1, Engraved, Fancy Checkering, Fancy Wood, *Modern*	2,000.00	2,700.00
☐ **Superposed**, 28 Ga. or .410 Ga., Lightning Skeet Model, Presentation Grade 4, Fancy Engraving, with Sideplates, Gold Inlays, Fancy Checkering, Fancy Wood, *Modern*	4,950.00	6,550.00
☐ **Superposed**, 28 Ga. or .410 Ga., Lightning Hunting Model, Presentation Grade 4, Fancy Engraving, with Sideplates, Gold Inlays, Fancy Checkering, Fancy Wood, *Modern*	4,900.00	6,500.00
☐ **Superposed**, 28 Ga. or .410 Ga., Lightning Skeet Model, Presentation Grade 4, Fancy Engraving, with Sideplates, Gold Inlays, Fancy Checkering, Fancy Wood, *Modern*	4,950.00	6,550.00
☐ **Superposed**, 28 Ga. or .410 Ga., Lightning Hunting Model, Presentation Grade 4, Fancy Engraving, with Sideplates, Gold Inlays, Fancy Checkering, Fancy Wood, *Modern*	4,900.00	6,500.00
☐ **Superposed**, 28 Ga. or .410 Ga., Lightning Skeet Model, Presentation Grade 4, Fancy Engraving, with Sideplates, Fancy Checkering, Fancy Wood, *Modern*	4,300.00	5,800.00
☐ **Superposed**, 28 Ga. or .410 Ga., Lightning Hunting Model, Presentation Grade 4, Fancy Engraving, with Sideplates, Fancy Checkering, Fancy Wood, *Modern*	4,300.00	5,700.00
☐ **Superposed**, 28 Ga. or .410 Ga., Lightning Skeet Model, Presentation Grade 3, Fancy Engraving, Gold Inlays, Fancy Checkering, Fancy Wood, *Modern*	3,800.00	5,000.00
☐ **Superposed**, 28 Ga. or .410 Ga., Lightning Hunting Model, Presentation Grade 3, Fancy Engraving, Gold Inlays, Fancy Checkering, Fancy Wood, *Modern*	3,750.00	4,950.00
☐ **Superposed**, 28 Ga. or .410 Ga., Lightning Skeet Model, Presentation Grade 2, Fancy Engraving, Fancy Checkering, Fancy Wood, *Modern*	2,600.00	3,450.00
☐ **Superposed**, 28 Ga. or .410 Ga., Lightning Hunting Model, Presentation Grade 2, Fancy Engraving, Fancy Checkering, Fancy Wood, *Modern*	2,550.00	3,400.00
☐ **Superposed**, 28 Ga. or .410 Ga., Lightning Skeet Model, Presentation Grade 2, Fancy Engraving, Gold Inlays, Fancy Checkering, Fancy Wood, *Modern*	3,100.00	4,150.00
☐ **Superposed**, 28 Ga. or .410 Ga., Lightning Hunting Model, Presentation Grade 2, Fancy Engraving, Gold Inlays, Fancy Checkering, Fancy Wood, *Modern*	3,000.00	4,100.00
☐ **Superposed**, 28 Ga. or .410 Ga., Lightning Skeet Model, Presentation Grade 1, Engraved, Gold Inlays, Fancy Checkering, Fancy Wood, *Modern*	2,450.00	3,250.00

84 / BROWNING

	V.G.	EXC.
☐ **Superposed**, 28 Ga. or .410 Ga., Lightning Hunting Model, Presentation Grade 1, Engraved, Gold Inlays, Fancy Checkering, Fancy Wood, *Modern*	2,400.00	3,200.00
☐ **Superposed**, 28 Ga. or .410 Ga., Lightning Skeet Model, Presentation Grade 1, Engraved, Fancy Checkering, Fancy Wood, *Modern*	2,150.00	2,900.00
☐ **Superposed**, 28 Ga. or .410 Ga., Lightning Hunting Model, Presentation Grade 1, Engraved, Fancy Checkering, Fancy Wood, *Modern*	2,000.00	2,750.00

☐ **Superposed**, Various Gauges, Presentation Grade 4, Extra Sets of Barrels, *Add for each:* **$1,100.00-$1,600.00**
☐ **Superposed**, Various Gauges, Presentation Grade 3, Extra Sets of Barrels, *Add for each:* **$950.00-$1,500.00**
☐ **Superposed**, Various Gauges, Presentation Grade 2, Extra Sets of Barrels, Add for each: **$850.00-$1,250.00**
☐ **Superposed**, Various Gauges, Presentation Grade 1, Extra Sets of Barrels, *Add for each:* **$800.00-$1,100.00**
☐ **Superposed**, Pre-1977, Lightning Skeet, *Add* **5%-10%**
☐ **Superposed**, Pre-1977, Extra Barrel, *Add* **35%-40%**
☐ **Superposed**, Pre-1977, 4-Barrel, Skeet Set, *Add* **275%-300%**
☐ **Superposed**, Pre-War, Raised Solid Rib, Add **$50.00-$75.00**
☐ **Superposed**, Pre-1977, Vent Rib, Pre-War, *Add* **10%-15%**
☐ **Superposed**, Pre-1977, Super-Light Lightning, *Add* **15%-20%**
☐ **Superposed**, Pre-1977, Lightning Trap Model, *Add* **5%-10%**
☐ **Superposed**, Pre-1977, Broadway Trap Model, *Add* **8%-13%**
☐ **Superposed**, For .410 or 28 Gauge, *Add* **15%-25%**
☐ **Superposed**, For 20 Gauge, *Add* **10%-15%**

	V.G.	EXC.
☐ **Superposed**, Various Gauges, Pre-1977, Super Exhibition Grade, Fancy Wood, Fancy Checkering, Fancy Engraving, Gold Inlays, *Modern*	23,500.00	30,000.00
☐ **Superposed**, Various Gauges, Pre-1977, Field Grade, Engraved, Checkered Stock, Vent Rib, Single Selective Trigger, *Modern*	950.00	1,450.00
☐ **Superposed**, Various Gauges, Pre-1977, Pointer Grade, Fancy Engraving, Fancy Checkering, Single Selective Trigger, *Modern*	2,250.00	2,850.00
☐ **Superposed**, Various Gauges, Pre-1977, Pigeon Grade Hunting Model, Satin Nickel-Plated Frame, Fancy Engraving, Fancy Checkering, Fancy Wood, *Modern*	1,850.00	2,500.00
☐ **Superposed**, Various Gauges, Pre-1977, Diana Grade Hunting Model, Satin Nickel-Plated Frame, Fancy Engraving, Fancy Checkering, Fancy Wood, *Modern*	2,550.00	3,200.00
☐ **Superposed**, Various Gauges, Pre-1977, Midas Grade Hunting Model, Fancy Engraving, Fancy Checkering, Fancy Wood, Gold Inlays, *Modern*	3,650.00	4,350.00
☐ **Superposed**, Various Gauges, Pre-1977, Exhibition Grade, Fancy Engraving, Fancy Checkering, Fancy Wood, Gold Inlays, *Modern*	7,000.00	10,000.00
☐ **Superposed Bicentennial**, Fancy Engraving, Gold Inlays, Fancy Wood, Fancy Checkering, Cased, Commemorative, *Modern*	7,000.00	10,000.00
☐ **Grand Liege**, 12 Ga., Engraved, Single Trigger, Checkered Stock, *Modern*	500.00	700.00
☐ **Liege**, 12 Ga., Engraved, Single Trigger, Checkered Stock, *Modern*	350.00	550.00
☐ **ST-100**, 12 Ga., Trap Special, Engraved, Checkered Stock, *Modern*	1,900.00	2,550.00

SHOTGUN, DOUBLE BARREL, SIDE-BY-SIDE

	V.G.	EXC.
☐ **B-SS**, 12 and 20 Gauges, Checkered Stock, Field Grade, *Modern*	325.00	425.00
☐ **B-SS**, 12 and 20 Gauges, Checkered Stock, Grade II, Engraved, *Modern*	575.00	725.00

	V.G.	EXC.

SHOTGUN, SEMI-AUTOMATIC
- ☐ **Auto-5**, For Belgian Make *Add,* **15%-25%**
- ☐ **Auto-5**, l2 Ga., Trap Grade, Vent Rib, Checkered Stock, *Modern* ... 350.00   465.00
- ☐ **Auto-5**, 12 and 20 Gauges, Magnum, Checkered Stock, Light Engraving, Plain Barrel, *Modern* 340.00   450.00
- ☐ **Auto-5**, 12 and 20 Gauges, Skeet Grade, Checkered Stock, Light Engraving, Vent Rib, *Modern* 355.00   465.00
- ☐ **Auto-5**, 16 Ga. 2 $9/_{16}$", Pre-WW2, Checkered Stock, Light Engraving, Plain Barrel, *Modern* 400.00   550.00
- ☐ **Auto-5**, 16 Gauge, Sweet Sixteen, Lightweight, Checkered Stock, Light Engraving, Plain Barrel, *Modern* 425.00   550.00
- ☐ **Auto-5**, Various Gauges, Lightweight, Checkered Stock, Light Engraving, Plain Barrel, *Modern* 340.00   450.00
- ☐ **Auto-5**, Various Gauges, Buck Special, Checkered Stock, Light Engraving, Plain Barrel, *Modern* 360.00   475.00
- ☐ **Auto-5**, Various Gauges, Vent Rib, *Add* **$35.00-$50.00**
- ☐ **Auto-5**, Various Gauges, Raised Solid Rib, *Add* **$25.00-$45.00**
- ☐ **Auto-5**, Various Gauges, Diana Grade, Pre-WW2, Plain Barrel, Fancy Engraving, *Modern* 750.00   1,100.00
- ☐ **Auto-5**, Various Gauges, Midas Grade, Pre-WW2, Plain Barrel, Fancy Engraving, Gold Inlays, *Modern* 950.00   1,500.00
- ☐ **Auto-5**, Various Gauges, Grade V, Plain Barrel, Fancy Engraving, *Modern* 1,950.00   2,800.00
- ☐ **Double-Auto**, l2 Ga., Trap Model, *Add* **10%-15%**
- ☐ **Double-Auto**, l2 Gauge, Checkered Stock, Engraved, Plain Barrel, *Modern* 215.00   300.00
- ☐ **Double-Auto**, l2 and 20 Gauges, Lightweight, Checkered Stock, Engraved, Plain Barrel, *Modern* 245.00   350.00
- ☐ **Double-Auto**, Vent Rib, *Add* **$35.00-$45.00**
- ☐ **Double-Auto**, Skeet Model, *Add* **10%-15%**
- ☐ **Model 2000**, l2 Ga., Trap Grade, Vent Rib, Tube Feed, Checkered Stock, *Modern* 285.00   375.00
- ☐ **Model 2000**, 12 and 20 Gauges, Vent Rib, Tube Feed, Checkered Stock, *Modern* 245.00   325.00
- ☐ **Model 2000**, 12 and 20 Gauges, Buck Special, Open Rear Sight, Tube Feed, Checkered Stock, *Modern* 260.00   335.00
- ☐ **Model 2000**, 12 and 20 Gauges, Skeet Grade, Vent Rib, Tube Feed, Checkered Stock, *Modern* 285.00   375.00
- ☐ **Model 2000 Montreal Olympic**, l2 Ga., Trap Grade, Vent Rib, Engraved, Gold Inlays, Commemorative, Tube Feed, Checkered Stock, *Modern* 1,375.00   1,900.00

SHOTGUN, SINGLESHOT
- ☐ **BT-99**, 12 Ga., Trap Grade, Vent Rib, with extra Single Trap Barrel, Checkered Stock, Engraved, *Modern* 500.00   675.00
- ☐ **BT-99**, 12 Ga., Pigeon Grade, Checkered Stock, Engraved, Vent Rib, *Modern* 750.00   1,050.00
- ☐ **BT-99**, 12 Ga., Trap Grade, Vent Rib, Checkered Stock, Engraved, *Modern* 350.00   450.00

SHOTGUN, SLIDE ACTION
- ☐ **BPS**, 12 Ga., Checkered Stock, Vent Rib, *Modern* 175.00   250.00
- ☐ **BPS**, 12 Ga., Buck Special, Rifle Sights, *Modern* 200.00   285.00

BRUTUS
Made by Hood Firearms Co. c. 1875-76

	V.G.	EXC.

HANDGUN, REVOLVER
- ☐ **.22 Short R.F.**, 7 Shot, Spur Trigger, Solid Frame, Single Action, Antique ... 95.00 ... 165.00

BSA
Birmingham Small Arms, Ltd, England. From 1885 to date.

AUTOMATIC WEAPON, LIGHT MACHINE GUN
- ☐ **Lewis Gun**, .303 British, Drum Magazine, Bipod, *Class 3* ... 1,500.00 ... 2,100.00

RIFLE, BOLT ACTION
- ☐ **Model CF-2**, Various Calibers, Sporting Rifle, Checkered Stock, Open Rear Sight, *Modern* ... 225.00 ... 345.00
- ☐ **Model CF-2**, Various Calibers, Sporting Rifle, Checkered Stock, Double Set Triggers, Open Rear Sight, *Modern* ... 245.00 ... 385.00
- ☐ **Imperial**, Various Calibers, Sporting Rifle, Muzzle Brake, Checkered Stock, Open Rear Sight, *Modern* ... 150.00 ... 250.00
- ☐ **Imperial**, Various Calibers, Sporting Rifle, Muzzle Brake, Checkered Stock, Open Rear Sight, Lightweight, *Modern* ... 175.00 ... 265.00
- ☐ **Majestic Deluxe**, .458 Win. Mag., Sporting Rifle, Muzzle Brake, Lightweight, Checkered Stock, Open Rear Sight, *Modern* ... 200.00 ... 310.00
- ☐ **Majestic Deluxe**, Various Calibers, Sporting Rifle, Muzzle Brake, Lightweight, Checkered Stock, Open Rear Sight, *Modern* ... 165.00 ... 260.00
- ☐ **Majestic Deluxe**, Various Calibers, Sporting Rifle, Checkered Stock, Open Rear Sight, *Modern* ... 155.00 ... 255.00
- ☐ **Monarch Deluxe**, Various Calibers, Sporting Rifle, Checkered Stock, Open Rear Sight, *Modern* ... 175.00 ... 275.00
- ☐ **Monarch Deluxe**, Various Calibers, Varmint, Heavy Barrel, Checkered Stock, Open Rear Sight, *Modern* ... 190.00 ... 275.00

RIFLE, SINGLESHOT
- ☐ **#12 Martini**, .22 L.R.R.F., Target, Target Sights, Checkered Stock, *Modern* ... 185.00 ... 275.00
- ☐ **#12/15 Martini**, .22 L.R.R.F., Target, Target Sights, Target Stock, *Modern* ... 235.00 ... 325.00
- ☐ **#12/15 Martini**, .22 L.R.R.F., Target, Target Sights, Target Stock, Heavy Barrel, *Modern* ... 240.00 ... 350.00
- ☐ **#13 Martini**, .22 Hornet, Sporting Rifle, Checkered Stock, *Modern* ... 250.00 ... 345.00
- ☐ **#13 Martini**, .22 L.R.R.F., Target, Target Sights, Checkered Stock, *Modern* ... 180.00 ... 250.00
- ☐ **#13 Martini**, .22 L.R.R.F., Sporting Rifle, Checkered Stock, *Modern* ... 170.00 ... 245.00
- ☐ **#15 Martini**, .22 L.R.R.F., Target, Target Sights, Target Stock, *Modern* ... 320.00 ... 415.00
- ☐ **Centurian Martini**, .22 L.R.R.F., Target, Target Sights, Target Stock, Target Barrel, *Modern* ... 225.00 ... 340.00
- ☐ **International Martini**, .22 L.R.R.F., Target, Target Sights, Heavy Barrel, Target Stock, *Modern* ... 235.00 ... 365.00
- ☐ **International MK 2 Martini**, .22 L.R.R.F., Target, Target Sights, Target Stock, *Modern* ... 235.00 ... 375.00
- ☐ **International MK 2 Martini**, .22 L.R.R.F., Target, Target Sights, Target Stock, Heavy Barrel, *Modern* ... 235.00 ... 355.00
- ☐ **International MK 3 Martini**, .22 L.R.R.F., Target, Target Sights, Target Stock, Heavy Barrel, *Modern* ... 260.00 ... 380.00
- ☐ **Mark V**, .22 L.R.R.F., Heavy Barrel, Target Rifle. Target Sights, Target Stock, *Modern* ... 315.00 ... 450.00
- ☐ **Martini I S U**, .22 L.R.R.F., Target Rifle, Target Sights, Target Stock, *Modern* ... 315.00 ... 450.00

	V.G.	EXC.

RIFLE, SLIDE ACTION
- ☐ **.22 L.R.R.F.**, Clip Fed, Takedown, *Modern* 70.00 130.00
- ☐ **.22 L.R.R.F.**, Tube Feed, Takedown, *Modern* 80.00 140.00

BUCHEL, ERNST FRIEDRICH
Zella Mehlis, Germany, 1919-1926

HANDGUN, SINGLESHOT
- ☐ **Luna**, .22 L.R.R.F., Rotary Breech, Free Pistol, Set Triggers, Light Engraving, *Curio* 675.00 925.00
- ☐ **Practice**, .22 Short R.F., Warnant Action, Hammer, Target Pistol, *Curio* 185.00 275.00
- ☐ **Model W.B.**, .22 L.R.R.F., Roux Action, Target Pistol, Hammerless, Tip-Down Barrel, *Curio* 320.00 450.00
- ☐ **Tell I**, .22 L.R.R.F., Rotary Breech, Free Pistol, Set Triggers, Light Engraving, *Curio* 675.00 925.00
- ☐ **Tell II**, .22 L.R.R.F., Rotary Breech, Free Pistol, Set Triggers, Light Engraving, *Curio* 675.00 925.00

BUDDY ARMS
Fort Worth, Tex. during the early 1960's.

HANDGUN, DOUBLE BARREL, OVER-UNDER
- ☐ **Double Deuce**, .22 L.R.R.F., Remington Derringer Copy, *Modern* 40.00 60.00

Budischowsky TP-70 .25

BUDISCHOWSKY
Made by Norton Armament (Norarmco), Mt. Clemens, Mich. 1973-1977.

HANDGUN, SEMI-AUTOMATIC
- ☐ **TP-70**, .22 L.R.R.F., Clip Fed, Double Action, Pocket Pistol, Stainless Steel, Hammer, *Modern* 250.00 350.00
- ☐ **TP-70**, .25 ACP, Clip Fed, Double Action, Pocket Pistol, Stainless Steel, Hammer, Presentation, Custom Serial Number, *Curio* 975.00 1,500.00
- ☐ **TP-70**, .25 ACP, Clip Fed, Double Action, Pocket Pistol, Stainless Steel, Hammer, *Modern* 200.00 300.00

BUFALO
Gabilondo y Cia., Elgoibar, Spain

HANDGUN, SEMI-AUTOMATIC
- ☐ **Model 1920**, .25 ACP, Clip Fed, *Modern* 75.00 125.00
- ☐ **Pocket**, .32 ACP, Clip Fed, *Modern* 75.00 125.00

BUFFALO ARMS
Tonawanda, N.Y.

88 / BUFFALO BILL

	V.G.	EXC.

HANDGUN, DOUBLE BARREL, OVER-UNDER
☐ **Model 1**, .357 Mag., Hammer, Blue or Nickel, *Modern* 60.00   95.00

BUFFALO BILL
Maker Unknown, Sold by Homer Fisher Co.
HANDGUN, REVOLVER
☐ **.22 Short R.F.**, 7 Shot, Spur Trigger, Solid Frame, Single Action, Antique 90.00   160.00

BUFFALO STAND
Tradename used by ManuFrance.
HANDGUN, SINGLESHOT
☐ **Bolt Action**, .22 L.R.R.F., Target Pistol, Modern 65.00   115.00

BUHAG
Buchsenmacher-Handwerkgenossenschaft M.B.H. of Suhl, East Germany.
HANDGUN, SEMI-AUTOMATIC
☐ **Olympia**, .22 Short R.F., Clip Fed, Target Pistol, *Modern* 350.00   525.00

BULL DOZER
Made by Norwich Pistol Co., Sold by J. McBride & Co. c. 1875-1883.
HANDGUN, REVOLVER
☐ **.22 Short R.F.**, 7 Shot, Spur Trigger, Solid Frame, Single Action, Antique 90.00   160.00
☐ **.38 Short R.F.**, 5 Shot, Spur Trigger, Solid Frame, Single Action, Antique 95.00   175.00
☐ **.41 Short R.F.**, 5 Shot, Spur Trigger, Solid Frame, Single Action, Antique 125.00   200.00
☐ **.44 Short R.F.**, 5 Shot, Spur Trigger, Solid Frame, Single Action, Antique 175.00   250.00

BULLARD REPEATING ARMS CO.
Springfield, Mass. 1887-1889
RIFLE, LEVER ACTION
☐ **Military**, Full Stocked, with Bayonet, Open Rear Sight, *Antique* ... 1,850.00   2,700.00
☐ **Military**, Full Stocked, with Bayonet, Open Rear Sight, Carbine, Antique 1,850.00   2,700.00
☐ **Various Calibers**, Small Frame, Tube Feed, Round Barrel, Plain, Open Rear Sight, Sporting Rifle, *Antique* 435.00   695.00
☐ **Various Calibers**, Tube Feed, Round Barrel, Plain, Open Rear Sight, Sporting Rifle, *Antique* 525.00   795.00
☐ **Various Calibers**, Light Engraving, *Add* **$50.00-$150.00**
☐ **Various Calibers**, Medium Engraving, *Add* **$200.00-$400.00**
☐ **Various Calibers**, Ornate Engraving, *Add* **$750.00-$1,000.00**
☐ **Various Calibers**, Full Nickel Plating, **$50.00-$75.00**
☐ **Various Calibers**, for Fancy Wood, *Add* **$25.00-$45.00**
☐ **Various Calibers**, for Standard Checkering, *Add* **$30.00-$45.00**
☐ **Various Calibers**, Fancy Checkering, *Add* **$70.00-$100.00**
☐ **Various Calibers**, Octagon Barrel, *Add* **$25.00-$50.00**
☐ **Various Calibers**, Half-Octagon Barrel, *Add* **$30.00-$60.00**
☐ **Various Calibers**, Target Sights, *Add* **$125.00-$175.00**
☐ **Various Calibers**, for Lyman Sights, *Add* **$40.00-$70.00**
☐ **Various Calibers**, for Express Sights, *Add* **$100.00-$150.00**

	V.G.	EXC.

RIFLE, SINGLESHOT
- ☐ **Military**, Full-Stocked, with Bayonet, Open Rear Sight, *Antique* ... 900.00 1,400.00
- ☐ **Military**, Full-Stocked, with Bayonet, Open Rear Sight, Carbine, *Antique* 900.00 1,400.00
- ☐ **Various Calibers**, Schuetzen Target Rifle, Octagon Barrel, Target Sights, Swiss Buttplate, Checkered Stock, *Antique* 995.00 1,850.00
- ☐ **Various Calibers**, Sporting Rifle, Octagon Barrel, Open Rear Sight, *Antique* 525.00 800.00
- ☐ **Various Rimfires**, Target Rifle, Octagon Barrel, Target Sights, Swiss Buttplate, Checkered Stock, *Antique* 575.00 900.00
- ☐ **Various Rimfires**, Sporting Rifle, Octagon Barrel, Open Rear Sight, *Antique* 500.00 850.00

BULLDOG
Made by Forehand & Wadsworth.

HANDGUN, REVOLVER
- ☐ **.32 S & W**, 7 Shot, Double Action, Solid Frame, *Modern* 55.00 95.00
- ☐ **.38 S & W**, 6 Shot, Double Action, Solid Frame, *Modern* 55.00 95.00
- ☐ **.44 S & W**, 5 Shot, Double Action, Solid Frame, *Modern* 70.00 125.00

BULLS EYE
Maker Unknown c. 1875.

HANDGUN, REVOLVER
- ☐ **.22 Short R.F.**, 7 Shot, Spur Trigger, Solid Frame, Single Action, *Antique* 90.00 150.00

BULWARK
Beistegui Hermanos, Eibar, Spain.

HANDGUN, SEMI-AUTOMATIC
- ☐ **.25 ACP**, External Hammer, Clip Fed, Blue, *Curio* 200.00 320.00
- ☐ **.25 ACP**, Hammerless, Clip Fed, Blue, *Curio* 85.00 140.00
- ☐ **.32 ACP**, External Hammer, Clip Fed, Blue, *Curio* 175.00 285.00
- ☐ **.32 ACP**, Hammerless, Clip Fed, Blue, *Curio* 95.00 145.00

BUMFORD
London, England 1730-1760.

HANDGUN, FLINTLOCK
- ☐ **.38**, Pocket Pistol, Boxlock, Queen Anne Style, Screw Barrel, Silver Inlay, *Antique* 500.00 725.00

BURGESS, ANDREW
Oswego, N.Y. 1874-1887

RIFLE, LEVER ACTION
- ☐ **Model 1876**, .45-70 Government, Tube Feed, Octagon Barrel, *Antique* 750.00 1,600.00

RIFLE, SLIDE ACTION
- ☐ **Various Calibers**, Folding Gun, With Case, *Antique* 800.00 1,250.00

SHOTGUN, SLIDE ACTION
- ☐ **12 Ga.**, Takedown, Solid Rib, Light Engraving, *Antique* 185.00 375.00
- ☐ **12 Ga.**, Folding Gun, With Case, *Antique* 425.00 675.00

BUSHMASTER
Gwinn Arms Co., Winston-Salem, N.C.

	V.G.	EXC.

AUTOMATIC WEAPON, MACHINE-PISTOL
☐ .223 Rem., Clip Fed, Commercial, *Class 3* 375.00   500.00

HANDGUN, SEMI—AUTOMATIC
☐ **Bushmaster**, .223 Rem., Clip Fed, *Modern* 225.00   325.00

RIFLE, SEMI—AUTOMATIC
☐ .223 Rem., Clip Fed, Wood Stock, *Modern* 200.00   300.00
☐ .223 Rem., Clip Fed, Folding Stock, *Modern* 220.00   330.00

BUSOMS
Spain c. 1780

HANDGUN, MIQUELET-LOCK
☐ .70 Pair, Belt Pistol, Belt Hook, Engraved, Brass Furniture, *Antique* **1,850.00 2,350.00**

BUSTINDUI, AUGUSTIN
Toledo, Spain c. 1765.

HANDGUN, MIQUELET-LOCK
☐ **Pair**, Locks by Guisasola, Half-Octagon Barrel, *Antique* 3,700.00 4,900.00

BUSTINDIU, JUAN ESTEBAN
Eibar, Spain c. 1775.

HANDGUN, MIQUELET-LOCK
☐ **Pair**, Half-Octagon Barrel, Silver Inlay, Light Decoration, *Antique*   2,850.00 3,850.00

C.A.C.

HANDGUN, SEMI-AUTOMATIC
☐ **Combat**, .45 ACP, Clip Fed, Stainless Steel, *Modern* 300.00   425.00

CADET
Sold by Maltby-Curtis Co.

HANDGUN, REVOLVER
☐ .22 Long R.F., 7 Shot, Single Action, Solid Frame, Spur Trigger, *Antique* 85.00   140.00

CALDERWOOD, WILLIAM
Phila., Pa. 1808-1816. See Kentucky Rifles and Pistols and U.S. Military

CANADIAN MILITARY

HANDGUN, SEMI-AUTOMATIC
☐ **Hi Power Inglis #1 Mk I**, 9mm, Tangent Sights, Slotted for Shoulder Stock, Military, *Modern* 675.00   995.00
☐ **Hi Power Inglis #1 Mk I***, 9mm, Tangent Sights, Slotted for Shoulder Stock, Military, *Modern* 575.00   900.00
☐ **Hi Power Inglis #2 Mk I**, 9mm, Fixed Sights, Military, *Modern* 500.00   750.00
☐ **Hi Power Inglis #2 Mk I***, 9mm, Tangent Sights, Slotted for Shoulder Stock, Military, *Modern* 375.00   585.00

RIFLE, BOLT ACTION
☐ **SMLE #4 Mk.1***, .303 British, Clip Fed, *Curio* 110.00   165.00
☐ **1907 MK 2 Ross**, .303 British, Full-Stocked, Military, *Modern* 145.00   200.00
☐ **1910 MK 3 Ross**, .303 British, Full-Stocked, Military, *Modern* 150.00   225.00

CAPT. JACK
Made by Hopkins & Allen 1871-1875.

	V.G.	EXC.

HANDGUN, REVOLVER
- ☐ **.22 Short R.F.**, 7 Shot, Spur Trigger, Solid Frame, Single Action, *Antique* 85.00 150.00

CAROLINE ARMS
Made by Crescent Firearms Co. 1892-1900.

SHOTGUN, DOUBLE BARREL, SIDE-BY-SIDE
- ☐ **Various Gauges**, Outside Hammers, Damascus Barrel, *Modern* 80.00 150.00
- ☐ **Various Gauges**, Hammerless, Steel Barrel, *Modern* 95.00 175.00
- ☐ **Various Gauges**, Hammerless, Damascus Barrel, *Modern* 75.00 150.00
- ☐ **Various Gauges**, Outside Hammers, Steel Barrel, *Modern* 90.00 175.00

SHOTGUN, SINGLESHOT
- ☐ **Various Gauges**, Hammer, Steel Barrel, *Modern* 45.00 75.00

CARPENTER, JOHN
Lancaster, Pa. 1771-1790. See Kentucky Rifles.

CARROLL, LAWRENCE
Philadelphia, Pa. 1786-1790. See Kentucky Rifles.

CARTRIDGE FIREARMS
Unknown Maker

HANDGUN, REVOLVER
- ☐ **11mm Pinfire**, Lefaucheux Military Style, *Antique* 150.00 225.00
- ☐ **11mm Pinfire**, Lefaucheux Military Style, Engraved, *Antique* 200.00 350.00
- ☐ **7mm Pinfire**, Pocket Pistol, Folding Trigger, Engraved, *Antique* 75.00 125.00
- ☐ **.22 Short**, Small Pocket Pistol, Folding Trigger, *Modern* 60.00 110.00
- ☐ **.22 Short**, Small Pocket Pistol, Double Action, *Modern* 45.00 85.00
- ☐ **.25 A.C.P.**, Small Pocket Pistol, Folding Trigger, *Modern* 60.00 110.00
- ☐ **.22 A.C.P.**, Small Pocket Pistol, Double Action, *Modern* 45.00 85.00
- ☐ **Belgian Proofs**, Various Calibers, Top Break, Double Action, Medium Quality, *Modern* 60.00 90.00
- ☐ **Belgian Proofs**, Various Calibers, Top Break, Double Action, Engraved, Medium Quality, *Modern* 75.00 110.00
- ☐ **Belgian Proofs**, Various Calibers, Top Break, Double Action, Folding Trigger, Medium Quality, *Modern* 55.00 85.00
- ☐ **Chinese Copy of Colt Police Positive**, .38 Special, Double Action, Solid Frame, Swing-Out Cylinder, Low Quality, *Modern* 55.00 95.00
- ☐ **Chinese Copy of Police Positive**, 9mm Luger, Double Action, Solid Frame, Swing-Out Cylinder, Low Quality, *Modern* 45.00 80.00
- ☐ **Copy of Colt SAA**, Various Calibers, Western Style, Single Action, Low Quality, *Modern* 60.00 100.00
- ☐ **Copy of Colt SAA**, Various Calibers, Western Style, Single Action, Medium Quality, *Modern* 75.00 125.00
- ☐ **Chinese Copy of S&W M-10**, .38 Special, Double Action, Solid Frame, Swing-Out Cylinder, Low Quality, *Modern* 50.00 90.00
- ☐ **Spanish Copy of S&W M-10**, .38 Special, Double Action, Solid Frame, Swing-Out Cylinder, Low Quality, *Modern* 55.00 95.00
- ☐ **Copy of S&W Russian Model**, Various Calibers, Break, Single Action, Low Quality, *Antique* 65.00 125.00
- ☐ **Copy of S&W Russian Model**, Various Calibers, Top Break, Single Action, Medium Quality, *Antique* 100.00 200.00
- ☐ **Copy of S&W Russian Model**, Various Calibers, Top Break, Single Action, High Quality, *Antique* 325.00 475.00

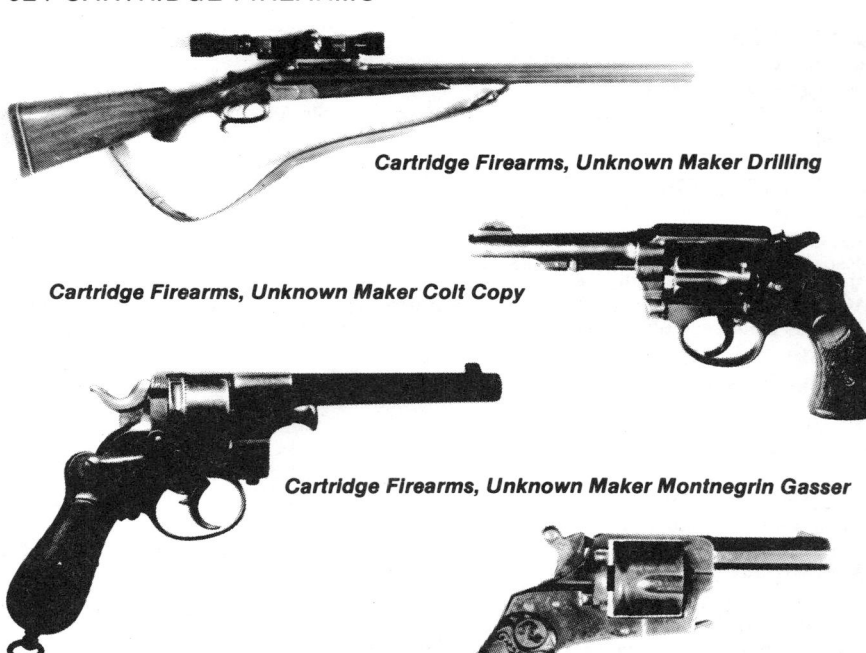

92 / CARTRIDGE FIREARMS

Cartridge Firearms, Unknown Maker Drilling

Cartridge Firearms, Unknown Maker Colt Copy

Cartridge Firearms, Unknown Maker Montnegrin Gasser

Cartridge Firearms, Unknown Maker 7mm Pinfire

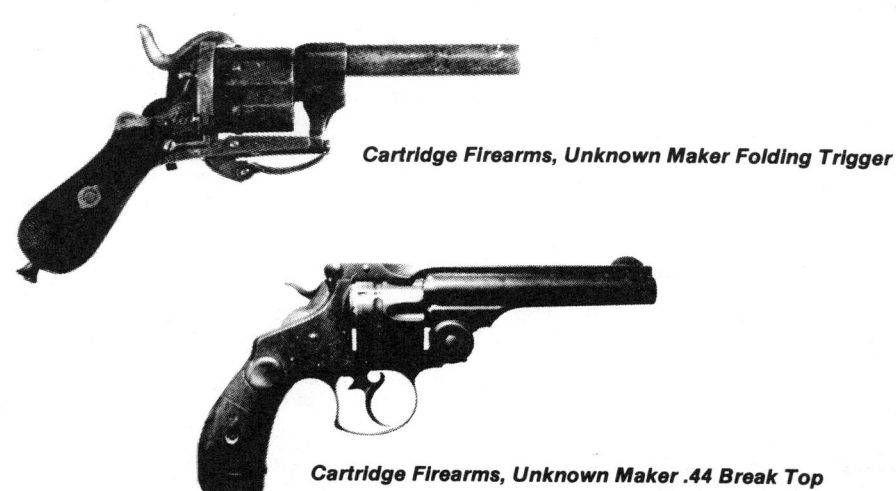

Cartridge Firearms, Unknown Maker Folding Trigger

Cartridge Firearms, Unknown Maker .44 Break Top

CARTRIDGE FIREARMS / 93

	V.G.	EXC.
☐ **Spanish Copy of S&W M-10**, .32-20 WCF, Double Action, Solid Frame, Swing-Out Cylinder, Low Quality, *Modern*	55.00	80.00
☐ **Spanish Copy of S&W M-10**, .38 Special, Double Action, Solid Frame, Swing-Out Cylinder, Low Quality, *Modern*	45.00	70.00
☐ **Various Centerfire Calibers**, Folding Trigger, Open Top Frame, *Modern*	60.00	100.00
☐ **Various Centerfire Calibers**, Bulldog Style, Double Action, Solid Frame, *Modern*	50.00	90.00
☐ **Various Centerfire Calibers**, Small Pocket Pistol, Hammerless, Folding Trigger, with Safety, *Modern*	60.00	100.00
☐ **7.62mm Nagent**, Nagent Style Gas Seal, Solid Frame, Double Action, *Modern*	75.00	150.00
☐ **Various Centerfire Calibers**, European Military Style, Double Action, Solid Frame, *Modern*	75.00	150.00
☐ **Various Centerfire Calibers**, Warnant Style, Top Break, Double Action, *Modern*	80.00	150.00
☐ **Various Centerfire Calibers**, Gasser Style, Solid Frame, Double Action, *Modern*	80.00	150.00
☐ **Velo-Dog Pistols**, Various Calibers, Double Action, Modern	80.00	125.00

HANDGUN, SEMI-AUTOMATIC

	V.G.	EXC.
☐ **Chinese Broomhandle**, 7.63 Mauser, Low Quality, Modern	85.00	160.00
☐ **Chinese Copy of FN 1900**, Various Calibers, Clip Fed, Low Quality, Modern	55.00	90.00
☐ **Chinese Pocket Pistols**, Various Calibers, Clip Fed, Low Quality, Modern	60.00	95.00
☐ **Copy of Colt M1911**, .45 ACP, Clip Fed, Military, High Quality, *Modern*	175.00	250.00
☐ **Spanish Pocket Pistols**, .25 ACP, Clip Fed, Low Quality, *Modern*	60.00	95.00
☐ **Spanish Pocket Pistols**, .32 ACP, Clip Fed, Low Quality, *Modern*	65.00	115.00
☐ **Spanish Pocket Pistols**, .32 ACP, Clip Fed, Low Quality, Ruby Style, *Modern*	65.00	115.00

HANDGUN, SINGLESHOT

	V.G.	EXC.
☐ **Flobert Style**, Various Configurations, *Modern*	45.00	85.00
☐ **.22 Short**, Target Pistol, Tip-Up Barrel, Plain, *Modern*	65.00	120.00
☐ **.22 Short**, Fancy German Target Pistol, Tip-Up Barrel, Engraved, Set Triggers, *Modern*	350.00	500.00
☐ **.22 R.F.**, Fancy Target Pistol, Hammerless, Set Triggers, *Modern*	250.00	400.00

RIFLE, BOLT ACTION

	V.G.	EXC.
☐ **Various Rimfire Calibers**, Singleshot, Checkered Stock, European, *Modern*	30.00	50.00
☐ **Various Centerfire Calibers**, Commercial Sporting Rifle, Low Quality, *Modern*	80.00	125.00
☐ **Arabian Copies**, Various Calibers, Military, Reproduction, Low Quality, *Modern*	55.00	90.00

RIFLE, SINGLESHOT

	V.G.	EXC.
☐ **Various Calibers**, Flobert Style, Checkered Stock, *Modern*	55.00	95.00
☐ **Various Calibers**, Warnant Style, Checkered Stock, *Modern*	70.00	125.00
☐ **Belgian Proofs**, .22 Long R.F., Tip-Up, Octagon Barrel, Medium Quality, *Antique*	70.00	95.00

SHOTGUN, DOUBLE BARREL, SIDE-BY-SIDE

	V.G.	EXC.
☐ **Belgian Proofs**, Various Gauges, Damascus Barrel, Low Quality, Outside Hammers, *Modern*	70.00	120.00
☐ **English Proofs**, Various Gauges, Damascus Barrel, Low Quality, Outside Hammers, *Modern*	80.00	125.00
☐ **No Proofs**, Various Gauges, Damascus Barrel, Low Quality, Outside Hammers, *Modern*	50.00	95.00

	V.G.	EXC.
☐ **Various Gauges**, American, Outside Hammers, Damascus Barrel, Modern	80.00	150.00
☐ **Various Gauges**, American, Hammerless, Steel Barrel, Modern	95.00	175.00
☐ **Various Gauges**, American, Hammerless, Damascus Barrel, Modern	75.00	150.00
☐ **Various Gauges**, American, Outside Hammers, Steel Barrel, Modern	90.00	175.00

SHOTGUN, SINGLESHOT

☐ **Various Gauges**, American, Hammer, Steel Barrel, Modern	45.00	75.00
☐ **Various Gauges**, Warnant Style, Checkered Stock, Modern	40.00	70.00
☐ **"Zulu"**, 12 Ga., Converted from Perc. Musket, Trap Door Action, Antique	75.00	125.00

COMBINATION WEAPON, DRILLING

☐ **German**, Various Calibers, **Light Engraving**, Modern	450.00	700.00

CEBRA
Arizmendi, Zulaika y Cia., Eibar, Spain.

HANDGUN, SEMI-AUTOMATIC

☐ **Pocket**, .25 ACP, Clip Fed, Curio	75.00	125.00

CELTA
Tomas de Urizar y Cia., Eibar, Spain c. 1935.

HANDGUN, SEMI-AUTOMATIC

☐ **Pocket**, .25 ACP, Clip Fed, Curio	75.00	125.00

CENTENNIAL
Made by Derringer Rifle & Pistol Works 1876.

HANDGUN, REVOLVER

☐ **.22 Short R.F.**, 7 Shot, Spur Trigger, Tip-Up, Antique	245.00	375.00
☐ **.32 Short R.F.**, 5 Shot, Spur Trigger, Solid Frame, Single Action, Antique	95.00	175.00
☐ **.38 Short R.F.**, 5 Shot, Spur Trigger, Solid Frame, Single Action, Antique	95.00	180.00
☐ **Centennial '76**, .38 Long R.F., 5 Shot, Single Action, Spur Trigger, Tip-Up, Antique	260.00	345.00
☐ **Model 2**, .32 R.F., 5 Shot, Single Action, Spur Trigger, Tip-Up, Antique	235.00	340.00

CENTRAL
Made by Stevens Arms.

SHOTGUN, DOUBLE BARREL, SIDE-BY-SIDE

☐ **Model 315**, Various Gauges, Hammerless, Steel Barrel, Modern	95.00	165.00
☐ **Model 215**, 12 and 16 Gauges, Outside Hammers, Steel Barrel, Modern	90.00	160.00
☐ **Model 311**, Various Gauges, Hammerless, Steel Barrel, Modern	95.00	175.00

SHOTGUN, SINGLESHOT

☐ **Model 94**, Various Gauges, Takedown, Automatic Ejector, Plain Hammer, Modern	40.00	65.00

CENTRAL ARMS CO.
Made by Crescent, For Shapleigh Hardware Co., c.1900.

SHOTGUN, DOUBLE BARREL, SIDE-BY-SIDE

☐ **Various Gauges**, Outside Hammers, Damascus Barrel, Modern	80.00	150.00
☐ **Various Gauges**, Hammerless, Steel Barrel, Modern	95.00	175.00

	V.G.	EXC.
☐ **Various Gauges**, Hammerless, Damascus Barrel, *Modern*	75.00	150.00
☐ **Various Gauges**, Outside Hammers, Steel Barrel, *Modern*	90.00	175.00

SHOTGUN, SINGLESHOT
☐ **Various Gauges**, Hammer, Steel Barrel, *Modern* 45.00   75.00

CHALLENGE
Made by Bliss & Goodyear, c. 1878.

HANDGUN, REVOLVER
☐ **.32 Short R.F.**, 5 Shot, Spur Trigger, Solid Frame, Single Action,
Antique 90.00   160.00

CHAMPION
Unknown Maker c. 1870.

HANDGUN, REVOLVER
☐ **.22 Short R.F.**, 7 Shot, Spur Trigger, Solid Frame, Single Action,
Antique 90.00   160.00

CHAMPLIN FIREARMS
Enid, Oklahoma.

RIFLE, BOLT ACTION
☐ **Basic Rifle**, with Quarter Rib, Express Sights, *Add* **$175.00-$250.00**
☐ **Basic Rifle**, Fancy Wood, *Add* **$50.00-$85.00**
☐ **Basic Rifle**, Fancy Checkering, *Add* **$25.00-$40.00**
☐ **Basic Rifle**, Various Calibers, Adjustable Trigger, Round or
Octagon Tapered Barrel, Checkered Stock, *Modern* 1,650.00 2,450.00

SHOTGUN, DOUBLE BARREL, OVER-UNDER
☐ **12 Ga.**, Extra Barrels, *Add* **$175.00-$250.00**
☐ **Model 100**, 12 Ga., Field Grade, Checkered Stock, Vent Rib, Single
Selective Trigger, Engraved, *Modern* 500.00   825.00
☐ **Model 100**, 12 Ga., Trap Grade, Checkered Stock, Vent Rib, Single
Selective Trigger, Engraved, *Modern* 550.00   875.00
☐ **Model 100**, 12 Ga., Skeet Grade, Checkered Stock, Vent Rib,
Single Selective Trigger, Engraved, *Modern* 550.00   875.00
☐ **Model 500**, 12 Ga., Field Grade, Checkered Stock, Vent Rib, Single
Selective Trigger, Engraved, *Modern* 825.00 1,300.00
☐ **Model 500**, 12 Ga., Skeet Grade, Checkered Stock, Vent Rib,
Single Selective Trigger, Engraved, *Modern* 875.00 1,400.00
☐ **Model 500**, 12 Ga., Trap Grade, Checkered Stock, Vent Rib, Single
Selective Trigger, Engraved, *Modern* 950.00 1,525.00

SHOTGUN, SINGLESHOT
☐ **Model SB 100**, 12 Ga., Trap Grade, Checkered Stock, Vent Rib,
Single Selective Trigger, Engraved, *Modern* 575.00   875.00
☐ **Model SB 500**, 12 Ga., Trap Grade, Checkered Stock, Vent Rib,
Single Selective Trigger, Engraved, *Modern* 875.00 1,350.00

CHAPUIS
St. Bonnet-le-Chateau, France.

SHOTGUN, DOUBLE BARREL, SIDE-BY-SIDE
☐ **Progress RBV, R20**, 12 or 20 Gauge, Automatic Ejectors,
Sideplates, Double Triggers, Checkered Stock, *Modern* 800.00 1,150.00
☐ **Progress RG**, 12 or 20 Gauge, Automatic Ejectors, Double
Triggers, Checkered Stock, *Modern* 450.00   650.00
☐ **Progress Slug**, 12 or 20 Gauge, Automatic Ejectors, Slug Barrel,
Double Triggers, Checkered Stock, *Modern* 575.00   800.00

CHARLES DALY
Tradename on guns made in Suhl, Germany prior to WWII, and by Miroku and Breda after WWII.

	V.G.	EXC.

COMBINATION WEAPON, DRILLING
- ☐ **Diamond**, Various Calibers, Fancy Engraving, Fancy Checkering, *Modern* 2,850.00 4,650.00
- ☐ **Regent Diamond**, Various Calibers, Fancy Engraving, Fancy Checkering, Fancy Wood, *Modern* 4,600.00 6,850.00
- ☐ **Superior**, Various Calibers, Engraved, *Modern* 2,550.00 3,350.00

RIFLE, BOLT ACTION
- ☐ **.22 Hornet**, 5 Shot Clip, Checkered Stock, *Modern* 600.00 950.00

SHOTGUN, DOUBLE BARREL, OVER-UNDER
- ☐ For 28 Ga., *Add 10%-15%*
- ☐ 12 Ga., for Wide Vent Rib, *Add $25.00-$40.00*
- ☐ **Various Gauges**, Field Grade, Light Engraving, Single Selective Trigger, Automatic Ejector, Post-War, *Modern* 285.00 400.00
- ☐ **Commander 100**, Various Gauges, Automatic Ejector, Checkered Stock, Double Trigger, *Modern* 320.00 420.00
- ☐ **Commander 100**, Various Gauges, Automatic Ejector, Checkered Stock, Single Trigger, *Modern* 360.00 465.00
- ☐ **Commander 200**, Various Gauges, Double Trigger, *Modern* 470.00 595.00
- ☐ **Commander 200**, Various Gauges, Automatic Ejector, Checkered Stock, Engraved, Single Trigger, *Modern* 520.00 675.00
- ☐ **Diamond**, 12 Ga., Trap Grade, Selective Ejector, Single Selective Trigger, Post-War, *Modern* 495.00 750.00
- ☐ **Diamond**, 12 and 20 Gauges, Field Grade, Trap Grade, Selective Ejector, Single Selective Trigger, Post-War, *Modern* 525.00 800.00
- ☐ **Diamond**, 12 and 20 Gauges, Skeet Grade, Trap Grade, Selective Ejector, Single Selective Trigger, Post-War, *Modern* 525.00 800.00
- ☐ **Diamond**, Various Gauges, Double Trigger, Automatic Ejector, Fancy Engraving, Fancy Checkering, *Modern* 3,000.00 5,200.00
- ☐ **Empire**, Various Gauges, Double Trigger, Automatic Ejector, Checkered Stock, Engraved, *Modern* 2,650.00 4,200.00
- ☐ **Superior**, 12 Ga., Trap Grade, Automatic Ejector, Single Selective Trigger, Post-War, *Modern* 335.00 465.00
- ☐ **Superior**, Various Gauges, Field Grade, Trap Grade, Automatic Ejector, Single Selective Trigger, Post-War, *Modern* 335.00 465.00
- ☐ **Superior**, Various Gauges, Skeet Grade, Trap Grade, Automatic Ejector, Single Selective Trigger, Post-War, *Modern* 335.00 465.00
- ☐ **Venture**, 12 Ga., Trap Grade, Single Trigger, Monte Carlo Stock, Post-War, *Modern* 260.00 375.00
- ☐ **Venture**, 12 and 20 Gauges, Field Grade, Single Trigger, Trap Grade, Post-War, *Modern* 255.00 365.00
- ☐ **Venture**, 12 and 20 Gauges, Skeet Grade, Single Trigger, Trap Grade, Post-War, *Modern* 260.00 375.00

SHOTGUN, DOUBLE BARREL, SIDE-BY-SIDE
- ☐ **Diamond**, Various Gauges, Double Trigger, Fancy Engraving, Fancy Checkering, Fancy Wood, Automatic Ejector, *Modern* 2,600.00 4,150.00
- ☐ **Empire**, Various Gauges, Double Trigger, Engraved, Checkered Stock, Automatic Ejector, *Modern* 1,850.00 2,600.00
- ☐ **Empire**, Various Gauges, Vent Rib, Single Trigger, Checkered Stock, Engraved, Post-War, *Modern* 235.00 340.00
- ☐ **Regent Diamond**, Various Gauges, Double Trigger, Fancy Engraving, Fancy Checkering, Fancy Wood, Automatic Ejector, *Modern* 3,100.00 5,350.00
- ☐ **Superior**, Various Gauges, Double Trigger, Light Engraving, Checkered Stock, *Modern* 875.00 1,650.00

	V.G.	EXC.

SHOTGUN, SEMI-AUTOMATIC
- ☐ **Novamatic**, 12 Ga., Takedown, Trap Grade, Vent Rib, Checkered Stock, Monte Carlo Stock, *Modern* 175.00 235.00
- ☐ **Novamatic**, 12 and 20 Gauges, Takedown, Plain Barrel, Checkered Stock, Lightweight, *Modern* 135.00 185.00
- ☐ **Novamatic**, 12 and 20 Gauges, Takedown, Vent Rib, Checkered Stock, Lightweight, *Modern* 150.00 195.00
- ☐ **Novamatic**, 12 and 20 Gauges, Takedown, Plain Barrel, Checkered Stock, Lightweight, Interchangeable Choke Tubes, *Modern* 140.00 190.00
- ☐ **Novamatic**, 12 and 20 Gauges, Takedown, Vent Rib, Checkered Stock, Lightweight, Interchangeable Choke Tubes, *Modern* 160.00 220.00
- ☐ **Novamatic**, 12 Ga. Mag. 3", Takedown, Vent Rib, Checkered Stock, Magnum, *Modern* 170.00 225.00
- ☐ **Novamatic**, 20 Ga., Takedown, Checkered Stock, Magnum, Lightweight, *Modern* 145.00 210.00
- ☐ **Novamatic Super Light**, 12 and 20 Gauges, Takedown, Plain Barrel, Checkered Stock, *Modern* 130.00 195.00
- ☐ **Novamatic Super Light**, 12 and 20 Gauges, Takedown, Plain Barrel, Checkered Stock, Interchangeable Choke Tubes, *Modern* 140.00 215.00
- ☐ **Novamatic Super Light**, 12 and 20 Gauges, Takedown, Vent Rib, Checkered Stock, *Modern* 150.00 230.00

SHOTGUN, SINGLESHOT
- ☐ **Empire**, 12 Ga., Trap Grade, Fancy Engraving, Fancy Wood, Automatic Ejector, *Modern* 3,600.00 4,850.00
- ☐ **Sextuple Empire**, 12 Ga., Trap Grade, Fancy Checkering, Fancy Engraving, Fancy Wood, Automatic Ejector, *Modern* 3,950.00 5,200.00
- ☐ **Sextuple Regent Diamond**, 12 Ga., Trap Grade, Fancy Checkering, Fancy Engraving, Fancy Wood, Automatic Ejector, *Modern* 5,200.00 6,750.00
- ☐ **Superior**, 12 Ga., Trap Grade, Monte Carlo Stock, Selective Ejector, Engraved, Post-War, *Modern* 275.00 385.00

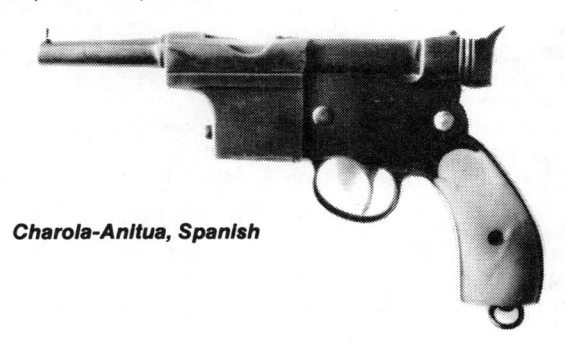

Charola-Anitua, Spanish

CHAROLA Y ANITUA
Garate, Anitua y Cia., Eibar, Spain c. 1898

HANDGUN, SEMI-AUTOMATIC
- ☐ **Charola**, 5mm Clement, Locked Breech, Box Magazine, Belgian Made, *Curio* 385.00 575.00
- ☐ **Charola**, 5mm Clement, Locked Breech, Box Magazine, Spanish Made, *Curio* 525.00 775.00

CHARTER ARMS
Stratford, Conn. since 1965.

98 / CHASE, WILLIAM

	V.G.	EXC.

HANDGUN, REVOLVER
- **Milestone Limited Edition**, .44 Special, Bulldog, Engraved, Silver Plated, Cased with Accessories, *Modern* 850.00 1,250.00
- **Bulldog Tracker**, .357 Magnum, Double Action, Blue, Adjustable Sights, *Modern* 110.00 150.00
- **Bulldog**, .44 Special, Double Action, Blue, *Modern* 95.00 145.00
- **Bulldog**, .44 Special, Double Action, Nickel Plated, *Modern* 110.00 155.00
- **Bulldog**, .44 Special, Double Action, Stainless, *Modern* 125.00 170.00
- **Pathfinder**, .22 L.R.R.F., Adjustable Sights, Bulldog Grips, Double Action, *Modern* 100.00 150.00
- **Pathfinder**, .22 L.R.R.F., Adjustable Sights, Bulldog Grips, Double Action, Stainless Steel, *Modern* 140.00 185.00
- **Pathfinder**, .22 L.R.R.F., Adjustable Sights, Square-Butt, Double Action, *Modern* 90.00 140.00
- **Pathfinder**, .22 WMR, Adjustable Sights, Double Action, Bulldog Grips, *Modern* 100.00 150.00
- **Pathfinder**, .22 WMR, Adjustable Sights, Double Action, Square-Butt, *Modern* 95.00 140.00
- **Police Bulldog**, .38 Special, Double Action, Blue, Adjustable Sights, *Modern* 95.00 135.00
- **Target Bulldog**, .357 Magnum, Double Action, Blue, Adjustable Sights, *Modern* 120.00 160.00
- **Target Bulldog**, .44 Special, Double Action, Blue, Adjustable Sights, *Modern* 125.00 165.00
- **Undercover**, .38 Special, Double Action, Blue, *Modern* 90.00 135.00
- **Undercover**, .38 Special, Double Action, Stainless Steel, *Modern* 140.00 180.00
- **Undercover**, .38 Special, Double Action, Blue, Bulldog Grips, *Modern* 95.00 145.00
- **Undercover**, .38 Special, Double Action, Nickel Plated, *Modern* ... 95.00 140.00
- **Undercover**, .38 Special, Double Action, Nickel Plated, Bulldog Grips, *Modern* 115.00 150.00
- **Undercoverette**, .32 S & W Long, Double Action, Blue, *Modern* 75.00 120.00
- **Undercoverette**, .32 S & W Long, Double Action, Blue, Bulldog Grips, *Modern* 85.00 125.00

HANDGUN, SEMI-AUTOMATIC
- **Explorer II**, .22 L.R.R.F., Clip Fed, Takedown, *Modern*............ 50.00 70.00

RIFLE, SEMI-AUTOMATIC
- **Explorer**, .22 L.R.R.F., Clip Fed, Takedown, *Modern* 50.00 70.00

CHASE, WILLIAM
Pandora, Ohio 1854-1860.

COMBINATION WEAPON, PERCUSSION
- **Various Calibers**, Double Barrel, *Antique*........................ 725.00 1,200.00

CHEROKEE ARMS CO.
Made by Crescent, C.M. McClung & Co. Tennessee c. 1900.

SHOTGUN, DOUBLE BARREL, SIDE-BY-SIDE
- **Various Gauges**, Outside Hammers, Damascus Barrel, *Modern* 80.00 150.00
- **Various Gauges**, Hammerless, Steel Barrel, *Modern* 95.00 175.00
- **Various Gauges**, Hammerless, Damascus Barrel, *Modern* 75.00 150.00
- **Various Gauges**, Outside Hammers, Steel Barrel, *Modern* 90.00 175.00

RIFLE, SINGLESHOT
- **Various Gauges**, Hammer, Steel Barrel, *Modern* 45.00 75.00

CHERRINGTON, THOMAS P.
Cattawissa, Pa. 1847-1858.
RIFLE, PILL LOCK
	V.G.	EXC.
☐ .40, Revolver, Octagon Barrel, *Antique*	1,850.00	2,525.00

CHESAPEAKE GUN CO.
Made by Crescent, c. 1900.
SHOTGUN, DOUBLE BARREL, SIDE-BY-SIDE
☐ **Various Gauges**, Outside Hammers, Damascus Barrel, *Modern* 80.00 150.00
☐ **Various Gauges**, Hammerless, Steel Barrel, *Modern* 95.00 175.00
☐ **Various Gauges**, Hammerless, Damascus Barrel, *Modern* 75.00 150.00
☐ **Various Gauges**, Outside Hammers, Steel Barrel, *Modern* 90.00 175.00
SHOTGUN, SINGLESHOT
☐ **Various Gauges**, Hammer, Steel Barrel, *Modern* 45.00 75.00

CHICAGO ARMS
HANDGUN, REVOLVER
☐ .38 S & W, Top Break, Hammerless, Double Action, Grip Safety, *Modern* 80.00 125.00

CHICAGO ARMS CO.
Sold by Fred Bifflar Co. Made by Meriden Firearms Co. 1870-1890.
HANDGUN, REVOLVER
☐ .32 S & W, 5 Shot, Double Action, Top Break, *Modern* 45.00 95.00
☐ .38 S & W, 5 Shot, Double Action, Top Break, *Modern* 45.00 95.00

Chicago Fire Arms Palm Pistol

CHICAGO FIRE ARMS CO.
Chicago, Ill. 1883-1894.
HANDGUN, PALM PISTOL
☐ .32 Extra Short R.F., Engraved, *Antique* 525.00 775.00

CHICNESTER
Made by Hopkins & Allen, c. 1880.
HANDGUN, REVOLVER
☐ .38 Short R.F., 5 Shot, Spur Trigger, Solid Frame, Single Action, *Antique* 95.00 170.00

CHIEFTAIN
Made by Norwich Pistol Co., c. 1880.
HANDGUN, REVOLVER
☐ .32 Short R.F., 5 Shot, Spur Trigger, Solid Frame, Single Action, *Antique* 90.00 160.00

CHILEAN MILITARY

	V.G.	EXC.

RIFLE, BOLT ACTION
- **M1895 Rifle**, 7mm Mauser, Military, *Curio* 80.00 140.00
- **M1895 Short Rifle**, 7mm Mauser, Military, *Curio* 95.00 150.00
- **M1895 Carbine**, 7mm Mauser, Military, *Curio* 85.00 145.00

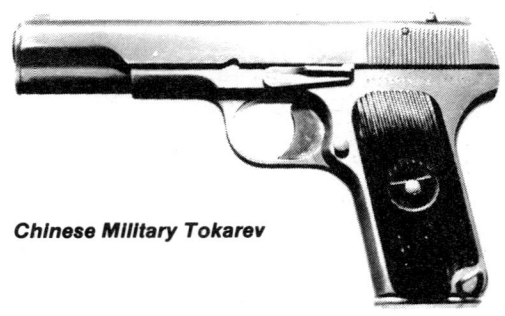

Chinese Military Tokarev

CHINESE MILITARY
AUTOMATIC WEAPON, HEAVY MACHINE GUN
- **Type 24**, 8mm Mauser, Belt Fed, Tripod, *Class 3* 3,500.00 4,700.00

HANDGUN, SEMI-AUTOMATIC
- **Makarov**, 9mm Mak., Clip Fed, *Modern* 550.00 850.00
- **Tokarev**, 7.62mm Tokarev, Clip Fed, *Modern* 160.00 245.00
- **Walther PPk Type**, .32 A.C.P., Double Action, Blue, Clip Fed, Military, *Modern* 1,000.00 1,650.00

RIFLE, BOLT ACTION
- **Type 53 (Nagent)**, 7.62 x 54R Russian, *Modern* 85.00 155.00

RIFLE, SEMI-AUTOMATIC
- **SKS**, 7.62 x 39 Russian, Folding Bayonet, Military, *Modern* 250.00 365.00

CHINESE NATIONALIST MILITARY
AUTOMATIC WEAPON, SUBMACHINE GUN
- **Sten MK II**, 9mm Luger, all Metal, Clip Fed, *Class 3* 550.00 775.00

HANDGUN, SEMI-AUTOMATIC
- **Hi Power**, 9mm Luger, Clip Fed, Military, Tangent Sights, *Curio* ... 475.00 700.00
- **Hi Power**, 9mm Luger, Clip Fed, Military, Tangent Sight, with Detachable Shoulder Stock, *Curio* 650.00 925.00

RIFLE, BOLT ACTION
- **Kar 98k Type 79**, 8mm Mauser, *Modern* 120.00 175.00
- **M1871 Mauser**, .43 Mauser, Carbine, *Antique* 95.00 160.00
- **M1888 Hanyang**, 8mm Mauser, 5 Shot, *Curio* 95.00 150.00
- **M98 Mukden**, 8mm Mauser, *Modern* 155.00 240.00

CHURCHILL, E.J. & ROBERT
London, England 1892 to Date.

RIFLE, BOLT ACTION
- **One of 1,000**, Various Calibers, Checkered Stock, Recoil Pad, Express Sights, Cartridge Trap, *Modern* 700.00 875.00
- **One of 1,000**, Various Calibers, Fancy Checkering, Engraved Express Sights, Cartridge Trap, Cased with Accessories, *Modern* .. 1,600.00 2,250.00

	V.G.	EXC.

SHOTGUN, DOUBLE BARREL, SIDE-BY-SIDE
- ☐ **Utility Model**, Various Gauges, Boxlock, Double Triggers, Color Case Hardened Frame, Engraved, *Modern* 2,400.00 3,300.00
- ☐ **Hercules Model XXV**, Various Gauges, Hammerless Sidelock, Engraved, Fancy Checkering, Fancy Wood, Cased, *Modern* 3,750.00 5,200.00
- ☐ **Field Model**, Various Gauges, Hammerless Sidelock, Fancy Checkering, Automatic Ejectors, Engraved, *Modern* 6,500.00 7,900.00
- ☐ **Imperial Model XXV**, Various Gauges, Hammerless Sidelock, Fancy Checkering, Automatic Ejectors, Engraved, *Modern* 6,500.00 7,825.00
- ☐ **Premier Quality**, Various Gauges, Hammerless Sidelock, Fancy Checkering, Automatic Ejectors, Engraved, *Modern* 7,500.00 8,800.00
- ☐ **Regal Model XXV**, Various Gauges, Hammerless Sidelock, Fancy Checkering, Automatic Ejectors, Engraved, *Modern* 3,000.00 4,250.00
- ☐ **For Single Selective Trigger** *Add* $350.00-$500.00

SHOTGUN, DOUBLE BARREL, OVER-UNDER
- ☐ **Premier Quality**, Various Gauges, Hammerless Sidelock, Fancy Checkering, Automatic Ejectors, Engraved, *Modern* 10,000.00 13,500.00
- ☐ **Premier Quality**, for Single Selective Trigger, *Add* $400.00-$500.00
- ☐ **Premier Quality**, for Raised Vent Rib, *Add* $350.00-$500.00

Chysewski .25

CHYLEWSKI, WITOLD
Austria, 1910-1918. Pistols made by S.I.G.
HANDGUN, SEMI-AUTOMATIC
- ☐ **Einhand**, .25 ACP, Clip Fed, Blue, *Curio* 525.00 675.00

CLARK, F.H.
Memphis, Tenn. c. 1860.
HANDGUN, PERCUSSION
- ☐ **Deringer**, .41, German Silver Mountings, *Antique* 475.00 725.00
- ☐ **Deringer Copy**, .41, German Silver Mountings, *Antique* 550.00 835.00

CLARKSON, J.
London, England 1680-1740.
HANDGUN, FLINTLOCK
- ☐ **.32**, Pocket Pistol, Queen Anne Style, Box Lock, Screw Barrel, Silver Furniture, *Antique* 450.00 675.00

CLASSIC ARMS
Palmer, Mass.
HANDGUN, PERCUSSION
- ☐ **.36 Duckfoot**, 3 Shot, Brass Frame, Reproduction, *Antique* 25.00 40.00
- ☐ **.36 Twister**, 2 Shot, Brass Frame, Reproduction, *Antique* 25.00 40.00
- ☐ **.36 Ethan Allen**, Pepperbox, 4 Shot, Brass Frame, Reproduction, *Antique* 25.00 40.00

102 / CLEMENT, CHARLES

	V.G.	EXC.
☐ **.36 Snake-Eyes**, Double Barrel, Side by Side, Brass Frame, Reproduction, *Antique*	20.00	35.00
☐ **.44 Ace**, Rifled, Brass Frame, Reproduction, *Antique*	15.00	25.00
☐ **.44 Ace**, Smoothbore, Brass Frame, Reproduction, *Antique*	15.00	25.00

Clement M1909 .25

Clement M1903 5mm

CLEMENT, CHARLES
Liege, Belgium 1886-1914.

HANDGUN, SEMI-AUTOMATIC
☐ **M1903**, 5mm Clement, Clip Fed, *Curio*	345.00	485.00
☐ **M1907**, .25 ACP, Clip Fed, *Curio*	185.00	290.00
☐ **M1907**, .32 ACP, Clip Fed, *Curio*	235.00	370.00
☐ **M1908**, .25 ACP, Clip Fed, *Curio*	235.00	370.00
☐ **M1909**, .25 ACP, Clip Fed, *Curio*	185.00	290.00
☐ **M1909**, .32 ACP, Clip Fed, *Curio*	235.00	370.00
☐ **M1912 Fulgor**, .32 ACP, Clip Fed, *Curio*	425.00	675.00

RIFLE, SEMI-AUTOMATIC
☐ **Clement-Neumann**, .401 Win., Clip Fed, Checkered Stock, Matted Rib, *Curio*	450.00	625.00

SHOTGUN, DOUBLE BARREL, SIDE-BY-SIDE
☐ **Various Gauges**, Outside Hammers, Damascus Barrel, *Curio*	100.00	175.00
☐ **Various Gauges**, Hammerless, Steel Barrel, *Curio*	135.00	200.00
☐ **Various Gauges**, Hammerless, Damascus Barrel, *Curio*	100.00	175.00
☐ **Various Gauges**, Outside Hammers, Steel Barrel, *Curio*	125.00	190.00

CLEMENT, J.B.
Belgium.

SHOTGUN, DOUBLE BARREL, SIDE-BY-SIDE
☐ **Various Gauges**, Hammerless, Steel Barrel, *Modern*	135.00	200.00
☐ **Various Gauges**, Outside Hammers, Steel Barrel, *Modern*	125.00	190.00

CLERKE
Santa Monica, Calif.

HANDGUN, REVOLVER
☐ **32-200**, .32 S & W, Nickel Plated, *Modern*	15.00	25.00

	V.G.	EXC.
☐ CF200, .22 L.R.R.F., Nickel Plated, *Modern*	15.00	25.00

RIFLE, SINGLESHOT
☐ **Hi-Wall**, Various Calibers, Fancy Wood, *Modern*	185.00	295.00
☐ **Hi-Wall Deluxe**, Various Calibers, Octagon Barrel, Fancy Wood, *Modern*	275.00	395.00
☐ **Hi-Wall Deluxe**, Various Calibers, Octagon Barrel, Set Trigger, Fancy Wood, *Modern*	295.00	435.00

CLIMAS
Made by Stevens Arms.

SHOTGUN, SINGLESHOT
☐ **Model 90**, Various Gauges, Takedown, Automatic Ejector, Plain Hammer, *Modern*	40.00	60.00

CLIPPER
Maker Unknown c. 1880.

HANDGUN, REVOLVER
☐ **.22 Short R.F.**, 7 Shot, Spur Trigger, Solid Frame, Single Action, *Antique*	85.00	150.00

CODY MANUFACTURING CO.
Chicopee, Mass. 1957-1959.

HANDGUN, REVOLVER
☐ **Thunderbird**, .22 R.F., 6 Shot, Double Action, Aluminium with Steel Liners, *Modern*	110.00	175.00

COGSWELL & HARRISON
London, England 1770 to Date; Branch in Paris 1924-1938.

HANDGUN, REVOLVER
☐ **S & W Victory**, .38 Special, Double Action, Swing-Out Cylinder, Refinished and Customized. Rebored from .38 S & W and may be unsafe with .38 Spec., *Modern*	75.00	135.00

RIFLE, BOLT ACTION
☐ **BSA-Lee Speed**, .303 British, Sporting Rifle, Express Sights, Engraved, Checkered Stock, Commercial, *Modern*	525.00	800.00

SHOTGUN, DOUBLE BARREL, SIDE-BY-SIDE
☐ **Avant Tout (Konor)**, Various Gauges, Box Lock, Automatic Ejector, Fancy Checkering, Fancy Engraving, Double Trigger, *Modern*	2,100.00	2,975.00
☐ **Avant Tout (Konor)**, Various Gauges, Box Lock, Automatic Ejector, Fancy Checkering, Fancy Engraving, Single Trigger, *Modern*	2,375.00	3,275.00
☐ **Avant Tout (Konor)**, Various Gauges, Box Lock, Automatic Ejector, Fancy Checkering, Fancy Engraving, Single Selective Trigger, *Modern*	2,600.00	3,475.00
☐ **Avant Tout (Rex)**, Various Gauges, Box Lock, Automatic Ejector, Checkered Stock, Light Engraving, Double Trigger, *Modern*	1,250.00	2,175.00
☐ **Avant Tout (Rex)**, Various Gauges, Box Lock, Automatic Ejector, Checkered Stock, Light Engraving, Single Trigger, *Modern*	1,400.00	2,375.00
☐ **Avant Tout (Rex)**, Various Gauges, Box Lock, Automatic Ejector, Checkered Stock, Light Engraving, Single Selective Trigger, *Modern*	1,550.00	2,575.00
☐ **Avant Tout (Sandhurst)**, Various Gauges, Box Lock, Automatic Ejector, Fancy Checkering, Engraved, Double Trigger, *Modern*	1,850.00	2,775.00

104 / COLON

Cogswell & Harrison Lee Speed

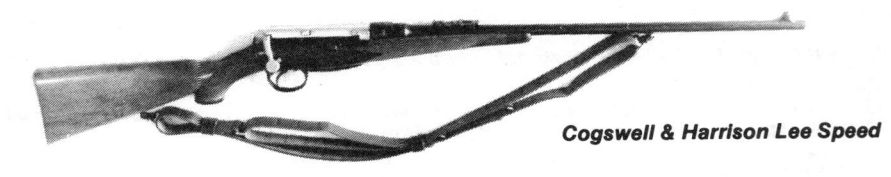

	V.G.	EXC.
☐ **Avant Tout (Sandhurst)**, Various Gauges, Box Lock, Automatic Ejector, Fancy Checkering, Engraved, Single Trigger, *Modern*	2,100.00	2,975.00
☐ **Avant Tout (Sandhurst)**, Various Gauges, Box Lock, Automatic Ejector, Fancy Checkering, Engraved, Single Selective Trigger, *Modern*	2,250.00	3,150.00
☐ **Huntic**, Various Gauges, Sidelock, Automatic Ejector, Checkered Stock, Double Trigger, *Modern*	2,350.00	3,450.00
☐ **Huntic**, Various Gauges, Sidelock, Automatic Ejector, Checkered Stock, Single Trigger, *Modern*	2,600.00	3,675.00
☐ **Huntic**, Various Gauges, Sidelock, Automatic Ejector, Checkered Stock, Single Selective Trigger, *Modern*	2,700.00	3,775.00
☐ **Markor**, Various Gauges, Box Lock, Automatic Ejector, Checkered Stock, Double Trigger, *Modern*	1,100.00	2,175.00
☐ **Markor**, Various Gauges, Box Lock, Checkered Stock, Double Trigger, *Modern*	850.00	1,850.00
☐ **Primic**, Various Gauges, Sidelock, Automatic Ejector, Fancy Engraving, Fancy Checkering, Double Trigger, *Modern*	3,200.00	4,450.00
☐ **Primic**, Various Gauges, Sidelock, Automatic Ejector, Fancy Engraving, Fancy Checkering, Single Trigger, *Modern*	3,400.00	4,650.00
☐ **Primic**, Various Gauges, Sidelock, Automatic Ejector, Fancy Engraving, Fancy Checkering, Single Selective Trigger, *Modern*	3,450.00	4,675.00
☐ **Victor**, Various Gauges, Sidelock, Automatic Ejector, Engraved, Checkered Stock, Double Trigger, *Modern*	5,100.00	6,575.00
☐ **Victor**, Various Gauges, Sidelock, Automatic Ejector, Engraved, Checkered Stock, Single Trigger, *Modern*	5,400.00	6,850.00
☐ **Victor**, Various Gauges, Sidelock, Automatic Ejector, Engraved, Checkered Stock, Single Selective Trigger, *Modern*	5,450.00	6,875.00

COLON
Antonio Azpiri y Cia. Eibar, Spain 1914-1918.

HANDGUN, SEMI-AUTOMATIC
☐ **Pocket**, .25 ACP, Clip Fed, *Curio*	80.00	120.00

COLON
Made by Orbea Hermanos Eibar, Spain c. 1925.

HANDGUN, REVOLVER
☐ **Colt Police Positive Copy**, .32/20, Double Action, Blue, *Curio*	80.00	135.00

COLONIAL
Fabrique d'Armes de Guerre de Grand Precision, Eibar, Spain.

HANDGUN, SEMI-AUTOMATIC
☐ **.25 ACP**, Clip Fed, Blue, *Modern*	70.00	115.00
☐ **.32 ACP**, Clip Fed, Blue, *Modern*	95.00	145.00

COLT
Patterson N.J. 1836-1841. Whitneyville, Conn. 1847-1848. Hartford, Conn. l848 to Date; London, England l853-1864. Also See U.S. Military.

COLT / 105

	V.G.	EXC.

AUTOMATIC WEAPON, ASSAULT RIFLE
☐ **AR-15**, .223 Rem., Clip Fed, Early Model, *Class 3* 700.00   1,100.00
☐ **M16-M A C**, .22 L.R.R.F., Clip Fed, Conversion Unit only, *Class 3*   70.00   110.00
☐ **MI6A1**, .223 Rem., Clip Fed, Commercial, *Class 3* 575.00   850.00
☐ **M1919 BAR**, .30-06 Springfield, Clip Fed, Commercial, Finned Barrel, with Compensator, Curio, *Class 3* 2,850.00 3,650.00

AUTOMATIC WEAPON, HEAVY MACHINE GUN
☐ **M1906 Colt**, .30-06 Springfield, Belt Fed, Tripod Potato Digger, Military, *Class 3* 1,850.00 2,500.00
☐ **M2 Browning**, .50 BMG, Belt Fed, Heavy Barrel, Military, *Class 3* ... 1,950.00 2,600.00
☐ **M2 Browning**, .50 BMG, Belt Fed, Heavy Barrel, Commercial, *Class 3* 3,500.00 4,450.00

AUTOMATIC WEAPON, LIGHT MACHINE GUN
☐ **Benet-Mercie U.S.N. 1912**, .30-06 Springfield, Clip Fed, Dewat, *Class 3* 2,700.00 3,750.00

AUTOMATIC WEAPON, SUBMACHINE GUN
☐ **XM177E2**, .223 Rem., Clip Fed, Folding Stock, Silencer, Short Rifle, Military, *Class 3* 1,550.00 2,250.00

COMBINATION WEAPON, DRILLING
☐ **Various Calibers**, Engraved, Fancy Checkering, *Modern* 1,650.00 2,550.00

HANDGUN, PERCUSSION
☐ **.28 Model 1855 Root**, Full Fluted Cylinder, Side Hammer, Spur Trigger, Revolver, Octagon Barrel, *Antique* 425.00   700.00
☐ **.28 Model 1855 Root**, Full Fluted Cylinder, Side Hammer, Spur Trigger, Revolver, Round Barrel, *Antique* 450.00   725.00
☐ **.28 Model 1855 Root**, Round Cylinder, Side Hammer, Spur Trigger, Revolver, Octagon Barrel, *Antique* 375.00   675.00
☐ **.28 Model 1855 Root**, Round Cylinder, Side Hammer, Spur Trigger, Revolver, Round Barrel, *Antique* 425.00   725.00
☐ **.28 Model Patterson (Baby)**, 5 Shot, Various Barrel Lengths, Octagon Barrel, no Loading Lever, *Antique* 2,450.00 3,750.00
☐ **.28 Model Patterson (Baby)**, 5 Shot, Various Barrel Lengths, Octagon Barrel, with Factory Loading Lever, *Antique* 2,850.00 4,100.00
☐ **.31 Model 1848 Revolver**, Baby Dragoon, 5 Shot, Various Barrels Lengths, no Loading Lever, no Capping Groove, *Antique* 1,950.00 3,000.00
☐ **.31 Model 1848 Revolver**, Baby Dragoon, 5 Shot, Various Barrels Lengths, no Loading Lever, Stagecoach Cylinder, *Antique* 1,150.00 2,250.00
☐ **.31 Model 1848 Revolver**, Baby Dragoon, 5 Shot, Various Barrels Lengths, no Loading Lever, *Antique* 1,500.00 2,650.00
☐ **.31 Model 1848 Revolver**, Baby Dragoon, 5 Shot, Various Barrel Lengths, with Loading Lever, *Antique* 1,700.00 2,850.00
☐ **.31 Model 1849 Revolver**, Wells Fargo, 5 Shot, no Loading Lever, Pocket Pistol, *Antique* 1,250.00 1,875.00
☐ **.31 Model 1849 Revolver**, Pocket Pistol, with Loading Lever, 5 Shot, Round-backed Trigger Guard, Large, 1-Line N.Y. Address, Brass Frame, *Antique* 425.00   600.00
☐ **.31 Model 1849 Revolver**, Pocket Pistol, with Loading Lever, 5 Shot, Large Round-Backed Trigger Guard, 1-Line Hartford Address, Brass Frame, *Antique* 495.00   725.00
☐ **.31 Model 1849 Revolver**, Pocket Pistol, with Loading Lever, 5 Shot, Round-backed Trigger Guard, Large, 1-Line Hartford Address, Iron Frame, *Antique* 500.00   750.00
☐ **.31 Model 1849 Revolver**, Pocket Pistol, with Loading Lever, 5 Shot, Large Round-backed Trigger Guard, 1-Line London Address, Iron Frame, *Antique* 675.00   950.00

106 / COLT

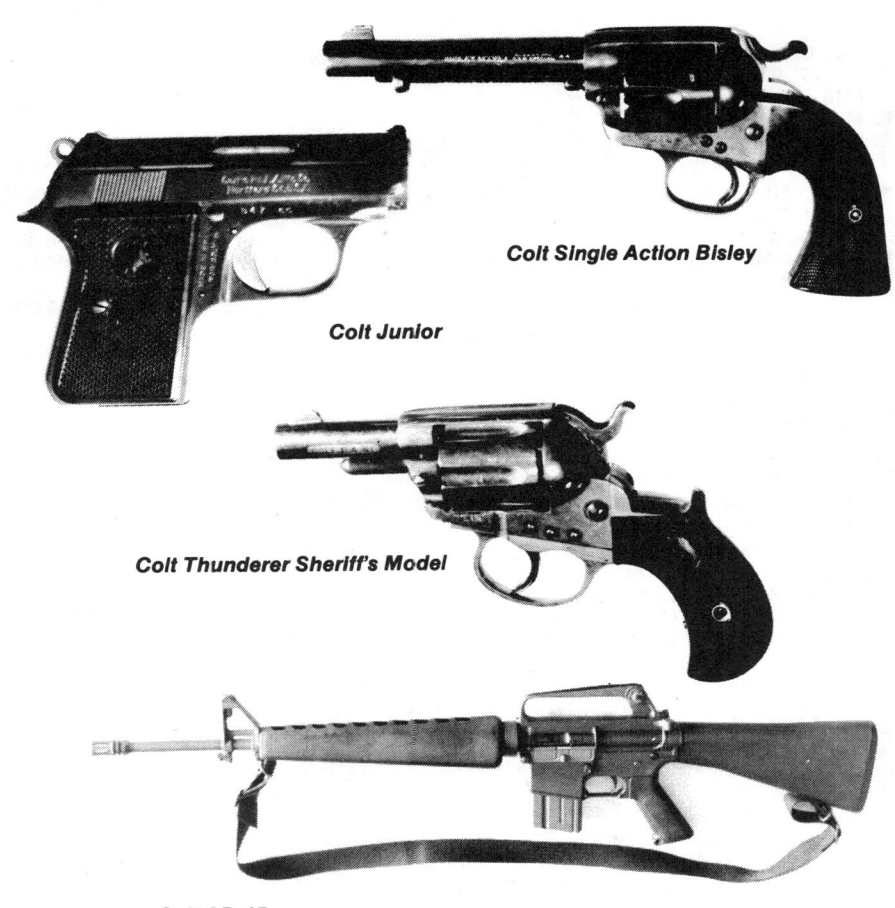

Colt Single Action Bisley

Colt Junior

Colt Thunderer Sheriff's Model

Colt AR-15

Colt Lightning Rifle Small Frame

Colt New Line

COLT / 107

	V.G.	EXC.
☐ **.31 Model 1849 Revolver**, Pocket Pistol, with Loading Lever, 5 Shot, Round-backed Trigger Guard, Small, 2-Line N.Y. Address, Iron Frame, *Antique*	425.00	575.00
☐ **.31 Model 1849 Revolver**, Pocket Pistol, with Loading Lever, 5 Shot, Round-Backed Trigger Guard, Small, 2-Line N.Y. Address, Brass Frame, *Antique*	425.00	575.00
☐ **.31 Model 1849 Revolver**, Pocket Pistol, with Loading Lever, 5 Shot, Square-Backed Trigger Guard, Small, 2-Line N.Y. Address, *Antique*	875.00	1,500.00
☐ **.31 Model 1849**, For 5" Barrel, *Add* **10%-15%**		
☐ **.31 Model 1849**, For 6" Barrel, *Add* **15%-25%**		
☐ **.31 Model 1849**, 6 Shot (Model 1850), *Add* **15%-25%**		
☐ **.31 Baby Dragoon**, Late, Unfluted Cylinder, Reproduction, *Antique*	125.00	200.00
☐ **.31 Model 1855 Root**, Full Fluted Cylinder, Side Hammer, Spur Trigger, Revolver, Octagon Barrel, *Antique*	500.00	800.00
☐ **.31 Model 1855 Root**, Full Fluted Cylinder, Side Hammer, Spur Trigger, Revolver, Round Barrel, *Antique*	525.00	825.00
☐ **.31 Model 1855 Root**, Round Fluted Cylinder, Side Hammer, Spur Trigger, Revolver, Octagon Barrel, *Antique*	525.00	825.00
☐ **.31 Model 1855 Root**, Round Fluted Cylinder, Side Hammer, Spur Trigger, Revolver, Round Barrel, *Antique*	600.00	925.00
☐ **.31 Model 1855**, For 4½" Barrel, *Add* **10%-15%**		
☐ **.31, .28 Model 1855**, London Markings, *Add* **50%-75%**		
☐ **.31 Model Patterson (Baby)**, 5 Shot, Octagon Barrel, Various Barrel Lengths, no Loading Lever, no Capping Groove, *Antique*	2,150.00	3,700.00
☐ **.31 Model Patterson (Baby)**, 5 Shot, Octagon Barrel, Various Barrel Lengths, with Factory Loading Lever, *Antique*	2,650.00	4,150.00
☐ **.31, .34 Model Patterson (Pocket)**, 5 Shot Octagon Barrel, Various Barrel Lengths, no Loading Lever, no Capping Groove, *Antique*	2,875.00	4,150.00
☐ **.31 Model Patterson (Pocket)**, 5 Shot, Octagon Barrel, Various Barrel Lengths, with Factory Loading Lever, *Antique*	3,450.00	4,750.00
☐ **.31 Model Patterson (Belt)**, 5 Shot, Octagon Barrel, Various Barrel Lengths, no Loading Lever, no Capping Groove, Straight Grip, *Antique*	2,850.00	4,450.00
☐ **.31 Model Patterson (Belt)**, 5 Shot, Octagon Barrel, Various Barrel Lengths, no Loading Lever, no Capping Groove, Flared Grip, *Antique*	3,450.00	4,950.00
☐ **.31 Model Patterson (Belt)**, Factory Loading Lever *Add* **10%-15%**		
☐ **.36 M1851 Grant-Lee Set**, Revolver, Commemorative, Cased Reproduction, *Antique*	750.00	1,100.00
☐ **.36 M1851 Late**, Revolver, 6 Shot, Reproduction, *Antique*	125.00	225.00
☐ **.36 M1851 R.E. Lee**, Revolver, Commemorative, Cased Reproduction, *Antique*	225.00	375.00
☐ **.36 M1851 U.S. Grant**, Revolver, Commemorative, Cased Reproduction, *Antique*	225.00	375.00
☐ **.36 Model 1851**, Half-Fluted, Rebated Cylinder, *Add* **25%-40%**		
☐ **.36 Model 1851 Navy**, Revolver, with Loading Lever, Square-Backed Trigger Guard, 1st Type, Under #1250, 6 Shot, *Antique*	2,450.00	3,650.00
☐ **.36 Model 1851 Navy**, Revolver, with Loading Lever, Square-Backed Trigger Guard, 2nd Type, #1250 to #3500, 6 Shot, *Antique*	1,400.00	2,200.00
☐ **.36 Model 1851 Navy**, Revolver, with Loading Lever, 6 Shot, Small Round-Backed Guard, Small Loading Cut, *Antique*	725.00	1,375.00
☐ **.36 Model 1851 Navy**, Revolver, with Loading Lever, 6 Shot, Small Round-Backed Guard, Large Loading Cut, *Antique*	725.00	1,350.00
☐ **.36 Model 1851 Navy**, Revolver, with Loading Lever, 6 Shot, Round-Backed Trigger Guard, Large Loading Cut, London Address, Iron Frame, *Antique*	725.00	1,450.00

108 / COLT

	V.G.	EXC.
☐ .36 **Model 1851 Navy**, Revolver, with Loading Lever, 6 Shot, Round-Backed Trigger Guard, Small Loading Cut, London Address, Iron Frame, *Antique*	950.00	1,750.00
☐ .36 **Model 1851 Navy**, Revolver, with Loading Lever, 6 Shot, Large Round-Backed Guard, Large Loading Cut, N.Y. Address, *Antique*	525.00	925.00
☐ .36 **Model 1851 Navy**, Revolver, with Loading Lever, 6 Shot, Large Round-Backed Guard, Large Loading Cut, Hartford Address, *Antique*	600.00	1,100.00
☐ .36 **Model 1851 Navy**, Revolver, with Loading Lever, 6 Shot, Large Round-Backed Guard, Cut for Shoulder Stock, Iron Backstrap, *Antique*	1,850.00	3,150.00
☐ .36 **Model 1851 Navy**, Revolver, with Loading Lever, 6 Shot, Large Round-Backed Guard, with Detachable Shoulder Stock, Iron Backstrap, *Antique*	3,650.00	5,750.00
☐ .36 **Model 1862 Navy**, Revolver, New Navy Pocket Pistol 4½" Barrel, Rebated Cylinder, *Antique*	525.00	875.00
☐ .36 **Model 1862 Navy**, Revolver, New Navy Pocket Pistol 5½" Barrel, Rebated Cylinder, *Antique*	575.00	925.00
☐ .36 **Model 1862 Navy**, Revolver, Late New Navy Pocket Pistol 5½" Barrel, Rebated Cylinder, Reproduction, *Antique*	125.00	200.00
☐ .36 **Model 1862 Navy**, Revolver, New Navy Pocket Pistol 1861, 6½" Barrel, Rebated Cylinder, *Antique*	575.00	875.00
☐ .36 **Model 1861 Navy**, Revolver, Round Barrel, Military Model, no Cuts for Shoulder Stock, *Antique*	1,775.00	2,950.00
☐ .36 **Model 1861 Navy**, Revolver, Round Barrel, Civilian Model, no Cuts for Shoulder Stock, *Antique*	775.00	1,375.00
☐ .36 **Model 1861 Navy**, Revolver, Late, Round Barrel, Civilian Model, no Cuts for Shoulder Stock, Reproduction, *Antique*	125.00	225.00
☐ .36 **Model 1861 Navy**, Revolver, Round Barrel, Military, Cut for Shoulder Stock, *Antique*	2,150.00	3,950.00
☐ .36 **Model 1861 Navy**, Revolver, Round Barrel, Military, With Shoulder Stock, *Antique*	2,950.00	6,475.00
☐ .36 **Model 1862 Police**, Revolver, Half-Fluted Rebated Cylinder, *Antique*	475.00	850.00
☐ .36 **Model 1862 Police**, Revolver, Late, Half-Fluted Rebated Cylinder, Reproduction, *Antique*	125.00	200.00
☐ .36 **Model 1862 Police**, for Hartford Marks Add 10%-20%		
☐ .36 **Model 1862 Police**, for London Marks Add 10%-20%		
☐ .36 **Model Patterson (Holster)**, 5 Shot, Octagon Barrel, Various Barrel Lengths, no Loading Lever, no Capping Groove, *Antique*	6,500.00	9,975.00
☐ .36 **Model Patterson (Holster)**, 5 Shot, Octagon Barrel, Various Barrel Lengths, with Factory Loading Lever, *Antique*	9,250.00	17,000.00
☐ .44 **Model 1847**, Revolver, Whitneyville Walker (U.S.M.R.), Square-Backed Trigger Guard, 6 Shot, *Antique*	17,750.00	27,500.00
☐ .44 **Model 1847 Revolver**, Dragoon, (Hartford) Horizontal Loading Lever Latch, 6 Shot, *Antique*	5,250.00	9,750.00
☐ .44 **Model 1847**, Revolver, Dragoon, (Hartford) Vertical Loading Lever Latch, Square-Backed Trigger Guard, 6 Shot, *Antique*	3,000.00	4,950.00
☐ .44 **Dragoon 1st Model**, Revolver, 6 Shot, Civilian, *Antique*	1,750.00	3,900.00
☐ .44 **Dragoon 1st Model**, Revolver, 6 Shot, Military, *Antique*	1,975.00	4,500.00
☐ .44 **Dragoon 1st Model**, Revolver, 6 Shot, Military, Cut for Shoulder Stock, *Antique*	2,200.00	4,950.00
☐ .44 **Dragoon 1st Model**, Revolver, 6 Shot, Military, With Shoulder Stock, *Antique*	3,875.00	7,750.00
☐ .44 **Dragoon 1st Model**, Revolver, 6 Shot, Reproduction, *Antique*	165.00	235.00
☐ .44 **Dragoon 1st Model**, Revolver, 6 Shot, Fluck Variation, *Antique*	2,650.00	4,500.00
☐ .44 **Dragoon 2nd Model**, Revolver, 6 Shot, Civilian, *Antique*	1,450.00	3,500.00

COLT / 109

	V.G.	EXC.
☐ .44 Dragoon 2nd Model, Revolver, 6 Shot, Military, *Antique*	1,600.00	3,750.00
☐ .44 Dragoon 2nd Model, Revolver, 6 Shot, Military, Cut for Shoulder Stock, *Antique*	2,500.00	5,000.00
☐ .44 Dragoon 2nd Model, Revolver, 6 Shot, Military, With Shoulder Stock, *Antique*	5,000.00	8,700.00
☐ .44 Dragoon 2nd Model, Revolver, 6 Shot, Militia, *Antique*	1,850.00	4,500.00
☐ .44 Dragoon 3rd Model, Revolver, 6 Shot, Civilian, *Antique*	1,100.00	2,750.00
☐ .44 Dragoon 3rd Model, Revolver, 6 Shot, Military, *Antique*	1,450.00	2,950.00
☐ .44 Dragoon 3rd Model, Revolver, 6 Shot, Military, Cut for Shoulder Stock, *Antique*	1,850.00	3,750.00
☐ .44 Dragoon 3rd Model, Revolver, 6 Shot, Military, With Shoulder Stock, *Antique*	2,850.00	5,700.00
☐ .44 Statehood Dragoon 3rd Model, Revolver, 6 Shot, Fancy Engraving, Gold Inlays, Ivory Stocks, Commemorative, Reproduction, *Antique*	10,500.00	14,500.00
☐ .44 Model 1860 Army, Revolver, Cut for Shoulder Stock, *Antique*	700.00	1,150.00
☐ .44 Model 1860 Army, Revolver, Cut for Shoulder Stock, Four-Screw Frame, *Antique*	825.00	1,450.00
☐ .44 Model 1860 Army, Revolver, Cut for Shoulder Stock, Four-Screw Frame, with Shoulder Stock, *Antique*	2,750.00	3,750.00
☐ .44 Model 1860 Army, Revolver, Cut for Shoulder Stock, Four-Screw Frame, Fluted Cylinder, *Antique*	1,200.00	1,850.00
☐ .44 Model 1860 Army, Revolver, Cut for Shoulder Stock, Four-Screw Frame, Fluted Cylinder, Hartford Address, *Antique*	1,650.00	2,350.00
☐ .44 Model 1860 Army, Revolver, Cut for Shoulder Stock, Four-Screw Frame, Fluted Cylinder, Hartford Address, with Shoulder Stock, *Antique*	3,200.00	4,500.00
☐ .44 Model 1860 Army, Revolver, Fluted Cylinder, Reproduction, *Antique*	175.00	250.00
☐ .44 Model 1860 Army, Revolver, Butterfield Overland Express Commemorative, Two Cylinders, Reproduction, *Antique*	400.00	625.00
☐ .44 Model 1860 Army, Revolver, Cut for Shoulder Stock, Civilian Model, *Antique*	650.00	1,150.00
☐ .44 Model 1860 Army, Revolver, Cut for Shoulder Stock, London Markings, *Add 50%-75%*		

HANDGUN, CARTRIDGE CONVERSIONS

	V.G.	EXC.
☐ Model 1851 Navy, .38 R.F or C.F., Richards-Mason, *Antique*	400.00	675.00
☐ Model 1851 Navy, .36 Thuer, Thuer Style, *Antique*	1,850.00	3,300.00
☐ Model 1860 Army, .44 Thuer, Theur Style, *Antique*	1,850.00	3,300.00
☐ Model 1860 Army, .44 Colt, Richards, *Antique*	500.00	825.00
☐ Model 1860 Army, .44 Colt, Richards-Mason, *Antique*	675.00	1,100.00
☐ Model 1861 Navy, .36 Thuer, Theur Style, *Antique*	2,375.00	4,500.00
☐ Model 1862 Pocket Navy, .36 Thuer, Theur Style, *Antique*	1,950.00	3,750.00
☐ Model 1862 Pocket Navy, .38 R.F., no Ejector, Octagon Barrel, *Antique*	325.00	600.00
☐ Model 1862 Pocket Navy, .38 R.F., no Ejector, Round Barrel, *Antique*	275.00	550.00
☐ Model 1862 Pocket Navy, .38 R.F., with Ejector, Round Barrel, *Antique*	425.00	750.00

HANDGUN, REVOLVER
☐ for Nickel Plating *Add $20.00-$30.00*

	V.G.	EXC.
☐ ".357 Magnum", .357 Magnum, 6 Shot, Various Barrel Lengths, Adjustable Sights, Target Hammer, Target Grips, *Modern*	275.00	425.00
☐ ".357 Magnum", .357 Magnum, 6 Shot, Various Barrel Lengths, Adjustable Sights, *Modern*	250.00	375.00
☐ 125th Anniversary, .45 Colt, Single Action Army, Commemorative, Blue, with Gold Plating, Cased, *Curio*	450.00	700.00

110 / COLT

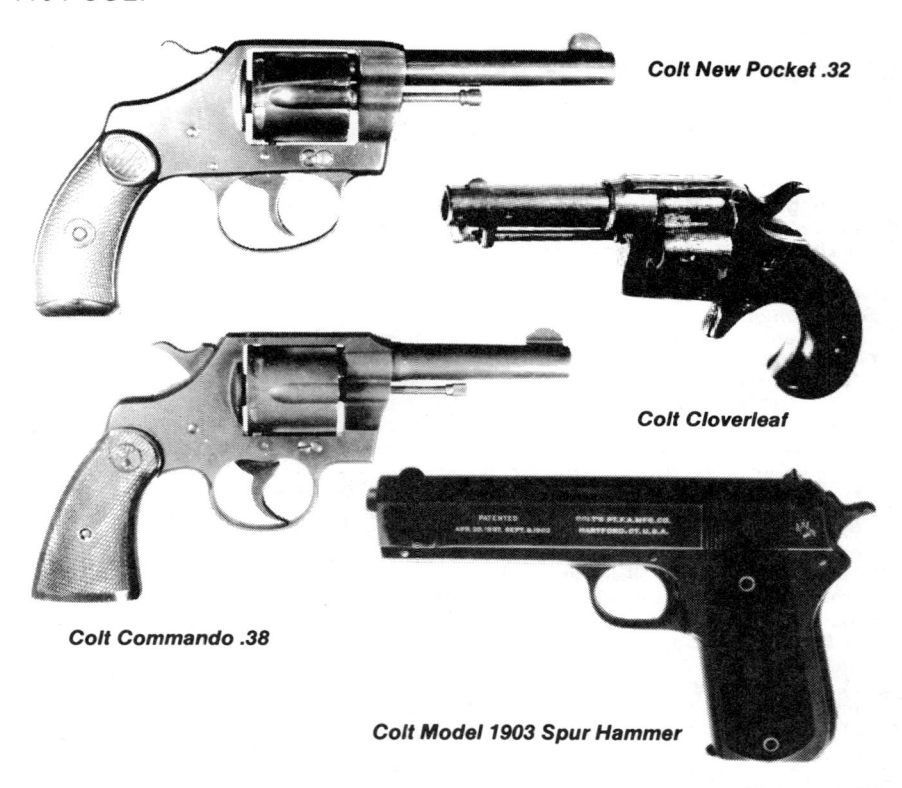

Colt New Pocket .32

Colt Cloverleaf

Colt Commando .38

Colt Model 1903 Spur Hammer

	V.G.	EXC.
☐ **Agent**, .38 Special, 6 Shot, Parkerized, 2" Barrel, Lightweight, *Modern*	115.00	150.00
☐ **Agent**, .38 Special, 6 Shot, Blue, 2" Barrel, Lightweight, *Modern*	145.00	200.00
☐ **Agent**, .38 Special, 6 Shot, Nickel Plated, 2" Barrel, Lightweight, *Modern*	155.00	220.00
☐ **Agent Early**, .38 Special, 6 Shot, 2" Barrel, Lightweight, *Modern*	155.00	225.00
☐ **Alabama Sesquicentennial**, .22 L.R.R.F., Frontier Scout S.A., Commemorative, Gold Plated, with Nickel Plating, 4¾" Barrel, Cased, *Curio*	225.00	300.00
☐ **Alamo Model**, .22 L.R.R.F., Frontier Scout S.A., Commemorative, Blue, with Gold Plating, 4¾" Barrel, Cased, *Curio*	200.00	275.00
☐ **Alamo Model**, .22 L.R.R.F., and .45 Colt Set, Frontier Scout and S.A.A., Commemorative, Blue, with Gold Plating, Cased, *Curio*	750.00	1,100.00
☐ **Alamo Model**, .45 Colt, Single Action Army, Commemorative, Blue, with Gold Plating, 5½" Barrel, Cased, *Curio*	575.00	800.00
☐ **Abercrombie & Fitch**, .45 Colt, Trailblazer New Frontier S.A., Commemorative, New York, 7½" Barrel, Cased, *Curio*	1,400.00	1,950.00
☐ **Abercrombie & Fitch**, .45 Colt, Trailblazer New Frontier S.A., Commemorative, Chicago, 7½" Barrel, Cased, *Curio*	1,400.00	1,950.00
☐ **Abercrombie & Fitch**, 45. Colt, Trailblazer New Frontier S.A., Commemorative, San Francisco, 7½" Barrel, Cased, *Curio*	1,400.00	1,950.00

COLT / 111

	V.G.	EXC.
☐ **Appomattox Centennial**, .22 L.R.R.F., Frontier Scout S.A., Commemorative, Blue, With Nickel Plating, 4¾" Barrel, Cased, *Curio*	195.00	275.00
☐ **Appomattox Centennial**, .22 L.R.R.F., and .45 Colt Set, Frontier Scout and S.A.A., Commemorative, Blue, with Nickel Plating, Cased, *Curio*	725.00	1,075.00
☐ **Appomattox Centennial**, .45 Colt, Single Action Army, Commemorative, Blue, with Nickel Plating, 5½" Barrel, Cased, *Curio*	500.00	800.00
☐ **Argentine M1895**, .38, Double Action, Solid Frame, Swing-Out Cylinder, Military, *Curio*	100.00	170.00
☐ **Arizona Ranger**, .22 L.R.R.F., Frontier Scout S.A., Commemorative, Blue, Color Case Hardened Frame, 4¾" Barrel, Cased, *Curio*	200.00	300.00
☐ **Arizona Territorial Centennial**, .22 L.R.R.F., Frontier Scout S.A., Commemorative, Blue, with Gold Plating, 4¾" Barrel, Cased, *Curio*	225.00	300.00
☐ **Arizona Territorial Centennial**, .45 Colt, Single Action Army, Commemorative, Blue, with Gold Plating, 4¾" Barrel, Cased, *Curio*	550.00	800.00
☐ **Arkansas Territorial Sesquicentennial**, .22 L.R.R.F., Frontier Scout S.A., Commemorative, Blue, 4¾" Barrel, Cased, *Curio*	175.00	235.00
☐ **Army Special**, .32-20 WCF, 6 Shot, Various Barrel Lengths, *Curio*	195.00	325.00
☐ **Army Special**, .38 Special, 6 Shot, Various Barrel Lengths, *Curio*	185.00	275.00
☐ **Army Special**, .41 Long Colt, 6 Shot, Various Barrel Lengths, *Curio*	155.00	235.00
☐ **Banker's Special**, .22 L.R.R.F., 6 Shot, 2" Barrel, *Modern*	475.00	750.00
☐ **Banker's Special**, Fitzgerald Trigger Guard Add **$150.00-$250.00**		
☐ **Banker's Special**, .38 S & W, 6 Shot, 2" Barrel, *Modern*	300.00	425.00
☐ **Battle of Gettysburg Centennial**, .22 L.R.R.F., Frontier Scout S.A., Nickel Plated, Blue, with Gold Plating, 4¾" Barrel, Cased, *Curio*	220.00	300.00
☐ **Bicentennial Set**, Python, SAA, Dragoon, Commemorative, Cased, *Curio*	1,900.00	2,500.00
☐ **California Bicentennial**, .22 L.R.R.F., Frontier Scout S.A., Commemorative, Gold Plated, with Nickel Plating, 6" Barrel, Cased, *Curio*	190.00	275.00
☐ **California Gold Rush**, .22 L.R.R.F., Frontier Scout S.A., Commemorative, Gold Plated, 4¾" Barrel, Cased, *Curio*	250.00	350.00
☐ **California Gold Rush**, .45 Colt, Single Action Army, Commemorative, Gold Plated, 5½" Barrel, Cased, *Curio*	850.00	1,100.00
☐ **Carolina Charter Tercentennial**, .22 L.R.R.F., Frontier Scout S.A., Commemorative, Blue, with Gold Plating, 4¾" Barrel, Cased, *Curio*	300.00	400.00
☐ **Carolina Charter Tercentennial**, .22 L.R.R.F., and .45 Colt Set, Frontier Scout & S.A.A., Commemorative, Blue, with Gold Plating, 4¾" Barrel, Cased, *Curio*	700.00	1,000.00
☐ **Chamizal Treaty**, .22 L.R.R.F., Frontier Scout S.A., Commemorative, Blue, with Gold Plating, 4¾" Barrel, Cased, *Curio*	220.00	300.00
☐ **Chamizal Treaty**, .22 L.R.R.F., and .45 Colt Set, Frontier Scout and S.A.A., Commemorative, Blue, with Gold Plating, Cased, *Curio*	1,300.00	1,950.00
☐ **Chamizal Treaty**, .45 Colt, Single Action Army, Commemorative, Blue, with Gold Plating, 5½" Barrel, Cased, *Curio*	800.00	1,150.00
☐ **Cherry's 35th Anniversary**, .22 L.R.R.F., and .45 Colt Set, Frontier Scout and S.A.A., Nickel Plated, Gold Plated, 4¾" Barrel, Cased, *Curio*	925.00	1,450.00
☐ **Cobra**, .38 Special, Blue, 2" Barrel, 6 Shot, Lightweight, *Modern*	145.00	220.00
☐ **Cobra**, .38 Special, Nickel Plated, 2" Barrel, 6 Shot, Lightweight, *Modern*	165.00	235.00
☐ **Cobra**, .38 Special, 6 Shot, 5" Barrel Military, Lightweight, *Modern*	135.00	195.00
☐ **Cobra Early**, .38 Special, 6 Shot, 2" Barrel, Lightweight, *Modern*	145.00	220.00
☐ **Cobra Early**, .38 Special, 6 Shot, 4" Barrel, Lightweight, *Modern*	155.00	235.00

112 / COLT

	V.G.	EXC.
☐ **Cobra Early**, .38 Special, 6 Shot, 2" Barrel, Lightweight, Hammer Shroud, *Modern*	165.00	255.00
☐ **Cobra Early**, .38 Special, 6 Shot, 4" Barrel, Lightweight, Hammer Shroud, *Modern*	185.00	265.00
☐ **Col. Sam Colt Sesquicentennial**, .45 Colt, Single Action Army, Commemorative, Blue, Silver-Plated Gripframe, 7½" Barrel, Cased, *Curio*	675.00	900.00
☐ **Col. Sam Colt Sesquicentennial**, .45 Colt, Single Action Army, Commemorative, Deluxe, Blue, Silver-Plated Gripframe, 7½" Barrel, Cased, *Curio*	1,350.00	1,950.00
☐ **Col. Sam Colt Sesquicentennial**, .45 Colt, Single Action Army, Commemorative, Special Deluxe, Blue, Silver-Plated Gripframe, 7½" Barrel, Cased, *Curio*	2,250.00	2,950.00
☐ **Colorado Gold Rush**, .22 L.R.R.F., Frontier Scout S.A., Commemorative, Gold Plated, with Nickel Plating, 4¾" Barrel, Cased, *Curio*	200.00	300.00
☐ **Columbus Sesquicentennial**, .22 L.R.R.F., Frontier Scout S.A., Commemorative, Gold Plated, 4¾" Barrel, Cased, *Curio*	400.00	550.00
☐ **Commando**, .38 Special, 6 Shot, Military, *Curio*	125.00	185.00
☐ **Courier**, .22 L.R.R.F., 6 Shot, 2" Barrel, Lightweight, *Modern*	475.00	700.00
☐ **Courier**, .32 S & W Long, 6 Shot, 2" Barrel, Lightweight, *Modern*	445.00	650.00
☐ **Dakota Territory**, .22 L.R.R.F., Frontier Scout S.A., Commemorative, Blue, with Gold Plating, 4¾" Barrel Cased, *Curio*	220.00	300.00
☐ **Detective Special**, .38 Special, 6 Shot, 4" Barrel, Heavy Barrel, *Modern*	200.00	300.00
☐ **Detective Special Early**, .32 S & W, 6 Shot, 2" Barrel, *Modern*	130.00	185.00
☐ **Detective Special Early**, .38 S & W, 6 Shot, 2" Barrel, *Modern*	140.00	190.00
☐ **Detective Special Early**, .38 Special, 6 Shot, 2" Barrel, *Modern*	160.00	225.00
☐ **Detective Special Late**, .38 Special, 6 Shot, 2" Barrel, Blue, *Modern*	180.00	240.00
☐ **Detective Special Late**, .38 Special, 6 Shot, 2" Barrel, Nickel Plated, *Modern*	190.00	265.00
☐ **Detective Special Late**, .38 Special, 6 Shot, 2" Barrel, Electroless Nickel Plated, *Modern*	220.00	300.00
☐ **Diamondback**, .22 L.R.R.F., Blue, Vent Rib, 6 Shot, *Modern*	195.00	275.00
☐ **Diamondback**, .22 L.R.R.F., Electroless Nickel Plated, Vent Rib, 6 Shot, *Modern*	235.00	325.00
☐ **Diamondback**, .38 Special, Blue, Vent Rib, 6 Shot, *Modern*	185.00	260.00
☐ **Diamondback**, .38 Special, Electroless Nickel Plated, Vent Rib, 6 Shot, *Modern*	245.00	340.00
☐ **Diamondback**, .38 Special, Nickel Plated, Vent Rib, 6 Shot, *Modern*	215.00	285.00
☐ **Florida Sesquicentennial**, .22 L.R.R.F., Frontier Scout S.A., Commemorative, Blue, Color Case, Hardened Frame, 4¾" Barrel, Cased, *Curio*	195.00	285.00
☐ **Fort Findlay Sesquicentennial**, .22 L.R.R.F., Frontier Scout S.A., Commemorative, Gold Plated, 4¾" Barrel, Cased, *Curio*	425.00	550.00
☐ **Fort Findlay Sesquicentennial Pair**, .22LR/.22 WMR Combo, Frontier Scout S.A., Commemorative, Gold Plated, 4¾" Barrel, Cased, *Curio*	1,750.00	2,500.00
☐ **Fort Stephenson Sesquicentennial**, .22 L.R.R.F., Frontier Scout S.A. Nickel Plated, Blue, with Nickel Plating, 4¾" Barrel, Cased, *Curio*	425.00	550.00
☐ **Forty-Niner Miner**, .22 L.R.R.F., Frontier Scout S.A., Commemorative, Blue with Gold Plating, 4¾" Barrel, Cased, *Curio*	210.00	300.00
☐ **Frontier Scout**, .22 L.R.R.F., Single Action, Western Style, 6 Shot, Various Barrel Lengths, *Modern*	125.00	180.00

COLT / 113

	V.G.	EXC.
☐ **Frontier Model 1878 Double Action**, Various Calibers, Various Barrel Lengths, with Ejector, *Curio*	285.00	500.00
☐ **Frontier Model 1878 Double Action**, Sheriff's Model, Various Calibers, Various Barrel Lengths, no Ejector, *Curio*	325.00	525.00
☐ **Frontier Model 1878 Double Action**, Phillipine Model, .45 Colt, 6" Barrel, Large Trigger Guard, *Curio*	365.00	675.00
☐ **Frontier Model 1878**, Serial #'s under 39,000 are *Antique*		
☐ **Gen. J.H. Morgan Indian Raid**, .22 L.R.R.F., Frontier Scout S.A., Nickel Plated, Blue, with Gold Plating, 4¾" Barrel, Cased, *Curio*	450.00	675.00
☐ **Gen. Nathan Bedford Forrest**, .22 L.R.R.F., Frontier Scout S.A., Commemorative, Blue, with Gold Plating, 4¾" Barrel, Cased, *Curio*	220.00	300.00
☐ **Gen Hood Centennial**, .22 L.R.R.F., Frontier Scout S.A., Commemorative, Blue, with Gold Plating, 4¾" Barrel Cased, *Curio*	220.00	300.00
☐ **Gen. Meade Campaign**, .22 L.R.R.F., Frontier Scout S.A., Commemorative, Blue, with Gold Plating, 4¾" Barrel, Cased, *Curio*	220.00	300.00
☐ **Gen. Meade Campaign**, .45 Colt, Single Action Army, Commemorative, Blue, with Gold PLating, 5½" Barrel Cased, *Curio*	625.00	900.00
☐ **Golden Spike**, .22 L.R.R.F., Frontier Scout S.A., Commemorative, Blue, with Gold Plating, 6" Barrel, Cased, *Curio*	220.00	300.00
☐ **H. Cook 1 of 100**, .22 L.R.R.F., and .45 Colt Set, Commemorative, Nickel Plated, Blue Frame, Cased, *Curio*	775.00	1,100.00
☐ **House Pistol**, .41 Short R.F., Cloverleaf-Cylinder, Model 1871, 4 Shot, 3" Barrel, Round Barrel, Spur Trigger, *Antique*	325.00	450.00
☐ **House Pistol**, .41 Short R.F., Cloverleaf-Cylinder Model 1871, 4 Shot, 1½" Barrel, Round Barrel, Spur Trigger, *Antique*	475.00	650.00
☐ **House Pistol**, .41 Short R.F., Cloverleaf-Cylinder Model 1871, 4 Shot, 1½" Barrel, Octagon Barrel, Spur Trigger, *Antique*	625.00	875.00
☐ **House, Pistol**, .41 Short R.F., Round Cylinder Model of 1871, 5 Shot, 2⅝" Barrel, Round Barrel, Spur Trigger, *Antique*	350.00	485.00
☐ **Idaho Territorial Centennial**, .22 L.R.R.F., Frontier Scout S.A., Nickel Plated, Blue, with Nickel Plating, 4¾" Barrel, Cased, *Curio*	275.00	375.00
☐ **Indiana Sesquicentennial**, .22 L.R.R.F., Frontier Scout S.A., Commemorative, Blue, with Gold Plating, 4¾" Barrel, Cased, *Curio*	200.00	280.00
☐ **Joaquin Murietta**, .22 L.R.R.F., and .45 Colt Set, Frontier Scout and S.A.A., Commemorative, Blue, with Gold Plating, Cased, *Curio*	875.00	1,450.00
☐ **Kansas Centennial**, .22 L.R.R.F., Frontier Scout S.A., Commemorative, Gold Plated, Walnut Grips, Cased, *Curio*	200.00	280.00
☐ **Kansas Cowtown: Abilene**, .22 L.R.R.F., Frontier Scout S.A., Commemorative, Gold Plated, 4¾" Barrel, Cased, *Curio*	220.00	300.00
☐ **Kansas Cowtown: Coffyville**, .22 L.R.R.F., Frontier Scout S.A., Commemorative, Blue, with Gold Plating, 4¾" Barrel, Cased, *Curio*	220.00	300.00
☐ **Kansas Cowtown: Dodge City**, .22 L.R.R.F., Frontier Scout S.A., Commemorative, Blue, with Gold Plating, 4¾" Barrel, Cased, *Curio*	220.00	300.00
☐ **Kansas Cowtown: Wichita**, .22 L.R.R.F., Frontier Scout S.A., Commemorative, Gold Plated, 4¾" Barrel, Cased, *Curio*	220.00	300.00
☐ **Kansas Fort Hays**, .22 L.R.R.F., Frontier Scout S.A., Commemorative, Blue, with Nickel Plating, 4¾" Barrel, Cased, *Curio*	220.00	300.00
☐ **Kansas Fort Learned**, .22 L.R.R.F., Frontier Scout S.A., Commemorative, Blue, with Nickel Plating, Cased, *Curio*	200.00	275.00
☐ **Kansas Fort Riley**, .22 L.R.R.F., Frontier Scout S.A., Commemorative, Blue, with Nickel Plating, 4¾" Barrel, Cased, *Curio*	200.00	275.00
☐ **Kansas Fort Scott**, .22 L.R.R.F., Frontier Scout S.A., Commemorative, Blue, with Nickel Plating, 4¾" Barrel, Cased, *Curio*	220.00	300.00

114 / COLT

	V.G.	EXC.
☐ **Kansas: Chisholm Trail**, .22 L.R.R.F., Frontier Scout S.A., Commemorative, Blue, with Nickel Plating, 4¾" Barrel, Cased, *Curio*	200.00	275.00
☐ **Kansas: Pawnee Trail**, .22 L.R.R.F., Frontier Scout S.A., Commemorative, Blue, with Nickel Plating, 4¾" Barrel, Cased, *Curio*	200.00	275.00
☐ **Kansas: Santa Fe Trail**, .22 L.R.R.F., Frontier Scout S.A., Commemorative, Blue, with Nickel Plating, 4¾" Barrel, Cased, *Curio*	200.00	275.00
☐ **Kansas: Shawnee Trail**, .22 L.R.R.F., Frontier Scout S.A., Commemorative, Blue, with Nickel Plating, 4¾" Barrel, Cased, *Curio*	200.00	275.00
☐ **Lawman MK III**, .357 Magnum, Various Barrel Lengths, Blue, 6 Shot, *Modern*	135.00	175.00
☐ **Lawman MK III**, .357 Magnum, Various Barrel Lengths, Nickel Plated, 6 Shot, *Modern*	140.00	180.00
☐ **Lawman MK V**, .357 Magnum, Various Barrel Lengths, Blue, 6 Shot, *Modern*	165.00	230.00
☐ **Lawman MK V**, .357 Magnum, Various Barrel Lengths, Nickel Plated, 6 Shot, *Modern*	170.00	245.00
☐ **Lawman: Bat Masterson**, .22 L.R.R.F., Frontier Scout S.A., Commemorative, Nickel Plated, 4¾" Barrel, Cased, *Curio*	250.00	325.00
☐ **Lawman: Bat Masterson**, .45 Colt, Single Action Army, Commemorative, Nickel Plated, 4¾" Barrel, Cased, *Curio*	575.00	850.00
☐ **Lawman: Pat Garrett**, .22 L.R.R.F., Frontier Scout S.A., Commemorative, Gold Plated, with Nickel Plating, 4¾" Barrel, Cased, *Curio*	250.00	325.00
☐ **Lawman: Pat Garrett**, .45 Colt, Single Action Army, Commemorative, Gold Plated, with Nickel Plating, 5½" Barrel, Cased, *Curio*	575.00	850.00
☐ **Lawman: Wild Bill Hickock**, .22 L.R.R.F., Frontier Scout S.A., Commemorative, Blue, with Nickel Plating, 6" Barrel, Cased, *Curio*	250.00	325.00
☐ **Lawman: Wild Bill Hickock**, .45 Colt, Single Action Army, Commemorative, Blue, with Nickel Plating, 7½" Barrel, Cased, *Curio*	575.00	850.00
☐ **Lawman: Wyatt Earp**, .22 L.R.R.F., Frontier Scout S.A., Commemorative, Blue, with Nickel Plating, Cased, *Curio*	300.00	400.00
☐ **Lawman: Wyatt Earp**, .45 Colt, Single Action Army, Commemorative, Blue, with Nickel Plating, 16⅛" Barrel, Cased, *Curio*	925.00	1,350.00
☐ **Lightning Model 1877**, .38 Colt, 6 Shot, Double Action, Standard Model, *Curio*	225.00	400.00
☐ **Lightning Model 1877**, .38 Colt, 6 Shot, Double Action, Sheriff's Model, *Curio*	245.00	430.00
☐ **Lightning Model 1877**, Serial Numbers under 105, 123 are *Antique*		
☐ **Maine Sesquicentennial**, .22 L.R.R.F., Frontier Scout S.A., Commemorative, Gold Plated, with Nickel Plating, 4¾" Barrel, Cased, *Curio*	200.00	275.00
☐ **Marshal**, .38 Special, 6 Shot, Round Butt, *Modern*	195.00	275.00
☐ **Metropolitan MK III**, .38 Special, 4" Barrel, 6 Shot, *Modern*	150.00	225.00
☐ **Missouri Sesquicentennial**, .22 L.R.R.F., Frontier Scout S.A., Commemorative, Blue, with Gold Plating, 4¾" Barrel, Cased, *Curio*	200.00	275.00
☐ **Missouri Sesquicentennial**, .45 Colt, Single Action Army, Commemorative, Blue, with Gold Plating, 5½" Barrel, Cased, *Curio*	475.00	700.00
☐ **Model 1872 Army**, .44 Henry R.F., Open-Top Frontier Single Action, Army Style Gripframe, *Antique*	1,600.00	2,500.00

COLT / 115

Colt New Police

Colt Old Line .22

Colt .22 Banker's Special

Colt Ace .22

Colt Model 1855 Root Revolver

Colt Model 1855 Root Fluted Cylinder

Colt Model 1903 Pocket Military

116 / COLT

	V.G.	EXC.
☐ **Model 1872 Army**, .44 Henry R.F., Open-Top Frontier Single Action, Navy Style Gripframe, *Antique*	1,800.00	2,750.00
☐ **Model 1889**, .38 Long Colt, 6 Shot, Commercial, Various Barrel Lengths, Double Action, Swing-Out Cylinder, *Antique*	200.00	375.00
☐ **Model 1889**, .41 Long Colt, 6 Shot, Commercial, Various Barrel Lengths, Double Action, Swing-Out Cylinder, *Antique*	175.00	365.00
☐ **Model 1889 Navy**, .38 Long Colt, 6 Shot, Military, 6" Barrel, Double Action, Swing-Out Cylinder, *Antique*	270.00	485.00
☐ **Model 1892 New Army**, .38 Long Colt, 6 Shot, Military, 6" Barrel, Double Action, Swing-Out Cylinder, *Antique*	165.00	275.00
☐ **Model 1892 New Navy**, .38 Long Colt, 6 Shot, Military, 6" Barrel, Double Action, Swing-Out Cylinder, *Antique*	195.00	325.00
☐ **Model 1892 New Navy**, .38 Long Colt, 6 Shot, Commercial, Various Barrel Lengths, Double Action, Swing-Out Cylinder, *Antique*	135.00	225.00
☐ **Model 1892 New Navy**, .41 Long Colt, 6 Shot, Commercial, Various Barrel Lengths, Double Action, Swing-Out Cylinder, *Antique*	135.00	225.00
☐ **Model 1894 New Army**, .38 Long Colt, 6 Shot, Military, 6" Barrel, Double Action, Swing-Out Cylinder, *Antique*	160.00	265.00
☐ **Model 1894 New Navy**, .38 Long Colt, 6 Shot, Military, 6" Barrel, Double Action, Swing-Out Cylinder, *Antique*	185.00	275.00
☐ **Model 1895 New Army**, .38 Long Colt, 6 Shot, Military, 6" Barrel, Double Action, Swing-Out Cylinder, *Antique*	145.00	240.00
☐ **Model 1895 New Navy**, .38 Long Colt, 6 Shot, Military, 6" Barrel, Double Action, Swing-Out Cylinder, *Antique*	195.00	325.00
☐ **Model 1896 New Army**, .38 Long Colt, 6 Shot, Military, 6" Barrel, Double Action, Swing-Out Cylinder, *Curio*	180.00	265.00
☐ **Model 1896 New Navy**, .38 Long Colt, 6 Shot, Military, 6" Barrel, Double Action, Swing-Out Cylinder, *Curio*	180.00	265.00
☐ **Model 1901 New Army**, .38 Long Colt, 6 Shot, Military, 6" Barrel, Double Action, Swing-Out Cylinder, *Curio*	150.00	235.00
☐ **Model 1902 Army**, .45 Colt, 6 Shot, Military, 6" Barrel, Double Action, *Curio*	320.00	475.00
☐ **Model 1903 New Army**, .38 Long Colt, 6 Shot, Military, 6" Barrel, Double Action, Swing-Out Cylinder, *Curio*	150.00	225.00
☐ **Model 1903 New Navy**, .32-20 WCF, 6 Shot Commercial, Various Barrel Lengths, Double Action, Swing-Out Cylinder, *Curio*	195.00	330.00
☐ **Model 1903 New Navy**, .38 Long Colt, 6 Shot, Commercial, Various Barrel Lengths, Double Action, Swing-Out Cylinder, *Curio*	180.00	285.00
☐ **Model 1903 New Navy**, .38 Long Colt, 6 Shot, Commercial, Various Barrel Lengths, Double Action, Swing-Out Cylinder, *Curio*	160.00	275.00
☐ **Model 1905 U.S.M.C.**, .38 Long Colt, 6 Shot, Military, 6" Barrel, Swing-Out Cylinder, *Curio*	625.00	1,250.00
☐ **Model 1905 U.S.M.C.**, .38 Long Colt, 6 Shot, Commercial, 6" Barrel, Swing-Out Cylinder, *Curio*	650.00	1,350.00
☐ **Model 1909 Army**, .45 Colt, 6 Shot, Military, 5½" Barrel, *Curio*	265.00	450.00
☐ **Model 1909 U.S.M.C.**, .45 Colt, 6 Shot, 5½" Barrel, *Modern*	525.00	825.00
☐ **Model 1909 U.S.N.**, .45 Colt, 6 Shot, Military, 5½" Barrel, *Modern*	340.00	575.00
☐ **Model 1917 Army**, .45 Auto-Rim, 6 Shot, Military, 5½" Barrel, *Modern*	250.00	350.00
☐ **Montana Territory Centennial**, .22 L.R.R.F., Frontier Scout S.A., Commemorative, Blue, with Gold Plating, 4¾" Barrel, Cased, *Curio*	220.00	300.00
☐ **Montana Territory Centennial**, .45 Colt, Single Action Army, Commemorative, Blue, with Gold Plating, 7½" Barrel, Cased, *Curio*	575.00	800.00
☐ **Nebraska Centennial**, .22 L.R.R.F., Frontier Scout S.A., Commemorative, Gold Plated, 4¾" Barrel, Cased, *Curio*	200.00	275.00
☐ **Ned Buntline**, .45 Colt, New Frontier Single Action Army, 12" Barrel, Commemorative, *Modern*	700.00	950.00

	V.G.	EXC.
☐ **Nevada Battle Born**, .22 L.R.R.F., Frontier Scout S.A., Commemorative, Blue, with Nickel Plating, 4¾" Barrel, Cased, Curio	220.00	300.00
☐ **Nevada Battle Born**, .22 L.R.R.F. and .45 Colt Set, Frontier Scout and S.A.A., Commemorative, Blue, with Nickel Plating, Cased, Curio	1,350.00	2,000.00
☐ **Nevada Battle Born**, .45 Colt, Single Action Army, Commemorative, Blue, with Nickel Plating, 5½" Barrel, Cased, Curio	850.00	1,200.00
☐ **Nevada Centennial**, .22 L.R.R.F., Frontier Scout S.A., Commemorative, Blue, with Nickel Plating, 4¾" Barrel, Cased, Curio	200.00	275.00
☐ **Nevada Centennial**, .22 L.R.R.F. and .45 Colt Set, Frontier Scout and S.A.A., Nickel Plated, Blue, with Nickel Plating, Cased, Curio	525.00	775.00
☐ **Nevada Centennial**, .22 L.R.R.F. and .45 Colt Set, Frontier Scout and S.A.A., Commemorative, Blue, with Nickel Plating, with Extra Engraved Cylinder, Cased, Curio	825.00	1,275.00
☐ **Nevada Centennial**, .45 Colt, Single Action Army, Nickel Plated, Blue, with Nickel Plating, 5½" Barrel, Cased, Curio	700.00	1,100.00
☐ **New Frontier**, .22 L.R.R.F., Various Barrel Lengths, Blue, 6 Shot, Adjustable Sights, *Modern*	135.00	180.00
☐ **New Frontier**, .22 L.R.R.F., 7½" Barrel, Blue, 6 Shot, Adjustable Sights, *Modern*	140.00	190.00
☐ **New Frontier**, .22LR/.22WMR Combo, Various Barrel Lengths, Blue, 6 Shot, Adjustable Sights, *Modern*	140.00	200.00
☐ **New Frontier**, .22R/.22 WRM Combo, 7½" Barrel, Blue, 6 Shot, Adjustable Sights, *Modern*	150.00	225.00
☐ **New Jersey Tercentenary**, .22 L.R.R.F., Frontier Scout S.A., Commemorative, Blue, with Nickel Plating, 4¾" Barrel, Cased, Curio	200.00	275.00
☐ **New Jersey Tercentenary**, .45 Colt, Single Action Army, Commemorative, Blue, with Nickel Plating, 5½" Barrel, Cased, Curio	575.00	850.00
☐ **New Line**, .38 Long Colt, Police and Thug Model, with Ejector, 5 Shot, Spur Trigger, Standard, *Antique*	425.00	675.00
☐ **New Line**, .32 or .41 C.F., Police and Thug Model, with Ejector, 5 Shot, Spur Trigger, *Antique*	550.00	900.00
☐ **New Line**, .38 Long Colt, House Civilian Model, with Ejector, 5 Shot, Spur Trigger, *Antique*	235.00	370.00
☐ **New Line**, .38 Long Colt, House Civilian Model, no Ejector, 5 Shot, Spur Trigger, *Antique*	235.00	370.00
☐ **New Line**, .41 Short C.F., House Civilian Model, with Ejector, 5 Shot, Spur Trigger, *Antique*	260.00	425.00
☐ **New Line**, .41 Short C.F., House Civilian Model, no Ejector, 5 Shot, Spur Trigger, *Antique*	220.00	375.00
☐ **New Line Pocket**, Locking Notches on Cylinder Periphery, *Add* **20%-30%**		
☐ **New Line Pocket**, .22 Long R.F., "the Little Colt," 7 Shot, Spur Trigger, *Antique*	170.00	295.00
☐ **New Line Pocket**, .30 Long R.F., "the Pony Colt," 5 Shot, Spur Trigger, *Antique*	185.00	325.00
☐ **New Line Pocket**, .32 Long R.F. or .32 Long Colt, for 4" Barrel, *Add* **100%-150%**		
☐ **New Line Pocket**, .32 Long Colt, "the Ladies Colt," 5 Shot, Spur Trigger, *Antique*	175.00	270.00

	V.G.	EXC.
☐ **New Line Pocket**, .32 Long R.F., "the Ladies Colt," 5 Shot, Spur Trigger, *Antique*	175.00	270.00
☐ **New Line Pocket**, .38 Long Colt, "the Pet Colt," 5 Shot, Spur Trigger, *Antique*	220.00	325.00
☐ **New Line Pocket**, .38 Long R.F., "the Pet Colt," 5 Shot, Spur Trigger, *Antique*	195.00	285.00
☐ **New Line Pocket**, .41 Long R.F., "the Big Colt," 5 Shot, Spur Trigger, *Antique*	260.00	365.00
☐ **New Line Pocket**, .41 Short C.F., "the Big Colt," 5 Shot, Spur Trigger, *Antique*	265.00	385.00
☐ **New Mexico Golden Anniversary**, .22 L.R.R.F., Frontier Scout S.A., Commemorative, Blue, with Gold Plating, 4 3/4" Barrel, Cased, *Curio*	250.00	325.00
☐ **New Pocket**, .32 Long Colt, 6 Shot, Various Barrel Lengths, *Curio*	185.00	275.00
☐ **New Pocket**, .32 S & W Long, 6 Shot, Various Barrel Lengths, *Curio*	195.00	285.00
☐ **New Police**, .32 Long Colt, 6 Shot, Various Barrel Lengths, *Curio*	165.00	265.00
☐ **New Police**, Serial Numbers under 7,300 are *Antique*		
☐ **New Police**, .32 S & W Long, 6 Shot, Various Barrel Lengths, *Curio*	155.00	250.00
☐ **New Police Target**, .32 Long Colt, 6 Shot, 6" Barrel, Adjustable, *Modern*	235.00	375.00
☐ **New Police Target**, .32 S & W Long, 6 Shot, 6" Barrel, Adjustable Sights, *Modern*	235.00	375.00
☐ **New Service**, .357 Magnum, 6 Shot, Commercial, Various Barrel Lengths, *Modern*	350.00	525.00
☐ **New Service**, .38 Special, 6 Shot, Commercial, Various Barrel Lengths, *Modern*	250.00	375.00
☐ **New Service**, .38-40 WCF, 6 Shot, Commercial, Various Barrel Lengths, *Modern*	275.00	425.00
☐ **New Service**, .38-44, 6 Shot, Commercial, Various Barrel Lengths, *Modern*	300.00	475.00
☐ **New Service**, .44 Special, 6 Shot, Commercial, Various Barrel Lengths, *Modern*	325.00	495.00
☐ **New Service**, .44-40 WCF, 6 Shot, Commercial, Various Barrel Lengths, *Modern*	325.00	485.00
☐ **New Service**, .45 Auto-Rim, 6 Shot, Commercial, Various Barrel Lengths, *Modern*	225.00	375.00
☐ **New Service**, .45 Colt, 6 Shot, Commercial, Various Barrel Lengths, *Modern*	300.00	450.00
☐ **New Service**, .455 Colt, 6 Shot, Commercial, Various Barrel Lengths, *Modern*	300.00	425.00
☐ **New Service Target**, .44 Special, 6 Shot, Commercial, 7½" Barrel, Adjustable Sights, *Modern*	475.00	750.00
☐ **New Service Target**, .45 Auto-Rim, 6 Shot, Commercial, 7½" Barrel, Adjustable Sights, *Modern*	450.00	700.00
☐ **New Service Target**, .45 Colt, 6 Shot, Commercial, 7½" Barrel, Adjustable Sights, *Modern*	500.00	800.00
☐ **New Service Target**, .455 Colt, 6 Shot, Commercial, 7½" Barrel, Adjustable Sights, *Modern*	475.00	775.00
☐ **NRA Centennial**, .357 Mag. or .45 Colt, Single Action Army, Commemorative, Blue, Color Case, Hardened Frame, Various Barrel Lengths, Cased, *Curio*	475.00	700.00
☐ **Officer's Model**, .38 Special, 6 Shot, Adjustable Sights, with Detachable Shoulder Stock, *Curio*	875.00	1,450.00
☐ **Officer's Model Match**, .22 L.R.R.F., 6 Shot, Adjustable Sights, 6" Barrel, Target Grips, Target Hammer, *Modern*	245.00	350.00

	V.G.	EXC.
☐ **Officer's Model Match**, .22 W.M.R., 6 Shot, Adjustable Sights, 6" Barrel, Target Grips, Target Hammer, *Modern*	465.00	675.00
☐ **Officer's Model Match**, .32 S&W Long, 6 Shot, Adjustable Sights, 6" Barrel, Target Grips, Target Hammer, *Modern*	450.00	650.00
☐ **Officer's Model Match**, .38 Special, 6 Shot, Adjustable Sights, 6" Barrel, Target Grips, Target Hammer, *Modern*	195.00	300.00
☐ **Officer's Model Special**, .22 L.R.R.F., 6 Shot, Adjustable Sights, 6" Barrel, Heavy Barrel, *Modern*	185.00	295.00
☐ **Officer's Model Special**, .38 Special, 6 Shot, Adjustable Sights, 6" Barrel, Heavy Barrel, *Modern*	195.00	315.00
☐ **Officer's Model Target**, .22 L.R.R.F., 6 Shot, Adjustable Sights, 6" Barrel, Second Issue, *Modern*	275.00	395.00
☐ **Officer's Model Target**, .32 S & W Long, 6 Shot, Adjustable Sights, 6" Barrel, Second Issue, *Modern*	295.00	425.00
☐ **Officer's Model Target**, .38 Special, 6 Shot, Adjustable Sights, 6" Barrel, *Modern*	235.00	375.00
☐ **Officer's Model Target**, .38 Special, 6 Shot, Adjustable Sights, 6" Barrel, Second Issue, *Modern*	265.00	425.00
☐ **Official Police**, .22 L.R.R.F., 6 Shot, Various Barrel Lengths, *Modern*	190.00	275.00
☐ **Official Police**, .32-20 WCF, 6 Shot, *Modern*	225.00	350.00
☐ **Official Police**, .38 Special, 6 Shot, *Modern*	150.00	215.00
☐ **Official Police Mk.III**, .38 Special, 6 Shot, *Modern*	170.00	235.00
☐ **Official Police**, .41 Long Colt, 6 Shot, *Modern*	175.00	250.00
☐ **Oklahoma Territory**, .22 L.R.R.F., Frontier Scout S.A., Commemorative, Blue, with Gold Plating, 4¾" Barrel, Cased, *Curio*	220.00	300.00
☐ **Old Fort Des Moines**, .22 L.R.R.F., Frontier Scout S.A., Commemorative, Gold Plated, 4¾" Barrel, Cased, *Curio*	250.00	350.00
☐ **Old Fort Des Moines**, .22 L.R.R.F. and .45 Colt Set, Frontier Scout S.A. and S.A.A., Commemorative, Gold Plated, Cased, *Curio*	800.00	1,250.00
☐ **Old Fort Des Moines**, .45 Colt, Single Action Army, Commemorative, Gold Plated, 5½" Barrel, Cased, *Curio*	575.00	850.00
☐ **Old Line Pocket**, .22 Short R.F., Open Top, First Model with Ejector, 7 Shot, Spur Trigger, *Antique*	525.00	775.00
☐ **Old Line Pocket**, .22 Short R.F., Open Top, Second Model, No Ejector, 7 Shot, Spur Trigger, *Antique*	195.00	325.00
☐ **Oregon Trail**, .22 L.R.R.F., Frontier Scout S.A., Commemorative, Blue, with Gold Plating, 4¾" Barrel, Cased, *Curio*	200.00	275.00
☐ **Peacemaker**, .22LR/.22 WMR Combo, Various Barrel Lengths, Blue, 6 Shot, *Modern*	120.00	180.00
☐ **Peace Maker**, .22LR/.22 WMR Combo, 7½" Barrel, Blue, 6 Shot, *Modern*	125.00	190.00
☐ **Peacemaker Centennial**, .44-40 WCF, Single Action Army, Commemorative, Blue, Color Case, Hardened Frame, 7½" Barrel, Cased, *Curio*	525.00	750.00
☐ **Peacemaker Centennial**, .44-40 and .45 Colt Set, Single Action Army, Commemorative, Blue, Color Case, Hardened Frame, 7½" Barrel, Cased, *Curio*	1,275.00	1,650.00
☐ **Peacemaker Centennial**, .45 Colt, Single Action Army, Commemorative, Blue, Color Case, Hardened Frame, 7½" Barrel, Cased, *Curio*	525.00	750.00
☐ **Pocket Positive**, .32 Long Colt, 6 Shot, Various Barrel Lengths, *Modern*	175.00	250.00
☐ **Pocket Positive**, .32 S & W Long, 6 Shot, Various Barrel Lengths, *Modern*	195.00	275.00

120 / COLT

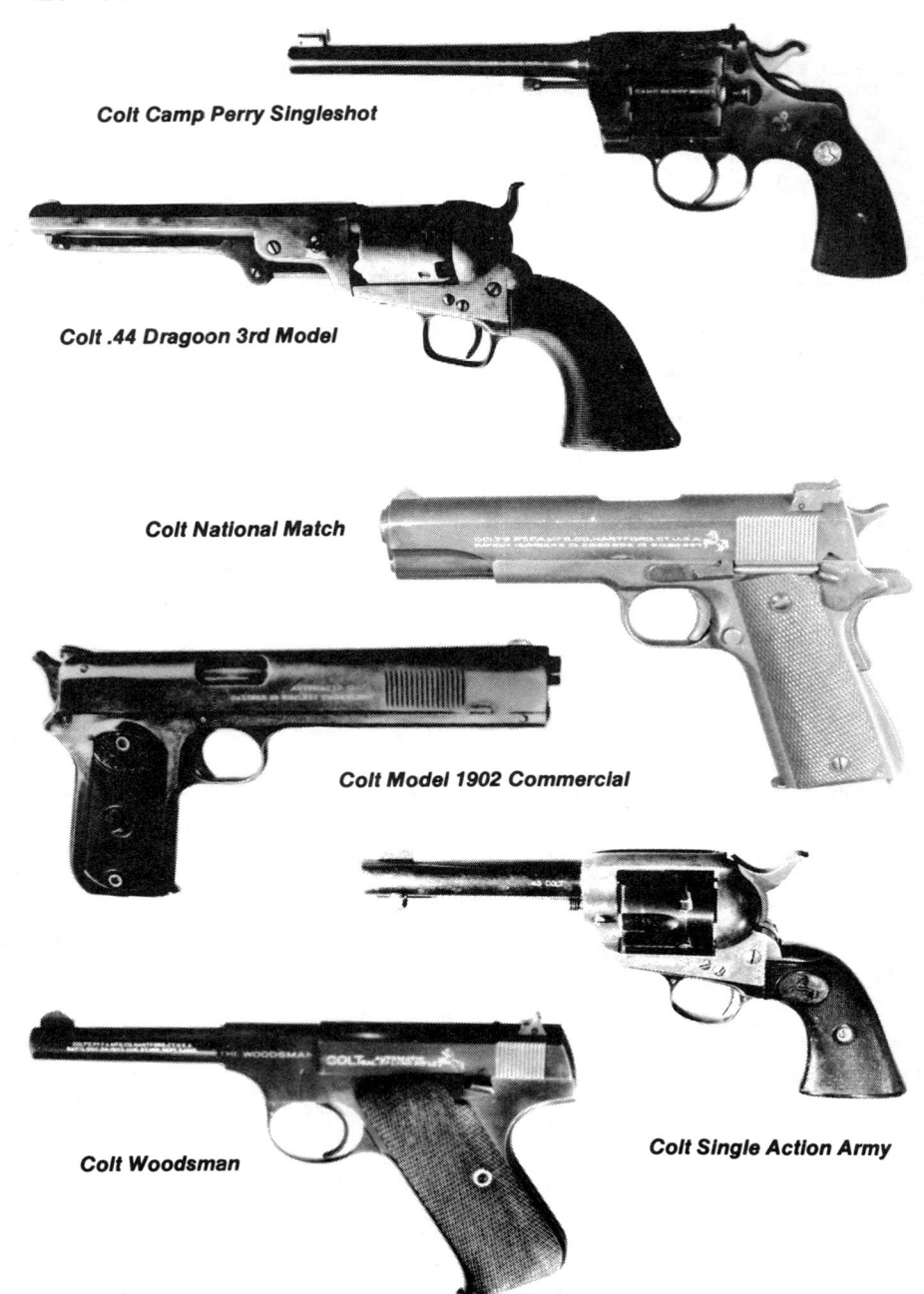

Colt Camp Perry Singleshot

Colt .44 Dragoon 3rd Model

Colt National Match

Colt Model 1902 Commercial

Colt Woodsman

Colt Single Action Army

COLT / 121

	V.G.	EXC.
☐ **Police Positive**, .22 L.R.R.F., 6 Shot, Various Barrel Lengths, *Modern*	150.00	225.00
☐ **Police Positive**, .22 WRF, 6 Shot, Various Barrel Lengths, *Modern*	185.00	250.00
☐ **Police Positive**, .32 Long Colt, 6 Shot, Various Barrel Lengths, *Modern*	120.00	175.00
☐ **Police Positive**, .32 S & W Long, 6 Shot, Various Barrel Lengths, *Modern*	125.00	180.00
☐ **Police Positive**, .38 S & W, 6 Shot, Various Barrel Lengths, *Modern*	125.00	185.00
☐ **Police Positive Late**, .38 Special, Blue, 4" Barrel, *Modern*	145.00	200.00
☐ **Police Positive Late**, .38 Special, Nickel Plated, 4" Barrel, 6 Shot, *Modern*	150.00	225.00
☐ **Police Positive Special**, .32 S & W Long, 6 Shot, Various Barrel Lengths, *Modern*	130.00	185.00
☐ **Police Positive Special**, .32-20 WCF, 6 Shot, Various Barrel Lengths, *Modern*	165.00	275.00
☐ **Police Positive Special**, .38 S & W, 6 Shot, Various Barrel Lengths, *Modern*	100.00	165.00
☐ **Police Positive Special**, .38 Special, Shot, Various Barrel Lengths, *Modern*	135.00	200.00
☐ **Police Positive Target**, .22 L.R.R.F., 6 Shot, 6" Barrel, Adjustable Sights, *Modern*	195.00	375.00
☐ **Police Positive Target**, .22 WRF, 6 Shot, 6" Barrel, Adjustable Sights, *Modern*	225.00	400.00
☐ **Police Positive Target**, .32 Long Colt, 6 Shot, 6" Barrel, Adjustable Sights, *Modern*	225.00	325.00
☐ **Police Positive Target**, .32 S & W Long, 6 Shot, 6" Barrel, Adjustable Sights, *Modern*	225.00	325.00
☐ **Police Positive Target**, .38 S & W Long, 6 Shot, 6" Barrel, Adjustable Sights, *Modern*	215.00	315.00
☐ **Pony Express Centennial**, .22 L.R.R.F., Frontier Scout S.A., Commemorative, 4¾" Barrel, Gold Plated, Cased, *Curio*	325.00	475.00
☐ **Pony Express Presentation**, .45 Colt, Single Action Army, Commemorative, Nickel Plated, 7½" Barrel, Cased, *Curio*	700.00	950.00
☐ **Pony Express Presentation 4 Gun Set**, .45 Colt, Single Action Army, Commemorative, Nickel Plated, 7½" Barrel, Cased, *Curio*	2,700.00	3,850.00
☐ **Python**, .357 Magnum, 2" Barrel, Blue, Vent Rib, Adjustable Sights, 6 Shot, *Modern*	275.00	375.00
☐ **Python**, .357 Magnum, 4" Barrel, Blue, Vent Rib, 6 Shot, Adjustable Sights, *Modern*	265.00	365.00
☐ **Python**, .357 Magnum, 4" Barrel, Nickel, Vent Rib, 6 Shot, Adjustable Sights, *Modern*	275.00	375.00
☐ **Python**, .357 Magnum, 6" Barrel, Blue, Vent Rib, 6 Shot, Adjustable Sights, *Modern*	275.00	375.00
☐ **Python**, .357 Magnum, 6" Barrel, Nickel, Vent Rib, 6 Shot, Adjustable Sights, *Modern*	300.00	400.00
☐ **Python**, .357 Magnum, 8" Barrel, Blue, Vent Rib, 6 Shot, Adjustable Sights, *Modern*	300.00	390.00
☐ **Python**, .357 Magnum, 8" Barrel, Nickel, Vent Rib, 6 Shot, Adjustable Sights, *Modern*	330.00	420.00
☐ **Sheriff's Model**, .45 Colt, Single Action Army, Commemorative, Blue, Color Case, Hardened Frame, 3" Barrel, *Curio*	950.00	1,450.00
☐ **Sheriff's Model**, .45 Colt, Single Action Army, Commemorative, Nickel Plated, 3" Barrel, *Curio*	2,500.00	3,450.00
☐ **Shooting Master**, .357 Magnum, 6 Shot, Commercial, 6" Barrel, Adjustable Sights, *Modern*	495.00	675.00

	V.G.	EXC.
☐ **Shooting Master**, .38 Special, 6 Shot, Commercial, 6" Barrel, Adjustable Sights, *Modern*	425.00	550.00
☐ **Shooting Master**, .44 Special, 6 Shot, Commercial, 6" Barrel, Adjustable Sights, *Modern*	495.00	650.00
☐ **Shooting Master**, .45 Auto-Rim, 6 Shot, Commercial, 6" Barrel, Adjustable Sights, *Modern*	425.00	550.00
☐ **Shooting Master**, .45 Colt, 6 Shot, Commercial, 6" Barrel, Adjustable Sights, *Modern*	450.00	625.00
☐ **Single Action Army Late**, .357 Magnum, Various Barrel Lengths, Blue, 6 Shot, *Modern*	315.00	420.00
☐ **Single Action Army Late**, .357 Magnum, 7½" Barrel, Blue, 6 Shot, *Modern*	275.00	375.00
☐ **Single Action Army Late**, .44 Special, 7½" Barrel, Blue, 6 Shot, *Modern*	290.00	385.00
☐ **Single Action Army Late**, .45 Colt, 7½" Barrel, Blue, 6 Shot, *Modern*	280.00	370.00
☐ **Single Action Army Late**, .45 Colt, Various Barrel Lengths, Blue, 6 Shot, *Modern*	280.00	375.00
☐ **Single Action Army Buntline Late**, .45 Colt, 12" Barrel, Blue, 6 Shot, *Modern*	375.00	500.00
☐ **Single Action Army Late**, .45 Colt, 7½" Barrel, Nickel Plated, 6 Shot, *Modern*	300.00	390.00
☐ **Single Action Army New Frontier**, .357 Magnum, Various Barrel Lengths, Blue, 6 Shot, Adjustable Sights, *Modern*	325.00	435.00
☐ **Single Action Army New Frontier**, .44 Special, 7½" Barrel, Blue, 6 Shot, Adjustable Sights, *Modern*	335.00	450.00
☐ **Single Action Army New Frontier**, .45 Colt, Various Barrel Lengths, Blue, 6 Shot, Adjustable Sights, *Modern*	340.00	450.00
☐ **Single Action Army Buntline New Frontier**, .45 Colt, 12" Barrel, Blue, 6 Shot, Adjustable Sights, *Modern*	400.00	600.00
☐ **Single Action Army**, .45 Colt, Standard Cavalry Model # Under 15,000, Screw-Retained Cylinder Pin, Blue, Military, 7½" Barrel, *Antique*	1,450.00	2,650.00
☐ **Single Action Army**, .45 Colt, Indian Scout Model, #'s Under 30000, Screw-Retained Cylinder Pin, Nickel Plated, Military, 7½" Barrel, *Antique*	1,850.00	3,250.00
☐ **Single Action Army**, .45 Colt, Artillery Model, Screw-Retained Cylinder Pin, Military, 5½" Barrel, *Antique*	995.00	1,900.00
☐ **Single Action Army**, Various Calibers, Storekeeper's Model, No Ejector, Short Barrel, Commercial, *Antique*	1,750.00	2,950.00
☐ **Single Action Army**, Various Calibers, Standard Peacemaker, Calibers: .45 Colt, .44-40, .38-40, .41, .32-20, Commercial, *Antique*	650.00	1,150.00

☐ **Single Action Army**, for Rare Calibers *Add* **50%-200%**
☐ **Single Action Army**, Folding Rear Sight, Long Barrel, *Add* **$1,950.00-$2,950.00**
☐ **Single Action Army**, Target Model (Flat-Top), *Add* **$950.00-$1,850.00**
☐ **Single Action Army**, 8" or 9" Barrel, *Add* **$350.00-$575.00**
☐ **Single Action Army**, for 12" Barrel, *Add* **$425.00-$675.00**
☐ **Single Action Army**, for 16" Barrel, Add **$575.00-$975.00**
☐ **Single Action Army**, Shoulder Stock, *Add* **$975.00-$1,775.00**
☐ **Single Action Army**, #'s over 182,000 are *Modern*, #'s under 165,000 are Black Powder Only
☐ **Single Action Army**, Nickel Plating, *Add* **15%-25%**
☐ **Single Action Army**, Rimfire Calibers *Add* **100%-125%**

COLT / 123

	V.G.	EXC.
☐ **Single Action Army**, Long-Fluted Cylinder #'s 330,000 to 331,379, Commercial, *Curio*	950.00	1,575.00
☐ **Single Action Bisley**, Various Calibers, Standard Model, Calibers:, 32-20, 38-40, 41, 41-40, 45, Target Trigger, *Modern*	575.00	950.00
☐ **Single Action Bisley**, Various Calibers, Target Model, (Flat-Top), *Modern*	995.00	1,875.00
☐ **Single Action Bisley**, other than Standard Calibers, Add **50%-100%**		
☐ **Single Action Bisley**, Non-Standard Barrel Lengths, Add **20%-30%**		
☐ **Single Action Bisley**, No Ejector Housing, Add **25%-35%**		
☐ **Second Amendment**, .22 L.R.R.F., Frontier Scout, Cased, *Curio*	230.00	325.00
☐ **St. Augustine Quadricentennial**, .22 L.R.R.F., Frontier Scout S.A., Commemorative, Blue, with Gold Plating, 4¾" Barrel, Cased, *Curio*	225.00	325.00
☐ **St. Louis Bicentennial**, .22 L.R.R.F., Frontier Scout S.A., Commemorative, Blue, with Gold Plating, 4¾" Barrel, Cased, *Curio*	220.00	300.00
☐ **St. Louis Scout**, .22 L.R.R.F. and .45 Colt Set, Frontier Scout and S.A.A., Commemorative, Blue, with Gold Plating, Cased, *Curio*	750.00	1,100.00
☐ **St. Louis Bicentennial**, .45 Colt, Single Action Army, Commemorative, Blue, with Gold Plating, 5½" Barrel, Cased, *Curio*	550.00	800.00
☐ **Texas Ranger**, Standard, .45 Colt, Single Action Army, Commemorative, Blue, Color Case Hardened Frame, Cased, *Curio*	950.00	1,450.00
☐ **Thunderer Model 1877**, .41 Colt, 6 Shots, Double Action, Standard Model, *Modern*	275.00	400.00
☐ **Thunderer Model 1877**, .41 Colt, 6 Shots, Double Action, Sheriff's Model, *Modern*	295.00	425.00
☐ **Trooper**, .22 L.R.R.F., 6 Shot, Adjustable Sights, Target Grips, Target Hammer, *Modern*	185.00	275.00
☐ **Trooper**, .357 Magnum, 6 Shot, 4" Barrel, Adjustable Sights, *Modern*	185.00	275.00
☐ **Trooper**, .357 Magnum, 6 Shot, Adjustable Sights, Target Grips, Target Hammer, *Modern*	200.00	290.00
☐ **Trooper**, .38 Special, 6 Shot, 4" Barrel, Adjustable Sights, *Modern*	185.00	275.00
☐ **Trooper**, .38 Special, 6 Shot, Adjustable Sights, Target Grips, Target Hammer, *Modern*	195.00	280.00
☐ **Trooper MK III**, .22 L.R.R.F., 4" Barrel, Blue, 6 Shot, Adjustable Sights, *Modern*	140.00	185.00
☐ **Trooper MK III**, .22 L.R.R.F., 8" Barrel, Blue, 6 Shot, Adjustable Sights, *Modern*	180.00	250.00
☐ **Trooper MK III**, .22 L.R.R.F., 6" Barrel, 6 Shot, Adjustable Sights, *Modern*	140.00	180.00
☐ **Trooper MK III**, .357 Magnum, 4" Barrel, Blue, 6 Shot, Adjustable Sights, *Modern*	145.00	175.00
☐ **Trooper MK III**, .357 Magnum, 4" Barrel, Nickel Plated, 6 Shot, Adjustable Sights, *Modern*	150.00	180.00
☐ **Trooper MK III**, .357 Magnum, 6" Barrel, 6 Shot, Adjustable Sights, *Modern*	160.00	195.00
☐ **Trooper MK III**, .357 Magnum, 6" Barrel, Nickel Plated, 6 Shot, Adjustable Sights, *Modern*	160.00	200.00
☐ **Trooper MK III**, .357 Magnum, 8" Barrel, 6 Shot, Adjustable Sights, *Modern*	160.00	200.00
☐ **Trooper MK III**, .357 Magnum, 8" Barrel, Nickel Plated, 6 Shot, Adjustable Sights, *Modern*	165.00	210.00
☐ **Trooper MK IV**, .22 W.M.R., 4" Barrel, Blue, 6 Shot, Adjustable Sights, *Modern*	150.00	215.00
☐ **Trooper MK IV**, .22 W.M.R., 6" Barrel, 6 Shot, Adjustable Sights, *Modern*	150.00	215.00

	V.G.	EXC.
☐ **Trooper MK IV**, .357 Magnum, 6" Barrel, 6 Shot, Adjustable Sights, *Modern*	165.00	225.00
☐ **Trooper MK V**, .357 Magnum, Vent Rib Barrel, Blue, 6 Shot, Adjustable Sights, *Modern*	175.00	235.00
☐ **Trooper MK V**, .357 Magnum, 4" Vent Rib Barrel, Nickel Plated, 6 Shot, Adjustable Sights, *Modern*	185.00	250.00
☐ **Viper**, .38 Special, Nickel Plated, 4" Barrel, 6 Shot, Lightweight, *Modern*	160.00	225.00
☐ **Viper**, .38 Special, Blue, 4" Barrel, 6 Shot, Lightweight, *Modern*	145.00	200.00
☐ **West Virginia Centennial**, .22 L.R.R.F., Frontier Scout S.A., Commemorative, Blue, with Gold Plating, 4¾" Barrel, Cased, *Curio*	220.00	300.00
☐ **West Virginia Centennial**, .45 Colt, Single Action Army, Commemorative, Blue, with Gold Plating, 4¾" Barrel, Cased, *Curio*	575.00	800.00
☐ **Wyatt Earp Buntline**, .45 Colt, Single Action Army, Commemorative, Gold Plated, 12" Barrel, Cased, *Curio*	1,250.00	1,750.00
☐ **Wyoming Diamond Jubilee**, .22 L.R.R.F., Frontier Scout S.A., Commemorative, Blue, with Nickel Plating, 4¾" Barrel, Cased, *Curio*	220.00	300.00

HANDGUN, SEMI-AUTOMATIC

	V.G.	EXC.
☐ **Ace**, .22 L.R.R.F., Clip Fed, Adjustable Sights, Target Pistol, *Curio*	450.00	700.00
☐ **Ace, New Type**, .22 L.R.R.F., Clip Fed, Adjustable Sights, Target Pistol, *Modern*	220.00	295.00
☐ **Ace, New Type**, .22 L.R.R.F., Clip Fed, Adjustable Sights, Target Pistol, Nickel Plated, *Modern*	260.00	345.00
☐ **Ace Signature**, .22 L.R.R.F., Clip Fed, Adjustable Sights, Target Pistol, Etched and Gold Plated, *Modern*	425.00	650.00
☐ **Ace 45-22 Conversion Unit**, .45 ACP, Clip Fed, Adjustable Sights, Target Pistol, *Curio*	175.00	275.00
☐ **Ace Service Model**, .22 L.R.R.F., Clip Fed, Adjustable Sights, Target Pistol, *Curio*	675.00	975.00
☐ **Challenger**, .22 L.R.R.F., Clip Fed, *Modern*	150.00	225.00
☐ **Combat Commander**, .38 Super, Clip Fed, Blue, *Modern*	200.00	285.00
☐ **Combat Commander**, .45 ACP, Clip Fed, Blue, *Modern*	200.00	285.00
☐ **Combat Commander**, .45 ACP, Clip Fed, Satin Nickel, *Modern*	220.00	300.00
☐ **Combat Commander**, 9mm Luger, Clip Fed, Blue, *Modern*	195.00	280.00
☐ **Commander**, .45 ACP, Clip Fed, Blue, Lightweight, *Modern*	200.00	285.00
☐ **Conversion Unit**, .22 L.R.R.F., Clip Fed, Blue, Adjustable Sights, *Modern*	95.00	175.00
☐ **Conversion Unit, Service Ace**, .22 L.R.R.F., Clip Fed, Blue, Adjustable Sights, *Modern*	800.00	1,450.00
☐ **Gold Cup**, .45 ACP, Clip Fed, Adjustable Sights, Target Pistol, Military Style Stock, *Modern*	300.00	425.00
☐ **Gold Cup MK III**, .38 Special, Clip Fed, Adjustable Sights, Target Pistol, Military Style Stock, *Modern*	355.00	470.00
☐ **Gold Cup MK IV**, .45 ACP, Clip Fed, Blue, Target Trigger, *Modern*	295.00	400.00
☐ **Gold Cup Camp Perry**, .45 ACP, Commemorative, Target Pistol, Light Engraving, Cased, *Modern*	550.00	775.00
☐ **Gold Cup NRA Centennial**, .45 ACP, Commemorative, Target Pistol, Light Engraving, Cased, *Curio*	450.00	600.00
☐ **Gold Cup D.E.A. Commemorative**, .45 A.C.P., Clip Fed, Adjustable Sights, Comemorative, Cased, *Modern*	800.00	1,200.00
☐ **Government**, .45 ACP, Clip Fed, Commercial, *Modern*	240.00	325.00
☐ **Government John Browning M1911**, .45 ACP, Commemorative, Light Engraving, Cased, *Modern*	750.00	1,100.00

COLT / 125

Colt Model 1902 Military

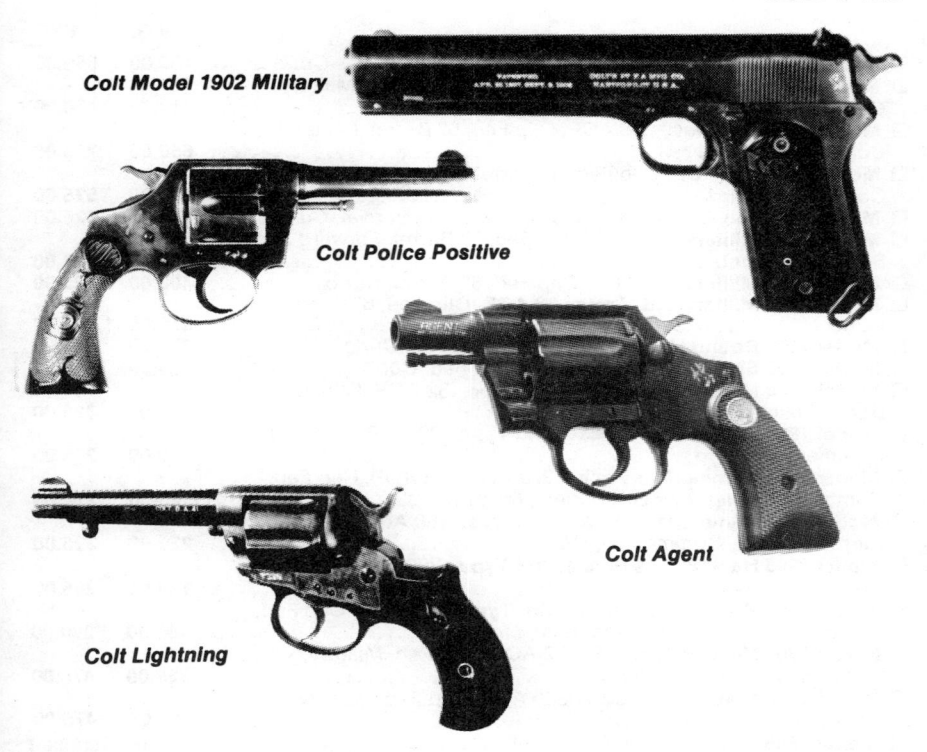

Colt Police Positive

Colt Agent

Colt Lightning

	V.G.	EXC.
☐ **Government 1911 English**, .455 Webley Auto., Clip Fed, Military, *Curio*	475.00	700.00
☐ **Government 1911 English**, .455 Webley Auto., Clip Fed, Military, R.A.F. Markings, *Curio*	625.00	900.00
☐ **Government BB 1911A1**, .45 ACP. Clip Fed, *Curio*	345.00	450.00
☐ **Government M1911**, M1911A1, .45 ACP, *Also See U.S. Military*		
☐ **Government M1911**, .45 ACP, Clip Fed, Commercial, *Curio*	525.00	775.00
☐ **Government M1911**, .45 ACP, Clip Fed, Military, *Curio*	575.00	850.00
☐ **Government M1911A1**, .45 ACP, Clip Fed, Military, *Modern*	325.00	500.00
☐ **Government M1911A1**, .45 ACP, Clip Fed, Military, with Detachable Shoulder Stock, *Class 3*	975.00	1,750.00
☐ **Government MK IV**, .38 Super, Clip Fed, Blue, *Modern*	195.00	295.00
☐ **Government MK IV**, .45 ACP, Clip Fed, Blue, *Modern*	190.00	280.00
☐ **Government MK IV**, .45 ACP, Clip Fed, Nickel Plated, *Modern*	220.00	300.00
☐ **Government MK IV**, 9mm Luger, Clip Fed, Blue, *Modern*	185.00	275.00
☐ **Government MK IV U.S.M.C. Limited Edition**, .45 A.C.P., Clip Fed, Cased, Commemorative, *Modern*	550.00	725.00
☐ **M 1911A1 (British)**, .455 Webley Auto., Clip Fed, Military, *Modern*	475.00	700.00
☐ **Junior**, .22 Short R.F., Clip Fed, *Modern*	115.00	185.00
☐ **Junior**, .25 ACP, Clip Fed, *Modern*	95.00	170.00
☐ **Model 1900**, .38 ACP, Clip Fed, 6" Barrel, Commercial, Safety Sight, *Curio*	675.00	1,250.00
☐ **Model 1900**, .38 ACP, Clip Fed, 6" Barrel, Commercial, Forward Slide Serrations, *Curio*	585.00	850.00

126 / COLT

	V.G.	EXC.
☐ **Model 1900**, .38 ACP, Clip Fed, 6" Barrel, Commercial, *Curio*	465.00	650.00
☐ **Model 1900 U.S. Army**, .38 ACP, Clip Fed, 6" Barrel, Military, *Curio*	750.00	1,450.00
☐ **Model 1900 U.S. Navy**, .38 ACP, Clip Fed, 6" Barrel, Military, *Curio*	650.00	1,275.00
☐ **Model 1902**, .38 ACP, Clip Fed, 6" Barrel, Forward Slide Serrations, Commercial, *Curio*	375.00	525.00
☐ **Model 1902**, .38 ACP, Clip Fed, 6" Barrel, Commercial, *Curio*	475.00	625.00
☐ **Model 1902 Military**, .38 ACP, Clip Fed, 6" Barrel, Forward Slide Serrations, *Curio*	475.00	600.00
☐ **Model 1902 Military**, .38 ACP, Clip Fed, 6" Barrel, *Curio*	400.00	525.00
☐ **Model 1902 Military U.S. Army**, .38 ACP, Clip Fed, 6" Barrel, *Curio*	875.00	1,400.00
☐ **Model 1903 Round Hammer**, .38 ACP, Clip Fed, *Curio*	250.00	375.00
☐ **Model 1903 Spur Hammer**, .38 ACP, Clip Fed, *Curio*	225.00	350.00
☐ **Model 1903 Hammerless Pocket 1st Type**, .32 ACP, Clip Fed, Barrel Bushing, Commercial, *Curio*	225.00	325.00
☐ **Model 1903 Hammerless Pocket 2nd Type**, .32 ACP, Clip Fed, Commercial, *Curio*	170.00	265.00
☐ **Model 1903 Hammerless Pocket 3rd Type**, .32 ACP, Clip Fed, Commercial, Magazine Disconnect, *Modern*	165.00	270.00
☐ **Model 1903 Hammerless Pocket 1st Type**, .380 ACP, Clip Fed, Barrel Bushing, Commercial, *Curio*	225.00	325.00
☐ **Model 1903 Hammerless Pocket 2nd Type**, .380 ACP, Clip Fed, Commercial, *Curio*	180.00	285.00
☐ **Model 1903 Hammerless Pocket 3rd Type**, .380 ACP, Clip Fed, Commercial, Magazine Disconnect, *Modern*	190.00	290.00
☐ **Model 1903 Hammerless U.S.**, .32 ACP, Clip Fed, Military, Magazine Disconnect, *Curio*	325.00	475.00
☐ **Model 1903 Hammerless U.S.**, .380 ACP, Clip Fed, Military, Magazine Disconnect, *Curio*	325.00	475.00
☐ **Model 1905**, .45 ACP, Clip Fed, *Curio*	675.00	1,150.00
☐ **Model 1905**, .45 ACP, Clip Fed, Adjustable Sights, with Detachable Shoulder Stock, *Curio*	2,550.00	3,875.00
☐ **Model 1905/07 U.S.**, .45 ACP, Clip Fed, Blue, Military, *Curio*	1,550.00	2,150.00
☐ **Model 1908 Pocket**, .25 ACP, Clip Fed, Hammerless, *Curio*	185.00	265.00
☐ **Model 1908 Pocket**, .25 ACP, Clip Fed, Hammerless, Magazine Disconnect, *Modern*	170.00	245.00
☐ **Model 1908 Pocket**, .25 ACP, Clip Fed, Hammerless, Magazine Disconnect, Military, *Curio*	275.00	400.00
☐ **National Match**, .45 ACP, Clip Fed, Target Pistol, Adjustable Sights, *Modern*	575.00	825.00
☐ **National Match**, .45 ACP, Clip Fed, Target Pistol, *Modern*	500.00	725.00
☐ **Pony**, .380 ACP, Clip Fed, Hammer, *Modern*	850.00	1,400.00
☐ **Super**, .38 Super, Clip Fed, Commercial, *Modern*	300.00	425.00
☐ **Super Match**, .38 Super, Clip Fed, Adjustable Sights, Target Pistol, *Modern*	500.00	700.00
☐ **Super Match**, .38 Super, Clip Fed, Target Pistol, *Modern*	400.00	550.00
☐ **Super Mexican Police**, .38 Super, Clip Fed, Military, *Modern*	375.00	525.00
☐ **WWI Battle of 2nd Marne**, .45 ACP, Commemorative, M1911, Light Engraving, Cased, *Curio*	375.00	500.00
☐ **WWI Battle of 2nd Marne Deluxe**, .45 ACP, Commemorative, M1911, Engraved, Cased, *Curio*	875.00	1,350.00
☐ **WWI Battle of 2nd Marne Special Deluxe**, .45 ACP., Commemorative, M1911, Fancy Engraving, Cased, *Curio*	1,550.00	2,250.00
☐ **WWI Belleau Wood**, .45 ACP, Commemorative, M1911, Light Engraving, Cased, *Curio*	375.00	500.00

	V.G.	EXC.
☐ **WWI Belleau Wood Special Deluxe**, .45 ACP, Commemorative, M1911, Fancy Engraving, Cased, *Curio*	1,550.00	2,250.00
☐ **WWI Belleau Wood Deluxe**, .45 ACP, Commemorative, M1911, Engraved, Cased, *Curio*	875.00	1,350.00
☐ **WWI Chateau Thierry**, .45 ACP, Commemorative, M1911, Light Engraving, Cased, *Curio*	375.00	500.00
☐ **WWI Chateau Thierry Deluxe**, .45 ACP, Commemorative, M1911, Engraved, Cased, *Curio*	875.00	1,375.00
☐ **WWI Chateau Thierry Special Deluxe**, .45 ACP, Commemorative, M1911, Fancy Engraving, Cased, *Curio*	1,550.00	2,250.00
☐ **WWI Meuse-Argonne**, .45 ACP, Commemorative, M1911, Light Engraving, Cased, *Curio*	375.00	500.00
☐ **WWI Meuse-Argonne Deluxe**, .45 ACP, Commemorative, M1911, Engraved, Cased, *Curio*	875.00	1,350.00
☐ **WWI Meuse-Argonne Special Deluxe**, .45 ACP, Commemorative, M1911, Fancy Engraving, Cased, *Curio*	1,550.00	2,250.00
☐ **WWII E.T.O.**, .45 ACP, Commemorative, M1911A1, Light Engraving, Cased, *Curio*	350.00	500.00
☐ **WWII P.T.O.**, .45 ACP, Commemorative, M1911A1, Light Engraving, Cased, *Curio*	350.00	500.00
☐ **Woodsman**, .22 L.R.R.F., Clip Fed, Adjustable Sights, with Detachable Shoulder Stock, *Curio*	975.00	1,600.00
☐ **Woodsman Huntsman**, .22 L.R.R.F., Clip Fed, Blue, Adjustable Sights, *Modern*	165.00	250.00
☐ **Woodsman Match Target 1st Type**, .22 L.R.R.F., Clip Fed, Extended Target Grips, *Modern*	425.00	650.00
☐ **Woodsman Match Target 2nd Type**, .22 L.R.R.F., Clip Fed, Blue, Adjustable Sights, *Modern*	210.00	300.00
☐ **Woodsman N & S**, .22 L.R.R.F., Clip Fed, Adjustable Sights, with Detachable Shoulder Stock, *Curio*	975.00	1,850.00
☐ **Woodsman Sport 1st. Type**, .22 L.R.R.F., Clip Fed, Adjustable Sights, *Modern*	295.00	395.00
☐ **Woodsman Sport**, .22 L.R.R.F., Clip Fed, Blue, Adjustable Sights, *Modern*	215.00	320.00
☐ **Woodsman Target 1st Type**, .22 L.R.R.F., Clip Fed, Adjustable Sights, *Modern*	195.00	315.00
☐ **Woodsman Target 1st. Type**, .22 L.R.R.F., Clip Fed, Adjustable Sights, with Extra Mainspring Housing, *Modern*	295.00	400.00
☐ **Woodsman Target 2nd. Type**, .22 L.R.R.F., Clip Fed, Adjustable Sights, *Modern*	260.00	345.00
☐ **Woodsman Target 3rd. Type**, .22 L.R.R.F., Clip Fed, Blue, Adjustable Sights, *Modern*	220.00	350.00
☐ **Woodsman Targetsman**, .22 L.R.R.F., Clip Fed, Blue, Adjustable Sights, *Modern*	160.00	225.00

HANDGUN, SINGLESHOT

	V.G.	EXC.
☐ **#1 Deringer**, .41 Short R.F., all Metal, Spur Trigger, Light Engraving, *Antique*	575.00	800.00
☐ **#2 Deringer**, .41 Short R.F., "Address Col. Colt", Wood Grips, Spur Trigger, Light Engraving, *Antique*	600.00	950.00
☐ **#2 Deringer**, .41 Short R.F., Wood Grips, Spur Trigger, Light Engraving, *Antique*	400.00	575.00
☐ **#3 Deringer Thuer**, .41 Short R.F., Wood Grips, Spur Trigger, 1st Issue, Contoured Swell at Pivot, High-Angled Hammer, *Antique*	595.00	950.00
☐ **#3 Deringer Thuer**, .41 Short R.F., Wood Grips, Spur Trigger, 2nd Issue, Angled Frame, no Swell, High Angled Hammer, *Antique*	350.00	500.00
☐ **#3 Deringer Thuer**, .41 Short R.F., Wood Grips, Spur Trigger, 3rd Issue, Straight Thick Frame, High-Angled Hammer, *Antique*	295.00	400.00

128 / COLT

	V.G.	EXC.
☐ **#3 Deringer Thuer**, .41 Short R.F., Wood Grips, Spur Trigger, London Marked, *Antique*	600.00	800.00
☐ **#4 Deringer**, .22 Short R.F., Geneseo Anniversary Commemorative, Spur Trigger, *Curio*	300.00	450.00
☐ **#4 Deringer**, .22 Short R.F., Fort McPherson Commemorative, Spur Trigger, *Curio*	220.00	300.00
☐ **#4 Deringer**, .22 Short R.F., Spur Trigger, *Modern*	50.00	75.00
☐ **#4 Deringer**, .22 Short R.F., Spur Trigger, Cased Pair, *Modern*	95.00	160.00
☐ **#4 Lord Deringer**, .22 Short R.F., Spur Trigger, Cased Pair, *Modern*	90.00	150.00
☐ **#4 Lady Deringer**, .22 Short R.F., Spur Trigger, Cased Pair, *Modern*	95.00	155.00
☐ **#4 Lord and Lady Deringers**, .22 Short R.F., Spur Trigger, Cased Pair, *Modern*	90.00	150.00
☐ **Camp Perry 1st Issue**, .22 L.R.R.F., Adjustable Sights, Target Pistol, *Modern*	600.00	800.00
☐ **Camp Perry 2nd Issue**, .22 L.R.R.F., Adjustable Sights, Target Pistol, *Modern*	700.00	1,100.00
☐ **Civil War Centennial**, .22 Short R.F., ⅞ Scale 1860 Army Replica, Commemorative, 6" Barrel, Blue, Cased, *Curio*	45.00	85.00
☐ **Civil War Centennial Pair**, .22 Short R.F., ⅞ Scale 1860 Army Replica, Commemorative, 6" Barrel, Blue, Cased, *Curio*	110.00	180.00
☐ **Rock Island Arsenal Centennial**, .22 Short R.F., ⅞ Scale 1860 Army Replica, Commemorative, 6" Barrel, Blue, Cased, *Curio*	95.00	175.00

RIFLE, BOLT ACTION

☐ **Colteer 1-22**, .22 L.R.R.F., Singleshot, Plain, *Modern*	35.00	55.00
☐ **Colteer 1-22**, .22 WMR, Singleshot, Plain, *Modern*	45.00	65.00
☐ **Coltsman Custom (FN)**, Various Calibers, Sporting Rifle, Fancy Wood, Light Engraving, Checkered Stock, Monte Carlo Stock, *Modern*	290.00	395.00
☐ **Coltsman Custom (Sako)**, Various Calibers, Sporting Rifle, Fancy Wood, Checkered Stock, Monte Carlo Stock, *Modern*	345.00	450.00
☐ **Coltsman Deluxe (FN)**, Various Calibers, Sporting Rifle, Checkered Stock, Monte Carlo Stock, *Modern*	270.00	365.00
☐ **Coltsman Deluxe (Sako)**, Various Calibers, Sporting Rifle, Checkered Stock, Monte Carlo Stock, *Modern*	285.00	395.00
☐ **Coltsman Standard (FN)**, Various Calibers, Sporting Rifle, Checkered Stock, *Modern*	215.00	295.00
☐ **Coltsman Standard (Sako)**, Various Calibers, Sporting Rifle, Checkered Stock, *Modern*	235.00	350.00
☐ **Sauer**, Various Calibers, Clip Fed, Checkered Stock, Short Action, *Modern*	500.00	775.00
☐ **Sauer**, Various Calibers, Clip Fed, Checkered Stock, Magnum *Modern*	575.00	845.00
☐ **Sauer**, Various Calibers, Clip Fed, Checkered Stock, *Modern*	525.00	800.00
☐ **Sauer Grand African**, .458 Win. Mag., Clip Fed, Fancy Wood, *Modern*	600.00	900.00
☐ **Sauer Grand Alaskan**, .375 H & H Mag., Clip Fed, Checkered Stock, Magnum, *Modern*	585.00	875.00

RIFLE, SEMI-AUTOMATIC

☐ **AR-l5**, .223 Rem., Clip Fed, *Modern*	335.00	425.00
☐ **AR-l5**, .223 Rem., Clip Fed, Collapsible Stock, *Modern*	360.00	455.00
☐ **Colteer 22 Autoloader**, .22 L.R.R.F., Tube Feed, Plain, *Modern*	90.00	130.00
☐ **Colteer Stagecoach**, .22 L.R.R.F., Tube Feed, Light Engraving, *Modern*	95.00	140.00

RIFLE, PERCUSSION

☐ **1st Model Ring Lever**, Various Calibers, 8 or 10 Shot Revolving Cylinder, with Topstrap, *Antique*	4,200.00	6,950.00

	V.G.	EXC.
☐ **2nd Model Ring Lever**, .44, 8 or 10 Shot Revolving Cylinder, no Topstrap, *Antique*	3,650.00	6,400.00
☐ **Model 1839**, 6 Shot Cylinder, with Hammer, *Antique*	2,950.00	4,750.00
☐ **Model 1855 Sporting Rifle**, .36, 6 Shot Revolving Cylinder, Sidehammer, no Forestock, Spur Triggerguard, *Antique*	1,650.00	3,200.00
☐ **Model 1855 Sporting Rifle**, Various Calibers, 6 Shot Revolving Cylinder, Sidehammer, Halfstock, Scroll Triggerguard, *Antique*	1,350.00	2,650.00
☐ **Model 1855 Sporting Rifle**, Various Calibers, 6 Shot Revolving Cylinder, Sidehammer, Full Stock, Scroll Triggerguard, *Antique*	1,550.00	2,650.00
☐ **Model 1855 Carbine**, Various Calibers, 6 Shot Revolving Cylinder, Sidehammer, no Forestock, *Antique*	1,550.00	2,650.00
☐ **Model 1855 Military Rifle**, Various Calibers, 6 Shot Revolving Cylinder, Sidehammer, Full Stock, U.S. Military, *Antique*	2,200.00	4,300.00
☐ **Model 1861 Musket**, .58, Military Contract Musket, *Antique*	535.00	850.00

RIFLE, SINGLESHOT
☐ **Sharps**, Various Calibers, Fancy Wood, Fancy Checkering, Cased with Accessories, *Modern*	1,300.00	1,900.00

RIFLE, SLIDE ACTION
☐ **Lightning**, .22 R.F., Small Frame (Numbers over 35,300 are Modern), *Antique*	250.00	465.00
☐ **Lightning**, Various Calibers, Medium Frame (Numbers over 84,000 are Modern), *Antique*	300.00	475.00
☐ **Lightning Carbine**, Various Calibers, Medium Frame (Numbers over 84,000 are Modern), *Antique*	550.00	775.00
☐ **Lightning Baby Carbine**, Various Calibers, Medium Frame (Numbers over 84,000 are Modern), *Antique*	650.00	875.00
☐ **Lightning**, Various Calibers, Large Frame, *Antique*	475.00	625.00
☐ **Lightning Carbine**, Various Calibers, Large Frame, *Antique*	825.00	1,300.00
☐ **Lightning Baby Carbine**, Various Calibers, Large Frame, *Antique*	995.00	1,750.00

SHOTGUN, DOUBLE BARREL, SIDE-BY-SIDE
☐ **Custom**, 12 and 16 Gauges, Double Trigger, Automatic Ejector, Checkered Stock, Beavertail Forend, Hammerless, *Modern*	245.00	375.00
☐ **Model 1878 Standard**, Various Gauges, Outside Hammers, Damascus Barrel, *Antique*	395.00	550.00
☐ **Model I883 Standard**, Various Gauges, Hammerless, Damascus Barrel, *Antique*	450.00	650.00

SHOTGUN, SEMI-AUTOMATIC
☐ **Various Gauges**, for Solid Rib, *Add* **$15.00-$25.00**		
☐ **Various Gauges**, for Vent Rib, *Add* **$25.00-$35.00**		
☐ **Ultra-Light**, 12 and 20 Gauges, Checkered Stock, Takedown, *Modern*	145.00	195.00
☐ **Ultra-Light Custom**, I2 and 20 Gauges, Checkered Stock, Light Engraving, Takedown, *Modern*	165.00	235.00
☐ **Ultra-Light Magnum**, I2 and 20 Gauges 3", Checkered Stock, Takedown, *Modern*	165.00	235.00
☐ **Ultra-Light Magnum Custom**, I2 and 20 Gauges 3", Checkered Stock, Light Engraving, Takedown, *Modern*	185.00	250.00

SHOTGUN, SLIDE ACTION
☐ **Coltsman Custom**, Various Gauges, Takedown, Checkered Stock, Vent Rib, *Modern*	155.00	225.00
☐ **Coltsman Standard**, Various Gauges, Takedown, Plain, *Modern*	115.00	175.00

COLUMBIA ARMORY
Tenn., Maltby & Henley Distributers c. 1890.

HANDGUN, REVOLVER

	V.G.	EXC.
☐ **New Safety**, .22 L.R.R.F., 7 Shot, Double Action, Solid Frame, Grip Safety, *Modern*	70.00	115.00
☐ **New Safety**, .32 S & W, 5 Shot, Double Action, Solid Frame, Grip Safety, *Modern*	80.00	135.00
☐ **New Safety**, .38 S & W, 5 Shot, Double Action, Solid Frame, Grip Safety, *Modern*	85.00	140.00

COLUMBIAN
Made by Foehl & Weeks, Philadelphia, Pa. c. 1890.

HANDGUN, REVOLVER

☐ .32 S & W, 5 Shot, Double Action, Solid Frame, *Modern*	55.00	90.00
☐ .38 S & W, 5 Shot, Double Action, Solid Frame, *Modern*	55.00	90.00

COMET

HANDGUN, REVOLVER

☐ **.32 Long R.F.**, 7 Shot, Single Action, Spur Trigger, Solid Frame, *Antique*	85.00	150.00

COMINAZZO OR COMINAZZI
Family of armorers in Brescia, Italy from about 1593 to about 1875.

HANDGUN, FLINTLOCK

☐ .54, Mid-l600's, Belt Pistol, Brass Furniture, Ornate *Antique*	3,750.00	5,250.00

HANDGUN, WHEEL-LOCK

☐ **Ebony Full Stock**, Ivory Pom, Holster Pistol, German Style, Military, Engraved, *Antique*	3,950.00	5,450.00

COMMANDO ARMS
Made by Volunteer Enterprises in Knoxville, Tenn. since 1969.

RIFLE, SEMI-AUTOMATIC

☐ **Commando MK III**, .45 ACP, Clip Fed, Horizontal Forend, with Compensator, Carbine, *Modern*	90.00	135.00
☐ **Commando MK III**, .45 ACP, Clip Fed, Vertical Forend, with Compensator, Carbine, *Modern*	95.00	145.00
☐ **Commando MK 9**, 9mm Luger, Clip Fed, Horizontal Forend, with Compensator, Carbine, *Modern*	95.00	145.00
☐ **Commando MK 9**, 9mm Luger, Clip Fed, Vertical Forend, with Compensator, Carbine, *Modern*	110.00	150.00
☐ **Commando MK 45**, .45 ACP, Clip Fed, Horizontal Forend, with Compensator, Carbine, *Modern*	95.00	145.00
☐ **Commando MK 45**, .45 ACP, Clip Fed, Vertical Forend, with Compensator, Carbine, *Modern*	110.00	150.00

COMMANDER

HANDGUN, REVOLVER

☐ **.32 Long R.F.**, 7 Shot, Single Action, Spur Trigger Solid Frame, *Antique*	85.00	145.00

COMMERCIAL
See Smith, Otis A.

COMPEER
Made by Crescent for Van Camp Hardware c. 1900.

	V.G.	EXC.

SHOTGUN, DOUBLE BARREL, SIDE-BY-SIDE
- ☐ **Various Gauges**, Outside Hammers, Damascus Barrel, *Modern* 80.00 150.00
- ☐ **Various Gauges**, Hammerless, Steel Barrel, *Modern* 95.00 175.00
- ☐ **Various Gauges**, Hammerless, Damascus Barrel, *Modern* 75.00 150.00
- ☐ **Various Gauges**, Outside Hammers, Steel Barrel, *Modern* 90.00 175.00

SHOTGUN, SINGLESHOT
- ☐ **Various Gauges**, Hammer, Steel Barrel, *Modern* 45.00 75.00

CONE, D.D.
Washington, D.C. c. 1865.

HANDGUN, REVOLVER
- ☐ **.22 Long R.F.**, 7 Shot, Single Action, Spur Trigger, Solid Frame, *Antique* 95.00 175.00
- ☐ **.32 Long R.F.**, 6 Shot, Single Action, Spur Trigger, Solid Frame, *Antique* 125.00 200.00

CONFEDERATE MILITARY

HANDGUN, PERCUSSION
- ☐ **.36 Columbus**, Revolver, Brass Trigger Guard, 6 Shot, *Antique* 3,950.00 9,750.00
- ☐ **.36 Dance Bros.**, Revolver, Iron Frame, 6 Shot, *Antique* 3,400.00 7,750.00
- ☐ **.36 Griswald & Gunnison**, Revolver, Brass Frame, 6 Shot, Serial No. is the Only Marking, *Antique* 2,750.00 4,000.00
- ☐ **.36 Leech & Co.**, Revolver, Brass Grip Frame, 6 Shot, *Antique* 3,000.00 4,350.00
- ☐ **.36 Leech & Rigdon**, Revolver, Brass Grip Frame, 6 Shot, *Antique* 1,950.00 3,150.00
- ☐ **.36 Rigdon & Ansley**, Revolver, Brass Grip Frame, 6 Shot, *Antique* 2,350.00 3,850.00
- ☐ **.36 Shawk & McLanahan**, Revolver, Brass Frame, 6 Shot, *Antique* 3,975.00 8,500.00
- ☐ **.36 Spiller & Burr**, Revolver, Brass Frame, 6 Shot, *Antique* 2,200.00 3,850.00
- ☐ **.36 T.W. Cofer**, Revolver, Brass Frame, 6 Shot, *Antique* 7,700.00 16,000.00
- ☐ **.44 Dance Bros.**, Revolver, Brass Grip Frame, 6 Shot, *Antique* 3,200.00 4,700.00
- ☐ **.44 Tucker & Sherrod**, Revolver, Copy of Colt Dragoon, Serial Number is the Only Marking, *Antique* 4,250.00 9,400.00
- ☐ **.54 Palmetto**, Singleshot, Brass Furniture, *Antique* 850.00 1,700.00
- ☐ **.58 Fayetteville**, Singleshot, Rifled, *Antique* 975.00 1,750.00
- ☐ **.58 Fayetteville**, Singleshot, Rifled, with Shoulder Stock, *Antique* 1,600.00 2,650.00
- ☐ **.60 Sutherland**, Singleshot, Brass Barrel, Converted from Flintlock, *Antique* 600.00 975.00

RIFLE, PERCUSSION
- ☐ **.52, "P," Tallahassee**, Breech Loader, Carbine, *Antique* 2,350.00 4,150.00
- ☐ **.52, Tarpley**, Breech Loader, Carbine, Brass Breech, *Antique* 3,500.00 7,950.00
- ☐ **.54, L.G. Sturdivant**, Brass Furniture, Rifled, Serial No. is the Only Marking, *Antique* 1,100.00 1,900.00
- ☐ **.54, Wytheville-Hall**, Muzzle Loader, Rifled, Brass Frame, *Antique* 1,300.00 2,150.00
- ☐ **.57, Texas Enfield**, Brass Furniture, *Antique* 2,700.00 4,200.00
- ☐ **.58, Musketoon**, Brass Furniture, Military, Cook & Brother, *Antique* 1,600.00 2,850.00
- ☐ **.58, Military, Carbine**, Dickson, Nelson & Co., *Antique*, ... 1,850.00 4,375.00
- ☐ **.58, Military**, Dickson, Nelson & Co., *Antique*, ... 1,650.00 2,700.00
- ☐ **.58, Artillery**, Brass Furniture, Military, Cook & Brother, *Antique* ... 1,875.00 3,300.00
- ☐ **.58, D.C. Hodgkins & Co.**, Iron Mounts, Rifled, Carbine, *Antique* ... 1,900.00 3,700.00
- ☐ **.58, Enfield Type**, Brass Furniture, Military, Cook & Brother, *Antique* 1,450.00 2,650.00
- ☐ **.58, Enfield Type**, Rifled, Brass Furniture, Military, *Antique* 1,350.00 2,325.00
- ☐ **.58, Fayetteville**, Brass Furniture, 2 Bands, Rifled, *Antique* 1,400.00 2,875.00
- ☐ **.58, Georgia**, Brass Furniture, Rifled, *Antique* 1,350.00 2,600.00
- ☐ **.58, H.C. Lamb & Co.**, Brass Furniture, 2 Bands, Rifled, *Antique* .. 2,350.00 4,200.00

132 / CONN. ARMS CO.

	V.G.	EXC.
☐ .58, Palmetto, Musket, *Antique*	1,100.00	2,150.00
☐ .58, Richmond, Carbine, *Antique*	975.00	1,800.00
☐ .58, Richmond, Musket, Rifled, *Antique*	800.00	1,600.00
☐ .58, Tallahassee, Carbine, Brass Furniture, 2 Bands, *Antique*	2,675.00	4,650.00
☐ .58, Whitney, Rifled, Musket, *Antique*	375.00	650.00
☐ .61, Whitney Enfield, Rifled, Brass Furniture, *Antique*	375.00	750.00
☐ .62, Richmond Navy, Musketoon, Smoothbore, *Antique*	975.00	2,150.00
☐ .69, Prussian Musket, Brass Furniture, Military, *Antique*	350.00	550.00

RIFLE, SINGLESHOT
☐ .50, S.C. Robinson, Brass Furniture, Breech Loader, Carbine, Imitation Sharps, *Antique*	975.00	2,100.00
☐ .69, Morse, Smoothbore, Carbine, Breech Loader, *Antique*	1,550.00	2,650.00
☐ .69, Morse, Smoothbore, Breech Loader, *Antique*	975.00	2,100.00

CONN. ARMS CO.
Norfolk, Conn. 1862-1869.

HANDGUN, REVOLVER
☐ **Wood's Patent**, .28 T.F., Tip-Up Barrel, 6 Shot, Spur Trigger, *Antique*	140.00	290.00

CONN. ARMS & MFG. CO.
Naubuc, Conn. 1863-1869.

HANDGUN, SINGLESHOT
☐ **Hammond Patent Bulldog**, .44 R.F., Pivoting Breechblock, Hammer, Spur Trigger, *Antique*	165.00	275.00
☐ **Hammond Patent Bulldog**, .44 R.F., Pivoting Breechblock, Hammer, Spur Trigger, Very Long Barrel, *Antique*	250.00	400.00
☐ **Hammond Patent Bull-Dozer**, .44 R.F., Pivoting Breechblock, Hammer, Spur Trigger, *Antique*	185.00	290.00

CONQUERER
Made by Bacon Arms Co. c. 1880.

HANDGUN, REVOLVER
☐ .22 Short R.F., 7 Shot, Spur Trigger, Solid Frame, Single Action, *Antique*	85.00	160.00
☐ .32 Short R.F., 5 Shot, Spur Trigger, Solid Frame, Single Action, *Antique*	85.00	160.00

CONSTABLE, RICHARD
Philadelphia, Pa. 1817-1851.

HANDGUN, PERCUSSION
☐ **Dueling Pistols**, Cased Pair, with Accessories, *Antique*	1,750.00	3,450.00

RIFLE, PERCUSSION
☐ .44, Octagon Barrel, Brass Furniture, *Antique*	925.00	1,750.00

CONTENTO
See Ventura Imports

CONTINENTAL
Made by Jules Bertrand, Liege, Belgium c. 1910.

HANDGUN, SEMI-AUTOMATIC
☐ **Pocket**, .25 ACP, Clip Fed, *Curio*	150.00	225.00

CONTINENTAL
Rheinische Waffen u. Munitionsfabrik. Possibly a tradename used by Arizmendi c. 1910.

V.G. EXC.

HANDGUN, SEMI-AUTOMATIC
- ☐ **.25 ACP**, Clip Fed, Blue, *Curio* 85.00   125.00
- ☐ **.32 ACP**, Clip Fed, Webley Copy, Blue, *Curio* 110.00 165.00

CONTINENTAL
Made by Stevens Arms.

RIFLE, BOLT ACTION
- ☐ **Model 52**, .22 L.R.R.F., Singleshot, Takedown, *Modern* 35.00   50.00

SHOTGUN, DOUBLE BARREL, SIDE-BY-SIDE
- ☐ **Model 315**, Various Gauges, Hammerless, Steel Barrel, *Modern* 95.00   175.00
- ☐ **Model 215**, 12 and 16 Gauges, Outside Hammers, Steel Barrel, *Modern* 95.00   165.00
- ☐ **Model 311**, Various Gauges, Hammerless, Steel Barrel, *Modern* 120.00 190.00

SHOTGUN, SINGLESHOT
- ☐ **Model 90**, Various Gauges, Takedown, Automatic Ejector, Plain Hammer, *Modern* 40.00   60.00

CONTINENTAL
Made by Hood Firearms Co., Successors to Continental Arms Co.; Sold by Marshall Wells Co., Duluth, Minn. c. 1870.

HANDGUN, REVOLVER
- ☐ **.22 Short R.F.**, 7 Shot, Spur Trigger, Solid Frame, Single Action, *Antique* 85.00   160.00
- ☐ **.32 Short R.F.**, 5 Shot, Spur Trigger, Solid Frame, Single Action, *Antique* 90.00   170.00

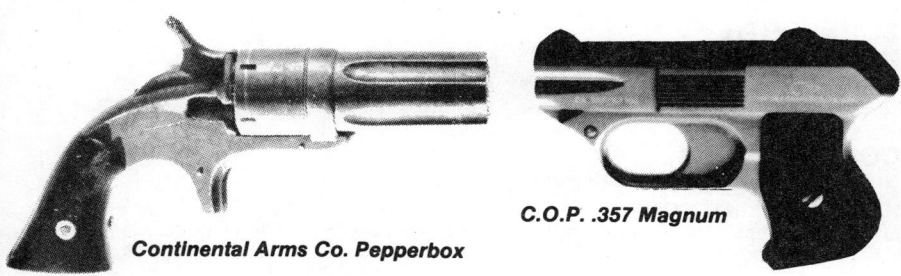

Continental Arms Co. Pepperbox

C.O.P. .357 Magnum

CONTINENTAL ARMS CO.
Norwich, Conn. 1866-1867.

HANDGUN, PEPPERBOX
- ☐ **Continental 1**, .22 R.F., 7 Shot, Spur Trigger, Solid Frame, *Antique* 275.00 425.00
- ☐ **Continental 2**, .32 R.F., 5 Shot, Spur Trigger, Solid Frame, *Antique* 325.00 525.00

COOPER FIREARMS MFG. CO.
Philadelphia, Pa. 1851-1869.

HANDGUN, PERCUSSION
- ☐ **Pocket**, .31, 5 or 6 Shots, Double Action, *Antique* 275.00 450.00
- ☐ **Navy**, .31, 5 Shots, Double Action, *Antique* 335.00 550.00

C.O.P.
M & N *Distributers, Torrance, Calif.*

	V.G.	EXC.

HANDGUN, REPEATER
- **Model SS-1**, .357 Mag., Four Barrels, Stainless Steel, Hammerless, Double Action, *Modern* 140.00 180.00
- **Model Mini**, .22 W.M.R., Four Barrels, Stainless Steel, Hammerless, Double Action, *Modern* 160.00 220.00
- **Model Mini**, .22 L.R.R.F., Four Barrels, Aluminium Frame, Hammerless, Double Action, *Modern* 115.00 150.00

HANDGUN, SEMI-AUTOMATIC
- **TP-70 AAI**, .22 L.R.R.F., Double Action, Clip Fed, Stainless Steel, Hammer, *Modern* 115.00 165.00
- **TP-70 AAI**, .25 A.C.P., Double Action, Clip Fed, Stainless Steel, Hammer, *Modern* 110.00 160.00

COPELAND, F.
Made by Frank Copeland, Worcester, Mass. 1868-1874.

HANDGUN, REVOLVER
- **.22 Short R.F.**, 7 Shot, Spur Trigger, Solid Frame, Single Action, *Antique* 125.00 195.00
- **.32 Short R.F.**, 5 Shot, Spur Trigger, Solid Frame, Single Action, *Antique* 140.00 220.00

COQ
Spain, Unknown Maker c. 1900.

HANDGUN, SEMI-AUTOMATIC
- **K-25**, .25 ACP, Clip Fed, *Modern* 70.00 115.00

CORNFORTH
London, England 1725-1760.

HANDGUN, FLINTLOCK
- **Pair**, Belt Pistol, Brass Barrel, Brass Furniture, Plain, *Antique* 2,650.00 3,950.00

COSENS, JAMES
Gunmaker in Ordinary to Charles II England, Late 1600's.

HANDGUN, FLINTLOCK
- **Pair**, Holster Pistol, Silver Furniture, Engraved Silver Inlay, High Quality, *Antique* 9,000.00 15,000.00

COSMI
Made for Abercrombie & Fitch c. 1960.

SHOTGUN, SEMI-AUTOMATIC
- **12 or 20 Gauge**, Top Break, Engraved, Checkered Stock, Vent Rib, *Modern* 1,250.00 1,950.00

COSMOPOLITAN ARMS CO.
Hamilton, Ohio 1860-1865. Also see U.S. Military.

RIFLE, PERCUSSION
- **.45**, Sporting Rifle, *Antique* 750.00 1,100.00
- **.50**, Carbine, *Antique* 635.00 950.00

COWLES & SON
V.G.   EXC.

Cowles & Smith, 1866-1871, Cowles & Son 1871-1876 in Chicopee Falls, Mass.

HANDGUN, SINGLESHOT
☐ **.22 Short R.F.**, Brass Frame, Side Swing Barrel, *Antique* 150.00   225.00

CRAFT PRODUCTS

HANDGUN, SEMI—AUTOMATIC
☐ **.25 ACP**, Clip Fed, *Modern* 65.00   110.00

COWELS & SMITH
Chicopee Falls, Mass. 1863-1876. Became Cowels & Son in 1871.

HANDGUN, SINGLESHOT
☐ **.22 R.F.**, Side-Swing Barrel, Hammer, Spur Trigger, *Antique* 125.00   200.00
☐ **.30 R.F.**, Side-Swing Barrel, Hammer, Spur Trigger, *Antique* 140.00   220.00

CRESCENT
Made by Norwich Falls Pistol Co. c. 1880.

HANDGUN, REVOLVER
☐ **.32 Short R.F.**, 5 Shot, Spur Trigger, Solid Frame, Single Action, *Antique* 85.00   160.00

CRESCENT FIRE ARMS CO.
Norwich, Conn., 1892; Purchased by H & D Folsom in 1893, and Absorbed by Stevens Arms & Tool 1926.

HANDGUN, SINGLESHOT
☐ **.410 Ga.**, Top Break, *Class 3* 145.00   250.00

SHOTGUN, DOUBLE BARREL, SIDE-BY-SIDE
☐ **Various Gauges**, Outside Hammers, Damascus Barrel, *Modern* 80.00   150.00
☐ **Various Gauges**, Hammerless, Steel Barrel, *Modern* 95.00   175.00
☐ **Various Gauges**, Hammerless, Damascus Barrel, *Modern* 75.00   150.00
☐ **Various Gauges**, Outside Hammers, Steel Barrel, *Modern* 90.00   175.00

SHOTGUN, SINGLESHOT
☐ **Various Gauges**, Hammer, Steel Barrel, *Modern* 45.00   75.00

CREEDMORE
Made by Hopkins & Allen c. 1870.

HANDGUN, REVOLVER
☐ **#1**, .22 Short R.F., 7 Shot, Spur Trigger, Solid Frame, Single Action, *Antique* 85.00   160.00

CRIOLLA
Hispano Argentine Automoviles, Buenos Aires, Argentina c. 1935.

HANDGUN, SEMI-AUTOMATIC
☐ **La Criolla**, .22 L.R.R.F., Colt M1911 Ace Copy, Clip Fed, Blue, *Modern* 230.00   325.00

CROWN JEWEL
Made by Norwich Falls Pistol Co. c.1880.

HANDGUN, REVOLVER
☐ **.32 Short R.F.**, 5 Shot, Spur Trigger, Solid Frame, Single Action, *Antique* 85.00   160.00

CRUCELEGUI
Spain, Imported by Mandall Shooting Supplies, Scotsdale, Ariz.

	V.G.	EXC.

SHOTGUN, DOUBLE BARREL, SIDE-BY-SIDE
☐ **Model 150**, 12 and 20 Gauges, Outside Hammers, Double Trigger, Modern ... 130.00   180.00

CRUSO
Made by Stevens Arms

RIFLE, BOLT ACTION
☐ **Model 53**, .22 L.R.R.F., Singleshot, Takedown, Modern ... 35.00   50.00

SHOTGUN, SINGLESHOT
☐ **Model 90**, Various Gauges, Takedown, Automatic Ejector, Plain Hammer, Modern ... 40.00   60.00

CUMBERLAND ARMS CO.
Made by Crescent for Hibbard-Spencer Bartlett Co. c. 1900.

SHOTGUN, DOUBLE BARREL, SIDE-BY-SIDE
☐ **Various Gauges**, Outside Hammers, Damascus Barrel, Modern ... 100.00   175.00
☐ **Various Gauges**, Hammerless, Steel Barrel, Modern ... 135.00   200.00
☐ **Various Gauges**, Hammerless, Damascus Barrel, Modern ... 100.00   175.00
☐ **Various Gauges**, Outside Hammers, Steel Barrel, Modern ... 125.00   190.00

SHOTGUN, SINGLESHOT
☐ **Various Gauges**, Hammer, Steel Barrel, Modern ... 55.00   85.00

C.V.A. (CONNECTICUT VALLEY ARMS)
Haddon, Conn. Current (Prices reflect Factory Assembled Guns, not Kits)

HANDGUN, FLINTLOCK
☐ **.50 Hawkin**, Brass Furniture, Set Triggers, Reproduction, Antique   55.00   80.00
☐ **.45 Kentucky**, Brass Furniture, Reproduction, Antique ...   45.00   60.00

HANDGUN, PERCUSSION
☐ **.50 Hawkin**, Brass Furniture, Set Triggers, Reproduction, Antique   55.00   75.00
☐ **.45 or .50 Mountain Pistol**, Brass Furniture, Reproduction, Antique   55.00   80.00
☐ **.45 Kentucky**, Brass Furniture, Reproduction, Antique ...   40.00   55.00
☐ **.45 Tower Pistol**, Brass Furniture, Reproduction, Antique ...   35.00   55.00
☐ **.45 Colonial Pistol**, Brass Furniture, Reproduction, Antique ...   30.00   45.00
☐ **.45 Philadelphia Derringer**, Reproduction, Antique ...   25.00   40.00

RIFLE, FLINTLOCK
☐ **.50 Frontier Rifle**, Brass Furniture, Reproduction, Antique ...   95.00   145.00
☐ **.50 or .54 Hawkin Rifle**, Brass Furniture, Reproduction, Antique ...   115.00   170.00
☐ **.45 or .50 Mountain Rifle**, German Silver Furniture, Reproduction, Antique ...   120.00   180.00
☐ **.45 Kentucky Rifle**, Brass Furniture, Reproduction, Antique ...   90.00   130.00

RIFLE, PERCUSSION
☐ **.50 or .54 Hawkin Rifle**, Brass Furniture, Reproduction, Antique ...   110.00   165.00
☐ **.45, .50, .54, or .58 Mountain Rifle**, German Silver Furniture, Reproduction, Antique ...   120.00   180.00
☐ **.45 or .50 Frontier Rifle**, Brass Furniture, Reproduction, Antique ...   90.00   140.00
☐ **.45 Kentucky Rifle**, Brass Furniture, Reproduction, Antique ...   85.00   130.00
☐ **.58 Zouave**, Brass Furniture, Reproduction, Antique ...   95.00   155.00

CZ
Czechoslovakia from 1918 to date. This listing includes both Ceska Zbrojovka Brno and Ceskslovenska Zbrojovka. Also see BRNO.

CZ / 137

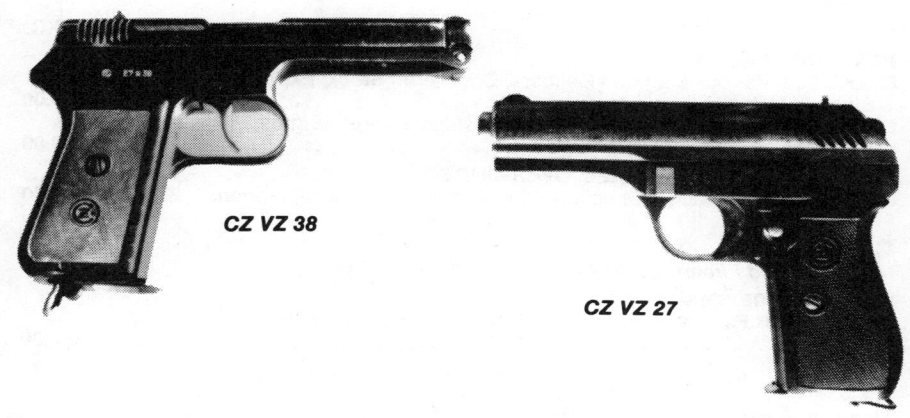

CZ VZ 38

CZ VZ 27

	V.G.	EXC.
HANDGUN, REVOLVER		
☐ **Grand**, .38 Spec., Double Action, Swing-Out Cylinder, *Modern*	110.00	160.00
☐ **Grand**, .357 Mag., Double Action, Swing-Out Cylinder, *Modern* ...	125.00	175.00
☐ **ZKR 551**, .38 Spec., Single Action, Swing-Out Cylinder, Target Pistol, *Modern*	160.00	235.00
HANDGUN, SEMI-AUTOMATIC		
☐ **CZ1922**, .25 ACP, Clip Fed, *Curio*	275.00	375.00
☐ **CZ1922**, .380 ACP, Clip Fed, *Curio*	155.00	240.00
☐ **CZ1936**, .25 ACP, Clip Fed, *Curio*	115.00	165.00
☐ **CZ 70**, .32 ACP, CLip Fed, Blue, Double Action, *Modern*	135.00	190.00
☐ **CZ 75**, 9mm P, Clip Fed, Double Action, Blue, *Modern*	350.00	450.00
☐ **Duo**, .25 ACP, Clip Fed, *Modern*	100.00	175.00
☐ **Fox**, .25 ACP, Clip Fed, *Curio*	250.00	350.00
☐ **M1938**, .380 ACP, Clip Fed, Double Action, *Curio*	120.00	200.00
☐ **Niva**, .25 ACP, Clip Fed, *Curio*	200.00	285.00
☐ **PZK**, .25 ACP, Clip Fed, *Modern*	180.00	275.00
☐ **Vest Pocket CZ 1945**, .25 ACP, Clip Fed, *Modern*	125.00	185.00
☐ **VZ NB 50 Police**, .32 ACP, Clip Fed, Double Action, *Curio*	225.00	325.00
☐ **VZ1922**, .380 ACP, Clip Fed, *Curio*	150.00	240.00
☐ **VZ1924**, .380 ACP, Clip Fed, *Curio*	120.00	185.00
☐ **VZ1924 Navy**, .380 ACP, Clip Fed, Nazi-Proofed, *Curio*	185.00	275.00
☐ **VZ1938**, .380 ACP, Clip Fed, Double Action, Nazi-Proofed, *Curio*	170.00	265.00
☐ **VZ1938**, .380 ACP, Clip Fed, Double Action, *Curio*	160.00	250.00
☐ **VZ27**, .22 L.R.R.F., Clip Fed, Nazi-Proofed, *Curio*	450.00	600.00
☐ **VZ27**, .32 ACP, Clip Fed, Commercial, *Curio*	135.00	200.00
☐ **VZ27**, .32 ACP, Clip Fed, Barrel Extension for Silencer, *Curio*, Class 3	400.00	575.00
☐ **VZ27 Luftwaffe**, .32 ACP, Clip Fed, Nazi-Proofed, *Modern*	140.00	245.00
☐ **VZ27 Navy**, .32 ACP, Clip Fed, Nazi-Proofed, *Curio*	175.00	265.00
☐ **VZ27 Police**, .32 ACP, Clip Fed, Nazi-Proofed, *Curio*	150.00	250.00
☐ **VZ50**, .32 ACP, Clip Fed, Double Action, Military, *Modern*	165.00	225.00
☐ **VZ52**, 7.62mm Tokarev, Clip Fed, Double Action, *Curio*	500.00	950.00
HANDGUN, SINGLESHOT		
☐ **Drulov**, .22 L.R.R.F., Top Break, Target Pistol, Target Sights, *Modern*	300.00	400.00
☐ **Model P**, .22 L.R.R.F., Top Break, Target Pistol, *Modern*	175.00	250.00
☐ **Model P**, 6mm Flobert, Top Break, Target Pistol, *Modern*	145.00	225.00

138 / CZAR

	V.G.	EXC.

RIFLE, BOLT ACTION
☐ **ZKK 602**, Various Magnum Calibers, Checkered Stock, Express Sights, *Modern* 300.00 450.00
☐ **ZKK 600**, Various Calibers, Checkered Stock, Express Sights, *Modern* 250.00 350.00

SHOTGUN, DOUBLE BARREL, OVER-UNDER
☐ **Model 581**, 12 Gauge, Checkered Stock with Cheekpiece, *Modern* 275.00 400.00

CZAR
Made by Hood Firearms c. 1876.

HANDGUN, REVOLVER
☐ **.22 Short R.F.**, 7 Shot, Spur Trigger, Solid Frame, Single Action, Antique 85.00 160.00

CZAR
Made by Hopkins & Allen c. 1880.

HANDGUN, REVOLVER
☐ **.22 Short R.F.**, 7 Shot, Spur Trigger, Solid Frame, Single Action, Antique 85.00 160.00
☐ **.32 Short R.F.**, 5 Shot, Spur Trigger, Solid Frame, Single Action, Antique 90.00 170.00

CZECHOSLAVAKIAN MILITARY
Also see German Military, CZ.

AUTOMATIC WEAPON, LIGHT MACHINE GUN
☐ **ZB-VZ26**, 8mm Mauser, Finned Barrel, Clip Fed, Bipod, *Class 3* ... 2,700.00 3,500.00

RIFLE, BOLT ACTION
☐ **GEW 33/40**, 8mm Mauser, Military, Nazi-Proofed, Carbine, *Modern* 170.00 275.00
☐ **Gewehr 24 T**, 8mm Mauser, Military, Nazi-Proofed, *Curio* 150.00 240.00
☐ **VZ 24**, 8mm Mauser, Military, *Modern* 120.00 195.00
☐ **VZ 33**, 8mm Mauser, Military, Carbine, *Modern* 120.00 195.00

DAISY
Made by Bacon Arms Co., c. 1880.

HANDGUN, REVOLVER
☐ **.22 Short R.F.**, 7 Shot, Spur Trigger, Solid Frame, Single Action, Antique 85.00 160.00

DAKIN GUN CO.
San Francisco, Calif., c. 1960.

SHOTGUN, DOUBLE BARREL, OVER-UNDER
☐ **Model 170**, Various Gauges, Light Engraving, Checkered Stock, Double Triggers, Vent Rib, *Modern* 265.00 425.00

SHOTGUN, DOUBLE BARREL, SIDE-BY-SIDE
☐ **Model 100**, 12 or 20 Gauges, Boxlock, Light Engraving, Double Triggers, *Modern* 150.00 235.00
☐ **Model 147**, Various Magnum Gauges, Boxlock, Light Engraving, Double Triggers, Vent Rib, *Modern* 175.00 285.00
☐ **Model 160**, 12 or 20 Gauges, Single Selective Trigger, Ejectors, Vent Rib, *Modern* 225.00 360.00
☐ **Model 215**, 12 or 20 Gauges, Sidelock, Fancy Engraving, Fancy Wood, Ejectors, Single Selective Trigger, Vent Rib, *Modern* 400.00 725.00

DALBY, DAVID
Lincolnshire, England, c. 1835.

HANDGUN, FLINTLOCK
- ☐ **.50**, Pocket Pistol, Box Lock, Screw Barrel, Folding Trigger, Silver Inlay, *Antique* 525.00   800.00

DALY ARMS CO.
N.Y.C., c. 1890.

HANDGUN, REVOLVER
- ☐ **.22 Long R.F.**, 6 Shot, Double Action, Ring Trigger, Solid Frame, *Antique* 160.00   225.00
- ☐ **Peacemaker**, .32 Short R.F., 5 Shot, Spur Trigger, Solid Frame, Single Action, *Antique* 90.00   160.00

DANIELS, HENRY & CHARLES
Chester, Conn., 1838-1850.

RIFLE, PERCUSSION
- ☐ **Turret Rifle**, .40, Underhammer, 8 Shot, Manual Repeater, Octagon Barrel, *Antique* 3,650.00   6,750

DANISH MILITARY

AUTOMATIC WEAPON, SUBMACHINE GUN
- ☐ **Madsen M50B**, 9mm Luger, Clip Fed, Wood Stock, Military, *Class 3*   625.00   950.00

HANDGUN, REVOLVER
- ☐ **9.1mm Ronge 1891**, Military, Top Break, Hammer-Like Latch, *Antique* 200.00   320.00

HANDGUN, SEMI-AUTOMATIC
- ☐ **M1910**, 9mm B, Made by Pieper, Clip Fed, *Curio* 475.00   850.00
- ☐ **M1910/21**, 9mm B, Converted From M1910, Clip Fed, *Curio* 425.00   675.00
- ☐ **M1910/21**, 9mm B, Made by Danish Army Arsenal, Clip Fed, *Curio*   575.00   950.00
- ☐ **S.I.G. SG/8 9mm Luger**, Clip Fed, Military, *Modern* 1,200.00   1,950.00

RIFLE, BOLT ACTION
- ☐ **M98 Mauser**, 6.5 x 57, Haerens Vabenarsenal, *Curio* 300.00   400.00
- ☐ **M1889 Krag**, 8 x 54 Krag-Jorgensen, Carbine, *Antique* 350.00   500.00

RIFLE, SINGLESHOT
- ☐ **M1867**, Remington Rolling Block, Full Stock, *Antique* 375.00   550.00

Danton .25

DANTON

Made By Gabilondo y Cia., Elgoibar, Spain, 1925-1933.

	V.G.	EXC.
HANDGUN, SEMI-AUTOMATIC		
☐ **Pocket**, .25 ACP, Clip Fed, *Modern*	85.00	140.00
☐ **Pocket**, .32 ACP, Clip Fed, *Modern*	95.00	155.00
☐ **Pocket**, .25 ACP, Grip Safety, Clip Fed, *Modern*	100.00	155.00
☐ **Pocket**, .32 ACP, Grip Safety, Clip Fed, *Modern*	110.00	165.00

DAN WESSON ARMS

Monson, Mass. since 1970.

	V.G.	EXC.
HANDGUN, REVOLVER		
☐ **Model 11**, .357 Magnum, Double Action, 3-Barrel Set, Satin Blue, *Modern*	160.00	210.00
☐ **Model 11**, .357 Magnum, Double Action, 3-Barrel Set, Nickel Plated, *Modern*	170.00	225.00
☐ **Model 11**, .357 Magnum, Various Barrel Lengths, Satin Blue, Double Action, *Modern*	100.00	135.00
☐ **Model 11**, .357 Magnum, Various Barrel Lengths, Nickel Plated, Double Action, *Modern*	115.00	150.00
☐ **Model 11**, .38 Special, Various Barrel Lengths, Satin Blue, Double Action, *Modern*	90.00	125.00
☐ **Model 11**, .38 Special, Various Barrel Lengths, Nickel Plated, Double Action, *Modern*	85.00	120.00
☐ **Model 12**, .357 Magnum, Double Action, 3-Barrel Set, Satin Blue, Adjustable Sights, *Modern*	165.00	225.00
☐ **Model 12**, .357 Magnum, Double Action, 3-Barrel Set, Nickel Plated, Adjustable Sights, *Modern*	225.00	325.00
☐ **Model 12**, .357 Magnum, Various Barrel Lengths, Double Action, Blue, Adjustable Sights, *Modern*	100.00	135.00
☐ **Model 12**, .357 Magnum, Various Barrel Lengths, Double Action, Nickel Plated, Adjustable Sights, *Modern*	110.00	145.00
☐ **Model 12**, .38 Special, Various Barrel Lengths, Double Action, Blue, Adjustable Sights, *Modern*	95.00	125.00
☐ **Model 12**, .38 Special, Various Barrel Lengths, Double Action, Nickel Plated, Adjustable Sights, *Modern*	105.00	140.00
☐ **Model 14**, .357 Magnum, Double Action, 3-Barrel Set, Satin Blue, *Modern*	200.00	285.00
☐ **Model 14**, .357 Magnum, Double Action, 3-Barrel Set, Nickel Plated, *Modern*	225.00	315.00
☐ **Model 14**, .357 Magnum, Various Barrel Lengths, Double Action, Satin Blue, *Modern*	95.00	135.00
☐ **Model 14**, .357 Magnum, Various Barrel Lengths, Double Action, Nickel Plated, *Modern*	115.00	155.00
☐ **Model 14**, .38 Special, Various Barrel Lengths, Double Action, Satin Blue, *Modern*	90.00	130.00
☐ **Model 14**, .38 Special, Various Barrel Lengths, Double Action, Nickel Plated, *Modern*	110.00	150.00
☐ **Model 14-2**, .357 Magnum, Various Barrel Lengths, Double Action, Satin Blue, *Modern*	95.00	135.00
☐ **Model 14-2**, .357 Magnum, Double Action, 4-Barrel Set, Blue, *Modern*	225.00	325.00
☐ **Model 14-2B**, .357 Magnum, Various Barrel Lengths, Double Action, Brite Blue, *Modern*	110.00	145.00
☐ **Model 14-2B**, .357 Magnum, Double Action, 4-Barrel Set, Brite Blue, *Modern*	245.00	350.00
☐ **Model 15**, .357 Magnum, Various Barrel Lengths, Double Action, Nickel Plated, Adjustable Sights, *Modern*	115.00	155.00

DAN WESSON ARMS / 141

	V.G.	EXC.
☐ **Model 15**, .357 Magnum, Double Action, 3-Barrel Set, Satin Blue, Adjustable Sights, *Modern*	215.00	290.00
☐ **Model 15**, .357 Magnum, Double Action, 3-Barrel Set, Nickel Plated, Adjustable Sights, *Modern*	235.00	335.00
☐ **Model 15**, .357 Magnum, Double Action, 3-Barrel Set, Blue, Adjustable Sights, *Modern*	220.00	300.00
☐ **Model 15**, .357 Magnum, Various Barrel Lengths, Double Action, Satin Blue, Adjustable Sights, *Modern*	110.00	155.00
☐ **Model 15**, .357 Magnum, Various Barrel Lengths, Double Action, Blue, Adjustable Sights, *Modern*	115.00	165.00
☐ **Model 15**, .38 Special, Various Barrel Lengths, Double Action, Nickel Plated, Adjustble Sights, *Modern*	115.00	160.00
☐ **Model 15**, .38 Special, Various Barrel Lengths, Double Action, Satin Blue, Adjustable Sights, *Modern*	95.00	140.00
☐ **Model 15**, .38 Special, Various Barrel Lengths, Double Action, Blue, Adjustable Sights, *Modern*	105.00	145.00
☐ **Model 15-2**, .357 Magnum or .22 L.R.R.F., Various Barrel Lengths, Double Action, Blue, Adjustable Sights, *Modern*	135.00	185.00
☐ **Model 15-2**, .357 Magnum or .22 L.R.R.F., Double Action, 4-Barrel Set, Blue, Adjustable Sights, *Modern*	245.00	325.00
☐ **Model 15-2H**, .357 Magnum or .22 L.R.R.F., Various Barrel Lengths, Double Action, Blue, Adjustable Sights, Heavy Barrel, *Modern*	140.00	200.00
☐ **Model 15-2H**, .357 Magnum or .22 L.R.R.F., Double Action, 4-Barrel Set, Blue, Adjustable Sights, Heavy Barrel, *Modern*	285.00	375.00
☐ **Model 15-2V**, .357 Magnum or .22 L.R.R.F., Various Barrel Lengths, Double Action, Blue, Adjustable Sights, Vent Rib, *Modern*	150.00	210.00
☐ **Model 15-2V**, .357 Magnum or .22 L.R.R.F., Double Action, 4-Barrel Set, Blue, Adjustable Sights, Vent Rib, *Modern*	300.00	400.00
☐ **Model 15-2VH**, .357 Magnum or .22 L.R.R.F., Various Barrel Lengths, Double Action, Adjustable Sights, Heavy Barrel, Vent Rib, *Modern*	160.00	225.00
☐ **Model 15-2VH**, .357 Magnum or .22 L.R.R.F., Double Action, 4-Barrel Set, Blue, Adjustable Sights, Heavy Barrel, Vent Rib, *Modern*	320.00	450.00
☐ **Model 714-2**, .357 Magnum, Various Barrel Lengths, Double Action, Stainless Steel, , Fixed Sights, *Modern*	130.00	180.00
☐ **Model 714-2**, .357 Magnum, Double Action, 4-Barrel Set, Stainless Steel, Fixed Sights, *Modern*	215.00	300.00
☐ **Model 715-2**, .357 Magnum, Various Barrel Lengths, Double Action, Stainless Steel, Adjustable Sights, *Modern*	160.00	225.00
☐ **Model 715-2**, .357 Magnum, Double Action, 4-Barrel Set, Stainless Steel, Adjustable Sights, *Modern*	320.00	400.00
☐ **Model 715-2V**, .357 Magnum, Various Barrel Lengths, Double Action, Stainless Steel, Adjustable Sights, Vent Rib, *Modern*	180.00	245.00
☐ **Model 715-2V**, .357 Magnum, Double Action, 4-Barrel Set, Stainless Steel, Adjustable Sights, Vent Rib, *Modern*	380.00	470.00
☐ **Model 715-2VH**, .357 Magnum, Various Barrel Lengths, Double Action, Stainless Steel, Adjustable Sights, Vent Rib, Heavy Barrel, *Modern*	190.00	260.00
☐ **Model 715-2VH**, .357 Magnum, Double Action, 4-Barrel Set, Stainless Steel, Adjustable Sights, Vent Rib, Heavy Barrel, *Modern*	400.00	525.00
☐ **Model 44-V**, .44 Magnum, Various Barrel Lengths, Double Action, Blue, Adjustable Sights, Vent Rib, *Modern*	200.00	275.00
☐ **Model 44-V**, .44 Magnum, Double Action, 4-Barrel Set, Blue, Adjustable Sights, Vent Rib, *Modern*	340.00	435.00
☐ **Model 44-VH**, .44 Magnum, Various Barrel Lengths, Double Action, Adjustable Sights, Heavy Barrel, Vent Rib, *Modern*	220.00	315.00

142 / DARDICK

	V.G.	EXC.
☐ **Model 44-VH**, .44 Magnum, Double Action, 4-Barrel Set, Blue, Adjustable Sights, Heavy Barrel, Vent Rib, *Modern*	360.00	470.00

☐ **Extra Barrel Assemblies** *Add:*
   15" 15-2 **$75.00-$110.00**; 15-2H **$95.00-$135.00**; 15-2V **$95.00-$135.00**; 15-2VH **$120.00-$160.00**
   12" 15-2 **$50.00-$80.00**; 15-2H **$75.00-$110.00**; 15-2V **$75.00-$110.00**; 15-2VH **$80.00-$120.00**
   10" 15-2 **$45.00-$70.00**; 15-2H **$55.00-$85.00**; 15-2V **$55.00-$85.00**; 15-2VH **$70.00-$100.00**; 44-V **$60.00-$100.00**; 44-VH **$80.00-$120.00**
   Others 15-2, **$20.00-$40.00**; 15-2H, **$35.00-$55.00**; 15-2V, **$35.00-$55.00**; 15-2VH, **$40.00-$70.00**; 44-V **$55.00-$85.00**; 44-VH

DARDICK
Hamden, Conn., 1954-1962.

HANDGUN, REVOLVER

	V.G.	EXC.
☐ **Series 1100**, .38 Dardick Tround, Double Action, Clip Fed, 3" Barrel, 11 Shot, *Modern*	400.00	550.00
☐ **Series 1500**, .30, Double Action, Clip Fed, 4¾" Barrel, *Modern*	625.00	850.00
☐ **Series 1500**, .38 Dardick Tround, Double Action, Clip Fed, 6" Barrel, 15 Shot, *Modern*	375.00	550.00
☐ **Series 1500**, .22, Double Action, Clip Fed, 2" and 11" Barrels, *Modern*	650.00	900.00
☐ **For Carbine Conversion Unit .38**, *Add* **$200.00-$300.00**		
☐ **For Carbine Conversion Unit .22**, *Add* **$225.00-$375.00**		

DARNE
St. Etienne, France.

SHOTGUN, DOUBLE BARREL, SIDE-BY-SIDE

	V.G.	EXC.
☐ **Bird Hunter**, Various Gauges, Sliding Breech, Ejectors, Double Triggers, Checkered Stock, *Modern*	525.00	775.00
☐ **Hors Serie #1**, Various Gauges, Sliding Breech, Ejectors, Fancy Engraving, Checkered Stock, *Modern*	3,450.00	4,350.00
☐ **Magnum**, 12 or 20 Gauges 3", Sliding Breech, Ejectors, Double Triggers, Checkered Stock, *Modern*	850.00	1,400.00
☐ **Pheasant Hunter**, Various Gauges, Sliding Breech, Ejectors, Light Engraving, Checkered Stock, *Modern*	775.00	1,150.00
☐ **Quail Hunter**, Various Gauges, Sliding Breech, Ejectors, Engraved, Checkered Stock, *Modern*	1,250.00	1,800.00

DAVENPORT, W.H.
Providence, R.I. 1880-1883, Norwich, Conn. 1890-1900.

SHOTGUN, DOUBLE BARREL, SIDE-BY-SIDE

	V.G.	EXC.
☐ **8 Ga.**, *Modern*	375.00	525.00

SHOTGUN, SINGLESHOT

	V.G.	EXC.
☐ **Various Gauges**, Hammer, Steel Barrel, *Modern*	50.00	75.00

DAVIDSON
Spain Mfg. by Fabrica de Armas, Imported by Davidson Firearms Co., Greensboro, N.C.

SHOTGUN, DOUBLE BARREL, SIDE-BY-SIDE

	V.G.	EXC.
☐ **73 Stagecoach**, 12 or 20 Gauges, Magnum, Checkered Stock, *Modern*	125.00	170.00
☐ **Model 63B**, 10 Ga. 3½", Magnum, Engraved, Nickel Plated, Checkered Stock, *Modern*	150.00	200.00

	V.G.	EXC.
☐ **Model 63B**, 12 and 20 Gauges, Magnum, Engraved, Nickel Plated, Checkered Stock, *Modern*	135.00	180.00
☐ **Model 63B**, Various Gauges, Engraved, Nickel Plated, Checkered Stock, *Modern*	130.00	175.00
☐ **Model 69 SL**, 12 and 20 Gauges, Sidelock, Light Engraving, Checkered Stock, *Modern*	145.00	220.00

DAVIS, N.R. & CO.
Freetown, Mass. 1853-1917. Merged with Warner Co. of Norwich, Conn. and became Davis-Warner Arms Co. It was not active between 1920-1922, but in 1930 started again as Crescent-Davis Arms Co., Norwich. This included Crescent Firearms Co. They relocated in Springfield, Mass. 1931-1932. and was taken over in 1932 by Stevens Arms.

RIFLE, PERCUSSION
☐ **.45**, Octagon Barrel, *Antique*	400.00	625.00

SHOTGUN, PERCUSSION
☐ **#1 Various Gauges**, Double Barrel, Side by Side Damascus Barrel, Outside Hammers, *Antique*	300.00	450.00
☐ **#3**, Various Gauges, Double Barrel, Side by Side Damascus Barrel, Outside Hammers, *Antique*	240.00	365.00

SHOTGUN, DOUBLE BARREL, SIDE-BY-SIDE
☐ **Various Gauges**, Outside Hammers, Damascus Barrel, *Modern*	100.00	175.00
☐ **Various Gauges**, Hammerless, Steel Barrel, *Modern*	135.00	200.00
☐ **Various Gauges**, Hammerless, Damascus Barrel, *Modern*	100.00	175.00
☐ **Various Gauges**, Outside Hammers, Steel Barrel, *Modern*	125.00	190.00

SHOTGUN, SINGLESHOT
☐ **Various Gauges**, Hammer, Steel Barrel, *Modern*	55.00	85.00

DAY ARMS CO.
San Antonio, Tex.

HANDGUN, SEMI-AUTOMATIC
☐ **Conversion Unit Only**, .22 L.R.R.F., For Colt M1911, Clip Fed, *Modern*	90.00	145.00

DEAD SHOT
L.W. Pond Co.

HANDGUN, REVOLVER
☐ **.22 Long R.F.**, 6 Shot, Single Action, Solid Frame, Spur Trigger, *Antique*	170.00	250.00

Debatir .25

DEBATIR

	V.G.	EXC.
HANDGUN, SEMI-AUTOMATIC		
☐ .25 ACP, Clip Fed, Modern	135.00	195.00
☐ .32 ACP, Clip Fed, Modern	150.00	240.00

DEBERIERE, HENRY
Phila., Pa. 1769-1774, See Kentucky Rifles & Pistols.

DECKER, WILHELM
Zella St. Blasii, Germany, c. 1913.

HANDGUN, REVOLVER
- ☐ **Decker**, .25 ACP, Hammerless, 6 Shot, Curio 500.00   850.00
- ☐ **Mueller Special**, .25 ACP, Hammerless, 6 Shot, Curio 600.00   950.00

DEFENDER
Made by Iver-Johnson, Sold by J.P. Lovell Arms 1875-1895.

HANDGUN, REVOLVER
- ☐ .22 Short R.F., 7 Shot, Spur Trigger, Solid Frame, Single Action, Antique 95.00   160.00
- ☐ .32 Short R.F., 5 Shot, Spur Trigger, Solid Frame, Single Action, Antique 95.00   170.00
- ☐ **#89**, .22 Short R.F., 7 Shot, Spur Trigger, Solid Frame, Single Action, Antique 90.00   155.00
- ☐ **#89**, .32 Short R.F., 5 Shot, Spur Trigger, Solid Frame, Single Action, Antique 90.00   165.00

DEFENDER
N. Shore & Co., Chicago, Ill., c.1922

HANDGUN, KNIFE PISTOL
- ☐ **#215**, .22 R.F., 3" Over All Length, 1 Blade, Class 3 ..... 90.00   140.00

DEFIANCE
Made By Norwich Falls Pistol Co., c. 1880.

HANDGUN, REVOLVER
- ☐ .22 Short R.F., 7 Shot, Spur Trigger, Solid Frame, Single Action, Antique 85.00   150.00

DEHUFF, ABRAHAM
Lancaster, Pa., c. 1779. See Kentucky rifles & pistols

DEK-DU
Tomas de Urizar y Cia., Eibar, Spain, c. 1910.

HANDGUN, REVOLVER
- ☐ **Velo Dog**, 5.5mm Velo Dog, 12 Shots, Folding Trigger, Curio 95.00   145.00
- ☐ **Velo Dog**, .25 ACP, 12 Shots, Folding Trigger, Curio 100.00   150.00

DELPHIAN
Made by Stevens Arms.

SHOTGUN, SINGLESHOT
- ☐ **Model 90**, Various Gauges, Takedown, Automatic Ejector, Plain Hammer, Modern 40.00   60.00

DELU
Fab. d'Armes Delu & Co.

HANDGUN, SEMI-AUTOMATIC

	V.G.	EXC.
☐ **.25 ACP**, Clip Fed, *Curio*	135.00	185.00

DEMRO
Manchester, Conn.

HANDGUN, SEMI-AUTOMATIC
☐ **T.A.C. XF-7 Wasp**, .45 ACP or 9mm Luger, Clip Fed, *Modern* 280.00   370.00

RIFLE, SEMI-AUTOMATIC
☐ **T.A.C. Model 1**, .45 ACP or 9mm Luger, Clip Fed, *Modern* 220.00   325.00
☐ **T.A.C. Model 1M**, .45 ACP or 9mm Luger, Clip Fed, *Modern* 220.00   325.00
☐ **T.A.C. XF-7 Wasp**, .45 ACP or 9mm Luger, Clip Fed, Folding Stock, *Modern* 290.00   380.00

DERR, JOHN
Lancaster, Pa. 1810-1844. See Kentucky Rifles & Pistols.

DERINGER, HENRY, SR.
Richmond, Va. & Philadelphia, Pa. 1768-1814. See Kentucky Rifles & Pistols; U.S. Military.

DERINGER, HENRY, JR.
Philadelphia, Pa. 1806-1868. Also see U.S. Military.

HANDGUN, PERCUSSION
☐ **Pocket**, .41, Back Lock, German Silver Mounts, *Antique* 375.00   725.00
☐ **Medium Pocket**, .41, Back Lock, German Silver Mounts, *Antique* .. 425.00   775.00
☐ **Dueller**, .41, Back Lock, German Silver Mounts, Cased Pair, *Antique* 575.00 1,450.00
☐ **Dueller**, .41, Back Lock, Silver Mounts, Cased Pair, *Antique* 975.00 1,950.00
☐ **Dueller**, .41, Back Lock, Gold Mounts, Cased Pair, *Antique* 3,600.00 5,450.00

DERINGER RIFLE AND PISTOL WORKS
Philadelphia, Pa. 1870-1880.

HANDGUN, REVOLVER
☐ **Centennial '76**, .38 Long R.F., 5 Shot, Single Action, Spur Trigger, Tip-up, *Antique* 245.00   350.00
☐ **Model 1**, .22 Short R.F., 7 Shot, Spur Trigger, Tip-up, *Antique* 220.00   325.00
☐ **Model 2**, .22 Short R.F., 7 Shot, Spur Trigger, Tip-up, *Antique* 200.00   295.00
☐ **Model 2**, .32 Long R.F., 5 Shot, Single Action, Spur Trigger, Tip-up, *Antique* 200.00   295.00

DESPATCH
Made by Hopkins & Allen, c. 1875.

HANDGUN, REVOLVER
☐ **.22 Short R.F.**, 7 Shot, Spur Trigger, Solid Frame, Single Action, *Antique* 85.00   160.00

DESTROYER
Made in Spain by Isidro Gaztanaga 1914-1933, reorganized as Gaztanaga, Trocaola y Ibarzabal 1933-1936.

HANDGUN, SEMI-AUTOMATIC
☐ **Model 1913**, .25 ACP, Clip Fed, *Modern* 85.00   150.00

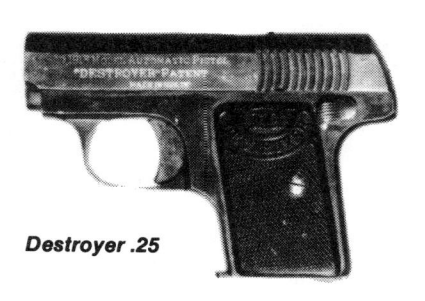

Destroyer .25

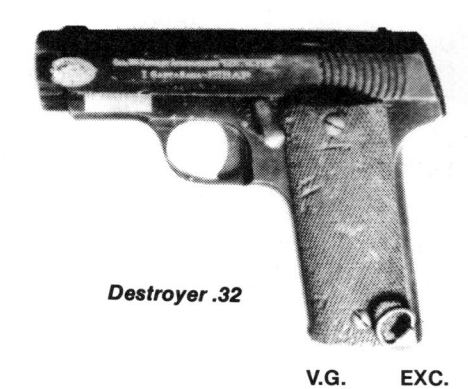

Destroyer .32

	V.G.	EXC.
☐ **Destroyer**, .25 ACP, Clip Fed, *Curio*	90.00	155.00
☐ **Model 1919**, .32 ACP, Clip Fed, *Modern*	90.00	155.00
☐ **Destroyer**, .32 ACP, Clip Fed, Long Grip, *Curio*	110.00	170.00
☐ **Super Destroyer**, .32 ACP, Clip Fed, *Modern*	150.00	220.00

DESTRUCTOR
Iraola Salaverria, Eibar, Spain.
HANDGUN, SEMI—AUTOMATIC
☐ **.25 ACP**, Clip Fed, *Modern*	85.00	145.00
☐ **.32 ACP**, Clip Fed, *Modern*	95.00	165.00

DETONICS
Seattle, Washington.
HANDGUN, SEMI-AUTOMATIC
☐ **"45" Combat**, .45 ACP, Combat Modifications, Clip Fed, Pocket Pistol, Blue, *Modern*	265.00	370.00
☐ **"45" Combat**, .45 ACP, Combat Modifications, Clip Fed, Pocket Pistol, Nickel, *Modern*	290.00	395.00
☐ **Combat MC-1**, .45 ACP, Combat Modifications, Clip Fed, Pocket Pistol, Matt Blue, *Modern*	300.00	400.00
☐ **Combat MC-1**, 9mm P., Combat Modifications, Clip Fed, Pocket Pistol, Matt Blue, *Modern*	350.00	440.00
☐ **Combat Master Mk.I**, .45 ACP, Combat Modifications, Clip Fed, Pocket Pistol, Matt Blue, *Modern*	295.00	395.00
☐ **Combat Master Mk.IV**, .45 ACP, Combat Modifications, Clip Fed, Pocket Pistol, Matt Blue, Adjustable Sights, *Modern*	300.00	400.00
☐ **Combat Master Mk.V**, .45 ACP, Combat Modifications, Clip Fed, Pocket Pistol, Matt Stainless, *Modern*	330.00	425.00
☐ **Combat Master Mk.V**, 9mm P., Combat Modifications, Clip Fed, Pocket Pistol, Matt Stainless, *Modern*	350.00	445.00
☐ **Combat Master Mk.VI**, .45 ACP, Combat Modifications, Clip Fed, Pocket Pistol, Polished Stainless, Adjustable Sights, *Modern*	380.00	475.00
☐ **Combat Master Mk.VI**, 9mm P., Combat Modifications, Clip Fed, Pocket Pistol, Polished Stainless, Adjustable Sights, *Modern*	385.00	500.00
☐ **Combat Master Mk.VI**, .38 Super, Combat Modifications, Clip Fed, Pocket Pistol, Polished Stainless, Adjustable Sights, *Modern*	385.00	500.00
☐ **Combat Master Mk.VII**, .45 ACP, Combat Modifications, Clip Fed, Pocket Pistol, Matt Stainless, No Sights, Lightweight, *Modern*	380.00	490.00
☐ **Combat Master Mk.VII**, 9mm P., Combat Modifications, Clip Fed, Pocket Pistol, Matt Stainless, No Sights, Lightweight, *Modern*	400.00	525.00

	V.G.	EXC.
☐ **Combat Master Mk.VII**, .38 Super, Combat Modifications, Clip Fed, Pocket Pistol, Matt Stainless, No Sights, Lightweight, *Modern*	400.00	525.00
☐ **Green Beret Series**, .45 ACP, Combat Modifications, Clip Fed, Pocket Pistol, Engraved, Cased, *Modern*	1,000.00	1,500.00
☐ **Royalty Series**, .45 ACP, Combat Modifications, Clip Fed, Pocket Pistol, Fancy Engraving, Cased, *Modern*	3,000.00	4,500.00
☐ **Signature Series**, .45 ACP, Combat Modifications, Clip Fed, Pocket Pistol, Customized, *Modern*	450.00	650.00

DIAMOND
Made by Stevens Arms.

SHOTGUN, SINGLESHOT

☐ **Model 89 Dreadnaught**, Various Gauges, Hammer, *Modern*	50.00	65.00
☐ **Model 90**, Various Gauges, Takedown, Automatic Ejector, Plain Hammer, *Modern*	40.00	60.00
☐ **Model 95**, 12 and 16 Gauge, Takedown, *Modern*	40.00	60.00

DIANE
Made by Wilkinson Arms, Covina, Calif.

HANDGUN, SEMI-AUTOMATIC

☐ **Standard Model**, .25 ACP, Clip Fed, *Modern*	150.00	250.00
☐ **Lightweight Model**, .25 ACP, Clip Fed, *Modern*	550.00	800.00

DEANE, ADAMS & DEANE
See Adams

DIANE
Erquiaga, Muguruzu, y Cia., Eibar, Spain, c. 1923.

HANDGUN, SEMI-AUTOMATIC

☐ **.25 ACP**, Clip Fed, Blue, *Curio*	175.00	265.00

DICKINSON, J. & L.
Also E. L. & J. Dickinson, Springfield, Mass. 1863-1880.

HANDGUN, SINGLESHOT

☐ **.22 R.F.**, Brass Frame, Pivoting Barrel, Rack Ejector, *Antique*	250.00	375.00
☐ **.32 R.F.**, Brass Frame, Pivoting Barrel, Rack Ejector, *Antique*	175.00	275.00

DICKSON
Made in Italy for American Import Co. until 1968.

HANDGUN, SEMI-AUTOMATIC

☐ **Detective**, .25 ACP, Clip Fed, *Modern*	85.00	125.00

DICTATOR
Made by Hopkins & Allen, c. 1880.

HANDGUN, REVOLVER

☐ **.22 Short R.F.**, 7 Shot, Spur Trigger, Solid Frame, Single Action, *Antique*	85.00	160.00
☐ **.32 Short R.F.**, 5 Shot, Spur Trigger, Solid Frame, Single Action, *Antique*	85.00	160.00
☐ **#2**, .32 Short R.F., 5 Shot, Spur Trigger, Solid Frame, Single Action, *Antique*	85.00	175.00

DIXIE GUN WORKS
Union City, Tenn.

	V.G.	EXC.

HANDGUN, FLINTLOCK
☐ **Tower**, .67, Brass Furniture, Reproduction, *Antique*	15.00	30.00

HANDGUN, PERCUSSION
☐ **Army**, .44, Revolver, Buntline, Reproduction, *Antique*	55.00	75.00
☐ **Navy**, .36, Revolver, Buntline, Brass Frame, Reproduction, *Antique*	20.00	40.00
☐ **Navy**, .36, Revolver, Buntline, Brass Frame, Engraved, Reproduction, *Antique*	25.00	45.00
☐ **Spiller & Burr**, .36, Revolver, Buntline, Brass Frame, Reproduction, *Antique*	35.00	60.00
☐ **Wyatt Earp**, .44 Revolver, Buntline, Brass Frame, Reproduction, *Antique*	35.00	55.00
☐ **Wyatt Earp**, .44 Revolver, Buntline, Brass Frame, With Shoulder Stock, Reproduction, *Antique*.	55.00	85.00

RIFLE, FLINTLOCK
☐ **1st. Model Brown Bess**, .75, Military, Reproduction, *Antique*	260.00	365.00
☐ **2nd. Model Brown Bess**, .74, Military, Reproduction, *Antique*	140.00	215.00
☐ **Coach Guard**, .95, Blunderbuss, Brass Furniture, Reproduction, *Antique*	80.00	125.00
☐ **Day Rifle**, .45, Double Barrel, Over-under, Swivel Breech, Brass Furniture, Reproduction, *Antique*	265.00	360.00
☐ **Deluxe Pennsylvania**, .45, Kentucky Rifle, Full-Stocked, Brass Furniture, Light Engraving, Reproduction, *Antique*	190.00	265.00
☐ **Deluxe Pennsylvania**, .45, Kentucky Rifle, Full-Stocked, Brass Furniture, Reproduction, *Antique*	180.00	275.00
☐ **Kentuckian**, .45, Kentucky Rifle, Full-Stocked, Brass Furniture, Reproduction, *Antique*	85.00	125.00
☐ **Kentuckian**, .45, Kentucky Rifle, Full-Stocked, Brass Furniture, Reproduction, Carbine, *Antique*	85.00	125.00
☐ **Musket**, .67 Smoothbore, Reproduction, Carbine, *Antique*	50.00	85.00
☐ **Squirrel Rifle**, .45, Kentucky Rifles, Full-Stocked, Brass Furniture, Reproduction, *Antique*	160.00	215.00
☐ **York County**, .45, Kentucky Rifle, Full-Stocked, Brass Furniture, Reproduction, *Antique*	90.00	135.00

RIFLE, LEVER ACTION
☐ **Win. 73 (Italian)**, .44-40 WCF, Tube Feed, Octagon Barrel, Carbine, *Modern*	170.00	275.00
☐ **Win 73 (Italian)**, .44-40 WCF, Tube Feed, Octagon Barrel, Color Cased Hardened Frame, Engraved, *Modern*	200.00	300.00

RIFLE, PERCUSSION
☐ **Day Rifle**, .45, Double Barrel, Over-under, Swivel Breech, Brass Furniture, Reproduction, *Antique*	160.00	245.00
☐ **Deluxe Pennsylvania**, .45, Kentucky Rifle, Full-Stocked, Brass Furniture, Reproduction, *Antique*	170.00	240.00
☐ **Deluxe Pennsylvania**, .45, Kentucky Rifle, Full-Stocked, Brass Furniture, Light Engraving, Reproduction, *Antique*	185.00	260.00
☐ **Dixie Hawkin**, .45, Half-Stocked, Octagon Barrel, Set Trigger, Brass Furniture, Reproduction, *Antique*	110.00	155.00
☐ **Dixie Hawkin**, .50, Half-Stocked, Octagon Barrel, Set Trigger, Brass Furniture, Reproduction, *Antique*	110.00	155.00
☐ **Enfield Two-Band**, .577, Musketoon, Military, Reproduction, *Antique*	85.00	150.00
☐ **Kentuckian**, .45, Kentucky Rifle, Full-Stocked, Brass Furniture, Reproduction, *Antique*	75.00	125.00
☐ **Kentuckian**, .45, Kentucky Rifle, Full-Stocked, Brass Furniture, Reproduction, Carbine, *Antique*	75.00	125.00

	V.G.	EXC.
☐ **Musket**, .66, Smoothbore, Reproduction, *Antique*	45.00	75.00
☐ **Plainsman**, .45, Half-Stocked, Octagon Barrel, Reproduction, *Antique*	85.00	145.00
☐ **Plainsman**, .50, Half-Stocked, Octagon Barrel, Reproduction, *Antique*	85.00	145.00
☐ **Squirrel Rifle**, .45, Kentucky Rifle, Full-Stocked, Brass Furniture, Reproduction, *Antique*	145.00	200.00
☐ **Target**, .45, Half-Stocked, Octagon Barrel, Reproduction, *Antique*	45.00	75.00
☐ **York County**, .45, Kentucky Rifle, Full-Stocked, Brass Furniture, Reproduction, *Antique*	80.00	125.00
☐ **Zouave M 1863**, .58, Military, Reproduction, *Antique*	75.00	125.00

SHOTGUN, FLINTLOCK
☐ **Fowling Piece**, 14 Gauge, Single Barrel, Reproduction, *Antique*	50.00	85.00

SHOTGUN, PERCUSSION
☐ **12 Gauge**, Double Barrel, Side by Side, Double Trigger, Reproduction, *Antique*	90.00	135.00
☐ **28 Gauge**, Single Barrel, Reproduction, *Antique*	25.00	45.00

DOBSON, T.
London, England, c. 1780.

HANDGUN, FLINTLOCK
☐ **.64**, Presentation, Holster Pistol, Gold Inlays, Engraved, Half-Octagon Barrel, High Quality, *Antique*	2,600.00	3,750.00

DOMINO
Made in Italy, Imported by Mandell Shooting Sports

HANDGUN, SEMI—AUTOMATIC
☐ **Model O.P. 601**, .22 Short, Target Pistol, Adjustable Sights, Target Grips, *Modern*	450.00	675.00
☐ **Model O.P. 601**, .22 Short, Target Pistol, Adjustable Sights, Target Grips, *Modern*	450.00	675.00

DREADNAUGHT
Made by Hopkins & Allen, c. 1880.

HANDGUN, REVOLVER
☐ **.22 Short R.F.**, 7 Shot, Spur Trigger, Solid Frame, Single Action, *Antique*	90.00	150.00
☐ **.32 Short R.F.**, 5 Shot, Spur Trigger, Solid Frame, Single Action, *Antique*	95.00	170.00

DREYSE
Dreyse Rheinische Metallwaren Machinenfabrik, Sommerda, Germany since 1889. In 1936 merged and became Rheinmetall-Borsig, Dusseldorf, Germany.

HANDGUN, SEMI-AUTOMATIC
☐ **M1907**, .32 ACP, Clip Fed, Early Model, *Modern*	145.00	225.00
☐ **M1907**, .32 ACP, Clip Fed, *Modern*	115.00	165.00
☐ **M1910**, 9mm Luger, Clip Fed, *Curio*	575.00	800.00
☐ **Rheinmetall**, .32 ACP, Clip Fed, *Modern*	185.00	295.00
☐ **Vest Pocket**, .25 ACP, Clip Fed *Modern*	125.00	195.00

RIFLE, SEMI-AUTOMATIC
☐ **Carbine**, .32 ACP, Clip Fed, Checkered Stock, *Curio*	265.00	400.00

150 / DRIPPARD, F.

Dreyse Model 2

Dreyse Model 1907

DRIPPARD, F.
Lancaster, Pa. 1767-1773, See Kentucky Rifles & Pistols.

V.G.   EXC.

DRISCOLL, J.B.
Springfield, Mass., c. 1870.
HANDGUN, SINGLESHOT
- ☐ .22 R.F., Brass Frame, Spur Trigger, *Antique* 165.00   285.00

DUMARESD, B.
Marseille, France, probably c. 1730.
HANDGUN, FLINTLOCK
- ☐ **Holster Pistol**, Engraved, Horn Inlays, Ornate, Silver Furniture, *Antique* 975.00 1,950.00

DUBIEL ARMS CO.
Sherman, Tex. since 1975.
RIFLE, BOLT ACTION
- ☐ **Custom Rifle**, Various Calibers, Various Styles, Fancy Wood, *Modern* 1,200.00 1,750.00

DUMOULIN FRERES ET CIE
Milmort, Belgium since 1849.
RIFLE, BOLT ACTION
- ☐ **Grade I**, Various Calibers, Fancy Checkering, Engraved, *Modern*   875.00 1,400.00
- ☐ **Grade II**, Various Calibers, Fancy Checkering, Engraved, Fance Wood, *Modern* 1,350.00 1,975.00
- ☐ **Grade III**, Various Calibers, Fancy Checkering, Fancy Engraving, Fancy Wood, *Modern* 1,750.00 2,500.00

RIFLE, DOUBLE BARREL, SIDE-BY-SIDE
- ☐ **Various Calibers**, Fancy Checkering, Engraved, Fancy Wood, *Modern* 1,650.00 2,200.00

DUO
Frantisek Dusek, Opocno, Czechoslovakia 1926-1948. Ceska Zbrojovka from 1948 to date.
HANDGUN, SEMI-AUTOMATIC
- ☐ **.25 ACP**, Clip Fed, *Modern* 100.00   175.00

Dutch Military 1871 Hemburg Revolver

DUTCH MILITARY

	V.G.	EXC.
HANDGUN, REVOLVER		
☐ **Model 1871 Hemberg**, 9.4mm, Military, *Antique*	85.00	145.00
RIFLE, BOLT ACTION		
☐ **Model 95**, 6.5mm Mannlicher, Full Stock, *Curio*	65.00	100.00
☐ **Model 95**, 6.5mm Mannlicher, Carbine, Full Stock, *Curio*	65.00	100.00
☐ **Beaumont-Vitale M1871/88**, Military, *Antique*	90.00	145.00
RIFLE, FLINTLOCK		
☐ **.70**, Officers Type, Musket, Brass Furniture, *Antique*	650.00	950.00

DUTTON, JOHN S.
Jaffrey, N.H. 1855-1870.

RIFLE, PERCUSSION
☐ **.36**, Target Rifle, Swiss Buttplate, Octagon Barrel, Target Sights, *Antique* ... 775.00 1,400.00

DWM
Deutche Waffen und Munitionsfabrik, Berlin, Germany 1896-1945. Also see Luger and Borchardt.

HANDGUN, SEMI-AUTOMATIC
☐ **Pocket**, .32 ACP, Clip Fed, *Curio* ... 245.00 375.00

E.A.
Echava y Arizmendi, Eibar, Spain 1911-1975.

HANDGUN, SEMI-AUTOMATIC
☐ **1916 Model**, .25 ACP, Clip Fed, *Curio* ... 75.00 120.00

E.A.
Eulogio Arostegui, Eibar, Spain, c. 1930.

HANDGUN, SEMI-AUTOMATIC
☐ **.25 ACP**, Clip Fed, Dog Logo on Grips, *Modern* ... 70.00 115.00

EAGLE
Made by Iver-Johnson, c. 1879-1886.

HANDGUN, REVOLVER
☐ **.22 Short R.F.**, 7 Shot, Spur Trigger, Solid Frame, Single Action, *Antique* ... 85.00 150.00
☐ **.32 Short R.F.**, 5 Shot, Spur Trigger, Solid Frame, Single Action, *Antique* ... 85.00 150.00
☐ **.38 Short R.F.**, 5 Shot, Spur Trigger, Solid Frame, Single Action, *Antique* ... 95.00 175.00
☐ **.44 Short R.F.**, 5 Shot, Spur Trigger, Solid Frame, Single Action, *Antique* ... 170.00 250.00

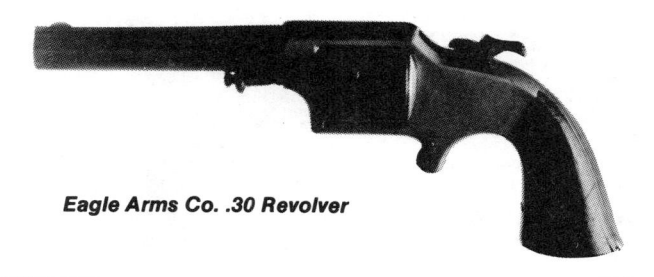

Eagle Arms Co. .30 Revolver

EAGLE ARMS CO.
N.Y.C., c. 1865.

                                                                                   V.G.   EXC.

HANDGUN, REVOLVER
- ☐ **.28 Cup Primed Cartridge**, 6 Shot, Single Action, Spur Trigger, Solid Frame, *Antique* 175.00   325.00
- ☐ **.28 Cup Primed Cartridge**, 6 Shot, Single Action, Spur Trigger, Tip-up, *Antique* 200.00   325.00
- ☐ **.30 Cup Primed Cartridge**, 6 Shot, Single Action, Spur Trigger, Solid Frame, *Antique* 175.00   295.00
- ☐ **.30 Cup Primed Cartridge**, 6 Shot, Single Action, Spur Trigger, Tip-up, *Antique* 220.00   345.00
- ☐ **.42 Cup Primed Cartridge**, 6 Shot, Single Action, Spur Trigger, Solid Frame, *Antique* 165.00   285.00
- ☐ **.42 Cup Primed Cartridge**, 6 Shot, Single Action, Spur Trigger, Tip-up, *Antique* 235.00   385.00

EAGLE GUN CO.
Stratford, Conn., c. 1965.

RIFLE, SEMI-AUTOMATIC
- ☐ **.45 ACP**, Clip Fed, Carbine, *Class 3* 110.00   175.00
- ☐ **9mm Luger, Clip Fed**, Carbine, *Class 3* 160.00   225.00

EARLHOOD
Made by E.L. Dickinson Co. Springfield, Mass. 1870-1880.

HANDGUN, REVOLVER
- ☐ **.32 Short R.F.**, 5 Shot, Spur Trigger, Solid Frame, Single Action, *Antique* 90.00   165.00

EARLY, AMOS
Dauphin Co. Pa. See Kentucky Rifles.

EARLY, JACOB
Dauphin Co. Pa. See Kentucky Rifles.

EARTHQUAKE
Made by E.L. Dickinson Co. Springfield, Mass. 1870-1880.

HANDGUN, REVOLVER
- ☐ **.32 Short R.F.**, 5 Shot, Spur Trigger, Solid Frame, Single Action, *Antique* 90.00   170.00

EASTERN
Made by Stevens Arms.

SHOTGUN, DOUBLE BARREL, SIDE-BY-SIDE

	V.G.	EXC.
☐ **Model 311**, Various Gauges, Hammerless, Steel Barrel, *Modern*....	125.00	175.00

SHOTGUN, SINGLESHOT
☐ **Model 94**, Various Gauges, Takedown, Automatic Ejector, Plain Hammer, *Modern* 40.00 55.00

EASTERN ARMS CO.
Made by Meriden Firearms and sold by Sears-Roebuck.

HANDGUN, REVOLVER
☐ **.32 S & W**, 5 Shot, Double Action, Top Break, *Modern*............. 55.00 95.00
☐ **.38 S & W**, 5 Shot, Double Action, Top Break, *Modern*............. 60.00 100.00

EASTFIELD
See Smith & Wesson.

ECHABERRIA, ARTURA
Spain, c. 1790.

HANDGUN, MIQUELET-LOCK
☐ **Pair**, Holster Pistol, Plain, Brass Furniture, *Antique* 2,850.00 4,200.00

Echasa GZ-MAB

ECHASA
Tradename used in the 1950's by Echave, Arizmendi y Cia., Eibar, Spain.

HANDGUN, SEMI-AUTOMATIC
☐ **Model GZ MAB**, .22 L.R.R.F., Clip Fed, Hammer *Modern* 85.00 130.00
☐ **Model GZ MAB**, .25 ACP, Clip Fed, Hammer, *Modern* 90.00 140.00
☐ **Model GZ MAB**, .32 ACP, Clip Fed, Hammer, *Modern* 95.00 150.00

ECLIPSE
Made by Johnson, Bye & Co., c. 1875.

HANDGUN, SINGLESHOT
☐ **.25 Short R.F.**, Derringer, Spur Trigger, *Antique* 70.00 115.00

EDGESON
Lincolnshire, England, 1810-1830.

HANDGUN, FLINTLOCK
☐ **.45**, Pair, Box Lock, Screw Barrel, Pocket Pistol, Folding Trigger, Plain *Antique* 950.00 1,650.00

EDMONDS, J.
See Kentucky Rifles.

EGG, CHARLES
London, England, c. 1850.

HANDGUN, PERCUSSION

	V.G.	EXC.
☐ **Pepperbox**, .36, 6 Shot, 3½" Barrels, *Antique*	220.00	370.00

EGG, DURS
London, England 1770-1840. Also see British Military.

HANDGUN, FLINTLOCK
- ☐ **.50**, Duelling Type, Holster Pistol, Octagon Barrel, Steel Furniture, Light Ornamentation, *Antique* ... 925.00 1,550.00

HANDGUN, PERCUSSION
- ☐ **6 Shot**, Pepperbox, Fluted Barrel, Pocket Pistol, Engraved, *Antique* 975.00 1,600.00

EGYPTIAN MILITARY

HANDGUN, SEMI-AUTOMATIC
- ☐ **Tokagypt M-58**, 9mm Luger, Clip Fed, *Curio* ... 325.00 475.00

RIFLE, SEMI-AUTOMATIC
- ☐ **Hakim**, .22 L.R.R.F., Training Rifle, Military, *Modern* ... 200.00 325.00
- ☐ **Hakim**, 8mm Mauser, Military, *Modern* ... 450.00 600.00

84 GUN CO.
Eighty Four, Pa., c. 1973.

RIFLE, BOLT ACTION
- ☐ **Classic Rifle**, Various Calibers, Checkered Stock, Standard Grade, *Modern* ... 200.00 300.00
- ☐ **Classic Rifle**, Various Calibers, Checkered Stock, Grade 1, *Modern* 275.00 400.00
- ☐ **Classic Rifle**, Various Calibers, Checkered Stock, Grade 2, *Modern* 400.00 600.00
- ☐ **Classic Rifle**, Various Calibers, Checkered Stock, Grade 3, *Modern* 800.00 1,300.00
- ☐ **Classic Rifle**, Various Calibers, Checkered Stock, Grade 4, *Modern* 1,200.00 2,000.00
- ☐ **Lobo Rifle**, Various Calibers, Checkered Stock, Standard Grade, *Modern* ... 200.00 300.00
- ☐ **Lobo Rifle**, Various Calibers, Checkered Stock, Grade 1, *Modern* 275.00 400.00
- ☐ **Lobo Rifle**, Various Calibers, Checkered Stock, Grade 2, *Modern* 400.00 600.00
- ☐ **Lobo Rifle**, Various Calibers, Checkered Stock, Grade 3, *Modern* 800.00 1,300.00
- ☐ **Lobo Rifle**, Various Calibers, Checkered Stock, Grade 4, *Modern* 1,200.00 2,000.00
- ☐ **Pennsy Rifle**, Various Calibers, Checkered Stock, Standard Grade, *Modern* ... 200.00 300.00
- ☐ **Pennsy Rifle**, Various Calibers, Checkered Stock, Grade 1, *Modern* 275.00 400.00
- ☐ **Pennsy Rifle**, Various Calibers, Checkered Stock, Grade 2, *Modern* 400.00 600.00
- ☐ **Pennsy Rifle**, Various Calibers, Checkered Stock, Grade 3, *Modern* 800.00 1,300.00
- ☐ **Pennsy Rifle**, Various Calibers, Checkered Stock, Grade 4, *Modern* 1,200.00 2,000.00

ELECTOR
Made by Hopkins & Allen, c. 1880.

HANDGUN, REVOLVER
- ☐ **.22 Short R.F.**, 7 Shot, Spur Trigger, Solid Frame, Single Action, *Antique* ... 90.00 160.00
- ☐ **.32 Short R.F.**, 5 Shot, Spur Trigger, Solid Frame, Single Action, *Antique* ... 95.00 170.00

ELECTRIC
Made by Forehand & Wadsworth 1871-1880.

HANDGUN, REVOLVER
- ☐ **.32 Short R.F.**, 5 Shot, Spur Trigger, Solid Frame, Single Action, *Antique* ... 90.00 160.00

EL FAISAN

	V.G.	EXC.

SHOTGUN, DOUBLE BARREL, SIDE-BY-SIDE
☐ **El Faisan**, .410 Gauge, Folding Gun, Double Trigger, Outside
Hammers, *Modern* 70.00   100.00

ELGIN ARMS CO.
Made by Crescent for Fred Bifflar & Co., Chicago, Ill.

SHOTGUN, DOUBLE BARREL, SIDE-BY-SIDE
☐ **Various Gauges**, Outside Hammers, Damascus Barrel, *Modern* 80.00   150.00
☐ **Various Gauges**, Hammerless, Steel Barrel, *Modern* 95.00   175.00
☐ **Various Gauges**, Hammerless, Damascus Barrel, *Modern* 75.00   150.00
☐ **Various Gauges**, Outside Hammers, Steel Barrel, *Modern* 90.00   175.00

SHOTGUN, SINGLESHOT
☐ **Various Gauges**, Hammer, Steel Barrel, *Modern* 45.00   75.00

ELLIS, REUBEN
Albany, N.Y. 1808-1829.

RIFLE, FLINTLOCK
☐ **Ellis-Jennings**, .69, Sliding Lock for Multiple Loadings, 4 shot,
Antique 5,300.00 8,850.00
☐ **Ellis-Jennings**, .69, Sliding Lock for Multiple Loadings, 10 shot,
Antique 7,800.00 15,500.00

EL TIGRE

RIFLE, LEVER ACTION
☐ **Copy of Winchester M1892**, .44-40 WCF, Tube Feed, *Modern* 165.00   255.00

E.M.F.
(Early and Modern Firearms) Santa Ana, Calif.

HANDGUN, REVOLVER
☐ **California Dragoon**, .44 Magnum, Single Action, Western Style,
Engraved, *Modern* 175.00   225.00
☐ **Dakota**, Various Calibers, Single Action, Western Style, *Modern* ... 115.00   155.00
☐ **Dakota**, Various Calibers, Single Action, Western Style, Engraved,
Modern 145.00   220.00
☐ **Dakota**, Various Calibers, Single Action, Western Style, Nickel
Plated, *Modern* 125.00   185.00
☐ **Dakota**, Various Calibers, Single Action, Western Style, Nickel
Plated, Engraved, *Modern* 175.00   245.00
☐ **Dakota Buntline**, Various Calibers, 12" Barrel, Single Action,
Western Style, *Modern* 130.00   165.00
☐ **Dakota Buckhorn**, Various Calibers, 16¼" Barrel, Single Action,
Western Style, *Modern* 140.00   180.00
☐ **Dakota Buckhorn**, Various Calibers, 16¼" Barrel, Single Action,
Western Style, with Shoulder Stock, *Modern* 170.00   215.00
☐ **Super Dakota**, Various Calibers, Single Action, Western Style,
Magnum, *Modern* 125.00   190.00
☐ **Outlaw 1875**, Various Calibers, Single Action, Remington Style,
Modern 120.00   160.00
☐ **Outlaw 1875**, Various Calibers, Single Action, Remington Style,
Engraved, *Modern* 165.00   220.00
☐ **Thermodynamics**, .357 Magnum, Solid Frame, Swing-out Cylinder,
Vent Rib, Stainless Steel, *Modern* 125.00   175.00

E.M.F. Super Dakota

	V.G.	EXC.
HANDGUN, SINGLESHOT		
☐ **Baron**, .22 Short R.F., Derringer, Gold Frame, Blue Barrel, Wood Grips, *Modern*	25.00	40.00
☐ **Baron**, Count, Etc., Derringer, if Cased *Add* **$10.00-$15.00**		
☐ **Baroness**, .22 Short R.F., Derringer, Gold Plated, Pearl Grips, *Modern*	30.00	50.00
☐ **Count**, .22 Short R.F., Derringer, Blue, Wood Grips, *Modern*	25.00	40.00
☐ **Countess**, .22 Short R.F., Derringer, Chrome, Pearl Grips, *Modern*	30.00	50.00
☐ **Rolling Block**, .357 Magnum, Remington Copy, *Modern*	80.00	125.00
RIFLE, LEVER ACTION		
☐ **1866 Yellowboy**, Various Calibers, Brass Frame, Winchester Copy, *Modern*	175.00	230.00
☐ **1866 Yellowboy**, Various Calibers, Brass Frame, Winchester Copy, Engraved, *Modern*	215.00	295.00
☐ **1873 Carbine**, Various Calibers, Winchester Copy, *Modern*	250.00	350.00
☐ **1873 Rifle**, Various Calibers, Winchester Copy, *Modern*	290.00	385.00
☐ **1873 Rifle**, Various Calibers, Winchester Copy, Engraved, *Modern*	325.00	450.00
RIFLE, SEMI-AUTOMATIC		
☐ **AP-74 Military**, .22 L.R.R.F., Clip Fed, Carbine, *Modern*	80.00	125.00
☐ **AP-74 Sport**, .22 L.R.R.F., Clip Fed, Wood Stock, Carbine, *Modern*	90.00	135.00
☐ **AP-74 Military**, .32 ACP, Clip Fed, Carbine, *Modern*	90.00	135.00
☐ **AP-74 Sport**, .32 ACP, Clip Fed, Carbine, *Modern*	85.00	130.00

EM-GE
Gerstenberger & Eberwein, Gussenstadt, West Germany.

HANDGUN, REVOLVER		
☐ **Model 220 KS**, .22 L.R.R.F., Double Action, *Modern*	20.00	35.00
☐ **Model 223**, .22 W.M.R., Double Action, *Modern*	30.00	55.00
☐ **Target Model 200**, .22 L.R.R.F., Double Action, Target Sights, Vent Rib, *Modern*	35.00	60.00

EMPIRE
Made by Jacob Rupertus 1858-1888.

HANDGUN, REVOLVER		
☐ **.22 Short R.F.**, 7 Shot, Spur Trigger, Solid Frame, Single Action, Antique	90.00	160.00
☐ **.38 Short R.F.**, 5 Shot, Spur Trigger, Solid Frame, Single Action, Antique	95.00	190.00
☐ **.41 Short R.F.**, 5 Shot, Spur Trigger, Solid Frame, Single Action, Antique	125.00	220.00

EMPIRE ARMS
Made by Meriden, and distributed by H. & D. Folsom.

	V.G.	EXC.
HANDGUN, REVOLVER		
☐ **.32 S & W**, 5 Shot, Double Action, Top Break, *Modern*	45.00	95.00
☐ **.38 S & W**, 5 Shot, Double Action, Top Break, *Modern*	45.00	95.00

EMPIRE ARMS CO.
Made by Crescent for Sears Roebuck & Co., c. 1900.

SHOTGUN, DOUBLE BARREL, SIDE-BY-SIDE
☐ **Various Gauges**, Outside Hammers, Damascus Barrel, *Modern*	80.00	150.00
☐ **Various Gauges**, Hammerless, Steel Barrel, *Modern*	95.00	175.00
☐ **Various Gauges**, Hammerless, Damascus Barrel, *Modern*	75.00	150.00
☐ **Various Gauges**, Outside Hammers, Steel Barrel, *Modern*	90.00	175.00

SHOTGUN, SINGLESHOT
☐ **Various Gauges**, Hammer, Steel Barrel, *Modern*	45.00	75.00

EMPIRE STATE
Made by Meriden Firearms, and distributed by H & D Folsom.

HANDGUN, REVOLVER
☐ **.32 S & W**, 5 Shot, Double Action, Top Break, *Modern*	45.00	95.00
☐ **.38 S & W**, 5 Shot, Double Action, Top Break, *Modern*	45.00	95.00

EMPRESS
Made by Jacob Rupertus 1858-1888.

HANDGUN, REVOLVER
☐ **.32 Short R.F.**, 5 Shot, Spur Trigger, Solid Frame, Single Action, *Antique*	95.00	170.00

ENCORE
Made by Johnson-Bye, also by Hopkins & Allen 1847-1887.

HANDGUN, REVOLVER
☐ **.22 Short R.F.**, 7 Shot, Spur Trigger, Solid Frame, Single Action, *Antique*	90.00	160.00
☐ **.32 Short R.F.**, 5 Shot, Spur Trigger, Solid Frame, Single Action, *Antique*	95.00	170.00
☐ **.38 R.F.**, 5 Shot, Spur Trigger, Solid Frame, Single Action, *Antique*	95.00	190.00

ENDERS OAKLEAF
Made by Crescent for Shapleigh Hardware Co., St. Louis, Mo.

SHOTGUN, DOUBLE BARREL, SIDE-BY-SIDE
☐ **Various Gauges**, Outside Hammers, Damascus Barrel, *Modern*	80.00	150.00
☐ **Various Gauges**, Hammerless, Steel Barrel, *Modern*	95.00	175.00
☐ **Various Gauges**, Hammerless, Damascus Barrel, *Modern*	75.00	150.00
☐ **Various Gauges**, Outside Hammers, Steel Barrel, *Modern*	90.00	175.00

SHOTGUN, SINGLESHOT
☐ **Various Gauges**, Hammer, Steel Barrel, *Modern*	45.00	75.00

ENDERS ROYAL SERVICE
Made by Crescent for Shapleigh Hardware Co., St. Louis, Mo.

SHOTGUN, DOUBLE BARREL, SIDE-BY-SIDE
☐ **Various Gauges**, Outside Hammers, Damascus Barrel, *Modern*	80.00	150.00
☐ **Various Gauges**, Hammerless, Steel Barrel, *Modern*	95.00	175.00
☐ **Various Gauges**, Hammerless, Damascus Barrel, *Modern*	75.00	150.00

	V.G.	EXC.
☐ **Various Gauges**, Outside Hammers, Steel Barrel, *Modern*	90.00	175.00

SHOTGUN, SINGLESHOT
☐ **Various Gauges**, Hammer, Steel Barrel, *Modern*	45.00	75.00

ENTERPRISE
Made by Enterprise Gun Works, Pittsburgh, Pa., c. 1875.

HANDGUN, REVOLVER
☐ **#1**, .22 Short R.F., 7 Shot, Spur Trigger, Solid Frame, Single Action, *Antique*	95.00	170.00
☐ **#2**, .32 Short R.F., 5 Shot, Spur Trigger, Solid Frame, Single Action, *Antique*	110.00	185.00
☐ **#3**, .38 Short R.F., 5 Shot, Spur Trigger, Solid Frame, Single Action, *Antique*	115.00	200.00
☐ **#4**, .41 Short R.F., 5 Shot, Spur Trigger, Solid Frame, Single Action, *Antique*	135.00	235.00

ERBI

SHOTGUN, DOUBLE BARREL, SIDE-BY-SIDE
☐ **Deluxe Ejector Grade**, 12 and 20 Gauge, Raised Matted Rib, Double Trigger, Checkered Stock, Beavertail Forend, Automatic Ejector, *Modern*	160.00	230.00
☐ **Field Grade**, 12 and 20 Gauge, Raised Matted Rib, Double Trigger, Checkered Stock, *Modern*	140.00	185.00

ERIKA
Francois Pfannl, Krems, Austria 1913-1926.

HANDGUN, SEMI-AUTOMATIC
☐ **4.25mm**, Clip Fed, Blue, *Curio*	400.00	600.00

ERMA
Erfurter Maschinen u. Werkzeugfabrik, Erfurt, Germany prior to WW-II, and after the war became Erma-Werke, Munich-Dachau, West Germany.

AUTOMATIC WEAPON, SUBMACHINE GUN
☐ **EMP**, 9mm Luger, Clip Fed, *Class 3*	700.00	975.00

HANDGUN, SEMI-AUTOMATIC
☐ **EP-22**, .22 L.R.R.F., Clip Fed, *Modern*	95.00	150.00
☐ **EP-25**, .25 ACP, Clip Fed, *Modern*	90.00	140.00
☐ **ET-22 Navy**, .22 L.R.R.F., Clip Fed, *Modern*	150.00	225.00
☐ **ET-22 Navy**, .22 L.R.R.F., Clip Fed, With Conversion Kit, Cased With Accessories, *Modern*	195.00	325.00
☐ **FB-1**, .25 ACP, Clip, *Modern*	45.00	75.00
☐ **KGP-68 (Baby)**, .32 ACP, Clip Fed, *Modern*	120.00	165.00
☐ **KGP-68 (Baby)**, .380 ACP, Clip Fed, *Modern*	125.00	175.00
☐ **KGP-69**, .22 L.R.R.F., Clip Fed, *Modern*	95.00	145.00
☐ **LA-22 PO 8**, .22 L.R.R.F., Clip Fed, *Modern*	95.00	155.00
☐ **RX-22**, .22 L.R.R.F., Double Action, Clip Fed, *Modern*	95.00	145.00
☐ **Old Model Target**, .22 L.R.R.F., Clip Fed, *Modern*	145.00	220.00
☐ **New Model Target**, .22 L.R.R.F., Clip Fed, *Modern*	165.00	240.00

HANDGUN, REVOLVER
☐ **Model 442**, .22 L.R.R.F., Double Action, Swing-Out Cylinder, Blue, *Modern*	95.00	140.00
☐ **Model 443**, .22 W.M.R., Double Action, Swing-Out Cylinder, Blue, *Modern*	100.00	145.00

	V.G.	EXC.
☐ **Model 440**, .38 Spec., Double Action, Swing-Out Cylinder, Stainless, *Modern*	140.00	190.00

RIFLE, BOLT ACTION
☐ **M98 Conversion Unit**, .22 L.R.R.F., Clip Fed, Cased, *Modern*	185.00	260.00
☐ **EG-61**, .22 L.R.R.F., Singleshot, Open Sights, *Modern*	45.00	75.00
☐ **M1957 KK**, .22 L.R.R.F., Military Style Training Rifle, *Modern*	55.00	85.00
☐ **Master Target**, .22 L.R.R.F., Checkered Stock, Peep Sights, *Modern*	90.00	145.00

RIFLE, LEVER ACTION
☐ **EG-71**, .22 L.R.R.F., Tube Feed, *Modern*	90.00	140.00
☐ **EG-712**, .22 L.R.R.F., Tube Feed, *Modern*	95.00	150.00
☐ **EG-712 L**, .22 L.R.R.F., Tube Feed, Octagon Barrel, Nickel Silver Receiver, *Modern*	170.00	255.00
☐ **EG-73**, .22 W.M.R., Tube Feed, *Modern*	125.00	170.00

RIFLE, SEMI-AUTOMATIC
☐ **EM-1**, .22 L.R.R.F., Clip Fed, *Modern*	85.00	140.00
☐ **EGM-1**, .22 L.R.R.F., Clip Fed, *Modern*	85.00	140.00
☐ **ESG22**, .22 L.R.R.F., Clip Fed, *Modern*	95.00	150.00
☐ **ESG22**, .22 W.M.R., Clip Fed, *Modern*	175.00	245.00

ESSEX
Made by Crescent for Belknap Hardware Co. Louisville, Ky.

SHOTGUN, DOUBLE BARREL, SIDE-BY-SIDE
☐ **Various Gauges**, Outside Hammers, Damascus Barrel, *Modern*	80.00	150.00
☐ **Various Gauges**, Hammerless, Steel Barrel, *Modern*	95.00	175.00
☐ **Various Gauges**, Hammerless, Damascus Barrel, *Modern*	75.00	150.00
☐ **Various Gauges**, Outside Hammers, Steel Barrel, *Modern*	90.00	175.00

SHOTGUN, SINGLESHOT
☐ **Various Gauges**, Hammer, Steel Barrel, *Modern*	45.00	75.00

ESSEX
Made by Stevens Arms.

RIFLE, BOLT ACTION
☐ **Model 50**, .22 L.R.R.F., Singleshot, Takedown, *Modern*	30.00	40.00
☐ **Model 53**, .22 L.R.R.F., Singleshot, Takedown, *Modern*	30.00	40.00
☐ **Model 56 Buckhorn**, .22 L.R.R.F., 5 Shot Clip, Open Rear Sight, *Modern*	35.00	50.00

SHOTGUN, DOUBLE BARREL, SIDE—BY—SIDE
☐ **Model 515**, Various Gauges, Hammerless, *Modern*	90.00	140.00

ESSEX
Makers of pistol frames in Island Pond, Vt.

HANDGUN, SEMI-AUTOMATIC
☐ **Colt M1911 Copy**, .45 ACP, Parts Gun, *Modern*	185.00	250.00

ESTEVA, PEDRO
Spain, c. 1740.

HANDGUN, FLINTLOCK
☐ **Pair**, Belt Pistol, Silver Inlay, Silver Furniture, Engraved, Half-Octagon Barrel, *Antique*	6,750.00	8,500.00

EVANS RIFLE MFG. CO.
Mechanic Falls, Maine 1868-1880

	V.G.	EXC.
RIFLE, LEVER ACTION		
☐ **Old Model**, .44 C.F., Upper Buttstock Only, Tube Feed, Sporting Rifle, *Antique*	600.00	975.00
☐ **New Model**, .44 C.F., Tube Feed, Dust Cover, Sporting Rifle, *Antique*	450.00	775.00
☐ **New Model**, .44 C.F., Tube Feed, Dust Cover, Military Style, *Antique*	575.00	950.00
☐ **New Model**, .44 C.F., Tube Feed, Dust Cover, Carbine, *Antique*	500.00	800.00

EVANS, STEPHEN
Valley Forge, Pa. 1742-1797. See Kentucky Rifles and U. S. Military.

EVANS, WILLIAM
London, England 1883-1900.

	V.G.	EXC.
SHOTGUN, DOUBLE BARREL, SIDE-BY-SIDE		
☐ **Pair**, 12 Gauge, Double Trigger, Plain, Cased *Modern*	4,000.00	5,500.00
☐ **Pair**, 12 Gauge, Double Trigger, Straight Grip, Cased, *Modern*	5,000.00	6,500.00

EXCAM
Importers, Hialeah, Fla. Also see Erma and Tanarmi.

	V.G.	EXC.
HANDGUN, DOUBLE BARREL, OVER-UNDER		
☐ **TA-38**, .38 Special, 2 Shot, Derringer, *Modern*	35.00	55.00
HANDGUN, REVOLVER		
☐ **Buffalo Scout TA-76**, .22LR/.22 WMR Combo, Western Style, Single Action, *Modern*	35.00	55.00
☐ **Buffalo Scout TA-76**, .22 L.R.R.F., Western Style, Single Action, *Modern*	25.00	45.00
☐ **Buffalo Scout TA-22**, .22LR/.22 WMR Combo, Western Style, Single Action, Brass Backstrap, *Modern*	40.00	65.00
☐ **Buffalo Scout TA-22**, .22LR/.22 WMR Combo, Western Style, Single Action, Brass Backstrap, Target Sights, *Modern*	45.00	75.00
☐ **Buffalo Scout TA-22**, .22 L.R.R.F., Western Style, Single Action, Brass Backstrap, *Modern*	30.00	50.00
☐ **Warrior**, .22 L.R.R.F., Double Action, Blue, Vent Rib, *Modern*	45.00	70.00
☐ **Warrior**, .22 LR/.22 WMR Combo, Double Action, Blue, Vent Rib, *Modern*	65.00	100.00
☐ **Warrior**, .38 Spec., Double Action, Blue, Vent Rib, Target Sights, *Modern*	65.00	100.00
☐ **Warrior**, .357 Mag., Double Action, Blue, Vent Rib, Target Sights, *Modern*	85.00	135.00
HANDGUN, SEMI-AUTOMATIC		
☐ **GT-22**, .22 L.R.R.F., Clip Fed, *Modern*	60.00	95.00
☐ **GT-27**, .25 ACP, Clip Fed, *Modern*	30.00	45.00
☐ **GT-27**, .25 ACP, Clip Fed, Steel Frame, *Modern*	65.00	100.00
☐ **GT-32**, .32 ACP, Clip Fed, *Modern*	60.00	95.00
☐ **GT-380**, .380 ACP, Clip Fed, *Modern*	70.00	110.00
☐ **GT-380**, .25 ACP, Clip Fed, Engraved, *Modern*	90.00	140.00
☐ **GT-32**, .32 ACP, Clip Fed, 12 Shot, *Modern*	90.00	135.00
☐ **GT-380**, .380 ACP, Clip Fed, 11 Shot, *Modern*	110.00	150.00
☐ **RX-22**, .22 L.R.R.F., Clip Fed, *Modern*	75.00	110.00

EXCELSIOR
Made by Norwich Pistol Co., c. 1880.

	V.G.	EXC.

HANDGUN, REVOLVER
☐ **.32 Short R.F.**, 5 Shot, Spur Trigger, Solid Frame, Single Action, Antique 90.00 160.00

EXCELSIOR
Made in Italy.

SHOTGUN, DOUBLE BARREL, SIDE-BY-SIDE
☐ **Super 88**, 12 Ga. Mag. 3", Boxlock, Checkered Stock, *Modern* 225.00 320.00

EXPRESS
Made by Bacon Arms Co., c. 1880.

HANDGUN, REVOLVER
☐ **.22 Short R.F.**, 7 Shot, Spur Trigger, Solid Frame, Single Action, Antique 90.00 160.00

EXPRESS
Tomas de Urizar y Cia., Eibar, Spain, c. 1905-1921.

HANDGUN, SEMI-AUTOMATIC
☐ **Type 1**, .25 ACP, Clip Fed, Fixed Ribbed Barrel, *Curio* 165.00 235.00
☐ **Type 1**, .32 ACP, Clip Fed, 4" Fixed Barrel, *Curio* 155.00 225.00
☐ **Type 2**, .25 ACP, Clip Fed, Hammerless, Eibar Style, *Curio* 85.00 125.00
☐ **Type 2**, .32 ACP, Clip Fed, Hammerless, Eibar Style, *Curio* 90.00 135.00
☐ **Type 3**, .25 ACP, Clip Fed, Hammer, Eibar Style, *Curio* 95.00 140.00
☐ **Type 3**, .32 ACP, Clip Fed, Hammer, Eibar Style, *Curio* 95.00 145.00

FABRIQUE D'ARMES DE GUERRE
Spain, unknown maker, c. 1900.

HANDGUN, SEMI-AUTOMATIC
☐ **Paramount**, .25 ACP, Clip Fed, *Curio* 80.00 130.00

FABRIQUE D'ARMES DE GUERRE DE GRAND PRECISION
Tradename used by Etxezagarra & Abitua, Eibar, Spain, c. 1920.

HANDGUN, SEMI-AUTOMATIC
☐ **Bulwark**, .25 ACP, Clip Fed, *Modern* 85.00 135.00
☐ **Colonial**, .25 ACP, Clip Fed, *Modern* 90.00 145.00
☐ **Colonial**, .32 ACP, Clip Fed, *Modern* 115.00 180.00
☐ **Helvece**, .25 ACP, Clip Fed, *Modern* 75.00 125.00

Fabrique De Guerre De Grand Precision Bulwark

	V.G.	EXC.
☐ **Jupiter**, .32 ACP, Clip Fed, *Modern*	90.00	145.00
☐ **Libia**, .32 ACP, Clip Fed, *Modern*	110.00	160.00
☐ **Looking Glass**, .32 ACP, Clip Fed, *Modern*	90.00	145.00
☐ **Looking Glass**, .32 ACP, Clip Fed, Grip Safety, *Modern*	115.00	175.00
☐ **Trust**, .25 ACP, Clip Fed, *Modern*	80.00	140.00

FALCON
HANDGUN, SEMI-AUTOMATIC
☐ **.25 ACP**, Clip Fed, Blue, *Modern* 50.00 80.00

FAMARS
Brescia, Italy.
SHOTGUN, DOUBLE BARREL, SIDE-BY-SIDE
☐ **Hammer Gun**, Various Gauges, Automatic Ejector, Fancy Wood, Fancy Engraving, Double Triggers, *Modern* 4,300.00 6,500.00
☐ **Sidelock Gun**, Various Gauges, Automatic Ejector, Double Trigger, Fancy Engraving, Fancy Wood, *Modern* 6,800.00 9,750.00

FARNOT, FRANK
Lancaster, Pa. 1779-1783. See Kentucky Rifles and Pistols.

FARNOT, FREDERICK
Lancaster, Pa. 1779-1782. See Kentucky Rifles and Pistols.

FARROW ARMS CO.
Holyoke, Mass. Established by William Farrow 1878-1885. Became Farrow Arms Co. About 1885 and moved to Mason, Tenn. to 1904, then to Washington, D.C. 1904-1917.
RIFLE, SINGLESHOT
☐ **#1**, .30 Long R.F., Target Rifle, Octagon Barrel, Target Sights, Fancy Wood, *Antique* 1,250.00 2,950.00
☐ **#2**, .30 Long R.F., Target Rifle, Octagon Barrel, Target Sights, *Antique* 950.00 2,000.00

FAST
Echave, Arizmendi y Cia., Eibar, Spain.
HANDGUN, SEMI-AUTOMATIC
☐ **.22 L.R.R.F.**, Clip Fed, *Modern* 90.00 150.00
☐ **.25 ACP**, Clip Fed, *Modern* 85.00 140.00
☐ **.32 ACP**, Clip Fed, *Modern* 90.00 150.00
☐ **.380 ACP**, Clip Fed, *Modern* 95.00 160.00

FAULTLESS
Made by Crescent for John M. Smythe Hdw. Co., Chicago, Ill.
SHOTGUN, DOUBLE BARREL, SIDE-BY-SIDE
☐ **Various Gauges**, Outside Hammers, Damascus Barrel, *Modern* 80.00 150.00
☐ **Various Gauges**, Hammerless, Steel Barrel, *Modern* 95.00 175.00
☐ **Various Gauges**, Hammerless, Damascus Barrel, *Modern* 75.00 150.00
☐ **Various Gauges**, Outside Hammers, Steel Barrel, *Modern* 90.00 175.00
SHOTGUN, SINGLESHOT
☐ **Various Gauges**, Hammer, Steel Barrel, *Modern* 45.00 75.00

FAULTLESS GOOSE GUN
Made by Crescent for John M. Smythe Hdw. Co., Chicago, Ill.

V.G.   EXC.

SHOTGUN, DOUBLE BARREL, SIDE-BY-SIDE
- ☐ **Various Gauges**, Outside Hammers, Damascus Barrel, *Modern* 80.00   150.00
- ☐ **Various Gauges**, Hammerless, Steel Barrel, *Modern* 95.00   175.00
- ☐ **Various Gauges**, Hammerless, Damascus Barrel, *Modern* 75.00   150.00
- ☐ **Various Gauges**, Outside Hammers, Steel Barrel, *Modern* 90.00   175.00

SHOTGUN, SINGLESHOT
- ☐ **Various Gauges**, Hammer, Steel Barrel, *Modern* 45.00   75.00

FAVORITE
Made by Johnson-Bye Co., c. 1874-1884.

HANDGUN, REVOLVER
- ☐ **#1**, .22 Short R.F., 7 Shot, Spur Trigger, Solid Frame, Single Action, *Antique* 90.00   160.00
- ☐ **#2**, .32 Short R.F., 5 Shot, Spur Trigger, Solid Frame, Single Action, *Antique* 95.00   170.00
- ☐ **#3**, .38 Short R.F., 5 Shot, Spur Trigger, Solid Frame, Single Action, *Antique* 95.00   190.00
- ☐ **#4**, .41 Short R.F., 5 Shot, Spur Trigger, Solid Frame, Single Action, *Antique* 125.00   200.00

FAVORITE NAVY
Made by Johnson-Bye Co., c. 1874-1884.

HANDGUN, REVOLVER
- ☐ **.44 Short R.F.**, 5 Shot, Spur Trigger, Solid Frame, Single Action, *Antique* 175.00   275.00

FAY, HENRY C.
Lancaster, Mass., c. 1837.

RIFLE, PERCUSSION
- ☐ **.58**, Military, *Antique* 1,450.00   2,750.00

FECHT, G. VAN DER
Berlin, Germany, c. 1733.

RIFLE, FLINTLOCK
- ☐ **Yaeger**, Half-Octagon Barrel, Brass Furniture, Engraved, Carved, *Antique* 3,450.00   4,750.00

FEDERAL ARMS
Made by Meriden Firearms, sold by Sears-Roebuck.

HANDGUN, REVOLVER
- ☐ **.32 S & W**, 5 Shot, Double Action, Top Break, *Modern* 45.00   95.00
- ☐ **.38 S & W**, 5 Shot, Double Action, Top Break, *Modern* 45.00   95.00

FEMARU
Made by Femaru Fegyver es Gepgyar (Fegyvergyar) Pre-War; Post War Made by Femaru es Szerszamgepgyar, N.V., Budapest, Hungary. Also see Frommer.

HANDGUN, SEMI-AUTOMATIC
- ☐ **M 29**, .380 ACP, Clip Fed, Military, *Curio* 140.00   195.00
- ☐ **M 37**, .380 ACP, Clip Fed, Military, *Modern* 150.00   220.00
- ☐ **M 37**, .32 ACP, Clip Fed, Nazi-Proofed, *Modern* 150.00   220.00
- ☐ **M 37**, .380 ACP, Clip Fed, Nazi-Proofed, *Modern* 165.00   250.00

Femaru M.29

FENNO
Lancaster, Pa. 1790-1800. See Kentucky Rifles and Pistols.

V.G.   EXC.

FERLACH
Genossenschaft der Buchsenmachermeister, Ferlach, Austria.
COMBINATION WEAPON, OVER-UNDER
☐ **Turkey Gun**, Various Rifle and Shotgun Calibers, Hammerless,
  Vent Rib, Double Set Triggers, Automatic Ejectors, *Modern* 425.00   650.00
RIFLE, DOUBLE BARREL, SIDE-BY-SIDE
☐ **Standard Grade**, Various Calibers, Boxlock, Engraved, Checkered
  Stock, Fancy Wood, *Modern* 2,000.00 2,900.00
☐ **Standard Grade**, Various Calibers, Sidelock, Engraved, Checkered
  Stock, Fancy Wood, *Modern* 3,500.00 4,350.00

FERREE, JACOB
Lancaster, Pa. 1774-1784, see Kentucky Rifles and U.S. Military.

FESIG, CONRAD
Reading, Pa. 1779-1790, see Kentucky Rifles and Pistols.

FIALA
Made for Fiala Arms & Equipment Co. by Blakslee Forging Co., New Haven, Conn.
HANDGUN, MANUAL REPEATER
☐ **.22 L.R.R.F.**, Clip Fed, Target Pistol, *Curio* 235.00   370.00
☐ **.22 L.R.R.F.**, Clip Fed, Target Pistol, With Shoulder Stock, 20"
  Barrel, 3" Barrel, Cased, *Curio* 400.00   625.00

F.I.E.
Firearms Import & Export, Miami, Fla.
HANDGUN, DOUBLE BARREL, OVER-UNDER
☐ **.38 S & W**, Derringer, *Modern* 30.00   50.00
☐ **.38 Special**, Derringer, *Modern* 35.00   55.00
HANDGUN, FLINTLOCK
☐ **Kentucky**, .44, Belt Pistol, Reproduction, *Antique* 35.00   50.00
☐ **Kentucky**, .44, Belt Pistol, Engraved, Reproduction, *Antique* 40.00   55.00
☐ **Tower**, .69, *Antique* 15.00   28.00

	V.G.	EXC.

HANDGUN, PERCUSSION
- ☐ **Baby Dragoon**, .31, Revolver, Reproduction, *Antique* 25.00 40.00
- ☐ **Baby Dragoon**, .31, Revolver, Engraved, Reproduction, *Antique* ... 30.00 45.00
- ☐ **Kentucky**, .44, Belt Pistol, Reproduction, *Antique* 30.00 45.00
- ☐ **Kentucky**, .44, Belt Pistol, Engraved, Reproduction, *Antique* 35.00 50.00
- ☐ **Navy**, .36, Revolver, Reproduction, *Antique* 25.00 35.00
- ☐ **Navy**, .36, Revolver, Engraved, Reproduction, *Antique* 30.00 40.00
- ☐ **Navy**, .44, Revolver, Reproduction, *Antique* 25.00 40.00
- ☐ **Navy**, .44, Revolver, Engraved, Reproduction, *Antique* 30.00 45.00
- ☐ **Remington**, .36, Revolver, Reproduction, *Antique* 30.00 45.00
- ☐ **Remington**, .36, Revolver, Engraved, Reproduction, *Antique* 35.00 55.00
- ☐ **Remington**, .44, Revolver, Reproduction, *Antique* 30.00 45.00
- ☐ **Remington**, .44, Revolver, Engraved, Reproduction, *Antique* 35.00 55.00

HANDGUN, REVOLVER
- ☐ **Arminius**, .22 L.R.R.F., Double Action, Swing-out Cylinder, Fixed Sights, Chrome, *Modern* 40.00 65.00
- ☐ **Arminius**, .22 LR/.22 WMR Combo, Double Action, Swing-out Cylinder, Fixed Sights, Chrome, *Modern* 50.00 85.00
- ☐ **Arminius**, .22 LR/.22 WMR Combo, Double Action, Swing-out Cylinder, Adjustable Sights, Chrome, *Modern* 60.00 90.00
- ☐ **Arminius**, .22 LR/.22 WMR Combo, Double Action, Swing-out Cylinder, Adjustable Sights, Blue, *Modern* 55.00 85.00
- ☐ **Arminius**, .22 LR/.22 WMR Combo, Double Action, Swing-out Cylinder, Adjustable Sights, Blue, Target, *Modern* 50.00 70.00
- ☐ **Arminius**, .22 L.R.R.F., Double Action, Swing-out Cylinder, Adjustable Sights, Blue, *Modern* 45.00 65.00
- ☐ **Arminius**, .22 L.R.R.F., Double Action, Swing-out Cylinder, Adjustable Sights, Chrome, *Modern* 45.00 75.00
- ☐ **Arminius**, .22 L.R.R.F., Double Action, Swing-out Cylinder, Adjustable Sights, Blue, Target, *Modern* 45.00 75.00
- ☐ **Arminius**, .22 L.R.R.F., Double Action, Swing-out Cylinder, Adjustable Sights, Chrome, Target, *Modern* 45.00 75.00
- ☐ **Arminius**, .32 S & W, Double Action, Swing-out Cylinder, Adjustable Sights, Blue, Target, *Modern* 45.00 75.00
- ☐ **Arminius**, .32 S & W, Double Action, Swing-out Cylinder, Adjustable Sights, Chrome, Target, *Modern* 45.00 75.00
- ☐ **Arminius**, .357 Magnum, Double Action, Swing-out Cylinder, Adjustable Sights, Chrome, Target, *Modern* 75.00 110.00
- ☐ **Arminius**, .357 Magnum, Double Action, Swing-out Cylinder, Adjustable Sights, Blue, Target, *Modern* 75.00 110.00
- ☐ **Arminius**, .38 Special, Double Action, Swing-out Cylinder, Adjustable Sights, Blue, Target, *Modern* 55.00 75.00
- ☐ **Arminius**, .38 Special, Double Action, Swing-out Cylinder, Adjustable Sights, Chrome, Target, *Modern* 55.00 75.00
- ☐ **Arminius**, .38 Special, Double Action, Swing-out Cylinder, Blue, *Modern* 40.00 60.00
- ☐ **Arminius**, .38 Special, Double Action, Swing-out Cylinder, Chrome, *Modern* 40.00 60.00
- ☐ **Buffalo Scout**, .22LR/.22 WMR Combo, Single Action, Western Style, *Modern* 35.00 55.00
- ☐ **Buffalo**, .22 L.R.R.F., Single Action, Western Style, *Modern* 30.00 45.00
- ☐ **Guardian**, .22 L.R.R.F., Double Action, Swing-out Cylinger, *Modern* 25.00 40.00
- ☐ **Guardian**, .22 L.R.R.F., Double Action, Swing-out Cylinder, Chrome, *Modern* 30.00 45.00
- ☐ **Guardian**, .32 S & W, Double Action, Swing-out Cylinder, *Modern* 25.00 40.00

	V.G.	EXC.
☐ **Guardian**, .32 S & W, Double Action, Swing-out Cylinder, Chrome, *Modern*	30.00	45.00
☐ **Hombre**, .357 Mag, Single Action, Western Style, Steel Frame, *Modern*	75.00	110.00
☐ **Hombre**, .44 Mag, Single Action, Western Style, Steel Frame, *Modern*	85.00	130.00
☐ **Hombre**, .45 L.C., Single Action, Western Style, Steel Frame, *Modern*	75.00	110.00
☐ **Legend**, .22LR/.22 WMR Combo, Single Action, Western Style, Steel Frame, *Modern*	45.00	65.00
☐ **Legend**, .22 L.R.R.F., Single Action, Western Style, Steel Frame, *Modern*	30.00	45.00
☐ **Titan Tiger**, .38 Spec., Double Action, Blue, *Modern*	50.00	75.00

HANDGUN, SEMI-AUTOMATIC

	V.G.	EXC.
☐ **Best**, .25 ACP, Hammer, Steel Frame, Blue, *Modern*	60.00	95.00
☐ **Best**, .32 ACP, Hammer, Steel Frame, Blue, *Modern*	70.00	105.00
☐ **Guardian**, .25 ACP, Hammer, Blue, *Modern*	25.00	35.00
☐ **Guardian**, .25 ACP, Hammer, Chrome, *Modern*	25.00	35.00
☐ **Guardian**, .25 ACP, Hammer, Gold Plated, *Modern*	25.00	40.00
☐ **Interdynamics KG-9**, 9mm Luger, Clip Fed, *Modern*	225.00	325.00
☐ **Titan**, .25 ACP, Hammer, Blue, *Modern*	25.00	35.00
☐ **Titan**, .25 ACP, Hammer, Chrome, *Modern*	25.00	40.00
☐ **Super Titan II**, .32 ACP, Hammer, Steel Frame, Blue, 13 Shot, *Modern*	85.00	125.00
☐ **Titan**, .32 ACP, Hammer, Steel Frame, Blue, *Modern*	50.00	75.00
☐ **Titan**, .32 ACP, Hammer, Steel Frame, Chrome, *Modern*	55.00	80.00
☐ **Titan**, .32 ACP, Hammer, Steel Frame, Engraved, Chrome, *Modern*	65.00	90.00
☐ **Titan**, .32 ACP, Hammer, Steel Frame, Engraved, Blue, *Modern*	60.00	85.00
☐ **Super Titan II**, .380 ACP, Hammer, Steel Frame, Blue, 12 Shot, *Modern*	95.00	135.00
☐ **Titan**, .380 ACP, Hammer, Steel Frame, Blue, *Modern*	65.00	95.00
☐ **Titan**, .380 ACP, Hammer, Steel Frame, Chrome, *Modern*	75.00	110.00
☐ **Titan**, .380 ACP, Hammer, Steel Frame, Engraved, Blue, *Modern*	90.00	130.00
☐ **Titan**, .380 ACP, Hammer, Steel Frame, Engraved, Chrome, *Modern*	95.00	135.00

RIFLE, FLINTLOCK

	V.G.	EXC.
☐ **Kentucky**, .45, Reproduction, *Antique*	55.00	85.00
☐ **Kentucky**, .45, Engraved, Reproduction, *Antique*	60.00	85.00

RIFLE, PERCUSSION

	V.G.	EXC.
☐ **Berdan**, .45, Reproduction, *Antique*	50.00	80.00
☐ **Kentucky**, .45, Reproduction, *Antique*	50.00	80.00
☐ **Kentucky**, .45, Engraved, Reproduction, *Antique*	55.00	80.00
☐ **Zoave**, .58, Reproduction, *Antique*	60.00	95.00

COMBINATION WEAPON, OVER-UNDER

	V.G.	EXC.
☐ **Combo**, 30/30-20 Ga., *Modern*	45.00	75.00

SHOTGUN, DOUBLE BARREL, OVER-UNDER

	V.G.	EXC.
☐ **OU**, 12 and 20 Ga., Field Grade, Vent Rib, *Modern*	110.00	160.00
☐ **OU 12 T**, 12 Ga., Trap Grade, Vent Rib, *Modern*	135.00	170.00
☐ **OU-S**, 12 and 20 Ga., Skeet Grade, Vent Rib, *Modern*	135.00	170.00

SHOTGUN, DOUBLE BARREL, SIDE-BY-SIDE

	V.G.	EXC.
☐ **DB**, Various Gauges, Hammerless, *Modern*	65.00	110.00
☐ **DB Riot**, Various Gauges, Hammerless, *Modern*	65.00	110.00
☐ **Brute**, Various Gauges, Short Barrels, Short Stock, *Modern*	90.00	150.00

SHOTGUN, SINGLESHOT

	V.G.	EXC.
☐ **SB 40**, 12 Ga., Hammer, Button Break, *Modern*	25.00	45.00

	V.G.	EXC.
☐ **SB 41**, 20 Ga., Hammer, Button Break, *Modern*	25.00	45.00
☐ **SB 42**, .410 Ga., Hammer, Button Break, *Modern*	25.00	45.00
☐ **SB Youth**, Various Gauges, Hammer, *Modern*	25.00	35.00
☐ **SB 12 16 20 .410**, Various Gauges, Hammer, *Modern*	25.00	40.00
☐ **S.O.B.**, 12 and 20 Gauges, Short Barrel, Short Stock, *Modern*	35.00	55.00

FIEHL & WEEKS FIRE ARMS MFG. CO.
Philadelphia, Pa., c. 1895.

HANDGUN, REVOLVER
☐ **.32 S & W**, 5 Shot, Top Break, Hammerless, Double Action, *Modern*	55.00	95.00

FIEL
Erquiaga, Muguruzu y Cia., Eibar, Spain, c. 1920.

HANDGUN, SEMI-AUTOMATIC
☐ **Fiel #1**, .25 ACP, Clip Fed, Eibar Style, *Curio*	90.00	125.00
☐ **Fiel #1**, .32 ACP, Clip Fed, Eibar Style, *Curio*	95.00	140.00
☐ **Fiel #2**, .25 ACP, Clip Fed, Breech Bolt, *Curio*	130.00	195.00

FIGTHORN, ANDREW
Reading, Pa. 1779-1790, see Kentucky Rifles.

FINNISH LION
Made by Valmet, Jyvaskyla, Finland

RIFLE, BOLT ACTION
☐ **Standard**, .22 L.R.R.F., Singleshot, Target Rifle, Target Stock, Target Sights, U.I.T. Rifle, *Modern*	320.00	440.00
☐ **Match**, .22 L.R.R.F., Singleshot, Target Rifle, Thumbhole Stock, Target Sights, *Modern*	365.00	525.00
☐ **Champion**, 22 L.R.R.F., Singleshot, Free Rifle, Thumbhole Stock, Target Sights, Heavy Barrel, *Modern*	385.00	595.00

FIREARMS, CUSTOM MADE
This catagory covers some of the myriad special firearms that are built to an individual's specifications by a competent gunsmith, and not by the original factory. Most firearms in this class will appeal only to a person who happens to want the same special features, and because of this most of these guns sell for less than the cost of the conversion.

HANDGUN, REVOLVER
☐ **P.P.C. Conversion**, .38 Special, Heavy Barrel, Rib with Target Sights, Target Trigger, Target Grips, *Modern*	175.00	300.00
☐ **"F.B.I." Conversion**, .38 Special, Cut Trigger Guard, Spurless Hammer, Short Barrel, *Modern*	145.00	235.00
☐ **Recoil Compensation Devices or Ports**, *Add $25.00-$45.00*		

HANDGUN, SEMI-AUTOMATIC
☐ **M1911A1**, Double Action Conversion, *Add $95.00-$175.00*		
☐ **M1911A1**, Combat Conversion, Extended Trigger Guard, Ambidextrous Safety, Special Slide Release, Ported, Combat Sights, *Modern*	275.00	400.00

HANDGUN, SINGLESHOT
☐ **Silhouette Pistol**, Various Calibers, Bolt Action, Thumbhole Stock, Target Sights, Target Trigger, *Modern*	250.00	400.00

HANDGUN, PERCUSSION
☐ **Target Revolver**, Various Calibers, Tuned, Target Sights, Reproduction, *Antique*	90.00	145.00

	V.G.	EXC.

RIFLE, BOLT ACTION
- **Sporting Rifle**, Various Calibers, Checkered Stock, Recoil Pad, Simple Military Conversion, *Modern* .... 85.00 — 140.00
- **Sporting Rifle**, Various Calibers, Fancy Wood, Recoil Pad, Fancy Military Conversion, *Modern* .... 250.00 — 400.00
- **Sporting Rifle**, Various Calibers, Plain Stock, Commercial Parts, *Modern* .... 90.00 — 165.00
- **Sporting Rifle**, Various Calibers, Fancy Stock, High Quality Commercial Parts, Fancy Checkering, Stock Inlays, *Modern* .... 450.00 — 950.00
- **Sporting Rifle**, Various Calibers, Fancy Stock, High Quality Commercial Parts, Fancy Checkering, Stock Inlays, Engraved, *Modern* .... 750.00 — 1,500.00
- **Sporting Rifle**, Various Calibers, Fancy Stock, High Quality Commercial Parts, Fancy Checkering, Stock Inlays, Engraved, Gold Inlays, *Modern* .... 950.00 — 2,500.00
- **Sporting Rifle**, Various Calibers, Mauser 1871 Action, Checkered Stock, *Antique* .... 150.00 — 250.00

RIFLE, SINGLESHOT
- **Target Rifle**, Centerfire Calibers, Plain, Target Sights, Built on Various Bolt Actions, *Modern* .... 250.00 — 375.00
- **Target Rifle**, Centerfire Calibers, Plain, Target Sights, Built on Various Moving Block Actions, *Modern* .... 175.00 — 275.00
- **Target Rifle**, Centerfire Calibers, Fancy, Target Sights, Built on Various Moving Block Actions, *Modern* .... 275.00 — 400.00
- **Target Rifle**, Rimfire Calibers, Plain, Target Sights, Built on Various Moving Block Actions, *Modern* .... 150.00 — 250.00

SHOTGUN, SLIDE ACTION
- **Combat Conversion**, 12 Ga., Short Barrel, Extended Magazine Tube, Folding Stock, Rifle Sights, *Modern* .... 135.00 — 250.00
- **Competition Conversion**, Various Gauges, High Rib, Recoil Reducer in Stock, Fancy Wood, *Modern* .... 225.00 — 350.00

SHOTGUN, DOUBLE BARREL, OVER-UNDER
- **Trap Conversion**, 12 Ga., Recoil Reducer in Stock, Release Triggers, Throated Chambers, Trap Pad, *Add* **$275.00-$400.00**

FIREARMS CO. LTD.
Made in England for Mandall Shooting Supplies.

RIFLE, BOLT ACTION
- **Alpine Standard**, Various Calibers, Checkered Stock, Recoil Pad, Open Rear Sight, *Modern* .... 175.00 — 275.00
- **Alpine Custom**, Various Calibers, Checkered Stock, Recoil Pad, Open Rear Sight, *Modern* .... 200.00 — 300.00

FIREARMS INTERNATIONAL
Washington, D.C.

HANDGUN, REVOLVER
- **Regent**, .22 L.R.R.F., 8 Shot, Various Barrel Lengths, Blue, *Modern* — 40.00 — 60.00
- **Regent**, .22 L.R.R.F., 7 Shot, Various Barrel Lengths, Blue, *Modern* — 45.00 — 65.00

HANDGUN, SEMI-AUTOMATIC
- **Combo**, .22 L.R.R.F., Unique Model L Pistol with Conversion Kit for Stocked Rifle, *Modern* .... 75.00 — 130.00
- **Model D**, .380 ACP, Clip Fed, Adjustable Sights, Blue, *Modern* .... 90.00 — 140.00
- **Model D**, .380 ACP, Clip Fed, Adjustable Sights, Chrome *Modern* — 95.00 — 150.00
- **Model D**, .380 ACP, Clip Fed, Adjustable Sights, Matt Blue, *Modern* — 90.00 — 140.00

	V.G.	EXC.

SHOTGUN, DOUBLE BARREL, SIDE-BY-SIDE
- ☐ **Model 400**, Various Gauges, Single Trigger, Checkered Stock, *Modern* 150.00 200.00
- ☐ **Model 400E**, Various Gauges, Single Selective Trigger, Checkered Stock, Selective Ejector, Vent Rib, *Modern* 180.00 250.00
- ☐ **Model 400E**, Various Gauges, Single Selective Trigger, Selective Ejector, *Modern* 160.00 240.00

FIREARMS SPECIALTIES
Owosso, Mich., c. 1972.

HANDGUN, REVOLVER
- ☐ **.45/70 Custom Revolver**, Brass Frame, Single Action, Western Style, *Modern* 350.00 550.00

FLINTLOCK, UNKNOWN MAKER
Also see Miquelet-Lock, Unknown Maker and Snaphaunce, Unknown Maker.

HANDGUN, FLINTLOCK
- ☐ **.28**, English, Pocket Pistol, Queen Anne Style, Box Lock, Screw Barrel, Plain, *Antique* 250.00 425.00
- ☐ **.40**, India Herdsman Pistol, Long Tapered Round Barrel, Silver Furniture, *Antique* 400.00 625.00
- ☐ **.45**, French, Mid-1700's, Screw Barrel, Long Cannon Barrel, Silver Furniture, *Antique* 800.00 1,200.00
- ☐ **.60**, Continental, Early 1700's, Holster Pistol, Half-Octagon Barrel, Engraved, High Quality, *Antique* 1,500.00 2,200.00
- ☐ **.60**, Oval Bore, Box Lock, Pocket Pistol, Steel Furniture, *Antique* 500.00 775.00
- ☐ **.62**, Crantham English, Holster Pistol, Brass Furniture, Plain, *Antique* 300.00 400.00
- ☐ **.63**, Spanish, Mid-1600's, Holster Pistol, Silver Inlay, Engraved, *Antique* 2,000.00 3,300.00
- ☐ **.68**, Tower, Continental, Plain, *Antique* 225.00 325.00
- ☐ **.65**, Arabian, Holster Pistol, Flared, Round Barrel, Low Quality, *Antique* 175.00 250.00
- ☐ **English Lock**, Mid-1600's, Military, Holster Pistol, Iron Mounts, Plain, *Antique* 2,500.00 4,400.00
- ☐ **English**, Early 1700's, Pocket Pistol, Queen Anne Style, Box Lock, Screw Barrel, All Metal, *Antique* 300.00 525.00
- ☐ **English**, Early 1700's, Pocket Pistol, Box Lock, Double Barrel, Screw Barrel, Low Quality, *Antique* 350.00 525.00
- ☐ **English**, Mid-1600's, Button Triger, Brass Barrel, Octagon Fish-tail Butt, *Antique* 1,200.00 2,250.00
- ☐ **French Officers Type c. 1650**, Steel Furniture, Rifled, *Antique* 1,200.00 2,250.00
- ☐ **French Sedan Mid-1600's**, Long Screw Barrel, Rifled, Plain, *Antique* 1,500.00 2,450.00

RIFLE, FLINTLOCK
- ☐ **.64**, Continental, Carbine, Musket, Brass Furniture, *Antique* 300.00 475.00
- ☐ **.72**, Continental, 1650, Musket, Brass Furniture, Plain, *Antique* 650.00 950.00

SHOTGUN, FLINTLOCK
- ☐ **.65**, American Hudson Valley, *Antique* 700.00 1,250.00

F.N.
Fabrique Nationale, Herstal, Belgium from 1889. Also see Browning.

AUTOMATIC WEAPON, ASSAULT RIFLE
- ☐ **FN-CAL**, .223 Rem., Clip Fed, Commercial, *Class 3* 1,200.00 1,850.00

170 / FOLGER, WILLIAM H.

	V.G.	EXC.
☐ FN-FAL, .308 Win., Clip Fed, Commercial, *Class 3*	950.00	1,400.00
☐ FN-FAL, .308 Win., Clip Fed, Folding Stock, Commercial, *Class 3*	1,200.00	1,800.00
☐ FN-FAL G-1, .308 Win., Clip Fed, Heavy Barrel, Bipod, Sniper, with Scope, *Class 3*	2,000.00	3,500.00
☐ FN-FAL L2A1, .308 Win., Clip Fed, Heavy Barrel, Bipod, Commercial, *Class 3*	1,200.00	1,900.00
☐ FN-FAL "Para", .308 Win., Clip Fed, Folding Stock, Lightweight, Commercial, *Class 3*	1,300.00	1,750.00

AUTOMATIC WEAPON, LIGHT MACHINE GUN

☐ FN M.A.G. 58, .308 Win., Belt Fed, Bipod, *Class 3*	2,750.00	3,650.00
☐ FN M.A.G. 58, .308 Win., Belt Fed, Tripod, *Class 3*	3,800.00	4,950.00

RIFLE, BOLT ACTION

☐ Model 1925, .22 L.R.R.F., Singleshot, *Modern*	40.00	55.00
☐ Model 1925 Deluxe, .22 L.R.R.F., Singleshot, Checkered Stock, *Modern*	55.00	80.00
☐ Mauser 98 Military Style, 30/06, Military Finish, Military Stock, Commercial, *Modern*	125.00	230.00
☐ Mauser 98 Military Style, Various Military Calibers, Military Finish, Military Stock, Commercial, *Modern*	110.00	175.00
☐ Mauser Deluxe, Various Calibers, Sporting Rifle, Checkered Stock, *Modern*	300.00	475.00
☐ Mauser Deluxe Presentation, Various Calibers, Sporting Rifle, Fancy Wood, Engraved, *Modern*	650.00	950.00
☐ Mauser Supreme, Various Calibers, Sporting Rifle, Checkered Stock, *Modern*	375.00	550.00
☐ Mauser Supreme, Various Calibers, Sporting Rifle, Checkered Stock, Magnum, *Modern*	400.00	600.00

RIFLE, SEMI-AUTOMATIC

☐ FN FAL, .308 Win., Clip Fed, Commercial, *Modern*	750.00	1,100.00
☐ FN LAR Competition, .308 Win., Clip Fed, Commercial, Flash Hider, *Modern*	775.00	1,200.00
☐ FN LAR Paratrooper, .308 Win., Clip Fed, Commercial, Folding Stock, *Modern*	875.00	1,300.00
☐ FN LAR Heavy Barrel, .308 Win., Clip Fed, Commercial, Synthetic Stock, Bipod, *Modern*	925.00	1,500.00
☐ FN LAR Heavy Barrel, .308 Win., Clip Fed, Commercial, Wood Stock, Bipod, *Modern*	995.00	1,600.00
☐ Model 1949, 30/06, Clip Fed, Military, *Modern*	325.00	475.00
☐ Model 1949, 7mm or 8mm Mauser, Clip Fed, Military, *Modern*	225.00	360.00
☐ M-49 Egyptian, 8mm Mauser, Clip Fed, Military, *Modern*	245.00	375.00

SHOTGUN, BOLT ACTION

☐ 9mm Shotshell, *Modern*	80.00	120.00

FOLGER, WILLIAM H.
Barnsville, Ohio 1830-1854, also See Kentucky Rifles.

FOLK'S GUN WORKS
Bryan, Ohio 1860-1891.

RIFLE, SINGLESHOT

☐ .32 L.R.R.F., Side Lever, Octagon Barrel, *Antique*	225.00	355.00

FONDERSMITH, JOHN
Strasburg, Pa. 1749-1801. See Kentucky Rifles, U.S. Military.

FORBES, F.F.
Made by Crescent, c. 1900.
SHOTGUN, DOUBLE BARREL, SIDE-BY-SIDE
☐ **Various Gauges**, Outside Hammers, Damascus Barrel, *Modern* 80.00 150.00
☐ **Various Gauges**, Hammerless, Steel Barrel, *Modern* 95.00 175.00
☐ **Various Gauges**, Hammerless, Damascus Barrel, *Modern* 75.00 150.00
☐ **Various Gauges**, Outside Hammers, Steel Barrel, *Modern* 90.00 175.00
SHOTGUN, SINGLESHOT
☐ **Various Gauges**, Hammer, Steel Barrel, *Modern* 45.00 75.00

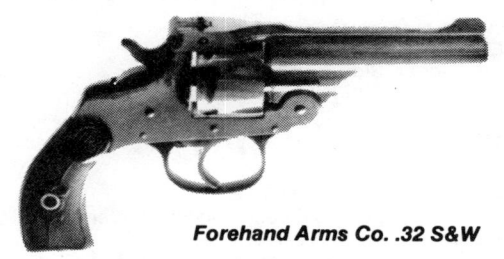

Forehand Arms Co. .32 S&W

FOREHAND ARMS CO.
HANDGUN, REVOLVER
☐ **.32 S & W**, 5 Shot, Double Action, Solid Frame, 2" Barrel, *Antique* 50.00 90.00
☐ **.38 S & W**, 5 Shot, Double Action, Solid Frame, 2" Barrel, *Antique* 50.00 90.00
☐ **Perfection Automatic**, .32 S & W, 5 Shot, Double Action, Top Break, Hammerless, *Antique* 70.00 120.00
☐ **Perfection Automatic**, .32 S & W, 5 Shot, Double Action, Top Break, *Antique* 60.00 100.00

FOREHAND & WADSWORTH
Worcester, Mass. Successors and sons-in-law To Ethan Allen 1871-1902. In 1872 name was changed to Forehand & Wadsworth, in 1890 to Forehand Arms Co.
HANDGUN, REVOLVER
☐ **.22 Short R.F.**, Single Action, Spur Trigger, Solid Frame, Side Hammer, *Antique* 95.00 185.00
☐ **.22 Short R.F.**, 7 Shot, Single Action, Solid Frame, *Antique* 85.00 145.00
☐ **.30 Short R.F.**, Single Action, Spur Trigger, Solid Frame, Side Hammer, *Antique* 90.00 170.00
☐ **.32 Short R.F.**, Single Action, Spur Trigger, Solid Frame, Side Hammer, *Antique* 95.00 185.00
☐ **.44 Short R.F.**, Single Action, Spur Trigger, Solid Frame, Side Hammer, *Antique* 135.00 215.00
☐ **Army**, .38 Long R.F., 6 Shot, Single Action, Solid Frame, *Antique* .. 350.00 495.00
☐ **British Bulldog**, .32 S & W, 7 Shot, Double Action, Solid Frame, *Antique* 55.00 95.00
☐ **British Bulldog**, .38 S & W, 6 Shot, Double Action, Solid Frame, *Antique* 55.00 95.00
☐ **British Bulldog**, .44 S & W, 5 Shot, Double Action, Solid Frame, *Antique* 70.00 120.00
☐ **Bulldog**, .38 Long R.F., 5 Shot, Single Action, Solid Frame, 2" Barrel, *Antique* 85.00 150.00
☐ **Bulldog**, .44 S & W, 5 Shot, Double Action, Solid Frame, 2" Barrel, *Antique* 70.00 120.00
☐ **New Navy**, .44 Russian, 6 Shot, Double Action, Solid Frame, 6" Barrel, *Antique* 325.00 495.00

172 / FOREVER YOURS

	V.G.	EXC.
☐ **Old Army**, .44 Russian, 6 Shot, Single Action, Solid Frame, 7" Barrel, *Antique*	395.00	550.00
☐ **Pocket Model**, .32 S & W Long, 6 Shot, Double Action, Top Break, *Antique*	55.00	95.00
☐ **Russian Model**, .32, .32 Short R.F., 5 Shot, Single Action, Solid Frame, Spur Trigger, *Antique*	125.00	185.00
☐ **Swamp Angel**, .41 Short R.F., 5 Shot, Single Action, Solid Frame, Spur Trigger, *Antique*	120.00	200.00
☐ **Terror**, .32 Short R.F., 5 Shot, Single Action, Solid Frame, Spur Trigger, *Antique*	85.00	160.00

HANDGUN, SINGLESHOT

	V.G.	EXC.
☐ **.22 Short R.F.**, Spur Trigger, Side-swing Barrel, *Antique*	165.00	250.00
☐ **.41 Short R.F.**, Spur Trigger, Side-swing Barrel, *Antique*	220.00	350.00

FOREVER YOURS
Flaig's Lodge, Millvale, Pa.

SHOTGUN, DOUBLE BARREL, OVER-UNDER

	V.G.	EXC.
☐ **Various Gauges**, Automatic Ejector, Checkered Stock, Vent Rib, Double Trigger, *Modern*	400.00	625.00
☐ **Various Gauges**, Automatic Ejector, Checkered Stock, Vent Rib, Single Trigger, *Modern*	450.00	675.00

FOULKES, ADAM
Easton & Allentown, Pa. 1773-1794. See Kentucky Rifles and U.S. Military.

FOUR ACE CO.
Brownsville, Texas.

HANDGUN, SINGLESHOT

	V.G.	EXC.
☐ **Four Ace**, Derringer, Presentation Case *Add* **$10.00-$15.00**		
☐ **Four Ace Model 200**, .22 Short R.F., Derringer, 4 Shot, Spur Trigger, *Modern*	30.00	45.00
☐ **Four Ace Model 200**, .22 Short R.F., Derringer, 4 Shot, Spur Trigger, Nickel Plated, Gold Plated, *Modern*	40.00	55.00
☐ **Four Ace Model 202**, .22 L.R.R.F., Derringer, 4 Shot, Spur Trigger, Nickel Plated, Gold Plated, *Modern*	45.00	60.00
☐ **Four Ace Model**, 202, .22 L.R.R.F., Derringer, 4 Shot, Spur Trigger, *Modern*	35.00	50.00
☐ **Four Ace Model 204**, .22 L.R.R.F., Derringer, 4 Shot, Spur Trigger, Stainless Steel, *Modern*	45.00	65.00
☐ **Little Ace Model 300**, .22 Short R.F., Derringer, Side-swing Barrel, Spur Trigger, *Modern*	25.00	40.00

FOX
Foxco Products, Inc. Manchester, Conn. Also see Demro, T.A.C.

RIFLE, SEMI-AUTOMATIC

	V.G.	EXC.
☐ **9mm Luger or .45 ACP**, Clip Fed, *Modern*	165.00	250.00

FOX, A.H. GUN CO.
Philadelphia, Pa. Formerly Philadelphia Arms Co., now a subsidiary of Savage Arms Co., 1930 to date. Also see Savage Arms Co.

SHOTGUN, DOUBLE BARREL, SIDE-BY-SIDE
☐ **Various Gauges**, Single Selective Trigger *Add* **$165.00-$275.00**
☐ **Various Gauges**, For Vent Rib *Add* **$165.00-$275.00**

	V.G.	EXC.

- ☐ **Various Gauges**, Beavertail Forend *Add* 10%-15%
- ☐ **Various Gauges**, For Single Trigger *Add* $110.00-$190.00
- ☐ **Various Grades**, for 20 Ga. *Add* 50%-75%
- ☐ **A Grade**, Various Gauges, Box Lock, Light Engraving, Checkered Stock, *Modern* 525.00 725.00
- ☐ **AE Grade**, Various Gauges, Box Lock, Light Engraving, Checkered Stock, Automatic Ejector, *Modern* 675.00 950.00
- ☐ **BE Grade**, Various Gauges, Box Lock, Engraved, Checkered Stock, Automatic Ejector, *Modern* 850.00 1,200.00
- ☐ **CE Grade**, Various Gauges, Box Lock, Engraved, Fancy Checkering, Automatic Ejector, *Modern* 1,000.00 1,650.00
- ☐ **DE Grade**, Various Gauges, Box Lock, Fancy Engraving, Fancy Checkering, Fancy Wood, Automatic Ejector, *Modern* 3,750.00 5,500.00
- ☐ **FE Grade**, Various Gauges, Box Lock, Fancy Engraving, Fancy Checkering, Fancy Wood, Automatic Ejector, *Modern* 6,250.00 9,250.00
- ☐ **GE Grade**, Various Gauges, Box Lock, Fancy Engraving, Fancy Checkering, Fancy Wood, Automatic Ejector, *Modern* 9,750.00 15,750.00
- ☐ **HE Grade**, 12 and 20 Gauge, Box Lock, Light Engraving, Checkered Stock, Automatic Ejector, *Modern* 650.00 925.00
- ☐ **Skeeter Grade**, 12 and 20 Gauge, Box Lock, Skeet Grade, Beavertail Forend, Vent Rib, Automatic Ejector, *Modern* 925.00 1,400.00
- ☐ **SP Grade**, Various Gauges, Box Lock, Checkered Stock, *Modern* 350.00 500.00
- ☐ **SP Grade**, Various Gauges, Box Lock, Checkered Stock, Automatic Ejector, *Modern* 375.00 550.00
- ☐ **SP Grade**, Various Gauges, Box Lock, Skeet Grade, Checkered Stock, *Modern* 375.00 550.00
- ☐ **SP Grade**, Various Gauges, Box Lock, Skeet Grade, Automatic Ejector, Checkered Stock, *Modern* 450.00 625.00
- ☐ **Sterlingworth**, Various Gauges, Box Lock, Checkered Stock, Hammerless, *Modern* 325.00 475.00
- ☐ **Sterlingworth**, Various Gauges, Box Lock, Checkered Stock, Hammerless, Automatic Ejector, *Modern* 450.00 625.00
- ☐ **Sterlingworth**, Various Gauges, Box Lock, Skeet Grade, Checkered Stock, *Modern* 400.00 550.00
- ☐ **Sterlingworth**, Various Gauges, Box Lock, Skeet Grade, Checkered Stock, Automatic Ejector, *Modern* 525.00 775.00
- ☐ **Sterlingworth Deluxe**, Various Gauges, Box Lock, Checkered Stock, Hammerless, Recoil Pad, *Modern* 425.00 575.00
- ☐ **Sterlingworth Deluxe**, Various Gauges, Box Lock, Checkered Stock, Hammerless, Recoil Pad, Automatic Ejector, *Modern* 550.00 775.00
- ☐ **XE Grade**, Various Gauges, Box Lock, Fancy Engraving, Fancy Checkering, Fancy Wood, Automatic Ejector, *Modern* 1,975.00 2,750.00

SHOTGUN, SINGLESHOT
- ☐ **JE Grade**, 12 Gauge, Trap Grade, Vent Rib, Automatic Ejector, Engraved, Fancy Checkering, *Modern* 1,250.00 1,675.00
- ☐ **KE Grade**, 12 Gauge, Trap Grade, Vent Rib, Automatic Ejector, Engraved, Fancy Checkering, *Modern* 1,650.00 2,275.00
- ☐ **LE Grade**, 12 Gauge, Trap Grade, Vent Rib, Automatic Ejector, Fancy Engraving, Fancy Checkering, *Modern* 2,250.00 3,175.00
- ☐ **ME Grade**, 12 Gauge, Trap Grade, Vent Rib, Automatic Ejector, Fancy Engraving, Fancy Checkering, *Modern* 4,500.00 6,750.00

FRANCAIS
France, made by Manufacture D'Armes Automatiques Francaise.
HANDGUN, SEMI-AUTOMATIC
- ☐ **Prima**, .25 ACP, Clip Fed, *Modern* 85.00 140.00

FRANCHI
Brescia, Italy, now imported by F.I.E.

	V.G.	EXC.

RIFLE, SEMI-AUTOMATIC
- ☐ **Centennial**, .22 L.R.R.F., Checkered Stock, Tube Feed, Takedown, *Modern* 145.00 220.00
- ☐ **Centennial Deluxe**, .22 L.R.R.F., Checkered Stock, Tube Feed, Takedown, Light Engraving, *Modern* 220.00 325.00
- ☐ **Centennial Gallery**, .22 Short R.F., Checkered Stock, Tube Feed, Takedown, *Modern* 135.00 200.00

SHOTGUN, DOUBLE BARREL, OVER-UNDER
- ☐ **Alcione Super**, 12, Vent Rib, Single Selective Trigger, Automatic Ejector, Engraved, *Modern* 295.00 450.00
- ☐ **Alcione Super Deluxe**, 12, Vent Rib, Single Selective Trigger, Automatic Ejector, Engraved, *Modern* 445.00 625.00
- ☐ **Aristocrat**, 12 Ga., Field Grade, Automatic Ejectors, Single Selective Trigger, Vent Rib, *Modern* 375.00 575.00
- ☐ **Aristocrat**, 12 Ga., Imperial Grade, Automatic Ejectors, Single Selective Trigger, Vent Rib, *Modern* 1,250.00 1,750.00
- ☐ **Aristocrat**, 12 Ga., Monte Carlo Grade, Automatic Ejectors, Single Selective Trigger, Vent Rib, *Modern* 1,800.00 2,600.00
- ☐ **Barrage Skeet**, 12 Ga., Vent Rib, Single Selective Trigger, Automatic Ejector, Recoil Pad, *Modern* 640.00 900.00
- ☐ **Barrage Trap**, 12 Ga., Vent Rib, Single Selective Trigger, Automatic Ejector, Recoil Pad, *Modern* 635.00 900.00
- ☐ **Dragon Skeet**, 12 Ga., Vent Rib, Single Selective Trigger, Automatic Ejector, Recoil Pad, *Modern* 450.00 625.00
- ☐ **Dragon Trap**, 12 Ga., Vent Rib, Single Selective Trigger, Automatic Ejector, Recoil Pad, *Modern* 450.00 625.00
- ☐ **Falconet Buckskin**, 12 and 20 Ga., Vent Rib, Single Selective Trigger, Automatic Ejector, *Modern* 300.00 435.00
- ☐ **Falconet Ebony**, 12 and 20 Ga., Vent Rib, Single Selective Trigger, Automatic Ejector, *Modern* 285.00 415.00
- ☐ **Falconet Peregrine 400**, 12 and 20 Ga., Vent Rib, Single Selective Trigger, Automatic Ejector, *Modern* 300.00 415.00
- ☐ **Falconet Peregrine 451**, 12 and 20 Ga., Vent Rib, Single Selective Trigger, Automatic Ejector, *Modern* 340.00 450.00
- ☐ **Falconet Pigeon**, 12 Ga. Vent Rib, Single Selective Trigger, Automatic Ejector, Fancy Engraving, Fancy Checkering, *Modern* ... 950.00 1,350.00
- ☐ **Falconet Silver**, 12 Ga., Vent Rib, Single Selective Trigger, Automatic Ejector, *Modern* 325.00 465.00
- ☐ **Falconet Super**, 12 Ga., Vent Rib, Single Selective Trigger, Automatic Ejector, *Modern* 345.00 485.00
- ☐ **Falconet Super Deluxe**, 12 Ga., Vent Rib, Single Selective Trigger, Automatic Ejector, *Modern* 445.00 625.00
- ☐ **Model 255**, 12 Ga., Vent Rib, Single Selective Trigger, Automatic Ejector, *Modern* 275.00 410.00
- ☐ **Model 2003**, 12 Ga. Trap Grade, Vent Rib, Single Selective Trigger, Automatic Ejector, *Modern* 750.00 1,050.00
- ☐ **Model 2005/2**, 12 Ga., Trap Grade, Vent Rib, Single Selective Trigger, Automatic Ejector, Extra Shotgun Barrel, *Modern* 995.00 1,750.00
- ☐ **Model 2005/3**, 12 Ga., Trap Grade, Vent Rib, Single Selective Trigger, Automatic Ejector, Extra Shotgun Barrel, Custom Choke, *Modern* 1,550.00 2,150.00

SHOTGUN, DOUBLE BARREL, SIDE-BY-SIDE
- ☐ **Airone**, 12 Ga., Box Lock, Hammerless, Checkered Stock, Automatic Ejector, *Modern* 540.00 750.00
- ☐ **Astore**, 12 Ga., Box Lock, Hammerless, Checkered Stock, *Modern* 435.00 575.00

	V.G.	EXC.
☐ **Astore S**, 12 Ga., Box Lock, Hammerless, Checkered Stock, Light Engraving, *Modern*	900.00	1,350.00
☐ **Condor**, Various Gauges, Sidelock, Engraved, Checkered Stock, Automatic Ejector, *Modern*	2,350.00	3,200.00
☐ **Imperial**, Various Gauges, Sidelock, Engraved, Checkered Stock, Automatic Ejector, *Modern*	3,50.00	4,500.00
☐ **Imperial Monte Carlo #11**, Various Gauges, Sidelock, Fancy Engraving, Fancy Checkering, Automatic Ejector, *Modern*	7,300.00	9,500.00
☐ **Imperial Monte Carlo Extra**, Various Gauges, Sidelock, Fancy Engraving, Fancy Checkering, Automatic Ejector, *Modern*	8,700.00	11,500.00
☐ **Imperial Monte Carlo #5**, Various Gauges, Sidelock, Fancy Engraving, Fancy Checkering, Automatic Ejector, *Modern*	7,400.00	9,750.00
☐ **Imperial S**, Various Gauges, Sidelock, Engraved, Checkered Stock, Automatic Ejector, *Modern*	3,400.00	4,550.00

SHOTGUN, SEMI-AUTOMATIC

	V.G.	EXC.
☐ **Dynamic (Heavy)**, 12 Ga., Plain Barrel, *Modern*	165.00	240.00
☐ **Dynamic (Heavy)**, 12 Ga., Vent Rib, *Modern*	160.00	250.00
☐ **Dynamic (Heavy)**, 12 Ga., Skeet Grade, Vent Rib, Checkered Stock, *Modern*	185.00	270.00
☐ **Dynamic (Heavy)**, 12 Ga., Checkered Stock, Slug, Open Rear Sight, *Modern*	190.00	275.00
☐ **Eldorado**, 12 and 20 Ga., Vent Rib, Engraved, Fancy Checkering, Lightweight, *Modern*	285.00	375.00
☐ **Hunter**, 12 and 20 Ga., Vent Rib, Engraved, Checkered Stock, Lightweight, *Modern*	230.00	340.00
☐ **Model 500**, 12 Ga., Vent Rib, Checkered Stock, Engraved, *Modern*	245.00	325.00
☐ **Model 500**, 12 Ga., Vent Rib, Checkered Stock, *Modern*	190.00	245.00
☐ **Slug Gun**, 12 and 20 Ga., Open Rear Sight, Sling Swivels, *Modern*	190.00	275.00
☐ **Standard**, 12 and 20 Ga., Plain Barrel, Lightweight, Checkered Stock, *Modern*	185.00	260.00
☐ **Standard**, 12 and 20 Ga., Solid Rib, Lightweight, Checkered Stock, *Modern*	180.00	250.00
☐ **Standard**, 12 and 20 Ga., Vent Rib, Lightweight, Checkered Stock, *Modern*	190.00	275.00
☐ **Standard Magnum**, 12 and 20 Gauges, Vent Rib, Lightweight, Checkered Stock, *Modern*	225.00	310.00
☐ **Superange (Heavy)**, 12 and 20 Gauges, Magnum, Plain Barrel, Checkered Stock, *Modern*	175.00	250.00
☐ **Superange (Heavy)**, 12 and 20 Gauges, Magnum, Vent Rib, Checkered Stock, *Modern*	190.00	285.00
☐ **Wildfowler (Heavy)**, 12 and 20 Gauges, Magnum, Vent Rib, Checkered Stock, Engraved, *Modern*	250.00	340.00

SHOTGUN, SINGLESHOT

	V.G.	EXC.
☐ **Model 2004**, 12 Ga., Trap Grade, Vent Rib, Automatic Ejector, *Modern*	765.00	1,075.00
☐ **Model 3000/2**, 12 Ga., Trap Grade, Vent Rib, Automatic Ejector, with Choke Tubes, *Modern*	1,300.00	2,000.00

FRANCI, PIERO INZI
Brescia, Italy, c. 1640.

HANDGUN, WHEEL-LOCK

	V.G.	EXC.
☐ **Octagon-Barrel**, Dagger Handle Butt, *Antique*	2,500.00	3,650.00

FRANCOTTE, AUGUST
Liege, Belgium 1844 to date, also London, England 1877-1893.

176 / FRANCOTTE, AUGUST

Francotte .25 ACP pistol

Francotte Bulldog Revolver

	V.G.	EXC.
HANDGUN, REVOLVER		
☐ **Military Style, Various Calibers, Double Action,** *Antique*	80.00	135.00
☐ **Bulldog,** Various Calibers, Double Action, Solid Frame, *Curio*	75.00	125.00
HANDGUN, SEMI-AUTOMATIC		
☐ **Vest Pocket,** .25 ACP, Clip Fed, *Curio*	195.00	295.00
HANDGUN, SINGLESHOT		
☐ **Target Pistol,** .22 L.R.R.F., Toggle Breech, *Modern*	225.00	350.00
RIFLE, DOUBLE BARREL, SIDE-BY-SIDE		
☐ **Luxury Double,** .458 Win., Sidelock, Hammerless, Double Triggers, Fancy Engraving, *Modern*	9,950.00	15,000.00
SHOTGUN, DOUBLE BARREL, SIDE-BY-SIDE		
☐ **A & F #14,** Various Gauges, Box Lock, Automatic Ejector, Checkered Stock, Engraved, Hammerless, *Modern*	2,250.00	2,950.00
☐ **A & F #20,** Various Gauges, Box Lock, Automatic Ejector, Checkered Stock, Engraved, Hammerless, *Modern*	2,700.00	3,450.00
☐ **A & F #25,** Various Gauges, Box Lock, Automatic Ejector, Checkered Stock, Engraved, Hammerless, *Modern*	3,200.00	4,000.00
☐ **A & F #30,** Various Gauges, Box Lock, Automatic Ejector, Checkered Stock, Fancy Engraving, Hammerless, *Modern*	3,600.00	4,450.00
☐ **A & F #45,** Various Gauges, Box Lock, Automatic Ejector, Checkered Stock, Fancy Engraving, Hammerless, *Modern*	4,250.00	5,250.00
☐ **A & F Jubilee,** Various Gauges, Box Lock, Automatic Ejector, Checkered Stock, Light Engraving, Hammerless, *Modern*	2,150.00	3,000.00
☐ **A & F Knockabout,** Various Gauges, Box Lock, Automatic Ejector, Checkered Stock, Hammerless, *Modern*	1,450.00	2,250.00
☐ **Francotte Original,** Various Gauges, Box Lock, Automatic Ejector, Checkered Stock, Hammerless, Engraved, *Modern*	2,150.00	2,900.00
☐ **Francotte Special,** Various Gauges, Box Lock, Automatic Ejector, Checkered Stock, Hammerless, Light Engraving, *Modern*	1,600.00	2,400.00
☐ **Model 10/18E/628,** Various Gauges, Box Lock, Automatic Ejector, Checkered Stock, Hammerless, Light Engraving, *Modern*	2,950.00	3,750.00
☐ **Model 10594,** Various Gauges, Box Lock, Automatic Ejector, Checkered Stock, Hammerless, Engraved, *Modern*	2,300.00	3,100.00
☐ **Model 11/18E,** Various Gauges, Box Lock, Automatic Ejector, Checkered Stock, Hammerless, Engraved, *Modern*	2,300.00	3,100.00
☐ **Model 120.HE/328,** Various Gauges, Sidelock, Automatic Ejector, Checkered Stock, Hammerless, Fancy Engraving, *Modern*	6,750.00	8,500.00
☐ **Model 4996,** Various Gauges, Box Lock, Automatic Ejector, Checkered Stock, Hammerless, Light Engraving, *Modern*	1,650.00	2,450.00
☐ **Model 6886,** Various Gauges, Box Lock, Automatic Ejector, Checkered Stock, Hammerless, *Modern*	1,450.00	2,300.00

	V.G.	EXC.
☐ **Model 6930**, Various Gauges, Box Lock, Automatic Ejector, Checkered Stock, Hammerless, Light Engraving, *Modern*	1,600.00	2,400.00
☐ **Model 6982**, Various Gauges, Box Lock, Automatic Ejector, Checkered Stock, Hammerless, Engraved, *Modern*	2,500.00	3,300.00
☐ **Model 8455**, Various Gauges, Box Lock, Automatic Ejector, Checkered Stock, Hammerless, *Modern*	2,600.00	3,450.00
☐ **Model 8457**, Various Gauges, Box Lock, Automatic Ejector, Checkered Stock, Hammerless, Engraved, *Modern*	2,350.00	3,000.00
☐ **Model 9/40.SE**, Various Gauges, Box Lock, Automatic Ejector, Checkered Stock, Hammerless, Fancy Engraving, *Modern*	6,750.00	9,500.00
☐ **Model 9/40E/38321**, Various Gauges, Box Lock, Automatic Ejector, Checkered Stock, Hammerless, Engraved, *Modern*	3,000.00	3,900.00
☐ **Model SOB.E/11082**, Various Gauges, Box Lock, Automatic Ejector, Checkered Stock, Hammerless, Engraved, *Modern*	4,450.00	5,850.00

FRANKLIN, C.W.
Belgium, c. 1900.

SHOTGUN, DOUBLE BARREL, SIDE-BY-SIDE
☐ **Various Gauges**, Outside Hammers, Damascus Barrel, *Modern*	100.00	175.00
☐ **Various Gauges**, Hammerless, Steel Barrel, *Modern*	135.00	200.00
☐ **Various Gauges**, Hammerless, Damascus Barrel, *Modern*	100.00	175.00
☐ **Various Gauges**, Outside Hammers, Steel Barrel, *Modern*	125.00	190.00

SHOTGUN, SINGLESHOT
☐ **Various Gauges**, Hammer, Steel Barrel, *Modern*	55.00	85.00

FRANKONIA
Franconia Jagd, arms dealers and manufacturers in West Germany.

RIFLE, SINGLESHOT
☐ **Heeren Rifle**, Various Calibers, Fancy Engraving, Fancy wood, Octagon Barrel, *Modern*	1,550.00	2,400.00
☐ **Heeren Rifle**, Various Calibers, Fancy Engraving, Fancy wood, Round Barrel, *Modern*	1,150.00	1,850.00

RIFLE, BOLT ACTION
☐ **Favorit**, Various Calibers, Set Triggers, Checkered Stock, *Modern*	160.00	250.00
☐ **Favorit Deluxe**, Various Calibers, Set Triggers, Checkered Stock, *Modern*	195.00	270.00
☐ **Favorit Leichtmodell**, Various Calibers, Lightweight, Set Triggers, Checkered Stock, *Modern*	245.00	370.00
☐ **Safari**, Various Calibers, Target Trigger, Checkered Stock, *Modern*	260.00	385.00
☐ **Stutzen**, Various Calibers, Carbine, Set Triggers, Full Stock, *Modern*	195.00	265.00

FRASER, D. & J.
Edinburgh, Scotland 1870-1900.

RIFLE, DOUBLE BARREL, SIDE-BY-SIDE
☐ **.360 N.E. #2**, Automatic Ejector, Express Sights, Engraved, Extra Set of Barrels, Cased with Accessories, *Modern*	6,250.00	8,300.00

FRAZIER, CLARK K.
Rawson, Ohio.

RIFLE, PERCUSSION
		V.G.	EXC.
☐ **Matchmate Offhand**, Various Calibers, Under-Hammer, Thumbhole Stock, Heavy Barrel, Reproduction, *Antique*		400.00	625.00

FRAZIER, JAY
Tyler, Wash., c. 1974.

RIFLE, SINGLESHOT
- ☐ **Creedmore Rifle**, Various Calibers, Single Set Trigger, Vernier Sights, Skeleton Buttplate, Pistol Grip Stock, *Modern* 550.00   750.00
- ☐ **Schuetzen Rifle**, Various Calibers, Single Set Trigger, Vernier Sights, Helm Buttplate, Palm Rest, False Muzzle, *Modern* 550.00   750.00

FREEDOM ARMS
Freedom, Wyo.

HANDGUN, REVOLVER
- ☐ **FA-S**, .22 L.R.R.F., Stainless Steel, Matt Finish, Spur Trigger, 1" Barrel, Single Action, *Modern* 55.00   80.00
- ☐ **FA-L**, .22 L.R.R.F., Stainless Steel, Matt Finish, Spur Trigger, 1¾" Barrel, Single Action, *Modern* 60.00   85.00
- ☐ **FA-S**, .22 W.M.R., Stainless Steel, Matt Finish, Spur Trigger, 1" Barrel, Single Action, *Modern* 65.00   95.00
- ☐ **FA-L**, .22 W.M.R., Stainless Steel, Matt Finish, Spur Trigger, 1¾" Barrel, Single Action, *Modern* 70.00   100.00
- ☐ **FA-BG**, .22 W.M.R., Stainless Steel, Spur Trigger, 3" Barrel, Single Action, *Modern* 70.00   110.00
- ☐ **For High Gloss Finish** *Add* $5.00-$10.00

FRENCH MILITARY

AUTOMATIC WEAPON, LIGHT MACHINE GUN
- ☐ **CSRG 1915 Chauchat**, 8 x 50R Lebel, Clip Fed, Bipod, *Class 3* 650.00   900.00

AUTOMATIC WEAPON, SUBMACHINE GUN
- ☐ **MAS 38**, 7.65 MAS, Clip Fed, Wood Stock, Dewat, *Class 3* 475.00   725.00
- ☐ **MAS 38**, 7.65 MAS, Clip Fed, Wood Stock, *Class 3* 900.00   1,350.00

HANDGUN, FLINTLOCK
- ☐ **.69 Charleville 1810**, Cavalry Pistol, Brass Furniture, Plain, *Antique* 525.00   800.00
- ☐ **.69 Charleville 1777**, Cavalry Pistol, Brass Frame, Belt Hook, *Antique* 625.00   950.00
- ☐ **.69**, Model 1763, Belt Pistol, Military, *Antique* 925.00   1,475.00

HANDGUN, PERCUSSION
- ☐ **.69 AN XIII**, Officer's Pistol, Made in France, *Antique* 275.00   450.00
- ☐ **.69 AN XIII**, Officer's Pistol, Made in Occupied Country, *Antique*... 375.00   550.00
- ☐ **.69 Charleville 1810 Cavalry Pistol**, Brass Furniture, Converted from Flintlock, Plain, *Antique* 350.00   475.00

HANDGUN, REVOLVER
- ☐ **Model 1873**, 11mm French Ordnance, Double Action, Solid Frame, *Antique* 140.00   225.00
- ☐ **Model 1892**, 8mm Lebel Revolver, Double Action, Solid Frame, *Curio* 100.00   175.00
- ☐ **Model 1915**, 8mm Lebel Revolver, Double Action, Solid Frame, Spanish Contract, *Curio* 90.00   160.00

FRENCH MILITARY / 179

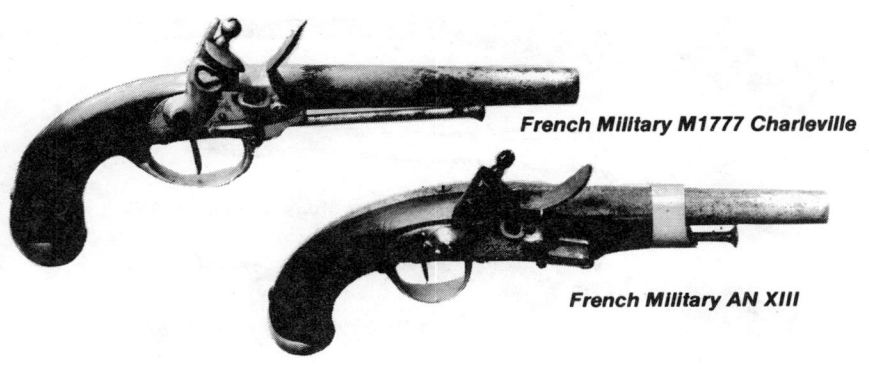

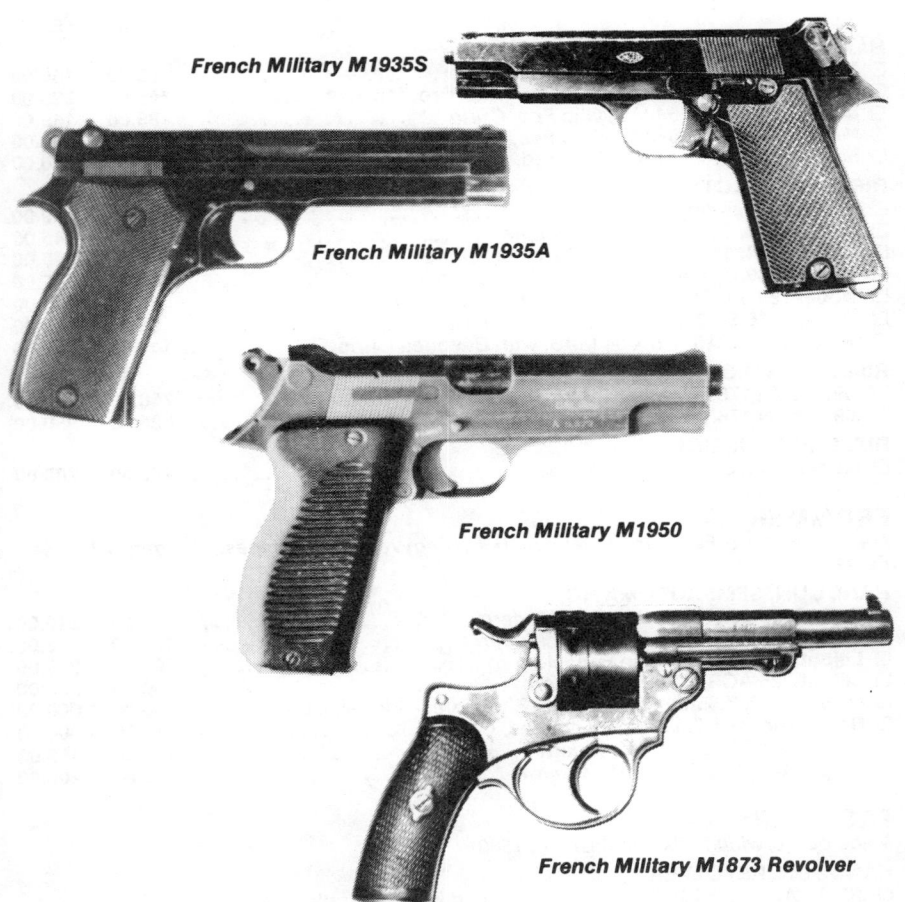

French Military M1777 Charleville

French Military AN XIII

French Military M1935S

French Military M1935A

French Military M1950

French Military M1873 Revolver

180 / FROMMER

French Military Daudetau Rifle

French Military Model 1936 MAS Rifle

French Military Model 1916 Carbine

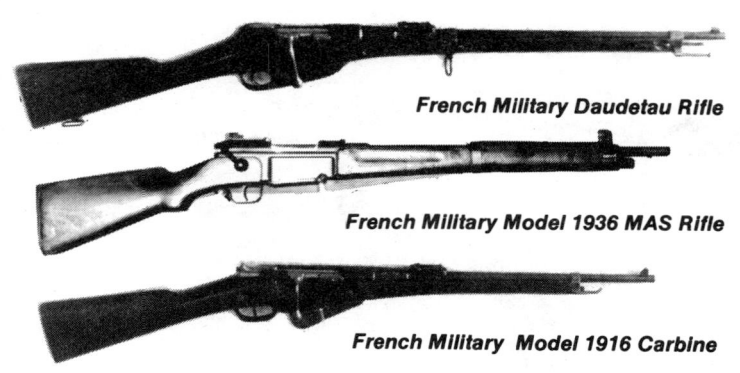

	V.G.	EXC.
HANDGUN, SEMI-AUTOMATIC		
☐ **Model 1935-A**, 7.65 MAS, Clip Fed, *Curio*	85.00	165.00
☐ **Model 1935-A**, 7.65 MAS, Clip Fed, Nazi Proofed, *Curio*	145.00	225.00
☐ **Model 1935-S**, 7.65 MAS, Clip Fed, *Curio*	85.00	155.00
☐ **Model 1935-S**, 7.65 MAS, Clip Fed, Nazi Proofed, *Curio*	135.00	200.00
☐ **Model 1950**, 9mm Luger, Clip Fed, *Modern*	300.00	450.00
RIFLE, BOLT ACTION		
☐ **6.5 x 53.5 Daudetau**, Carbine, *Curio*	135.00	200.00
☐ **Model 1874**, 11 x 59R Gras, *Antique*	90.00	145.00
☐ **Model 1874**, 11 x 59R Gras, Carbine, *Antique*	115.00	170.00
☐ **Model 1886/93 Lebel**, 8 x 50R Lebel, *Curio*	80.00	135.00
☐ **Model 1907/15 Remington**, 8 x 50R Lebel, *Curio*	85.00	145.00
☐ **Model 1916 St. Etienne**, 8 x 50R Lebel, Carbine, *Curio*	95.00	155.00
☐ **Model 1936 MAS**, 7.5 x 54 MAS, with Bayonet, *Curio*	140.00	195.00
RIFLE, FLINTLOCK		
☐ **.69**, Model 1763 Charleville 1st. Type, Musket, *Antique*	750.00	1,250.00
☐ **.69**, Model 1763/66 Charleville, Musket, *Antique*	625.00	950.00
RIFLE, PERCUSSION		
☐ **Model 1840**, Short Rifle, *Antique*	450.00	700.00

FROMMER

Made by Femaru-Fegyver-Es Gepgyar R.T., (Fegyvergyar) Budapest, Hungary. Also see Femaru.

HANDGUN, SEMI-AUTOMATIC		
☐ **Baby Stop**, .32 ACP, Clip Fed, *Modern*	145.00	210.00
☐ **Baby Stop**, .380 ACP, Clip Fed, *Modern*	175.00	265.00
☐ **Liliput**, .22 L.R.R.F., Clip Fed, *Modern*	265.00	395.00
☐ **Liliput**, .25 ACP, Clip Fed, *Modern*	180.00	260.00
☐ **Model 1910**, 7.65mm K, Clip Fed, Blue, Police Model, *Curio*	950.00	1,600.00
☐ **Roth-Frommer**, 7.65mm K, Clip Fed, *Curio*	750.00	1,300.00
☐ **Stop**, .32 ACP, Clip Fed, *Modern*	120.00	165.00
☐ **Stop**, .380 ACP, Clip, Fed, *Modern*	135.00	200.00

FRONTIER

Made by Norwich Falls Pistol Co., c. 1880.

HANDGUN, REVOLVER		
☐ **.32 Short R.F.**, 5 Shot, Spur Trigger, Solid Frame, Single Action, *Antique*	95.00	170.00

Frommer Roth Frommer

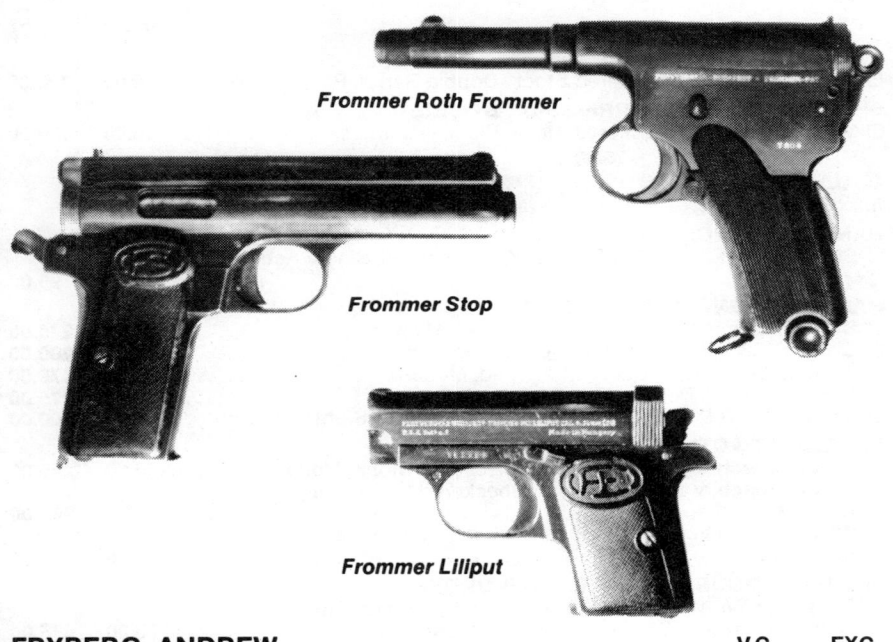

Frommer Stop

Frommer Liliput

FRYBERG, ANDREW
Hopkintown, Mass., c. 1905.

HANDGUN, REVOLVER

	V.G.	EXC.
☐ **.32 S & W**, 5 Shot, Top Break, Hammerless, Double Action, *Modern*	55.00	95.00
☐ **.32 S & W**, 5 Shot, Top Break, Double Action, *Modern*	45.00	95.00
☐ **.38 S & W**, 5 Shot, Top Break, Double Action, Hammerless, *Modern*	55.00	95.00
☐ **.38 S & W**, 5 Shot, Top Break, Double Action, *Modern*	45.00	95.00

FTL
Covina, Calif.

HANDGUN, SEMI-AUTOMATIC

☐ **.22 L.R.R.F.**, Clip Fed, Chrome Plated, *Modern*	80.00	130.00

GALAND, CHARLES FRANCOIS
From 1865 until about 1910 with plants in London, England, Paris, France, and Liege, Belgium.

HANDGUN, REVOLVER

☐ **Galand**, Various Calibers, Double Action, Underlever Extraction, *Curio*	160.00	275.00
☐ **Galand-Perrin**, Various Calibers, Double Action, Underlever Extraction, *Curio*	150.00	270.00
☐ **Galand & Sommerville**, .38 C.F., Double Action, Underlever Extraction, *Curio*	160.00	275.00
☐ **Galand & Sommerville**, .450 C.F., Double Action, Underlever Extraction, *Curio*	175.00	300.00
☐ **Le Novo**, .25 ACP, Double Action, Folding Trigger, *Curio*	80.00	130.00

	V.G.	EXC.
SHOTGUN, PERCUSSION		
☐ **Various Gauges**, Checkered Stock, Double Barrel, Plain, *Antique*	125.00	200.00
SHOTGUN, DOUBLE BARREL, SIDE-BY-SIDE		
☐ **Various Gauges**, Checkered Stock, Plain, Hammers, *Curio*	90.00	150.00

GALEF
Importers in N.Y.C.

	V.G.	EXC.
HANDGUN, REVOLVER		
☐ **Stallion**, .22LR/.22 WMR Combo, Western Style, Single Action, *Modern*	65.00	95.00
HANDGUN, SEMI-AUTOMATIC		
☐ **Brigadier**, 9mm Luger, Beretta, Clip Fed, *Modern*	175.00	275.00
☐ **Cougar**, .380 ACP, Beretta, Clip Fed, *Modern*	125.00	200.00
☐ **Jaguar**, .22 L.R.R.F., Beretta, Clip Fed, *Modern*	95.00	175.00
☐ **Puma**, .32 ACP, Beretta, Clip Fed, *Modern*	95.00	175.00
☐ **Sable**, .22 L.R.R.F., Beretta, Clip Fed, Adjustable Sights, *Modern*	135.00	200.00
RIFLE, BOLT ACTION		
☐ **BSA Monarch**, Various Calibers, Checkered Stock, *Modern*	155.00	245.00
☐ **BSA Monarch**, Various Calibers, Checkered Stock, Magnum Action, *Modern*	175.00	265.00
☐ **BSA Monarch Varmint**, Various Calibers, Checkered Stock, Heavy Barrel, *Modern*	190.00	275.00
SHOTGUN, DOUBLE BARREL, OVER-UNDER		
☐ **Golden Snipe**, 12 Ga., Trap Grade, Single Trigger, Automatic Ejector, Engraved, Checkered Stock, *Modern*	365.00	475.00
☐ **Golden Snipe**, 12 and 20 Gauges, Beretta, Single Trigger, Automatic Ejector, Engraved, Fancy Checkering, *Modern*	295.00	390.00
☐ **Golden Snipe**, 12 and 20 Gauges, Beretta, Single Selective Trigger, Automatic Ejector, Engraved, Fancy Checkering, *Modern*	350.00	465.00
☐ **Golden Snipe**, 12 and 20 Gauges, Skeet Grade, Single Trigger, Automatic Ejector, Engraved, Checkered Stock, *Modern*	355.00	475.00
☐ **Golden Snipe Deluxe**, 12 and 20 Gauges, Beretta, Single Selective Trigger, Automatic Ejector, Fancy Engraving, Fancy Checkering, *Modern*	375.00	500.00
☐ **Silver Snipe**, 12 Ga., Trap Grade, Single Trigger, Vent Rib, Engraved, Checkered Stock, *Modern*	300.00	400.00
☐ **Silver Snipe**, 12 and 20 Gauges, Skeet Grade, Single Trigger, Vent Rib, Engraved, Checkered Stock, *Modern*	300.00	400.00
☐ **Silver Snipe**, 12 and 20 Gauges, Beretta, Single Trigger, Checkered Stock, *Modern*	240.00	325.00
☐ **Silver Snipe**, 12 and 20 Gauges, Beretta, Single Selective Trigger, Checkered Stock, Light Engraving, *Modern*	275.00	365.00
☐ **Zoli Golden Snipe**, 12 and 20 Gauges, Vent Rib, Single Trigger, Adjustable Choke, Engraved, Checkered Stock, *Modern*	325.00	435.00
☐ **Zoli Silver Snipe**, 12 and 20 Gauges, Vent Rib, Single Trigger, Engraved, Checkered Stock, *Modern*	275.00	370.00
SHOTGUN, DOUBLE BARREL, SIDE-BY-SIDE		
☐ **M213CH**, 10 Ga. 3½", Double Trigger, Checkered Stock, Light Engraving, Recoil Pad, *Modern*	160.00	235.00
☐ **M213CH**, Various Gauges, Double Trigger, Checkered Stock, Light Engraving, Recoil Pad, *Modern*	125.00	165.00
☐ **Silver Hawk**, 10 Ga. 3½", Beretta, Double Trigger, Magnum, *Modern*	365.00	475.00
☐ **Silver Hawk**, 12 and 20 Gauges, Double Trigger, Engraved, Checkered Stock, *Modern*	275.00	365.00

	V.G.	EXC.
☐ **Silver Hawk**, 12 Ga. Mag. 3", Beretta, Double Trigger, Magnum, *Modern*	275.00	365.00
☐ **Silver Hawk**, 12 Ga. Mag. 3", Beretta, Single Trigger, Magnum, *Modern*	330.00	425.00
☐ **Silver Hawk**, Various Gauges, Beretta, Double Trigger, Lightweight, *Modern*	225.00	315.00
☐ **Silver Hawk**, Various Gauges, Beretta, Double Trigger, Lightweight, *Modern*	275.00	375.00
☐ **Zabala 213**, 10 Ga. 3½", Double Trigger, *Modern*	140.00	200.00
☐ **Zabala 213**, 12 and 20 Gauges, Double Trigger, *Modern*	115.00	160.00
☐ **Zabala 213**, 12 and 20 Gauges, Double Trigger, Vent Rib, *Modern*	120.00	170.00
☐ **Zabala Police**, 12 and 20 Gauges, Double Trigger, *Modern*	120.00	175.00

SHOTGUN, SEMI-AUTOMATIC

	V.G.	EXC.
☐ **Gold Lark**, 12 Ga., Beretta, Vent Rib, Light Engraving, Checkered Stock, *Modern*	145.00	225.00
☐ **Ruby Lark**, 12 Ga., Beretta, Vent Rib, Fancy Engraving, Fancy Checkering, *Modern*	235.00	350.00
☐ **Silver Gyrfalcon**, 12 Ga., Beretta, Checkered Stock, *Modern*	70.00	120.00
☐ **Silver Lark**, 12 Ga., Beretta, Checkered Stock, *Modern*	95.00	165.00

SHOTGUN, SINGLESHOT

	V.G.	EXC.
☐ **Companion**, Various Gauges, Folding Gun, Checkered Stock, *Modern*	35.00	55.00
☐ **Companion**, Various Gauges, Folding Gun, Checkered Stock, Vent Rib, *Modern*	45.00	65.00
☐ **Monte Carlo**, 12 Ga., Trap Grade, Vent Rib, Engraved, Checkered Stock, *Modern*	140.00	200.00

SHOTGUN, SLIDE ACTION

	V.G.	EXC.
☐ **Gold Pigeon**, 12 Ga., Beretta, Vent Rib, Fancy Engraving, Fancy Checkering, *Modern*	225.00	350.00
☐ **Ruby Pigeon**, 12 Ga., Beretta, Vent Rib, Fancy Engraving, Fancy Checkering, *Modern*	345.00	450.00
☐ **Silver Pigeon**, 12 Ga., Beretta, Light Engraving, Checkered Stock, *Modern*	95.00	135.00

GALESI
Industria Armi Galesi, Brescia, Italy since 1910.

HANDGUN, SEMI-AUTOMATIC

	V.G.	EXC.
☐ **Model 506**, .22 L.R.R.F., Clip Fed, *Modern*	70.00	120.00
☐ **Model 6**, .22 Long R.F., Clip Fed, *Modern*	65.00	95.00
☐ **Model 6**, .25 ACP, Clip Fed, *Modern*	60.00	90.00
☐ **Model 9**, .22 L.R.R.F., Clip Fed, *Modern*	75.00	125.00
☐ **Model 9**, .32 ACP, Clip Fed, *Modern*	80.00	135.00
☐ **Model 9**, .380 ACP, Clip Fed, *Modern*	85.00	150.00

GALLATIN, ALBERT
See Kentucky Rifles and Pistols

GALLUS
Retoloza Hermanos, Eibar, Spain, c. 1920.

HANDGUN, SEMI-AUTOMATIC

	V.G.	EXC.
☐ **.25 ACP**, Clip Fed, Blue, *Modern*	80.00	125.00

Galesi Revolver

Galesi Model 9 Pistol

GAMBA
V.G.   EXC.

Renato Gamba, Brescia, Italy.

RIFLE, SINGLESHOT
☐ **Mustang**, Various Calibers, Holland Type Sidelock Action, Set Triggers, Checkered Stock, Engraved, Zeiss Scope, *Modern* 4,000.00 6,250.00

RIFLE, DOUBLE BARREL, OVER-UNDER
☐ **Safari**, Various Calibers, Boxlock, Checkered Stock, Engraved, Double Triggers, *Modern* 3,500.00 5,750.00

SHOTGUN, DOUBLE BARREL, SIDE-BY-SIDE
☐ **London**, 12 or 20 Ga., Sidelock, Checkered Stock, Engraved, *Modern* 1,800.00 2.450.00
☐ **Oxford**, 12 or 20 Ga., Boxlock, Checkered Stock, Engraved, *Modern* 700.00 1,050.00

GANDER. PETER
Lancaster, Pa. 1779-1782, see Kentucky Rifles.

GARATE, ANITUA
Eibar, Spain, c. 1915.

HANDGUN, REVOLVER
☐ **Pistol O.P. #1 Mk.I**, .455 Webley, British Military, *Curio* 150.00 250.00

HANDGUN, SEMI-AUTOMATIC
☐ **.32 ACP**, Clip Fed, Long Grip, *Modern* 125.00 185.00

GARBI
Armas Garbi, Eibar, Spain.

☐ **Model 51**, Various Gauges, Boxlock, Checkered Stock, Engraved, *Modern* 260.00 375.00
☐ **Model 60**, Various Gauges, Sidelock, Checkered Stock, Engraved, *Modern* 400.00 550.00
☐ **Model 60**, Various Gauges, Sidelock, Checkered Stock, Engraved, Automatic Ejectors, *Modern* 575.00 750.00

GARRISON
Made by Hopkins & Allen, c. 1880-1890.

HANDGUN, REVOLVER
☐ **.22 Short R.F.**, 7 Shot, Spur Trigger, Solid Frame, Single Action, *Antique* 95.00 170.00

GARRUCHA
Made by Amadeo Rossi, Sao Leopoldo, Brazil.
HANDGUN, DOUBLE BARREL, SIDE-BY-SIDE
- ☐ **.22 L.R.R.F.**, Double Triggers, Outside Hammers, *Modern* 30.00 55.00

GASSER
Leopold Gasser, Vienna, Austria.
HANDGUŃ, REVOLVER
- ☐ **Montenegrin Gasser**, 11mm Montenegrin, Double Action, Break Top, Ring Extractor, *Antique* 185.00 275.00
- ☐ **Rast & Gasser**, 8mm R&G, Double Action, Solid Frame, *Curio* 135.00 220.00

GATLING ARMS & AMMUNITION CO.
Birmingham, England, c. 1890.
HANDGUN, REVOLVER
- ☐ **Dimancea**, .450 C.F., Hammerless, Twist Opening, Double Action, *Antique* 450.00 725.00

Gaulois Palm Pistol

Gavage .32 Pistol

GAULOIS
Tradename used by Mre. Francaise de Armes et Cycles de St. Etienne, France 1897-1910.
HANDGUN, MANUAL REPEATER
- ☐ **Palm Pistol**, 8mm, Engraved, *Curio* 300.00 475.00

GAUTEC, PETER
Lancaster, Pa. c. 1780 Kentucky Rifles & Pistols

GAVAGE
Fab. d'Armes de Guerre de Haute Precision Armand Gavage, Leige, Belgium, c. 1940.
HANDGUN, SEMI-AUTOMATIC
- ☐ **.32 ACP**, Clip Fed, Blue, *Modern* 160.00 265.00
- ☐ **.32 ACP**, Clip Fed, Blue, Nazi-Proofed, *Modern* 225.00 335.00

GECADO
Suhl, Germany, by G.C. Dornheim
HANDGUN, SEMI—AUTOMATIC
- ☐ **Model 11**, .25 ACP, Clip Fed, *Modern* 75.00 125.00

GECO
Tradename used by Gustav Genschow, Hamburg, Germany.

	V.G.	EXC.
HANDGUN, REVOLVER		
☐ **Velo Dog**, .25 ACP, Double Action, *Modern*	65.00	100.00
☐ **Bulldog**, .32 ACP, Double Action, *Modern*	70.00	110.00
SHOTGUN, DOUBLE BARREL, SIDE-BY-SIDE		
☐ **12 Gauge**, Checkered Stock, Double Triggers, Plain, *Modern*	90.00	145.00

GEM
Made by Bacon Arms Co., c. 1880.

	V.G.	EXC.
HANDGUN, REVOLVER		
☐ **.22 Short R.F.**, 7 Shot, Spur Trigger, Solid Frame, Single Action, *Antique*	135.00	200.00

GEM
Made by J. Stevens Arms & Tool, Chicopee Falls, Mass.

	V.G.	EXC.
HANDGUN, SINGLESHOT		
☐ **.22 or .30 R.F.**, Side-Swing Barrel, Spur Trigger, *Antique*	100.00	175.00

GERMAN MILITARY
Also See: Walther, Mauser, Luger.

	V.G.	EXC.
AUTOMATIC WEAPON, ASSAULT RIFLE		
☐ **FG 42 (Type 2)**, 8mm Mauser, Clip Fed, Wood Stock, *Class 3*	7,000.00	8,500.00
☐ **MP43**, 8mm Mauser, Clip Fed, *Class 3*	525.00	800.00
☐ **MP44**, 8mm Mauser, Clip Fed, *Class 3*	575.00	850.00
AUTOMATIC WEAPON, HEAVY MACHINE GUN		
☐ **MG-08 Sledge Mount**, 8mm Mauser, Belt Fed, *Class 3*	1,700.00	2,350.00
☐ **MG-08/15**, 8mm Mauser, Belt Fed, Bipod, *Class 3*	800.00	1,350.00
☐ **MG-42**, 8mm Mauser, Belt Fed, Bipod, *Class 3*	675.00	975.00
AUTOMATIC WEAPON, LIGHT MACHINE GUN		
☐ **MG-34**, 8mm Mauser, Belt Fed, High Quality, Bipod, *Class 3*	1,700.00	2,550.00
AUTOMATIC WEAPON, SUBMACHINE GUN		
☐ **EMP**, 9mm Luger, Clip Fed, *Class 3*	775.00	1,300.00
☐ **MP 18/1**, 9mm Luger, Drum Magazine, Bergmann, Wood Stock, Military, *Class 3*	1,350.00	2,200.00
☐ **MP 18/1**, 9mm Luger, Drum Magazine, Bergmann, Wood Stock, Military, Dewat, *Class 3*	375.00	525.00
☐ **MP 18/1 (Modified)**, 9mm Luger, Clip Fed, Bergmann, Wood Stock, Military, *Class 3*	875.00	1,500.00
☐ **MP 3008**, 9mm Luger, Clip Fed, Military, *Class 3*	1,650.00	2,400.00
☐ **MP 35/1**, 9mm Luger, Clip Fed, Bergmann, Wood Stock, Military, *Class 3*	975.00	1,675.00
☐ **MP 38**, 9mm Luger, Clip Fed, Schmeisser, Military, Folding Stock, *Class 3*	1,500.00	2,300.00
☐ **MP 38/40**, 9mm Luger, Clip Fed, Schmeisser, Military, Folding Stock, *Class 3*	1,500.00	2,450.00
☐ **MP 40**, 9mm Luger, Clip Fed, Schmeisser, Military, Folding Stock, *Class 3*	800.00	1,200.00
☐ **MP 40/1**, 9mm Luger, Clip Fed, Schmeisser, Military, Folding Stock, *Class 3*	700.00	1,100.00
HANDGUN, FLINTLOCK		
☐ **Model 1830**, .63, Military, *Antique*	375.00	550.00

GERMAN MILITARY / 187

German Military Model 1883 Revolver

German Military Model 1879 Revolver

German Military Model 1871 Rifle

German Military Model 1871/84 Rifle

	V.G.	EXC.
HANDGUN, PERCUSSION		
☐ **Model 1860**, .63, Military, *Antique*	235.00	350.00
HANDGUN, REVOLVER		
☐ **Model 1879 Troopers Model**, 11mm German Service, Solid Frame, Single Action, Safety, 7″ Barrel, 6 Shot, *Antique*	225.00	350.00
☐ **Model 1883 Officers' Model**, 11mm German Service, Solid Frame, Single Action, Safety, 5″ Barrel, 6 Shot, *Antique*	200.00	300.00
RIFLE, BOLT ACTION		
☐ **GEW 88 Commission**, 8 x 57 JRS, Clip Fed, *Antique*	45.00	75.00
☐ **GEW 98 (Average)**, 8mm Mauser, Military, *Curio*	100.00	185.00
☐ **GEW 98 Sniper**, 8mm Mauser, Scope Mounted, Military, *Curio*	650.00	950.00
☐ **K98K Sniper**, 8mm Mauser, Scope Mounted, Military, *Curio*	400.00	575.00
☐ **KAR 98 (Average)**, 8mm Mauser, Military, Carbine, *Curio*	100.00	190.00
☐ **KAR 98A (Average)**, 8mm Mauser, Military, Carbine, *Curio*	100.00	190.00
☐ **M-95**, 8mm Mauser, Steyr-Mannlicher, German Military, Nazi-Proofed, *Curio*	90.00	160.00
☐ **M-95**, 8mm Mauser, Steyr-Mannlicher, German Military, Carbine, Nazi-Proofed, *Curio*	85.00	150.00
☐ **Model 1871 Mauser**, .43 Mauser, Singleshot, Military, *Antique*	175.00	275.00
☐ **Model 1871 Mauser**, .43 Mauser, Carbine, Singleshot, Military, *Antique*	250.00	375.00
☐ **Model 71/84 Mauser**, .43 Mauser, Tube Feed, Military, *Antique*	190.00	295.00
☐ **Model 45 Mauser**, .22 L.R.R.F., Training Rifle, Military, *Curio*	175.00	225.00

188 / GESSCER, GEORG

	V.G.	EXC.
☐ **Model 1936 Falke KK**, .22 L.R.R.F., Training Rifle, Military, *Curio*	65.00	100.00
☐ **Model 29/40**, 8mm Mauser, Nazi-Proofed, Military, *Curio*	95.00	175.00
☐ **Model 33/40**, 8mm Mauser, Nazi-Proofed, Military, *Curio*	125.00	215.00
☐ **VK-98**, 8mm Mauser, Nazi-Proofed, Military, *Curio*	150.00	250.00
☐ **VZ-24 BRNO**, 8mm Mauser, Nazi-Proofed, Military, *Curio*	95.00	170.00
☐ **Needle Gun**, 11mm, Singleshot, Military, *Antique*	250.00	475.00

RIFLE, PERCUSSION
☐ **M1839**, .69, Musket, Brass Furniture, Military, *Antique*	240.00	375.00
☐ **M1842**, .75, Musket, Brass Furniture, Military, *Antique*	200.00	300.00

RIFLE, SEMI-AUTOMATIC
☐ **G43**, 8mm Mauser, Clip Fed, 10 Shot, Military, *Curio*	225.00	325.00
☐ **GEW 41**, 8mm Mauser, 10 Shot, Military, *Curio*	325.00	450.00
☐ **GEW 41 (W)**, 8mm Mauser, 10 Shot, Military, *Curio*	300.00	425.00
☐ **KAR 43 Sniper**, 8mm Mauser, Scope Mounted, Clip Fed, 10 Shot, Military, *Curio*	450.00	700.00
☐ **VG 2**, 8mm Mauser, Clip Fed, 10 Shot, Military, *Curio*	275.00	425.00

RIFLE, SINGLESHOT
☐ **Model 1869 Werder**, 11.5mm, Bavarian, *Antique*	400.00	650.00

GESSCER, GEORG
Saxony, 1591-1611.

HANDGUN, WHEEL—LOCK
☐ **Pair**, Military, Inlays, Pear Pommel, Medium Ornamentation, *Antique*	15,000.00	20,000.00

GEVARM
Gevelot, St. Etienne, France.

RIFLE, SEMI-AUTOMATIC
☐ **Model A3**, .22 L.R.R.F., Target Sights, Clip Fed, *Modern*	95.00	160.00
☐ **Model A6**, .22 L.R.R.F., Open Sights, Clip Fed, *Modern*	75.00	125.00
☐ **Model A7**, .22 L.R.R.F., Target Sights, Clip Fed, *Modern*	110.00	185.00
☐ **Model E1**, .22 L.R.R.F., Target Sights, Clip Fed, *Modern*	75.00	120.00

GIBRALTER
Possibly Meriden Firearms. Brand Name for Sears-Roebuck.

HANDGUN, REVOLVER
☐ **.32 S & W**, 5 Shot, Double Action, Top Break, *Modern*	45.00	95.00
☐ **.38 S & W**, 5 Shot, Double Action, Top Break, *Modern*	45.00	95.00

GIBRALTER
Made by Stevens Arms.

SHOTGUN, SINGLESHOT
☐ **Model 116**, Various Gauges, Hammer, Automatic Ejector, Raised Matted Rib, *Modern*	45.00	65.00

GILL, THOMAS
London, England 1770-1812.

HANDGUN, FLINTLOCK
☐ **.68**, Pocket Pistol, Octagon Barrel, Plain, High Quality, *Antique*	650.00	950.00

GLASER WAFFEN
Zurich, Switzerland.

HANDGUN, SINGLESHOT
☐ **Target Pistol**, .22 L.R.R.F., Toggle Breech, Francotte, *Modern*	225.00	350.00

Glaser Waffen .22 Pistol

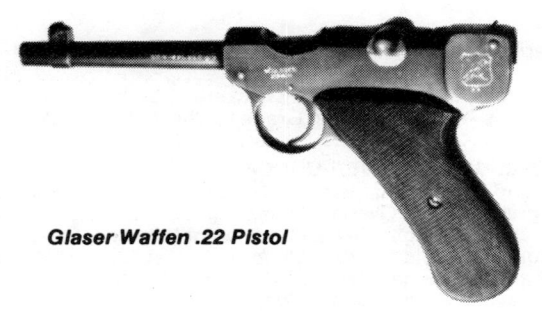

	V.G.	EXC.

RIFLE, BOLT ACTION
☐ **Custom Rifle**, Various Calibers, Fancy Wood, *Modern* 600.00 1,000.00
RIFLE, SINGLESHOT
☐ **Heeren Rifle**, Various Calibers, Engraved, Fancy Wood, *Modern* ... 1,500.00 2,400.00

GLASSBRENNER, DAVID
Lancaster, Pa., c. 1800. See Kentucky Rifles.

GLAZIER, JOHN
Belleville, Ind., c. 1820. See Kentucky Rifles.

GLENFIELD
See Marlin.

GLENN, ROBERT
Edinburgh, Scotland, c. 1860. Made Fine Copies of Highland Pistols.

HANDGUN, SNAPHAUNCE
☐ **Replica Highland**, All Brass, Engraved, Ovoid Pommel, *Antique* ... 1,800.00 2,850.00

GLISENTI
Soc. Siderugica Glisenti, Turin, Italy, c. 1889-1930.

HANDGUN, REVOLVER
☐ **MI889**, 10.4mm Glisenti, Double Action, Folding Trigger, Military, *Curio* 90.00 135.00
☐ **MI889**, 10.4mm Glisenti, Double Action, Trigger Guard, Military, *Curio* 85.00 130.00

HANDGUN, SEMI-AUTOMATIC
☐ **M1910 Army**, 9mm Glisenti, Clip Fed, Wood Grips, *Modern* 225.00 375.00
☐ **M1910 Navy**, 9mm Glisenti, Clip Fed, Plastic Stock, *Modern* 200.00 350.00
☐ **M906**, 7.63 Mauser, Clip Fed, Military, *Modern* 275.00 425.00

GOFF, DANIEL
London, England 1779-1810.

HANDGUN, FLINTLOCK
☐ **Duelling Pistols**, .50, Cased pair, with Accessories, *Antique* 1,450.00 2,350

GOLDEN EAGLE
Nikko Arms Co. Ltd., Japan

RIFLE, BOLT ACTION
☐ **Model 7000**, Various Calibers, Grade 1, Checkered Stock, *Modern* 240.00 375.00

190 / GONTER, PETER

	V.G.	EXC.
☐ **Model 7000**, Various African Calibers, Grade 1, Checkered Stock, *Modern*	275.00	400.00
☐ **Model 7000**, Various Calibers, Grade 2, Checkered Stock, *Modern*	275.00	400.00
☐ **Model 7000**, Various African Calibers, Grade 2, Checkered Stock, *Modern*	325.00	450.00

SHOTGUN, DOUBLE BARREL, OVER-UNDER

	V.G.	EXC.
☐ **Model 5000**, 12 and 20 Gauges, Field Grade, Vent Rib, Checkered Stock, Light Engraving, Gold Overlay, *Modern*	400.00	575.00
☐ **Model 5000**, 12 and 20 Gauges, Skeet Grade, Vent Rib, Checkered Stock, Light Engraving, Gold Overlay, *Modern*	475.00	675.00
☐ **Model 5000**, 12 and 20 Gauges, Trap Grade, Vent Rib, Checkered Stock, Light Engraving, Gold Overlay, *Modern*	425.00	675.00
☐ **Model 5000**, 12 and 20 Gauges, Field Grade 2, Vent Rib, Checkered Stock, Light Engraving, Gold Overlay, *Modern*	500.00	675.00
☐ **Model 5000**, 12 and 20 Gauges, Skeet Grade 2, Vent Rib, Checkered Stock, Light Engraving, Gold Overlay, *Modern*	575.00	750.00
☐ **Model 5000**, 12 and 20 Gauges, Trap Grade 2, Vent Rib, Checkered Stock, Light Engraving, Gold Overlay, *Modern*	550.00	700.00
☐ **Model 5000 Grandee**, 12 and 20 Gauges, Field Grade 3, Vent Rib, Checkered Stock, Fancy Engraving, Gold Overlay, *Modern*	1,650.00	2,500.00
☐ **Model 5000 Grandee**, 12 and 20 Gauges, Skeet Grade 3, Vent Rib, Checkered Stock, Fancy Engraving, Gold Overlay, *Modern*	1,850.00	2,750.00
☐ **Model 5000 Grandee**, 12 Ga., Trap Grade 3, Vent Rib, Checkered Stock, Fancy Engraving, Gold Overlay, *Modern*	1,850.00	2,750.00

GONTER, PETER
Lancaster, Pa. 1770-1778. See Kentucky Rifles.

GOLCHER, JAMES
Philadelphia, Pa. 1820-1833.

GOLCHER, JOHN
Easton, Pa., c. 1775.

GOLCHER, JOSEPH
Philadelphia, Pa., c. 1800.

GOOSE GUN
Made by Stevens Arms.

SHOTGUN, SINGLESHOT

	V.G.	EXC.
☐ **Model 89 Dreadnaught**, Various Gauges, Hammer, *Modern*	45.00	65.00

GOVERNOR
Made by Bacon Arms Co.

HANDGUN, REVOLVER

	V.G.	EXC.
☐ **.22 Short R.F.**, 7 Shot, Spur Trigger, Solid Frame, Single Action, *Antique*	90.00	160.00

GOVERNOR
Various Makers, c. 1880.

HANDGUN, REVOLVER

	V.G.	EXC.
☐ **.32 S & W**, 5 Shot, Double Action, Top Break, *Modern*	45.00	95.00
☐ **.38 S & W**, 5 Shot, Double Action, Top Break, *Modern*	45.00	95.00

GRAEFF, WM.
Reading, Pa. 1751-1784. Also See Kentucky Rifles.

	V.G.	EXC.

GRANT, W.L.
HANDGUN, REVOLVER
☐ **.22 Long R.F.**, 6 Shot, Single Action, Solid Frame, Spur Trigger,
  Antique 135.00   220.00
☐ **.32 Short R.F.**, 6 Shot, Single Action, Solid Frame, Spur Trigger,
  Antique 155.00   235.00

GRAVE, JOHN
Lancaster, Pa. 1769-1773. See Kentucky Rifles.

GREAT WESTERN
Venice, Calif. 1954-1962. Moved to North Hollywood, Calif. in 1959.
HANDGUN, REVOLVER
☐ **Frontier**, .22 L.R.R.F., Single Action, Western Style, *Modern*   30.00   50.00
☐ **Frontier**, Various Calibers, Single Action, Western Style, *Modern* 40.00   65.00
☐ **Deputy**, .22 L.R.R.F., Single Action, Western Style, *Modern*   30.00   50.00
☐ **Deputy**, .22 L.R.R.F., Single Action, Western Style, *Modern*   30.00   50.00
☐ **Buntline**, Various Calibers, Single Action, Western Style, *Modern* 45.00   70.00

HANDGUN, DOUBLE BARREL, OVER-UNDER
☐ **Double Derringer**, .38 Spec., Remington Copy, *Modern* 30.00   45.00

GREAT WESTERN GUN WORKS
Pittsburg, Pa. 1860 to about 1923.
HANDGUN, REVOLVER
☐ **.22 Short R.F.**, 7 Shot, Spur Trigger, Solid Frame, Single Action,
  Antique 90.00   160.00

RIFLE, PERCUSSION
☐ **No. 5**, Various Calibers, Various Barrel Lengths, Plains Rifle,
  Octagon Barrel, Brass Fittings, *Antique* 350.00 550.00

GREEK MILITARY
RIFLE, BOLT ACTION
☐ **M 1903 Mannlicher Schoenauer**, 6.5mm M.S., Military, *Curio* 80.00 125.00
☐ **M 1903 Mannlicher Schoenauer**, 8mm Mauser, Military, *Curio* 90.00 135.00
☐ **M 1930 Greek**, 8mm Mauser, Military, *Curio* 95.00 155.00

GREENER, W.W.
Established in 1829 in Northumberland, England as W. Greener, moved to Birmingham, England in 1844; name changed to W.W. Greener in 1860, and to W.W. Greener & Son in 1879.

SHOTGUN, DOUBLE BARREL, SIDE-BY-SIDE
☐ **Various Gauges**, Single Non-Selective Trigger *Add* **$185.00-$275.00**
☐ **Various Gauges**, Single Selective Trigger *Add* **$265.00-$385.00**
☐ **Crown DH-55**, Various Gauges, Box Lock, Automatic Ejector,
  Checkered Stock, Fancy Engraving, *Modern* 1,850.00 2,675.00
☐ **Empire**, 12 Ga. Mag. 3", Box Lock, Hammerless, Light Engraving,
  Checkered Stock, *Modern* 875.00 1,375.00
☐ **Empire**, 12 Ga. Mag. 3", Box Lock, Hammerless, Light Engraving,
  Checkered Stock, Automatic Ejector, *Modern* 995.00 1,775.00
☐ **Empire Deluxe**, 12 Ga. Mag. 3", Box Lock, Hammerless, Engraved,
  Checkered Stock, *Modern* 1,050.00 1,775.00

	V.G.	EXC.
☐ **Empire Deluxe**, 12 Ga. Mag. 3", Box Lock, Hammerless, Engraved, Checkered Stock, Automatic Ejector, *Modern*	1,200.00	1,975.00
☐ **Far-Killer F35**, 10 Ga. 3½", Box Lock, Hammerless, Engraved, Checkered Stock, *Modern*	1,150.00	1,900.00
☐ **Far-Killer F35**, 10 Ga. 3½", Box Lock, Hammerless, Engraved, Checkered Stock, Automatic Ejector, *Modern*	1,850.00	2,750.00
☐ **Far-Killer F35**, 12 Ga. Mag. 3", Box Lock, Hammerless, Engraved, Checkered Stock, *Modern*	1,600.00	2,275.00
☐ **Far-Killer F35**, 12 Ga. Mag. 3", Box Lock, Hammerless, Engraved, Checkered Stock, Automatic Ejector, *Modern*	1,875.00	2,775.00
☐ **Far-Killer F35**, 8 Ga., Box Lock, Hammerless, Engraved, Checkered Stock, *Modern*	1,400.00	2,275.00
☐ **Far-Killer F35**, 8 Ga., Box Lock, Hammerless, Engraved, Checkered Stock, Automatic Ejector, *Modern*	1,975.00	2,975.00
☐ **Jubilee DH-35**, Various Gauges, Box Lock, Automatic Ejector, Checkered Stock, Engraved, *Modern*	1,200.00	1,975.00
☐ **Royal DH-75**, Various Gauges, Box Lock, Automatic Ejector, Checkered Stock, Fancy Engraving, *Modern*	2,500.00	3,475.00
☐ **Sovereign DH-40**, Various Gauges, Box Lock, Automatic Ejector, Checkered Stock, Engraved, *Modern*	1,650.00	2,525.00

SHOTGUN, SINGLESHOT
☐ **G. P. Martini**, 12 Ga., Checkered Stock, Takedown, *Modern*	165.00	275.00

GREGORY
Mt. Vernon, Ohio 1837-1842. See Kentucky Rifles.

GREIFELT & CO.
Suhl, Germany from 1885.

COMBINATION WEAPON, DOUBLE BARREL, OVER-UNDER
☐ **Various Calibers**, Solid Rib, Engraved, Checkered Stock, *Modern*	2,900.00	3,950.00
☐ **Various Calibers**, Solid Rib, Engraved, Checkered Stock, Automatic Ejector, *Modern*	3,850.00	4,950.00

COMBINATION WEAPON, DRILLING
☐ **Various Calibers**, Fancy Wood, Fancy Checkering, Engraved, *Modern*	3,450.00	4,650.00
☐ **Various Calibers**, Engraved, Checkered Stock, *Modern*	2,550.00	3,600.00

RIFLE, BOLT ACTION
☐ **Sport**, .22 Hornet, Checkered Stock, Express Sights, *Modern*	500.00	775.00

SHOTGUN, DOUBLE BARREL, OVER-UNDER
☐ **Various Gauges**, Single Trigger *Add* **$245.00-$350.00**
☐ **Various Gauges**, For Vent Rib *Add* **$190.00-$300.00**

☐ **#1**, .410 Ga., Automatic Ejector, Fancy Engraving, Checkered Stock, Fancy Wood, Solid Rib, *Modern*	4,000.00	5,500.00
☐ **#1**, Various Gauges, Automatic Ejector, Fancy Engraving, Checkered Stock, Fancy Wood, Solid Rib, *Modern*	2,900.00	3,800.00
☐ **#3**, .410 Ga., Automatic Ejector, Engraved, Checkered Stock, Solid Rib, *Modern*	2,950.00	3,850.00
☐ **#3**, Various Gauges, Automatic Ejector, Engraved, Checkered Stock, Solid Rib, *Modern*	1,800.00	2,400.00
☐ **Model 143E**, Various Gauges, Automatic Ejector, Engraved, Checkered Stock, Solid Rib, Double Trigger, *Modern*	1,200.00	1,950.00
☐ **Model 143E**, Various Gauges, Automatic Ejector, Engraved, Checkered Stock, Vent Rib, Single Selective Trigger, *Modern*	1,600.00	2,250.00

	V.G.	EXC.

SHOTGUN, DOUBLE BARREL, SIDE-BY-SIDE
- ☐ **Model 103**, 12 and 16 Gauges, Box Lock, Double Trigger, Checkered Stock, Light Engraving, *Modern* 750.00 1,050.00
- ☐ **Model 103E**, 12 and 16 Gauges, Box Lock, Double Trigger, Checkered Stock, Light Engraving, Automatic Ejector, *Modern* 975.00 1,375.00
- ☐ **Model 22**, 12 and 16 Gauges, Box Lock, Double Trigger, Checkered Stock, Engraved, *Modern* 675.00 1,000.00
- ☐ **Model 22E**, 12 and 16 Gauges, Box Lock, Double Trigger, Checkered Stock, Engraved, Automatic Ejector, *Modern* 975.00 1,450.00

GRANT HAMMOND
New Haven, Conn. 1915-1917.

HANDGUN, SEMI-AUTOMATIC
- ☐ **U.S. Test**, .45 ACP, Clip Fed, Hammer, *Curio* 4,500.00 7,500.00

GREYHAWK ARMS CORP.
South El Monte, Calif., c. 1975.

RIFLE, SINGLESHOT
- ☐ **Model 74**, Various Calibers, Rolling Block, Octagon Barrel, Open Rear Sight, Reproduction, *Modern* 85.00 125.00

GRIFFEN & HOWE
N.Y.C. 1923, absorbed by Abercrombie & Fitch 1930.

RIFLE, BOLT ACTION
- ☐ **Mauser 98**, .30/06, Sporterized, Engraved, Fancy Wood, Fancy Checkering, *Modern* 975.00 1,750.00
- ☐ **Mauser 98**, .30/06, Sporterized, Fancy Engraving, Fancy Wood, Fancy Checkering, Gold Inlays, *Modern* 3,000.00 4,500.00
- ☐ **Springfield**, .30/06, Sporterized, Engraved, Fancy Wood, Fancy Checkering, *Modern* 975.00 1,750.00
- ☐ **Springfield**, .30/06, Sporterized, Fancy Engraving, Fancy Wood, Fancy Checkering, *Modern* 1,950.00 3,250.00
- ☐ **Winchester M70**, .30/06, Sporterized, Engraved, Fancy Wood, Fancy Checkering, *Modern* 1,200.00 1,950.00

GROOM, RICHARD
London, England, c. 1855.

HANDGUN, FLINTLOCK
- ☐ **.68**, East India Company, Calvary Pistol, Military, Tapered Round Barrel, Brass Furniture, *Antique* 975.00 1,800.00

GROSS ARMS CO.
Tiffin, Ohio 1862-1865.

HANDGUN, REVOLVER
- ☐ **.22 Short R.F.**, 7 Shot, Spur Trigger, Tip-Up, *Antique* 350.00 600.00
- ☐ **.25 Short R.F.**, 6 Shot, Single Action, Spur Trigger, Tip-Up, *Antique* 350.00 625.00
- ☐ **.32 Short R.F.**, 5 Shot, Spur Trigger, Tip-Up, *Antique* 350.00 600.00

GRUENEL
Gruenig & Elmiger, Malters, Switzerland.

RIFLE, BOLT ACTION
- ☐ **Model K 31**, .308 Win., U.I.T. Target Rifle, Target Sights, Ventilated Forestock, *Modern* 525.00 850.00

194 / GUARDIAN

	V.G.	EXC.
☐ **Match 300m**, Various Calibers, Offhand Target Rifle, Target Sights, Ventilated Forestock, Palm Rest, Hook Buttplate, *Modern*	675.00	1,075.00
☐ **U.I.T. Standard**, .308 Win., Target Rifle, Target Sights, Ventilated Forestock, *Modern*	475.00	725.00

GUARDIAN
Made by Bacon Arms Co., c. 1880.
HANDGUN, REVOLVER
☐ **.22 Short R.F.**, 7 Shot, Spur Trigger, Solid Frame, Single Action, Antique 90.00 160.00
☐ **.32 Short R.F.**, 5 Shot, Spur Trigger, Solid Frame, Single Action, Antique 95.00 170.00

GUMPH, CHRISTOPHER
Lancaster, Pa. 1779-1803. See Kentucky Rifles and Pistols.

GUSTAF, CARL
See Husqvarna.

Gustloff Werke .32 Pistol

GUSTLOFF WERKE
Suhl, Germany
HANDGUN, SEMI-AUTOMATIC
☐ **.32 ACP**, Clip Fed, Hammer, Single Action, *Modern* 1,150.00 2,000.00
☐ **.380 ACP**, Clip Fed, Hammer, Single Action, *Modern* 2,000.00 3,500.00
RIFLE, BOLT ACTION
☐ **Mauser M98**, 8mm Mauser, Military, *Curio* 95.00 150.00
☐ **Model KKW**, .22 L.R.R.F., Pre-WW2, Singleshot, Tangent Sights, Military Style Stock, *Modern* 300.00 425.00
SHOTGUN, DOUBLE BARREL, SIDE-BY-SIDE
☐ **16 Ga.**, Engraved, Color Case Hardened Frame, *Modern* 375.00 500.00

GYROJET
See M.B. Associates.

HACKETT, EDWIN AND GEORGE
London, England, c. 1870.
SHOTGUN, DOUBLE BARREL, SIDE-BY-SIDE
☐ **10 Ga. 2⅞"**, Damascus Barrel, Plain, *Antique* 125.00 190.00

HADDEN, JAMES
Philadelphia, Pa., c. 1769. See Kentucky Rifles and Pistols.

HAEFFER, JOHN
Lancaster, Pa., c. 1800. See Kentucky Rifles and Pistols.

HAENEL, C.G.
C.G. Haenel Waffen und Fahrradfabrik, Suhl, Germany 1840-1945

HANDGUN, SEMI-AUTOMATIC
	V.G.	EXC.
☐ **Schmiesser Model 1**, .25 ACP, Clip Fed, *Modern*	145.00	225.00
☐ **Schmiesser Model 2**, .25 ACP, Clip Fed, *Modern*	165.00	275.00

RIFLE, BOLT ACTION
☐ **Model 88**, Various Calibers, Sporting Rifle, Half-Octagon Barrel, Open Rear Sight, *Modern* 200.00 335.00
☐ **Model 88 Sporter**, Various Calibers, 5 Shot Clip, Half-Octagon Barrel, Open Rear Sight, *Modern* 225.00 375.00

Haenel Schmeisser Model 1

Hafdasa .22

HAFDASA
Hispano Argentina Fab. de Automoviles, Buenos Aires, Argentina, c. 1935.

HANDGUN, SINGLESHOT
☐ **.22 L.R.R.F.**, Blowback, *Modern* 225.00 325.00

HALF-BREED
Made by Hopkins & Allen, c. 1880.

HANDGUN, REVOLVER
☐ **.32 Short R.F.**, 5 Shot, Spur Trigger, Solid Frame, Single Action, *Antique* 90.00 170.00

HAMMERLI
Lenzburg, Switzerland

	V.G.	EXC.
HANDGUN, REVOLVER		
☐ **Virginian**, .357 Magnum, Single Action, Western Style, *Modern*	145.00	200.00
☐ **Virginian**, .45 Colt, Single Action, Western Style, *Modern*	145.00	225.00
HANDGUN, SEMI-AUTOMATIC		
☐ **Model 200 Walther Olympia**, .22 L.R.R.F., Target Pistol, *Modern*	350.00	500.00
☐ **Model 200 Walther Olympia**, .22 L.R.R.F., Target Pistol, Muzzle Brake, *Modern*	400.00	550.00
☐ **Model 201 Walther Olympia**, .22 L.R.R.F., Target Pistol, Adjustable Grips, *Modern*	350.00	500.00
☐ **Model 202 Walther Olympia**, .22 L.R.R.F., Target Pistol, Adjustable Grips, *Modern*	400.00	550.00
☐ **Model 203 Walther Olympia**, .22 L.R.R.F., Target Pistol, Adjustable Grips, *Modern*	450.00	600.00
☐ **Model 203 Walther Olympia**, .22 L.R.R.F., Target Pistol, Adjustable Grips, Muzzle Brake, *Modern*	475.00	675.00
☐ **Model 204 Walther Olympia**, .22 L.R.R.F., Target Pistol, *Modern*	475.00	675.00
☐ **Model 204 Walther Olympia**, .22 L.R.R.F., Target Pistol, Muzzle Brake, *Modern*	550.00	725.00
☐ **Model 205 Walther Olympia**, .22 L.R.R.F., Target Pistol, Fancy Wood, *Modern*	550.00	725.00
☐ **Model 205 Walther Olympia**, .22 L.R.R.F., Target Pistol, Fancy Wood, Muzzle Brake, *Modern*	600.00	785.00
☐ **Model 206**, .22 L.R.R.F., Target Pistol, *Modern*	400.00	575.00
☐ **Model 207**, .22 L.R.R.F., Target Pistol, Adjustable Grips, *Modern*	525.00	650.00
☐ **Model 208**, .22 L.R.R.F., Target Pistol, Clip Fed, Adjustable Grips, *Modern*	525.00	775.00
☐ **Model 208**, .22 L.R.R.F., Target Pistol, Clip Fed, Adjustable Grips, Left-Hand, *Modern*	550.00	785.00
☐ **Model 209**, .22 Short R.F., Target Pistol, 5 Shot Clip, Muzzle Brake, *Modern*	475.00	650.00
☐ **Model 210**, .22 L.R.R.F., Target Pistol, *Modern*	450.00	625.00
☐ **Model 210**, .22 L.R.R.F., Target Pistol, Adjustable Grips, *Modern*	475.00	650.00
☐ **Model 211**, .22 L.R.R.F., Target Pistol, Clip Fed, *Modern*	500.00	750.00
☐ **Model 212 SIG**, .22 L.R.R.F., Target Pistol, Clip Fed, *Modern*	600.00	790.00
☐ **Model 215**, .22 L.R.R.F., Target Pistol, Clip Fed, *Modern*	475.00	675.00
☐ **Model 230-1**, .22 Short R.F., Target Pistol, 5 Shot Clip, *Modern*	500.00	700.00
☐ **Model 230-2**, .22 Short R.F., Target Pistol, 5 Shot Clip, Adjustable Grips, *Modern*	550.00	770.00
☐ **Model 230-2**, .22 Short R.F., Target Pistol, 5 Shot Clip, Adjustable Grips, Left-Hand, *Modern*	575.00	785.00
☐ **Model P-240 SIG**, .22 L.R.R.F., Target Pistol, Clip Fed, Conversion Unit Only, *Modern*	375.00	525.00
☐ **Model P-240 SIG**, .32 S & W Long, Clip Fed, Target Pistol, Cased with Accessories, *Modern*	525.00	775.00
☐ **Model P-240 SIG**, .38 Special, Clip Fed, Target Pistol, Cased with Accessories, *Modern*	550.00	825.00
HANDGUN, SINGLESHOT		
☐ **Model 100**, .22 L.R.R.F., Target Pistol, *Modern*	450.00	575.00
☐ **Model 100 Deluxe**, .22 L.R.R.F., Target Pistol, *Modern*	475.00	650.00
☐ **Model 101**, .22 L.R.R.F., Target Pistol, *Modern*	475.00	625.00
☐ **Model 102**, .22 L.R.R.F., Target Pistol, *Modern*	450.00	600.00
☐ **Model 102 Deluxe**, .22 L.R.R.F., Target Pistol, *Modern*	500.00	675.00
☐ **Model 103**, .22 L.R.R.F., Target Pistol, Carved, Inlays, *Modern*	500.00	725.00
☐ **Model 103**, .22 L.R.R.F., Target Pistol, Carved, *Modern*	450.00	650.00
☐ **Model 104**, .22 L.R.R.F., Target Pistol, Round Barrel, *Modern*	350.00	600.00

HARRINGTON AND RICHARDSON ARMS COMPANY / 197

	V.G.	EXC.
☐ **Model 105**, .22 L.R.R.F., Target Pistol, Octagon Barrel, *Modern*	475.00	650.00
☐ **Model 106**, .22 L.R.R.F., Target Pistol, Round Barrel, *Modern*	450.00	625.00
☐ **Model 107**, .22 L.R.R.F., Target Pistol, Octagon Barrel, *Modern*	525.00	725.00
☐ **Model 107 Deluxe**, .22 L.R.R.F., Target Pistol, Octagon Barrel, Engraved, *Modern*	625.00	950.00
☐ **Model 110**, .22 L.R.R.F., Target Pistol, *Modern*	425.00	600.00
☐ **Model 120**, .22 L.R.R.F., Target Pistol, Heavy Barrel, *Modern*	350.00	500.00
☐ **Model 120**, .22 L.R.R.F., Target Pistol, Heavy Barrel, Adjustable Grips, *Modern*	375.00	525.00
☐ **Model 120**, .22 L.R.R.F., Target Pistol, Heavy Barrel, Left-Hand, Adjustable Grips, *Modern*	375.00	535.00
☐ **Model 120-1**, .22 L.R.R.F., Target Pistol, *Modern*	350.00	500.00
☐ **Model 120-2**, .22 L.R.R.F., Target Pistol, Adjustable Grips, *Modern*	375.00	525.00
☐ **Model 120-2**, .22 L.R.R.F., Target Pistol, Adjustable Grips, Left-Hand, *Modern*	375.00	535.00
☐ **Model 150**, .22 L.R.R.F., Target Pistol, *Modern*	650.00	900.00
☐ **Model 152 Electronic**, .22 L.R.R.F., Target Pistol, *Modern*	550.00	850.00

RIFLE, BOLT ACTION

	V.G.	EXC.
☐ **Model 45**, .22 L.R.R.F., Singleshot, Thumbhole Stock, Target Sights, with Accessories, *Modern*	400.00	575.00
☐ **Model 54**, .22 L.R.R.F., Singleshot, Thumbhole Stock, Target Sights, with Accessories, *Modern*	400.00	575.00
☐ **Model 503**, .22 L.R.R.F., Singleshot, Thumbhole Stock, Target Sights, with Accessories, *Modern*	400.00	575.00
☐ **Model 506**, .22 L.R.R.F., Singleshot, Thumbhole Stock, Target Sights, with Accessories, *Modern*	425.00	600.00
☐ **Olympia 300 Meter**, Various Calibers, Singleshot, Thumbhole Stock, Target Sights, with Accessories, *Modern*	475.00	700.00
☐ **Tanner**, Various Calibers, Singleshot, Thumbhole Stock, Target Sights, with Accessories, *Modern*	575.00	825.00
☐ **Sporting Rifle**, Various Calibers, Set Triggers, Fancy Wood, Checkered Stock, Open Sights, *Modern*	375.00	575.00

HAMPTON, JOHN
Dauphin County, Pa. See Kentucky Rifles and Pistols.

HARD PAN
Made by Hood Firearms, c. 1875.

HANDGUN, REVOLVER

	V.G.	EXC.
☐ **.22 Short R.F.**, 7 Shot, Spur Trigger, Solid Frame, Single Action, *Antique*	90.00	160.00
☐ **.32 Short R.F.**, 5 Shot, Spur Trigger, Solid Frame, Single Action, *Antique*	95.00	170.00

HARPERS FERRY ARMS CO.

RIFLE, FLINTLOCK

	V.G.	EXC.
☐ **.72 Lafayette**, Musket, Reproduction, *Antique*	175.00	275.00

RIFLE, PERCUSSION

	V.G.	EXC.
☐ **.51 Maynard**, Carbine, Breech Loader, Reproduction, *Antique*	140.00	185.00
☐ **.58 1861 Springfield**, Rifled Musket, Reproduction, *Antique*	140.00	185.00

HARRINGTON & RICHARDSON ARMS CO.
Worcester, Mass. Successors to Wesson & Harrington, 1874 to Date.

HARRINGTON AND RICHARDSON ARMS COMPANY

	V.G.	EXC.

AUTOMATIC WEAPON, ASSAULT RIFLE
☐ **T-48**, .308 Win., Clip Fed, Military, *Class 3* 2,500.00 3,500.00

AUTOMATIC WEAPON, SUBMACHINE GUN
☐ **Riesing M50**, .45 ACP, Commercial, Clip Fed, *Class 3* 250.00 400.00

HANDGUN, REVOLVER
☐ **Abilene Anniversary**, .22 L.R.R.F., Commemorative, *Curio* 70.00 105.00
☐ **American**, Various Calibers, Double Action, Solid Frame, *Modern* 40.00 75.00
☐ **Auto Ejecting**, Various Calibers, Top Break, Hammer, Double Action, *Modern* 65.00 110.00
☐ **Bobby**, Various Calibers, 6 Shot, Top Break, Double Action, *Modern* 60.00 90.00
☐ **Bulldog**, Various Calibers, Double Action, Solid Frame, *Modern* 40.00 75.00
☐ **Defender**, .38 S & W, Top Break, 6 Shot, Double Action, Adjustable Sights, *Modern* 60.00 95.00
☐ **Expert**, .22 L.R.R.F., Top Break, 9 Shot, Double Action, Wood Grips, *Modern* 85.00 135.00
☐ **Expert**, .22 W.R.F., Top Break, 9 Shot, Double Action, Wood Grips, *Modern* 90.00 145.00
☐ **Hammerless**, Various Calibers, Double Action, Solid Frame, *Modern* 50.00 90.00
☐ **Hunter (Early)**, .22 L.R.R.F., 7 Shot, Solid Frame, Wood Grips, Double Action, *Modern* 65.00 95.00
☐ **Hunter (Later)**, .22 L.R.R.F., 9 Shot, Solid Frame, Wood Grips, Double Action, *Modern* 60.00 90.00
☐ **Model 199**, .22 L.R.R.F., Single Action, 9 Shot, Top Break, Adjustable Sights, *Modern* 55.00 90.00
☐ **Model 4**, Various Calibers, Double Action, Solid Frame, *Modern* ... 45.00 85.00
☐ **Model 40**, Various Calibers, Top Break, Hammerless, Double Action, *Modern* 65.00 110.00
☐ **Model 5**, .32 S & W, Double Action, 5 Shot, Solid Frame, *Modern* 45.00 80.00
☐ **Model 6**, .22 L.R.R.F., Double Action, 7 Shot, Solid Frame, *Modern* 45.00 80.00
☐ **Model 603**, .22 W.M.R., 9 Shot, Solid Frame, Double Action, Swing-Out Cylinder, Adjustable Sights, *Modern* 65.00 95.00
☐ **Model 604**, .22 W.M.R., 9 Shot, Solid Frame, Double Action, Swing-Out Cylinder, Adjustable Sights, *Modern* 65.00 95.00
☐ **Model 622**, .22 L.R.R.F., Solid Frame, 6 Shot, Double Action, *Modern* 40.00 60.00
☐ **Model 632**, .32 S & W Long, Solid Frame, 6 Shot, Double Action, *Modern* 40.00 60.00
☐ **Model 633**, .32 S & W Long, Solid Frame, 6 Shot, Chrome, Double Action, *Modern* 40.00 65.00
☐ **Model 649**, .22LR/.22 W.M.R. Combo, Western Style, 9 Shot, Double Action, Adjustable Sights, *Modern* 45.00 65.00
☐ **Model 650**, .22LR/.22 W.M.R. Combo, Western Style, 9 Shot, Double Action, Adjustable Sights, *Modern* 50.00 70.00
☐ **Model 666**, .22LR/.22 W.M.R. Combo, Solid Frame, 9 Shot, Double Action, *Modern* 40.00 65.00
☐ **Model 676**, .22LR/.22 W.M.R. Combo, Western Style, 9 Shot, Double Action, Adjustable Sights, *Modern* 60.00 85.00
☐ **Model 676-12"**, .22LR/.22 W.M.R. Combo, Western Style, 9 Shot, Double Action, Adjustable Sights, *Modern* 55.00 75.00
☐ **Model 686**, .22LR/.22 W.M.R. Combo, Western Style, 9 Shot, Double Action, Adjustable Sights, *Modern* 60.00 90.00
☐ **Model 732**, .32 S & W Long, Solid Frame, 6 Shot, Double Action, Swing-Out Cylinder, *Modern* 45.00 65.00

HARRINGTON AND RICHARDSON ARMS COMPANY / 199

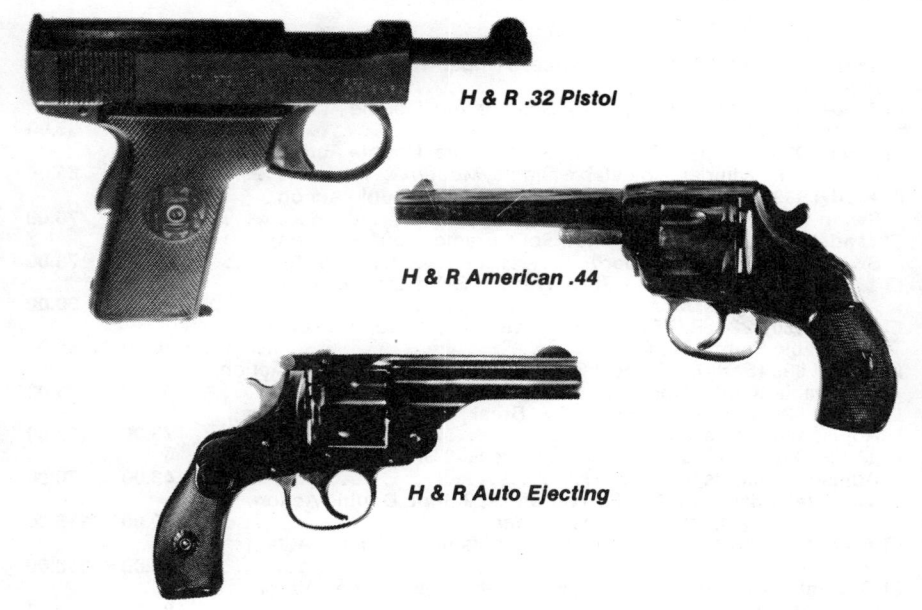

H & R .32 Pistol

H & R American .44

H & R Auto Ejecting

	V.G.	EXC.
☐ **Model 733**, .32 S & W Long, Solid Frame, 6 Shot, Double Action, Swing-Out Cylinder, *Modern*	50.00	70.00
☐ **Model 766**, .22 L.R.R.F., Top Break, 7 Shot, Double Action, Wood Grips, *Modern*	75.00	120.00
☐ **Model 766**, .22 W.R.F., Top Break, 7 Shot, Double Action, Wood Grips, *Modern*	85.00	140.00
☐ **Model 826**, .22 W.M.R., 6 Shot, Double Action, Adjustable Sights, Swing Out Cylinder, *Modern*	60.00	95.00
☐ **Model 829**, .22 L.R.R.F., 9 Shot, Double Action, Adjustable Sights, Swing Out Cylinder, *Modern*	60.00	95.00
☐ **Model 832**, .32 S & W, 6 Shot, Double Action, Adjustable Sights, Swing Out Cylinder, *Modern*	60.00	95.00
☐ **Model 900**, .22 L.R.R.F., Solid Frame, 9 Shot, Double Action, *Modern*	35.00	55.00
☐ **Model 901**, .22 L.R.R.F., Solid Frame, 9 Shot, Double Action, *Modern*	35.00	55.00
☐ **Model 922 (Early)**, .22 L.R.R.F., 9 Shot, Solid Frame, Wood Grips, Octagon Barrel, Double Action, *Modern*	65.00	90.00
☐ **Model 922 (Early)**, .22 L.R.R.F., 9 Shot, Solid Frame, Double Action, *Modern*	55.00	85.00
☐ **Model 922 (Early)**, .22 L.R.R.F., 9 Shot, Solid Frame, Pocket Pistol, Double Action, *Modern*	55.00	85.00
☐ **Model 922 (Late)**, .22 L.R.R.F., 9 Shot, Solid Frame, Swing-Out Cylinder, Double Action, *Modern*	35.00	55.00
☐ **Model 925**, .22 L.R.R.F., 9 Shot, Solid Frame, Double Action, Swing-Out Cylinder, *Modern*	45.00	70.00
☐ **Model 925**, .38 S & W, Solid Frame, 5 Shot, Adjustable Sights, *Modern*	50.00	75.00
☐ **Model 926**, .22 L.R.R.F., 5 Shot, Solid Frame, Adjustable Sights, *Modern*	50.00	75.00

HARRINGTON AND RICHARDSON ARMS COMPANY

	V.G.	EXC.
☐ **Model 926**, .38 S & W, Solid Frame, 5 Shot, Adjustable Sights, *Modern*	50.00	75.00
☐ **Model 929**, .22 L.R.R.F., 9 Shot, Solid Frame, Double Action, Swing-Out Cylinder, *Modern*	40.00	55.00
☐ **Model 930**, .22 L.R.R.F., 9 Shot, Solid Frame, Double Action, Swing-Out Cylinder, Adjustable Sights, *Modern*	45.00	65.00
☐ **Model 939**, .22 L.R.R.F., 9 Shot, Solid Frame, Double Action, Swing-Out Cylinder, Adjustable Sights, *Modern*	45.00	70.00
☐ **Model 940**, .22 L.R.R.F., 9 Shot, Solid Frame, Double Action, Swing-Out Cylinder, *Modern*	45.00	70.00
☐ **Model 949**, .22 L.R.R.F., 9 Shot, Western Style, Double Action, Adjustable Sights, *Modern*	40.00	60.00
☐ **Model 950**, .22 L.R.R.F., 9 Shot, Western Style, Double Action, Adjustable Sights, *Modern*	40.00	60.00
☐ **Model 999 (Early)**, .22 L.R.R.F., 9 Shot, Top Break, Double Action, Adjustable Sights, *Modern*	55.00	85.00
☐ **Model 999 (Early)**, .22 W.R.F., Top Break, 9 Shot, Double Action, Adjustable Sights, *Modern*	75.00	130.00
☐ **Model 999 (Late)**, .22 L.R.R.F, Top Break, 9 Shot, Double Action, Adjustable Sights, *Modern*	45.00	70.00
☐ **New Defender**, .22 L.R.R.F., Top Break, 9 Shot, Double Action, Wood Grips, Adjustable Sights, *Modern*	80.00	115.00
☐ **Premier**, Various Calibers, Top Break, Hammer, Double Action, *Modern*	65.00	110.00
☐ **Special**, .22 L.R.R.F., Top Break, 9 Shot, Double Action, Wood Grips, *Modern*	80.00	120.00
☐ **Special**, .22 W.R.F., Top Break, 9 Shot, Double Action, Wood Grips, *Modern*	85.00	135.00
☐ **Target (Early)**, .22 L.R.R.F., Top Break, 9 Shot, Double Action, Wood Grips, *Modern*	75.00	110.00
☐ **Target (Early)**, .22 W.R.F., Top Break, 9 Shot, Double Action, Wood Grips, *Modern*	80.00	120.00
☐ **Target (Hi Speed)**, .22 W.R.F., Top Break, 9 Shot, Double Action, Wood Grips, *Modern*	85.00	130.00
☐ **Target (Hi Speed)**, .22 L.R.R.F., Top break, 9 Shot, Double Action, Wood Grips, *Modern*	75.00	120.00
☐ **Trapper**, .22 L.R.R.F., 7 Shot, Solid Frame, Wood Grips, Double Action, *Modern*	60.00	90.00
☐ **Vest Pocket**, Various Calibers, Double Action, Solid Frame, Spurless Hammer, *Modern*	45.00	80.00
☐ **Young America**, Various Calibers, Double Action, Solid Frame, *Modern*	45.00	80.00

HANDGUN, SEMI-AUTOMATIC

	V.G.	EXC.
☐ **Self-Loading**, .25 ACP, Clip Fed, *Modern*	150.00	250.00
☐ **Self-Loading**, .32 ACP, Clip Fed, *Modern*	150.00	225.00

HANDGUN, SINGLESHOT

	V.G.	EXC.
☐ **U.S.R.A. Target**, .22 L.R.R.F., Top Break, Adjustable Sights, Wood Grips, *Modern*	195.00	325.00

RIFLE, BOLT ACTION

	V.G.	EXC.
☐ **Model 250 Sportster**, .22 L.R.R.F., 5 Shot Clip, Open Rear Sight, *Modern*	30.00	45.00
☐ **Model 251 Sportster**, .22 L.R.R.F., 5 Shot Clip, Lyman Sights, *Modern*	35.00	55.00
☐ **Model 265 Reg'lar**, .22 L.R.R.F., Clip Fed, Peep Sights, *Modern*	35.00	50.00
☐ **Model 300**, Various Calibers, Cheekpiece, Monte Carlo Stock, Checkered Stock, *Modern*	220.00	300.00

HARRINGTON AND RICHARDSON ARMS COMPANY / 201

	V.G.	EXC.
☐ **Model 301**, Various Calibers, Checkered Stock, Mannlicher, *Modern*	250.00	375.00
☐ **Model 317**, Various Calibers, Checkered Stock, Monte Carlo Stock, *Modern*	220.00	300.00
☐ **Model 317P**, .223 Rem., Fancy Checkering, Monte Carlo Stock, Fancy Wood, *Modern*	325.00	475.00
☐ **Model 330**, Various Calibers, Checkered Stock, Monte Carlo Stock, *Modern*	175.00	250.00
☐ **Model 333**, Various Calibers, Monte Carlo Stock, *Modern*	175.00	250.00
☐ **Model 365 ACE**, .22 L.R.R.F., Singleshot, Peep Sights, *Modern*	25.00	40.00
☐ **Model 370**, Various Calibers, Target Stock, Heavy Barrel, *Modern*	200.00	325.00
☐ **Model 450 Medalist**, .22 L.R.R.F., 5 Shot Clip, No Sights, Target Stock, *Modern*	95.00	130.00
☐ **Model 451 Medalist**, .22 L.R.R.F., 5 Shot Clip, Lyman Sights, Target Stock, *Modern*	110.00	150.00
☐ **Model 465 Targeteer**, .22 L.R.R.F., Clip Fed, Peep Sights, *Modern*	55.00	75.00
☐ **Model 465 Targeteer Jr**, .22 L.R.R.F., Clip Fed, Peep Sights, *Modern*	55.00	75.00
☐ **Model 750 Pioneer**, .22 L.R.R.F., Singleshot, Open Rear Sight, *Modern*	25.00	40.00
☐ **Model 751 Pioneer**, .22 L.R.R.F., Singleshot, Open Rear Sight, Mannlicher, *Modern*	35.00	50.00
☐ **Model 765 Pioneer**, .22 L.R.R.F., Singleshot, Open Rear Sight, *Modern*	20.00	30.00
☐ **Model 852 Fieldsman**, .22 L.R.R.F., Tube Feed, Open Rear Sight, *Modern*	40.00	55.00
☐ **Model 865 Plainsman**, .22 L.R.R.F., 5 Shot Clip, Open Rear Sight, *Modern*	40.00	55.00
☐ **Model 866 Plainsman**, .22 L.R.R.F., 5 Shot Clip, Open Rear Sight, Mannlicher, *Modern*	40.00	60.00

RIFLE, PERCUSSION

	V.G.	EXC.
☐ **Huntsman .45**, Top Break, Side Lever, Rifled, Reproduction, *Antique*	55.00	85.00
☐ **Huntsman .50**, Top Break, Side Lever, Rifled, Reproduction, *Antique*	50.00	75.00
☐ **Model 175**, .45 or .58 Caliber, Springfield Style, Open Sights, Reproduction, *Antique*	95.00	155.00
☐ **Model 175 Deluxe**, .45 or .58 Caliber, Springfield Style, Open Sights, Checkered Stock, Reproduction, *Antique*	155.00	245.00

RIFLE, SEMI-AUTOMATIC

	V.G.	EXC.
☐ **Model 150 Leatherneck**, .22 L.R.R.F., 5 Shot Clip, Open Rear Sight, *Modern*	45.00	65.00
☐ **Model 151 Leatherneck**, .22 L.R.R.F., 5 Shot Clip, Peep Sights, *Modern*	55.00	75.00
☐ **Model 165 Leatherneck**, .22 L.R.R.F., Clip Fed, Heavy Barrel, Peep Sights, *Modern*	75.00	110.00
☐ **Model 308**, Various Calibers, Checkered Stock, Monte Carlo Stock, *Modern*	200.00	285.00
☐ **Model 360**, Various Calibers, Checkered Stock, Monte Carlo Stock, *Modern*	190.00	275.00
☐ **Model 361**, Various Calibers, Checkered Stock, Monte Carlo Stock, *Modern*	200.00	300.00
☐ **Model 60 Reising**, .45 ACP, Clip Fed, Carbine, Open Rear Sight, *Modern*	275.00	375.00
☐ **Model 65 General**, .22 L.R.R.F., Clip Fed, Heavy Barrel, Peep Sights, *Modern*	135.00	225.00

HARRINGTON AND RICHARDSON ARMS COMPANY

	V.G.	EXC.
☐ **Model 700**, .22 W.M.R., Monte Carlo Stock, 5 Shot Clip, *Modern* ...	85.00	135.00
☐ **Model 700 Deluxe**, .22 W.M.R., Monte Carlo Stock, 5 Shot Clip, *Modern*	150.00	225.00
☐ **Model 755 Sahara**, .22 L.R.R.F., Singleshot, Open Rear Sight, Mannlicher, *Modern*	30.00	45.00
☐ **Model 760 Sahara**, .22 L.R.R.F., Singleshot, Open Rear Sight, *Modern*	25.00	40.00
☐ **Model 800 Lynx**, .22 L.R.R.F., Clip Fed, Open Rear Sight, *Modern*	40.00	60.00

RIFLE, SINGLESHOT

	V.G.	EXC.
☐ **1871 Springfield Deluxe**, .45-70 Government, Trap Door Action, Carbine, Light Engraving, *Modern*	160.00	190.00
☐ **1871 Springfield Officers'**, .45-70 Government, Commemorative, Trap Door Action, *Curio*	175.00	300.00
☐ **1871 Springfield Standard**, .45-70 Government, Trap Door Action, Carbine, *Modern*	100.00	160.00
☐ **1873 Springfield Officers'**, .45-70 Government, Trap Door Action, Light Engraving, Peep Sights, *Modern*	175.00	250.00
☐ **1873 Springfield Standard**, .45-70 Government, Trap Door Action, Commemorative, *Modern*	175.00	215.00
☐ **Custer Memorial Enlisted Model**, .45-70 Government, Commemorative, Trap Door Action, Carbine, Fancy Engraving, Fancy Wood, *Curio*	1,400.00	2,000.00
☐ **Custer Memorial Officers' Model**, .45-70 Government, Commemorative, Trap Door Action, Carbine, Fancy Engraving, Fancy Wood, *Curio*	2,200.00	3,000.00
☐ **Little Big Horn Springfield Officers'**, .45-70 Government, Commemorative, Trap Door Action, Carbine, *Curio*	175.00	250.00
☐ **Little Big Horn Springfield Standard**, .45-70 Government, Commemorative, Trap Door Action, Carbine, *Curio*	150.00	200.00
☐ **Model 172 Springfield**, .45-70 Government, Trap Door Action, Carbine, Engraved, Silver Plated, Tang Sights, Checkered Stock, *Modern*	600.00	800.00
☐ **Model 157**, Various Calibers, Top Break, Side Lever, Automatic Ejector, Open Rear Sight, Mannlicher, *Modern*	45.00	65.00
☐ **Model 158 Topper**, Various Calibers, Top Break, Side Lever, Automatic Ejector, Open Rear Sight, *Modern*	35.00	55.00
☐ **Model 158 Topper**, Various Calibers, Top Break, Side Lever, Automatic Ejector, Open Rear Sight, Extra Set of Rifle Barrels, *Modern*	55.00	75.00
☐ **Model 158 Topper**, Various Calibers, Top Break, Side Lever, Automatic Ejector, Open Rear Sight, Extra Set of Shotgun Barrels, *Modern*	50.00	70.00
☐ **Shikari**, .44 Magnum, Top Break, Side Lever, Automatic Ejector, *Modern*	45.00	65.00
☐ **Shikari**, .45-70 Government, Top Break, Side Lever, Automatic Ejector, *Modern*	50.00	75.00

RIFLE, SLIDE ACTION

	V.G.	EXC.
☐ **Model 422**, .22 L.R.R.F., Tube Feed, Open Rear Sight, *Modern*	55.00	85.00

SHOTGUN, BOLT ACTION

	V.G.	EXC.
☐ **Model 348 Gamemaster**, 12 and 16 Gauges, Tube Feed, Takedown, *Modern*	35.00	50.00
☐ **Model 349 Deluxe**, 12 and 16 Gauges, Tube Feed, Takedown, Adjustable Choke, *Modern*	45.00	60.00
☐ **Model 351 Huntsman**, 12 and 16 Gauges, Tube Feed, Takedown, Monte Carlo Stock, Adjustable Choke, *Modern*	45.00	60.00

HARRINGTON AND RICHARDSON ARMS COMPANY / 203

	V.G.	EXC.
SHOTGUN, DOUBLE BARREL, OVER-UNDER		
☐ **Model 1212**, 12 Ga., Field Grade, Vent Rib, Single Selective Trigger, *Modern*	240.00	345.00
☐ **Model 1212 Waterfowl**, 12 Ga. Mag. 3", Field Grade, Vent Rib, Single Selective Trigger, *Modern*	255.00	365.00
SHOTGUN, DOUBLE BARREL, SIDE-BY-SIDE		
☐ **Model 404**, Various Gauges, Hammerless, *Modern*	125.00	165.00
☐ **Model 404C**, Various Gauges, Hammerless, Checkered Stock, *Modern*	125.00	165.00
SHOTGUN, PERCUSSION		
☐ **Huntsman 12 Ga.**, Top Break, Side Lever, Reproduction, *Antique*	55.00	80.00
SHOTGUN, SEMI-AUTOMATIC		
☐ **Model 403**, .410 Ga., Takedown, *Modern*	120.00	160.00
SHOTGUN, SINGLESHOT		
☐ **Folding Gun**, Various Gauges, Top Break, Hammer, Automatic Ejector, *Modern*	40.00	40.00
☐ **Model #1 Harrich**, 12 Ga., Vent Rib, Engraved, Fancy Checkering, *Modern*	1,100.00	1,500.00
☐ **Model 148**, Various Gauges, Top Break, Side Lever, Automatic Ejector, *Modern*	30.00	50.00
☐ **Model 158**, Various Gauges, Top Break, Side Lever, Automatic Ejector, *Modern*	30.00	50.00
☐ **Model 159**, Various Gauges, Top Break, Side Lever, Automatic Ejector, *Modern*	40.00	60.00
☐ **Model 162 Buck**, 12 Ga., Top Break, Side Lever, Automatic Ejector, Peep Sights, *Modern*	35.00	60.00
☐ **Model 176**, 10 Ga. 3½", Top Break, Side Lever, Automatic Ejector, *Modern*	35.00	60.00
☐ **Model 188 Deluxe**, Various Gauges, Top Break, Side Lever, Automatic Ejector, *Modern*	25.00	45.00
☐ **Model 198 Deluxe**, Various Gauges, Top Break, Side Lever, Automatic Ejector, *Modern*	25.00	45.00
☐ **Model 3**, Various Gauges, Top Break, Hammerless, Automatic Ejector, *Modern*	35.00	60.00
☐ **Model 459 Youth**, Various Gauges, Top Break, Side Lever, Automatic Ejector, *Modern*	30.00	50.00
☐ **Model 48**, Various Gauges, Top Break, Hammer, Automatic Ejector, *Modern*	30.00	45.00
☐ **Model 480 Youth**, Various Gauges, Top Break, Side Lever, Automatic Ejector, *Modern*	25.00	40.00
☐ **Model 488 Deluxe**, Various Gauges, Top Break, Hammer, Automatic Ejector, *Modern*	35.00	50.00
☐ **Model 490 Youth**, Various Gauges, Top Break, Side Lever, Automatic Ejector, *Modern*	30.00	45.00
☐ **Model 5**, Various Gauges, Top Break, Lightweight, Automatic Ejector, *Modern*	45.00	70.00
☐ **Model 6**, Various Gauges, Top Break, Heavyweight, Automatic Ejector, *Modern*	45.00	70.00
☐ **Model 7**, Various Gauges, Top Break, Automatic Ejector, *Modern*	35.00	55.00
☐ **Model 8 Standard**, Various Gauges, Top Break, Automatic Ejector, *Modern*	35.00	55.00
☐ **Model 9**, Various Gauges, Top Break, Automatic Ejector, *Modern*	35.00	55.00
☐ **Model 98**, Various Gauges, Top Break, Side Lever, Automatic Ejector, *Modern*	35.00	50.00

	V.G.	EXC.
SHOTGUN, SLIDE ACTION		
☐ **Model 400**, Various Gauges, Solid Frame, *Modern*	85.00	145.00
☐ **Model 401**, Various Gauges, Solid Frame, Adjustable Choke, *Modern*	95.00	150.00
☐ **Model 402**, .410 Ga., Solid Frame, *Modern*	85.00	145.00
☐ **Model 440**, Various Gauges, Solid Frame, *Modern*	95.00	150.00
☐ **Model 400**, Various Gauges, Solid Frame, Vent Rib, *Modern*	95.00	160.00

HARRIS, HENRY
Payton, Pa. 1779-1783. See Kentucky Rifles.

HARRISON ARMS CO.
Made in Belgium for Sickles & Preston, Davenport, Iowa.

	V.G.	EXC.
SHOTGUN, DOUBLE BARREL, SIDE-BY-SIDE		
☐ **Various Gauges**, Outside Hammers, Damascus Barrel, *Modern*	80.00	150.00
☐ **Various Gauges**, Hammerless, Steel Barrel, *Modern*	95.00	175.00
☐ **Various Gauges**, Hammerless, Damascus Barrel, *Modern*	75.00	150.00
☐ **Various Gauges**, Outside Hammers, Steel Barrel, *Modern*	90.00	175.00
SHOTGUN, SINGLESHOT		
☐ **Various Gauges**, Hammer, Steel Barrel, *Modern*	45.00	75.00

HARTFORD ARMS & EQUIPMENT CO.
Hartford, Conn. 1929-1930.

	V.G.	EXC.
HANDGUN, MANUAL REPEATER		
☐ **.22 L.R.R.F.**, Clip Fed, Target Pistol, *Curio*	295.00	425.00
HANDGUN, SEMI-AUTOMATIC		
☐ **Model 1928**, .22 L.R.R.F., Clip Fed, Target Pistol, *Curio*	270.00	390.00
HANDGUN, SINGLESHOT		
☐ **.22 L.R.R.F.**, Target Pistol, *Curio*	300.00	400.00

HARTFORD ARMS CO.
Made by Norwich Falls Pistol Co., c. 1880.

	V.G.	EXC.
HANDGUN, REVOLVER		
☐ **.32 Short R.F.**, 5 Shot, Spur Trigger, Solid Frame, Single Action, *Antique*	90.00	160.00

HARTFORD ARMS CO.
Made by Crescent for Simmons Hardware Co., St. Louis, Mo.

	V.G.	EXC.
SHOTGUN, DOUBLE BARREL, SIDE-BY-SIDE		
☐ **Various Gauges**, Outside Hammers, Damascus Barrel, *Modern*	100.00	175.00
☐ **Various Gauges**, Hammerless, Steel Barrel, *Modern*	135.00	200.00
☐ **Various Gauges**, Hammerless, Damascus Barrel, *Modern*	100.00	175.00
☐ **Various Gauges**, Outside Hammers, Steel Barrel, *Modern*	125.00	190.00
SHOTGUN, SINGLESHOT		
☐ **Various Gauges**, Hammer, Steel Barrel, *Modern*	55.00	85.00

HARVARD
Made by Crescent, c. 1900.

	V.G.	EXC.
SHOTGUN, DOUBLE BARREL, SIDE-BY-SIDE		
☐ **Various Gauges**, Outside Hammers, Damascus Barrel, *Modern*	100.00	175.00
☐ **Various Gauges**, Hammerless, Steel Barrel, *Modern*	135.00	200.00

	V.G.	EXC.
☐ **Various Gauges**, Hammerless, Damascus Barrel, *Modern*	100.00	175.00
☐ **Various Gauges**, Outside Hammers, Steel Barrel, *Modern*	125.00	190.00

SHOTGUN, SINGLESHOT

☐ **Various Gauges**, Hammer, Steel Barrel, *Modern*	55.00	85.00

HAUCK, WILBUR
West Arlington, Vt., c. 1950.

RIFLE, SINGLESHOT

☐ **Target Rifle**, Various Calibers, Target Sights, Target Stock, Adjustable Trigger, *Modern*	300.00	475.00

HAWES FIREARMS
Van Nuys, Calif.

HANDGUN, REVOLVER

	V.G.	EXC.
☐ **Montana Marshall**, .22 L.R.R.F./.22 W.M.R. Combo, Western Style, Single Action, Brass Grip Frame, *Modern*	55.00	80.00
☐ **Montana Marshall**, .22 L.R.R.F., Western Style, Single Action, Brass Grip Frame, *Modern*	45.00	75.00
☐ **Montana Marshall**, .357 Magnum/9mm Combo, Western Style, Single Action, Brass Grip Frame, *Modern*	125.00	165.00
☐ **Montana Marshall**, .44 Magnum, Western Style, Single Action, Brass Grip Frame, *Modern*	110.00	140.00
☐ **Montana Marshall**, .44 Magnum/.44-40 Combo, Western Style, Single Action, Brass Grip Frame, *Modern*	135.00	175.00
☐ **Montana Marshall**, .45 Colt, Western Style, Single Action, Brass Grip Frame, *Modern*	110.00	145.00
☐ **Montana Marshall**, .45 Colt/.45 ACP Combo, Western Style, Single Action, Brass Grip Frame, *Modern*	145.00	190.00
☐ **Silver City Marshall**, .22 L.R.R.F./.22 W.M.R. Combo, Western Style, Single Action, Brass Grip Frame, *Modern*	50.00	85.00
☐ **Silver City Marshall**, .22 L.R.R.F., Western Style, Single Action, Brass Grip Frame, *Modern*	45.00	75.00
☐ **Silver City Marshall**, .357 Magnum/9mm Combo, Western Style, Single Action, Brass Grip Frame, *Modern*	125.00	170.00
☐ **Silver City Marshall**, .44 Magnum, Western Style, Single Action, Brass Grip Frame, *Modern*	110.00	155.00
☐ **Silver City Marshall**, .44 Magnum/.44-40 Combo, Western Style, Single Action, Brass Grip Frame, *Modern*	125.00	170.00
☐ **Silver City Marshall**, .45 Colt, Western Style, Single Action, Brass Grip Frame, *Modern*	110.00	155.00
☐ **Silver City Marshall**, .45 Colt/.45 ACP Combo, Western Style, Single Action, Brass Grip Frame, *Modern*	145.00	195.00
☐ **Texas Marshall**, .22 L.R.R.F./.22 W.M.R. Combo, Western Style, Single Action, Nickel Plated, *Modern*	50.00	85.00
☐ **Texas Marshall**, .22 L.R.R.F., Western Style, Single Action, Nickel Plated, *Modern*	45.00	75.00
☐ **Texas Marshall**, .357 Magnum, Western Style, Single Action, Nickel Plated, *Modern*	110.00	150.00
☐ **Texas Marshall**, .357 Magnum/9mm Combo, Western Style, Single Action, Nickel Plated, *Modern*	125.00	180.00
☐ **Texas Marshall**, .44 Magnum, Western Style, Single Action, Nickel Plated, *Modern*	125.00	170.00
☐ **Texas Marshall**, .44 Magnum/.44-40 Combo, Western Style, Single Action, Nickel Plated, *Modern*	140.00	190.00
☐ **Texas Marshall**, .45 Colt, Western Style, Single Action, Nickel Plated, *Modern*	110.00	150.00

	V.G.	EXC.
☐ **Texas Marshall**, .45 Colt/.45 ACP Combo, Western Style, Single Action, Nickel Plated, *Modern*	150.00	195.00
☐ **Denver Marshall**, .22 L.R.R.F./.22 W.M.R. Combo, Western Style, Single Action, Adjustable Sights, *Modern*	50.00	85.00
☐ **Denver Marshall**, .22 L.R.R.F., Western Style, Single Action, Brass Grip Frame, Adjustable Sights, *Modern*	45.00	75.00
☐ **Chief Marshall**, .357 Magnum, Western Style, Single Action, Brass Grip Frame, Adjustable Sights, *Modern*	110.00	145.00
☐ **Chief Marshall**, .44 Magnum, Western Style, Single Action, Brass Grip Frame, Adjustable Sights, *Modern*	110.00	155.00
☐ **Chief City Marshall**, .45 Colt, Western Style, Single Action, Brass Grip Frame, Adjustable Sights, *Modern*	110.00	155.00

HANDGUN, SINGLESHOT

☐ **Stevens Favorite Copy**, .22 L.R.R.F., Tip-Up, Rosewood Grips, *Modern*	45.00	75.00
☐ **Stevens Favorite Copy**, .22 L.R.R.F., Tip-Up, Plastic Grips, *Modern*	45.00	75.00
☐ **Stevens Favorite Copy**, .22 L.R.R.F., Tip-Up, Plastic Grips, Target Sights, *Modern*	45.00	80.00

HANDGUN, SEMI-AUTOMATIC

☐ **.25 ACP**, Clip Fed, *Modern*	60.00	95.00

HAWKIN, J. & S.
Jacob and Samuel Hawkin, St. Louis, Mo. 1822-1862. John Gemmer purchased the business and continued it until 1890.

RIFLE, PERCUSSION

☐ **Hawkin Plains Rifle**, Various Calibers, Hawkin Style, *Antique*	3,300.00	6,500.00
☐ **Gemmer Plains Rifle**, Various Calibers, Hawkin Style, *Antique*	2,500.00	4,500.00

HAWKINS, HENRY
Schenectady, N.Y. 1769-1775. See Kentucky Rifles.

H & D
Henrion & Dassy, Liege, Belgium, c. 1900.

HANDGUN, SEMI-AUTOMATIC

☐ **H & D Patent**, .25 ACP, Clip Fed, *Curio*	350.00	575.00

HDH 10 Shot Revolver

H.D.H.
Mre. D'Armes HDH, Liege, Belgium, c. 1910.
HANDGUN, REVOLVER
☐ **20 Shot**, Various Calibers, Over-Under Barrels, Two Row Cylinder,
  Double Action, *Curio* 150.00   250.00
☐ **10 Shot**, Various Calibers, Double Action, *Curio* 95.00   165.00
☐ **Ordnance Type**, Various Calibers, Double Action *Curio* 115.00   165.00
☐ **Constabulary Type**, Various Calibers, Double Action, *Curio* 80.00   130.00
☐ **Velo-Dog**, Various Calibers, Folding Trigger, Double Action, *Curio* 70.00   110.00
☐ **Velo-Dog**, Various Calibers, Folding Trigger, Double Action,
  Hammerless, *Curio* 70.00   110.00

HECKERT, PHILIP
York, Pa. 1769-1779. See Kentucky Rifles and Pistols.

HECKLER & KOCH
Oberndorf/Neckar, Germany
AUTOMATIC WEAPON, ASSAULT RIFLE
☐ **Model G3**, .308 Win., Clip Fed, *Class 3* 475.00   700.00
☐ **Model G3A3**, .308 Win., Clip Fed, *Class 3* 575.00   825.00
☐ **Model G3A4**, .308 Win., Clip Fed, *Class 3* 675.00   900.00
☐ **Model G3A4**, .308 Win., Clip Fed, with Conversion Kit, *Class 3* 750.00 1,050.00
☐ **Model HK33**, .223 Rem., Clip Fed, *Class 3* 325.00   450.00
AUTOMATIC WEAPON, SUBMACHINE GUN
☐ **Model MP5A2**, 9mm Luger, Clip Fed, *Class 3* 450.00   675.00
☐ **Model MP5A3**, 9mm Luger, Clip Fed, Folding Stock, *Class 3* 600.00   825.00
HANDGUN, SEMI-AUTOMATIC
☐ **HK-4**, .22 L.R.R.F., Clip Fed, Double Action, *Modern* 225.00   300.00
☐ **HK-4**, .25 ACP, Clip Fed, Double Action, *Modern* 210.00   290.00
☐ **HK-4**, .32 ACP, Clip Fed, Double Action, *Modern* 225.00   300.00
☐ **HK-4**, .380 ACP, Clip Fed, Double Action, *Modern* 230.00   325.00
☐ **HK-4**, Various Calibers, Clip Fed, Conversion Kit Only, Each 50.00   70.00
☐ **HK-4**, Various Calibers, Clip Fed, Double Action, with Conversion
  Kits All 4 Calibers, *Modern* 325.00   450.00
☐ **HK P-7 (PSP)**, 9mm Luger, Squeeze Cocking, *Modern* 300.00   440.00
☐ **HK P-9S**, .45 ACP, Clip Fed, Double Action, *Modern* 375.00   500.00
☐ **HK P-9S**, .45 ACP, Target Model, Clip Fed, Double Action, *Modern* 450.00   575.00
☐ **HK P-9S**, .45 ACP, with Extra 8" Barrel, Clip Fed, Double Action,
  Modern 475.00   625.00
☐ **P-9S Competition Kit**, 9mm Luger, Clip Fed, Double Action, Extra
  Barrel, Target Sights, Target Grips, *Modern* 575.00   850.00
☐ **P-9S Target**, 9mm Luger, Clip Fed, Double Action, 5½" Barrel,
  Target Sights, *Modern* 450.00   575.00
☐ **P-9S Combat**, 9mm Luger, Clip Fed, Double Action, 4" Barrel,
  Modern 375.00   500.00
☐ **P-9S Combat**, 9mm Luger, Clip Fed, Double Action, 4" Barrel, with
  .30 Luger Conversion Kit, *Modern* 475.00   650.00
☐ **VP-70Z**, 9mm Luger, Clip Fed, Double Action, 18 Shot Clip,
  Modern 250.00   350.00
RIFLE, SEMI-AUTOMATIC
☐ **HK 91**, .22 L.R.R.F., Clip Fed, Conversion Unit Only 175.00   240.00
☐ **HK 91 A-2**, .308 Win., Clip Fed, Sporting Version of Military Rifle,
  with Compensator, *Modern* 450.00   525.00
☐ **HK 91 A-3**, .308 Win., Clip Fed, Sporting Version of Military Rifle,
  Folding Stock with Compensator, *Modern* 490.00   650.00

	V.G.	EXC.
☐ **HK 91 A-4**, .308 Win., Clip Fed, Sporting Version of Military Rifle, with Compensator, Polygonal Rifling, *Modern*	475.00	675.00
☐ **HK 91 A-5**, .308 Win., Clip Fed, Sporting Version of Military Rifle, Folding Stock with Compensator, Polygonal Rifling, *Modern*	575.00	825.00
☐ **HK 91/93**, Light Bipod, *Add* **$60.00-$90.00**		
☐ **HK 91/93**, For Scope Mount *Add* **$95.00-$150.00**		
☐ **HK 93 A-2**, .223 Rem., Clip Fed, Sporting Version of Military Rifle, with Compensator, *Modern*	375.00	500.00
☐ **HK 93 A-3**, .223 Rem., Clip Fed, Sporting Version of Military Rifle, Folding Stock, with Compensator, *Modern*	450.00	625.00
☐ **Model 270**, .22 L.R.R.F., Clip Fed, Checkered Stock, Open Rear Sight, *Modern*	175.00	250.00
☐ **Model 300**, .22 WMR, Clip Fed, Checkered Stock, Open Rear Sight, *Modern*	200.00	300.00
☐ **Model 630**, .223 Rem., Clip Fed, Checkered Stock, Open Rear Sight, *Modern*	325.00	450.00
☐ **HK 770**, .308 Win., Sporting Rifle, Checkered Stock, Monte Carlo Stock, *Modern*	325.00	450.00
☐ **Model 940**, .30/06, Clip Fed, Checkered Stock, Open Rear Sight, *Modern*	425.00	550.00

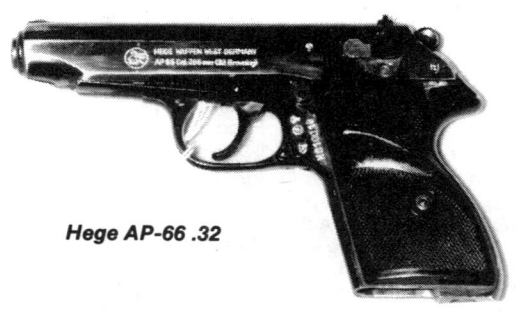

Hege AP-66 .32

HEGE
Tradename of Hebsacker Gesellschaft and Hege GmbH, Schwabisch Hall, West Germany.

COMBINATION WEAPON, DOUBLE BARREL, OVER-UNDER
☐ **President**, Various Calibers, Box Lock, Solid Rib, Double Trigger, Checkered Stock, *Modern*	475.00	675.00

HANDGUN, SEMI-AUTOMATIC
☐ **AP-63**, .32 ACP, Clip Fed, Double Action, *Modern*	215.00	295.00
☐ **AP-66**, .32 ACP, Clip Fed, Double Action, *Modern*	150.00	225.00
☐ **AP-66**, .380 ACP, Clip Fed, Double Action, *Modern*	175.00	250.00

HEINZELMANN, C.E.
Plochingen, Germany 1921-1928.

HANDGUN, SEMI-AUTOMATIC
☐ **Heim**, .25 ACP, Clip Fed, Blue, *Curio*	375.00	550.00

HELFRICHT
Alfred Krauser Waffenfabrik, Zella Mehlis, Germany 1921-1929.

HANDGUN, SEMI-AUTOMATIC
☐ **Model 1**, .25 ACP, Clip Fed, *Curio*	295.00	425.00

	V.G.	EXC.
☐ **Model 2**, .25 ACP, Clip Fed, *Curio*	275.00	400.00
☐ **Model 3**, .25 ACP, Clip Fed, *Curio*	275.00	400.00
☐ **Model 4**, .25 ACP, Clip Fed, *Curio*	250.00	375.00

HELVICE
Fab. D'Armes de Guerre de Grand Precision, Eibar Spain.
HANDGUN, SEMI-AUTOMATIC
☐ **.25 ACP**, Clip Fed, *Modern* 80.00 125.00

HENNCH, PETER
Lancaster, Pa. 1770-1774. See Kentucky Rifles.

HENRY, ALEXANDER
Edinburgh, Scotland 1869-1895.
RIFLE, DOUBLE BARREL, SIDE-BY-SIDE
☐ **.500/450 Mag. BPE**, Damascus Barrel, Engraved, Fancy Checkering, Ornate, Cased with Accessories, Hammerless, *Antique* 3,250.00 4,500.00

HENRY GUN CO.
Belgium, c. 1900.
SHOTGUN, DOUBLE BARREL, SIDE-BY-SIDE
☐ **Various Gauges**, Outside Hammers, Damascus Barrel, *Modern* 100.00 175.00
☐ **Various Gauges**, Hammerless, Steel Barrel, *Modern* 135.00 200.00
☐ **Various Gauges**, Hammerless, Damascus Barrel, *Modern* 100.00 175.00
☐ **Various Gauges**, Outside Hammers, Steel Barrel, *Modern* 125.00 190.00

SHOTGUN, SINGLESHOT
☐ **Various Gauges**, Hammer, Steel Barrel, *Modern* 55.00 85.00

HERCULES
Made by Stevens Arms.
SHOTGUN, DOUBLE BARREL, SIDE-BY-SIDE
☐ **M 315**, Various Gauges, Hammerless, Steel Barrel, *Modern* 95.00 170.00
☐ **Model 215**, 12 and 16 Gauges, Outside Hammers, Steel Barrel, *Modern* 95.00 160.00
☐ **Model 311**, Various Gauges, Hammerless, Steel Barrel, *Modern*.... 95.00 175.00
☐ **Model 3151**, Various Gauges, Hammerless, Recoil Pad, Front & Rear Bead Sights, *Modern* 110.00 185.00
☐ **Model 5151**, Various Gauges, Hammerless, Steel Barrel, *Modern* .. 95.00 175.00

SHOTGUN, SINGLESHOT
☐ **Model 94**, Various Gauges, Takedown, Automatic Ejector, Plain Hammer, *Modern* 40.00 60.00

HERMETIC
Tradename used by Bernadon-Martin, St. Etienne, France, c. 1912.
HANDGUN, SEMI-AUTOMATIC
☐ **B.M.**, .32 ACP, Clip Fed, *Curio* 220.00 295.00

HERMITAGE
Made by Stevens Arms.
SHOTGUN, SINGLESHOT
☐ **Model 90**, Various Gauges, Takedown, Automatic Ejector, Plain Hammer, *Modern* 40.00 60.00

HERMITAGE ARMS CO.
Made by Crescent for Grey & Dudley Hdw. Co., Nashville, Tenn.

	V.G.	EXC.

SHOTGUN, DOUBLE BARREL, SIDE-BY-SIDE
- ☐ **Various Gauges**, Outside Hammers, Damascus Barrel, *Modern* 100.00 175.00
- ☐ **Various Gauges**, Hammerless, Steel Barrel, *Modern* 135.00 200.00
- ☐ **Various Gauges**, Hammerless, Damascus Barrel, *Modern* 100.00 175.00
- ☐ **Various Gauges**, Outside Hammers, Steel Barrel, *Modern* 125.00 190.00

SHOTGUN, SINGLESHOT
- ☐ **Various Gauges**, Hammer, Steel Barrel, *Modern* 55.00 85.00

HERMITAGE GUN CO.
Made by Crescent for Grey & Dudley Hdw. Co., Nashville, Tenn.

SHOTGUN, DOUBLE BARREL, SIDE-BY-SIDE
- ☐ **Various Gauges**, Outside Hammers, Damascus Barrel, *Modern* 100.00 175.00
- ☐ **Various Gauges**, Hammerless, Steel Barrel, *Modern* 135.00 200.00
- ☐ **Various Gauges**, Hammerless, Damascus Barrel, *Modern* 100.00 175.00
- ☐ **Various Gauges**, Outside Hammers, Steel Barrel, *Modern* 125.00 190.00

SHOTGUN, SINGLESHOT
- ☐ **Various Gauges**, Hammer, Steel Barrel, *Modern* 55.00 85.00

HERO
Made by Rupertus Arms for Tryon Bros. Co., c. 1880.

HANDGUN, REVOLVER
- ☐ **.22 Short R.F.**, 7 Shot, Spur Trigger, Solid Frame, Single Action, Antique 90.00 160.00
- ☐ **.32 Short R.F.**, 5 Shot, Spur Trigger, Solid Frame, Single Action, Antique 95.00 170.00
- ☐ **.38 Short R.F.**, 5 Shot, Spur Trigger, Solid Frame, Single Action, Antique 95.00 180.00
- ☐ **.41 Short R.F.**, 5 Shot, Spur Trigger, Solid Frame, Single Action, Antique 120.00 200.00

HEROLD
Tradename of Franz Jager & Co., Suhl, Germany 1923-1939.

- **Herold Repetierbuchse**, .22 Hornet, Set Triggers, Checkered Stock, *Modern* 500.00 750.00

HERTERS
Distributer & Importer in Waseca, Minn.

HANDGUN, REVOLVER
- ☐ **Guide**, .22 L.R.R.F., Swing-Out Cylinder, Double Action, *Modern* 25.00 45.00
- ☐ **Power-Mag**, .357 Magnum, Western Style, Single Action, *Modern* 50.00 80.00
- ☐ **Power-Mag**, .401 Herter Mag., Western Style, Single Action, *Modern* 50.00 80.00
- ☐ **Power-Mag**, .44 Magnum, Western Style, Single Action, *Modern* ... 60.00 95.00
- ☐ **Western**, .22 L.R.R.F., Single Action, Western Style, *Modern* 25.00 45.00

RIFLE, BOLT ACTION
- ☐ **Model J-9 Hunter**, Various Calibers, Plain, Monte Carlo Stock, *Modern* 135.00 195.00
- ☐ **Model J-9 Presentation**, Various Calibers, Checkered Stock, Monte Carlo Stock, Sling Swivels, *Modern* 150.00 220.00
- ☐ **Model J-9 Supreme**, Various Calibers, Checkered Stock, Monte Carlo Stock, Sling Swivels, *Modern* 150.00 220.00
- ☐ **Model U-9 Hunter**, Various Calibers, Plain, Monte Carlo Stock, *Modern* 135.00 185.00

	V.G.	EXC.
☐ **Model U-9 Presentation**, Various Calibers, Checkered Stock, Sling Swivels, Monte Carlo Stock, *Modern*	150.00	220.00
☐ **Model U-9 Supreme**, Various Calibers, Checkered Stock, Sling Swivels, Monte Carlo Stock, *Modern*	145.00	190.00

SHOTGUN, SINGLESHOT
☐ **Model 151**, Various Gauges, Hammer, *Modern* 25.00   40.00

SHOTGUN, SEMI-AUTOMATIC
☐ **Model SL-18**, 12 Ga. 3", Checkered Stock, *Modern* 175.00   250.00

HESS, JACOB
Stark Co., Ohio 1842-1860. See Kentucky Rifles.

HESS, SAMUEL
Lancaster, Pa., c. 1771. See Kentucky Rifles.

HEYM
Franz W. Heym, 1934-1945 in Suhl, Germany, now in Munnerstadt, West Germany.

COMBINATION WEAPON, DRILLING
☐ **Model 33**, Various Calibers, Hammerless, Double Triggers, Engraved, Checkered Stock, Express Sights, *Modern* 2,600.00   3,500.00
☐ **Model 37**, Various Calibers, Hammerless, Sidelock, Engraved, Checkered Stock, *Modern* 2,950.00   3,950.00
☐ **Model 37**, Various Calibers, Hammerless, Sidelock, Double Rifle Barrels, Engraved, Checkered Stock, *Modern* 3,750.00   5,400.00
☐ **Model 37 Deluxe**, Various Calibers, Hammerless, Sidelock, Double Rifle Barrels, Engraved, Checkered Stock, *Modern* 4,250.00   5,800.00

COMBINATION WEAPON, DOUBLE BARREL, OVER-UNDER
☐ **Model 22S**, Various Calibers, Single Set Trigger, Checkered Stock, Light Engraving, *Modern* 750.00   1,150.00
☐ **Model 55BF (77BF)**, Various Calibers, Boxlock, Double Triggers, Checkered Stock, Engraved, *Modern* 1,700.00   2,500.00
☐ **Model 55BFSS (77BFSS)**, Various Calibers, Sidelock, Double Triggers, Checkered Stock, *Modern* 3,400.00   4,200.00

RIFLE, DOUBLE BARREL, OVER-UNDER
☐ **Model 55B (77B)**, Various Calibers, Boxlock, Engraved, Checkered Stock, *Modern* 1,850.00   2,700.00
☐ **Model 55BSS (77BSS)**, Various Calibers, Sidelock, Engraved, Checkered Stock, *Modern* 3,300.00   4,300.00

SHOTGUN, DOUBLE BARREL, OVER-UNDER
☐ **Model 55F (77F)**, Various Gauges, Boxlock, Engraved, Checkered Stock, Double Triggers, *Modern* 1,650.00   2,500.00
☐ **Model 55FSS (77FSS)**, Various Gauges, Sidelock, Engraved, Checkered Stock, Double Triggers, *Modern* 2,600.00   3,500.00

RIFLE, BOLT ACTION
☐ **Model SR-20**, Various Calibers, Fancy Wood, Double Set Triggers, *Modern* 425.00   595.00
☐ **Model SR-20**, Various Calibers, Fancy Wood, Double Set Triggers, Left Hand, *Modern* 525.00   695.00

RIFLE, SINGLESHOT
☐ **Model HR-30**, Various Calibers, Fancy Wood, Engraved, Single Set Trigger, Ruger Action, Round Barrel, *Modern* 950.00   1,500.00
☐ **Model HR-38**, Various Calibers, Fancy Wood, Engraved, Single Set Trigger, Ruger Action, Octagon Barrel, *Modern* 1,100.00   1,700.00

HIGGINS, J.C.
Trade Name used by Sears-Roebuck.

	V.G.	EXC.

HANDGUN, REVOLVER
- ☐ **Model 88**, .22 L.R.R.F., *Modern* .... 40.00 / 65.00
- ☐ **Model 88 Fisherman**, .22 L.R.R.F., *Modern* .... 40.00 / 65.00
- ☐ **Ranger**, .22 L.R.R.F., *Modern* .... 40.00 / 65.00

HANDGUN, SEMI-AUTOMATIC
- ☐ **Model 80**, .22 L.R.R.F., Clip Fed, Hammerless, *Modern* .... 65.00 / 95.00
- ☐ **Model 85**, .22 L.R.R.F., Clip Fed, Hammer, *Modern* .... 75.00 / 120.00

RIFLE, BOLT ACTION
- ☐ **Model 228**, .22 L.R.R.F., Clip Fed, *Modern* .... 30.00 / 45.00
- ☐ **Model 229**, .22 L.R.R.F., Tube Feed, *Modern* .... 35.00 / 50.00
- ☐ **Model 245**, .22 L.R.R.F., Singleshot, *Modern* .... 20.00 / 35.00
- ☐ **Model 51**, Various Calibers, Checkered Stock, *Modern* .... 160.00 / 225.00
- ☐ **Model 51 Special**, Various Calibers, Checkered Stock, Light Engraving, *Modern* .... 220.00 / 300.00

RIFLE, LEVER ACTION
- ☐ **.22 WMR**, *Modern* .... 50.00 / 80.00
- ☐ **Model 45**, Various Calibers, Tube Feed, Carbine, *Modern* .... 50.00 / 75.00

RIFLE, SEMI-AUTOMATIC
- ☐ **Model 25**, .22 L.R.R.F., Clip Fed, *Modern* .... 30.00 / 50.00
- ☐ **Model 31**, .22 L.R.R.F., Tube Feed, *Modern* .... 40.00 / 65.00

RIFLE, SLIDE ACTION
- ☐ **Model 33**, .22 L.R.R.F., Tube Feed, *Modern* .... 35.00 / 55.00

SHOTGUN, BOLT ACTION
- ☐ **Model 10**, Various Gauges, Tube Feed, 5 Shot, *Modern* .... 40.00 / 60.00
- ☐ **Model 11**, Various Gauges, Tube Feed, 3 Shot, *Modern* .... 30.00 / 50.00

SHOTGUN, DOUBLE BARREL, SIDE-BY-SIDE
- ☐ **Various Calibers**, Plain, Takedown, Hammerless, *Modern* .... 95.00 / 165.00

SHOTGUN, SEMI-AUTOMATIC
- ☐ **Model 66**, 12 Ga., Plain Barrel, *Modern* .... 90.00 / 155.00
- ☐ **Model 66**, 12 Ga., Plain Barrel, Adjustable Choke, *Modern* .... 95.00 / 165.00
- ☐ **Model 66**, 12 Ga., Vent Rib, Adjustable Choke, *Modern* .... 95.00 / 170.00
- ☐ **Model 66 Deluxe**, 12 Ga., *Modern* .... 95.00 / 175.00

SHOTGUN, SINGLESHOT
- ☐ **Various Calibers**, Takedown, Adjustable Choke, Plain, Hammer, *Modern* .... 30.00 / 50.00

SHOTGUN, SLIDE ACTION
- ☐ **Model 20 Deluxe**, 12 Ga., *Modern* .... 85.00 / 140.00
- ☐ **Model 20 Deluxe**, 12 Ga., Vent Rib, Adjustable Choke, *Modern* .... 95.00 / 155.00
- ☐ **Model 20 Special**, 12 Ga., Vent Rib, Adjustable Choke, *Modern* ... 135.00 / 190.00
- ☐ **Model 20 Standard**, 12 Ga., *Modern* .... 85.00 / 130.00

HIGH STANDARD
High Standard Mfg. Co. 1926 to the present, first in New Haven, Conn., then as High Standard Sporting Firearms in Hamden, Conn., now as High Standard, Inc. in East Hartford, Conn.

HANDGUN, DOUBLE BARREL, OVER-UNDER
- ☐ **Derringer**, .22 L.R.R.F., Double Action, 2 Shot, *Modern* .... 60.00 / 110.00
- ☐ **Derringer**, .22 WMR, Double Action, 2 Shot, *Modern* .... 65.00 / 115.00
- ☐ **Derringer**, .22 L.R.R.F., Double Action, Top Break, Nickel Plated, Hammerless, Cased, *Modern* .... 70.00 / 120.00
- ☐ **Derringer**, .22 WMR, Double Action, Top Break, Nickel Plated, Hammerless, Cased, *Modern* .... 75.00 / 125.00

HIGH STANDARD / 213

	V.G.	EXC.
☐ **Derringer**, .22 L.R.R.F., Double Action, Top Break, Electroless Nickel Plated, Hammerless, Walnut Grips, Cased, *Modern*	70.00	120.00
☐ **Derringer**, .22 WMR, Double Action, Top Break, Electroless Nickel Plated, Hammerless, Walnut Grips, Cased, *Modern*	75.00	125.00
☐ **Gold Derringer**, .22 WMR, Double Action, 2 Shot, *Modern*	120.00	165.00
☐ **Presidential Derringer**, .22 WMR, Double Action, Top Break, Gold Plated, Hammerless, Cased, *Modern*	130.00	185.00

HANDGUN, PERCUSSION

	V.G.	EXC.
☐ **.36**, Griswald & Gunnison, Revolver, Commemorative, Cased, Reproduction, *Antique*	170.00	250.00
☐ **.36 Leech & Rigdon**, Revolver, Commemorative, Cased, Reproduction, *Antique*	170.00	250.00
☐ **.36 Schneider & Glassick**, Revolver, Commemorative, Cased, Reproduction, *Antique*	260.00	365.00

HANDGUN, REVOLVER

	V.G.	EXC.
☐ **For Nickel Plating**, Add **$5.00-$10.00**		
☐ **Camp Gun**, .22 L.R.R.F., Double Action, Swing-Out Cylinder, Adjustable Sights, *Modern*	75.00	90.00
☐ **Camp Gun**, .22 WMR, Double Action, Swing-Out Cylinder, Adjustable Sights, *Modern*	80.00	100.00
☐ **Crusader**, Deluxe Pair, .44 Mag. & .45 Colt, Commemorative, Double Action, Swing-Out Cylinder, Gold Inlays, Engraved, *Modern*	1,400.00	2,950.00
☐ **Double-Nine**, .22LR/.22 WMR Combo, Double Action, Western Style, Alloy Frame, *Modern*	60.00	85.00
☐ **Double-Nine**, .22LR/.22 WMR Combo, Double Action, Western Style, *Modern*	85.00	120.00
☐ **Double-Nine**, .22 L.R.R.F., Double Action, Western Style, *Modern*	65.00	95.00
☐ **Double-Nine Deluxe**, .22LR/.22 WMR Combo, Double Action, Western Style, Adjustable Sights, *Modern*	95.00	140.00
☐ **Durango**, .22 L.R.R.F., Double Action, Western Style, *Modern*	65.00	95.00
☐ **High Sierra**, .22LR/.22 WMR Combo, Double Action, Western Style, Octagon Barrel, *Modern*	85.00	135.00
☐ **High Sierra Deluxe**, .22LR/.22 WMR Combo, Double Action, Western Style, Octagon Barrel, Adjustable Sights, *Modern*	95.00	155.00
☐ **Longhorn**, .22LR/.22 WMR Combo, Double Action, Western Style, Alloy Frame, *Modern*	65.00	90.00
☐ **Longhorn**, .22LR/.22 WMR Combo, Double Action, Western Style, *Modern*	90.00	135.00
☐ **Longhorn**, .22LR/.22 WMR Combo, Double Action, Adjustable Sights, Western Style, *Modern*	95.00	155.00
☐ **Natchez**, .22LR/.22 WMR Combo, Double Action, Western Style, Birdshead Grip, Alloy Frame, *Modern*	65.00	90.00
☐ **Posse**, .22LR/.22 WMR Combo, Double Action, Western Style, Brass Gripframe, *Modern*	80.00	120.00
☐ **Sentinel**, .22 L.R.R.F., Double Action, Swing-Out Cylinder, *Modern*	50.00	85.00
☐ **Sentinel Deluxe**, .22 L.R.R.F., Double Action, Swing-Out Cylinder, *Modern*	55.00	90.00
☐ **Sentinel Imperial**, .22 L.R.R.F., Double Action, Swing-Out Cylinder, *Modern*	55.00	90.00
☐ **Sentinel Mk III**, .357 Magnum, Double Action, Swing-Out Cylinder, Adjustable Sights, *Modern*	120.00	165.00
☐ **Sentinel Mk II**, .357 Magnum, Double Action, Swing-Out Cylinder, *Modern*	95.00	145.00
☐ **Sentinel Mk. I**, .22 L.R.R.F., Double Action, Swing-Out Cylinder, *Modern*	70.00	100.00

214 / HIGH STANDARD

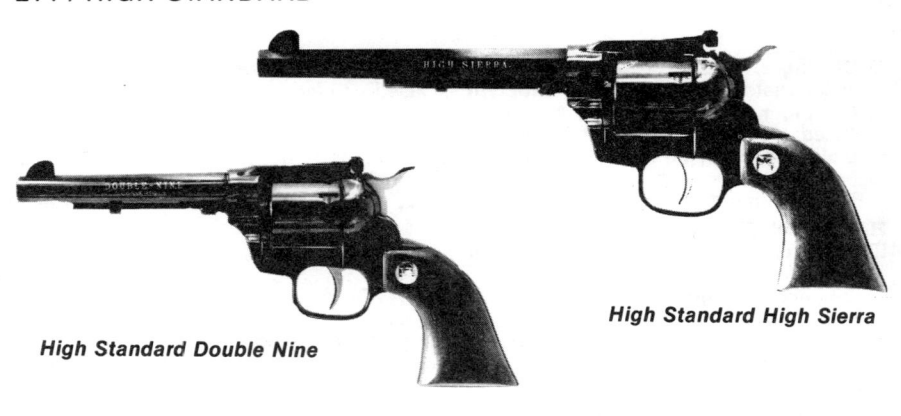

High Standard High Sierra

High Standard Double Nine

High Standard Sentinel

High Standard Sport King

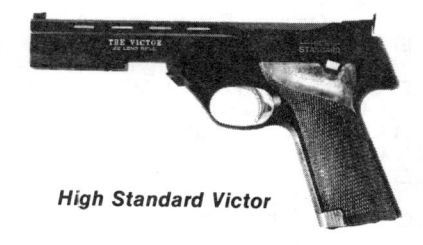

High Standard Sharpshooter

High Standard Victor

High Standard Trophy

High Standard Derringer

HIGH STANDARD / 215

	V.G.	EXC.
☐ **Sentinel Mk. I**, .22 L.R.R.F., Double Action, Swing-Out Cylinder, Adjustable Sights, *Modern*	80.00	115.00
☐ **Sentinel Mk. IV**, .22 L.R.R.F., Double Action, Swing-Out Cylinder, Adjustable Sights, *Modern*	115.00	155.00
☐ **Sentinel Mk. IV**, .22 WMR, Double Action, Swing-Out Cylinder, Adjustable Sights, *Modern*	120.00	160.00
☐ **Sentinel Mk. IV**, .22 WMR, Double Action, Swing-Out Cylinder, *Modern*	85.00	120.00
☐ **Sentinel Snub**, .22 L.R.R.F., Double Action, Swing-Out Cylinder, *Modern*	55.00	85.00

HANDGUN, SEMI-AUTOMATIC
☐ **For Nickel Plating**, *Add* **$20.00-$35.00**

	V.G.	EXC.
☐ **"Benner Olympic"**, .22 L.R.R.F., Supermatic, Military, Engraved, *Curio*	600.00	950.00
☐ **Citation (Early)**, .22 L.R.R.F., Supermatic, Clip Fed, Hammerless, Tapered Barrel, *Modern*	140.00	180.00
☐ **Citation (Early)**, .22 L.R.R.F., Supermatic, Clip Fed, Hammerless, Heavy Barrel, *Modern*	130.00	170.00
☐ **Citation (Late)**, .22 L.R.R.F., Supermatic, Military, Hammerless, Frame-Mounted Rear Sight, Fluted Barrel, *Modern*	160.00	245.00
☐ **Citation (Late)**, .22 L.R.R.F., Supermatic, Military, Hammerless, Frame-Mounted Rear Sight, Heavy Barrel, *Modern*	155.00	225.00
☐ **Citation (Late)**, .22 L.R.R.F., Supermatic, Clip Fed, Hammerless, Frame-Mounted Rear Sight, Heavy Barrel, *Modern*	145.00	215.00
☐ **Dura-Matic**, .22 L.R.R.F., Clip Fed, Hammerless, *Modern*	70.00	120.00
☐ **Field King**, .22 L.R.R.F., Clip Fed, Hammerless, Heavy Barrel, *Modern*	90.00	135.00
☐ **Flight King**, .22 Short R.F., Clip Fed, Hammerless, Lightweight, *Modern*	85.00	125.00
☐ **Flight King**, .22 Short R.F., Clip Fed, Hammerless, Lightweight, Extra Barrel, *Modern*	110.00	160.00
☐ **Flight King**, .22 Short R.F., Clip Fed, Hammerless, *Modern*	80.00	135.00
☐ **Flight King**, .22 Short R.F., Clip Fed, Hammerless, Extra Barrel, *Modern*	120.00	160.00
☐ **H-DM (O.S.S.)**, .22 Short R.F., Clip Fed, Silencer, Hammer, *Class 3*	525.00	750.00
☐ **Model A**, .22 L.R.R.F., Clip Fed, Hammerless, *Curio*	145.00	190.00
☐ **Model B**, .22 L.R.R.F., Clip Fed, Hammerless, *Curio*	165.00	210.00
☐ **Model C**, .22 Short R.F., Clip Fed, Hammerless, *Curio*	170.00	220.00
☐ **Model D**, .22 L.R.R.F., Clip Fed, Hammerless, Heavy Barrel, *Curio*	175.00	225.00
☐ **Model E**, .22 L.R.R.F., Clip Fed, Hammerless, Heavy Barrel, Target Grips, *Curio*	190.00	270.00
☐ **Model G-380**, .380 ACP, Clip Fed, Hammer, Takedown, *Curio*	240.00	325.00
☐ **Model G-B**, .22 L.R.R.F., Clip Fed, Hammerless, Takedown, *Curio*	135.00	175.00
☐ **Model G-B**, .22 L.R.R.F., Clip Fed, Hammerless, Takedown, Extra Barrel, *Curio*	160.00	200.00
☐ **Model G-D**, .22 L.R.R.F., Clip Fed, Hammerless, Takedown, *Curio*	160.00	225.00
☐ **Model G-D**, .22 L.R.R.F., Clip Fed, Hammerless, Takedown, Extra Barrel, *Curio*	185.00	265.00
☐ **Model G-E**, .22 L.R.R.F., Clip Fed, Hammerless, Takedown, Extra Barrel, *Curio*	225.00	300.00
☐ **Model G-E**, .22 L.R.R.F., Clip Fed, Hammerless, Takedown, *Curio*	175.00	250.00
☐ **Model G-O**, .22 Short R.F., Clip Fed, Hammerless, Takedown, Extra Barrel, *Curio*	275.00	350.00
☐ **Model G-O**, .22 Short R.F., Clip Fed, Hammerless, Takedown, *Curio*	245.00	300.00
☐ **Model H-A**, .22 L.R.R.F., Clip Fed, Hammer, *Curio*	130.00	185.00

216 / HIGH STANDARD

High Standard Supermatic

High Standard HD Military

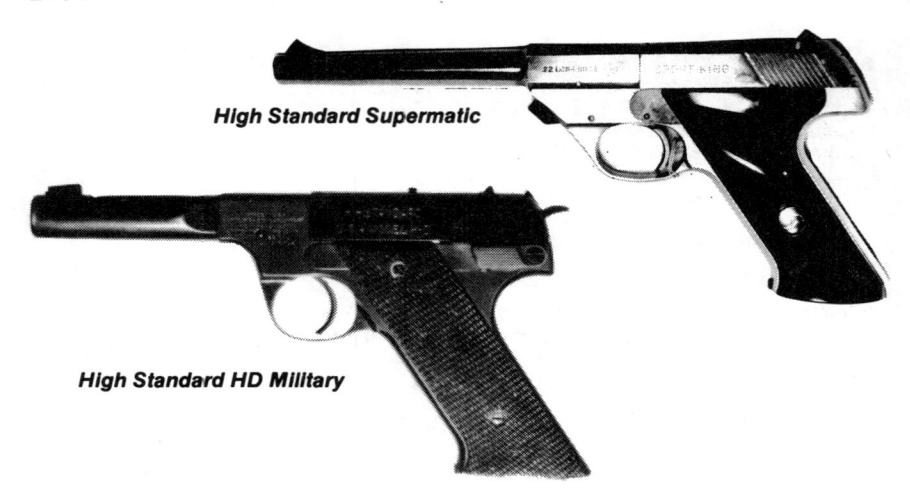

	V.G.	EXC.
☐ **Model H-B**, .22 L.R.R.F., Clip Fed, Hammer, *Curio*	140.00	175.00
☐ **Model H-D**, .22 L.R.R.F., Clip Fed, Hammer, Heavy Barrel, *Curio*	145.00	200.00
☐ **Model H-D Military**, .22 L.R.R.F., Clip Fed, Hammer, Heavy Barrel, Thumb Safety, *Curio*	175.00	245.00
☐ **Model H-E**, .22 L.R.R.F., Clip Fed, Hammer, Heavy Barrel, Target Grips, *Curio*	190.00	275.00
☐ **Model SB**, .22 L.R.R.F., Clip Fed, Hammerless, Smoothbore, Class 3	125.00	175.00
☐ **Olympic**, .22 Short R.F., Clip Fed, Hammerless, *Modern*	165.00	220.00
☐ **Olympic**, .22 Short R.F., Clip Fed, Hammerless, Extra Barrel, *Modern*	190.00	250.00
☐ **Olympic I.S.U.**, .22 Short R.F., Supermatic, Clip Fed, Hammerless, Military, *Modern*	175.00	225.00
☐ **Olympic I.S.U.**, .22 Short R.F., Supermatic, Clip Fed, Hammerless, *Modern*	175.00	225.00
☐ **Olympic I.S.U.**, .22 Short R.F., Clip Fed, Hammerless, Military, Frame-Mounted Rear Sight, *Modern*	185.00	240.00
☐ **Olympic I.S.U.**, .22 Short R.F., Clip Fed, Hammerless, Frame-Mounted Rear Sight, *Modern*	185.00	245.00
☐ **Plinker**, .22 L.R.R.F., Clip Fed, Hammer, *Modern*	70.00	110.00
☐ **Sharpshooter**, .22 L.R.R.F., Clip Fed, Hammerless, *Modern*	95.00	150.00
☐ **Sharpshooter (Late)**, .22 L.R.R.F., Military Grip, Clip Fed, Hammerless, *Modern*	150.00	200.00
☐ **Sport King**, .22 L.R.R.F., Clip Fed, Hammerless, Lightweight, *Modern*	80.00	125.00
☐ **Sport King**, .22 L.R.R.F., Clip Fed, Hammerless, Lightweight, Extra Barrel, *Modern*	110.00	150.00
☐ **Sport King**, .22 L.R.R.F., Clip Fed, Hammerless, *Modern*	115.00	150.00
☐ **Sport King**, .22 L.R.R.F., Clip Fed, Hammerless, Extra Barrel, *Modern*	110.00	150.00
☐ **Sport King (Late)**, .22 L.R.R.F., Military Grip, Clip Fed, Hammerless, *Modern*	135.00	160.00
☐ **Supermatic**, .22 L.R.R.F., Clip Fed, Hammerless, *Modern*	125.00	160.00
☐ **Supermatic**, .22 L.R.R.F., Clip Fed, Hammerless, Extra Barrel, *Modern*	145.00	200.00

HIGH STANDARD / 217

	V.G.	EXC.
☐ **Survival Pack, (Late)**, .22 L.R.R.F., Sharpshooter, Electroless Nickel, Cased with Accessories, *Modern*	165.00	245.00
☐ **Tournament**, .22 L.R.R.F., Supermatic, Clip Fed, Hammerless, *Modern*	125.00	165.00
☐ **Tournament**, .22 L.R.R.F., Supermatic, Clip Fed, Hammerless, Military, *Modern*	140.00	185.00
☐ **Trophy (Early)**, .22 L.R.R.F., Supermatic, Clip Fed, Hammerless, *Modern*	150.00	190.00
☐ **Trophy (Late)**, .22 L.R.R.F., Supermatic, Military, Hammerless, Frame-Mounted Rear Sight, Fluted Barrel, *Modern*	170.00	225.00
☐ **Trophy (Late)**, .22 L.R.R.F., Supermatic, Military, Hammerless, Frame-Mounted Rear Sight, Heavy Barrel, *Modern*	170.00	255.00
☐ **Victor**, .22 L.R.R.F., Heavy Barrel, Military Grip, Solid Rib, Target Sights, *Modern*	200.00	290.00
☐ **Victor**, .22 L.R.R.F., Heavy Barrel, Military Grip, Vent Rib, Target Sights, *Modern*	225.00	310.00
☐ **10-X Custom**, .22 L.R.R.F., Heavy Barrel, Military Grip, Target Sights, *Modern*	375.00	500.00

RIFLE, BOLT ACTION

	V.G.	EXC.
☐ **Hi Power**, Various Calibers, Field Grade, *Modern*	160.00	200.00
☐ **Hi Power Deluxe**, Various Calibers, Monte Carlo Stock, Checkered Stock, *Modern*	185.00	235.00

RIFLE, SLIDE ACTION

	V.G.	EXC.
☐ **.22 L.R.R.F.**, Flight-King, Tube Feed, Monte Carlo Stock, *Modern*	65.00	95.00

RIFLE, SEMI-AUTOMATIC

	V.G.	EXC.
☐ **Sport King**, .22 L.R.R.F., Field Grade, Tube Feed, *Modern*	65.00	90.00
☐ **Sport King**, .22 L.R.R.F., Field Grade, Carbine, Tube Feed, *Modern*	70.00	95.00
☐ **Sport King Deluxe**, .22 L.R.R.F., Tube Feed, Monte Carlo Stock, Checkered Stock, *Modern*	70.00	95.00
☐ **Sport King Special**, .22 L.R.R.F., Tube Feed, Monte Carlo Stock, *Modern*	65.00	90.00

SHOTGUN, SEMI-AUTOMATIC

	V.G.	EXC.
☐ **Trap Grade**, Vent Rib, Recoil Pad, *Modern*	145.00	190.00
☐ **Skeet Grade**, Vent Rib, Recoil Pad, *Modern*	145.00	190.00
☐ **12 Ga.**, Supermatic, Field Grade, *Modern*	110.00	155.00
☐ **20 Ga.**, Mag., Supermatic, Field Grade, *Modern*	115.00	160.00
☐ **20 Ga.**, Mag., Supermatic, Skeet Grade, Vent Rib, *Modern*	145.00	190.00
☐ **Deer Gun**, 12 Ga., Supermatic, Open Rear Sight, Recoil Pad, *Modern*	135.00	185.00
☐ **Deluxe**, Recoil Pad, *Modern*	120.00	165.00
☐ **Deluxe**, Recoil Pad, Vent Rib, *Modern*	145.00	185.00
☐ **Deluxe**, 20 Ga. Mag., Supermatic, Recoil Pad, *Modern*	120.00	165.00
☐ **Deluxe**, 20 Ga. Mag., Supermatic, Recoil Pad, Vent Rib, *Modern*	145.00	190.00
☐ **Duck Gun**, 12 Ga. Mag. 3", Supermatic, Recoil Pad, Field Grade, *Modern*	145.00	195.00
☐ **Duck Gun**, 12 Ga. Mag. 3", Supermatic, Vent Rib, Recoil Pad, *Modern*	150.00	195.00
☐ **Model 10**, 12 Ga., Riot Gun, *Modern*	225.00	350.00
☐ **Special**, 12 Ga., Field Grade, Adjustable Choke, *Modern*	135.00	185.00
☐ **Special**, 20 Ga. Mag., Supermatic, Field Grade, Adjustable Choke, *Modern*	140.00	190.00
☐ **Trophy**, Recoil Pad, Vent Rib, Adjustable Choke, *Modern*	165.00	215.00
☐ **Trophy**, 20 Ga. Mag., Supermatic, Recoil Pad, Vent Rib, Adjustable Choke, *Modern*	170.00	220.00

	V.G.	EXC.
SHOTGUN, SLIDE ACTION		
☐ .410 Ga. 3", Flight-King, Field Grade, *Modern*	95.00	140.00
☐ .410 Ga. 3", Flight-King, Skeet Grade, *Modern*	125.00	165.00
☐ 12 Ga., Flight-King, Trap Grade, Vent Rib, Recoil Pad, *Modern*	125.00	165.00
☐ 12 Ga., Flight-King, Skeet Grade, Vent Rib, Recoil Pad, *Modern*	120.00	160.00
☐ 12 and 20 Gauges, Flight-King, Field Grade, *Modern*	90.00	135.00
☐ 28 Ga., Flight-King, Field Grade, *Modern*	95.00	140.00
☐ 28 Ga., Flight-King, Skeet Grade, Vent Rib, *Modern*	120.00	165.00
☐ **Brush Gun**, 12 Ga., Flight-King, Open Rear Sight, *Modern*	95.00	145.00
☐ **Deluxe**, .410 Ga. 3", Flight-King, Vent Rib, *Modern*	100.00	145.00
☐ **Deluxe**, 12 and 20 Gauges, Flight-King, Recoil Pad, *Modern*	85.00	125.00
☐ **Deluxe**, 12 and 20 Gauges, Flight-King, Recoil Pad, Vent Rib, *Modern*	100.00	145.00
☐ **Deluxe**, 28 Ga., Flight-King, Vent Rib, *Modern*	110.00	155.00
☐ **Deluxe Brush Gun**, 12 Ga., Flight-King, Peep Sights, Sling Swivels, *Modern*	115.00	160.00
☐ **Riot**, 12 Ga., Flight-King, Plain Barrel, *Modern*	110.00	150.00
☐ **Riot**, 12 Ga., Flight-King, Open Rear Sight, *Modern*	120.00	165.00
☐ **Special**, 12 and 20 Gauges, Flight-King, Field Grade, Adjustable Choke, *Modern*	95.00	140.00
☐ **Trophy**, 12 and 20 Gauges, Flight-King, Recoil Pad, Vent Rib, Adjustable Choke, *Modern*	120.00	165.00
SHOTGUN, DOUBLE BARREL, OVER-UNDER		
☐ **Shadow Indy**, 12 Ga., Single Selective Trigger, Selective Ejectors, Checkered Stock, Engraved, *Modern*	450.00	575.00
☐ **Shadow Seven**, 12 Ga., Single Selective Trigger, Selective Ejectors, Checkered Stock, Light Engraving, *Modern*	340.00	485.00

HIJO
Tradename used by Sloan's of N.Y.C.

HANDGUN, SEMI-AUTOMATIC

☐ **Hijo**, .25 ACP, Clip Fed, *Modern*	60.00	95.00
☐ **Hijo Military**, .22 L.R.R.F., Clip Fed, *Modern*	65.00	100.00

HILL, S.W.
See Kentucky Rifles and Pistols.

HILLEGAS, J.
Pottsville, Pa. 1810-1830. See Kentucky Rifles.

HILLIARD, D.H. & GEORGE C.
D.H. Hilliard, Cornish, New Hampshire, 1842-1877, taken over by George C. Hilliard and operated 1877-1880.

HANDGUN, PERCUSSION

☐ .34, Underhammer Target Pistol, *Antique*	200.00	300.00

HINO-KOMORO
Kumaso Hino and Tomisiro Komoro, Tokyo, Japan, c. 1910.

HANDGUN, SEMI-AUTOMATIC

☐ **Blow-Forward**, .32 ACP, Clip Fed, *Curio*	1,550.00	2,500

HOCKLEY, JAMES
Chester County, Pa. 1769-1771. See Kentucky Rifles.

HOLDEN, CYRUS B.
Worcester, Mass., c. 1861-1880.

	V.G.	EXC.

SHOTGUN, SINGLESHOT
- ☐ **Model 1862**, .44 Henry, Octagon Barrel, *Antique* 300.00 550.00
- ☐ **Tip-Up**, .22 R.F., Nickel Plated Frame, Blued Barrel, *Antique* 300.00 450.00

HOLLAND & HOLLAND
London, England since 1835.

RIFLE, BOLT ACTION
- ☐ **Best Quality**, Various Calibers, Express Sights, Fancy Checkering, Engraved, *Modern* 1,700.00 2,850.00
- ☐ **Best Quality**, Various Calibers, Express Sights, Checkered Stock, *Modern* 1,250.00 1,975.00

RIFLE, DOUBLE BARREL, SIDE-BY-SIDE
- ☐ **#2**, Various Calibers, Sidelock, Checkered Stock, Engraved, Hammerless, *Modern* 5,500.00 8,775.00
- ☐ **Deluxe**, Various Calibers, Sidelock, Automatic Ejector, Fancy Engraving, Fancy Checkering, Double Trigger, *Modern* 12,500.00 16,500.00
- ☐ **Royal**, Various Calibers, Sidelock, Automatic Ejector, Fancy Engraving, Fancy Checkering, Double Trigger, *Modern* 6,750.00 10,500.00
- ☐ **Special Order**, Various Calibers, Sidelock, Fancy Checkering, Fancy Engraving, Hammerless, *Modern* 11,000.00 16,500.00

SHOTGUN, DOUBLE BARREL, OVER-UNDER
- ☐ **Deluxe Royal**, 12 Ga., Sidelock, Automatic Ejector, Fancy Engraving, Fancy Checkering, Double Triggers, *Modern* 12,000.00 17,000.00
- ☐ **Deluxe Royal**, 12 Ga., Sidelock, Automatic Ejector, Fancy Engraving, Fancy Checkering, Double Triggers, *Modern* 12,000.00 17,000.00
- ☐ **Royal Model (Late)**, 12 Ga., Sidelock, Automatic Ejector, Fancy Engraving, Fancy Checkering, Double Triggers, *Modern*............ 9,500.00 14,500.00
- ☐ **Royal Model (Late)**, 12 Ga., Sidelock, Automatic Ejector, Fancy Engraving, Fancy Checkering, Single Trigger, *Modern* 10,000.00 15,000.00
- ☐ **Royal Model (Old)**, 12 Ga., Sidelock, Automatic Ejector, Fancy Engraving, Fancy Checkering, Double Triggers, *Modern* 8,000.00 11,500.00
- ☐ **Royal Model (Old)**, 12 Ga., Sidelock, Automatic Ejector, Fancy Engraving, Fancy Checkering, Single Trigger, *Modern* 9,000.00 13,000.00

SHOTGUN, DOUBLE BARREL, SIDE-BY-SIDE
- ☐ **Badminton**, Various Gauges, Sidelock, Automatic Ejector, Fancy Engraving, Fancy Checkering, Double Triggers, *Modern*........... 5,000.00 7,750.00
- ☐ **Badminton**, Various Gauges, Sidelock, Automatic Ejector, Fancy Engraving, Fancy Checkering, Single Trigger, *Modern* 5,500.00 8,250.00
- ☐ **Centenary Badminton**, 12 Ga. 2", Sidelock, Automatic Ejector, Fancy Engraving, Fancy Checkering, Double Triggers, *Modern* 5,000.00 7,250.00
- ☐ **Centenary Deluxe**, 12 Ga. 2", Sidelock, Automatic Ejector, Fancy Engraving, Fancy Checkering, Double Triggers, *Modern*........... 8,750.00 13,500.00
- ☐ **Centenary Dominion**, 12 Ga. 2", Sidelock, Automatic Ejector, Engraved, Checkered Stock, Double Triggers, *Modern* 2,750.00 4,650.00
- ☐ **Cententary Royal**, 12 Ga. 2", Sidelock, Automatic Ejector, Fancy Engraving, Fancy Checkering, Double Triggers, *Modern*........... 8,500.00 11,750.00
- ☐ **Deluxe**, Various Gauges, Sidelock, Automatic Ejector, Fancy Engraving, Fancy Checkering, Double Triggers, *Modern*........... 8,750.00 13,250.00
- ☐ **Deluxe**, Various Gauges, Sidelock, Automatic Ejector, Fancy Engraving, Fancy Checkering, Single Trigger, *Modern* 9,250.00 14,000.00
- ☐ **Dominion**, Various Gauges, Sidelock, Automatic Ejector, Engraved, Checkered Stock, Double Triggers, *Modern* 2,800.00 4,700.00
- ☐ **Northwood**, Various Gauges, Boxlock, Automatic Ejector, Checkered Stock, Engraved, *Modern* 1,750.00 2,650.00

	V.G.	EXC.
☐ **Riviera**, Various Gauges, Extra Shotgun Barrel, Automatic Ejector, Fancy Engraving, Fancy Checkering, Double Triggers, *Modern*	6,000.00	9,750.00
☐ **Royal**, Various Gauges, Sidelock, Automatic Ejector, Fancy Engraving, Fancy Checkering, Double Triggers, *Modern*	8,500.00	12,000.00
☐ **Royal**, Various Gauges, Sidelock, Automatic Ejector, Fancy Engraving, Fancy Checkering, Single Trigger, *Modern*	8,750.00	14,000.00
☐ **Royal Ejector Grade**, 12 Ga. Mag. 3", Single Selective Trigger, Vent Rib, Pistol-Grip Stock, Cased with Accessories, *Modern*	11,000.00	16,500.00

SHOTGUN, SINGLESHOT

	V.G.	EXC.
☐ **Standard Super Trap**, 12 Ga., Boxlock, Automatic Ejector, Vent Rib, Fancy Engraving, Checkered Stock, *Modern*	5,500.00	8,250.00
☐ **Deluxe Super Trap**, 12 Ga., Boxlock, Automatic Ejector, Vent Rib, Fancy Engraving, Checkered Stock, *Modern*	6,500.00	9,000.00
☐ **Exhibition Super Trap**, 12 Ga., Boxlock, Automatic Ejector, Vent Rib, Fancy Engraving, Checkered Stock, *Modern*	7,750.00	12,000.00

HOLLIS, CHAS. & SONS
London, England.

SHOTGUN, DOUBLE BARREL, SIDE-BY-SIDE

	V.G.	EXC.
☐ **12 Ga.**, Hammerless, Engraved, Fancy Checkering, Fancy Wood, *Modern*	2,150.00	2,875.00

HOLLIS, RICHARD
London, England 1800-1850.

HANDGUN, FLINTLOCK

	V.G.	EXC.
☐ **.68**, Holster Pistol, Round Barrel, Brass Furniture, Plain, *Antique*	500.00	750.00

SHOTGUN, PERCUSSION

	V.G.	EXC.
☐ **12 Ga.**, Double Barrels, Double Triggers, Hook Breech, Light Engraving, Checkered Stock, *Antique*	325.00	500.00

HOLMES, BILL
Fayetteville, Ark.

SHOTGUN, SINGLESHOT

	V.G.	EXC.
☐ **Supertrap**, 12 Ga., Various Action Types, Checkered Stock, *Modern*	1,100.00	1,750.00

HOOD FIRE ARMS CO.
Norwich, Conn., c. 1875

HANDGUN, REVOLVER

	V.G.	EXC.
☐ **.32 Short R.F.**, 5 Shot, Spur Trigger, Solid Frame, Single Action, *Antique*	90.00	160.00

HOPKINS & ALLEN
Norwich, Conn. 1868-1917, taken over by Marlin-Rockwell in 1917. Later purchased by Numrich Arms Corp., West Hurley, N.Y., and now in Hawthorne, N.J.

HANDGUN, PERCUSSION

	V.G.	EXC.
☐ **"Boot Pistol"**, .36, Under-Hammer, Octagon Barrel, Reproduction, (Numrich), *Antique*	25.00	45.00

HANDGUN, REVOLVER

	V.G.	EXC.
☐ **Model 1876 Army**, .44-40 WCF, Solid Frame, Single Action, 6 Shot, Finger-Rest Trigger Guard, *Antique*	325.00	550.00

	V.G.	EXC.
☐ **Safety Police**, .22 L.R.R.F., Top Break, Double Action, Various Barrel Lengths, *Modern*	70.00	125.00
☐ **Safety Police**, .32 S & W, Top Break, Double Action, Various Barrel Lengths, *Modern*	65.00	115.00
☐ **Safety Police**, .38 S & W, Top Break, Double Action, Various Barrel Lengths, *Modern*	65.00	115.00
☐ **XL .30 Long**, .30 Long R.F., Solid Frame, Spur Trigger, Single Action, 5 Shot, *Antique*	95.00	155.00
☐ **XL 1 Double Action**, .22 Short R.F., Solid Frame, Folding Hammer, *Modern*	60.00	95.00
☐ **XL 3 Double Action**, .32 S & W, Solid Frame, Folding Hammer, *Modern*	60.00	95.00
☐ **XL Bulldog**, .32 S & W, Solid Frame, Folding Hammer, *Modern*	60.00	95.00
☐ **XL Bulldog**, .32 Short R.F., Solid Frame, Folding Hammer, *Modern*	50.00	85.00
☐ **XL Bulldog**, .38 S & W, Solid Frame, Folding Hammer, *Modern*	60.00	95.00
☐ **XL CR .22 Short R.F.**, Solid Frame, Spur Trigger, Single Action, 7 Shot, *Antique*	95.00	150.00
☐ **XL Double Action**, .32 S & W, Solid Frame, Folding Hammer, *Modern*	60.00	95.00
☐ **XL Double Action**, .38 S & W, Solid Frame, Folding Hammer, *Modern*	60.00	95.00
☐ **XL Navy**, .38 Short R.F., Solid Frame, Single Action, 6 Shot, *Antique*	285.00	425.00
☐ **XL No. 1**, .22 Short R.F., Solid Frame, Spur Trigger, Single Action, 7 Shot, *Antique*	125.00	170.00
☐ **XL No. 2**, .30 Short R.F., Solid Frame, Spur Trigger, Single Action, 5 Shot, *Antique*	125.00	180.00

Hopkins & Allen New Target

Hopkins & Allen XL #3

	V.G.	EXC.
☐ **XL No. 3**, .32 Short R.F., Solid Frame, Spur Trigger, Single Action, 5 Shot, Safety Cylinder, *Antique*	135.00	185.00
☐ **XL No. 4**, .38 Short R.F., Solid Frame, Spur Trigger, Single Action, 5 Shot, *Antique*	135.00	185.00
☐ **XL No. 5**, .38 S & W, Solid Frame, Spur Trigger, Single Action, 5 Shot, *Antique*	200.00	360.00
☐ **XL No. 5**, .38 Short R.F., Solid Frame, Spur Trigger, Single Action, 5 Shot, Safety Cylinder, Engraved, *Antique*	315.00	475.00
☐ **XL No. 6**, .41 Short R.F., Solid Frame, Spur Trigger, Single Action, 5 Shot, *Antique*	135.00	215.00
☐ **XL No. 7**, .41 Short R.F., Solid Frame, Spur Trigger, Single Action, 5 Shot, Swing-Out Cylinder, *Antique*	145.00	250.00
☐ **XL No. 8 (Army)**, .44 R.F., Solid Frame, Single Action, 6 Shot, *Antique*	350.00	525.00
☐ **XL Police**, .38 Short R.F., Solid Frame, Single Action, 6 Shot, *Antique*	120.00	170.00

222 / HOPKINS AND ALLEN

	V.G.	EXC.
HANDGUN, SINGLESHOT		
☐ **Ladies Garter Pistol**, .22 Short R.F., Tip-Up, Folding Trigger, Single Action, *Antique*	85.00	130.00
☐ **New Model Target**, .22 L.R.R.F., Top Break, 10" Barrel, Adjustable Sights, Target Grips, *Modern*	225.00	325.00
☐ **XL Derringer**, .41 Short R.F., Spur Trigger, Single Action, *Antique*	350.00	550.00
RIFLE, BOLT ACTION		
☐ **American Military**, .22 L.R.R.F., Singleshot, Takedown, Open Rear Sight, Round Barrel, *Modern*	135.00	185.00
RIFLE, FLINTLOCK		
☐ **"Kentucky"**, .31, Octagon Barrel, Full-Stocked, Brass Furniture, Reproduction, (Numrich), *Antique*	135.00	180.00
☐ **"Kentucky"**, .36, Octagon Barrel, Full-Stocked, Brass Furniture, Reproduction, (Numrich), *Antique*	140.00	180.00
☐ **"Kentucky"**, .45, Octagon Barrel, Full-Stocked, Brass Furniture, Reproduction, (Numrich), *Antique*	150.00	190.00
☐ **"Minuteman Brush"**, .45, Octagon Barrel, Full-Stocked, Carbine, Reproduction, (Numrich), *Antique*	140.00	190.00
☐ **"Minuteman Brush"**, .50, Octagon Barrel, Full-Stocked, Carbine, Reproduction, (Numrich), *Antique*	140.00	190.00
☐ **"Minuteman"**, .31, Octagon Barrel, Full-Stocked, Brass Furniture, Reproduction, (Numrich), *Antique*	135.00	180.00
☐ **"Minuteman"**, .36, Octagon Barrel, Full-Stocked, Brass Furniture, Reproduction, (Numrich), *Antique*	140.00	180.00
☐ **"Minuteman"**, .45, Octagon Barrel, Full-Stocked, Brass Furniture, Reproduction, (Numrich), *Antique*	150.00	190.00
☐ **"Minuteman"**, .50, Octagon Barrel, Full-Stocked, Brass Furniture, Reproduction, (Numrich), *Antique*	155.00	190.00
☐ **"Pennsylvania"**, .31, Octagon Barrel, Half-Stocked, Brass Furniture, Reproduction, (Numrich), *Antique*	130.00	175.00
☐ **"Pennsylvania"**, .36, Octagon Barrel, Half-Stocked, Brass Furniture, Reproduction, (Numrich), *Antique*	135.00	175.00
☐ **"Pennsylvania"**, .45, Octagon Barrel, Half-Stocked, Brass Furniture, Reproduction, (Numrich), *Antique*	135.00	185.00
☐ **"Pennsylvania"**, .50, Octagon Barrel, Half-Stocked, Brass Furniture, Reproduction, (Numrich), *Antique*	140.00	185.00
RIFLE, PERCUSSION		
☐ **"Buggy Deluxe"**, .36, Under-Hammer, Octagon Barrel, Carbine, Reproduction, (Numrich), *Antique*	70.00	100.00
☐ **"Buggy Deluxe"**, .45, Under-Hammer, Octagon Barrel, Carbine, Reproduction, (Numrich), *Antique*	75.00	110.00
☐ **"Deer Stalker"**, .58, Under-Hammer, Octagon Barrel, Reproduction, (Numrich), *Antique*	75.00	100.00
☐ **"Heritage"**, .36, Under-Hammer, Octagon Barrel, Brass Furniture, Reproduction, (Numrich), *Antique*	70.00	110.00
☐ **"Heritage"**, .45, Under-Hammer, Octagon Barrel, Brass Furniture, Reproduction, (Numrich), *Antique*	75.00	115.00
☐ **"Kentucky"**, .31, Full-Stocked, Octagon Barrel, Brass Furniture, Reproduction, (Numrich), *Antique*	130.00	175.00
☐ **"Kentucky"**, .36, Full-Stocked, Octagon Barrel, Brass Furniture, Reproduction, (Numrich), *Antique*	135.00	175.00
☐ **"Kentucky"**, .45, Full-Stocked, Octagon Barrel, Brass Furniture, Reproduction, (Numrich), *Antique*	140.00	180.00
☐ **"Minuteman Brush"**, .45, Full-Stocked, Octagon Barrel, Carbine, Reproduction, (Numrich), *Antique*	130.00	180.00

HOPKINS AND ALLEN / 223

	V.G.	EXC.
☐ **"Minuteman Brush"**, .50, Full-Stocked, Octagon Barrel, Carbine, Reproduction, (Numrich), *Antique*	130.00	180.00
☐ **"Minuteman"**, .31, Full-Stocked, Octagon Barrel, Brass Furniture, Reproduction, (Numrich), *Antique*	125.00	175.00
☐ **"Minuteman"**, .36, Full-Stocked, Octagon Barrel, Brass Furniture, Reproduction, (Numrich), *Antique*	130.00	175.00
☐ **"Minuteman"**, .45, Full-Stocked, Octagon Barrel, Brass Furniture, Reproduction, (Numrich), *Antique*	130.00	180.00
☐ **"Minuteman"**, .50, Full-Stocked, Octagon Barrel, Brass Furniture, Reproduction, (Numrich), *Antique*	135.00	180.00
☐ **"Offhand Deluxe"**, .36, Under-Hammer, Octagon Barrel, Reproduction, (Numrich), *Antique*	60.00	100.00
☐ **"Offhand Deluxe"**, .45, Under-Hammer, Octagon Barrel, Reproduction, (Numrich), *Antique*	65.00	100.00
☐ **"Offhand Deluxe"**, .45, Under-Hammer, Octagon Barrel, Reproduction, (Numrich), *Antique*	65.00	100.00
☐ **"Pennsylvania"**, .31, Half-Stocked, Octagon Barrel, Brass Furniture, Reproduction, (Numrich), *Antique*	125.00	165.00
☐ **"Pennsylvania"**, .36, Half-Stocked, Octagon Barrel, Brass Furniture, Reproduction, (Numrich), *Antique*	130.00	165.00
☐ **"Pennsylvania"**, .45, Half-Stocked, Octagon Barrel, Brass Furniture, Reproduction, (Numrich), *Antique*	130.00	170.00
☐ **"Pennsylvania"**, .50, Half-Stocked, Octagon Barrel, Brass Furniture, Reproduction, (Numrich), *Antique*	135.00	170.00
☐ **"Target"**, .45, Under-Hammer, Octagon Barrel, Reproduction, (Numrich), *Antique*	60.00	95.00
☐ **.45**, Double Barrel, Over-Under, Swivel Breech, Brass Furniture, Reproduction, (Numrich), *Antique*	80.00	120.00

RIFLE, SINGLESHOT

	V.G.	EXC.
☐ **Model 1888 (XL)**, Various Calibers, Falling Block, Takedown, Lever Action, Round Barrel, Open Rear Sight, *Antique*	200.00	325.00
☐ **Model 1888 Junior**, .22 L.R.R.F., Falling Block, Takedown, Lever Action, Round Barrel, Open Rear Sight, *Antique*	90.00	145.00
☐ **No. 1922 New Model Junior**, .22 L.R.R.F., Falling Block, Takedown, Lever Action, Octagon Barrel, Open Rear Sight, *Modern*	125.00	200.00
☐ **No. 1925 New Model Junior**, .25 Short R.F., Falling Block, Takedown, Lever Action, Octagon Barrel, Open Rear Sight, *Modern*	145.00	225.00
☐ **No. 1932 New Model Junior**, .32 Long R.F., Falling Block, Takedown, Lever Action, Octagon Barrel, Open Rear Sight, *Modern*	140.00	230.00
☐ **No. 1938 New Model Junior**, .38 S & W, Falling Block, Takedown, Lever Action, Octagon Barrel, Open Rear Sight, *Modern*	165.00	245.00
☐ **No. 2922 New Model Junior**, .22 L.R.R.F., Falling Block, Takedown, Lever Action, Octagon Barrel, Checkered Stock, Open Rear Sight, *Modern*	145.00	225.00
☐ **No. 2925 New Model Junior**, .25 Short R.F., Falling Block, Takedown, Lever Action, Octagon Barrel, Checkered Stock, Open Rear Sight, *Modern*	165.00	245.00
☐ **No. 2932 New Model Junior**, .32 Long R.F., Falling Block, Takedown, Lever Action, Octagon Barrel, Checkered Stock, Open Rear Sight, *Modern*	165.00	245.00
☐ **No. 2938 New Model Junior**, .38 S & W, Falling Block, Takedown, Lever Action, Octagon Barrel, Checkered Stock, Open Rear Sight, *Modern*	195.00	290.00
☐ **No. 3922 Schuetzen Target**, .22 L.R.R.F., Falling Block, Takedown, Lever Action, Octagon Barrel, Checkered Stock, Swiss Buttplate, *Modern*	400.00	600.00

	V.G.	EXC.
☐ **No. 3925 Schuetzen Target**, .25-20 WCF, Falling Block, Takedown, Lever Action, Octagon Barrel, Checkered Stock, Swiss Buttplate, *Modern*	475.00	700.00
☐ **No. 722**, .22 L.R.R.F., Rolling Block, Takedown, Round Barrel, Open Rear Sight, *Modern*	70.00	115.00
☐ **No. 822**, .22 L.R.R.F., Rolling Block, Takedown, Lever Action, Round Barrel, Open Rear Sight, *Modern*	85.00	140.00
☐ **No. 832**, .32 Short R.F., Rolling Block, Takedown, Lever Action, Round Barrel, Open Rear Sight, *Modern*	90.00	150.00
☐ **No. 922 New Model Junior**, .22 L.R.R.F., Falling Block, Takedown, Lever Action, Round Barrel, Open Rear Sight, *Modern*	100.00	155.00
☐ **No. 925 New Model Junior**, .25 Short R.F., Falling Block, Takedown, Lever Action, Round Barrel, Open Rear Sight, *Modern*	95.00	150.00
☐ **No. 932 New Model Junior**, .32 Long R.F., Falling Block, Takedown, Lever Action, Round Barrel, Open Rear Sight, *Modern*	95.00	150.00
☐ **No. 938 New Model Junior**, .38 S & W, Falling Block, Takedown, Lever Action, Round Barrel, Open Rear Sight, *Modern*	140.00	200.00
☐ **Noiseless**, .22 L.R.R.F., Falling Block, Takedown, Lever Action, Round Barrel, Silencer, *Class 3*	275.00	400.00

SHOTGUN, DOUBLE BARREL, SIDE-BY-SIDE

	V.G.	EXC.
☐ **No. 100**, 12 and 16 Ga., Double Trigger, Outside Hammers, Checkered Stock, Steel Barrel, *Modern*	95.00	150.00
☐ **No. 110**, 12 and 16 Ga., Double Trigger, Hammerless, Checkered Stock, Steel Barrel, *Modern*	120.00	165.00

SHOTGUN, SINGLESHOT

	V.G.	EXC.
☐ **New Model**, Various Gauges, Hammer, Top Break, Steel Barrel, *Modern*	45.00	65.00
☐ **New Model**, Various Gauges, Hammer, Top Break, Steel Barrel, Automatic Ejector, Checkered Stock, *Modern*	50.00	85.00
☐ **New Model**, Various Gauges, Hammer, Top Break, Damascus Barrel, Checkered Stock, *Modern*	45.00	70.00

HOPKINS, C.W.
Made by Bacon Mfg. Co., Norwich, Conn.

HANDGUN, REVOLVER

	V.G.	EXC.
☐ **.32 Short R.F.**, Single Action, Solid Frame, Swing-Out Cylinder, *Antique*	200.00	325.00
☐ **.38 Long R.F.**, Single Action, Solid Frame, Swing-Out Cylinder, *Antique*	350.00	600.00

HOROLT, LORENZ
Nuremberg, Germany, c. 1600.

HANDGUN, WHEEL-LOCK

	V.G.	EXC.
☐ **Long Barreled**, Holster Pistol, Hexagonal Ball Pommel, Light Ornamentation, *Antique*	6,000.00	7,750.00

HOWARD ARMS
Made by Meriden Firearms Co.

HANDGUN, REVOLVER

	V.G.	EXC.
☐ **.32 S & W**, 5 Shot, Double Action, Top Break, *Modern*	55.00	95.00
☐ **.38 S & W**, 5 Shot, Double Action, Top Break, *Modern*	55.00	95.00

HOWARD ARMS
Made by Cresent for Fred Bifflar & Co.

	V.G.	EXC.
SHOTGUN, DOUBLE BARREL, SIDE-BY-SIDE		
☐ **Various Gauges**, Outside Hammers, Damascus Barrel, *Modern*	100.00	175.00
☐ **Various Gauges**, Hammerless, Steel Barrel, *Modern*	135.00	200.00
☐ **Various Gauges**, Hammerless, Damascus Barrel, *Modern*	100.00	175.00
☐ **Various Gauges**, Outside Hammers, Steel Barrel, *Modern*	125.00	190.00
SHOTGUN, SINGLESHOT		
☐ **Various Gauges**, Hammer, Steel Barrel, *Modern*	55.00	85.00

HOWARD BROTHERS
Detroit, Mich., c. 1868.

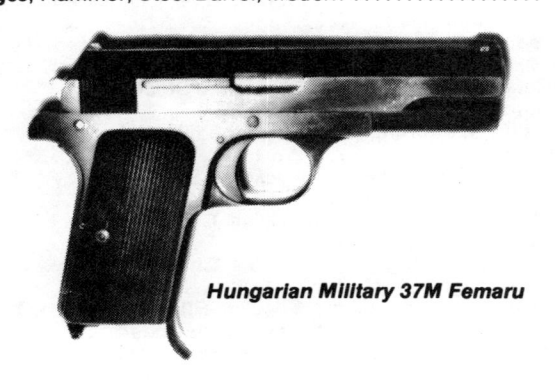

RIFLE, SINGLESHOT
☐ **.44 Henry R.F., Round Barrel,** *Antique* 300.00   475.00

HOUILLER, BLANCHAR
Paris, France, c. 1845.

HANDGUN, PERCUSSION
☐ **Pepperbox**, .48, 6 Shot, *Antique* 350.00   475.00

HUMBERGER, PETER JR.
Ohio 1791-1852. See Kentucky Rifles.

HUMBERGER, PETER SR.
Pa. 1774-1791, then Ohio 1791-1811. See Kentucky Rifles.

HUMMER
Belgium, for Lee Hdw., Kansas.

SHOTGUN, DOUBLE BARREL, SIDE—BY—SIDE
☐ **Various Gauges**, Outside Hammers, Damascus Barrel, *Modern* 100.00   175.00
☐ **Various Gauges**, Hammerless, Steel Barrel, *Modern* 135.00   200.00
☐ **Various Gauges**, Hammerless, Damascus Barrel, *Modern* 100.00   175.00
☐ **Various Gauges**, Outside Hammers, Steel Barrel, *Modern* 125.00   190.00

SHOTGUN, SINGLESHOT
☐ **Various Gauges**, Hammer, Steel Barrel, *Modern* 55.00   85.00

Hungarian Military 37M Femaru

HUNGARIAN MILITARY

	V.G.	EXC.
AUTOMATIC WEAPON, SUBMACHINE GUN		
☐ **43M**, 9mm Mauser Export, Clip Fed, Retarded Blowback, *Class 3*	750.00	1,100.00
HANDGUN, SEMI-AUTOMATIC		
☐ **19M Frommer Stop**, .380 ACP, Clip Fed, Blue, Military, *Curio*	165.00	250.00
☐ **29M Femaru**, .380 ACP, Clip Fed, Blue, Military, *Curio*	150.00	220.00
☐ **37M Femaru**, .380 ACP, Clip Fed, Blue, Military, *Curio*	145.00	195.00
RIFLE, BOLT ACTION		
☐ **1943M**, 8mm Mauser, Mannlicher, Military, *Curio*	100.00	175.00
☐ **8mm 1935M**, Mannlicher, Military, *Curio*	90.00	145.00

HUNTER ARMS
See L.C. Smith.

HUNTING WORLD
N.Y.C.

SHOTGUN, DOUBLE BARREL, SIDE-BY-SIDE
☐ **Royal Deluxe Game Gun**, 12 or 20 Gauges, Sidelock, Fancy Wood, Engraved, *Modern* 3,500.00 4,500.00

HUSQVARNA VAPENFABRIK AKITIEBOLAG
Sweden

	V.G.	EXC.
HANDGUN, REVOLVER		
☐ **Model 1887 Swedish Nagent**, 7.5mm, Double Action, Blue, Military, Antique	165.00	250.00
HANDGUN, SEMI-AUTOMATIC		
☐ **Model 07**, 9mm Browning Long, Clip Fed, Military, *Modern*	165.00	250.00
RIFLE, BOLT ACTION		
☐ **Various Calibers**, Sporting Rifle, Checkered Stock, *Modern*	200.00	285.00
☐ **1000 Super Grade**, Various Calibers, Sporting Rifle, Checkered Stock, Monte Carlo Stock, *Modern*	225.00	325.00
☐ **1100 Deluxe**, Various Calibers, Sporting Rifle, Checkered Stock, *Modern*	225.00	325.00
☐ **1622**, .22 L.R.R.F., Clip Fed, Sling Swivels, *Modern*	50.00	75.00
☐ **1951**, Various Calibers, Sporting Rifle, Checkered Stock, *Modern*	200.00	275.00
☐ **3000 Crown Grade**, Various Calibers, Sporting Rifle, Checkered Stock, Monte Carlo Stock, *Modern*	275.00	375.00
☐ **3100 Crown Grade**, Various Calibers, Sporting Rifle, Checkered Stock, *Modern*	275.00	375.00
☐ **4000**, Various Calibers, Sporting Rifle, Checkered Stock, Lightweight, Monte Carlo Stock, *Modern*	275.00	375.00
☐ **4100**, Various Calibers, Sporting Rifle, Checkered Stock, Lightweight, *Modern*	275.00	375.00
☐ **456**, Various Calibers, Sporting Rifle, Checkered Stock, Lightweight, Full-Stocked, *Modern*	300.00	400.00
☐ **6000 Imperial**, Various Calibers, Sporting Rifle, Checkered Stock, Fancy Wood, Express Sights, *Modern*	325.00	450.00
☐ **7000 Imperial**, Various Calibers, Sporting Rifle, Checkered Stock, Lightweight, Express Sights, *Modern*	325.00	450.00
☐ **8000 Imperial Grade**, Various Calibers, Sporting Rifle, Checkered Stock, Engraved, Monte Carlo Stock, Fancy Wood, *Modern*	350.00	475.00
☐ **9000 Crown Grade**, Various Calibers, Sporting Rifle, Checkered Stock, Monte Carlo Stock, *Modern*	275.00	375.00
☐ **Gustav CG-T**, Various Calibers, Singleshot, Target Stock, Heavy Barrel, *Modern*	200.00	270.00

Husqvarna M1907 Pistol

Husqvarna M1887 Revolver

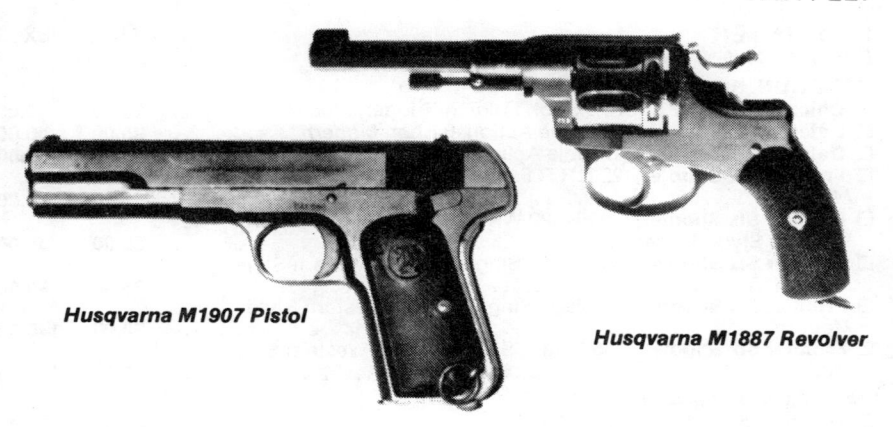

	V.G.	EXC.
☐ **Gustav Grade II**, Various Calibers, Sporting Rifle, Checkered Stock, *Modern*	280.00	400.00
☐ **Gustav Grade II**, Various Calibers, Sporting Rifle, Checkered Stock, Left-Hand, *Modern*	290.00	420.00
☐ **Gustav Grade II**, Various Calibers, Sporting Rifle, Checkered Stock, Magnum Action, *Modern*	285.00	410.00
☐ **Gustav Grade III**, Various Calibers, Sporting Rifle, Checkered Stock, Magnum Action, Left-Hand, *Modern*	285.00	425.00
☐ **Gustav Grade III**, Various Calibers, Sporting Rifle, Checkered Stock, Magnum Action, Light Engraving, Left-Hand, *Modern*	325.00	475.00
☐ **Gustav Grade III**, Various Calibers, Sporting Rifle, Checkered Stock, Magnum Action, Light Engraving, *Modern*	325.00	475.00
☐ **Gustav Grade III**, Various Calibers, Sporting Rifle, Checkered Stock, Light Engraving, *Modern*	325.00	475.00
☐ **Gustav Grade III**, Various Calibers, Sporting Rifle, Checkered Stock, Light Engraving, Left-Hand, *Modern*	325.00	475.00
☐ **Gustav Grade V**, Various Calibers, Sporting Rifle, Checkered Stock, Engraved, *Modern*	450.00	650.00
☐ **Gustav Grade V**, Various Calibers, Sporting Rifle, Checkered Stock, Engraved, Left-Hand, *Modern*	450.00	650.00
☐ **Gustav Grade V**, Various Calibers, Sporting Rifle, Checkered Stock, Engraved, Magnum Action, *Modern*	450.00	650.00
☐ **Gustav Grade V**, Various Calibers, Sporting Rifle, Checkered Stock, Engraved, Magnum Action, Left-Hand, *Modern*	450.00	650.00
☐ **Gustav Swede**, Various Calibers, Sporting Rifle, Checkered Stock, *Modern*	200.00	300.00
☐ **Gustav Swede Deluxe**, Various Calibers, Sporting Rifle, Checkered Stock, Light Engraving, *Modern*	265.00	335.00
☐ **Gustav V-T**, Various Calibers, Varmint, Target Stock, Heavy Barrel, *Modern*	300.00	425.00
☐ **P 3000 Presentation**, Various Calibers, Sporting Rifle, Checkered Stock, Engraved, Fancy Wood, *Modern*	460.00	650.00

HUTZ, BENJAMIN
Lancaster, Pa. c. 1802. See Kentucky Rifles.

HVA
See Husqvarna.

HY HUNTER
Burbank, Calif.

	V.G.	EXC.
HANDGUN, REVOLVER		
☐ **Chicago Cub**, .22 Short, 6 Shot, Folding Trigger, *Modern*	20.00	35.00
☐ **Detective**, .22 L.R.R.F., Double Action, 6 Shot, *Modern*	25.00	40.00
☐ **Detective**, .22 W.M.R., Double Action, 6 Shot, *Modern*	25.00	40.00
☐ **Frontier Six Shooter**, .22 L.R.R.F., Single Action, Western Style, *Modern*	35.00	55.00
☐ **Frontier Six Shooter**, .22 LR/.22 WRF Combo, Single Action, Western Style, *Modern*	35.00	55.00
☐ **Frontier Six Shooter**, .357 Mag., Single Action, Western Style, *Modern*	65.00	90.00
☐ **Frontier Six Shooter**, .44 Mag., Single Action, Western Style, *Modern*	90.00	135.00
☐ **Frontier Six Shooter**, ".45 Mag.", Single Action, Western Style, *Modern*	75.00	120.00
HANDGUN, SEMI-AUTOMATIC		
☐ **Maxim**, .25 ACP, Clip Fed, *Modern*	45.00	70.00
☐ **Militar**, .22 L.R.R.F., Double Action, Hammer, Clip Fed, Blue, *Modern*	50.00	80.00
☐ **Militar**, .32 ACP, Double Action, Hammer, Clip Fed, Blue, *Modern*	60.00	95.00
☐ **Militar**, .380 ACP, Double Action, Hammer, Clip Fed, Blue, *Modern*	65.00	95.00
☐ **Panzer**, .22 L.R.R.F., Clip Fed, Blue, *Modern*	40.00	65.00
☐ **Stingray**, .25 ACP, Clip Fed, Blue, *Modern*	40.00	65.00
☐ **Stuka**, .22 Long, Clip Fed, Blue, *Modern*	40.00	65.00
HANDGUN, DOUBLE BARREL, OVER-UNDER		
☐ **Automatic Derringer**, .22 L.R.R.F., Blue, *Modern*	25.00	40.00
HANDGUN, SINGLESHOT		
☐ **Accurate Ace**, .22 Short, Flobert Type, Chrome Plated, *Modern*	20.00	40.00
☐ **Favorite**, .22 L.R.R.F., Stevens Copy, *Modern*	35.00	55.00
☐ **Favorite**, .22 W.M.R., Stevens Copy, *Modern*	40.00	65.00
☐ **Gold Rush Derringer**, .22 L.R.R.F., Spur Trigger, *Modern*	25.00	40.00
☐ **Target**, .22 L.R.R.F., Bolt Action, *Modern*	30.00	45.00
☐ **Target**, .22 W.M.R., Bolt Action, *Modern*	35.00	50.00
RIFLE, BOLT ACTION		
☐ **Maharaja**, Various Calibers, Various Actions, Custom Made, Fancy Engraving, Fancy Wood, Fancy Inlays, Gold Plated, *Modern*	3,750.00	5,500.00

HYPER
Jenks, Okla.

	V.G.	EXC.
RIFLE, SINGLESHOT		
☐ **Hyper-Single Rifle**, Various Calibers, Fancy Wood, No Sights, Falling Block, Fancy Checkering, *Modern*	750.00	1,000.00
☐ **Hyper-Single Rifle**, Various Calibers, Fancy Wood, No Sights, Falling Block, Fancy Checkering, Stainless Steel Barrel, *Modern*	775.00	1,100.00

HY SCORE ARMS
Brooklyn, N.Y.

	V.G.	EXC.
HANDGUN, REVOLVER		
☐ **.22 L.R.R.F., Double Action**, *Modern*	20.00	35.00

IAB
Puccinelli Co., San Anselmo, Calif.

SHOTGUN, DOUBLE BARREL, OVER-UNDER
☐ **C-300 Combo**, 12 Ga., Vent Rib, Single Selective Trigger,
Checkered Stock, with 2 Extra Single Barrels, *Modern* 1,650.00 2,450.00
☐ **C-300 Super Combo**, 12 Ga., Vent Rib, Single Selective Trigger,
Checkered Stock, with 2 Extra Single Barrels, *Modern* 2,200.00 2,975.00

SHOTGUN, SINGLESHOT
☐ **S-300**, 12 Ga., Vent Rib, Checkered Stock, Trap Grade, *Modern* ... 875.00 1,300.00

I G
Grey, of Dundee, c. 1630.

HANDGUN, SNAPHAUNCE
☐ **Belt Pistol**, Engraved, Ovoid Pommel, All Metal, *Antique* 15,000.00 20,000.00

IMPERIAL
Maker unknown, c. 1880.

HANDGUN, REVOLVER
☐ **.22 Short R.F.**, 7 Shot, Spur Trigger, Solid Frame, Single Action,
Antique 90.00 160.00
☐ **.32 Short R.F.**, 5 Shot, Spur Trigger, Solid Frame, Single Action,
Antique 95.00 170.00

IMPERIAL ARMS
Made by Hopkins & Allen, c. 1880.

HANDGUN, REVOLVER
☐ **.32 Short R.F.**, 5 Shot, Spur Trigger, Solid Frame, Single Action,
Antique 90.00 160.00
☐ **.38 Short R.F.**, 5 Shot, Spur Trigger, Solid Frame, Single Action,
Antique 95.00 175.00

I.N.A.
Industria Nacional de Armas, Sao Paulo, Brazil.

HANDGUN, REVOLVER
☐ **Tiger**, .22 L.R.R.F., Single Action, Western Style, *Modern* 40.00 65.00
☐ **Tiger**, .32 S&W Long, Single Action, Western Style, *Modern* 45.00 70.00

INDIA MILITARY
AUTOMATIC WEAPON, HEAVY MACHINE GUN
☐ **Bira Gun**, .450/.577 Martini-Henry, Drum Magazine, Carriage
Mount, Twin Barrels, *Antique* 7,000.00 10,000.00

RIFLE, BOLT ACTION
☐ **S.M.L.E. No. 1 Mk.III**, .303 British, Clip Fed, Ishapore, *Curio* 90.00 140.00

India Military #1 Mk.III Rifle

INDIAN ARMS
Detroit, Mich.

	V.G.	EXC.

HANDGUN, SEMI-AUTOMATIC
☐ **.380 ACP**, Clip Fed, Stainless Steel, Vent Rib, Double Action, Modern 275.00   425.00

INDIAN SALES
Cheyenne, Wyo.

HANDGUN, REVOLVER
☐ **HS-21**, .22 L.R.R.F., Double Action, Blue, *Modern* 20.00   30.00

HANDGUN, SEMI-AUTOMATIC
☐ **Model 4**, .25 ACP, Clip Fed, Blue, *Modern* 55.00   80.00

INGRAM
Invented by Gordon Ingram. Made by Police Ordnance Co., Los Angeles, Calif. and Military Armament Corp., Georgia.

AUTOMATIC WEAPON, SUBMACHINE GUN
☐ **M-10 M A C**, .45 ACP, Clip Fed, Folding Stock, Commercial, *Class 3* 125.00   175.00
☐ **M-10 M A C**, .45 ACP, Clip Fed, Folding Stock, Commercial, Silencer, *Class 3* 200.00   275.00
☐ **M-10 M A C**, 9mm Luger, Clip Fed, Folding Stock, Commercial, *Class 3* 125.00   175.00
☐ **M-10 M A C**, 9mm Luger, Clip Fed, Folding Stock, Commercial, Silencer, *Class 3* 200.00   275.00
☐ **M-11 M A C**, .380 ACP, Clip Fed, Folding Stock, Commercial, *Class 3* 300.00   375.00
☐ **M-11 M A C**, .380 ACP, Clip Fed, Folding Stock, Commercial, Silencer, *Class 3* 400.00   500.00
☐ **M6 Ingram**, .45 ACP, Clip Fed, Commercial, *Class 3* 275.00   375.00

INGRAM, CHARLES
Glasgow, Scotland, c. 1860.

SHOTGUN, DOUBLE BARREL, SIDE-BY-SIDE
☐ **Extra Set of Rifle Barrels**, High Quality, Cased with Accessories, Engraved, Checkered Stock, *Antique* 5,000.00   7,000.00

INHOFF, BENEDICT
Berks County, Pa. 1781-1783. See Kentucky Rifles.

INTERCHANGEABLE
Belgium, Trade Name Schoverlin-Daley & Gales, c. 1880.

SHOTGUN, DOUBLE BARREL, SIDE-BY-SIDE
☐ **Various Gauges**, Outside Hammers, Damascus Barrel, *Modern* 90.00   150.00

INTERDYNAMIC

HANDGUN, SEMI-AUTOMATIC
☐ **KG-9**, 9mm Luger, Clip Fed, SMG Styling, *Modern* 220.00   325.00
☐ **KG-9**, 9mm Luger, Clip Fed, SMG Styling, Serial Number Higher Than 4089, *Class 3* 185.00   250.00

INTERNATIONAL
Made by Hood Firearms, c. 1875.

	V.G.	EXC.
HANDGUN, REVOLVER		
☐ **.22 Short R.F.**, 7 Shot, Spur Trigger, Solid Frame, Single Action, Antique	90.00	160.00
☐ **.32 Short R.F.**, 5 Shot, Spur Trigger, Solid Frame, Single Action, Antique	95.00	170.00

INTERNATIONAL DISTRIBUTERS
Miami, Florida.

RIFLE, BOLT ACTION
☐ **Mauser Type**, Various Calibers, Checkered Stock, Sling Swivels, Recoil Pad, *Modern* 140.00 200.00

INTERSTATE ARMS CO.
Made by Crescent for Townley Metal & Hdw., Kansas City, Mo.

SHOTGUN, DOUBLE BARREL, SIDE-BY-SIDE
☐ **Various Gauges**, Outside Hammers, Damascus Barrel, *Modern* 100.00 175.00
☐ **Various Gauges**, Hammerless, Steel Barrel, *Modern* 135.00 200.00
☐ **Various Gauges**, Hammerless, Damascus Barrel, *Modern* 100.00 175.00
☐ **Various Gauges**, Outside Hammers, Steel Barrel, *Modern* 125.00 190.00

SHOTGUN, SINGLESHOT
☐ **Various Gauges**, Hammer, Steel Barrel, *Modern* 55.00 85.00

I P
Probably German, 1580-1600.

RIFLE, WHEEL-LOCK
☐ **.60**, German Style, Brass Furniture, Light Ornamentation, Horn Inlays, Set Trigger, *Antique* 3,000.00 4,000.00

ISRAELI MILITARY
This list includes both military arms and the commercial arms made by Israeli Military Industries (I.M.I.).

AUTOMATIC WEAPON, SUBMACHINE GUN
☐ **UZI**, 9mm Luger, Clip Fed, Silencer, *Class 3* 700.00 850.00
☐ **UZI**, 9mm Luger, Clip Fed, Folding Stock, *Class 3* 500.00 650.00
☐ **UZI**, 9mm Luger, Clip Fed, Folding Stock, Commercial Conversion, *Class 3* 300.00 450.00

HANDGUN, REVOLVER
☐ **S & W Model 10 Copy**, 9mm Luger, Solid Frame, Swing-Out Cylinder, Double Action, Military, *Modern* 400.00 575.00

RIFLE, SEMI-AUTOMATIC
☐ **Galil**, .223 Rem., Clip Fed, Assault Rifle, Folding Stock, *Modern* ... 650.00 900.00
☐ **Galil**, .308 Win., Clip Fed, Assault Rifle, Folding Stock, *Modern* 700.00 1,000.00
☐ **UZI**, 9mm Luger, Clip Fed, Folding Stock, Commercial, *Modern* ... 300.00 450.00

ITALGUNS INTERNATIONAL
Cusago, Italy

COMBINATION WEAPON, OVER-UNDER
☐ **Various Calibers**, Checkered Stock, Double Triggers, *Modern* 200.00 300.00

HANDGUN, REVOLVER
☐ **Western Style**, Various Calibers, Single Action, *Modern* 90.00 125.00
☐ **Western Style**, Various Calibers, Single Action, Automatic Hammer Safety, *Modern* 95.00 135.00

232 / ITALIAN MILITARY

	V.G.	EXC.

SHOTGUN, DOUBLE BARREL, OVER-UNDER
☐ **Model 125**, 12 Gauge, Checkered Stock, Vent Rib, Double Triggers, *Modern* 150.00 200.00
☐ **Model 150**, 12 or 20 Gauges, Checkered Stock, Vent Rib, Single Trigger, *Modern* 175.00 225.00

Italian Military Service Revolver, Folding Trigger

Italian Military M910

Italian Military M91/24 Rifle

Italian Military M91 Rifle

ITALIAN MILITARY
Also See Beretta.

AUTOMATIC WEAPON, ASSAULT RIFLE
☐ **BM59**, .308 Win., Clip Fed, Bipod, *Class 3* 650.00 875.00

AUTOMATIC WEAPON, SUBMACHINE GUN
☐ **MP 38/44**, 9mm Luger, Clip Fed, Military, *Class 3* 650.00 800.00
☐ **MP 38/49**, 9mm Luger, Clip Fed, Wood Stock, Military, *Class 3* 275.00 375.00
☐ **MP 38A**, 9mm Luger, Clip Fed, Military, *Class 3* 550.00 725.00

HANDGUN, REVOLVER
☐ **Service Revolver**, 10.4mm, Double Action, 6 Shot, Folding Trigger, *Curio* 85.00 145.00
☐ **Service Revolver**, 10.4mm, Double Action, 6 Shot, Trigger Guard, *Curio* 85.00 145.00

HANDGUN, SEMI-AUTOMATIC
☐ **Brixia**, 9mm Glisenti, Clip Fed, Military, *Curio* 265.00 375.00
☐ **M910 Army**, 9mm Glisenti, Clip Fed, Military, *Curio* 250.00 350.00
☐ **M 1934 Beretta**, .380 ACP, Clip Fed, Military, *Modern* 120.00 175.00

RIFLE, BOLT ACTION
☐ **M1891**, 6.5 x 52 Mannlicher-Carcano, Military, *Modern* 65.00 100.00
☐ **M 38**, 7.35mm Carcano, Military, *Modern* 65.00 100.00

	V.G.	EXC.
☐ **M91 T.S.**, 6.5 x 52 Mannlicher-Carcano, Carbine, Folding Bayonet, Military, *Modern*	70.00	110.00
☐ **M91 T.S. (Late)**, 6.5 x 52 Mannlicher-Carcano, Carbine, Folding Bayonet, Military, *Modern*	55.00	95.00
☐ **M91/24**, 6.5 x 52 Mannlicher-Carcano, Carbine, Military, *Modern*	55.00	95.00
☐ **M91/24**, 6.5 x 52 Mannlicher-Carcano, Military, *Modern*	55.00	90.00
☐ **Vetterli M1870/1887**, 10.4 x 47R Italian Vetterli, *Antique*	60.00	95.00
☐ **Vetterli M1870/87/15**, 6.5 x 52 Mannlicher-Carcano, *Antique*	65.00	100.00

ITHACA GUN CO.
Ithaca, N.Y. 1873 to Date. Absorbed Lefever Arms Co., Syracuse Arms Co., Union Firearms Co., and Wilkes Barre Gun Co.

COMBINATION WEAPON, DOUBLE BARREL, OVER-UNDER
☐ **LSA 55 Turkey Gun**, 12 Ga./.222, Open Rear Sight, Monte Carlo Stock, *Modern*	275.00	375.00

RIFLE, BOLT ACTION
☐ **BSA CF 2**, Various Calibers, Magnum Action, Monte Carlo Stock, Checkered Stock, *Modern*	190.00	275.00
☐ **LSA 55**, Various Calibers, Monte Carlo Stock, Cheekpiece, Heavy Barrel, *Modern*	275.00	350.00
☐ **LSA-55**, Various Calibers, Monte Carlo Stock, Open Rear Sight, *Modern*	210.00	285.00
☐ **LSA-55 Deluxe**, Various Calibers, Monte Carlo Stock, Cheekpiece, No Sights, Scope Mounts, *Modern*	265.00	335.00
☐ **LSA-65**, Various Calibers, Monte Carlo Stock, Open Rear Sight, *Modern*	225.00	300.00
☐ **LSA-65 Deluxe**, Various Calibers, Monte Carlo Stock, Cheekpiece, No Sights, Scope Mounts, *Modern*	255.00	340.00

RIFLE, LEVER ACTION
☐ **Model 49**, .22 L.R.R.F., Singleshot, *Modern*	30.00	45.00
☐ **Model 49**, .22 WMR, Singleshot, *Modern*	35.00	50.00
☐ **Model 49 Deluxe**, .22 L.R.R.F., Singleshot, Fancy Wood, *Modern*	45.00	60.00
☐ **Model 49 Presentation**, .22 L.R.R.F., Singleshot, Engraved, Fancy Checkering, *Modern*	120.00	170.00
☐ **Model 49 R**, .22 L.R.R.F., Tube Feed, *Modern*	50.00	75.00
☐ **Model 49 St. Louis**, .22 L.R.R.F., Bicentennial, Singleshot, Fancy Wood, *Curio*	100.00	150.00
☐ **Model 49 Youth**, .22 L.R.R.F., Singleshot, *Modern*	30.00	45.00
☐ **Model 72**, .22 L.R.R.F., Tube Feed, *Modern*	85.00	120.00
☐ **Model 72**, .22 WMR, Tube Feed, *Modern*	95.00	140.00
☐ **Model 72 Deluxe**, .22 L.R.R.F., Tube Feed, Octagon Barrel, *Modern*	115.00	165.00

RIFLE, SEMI-AUTOMATIC
☐ **X-15 Lightning**, .22 L.R.R.F., Clip Fed, *Modern*	50.00	75.00
☐ **X5 C Lightning**, .22 L.R.R.F., Clip Fed, *Modern*	55.00	80.00
☐ **X5 T Lightning**, .22 L.R.R.F., Tube Feed, *Modern*	55.00	80.00

SHOTGUN, DOUBLE BARREL, OVER-UNDER
☐ **Model 500**, 12 and 20 Gauges, Field Grade, Selective Ejector, Vent Rib, *Modern*	275.00	375.00
☐ **Model 500**, 12 Ga. Mag. 3", Field Grade, Selective Ejector, Vent Rib, *Modern*	285.00	390.00
☐ **Model 600**, 12 Ga., Trap Grade, Selective Ejector, Vent Rib, *Modern*	375.00	500.00
☐ **Model 600**, 12 Ga., Trap Grade, Selective Ejector, Vent Rib, Monte Carlo Stock, *Modern*	375.00	500.00

234 / ITHACA GUN CO.

	V.G.	EXC.
☐ **Model 600**, 12 and 20 Gauges, Field Grade, Selective Ejector, Vent Rib, *Modern*	365.00	480.00
☐ **Model 600**, 12 and 20 Gauges, Skeet Grade, Selective Ejector, Vent Rib, *Modern*	375.00	500.00
☐ **Model 600**, 20 and .410 Gauges, Skeet Grade, Selective Ejector, Vent Rib, *Modern*	390.00	520.00
☐ **Model 600 Combo Set**, Various Gauges, Skeet Grade, Selective Ejector, Vent Rib, Cased, *Modern*	850.00	1,200.00
☐ **Model 680 English**, 12 and 20 Gauges, Field Grade, Selective Ejector, Vent Rib, *Modern*	400.00	515.00
☐ **Model 700**, 12 Ga., Trap Grade, Selective Ejector, Vent Rib, *Modern*	450.00	600.00
☐ **Model 700**, 12 Ga., Trap Grade, Selective Ejector, Vent Rib, Monte Carlo Stock, *Modern*	450.00	600.00
☐ **Model 700**, 12 and 20 Gauges, Skeet Grade, Selective Ejector, Vent Rib, *Modern*	450.00	600.00
☐ **Model 700 Combo Set**, Various Gauges, Skeet Grade, Selective Ejector, Vent Rib, Cased, *Modern*	975.00	1,600.00
☐ **Perazzi Light Game Model**, 12 Ga., Automatic Ejector, Vent Rib, Single Trigger, *Modern*	875.00	1,300.00
☐ **Perazzi Competition 1**, 12 Ga., Trap Grade, Automatic Ejector, Vent Rib, Single Trigger, Cased, *Modern*	875.00	1,300.00
☐ **Perazzi Competition 1**, 12 Ga., Skeet Grade, Automatic Ejector, Vent Rib, Single Trigger, Cased, *Modern*	875.00	1,300.00
☐ **Perazzi Mirage**, 12 Ga., Trap Grade, Automatic Ejector, Vent Rib, Cased, *Modern*	1,350.00	1,850.00
☐ **Perazzi Mirage 4-Barrel Set**, Various Gauges, Skeet Grade, Automatic Ejector, Vent Rib, Cased, *Modern*	3,400.00	4,400.00
☐ **Perazzi MT-6**, 12 Ga., Trap Grade, Automatic Ejector, Vent Rib, Cased, *Modern*	1,750.00	2,450.00
☐ **Perazzi MT-6**, 12 Ga., Skeet Grade, Automatic Ejector, Vent Rib, Cased, *Modern*	1,800.00	2,500.00
☐ **Perazzi MX-8**, 12 Ga., Trap Grade, Automatic Ejector, Vent Rib, Cased, *Modern*	1,350.00	1,950.00
☐ **Perazzi MX-8 Combo**, 12 Ga., Trap Grade, Automatic Ejector, Vent Rib, Cased, *Modern*	2,000.00	2,750.00

SHOTGUN, DOUBLE BARREL, SIDE-BY-SIDE

	V.G.	EXC.
☐ **Early Model**, Serial Numbers under 425,000 *Deduct 50%*		
☐ **Outside Hammers**, *Deduct Another 20%-30%*		
☐ **Various Gauges**, Field Grade, Hammerless, Magnum, Beavertail Forend, *Modern*	600.00	775.00
☐ **Various Gauges**, Field Grade, Hammerless, Beavertail Forend, Double Trigger, *Modern*	550.00	700.00
☐ **Various Gauges**, Field Grade, Hammerless, Double Trigger, Checkered Stock, *Modern*	375.00	525.00
☐ **Various Gauges**, Field Grade, Hammerless, Magnum, Double Trigger, *Modern*	425.00	575.00
☐ **#1 E Grade**, Various Gauges, Hammerless, Automatic Ejector, Beavertail Forend, Double Trigger, *Modern*	725.00	975.00
☐ **#1 E Grade**, Various Gauges, Hammerless, Automatic Ejector, Magnum, Beavertail Forend, Double Trigger, *Modern*	850.00	1,200.00
☐ **#1 E Grade**, Various Gauges, Hammerless, Automatic Ejector, Magnum, Double Trigger, *Modern*	750.00	1,050.00
☐ **#1 E Grade**, Various Gauges, Hammerless, Automatic Ejector, Light Engraving, Checkered Stock, Double Trigger, *Modern*	625.00	850.00
☐ **#1 Grade**, Various Gauges, Hammerless, Magnum, Double Trigger, Light Engraving, Checkered Stock, *Modern*	550.00	775.00

	V.G.	EXC.
☐ **#1 Grade**, Various Gauges, Hammerless, Double Trigger, Checkered Stock, Light Engraving, *Modern*	450.00	635.00
☐ **#1 Grade**, Various Gauges, Hammerless, Magnum, Beavertail Forend, Double Trigger, *Modern*	650.00	900.00
☐ **#1 Grade**, Various Gauges, Hammerless, Beavertail Forend, Light Engraving, Checkered Stock, Double Trigger, *Modern*	550.00	775.00
☐ **#2 E Grade**, Various Gauges, Hammerless, Automatic Ejector, Magnum, Beavertail Forend, Double Trigger, *Modern*	950.00	1,300.00
☐ **#2 E Grade**, Various Gauges, Hammerless, Automatic Ejector, Magnum, Double Trigger, *Modern*	750.00	1,050.00
☐ **#2 E Grade**, Various Gauges, Hammerless, Automatic Ejector, Beavertail Forend, Double Trigger, *Modern*	800.00	1,150.00
☐ **#2 E Grade**, Various Gauges, Hammerless, Automatic Ejector, Double Trigger, Engraved, Checkered Stock, *Modern*	700.00	975.00
☐ **#2 Grade**, Various Gauges, Hammerless, Magnum, Beavertail Forend, Double Trigger, *Modern*	725.00	1,000.00
☐ **#2 Grade**, Various Gauges, Hammerless, Beavertail Forend, Double Trigger, Engraved, Checkered Stock, *Modern*	625.00	800.00
☐ **#2 Grade**, Various Gauges, Hammerless, Magnum, Double Trigger, Engraved, Checkered Stock, *Modern*	650.00	825.00
☐ **#2 Grade**, Various Gauges, Hammerless, Double Trigger, Engraved, Checkered Stock, *Modern*	450.00	650.00
☐ **#3 E Grade**, Various Gauges, Hammerless, Magnum, Beavertail Forend, Automatic Ejector, Double Trigger, *Modern*	1,100.00	1,550.00
☐ **#3 E Grade**, Various Gauges, Hammerless, Magnum, Double Trigger, Engraved, Checkered Stock, *Modern*	950.00	1,375.00
☐ **#3 E Grade**, Various Gauges, Hammerless, Beavertail Forend, Automatic Ejector, Double Trigger, *Modern*	900.00	1,300.00
☐ **#3 E Grade**, Various Gauges, Hammerless, Double Trigger, Engraved, Checkered Stock, Automatic Ejector, *Modern*	825.00	1,250.00
☐ **#3 Grade**, Various Gauges, Hammerless, Magnum, Beavertail Forend, Double Trigger, *Modern*	825.00	1,250.00
☐ **#3 Grade**, Various Gauges, Hammerless, Magnum, Double Trigger, Engraved, Checkered Stock, *Modern*	750.00	1,150.00
☐ **#3 Grade**, Various Gauges, Hammerless, Beavertail Forend, Engraved, Checkered Stock, Double Trigger, *Modern*	725.00	1,050.00
☐ **#3 Grade**, Various Gauges, Hammerless, Double Trigger, Engraved, Checkered Stock, *Modern*	775.00	1,100.00
☐ **#4 E Grade**, Various Gauges, Hammerless, Automatic Ejector, Vent Rib, Beavertail Forend, *Modern*	2,200.00	2,800.00
☐ **#4 E Grade**, Various Gauges, Hammerless, Automatic Ejector, Vent Rib, Fancy Checkering, Fancy Engraving, *Modern*	1,975.00	2,550.00
☐ **#4 E Grade**, Various Gauges, Hammerless, Automatic Ejector, Beavertail Forend, Fancy Checkering, Fancy Engraving, *Modern*	1,700.00	2,200.00
☐ **#4 E Grade**, Various Gauges, Hammerless, Automatic Ejector, Fancy Checkering, Fancy Engraving, Double Trigger, *Modern*	1,350.00	1,950.00
☐ **#5 E Grade**, Various Gauges, Hammerless, Automatic Ejector, Vent Rib, Beavertail Forend, *Modern*	3,200.00	3,850.00
☐ **#5 E Grade**, Various Gauges, Hammerless, Automatic Ejector, Vent Rib, Fancy Checkering, Fancy Engraving, *Modern*	3,000.00	3,800.00
☐ **#5 E Grade**, Various Gauges, Hammerless, Automatic Ejector, Beavertail Forend, Fancy Checkering, Fancy Engraving, *Modern*	2,800.00	3,500.00
☐ **#5 E Grade**, Various Gauges, Hammerless, Automatic Ejector, Fancy Checkering, Fancy Engraving, Double Trigger, *Modern*	2,750.00	3,400.00
☐ **#7 E Grade**, Various Gauges, Hammerless, Automatic Ejector, Vent Rib, Beavertail Forend, *Modern*	6,850.00	8,550.00

236 / ITHACA GUN CO.

	V.G.	EXC.
☐ **#7 E Grade**, Various Gauges, Hammerless, Automatic Ejector, Vent Rib, Fancy Checkering, Fancy Engraving, *Modern*	6,650.00	8,200.00
☐ **#7 E Grade**, Various Gauges, Hammerless, Automatic Ejector, Beavertail Forend, Fancy Checkering, Fancy Engraving, *Modern*	6,500.00	7,900.00
☐ **#7 E Grade**, Various Gauges, Hammerless, Automatic Ejector, Fancy Checkering, Fancy Engraving, Double Trigger, *Modern*	6,300.00	7,750.00
☐ **$2000 Grade**, Various Gauges, Hammerless, Automatic Ejector, Single Selective Trigger, Ornate, *Modern*	7,500.00	10,500.00
☐ **$2000 Grade**, Various Gauges, Hammerless, Automatic Ejector, Single Selective Trigger, Vent Rib, Ornate, *Modern*	8,200.00	11,500.00
☐ **$2000 Grade**, Various Gauges, Hammerless, Automatic Ejector, Single Selective Trigger, Beavertail Forend, Ornate, *Modern*	7,700.00	10,500.00
☐ **$2000 Grade**, Various Gauges, Hammerless, Automatic Ejector, Single Selective Trigger, Vent Rib, Beavertail Forend, *Modern*	8,250.00	12,000.00
☐ **Model 100**, 12 and 20 Gauges, Hammerless, Field Grade, *Modern*	200.00	275.00
☐ **Model 200 E**, 12 and 20 Gauges, Hammerless, Selective Ejector, Field Grade, *Modern*	285.00	375.00
☐ **Model 200 E**, 12 and 20 Gauges, Hammerless, Selective Ejector, Skeet Grade, *Modern*	300.00	380.00
☐ **Model 280 English**, 12 and 20 Gauges, Hammerless, Selective Ejector, Field Grade, *Modern*	300.00	400.00

SHOTGUN, LEVER ACTION

	V.G.	EXC.
☐ **Model 66 Supersingle**, Various Gauges, Singleshot, *Modern*	40.00	55.00
☐ **Model 66 Buck**, Various Gauges, Singleshot, Open Rear Sight, *Modern*	40.00	60.00
☐ **Model 66 Youth**, Various Gauges, Singleshot, *Modern*	35.00	55.00

SHOTGUN, PISTOL

	V.G.	EXC.
☐ **Auto Burglar**, Various Gauges, Double Barrel, Side by Side, Short Shotgun, *Class 3*	425.00	600.00

SHOTGUN, SEMI-AUTOMATIC

	V.G.	EXC.
☐ **300 Standard**, 12 and 20 Gauges, *Modern*	145.00	180.00
☐ **300 Standard**, 12 and 20 Gauges, Vent Rib, *Modern*	150.00	190.00
☐ **300 XL Standard**, 12 and 20 Gauges, *Modern*	155.00	195.00
☐ **300 XL Standard**, 12 and 20 Gauges, Vent Rib, *Modern*	170.00	220.00
☐ **900 Deluxe**, 12 and 20 Gauges, Vent Rib, *Modern*	160.00	950.00
☐ **900 XL**, 12 Ga., Trap Grade, *Modern*	185.00	245.00
☐ **900 XL**, 12 Ga., Trap Grade, Monte Carlo Stock, *Modern*	185.00	250.00
☐ **900 XL**, 12 and 20 Gauges, Skeet Grade, *Modern*	180.00	235.00
☐ **900 XL Deluxe**, 12 and 20 Gauges, Vent Rib, *Modern*	180.00	225.00
☐ **900 XL Slug**, 12 and 20 Gauges, Open Rear Sight, *Modern*	170.00	220.00
☐ **Mag 10 Deluxe**, 10 Ga. 3½", Takedown, Vent Rib, Fancy Wood, Checkered Stock, *Modern*	400.00	485.00
☐ **Mag 10 Standard**, 10 Ga. 3½", Takedown, Vent Rib, Recoil Pad, Checkered Stock, Sling Swivels, *Modern*	300.00	395.00
☐ **Mag 10 Standard**, 10 Ga. 3½", Takedown, Recoil Pad, Checkered Stock, Sling Swivels, *Modern*	260.00	340.00
☐ **Mag 10 Supreme**, 10 Ga. 3½", Takedown, Vent Rib, Fancy Wood, Engraved, Checkered Stock, *Modern*	500.00	620.00
☐ **Model 51**, 12 and 20 Gauges, Takedown, Vent Rib, Recoil Pad, Magnum, *Modern*	195.00	260.00
☐ **Model 51 Deerslayer**, 12 Ga., Takedown, Open Rear Sight, Sling Swivels, *Modern*	190.00	250.00
☐ **Model 51 Deluxe**, 12 Ga., Trap Grade, Takedown, Checkered Stock, Fancy Wood, Recoil Pad, *Modern*	270.00	325.00
☐ **Model 51 Deluxe**, 12 Ga., Trap Grade, Monte Carlo Stock, Fancy Wood, Recoil Pad, *Modern*	280.00	335.00

ITHACA GUN CO. / 237

	V.G.	EXC.
☐ **Model 51 Deluxe**, 12 and 20 Gauges, Skeet Grade, Takedown, Checkered Stock, Fancy Wood, Recoil Pad, *Modern*	220.00	285.00
☐ **Model 51 Standard**, 12 and 20 Gauges, Takedown, Checkered Stock, *Modern*	170.00	220.00
☐ **Model 51 Standard**, 12 and 20 Gauges, Takedown, Vent Rib, Checkered Stock, *Modern*	190.00	245.00

SHOTGUN, SINGLESHOT

	V.G.	EXC.
☐ **$5000 Grade**, 12 Ga., Trap Grade, Automatic Ejector, Ornate, *Modern*	4,100.00	4,800.00
☐ **4 E Grade**, 12 Gauge, Trap Grade, Automatic Ejector, Engraved, Fancy Checkering, *Modern*	2,200.00	2,850.00
☐ **5 E Grade**, 12 Gauge, Trap Grade, Automatic Ejector, Fancy Engraving, Fancy Checkering, *Modern*	3,000.00	3,700.00
☐ **7 E Grade**, 12 Gauge, Trap Grade, Automatic Ejector, Fancy Engraving, Fancy Checkering, *Modern*	3,300.00	4,100.00
☐ **Century 12 Ga.**, Trap Grade, Automatic Ejector, Engraved, Checkered Stock, *Modern*	330.00	440.00
☐ **Century II**, 12 Ga., Trap Grade, Automatic Ejector, Engraved, Checkered Stock, *Modern*	350.00	465.00
☐ **Perazzi Competition 1**, 12 Ga., Trap Grade, Automatic Ejector, Vent Rib, Cased, *Modern*	995.00	1,450.00
☐ **Victory Grade**, 12 Ga., Automatic Ejector, Checkered Stock, Vent Rib, Trap Grade, *Modern*	750.00	1,100.00

SHOTGUN, SLIDE ACTION

☐ **Model 37**, for Extra Barrel *Add* **$45.00-$70.00**
☐ **Model 37**, Extra Vent Rib Barrel *Add* **$60.00-$85.00**

	V.G.	EXC.
☐ **Model 37**, 12 Ga., Takedown, Bicentennial, Engraved, Fancy Wood, Checkered Stock, *Modern*	450.00	550.00
☐ **Model 37**, Various Gauges, Takedown, Plain, *Modern*	95.00	135.00
☐ **Model 37 Deerslayer**, Various Gauges, Takedown, Checkered Stock, Recoil Pad, Open Rear Sight, *Modern*	140.00	175.00
☐ **Model 37 Deerslayer**, Various Gauges, Takedown, Fancy Wood, Checkered Stock, Recoil Pad, Open Rear Sight, *Modern*	150.00	200.00
☐ **Model 37 DSPS**, 12 Ga., Takedown, Checkered Stock, 8 Shot, Open Rear Sight, *Modern*	150.00	200.00
☐ **Model 37 DSPS**, 12 Ga., Takedown, Checkered Stock, 5 Shot, Open Rear Sight, *Modern*	145.00	190.00
☐ **Model 37 M & P**, 12 Ga., Takedown, Parkerized, 5 Shot, *Modern*	125.00	185.00

☐ **Model 37 M & P**, Bayonet & Adapter *Add* **$25.00-$45.00**

	V.G.	EXC.
☐ **Model 37-V Standard**, Various Gauges, Takedown, Checkered Stock, Vent Rib, *Modern*	140.00	185.00
☐ **Model 37 Standard**, Various Gauges, Takedown, Checkered Stock, *Modern*	120.00	165.00
☐ **Model 37 Supreme**, Various Gauges, Takedown, Trap Grade, Fancy Wood, Checkered Stock, *Modern*	250.00	350.00
☐ **Model 37 Supreme**, Various Gauges, Takedown, Skeet Grade, Fancy Wood, Checkered Stock, *Modern*	250.00	350.00
☐ **Model 37-$1000 Grade**, Various Gauges, Takedown, Fancy Wood, Fancy Checkering, Fancy Engraving, Gold Inlays, *Modern*	2,700.00	3,800.00
☐ **Model 37-$3000 Grade**, Various Gauges, Takedown, Fancy Wood, Fancy Checkering, Fancy Engraving, Gold Inlays, *Modern*	3,000.00	3,800.00
☐ **Model 37-D**, Various Gauges, Takedown, Checkered Stock, Beavertail Forend, *Modern*	120.00	155.00
☐ **Model 37-Deluxe**, Various Gauges, Takedown, Checkered Stock, Recoil Pad, *Modern*	130.00	165.00

238 / IVER JOHNSON

	V.G.	EXC.
☐ **Model 37-Deluxe**, Various Gauges, Takedown, Checkered Stock, Recoil Pad, Vent Rib, *Modern*	160.00	200.00
☐ **Model 37-R**, Various Gauges, Takedown, Solid Rib, Checkered Stock, *Modern*	125.00	165.00
☐ **Model 37-R**, Various Gauges, Takedown, Solid Rib, Plain, *Modern*	115.00	155.00
☐ **Model 37-R Deluxe**, Various Gauges, Takedown, Solid Rib, Fancy Wood, Checkered Stock, *Modern*	160.00	200.00
☐ **Model 37-S**, Various Gauges, Takedown, Skeet Grade, Checkered Stock, Fancy Wood, *Modern*	225.00	300.00
☐ **Model 37-T**, Various Gauges, Takedown, Trap Grade, Checkered Stock, Fancy Wood, *Modern*	225.00	300.00

IVER JOHNSON

Started as Johnson & Bye 1871 in Worcester, Mass. In 1883 became Iver Johnson's Arms & Cycle Works. 1891 to date at Fitchburg, Mass.

HANDGUN, PERCUSSION

	V.G.	EXC.
☐ **.36 1861 Navy**, Revolver, Reproduction, *Antique*	50.00	75.00
☐ **.36 New Model Navy**, Revolver, Reproduction, *Antique*	35.00	60.00
☐ **.36 Pocket Model**, Revolver, Reproduction, *Antique*	50.00	75.00
☐ **.36 Remington Army**, Revolver, Reproduction, *Antique*	50.00	75.00
☐ **.44 1860 Army**, Revolver, Reproduction, *Antique*	50.00	75.00
☐ **.44 Confederate Army**, Revolver, Reproduction, *Antique*	30.00	50.00
☐ **.44 Remington Army**, Revolver, Reproduction, *Antique*	50.00	75.00
☐ **.44 Remington Target**, Revolver, Reproduction, *Antique*	60.00	90.00

HANDGUN, REVOLVER

	V.G.	EXC.
☐ **.22 Supershot**, .22 L.R.R.F., 7 Shot, Blue, Wood Grips, Top Break, Double Action, *Modern*	50.00	85.00
☐ **Armsworth M855**, .22 L.R.R.F., 8 Shot, Single Action, Top Break, Adjustable Sights, Wood Grips, *Modern*	60.00	100.00
☐ **Cadet**, .22 WMR, 8 Shot, Solid Frame, Double Action, Plastic Stock, Blue, *Modern*	35.00	60.00
☐ **Cadet**, .32 S & W Long, 5 Shot, Solid Frame, Double Action, Plastic Stock, Nickel Plated, *Modern*	40.00	65.00
☐ **Cadet**, .32 S & W, 5 Shot, Solid Frame, Double Action, Plastic Stock, Blue, *Modern*	35.00	60.00
☐ **Cadet**, .38 Special, 5 Shot, Solid Frame, Double Action, Plastic Stock, Blue, *Modern*	40.00	65.00
☐ **Cadet**, .38 Special, 5 Shot, Solid Frame, Double Action, Plastic Stock, Nickel Plated, *Modern*	45.00	70.00
☐ **Cattleman**, .357 Magnum, Single Action, Western Style, Color Case Hardened Frame, Various Barrel Lengths, *Modern*	95.00	140.00
☐ **Cattleman**, .44 Magnum, Single Action, Western Style, Color Case Hardened Frame, Various Barrel Lengths, *Modern*	125.00	165.00
☐ **Cattleman**, .45 Colt, Single Action, Western Style, Color Case Hardened Frame, Various Barrel Lengths, *Modern*	95.00	145.00
☐ **Cattleman Buckhorn**, .357 Magnum, Single Action, Western Style, Color Case Hardened Frame, Adjustable Sights, Various Barrel Lengths, *Modern*	95.00	140.00
☐ **Cattleman Buckhorn**, .357 Magnum, Single Action, Western Style, Color Case Hardened Frame, Adjustable Sights, 12" Barrel, *Modern*	125.00	175.00
☐ **Cattleman Buckhorn**, .44 Magnum, Single Action, Western Style, Color Case Hardened Frame, Adjustable Sights, Various Barrel Lengths, *Modern*	135.00	175.00
☐ **Cattleman Buckhorn**, .44 Magnum, Single Action, Western Style, Color Case Hardened Frame, *Modern*	115.00	160.00

IVER JOHNSON / 239

	V.G.	EXC.
☐ **Cattleman Buckhorn**, .45 Colt, Single Action, Western Style, Color Case Hardened Frame, Adjustable Sights, Various Barrel Lengths, *Modern*	95.00	155.00
☐ **Cattleman Buckhorn**, .45 Colt, Single Action, Western Style, Color Case Hardened Frame, Adjustable Sights, 12" Barrel, *Modern*	135.00	185.00
☐ **Cattleman Buntline**, .357 Magnum, Single Action, Western Style, with Detachable Shoulder Stock, Adjustable Sights, 18" Barrel, *Modern*	200.00	275.00
☐ **Cattleman Buntline**, .44 Magnum, Single Action, Western Style, with Detachable Shoulder Stock, Adjustable Sights, 18" Barrel, *Modern*	210.00	290.00
☐ **Cattleman Buntline**, .45 Colt, Single Action, Western Style, with Detachable Shoulder Stock, Adjustable Sights, 18" Barrel, *Modern*	200.00	280.00
☐ **Cattleman Trailblazer**, .22LR/.22 WMR Combo, Single Action, Western Style, Color Case Hardened Frame, Adjustable Sights, *Modern*	90.00	135.00
☐ **Champion Target**, .22 L.R.R.F., 8 Shot, Single Action, Top Break, Adjustable Sights, Wood Grips, *Modern*	75.00	120.00
☐ **Model 1900**, .22 L.R.R.F., 7 Shot, Blue, Double Action, Solid Frame, *Modern*	55.00	95.00
☐ **Model 1900**, .22 L.R.R.F., 7 Shot, Nickel Plated, Double Action, Solid Frame, *Modern*	50.00	95.00
☐ **Model 1900**, .32 S & W Long, 6 Shot, Blue, Double Action, Solid Frame, *Modern*	55.00	95.00
☐ **Model 1900**, .32 S & W Long, 6 Shot, Nickel Plated, Double Action, Solid Frame, *Modern*	55.00	95.00
☐ **Model 1900**, .32 Short R.F., 6 Shot, Blue, Double Action, Solid Frame, *Modern*	50.00	90.00
☐ **Model 1900**, .32 Short RF., 6 Shot, Nickel Plated, Double Action, Solid Frame, *Modern*	55.00	95.00
☐ **Model 1900**, .38 S & W, 5 Shot, Blue, Double Action, Solid Frame, *Modern*	55.00	95.00
☐ **Model 1900**, .38 S & W, 5 Shot, Nickel Plated, Double Action, Solid Frame, *Modern*	60.00	110.00
☐ **Model 1900 Target**, .22 L.R.R.F., 7 Shot, Blue, Wood Grips, Solid Frame, Double Action, *Modern*	65.00	120.00
☐ **Model 50A Sidewinder**, .22L.R.R.F., 8 Shot, Solid Frame, Double Action, Plastic Stock, Western Style, *Modern*	45.00	65.00
☐ **Model 50A Sidewinder**, .22L.R.R.F., 8 Shot, Solid Frame, Double Action, Wood Grips, Western Style, *Modern*	50.00	70.00
☐ **Model 55**, .22 L.R.R.F., 8 Shot, Solid Frame, Double Action, Wood Grips, Blue, *Modern*	40.00	65.00
☐ **Model 55-S Cadet**, .32 S & W, 5 Shot, Solid Frame, Double Action, Plastic Stock, Blue, *Modern*	40.00	65.00
☐ **Model 55-S Cadet**, .38 S & W, 5 Shot, Solid Frame, Double Action, Plastic Stock, Blue, *Modern*	40.00	65.00
☐ **Model 55-SA Cadet**, .22 L.R.R.F., 8 Shot, Solid Frame, Double Action, Plastic, Blue, *Modern*	40.00	65.00
☐ **Model 55-SA Cadet**, .32 S & W, 5 Shot, Solid Frame, Double Action, Plastic Stock, Blue, *Modern*	40.00	65.00
☐ **Model 55-SA Cadet**, .38 S & W, 5 Shot, Solid Frame, Double Action, Plastic Stock, Blue, *Modern*	40.00	65.00
☐ **Model 55A**, .22 L.R.R.F., 8 Shot, Solid Frame, Double Action, Wood Grips, Blue, *Modern*	40.00	65.00
☐ **Model 55A**, .22 L.R.R.F., 8 Shot, Solid Frame, Double Action, Wood Grips, Blue, *Modern*	40.00	65.00

240 / IVER JOHNSON

	V.G.	EXC.
☐ **Model 55A**, .22 L.R.R.F., 8 Shot, Solid Frame, Double Action, Plastic Stock, Blue, *Modern*	40.00	65.00
☐ **Model 55S**, .22 L.R.R.F., 8 Shot Solid Frame, Double Action, Plastic Stock, Blue, *Modern*	40.00	65.00
☐ **Model 57 Target**, .22 L.R.R.F., 8 Shot, Solid Frame, Double Action, Plastic Stock, Adjustable Sights, *Modern*	40.00	65.00
☐ **Model 57 Target**, .22 L.R.R.F., 8 Shot, Solid Frame, Double Action, Wood Grips, Adjustable Sights, *Modern*	40.00	65.00
☐ **Model 57-A Target**, .22 L.R.R.F., 8 Shot, Solid Frame, Double Action, Plastic Stock, Adjustable Sights, *Modern*	45.00	70.00
☐ **Model 57-A Target**, .22 L.R.R.F., 8 Shot, Solid Frame, Double Action, Wood Grips, Adjustable Sights, *Modern*	45.00	70.00
☐ **Model 66 Trailsman**, .22 L.R.R.F., 8 Shot, Top Break, Double Action, Wood Grips, Adjustable Sights, *Modern*	50.00	75.00
☐ **Model 67 Viking**, .22 L.R.R.F., 8 Shot, Top Break, Double Action, Plastic Stock, Adjustable Sights, *Modern*	55.00	75.00
☐ **Model 76S Viking**, .22 L.R.R.F., 8 Shot, Top Break, Double Action, Plastic Stock, Adjustable Sights, *Modern*	50.00	70.00
☐ **Model 67S Viking**, .32 S & W, 5 Shot, Top Break, Double Action, Plastic Stock, Adjustable Sights, *Modern*	50.00	70.00
☐ **Model 67S Viking**, .38 S & W, 5 Shot Top Break, Double Action, Plastic Stock, Adjustable Sights, *Modern*	40.00	55.00
☐ **Safety**, .22 L.R.R.F., 7 Shot, Top Break, Double Action, Hammer, Blue, *Modern*	60.00	95.00
☐ **Safety**, .22 L.R.R.F., 7 Shot, Top Break, Double Action, Hammer, Nickel Plated, *Modern*	70.00	110.00
☐ **Safety**, .22 L.R.R.F., 7 Shot, Top Break, Double Action, Hammerless, Blue, *Modern*	70.00	110.00
☐ **Safety**, .22 L.R.R.F., 7 Shot, Top Break, Double Action, Hammerless, Nickel Plated, *Modern*	75.00	120.00
☐ **Safety**, .32 S & W, 5 Shot, Top Break, Double Action, Hammer, Nickel Plated, *Modern*	70.00	110.00
☐ **Safety**, .32 S & W, 5 Shot, Top Break, Double Action, Hammer, Blue, *Modern*	60.00	95.00
☐ **Safety**, .32 S & W, 5 Shot, Top Break, Double Action, Hammerless, Blue, *Modern*	70.00	110.00
☐ **Safety**, .32 S & W, 5 Shot, Top Break, Double Action, Hammerless, Nickel Plated, *Modern*	75.00	120.00
☐ **Safety**, .32 S & W Long, 6 Shot, Top Break, Double Action, Hammer, Blue, *Modern*	60.00	95.00
☐ **Safety**, .32 S & W Long, 6 Shot, Top Break, Double Action, Hammer, Nickel Plated, *Modern*	70.00	110.00
☐ **Safety**, .32 S & W Long, 6 Shot, Top Break, Double Action, Hammerless, Blue, *Modern*	70.00	110.00
☐ **Safety**, .38 S & W, 5 Shot, Top Break, Double Action, Hammerless, Nickel Plated, *Modern*	75.00	120.00
☐ **Sealed 8 Protector**, .22 L.R.R.F., 8 Shot, Blue Wood Grips, Top Break, Double Action, *Modern*	75.00	120.00
☐ **Sealed 8 Supershor**, .22 L.R.R.F., Adjustable Sights, Blue, Wood Grips, Top Break, Double Action, *Modern*	80.00	125.00
☐ **Sealed 8 Target**, .22 L.R.R.F., 8 Shot, Blue, Wood Grips, Solid Frame, Double Action, *Modern*	70.00	110.00
☐ **Sidewinder**, .22LR/.22WMR Combo, Western Style, 4" Barrel, Adjustable Sights, *Modern*	65.00	85.00
☐ **Sidewinder**, .22LR/.22WMR Combo, Western Style, 6" Barrel, Adjustable Sights, *Modern*	65.00	85.00

IVER JOHNSON / 241

	V.G.	EXC.
☐ **Supershot 9**, .22 L.R.R.F., 9 Shot, Adjustable Sights, Blue, Wood Grips, Top Break, *Modern*	75.00	110.00
☐ **Supershot M 844**, .22 L.R.R.F., 8 Shot, Double Action, Top Break, Adjustable Sights, Wood Grips, *Modern*	60.00	85.00
☐ **Swing Out**, .22 L.R.R.F., Swing-out Cylinder, Various Barrel Lengths, Double Action, Wood Grips, Blue, *Modern*	65.00	90.00
☐ **Swing Out**, .22 L.R.R.F., Swing-out Cylinder, 4" Barrel, Double Action, Wood Grips, Blue, *Modern*	70.00	95.00
☐ **Swing Out**, .22 L.R.R.F., Swing-Out Cylinder, 4" Barrel, Double Action, Adjustable Sights, Blue, *Modern*	90.00	130.00
☐ **Swing Out**, .22 L.R.R.F., Swing-out Cylinder, 6" Barrel, Double Action, Adjustable Sights, Blue, *Modern*	75.00	110.00
☐ **Swing Out**, .22 WMR, Swing-Out Cylinder, Various Barrel Lengths, Double Action, Wood Grips, Blue, *Modern*	65.00	85.00
☐ **Swing Out**, .22 WRM, Swing-out Cylinder, 4" Barrel, Double Action, Wood Grips, Blue, *Modern*	65.00	90.00
☐ **Swing Out**, .22 WRM, Swing-out Cylinder, 4" Barrel, Double Action, Adjustable Sights, Blue, *Modern*	90.00	130.00
☐ **Swing Out**, .22 WRM, Swing-Out Cylinder, 6" Barrel, Double Action, Adjustable Sights, Blue, *Modern*	70.00	110.00
☐ **Swing Out**, .32 S & W Long, Swing-Out Cylinder, Various Barrel Lengths, Double Action, Wood Grips, Blue, *Modern*	65.00	85.00
☐ **Swing Out**, .32 S & W Long, Swing-Out Cylinder, Various Barrel Lengths, Double Action, Wood Grips, Nickel Plated, *Modern*	65.00	95.00
☐ **Swing Out**, .32 S & W Long, Swing-Out Cylinder, 4" Barrel, Double Action, Wood Grips, Blue, *Modern*	65.00	95.00
☐ **Swing Out**, .32 S & W Long, Swing-Out Cylinder, 4" Barrel, Double Action, Adjustable Sights, Blue, *Modern*	90.00	130.00
☐ **Swing Out**, .32 S & W Long, Swing-Out Cylinder, 6" Barrel, Double Action, Adjustable Sights, Blue, *Modern*	75.00	110.00
☐ **Swing Out**, .38 Special, Swing-Out Cylinder, Various Barrel Lengths, Double Action, Wood Grips, Blue, *Modern*	65.00	90.00
☐ **Swing Out**, .38 Special, Swing-Out Cylinder, Various Barrel Lengths, Double Action, Wood Grips, Nickel Plated, *Modern*	65.00	95.00
☐ **Swing Out**, .38 Special, Swing-Out Cylinder, 4" Barrel, Double Action, Wood Grips, Blue, *Modern*	65.00	95.00
☐ **Swing Out**, .38 Special, Swing-Out Cylinder, 4" Barrel, Double Action, Adjustable Sights, Blue, *Modern*	90.00	130.00
☐ **Swing Out**, .38 Special, Swing-Out Cylinder, 6" Barrel, Double Action, Adjustable Sights, Blue, *Modern*	75.00	110.00
☐ **Target 9**, .22 L.R.R.F., 9 Shot, Blue, Solid Frame, Wood Grips, Double Action, *Modern*	60.00	95.00
☐ **Trigger-Cocking**, .22 L.R.R.F., 8 Shot, Single Action, Top Break, Adjustable Sights, Wood Grips, *Modern*	75.00	120.00

HANDGUN, SEMI-AUTOMATIC

	V.G.	EXC.
☐ **Model 22**, .22 L.R.R.F., Double Action, Hammer, Clip Fed, Blue, *Modern*	80.00	130.00
☐ **Model 25**, .25 ACP, Double Action, Hammer, Clip Fed, Blue, *Modern*	75.00	125.00
☐ **PP30 Enforcer**, .30 M1 Carbine, Clip Fed, Blue, *Modern*	125.00	195.00
☐ **PP30S Enforcer**, .30 M1 Carbine, Clip Fed, Stainless, *Modern*	145.00	225.00
☐ **X-300 Pony**, .380 ACP, Hammer, Clip Fed, Blue, *Modern*	95.00	135.00
☐ **X-300 Pony**, .380 ACP, Hammer, Clip Fed, Nickel Plated, *Modern*	95.00	140.00
☐ **X-300 Pony**, .380 ACP, Hammer, Clip Fed, Matt Blue, *Modern*	90.00	135.00

RIFLE, BOLT ACTION

	V.G.	EXC.
☐ **Model 2X**, .22 L.R.R.F., Singleshot, Takedown, *Modern*	30.00	50.00
☐ **Model X**, .22 L.R.R.F., Singleshot, Takedown, *Modern*	30.00	50.00

242 / IVER JOHNSON

Iver Johnson Safety Hammerless

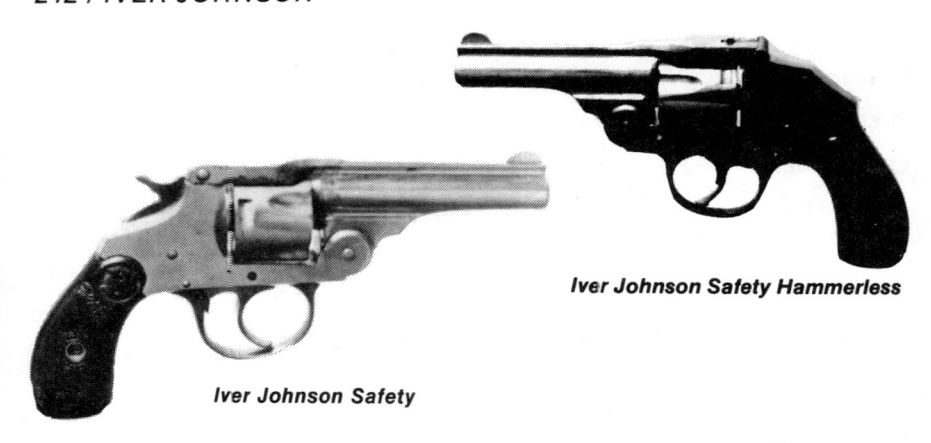

Iver Johnson Safety

	V.G.	EXC.
RIFLE, SEMI-AUTOMATIC		
☐ **PM30P**, .30 Carbine, Clip Fed, Telescoping Stock, Carbine, *Modern*	135.00	195.00
☐ **PM30G**, .30 Carbine, Clip Fed, Military Style, Carbine, *Modern*	125.00	175.00
☐ **PM5.7 Spitfire**, 5.7 Spitfire, Clip Fed, Military Style, *Modern*	110.00	155.00
☐ **PM30PS Paratrooper**, .30 M1 Carbine, Clip Fed, Stainless, *Modern*	165.00	225.00
☐ **PP30GS Standard**, .30 M1 Carbine, Clip Fed, Stainless, *Modern*	145.00	215.00
SHOTGUN, DOUBLE BARREL, OVER-UNDER		
☐ **Silver Shadow**, 12 Gauge, Single Trigger, Checkered Stock, *Modern*	190.00	250.00
☐ **Silver Shadow**, 12 Gauge, Double Trigger, Checkered Stock, *Modern*	170.00	225.00
☐ **Silver Shadow**, 12 Gauge, Double Trigger, Checkered Stock, Light Engraving, Vent Rib, *Modern*	160.00	220.00
☐ **Silver Shadow**, 12 Gauge, Single Trigger, Checkered Stock, Light Engraving, Vent Rib, *Modern*	180.00	240.00
SHOTGUN, DOUBLE BARREL, SIDE-BY-SIDE		
☐ **Hercules**, Various Gauges, Double Trigger, Checkered Stock, Hammerless, *Modern*	170.00	250.00
☐ **Hercules**, Various Gauges, Double Trigger, Automatic Ejector, Hammerless, Checkered Stock, *Modern*	200.00	295.00
☐ **Hercules**, Various Gauges, Single Trigger, Hammerless, Checkered Stock, *Modern*	235.00	345.00
☐ **Hercules**, Various Gauges, Single Trigger, Automatic Ejector, Hammerless, Checkered Stock, *Modern*	275.00	385.00
☐ **Hercules**, Various Gauges, Single Selective Trigger, Hammerless, Checkered Stock, *Modern*	275.00	400.00
☐ **Hercules**, Various Gauges, Single Selective Trigger, Automatic Ejector, Hammerless, Checkered Stock, *Modern*	325.00	435.00
☐ **Knox-All**, Various Gauges, Double Trigger, Hammer, Checkered Stock, *Modern*	170.00	245.00
☐ **Skeeter**, Various Gauges, Double Trigger, Hammerless, *Modern*	250.00	380.00
☐ **Skeeter**, Various Gauges, Skeet Grade, Double Trigger, Automatic Ejector, Hammerless, *Modern*	300.00	450.00
☐ **Skeeter**, Various Gauges, Skeet Grade, Single Trigger, Hammerless, *Modern*	290.00	430.00

	V.G.	EXC.
☐ **Skeeter**, Various Gauges, Skeet Grade, Single Trigger, Automatic Ejector, Hammerless, *Modern*	350.00	460.00
☐ **Skeeter**, Various Gauges, Skeet Grade, Single Selective Trigger, Hammerless, *Modern*	350.00	475.00
☐ **Skeeter**, Various Gauges, Skeet Grade, Single Selective Trigger, Automatic Ejector, Hammerless, *Modern*	380.00	495.00
☐ **Super**, 12 Gauge, Trap Grade, Double Trigger, Hammerless, *Modern*	400.00	525.00
☐ **Super**, 12 Gauge, Trap Grade, Single Trigger, Hammerless, *Modern*	450.00	575.00
☐ **Super**, 12 Gauge, Trap Grade, Single Selective Trigger, Hammerless, *Modern*	550.00	675.00

SHOTGUN, SINGLESHOT

	V.G.	EXC.
☐ **12 Gauge**, Trap Grade, Vent Rib, Checkered Stock, *Modern*	75.00	120.00
☐ **Champion**, Various Gauges, Automatic Ejector, *Modern*	45.00	60.00
☐ **Mat Rib Grade**, Various Gauges, Raised Matted Rib, Automatic Ejector, Checkered Stock, *Modern*	50.00	80.00

IZARRA
Made by Bonifacio Echeverra, Eibar, Spain, c. 1918.

HANDGUN, SEMI-AUTOMATIC

	V.G.	EXC.
☐ **.32 ACP**, Clip Fed, Long Grip, *Modern*	125.00	165.00

J & R
Burbank, Calif.

RIFLE, SEMI-AUTOMATIC

	V.G.	EXC.
☐ **Model 68**, 9mm Luger, Clip Fed, Flash Hider, Takedown, *Modern*	125.00	175.00

JACKRABBIT
Continental Arms Corp., N.Y.C., c. 1960.

RIFLE, SINGLESHOT

	V.G.	EXC.
☐ **Handy Gun**, .44 Magnum, Detachable Shoulder Stock, *Modern*	45.00	75.00

SHOTGUN, SINGLESHOT

	V.G.	EXC.
☐ **Handy Gun**, .410 3", Detachable Shoulder Stock, *Modern*	40.00	70.00

JACKSON ARMS CO.
Made by Crescent for C.M. McClung & Co., Knoxville, Tenn.

SHOTGUN, DOUBLE BARREL, SIDE-BY-SIDE

	V.G.	EXC.
☐ **Various Gauges**, Outside Hammers, Damascus Barrel, *Modern*	100.00	175.00
☐ **Various Gauges**, Hammerless, Steel Barrel, *Modern*	135.00	200.00
☐ **Various Gauges**, Hammerless, Damascus Barrel, *Modern*	100.00	175.00
☐ **Various Gauges**, Outside Hammers, Steel Barrel, *Modern*	125.00	190.00

SHOTGUN, SINGLESHOT

	V.G.	EXC.
☐ **Various Gauges**, Hammer, Steel Barrel, *Modern*	55.00	85.00

JACKSON HOLE RIFLE CO.
Jackson Hole, Wyo., c. 1970.

RIFLE, BOLT ACTION

	V.G.	EXC.
☐ **Sportsman**, Various Calibers, with 3 Interchangable Barrels, Checkered Stock, *Modern*	450.00	575.00
☐ **Custom**, Various Calibers, with 3 Interchangable Barrels, Fancy Checkering, Fancy Wood, *Modern*	600.00	845.00
☐ **Presentation**, Various Calibers, with 3 Interchangable Barrels, Fancy Checkering, Fancy Wood, Engraved, *Modern*	750.00	1,050.00

Jager .32 Pistol

JAGA
Frantisek Dusek. Opocno, Czechoslovakia, c. 1930.

HANDGUN, SEMI-AUTOMATIC

	V.G.	EXC.
☐ **.25 ACP**, Clip Fed, Blue, *Modern*	80.00	125.00

JAGER
Suhl, Germany.

HANDGUN, SEMI-AUTOMATIC

☐ **.32 ACP**, Clip Fed, *Modern*	250.00	400.00

JAGER

HANDGUN, REVOLVER

☐ **Jager**, .22LR/.22 WMR Combo, Single Action, Western Style, Adjustable Sights, *Modern*	70.00	95.00
☐ **Jager**, .22LR/.22 WMR Combo, Single Action, Western Style, *Modern*	65.00	90.00
☐ **Jager Centerfire**, Various Calibers, Single Action, Western Style, Adjustable Sights, *Modern*	85.00	125.00
☐ **Jager Centerfire**, Various Calibers, Single Action, Western Style, *Modern*	75.00	115.00

JAGER, F. & CO.
See Herold.

JANSSEN FRERES
Liege, Belgium, c. 1925

SHOTGUN, DOUBLE BARREL, SIDE-BY-SIDE

☐ **Various Gauges**, Hammerless, Steel Barrel, *Modern*	95.00	170.00

JAPANESE MILITARY

AUTOMATIC WEAPON, LIGHT MACHINE GUN

☐ **Type 92 (Lewis)**, 7.7mm Jap, Drum Magazine, Bipod, Military, *Class 3*	750.00	975.00
☐ **Type 96**, 6.5 x 50 Arisaka, Clip Fed, Bipod, Military, *Class 3*	700.00	925.00
☐ **Type 96**, 6.5 x 50 Arisaka, Clip Fed, Bipod, Military, Scope Mounted, *Class 3*	900.00	1,300.00
☐ **Type 99**, 7.7mm Jap, Clip Fed, Bipod, Scope Mounted, Military, *Class 3*	1,200.00	1,650.00
☐ **Type 99**, 7.7mm Jap, Clip Fed, Bipod, Military, *Class 3*	700.00	950.00

Japanese Military Type 99 Rifle

Japanese Military Type 14 Pistol

Japanese Military Type 26 Revolver

	V.G.	EXC.

AUTOMATIC WEAPON, SUBMACHINE GUN
☐ **Type 100**, 8mm Nambu, Clip Fed, Wood Stock, *Class 3* 850.00 1,400.00

HANDGUN, REVOLVER
☐ **Model 26**, 9mm, Military, *Curio* 135.00 195.00

HANDGUN, SEMI-AUTOMATIC
☐ **Baby Nambu**, 7mm Nambu, Clip Fed, Military, *Curio* 950.00 1,650.00
☐ **Baby Nambu**, 7mm Nambu, Presentation, Military, Clip Fed, Military, *Curio* 1,350.00 2,000.00
☐ **Type 14 Nambu**, 8mm Nambu, Clip Fed, Small Trigger Guard, Military, *Curio* 250.00 400.00
☐ **Type 14 Nambu**, 8mm Nambu, Clip Fed, Large Trigger Guard, Military, *Curio* 200.00 350.00
☐ **Type 1904**, 8mm Nambu, Clip Fed, Military, *Curio* 450.00 675.00
☐ **Type 94**, 8mm Nambu, Clip Fed, Military, *Curio* 175.00 275.00

RIFLE, BOLT ACTION
☐ **Model 38 (1905)**, 6.5 x 50 Arisaka, Military, *Curio* 85.00 135.00
☐ **Model 38 (1905)**, 6.5 x 50 Arisaka, Military, Carbine, *Curio* 85.00 135.00
☐ **Model 44 (1911)**, 6.5 x 50 Arisaka, Military, Carbine, *Curio* 85.00 135.00
☐ **Model 99 (1939)**, 7.7 x 58 Arisaka, Military, Open Rear Sight, *Curio* 85.00 135.00
☐ **Type 38**, 6.5 x 50 Arisaka, Late Model, Military, *Curio* 80.00 130.00
☐ **Type 44**, 6.5 x 50 Arisaka, Folding Bayonet, Military, *Curio* 85.00 140.00
☐ **Type 99**, 7.7 x 58 Arisaka, Aircraft Sights Dust Cover, Military, *Curio* 90.00 150.00

JENNINGS
☐ **Model J-22**, .22 L.R.R.F., Clip Fed, Satin Chrome Plate, *Modern* ... 45.00 65.00

JEWEL
Made by Hood Firearms Co., c. 1876.

HANDGUN, REVOLVER
☐ **#1**, .22 Short R.F., 7 Shot, Spur Trigger, Solid Frame, Single Action, *Antique* 90.00 160.00

JIEFFCO
Mre. Liegoise d'Armes a Feu Robar et Cie, Liege, Belgium, c. 1912-1914.

	V.G.	EXC.

HANDGUN, SEMI-AUTOMATIC
- ☐ **.25 ACP**, Clip Fed, Blue, *Curio* 195.00   275.00
- ☐ **.32 ACP**, Clip Fed, Blue, *Curio* 185.00   260.00

JIEFFCO
Tradename used by Davis-Warner on pistols made by Robar et Cie., c. 1920.

HANDGUN, SEMI-AUTOMATIC
- ☐ **New Model Melior**, .25 ACP, Clip Fed, *Curio* 110.00   155.00

J.G.L.
Jos. G. Landmann, Holstein, W. Germany, c. 1968.

RIFLE, SEMI-AUTOMATIC
- ☐ **JGL-68 Model 1**, .22 L.R.R.F., Clip Fed, Carbine Style, *Modern* 50.00   70.00
- ☐ **JGL-68 Model 2**, .22 L.R.R.F., Clip Fed, Vertical Grip & Foregrip, *Modern* 60.00   80.00
- ☐ **JGL-68 Model 3**, .22 L.R.R.F., Clip Fed, Vertical Grip, *Modern* 55.00   75.00

JOFFRE
Spain, Unknown Maker, c. 1900.

HANDGUN, SEMI-AUTOMATIC
- ☐ **M1916**, .32 ACP, Clip Fed, *Modern*............................... 80.00   125.00

JOHNSON AUTOMATICS
Providence, R.I. Also see U.S. Military.

RIFLE, BOLT ACTION
- ☐ **Diamond Cherry Featherweight**, Various Calibers, Engraved, Carved Cherry Stock, Muzzle Brake, *Modern* 750.00   1,100.00
- ☐ **Honey Featherweight**, Various Calibers, Engraved, Carved Stock, Muzzle Brake, Gold and Silver Inlays, *Modern* 1,250.00   2,000.00
- ☐ **Laminar Sporter**, Various Calibers, Laminated Stock, *Modern* 450.00   700.00

RIFLE, SEMI-AUTOMATIC
- ☐ **Model 1941**, .30-06 Springfield, Military, *Curio*.................... 450.00   650.00
- ☐ **Model 1941**, 7mm Mauser, Military, *Modern* 550.00   750.00

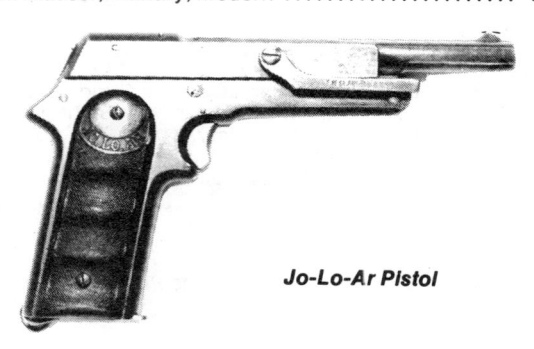

Jo-Lo-Ar Pistol

JO-LO-AR
Hijos de Arrizabalaga, Eibar, Spain, c. 1920.

HANDGUN, SEMI-AUTOMATIC

	V.G.	EXC.
☐ **.380 ACP**, Tip-up, Clip Fed, Hammer, Spur Trigger, Military, Modern	165.00	240.00
☐ **9mm Bergmann**, Tip-up, Clip Fed, Hammer, Spur Trigger, Military, Modern	135.00	200.00

JONES, CHARLES
Lancaster, Pa. 1780. See Kentucky Rifles.

JONES, J.N. & CO.
London, England, c. 1760.

HANDGUN, FLINTLOCK
- ☐ **.60**, George III, Navy Pistol, Brass Barrel, Brass Furniture, Military, *Antique* ...... 575.00 ... 950.00

HANDGUN, PERCUSSION
- ☐ **.58**, Holster Pistol, Converted from Flintlock, Brass Furniture, Plain, *Antique* ...... 450.00 ... 650.00

JUPITER
Fabrique d'Armes de Guerre de Grand Precision, Eibar, Spain.

HANDGUN, SEMI-AUTOMATIC
- ☐ **.32 ACP**. Clip Fed, Blue, *Curio* ...... 90.00 ... 135.00

KABA SPEZIAL
Made by August Menz, Suhl, Germany, for Karl Bauer & Co., Berlin, Germany, c. 1925.

HANDGUN, SEMI-AUTOMATIC
- ☐ **Liliput**, .25 ACP, Clip Fed, Blue, *Modern* ...... 165.00 ... 225.00
- ☐ **Liliput**, .32 ACP, Clip Fed, Blue, *Modern* ...... 175.00 ... 250.00

KABA SPEZIAL
Made by Francisco Arizmendi, Eibar, Spain.

HANDGUN, SEMI-AUTOMATIC
- ☐ **.25 ACP, Clip Fed, Blue,** *Modern* ...... 115.00 ... 155.00

KART

HANDGUN, SEMI-AUTOMATIC
- ☐ **Target**, .22 L.R.R.F., Clip Fed, M1911 Frame, 6" Barrel, *Modern* ... 425.00 ... 600.00
- ☐ **For Colt Government Target**, .22 L.R.R.F., Conversion Unit Only ... 140.00 ... 185.00

KASSNAR IMPORTS
Harrisburg, Pa.

RIFLE, BOLT ACTION
- ☐ **Model M-14S**, .22 L.R.R.F., Clip Fed, Checkered Stock, *Modern* .... 45.00 ... 60.00
- ☐ **Model M-15S**, .22 WMR, Clip Fed, Checkered Stock, *Modern* ...... 50.00 ... 75.00
- ☐ **Model M-1400**, .22 L.R.R.F., Clip Fed, Checkered Stock, *Modern* ... 50.00 ... 70.00
- ☐ **Model M-1500**, .22 WMR, Clip Fed, Checkered Stock, *Modern* ..... 55.00 ... 85.00
- ☐ **Parker Hale Midland**, Various Calibers, Checkered Stock, Open Sights, *Modern* ...... 150.00 ... 195.00
- ☐ **Parker Hale Super**, Various Calibers, Checkered Stock, Open Sights, Monte Carlo Stock, *Modern* ...... 190.00 ... 275.00
- ☐ **Parker Hale Varmint**, Various Calibers, Checkered Stock, Open Sights, Varmint Stock, *Modern* ...... 190.00 ... 275.00

	V.G.	EXC.
RIFLE, SEMI-AUTOMATIC		
☐ **Model M-16**, .22 L.R.R.F., Clip Fed, Military Style, *Modern*	55.00	75.00
☐ **Model M-20S**, .22 L.R.R.F., *Modern*	40.00	60.00
SHOTGUN, DOUBLE BARREL, OVER-UNDER		
☐ **Fias SK-1**, 12 and 20 Gauges, Double Trigger, Checkered Stock, *Modern*	225.00	320.00
☐ **Fias SK-3**, 12 and 20 Gauges, Single Selective Trigger, Checkered Stock, *Modern*	250.00	360.00
☐ **Fias SK-4**, 12 and 20 Gauges, Single Selective Trigger, Checkered Stock, Automatic Ejector, *Modern*	300.00	400.00
☐ **Fias SK-4D**, 12 and 20 Gauges, Single Selective Trigger, Fancy Checkering, Fancy Wood, Engraved, Automatic Ejector, *Modern*	325.00	425.00
☐ **Fias SK-4T**, 12 Ga., Trap Grade, Single Selective Trigger, Automatic Ejector, Checkered Stock, Wide Vent Rib, *Modern*	325.00	425.00
SHOTGUN, DOUBLE BARREL, SIDE-BY-SIDE		
☐ **Zabala**, Various Gauges, Checkered Stock, Double Triggers, *Modern*	170.00	245.00
SHOTGUN, SINGLESHOT		
☐ **Taiyojuki**, Various Gauges, Top Break, *Modern*	30.00	40.00

KEFFER, JACOB
Lancaster, Pa., c. 1802. See Kentucky Rifles and Pistols.

KEIM, JOHN
Reading, Pa. 1820-1839. See Kentucky Rifles and Pistols.

KENTUCKY RIFLES AND PISTOLS
The uniquely American "Kentucky" (or, as some prefer, "Pennsylvania") expressed in wood & metal the attitude of strength and independence that fostered our young nation. For the most part Kentuckys are custom guns, and, aside from general style similarities, virtually all are different, even those by the same maker. To add to the problem of price generalization, gunsmiths purchased parts from various makers and there may be three different names on a single gun or none at all. The main considerations in determining value are: 1. Type of ignition; 2. Quality of workmanship; 3. Decoration; 4. Orginality; 5. Condition. Except for orginality this list also applies to contemporary makers.

RIFLES, FLINTLOCK
☐ **Moderate Quality**, Plain, $675.00-$1,200.00
☐ **Moderate Quality**, Medium Decoration, $1,950.00-$4,200.00
☐ **High Quality**, Fancy Decoration, $3,500.00-$6,000.00
☐ **Over-Under**, Swivel-Breech, Plain, $850.00-$1,600.00
☐ **Over-Under**, Swivel-Breech, Medium Quality, $3,400.00-$5,600.00
☐ **Over-Under**, Swivel-Breech, High Quality, $4,500.00-$8,500.00
☐ **Deduct 30%-40%**, if Converted from Percussion

RIFLES, PERCUSSION
☐ **Moderate Quality**, Plain, $600.00-$1,200.00
☐ **Moderate Quality**, Medium Decoration, $850.00-$1,750.00
☐ **High Quality**, Fancy Decoration, $3,000.00-$5,500.00
☐ **Over-Under**, Medium Quality, Swivel Breech, Plain, $550.00-$1,100.00
☐ **Over-Under**, Medium Quality, Swivel-Breech, $1,300.00-$2,500.00
☐ **Over-Under**, High Quality, Swivel-Breech, $2,400.00-$4,000.00
☐ **Add 20%**, if converted from Flintlock to Percussion

PISTOLS, FLINTLOCK
☐ **Moderate Quality**, Medium Decoration, $1,750.00-$3,250.00
☐ **High Quality**, Fancy Decoration, $3,500.00-$6,750.00

	V.G.	EXC.

PISTOLS, PERCUSSION (ORIGINAL)
☐ **Moderate Quality**, Medium Decoration, $1,650.00-$2,400.00
☐ **High Quality**, Fancy Decoration, $2,750.00-$3,750.00

PISTOLS, PERCUSSION (CONVERTED FROM FLINTLOCK)
☐ **Moderate Quality,** Medium Decoration, $850.00-$1,450.00
☐ **High Quality,** Fancy Decoration, $1,650.00-$2,400.00

Arms with signatures are more desirable than those without markings. No name-deduct 10%-15%. If of recent vintage, and handmade, use this chart and deduct 50%.

KETLAND & CO.
Birmingham & London, England 1760-1831. Also See Kentucky Rifles.
HANDGUN, FLINTLOCK
☐ .58, Holster Pistol, Plain, Tapered Round Barrel, Brass Furniture, *Antique* 600.00   975.00
☐ .62, Belt Pistol, Brass Barrel, Brass Furniture, Light Ornamentation, *Antique* 625.00   995.00

KETLAND, T.
Birmingham, England 1750-1829.
HANDGUN, FLINTLOCK
☐ .69, Pair, Belt Pistol, Brass Furniture, Plain, *Antique* 1,450.00 2,250.00
RIFLE, FLINTLOCK
☐ .65, Officers Model Brown Bess, Musket, Military, *Antique* 2,250.00 3,250.00
☐ .73, 2nd. Model Brown Bess, Musket, Military, *Antique* 1,150.00 2,150.00

KETLAND, WILLIAM & CO.
HANDGUN, FLINTLOCK
☐ .63, Holster Pistol, Round Barrel, Plain, *Antique* 550.00   850.00

KETTNER, ED
Suhl, Thuringia, Germany 1922-1939
COMBINATION WEAPON, DRILLING
☐ **12x12 x 10.75x65R Collath**, Engraved, Checkered Stock, Sling Swivels, *Modern* 850.00 1,450.00

KIMBALL, J.M. ARMS CO.
Detroit, Mich., c. 1955.
HANDGUN, SEMI-AUTOMATIC
☐ **Standard Model**, .30 Carbine, Clip Fed, Blue, *Modern* 450.00   700.00
☐ **Standard Model**, .30 Carbine, Clip Fed, Blue, Grooved Chamber, *Modern* 500.00   800.00
☐ **Standard Model**, .22 Hornet, Clip Fed, Blue, *Modern* 1,100.00 1,650.00
☐ **Standard Model**, .38 Special, Clip Fed, Blue, *Modern* 800.00 1,200.00
☐ **Target Model**, .30 Carbine, Clip Fed, Blue, Adjustable Sights, *Modern* 500.00   800.00
☐ **Combat Model**, .30 Carbine, Clip Fed, Blue, Short Barrel, *Modern*   450.00   700.00

KIMBER
Clackamas, Ore.
RIFLE, BOLT ACTION
☐ **Model 82 Cascade**, .22 L.R.R.F., Checkered Stock, Clip Fed, No Sights, Monte Carlo Stock, *Modern* 240.00   325.00

250 / KIMEL INDUSTRIES

	V.G.	EXC.
☐ **Model 82 Cascade**, .22 W.M.R., Checkered Stock, Clip Fed, No Sights, Monte Carlo Stock, *Modern*	260.00	340.00
☐ **Model 82 Classic**, .22 L.R.R.F., Checkered Stock, Clip Fed, No Sights, *Modern*	240.00	315.00
☐ **Model 82 Classic**, .22 W.M.R., Checkered Stock, Clip Fed, No Sights, *Modern*	250.00	325.00

KIMEL INDUSTRIES
Matthews, N.C.

HANDGUN, DOUBLE BARREL, OVER-UNDER
| ☐ **Twist**, .22 Short R.F., Swivel Breech, Derringer, Spur Trigger, *Modern* | 20.00 | 35.00 |

Kimball Standard

Kimball Target

Kimball Combat

KINGLAND SPECIAL
Made by Crescent for Geller, Wards & Hasner St. Louis, Mo.

SHOTGUN, DOUBLE BARREL, SIDE-BY-SIDE
☐ **Various Gauges**, Outside Hammers, Damascus Barrel, *Modern*	100.00	175.00
☐ **Various Gauges**, Hammerless, Steel Barrel, *Modern*	135.00	200.00
☐ **Various Gauges**, Hammerless, Damascus Barrel, *Modern*	100.00	175.00
☐ **Various Gauges**, Outside Hammers, Steel Barrel, *Modern*	125.00	190.00

SHOTGUN, SINGLESHOT
| ☐ **Various Gauges**, Hammer, Steel Barrel, *Modern* | 55.00 | 85.00 |

KINGLAND 10-STAR
Made by Crescent for Geller, Wards & Hasner St. Louis, Mo.

	V.G.	EXC.
SHOTGUN, DOUBLE BARREL, SIDE-BY-SIDE		
☐ **Various Gauges**, Outside Hammers, Damascus Barrel, *Modern*	100.00	175.00
☐ **Various Gauges**, Hammerless, Steel Barrel, *Modern*	135.00	200.00
☐ **Various Gauges**, Hammerless, Damascus Barrel, *Modern*	100.00	175.00
☐ **Various Gauges**, Outside Hammers, Steel Barrel, *Modern*	125.00	190.00
SHOTGUN, SINGLESHOT		
☐ **Various Gauges**, Hammer, Steel Barrel, *Modern*	55.00	85.00

KING NITRO
Made by Stevens Arms.

RIFLE, BOLT ACTION
☐ **Model 53**, .22 L.R.R.F., Singleshot, Takedown, *Modern* .... 35.00 / 45.00

SHOTGUN, DOUBLE BARREL, SIDE-BY-SIDE
☐ **M 315 Various Gauges**, Hammerless, Steel Barrel, *Modern* .... 95.00 / 165.00

KIRIKKALE
Makina ve Kimya Endustrisi Kurumu Kirrikale, Ankara, Turkey.

HANDGUN, SEMI-AUTOMATIC
☐ **MKE**, .380 ACP, Clip Fed, Double Action, *Modern* .... 135.00 / 185.00

KITTEMAUG
Maker Unknown, c. 1880.

HANDGUN, REVOLVER
☐ **.32 Short R.F.**, 5 Shot, Spur Trigger, Solid Frame, Single Action, Antique .... 90.00 / 160.00

KLEINGUENTHER'S
Seguin, Texas.

HANDGUN, REVOLVER
☐ **Reck R-18**, .357 Magnum, Adjustable Sights, Western Style, Single Action, *Modern* .... 65.00 / 100.00

RIFLE, BOLT ACTION
☐ **K-10**, .22 L.R.R.F., Single Shot, Tangent Sights, *Modern*........... 30.00 / 45.00
☐ **K-12**, .22 L.R.R.F., Clip Fed, Checkered Stock, *Modern*........... 50.00 / 70.00
☐ **K-13**, .22 W.M.R., Clip Fed, Checkered Stock, *Modern* .... 75.00 / 110.00
☐ **K-14 Insta-fire**, Various Calibers, Checkered Stock, No Sights, Recoil Pad, *Modern* .... 285.00 / 395.00
☐ **K-15 Insta-fire**, Various Calibers, Checkered Stock, No Sights, Recoil Pad, *Modern* .... 350.00 / 575.00
☐ **K-15**, .22 L.R.R.F., Clip Fed, Checkered Stock, *Modern*........... 60.00 / 100.00
☐ **V2130**, Various Calibers, Checkered Stock, Recoil Pad, *Modern* ... 140.00 / 200.00

RIFLE, DOUBLE BARREL, OVER-UNDER
☐ **Model 222**, .22 WMR, Plain, *Modern* .... 75.00 / 120.00

SHOTGUN, DOUBLE BARREL, OVER-UNDER
☐ **Condor**, 12 Gauge, Skeet Grade, Single Selective Trigger, Automatic Ejector, Wide Vent Rib, *Modern*...................... 325.00 / 435.00
☐ **Condor**, 12 Gauge, Single Selective Trigger, Automatic Ejector, Vent Rib, *Modern* .... 300.00 / 400.00

SHOTGUN, DOUBLE BARREL, SIDE-BY-SIDE
☐ **Brescia**, 12 Gauge, Hammerless, Light Engraving, Double Trigger, *Modern* .... 165.00 / 225.00

252 / KLETT, SIMON

	V.G.	EXC.

SHOTGUN, SEMI-AUTOMATIC
- ☐ **12 Ga.**, Checkered Stock, Vent Rib, Engraved, Right Hand, *Modern* — 140.00 / 185.00
- ☐ **12 Ga.**, Checkered Stock, Vent Rib, Engraved, Left Hand, *Modern* — 150.00 / 200.00

KLETT, SIMON
Probably Leipzig, c. 1620.

RIFLE, WHEEL-LOCK
- ☐ **.54**, Rifled, Octagon Barrel, Brass Furniture, Medium Ornamentation, Engraved, High Quality, *Antique* — 6,000.00 / 9,500.00

KNICKERBOCKER
Made by Crescent for H & D Folsom, c. 1900.

SHOTGUN, DOUBLE BARREL, SIDE-BY-SIDE
- ☐ **Various Gauges**, Outside Hammers, Damascus Barrel, *Modern* — 100.00 / 175.00
- ☐ **Various Gauges**, Hammerless, Steel Barrel, *Modern* — 135.00 / 200.00
- ☐ **Various Gauges**, Hammerless, Damascus Barrel, *Modern* — 100.00 / 175.00
- ☐ **Various Gauges**, Outside Hammers, Steel Barrel, *Modern* — 125.00 / 190.00

SHOTGUN, SINGLESHOT
- ☐ **Various Gauges**, Hammer, Steel Barrel, *Modern* — 55.00 / 85.00

KNICKERBOCKER
Made by Stevens Arms.

SHOTGUN, DOUBLE BARREL, SIDE-BY-SIDE
- ☐ **Model 311**, Various Gauges, Hammerless, Steel Barrel, *Modern* — 95.00 / 165.00

KNOCKABOUT
Made by Stevens Arms.

SHOTGUN, DOUBLE BARREL, SIDE-BY-SIDE
- ☐ **Model 311**, Various Guages, Hammerless, Steel Barrel, *Modern* — 95.00 / 165.00

KNOXALL
Made by Crescent, c. 1900.

SHOTGUN, DOUBLE BARREL, SIDE-BY-SIDE
- ☐ **Various Gauges**, Outside Hammers, Damascus Barrel, *Modern* — 100.00 / 175.00
- ☐ **Various Gauges**, Hammerless, Steel Barrel, *Modern* — 135.00 / 200.00
- ☐ **Various Gauges**, Hammerless, Damascus Barrel, *Modern* — 100.00 / 175.00
- ☐ **Various Gauges**, Outside Hammers, Steel Barrel, *Modern* — 125.00 / 190.00

SHOTGUN, SINGLESHOT
- ☐ **Various Gauges**, Hammer, Steel Barrel, *Modern* — 55.00 / 85.00

KODIAK MFG. CO.
North Haven, Conn., c. 1965.

RIFLE, BOLT ACTION
- ☐ **Model 98 Brush Carbine**, Various Calibers, Checkered Stock, *Modern* — 90.00 / 145.00
- ☐ **Model 99 Deluxe Brush Carbine**, Various Calibers, Checkered Stock, *Modern* — 95.00 / 155.00
- ☐ **Model 100 Deluxe Rifle**, Various Calibers, Checkered Stock, *Modern* — 100.00 / 160.00
- ☐ **Model 100M Deluxe Rifle**, Various Magnum Calibers, Checkered Stock, *Modern* — 130.00 / 175.00
- ☐ **Model 101 Ultra**, Various Calibers, Monte Carlo Stock, *Modern* — 135.00 / 175.00

KOMMER, THEODOR / 253

	V.G.	EXC.
☐ **Model 101M Ultra**, Various Magnum Calibers, Monte Carlo Stock, *Modern*	145.00	190.00
☐ **Model 102 Ultra Varmint**, Various Calibers, Heavy Barrel, *Modern*	145.00	190.00

RIFLE, SEMI-AUTOMATIC

☐ **Model 260 Autoloader**, .22 L.R.R.F., Tube Feed, Open Sights, 22" Barrel, *Modern*	60.00	85.00
☐ **Model 260 Magnum**, .22 W.M.R., Tube Feed, Open Sights, 22" Barrel, *Modern*	80.00	125.00
☐ **Model 260 Autoloader Carbine**, .22 L.R.R.F., Tube Feed, Open Sights, 20" Barrel, *Modern*	75.00	90.00
☐ **Model 260 Magnum Carbine**, .22 W.M.R., Tube Feed, Open Sights, 20" Barrel, *Modern*	90.00	135.00

KOHOUT & SPOL
Kdyne, Czechoslovakia.

HANDGUN, SEMI-AUTOMATIC

☐ **Mars**, .25 ACP, Clip Fed, *Modern*	95.00	155.00
☐ **Mars**, .32 ACP, Clip Fed, *Modern*	120.00	165.00

Kommer Model 1

Kommer Model 2

Kommer Model 4

KOMMER, THEODOR
Zella Mehlis, Germany, c. 1920.

HANDGUN, SEMI-AUTOMATIC

☐ **Model I**, .25 ACP, Clip Fed, *Modern*	235.00	385.00
☐ **Model II**, .25 ACP, Clip Fed, *Modern*	175.00	265.00
☐ **Model III**, .25 ACP, Clip Fed, *Modern*	245.00	375.00
☐ **Model IV**, .32 ACP, Clip Fed, *Modern*	280.00	390.00

KORTH

	V.G.	EXC.
HANDGUN, REVOLVER
- ☐ **Target**, .22 L.R.R.F., 6 Shot, *Modern* 400.00 600.00
- ☐ **Target**, .22 L.R.R.F., 6 Shot, *Modern* 400.00 600.00

KRAFT, JACOB
Lancaster, Pa. 1771-1782. See Kentucky Rifles and Pistols.

KRICO
Stuttgart, West Germany.

RIFLE, BOLT ACTION
- ☐ **.222 Rem. Rifle**, Checkered Stock, Double Set Triggers, *Modern* ... 300.00 450.00
- ☐ **.222 Rem. Carbine**, Checkered Stock, Double Set, Triggers, *Modern* 325.00 475.00
- ☐ **Special Varmint**, .222 Rem., Checkered Stock, Heavy Barrel, Double Set Triggers, *Modern* 300.00 450.00
- ☐ **Model 311**, .22 L.R.R.F., Checkered Stock, Double Set Trigger, *Modern* 175.00 250.00
- ☐ **Model 351**, .22 WMR, Checkered Stock, Double Set Triggers, *Modern* 200.00 275.00
- ☐ **Model 354**, .22 WMR, Checkered Stock, Double Set Triggers, *Modern* 225.00 325.00
- ☐ **Model DJV**, .22 Various Calibers, Checkered Target Stock, Double Set Triggers, *Modern* 300.00 425.00
- ☐ **Model 600 Export**, Various Calibers, Checkered Stock, Double Set Triggers, *Modern* 200.00 275.00
- ☐ **Model 600 Luxus**, Various Calibers, Checkered Stock, Double Set Triggers, *Modern* 225.00 325.00
- ☐ **Model 620 Luxus**, Various Calibers, Checkered Stock, Double Set Triggers, *Modern* 275.00 375.00
- ☐ **Model 700 Export**, Various Calibers, Checkered Stock, Double Set Triggers, *Modern* 210.00 295.00
- ☐ **Model 700 Luxus**, Various Calibers, Checkered Stock, Double Set Triggers, *Modern* 250.00 345.00
- ☐ **Model 720 Luxus**, Various Calibers, Checkered Stock, Double Set Triggers, *Modern* 290.00 385.00

KRIEGHOFF GUN CO.
Suhl, Germany.

COMBINATION WEAPON, DOUBLE BARREL, OVER-UNDER
- ☐ **Teck**, Various Calibers, Hammerless, Engraved, Fancy Checkering, *Modern* 1,750.00 2,500.00
- ☐ **Teck Dural**, Various Calibers, Hammerless, Engraved, Fancy Checkering, Lightweight, *Modern* 1,850.00 2,600.00
- ☐ **Ulm**, Various Calibers, Hammerless, Engraved, Fancy Checkering, Sidelock, *Modern* 3,400.00 4,150.00
- ☐ **Ulm Dural**, Various Calibers, Hammerless, Engraved, Fancy Checkering, Sidelock, *Modern* 3,400.00 4,150.00
- ☐ **Ulm Primus**, Various Calibers, Hammerless, Engraved, Fancy Checkering, Sidelock, *Modern* 3,400.00 4,450.00
- ☐ **Ulm Primus**, Various Calibers, Hammerless, Engraved, Fancy Checkering, Sidelock, Lightweight, *Modern* 4,250.00 5,500.00

COMBINATION WEAPON, DRILLING
- ☐ **Neptun**, Various Calibers, Hammerless, Engraved, Fancy Checkering, Sidelock, *Modern* 3,300.00 4,350.00

KRIEGHOFF GUN COMPANY / 255

	V.G.	EXC.

- ☐ **Neptun Dural**, Various Calibers, Hammerless, Engraved, Fancy
  Checkering, Sidelock, *Modern* 3,400.00 4,350.00
- ☐ **Neptun Primus**, Various Calibers, Hammerless, Fancy Checkering,
  Fancy Engraving, Sidelock, *Modern* 4,100.00 5,250.00
- ☐ **Neptun Primus**, Various Calibers, Hammerless, Fancy Checkering,
  Fancy Engraving, Sidelock, Lightweight, *Modern* 4,100.00 5,250.00
- ☐ **Neptun Primus M**, Various Calibers, Hammerless, Fancy
  Engraving, Fancy Checkering, Sidelock, *Modern* 9,750.00 14,750.00
- ☐ **Trumpf**, Various Calibers, Hammerless, Engraved, Fancy
  Checkering, *Modern* 2,250.00 2,950.00
- ☐ **Trumpf Dural**, Various Calibers, Hammerless, Engraved, Fancy
  Checkering, Lightweight, *Modern* 2,250.00 2,950.00

RIFLE, DOUBLE BARREL, OVER-UNDER
- ☐ **Teck**, Various Calibers, Hammerless, Engraved, Fancy Checkering,
  Magnum, *Modern* 2,550.00 3,300.00
- ☐ **Teck**, Various Calibers, Hammerless, Engraved, Fancy Checkering,
  Modern 2,000.00 2,550.00
- ☐ **Ulm**, Various Calibers, Hammerless, Engraved, Fancy Checkering,
  Magnum, Sidelock, *Modern* 3,750.00 4,500.00
- ☐ **Ulm**, Various Calibers, Hammerless, Engraved, Fancy Checkering,
  Sidelock, *Modern* 3,350.00 4,150.00
- ☐ **Ulm Primus**, Various Calibers, Hammerless, Engraved, Fancy
  Checkering, Magnum, Sidelock, *Modern* 4,150.00 5,150.00
- ☐ **Ulm Primus**, Various Calibers, Hammerless, Engraved, Fancy
  Checkering, Sidelock, *Modern* 3,700.00 4,850.00

SHOTGUN, DOUBLE BARREL, OVER-UNDER
- ☐ **Extra Barrel**, Add $600.00-$775.00
- ☐ **Crown**, 12 Gauge, Trap Grade, *Modern* 7,500.00 9,950.00
- ☐ **Crown Combo**, Various Gauges, Skeet Grade, Four Barrel Set,
  Modern 13,500.00 17,500.00
- ☐ **Exhibition**, 12 Gauge, Trap Grade, *Modern* 19,500.00 25,500.00
- ☐ **Exhibition Combo**, Various Gauges, Skeet Grade, Four Barrel Set,
  Modern 25,500.00 29,500.00
- ☐ **Monte Carlo**, 12 Gauge, Trap Grade, *Modern* 6,750.00 9,000.00
- ☐ **Monte Carlo Combo**, Various Gauges, Skeet Grade, Four Barrel
  Set, *Modern* 9,750.00 14,000.00
- ☐ **Munchen Combo**, Various Gauges, Skeet Grade, Four Barrel Set,
  Modern 5,650.00 7,000.00
- ☐ **San Remo**, 12 Gauge, Trap Grade, *Modern* 3,300.00 4,250.00
- ☐ **San Remo Combo**, Various Gauges, Skeet Grade, Four Barrel Set,
  Modern 6,500.00 7,750.00
- ☐ **Standard**, 12 Gauge, Trap Grade, *Modern* 1,450.00 1,950.00
- ☐ **Standard**, 12 Gauge, Field Grade, *Modern* 1,700.00 2,250.00
- ☐ **Standard**, Various Gauges, Skeet Grade, *Modern* 1,700.00 2,250.00
- ☐ **Standard Combo**, 12 Gauge, Trap Grade, Two Barrel Set, *Modern* 2,200.00 2,850.00
- ☐ **Standard Combo**, Various Gauges, Skeet Grade, Four Barrel Set,
  Modern 4,200.00 5,500.00
- ☐ **Super Crown**, 12 Gauge, Trap Grade, *Modern* 9,950.00 13,500.00
- ☐ **Super Crown Combo**, Various Gauges, Skeet Grade, Four Barrel
  Set, *Modern* 14,500.00 19,500.00
- ☐ **Teck**, Various Gauges, Hammerless, Engraved, Fancy Checkering,
  Modern 1,800.00 2,400.00
- ☐ **Teck**, Various Gauges, Hammerless, Engraved, Fancy Checkering,
  Single Trigger, *Modern* 1,850.00 2,500.00
- ☐ **Teck Dural**, Various Gauges, Hammerless, Engraved, Fancy
  Checkering, Lightweight, *Modern* 1,750.00 2,450.00

	V.G.	EXC.
☐ **Ulm**, Various Gauges, Hammerless, Engraved, Fancy Checkering, Sidelock, *Modern*	2,750.00	3,400.00
☐ **Ulm**, Various Gauges, Hammerless, Engraved, Fancy Checkering, Sidelock, Lightweight, *Modern*	2,700.00	3,350.00
☐ **Ulm-Primus**, Various Gauges, Hammerless, Engraved, Fancy Checkering, Sidelock, *Modern*	3,550.00	4,350.00
☐ **Ulm-Primus**, Various Gauges, Hammerless, Engraved, Fancy Checkering, Sidelock, Lightweight, *Modern*	3,550.00	4,450.00
☐ **Vandalia Rib**, 12 Gauge, Trap Grade, *Modern*	1,800.00	2,450.00
☐ **Vandalia Rib Combo**, Various Gauges, Skeet Grade, Four Barrel Set, *Modern*	3,300.00	4,000.00

KRUSCHITZ
Vienna, Austria.

RIFLE, BOLT ACTION

☐ **Mauser 98**, .30/06, Checkered Stock, Double Set Triggers, *Modern*	200.00	280.00

KROYDEN

RIFLE, SEMI-AUTOMATIC

☐ **.22 L.R.R.F.**, Tube Feed, Plain Stock, *Modern*	40.00	55.00

Kynoch Schlund Revolver

Lahti M 40 Swedish

KYNOCH GUN FACTORY
Birmingham, England.

HANDGUN, REVOLVER

☐ **Schlund**, .476 Eley, Hammerless, Top Break, Double Trigger Cocking, *Antique*	450.00	700.00

LAHTI
Developed and made by Valtion Kivaarithedas, Jyvaskyla, Finland. Also made by Husqvarna in Sweden.

HANDGUN, SEMI-AUTOMATIC

☐ **L-35 Finnish**, 9mm Luger, Clip Fed, Military, *Curio*	550.00	850.00
☐ **M 40 Swedish**, 9mm Luger, Clip Fed, Military, *Modern*	175.00	275.00

LAKESIDE
Made by Crescent for Montgomery Ward & Co., c. 1900.

	V.G.	EXC.
SHOTGUN, DOUBLE BARREL, SIDE-BY-SIDE		
☐ **Various Gauges**, Outside Hammers, Damascus Barrel, *Modern*	100.00	175.00
☐ **Various Gauges**, Hammerless, Steel Barrel, *Modern*	135.00	200.00
☐ **Various Gauges**, Hammerless, Damascus Barrel, *Modern*	100.00	175.00
☐ **Various Gauges**, Outside Hammers, Steel Barrel, *Modern*	125.00	190.00
SHOTGUN, SINGLESHOT		
☐ **Various Gauges**, Hammer, Steel Barrel, *Modern*	55.00	85.00

LAMES
Chiavari, Italy.

SHOTGUN, DOUBLE BARREL, OVER-UNDER		
☐ **12 Gauge Mag. 3"**, Field Grade, Automatic Ejector, Single Selective Trigger, Vent Rib, Checkered Stock, *Modern*	270.00	350.00
☐ **12 Gauge Mag. 3"**, Skeet Grade, Automatic Ejector, Single Selective Trigger, Vent Rib, Checkered Stock, *Modern*	320.00	400.00
☐ **12 Gauge Mag. 3"**, Trap Grade, Automatic Ejector, Single Selective Trigger, Vent Rib, Checkered Stock, *Modern*.....................	320.00	400.00
☐ **12 Gauge Mag. 3"**, Trap Grade, Automatic Ejector, Single Selective Trigger, Vent Rib, Monte Carlo Stock, *Modern*	365.00	450.00
☐ **California**, 12 Gauge Mag. 3", Trap Grade, Automatic Ejector, Single Selective Trigger, Vent Rib, Checkered Stock, *Modern*	475.00	600.00

LANCASTER, CHARLES
London, England 1889-1936.

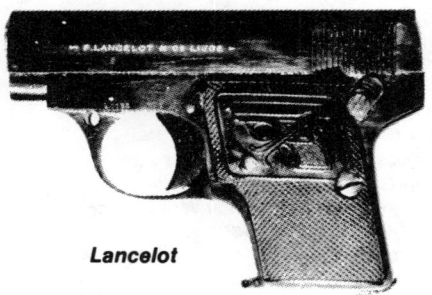

RIFLE, BOLT ACTION		
☐ **Various Calibers**, Sporting Rifle, *Modern*	575.00	875.00

Lancelot

LANCELOT

HANDGUN, SEMI-AUTOMATIC		
☐ **.25 ACP**, Clip Fed, Blue, *Modern*	135.00	185.00

LANE & READ
Boston, Mass. 1826-1835.

SHOTGUN, PERCUSSION		
☐ **28 Gauge**, Double Barrel, Side by Side, Light Engraving, Checkered Stock, *Antique*	325.00	445.00

LANG, JOSEPH
London, England, established in 1821.

258 / LANGENHAN

	V.G.	EXC.

HANDGUN, PERCUSSION
☐ **Pair**, Double Barrel, Over-Under, Officer's Belt Pistol, Light
   Engraving, Cased With Accessories, *Antique* 3,600.00 4,650.00
SHOTGUN, SINGLESHOT
☐ **12 Gauge**, Plain, Trap Grade, *Modern* 950.00 1,450.00

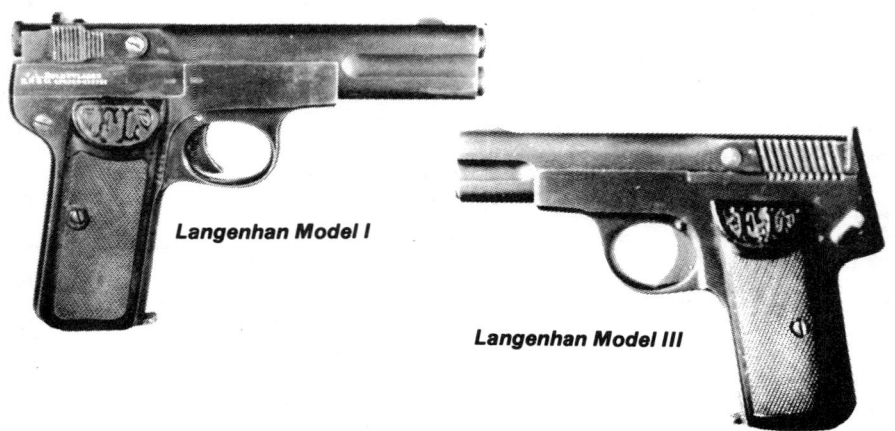

Langenhan Model I

Langenhan Model III

LANGENHAN
Friedrich Langenhan Gewehr u. Fahrradfabrik, Zella Mehlis, Germany.
HANDGUN, SEMI-AUTOMATIC
☐ **Model I**, .32 ACP, Clip Fed, Military, *Modern* 150.00 225.00
☐ **Model II**, .25 ACP, Clip Fed, *Modern* 175.00 275.00
☐ **Model III**, .25 ACP, Clip Fed, *Modern* 200.00 300.00

LA SALLE
Tradename used by Manufrance.
SHOTGUN, SLIDE ACTION
☐ **12 Gauge Mag. 3"**, Field Grade, Plain, *Modern*................... 85.00 135.00
☐ **12 Gauge Mag. 3"**, Checkered Stock, Fancy Wood, *Modern* 95.00 145.00
☐ **20 Gauge Mag.**, Field Grade, Plain, *Modern* 85.00 130.00
SHOTGUN, SEMI-AUTOMATIC
☐ **Custom**, 12 Ga., Checkered Stock, *Modern*...................... 125.00 175.00

LAURONA
Spain.
SHOTGUN, DOUBLE BARREL, OVER-UNDER
☐ **Model 67-G**, 12 Gauge 3", Checkered Stock, Vent Rib, Double
   Triggers, *Modern* 155.00 220.00

LE BARON
RIFLE, FLINTLOCK
☐ **.69 Presentation**, Silver Furniture, Fancy Wood, Fancy Checkering,
   Fancy Engraving, *Antique* 3,200.00 4,250.00

Le Francaise Military

Le Basque

Le Francaise Pocket

Le Francaise Policeman

	V.G.	EXC.
LE BASQUE		
HANDGUN, SEMI-AUTOMATIC		
☐ **.32 ACP**, Clip Fed, Blue, *Modern*	135.00	195.00
LE FRANCAISE		
Mre. Francaise de Armes et Cycles de St. Etienne, St. Etienne, France.		
HANDGUN, SEMI-AUTOMATIC		
☐ **Champion**, .25 ACP, Clip Fed, Long Grip, *Modern*	145.00	215.00
☐ **Le Francais**, .32 ACP, Clip Fed, *Modern*	275.00	400.00
☐ **Military Model**, 9mm French Long, Clip Fed, *Modern*	575.00	875.00
☐ **Pocket Model**, .25 ACP, Clip Fed, *Modern*	140.00	200.00
☐ **Policeman**, .25 ACP, Clip Fed, *Modern*	200.00	295.00
LE MARTINY		
HANDGUN, SEMI-AUTOMATIC		
☐ **.25 ACP**, Clip Fed, Blue, *Modern*	90.00	135.00
LE MONOBLOC		
Jules Jacquemart, Liege, Belgium, c. 1910.		
HANDGUN, SEMI-AUTOMATIC		
☐ **.25 ACP**, Clip Fed, *Modern*	265.00	375.00

LE SANS PARIEL
Mre. d'Armes des Pyrenees.

	V.G.	EXC.

HANDGUN, SEMI-AUTOMATIC
☐ **.25 ACP**, Clip Fed, Blue, *Modern* 90.00   135.00

LE TOUTACIER
Mre. d'Armes des Pyrenees.

HANDGUN, SEMI-AUTOMATIC
☐ **.25 ACP**, Clip Fed, Blue, *Modern* 90.00   135.00

LEADER
Possibly Hopkins & Allen, c. 1880.

HANDGUN, REVOLVER
☐ **.22 Short R.F.**, 7 Shot, Spur Trigger, Solid Frame, Single Action, Antique 90.00   160.00
☐ **.32 Short R.F.**, 5 Shot, Spur Trigger, Solid Frame, Single Action, Antique 95.00   170.00

LEADER GUN CO.
Made by Crescent for Charles William Stores of N.Y.C. c. 1900.

SHOTGUN, DOUBLE BARREL, SIDE-BY-SIDE
☐ **Various Gauges**, Outside Hammers, Damascus Barrel, *Modern* 100.00   175.00
☐ **Various Gauges**, Hammerless, Steel Barrel, *Modern* 135.00   200.00
☐ **Various Gauges**, Hammerless, Damascus Barrel, *Modern* 100.00   175.00
☐ **Various Gauges**, Outside Hammers, Steel Barrel, *Modern* 125.00   190.00

SHOTGUN, SINGLESHOT
☐ **Various Gauges**, Hammer, Steel Barrel, *Modern* 55.00   85.00

LEATHER, JACOB
York, Pa. 1779-1802. See U.S. Military, Kentucky Rifles

LEE ARMS CO.
Wilkes-Barre, Pa. c. 1870. Also See Red Jacket

HANDGUN, REVOLVER
☐ **.22 Short R.F.**, 7 Shot, Spur Trigger, Solid Frame, Single Action, Antique 90.00   160.00
☐ **.32 Short R.F.**, Spur Trigger, Nickel Plated, *Antique* 85.00   140.00
☐ **.32 Short R.F.**, 5 Shot, Spur Trigger, Solid Frame, Single Action, Antique 90.00   160.00

LEE SPECIAL
Made by Crescent for Lee Hardware, Salina, Kans. c. 1900

SHOTGUN, DOUBLE BARREL, SIDE-BY-SIDE
☐ **Various Gauges**, Outside Hammers, Damascus Barrel, *Modern* 100.00   175.00
☐ **Various Gauges**, Hammerless, Steel Barrel, *Modern* 135.00   200.00
☐ **Various Gauges**, Hammerless, Damascus Barrel, *Modern* 100.00   175.00
☐ **Various Gauges**, Outside Hammers, Steel Barrel, *Modern* 125.00   190.00

SHOTGUN, SINGLESHOT
☐ **Various Gauges**, Hammer, Steel Barrel, *Modern* 55.00   85.00

LEE'S MUNNER SPECIAL
Made by Crescent for Lee Hardware, Salina, Kans.

	V.G.	EXC.
SHOTGUN, DOUBLE BARREL, SIDE-BY-SIDE		
☐ **Various Gauges**, Outside Hammers, Damascus Barrel, *Modern*	100.00	175.00
☐ **Various Gauges**, Hammerless, Steel Barrel, *Modern*	135.00	200.00
☐ **Various Gauges**, Hammerless, Damascus Barrel, *Modern*	100.00	175.00
☐ **Various Gauges**, Outside Hammers, Steel Barrel, *Modern*	125.00	190.00
SHOTGUN, SINGLESHOT		
☐ **Various Gauges**, Hammer, Steel Barrel, *Modern*	55.00	85.00

LEFAUCHEUX
Paris, France

	V.G.	EXC.
HANDGUN, REVOLVER		
☐ **9mm Pinfire**, Double Action, Folding Trigger, Belgian, *Antique*	90.00	160.00
☐ **9mm Pinfire**, Double Action, Paris, *Antique*	175.00	275.00
☐ **12mm Pinfire**, Model 1863, Double Action, Finger Rest Trigger Guard, *Antique*	200.00	300.00
SHOTGUN, DOUBLE BARREL, SIDE-BY-SIDE		
☐ **Various Pinfire Gauges**, Double Triggers, Hammers, *Antique*	65.00	125.00

LEFEVER SONS & CO.
Syracuse, N.Y. Nichols & Lefever, 1876-1878; D.M. Lefever, 1879-1889; Lefever Arms Co. 1889-1899; Lefever, Sons & Co. 1899-1926. Purchased by Ithaca Gun Co. 1926.

	V.G.	EXC.
SHOTGUN, DOUBLE BARREL, SIDE-BY-SIDE		
☐ **#1000 Grade**, Various Gauges, Sidelock, Hammerless, Fancy Checkering, Fancy Engraving, Monte Carlo Stock, *Modern*	7,900.00	9,950.00
☐ **4AA**, Various Gauges, Box Lock, Hammerless, Automatic Ejector, Fancy Checkering, Fancy Engraving, Monte Carlo Stock, *Modern*	3,400.00	4,150.00
☐ **5BE**, Various Gauges, Box Lock, Hammerless, Fancy Checkering, Automatic Ejector, Fancy Engraving, *Modern*	2,350.00	3,150.00
☐ **6CE**, Various Gauges, Box Lock, Hammerless, Fancy Checkering, Automatic Ejector, Fancy Engraving, *Modern*	1,750.00	2,400.00
☐ **7DE**, Various Guages, Box Lock, Hammerless, Fancy Checkering, Automatic Ejector, Fancy Engraving, *Modern*	1,500.00	2,150.00
☐ **8EE**, Various Gauges, Box Lock, Hammerless, Checkered Stock, Automatic Ejector, Engraved, *Modern*	975.00	1,600.00
☐ **9FE**, Various Gauges, Box Lock, Hammerless, Checkered Stock, Automatic Ejector, Engraved, *Modern*	850.00	1,250.00
☐ **A**, Various Gauges, Sidelock, Hammerless, Fancy Checkering, Fancy Engraving, Monte Carlo Stock, *Modern*	2,600.00	3,450.00
☐ **AA**, Various Gauges, Sidelock, Hammerless, Fancy Checkering, Fancy Engraving, Monte Carlo Stock, *Modern*	3,400.00	4,100.00
☐ **B**, Various Gauges, Sidelock, Hammerless, Fancy Checkering, Fancy Engraving, Monte Carlo Stock, *Modern*	2,150.00	2,750.00
☐ **BE**, Various Gauges, Sidelock, Hammerless, Fancy Checkering, Fancy Engraving, Monte Carlo Stock, Automatic Ejector, *Modern*	2,400.00	2,950.00
☐ **C**, Various Gauges, Sidelock, Hammerless, Fancy Checkering, Fancy Engraving, Monte Carlo Stock, *Modern*	1,700.00	2,250.00
☐ **CE**, Various Gauges, Sidelock, Hammerless, Fancy Checkering, Fancy Engraving, Monte Carlo Stock, Automatic Ejector, *Modern*	1,750.00	2,350.00
☐ **D**, Various Gauges, Sidelock, Hammerless, Fancy Checkering, Engraved, Monte Carlo Stock, *Modern*	1,400.00	1,900.00
☐ **DE**, Various Gauges, Sidelock, Hammerless, Fancy Checkering, Engraved, Monte Carlo Stock, Automatic Ejector, *Modern*	1,500.00	2,150.00
☐ **D S**, Various Gauges, Sidelock, Hammerless, Checkered Stock, *Modern*	425.00	575.00

262 / LEFEVRE, PHILIP

	V.G.	EXC.
☐ **D SE**, Various Gauges, Sidelock, Hammerless, Checkered Stock, Automatic Ejector, *Modern*	525.00	750.00
☐ **E**, Various Gauges, Sidelock, Hammerless, Fancy Checkering, Engraved, *Modern*	975.00	1,500.00
☐ **EE**, Various Gauges, Sidelock, Hammerless, Fancy Checkering, Engraved, *Modern*	1,250.00	1,800.00
☐ **Excelsior**, Various Gauges, Box Lock, Hammerless, Checkered Stock, Automatic Ejector, Light Engraving, *Modern*	750.00	975.00
☐ **F**, Various Gauges, Sidelock, Hammerless, Checkered Stock, Engraved, *Modern*	925.00	1,350.00
☐ **FE**, Various Gauges, Sidelock, Hammerless, Checkered Stock, Engraved, Automatic Ejector, *Modern*	975.00	1,450.00
☐ **G**, Various Gauges, Sidelock, Hammerless, Checkered Stock, Light Engraving, *Modern*	625.00	850.00
☐ **GE**, Various Gauges, Sidelock, Hammerless, Checkered Stock, Light Engraving, Automatic Ejector, *Modern*	725.00	975.00
☐ **H**, Various Gauges, Sidelock, Hammerless, Checkered Stock, Light Engraving, *Modern*	525.00	675.00
☐ **HE**, Various Gauges, Sidelock, Hammerless, Checkered Stock, Light Engraving, Automatic Ejector, *Modern*	550.00	825.00
☐ **Nitro Special**, Various Gauges, Box Lock, Double Trigger, Checkered Stock, *Modern*	275.00	400.00
☐ **Nitro Special**, Various Gauges, Box Lock, Single Trigger, Checkered Stock, *Modern*	350.00	475.00
☐ **Optimus**, Various Gauges, Sidelock, Hammerless, Fancy Checkering, Fancy Engraving, Monte Carlo Stock, *Modern*	5,000.00	7,000.00
☐ **Uncle Dan**, Various Gauges, Box Lock, Hammerless, Automatic Ejector, Fancy Checkering, Fancy Engraving, Monte Carlo Stock, *Modern*	5,000.00	7,000.00

SHOTGUN, SINGLESHOT

	V.G.	EXC.
☐ **12 Gauge**, Trap Grade, Hammerless, Vent Rib, Checkered Stock, Automatic Ejector, *Modern*	215.00	300.00
☐ **D.M. Lefever**, 12 Gauge, Trap Grade, Hammerless, Vent Rib, Checkered Stock, Automatic Ejector, *Modern*	425.00	650.00
☐ **Long Range**, Various Gauges, Field Grade, Hammerless, Checkered Stock, *Modern*	95.00	140.00

LEFEVRE, PHILIP
Beaver Valley, Pa. 1731-1756. See Kentucky Rifles.

LEFEVRE, SAMUEL
Strasbourg, Pa. 1770-1771. See Kentucky Rifles and Pistols.

LEIGH, HENRY
Belgium, c. 1890.

SHOTGUN, DOUBLE BARREL, SIDE-BY-SIDE

☐ **Various Gauges**, Outside Hammers, Damascus Barrel, *Modern*	90.00	150.00

LEITNER, ADAM
York Co, Pa. See Kentucky Rifles and Pistols.

LENNARD
Lancaster, Pa. 1770-1772. See Kentucky Rifles and Pistols.

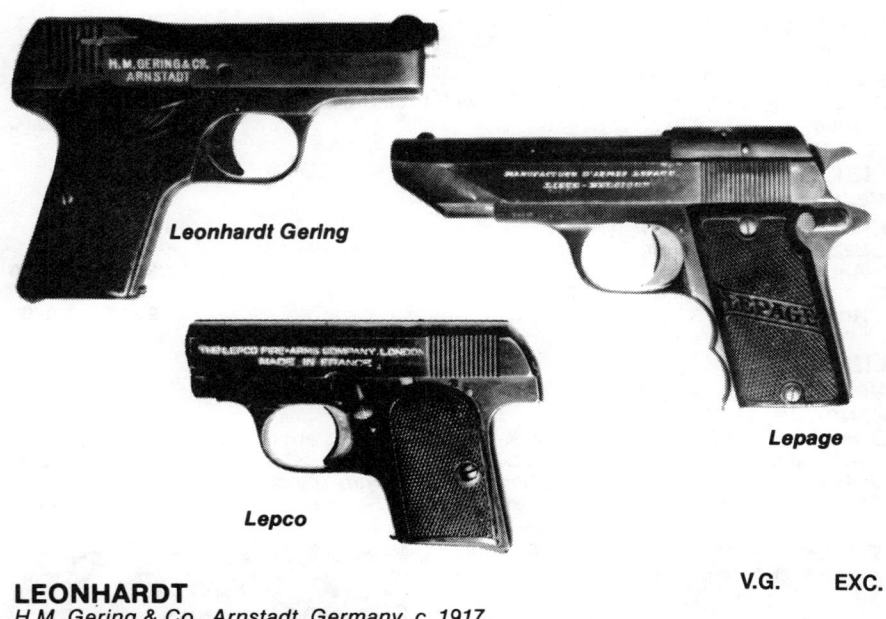

Leonhardt Gering

Lepage

Lepco

	V.G.	EXC.

LEONHARDT
H.M. Gering & Co., Arnstadt, Germany, c. 1917.

HANDGUN, SEMI-AUTOMATIC
- ☐ **Army**, .32 ACP, Clip Fed, *Modern* 115.00 175.00
- ☐ **Gering**, .32 ACP, Clip Fed, *Modern* 140.00 190.00

LEPAGE
Made by Manufacture D'Armes Le Page, Liege, Belgium.

HANDGUN, SEMI-AUTOMATIC
- ☐ **.25 ACP**, Clip Fed, *Modern* 160.00 245.00
- ☐ **.32 ACP**, Clip Fed, *Modern* 260.00 375.00
- ☐ **.380 ACP**, Clip Fed, Adjustable Sights, *Modern* 285.00 425.00
- ☐ **9mm Browning Long**, Clip Fed, Adjustable Sights, *Modern* 425.00 575.00
- ☐ **9mm Browning Long**, Clip Fed, Adjustable Sights, Detachable Shoulder Stock, *Class 3* 650.00 875.00

LEPCO

HANDGUN, SEMI-AUTOMATIC
- ☐ **.25 ACP**, Clip Fed, Blue, *Modern* 85.00 125.00

L.E.S.
Skokie, Ill.

HANDGUN, SEMI-AUTOMATIC
- ☐ **P-18**, 9mm Luger, Stainless Steel, Clip Fed, Hammer, Double Action, *Modern* 185.00 245.00
- ☐ **P-18 Deluxe**, 9mm Luger, Stainless Steel, Clip Fed, Hammer, Double Action, *Modern* 225.00 300.00

LESCHER
Philadelphia, Pa., c. 1730. See Kentucky Rifles and Pistols.

LESCONNE, A.
Maybe French, c. 1650.

V.G.   EXC.

HANDGUN, FLINTLOCK
☐ **Pair**, Engraved, Silver Inlay, Long Screw Barrel, Rifled, Belt Hook,
Antique 7,500.00 10,000.00

LIBERTY
Made by Hood Firearms, 1880-1900.

HANDGUN, REVOLVER
☐ **.22 Short R.F.**, 7 Shot, Spur Trigger, Solid Frame, Single Action,
Antique 90.00 160.00
☐ **.32 Short R.F.**, 5 Shot, Spur Trigger, Solid Frame, Single Action,
Antique 95.00 170.00

LIBERTY
Montrose, Calif.

HANDGUN, REVOLVER
☐ **Mustang**, .22LR/.22 WMR Combo, Single Action, Western Style,
Adjustable Sights, *Modern* 30.00 45.00
☐ **Mustang**, .22 L.R.R.F., Single Action, Western Style, Adjustable
Sights, *Modern* 25.00 40.00

Liberty M1924

Liberty Long Grip

LIBERTY
Retolaza Hermanos, Eibar, Spain, c. 1920.

HANDGUN, SEMI-AUTOMATIC
☐ **M1924**, .32 ACP, Clip Fed, *Modern* 90.00 130.00
☐ **.25 ACP**, Clip Fed, Blue, Long Grip, *Modern* 95.00 145.00

LIBERTY CHIEF
Miroku Firearms, Kochi, Japan.

HANDGUN, REVOLVER
☐ **Model 6**, .38 Spec., Double Action, Blue, *Modern* 80.00 125.00

LIBIA
Made by Beistegui Hermanos, c. 1920.

HANDGUN, SEMI-AUTOMATIC
☐ **.25 ACP**, Clip Fed, Blue, *Modern* 135.00 185.00
☐ **.32 ACP**, Clip Fed, Blue, *Modern* 155.00 215.00

LIEGEOISE D'ARMES A FEU
Robar et Cie., Liege, Belgium, c. 1920.

V.G.   EXC.

HANDGUN, SEMI-AUTOMATIC
- ☐ **Spanish Copy**, .25 ACP, Blue, Clip Fed, *Curio* 85.00   125.00
- ☐ **Spanish Copy**, .32 ACP, Blue, Clip Fed, *Curio* 90.00   135.00
- ☐ **New Model Melior**, .25 ACP, Clip Fed, Blue, *Curio* 125.00   170.00

LIGHTNING
Echave y Arizmendi, Eibar, Spain, c. 1920.

HANDGUN, SEMI-AUTOMATIC
- ☐ **.25 ACP**, Clip Fed, Blue, *Modern* 85.00   125.00

LIGNITZ, I.H.
Continental, c. 1650.

HANDGUN, WHEEL-LOCK
- ☐ **Brass Barrel**, Holster Pistol, Medium Ornamentation, *Antique* 5,000.00   6,750.00

Lignose 2A

Lignose 3A

LIGNOSE
Successors to Theodor Bergmann, Suhl, Germany, c. 1925.

HANDGUN, SEMI-AUTOMATIC
- ☐ **Model 2**, .25 ACP, Clip Fed, *Modern* 195.00   285.00
- ☐ **Model 2A**, .25 ACP, Clip Fed, Einhand, *Modern* 185.00   260.00
- ☐ **Model 3**, .25 ACP, Clip Fed, Long Grip, *Modern* 235.00   325.00
- ☐ **Model 3A**, .25 ACP, Clip Fed, Long Grip, Einhand, *Modern* 190.00   280.00

LILIPUT
August Menz, Suhl, Germany, c. 1920.

HANDGUN, SEMI-AUTOMATIC
- ☐ **4.25mm Liliput**, Clip Fed, Blue, *Curio* 375.00   545.00
- ☐ **25 ACP**, Clip Fed, Blue, *Modern* 175.00   265.00

LION
Made by Johnson Bye & Co., c. 1870-1880. Sold by J.P. Lovell, Boston, Mass.

HANDGUN, REVOLVER
- ☐ **#1**, .22 Short R.F., 7 Shot, Spur Trigger, Solid Frame, Single Action, *Antique* 90.00   160.00
- ☐ **#2**, .32 Short R.F., 5 Shot, Spur Trigger, Solid Frame, Single Action, *Antique* 95.00   170.00
- ☐ **#3**, .38 Short R.F., 5 Shot, Spur Trigger, Solid Frame, Single Action, *Antique* 95.00   175.00

LITTLE GIANT

	V.G.	EXC.
☐ **#4**, .41 Short R.F., 5 Shot, Spur Trigger, Solid Frame, Single Action, *Antique*	110.00	185.00

LITTLE GIANT
Made by Bacon Arms Co., c. 1880.
HANDGUN, REVOLVER
☐ **.22 Short R.F.**, 7 Shot, Spur Trigger, Solid Frame, Single Action, *Antique* 90.00 160.00

LITTLE JOHN
Made by Hood Firearms., c. 1876.
HANDGUN, REVOLVER
☐ **.22 Short R.F.**, 7 Shot, Spur Trigger, Solid Frame, Single Action, *Antique* 90.00 160.00

LITTLE JOKER
Made by John M. Marlin, New Haven, Conn. 1873-1875.
HANDGUN, REVOLVER
☐ **.22 Short R.F.**, 7 Shot, Spur Trigger, Solid Frame, Single Action, *Antique* 100.00 175.00

LITTLE PET
Made by Stevens Arms.
SHOTGUN, SINGLESHOT
☐ **Model 958**, .410 Gauge, Automatic Ejector, Hammer, *Modern* 35.00 55.00
☐ **Model 958**, 32 Gauge, Automatic Ejector, Hammer, *Modern* 45.00 65.00

LITTLE TOM
Alois Tomiska, Pilsen, Czechoslovakia 1909-1918.
HANDGUN, SEMI-AUTOMATIC
☐ **.25 ACP**, Clip Fed, Blue, Hammer, *Curio* 300.00 395.00
☐ **.32 ACP**, Clip Fed, Blue, Hammer, *Curio* 355.00 465.00

LITTLE TOM
Wiener Waffenfabrik, Vienna, Austria 1918-1925.
HANDGUN, SEMI-AUTOMATIC
☐ **.25 ACP**, Clip Fed, Blue, Hammer, *Curio* 265.00 350.00

LJUTIC INDUSTRIES, INC.
Yakima, Wash.
SHOTGUN, DOUBLE BARREL, OVER-UNDER
☐ **Bi Gun**, 12 Gauge, High Rib, Live Pigeon, Checkered Stock, Choke Tubes, *Modern* 3,300.00 4,250.00
☐ **Bi Gun**, 12 Gauge, Vent Rib, Trap Grade, Checkered Stock, *Modern* 3,250.00 4,000.00
☐ **Bi Gun Set**, Various Calibers, Vent Rib, Skeet Grade, Checkered Stock, With 4 Sets of Barrels, *Modern* 6,500.00 8,750.00

SHOTGUN, SEMI-AUTOMATIC
☐ **Bi Matic**, 12 Gauge, Vent Rib, Trap Grade, Checkered Stock, *Modern* 1,500.00 2,000.00

	V.G.	EXC.

SHOTGUN, SINGLESHOT
- ☐ **Dyn-A-Trap**, 12 Gauge, Trap Grade, Checkered Stock, Vent Rib, *Modern* 775.00   1,150.00
- ☐ **Dyn-A-Trap**, 12 Gauge, Release Trigger *Add* **$95.00-$140.00**
- ☐ **Dyn-A-Trap**, 12 Gauge, for Custom Stock *Add* **$115.00-$165.00**
- ☐ **Mono-Gun**, 12 Gauge, Trap Grade, Checkered Stock, Vent Rib, *Modern* 1,750.00   2,500.00
- ☐ **Mono-Gun**, 12 Gauge, Trap Grade, Checkered Stock, Olympic Rib, *Modern* 2,400.00   3,000.00
- ☐ **Mono-Gun**, 12 Gauge, For Extra Barrel *Add* **$350.00-$550.00**
- ☐ **Mono-Gun**, 12 Gauge, Release Trigger *Add* **$150.00-$200.00**
- ☐ **Mono-Gun**, 12 Gauge, Trap Grade, Checkered Stock, Vent Rib, Adjustable Pattern, *Modern* 2,400.00   3,000.00
- ☐ **X-73**, 12 Gauge, Trap Grade, Checkered Stock, Vent Rib, *Modern*   775.00   1,150.00
- ☐ **X-73**, 12 Gauge, For Extra Barrel *Add* **$300.00-$425.00**
- ☐ **X-73**, 12 Gauge, Release Trigger *Add* **$150.00-$200.00**

LLAMA
Gabilondo y Cia., Elgoibar, Spain from 1930 to date. Imported by Stoeger Arms.

HANDGUN, REVOLVER
- ☐ **Chrome Plate** *Add* **20%-30%**
- ☐ **Engraving** *Add* **25%-35%**
- ☐ **Gold Damascening** *Add* **300%-400%**
- ☐ **Commanche I**, .22 L.R.R.F., Swing-Out Cylinder, Double Action, Blue, *Modern* 125.00   175.00
- ☐ **Commanche II**, .38 Special, Swing-Out Cylinder, Double Action, Blue, *Modern* 125.00   175.00
- ☐ **Commanche III**, .357 Magnum, Swing-Out Cylinder, Double Action, Blue, *Modern* 140.00   200.00
- ☐ **Martial**, .22 L.R.R.F., Swing-Out Cylinder, Double Action, Blue, *Modern* 95.00   145.00
- ☐ **Martial**, .22 WMR, Swing-Out Cylinder, Double Action, Blue, *Modern* 115.00   160.00
- ☐ **Martial**, .38 Special, Swing-Out Cylinder, Double Action, Blue, *Modern* 100.00   145.00
- ☐ **Super Commanche**, .357 Magnum, Swing-Out Cylinder, Double Action, Blue, *Modern* 160.00   220.00
- ☐ **Super Commanche**, .44 Magnum, Swing-Out Cylinder, Double Action, Blue, *Modern* 240.00   325.00

HANDGUN, SEMI-AUTOMATIC
- ☐ **Chrome Plate** *Add* **20%-30%**
- ☐ **Engraving** *Add* **25%-35%**
- ☐ **Gold Damascening** *Add* **300%-400%**
- ☐ **Model I**, .32 ACP, Clip Fed, Blue, *Modern* 120.00   160.00
- ☐ **Model II**, .380 ACP, Clip Fed, Blue, *Modern* 120.00   175.00
- ☐ **Model III**, .380 ACP, Clip Fed, Blue, *Modern* 125.00   170.00
- ☐ **Model IIIA**, .380 ACP, Clip Fed, Grip Safety, Blue, *Modern* 145.00   190.00
- ☐ **Model IV**, 9mm Bergmann, Clip Fed, Blue, *Modern* 120.00   165.00
- ☐ **Model IX**, .45 ACP, Clip Fed, Blue, *Modern* 140.00   190.00
- ☐ **Model IXA**, .45 ACP, Clip Fed, Grip Safety, Blue, *Modern* 150.00   220.00
- ☐ **Model V**, .38 ACP, Clip Fed, Blue, *Modern* 140.00   185.00
- ☐ **Model VII**, .38 ACP, Clip Fed, Blue, *Modern* 145.00   190.00
- ☐ **Model VIII**, .38 ACP, Grip Safety, Blue, *Modern* 160.00   225.00
- ☐ **Model X**, .32 ACP, Clip Fed, Blue, *Modern* 120.00   165.00
- ☐ **Model XA**, .32 ACP, Clip Fed, Grip Safety, Blue, *Modern* 135.00   185.00

268 / LOBINGER, JOHANN

	V.G.	EXC.
☐ **Model XI**, 9mm Luger, Clip Fed, Blue, *Modern*	150.00	225.00
☐ **Model XV**, .22 L.R.R.F., Clip Fed, Grip Safety, Blue, *Modern*	130.00	180.00
☐ **Omni**, 9mm Luger or .45 ACP, Clip Fed, Double Action, Hammer, *Modern*	275.00	375.00

LOBINGER, JOHANN
Vienna, Austria, c. 1780.

RIFLE, FLINTLOCK
☐ **Yaeger**, Smoothbore, Half-Octagon Barrel, Silver Furniture, Carved, *Antique* 2,600.00 3,500.00

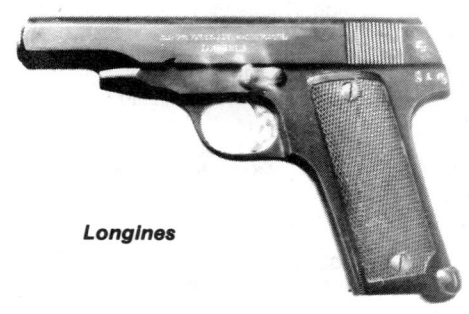

Longines

LONGINES
Cooperative Orbea, Eibar, Spain, c. 1920.

HANDGUN, SEMI-AUTOMATIC
☐ **.32 ACP**, Clip Fed, *Modern* 135.00   185.00

LONG RANGE WONDER
Tradename used by Sears, Roebuck & Co.

SHOTGUN, SINGLESHOT
☐ **12 Ga.**, Hammer, Break-Open, *Modern* 35.00   55.00

LONG TOM
Made by Stevens Arms.

SHOTGUN, SINGLESHOT
☐ **Model 90**, Various Gauges, Takedown, Automatic Ejector, Plain, Hammer, *Modern* 35.00   55.00
☐ **Model 95**, 12 and 16 Gauges, Hammer, Automatic Ejector, *Modern* 35.00   55.00

LOOKING GLASS
Domingo Acha and Acha Hermanos, Ermua, Spain, c. 1920.

HANDGUN, SEMI-AUTOMATIC
☐ **.25 ACP**, Clip Fed, Hammer, *Modern* 95.00   145.00
☐ **.25 ACP**, Clip Fed, Hammerless, *Modern* 85.00   125.00
☐ **.32 ACP**, Clip Fed, Long Grip, Hammerless, *Modern* 90.00   135.00
☐ **.32 ACP**, Clip Fed, Long Grip, Hammer, *Modern* 110.00   150.00

LORD, J.
Orwigsburg, Pa. 1842-55. See Kentucky Rifles.

Bache, Belt Pistol, *engraved, gold damascened, silver wire stock inlays, steel furniture, carved stock, antique . . . .* **$875.00-1,500.00**

Austrian Military, M1907 Roth Steyr, *8mm Roth-Steyr, curio* **$175.00-325.00**

Colt, Officer's Model Match, .38 Special, 6 shot, adjustable sights, 6" barrel, target grips, target hammer, modern . . . . **$195.00 - 300.00**

Sauer, J.P. & Sohn, Model 1913, early and late, .32 ACP, clip fed, modern **$175.00-250.00**

Top to bottom:
Savage Arms Co., Model 1907, (1914), .32 ACP, spur cocking piece, curio . . . . **$135.00 - 170.00**
Model 1907 (1918), .32 ACP, clip fed, no cartridge indicator, burr cocking piece, (after #175,000), curio . . . . **$120.00 - 155.00**
Model 1917, .32 ACP, clip fed, spur cocking piece, flared grip, curio . . . . . .
. . . . **$155.00 - 200.00**

Top to bottom:
Harrington & Richardson, Young America, *various calibers, double action, solid frame, modern*. . . . . **$45.00 - 80.00**
Forehand Arms Co., .32 S & W, *5 shot, double action, solid frame, 2" barrel, antique* . . . . **$50.00 - 90.00**

Forehand & Wadsworth, British Bulldog, .38 S & W, 6 shot, double action, solid frame, antique . . . . . **$55.00 - 95.00**

Kolb, Henry M., Baby Hammerless, .22 short R.F., folding trigger, nickel plated, round butt, curio . . . . **$90.00 - 150.00**

Red Jacket, .32 Short R.F., 5 shot, single action, solid frame, spur trigger, antique **$95.00-165.00**

Kolb, Henry M. Baby Hammerless, .22 short R.F., folding trigger, nickel plated, square butt, curio. . . . . **$90.00 - 150.00**

Kimball, J.M. Arms Co., standard Model, .30 carbine, clip fed, blue, modern. . . . . $450.00 - 700.00

LOWELL ARMS CO.
Lowell, Mass. 1864-68.
HANDGUN, REVOLVER
- ☐ **.22 Short R.F.**, 7 Shot, Spur Trigger, Tip-up, *Antique* 220.00   325.00
- ☐ **.32 Long R.F.**, 6 Shot, Spur Trigger, Tip-Up, Single Action, *Antique*   165.00   250.00
- ☐ **.38 Long R.F.**, 6 Shot, Spur Trigger, Tip-Up, Single Action, *Antique*   250.00   375.00

RIFLE, SINGLESHOT
- ☐ **.38 Long R.F.**, *Antique* 225.00   350.00

LOWER, J.P.
Philadelphia, Pa., c. 1875.
HANDGUN, REVOLVER
- ☐ **.22 Long R.F.**, 7 Shot, Single Action, Solid Frame, Spur Trigger, *Antique* 110.00   180.00
- ☐ **.32 Long R.F.**, 7 Shot, Single Action, Solid Frame, Spur Trigger, *Antique* 120.00   190.00

LUGER
Made by various companies for commercial and military use from 1900-45. Also see Mauser Parabellum.
HANDGUN, SEMI-AUTOMATIC
- ☐ **1900 Commercial**, .30 Luger, *Curio* 975.00   2,550.00
- ☐ **1900 Eagle**, .30 Luger, *Curio* 950.00   1,950.00
- ☐ **1900 Swiss Commercial**, .30 Luger, *Curio* 950.00   2,450.00
- ☐ **1900 Swiss Military**, .30 Luger, *Curio* 975.00   2,150.00
- ☐ **1900 Swiss Military**, .30 Luger, Wide Trigger, *Curio* 1,150.00 2,600.00
- ☐ **1902**, .30 Luger and 9mm Luger, Carbine, *Curio* 2,950.00 5,500.00
- ☐ **1902**, 9mm Luger, Cartridge Counter, *Curio* 4,950.00 7,500.00
- ☐ **1902 Commercial**, 9mm Luger, *Curio* 3,850.00 5,750.00
- ☐ **1902 Eagle**, 9mm Luger, *Curio* 2,975.00 4,500.00
- ☐ **1902 Prototype**, .30 Luger and 9mm Luger, *Curio* 7,500.00 14,500.00
- ☐ **1902 Test**, .30 Luger and 9mm Luger, *Curio* 2,400.00 4,500.00
- ☐ **1902-3 Presentation**, .30 Luger, Carbine, *Curio* 20,000.00 35,000.00
- ☐ **1903 Commercial**, .30 Luger, *Curio* 4,750.00 7,500.00
- ☐ **1904 Navy**, 9mm Luger, *Curio* 5,000.00 11,000.00
- ☐ **1906 Brazilian**, .30 Luger, *Curio* 750.00   1,750.00
- ☐ **1906 Bulgarian**, 9mm Luger, *Curio* 3,400.00 5,950.00
- ☐ **1906 Bulgarian**, .30 Luger, *Curio* 3,950.00 6,000.00
- ☐ **1906 Commercial**, .30 Luger, *Curio* 850.00   1,800.00
- ☐ **1906 Commercial**, 9mm Luger, *Curio* 1,200.00 2,400.00
- ☐ **1906 Dutch**, 9mm Luger, *Curio* 850.00   1,750.00
- ☐ **1906 Eagle**, .30 Luger, *Curio* 950.00   1,950.00
- ☐ **1906 Eagle**, 9mm Luger, *Curio* 1,250.00 2,200.00
- ☐ **1906 French**, .30 Luger, *Curio* 4,500.00 7,950.00
- ☐ **1906 Navy Commercial**, 9mm Luger, *Curio* 3,250.00 4,950.00
- ☐ **1906 Navy Military**, 9mm Luger, *Curio* 975.00   2,500.00
- ☐ **1906 Portuguese Army**, .30 Luger, *Curio* 850.00   1,400.00
- ☐ **1906 Portuguese Navy Crown**, .30 Luger and 9mm Luger, *Curio* ... 5,750.00 12,500.00
- ☐ **1906 Portuguese Navy**, RP, .30 Luger, *Curio* 3,100.00 5,000.00
- ☐ **1906 Russian**, 9mm Luger, *Curio* 4,750.00 9,750.00
- ☐ **1906 Swiss Commercial**, .30 Luger, *Curio* 1,500.00 3,650.00
- ☐ **1906 Swiss Military**, .30 Luger, *Curio* 875.00   1,650.00
- ☐ **1906 Swiss Police**, .30 Luger, *Curio* 950.00   1,950.00
- ☐ **1908 Bolivian**, 9mm Luger, *Curio* 5,750.00 9,000.00
- ☐ **1908 Bulgarian**, 9mm Luger, *Curio* 950.00   2,200.00
- ☐ **1908 DWM Commercial**, 9mm Luger, *Curio* 600.00   1,150.00

270 / LUGAR

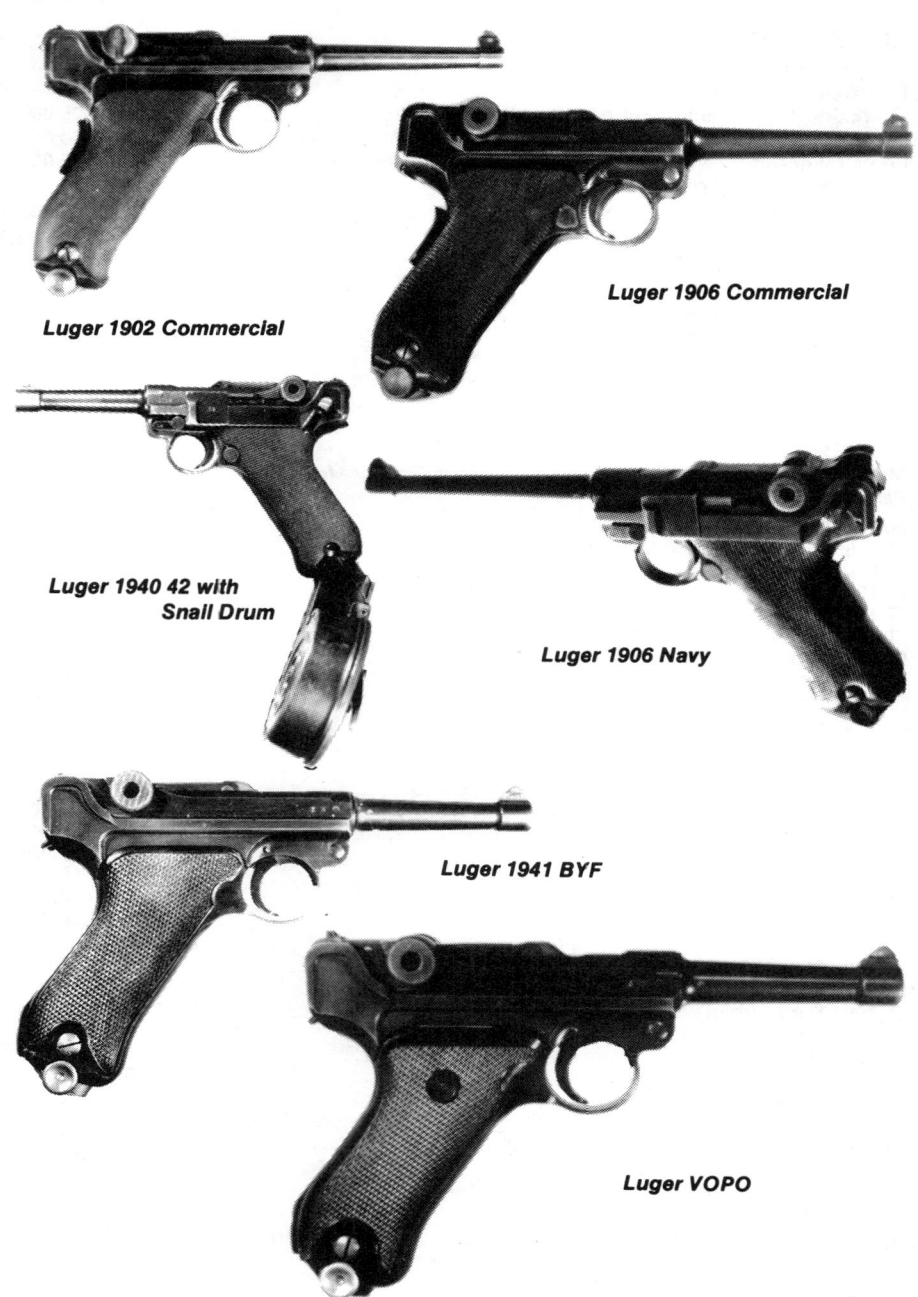

Luger 1902 Commercial

Luger 1906 Commercial

Luger 1940 42 with Snail Drum

Luger 1906 Navy

Luger 1941 BYF

Luger VOPO

	V.G.	EXC.
☐ 1908 **Military**, 9mm Luger, *Curio*	575.00	975.00
☐ 1908 **Navy Commercial**, .30 Luger, *Curio*	1,700.00	4,100.00
☐ 1908 **Navy Military**, 9mm Luger, *Curio*	975.00	2,100.00
☐ 1913 **Commercial**, 9mm Luger, *Curio*	700.00	1,775.00
☐ 1914 **Commercial**, 9mm Luger, *Curio*	700.00	1,775.00
☐ 1914 **Artillery**, 9mm Luger, *Curio*	700.00	1,800.00
☐ 1914 **Military**, 9mm Luger, *Curio*	600.00	975.00
☐ 1914 **Navy**, 9mm Luger, *Curio*	925.00	1,650.00
☐ 1918 **Spandau**, 9mm Luger, *Curio*	3,400.00	6,500.00
☐ 1920 **Abercrombie & Fitch**, .30 Luger and 9mm Luger, *Curio*	3,200.00	5,950.00
☐ 1920 **Artillery**, 9mm Luger, *Curio*	775.00	1,600.00
☐ 1920 **Commercial**, .30 Luger and 9mm Luger, *Curio*	475.00	975.00
☐ 1920 **Navy**, 9mm Luger, *Curio*	975.00	2,300.00
☐ 1920 **Simson**, 9mm Luger, *Curio*	535.00	1,100.00
☐ 1920 **Swiss Commercial**, .30 Luger and 9mm Luger, *Curio*	900.00	1,600.00
☐ 1920 **Swiss Rework**, .30 Luger and 9mm Luger, *Curio*	975.00	1,850.00
☐ 1920-22, .30 Luger and 9mm Luger, *Curio*	475.00	950.00
☐ 1921 **Krieghoff**, .30 Luger, *Curio*	800.00	1,750.00
☐ 1923 **Arabian**, .30 Luger, *Curio*	550.00	1,100.00
☐ 1923 **Commercial**, .30 Luger and 9mm Luger, *Curio*	475.00	1,100.00
☐ 1923 **Commercial Krieghoff**, 9mm Luger, *Curio*	650.00	1,350.00
☐ 1923 **Commercial "Safe-Loaded"**, .30 Luger and 9mm Luger, *Curio*	650.00	1,850.00
☐ 1923 **Dutch**, 9mm Luger, *Curio*	675.00	1,250.00
☐ 1923 **Russian**, .30 Luger, *Curio*	1,450.00	2,950.00
☐ 1923 **Simson Commercial**, 9mm Luger, *Curio*	650.00	2,100.00
☐ 1923 **Simson Military**, 9mm Luger, *Curio*	950.00	2,350.00
☐ 1923 **Stoeger**, .30 Luger and 9mm Luger, *Curio*	2,850.00	5,300.00
☐ 1924 **Bern**, .30 Luger, *Curio*	1,300.00	2,450.00
☐ 1924-7 **Simson**, 9mm Luger, *Curio*	950.00	2,300.00
☐ 1929 **Bern**, .30 Luger and 9mm Luger, *Curio*	1,300.00	3,550.00
☐ 1929-33 **Riff**, 9mm Luger, *Curio*	500.00	975.00
☐ 1929-33 **Sneak**, 9mm Luger, *Curio*	550.00	1,150.00
☐ 1930-33 **Death Head**, 9mm Luger, *Curio*	750.00	1,500.00
☐ 1933 **Finnish Army**, 9mm Luger, *Curio*	700.00	1,950.00
☐ 1933 **K.I.**, 9mm Luger, *Curio*	750.00	1,650.00
☐ 1933 **Stoeger**, .30 Luger and 9mm Luger, *Curio*	3,600.00	5,875.00
☐ 1933-35 **Dutch**, 9mm Luger, *Curio*	1,350.00	2,250.00
☐ 1933-35 **Mauser Commercial**, 9mm Luger, *Curio*	1,050.00	2,100.00
☐ 1934 **P Commercial, Krieghoff**, .30 Luger and 9mm Luger, *Curio*	1,550.00	3,250.00
☐ 1934 **P Commercial, Krieghoff**, 9mm Luger, *Curio*	1,450.00	2,900.00
☐ 1934 **Sidefrank, Krieghoff, 6" Barrel**, 9mm Luger, *Curio*	3,650.00	7,200.00
☐ 1934 **Sidefrank**, 9mm Luger, Krieghoff, 6" Barrel, *Curio*	3,200.00	5,750.00
☐ 1934 **Simson**, 9mm Luger, *Curio*	975.00	1,950.00
☐ 1935 **Portuguese**, .30 Luger, *Curio*	725.00	1,300.00
☐ 1936 **Persian**, 9mm Luger, *Curio*	3,950.00	8,500.00
☐ 1936-37, 9mm Luger, Krieghoff, *Curio*	975.00	2,650.00
☐ 1936-39, .30 Luger and 9mm Luger, 4" Barrel, *Curio*	575.00	1,200.00
☐ 1936-40 **Dutch Banner**, 9mm Luger, *Curio*	725.00	1,725.00
☐ 1936-9 **S/42**, 9mm Luger, *Curio*	575.00	975.00
☐ 1937-39 **Banner Commercial**, .30 Luger, 4" Barrel, *Curio*	1,500.00	2,700.00
☐ 1938, 9mm Luger, Krieghoff, *Curio*	2,650.00	4,250.00
☐ 1939-40 42, 9mm Luger, *Curio*	475.00	775.00
☐ 1940, 9mm Luger, Krieghoff, *Curio*	975.00	2,200.00
☐ 1940 42/42 **BYF**, 9mm Luger, *Curio*	650.00	2,100.00
☐ 1940 **Mauser Banner**, .30 Luger and 9mm Luger, *Curio*	700.00	1,500.00
☐ 1940-1 **S/42**, 9mm Luger, *Curio*	700.00	1,100.00
☐ 1941-2 **BYF**, 9mm Luger, *Curio*	475.00	750.00

	V.G.	EXC.
☐ **1941-4**, 9mm Luger, Krieghoff, *Curio*	1,850.00	2,900.00
☐ **1945**, 9mm Luger, Krieghoff, *Curio*	2,950.00	4,750.00
☐ **36**, 9mm Luger, Krieghoff, *Curio*	975.00	2,100.00
☐ **41 & 42 Banner**, 9mm Luger, *Curio*	675.00	1,250.00
☐ **42/41**, 9mm Luger, *Curio*	750.00	1,250.00
☐ **Artillery, Stock Only**, *Curio*	275.00	425.00
☐ **Austrian Banner**, 9mm Luger, *Curio*	650.00	1,250.00
☐ **Banner Commercial**, .30 Luger, 4" Barrel, *Curio*	1,600.00	2,350.00
☐ **Bulgarian**, .30 Luger, *Curio*	4,750.00	7,500.00
☐ **Cutaway**, 9mm Luger, *Curio*	1,900.00	4,250.00
☐ **Double Date**, 9mm Luger, *Curio*	550.00	975.00
☐ **Engraved Original**, 9mm Luger, *Curio*	4,200.00	6,750.00
☐ **Finnish Prison**, .30 Luger and 9mm Luger, *Curio*	3,650.00	5,950.00
☐ **G-S/42**, 9mm Luger, *Curio*	750.00	1,650.00
☐ **G-S/42**, DWM, 9mm Luger, *Curio*	850.00	1,850.00
☐ **G.L. Baby**, 9mm Luger, *Curio*	20,000.00	35,000.00
☐ **Ideal, Holster Stock**, *Curio*	375.00	650.00
☐ **K U**, 9mm Luger, *Curio*	775.00	1,600.00
☐ **K-S/42**, 9mm Luger, *Curio*	925.00	1,800.00
☐ **K-S/42 Navy**, 9mm Luger, *Curio*	1,500.00	2,850.00
☐ **Mauser Banner Commercial**, 9mm Luger, *Curio*	850.00	1,600.00
☐ **Navy, Stock Only**, *Curio*	325.00	875.00
☐ **Post War**, 9mm Luger, Krieghoff, *Curio*	975.00	2,500.00
☐ **S/42 Navy**, 9mm Luger, *Curio*	700.00	1,750.00
☐ **Snail Drum**, Magazine, *Curio*	250.00	425.00
☐ **Stoeger (New) STLR**, .22 L.R.R.F., Clip Fed, *Modern*	65.00	95.00
☐ **Stoeger (New) STLR**, .22 L.R.R.F., Clip Fed, Steel Frame, *Modern*	90.00	135.00
☐ **Stoeger (New) TLR.**, .22 L.R.R.F., Clip Fed, Adjustable Sights, *Modern*	80.00	120.00
☐ **Turkish**, 9mm Luger, *Curio*	7,750.00	15,000.00
☐ **U.S. Test Eagle**, .30 Luger, *Curio*	1,850.00	3,250.00
☐ **Vickers Commercial**, 9mm Luger, *Curio*	1,850.00	3,350.00
☐ **Vickers Military**, 9mm Luger, *Curio*	925.00	2,200.00
☐ **VOPO**, 9mm Luger, Clip Fed, *Modern*	450.00	675.00

LUR-PANZER
Echave y Arizmendi, Eibar, Spain.
HANDGUN, SEMI-AUTOMATIC
☐ **Luger Type**, .22 L.R.R.F., Toggle Action, Clip Fed, *Modern*	85.00	145.00

LYMAN GUN SIGHT CORP.
Middlefield, Conn.
HANDGUN, PERCUSSION
☐ **.36 1851 Navy**, Color Case Hardened Frame, Engraved Cylinder, Reproduction, *Antique*	65.00	95.00
☐ **.36 New Model Navy**, Brass Trigger Guard, Solid Frame, Reproduction, *Antique*	55.00	85.00
☐ **.44 1860 Army**, Color Case Hardened Frame, Engraved Cylinder, Reproduction, *Antique*	70.00	95.00
☐ **.44 New Model Army**, Brass Trigger Guard, Solid Frame, Reproduction, *Antique*	70.00	95.00

RIFLE, FLINTLOCK
☐ **Plains Rifle**, Various Calibers, Brass Furniture, Set Trigger, Reproduction, *Antique*	150.00	215.00

MAADI / 273

	V.G.	EXC.

RIFLE, PERCUSSION
- ☐ **Plains Rifle**, Various Calibers, Brass Furniture, Set Trigger, Reproduction, *Antique* **120.00 175.00**
- ☐ **Trade Rifle**, Various Calibers, Brass Furniture, Set Trigger, Reproduction, *Antique* **100.00 150.00**

RIFLE, SINGLESHOT
- ☐ **Centennial**, 45/70 Government, Ruger #1, Commemorative, Cased with Accessories, *Modern* **900.00 1,400.00**

MAADI
RIFLE, SEMI-AUTOMATIC
- ☐ **Paratrooper AKM**, 7.62 x 39mm, Clip Fed, Assault Rifle, *Modern* ... **625.00 975.00**
- ☐ **Standard AKM**, 7.62 x 39mm, Clip Fed, Assault Rifle, *Modern* **575.00 875.00**

MAB Modele A

MAB Modele D

MAB Modele Le Chasseur

MAB Modele F

MAB Modele E

MAB

Mre. d'Armes Automatiques Bayonne, Bayonne, France since 1921.

	V.G.	EXC.
HANDGUN, SEMI-AUTOMATIC		
☐ **Nazi Proofs** *Add* 20%-30%		
☐ **Nazi Navy Proofs** *Add* 40%-50%		
☐ **Modele A**, .25 ACP, Clip Fed, *Modern*	90.00	135.00
☐ **Modele B**, .25 ACP, Clip Fed, *Modern*	135.00	200.00
☐ **Modele C**, .32 ACP, Clip Fed, *Modern*	115.00	165.00
☐ **Modele C**, .380 ACP, Clip Fed, *Modern*	140.00	195.00
☐ **Modele C/D**, .32 ACP, Clip Fed, *Modern*	100.00	145.00
☐ **Modele C/D**, .380 ACP, Clip Fed, *Modern*	115.00	165.00
☐ **Modele D**, .32 ACP, Clip Fed, *Modern*	95.00	140.00
☐ **Modele D**, .380 ACP, Clip Fed, *Modern*	110.00	150.00
☐ **Modele E**, .25 ACP, Clip Fed, Long Grip, *Modern*	125.00	190.00
☐ **Modele F**, .22 L.R.R.F., Clip Fed, Hammer, *Modern*	120.00	185.00
☐ **Modele G**, .22 L.R.R.F., Clip Fed, *Modern*	90.00	135.00
☐ **Modele GZ**, .22 L.R.R.F., Clip Fed, Blue, *Modern*	110.00	150.00
☐ **Modele GZ**, .22 L.R.R.F., Clip Fed, Green, *Modern*	120.00	160.00
☐ **Modele GZ**, .25 ACP, Clip Fed, *Modern*	130.00	170.00
☐ **Modele Le Chasseur**, .22 L.R.R.F., Clip Fed, Hammer, Target Grips, *Modern*	135.00	190.00
☐ **Modele PA-15**, 9mm Luger, Clip Fed, Hammer, *Modern*	220.00	300.00
☐ **Modele R Para**, 9mm Luger, Clip Fed, Hammer, *Curio*	220.00	300.00
☐ **Modele R Court**, .32 ACP, Clip Fed, Hammer, *Modern*	160.00	240.00
☐ **Modele R Longue**, 7.65 MAS, Clip Fed, Hammer, *Modern*	160.00	220.00

M.A.C. (Military Armament Corp)

Also see Ingram. See Ruger and Remington for Silenced Adaptations.

	V.G.	EXC.
AUTOMATIC WEAPON, ASSAULT RIFLE		
☐ **M16-M.A.C.**, .22 L.R.R.F., Clip Fed, Conversion Unit Only, *Class 3*	90.00	125.00
AUTOMATIC WEAPON, SUBMACHINE GUN		
☐ **M-10 M A C**, .45 ACP, Clip Fed, Folding Stock, Commercial, *Class 3*	145.00	195.00
☐ **M-10 M A C**, .45 ACP, Clip Fed, Folding Stock, Commercial, Silencer, *Class 3*	225.00	300.00
☐ **M-10 M A C**, 9mm Luger, Clip Fed, Folding Stock, Commercial, *Class 3*	150.00	200.00
☐ **M-10 M A C**, 9 mm Luger, Clip Fed, Folding Stock, Commercial, Silencer, *Class 3*	225.00	300.00
☐ **M-11 M A C**, .380 ACP, Clip Fed, Folding Stock, Commercial, *Class 3*	325.00	400.00
☐ **M-11 M A C**, .380 ACP, Clip Fed, Folding Stock, Commercial, Silencer, *Class 3*	425.00	535.00
HANDGUN, SEMI-AUTOMATIC		
☐ **Model 200 S.A.P.**, 9mm Luger, Clip Fed, *Modern*	190.00	275.00
RIFLE, BOLT ACTION		
☐ **Model 40-XB Sniper (MAC)**, .308 Win., Heavy Barrel, Scope Mounted, Silencer, *Class 3*	550.00	750.00

MACLOED

Doune, Scotland 1711-1750.

	V.G.	EXC.
HANDGUN, FLINTLOCK		
☐ **.54**, All Steel, Engraved, Ram's Horn Butt, *Antique*	2,900.00	3,250.00

MAICHE, A.
France.
HANDGUN, FLINTLOCK

	V.G.	EXC.
☐ .56, Brass Mountings, Holster Pistol, *Antique*	375.00	550.00

MALTBY-CURTIS
Agent for Norwich Pistol Co. 1875-1881.
HANDGUN, REVOLVER
☐ .22 Short R.F., 7 Shot, Spur Trigger, Solid Frame, Single Action, *Antique* 90.00 160.00
☐ .32 Short R.F., 5 Shot, Spur Trigger, Solid Frame, Single Action, *Antique* 95.00 170.00

MALTBY—HENLEY & CO.
N.Y.C. 1878-1889. Made by Columbia Armory, Tenn.
HANDGUN, REVOLVER
☐ .22 L.R.R.F., 7 Shot, Double Action, Hammerless, Top Break, *Curio* 55.00 95.00
☐ .32 S & W, 5 Shot, Top Break, Hammerless, Double Action, *Curio* 55.00 95.00
☐ .38 S & W, 5 Shot, Top Break, Hammerless, Double Action, *Curio* 55.00 95.00

MAMBA
Made by Relay Products in Johannesburg, South Africa, and Navy Arms in the U.S.
HANDGUN, SEMI-AUTOMATIC
☐ **Relay Mamba**, 9mm Luger, Stainless, Double Action, *Modern* 325.00 450.00
☐ **Rhodesian Mamba**, 9mm Luger, Stainless, Double Action, *Modern* 1,350.00 2,000.00
☐ **Navy Mamba**, 9mm Luger, Stainless, Double Action, *Modern* 220.00 300.00

MANHATTAN FIREARMS MFG. CO.
N.Y.C. & Newark, N.J. 1849-1864.
HANDGUN, PERCUSSION
☐ **Hero**, Singleshot, Derringer, *Antique* 135.00 195.00
☐ **Bar Hammer**, Double Action, Screw Barrel, Singleshot, *Antique* 140.00 225.00
☐ **Pepperbox**, .28, 3 Shot, Double Action, *Antique* 250.00 475.00
☐ **Pepperbox**, .28, 6 Shot, Double Action, *Antique* 190.00 325.00
☐ **Revolver**, .36, Navy Model, Single Action, *Antique* 325.00 525.00
☐ **Revolver**, .36, Pocket Model, Single Action, *Antique* 185.00 335.00

MANHURIN
Mre. de Machines du Haut-Rhin, Mulhouse-Bourtzwiller, France. Also see Walther.
HANDGUN, REVOLVER
☐ **Model 73**, .357 Magnum, Police Model, Double Action, Swing-Out Cylinder, *Modern* 375.00 500.00
☐ **Model 73**, .357 Magnum, Target Model, Double Action, Swing-Out Cylinder, *Modern* 450.00 600.00

MANN
Fritz Mann Werkzeugfabrik, Suhl, Germany 1919-1924.
HANDGUN, SEMI-AUTOMATIC
☐ **Model Wt**, .25 ACP, Clip Fed, *Modern* 165.00 245.00
☐ **Pocket**, .32 ACP, Clip Fed, *Modern* 195.00 285.00
☐ **Pocket**, .380 ACP, Clip Fed, *Modern* 235.00 325.00

Mann Pocket

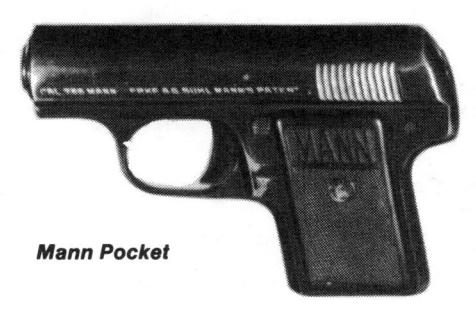

MANN, MICHEL
Uhlenberg, Germany, c. 1630.
HANDGUN, WHEEL-LOCK
☐ **Miniature**, All Metal, Gold Damascened, Ball Pommel, *Antique* 2,000.00 3,500.00

MANNLICHER-SCHOENAUER
Steyr-Daimler-Puch, Steyr, Austria.
RIFLE, DOUBLE BARREL, OVER-UNDER
☐ **Safari 72**, .375 H & H Mag., Checkered Stock, Engraved, Double Trigger, *Modern* 2,450.00 3,400.00
☐ **Safari 77**, Various Calibers, Checkered Stock, Engraved, Double Trigger, Automatic Ejector, *Modern* 3,500.00 4,400.00
RIFLE, BOLT ACTION
☐ **Alpine**, Various Caliber, Sporting Rifle, Full-Stocked, *Modern* 350.00   465.00
☐ **Custom M-S**, Various Calibers, Sporting Rifle, Scope Mounted, Carbine, *Modern* 380.00   675.00
☐ **Custom M-S**, Various Calibers, Sporting Rifle, Scope Mounted, *Modern* 380.00   675.00
☐ **High Velocity**, Various Calibers, Sporting Rifle, Set Trigger, *Modern* 525.00   800.00
☐ **High Velocity**, Various Calibers, Sporting Rifle, Takedown, Set Trigger, *Modern* 550.00   850.00
☐ **M-72 LM**, Various Calibers, Sporting Rifle, Full-Stocked, *Modern* 400.00   725.00
☐ **M-72 S**, Various Calibers, Sporting Rifle, *Modern* 500.00   800.00
☐ **M-72 T**, Various Calibers, Sporting Rifle, *Modern* 550.00   850.00
☐ **Magnum M-S**, Various Calibers, Sporting Rifle, Monte Carlo Stock, Set Trigger, *Modern*.. 550.00   850.00
☐ **MCA**, Various Calibers, Sporting Rifle, Carbine, Monte Carlo Stock, *Modern* 600.00   900.00
☐ **MCA**, Various Calibers, Sporting Rifle, Monte Carlo Stock, *Modern* 600.00   900.00
☐ **Model 1903**, Various Calibers, Sporting Rifle, Carbine, Set Trigger, Full-Stocked, *Modern* 550.00   800.00
☐ **Model 1905**, 9 x 56 M.S., Sporting Rifle, Carbine, Set Trigger, Full-Stocked, *Modern* 475.00   725.00
☐ **Model 1908**, Various Calibers, Sporting Rifle, Carbine, Set Trigger, Full-Stocked, *Modern* 425.00   700.00
☐ **Model 1910**, 9.5 x 57 M.S., Sporting Rifle, Carbine, Set Trigger, Full-Stocked, *Modern* 450.00   725.00
☐ **Model 1924**, .30-06 Springfield, Sporting Rifle, Carbine, Set Trigger, Full-Stocked, *Modern* 600.00   950.00
☐ **Model 1950**, 6.5 x 54 M.S., Sporting Rifle, Carbine, Set Trigger, Full-Stocked, *Modern* 400.00   675.00
☐ **Model 1950**, Various Calibers, Sporting Rifle, Set Trigger, *Modern* 450.00   750.00

	V.G.	EXC.
☐ **Model 1950**, Various Calibers, Sporting Rifle, Carbine, Set Trigger, Full-Stocked, *Modern*	475.00	750.00
☐ **Model 1952**, 6.5 x 54 M.S., Sporting Rifle, Carbine, Set Trigger, Full-Stocked, *Modern*	425.00	725.00
☐ **Model 1952**, Various Calibers, Sporting Rifle, Carbine, Set Trigger, Full-Stocked, *Modern*	450.00	750.00
☐ **Model 1952**, Various Calibers, Sporting Rifle, Set Trigger, *Modern*	450.00	750.00
☐ **Model 1956**, Various Calibers, Sporting Rifle, Carbine, Set Trigger, Full-Stocked, *Modern*	450.00	750.00
☐ **Model 1956**, Various Calibers, Sporting Rifle, Set Trigger, *Modern*	450.00	750.00
☐ **Premier**, Various Calibers, Sporting Rifle, Magnum Action, Fancy Checkering, Engraved, *Modern*	750.00	1,200.00
☐ **Premier**, Various Calibers, Sporting Rifle, Fancy Checkering, Engraved, *Modern*	450.00	600.00
☐ **Model SSG**, .308 Win., Synthetic Target Stock, Set Triggers, *Modern*	350.00	475.00
☐ **Model SSG Match**, .308 Win., Synthetic Target Stock, Set Triggers, Walther Peep Sights, *Modern*	450.00	600.00
☐ **Model ML 79**, Various Calibers, Checkered Stock, Set Trigger, *Modern*	475.00	700.00
☐ **Model L Varmint**, Various Calibers, Checkered Stock, Set Trigger, *Modern*	350.00	475.00
☐ **Model M**, Various Calibers, Checkered Stock, Set Trigger, *Modern*	375.00	550.00
☐ **Model M Professional**, Various Calibers, Checkered Stock, Set Trigger, *Modern*	250.00	375.00
☐ **Model S/T Magnum**, Various Calibers, Checkered Stock, Set Trigger, *Modern*	425.00	625.00
☐ **Model S**, Various Calibers, Checkered Stock, Set Trigger, *Modern*	425.00	625.00

RIFLE, DOUBLE BARREL, SIDE-BY-SIDE
☐ **Mustang**, Various Calibers, Standard, Checkered Stock, Sidelock, *Modern*	3,850.00	5,750.00
☐ **Mustang**, Various Calibers, Standard, Checkered Stock, Sidelock, Engraved, *Modern*	4,500.00	6,000.00

SHOTGUN, DOUBLE BARREL, OVER-UNDER
☐ **Edinbourgh**, 12 Ga., Checkered Stock, Vent Rib, *Modern*	950.00	1,400.00

SHOTGUN, DOUBLE BARREL, SIDE-BY-SIDE
☐ **Ambassador English**, 12 and 20 Gauges, Checkered Stock, Sidelock, Automatic Ejectors, Engraved, *Modern*	5,250.00	7,250.00
☐ **Ambassador Extra**, 12 and 20 Gauges, Checkered Stock, Sidelock, Automatic Ejectors, Engraved, *Modern*	5,000.00	7,000.00
☐ **Ambassador Golden Black**, 12 and 20 Gauges, Checkered Stock, Sidelock, Automatic Ejectors, Engraved, Gold Inlays, *Modern*	6,500.00	9,000.00
☐ **Ambassador Executive**, 12 and 20 Gauges, Checkered Stock, Sidelock, Automatic Ejectors, Fancy Engraving, *Modern*	11,000.00	15,000.00
☐ **Oxford Field**, 12 and 20 Gauges, Checkered Stock, Automatic Ejectors, Engraved, *Modern*	800.00	1,200.00
☐ **London**, 12 and 20 Gauges, Checkered Stock, Sidelock, Automatic Ejectors, Engraved, Cased, *Modern*	1,850.00	2,400.00

MANTON, J. & Co.
Belgium, c. 1900.

SHOTGUN, DOUBLE BARREL, SIDE-BY-SIDE
☐ **Various Gauges**, Outside Hammers, Damascus Barrel, *Modern*	100.00	175.00
☐ **Various Gauges**, Hammerless, Steel Barrel, *Modern*	135.00	200.00

278 / MANTON, JOSEPH

	V.G.	EXC.
☐ **Various Gauges**, Hammerless, Damascus Barrel, *Modern*	100.00	175.00
☐ **Various Gauges**, Outside Hammers, Steel Barrel, *Modern*	125.00	190.00
SHOTGUN, SINGLESHOT		
☐ **Various Gauges**, Hammer, Steel Barrel, *Modern*	55.00	85.00

MANTON, JOSEPH
London, England 1795-1835.

HANDGUN, FLINTLOCK
☐ **Pair**, Octagon Barrel, Duelling Pistols, Gold Inlays, Light Engraving, Cased with Accessories, *Antique* 3,500.00   4,500.00

HANDGUN, PERCUSSION
☐ **.55**, Pair, Duelling Pistols, Octagon Barrel, Light Ornamentation, Cased with Accessories, *Antique* 3,750.00   4,750.00

SHOTGUN, PERCUSSION
☐ **12 Ga. Double Barrel**, Side by Side, Damascus Barrels, Light Engraving, Gold Inlays, *Antique* 425.00   600.00

MANUFRANCE
Manufacture Francaise de Armes et Cycles de St. Etienne, St. Etienne, France.

HANDGUN, SEMI-AUTOMATIC
☐ **Model 1911 Astra-Manufrance**, .32 ACP, CLip Fed, Blue, *Curio* 90.00   155.00

RIFLE, SEMI-AUTOMATIC
☐ **Reina**, .22 L.R.R.F., Carbine, Clip Fed, *Modern* 90.00   145.00
☐ **Sniper**, .22 W.M.R., Carbine, Clip Fed, *Modern* 135.00   185.00

RIFLE, BOLT ACTION
☐ **Mauser K98 Sporter**, .270 Win., Sporterized, Plain, *Modern* 80.00   130.00
☐ **Mauser K98 Sporter**, .270 Win., Sporterized, Checkered Stock, *Modern* 95.00   140.00
☐ **Club**, .22 L.R.R.F., Singleshot, Carbine, *Modern* 55.00   85.00
☐ **Club**, .22 L.R.R.F., Singleshot, Carbine, Checkered Stock, *Modern*   65.00   95.00
☐ **Buffalo Match**, .22 L.R.R.F., Target Rifle, *Modern* 100.00   150.00
☐ **Rival**, 375 H & H Mag., Checkered Stock, *Modern* 175.00   275.00

SHOTGUN, DOUBLE BARREL, OVER-UNDER
☐ **Falcor Field**, 12 Ga., Vent Rib, Automatic Ejector, Single Selective Trigger, Checkered Stock, *Modern* 450.00   600.00
☐ **Falcor Trap**, 12 Ga., Vent Rib, Automatic Ejector, Single Selective Trigger, Checkered Stock, *Modern* 500.00   650.00
☐ **Falcor Sport**, 12 Ga., Vent Rib, Automatic Ejector, Single Selective Trigger, Checkered Stock, Extra Barrels, *Modern* 600.00   750.00

SHOTGUN, DOUBLE BARREL, SIDE-BY-SIDE
☐ **Ideal DeLuxe**, 12 Ga. 3", Fancy Engraving, Checkered Stock, Double Triggers, *Modern* 1,250.00   1,750.00
☐ **Ideal Prestige**, 12 Ga. 3", Fancy Engraving, Checkered Stock, Double Triggers, *Modern* 1,750.00   2,500.00
☐ **Robust**, 12 Ga. 3", Checkered Stock, Double Triggers, *Modern* 250.00   350.00
☐ **Robust Luxe**, 12 Ga. 3", Engraved, Automatic Ejectors, Checkered Stock, Double Triggers, *Modern* 400.00   600.00

SHOTGUN, SEMI-AUTOMATIC
☐ **Perfex Special**, 12 Ga. Mag. 3", Open Sights, Short Barrel, Checkered Stock, *Modern* 250.00   350.00
☐ **Perfex**, 12 Ga. Mag. 3", Checkered Stock, *Modern* 225.00   325.00

MARLIN FIREARMS COMPANY / 279

	V.G.	EXC.
SHOTGUN, SINGLESHOT		
☐ **Simplex**, 12 Gauge, Sling Swivels, *Modern*	80.00	120.00
SHOTGUN, SLIDE ACTION		
☐ **Rapid**, 12 or 16 Gauges, Plain, *Modern*	125.00	165.00

MARK X
Made in Zestavia, Yugoslavia. Imported by Interarms.

RIFLE, BOLT ACTION

	V.G.	EXC.
☐ **Alaskan**, Various Calibers, Magnum, Open Rear Sight, Checkered Stock, Sling Swivels, *Modern*	190.00	275.00
☐ **Cavalier**, Various Calibers, Cheekpiece, Checkered Stock, Open Rear Sight, Sling Swivels, *Modern*	175.00	260.00
☐ **Mannlicher**, Various Calibers, Carbine, Full-Stocked, Checkered Stock, Open Rear Sight, Sling Swivels, *Modern*	190.00	275.00
☐ **Standard**, Various Calibers, Checkered Stock, Open Rear Sight, Sling Swivels, *Modern*	150.00	225.00
☐ **Viscount**, Various Calibers, Plain, Open Rear Sight, Checkered Stock, Sling Swivels, *Modern*	125.00	175.00

MARKWELL ARMS CO.
Chicago, Ill.

HANDGUN, PERCUSSION

	V.G.	EXC.
☐ **.41 Derringer**, Singleshot, Brass Furniture, Reproduction, *Antique*	20.00	30.00
☐ **.44 C S A 1860**, Revolver, 6 Shot, Brass Frame, Reproduction, *Antique*	40.00	60.00
☐ **.44 New Army**, Revolver, 6 Shot, Brass Trigger Guard, Reproduction, *Antique*	40.00	65.00
☐ **.45 Colonial**, Singleshot, Brass Furniture, Reproduction, *Antique*	20.00	35.00
☐ **.45 Kentucky**, Singleshot, Brass Furniture, Reproduction, *Antique*	30.00	45.00
☐ **.45 Loyalist**, Singleshot, Brass Furniture, Set Trigger, Adjustable Sights, Reproduction, *Antique*	45.00	65.00

RIFLE, PERCUSSION

	V.G.	EXC.
☐ **.45 Hawken**, Brass Furniture, Reproduction, *Antique*	60.00	90.00
☐ **.45 Kentucky**, Brass Furniture, Reproduction, *Antique*	50.00	75.00
☐ **.45 Super Kentucky**, Brass Furniture, Set Trigger, Reproduction, *Antique*	70.00	110.00

MARLIN FIREARMS CO.
New Haven, Conn. J.M. Marlin from 1870-1881. Marlin Firearms from 1881-1915 Marlin-Rockwell Corp. 1915-1926. From 1926 to Date as Marlin Firearms Co. Also See Ballard.

AUTOMATIC WEAPON, HEAVY MACHINE GUN

	V.G.	EXC.
☐ **M1906 Marlin**, .30-06 Springfield, Belt Fed, Tripod, Potato Digger, Military, *Class 3*	1,600.00	2,300.00
☐ **M1906 Marlin**, .303 British, Belt Fed, Tripod, Potato Digger, Military, *Class 3*	1,500.00	2,250.00
☐ **M1906 Marlin**, .308 Win., Belt Fed, Tripod, Potato Digger, Military, *Class 3*	1,450.00	2,100.00
☐ **M1917 Marlin**, .30-06 Springfield, Belt Fed, Tripod, Potato Digger, Military, *Class 3*	1,650.00	2,250.00

HANDGUN, REVOLVER

	V.G.	EXC.
☐ **Standard 1875**, .30 R.F., Tip Up, Spur Trigger, *Antique*	95.00	175.00
☐ **XX Standard 1873**, .22 R.F., Tip Up, Spur Trigger, *Antique*	95.00	185.00
☐ **XX Standard 1873**, .22 R.F., Tip Up, Spur Trigger, Octagon Barrel, *Antique*	120.00	195.00

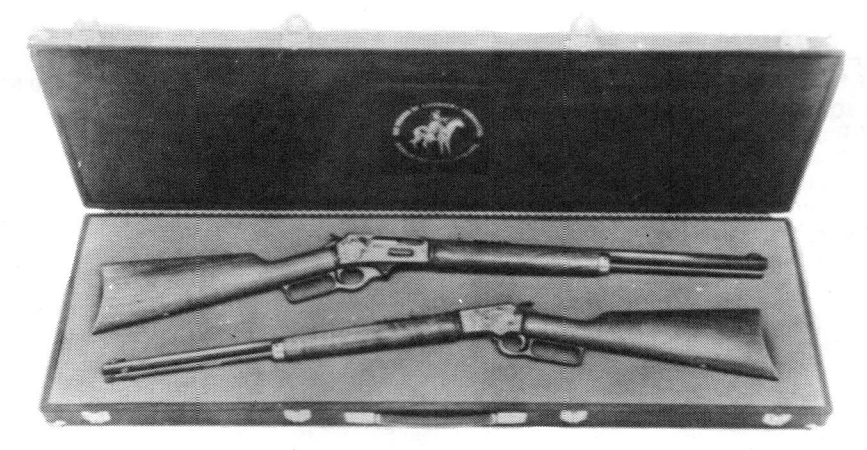

280 / MARLIN FIREARMS COMPANY

Marlin Cased Centennial Pair

Marlin Model 336A

Marlin Model 783

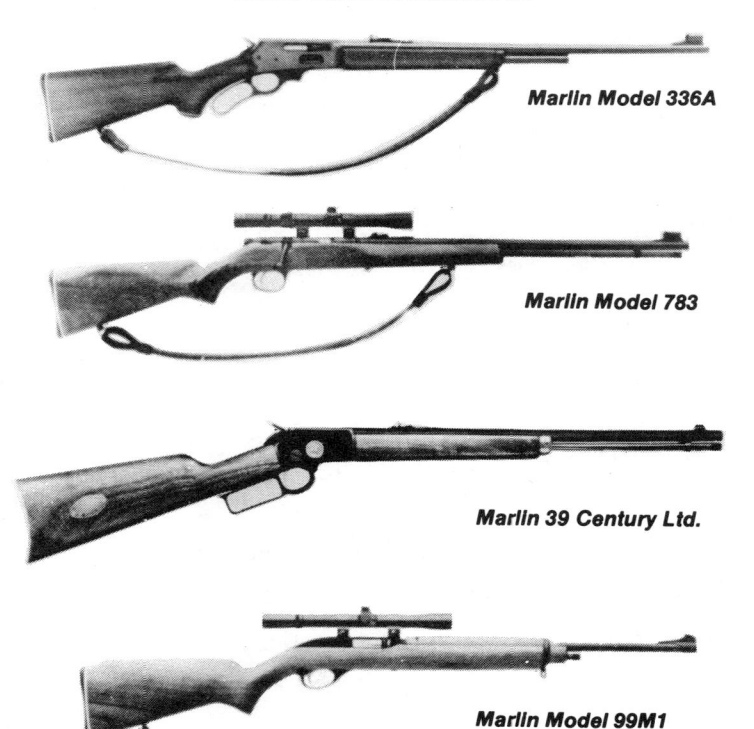

Marlin 39 Century Ltd.

Marlin Model 99M1

MARLIN FIREARMS COMPANY / 281

	V.G.	EXC.
☐ **XXX Standard 1872**, .30 R.F., Tip Up, Spur Trigger, *Antique*	110.00	180.00
☐ **XXX Standard 1872**, .30 R.F., Tip Up, Spur Trigger, Octagon Barrel, *Antique*	125.00	195.00
☐ **Model 1887**, .32 and .38, Double Action, Top Break, *Antique*	95.00	170.00

RIFLE, BOLT ACTION

	V.G.	EXC.
☐ **Glenfield M10**, .22 L.R.R.F., Singleshot, *Modern*	20.00	35.00
☐ **Glenfield M20**, .22 L.R.R.F., Clip Fed, *Modern*	30.00	45.00
☐ **Model 100**, .22 L.R.R.F., Singleshot, Open Rear Sight, Takedown, *Modern*	25.00	35.00
☐ **Model 100-S**, .22 L.R.R.F., Singleshot, Peep Sights, Takedown, *Modern*	45.00	65.00
☐ **Model 100-SB**, .22 L.R.R.F., Singleshot, Smoothbore, Takedown, *Modern*	25.00	35.00
☐ **Model 101**, .22 L.R.R.F., Singleshot, Open Rear Sight, Takedown, Beavertail Forend, *Modern*	25.00	40.00
☐ **Model 101-DL**, .22 L.R.R.F., Singleshot, Takedown, Peep Sights, Beavertail Forend, *Modern*	30.00	40.00
☐ **Model 122**, .22 L.R.R.F., Singleshot, Open Rear Sight, Monte Carlo Stock, *Modern*	25.00	40.00
☐ **Model 322 (Sako)**, .222 Rem., Clip Fed, Peep Sights, Checkered Stock, *Modern*	170.00	275.00
☐ **Model 455 (FN)**, Various Calibers, Peep Sights, Monte Carlo Stock, Checkered Stock, *Modern*	170.00	275.00
☐ **Model 65**, .22 L.R.R.F., Singleshot, Open Rear Sight, *Modern*	25.00	40.00
☐ **Model 65E**, .22 L.R.R.F., Singleshot, Peep Sights, *Modern*	25.00	40.00
☐ **Model 780**, .22 L.R.R.F., Clip Fed, Open Rear Sight, *Modern*	35.00	55.00
☐ **Model 781**, .22 L.R.R.F., Tube Feed, Open Rear Sight, *Modern*	40.00	60.00
☐ **Model 782**, .22 WMR, Clip Fed, Open Rear Sight, *Modern*	45.00	65.00
☐ **Model 783**, .22 WMR, Tube Feed, Open Rear Sight, *Modern*	45.00	65.00
☐ **Model 80**, .22 L.R.R.F., Clip Fed, Open Rear Sight, Takedown, *Modern*	35.00	50.00
☐ **Model 80 DL**, .22 L.R.R.F., Clip Fed, Beavertail Forend, Takedown, Peep Sights, *Modern*	35.00	60.00
☐ **Model 80C**, .22 L.R.R.F., Clip Fed, Beavertail Forend, Takedown, Open Rear Sight, *Modern*	40.00	55.00
☐ **Model 80E**, .22 L.R.R.F., Clip Fed, Peep Sights, Takedown, *Modern*	35.00	50.00
☐ **Model 81**, .22 L.R.R.F., Tube Feed, Takedown, Open Rear Sight, *Modern*	45.00	60.00
☐ **Model 81C**, .22 L.R.R.F., Tube Feed, Takedown, Open Rear Sight, Beavertail Forend, *Modern*	40.00	60.00
☐ **Model 81DL**, .22 L.R.R.F., Tube Feed, Takedown, Peep Sights, Beavertail Forend, *Modern*	35.00	55.00
☐ **Model 81E**, .22 L.R.R.F., Tube Feed, Takedown, Peep Sights, *Modern*	35.00	55.00
☐ **Model 81G**, .22 L.R.R.F., Tube Feed, Takedown, Open Rear Sight, Beavertail Forend, *Modern*	35.00	55.00
☐ **Model 980**, .22 WMR, Clip Fed, Monte Carlo Stock, Open Rear Sight, *Modern*	50.00	70.00

RIFLE, LEVER ACTION

	V.G.	EXC.
☐ **Centennial Set 336-39**, Fancy Checkering, Fancy Wood, Engraved, Brass Furniture, *Modern*	700.00	1,100.00
☐ **Glenfield M 30 A**, .30-30 Win., Tube Feed, *Modern*	95.00	135.00
☐ **M1894 (Late)**, .357 Magnum, Tube Feed, Open Rear Sight, *Modern*	130.00	165.00
☐ **M1894 (Late)**, .44 Magnum, Tube Feed, Open Rear Sight, *Modern*	95.00	145.00
☐ **M1895 (Late)**, .45-70 Government, Tube Feed, Open Rear Sight, *Modern*	140.00	

282 / MARLIN FIREARMS COMPANY

Marlin Model 49DL

Marlin Model 989M2

Marlin Model 39A

Marlin 55 Slug Gun

Marlin Model 1891

Marlin Model 780

MARLIN FIREARMS COMPANY / 283

	V.G.	EXC.
☐ **Model 1881 Standard**, Various Calibers, Tube Feed, Open Rear Sight, *Antique*	400.00	675.00
☐ **Model 1888**, Various Calibers, Tube Feed, Open Rear Sight, *Antique*	500.00	825.00
☐ **Model 1889 Standard**, Various Calibers, Tube Feed, Open Rear Sight, *Antique*	275.00	475.00
☐ **Model 1891**, .22 L.R.R.F., Tube Feed, Open Rear Sight, *Antique*	275.00	375.00
☐ **Model 1892**, Various Calibers, Tube Feed, Open Rear Sight, *Antique*	250.00	350.00
☐ **Model 1892 Over #177382**, Various Calibers, Tube Feed, *Modern*	225.00	300.00
☐ **Model 1893**, Various Calibers, Tube Feed, Solid Frame, Octagon Barrel, *Antique*	300.00	425.00
☐ **Model 1893**, Various Calibers, Tube Feed, Solid Frame, Round Barrel, *Antique*	250.00	375.00
☐ **Model 1893**, Various Calibers, Tube Feed, Solid Frame, Round Barrel, Carbine, *Antique*	400.00	525.00
☐ **Model 1893**, Various Calibers, Tube Feed, Takedown, Octagon Barrel, *Antique*	425.00	550.00
☐ **Model 1893**, Various Calibers, Tube Feed, Takedown, Round Barrel, *Antique*	325.00	450.00
☐ **Model 1893**, Various Calibers, Tube Feed, Sporting Carbine, 5 Shot, *Antique*	450.00	600.00
☐ **Model 1893**, Various Calibers, Tube Feed, Sporting Carbine, Takedown, 5 Shot, *Antique*	500.00	650.00
☐ **Model 1893**, Various Calibers, Tube Feed, Full-Stocked, with Bayonet, *Antique*	1,750.00	2,750.00
☐ **Model 1893 over #177304**, Various Calibers, Tube Feed, Solid Frame, Octagon Barrel, *Modern*	300.00	425.00
☐ **Model 1893 over #177304**, Various Calibers, Tube Feed, Solid Frame, Round Barrel, *Modern*	250.00	350.00
☐ **Model 1893 over #177304**, Various Calibers, Tube Feed, Solid Frame, Round Barrel, Carbine, *Modern*	375.00	475.00
☐ **Model 1893 over #177304**, Various Calibers, Tube Feed, Takedown, Octagon Barrel, *Modern*	350.00	450.00
☐ **Model 1893 over #177304**, Various Calibers, Tube Feed, Takedown, Round Barrel, *Modern*	275.00	350.00
☐ **Model 1893 over #177304**, Various Calibers, Tube Feed, Sporting Carbine, 5 Shot, *Modern*	375.00	450.00
☐ **Model 1893 over #177304**, Various Calibers, Tube Feed, Sporting Carbine, Takedown, 5 Shot, *Modern*	450.00	600.00
☐ **Model 1893 over #177304**, Various Calibers, Tube Feed, Full-Stocked, with Bayonet, *Modern*	1,600.00	2,750.00
☐ **Model 1894**, Various Calibers, Tube Feed, Takedown, Octagon Barrel, *Antique*	450.00	575.00
☐ **Model 1894**, Various Calibers, Tube Feed, Takedown, Round Barrel, *Antique*	400.00	525.00
☐ **Model 1894**, Various Calibers, Tube Feed, Solid Frame, Octagon Barrel, *Antique*	325.00	450.00
☐ **Model 1894**, Various Calibers, Tube Feed, Solid Frame, Round Barrel, *Antique*	275.00	375.00
☐ **Model 1894 over #175431**, Various Calibers, Tube Feed, Takedown, Octagon Barrel, *Antique*	450.00	575.00
☐ **Model 1894 over #175431**, Various Calibers, Tube Feed, Takedown, Round Barrel, *Modern*	300.00	425.00
☐ **Model 1894 over #175431**, Various Calibers, Tube Feed, Solid Frame, Octagon Barrel, *Modern*	300.00	425.00

284 / MARLIN FIREARMS COMPANY

	V.G.	EXC.
☐ **Model 1894 over #175431**, Various Calibers, Tube Feed, Solid Frame, Round Barrel, *Modern*	260.00	350.00
☐ **Model 1895**, Various Calibers, Tube Feed, Solid Frame, Round Barrel, *Antique*	500.00	775.00
☐ **Model 1895**, Various Calibers, Tube Feed, Solid Frame, Octagon Barrel, *Antique*	475.00	725.00
☐ **Model 1895**, Various Calibers, Tube Feed, Takedown, Octagon Barrel, *Antique*	500.00	850.00
☐ **Model 1895**, Various Calibers, Tube Feed, Takedown, Round Barrel, *Antique*	500.00	850.00
☐ **Model 1895 over #167531**, Various Calibers, Tube Feed, Solid Frame, Round Barrel, *Modern*	375.00	650.00
☐ **Model 1895 over #167531**, Various Calibers, Tube Feed, Solid Frame, Octagon Barrel, *Modern*	425.00	700.00
☐ **Model 1895 over #167531**, Various Calibers, Tube Feed, Takedown, Octagon Barrel, *Modern*	450.00	775.00

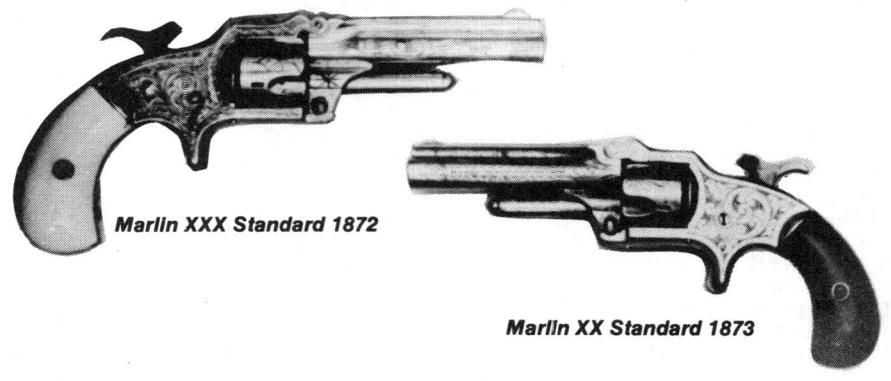

Marlin XXX Standard 1872

Marlin XX Standard 1873

	V.G.	EXC.
☐ **Model 1895 over #167531**, Various Calibers, Tube Feed, Takedown, Round Barrel, *Modern*	425.00	750.00
☐ **Model 1897**, .22 L.R.R.F., Tube Feed, Takedown, *Antique*	250.00	350.00
☐ **Model 1897 over #177197**, .22 L.R.R.F., Tube Feed, Takedown, *Modern*	225.00	325.00
☐ **Model 336**, .219 Zipper, Tube Feed, Sporting Carbine, Open Rear Sight, 5 Shot, *Modern*	200.00	300.00
☐ **Model 336**, Various Calibers, Tube Feed, Sporting Carbine, Open Rear Sight, 5 Shot, *Modern*	95.00	145.00
☐ **Model 336 Marauder**, Various Calibers, Tube Feed, Carbine, Open Rear Sight, Straight Grip, *Modern*	155.00	250.00
☐ **Model 336 Zane Grey**, .30-30 Win., Tube Feed, Octagon Barrel, Open Rear Sight, *Modern*	155.00	220.00
☐ **Model 336A**, Various Calibers, Tube Feed, Sporting Rifle, Open Rear Sight, 5 Shot, *Modern*	95.00	145.00
☐ **Model 336A-DL**, Various Calibers, Tube Feed, Sporting Rifle, Open Rear Sight, 5 Shot, Checkered Stock, *Modern*	115.00	155.00
☐ **Model 336C**, Various Calibers, Tube Feed, Carbine, Open Rear Sight, *Modern*	90.00	140.00
☐ **Model 336T**, .44 Magnum, Tube Feed, Carbine, Open Rear Sight, Straight Grip, *Modern*	120.00	165.00
☐ **Model 336T**, Various Calibers, Tube Feed, Carbine, Open Rear Sight, Straight Grip, *Modern*	90.00	140.00

	V.G.	EXC.
☐ **Model 36**, Various Calibers, Tube Feed, Beavertail Forend, Open Rear Sight, Carbine, *Modern*	145.00	200.00
☐ **Model 36**, Various Calibers, Tube Feed, Beavertail Forend, Open Rear Sight, Sporting Carbine, 5 Shot, *Modern*	145.00	200.00
☐ **Model 36A**, Various Calibers, Tube Feed, Beavertail Forend, Open Rear Sight, 5 Shot, *Modern*	145.00	200.00
☐ **Model 36DL**, Various Calibers, Tube Feed, Fancy Checkering, Open Rear Sight, 5 Shot, *Modern*	165.00	250.00
☐ **Model 39**, .22 L.R.R.F., Takedown, Tube Feed, Hammer, Octagon Barrel, *Modern*	165.00	250.00
☐ **Model 39 Article II**, .22 L.R.R.F., Takedown, Tube Feed, Hammer, Octagon Barrel, *Modern*	135.00	210.00
☐ **Model 39 Article II**, .22 L.R.R.F., Takedown, Tube Feed, Hammer, Octagon Barrel, Carbine, *Modern*	135.00	210.00
☐ **Model 39 Century**, ,22 L.R.R.F., Takedown, Tube Feed, Hammer, Octagon Barrel, *Modern*	135.00	200.00
☐ **Model 39 M**, .22 L.R.R.F., Takedown, Tube Feed, Hammer, Round Barrel, Carbine, *Modern*	85.00	125.00
☐ **Model 39A**, .22 L.R.R.F., Takedown, Tube Feed, Hammer, Round Barrel, *Modern*	80.00	125.00
☐ **Model 39A Mountie**, .22 L.R.R.F., Takedown, Tube Feed, Hammer, Round Barrel, *Modern*	90.00	130.00
☐ **Model 444**, .444 Marlin, Tube Feed, Monte Carlo Stock, Open Rear Sight, Straight Grip, *Modern*	120.00	165.00
☐ **Model 56**, .22 L.R.R.F., Clip Fed, Open Rear Sight, Monte Carlo Stock, *Modern*	55.00	85.00
☐ **Model 57**, .22 L.R.R.F., Tube Feed, Open Rear Sight, Monte Carlo Stock, *Modern*	55.00	85.00
☐ **Model 57M**, .22 WMR, Tube Feed, Open Rear Sight, Monte Carlo Stock, *Modern*	65.00	95.00
☐ **Model 62**, Various Calibers, Clip Fed, Open Rear Sight, Monte Carlo Stock, *Modern*	90.00	140.00

RIFLE, SEMI-AUTOMATIC

	V.G.	EXC.
☐ **Glenfield M40**, .22 L.R.R.F., Tube Feed, *Modern*	40.00	55.00
☐ **Glenfield M60**, .22 L.R.R.F., Tube Feed, *Modern*	30.00	45.00
☐ **Model 49 DL**, .22 L.R.R.F., Tube Feed, Open Rear Sight, *Modern*	35.00	55.00
☐ **Model 50**, .22 L.R.R.F., Clip Fed, Open Rear Sight, Takedown, *Modern*	35.00	55.00
☐ **Model 50E**, .22 L.R.R.F., Clip Fed, Peep Sights, Takedown, *Modern*	35.00	55.00
☐ **Model 88C**, .22 L.R.R.F., Tube Feed, Takedown, Open Rear Sight, *Modern*	40.00	55.00
☐ **Model 88DL**, .22 L.R.R.F., Tube Feed, Takedown, Peep Sights, *Modern*	40.00	60.00
☐ **Model 89 DL**, .22 L.R.R.F., Clip Fed, Takedown, Peep Sights, *Modern*	40.00	60.00
☐ **Model 89C**, .22 L.R.R.F., Clip Fed, Takedown, Open Rear Sight, *Modern*	40.00	60.00
☐ **Model 98**, .22 L.R.R.F., Tube Feed, Solid Frame, Open Rear Sight, Monte Carlo Stock, *Modern*	40.00	60.00
☐ **Model 989**, .22 L.R.R.F., Clip Fed, Open Rear Sight, Monte Carlo Stock, *Modern*	40.00	55.00
☐ **Model 989 G**, .22 L.R.R.F., Clip Fed, Open Rear Sight, Monte Carlo Stock, *Modern*	40.00	60.00
☐ **Model 990**, .22 L.R.R.F., Tube Feed, Open Rear Sight, Monte Carlo Stock, *Modern*	40.00	60.00
☐ **Model 995**, .22 L.R.R.F., Clip Fed, Open Rear Sight, *Modern*	40.00	55.00

286 / MARLIN FIREARMS COMPANY

	V.G.	EXC.
☐ **Model 99**, .22 L.R.R.F., Tube Feed, Open Rear Sight, *Modern*	35.00	55.00
☐ **Model 99 M-1**, .22 L.R.R.F., Tube Feed, Open Rear Sight, Monte Carlo Stock, *Modern*	40.00	55.00
☐ **Model 99 M-2**, .22 L.R.R.F., Clip Fed, Open Rear Sight, *Modern*	35.00	50.00
☐ **Model 99C**, .22 L.R.R.F., Tube Feed, Open Rear Sight, Monte Carlo Stock, *Modern*	40.00	50.00
☐ **Model 99DL**, .22 L.R.R.F., Tube Feed, Open Rear Sight, Monte Carlo Stock, *Modern*	40.00	50.00
☐ **Model A-1**, .22 L.R.R.F., Clip Fed, Takedown, Open Rear Sight, *Modern*	35.00	50.00
☐ **Model A-1E**, .22 L.R.R.F., Clip Fed, Takedown, Peep Sights, *Modern*	35.00	50.00

RIFLE, SLIDE ACTION

	V.G.	EXC.
☐ **Model 18**, .22 L.R.R.F., Solid Frame, Tube Feed, Hammer, *Modern*	140.00	225.00
☐ **Model 20**, .22 L.R.R.F., Takedown, Tube Feed, Hammer, Octagon Barrel, *Modern*	145.00	210.00
☐ **Model 25**, .22 Short R.F., Takedown, Tube Feed, Hammer, *Modern*	165.00	275.00
☐ **Model 27**, Various Calibers, Takedown, Tube Feed, Hammer, Octagon Barrel, *Modern*	165.00	250.00
☐ **Model 27-S**, Various Calibers, Takedown, Tube Feed, Hammer, Round Barrel, *Modern*	165.00	245.00
☐ **Model 29**, .22 L.R.R.F., Takedown, Tube Feed, Hammer, Round Barrel, *Modern*	145.00	225.00
☐ **Model 32**, .22 L.R.R.F., Takedown, Tube Feed, Hammerless, Octagon Barrel, *Modern*	145.00	220.00
☐ **Model 38**, .22 L.R.R.F., Takedown, Tube Feed, Hammerless, Octagon Barrel, *Modern*	145.00	220.00

SHOTGUN, LEVER ACTION

	V.G.	EXC.
☐ **Four-Tenner**, .410 Ga., Tube Feed, *Modern*	350.00	500.00

SHOTGUN, SLIDE ACTION

	V.G.	EXC.
☐ **Model 1898 Field**, 12 Ga., Hammer, Tube Feed, *Modern*	145.00	300.00
☐ **Model 1898 B**, 12 Ga., Hammer, Tube Feed, Checkered Stock, *Modern*	165.00	350.00
☐ **Model 1898 C**, 12 Ga., Hammer, Tube Feed, Checkered Stock, Fancy Wood, Light Engraving, *Modern*	450.00	700.00
☐ **Model 1898 D**, 12 Ga., Hammer, Tube Feed, Checkered Stock, Fancy Wood, Engraved, *Modern*	850.00	1,450.00
☐ **Model 19 Field**, 12 Ga., Hammer, Tube Feed, *Modern*	120.00	245.00
☐ **Model 19 B**, 12 Ga., Hammer, Tube Feed, Checkered Stock, *Modern*	170.00	350.00
☐ **Model 19 C**, 12 Ga., Hammer, Tube Feed, Checkered Stock, Fancy Wood, Light Engraving, *Modern*	350.00	500.00
☐ **Model 19 D**, 12 Ga., Hammer, Tube Feed, Checkered Stock, Fancy Wood, Engraved, *Modern*	750.00	1,100.00
☐ **Model 21 Field**, 12 Ga., Hammer, Tube Feed, *Modern*	120.00	250.00
☐ **Model 21 B**, 12 Ga., Hammer, Tube Feed, Checkered Stock, *Modern*	170.00	350.00
☐ **Model 21 C**, 12 Ga., Hammer, Tube Feed, Checkered Stock, Fancy Wood, Light Engraving, *Modern*	350.00	500.00
☐ **Model 21 D**, 12 Ga., Hammer, Tube Feed, Checkered Stock, Fancy Wood, Engraved, *Modern*	750.00	1,100.00
☐ **Model 24 Field**, 12 Ga., Hammer, Tube Feed, *Modern*	140.00	275.00
☐ **Model 24 B**, 12 Ga., Hammer, Tube Feed, Checkered Stock, *Modern*	225.00	375.00
☐ **Model 24 C**, 12 Ga., Hammer, Tube Feed, Checkered Stock, Fancy Wood, Light Engraving, *Modern*	350.00	500.00

MARLIN FIREARMS COMPANY / 287

	V.G.	EXC.
☐ **Model 24 D**, 12 Ga., Hammer, Tube Feed, Checkered Stock, Fancy Wood, Engraved, *Modern*	750.00	1,200.00
☐ **Model 16 Field**, 12 Ga., Hammer, Tube Feed, *Modern*	140.00	275.00
☐ **Model 16 B**, 12 Ga., Hammer, Tube Feed, Checkered Stock, *Modern*	225.00	375.00
☐ **Model 16 C**, 12 Ga., Hammer, Tube Feed, Checkered Stock, Fancy Wood, Light Engraving, *Modern*	350.00	500.00
☐ **Model 16 D**, 12 Ga., Hammer, Tube Feed, Checkered Stock, Fancy Wood, Engraved, *Modern*	750.00	1,200.00
☐ **Model 30 Field**, 12 Ga., Hammer, Tube Feed, *Modern*	140.00	275.00
☐ **Model 30 B**, 12 Ga., Hammer, Tube Feed, Checkered Stock, *Modern*	225.00	375.00
☐ **Model 30 C**, 12 Ga., Hammer, Tube Feed, Checkered Stock, Fancy Wood, Light Engraving, *Modern*	350.00	500.00
☐ **Model 30 D**, 12 Ga., Hammer, Tube Feed, Checkered Stock, Fancy Wood, Engraved, *Modern*	750.00	1,200.00
☐ **Model 28 Field**, 12 Ga., Hammerless, Tube Feed, *Modern*	165.00	300.00
☐ **Model 28 B**, 12 Ga., Hammerless, Tube Feed, Checkered Stock, *Modern*	275.00	450.00
☐ **Model 28 C**, 12 Ga., Hammerless, Tube Feed, Checkered Stock, Fancy Wood, Light Engraving, *Modern*	425.00	625.00
☐ **Model 28 D**, 12 Ga., Hammerless, Tube Feed, Checkered Stock, Fancy Wood, Engraved, *Modern*	800.00	1,350.00
☐ **Model 28 Trap**, 12 Ga., Hammerless, Tube Feed, *Modern*	325.00	450.00
☐ **Model 31 Field**, 12 Ga., Hammerless, Tube Feed, *Modern*	165.00	325.00
☐ **Model 31 B**, 12 Ga., Hammerless, Tube Feed, Checkered Stock, *Modern*	275.00	450.00
☐ **Model 31 C**, 12 Ga., Hammerless, Tube Feed, Checkered Stock, Fancy Wood, Light Engraving, *Modern*	425.00	625.00
☐ **Model 31 D**, 12 Ga., Hammerless, Tube Feed, Checkered Stock, Fancy Wood, Engraved, *Modern*	800.00	1,350.00
☐ **Model 17 Field**, 12 Ga., Hammer, Tube Feed, *Modern*	165.00	300.00
☐ **Model 26 Field**, 12 Ga., Hammer, Tube Feed, *Modern*	160.00	275.00
☐ **Model 44 Field**, 12 Ga., Hammerless, Tube Feed, *Modern*	185.00	300.00
☐ **Model 63 Field**, 12 Ga., Hammerless, Tube Feed, *Modern*	150.00	255.00
☐ **Premier Mark I**, 12 Ga., Hammerless, Tube Feed, *Modern*	100.00	145.00
☐ **Premier Mark II**, 12 Ga., Hammerless, Tube Feed, *Modern*	125.00	175.00
☐ **Premier Mark IV**, 12 Ga., Hammerless, Tube Feed, Vent Rib, *Modern*	185.00	270.00
☐ **Model 120**, 12 Ga. 3″, Hammerless, Tube Feed, *Modern*	120.00	160.00
☐ **Glenfield Model 778**, 12 Ga., Hammerless, Tube Feed, *Modern*	85.00	135.00

SHOTGUN, DOUBLE BARREL, OVER-UNDER

	V.G.	EXC.
☐ **Model 90**, 12 and 16 Gauges, Checkered Stock, Double Triggers, *Modern*	225.00	350.00
☐ **Model 90**, 20 and .410 Gauges, Checkered Stock, Double Triggers, *Modern*	275.00	400.00
☐ **Model 90**, 12 and 16 Gauges, Checkered Stock, Single Triggers, *Modern*	275.00	400.00
☐ **Model 90**, 20 and 16 Gauges, Checkered Stock, Single Triggers, *Modern*	350.00	475.00

SHOTGUN, BOLT ACTION

	V.G.	EXC.
☐ **Model 55**, Various Gauges, Clip Fed, *Modern*	45.00	60.00
☐ **Model 55**, Various Gauges, Clip Fed, Adjustable Choke, *Modern*	50.00	70.00
☐ **Model 55 Goose Gun**, 12 Ga. 3″, Clip Fed, *Modern*	50.00	70.00
☐ **Model 55**, 12 Ga. 3″, Clip Fed, Adjustable Choke, *Modern*	50.00	70.00

	V.G.	EXC.
☐ **Model 55S**, 12 Ga. 3", Clip Fed, *Modern*	50.00	70.00
☐ **Model Super Goose**, 10 Ga. 3½", Clip Fed, *Modern*	85.00	135.00
☐ **Glenfield 50**, 12 Ga. 3", Clip Fed, *Modern*	45.00	65.00

MARQUIS OF LORNE
Made by Hood Arms Co. Norwich, Conn., c. 1880.

HANDGUN, REVOLVER
☐ **.22 Short R.F.**, 7 Shot, Spur Trigger, Solid Frame, Single Action, *Antique* 90.00   160.00
☐ **.32 Short R.F.**, 5 Shot, Spur Trigger, Solid Frame, Single Action, *Antique* 95.00   170.00

MARS
Unknown maker, Spain, c. 1920.

HANDGUN, SEMI-AUTOMATIC
☐ **Automat Pistole Mars**, .25 ACP, Clip Fed, *Modern* 135.00   190.00

MARS
Kohout & Spolecnost, Kydne, Czechoslovakia, c. 1925.

HANDGUN, SEMI-AUTOMATIC
☐ **Mars**, .25 ACP, Clip Fed, Blue, *Modern* 155.00   235.00
☐ **Mars**, .32 ACP, Clip Fed, Blue, *Modern* 175.00   265.00

MARS AUTOMATIC PISTOL SYNDICATE
Distributers of the Gabbet-Fairfax pistol made by Webley & Scott, Birmingham, England, c. 1902.

HANDGUN, SEMI-AUTOMATIC
☐ **9mm**, Clip Fed, Blue, Hammer, *Curio* 2,500.00   3,500.00
☐ **.45 Long**, Clip Fed, Blue, Hammer, *Curio* 3,500.00   4,500.00

MARSHWOOD
Made by Stevens Arms.

SHOTGUN, DOUBLE BARREL, SIDE-BY-SIDE
☐ **M 315**, Various Gauges, Hammerless, Steel Barrel, *Modern* 95.00   160.00

MARSTON, STANHOPE
N.Y.C., c. 1850.

HANDGUN, PERCUSSION
☐ **Swivel Breech**, .31, Two Barrels, Ring Trigger, Bar Hammer, *Antique* 425.00   675.00

MARSTON, WILLIAM W.
N.Y.C. 1850-1863

HANDGUN, PERCUSSION
☐ **Pepperbox**, .31, Double Action, 6 Shot, Bar Hammer, *Antique* 220.00   385.00
☐ **Single Shot**, .36, Bar Hammer, Double Action, Screw Barrel, *Antique* 150.00   220.00
☐ **Single Shot**, .36, Bar Hammer, Single Action, Screw Barrel, *Antique* 170.00   235.00
☐ **Breech Loader**, .36, Half Octagon Barrel, Engraved, *Antique* 725.00   1,275.00

Martian

MARTE
Erquiaga, Muguruzu y Cia., Eibar, Spain, c. 1920.

HANDGUN, SEMI-AUTOMATIC

	V.G.	EXC.
☐ **.25 ACP**, Clip Fed, Blue, *Curio*	85.00	125.00

MARTIAN
Martin A Bascaran, Eibar, Spain 1916-1927.

HANDGUN, SEMI-AUTOMATIC
- ☐ **.25 ACP**, Clip Fed, Trigger Guard Takedown, *Curio* 170.00 225.00
- ☐ **.32 ACP**, Clip Fed, Trigger Guard Takedown, *Curio* 175.00 260.00
- ☐ **.25 ACP**, Clip Fed, Eibar Type, *Modern* 90.00 125.00
- ☐ **.32 ACP**, Clip Fed, Eibar Type, *Modern* 100.00 155.00

MARTIAN COMMERCIAL
Martin A Bascaran, Eibar, Spain 1919-1927.

HANDGUN, SEMI-AUTOMATIC
- ☐ **.25 ACP**, Clip Fed, Eibar Type, *Modern* 85.00 125.00
- ☐ **.25 ACP**, Clip Fed, Eibar Type, *Modern* 95.00 150.00

MARTIN, ALEXANDER
Glasgow & Aberdeen, Scotland 1922-1928.

RIFLE, BOLT ACTION
- ☐ **.303 British**, Sporting Rifle, Express Sights, Engraved, Fancy Wood, Cased, *Modern* 750.00 1,200.00

MASSACHUSETTS ARMS
Made by Stevens Arms.

SHOTGUN, DOUBLE BARREL, SIDE-BY-SIDE
- ☐ **Model 311**, Various Gauges, Hammerless, Steel Barrel, *Modern* 95.00 165.00

SHOTGUN, SINGLESHOT
- ☐ **Model 90**, Various Gauges, Takedown, Automatic Ejector, Plain, Hammer, *Modern* 40.00 60.00
- ☐ **Model 94**, Various Gauges, Takedown, Automatic Ejector, Plain, Hammer, *Modern* 40.00 60.00

MASSACHUSETTS ARMS CO.
Chicopee Falls, Mass. 1850-1866. Also see Adams.

HANDGUN, PERCUSSION
- ☐ **Maynard Pocket Revolver**, .28, 6 Shot, *Antique* 250.00 350.00
- ☐ **Maynard Belt Revolver**, .31, 6 Shot, *Antique* 375.00 500.00
- ☐ **Wesson & Leavitt Belt Revolver**, .31, 6 Shot, *Antique* 300.00 475.00
- ☐ **Wesson & Leavitt Dragoon Revolver**, .40, 6 Shot, *Antique* 700.00 1,200.00

MATCHLOCK ARMS, UNKNOWN MAKER

	V.G.	EXC.

RIFLE, MATCHLOCK
- ☐ **.45**, India Mid-1600's, 4 Shot, Revolving Cylinder, Light Ornamentation, Brass Furniture, *Antique* 1,000.00 1,700.00
- ☐ **.57**, Japanese Full Stock Musket, Octagon Barrel, Silver Inlay, Brass Furniture, *Antique* 500.00 750.00

MATADOR
Made in Spain for Firearms International, Washington, D.C.

SHOTGUN, DOUBLE BARREL, SIDE-BY-SIDE
- ☐ **Matador II**, 12 or 20 Gauges, Checkered Stock, Single Trigger, Selective Ejectors, *Modern* 150.00 225.00

MAUSER
Germany Gebruder Mauser et Cie from 1864-1890. From 1890 to date is known as Mauser Werke. Also See German Military, Luger.

AUTOMATIC WEAPON, MACHINE-PISTOL
- ☐ **M1912**, 7.63 Mauser, with Detachable Shoulder Stock, *Class 3* 750.00 1,350.00
- ☐ **M1930**, 7.63 Mauser, with Detachable Shoulder Stock, *Class 3* 3,200.00 4,000.00
- ☐ **MP1932**, 7.63 Mauser, with Detachable Shoulder Stock, *Class 3* ... 3,200.00 4,000.00

HANDGUN, REVOLVER
- ☐ **Colt Type**, .38 Spec., Double Action, 6 Shot, 2" Barrel, *Modern* ... 145.00 210.00
- ☐ **M 78 Zig Zag**, Tip-Up, Fancy Engraving, *Antique* 3,300.00 4,750.00
- ☐ **M 78 Zig Zag**, 9mm Mauser, Tip-Up, *Antique* 1,300.00 2,600.00
- ☐ **M 78 Zig Zag**, 10.6mm, Tip-Up, *Antique* 2,450.00 3,400.00
- ☐ **M 78 Zig Zag**, 7.6mm, Tip-Up, *Antique* 1,950.00 2,750.00

HANDGUN, SEMI-AUTOMATIC
- ☐ **Chinese Shansei**, .45 ACP, With Shoulder Stock, *Curio* 3,650.00 4,950.00
- ☐ **HSC**, .32 ACP, Pre-War, Prototype, Commercial, *Modern* 750.00 1,100.00
- ☐ **HSC**, .32 ACP, Post-War, Prototype, Commercial, *Modern* 450.00 600.00
- ☐ **HSC**, .32 ACP, Pre-War, Nazi-Proofed, Commercial, *Modern* 225.00 325.00
- ☐ **HSC**, .32 ACP, Post-War, Blue, *Modern* 175.00 250.00
- ☐ **HSC**, .32 ACP, Nickel Plated, Post-War, *Modern* 180.00 275.00
- ☐ **HSC**, .380 ACP, Blue, Post-War, *Modern* 185.00 260.00
- ☐ **HSC**, .380 ACP, Nickel Plated, Post-War, *Modern* 200.00 285.00
- ☐ **HSC 1 of 5,000**, .380 ACP, Blue, Post-War, Cased, *Modern* 195.00 265.00
- ☐ **HSC French**, .32 ACP, Nazi-Proofed, *Curio* 200.00 320.00
- ☐ **HSC Navy**, .32 ACP, Nazi-Proofed, *Curio* 350.00 475.00
- ☐ **HSC NSDAP SA**, .32 ACP, Nazi-Proofed, *Curio* 375.00 550.00
- ☐ **HSC Police**, .32 ACP, Nazi-Proofed, *Curio* 265.00 350.00
- ☐ **HSC Swiss**, .32 ACP, Nazi-Proofed, *Curio* 600.00 850.00
- ☐ **M 1896**, 7.63 Mauser, 10 Shot, Conehammer, *Curio* 1,100.00 1,950.00
- ☐ **M 1896**, 7.63 Mauser, 10 Shot, with Loading Lever, *Curio* 950.00 1,650.00
- ☐ **M 1896**, 7.63 Mauser, Conehammer, with Shoulder Stock, *Curio* ... 1,650.00 2,500.00
- ☐ **M 1896**, 7.63 Mauser, with Loading Lever, with Shoulder Stock, *Curio* 1,250.00 2,000.00
- ☐ **M 1896**, 7.63 Mauser, with Loading Lever, Transitional, *Curio* 950.00 1,550.00
- ☐ **M 1896**, 7.63 Mauser, Slabside, *Curio* 800.00 1,250.00
- ☐ **M 1896 (Early)**, 7.63 Mauser, Small Ring, *Curio* 800.00 1,250.00
- ☐ **M 1896 Italian**, 7.63 Mauser, Slabside, *Curio* 1,300.00 1,850.00
- ☐ **M 1896 Shallow Mill**, 7.63 Mauser, with Loading Lever, *Curio* 975.00 1,600.00
- ☐ **M 1896 Turkish**, 7.63 Mauser, Conehammer, *Curio* 1,700.00 2,500.00
- ☐ **M 1912**, .45 ACP, Clip Fed, *Curio* 4,250.00 5,500.00
- ☐ **M 1921**, .45 ACP, Clip Fed, *Curio* 2,250.00 3,250.00
- ☐ **M 1921**, 9mm Luger, Clip Fed, *Curio* 3,400.00 4,500.00
- ☐ **M 1895**, 7.65 Borchardt, *Antique* 2,300.00 3,400.00

Mauser M 78 Zig Zag

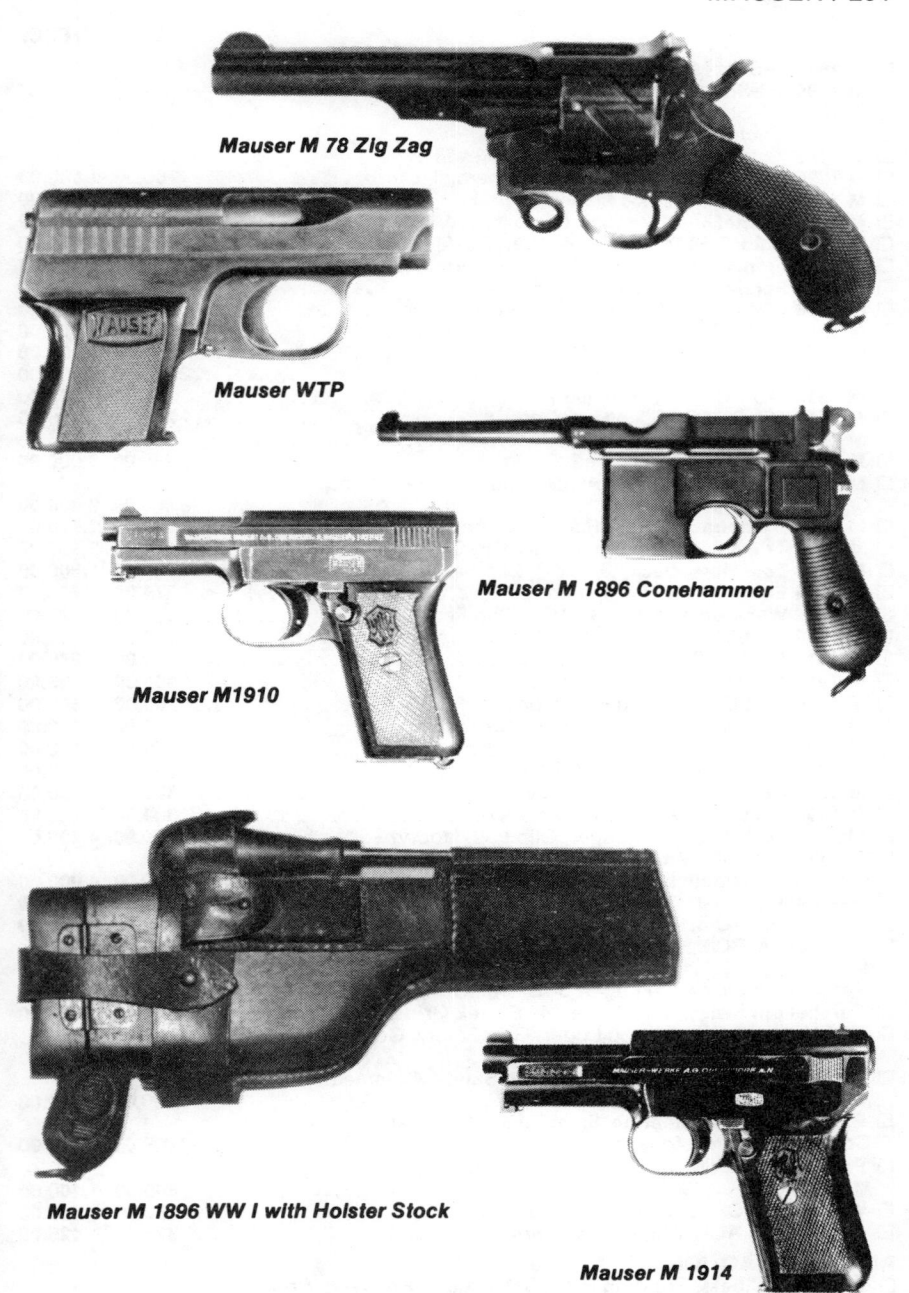

Mauser WTP

Mauser M 1896 Conehammer

Mauser M1910

Mauser M 1896 WW I with Holster Stock

Mauser M 1914

292 / MAUSER

	V.G.	EXC.
☐ **M 1896**, 6-Shot Model *Add* **75%-100%**		
☐ **M 1896**, 20-Shot Model *Add* **50%-80%**		
☐ **M 1896**, 40-Shot Model *Add* **100%**		
☐ **M 1896**, Factory Engraving *Add* **300%**		
☐ **M 1896**, Original Holster Stock *Add* **20%-35%**		
☐ **M 1896**, 7.63 Mauser, Pre-War, Commercial, *Curio*	700.00	1,100.00
☐ **M 1896 1920 Police**, 7.63 Mauser, *Curio*	600.00	1,000.00
☐ **M 1896 Banner**, 7.63 Mauser, *Curio*	900.00	1,450.00
☐ **M 1896 Bolo**, 7.63 Mauser, Post-War, *Curio*	900.00	1,450.00
☐ **M 1896 French Police**, 7.63 Mauser, *Curio*	1,350.00	2,000.00
☐ **M 1896 Persian**, 7.63 Mauser, *Curio*	1,500.00	2,350.00
☐ **M 1896 WW I**, 7.63 Mauser, Commercial, *Curio*	600.00	1,000.00
☐ **M 1896 WW I**, 7.63 Mauser, Military, *Curio*	600.00	1,000.00
☐ **M 1896 WW I**, 9mm Luger, Military, *Curio*	650.00	1,100.00
☐ **M 1906/08**, 7.63 Mauser, Clip Fed, *Curio*	2,550.00	3,500.00
☐ **M 1910**, .25 ACP, Clip Fed, *Curio*	200.00	300.00
☐ **M 1910/14**, .25 ACP, Clip Fed, *Curio*	225.00	325.00
☐ **M 1910/34**, .25 ACP, Clip Fed, *Modern*	350.00	475.00
☐ **M 1912**, 9mm Luger, Clip Fed, *Curio*	2,250.00	3,000.00
☐ **M 1914 Presentation Humpback**, 4mm, Clip Fed, Fancy Grips, *Curio*	6,000.00	9,000.00
☐ **M 1914 Humpback**, .32 ACP, Long Barrel, Clip Fed, *Curio*	1,500.00	2,500.00
☐ **M 1914 Transition Humpback**, .32 ACP, Clip Fed, *Curio*	1,250.00	2,000.00
☐ **M 1914 Late Humpback**, .32 ACP, Clip Fed, *Curio*	1,000.00	1,800.00
☐ **M 1914 Early**, .32 ACP, Clip Fed, *Curio*	275.00	400.00
☐ **M 1914 War Commercial**, .32 ACP, Clip Fed, *Curio*	300.00	425.00
☐ **M 1914 Post-War**, .32 ACP, Clip Fed, *Modern*	200.00	300.00
☐ **M 1914 Army**, .32 ACP, Clip Fed, *Curio*	190.00	275.00
☐ **M 1914 Navy**, .32 ACP, Clip Fed, *Curio*	400.00	525.00
☐ **M 1914/34**, .32 ACP, Clip Fed, *Modern*	200.00	300.00
☐ **M 1930**, 7.63 Mauser, Commercial, *Curio*	800.00	1,250.00
☐ **M 1930**, 9mm Luger, Commercial, *Curio*	750.00	1,150.00
☐ **M 1934**, .32 ACP, Clip Fed, *Modern*	200.00	300.00
☐ **M 1934 Navy**, .32 ACP, Clip Fed, *Curio*	325.00	450.00
☐ **M 1934 Police**, .32 ACP, Clip Fed, *Curio*	300.00	425.00
☐ **Model Nickl HSV**, 9mm Luger, Clip Fed, *Modern*	3,500.00	4,500.00
☐ **Parabellum 75th. Anniversary**, 9mm Luger, 12" Barrel, Grip Safety, Forestock, Detachable Buttstock, *Modern*	3,000.00	4,000.00
☐ **Parabellum PO 8**, .30 Luger, 6" Barrel, Grip Safety, *Modern*	425.00	525.00
☐ **Parabellum PO 8**, .30 Luger, 4" Barrel, Grip Safety, *Modern*	450.00	550.00
☐ **Parabellum PO 8**, 9mm Luger, Various Barrel Lengths, Grip Safety, *Modern*	425.00	500.00
☐ **Parabellum Swiss**, .30 Luger, 6" Barrel, Grip Safety, *Modern*	350.00	450.00
☐ **Parabellum Swiss**, 9mm Luger, 4" Barrel, Grip Safety, *Modern*	350.00	450.00
☐ **Parabellum Bulgarian**, .30 Luger, Grip Safety, Commemorative, *Modern*	1,000.00	1,800.00
☐ **Parabellum Russian**, .30 Luger, Grip Safety, Commemorative, *Modern*	1,000.00	1,800.00
☐ **Parabellum Kriegsmarine**, 9mm Luger, Grip Safety, Commemorative, *Modern*	2,000.00	3,000.00
☐ **Parabellum Sport**, .30 or 9mm Luger, Heavy Barrel, Target Sights, *Modern*	800.00	1,400.00
☐ **W T P**, .25 ACP, Clip Fed, *Modern*	250.00	350.00
☐ **W T P 2**, .25 ACP, Clip Fed, *Modern*	325.00	425.00

RIFLE, BOLT ACTION
☐ **Various Calibers**, Sporting Rifle, Set Trigger, Pre-WWI, Short Action, *Modern* 450.00   600.00

	V.G.	EXC.
☐ **Various Calibers**, Sporting Rifle, Set Trigger, Pre-WWI, Carbine, Full-Stocked, *Modern*	450.00	600.00
☐ **Various Calibers**, Sporting Rifle, Pre-WWI, Military, Commercial, *Modern*	375.00	500.00
☐ **Model 10 Varminter**, .22-250, Post-War, Heavy Barrel, Monte Carlo Stock, Checkered Stock, *Modern*	250.00	375.00
☐ **Model 2000**, Various Calibers, Post-War, Monte Carlo Stock, Checkered Stock, *Modern*	250.00	350.00
☐ **Model 3000**, Various Calibers, Post-War, Monte Carlo Stock, *Modern*	300.00	400.00
☐ **Model 3000**, Various Calibers, Post-War, Left-Hand, Monte Carlo Stock, Checkered Stock, *Modern*	300.00	415.00
☐ **Model 3000**, Various Calibers, Post-War, Magnum Action, Monte Carlo Stock, Checkered Stock, *Modern*	300.00	415.00
☐ **Model 3000**, Various Calibers, Post-War, Left-Hand, Magnum Action, Monte Carlo Stock, Checkered Stock, *Modern*	315.00	425.00
☐ **Model 4000**, Various Calibers, Varmint, Fancy Checkering, Flared, *Modern*	320.00	420.00
☐ **Model 660**, Various Calibers, Post-War, Takedown, Monte Carlo Stock, Checkered Stock, *Modern*	675.00	825.00
☐ **Model 660 Safari**, Various Calibers, Post-War, Takedown, Monte Carlo Stock, Checkered Stock, Magnum, *Modern*	750.00	950.00
☐ **Model 98**, Various Calibers, Sporting Rifle, Full-Stocked, Pre-WW2, Military, Commercial, *Modern*	400.00	525.00
☐ **Model A**, Various Calibers, Sporting Rifle, Pre-WW2, Short Action, *Modern*	600.00	750.00
☐ **Model A**, Various Calibers, Sporting Rifle, Pre-WW2, Magnum Action, *Modern*	625.00	775.00
☐ **Model A British**, Various Calibers, Sporting Rifle, Express Sights, Pre-WW2, *Modern*	425.00	650.00
☐ **Model A British**, Various Calibers, Sporting Rifle, Peep Sights, Pre-WW2, Octagon Barrel, Set Trigger, *Modern*	600.00	800.00
☐ **Model B**, Various Calibers, Sporting Rifle, Pre-WW2, Set Trigger, Express Sights, *Modern*	475.00	625.00
☐ **Model B**, Various Calibers, Sporting Rifle, Pre-WW2, Octagon Barrel, Set Trigger, *Modern*	500.00	725.00
☐ **Model DSM 34**, .22 L.R.R.F., Pre-WW2, Singleshot, Tangent Sights, Miltiary Style Stock, *Modern*	325.00	450.00
☐ **Model EL 320**, .22 L.R.R.F., Pre-WW2, Singleshot, Sporting Rifle, Adjustable Sights, *Modern*	220.00	325.00
☐ **Model EN 310**, .22 L.R.R.F., Pre-WW2, Singleshot, Open Rear Sight, *Modern*	175.00	260.00
☐ **Model ES 340**, .22 L.R.R.F., Pre-WW2, Singleshot, Tangent Sights, Sporting Rifle, *Modern*	200.00	290.00
☐ **Model ES 340B**, .22 L.R.R.F., Pre-WW2, Singleshot, Tangent Sights, Sporting Rifle, *Modern*	200.00	295.00
☐ **Model ES 350**, .22 L.R.R.F., Pre-WW2, Singleshot, Target Sights, Target Stock, *Modern*	365.00	475.00
☐ **Model ES 350B**, .22 L.R.R.F., Pre-WW2, Singleshot, Target Sights, Target Stock, *Modern*	300.00	425.00
☐ **Model K**, Various Calibers, Sporting Rifle, Pre-WW2, Short Action, *Modern*	450.00	575.00
☐ **Model KKW**, .22 L.R.R.F., Pre-WW2, Singleshot, Tangent Sights, Military Style Stock, *Modern*	335.00	450.00
☐ **Model M**, Various Calibers, Sporting Rifle, Full-Stocked, Set Trigger, Express Sights, Carbine, *Modern*	525.00	675.00

294 / MAUSER

	V.G.	EXC.
☐ **Model M**, Various Calibers, Sporting Rifle, Pre-WW2, Full-Stocked, Tangent Sights, Carbine, *Modern*	425.00	575.00
☐ **Model MM 410**, .22 L.R.R.F., Pre-WW2, 5 Shot Clip, Tangent Sights, Sporting Rifle, *Modern*	250.00	340.00
☐ **Model MM 410B**, .22 L.R.R.F., Pre-WW2, 5 Shot Clip, Tangent Sights, Sporting Rifle, *Modern*	350.00	475.00
☐ **Model MS 350B**, .22 L.R.R.F., Pre-WW2, 5 Shot Clip, Target Sights, Target Stock, *Modern*	400.00	525.00
☐ **Model MS 420**, .22 L.R.R.F., Pre-WW2, 5 Shot Clip, Tangent Sights, Sporting Rifle, *Modern*	250.00	350.00
☐ **Model MS 420B**, .22 L.R.R.F., Pre-WW2, 5 Shot Clip, Tangent Sights, Target Stock, *Modern*	375.00	465.00
☐ **Model S**, Various Calibers, Sporting Rifle, Pre-WW2, Full-Stocked, Set Trigger, Carbine, *Modern*	450.00	575.00
☐ **Standard**, Various Calibers, Sporting Rifle, Set Trigger, Pre-WW1, *Modern*	475.00	650.00

RIFLE, DOUBLE BARREL, OVER-UNDER

	V.G.	EXC.
☐ **Model Aristocrat**, .375 H & H Magnum, Fancy Checkering, Engraved, Open Rear Sight, Cheekpiece, Double Trigger, *Modern*	1,250.00	1,900.00
☐ **Model Aristocrat**, Various Calibers, Fancy Checkering, Engraved, Open Rear Sight, Cheekpiece, Double Trigger, *Modern*	1,000.00	1,450.00

RIFLE, SEMI-AUTOMATIC

	V.G.	EXC.
☐ **M1896**, 7.63 Mauser, Carbine, *Curio*	3,500.00	5.000.00

SHOTGUN, BOLT ACTION

	V.G.	EXC.
☐ **16 Gauge**, *Modern*	85.00	130.00

SHOTGUN, DOUBLE BARREL, OVER-UNDER

	V.G.	EXC.
☐ **Model 610**, 12 Gauge, Trap Grade, Vent Rib, Checkered Stock, *Modern*	600.00	875.00
☐ **Model 610**, 12 Gauge, Skeet Grade, with Conversion Kit, Vent Rib, Checkered Stock, *Modern*	1,100.00	1,500.00
☐ **Model 620**, 12 Gauge, Automatic Ejector, Single Selective Trigger, Vent Rib, Fancy Wood, *Modern*	650.00	925.00
☐ **Model 620**, 12 Gauge, Automatic Ejector, Single Trigger, Vent Rib, Fancy Wood, *Modern*	625.00	875.00
☐ **Model 620**, 12 Gauge, Automatic Ejector, Double Trigger, Vent Rib, Fancy Wood, *Modern*	575.00	825.00
☐ **Model 71E**, 12 Gauge, Field Grade, Double Trigger, Checkered Stock, *Modern*	275.00	350.00
☐ **Model 72E**, 12 Gauge, Trap Grade, Checkered Stock, Light Engraving, *Modern*	350.00	475.00
☐ **Model 72E**, 12 Gauge, Skeet Grade, Checkered Stock, Light Engraving, *Modern*	350.00	475.00

SHOTGUN, DOUBLE BARREL, SIDE-BY-SIDE

	V.G.	EXC.
☐ **Model 496**, 12 Gauge, Trap Grade, Vent Rib, Single Trigger, Checkered Stock, Box Lock, *Modern*	375.00	500.00
☐ **Model 545**, 12 and 20 Gauges, Single Trigger, Recoil Pad, Checkered Stock, Box Lock, *Modern*	350.00	450.00
☐ **Model 580**, 12 Gauge, Engraved, Fancy Checkering, Fancy Wood, *Modern*	625.00	875.00

SHOTGUN, SINGLESHOT

	V.G.	EXC.
☐ **Model 496**, 12 Gauge, Trap Grade, Engraved, Checkered Stock, *Modern*	350.00	475.00
☐ **Model 496 Competition**, 12 Gauge, Trap Grade, Engraved, Fancy Wood, Fancy Checkering, *Modern*	475.00	650.00

	V.G.	EXC.

MAYESCH
Lancaster, Pa. 1760-1770. See Kentucky Rifles and Pistols.

MAYER & SOEHNE
Arnsberg, W. Germany.
HANDGUN, REVOLVER
☐ **Target**, .22 L.R.R.F., Break Top, 5 Shot, Target Sights, Double Action, *Modern* 75.00   115.00

MAYOR, FRANCOIS
Lausanne, Switzerland.
HANDGUN, SEMI-AUTOMATIC
☐ **Rochat**, .25 ACP, Clip Fed, *Modern* 450.00   600.00

M.B. ASSOCIATES
San Ramon, Calif.
HANDGUN, ROCKET PISTOL
☐ **Gyrojet**, For Nickel Plating, Add **10%-15%**
☐ **Gyrojet**, For U.S. Property Stamping Add **75%-100%**
☐ **Gyrojet Mark I Model A**, Clip Fed, *Modern* 700.00   875.00
☐ **Gyrojet Mark I Model A Exp.**, Clip Fed, *Modern* 925.00   1,400.00
☐ **Gyrojet Mark II Model B**, Clip Fed, *Modern* 525.00   700.00
☐ **Gyrojet Mark II Model B Exp.**, Clip Fed, *Modern* 775.00   1,200.00
☐ **Gyrojet Mark II Model B Snub**, Clip Fed, *Modern* 575.00   775.00
☐ **Gyrojet Mark II Model C**, Clip Fed, *Modern* 425.00   550.00
☐ **Gyrojet Mark II B**, Clip Fed, Presentation, Cased with Accessories, *Modern* 950.00   1,450.00

MCCOY, ALEXANDER
Philadelphia, Pa. 1779. See Kentucky Rifles.

MCCOY, KESTER
Lancaster County, Pa. See Kentucky Rifles and Pistols.

MCCULLOUGH, GEORGE
Lancaster, Pa. 1770-1773. See Kentucky Rifles.

MEIER, ADOLPHUS
St. Louis, Mo. 1845-1850.
RIFLE, PERCUSSION
☐ **.58 Plains Type**, Double Barrel, Side by Side, Half-Octagon Barrel, Rifled, Plain, *Antique* 1,250.00   1,850.00

MELIOR
Liege, Belgium. Made by Robar et Cie. 1900-1959.
HANDGUN, SEMI-AUTOMATIC
☐ **New Model Pocket**, .22 L.R.R.F., Clip Fed, *Modern* 130.00   185.00
☐ **New Model Pocket**, .32 ACP, Clip Fed, *Modern* 100.00   160.00
☐ **New Model Pocket**, .380 ACP, Clip Fed, *Modern* 115.00   175.00
☐ **New Model Vest Pocket**, .22 Long R.F., Clip Fed, *Modern* 100.00   160.00
☐ **New Model Vest Pocket**, .25 ACP, Clip Fed, *Modern* 100.00   160.00
☐ **Old Model Pocket**, .32 ACP, Clip Fed, *Modern* 115.00   165.00
☐ **Old Model Vest Pocket**, .25 ACP, Clip Fed, *Modern* 100.00   165.00
☐ **Target**, .22 L.R.R.F., Clip Fed, Long Barrel, *Modern* 150.00   225.00

MENDOZA
Mexico City, Mexico.

HANDGUN, SINGLESHOT
	V.G.	EXC.
☐ **K-62**, .22 L.R.R.F., *Modern*	65.00	115.00

RIFLE, BOLT ACTION
☐ **Modelo Conejo**, .22 L.R.R.F., 2 Shot, *Modern*	95.00	160.00

MENTA
Made by August Menz, Suhl, Germany, c. 1916.

☐ **.25 ACP**, Clip Fed, *Modern*	350.00	450.00
☐ **.32 ACP**, Clip Fed, *Modern*	145.00	215.00

MENZ, AUGUST
Suhl, Germany. 1912-1924

HANDGUN, SEMI-AUTOMATIC
☐ **Lilliput**, .25 ACP, Clip Fed. *Curio*	175.00	240.00
☐ **Model I**, .32 ACP, Clip Fed, *Curio*	185.00	265.00
☐ **Model II**, .32 ACP, Clip Fed, *Curio*	220.00	325.00
☐ **Model III**, .32 ACP, Clip Fed, Hammer, *Curio*	220.00	325.00
☐ **P & B Special**, .32 ACP, Clip Fed, Hammer, Double Action, *Curio*	350.00	475.00
☐ **P & B Special**, .380 ACP, Clip Fed, Hammer, Double Action, *Curio*	475.00	650.00

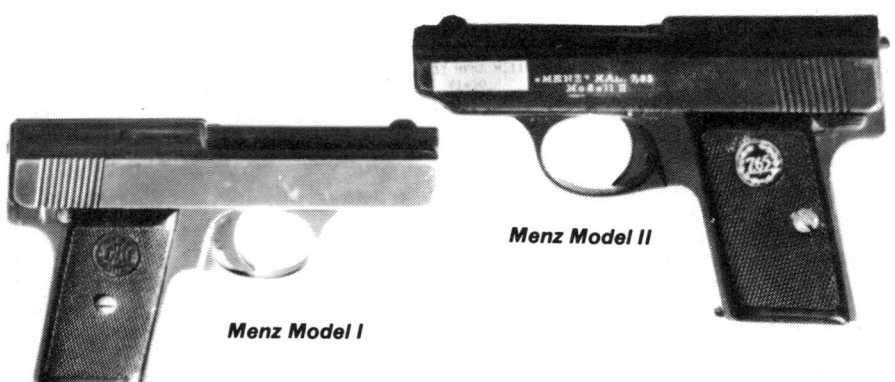

Menta .25

Menta .32

Menz Model I

Menz Model II

MERCURY
Made by Robar et Cie., Liege, Belgium for Tradewinds.

	V.G.	EXC.

HANDGUN, SEMI-AUTOMATIC
☐ **M 622 VP**, .22 L.R.R.F., Clip Fed, *Modern* 90.00   140.00

SHOTGUN, DOUBLE BARREL, SIDE-BY-SIDE
☐ **Mercury**, 10 Gauge 3", Hammerless, Magnum, Checkered Stock, Double Trigger, *Modern* 165.00   250.00
☐ **Mercury**, 12 and 20 Gauges, Hammerless, Magnum, Checkered Stock, Double Trigger, *Modern* 150.00   200.00

MERIDEN FIRE ARMS CO.
Meriden, Conn. 1907-1909.

HANDGUN, REVOLVER
☐ .38 S & W, 5 Shot, Top Break, Hammerless, Double Action, *Modern*   65.00   95.00

RIFLE, SINGLESHOT
☐ **Model 10**, .22 L.R.R.F., *Modern* 45.00   65.00

RIFLE, SLIDE ACTION
☐ **Model 15**, .22 L.R.R.F., Tube Feed, *Modern* 145.00   225.00

MERKEL
Gebruder Merkel, Suhl, Germany from 1920. After WW II, VEB Fahrzeug u. Jagdwaffenwerk Ernst Thalmann, Suhl, East Germany.

COMBINATION WEAPON, DOUBLE BARREL, OVER-UNDER
☐ **Model 210**, Various Calibers, Pre-WW2, Engraved, Checkered Stock, *Modern* 900.00   1,250.00
☐ **Model 210E**, Various Calibers, Engraved, Checkered Stock, Automatic Ejector, *Modern* 1,000.00   1,400.00
☐ **Model 211**, Various Calibers, Pre-WW2, Engraved, Checkered Stock, *Modern* 1,250.00   1,650.00
☐ **Model 211E**, Various Calibers, Engraved, Checkered Stock, Automatic Ejector, *Modern* 1,350.00   1,750.00
☐ **Model 212**, Various Calibers, Pre-WW2, Fancy Engraving, Fancy Checkering, *Modern* 1,400.00   1,750.00
☐ **Model 212E**, Various Calibers, Pre-WW2, Fancy Engraving, Fancy Checkering, Automatic Ejector, *Modern* 1,700.00   2,350.00
☐ **Model 213E**, Various Calibers, Sidelock, Fancy Checkering, Fancy Engraving, Automatic Ejector, *Modern* 2,350.00   3,000.00
☐ **Model 214E**, Various Calibers, Pre-WW2, Sidelock, Fancy Checkering, Fancy Engraving, Automatic Ejector, *Modern* 2,350.00   3,000.00
☐ **Model 310**, Various Calibers, Pre-WW2, Engraved, Checkered Stock, *Modern* 1,300.00   1,800.00
☐ **Model 310E**, Various Calibers, Pre-WW2, Engraved, Checkered Stock, Automatic Ejector, *Modern* 1,700.00   2,350.00
☐ **Model 311**, Various Calibers, Pre-WW2, Fancy Engraving, Fancy Checkering, *Modern* 1,500.00   2,100.00
☐ **Model 311E**, Various Calibers, Pre-WW2, Fancy Engraving, Fancy Checkering, Automatic Ejector, *Modern* 1,700.00   2,400.00
☐ **Model 312**, Various Calibers, Pre-WW2, Fancy Engraving, Fancy Checkering, Automatic Ejector, *Modern* 2,000.00   2,750.00
☐ **Model 313**, Various Calibers, Sidelock, Fancy Checkering, Fancy Engraving, Automatic Ejector, *Modern* 4,000.00   5,400.00
☐ **Model 314**, Various Calibers, Sidelock, Fancy Checkering, Fancy Engraving, Automatic Ejector, *Modern* 5,750.00   7,250.00
☐ **Model 410**, Various Calibers, Pre-WW2, Engraved, Checkered Stock, *Modern* 850.00   1,250.00

298 / MERKEL

	V.G.	EXC.
☐ **Model 410E**, Various Calibers, Pre-WW2, Engraved, Checkered Stock, Automatic Ejector, *Modern*	900.00	1,350.00
☐ **Model 411**, Various Calibers, Pre-WW2, Engraved, Checkered Stock, *Modern*	1,000.00	1,500.00
☐ **Model 411E**, Various Calibers, Pre-WW2, Engraved, Checkered Stock, Automatic Ejector, *Modern*	1,200.00	1,650.00

COMBINATION WEAPON, DRILLING

	V.G.	EXC.
☐ **Model 142**, Various Calibers, Pre-WW2, Double Trigger, Engraved, Checkered Stock, *Modern*	3,000.00	3,750.00
☐ **Model 144**, Various Calibers, Pre-WW2, Double Trigger, Engraved, Checkered Stock, *Modern*	3,100.00	3,800.00
☐ **Model 145**, Various Calibers, Pre-WW2, Double Trigger, Engraved, Checkered Stock, *Modern*	2,800.00	3,550.00

RIFLE, DOUBLE BARREL, OVER-UNDER

	V.G.	EXC.
☐ **Model 220**, Various Calibers, Pre-WW2, Checkered Stock, Engraved, *Modern*	875.00	1,250.00
☐ **Model 220E**, Various Calibers, Engraved, Checkered Stock, Automatic Ejector, *Modern*	975.00	1,350.00
☐ **Model 221**, Various Calibers, Pre-WW2, Checkered Stock, Engraved, *Modern*	975.00	1,350.00
☐ **Model 221E**, Various Calibers, Engraved, Checkered Stock, Automatic Ejector, *Modern*	1,350.00	1,850.00
☐ **Model 320**, Various Calibers, Pre-WW2, Checkered Stock, Engraved, *Modern*	1,350.00	1,850.00
☐ **Model 320E**, Various Calibers, Pre-WW2, Checkered Stock, Engraved, Automatic Ejector, *Modern*	1,750.00	2,400.00
☐ **Model 321**, Various Calibers, Pre-WW2, Fancy Engraving, Fancy Checkering, *Modern*	1,650.00	2,250.00
☐ **Model 321E**, Various Calibers, Pre-WW2, Fancy Engraving, Fancy Checkering, Automatic Ejector, *Modern*	1,900.00	2,500.00
☐ **Model 322**, Various Calibers, Pre-WW2, Fancy Engraving, Fancy Checkering, Automatic Ejector, *Modern*	2,000.00	2,800.00
☐ **Model 323**, Various Calibers, Sidelock, Fancy Checkering, Fancy Engraving, Automatic Ejector, *Modern*	4,400.00	5,750.00
☐ **Model 324**, Various Calibers, Sidelock, Fancy Checkering, Fancy Engraving, Automatic Ejector, *Modern*	6,000.00	7,500.00

SHOTGUN, DOUBLE BARREL, OVER-UNDER

	V.G.	EXC.
☐ **Model 100**, Various Gauges, Pre-WW2, Plain Barrel, Checkered Stock, *Modern*	575.00	725.00
☐ **Model 100**, Various Gauges, Pre-WW2, Raised Matted Rib, Checkered Stock, *Modern*	625.00	775.00
☐ **Model 101**, Various Gauges, Pre-WW2, Raised Matted Rib, Checkered Stock, Light Engraving, *Modern*	650.00	850.00
☐ **Model 101E**, Various Gauges, Pre-WW2, Raised Matted Rib, Checkered Stock, Light Engraving, Automatic Ejector, *Modern*	700.00	950.00
☐ **Model 200**, Various Gauges, Pre-WW2, Raised Matted Rib, Checkered Stock, Light Engraving, *Modern*	900.00	1,250.00
☐ **Model 200E**, Various Gauges, Pre-WW2, Raised Matted Rib, Checkered Stock, Light Engraving, Automatic Ejector, *Modern*	1,100.00	1,650.00
☐ **Model 201**, Various Gauges, Pre-WW2, Raised Matted Rib, Checkered Stock, Engraved, *Modern*	1,000.00	1,550.00
☐ **Model 201E**, Various Gauges, Pre-WW2, Raised Matted Rib, Checkered Stock, Engraved, Automatic Ejector, *Modern*	1,250.00	1,800.00
☐ **Model 202**, Various Gauges, Pre-WW2, Raised Matted Rib, Fancy Checkering, Fancy Engraving, *Modern*	1,300.00	1,850.00

MERRILL COMPANY / 299

	V.G.	EXC.

- ☐ **Model 202E**, Various Gauges, Pre-WW2, Raised Matted Rib, Fancy Checkering, Fancy Engraving, Automatic Ejector, *Modern* 1,750.00 2,400.00
- ☐ **Model 203E**, Various Gauges, Sidelock, Fancy Checkering, Fancy Engraving, Automatic Ejector, *Modern* 2,350.00 3,200.00
- ☐ **Model 203E**, Various Gauges, Sidelock, Single Selective Trigger, Automatic Ejector, Fancy Checkering, Fancy Engraving, *Modern*... 3,450.00 4,650.00
- ☐ **Model 204E**, Various Gauges, Pre-WW2, Sidelock, Fancy Checkering, Fancy Engraving, Automatic Ejector, *Modern* 2,600.00 3,500.00
- ☐ **Model 300**, Various Gauges, Pre-WW2, Raised Matted Rib, Checkered Stock, Engraved, *Modern* 1,450.00 1,900.00
- ☐ **Model 300E**, Various Gauges, Pre-WW2, Raised Matted Rib, Checkered Stock, Engraved, Automatic Ejector, *Modern* 1,750.00 2,400.00
- ☐ **Model 301**, Various Gauges, Pre-WW2, Raised Matted Rib, Fancy Checkering, Engraved, *Modern* 1,600.00 2,300.00
- ☐ **Model 301E**, Various Gauges, Pre-WW2, Raised Matted Rib, Fancy Checkering, Engraved, Automatic Ejector, *Modern* 1,950.00 2,550.00
- ☐ **Model 302**, Various Gauges, Pre-WW2, Raised Matted Rib, Fancy Checkering, Fancy Engraving, Automatic Ejector, *Modern* 2,350.00 3,100.00
- ☐ **Model 303E**, Various Gauges, Sidelock, Single Selective Trigger, Automatic Ejector, Fancy Engraving, Fancy Checkering, *Modern*... 4,250.00 5,600.00
- ☐ **Model 304E**, Various Gauges, Sidelock, Single Selective Trigger, Automatic Ejector, Fancy Engraving, Fancy Checkering, *Modern*... 6,000.00 7,500.00
- ☐ **Model 400**, Various Gauges, Pre-WW2, Raised Matted Rib, Checkered Stock, Engraved, *Modern* 775.00 1,050.00
- ☐ **Model 400E**, Various Gauges, Pre-WW2, Raised Matted Rib, Checkered Stock, Engraved, Automatic Ejector, *Modern* 850.00 1,300.00
- ☐ **Model 401**, Various Gauges, Pre-WW2, Raised Matted Rib, Checkered Stock, Fancy Engraving, *Modern* 975.00 1,425.00
- ☐ **Model 401E**, Various Gauges, Pre WW-2, Raised Matted Rib, Checkered Stock, Fancy Engraving, Automatic Ejector, *Modern*.... 1,100.00 1,600.00

SHOTGUN, DOUBLE BARREL, SIDE-BY-SIDE
- ☐ **Model 127**, Various Gauges, Pre-WW2, Sidelock, Fancy Engraving, Fancy Checkering, Automatic Ejector, *Modern* 5,500.00 7,000.00
- ☐ **Model 130**, Various Gauges, Pre-WW2, Fancy Engraving, Fancy Checkering, Automatic Ejector, *Modern* 2,900.00 3,700.00
- ☐ **Model 147E**, Various Gauges, Fancy Checkering, Fancy Engraving, *Modern* 850.00 1,100.00
- ☐ **Model 147E**, Various Gauges, Fancy Checkering, Fancy Engraving, Single Selective Trigger, *Modern*.............................. 950.00 1,300.00
- ☐ **Model 147S**, Various Gauges, Fancy Checkering, Fancy Engraving, Sidelock, *Modern* 1,850.00 2,500.00
- ☐ **Model 147S**, Various Gauges, Fancy Checkering, Fancy Engraving, Sidelock, Single Selective Trigger, *Modern* 1,950.00 2,800.00
- ☐ **Model 47E**, Various Gauges, Checkered Stock, Engraved, *Modern* 650.00 850.00
- ☐ **Model 47E**, Various Gauges, Single Selective Trigger, Checkered Stock, Engraved, *Modern*.. 700.00 975.00
- ☐ **Model 47S**, Various Gauges, Sidelock, Checkered Stock, Engraved, *Modern* 1,250.00 1,800.00
- ☐ **Model 47S**, Various Gauges, Sidelock, Single Selective Trigger, Checkered Stock, Engraved, *Modern* 1,400.00 2,000.00

MERRILL CO.
Formerly in Rockwell City, Iowa, now in Fullerton, Calif.
HANDGUN, SINGLESHOT
- ☐ **Sportsman**, For Extra Barrel *Add* **$70.00-$100.00**
- ☐ **Sportsman**, For Extra 14" Barrel and Dies *Add* **$120.00-$180.00**

	V.G.	EXC.
☐ **Sportsman**, Wrist Attachment *Add* **$15.00-$25.00**		
☐ **Sportsman**, Various Calibers, Target Pistol, Top Break, Adjustable Sights, Vent Rib, *Modern*	175.00	265.00

MERRIMAC ARMS & MFG. CO.
Newburyport, Mass. Absorbed by Brown Mfg. Co. Worcester, Mass. 1861-1866. Also see Ballard.

HANDGUN, SINGLESHOT
☐ **Southerner**, .41 Short R.F., Derringer, Iron Frame, Light Engraving, *Antique*	325.00	425.00

RIFLE, DOUBLE BARREL, SIDE-BY-SIDE
☐ **Various Calibers**, Octagon Barrel, *Antique*	750.00	1,000.00

SHOTGUN, SINGLESHOT
☐ **20 Gauge**, Falling Block, *Antique*	190.00	275.00

MERWIN & BRAY
Worcester, Mass. 1864-1868. Became Merwin & Simpkins in 1868 and also Merwin-Taylor & Simpkins the same year, also within the same year became Merwin, Hulbert & Co. Also see Ballard, Merwin, Hulbert & Co.

HANDGUN, REVOLVER
☐ **.22 Short R.F.**, 7 Shot, Single Action, Solid Frame, Spur Trigger, *Antique*	110.00	165.00
☐ **.28 Cup Primed Cartridge**, 6 Shot, Single Action, Spur Trigger, Solid Frame, *Antique*	110.00	175.00
☐ **.30 Cup Primed Cartridge**, 6 Shot, Single Action, Spur Trigger, Solid Frame, *Antique*	115.00	185.00
☐ **.31 R.F.**, 6 Shot, Single Action, Solid Frame, Spur Trigger, *Antique*	100.00	160.00
☐ **.32 Short R.F.**, 6 Shot, Single Action, Solid Frame, Spur Trigger, *Antique*	110.00	170.00
☐ **.42 Cup Primed Cartridge**, 6 Shot, Single Action, Spur Trigger, Solid Frame, *Antique*	145.00	225.00
☐ **.42 Cup Primed Cartridge**, 6 Shot, Single Action, Spur Trigger, Solid Frame, 6" Barrel, *Antique*	265.00	375.00
☐ **"Navy"**, .32 Short R.F., 6 Shot, Single Action, Solid Frame, Finger-Rest Trigger Guard, *Antique*	285.00	425.00
☐ **"Navy"**, .38 Short R.F., 6 Shot, Single Action, Solid Frame, Finger-Rest Trigger Guard, *Antique*	350.00	475.00
☐ **"Original"**, .28 Cup Primed Cartridge, 6 Shot, Single Action, Spur Trigger, Tip-Up, *Antique*	475.00	625.00
☐ **"Original"**, .30 Cup Primed Cartridge, 6 Shot, Single Action, Spur Trigger, Tip-Up, *Antique*	525.00	675.00
☐ **"Original"**, .42 Cup Primed Cartridge, 6 Shot, Single Action, Spur Trigger, Tip-Up, *Antique*	575.00	725.00
☐ **"Original"**, Various Cup-Primed Calibers, Extra Cylinder, Percussion, *Add* **$90.00-$150.00**		
☐ **Reynolds**, .25 Short R.F., 5 Shot, Single Action, Spur Trigger, 3" Barrel, *Antique*	110.00	175.00

HANDGUN, SINGLESHOT
☐ **.32 Short R.F.**, Side-Swing Barrel, Brass Frame, 3" Barrel, Spur Trigger, *Antique*	100.00	165.00

MERWIN, HULBERT & CO.
Successors to Merwin & Bray, et al. in 1868, and became Hulbert Bros. in 1892. Out of business in 1896.

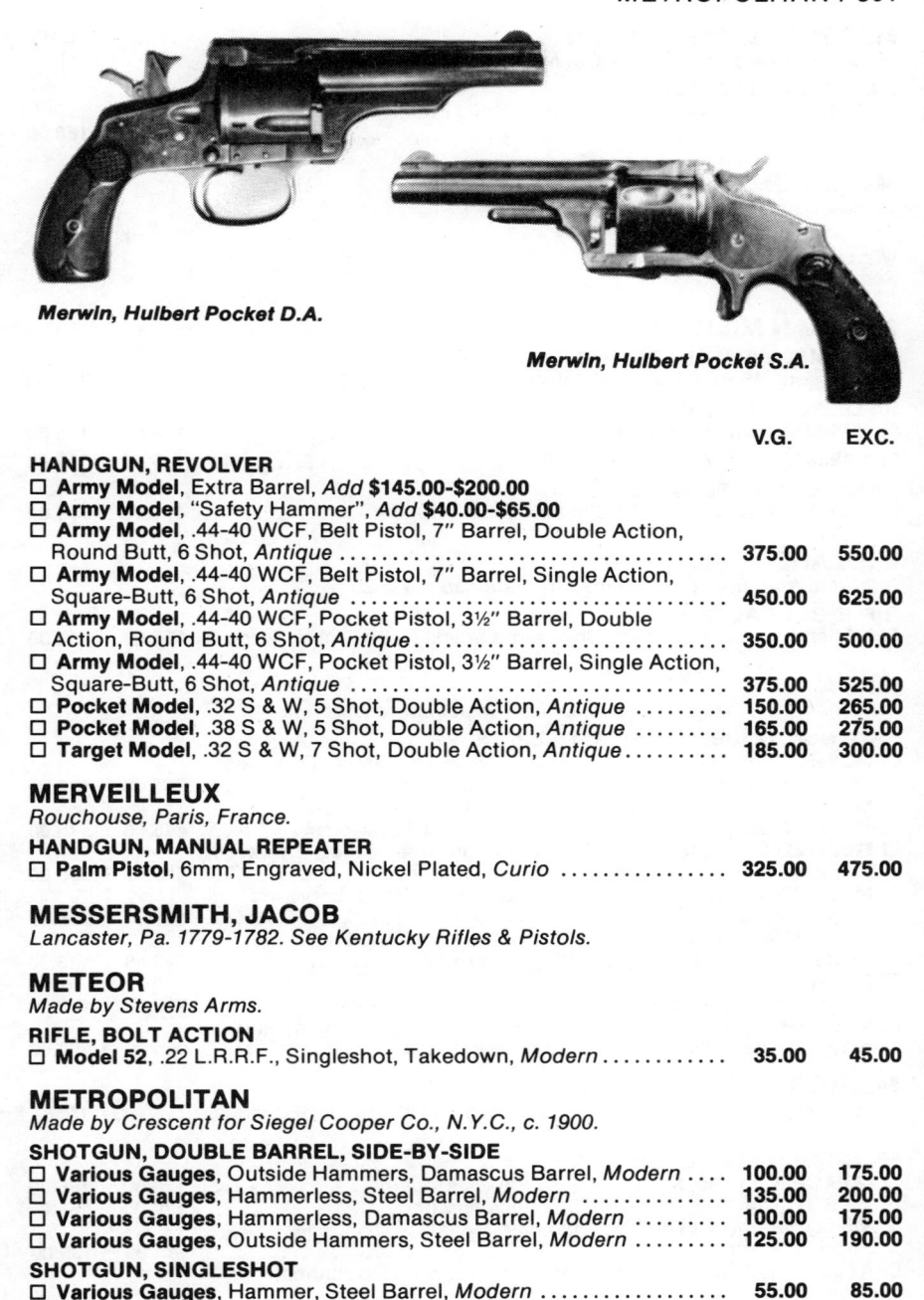

Merwin, Hulbert Pocket D.A.

Merwin, Hulbert Pocket S.A.

	V.G.	EXC.

HANDGUN, REVOLVER
- **Army Model**, Extra Barrel, *Add* **$145.00-$200.00**
- **Army Model**, "Safety Hammer", *Add* **$40.00-$65.00**
- **Army Model**, .44-40 WCF, Belt Pistol, 7" Barrel, Double Action, Round Butt, 6 Shot, *Antique* 375.00 550.00
- **Army Model**, .44-40 WCF, Belt Pistol, 7" Barrel, Single Action, Square-Butt, 6 Shot, *Antique* 450.00 625.00
- **Army Model**, .44-40 WCF, Pocket Pistol, 3½" Barrel, Double Action, Round Butt, 6 Shot, *Antique* 350.00 500.00
- **Army Model**, .44-40 WCF, Pocket Pistol, 3½" Barrel, Single Action, Square-Butt, 6 Shot, *Antique* 375.00 525.00
- **Pocket Model**, .32 S & W, 5 Shot, Double Action, *Antique* 150.00 265.00
- **Pocket Model**, .38 S & W, 5 Shot, Double Action, *Antique* 165.00 275.00
- **Target Model**, .32 S & W, 7 Shot, Double Action, *Antique* 185.00 300.00

MERVEILLEUX
Rouchouse, Paris, France.
HANDGUN, MANUAL REPEATER
- **Palm Pistol**, 6mm, Engraved, Nickel Plated, *Curio* 325.00 475.00

MESSERSMITH, JACOB
Lancaster, Pa. 1779-1782. See Kentucky Rifles & Pistols.

METEOR
Made by Stevens Arms.
RIFLE, BOLT ACTION
- **Model 52**, .22 L.R.R.F., Singleshot, Takedown, *Modern* 35.00 45.00

METROPOLITAN
Made by Crescent for Siegel Cooper Co., N.Y.C., c. 1900.
SHOTGUN, DOUBLE BARREL, SIDE-BY-SIDE
- **Various Gauges**, Outside Hammers, Damascus Barrel, *Modern* 100.00 175.00
- **Various Gauges**, Hammerless, Steel Barrel, *Modern* 135.00 200.00
- **Various Gauges**, Hammerless, Damascus Barrel, *Modern* 100.00 175.00
- **Various Gauges**, Outside Hammers, Steel Barrel, *Modern* 125.00 190.00

SHOTGUN, SINGLESHOT
- **Various Gauges**, Hammer, Steel Barrel, *Modern* 55.00 85.00

METROPOLITAN POLICE
Made by Norwich Falls Pistol Co. Norwich, Conn., c. 1885.

HANDGUN, REVOLVER

	V.G.	EXC.
☐ **.32 Short R.F.**, 5 Shot, Spur Trigger, Solid Frame, Single Action, Antique	90.00	160.00

METZGER, J.
Lancaster, Pa., c. 1728. See Kentucky Rifles.

MEUHIRTER, S.
See Kentucky Rifles.

MEXICAN MILITARY
HANDGUN, SEMI-AUTOMATIC

☐ **Obregon**, .45 ACP, Clip Fed, Military, *Modern*	225.00	350.00

RIFLE, BOLT ACTION

☐ **M1902 Mauser**, 7mm, Military, *Modern*	125.00	175.00
☐ **M1936 Mauser**, 7mm, Military, *Modern*	145.00	195.00

RIFLE, SEMI-AUTOMATIC

☐ **M1908 Mondragon**, 7mm, Clip Fed, S.I.G., *Curio*	475.00	775.00

MIDLAND
Imported from England by Jana International, c. 1973.

RIFLE, BOLT ACTION

☐ **Midland**, Various Calibers, Checkered Stock, Open Sights, *Modern*	175.00	250.00

MIIDA
Tradename of Marubeni America Corp. on Japanese shotguns.

SHOTGUN, DOUBLE BARREL, OVER-UNDER

☐ **Model 2100**, 12 Gauge, Skeet Grade, Checkered Stock, Engraved, Single Selective Trigger, Vent Rib, *Modern*	385.00	495.00
☐ **Model 2200 S**, 12 Gauge, Skeet Grade, Checkered Stock, Engraved, Single Selective Trigger, wide Vent Rib, *Modern*	445.00	575.00
☐ **Model 2200 T**, 12 Gauge, Trap Grade, Checkered Stock, Engraved, Single Selective Trigger, Wide Vent Rib, *Modern*	485.00	635.00
☐ **Model 2300 S**, 12 Gauge, Skeet Grade, Fancy Wood, Engraved, Single Selective Trigger, Vent Rib, *Modern*	485.00	635.00
☐ **Model 2300 T**, 12 Gauge, Trap Grade, Fancy Wood, Engraved, Single Selective Trigger, Vent Rib, *Modern*	520.00	685.00
☐ **Model 612**, 12 Gauge, Field Grade, Checkered Stock, Light Engraving, Single Selective Trigger, Vent Rib, *Modern*	390.00	485.00
☐ **Model Grandee**, 12 Gauge, Fancy Engraving, Fancy Wood, Gold Inlays, Single Selective Trigger, Vent Rib, *Modern*	950.00	1,400.00

MIKROS
Tradename of Manufacture D'Armes Des Pyrenees, Heydaye, France, 1934-1939, 1958 to date.

HANDGUN, SEMI-AUTOMATIC

☐ **.25 ACP**, Clip Fed, Magazine Disconnect, *Modern*	120.00	165.00
☐ **.32 ACP**, Clip Fed, Magazine Disconncet, *Modern*	120.00	165.00
☐ **KE**, .22 Short R.F., Clip Fed, Hammer, Magazine Disconnect, 2" Barrel, *Modern*	85.00	135.00
☐ **KE**, .22 Short R.F., Clip Fed, Hammer, Magazine Disconnect, 4" Barrel, *Modern*	95.00	140.00

	V.G.	EXC.
☐ **KE**, .22 Short R.F., Clip Fed, Hammer, Magazine Disconnect, 2" Barrel, Lightweight, *Modern*	85.00	125.00
☐ **KE**, .22 Short R.F., Clip Fed, Hammer, Magazine Disconnect, 4" Barrel, Lightweight, *Modern*	80.00	120.00
☐ **KN**, .25 ACP, Clip Fed, Hammer, Magazine Disconnect, 2" Barrel, *Modern*	85.00	120.00
☐ **KN**, .25 ACP, Clip Fed, Hammer, Magazine Disconncet, 2" Barrel, Lightweight, *Modern*	85.00	125.00

MILITARY
Retolaza Hermanos, Eibar, Spain, c. 1915.
HANDGUN, SEMI-AUTOMATIC
☐ **Model 1914**, .32 ACP, Clip Fed, *Modern* 90.00   135.00

MILLER, MATHIAS
Easton, Pa. 1771-1788. See Kentucky Rifles.

MILLS, BENJAMIN
Charlottesville, N.C. 1784-1790, 1790-1814 at Harrodsburg, Ky. See Kentucky Rifles, U.S. Military.

MINNEAPOLIS FIREARMS CO.
Minneapolis, Minn., c. 1883.
HANDGUN, PALM PISTOL
☐ **The Protector**, .32 Extra Short R.F., Nickel Plated, *Antique* 350.00   550.00

MIQUELET-LOCK, UNKNOWN MAKER
HANDGUN, MIQUELET-LOCK
☐ **.52 Arabian**, Holster Pistol, Tapered Round Barrel, Low Quality, *Antique* 225.00   325.00
☐ **.55**, Russian Cossack Type, Tapered Round Barrel, Steel Furniture, Silver Furniture, *Antique* 550.00   800.00
☐ **Central Italian 1700's**, Holster Pistol, Brass Furniture, Brass Overlay Stock, Medium Quality, *Antique* 1,500.00   2,350.00
☐ **Pair Late 1700's**, Pocket Pistol, Medium Quality, Brass Furniture, Light Ornamentation, *Antique* 1,000.00   1,600.00
☐ **Pair Spanish Late 1600's**, Belt Hook, Brass Overlay Stock, High Quality, *Antique* 14,000.00   20,000.00
☐ **Pair Cominazzo Early 1700's**, Steel Inlay, Medium Quality, Holster Pistol, *Antique* 2,300.00   3,500.00
☐ **Ripoll Type Late 1600's**, Blunderbuss, Brass Inlay, *Antique* 3,500.00   4,250.00
☐ **Ripoll Type Late 1600's**, Blunderbuss, Silver Inlay, *Antique* 5,500.00   7,000.00
RIFLE, MIQUELET-LOCK
☐ **Mid-Eastern**, Gold Inlays, Cannon Barrel, Front & Rear Bead Sights, Silver Overlay Stock, Silver Furniture, *Antique* 2,250.00   3,350.00
☐ **Mid-Eastern 1700's**, Damascus Barrel, Gold Inlays, Many Semi-Precious Gem Inlays, Silver Furniture, Ornate, *Antique* 4,000.00   6,500.00

MIROKU
Tokyo, Japan.
HANDGUN, REVOLVER
☐ **Model 6**, .38 Spec., Double Action, Swing-Out Cylinder, *Modern* ... 85.00   125.00

304 / MISSISSIPPI VALLEY ARMS COMPANY

Miroku .22 Auto

Miroku Model 3800

Miroku .22 Lever Action

	V.G.	EXC.
RIFLE, LEVER ACTION		
☐ **Center Fire**, Various Calibers, Checkered Stock, Clip Fed, *Modern*	145.00	220.00
☐ **.22 L.R.R.F.**, Tube Feed, Plain, *Modern*	145.00	225.00
RIFLE, SEMI-AUTOMATIC		
☐ **.22 L.R.R.F.**, Takedown, Tube Feed Through Butt, *Modern*	110.00	165.00
RIFLE, SINGLESHOT		
☐ **Model 78**, Various Calibers, Checkered Stock, Falling Block, *Modern*	200.00	300.00
SHOTGUN, DOUBLE BARREL, OVER-UNDER		
☐ **Model 3800**, 12 Ga., Checkered Stock, Vent Rib, *Modern*	300.00	425.00
☐ **Model H.S.W. DeLuxe**, 12 Ga., Checkered Stock, Vent Rib, Engraved, *Modern*	650.00	900.00

MISSISSIPPI VALLEY ARMS CO.
Made by Crescent for Shapleigh Hardware, St. Louis, Mo.

SHOTGUN, DOUBLE BARREL, SIDE-BY-SIDE
☐ **Various Gauges**, Outside Hammers, Damascus Barrel, *Modern* 100.00 175.00
☐ **Various Gauges**, Hammerless, Steel Barrel, *Modern* 135.00 200.00
☐ **Various Gauges**, Hammerless, Damascus Barrel, *Modern* 100.00 175.00
☐ **Various Gauges**, Outside Hammers, Steel Barrel, *Modern* 125.00 190.00

SHOTGUN, SINGLESHOT
☐ **Various Gauges**, Hammer, Steel Barrel, *Modern* 55.00 85.00

MITCHELL ARMS

HANDGUN, DOUBLE BARREL, OVER-UNDER
☐ **Derringer**, .357 Magnum, Spur Trigger, *Modern* 65.00 95.00

HANDGUN, REVOLVER
☐ **Army Target**, Various Calibers, Single Action, Western Style, *Modern* 100.00 150.00

MITRAILLEUSE
Mre. de Armes et Cycles de St. Etienne, St. Etienne, France, c. 1893-1897.

HANDGUN, PALM PISTOL
☐ **Mitrailleuse**, 8mm, Engraved, Nickel Plated, *Antique* 350.00 475.00

MOHAWK
Made by Crescent for Blish, Mize & Stillman, c. 1900.

	V.G.	EXC.
SHOTGUN, DOUBLE BARREL, SIDE-BY-SIDE		
☐ **Various Gauges**, Outside Hammers, Damascus Barrel, *Modern*	100.00	175.00
☐ **Various Gauges**, Hammerless, Steel Barrel, *Modern*	135.00	200.00
☐ **Various Gauges**, Hammerless, Damascus Barrel, *Modern*	100.00	175.00
☐ **Various Gauges**, Outside Hammers, Steel Barrel, *Modern*	125.00	190.00
SHOTGUN, SINGLESHOT		
☐ **Various Gauges**, Hammer, Steel Barrel, *Modern*	55.00	85.00

MOLL, DAVID
Hellerstown, Pa. 1814-1833. See Kentucky Rifles.

MOLL, JOHN
Hellerstown, Pa. 1770-1794. See Kentucky Rifles.

MOLL, JOHN III
Hellerstown, Pa. 1824-1863. See Kentucky Rifles.

MOLL, JOHN, JR.
Hellerstown, Pa. 1794-1824. See Kentucky Rifles.

MOLL, PETER
Hellerstown, Pa. 1804-1833 with Brother John Moll Jr. Made Some of the Finest Kentucky Rifles in Pa. See Kentucky Rifles.

MONARCH
Maker Unknown c. 1880

HANDGUN, REVOLVER
☐ .32 Short R.F., 5 Shot, Spur Trigger, Solid Frame, Single Action, *Antique* ... 90.00   160.00

MONARCH
Made by Hopkins & Allen, c. 1880.

HANDGUN, REVOLVER
☐ **#1**, .22 Short R.F., 7 Shot, Spur Trigger, Solid Frame, Single Action, *Antique* ... 90.00   160.00
☐ **#2**, .32 Short R.F., 5 Shot, Spur Trigger, Solid Frame, Single Action, *Antique* ... 95.00   170.00
☐ **#3**, .38 Short R.F., 5 Shot, Spur Trigger, Solid Frame, Single Action *Antique* ... 95.00   175.00
☐ **#4**, .41 Short R.F., 5 Shot, Spur Trigger, Solid Frame, Single Action, *Antique* ... 110.00   190.00

MONDIAL
Gaspar Arrizaga, Eibar, Spain.

HANDGUN, SEMI-AUTOMATIC
☐ **Model 1**, .25 ACP, Clip Fed, Grip Safety, Magazine Disconnect, *Modern* ... 160.00   235.00
☐ **Model 2**, .25 ACP, Clip Fed, Blue, *Modern* ... 130.00   175.00

MONITOR
Made by Stevens Arms.

306 / MOORE PATENT FIREARMS COMPANY

	V.G.	EXC.

SHOTGUN, DOUBLE BARREL, SIDE-BY-SIDE
☐ **Model 311**, Various Gauges, Hammerless, Steel Barrel, *Modern*.... 95.00   165.00
SHOTGUN, SINGLESHOT
☐ **Model 90**, Various Gauges, Takedown, Automatic Ejector, Plain, Hammer, *Modern* 40.00   60.00

Moore .32 T.F.

Mondial Model 2

MOORE PATENT FIRE ARMS CO.
Brooklyn, N.Y. 1863-1883.
HANDGUN, SINGLESHOT
☐ **.41 Short R.F.**, Derringer, Brass Frame, *Antique* 325.00   425.00
HANDGUN, REVOLVER
☐ **.32 T.F.**, Spur Trigger, Single Action, Brass Frame, No Extractor, *Antique* 175.00   275.00
☐ **.32 T.F.**, Spur Trigger, Single Action, Brass Frame, *Antique* 150.00   250.00
☐ **Williamson's Patent**, .32 T.F., Brass Frame, Hook Extractor, *Antique* 165.00   240.00

MORRONE
Rhode Island Arms Co., Hope Valley, R.I., c. 1951.
SHOTGUN, DOUBLE BARREL, OVER-UNDER
☐ **Model 46**, 12 Ga., Single Trigger, Plain Barrels, Checkered Stock, *Modern* 425.00   650.00
☐ **Model 46**, 20 Ga., Single Trigger, Vent Rib, Checkered Stock, *Modern* 675.00   950.00

MORTIMER, H.W. & SON
London, England 1800-1802.
HANDGUN, FLINTLOCK
☐ **.45**, 4 Barrel Duckfoot, Pocket Pistol, Steel Barrel and Frame, Plain, *Antique* 3,450.00 4,250.00

MOSSBERG, O.F. & SONS
New Haven, Conn. 1919 to date. Fitchburg & Chicopee Falls, Mass. 1892-1919 as Oscar F. Mossberg.
HANDGUN, MANUAL REPEATER
☐ **Brownie**, .22 L.R.R.F., Top Break, Double Action, Rotating Firing Pin, 4 Barrels, 4 Shot, *Modern* 145.00   225.00
HANDGUN, REVOLVER
☐ **Abilene**, .357 Mag., Single Action, Western Style, Adjustable Sights, Various Barrel Lengths, *Modern* 135.00   195.00

Mossberg Brownie

Mossberg 146B

	V.G.	EXC.
☐ **Abilene**, .44 Mag., Single Action, Western Style, Adjustable Sights, Various Barrel Lengths, *Modern*	155.00	220.00
☐ **Abilene Silhouette**, .357 Mag., Single Action, Western Style, Adjustable Sights, 10" Barrel, *Modern*	175.00	245.00

RIFLE, BOLT ACTION

	V.G.	EXC.
☐ **Model 10**, .22 L.R.R.F., Singleshot, Takedown, *Modern*	40.00	55.00
☐ **Model 14**, .22 L.R.R.F., Singleshot, Takedown, Peep Sights, *Modern*	45.00	60.00
☐ **Model 14OB**, .22 L.R.R.F., Clip Fed, Peep Sights, Monte Carlo Stock, *Modern*	45.00	70.00
☐ **Model 14OK**, .22 L.R.R.F., Clip Fed, Open Rear Sight, Monte Carlo Stock, *Modern*	40.00	65.00
☐ **Model 142A**, .22 L.R.R.F., Clip Fed, Peep Sights, *Modern*	50.00	75.00
☐ **Model 142A**, .22 L.R.R.F., Clip Fed, Carbine, Monte Carlo Stock, Peep Sights, *Modern*	45.00	75.00
☐ **Model 142K**, .22 L.R.R.F., Clip Fed, Open Rear Sight, *Modern*	50.00	75.00
☐ **Model 142K**, .22 L.R.R.F., Clip Fed, Carbine, Monte Carlo Stock, *Modern*	40.00	60.00
☐ **Model 144**, .22 L.R.R.F., Clip Fed, Heavy Barrel, Target Stock, Target Sights, *Modern*	75.00	110.00
☐ **Model 144LS**, .22 L.R.R.F., Clip Fed, Heavy Barrel, Lyman Sights, Target Stock, *Modern*	80.00	115.00
☐ **Model 146B**, .22 L.R.R.F., Takedown, Tube Feed, Monte Carlo Stock, Peep Sights, *Modern*	50.00	75.00
☐ **Model 20**, .22 L.R.R.F., Singleshot, Takedown, *Modern*	45.00	60.00
☐ **Model 25**, .22 L.R.R.F., Singleshot, Takedown, Peep Sights, *Modern*	45.00	60.00
☐ **Model 25A**, .22 L.R.R.F., Singleshot, Takedown, Peep Sights, *Modern*	45.00	65.00
☐ **Model 26B**, .22 L.R.R.F., Singleshot, Takedown, Peep Sights, *Modern*	35.00	55.00
☐ **Model 26C**, .22 L.R.R.F., Singleshot, Takedown, Open Rear Sight, *Modern*	35.00	50.00
☐ **Model 30**, .22 L.R.R.F., Singleshot, Takedown, Peep Sights, *Modern*	40.00	60.00
☐ **Model 32OB**, .22 L.R.R.F., Singleshot, Peep Sights, *Modern*	45.00	65.00
☐ **Model 32OK**, .22 L.R.R.F., Singleshot, Open Rear Sight, Monte Carlo Stock, *Modern*	35.00	50.00
☐ **Model 321K**, .22 L.R.R.F., Singleshot, Open Rear Sight, *Modern*	25.00	45.00
☐ **Model 340B**, .22 L.R.R.F., Clip Fed, Peep Sights, *Modern*	50.00	70.00
☐ **Model 340K**, .22 L.R.R.F., Clip Fed, Open Rear Sight, *Modern*	40.00	60.00
☐ **Model 340M**, .22 L.R.R.F., Clip Fed, Full-Stocked, Carbine, *Modern*	55.00	80.00
☐ **Model 341**, .22 L.R.R.F., Clip Fed, Open Rear Sight, *Modern*	45.00	65.00
☐ **Model 342K**, .22 L.R.R.F., Clip Fed, Open Rear Sight, *Modern*	40.00	60.00

MOSSBERG, O.F. AND SONS

	V.G.	EXC.
☐ **Model 346B**, .22 L.R.R.F., Tube Feed, Peep Sights, Monte Carlo Stock, *Modern*	50.00	75.00
☐ **Model 346K**, .22 L.R.R.F., Tube Feed, Monte Carlo Stock, Open Rear Sight, *Modern*	45.00	65.00
☐ **Model 35**, .22 L.R.R.F., Singleshot, Target Stock, Target Sights, *Modern*	75.00	115.00
☐ **Model 35A**, .22 L.R.R.F., Singleshot, Target Stock, Target Sights, *Modern*	65.00	110.00
☐ **Model 35A-LS**, .22 L.R.R.F., Singleshot, Target Stock, Lyman Sights, *Modern*	75.00	115.00
☐ **Model 35B**, .22 L.R.R.F., Singleshot, Target Sights, Heavy Barrel, Target Stock, *Modern*	75.00	110.00
☐ **Model 40**, .22 L.R.R.F., Takedown, Tube Feed, Open Rear Sight, *Modern*	45.00	65.00
☐ **Model 42**, .22 L.R.R.F., Takedown, Clip Fed, Open Rear Sight, *Modern*	45.00	65.00
☐ **Model 42A**, .22 L.R.R.F., Takedown, Clip Fed, Peep Sights, *Modern*	45.00	65.00
☐ **Model 42B**, .22 L.R.R.F., Takedown, 5 Shot Clip, Peep Sights, *Modern*	45.00	65.00
☐ **Model 42C**, .22 L.R.R.F., Takedown, 5 Shot Clip, Open Rear Sight, *Modern*	45.00	65.00
☐ **Model 42M**, .22 L.R.R.F., Takedown, Clip Fed, Full-Stocked, Peep Sights, *Modern*	50.00	75.00
☐ **Model 42MB (British)**, .22 L.R.R.F., Takedown, Clip Fed, Full-Stocked, Peep Sights, *Modern*	70.00	95.00
☐ **Model 43**, .22 L.R.R.F., Clip Fed, Heavy Barrel, Target Sights, Target Stock, *Modern*	70.00	100.00
☐ **Model 44**, .22 L.R.R.F., Takedown, Tube Feed, Open Rear Sight, *Modern*	50.00	70.00
☐ **Model 44 US**, .22 L.R.R.F., Clip Fed, Target Sights, Target Stock, Heavy Barrel, *Modern*	85.00	135.00
☐ **Model 448**, .22 L.R.R.F., Target Stock, Clip Fed, Target Sights, *Modern*	75.00	115.00
☐ **Model 45**, .22 L.R.R.F., Takedown, Tube Feed, Peep Sights, *Modern*	45.00	65.00
☐ **Model 45A**, .22 L.R.R.F., Takedown, Tube Feed, Peep Sights, *Modern*	50.00	65.00
☐ **Model 45AC**, .22 L.R.R.F., Takedown, Tube Feed, Open Rear Sight, *Modern*	50.00	65.00
☐ **Model 45B**, .22 L.R.R.F., Takedown, Tube Feed, Open Rear Sight, *Modern*	50.00	70.00
☐ **Model 45B**, .22 L.R.R.F., Takedown, Tube Feed, Open Rear Sight, *Modern*	55.00	75.00
☐ **Model 45C**, .22 L.R.R.F., Takedown, Tube Feed, no Sights, *Modern*	50.00	70.00
☐ **Model 46**, .22 L.R.R.F., Takedown, Tube Feed, Peep Sights, *Modern*	60.00	85.00
☐ **Model 46A-LS**, .22 L.R.R.F., Takedown, Tube Feed, Lyman Sights, *Modern*	60.00	95.00
☐ **Model 46AC**, .22 L.R.R.F., Takedown, Tube Feed, Open Rear Sight, *Modern*	50.00	70.00
☐ **Model 46B**, .22 L.R.R.F., Takedown, Tube Feed, Peep Sights, *Modern*	50.00	70.00
☐ **Model 46M**, .22 L.R.R.F., Takedown, Tube Feed, Full-Stocked, Peep Sights, *Modern*	55.00	95.00
☐ **Model 46T**, .22 L.R.R.F., Takedown, Tube Feed, Heavy Barrel, Target Stock, Peep Sights, *Modern*	60.00	95.00

	V.G.	EXC.
☐ **Model 64OK**, .22 WMR, 5 Shot Clip, Monte Carlo Stock, Open Rear Sight, *Modern*	60.00	80.00
☐ **Model 800**, Various Calibers, Open Rear Sight, Monte Carlo Stock, *Modern*	130.00	175.00
☐ **Model 800D**, Various Calibers, Monte Carlo Stock, Cheekpiece, Checkered Stock, Open Rear Sight, *Modern*	150.00	190.00
☐ **Model 800M**, Various Calibers, Open Rear Sight, Full-Stocked, *Modern*	145.00	190.00
☐ **Model 800SM**, Various Calibers, Scope Mounted, Monte Carlo Stock, *Modern*	160.00	215.00
☐ **Model 800V**, Various Calibers, no Sights, Monte Carlo Stock, Heavy Barrel, *Modern*	150.00	185.00
☐ **Model 810**, Various Calibers, Magnum Action, Open Rear Sight, Monte Carlo Stock, *Modern*	155.00	195.00
☐ **Model 810**, Various Calibers, Open Rear Sight, Long Action, Monte Carlo Stock, *Modern*	155.00	195.00
☐ **Model B**, .22 L.R.R.F., Singleshot, Takedown, *Modern*	25.00	45.00
☐ **Model L42A**, .22 L.R.R.F., Takedown, Clip Fed, Peep Sights, Left-Hand, *Modern*	50.00	80.00
☐ **Model L43**, .22 L.R.R.F., Clip Fed, Heavy Barrel, Target Sights, Target Stock, Left-Hand, *Modern*	85.00	120.00
☐ **Model L45A**, .22 L.R.R.F., Takedown, Tube Feed, Peep Sights, *Modern*	55.00	80.00
☐ **Model L46A-LS**, .22 L.R.R.F., Takedown, Tube Feed, Lyman Sights, Left-Hand, *Modern*	65.00	115.00
☐ **Model R**, .22 L.R.R.F., Takedown, Tube Feed, Open Rear Sight, *Modern*	35.00	55.00

RIFLE, LEVER ACTION

	V.G.	EXC.
☐ **Model 400**, .22 L.R.R.F., Tube Feed, Open Rear Sight, *Modern*	50.00	75.00
☐ **Model 402**, .22 L.R.R.F., Tube Feed, Open Rear Sight, Monte Carlo Stock, *Modern*	55.00	80.00
☐ **Model 472C**, Various Calibers, Straight Grip, Tube Feed, Open Rear Sight, Carbine, *Modern*	90.00	130.00
☐ **Model 472P**, Various Calibers, Pistol-Grip Stock, Tube Feed, Open Rear Sight, Carbine, *Modern*	85.00	125.00
☐ **RM-7**, Various Calibers, Open Sights, *Modern*	140.00	180.00

RIFLE, SEMI-AUTOMATIC

	V.G.	EXC.
☐ **Model 151K**, .22 L.R.R.F., Takedown, Tube Feed, Open Rear Sight, *Modern*	55.00	80.00
☐ **Model 151M**, .22 L.R.R.F., Takedown, Tube Feed, Peep Sights, Full-Stocked, *Modern*	60.00	80.00
☐ **Model 152**, .22 L.R.R.F., Clip Fed, Monte Carlo Stock, Peep Sights, Carbine, *Modern*	60.00	80.00
☐ **Model 152K**, .22 L.R.R.F., Clip Fed, Monte Carlo Stock, Open Rear Sight, Carbine, *Modern*	55.00	85.00
☐ **Model 350K**, .22 L.R.R.F., Clip Fed, Monte Carlo Stock, Open Rear Sight, *Modern*	50.00	75.00
☐ **Model 351C**, .22 L.R.R.F., Tube Feed, Monte Carlo Stock, Open Rear Sight, Carbine, *Modern*	50.00	75.00
☐ **Model 351K**, .22 L.R.R.F., Tube Feed, Monte Carlo Stock, Open Rear Sight, *Modern*	45.00	70.00
☐ **Model 352K**, .22 L.R.R.F., Clip Fed, Monte Carlo Stock, Open Rear Sight, Carbine, *Modern*	50.00	75.00
☐ **Model 450**, .22 L.R.R.F., Tube Feed, Monte Carlo Stock, Checkered Stock, Open Rear Sight, *Modern*	50.00	80.00

310 / MOSSBERG, O.F. AND SONS

	V.G.	EXC.
☐ **Model 432**, .22 L.R.R.F., Tube Feed, Western Style, Carbine, Modern	50.00	75.00
☐ **Model 50**, .22 L.R.R.F., Takedown, Tube Feed, Open Rear Sight, Modern	50.00	75.00
☐ **Model 51**, .22 L.R.R.F., Takedown, Tube Feed, Peep Sight, Modern	60.00	80.00
☐ **Model 51M**, .22 L.R.R.F., Takedown, Tube Feed, Peep Sight, Full-Stocked, Modern	60.00	80.00

RIFLE, SINGLESHOT
☐ **Model L**, .22 L.R.R.F., Lever Action, Falling Block, Takedown, Modern	155.00	215.00

RIFLE, SLIDE ACTION
☐ **Model K**, .22 L.R.R.F., Takedown, Tube Feed, Hammerless, Modern	55.00	80.00
☐ **Model M**, .22 L.R.R.F., Takedown, Tube Feed, Hammerless, Octagon Barrel, Modern	70.00	100.00

SHOTGUN, BOLT ACTION
☐ **Model 173**, .410 Ga., Takedown, Singleshot, Modern	35.00	55.00
☐ **Model 173Y**, .410 Ga., Clip Fed, Singleshot, Modern	35.00	55.00
☐ **Model 183D**, .410 Ga., Takedown, 3 Shot, Modern	40.00	60.00
☐ **Model 183K**, .410 Ga., Takedown, Adjustable Choke, Clip Fed, Modern	40.00	60.00
☐ **Model 183T**, .410 Ga., Clip Fed, Modern	40.00	65.00
☐ **Model 185D**, 20 Ga., Takedown, 3 Shot, Modern	40.00	60.00
☐ **Model 185K**, 20 Ga., Takedown, 3 Shot, Adjustable Choke, Modern	40.00	60.00
☐ **Model 190D**, 16 Ga., Takedown, Clip Fed, Modern	40.00	60.00
☐ **Model 190K**, 16 Ga., Takedown, Adjustable Choke, Clip Fed, Modern	40.00	60.00
☐ **Model 195D**, 12 Ga., Takedown, Clip Fed, Modern	45.00	65.00
☐ **Model 195K**, 12 Ga., Takedown, Adjustable Choke, Clip Fed, Modern	45.00	65.00
☐ **Model 385K**, 20 Ga., Clip Fed, Adjustable Choke, Modern	50.00	70.00
☐ **Model 385T**, 20 Ga., Clip Fed, Modern	45.00	65.00
☐ **Model 390K**, 16 Ga., Clip Fed, Adjustable Choke, Modern	50.00	70.00
☐ **Model 390T**, 16 Ga., Clip Fed, Modern	45.00	65.00
☐ **Model 395K**, 12 Ga. Mag. 3", Clip Fed, Adjustable Choke, Modern	50.00	70.00
☐ **Model 395S**, 12 Ga. Mag. 3", Clip Fed, Open Rear Sight, Modern	50.00	70.00
☐ **Model 395T**, 12 Ga., Clip Fed, Modern	45.00	65.00
☐ **Model 73**, .410 Ga., Takedown, Singleshot, Modern	35.00	50.00
☐ **Model 83D**, .410 Ga., Takedown, 3 Shot, Modern	40.00	60.00
☐ **Model 85D**, 20 Ga., Takedown, 3 Shot, Adjustable Choke, Modern	40.00	60.00

SHOTGUN, SLIDE ACTION
☐ **Cruiser**, 12 Ga., One-Hand Grip, Nickel Plated, Modern	140.00	190.00
☐ **Model 200D**, 12 Ga., Clip Fed, Adjustable Choke, Modern	55.00	85.00
☐ **Model 200K**, 12 Ga., Clip Fed, Adjustable Choke, Modern	60.00	90.00
☐ **Model 500 Super**, Checkered Stock, Vent Rib, Modern	125.00	175.00
☐ **Model 500A**, 12 Ga. Mag. 3", Field Grade, Modern	110.00	150.00
☐ **Model 500AA**, 12 Ga. Mag. 3", Trap Grade, Modern	140.00	190.00
☐ **Model 500AK**, Field Grade, Adjustable Choke, Modern	115.00	160.00
☐ **Model 500AKR**, Field Grade, Adjustable Choke, Vent Rib, Modern	125.00	170.00
☐ **Model 500AM**, Field Grade, Magnum, Modern	110.00	150.00
☐ **Model 500AMR**, Field Grade, Magnum, Vent Rib, Modern	120.00	160.00
☐ **Model 500AR**, Field Grade, Vent Rib, Modern	120.00	150.00
☐ **Model 500AS**, Field Grade, Open Rear Sight, Modern	125.00	160.00
☐ **Model 500ATR**, Trap Grade, Vent Rib, Modern	130.00	180.00
☐ **Model 500AHTD**, Trap Grade, High Vent Rib, with Choke Tubes, Modern	225.00	300.00
☐ **Model 500B**, 16 Ga., Field Grade, Modern	100.00	145.00

	V.G.	EXC.
☐ **Model 500BK**, 16 Ga., Adjustable Choke, *Modern*	100.00	140.00
☐ **Model 500BS**, 16 Ga., Open Rear Sight, *Modern*	110.00	150.00
☐ **Model 500C**, 20 Ga., Field Grade, *Modern*	100.00	145.00
☐ **Model 500CK**, 20 Ga., Field Grade, Adjustable Choke, *Modern*	110.00	150.00
☐ **Model 500CKR**, 20 Ga., Field Grade, Vent Rib, Adjustable Choke, *Modern*	110.00	160.00
☐ **Model 500CR**, 20 Ga., Field Grade, Vent Rib, *Modern*	110.00	150.00
☐ **Model 500CS**, 20 Ga., Field Grade, Open Rear Sight, *Modern*	110.00	150.00
☐ **Model 500E**, .410 Ga., Field Grade, *Modern*	100.00	140.00
☐ **Model 500EK**, .410 Ga., Field Grade, Adjustable Choke, *Modern*	110.00	145.00
☐ **Model 500EKR**, .410 Ga., Field Grade, Vent Rib, Adjustable Choke, *Modern*	115.00	160.00
☐ **Model 500ER**, .410 Ga., Field Grade, Vent Rib, *Modern*	110.00	150.00

MOSTER, GEO.
Lancaster, Pa. 1771-1779. See Kentucky Rifles and Pistols.

M.S.
Modesto Santos, Eibar, Spain, c. 1920.

HANDGUN, SEMI-AUTOMATIC
☐ **Model 1920**, .25 ACP, Clip Fed, Blue, *Curio*	85.00	130.00
☐ **Action**, .32 ACP, Clip Fed, Blue, *Curio*	95.00	135.00

MT. VERNON ARMS
Belgium, c. 1900.

SHOTGUN, DOUBLE BARREL, SIDE-BY-SIDE
☐ **Various Gauges**, Outside Hammers, Damascus Barrel, *Modern*	100.00	175.00
☐ **Various Gauges**, Hammerless, Steel Barrel, *Modern*	135.00	200.00
☐ **Various Gauges**, Hammerless, Damascus Barrel, *Modern*	100.00	175.00
☐ **Various Gauges**, Outside Hammers, Steel Barrel, *Modern*	125.00	190.00

SHOTGUN, SINGLESHOT
☐ **Various Gauges**, Hammer, Steel Barrel, *Modern*	55.00	85.00

MOUNTAIN EAGLE
Made by Hopkins & Allen, c. 1880.

HANDGUN, REVOLVER
☐ **.32 Short R.F.**, 5 Shot, Spur Trigger, Solid Frame, Single Action, *Antique*	90.00	160.00

MUGICA
Jose Mugica, Eibar, Spain, tradename on Llama pistols. See Llama for equivilent models.

MUSGRAVE
South Africa.

RIFLE, BOLT ACTION
☐ **Mk. III**, Various Calibers, Checkered Stock, *Modern*	165.00	225.00
☐ **Valiant NR6**, Various Calibers, Checkered Stock, *Modern*	160.00	200.00
☐ **Premier NR5**, Various Calibers, Checkered Stock, *Modern*	220.00	275.00

MUSKETEER
Tradename used by Firearms International, Washington, D.C., c. 1968.

312 / MUTTI, GEROLIMO

	V.G.	EXC.

RIFLE, BOLT ACTION
- ☐ **Carbine**, Various Calibers, Monte Carlo Stock, Checkered Stock, Sling Swivels, *Modern* 165.00   225.00
- ☐ **Deluxe**, Various Calibers, Monte Carlo Stock, Checkered Stock, Sling Swivels, *Modern* 190.00   250.00
- ☐ **Sporter**, Various Calibers, Monte Carlo Stock, Checkered Stock, Sling Swivels, *Modern* 175.00   235.00
- ☐ **Mannlicher**, Various Calibers, Full Stock, *Modern* 160.00   240.00

MUTTI, GEROLIMO
Brescia, c. 1680.

HANDGUN, SNAPHAUNCE
- ☐ **Pair**, Belt Pistol, Brass Mounts, Engraved, Ornate, *Antique* 8,500.00   15,000.00

MUTTI, GIESU
Brescia, c. 1790.

HANDGUN, SNAPHAUNCE
- ☐ **Pair**, Engraved, Belt Hook, Medium Ornamentation, *Antique* 6,750.00   9,750.00

NAPOLEON
Made by Thomas Ryan, Jr., Pistol Mfg. Co., c. 1870-1876.

HANDGUN, REVOLVER
- ☐ **.22 Short R.F.**, 7 Shot, Spur Trigger, Solid Frame, Single Action, *Antique* 90.00   160.00
- ☐ **.32 Short R.F.**, 5 Shot, Spur Trigger, Solid Frame, Single Action, *Antique* 95.00   170.00

NATIONAL
Made by Norwich Falls Pistol Co., c. 1880.

HANDGUN, REVOLVER
- ☐ **.32 Short R.F.**, 5 Shot, Spur Trigger, Solid Frame, Single Action, *Antique* 90.00   160.00
- ☐ **.38 Short R.F.**, 5 Shot, Spur Trigger, Solid Frame, Single Action, *Antique* 95.00   170.00

HANDGUN, SINGLESHOT
- ☐ **.41 Short R.F.**, Derringer, all Metal, Light Engraving, *Antique* 185.00   250.00

NATIONAL ARMS CO.
Made by Crescent, c. 1900.

SHOTGUN, DOUBLE BARREL, SIDE-BY-SIDE
- ☐ **Various Gauges**, Outside Hammers, Damascus Barrel, *Modern* 100.00   175.00
- ☐ **Various Gauges**, Hammerless, Steel Barrel, *Modern* 135.00   200.00
- ☐ **Various Gauges**, Hammerless, Damascus Barrel, *Modern* 100.00   175.00
- ☐ **Various Gauges**, Outside Hammers, Steel Barrel, *Modern* 125.00   190.00

SHOTGUN, SINGLESHOT
- ☐ **Various Gauges**, Hammer, Steel Barrel, *Modern* 55.00   85.00

NATIONAL ORDNANCE
South El Monte, Calif.

RIFLE, BOLT ACTION
- ☐ **1903A3**, .30-06 Springfield, Reweld, Military, *Modern* 85.00   125.00

	V.G.	EXC.
RIFLE, SEMI-AUTOMATIC		
☐ **Garand**, .30-06 Springfield, Reweld, Military, *Modern*	275.00	425.00
☐ **M-1 Carbine**, .30 Carbine, Clip Fed, Reweld, *Modern*	110.00	155.00
☐ **M-1 Carbine**, .30 Carbine, Clip Fed, Folding Stock, Reweld, *Modern*	125.00	165.00
☐ **Tanker Garand**, .308 Win., Reweld, Military, *Modern*	275.00	425.00

NAVY ARMS
Ridgefield, N.J.

- ☐ **Presentation Case Only**, *Add* $15.00-$25.00
- ☐ **A Engraving Pistol**, *Add* $70.00-$90.00
- ☐ **B Engraving Pistol**, *Add* $90.00-$130.00
- ☐ **C Engraving Pistol**, *Add* $185.00-$250.00
- ☐ **A Engraving Rifle**, *Add* $90.00-$135.00
- ☐ **B Engraving Rifle**, *Add* $145.00-$195.00
- ☐ **C Engraving Rifle**, *Add* $350.00-$475.00
- ☐ **Tiffany Grips Only**, *Add* $95.00-$150.00
- ☐ **Silver Plating**, *Add* $65.00-$95.00

HANDGUN, FLINTLOCK

	V.G.	EXC.
☐ .44 "**Kentucky**", Belt Pistol, Reproduction, Brass Furniture, *Antique*	60.00	80.00
☐ .44 "**Kentucky**", Belt Pistol, Reproduction, Brass Furniture, Brass Barrel, *Antique*	60.00	80.00
☐ .577 **Scotch Black Watch**, Military, Reproduction, Belt Pistol, all Metal, *Antique*	60.00	90.00
☐ .69 **M1763 Charleville**, Military, Reproduction, Belt Pistol, *Antique*	165.00	225.00
☐ .69 **M1763 Charleville**, Military, Reproduction, Belt Pistol, *Antique*	60.00	90.00
☐ .69 **M1777 Charleville**, Military, Reproduction, Belt Pistol, *Antique*	60.00	90.00
☐ .69 **Tower**, Military, Reproduction, Belt Pistol, *Antique*	30.00	40.00

HANDGUN, PERCUSSION

	V.G.	EXC.
☐ .36 **M1851 New Navy**, Revolver, Reproduction, Brass Grip Frame, *Antique*	65.00	85.00
☐ .36 **M1851 New Navy**, Revolver, Reproduction, Silver-Plated Grip Frame, *Antique*	65.00	85.00
☐ .36 **M1853**, Revolver, Reproduction, Pocket Pistol, 4½" Barrel, *Antique*	65.00	85.00
☐ .36 **M1853**, Revolver, Reproduction, Pocket Pistol, 5½" Barrel, *Antique*	65.00	85.00
☐ .36 **M1853**, Revolver, Reproduction, Pocket Pistol, 6½" Barrel, *Antique*	65.00	85.00
☐ .36 **M1860 Reb**, Revolver, Reproduction, Brass Frame, *Antique*	40.00	55.00
☐ .36 **M1860 Sheriff**, Revolver, Reproduction, Brass Frame, *Antique*	40.00	55.00
☐ .36 **M1861**, Revolver, Reproduction, Sheriff's Model, with Short Barrel, *Antique*	60.00	85.00
☐ .36 **M1861 Navy**, Revolver, Reproduction, Fluted Cylinder, *Antique*	60.00	85.00
☐ .36 **M1861 Navy**, Revolver, Reproduction, Engraved Cylinder, *Antique*	55.00	80.00
☐ .36 **M1862 Police**, Revolver, Reproduction, 5 Shot, Brass Grip Frame, Cased with Accessories, *Antique*	85.00	120.00
☐ .36 **M1862 Police**, Revolver, Reproduction, 5 Shot, Brass Grip Frame, 4½" Barrel, *Antique*	60.00	80.00
☐ .36 **M1862 Police**, Revolver, Reproduction, 5 Shot, Brass Grip Frame, 5½" Barrel, *Antique*	60.00	80.00
☐ .36 **M1862 Police**, Revolver, Reproduction, 5 Shot, Brass Grip Frame, 6½" Barrel, *Antique*	60.00	80.00
☐ .36 **M1862 Police**, Revolver, Reproduction, Fancy Engraving, Silver Plated, Gold Plated, *Antique*	350.00	450.00

	V.G.	EXC.
☐ **.36 M1863**, Revolver, Reproduction, Sheriff's Model, with Short Barrel, *Antique*	65.00	85.00
☐ **.36 Remington**, Revolver, Reproduction, Target Pistol, Adjustable Sights, *Antique*	75.00	110.00
☐ **.36 Remington**, Revolver, Reproduction, Solid Frame, *Antique*	65.00	85.00
☐ **.36 Spiller & Burr**, Revolver, Reproduction, Solid Frame, *Antique*	50.00	65.00
☐ **.44 "Kentucky"**, Belt Pistol, Reproduction, Brass Furniture, *Antique*	60.00	80.00
☐ **.44 "Kentucky"**, Belt Pistol, Reproduction, Brass Furniture, Brass Barrel, *Antique*	70.00	95.00
☐ **.44 First Model Dragoon**, Revolver, Reproduction, Brass Grip Frame, *Antique*	70.00	100.00
☐ **.44 M1847 Walker**, Revolver, Reproduction, Brass Grip Frame, *Antique*	80.00	110.00
☐ **.44 M1847 Walker**, Revolver, Reproduction, Brass Grip Frame, Engraved, Gold Inlays, *Antique*	175.00	225.00
☐ **.44 M1860**, Revolver, Reproduction, Sheriff's Model, with Short Barrel, *Antique*	65.00	85.00
☐ **.44 M1860 Army**, Revolver, Reproduction, Fluted Cylinder, *Antique*	65.00	85.00
☐ **.44 M1860 Army**, Revolver, Reproduction, Engraved Cylinder, *Antique*	65.00	85.00
☐ **.44 M1860 Reb**, Revolver, Reproduction, Brass Frame, *Antique*	40.00	55.00
☐ **.44 M1860 Reb**, Revolver, Reproduction, Shoulder Stock Only	30.00	40.00
☐ **.44 M1860 Sheriff**, Revolver, Reproduction, Brass Frame, *Antique*	40.00	55.00
☐ **.44 Remington**, Revolver, Reproduction, Target Pistol, Adjustable Sights, *Antique*	75.00	110.00
☐ **.44 Remington**, Revolver, Reproduction, Solid Frame, *Antique*	65.00	85.00
☐ **.44 Remington**, Revolver, Reproduction, Stainless Steel, *Antique*	95.00	135.00
☐ **.44 Remington Army**, Revolver, Reproduction, Nickel Plated, *Antique*	75.00	110.00
☐ **.44 Second Model**, Dragoon, Revolver, Reproduction, Brass Grip Frame, *Antique*	75.00	100.00
☐ **.44 Third Model Dragoon**, Revolver, Reproduction, Buntline, with Detachable Shoulder Stock, *Antique*	125.00	160.00
☐ **.44 Third Model Dragoon**, Revolver, Reproduction, Brass Grip Frame, *Antique*	80.00	110.00
☐ **.44 Third Model Dragoon**, Revolver, Reproduction, Brass Grip Frame, with Detachable Shoulder Stock, *Antique*	120.00	155.00
☐ **.58 M1806**, Harper's Ferry, Reproduction, Brass Furniture, Military, Belt Pistol, *Antique*	60.00	80.00
☐ **.58 M1855**, Harper's Ferry, Reproduction, Holster Pistol, Military, with Detachable Shoulder Stock, *Antique*	85.00	115.00
☐ **.58 M1855**, Harper's Ferry, Shoulder Stock Only	25.00	35.00

HANDGUN, REVOLVER

	V.G.	EXC.
☐ **Frontier**, Various Calibers, Color Case Hardened Frame, Single Action, Western Style, *Modern*	95.00	140.00
☐ **Frontier Target**, .357 Magnum, Color Case Hardened Frame, Single Action, Western Style, Adjustable Sights, with Detachable Shoulder Stock, *Modern*	145.00	195.00
☐ **Frontier Target**, .45 Colt, Color Case Hardened Frame, Single Action, Western Style, Adjustable Sights, with Detachable Shoulder Stock, *Modern*	150.00	190.00
☐ **Frontier Target**, Various Calibers, Color Case Hardened Frame, Single Action, Western Style, Adjustable Sights, *Modern*	95.00	145.00
☐ **M1875 Remington**, .357 Magnum, Color Case Hardened Frame, Western Style, Single Action, *Modern*	115.00	150.00

NAVY ARMS / 315

	V.G.	EXC.
☐ **M1875 Remington**, .357 Magnum, Nickel Plated, Western Style, Single Action, *Modern*	125.00	170.00
☐ **M1875 Remington**, .44-40 WCF, Color Case Hardened Frame, Western Style, Single Action, *Modern*	100.00	145.00
☐ **M1875 Remington**, .44-40 WCF, Nickel Plated, Western Style, Single Action, *Modern*	125.00	155.00
☐ **M1875 Remington**, .45 Colt, Color Case Hardened Frame, Western Style, Single Action, *Modern*	115.00	155.00
☐ **M1875 Remington**, .45 Colt, Stainless Steel, Western Style, Single Action, *Modern*	125.00	155.00
☐ **M1875 Remington**, .45 Colt, Nickel Plated, Western Style, Single Action, *Modern*	130.00	175.00

HANDGUN, SINGLESHOT

	V.G.	EXC.
☐ **Rolling Block**, .22 Hornet, Half-Octagon Barrel, Color Case Hardened Frame, Adjustable Sights, *Modern*	80.00	125.00
☐ **Rolling Block**, .22 L.R.R.F., Half-Octagon Barrel, Color Case Hardened Frame, Adjustable Sights, *Modern*	65.00	95.00
☐ **Rolling Block**, .357 Magnum, Half-Octagon Barrel, Color Case Hardened Frame, Adjustable Sights, *Modern*	80.00	120.00

RIFLE, BOLT ACTION

	V.G.	EXC.
☐ **Mauser '98**, .45-70 Government, Checkered Stock, *Modern*	90.00	130.00
☐ **Mauser '98**, .45-70 Government, Carbine, Checkered Stock, *Modern*	90.00	130.00

RIFLE, FLINTLOCK

	V.G.	EXC.
☐ **.45 "Kentucky"**, Long Rifle, Reproduction, Brass Furniture, *Antique*	115.00	155.00
☐ **.45 "Kentucky"**, Carbine, Reproduction, Brass Furniture, *Antique*	115.00	155.00
☐ **.58 M1803**, Harper's Ferry, Reproduction, Brass Furniture, Military, *Antique*	120.00	165.00
☐ **.69 M1795 Springfield**, Modern, Reproduction, Musket, *Antique*	165.00	225.00
☐ **.69 M1809 Springfield**, Modern, Reproduction, Musket, *Antique*	165.00	225.00
☐ **.75 Brown Bess**, Modern, Reproduction, Musket, *Antique*	185.00	240.00
☐ **.75 Brown Bess**, Modern, Reproduction, Carbine, *Antique*	185.00	240.00
☐ **.75 Brown Bess (Jap)**, Modern, Reproduction, Musket, *Antique*	150.00	190.00

RIFLE, LEVER ACTION

	V.G.	EXC.
☐ **M1873 1 of 1000**, .44-40 WCF, Blue Tube, Octagon Barrel, Steel Buttplate, Engraved, *Modern*	500.00	700.00
☐ **M1873-"101"**, .22 L.R.R.F., Color Case Hardened Frame, Tube Feed, Round Barrel, Steel Buttplate, Carbine, *Modern*	145.00	190.00
☐ **M1873-"101"**, .44-40 WCF, Color Case Hardened Frame, Tube Feed, Octagon Barrel, Steel Buttplate, *Modern*	165.00	215.00
☐ **M1873-"101"**, .44-40 WCF, Color Case Hardened Frame, Tube Feed, Round Barrel, Steel Buttplate, Carbine, *Modern*	145.00	190.00
☐ **M1873-"101"**, Trapper, .22 L.R.R.F., Color Case Hardened Frame, Tube Feed, Round Barrel, Steel Buttplate, *Modern*	145.00	190.00
☐ **M1873-"101"**, Trapper, .44-40 WCF, Color Case Hardened Frame, Tube Feed, Round Barrel, Steel Buttplate, *Modern*	145.00	190.00
☐ **Yellowboy**, .22 L.R.R.F., Brass Frame, Tube Feed, Round Barrel, Brass Buttplate, Saddle-Ring Carbine, *Modern*	130.00	180.00
☐ **Yellowboy**, .38 Special, Brass Frame, Tube Feed, Octagon Barrel, Brass Buttplate, *Modern*	145.00	190.00
☐ **Yellowboy**, .38 Special, Brass Frame, Tube Feed, Round Barrel, Brass Buttplate, Saddle-Ring Carbine, *Modern*	135.00	180.00
☐ **Yellowboy**, .44-40 WCF, Brass Frame, Tube Feed, Octagon Barrel, Brass Buttplate, *Modern*	145.00	190.00
☐ **Yellowboy**, .44-40 WCF, Brass Frame, Tube Feed, Round Barrel, Brass Buttplate, Saddle-Ring Carbine, *Modern*	135.00	180.00

316 / NAVY ARMS

	V.G.	EXC.
☐ **Yellowboy Trapper**, .22 L.R.R.F., Brass Frame, Tube Feed, Round Barrel, Brass Buttplate, *Modern*	135.00	180.00
☐ **Yellowboy Trapper**, .38 Special, Brass Frame, Tube Feed, Round Barrel, Brass Buttplate, *Modern*	135.00	180.00
☐ **Yellowboy Trapper**, .44-40 WCF, Brass Frame, Tube Feed, Round Barrel, Brass Buttplate, *Modern*	135.00	180.00

RIFLE, PERCUSSION

	V.G.	EXC.
☐ **.44 Remington**, Revolver, Reproduction, Carbine, Brass Furniture, *Antique*	100.00	135.00
☐ **.45 "Kentucky"**, Long Rifle, Reproduction, Brass Furniture, *Antique*	110.00	150.00
☐ **.45 "Kentucky"**, Carbine, Reproduction, Brass Furniture, *Antique*	110.00	145.00
☐ **.45 "Kentucky"**, Carbine, Reproduction, Brass Furniture, *Antique*	110.00	150.00
☐ **.45 Hawken Hurricane**, Octagon Barrel, Brass Furniture, Reproduction, *Antique*	130.00	165.00
☐ **.45 Morse**, Octagon Barrel, Brass Frame, Reproduction, *Antique*	80.00	110.00
☐ **.50 Hawken Hurricane**, Octagon Barrel, Brass Furniture, Reproduction, *Antique*	135.00	170.00
☐ **.50 Morse**, Octagon Barrel, Brass Frame, Reproduction, *Antique*	80.00	115.00
☐ **.54 Gallagher**, Carbine, Reproduction, Military, Steel Furniture, *Antique*	140.00	185.00
☐ **.577 M1853 3-Band**, Military, Reproduction, Musket, (Parker-Hale) *Antique*	185.00	240.00
☐ **.577 M1858 2-Band**, Military, Reproduction, Rifled, (Parker-Hale) *Antique*	135.00	180.00
☐ **.577 M1861**, Military, Reproduction, Musketoon, (Parker-Hale) *Antique*	135.00	180.00
☐ **.58 J.P. Murray Artillery Carbine**, Reproduction, Brass Furniture, Military, *Antique*	95.00	135.00
☐ **.58 Buffalo Hunter**, Round Barrel, Brass Furniture, Reproduction, *Antique*	110.00	150.00
☐ **.58 Hawken Hunter**, Octagon Barrel, Brass Furniture, Reproduction, *Antique*	130.00	170.00
☐ **.58 M1841 Mississippi Rifle**, Reproduction, Brass Furniture, Military, *Antique*	95.00	145.00
☐ **.58 M1863 Springfield**, Military, Reproduction, Rifled, Musket, *Antique*	125.00	165.00
☐ **.58 M1864 Springfield**, Military, Reproduction, Rifled, Musket, *Antique*	140.00	170.00
☐ **.58 Morse**, Octagon Barrel, Brass Frame, Reproduction, *Antique*	85.00	120.00
☐ **.58 Zouave**, Military, Reproduction, *Antique*	100.00	140.00
☐ **.58 Zouave 1864**, Military, Reproduction, Carbine, Brass Furniture, *Antique*	100.00	140.00

RIFLE, REVOLVER

	V.G.	EXC.
☐ **M1875 Remington**, .357 Magnum, Color Case Hardened Frame, Carbine, Single Action, Brass Furniture, *Modern*	135.00	175.00
☐ **M1875 Remington**, .44-40 WCF, Color Case Hardened Frame, Carbine, Single Action, Brass Furniture, *Modern*	135.00	175.00
☐ **M1875 Remington**, .45 Colt, Color Case Hardened Frame, Carbine, Single Action, Brass Furniture, *Modern*	135.00	175.00

RIFLE, SEMI-AUTOMATIC

	V.G.	EXC.
☐ **AP-74**, .22 L.R.R.F., Clip Fed, Plastic Stock, *Modern*	60.00	90.00
☐ **AP-74**, .22 L.R.R.F., Clip Fed, Wood Stock, *Modern*	70.00	100.00
☐ **AP-74**, .32 ACP, Clip Fed, Plastic Stock, *Modern*	70.00	100.00
☐ **AP-74 Commando**, .22 L.R.R.F., Clip Fed, Wood Stock, *Modern*	70.00	100.00

	V.G.	EXC.

RIFLE, SINGLESHOT
- ☐ **Buffalo**, .45-70 Government, Rolling Block, Color Case Hardened Frame, Octagon Barrel, Open Rear Sight, Various Barrel Lengths, *Modern* 120.00 150.00
- ☐ **Buffalo**, .45-70 Government, Rolling Block, Color Case Hardened Frame, Half-Octagon Barrel, Open Rear Sight, Various Barrel Lengths, *Modern* 115.00 145.00
- ☐ **Buffalo**, .50 U.S. Carbine, Rolling Block, Color Case Hardened Frame, Octagon Barrel, Open Rear Sight, Various Barrel Lengths, *Modern* 100.00 140.00
- ☐ **Buffalo**, .50 U.S. Carbine, Rolling Block, Color Case Hardened Frame, Half-Octagon Barrel, Open Rear Sight, Various Barrel Lengths, *Modern* 95.00 135.00
- ☐ **Creedmore**, .45-70 Government, Rolling Block, Color Case Hardened Frame, Octagon Barrel, Vernier Sights, 30" Barrel, *Modern* 140.00 195.00
- ☐ **Creedmore**, .45-70 Government, Rolling Block, Color Case Hardened Frame, Half-Octagon Barrel, Vernier Sights, 30" Barrel, *Modern* 135.00 185.00
- ☐ **Creedmore**, .50 U.S. Carbine, Rolling Block, Color Case Hardened Frame, Octagon Barrel, Vernier Sights, 30" Barrel, *Modern* 135.00 180.00
- ☐ **Creedmore**, .50 U.S. Carbine, Rolling Block, Color Case Hardened Frame, Half-Octagon Barrel, Vernier Sights, 30" Barrel, *Modern* ... 135.00 180.00
- ☐ **Creedmore**, .50-140 Sharps, Rolling Block, Color Case Hardened Frame, Octagon Barrel, Vernier Sights, 30" Barrel, *Modern* 135.00 185.00
- ☐ **Martini**, .45-70 Government, Color Case Hardened Frame, Half-Octagon Barrel, Open Rear Sight, Checkered Stock, *Modern* 170.00 225.00
- ☐ **Martini**, .45-70 Government, Color Case Hardened Frame, Octagon Barrel, Open Rear Sight, Checkered Stock, *Modern* 165.00 220.00
- ☐ **Rolling Block**, .22 Hornet, Carbine, Color Case Hardened Frame, Adjustable Sights, *Modern* 100.00 135.00
- ☐ **Rolling Block**, .22 L.R.R.F., Carbine, Color Case Hardened Frame, Adjustable Sights, *Modern* 85.00 120.00
- ☐ **Rolling Block**, .357 Magnum, Carbine, Color Case Hardened Frame, Adjustable Sights, *Modern* 100.00 135.00

SHOTGUN, PERCUSSION
- ☐ **Magnum Deluxe**, 12 Ga., Double Barrel, Side by Side, Reproduction, Outside Hammers, Checkered Stock, *Antique* 150.00 190.00
- ☐ **Morse/Navy**, 12 Ga., Singleshot, Reproduction, Brass Frame, *Antique* 85.00 125.00
- ☐ **Upland Deluxe**, 12 Ga., Double Barrel, Side by Side, Reproduction, Outside Hammers, Checkered Stock, *Antique* 85.00 125.00
- ☐ **Zouave**, 12 Ga., Brass Furniture, Reproduction, *Antique* 90.00 130.00

NEIHARD, PETER
Northhampton, Pa. 1785-1787. See Kentucky Rifles.

NERO
Made by J. Rupertus Arms Co., c. 1880. Sold by E. Tryon Co.

HANDGUN, REVOLVER
- ☐ **.22 Short R.F.**, 7 Shot, Spur Trigger, Solid Frame, Single Action, *Antique* 90.00 160.00
- ☐ **.32 Short R.F.**, 5 Shot, Spur Trigger, Solid Frame, Single Action, *Antique* 95.00 170.00

NERO
Made by Hopkins & Allen., c. 1880. Sold by C.L. Riker.

HANDGUN, REVOLVER

	V.G.	EXC.
☐ **.22 Short R.F.**, 7 Shot, Spur Trigger, Solid Frame, Single Action, Antique	90.00	160.00
☐ **.32 Short R.F.**, 5 Shot, Spur Trigger, Solid Frame, Single Action, Antique	95.00	170.00

NEW CHIEFTAIN
Made by Stevens Arms.

SHOTGUN, SINGLESHOT

☐ **Model 94**, Various Gauges, Takedown, Automatic Ejector, Plain, Hammer, *Modern*	40.00	60.00

NEW NAMBU
Shin Chuo Kogyo, Tokyo, Japan, c. 1960.

HANDGUN, REVOLVER

☐ **Model 58**, .38 Spec., Swing-Out Cylinder, Double Action, *Modern*	65.00	115.00

HANDGUN, SEMI-AUTOMATIC

☐ **Model 57A**, 9mm Luger, Clip Fed, Blue, *Modern*	135.00	195.00
☐ **Model 57B**, .32 ACP, Clip Fed, Blue, *Modern*	125.00	175.00

NEW RIVAL
Made by Crescent for Van Camp Hardwore & Iron Co., Indianapolis, Ind.

SHOTGUN, DOUBLE BARREL, SIDE-BY-SIDE

☐ **Various Gauges**, Outside Hammers, Damascus Barrel, *Modern*	100.00	175.00
☐ **Various Gauges**, Hammerless, Steel Barrel, *Modern*	135.00	200.00
☐ **Various Gauges**, Hammerless, Damascus Barrel, *Modern*	100.00	175.00
☐ **Various Gauges**, Outside Hammers, Steel Barrel, *Modern*	125.00	190.00

SHOTGUN, SINGLESHOT

☐ **Various Gauges**, Hammer, Steel Barrel, *Modern*	55.00	85.00

NEW YORK ARMS CO.
Made by Crescent for Garnet Carter Co. Tenn., c. 1900.

SHOTGUN, DOUBLE BARREL, SIDE-BY-SIDE

☐ **Various Gauges**, Outside Hammers, Damascus Barrel, *Modern*	100.00	175.00
☐ **Various Gauges**, Hammerless, Steel Barrel, *Modern*	135.00	200.00
☐ **Various Gauges**, Hammerless, Damascus Barrel, *Modern*	100.00	175.00
☐ **Various Gauges**, Outside Hammers, Steel Barrel, *Modern*	125.00	190.00

SHOTGUN, SINGLESHOT

☐ **Various Gauges**, Hammer, Steel Barrel, *Modern*	55.00	85.00

NEW YORK PISTOL CO.
N.Y.C., c. 1870.

HANDGUN, REVOLVER

☐ **.22 Short R.F.**, 7 Shot, Spur Trigger, Solid Frame, Single Action, Antique	90.00	160.00
☐ **.32 Short R.F.**, 5 Shot, Spur Trigger, Solid Frame, Single Action, Antique	90.00	165.00

NEWCOMER, JOHN
Lancaster, Pa. 1770-1772. See Kentucky Rifles.

NEWHARDT, JACOB
Allentown, Pa. 1770-1777. See Kentucky Rifles.

NEWPORT
Made by Stevens Arms.
SHOTGUN, DOUBLE BARREL, SIDE-BY-SIDE
	V.G.	EXC.
☐ **Model 311**, Various Gauges, Hammerless, Steel Barrel, *Modern*	95.00	165.00

NEWTON ARMS CO.
Buffalo, N.Y. 1914-1918, reorganized 1918-1930 as Newton Rifle Corp.
RIFLE, BOLT ACTION
	V.G.	EXC.
☐ **1st Type**, Various Calibers, Sporting Rifle, Set Trigger, Checkered Stock, Open Rear Sight, *Modern*	425.00	575.00
☐ **2nd Type**, Various Calibers, Sporting Rifle, Set Trigger, Checkered Stock, Open Rear Sight, *Modern*	450.00	625.00
☐ **Newton-Mauser**, Various Calibers, Sporting Rifle, Set Trigger, Checkered Stock, Open Rear Sight, *Modern*	325.00	475.00

NICHOLS, JOHN
Oxford, England 1730-1775.
HANDGUN, FLINTLOCK
	V.G.	EXC.
☐ **Holster Pistol**, Engraved, Brass Furniture, High Quality, *Antique*	2,500.00	3,450.00

NIKKO SPORTING FIREARMS
Japan Imported by Kanematsu-Gosho U.S.A. Inc., Arlington Heights, Ill.
RIFLE, BOLT ACTION
	V.G.	EXC.
☐ **Model 7000**, Various Calibers, Grade 1, Checkered Stock, *Modern*	200.00	300.00
☐ **Model 7000**, Various African Calibers, Grade 1, Checkered Stock, *Modern*	225.00	350.00

SHOTGUN, DOUBLE BARREL, OVER-UNDER
	V.G.	EXC.
☐ **Model 5000**, 12 and 20 Gauges, Field Grade, Vent Rib, Checkered Stock, Light Engraving, Gold Overlay, *Modern*	325.00	450.00
☐ **Model 5000**, 12 and 20 Gauges, Skeet Grade, Vent Rib, Checkered Stock, Light Engraving, Gold Overlay, *Modern*	400.00	550.00
☐ **Model 5000**, 12 and 20 Gauges, Trap Grade, Vent Rib, Checkered Stock, Light Engraving, Gold Overlay, *Modern*	400.00	550.00
☐ **Model 5000**, 12 and 20 Gauges, Field Grade 2, Vent Rib, Checkered Stock, Light Engraving, Gold Overlay, *Modern*	425.00	550.00
☐ **Model 5000**, 12 and 20 Gauges, Skeet Grade 2, Vent Rib, Checkered Stock, Light Engraving, Gold Overlay, *Modern*	475.00	600.00
☐ **Model 5000**, 12 and 20 Gauges, Trap Grade 2, Vent Rib, Checkered Stock, Light Engraving, Gold Overlay, *Modern*	475.00	600.00
☐ **Model 5000 Grandee**, 12 and 20 Gauges, Field Grade 3, Vent Rib, Checkered Stock, Fancy Engraving, Gold Overlay, *Modern*	1,250.00	2,000.00
☐ **Model 5000 Grandee**, 12 and 20 Gauges, Skeet Grade 3, Vent Rib, Checkered Stock, Fancy Engraving, Gold Overlay, *Modern*	1,250.00	2,000.00
☐ **Model 5000 Grandee**, 12 Ga., Trap Grade 3, Vent Rib, Checkered Stock, Fancy Engraving, Gold Overlay, *Modern*	1,250.00	2,000.00

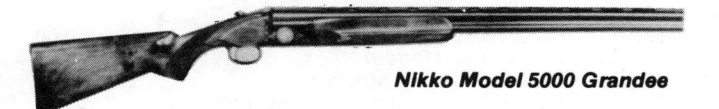

Nikko Model 5000 Grandee

NITRO PROOF
Made by Stevens Arms.

	V.G.	EXC.

SHOTGUN, SINGLESHOT
☐ **Model 115**, Various Gauges, Hammer, Automatic Ejector, *Modern* — 45.00 — 60.00

NIVA
Kohout & Spolecnost, Kydne, Czechoslovakia.

HANDGUN, SEMI-AUTOMATIC
☐ **Niva**, .25 ACP, Clip Fed, Blue, *Modern* — 120.00 — 185.00

NOBLE
Haydenville, Mass.1950-1971.

RIFLE, BOLT ACTION
☐ **98 Mauser**, .30-06 Springfield, Monte Carlo Stock, Open Rear Sight, *Modern* — 90.00 — 135.00
☐ **Model 10**, .22 L.R.R.F., Singleshot, *Modern* — 25.00 — 40.00
☐ **Model 20**, .22 L.R.R.F., Singleshot, *Modern* — 25.00 — 40.00
☐ **Model 222**, .22 L.R.R.F., Singleshot, *Modern* — 35.00 — 50.00

RIFLE, LEVER ACTION
☐ **Model 275**, .22 L.R.R.F., Tube Fed, *Modern* — 50.00 — 75.00

RIFLE, SEMI-AUTOMATIC
☐ **Model 285**, .22 L.R.R.F., Tube Fed, *Modern* — 55.00 — 80.00

RIFLE, SLIDE ACTION
☐ **Model 235**, .22 L.R.R.F., Wood Stock, *Modern* — 55.00 — 80.00
☐ **Model 33**, .22 L.R.R.F., Plastic Stock, *Modern* — 45.00 — 75.00
☐ **Model 33A**, .22 L.R.R.F., Wood Stock, *Modern* — 50.00 — 80.00

SHOTGUN, DOUBLE BARREL, SIDE-BY-SIDE
☐ **Model 420**, Various Gauges, Hammerless, Checkered Stock, Recoil Pad, *Modern* — 120.00 — 165.00
☐ **Model 420EK**, Various Gauges, Hammerless, Checkered Stock, Recoil Pad, Fancy Wood, *Modern* — 140.00 — 200.00
☐ **Model 450E**, Various Gauges, Hammerless, Checkered Stock, Recoil Pad, *Modern* — 175.00 — 285.00

SHOTGUN, SEMI-AUTOMATIC
☐ **Model 80**, .410 Ga., *Modern* — 100.00 — 150.00

SHOTGUN, SLIDE ACTION
☐ **Model 160 Deergun**, 12 and 20 Gauges, Peep Sights, *Modern* — 95.00 — 145.00
☐ **Model 166L Deergun**, 12 and 16 Gauges, Peep Sights, *Modern* — 95.00 — 145.00
☐ **Model 166LP Deergun**, 12 and 16 Gauges, Peep Sights, *Modern* — 95.00 — 150.00
☐ **Model 200**, 20 Ga., Vent Rib, Adjustable Choke, *Modern* — 90.00 — 140.00
☐ **Model 200**, 20 Ga., Adjustable Choke, *Modern* — 90.00 — 140.00
☐ **Model 200**, 20 Ga., *Modern* — 85.00 — 135.00
☐ **Model 200**, 20 Ga., Trap Grade, *Modern* — 95.00 — 150.00
☐ **Model 300**, 12 Ga., Vent Rib, Adjustable Choke, *Modern* — 110.00 — 160.00
☐ **Model 300**, 12 Ga., Adjustable Choke, *Modern* — 95.00 — 145.00
☐ **Model 300**, 12 Ga., *Modern* — 90.00 — 140.00
☐ **Model 300**, 12 Ga., Trap Grade, *Modern* — 115.00 — 160.00
☐ **Model 390**, 12 Ga., Peep Sights, *Modern* — 90.00 — 140.00
☐ **Model 40**, 12 Ga., Hammerless, Solid Frame, Adjustable Choke, *Modern* — 80.00 — 130.00
☐ **Model 400**, .410 Ga., Skeet Grade, *Modern* — 90.00 — 135.00
☐ **Model 400**, .410 Ga., Adjustable Choke, *Modern* — 90.00 — 135.00
☐ **Model 400**, .410 Ga., Skeet Grade, Adjustable Choke, *Modern* — 95.00 — 150.00
☐ **Model 400**, .410 Ga., *Modern* — 85.00 — 135.00

	V.G.	EXC.
☐ **Model 50**, 12 Ga., Hammerless, Solid Frame, *Modern*	65.00	110.00
☐ **Model 60**, 12 and 16 Gauges, Hammerless, Solid Frame, Adjustable Choke, *Modern*	85.00	125.00
☐ **Model 602**, 20 Ga., *Modern*	90.00	135.00
☐ **Model 602CLP**, 20 Ga., Adjustable Choke, *Modern*	95.00	145.00
☐ **Model 602RCLP**, 20 Ga., Adjustable Choke, Vent Rib, *Modern*	115.00	155.00
☐ **Model 602 RLP**, 20 Ga., Vent Rib, *Modern*	90.00	140.00
☐ **Model 60ACP**, 12 and 16 Gauges, Hammerless, Solid Frame, Adjustable Choke, Vent Rib, *Modern*	80.00	125.00
☐ **Model 60AF**, 12 and 16 Gauges, Hammerless, Solid Frame, Vent Rib, Adjustable Choke, *Modern*	85.00	130.00
☐ **Model 60 RCLP**, 12 and 16 Gauges, Hammerless, Solid Frame, Vent Rib, Adjustable Choke, Checkered Stock, *Modern*	85.00	135.00
☐ **Model 65**, 12 and 16 Gauges, Hammerless, Solid Frame, *Modern*	65.00	115.00
☐ **Model 662CR**, 20 Ga., Vent Rib, *Modern*	100.00	150.00
☐ **Model 66CLP**, 12 and 16 Gauges, Adjustable Choke, *Modern*	110.00	155.00
☐ **Model 66RCLP**, 12 and 16 Gauges, Hammerless, Solid Frame, Adjustable Choke, Vent Rib, *Modern*	110.00	155.00
☐ **Model 66RLP**, 12 and 16 Gauges, Hammerless, Solid Frame, Vent Rib, *Modern*	100.00	150.00
☐ **Model 66XLP**, 12 and 16 Gauges, Hammerless, Solid Frame, *Modern*	90.00	135.00
☐ **Model 70**, .410 Ga., *Modern*	70.00	100.00
☐ **Model 70CLP**, .410 Ga., Hammerless, Solid Frame, Adjustable Choke, *Modern*	90.00	135.00
☐ **Model 70RL**, .410 Ga., *Modern*	85.00	125.00
☐ **Model 70X**, .410 Ga., *Modern*	80.00	120.00
☐ **Model 70XL**, .410 Ga., *Modern*	80.00	125.00
☐ **Model 757**, 20 Ga., Adjustable Choke, Lightweight, *Modern*	115.00	160.00

NOCK, HENRY
London & Birmingham, England 1760-1810.

RIFLE, FLINTLOCK
☐ **.65**, Ellett Carbine, Musket, Military, *Antique* 975.00 1,650.00

SHOTGUN, PERCUSSION
☐ **Fowler**, Converted from Flintlock, Patent Breech, *Antique* 445.00 700.00

NONPAREIL
Made by Norwich Falls Pistols Co., c. 1880.

HANDGUN, REVOLVER
☐ **.32 Short R.F.**, 5 Shot, Spur Trigger, Solid Frame, Single Action, *Antique* 90.00 160.00

NORTH AMERICAN ARMS CO.
Freedom, Wyo.

HANDGUN, REVOLVER
☐ **.454 Casull Magnum**, Single Action, Western Style, Stainless Steel, 5 Shot, *Modern* 345.00 450.00
☐ **Mini**, .22 Short, 5 Shot, Single Action, Spur Trigger, 1″ Barrel, Derringer, *Modern* 65.00 85.00
☐ **Mini**, .22 L.R.R.F., 5 Shot, Single Action, Spur Trigger, 1″ Barrel, Derringer, *Modern* 65.00 85.00
☐ **Mini**, .22 L.R.R.F., 5 Shot, Single Action, Spur Trigger, 1½″ Barrel, Derringer, *Modern* 65.00 90.00
☐ **Mini**, .22 W.M.R., 5 Shot, Single Action, Spur Trigger, 1″ Barrel, Derringer, *Modern* 70.00 100.00

NORTH VIETNAM MILITARY

	V.G.	EXC.
AUTOMATIC WEAPON, SUBMACHINE GUN		
☐ **K50M**, 7.62mm Tokarev, Clip Fed, Folding Stock, *Class 3*	1,350.00	1,750.00

NORTHWESTERNER
Made by Stevens Arms.

RIFLE, BOLT ACTION
☐ **Model 52**, .22 L.R.R.F., Single Action, Takedown, *Modern* 35.00   45.00

SHOTGUN, SINGLESHOT
☐ **Model 94**, Various Gauges, Takedown, Automatic Ejector, Plain, Hammer, *Modern* 40.00   55.00

NORTON
See Budischowsky and American Arms & Ammunition Co.

Norwegian Military Model 1914 .45

NORWEGIAN MILITARY

HANDGUN, SEMI-AUTOMATIC
☐ **Mauser Model 1914**, .32 ACP, Blue, Clip Fed, *Modern* 525.00   775.00
☐ **Model 1914**, .45 ACP, Military, Clip Fed, *Modern* 250.00   400.00
☐ **Model 1914**, .45 ACP, Military, Clip Fed, Nazi-Proofed, *Modern* 400.00   550.00

RIFLE, BOLT ACTION
☐ **Model 1894 Krag**, 6.5 x 55mm, Military, *Curio* 135.00   195.00
☐ **Model 1925 Krag Sniper**, 6.5 x 55mm, Military, *Curio* 150.00   225.00

NORWICH ARMS CO.
Probably made by Norwich Falls Pistols Co.

HANDGUN, REVOLVER
☐ **.22 Short R.F.**, 7 Shot, Spur Trigger, Solid Frame, Single Action, Antique 90.00   160.00
☐ **.32 Short R.F.**, 5 Shot, Spur Trigger, Solid Frame, Single Action, Antique 95.00   170.00

NORWICH ARMS CO.
Made by Crescent, c. 1900.

SHOTGUN, DOUBLE BARREL, SIDE-BY-SIDE
☐ **Various Gauges**, Outside Hammers, Damascus Barrel, *Modern* 100.00   175.00
☐ **Various Gauges**, Hammerless, Steel Barrel, *Modern* 135.00   200.00
☐ **Various Gauges**, Hammerless, Damascus Barrel, *Modern* 100.00   175.00
☐ **Various Gauges**, Outside Hammers, Steel Barrel, *Modern* 125.00   190.00

	V.G.	EXC.

SHOTGUN, SINGLESHOT
☐ **Various Gauges**, Hammer, Steel Barrel, *Modern* 55.00 85.00

NOT-NAC MFG. CO.
Made by Crescent for Belknap Hardware Co., Louisville, Ky.

SHOTGUN, DOUBLE BARREL, SIDE-BY-SIDE
☐ **Various Gauges**, Outside Hammers, Damascus Barrel, *Modern* 100.00 175.00
☐ **Various Gauges**, Hammerless, Steel Barrel, *Modern* 135.00 200.00
☐ **Various Gauges**, Hammerless, Damascus Barrel, *Modern* 100.00 175.00
☐ **Various Gauges**, Outside Hammers, Steel Barrel, *Modern* 125.00 190.00

SHOTGUN, SINGLESHOT
☐ **Various Gauges**, Hammer, Steel Barrel, *Modern* 55.00 85.00

NOYS, R.
Wiltshire, England 1800-1830.

HANDGUN, FLINTLOCK
☐ **Pocket Pistol**, Screw Barrel, Box Lock, Steel Barrel and Frame, Plain, *Antique* 475.00 650.00

NUMRICH ARMS CO.
West Hurley, N.Y. Also see Thompson, Hopkins & Allen

HANDGUN, SEMI-AUTOMATIC
☐ **M1911A1**, .45 ACP, Clip Fed, Blue, Military Style, *Modern* 170.00 245.00
☐ **Model 27A5**, .45 ACP, Clip Fed, Finned Barrel, Adjustable Sights, with Compensator, (Numrich), *Modern* 250.00 350.00

RIFLE, SEMI-AUTOMATIC
☐ **Model 27A1**, .45 ACP, Clip Fed, without Compensator, *Modern* ... 250.00 350.00
☐ **Model 27A1**, .45 ACP, Clip Fed, without Compensator, Cased with Accessories, *Modern* 400.00 475.00
☐ **Model 27A1 Deluxe**, .45 ACP, Clip Fed, Finned Barrel, Adjustable Sights, with Compensator, *Modern* 265.00 370.00
☐ **Model 27A3**, .22 L.R.R.F., Clip Fed, Finned Barrel, Adjustable Sights, with Compensator, *Modern* 225.00 350.00

NUNNEMACHER, ABRAHAM
York, Pa. 1779-1783. See Kentucky Rifles.

OAK LEAF
Made by Stevens Arms.

SHOTGUN, SINGLESHOT
☐ **Model 90**, Various Gauges, Takedown, Automatic Ejector, Plain, Hammer, *Modern* 40.00 55.00

OCCIDENTAL
Belgium, c. 1880.

SHOTGUN, DOUBLE BARREL, SIDE-BY-SIDE
☐ **Various Gauges**, Outside Hammers, Damascus Barrel, *Modern* 90.00 150.00

OLD TIMER
Made by Stevens Arms.

SHOTGUN, SINGLESHOT
☐ **Model 94**, Various Gauges, Takedown, Automatic Ejector, Plain, Hammer, *Modern* 40.00 55.00

OLYMPIC
Made by Stevens Arms.

	V.G.	EXC.
SHOTGUN, DOUBLE BARREL, SIDE-BY-SIDE		
☐ **M 315**, Various Gauges, Hammerless, Steel Barrel, *Modern*	99.00	165.00
☐ **Model 311**, Various Gauges, Hammerless, Steel Barrel, *Modern*	95.00	165.00
SHOTGUN, SINGLESHOT		
☐ **Model 94**, Various Gauges, Takedown, Automatic Ejector, Plain, Hammer, *Modern*	40.00	55.00

O.M.
Ojanguren y Marcaido, Eibar, Spain, c. 1920.

HANDGUN, REVOLVER
☐ **S & W Type**, Various Calibers, Double Action, Swing-Out Cylinder, Blue, *Curio* 70.00 100.00

OMEGA
Armero Especialistas Reunidas, Eibar, Spain, c. 1925.

HANDGUN, SEMI-AUTOMATIC
☐ **.25 ACP**, Clip Fed, *Modern* 75.00 115.00
☐ **.32 ACP**, Clip Fed, Grip Safety, *Modern* 85.00 130.00

OMEGA
Torrance, Calif. Made by Hi-Shear Corp. Current

RIFLE, BOLT ACTION
☐ **Omega III**, Various Calibers, no Sights, Fancy Wood, Adjustable Trigger, *Modern* 275.00 400.00

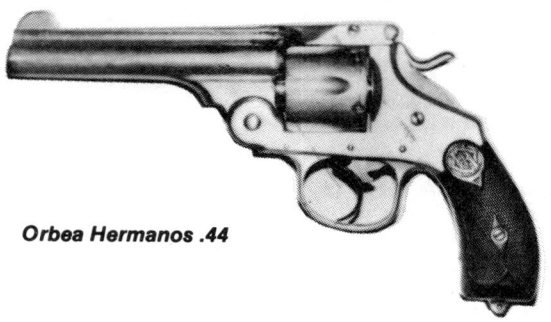

Orbea Hermanos .44

ORBEA HERMANOS
Orbea Hermanos and Orbea y Cia., Eibar, Spain, c. 1860-1935.

HANDGUN, REVOLVER
☐ **S & W Type**, .44 Russian, Double Action, Top-Break, *Antique* 85.00 125.00
☐ **S & W Type**, Various Calibers, Double Action, Swing-Out Cylinder, Blue, *Curio* 65.00 95.00

OREA
Orechowsky, Graz, Austria, c. 1930.

RIFLE, SINGLESHOT
☐ **Heeren Rifle**, Various Calibers, Checkered Stock, Engraved, Fancy Wood, *Modern* 900.00 1,500.00

Ortgies D Pocket

Ortgies H O Vest Pocket

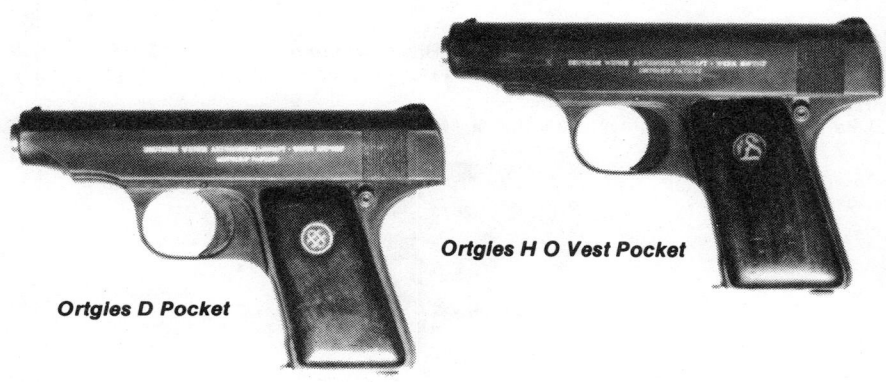

ORTGIES
Germany, 1918-1921, 1921 Taken over by Deutsche-Werke, Erfurt, Germany.

	V.G.	EXC.
HANDGUN, SEMI-AUTOMATIC		
☐ **D Pocket**, .380 ACP, Clip Fed, *Modern*	135.00	175.00
☐ **H O Pocket**, .380 ACP, Clip Fed, *Modern*	125.00	165.00
☐ **D Pocket**, .32 ACP, Clip Fed, *Modern*	110.00	150.00
☐ **H O Pocket**, .32 ACP, Clip Fed, *Modern*	120.00	160.00
☐ **D Vest Pocket**, .25 ACP, Clip Fed, *Modern*	130.00	170.00
☐ **H O Vest Pocket**, .25 ACP, Clip Fed, *Modern*	120.00	160.00

OSGOOD GUN WORKS
Norwich, Conn., c. 1880.

HANDGUN, REVOLVER
☐ **Duplex**, .22/.32 R.F., 8 Shot .22, Singleshot .32, Two Barrels, Spur Trigger, *Antique* 175.00   325.00

OUR JAKE
HANDGUN, REVOLVER
☐ **.32 R.F.**, Spur Trigger, Solid Frame, Hammer, *Antique* 85.00   140.00

OWA
Oesterreichische Werke Anstalt, Vienna, Austria, c. 1920-1925.

HANDGUN, SEMI-AUTOMATIC
☐ **Model 1921 Standard**, .25 ACP, Clip Fed, *Modern* 125.00   165.00
☐ **Model 1924**, .25 ACP, Clip Fed, Lightweight, *Modern* 145.00   190.00

OXFORD ARMS
Made by Stevens Arms.

SHOTGUN, DOUBLE BARREL, SIDE-BY-SIDE
☐ **Model 311**, Various Gauges, Hammerless, Steel Barrel, *Modern* 95.00   165.00

OXFORD ARMS CO.
Made by Crescent for Belknap Hdw. Co., Louisville, Ky.

SHOTGUN, DOUBLE BARREL, SIDE-BY-SIDE
☐ **Various Gauges**, Outside Hammers, Damascus Barrel, *Modern* 100.00   175.00
☐ **Various Gauges**, Hammerless, Steel Barrel, *Modern* 135.00   200.00

	V.G.	EXC.
☐ **Various Gauges**, Hammerless, Damascus Barrel, *Modern*	100.00	175.00
☐ **Various Gauges**, Outside Hammers, Steel Barrel, *Modern*	125.00	190.00

SHOTGUN, SINGLESHOT

☐ **Various Gauges**, Hammer, Steel Barrel, *Modern*	55.00	85.00

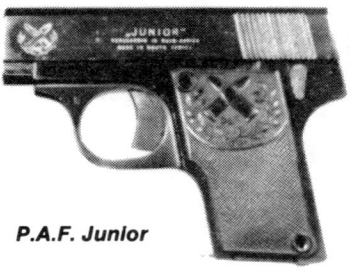

P.A.F. Junior

P.A.F.
Pretoria Arms Factory, Pretoria, South Africa, c. 1955.

HANDGUN, SEMI-AUTOMATIC

☐ **Junior**, For Cocking Indicator *Add* **10%-15%**

☐ **Junior**, .25 ACP, High Slide, Clip Fed, Blue, *Curio*	115.00	145.00
☐ **Junior**, .25 ACP, Sight Rib, Clip Fed, Blue, *Curio*	125.00	165.00
☐ **Junior**, .25 ACP, Low Slide, Clip Fed, Blue, *Curio*	110.00	150.00

PAGE, T.
Norwich, England, 1766-1776.

HANDGUN, FLINTLOCK

☐ **.60**, Queen Anne Style, Pocket Pistol, Screw Barrel, Box Lock, Brass Furniture, Engraved, *Antique*	950.00	1,450.00

PAGE-LEWIS ARMS CO.
See Stevens, J. Arms & Tool Co. for similar listings.

PALMER, THOMAS
Philadelphia, Pa. 1772-1776. See Kentucky Rifles and U.S. Military.

PALMETTO
Made by Stevens Arms.

SHOTGUN, SINGLESHOT

☐ **Model 90**, Various Gauges, Takedown, Automatic Ejector, Plain, Hammer, *Modern*	35.00	55.00
☐ **Model 94**, Various Gauges, Takedown, Automatic Ejector, Plain, Hammer, *Modern*	35.00	55.00

PANNABECKER, JEFFERSON
Lancaster, Pa. 1790-1810. See Kentucky Rifles.

PANNABECKER, JESSE
Lancaster, Pa. 1833-1860. See Kentucky Rifles.

PANTAX
Tradename used by E. Woerther, Buenos Aires, Argentina.

PARKER BROTHERS / 327

	V.G.	EXC.
HANDGUN, SEMI-AUTOMATIC		
☐ **.22 R.F.**, Clip Fed, Blue, *Modern*	85.00	125.00

PARAGON
Made by Stevens Arms.
SHOTGUN, DOUBLE BARREL, SIDE-BY-SIDE
☐ **Model 311**, Various Gauges, Hammerless, Steel Barrel, *Modern* 95.00 165.00

PANZER
G.M.F. Corp., Watertown, Ct.
HANDGUN, DOUBLE BARREL, OVER-UNDER
☐ **Panzer**, .22 L.R.R.F., Twist Barrel, Spur Trigger, *Modern* 20.00 35.00

PARAGON
Possibly made by Hopkins & Allen, c. 1880.
HANDGUN, REVOLVER
☐ **.32 Short R.F.**, 5 Shot, Spur Trigger, Solid Frame, Single Action, Antique 90.00 160.00

Paramount M1914

PARAMOUNT
Retolaza Hermanos, Eibar, Spain, c. 1920
HANDGUN, SEMI-AUTOMATIC
☐ **.32 ACP**, Clip Fed, *Modern* 80.00 120.00
☐ **M 1914**, .32 ACP, Clip Fed, Long Grip, *Modern* 80.00 125.00
☐ **Vest Pocket**, .25 ACP, Clip Fed, *Modern* 75.00 115.00

PARKER BROTHERS
Meriden, Conn. 1868-1934. In 1934 Parker Bros. was taken over by Remington Arms Co.
SHOTGUN, DOUBLE BARREL, SIDE-BY-SIDE
☐ **For Upgrades**, *Deduct 25%-30%*
☐ **For Plain Extractor**, *Deduct 30%-45%*
☐ **For Damascus Barrel**, *Deduct 60%-75%*
☐ **Single Selective Trigger**, *Add $200.00-$325.00*
☐ **Beavertail Forend**, for BHE through A-1, *Add $250.00-$350.00*
☐ **Beavertail Forend**, VHE through CHE, *Add $200.00-$300.00*
☐ **Extra Barrel**, *Add 30%-40%*
☐ **Vent Rib**, *Add $275.00-$350.00*
☐ **Trap Grade**, *Add 15%-25%*

328 / PARKER BROTHERS

	V.G.	EXC.

- ☐ **Skeet Grade,** *Add* **15%-25%**
- ☐ **Outside Hammers with Steel Barrels,** *Deduct* **20%-30%**
- ☐ **A-1 Special,** 12 Ga., Hammerless, Double Trigger, Automatic Ejector, *Modern* 15,000.00 25,000.00
- ☐ **A-1 Special,** 16 Ga., Hammerless, Double Trigger, Automatic Ejector, *Modern* 12,000.00 18,000.00
- ☐ **A-1 Special,** 20 Ga., Hammerless, Double Trigger, Automatic Ejector, *Modern* 20,000.00 30,000.00
- ☐ **A-1 Special,** 28 Ga., Hammerless, Double Trigger, Automatic Ejector, *Modern* 40,000.00 55,000.00
- ☐ **A-1 Upgrade,** .410 Ga., Hammerless, Double Trigger, Automatic Ejector, *Modern* 8,000.00 15,000.00
- ☐ **A-1 Upgrade,** 12 and 16 Gauges, Hammerless, Double Trigger, Automatic Ejector, *Modern* 6,500.00 10,000.00
- ☐ **A-1 Upgrade,** 20 Ga., Hammerless, Double Trigger, Automatic Ejector, *Modern* 6,000.00 9,000.00
- ☐ **A-1 Upgrade,** 28 Ga., Hammerless, Double Trigger, Automatic Ejector, *Modern* 9,000.00 15,000.00
- ☐ **AAHE,** 10 Ga., Hammerless, Double Trigger, Automatic Ejector, *Modern* 23,000.00 28,000.00
- ☐ **AAHE,** 12 Ga., Hammerless, Double Trigger, Automatic Ejector, *Modern* 9,000.00 15,000.00
- ☐ **AAHE,** 16 Ga., Hammerless, Double Trigger, Automatic Ejector, *Modern* 8,000.00 15,000.00
- ☐ **AAHE,** 20 Ga., Hammerless, Double Trigger, Automatic Ejector, *Modern* 12,000.00 18,000.00
- ☐ **AAHE,** 28 Ga., Hammerless, Double Trigger, Automatic Ejector, *Modern* 24,000.00 30,000.00
- ☐ **AHE,** .410 Ga., Hammerless, Double Trigger, Automatic Ejector, *Modern* 15,000.00 20,000.00
- ☐ **AHE,** 10 Ga., Hammerless, Double Trigger, Automatic Ejector, *Modern* 15,000.00 20,000.00
- ☐ **AHE,** 12 Ga., Hammerless, Double Trigger, Automatic Ejector, *Modern* 8,000.00 13,000.00
- ☐ **AHE,** 16 Ga., Hammerless, Double Trigger, Automatic Ejector, *Modern* 8,000.00 12,000.00
- ☐ **AHE,** 20 Ga., Hammerless, Double Trigger, Automatic Ejector, *Modern* 9,500.00 17,000.00
- ☐ **AHE,** 28 Ga., Hammerless, Double Trigger, Automatic Ejector, *Modern* 14,000.00 21,000.00
- ☐ **BHE,** .410 Ga., Hammerless, Double Trigger, Automatic Ejector, *Modern* 13,000.00 19,000.00
- ☐ **BHE,** 10 Ga., Hammerless, Double Trigger, Automatic Ejector, *Modern* 12,000.00 18,000.00
- ☐ **BHE,** 12 Ga., Hammerless, Double Trigger, Automatic Ejector, *Modern* 7,500.00 11,000.00
- ☐ **BHE,** 16 Ga., Hammerless, Double Trigger, Automatic Ejector, *Modern* 7,000.00 10,000.00
- ☐ **BHE,** 20 Ga., Hammerless, Double Trigger, Automatic Ejector, *Modern* 9,000.00 15,000.00
- ☐ **BHE,** 28 Ga., Hammerless, Double Trigger, Automatic Ejector, *Modern* 15,000.00 22,000.00
- ☐ **CHE,** .410 Ga., Hammerless, Double Trigger, Automatic Ejector, *Modern* 8,000.00 13,000.00
- ☐ **CHE,** 10 Ga., Hammerless, Double Trigger, Automatic Ejector, *Modern* 8,000.00 13,000.00

	V.G.	EXC.
☐ **CHE**, 12 Ga., Hammerless, Double Trigger, Automatic Ejector, *Modern*	6,000.00	9,000.00
☐ **CHE**, 16 Ga., Hammerless, Double Trigger, Automatic Ejector, *Modern*	5,500.00	8,500.00
☐ **CHE**, 20 Ga., Hammerless, Double Trigger, Automatic Ejector, *Modern*	8,000.00	11,000.00
☐ **CHE**, 28 Ga., Hammerless, Double Trigger, Automatic Ejector, *Modern*	9,500.00	14,000.00
☐ **DHE**, .410 Ga., Hammerless, Double Trigger, Automatic Ejector, *Modern*	6,500.00	9,750.00
☐ **DHE**, 10 Ga., Hammerless, Double Trigger, Automatic Ejector, *Modern*	5,500.00	9,000.00
☐ **DHE**, 12 Ga., Hammerless, Double Trigger, Automatic Ejector, *Modern*	5,000.00	8,500.00
☐ **DHE**, 16 Ga., Hammerless, Double Trigger, Automatic Ejector, *Modern*	4,500.00	8,000.00
☐ **DHE**, 20 Ga., Hammerless, Double Trigger, Automatic Ejector, *Modern*	7,000.00	10,000.00
☐ **DHE**, 28 Ga., Hammerless, Double Trigger, Automatic Ejector, *Modern*	9,000.00	14,000.00
☐ **Early Model**, Various Gauges, Outside Hammers, Damascus Barrel, Under-Lever, *Antique*	650.00	1,100.00
☐ **GHE**, .410 Ga., Hammerless, Double Trigger, Automatic Ejector, *Modern*	4,500.00	8,000.00
☐ **GHE**, 10 Ga. 3½", Hammerless, Double Trigger, Automatic Ejector, *Modern*	4,250.00	8,000.00
☐ **GHE**, 12 Ga., Hammerless, Double Trigger, Automatic Ejector, *Modern*	2,800.00	4,000.00
☐ **GHE**, 16 Ga., Hammerless, Double Trigger, Automatic Ejector, *Modern*	2,800.00	4,000.00
☐ **GHE**, 20 Ga., Hammerless, Double Trigger, Automatic Ejector, *Modern*	4,000.00	9,000.00
☐ **GHE**, 28 Ga., Hammerless, Double Trigger, Automatic Ejector, *Modern*	6,000.00	9,000.00
☐ **Invincible**, 12 Ga., Hammerless, Double Trigger, Automatic Ejector, *Modern*		120,000.00+
☐ **Invincible**, 16 Ga., Hammerless, Double Trigger, Automatic Ejector, *Modern*		65,000.00+
☐ **Trojan**, 12 and 16 Gauges, Hammerless, Double Trigger, *Modern*	600.00	950.00
☐ **Trojan**, 20 Ga., Hammerless, Double Trigger, *Modern*	900.00	1,500.00
☐ **Trojan**, 24 Ga., Hammerless, Double Trigger, *Modern*		20,000.00+
☐ **VHE**, .410 Ga., Hammerless, Double Trigger, Automatic Ejector, *Modern*	4,500.00	8,000.00
☐ **VHE**, 10 Ga. 3½", Hammerless, Double Trigger, Automatic Ejector, *Modern*	3,500.00	7,000.00
☐ **VHE**, 12 Ga., Hammerless, Double Trigger, Automatic Ejector, *Modern*	1,500.00	2,300.00
☐ **VHE**, 16 Ga., Hammerless, Double Trigger, Automatic Ejector, *Modern*	1,500.00	2,200.00
☐ **VHE**, 20 Ga., Hammerless, Double Trigger, Automatic Ejector, *Modern*	4,000.00	8,000.00
☐ **VHE**, 28 Ga., Hammerless, Double Trigger, Automatic Ejector, *Modern*	4,500.00	8,500.00

SHOTGUN, SINGLESHOT

	V.G.	EXC.
☐ **S.A.**, 12 Ga., Hammerless, Vent Rib, Automatic Ejector, *Modern*	5,000.00	7,500.00
☐ **S.A.-1 Special**, 12 Ga., Hammerless, Vent Rib, Automatic Ejector, *Modern*	8,000.00	12,000.00

330 / PARKER BROTHERS

	V.G.	EXC.
☐ **S.A.A.**, 12 Ga., Hammerless, Vent Rib, Automatic Ejector, *Modern*	6,000.00	9,000.00
☐ **S.B.**, 12 Ga., Hammerless, Vent Rib, Automatic Ejector, *Modern*	4,500.00	6,500.00
☐ **S.C.**, 12 Ga., Hammerless, Vent Rib, Automatic Ejector, *Modern*	3,500.00	5,500.00

PARKER BROTHERS
Imported from Italy by Jana International.

SHOTGUN, DOUBLE BARREL, OVER-UNDER
☐ **Field Model**, 12 Ga. 3", Single Selective Trigger, Automatic Ejectors, Checkered Stock, Engraved, Vent Rib, *Modern*	200.00	300.00
☐ **Skeet Model**, 12 Ga., Single Selective Trigger, Automatic Ejectors, Checkered Stock, Engraved, Vent Rib, *Modern*	230.00	325.00
☐ **Monte Carlo Trap Model**, 12 Ga., Single Selective Trigger, Automatic Ejectors, Checkered Stock, Engraved, Vent Rib, *Modern*	250.00	350.00
☐ **California Trap Model**, 12 Ga., Single Selective Trigger, Automatic Ejectors, Checkered Stock, Engraved, Double Vent Ribs, *Modern*	350.00	500.00

PARKER-HALE
Birmingham, England.

HANDGUN, REVOLVER
☐ **S & W Victory**, .22 L.R.R.F., Conversion, Adjustable Sights, *Modern*	80.00	125.00

RIFLE, BOLT ACTION
☐ **Model 1200**, Various Calibers, Checkered Stock, Open Rear Sight, Monte Carlo Stock, *Modern*	150.00	195.00
☐ **Model 1200M**, Various Calibers, Magnum, Checkered Stock, Open Rear Sight, Monte Carlo Stock, *Modern*	160.00	220.00
☐ **Model 1200V**, Various Calibers, Heavy Barrel, Checkered Stock, no Sights, Monte Carlo Stock, *Modern*	160.00	220.00

RIFLE, PERCUSSION
☐ **.54 Gallagher**, Breech Loader, Carbine, Brass Furniture, Reproduction, *Antique*	120.00	170.00
☐ **.58 M1853 Enfield**, Musket, Rifled, 2 Bands, Brass Furniture, Reproduction, *Antique*	135.00	185.00
☐ **.58 M1858 Enfield Rifle**, Rifled, Brass Furniture, Reproduction, *Antique*	130.00	190.00
☐ **.58 M1861 Enfield**, Musketoon, Rifled, 2 Bands, Brass Furniture, Reproduction, *Antique*	120.00	170.00
☐ **.451**, Whitworth Military Target Rifle, 3 Bands, Target Sights, Checkered Stock, Reproduction, *Antique*	250.00	350.00

SHOTGUN, SEMI-AUTOMATIC
☐ **Model 900**, 12 Ga., Checkered Stock, Vent Rib, *Modern*	140.00	200.00
☐ **Model 900**, 12 Ga. 3", Checkered Stock, Vent Rib, *Modern*	150.00	220.00

PARKER SAFETY HAMMERLESS
Made by Columbia Armory, Tenn., c. 1890.

HANDGUN, REVOLVER
☐ **.32 S & W**, 5 Shot, Top Break, Hammerless, Double Action, *Modern*	55.00	95.00

PARKER, WILLIAM
London, England 1790-1840.

SHOTGUN, FLINTLOCK
☐ **16 Ga.**, Double Barrel, Side by Side, Engraved, High Quality, *Antique*	2,450.00	3,950.00

	V.G.	EXC.

SHOTGUN, PERCUSSION
- [ ] **14 Ga.**, Single Barrel, Smoothbore, High Quality, Cased with Accessories, *Antique* 875.00 1,450.00

PARKHILL, ANDREW
Phila., Pa. 1778-1785. See Kentucky Rifles and Pistols.

PAROLE
Made by Hopkins & Allen, c. 1880.
HANDGUN, REVOLVER
- [ ] **.22 Short R.F.**, 7 Shot, Spur Trigger, Solid Frame, Single Action, *Antique* 90.00 160.00

PARR, J.
Liverpool, England, c. 1810.
RIFLE, FLINTLOCK
- [ ] **.75**, 3rd Model Brown Bess, Musket, Military, *Antique* 825.00 1,450.00

PARSONS, HIRAM
Baltimore, Md., c. 1819. See Kentucky Rifles.

PATRIOT
Made by Norwich Falls Pistol Co., c. 1880.
HANDGUN, REVOLVER
- [ ] **.32 Short R.F.**, 5 Shot, Spur Trigger, Solid Frame, Single Action, *Antique* 90.00 160.00

PECK, ABIJAH
Hartford, Conn. See U. S. Military.

PEERLESS
Made by Stevens.
RIFLE, BOLT ACTION
- [ ] **Model 056 Buckhorn**, .22 L.R.R.F., 5 Shot Clip, Peep Sights, *Modern* 45.00 65.00
- [ ] **Model 066 Buckhorn**, .22 L.R.R.F., Tube Feed, Peep Sights, *Modern* 45.00 65.00
- [ ] **Model 53**, .22 L.R.R.F., Singleshot, Takedown, *Modern* 30.00 45.00

PEERLESS
Made by Crescent H. & D. Folsom, c. 1900.
SHOTGUN, DOUBLE BARREL, SIDE-BY-SIDE
- [ ] **Various Gauges**, Outside Hammers, Damascus Barrel, *Modern* 100.00 175.00
- [ ] **Various Gauges**, Hammerless, Steel Barrel, *Modern* 135.00 200.00
- [ ] **Various Gauges**, Hammerless, Damascus Barrel, *Modern* 100.00 175.00
- [ ] **Various Gauges**, Outside Hammers, Steel Barrel, *Modern* 125.00 190.00

SHOTGUN, SINGLESHOT
- [ ] **Various Gauges**, Hammer, Steel Barrel, *Modern* 55.00 85.00

PENCE, JACOB
Lancaster, Pa. 1771. See Kentucky Rifles and Pistols.

332 / PENETRATOR

PENETRATOR
Made by Norwich Falls Pistol Co., c. 1880.

HANDGUN, REVOLVER

	V.G.	EXC.
☐ **.32 Short R.F.**, 5 Shot, Spur Trigger, Solid Frame, Single Action, Modern	90.00	160.00

PENNYPACKER, DANIEL
Berks County, Pa. 1773-1808. See Kentucky Rifles and Pistols.

PENNYPACKER, WM.
Berks County, Pa. 1808-1858. See Kentucky Rifles and Pistols.

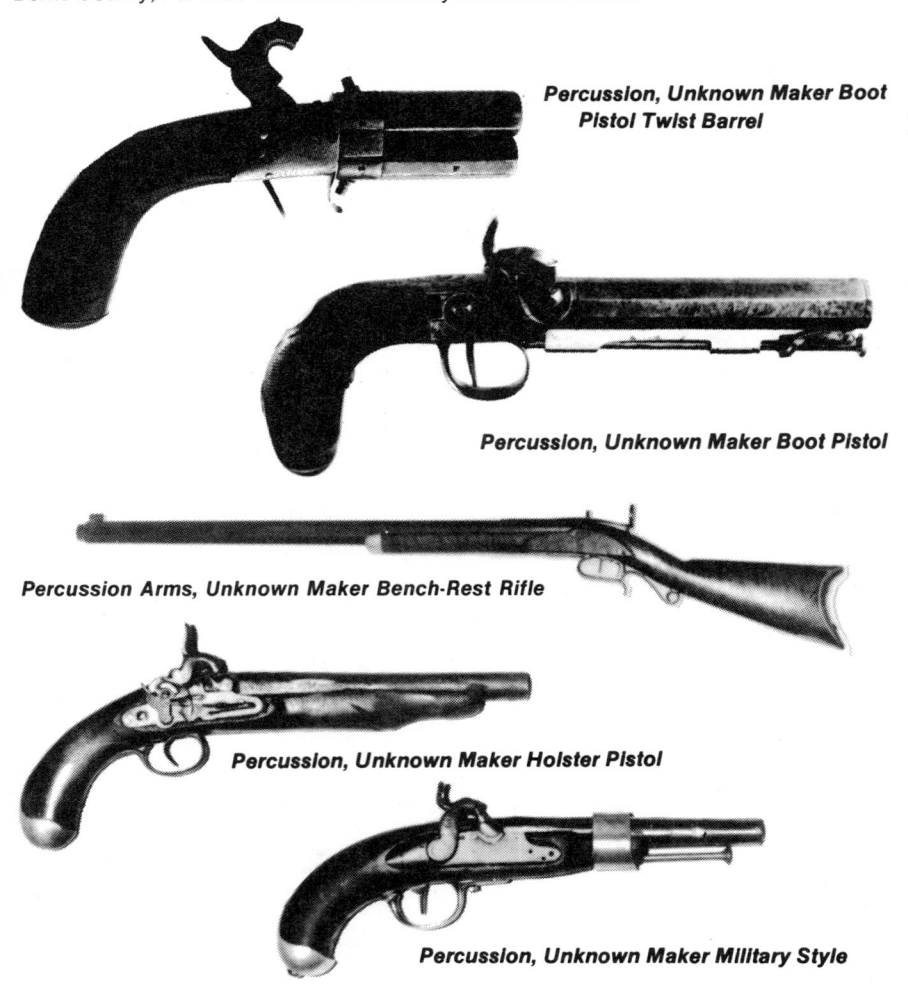

Percussion, Unknown Maker Boot Pistol Twist Barrel

Percussion, Unknown Maker Boot Pistol

Percussion Arms, Unknown Maker Bench-Rest Rifle

Percussion, Unknown Maker Holster Pistol

Percussion, Unknown Maker Military Style

PERCUSSION ARMS, UNKNOWN MAKER

	V.G.	EXC.

HANDGUN, PERCUSSION
- ☐ **.40 English**, 6 Shot, Pepperbox, Pocket Pistol, Light Engraving, German Silver Frame, Steel Barrel, *Antique* 250.00 375.00
- ☐ **.45**, Pair French, Target Pistol, Octagon Barrel, Single Set Trigger, Brass Furniture, Cased with Accessories, *Antique* 2,000.00 2,500.00
- ☐ **.70**, French Sotiau, Belt Pistol, Steel Furniture, Rifled, Octagon Barrel, *Antique* 400.00 550.00
- ☐ **Boot Pistol**, Bar Hammer, Screw Barrel, *Antique* 95.00 150.00
- ☐ **Boot Pistol**, Boxlock, Screw Barrel, *Antique* 95.00 150.00
- ☐ **Boot Pistol**, Sidelock, Derringer Style, *Antique* 120.00 180.00
- ☐ **Pair**, Duelling Pistols, Octagon Barrel, Single Set Trigger, German Silver Furniture, Medium Quality, Cased with Accessories, *Antique* 1,400.00 2,000.00

HANDGUN, REVOLVER
- ☐ **.36**, Navy Colt Type, Belgian Make, Medium Quality, *Antique* 100.00 175.00
- ☐ **.45**, Adams Type, Double Action, Octagon Barrel, Plain, Cased with Accessories, *Antique* 600.00 900.00

RIFLE, PERCUSSION
- ☐ **American Indian Trade Gun**, Belgian, Converted from Flintlock, Brass Furniture, *Antique* 500.00 900.00
- ☐ **Benchrest**, Various Calibers, Heavy Barrel, Set Triggers, Target Sights, Light Decoration, *Antique* 400.00 750.00
- ☐ **Benchrest**, Various Calibers, Heavy Barrel, Set Triggers, Target Sights, Medium Decoration, *Antique* 500.00 950.00
- ☐ **German**, Schutzen Rifle, Rifled, Ivory Inlays, Gold Inlays, Ornate, *Antique* 4,000.00 5,500.00

SHOTGUN, PERCUSSION
- ☐ **English**, 12 Ga., Double Barrel, Side by Side, Light Ornamentation, Medium Quality, *Antique* 300.00 450.00
- ☐ **English**, 12 Ga., Double Barrel, Side by Side, Light Ornamentation, High Quality, Cased with Accessories, *Antique* 500.00 800.00

PERFECT
Made by Foehl & Weeks. Phila, Pa., c. 1890.

HANDGUN, REVOLVER
- ☐ **.38 S & W**, 5 Shot, Double Action, Top Break, *Modern* 45.00 95.00

PERFECTION
Made by Crescent for H. & G. Lipscomb & Co., Nashville, Tenn.

SHOTGUN, DOUBLE BARREL, SIDE-BY-SIDE
- ☐ **Various Gauges**, Outside Hammers, Damascus Barrel, *Modern* 100.00 175.00
- ☐ **Various Gauges**, Hammerless, Steel Barrel, *Modern* 135.00 200.00
- ☐ **Various Gauges**, Hammerless, Damascus Barrel, *Modern* 100.00 175.00
- ☐ **Various Gauges**, Outside Hammers, Steel Barrel, *Modern* 125.00 190.00

SHOTGUN, SINGLESHOT
- ☐ **Various Gauges**, Hammer, Steel Barrel, *Modern* 55.00 85.00

PERFECTION AUTOMATIC REVOLVER
Made by Forehand Arms Co.

HANDGUN, REVOLVER
- ☐ **.32 S & W**, 5 Shot, Double Action, Top Break, *Antique* 55.00 85.00
- ☐ **.32 S & W**, 5 Shot, Double Action, Top Break, Hammerless, *Antique* 60.00 95.00

PERLA
Frantisek Dusek, Opocno, Czechoslovakia, c. 1935.
HANDGUN, SEMI-AUTOMATIC
☐ **.25 ACP**, Clip Fed, Blue, *Modern* 135.00 195.00

PETTIBONE, DANIEL
Philadelphia, Pa. 1799-1814.

PHILLIPINE MILITARY
SHOTGUN, SINGLESHOT
☐ **WW 2 Guerrilla Weapon**, 12 Ga., *Modern* 55.00 95.00

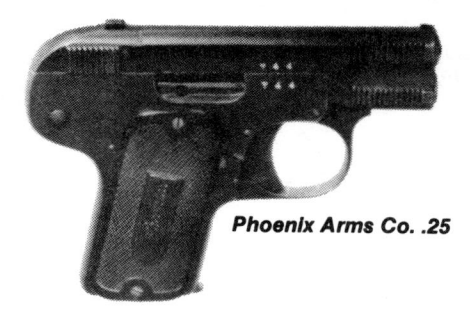

Phoenix Arms Co. .25

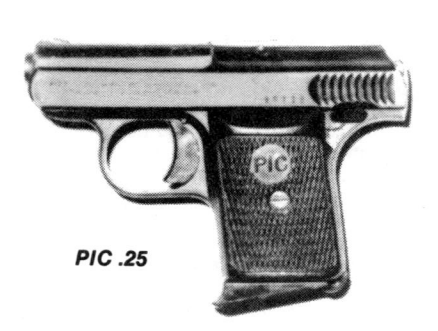

PIC .25

PHOENIX
Spain, Tomas de Urizar y Cia., c. 1920.
HANDGUN, SEMI-AUTOMATIC
☐ **Vest Pocket**, .25 ACP, Clip Fed, *Modern* 85.00 125.00

PHOENIX ARMS CO.
Lowell Arms Co., Lowell, Mass., c. 1920.
HANDGUN, SEMI-AUTOMATIC
☐ **Vest Pocket**, .25 ACP, Clip Fed, *Curio* 275.00 395.00

PIC
Made in West Germany for Precise Imports Corp., Suffern, N.Y.
HANDGUN, SEMI-AUTOMATIC
☐ **Vest Pocket**, .25 ACP, Clip Fed, *Modern* 55.00 75.00
☐ **Vest Pocket**, .22 Short R.F., Clip Fed, *Modern* 55.00 75.00
HANDGUN, REVOLVER
☐ **.22 L.R.R.F.**, Double Action, Blue, *Modern* 20.00 35.00

PICKFATT, HUMPHREY
London, England 1714-1730.
HANDGUN, FLINTLOCK
☐ **Pair**, Queen Anne Style, Box Lock, Pocket Pistol, Silver Furniture, *Antique* 2,000.00 2,750.00
☐ **Pair**, Holster Pistol, Engraved, Brass Furniture, High Quality, *Antique* 4,500.00 8,250.00

PIEDMONT
Made by Crescent for Piedmont Hdw. Danville, Pa.

	V.G.	EXC.
SHOTGUN, DOUBLE BARREL, SIDE-BY-SIDE		
☐ **Various Gauges**, Outside Hammers, Damascus Barrel, *Modern*	100.00	175.00
☐ **Various Gauges**, Hammerless, Steel Barrel, *Modern*	135.00	200.00
☐ **Various Gauges**, Hammerless, Damascus Barrel, *Modern*	100.00	175.00
☐ **Various Gauges**, Outside Hammers, Steel Barrel, *Modern*	125.00	190.00
SHOTGUN, SINGLESHOT		
☐ **Various Gauges**, Hammer, Steel Barrel, *Modern*	55.00	85.00

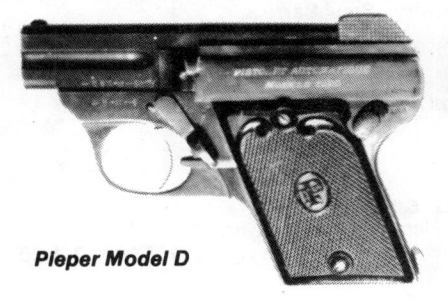

Pieper Model D

Pieper Legia

PIEPER
Henri Pieper, Herstal, Belgium 1884. Became Nicolas Pieper in 1898, and in 1905 became Anciens Etablissments Pieper.

	V.G.	EXC.
COMBINATION WEAPON, DOUBLE BARREL, SIDE-BY-SIDE		
☐ **Various Calibers**, Hammer, Open Rear Sight, Checkered Stock, Plain, *Modern*	275.00	375.00
HANDGUN, SEMI-AUTOMATIC		
☐ **Bayard Model 1908 Pocket**, .25 ACP, Blue, Clip Fed, *Modern*	125.00	175.00
☐ **Bayard Model 1908 Pocket**, .380 ACP, Blue, Clip Fed, *Modern*	95.00	155.00
☐ **Bayard Model 1923 Pocket**, .25 ACP, Blue, Clip Fed, *Modern*	95.00	160.00
☐ **Bayard Model 1923 Pocket**, .32 ACP, Blue, Clip Fed, *Modern*	130.00	195.00
☐ **Bayard Model 1930 Pocket**, .25 ACP, Blue, Clip Fed, *Modern*	130.00	195.00
☐ **Model A (Army)**, .32 ACP, Clip Fed, 7 Shot, *Modern*	95.00	140.00
☐ **Model B**, .32 ACP, Clip Fed, 6 Shot, *Modern*	80.00	120.00
☐ **Model C**, .25 ACP, Clip Fed, Long Grip, *Modern*	115.00	155.00
☐ **Model C**, .25 ACP, Clip Fed, *Modern*	95.00	135.00
☐ **Model D (1920)**, .25 ACP, Clip Fed, Tip-Up, *Modern*	110.00	150.00
☐ **Model Legia**, .25 ACP, Clip Fed, *Modern*	85.00	120.00
☐ **Model Legia**, .25 ACP, Clip Fed, Long Grip, *Modern*	95.00	135.00
☐ **Model N**, .32 ACP, Clip Fed, Tip-Up, 7 Shot, *Modern*	95.00	135.00
☐ **Model O**, .32 ACP, Clip Fed, Tip-Up, 6 Shot, *Modern*	85.00	120.00
☐ **Model P**, .25 ACP, Clip Fed, Tip-Up, *Modern*	120.00	160.00
RIFLE, BOLT ACTION		
☐ **Singleshot**, .22 L.R.R.F., Plain, *Curio*	35.00	55.00
RIFLE, SEMI-AUTOMATIC		
☐ **Pieper/Bayard Carbine**, .22 Short, Checkered Stock, Pistol Grip, *Curio*	45.00	75.00
☐ **Pieper/Bayard Carbine**, .22 Long, Checkered Stock, Pistol Grip, *Curio*	55.00	90.00
☐ **Pieper Carbine**, .22 L.R.R.F., Checkered Stock, English Grip, *Curio*	55.00	90.00

336 / PIEPER, ABRAHAM

	V.G.	EXC.
☐ **Pieper Musket**, .22 L.R.R.F., Military Style Stock, *Curio*	60.00	95.00
☐ **Pieper Musket**, .22 L.R.R.F., Military Style Stock, with Bayonet, *Curio*	80.00	120.00

SHOTGUN, DOUBLE BARREL, SIDE-BY-SIDE
☐ **Bayard**, Various Gauges, Hammerless, Boxlock, Light Engraving, Checkered Stock, *Modern*	100.00	175.00
☐ **Hammer Gun**, Various Gauges, Plain, Steel Barrels, *Modern*	75.00	135.00
☐ **Hammer Gun**, Various Gauges, Plain, Damascus Barrels, *Modern*	65.00	125.00
☐ **Hammer Gun**, Various Gauges, Light Engraving, Steel Barrels, *Modern*	95.00	165.00

PIEPER, ABRAHAM
Lancaster, Pa. 1801-1803. See Kentucky Rifles and Pistols.

PIEPER, HENRI
Also see Pieper

COMBINATION WEAPON, DOUBLE BARREL, SIDE-BY-SIDE
☐ **Various Calibers**, Double Trigger, Outside Hammers, Side Lever, *Antique*	265.00	375.00

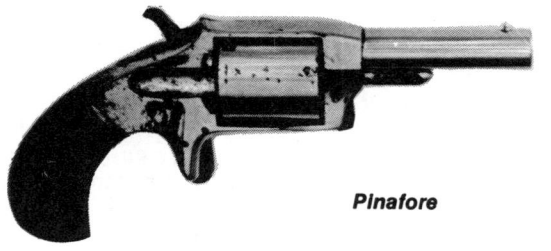

Pinafore

PINAFORE
Made by Norwich Falls Pistol Co., c. 1880.

HANDGUN, REVOLVER
☐ **.22 Short R.F.**, 7 Shot, Spur Trigger, Solid Frame, Single Action, *Antique*	90.00	160.00

PINKERTON
Gaspar Arizaga, Eibar, Spain, c. 1930.

HANDGUN, SEMI-AUTOMATIC
☐ **Browning Type**, .25 ACP, Clip Fed, Blue, *Modern*	90.00	125.00
☐ **Mondial Type**, .25 ACP, Clip Fed, Blue, *Modern*	130.00	175.00

PIONEER
Made by Stevens Arms.

RIFLE, SEMI-AUTOMATIC
☐ **Model 87**, .22 L.R.R.F., Tube Feed, Open Rear Sight, *Modern*	50.00	70.00

PIONEER
Maker unknown, c. 1880.

HANDGUN, REVOLVER
☐ **.38 Short R.F.**, 5 Shot, Spur Trigger, Solid Frame, Single Action, *Antique*	95.00	170.00

PIONEER ARMS CO.
Made by Crescent for Kruse Hardware Co. Cincinnati, Ohio.
SHOTGUN, DOUBLE BARREL, SIDE-BY-SIDE
☐ **Various Gauges**, Outside Hammers, Damascus Barrel, *Modern* 100.00 175.00
☐ **Various Gauges**, Hammerless, Steel Barrel, *Modern* 135.00 200.00
☐ **Various Gauges**, Hammerless, Damascus Barrel, *Modern* 100.00 175.00
☐ **Various Gauges**, Outside Hammers, Steel Barrel, *Modern* 125.00 190.00
SHOTGUN, SINGLESHOT
☐ **Various Gauges**, Hammer, Steel Barrel, *Modern* 55.00 85.00

PIOTTI
Brescia, Italy. Currently Imported by Ventura Imports.
SHOTGUN, DOUBLE BARREL, SIDE-BY-SIDE
☐ **Gardone**, 12 and 20 Gauges, Sidelock, Automatic Ejector, Double Trigger, Fancy Checkering, Fancy Engraving, *Modern* 1,250.00 1,750.00
☐ **Val Trompia Crown**, 12 and 20 Gauges, Sidelock, Automatic Ejector, Single Selective Trigger, Fancy Checkering, Fancy Engraving, *Modern* 2,600.00 3,750.00

PJK
Bradbury, Calif.
RIFLE, SEMI-AUTOMATIC
☐ **M-68**, 9mm Luger, Clip Fed, Carbine, Flash Hider, *Modern* 125.00 175.00

PLAINFIELD MACHINE CO.
Dunellen, N.J., Also see Iver Johnson.
AUTOMATIC WEAPON, SUBMACHINE GUN
☐ **M-2**, .30 Carbine, Carbine, Commercial, *Class 3* 150.00 195.00
HANDGUN, SEMI-AUTOMATIC
☐ **Super Enforcer**, .30 Carbine, Clip Fed, *Modern* 125.00 165.00
RIFLE, SEMI-AUTOMATIC
☐ **M-1**, .30 Carbine, Carbine, *Modern* 120.00 165.00
☐ **M-1**, .30 Carbine, Carbine, Sporting Rifle, *Modern* 115.00 160.00
☐ **M-1**, 5.7mm Carbine, Carbine, *Modern* 115.00 155.00
☐ **M-1 Deluxe**, .30 Carbine, Carbine, Sporting Rifle, Monte Carlo Stock, Checkered Stock, *Modern* 135.00 180.00
☐ **M-1 Paratrooper**, .30 Carbine, Carbine, Folding Stock, *Modern* 135.00 180.00
☐ **M-1 Presentation**, .30 Carbine, Carbine, Sporting Rifle, Monte Carlo Stock, Fancy Wood, *Modern* 135.00 185.00

PLAINFIELD ORDNANCE CO.
Middlesex, N.J.
HANDGUN, SEMI-AUTOMATIC
☐ **Model 71**, .22 L.R.R.F., Clip Fed, Stainless Steel, *Modern* 70.00 95.00
☐ **Model 71**, .22 L.R.R.F. and .25 ACP, Clip Fed, Stainless Steel, with Conversion Kit, *Modern* 80.00 120.00
☐ **Model 71**, .25 ACP, Clip Fed, Stainless Steel, *Modern* 70.00 110.00
☐ **Model 72**, .22 L.R.R.F., Clip Fed, Lightweight, *Modern* 70.00 110.00
☐ **Model 72**, .22 L.R.R.F. and .25 ACP, Clip Fed, Lightweight, with Conversion Kit, *Modern* 90.00 130.00
☐ **Model 72**, .25 ACP, Clip Fed, Lightweight, *Modern* 60.00 95.00

Plant's .42 C.P.

Plant's .28 C.P.

PLANT'S MFG. CO.
New Haven, Conn. 1860-1866.

	V.G.	EXC.

HANDGUN, REVOLVER
- ☐ **.28 Cup Primed Cartridge**, 6 Shot, Single Action, Spur Trigger, Solid Frame, *Antique* 130.00   195.00
- ☐ **.30 Cup Primed Cartridge**, 6 Shot, Single Action, Spur Trigger, Solid Frame, *Antique* 135.00   210.00
- ☐ **.31 R.F.**, 6 Shot, Single Action, Solid Frame, Spur Trigger, *Antique* ... 125.00   180.00
- ☐ **.32 Short R.F.**, 6 Shot, Single Action, Solid Frame, Spur Trigger, *Antique* 125.00   180.00
- ☐ **.42 Cup Primed Cartridge**, 6 Shot, Single Action, Spur Trigger, Solid Frame, *Antique* 155.00   240.00
- ☐ **.42 Cup Primed Cartridge**, 6 Shot, Single Action, Spur Trigger, Solid Frame, 6" Barrel, *Antique* 255.00   395.00
- ☐ **"Original"**, .28 Cup Primed Cartridge, 6 Shot, Single Action, Spur Trigger, Tip-Up, *Antique* 475.00   650.00
- ☐ **"Original"**, .30 Cup Primed Cartridge, 6 Shot, Single Action, Spur Trigger, Tip-Up, *Antique* 495.00   675.00
- ☐ **"Original"**, .42 Cup Primed Cartridge, 6 Shot, Single Action, Spur Trigger, Tip-Up, *Antique* 550.00   695.00
- ☐ **"Original"**, Various Cup-Primed Calibers, Extra Cylinder, Percussion, *Add* **$95.00-$175.00**
- ☐ **Reynolds**, .25 Short R.F., 5 Shot, Single Action, Spur Trigger, 3" Barrel, *Antique* 120.00   180.00

PLUS ULTRA
Gabilondo y Cia., Eibar, Spain, c. 1930.

HANDGUN, SEMI-AUTOMATIC
- ☐ **.32 ACP**, Extra Long Grip, Military, *Modern* 375.00   550.00

PORTUGUESE MILITARY

RIFLE, BOLT ACTION
- ☐ **Kropatchek M1886**, 8mm, Tube Feed, *Antique* 60.00   95.00
- ☐ **Mauser-Vergueiro**, 6.5mm, Rifle, *Curio* 80.00   125.00

POUS, EUDAL
Spain, c. 1790.

HANDGUN, MIQUELET-LOCK
- ☐ **Pair**, Holster Pistol, Low Quality, Light Brass Furniture, *Antique* ... **1,500.00   2,750.00**

PRAGA
Zbrojovka Praga, Prague, Czechoslovakia 1918-1926.

Portuguese Kropatchek

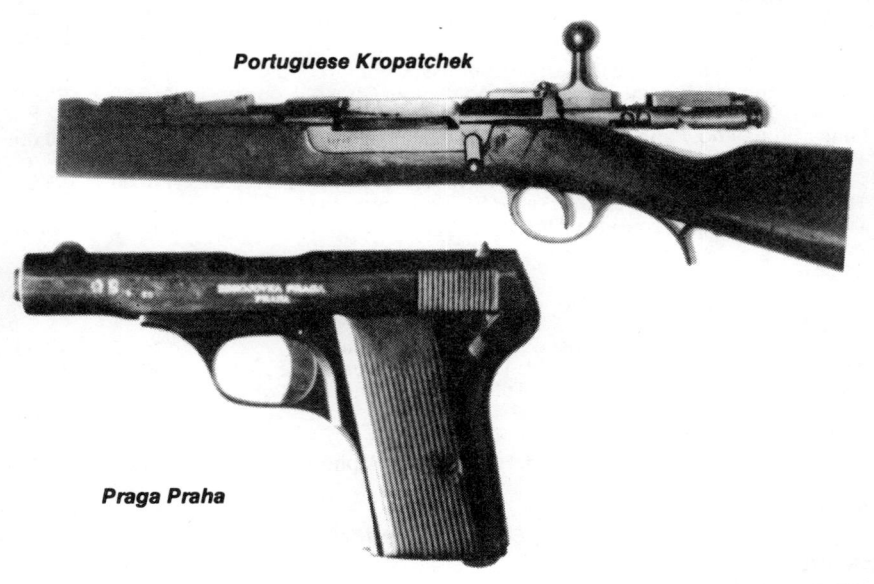

Praga Praha

	V.G.	EXC.
HANDGUN, SEMI-AUTOMATIC		
☐ **Praga**, .25 ACP, Clip Fed, Folding Trigger, *Curio*	135.00	180.00
☐ **Praha**, .32 ACP, Clip Fed, *Curio*	190.00	250.00

PRAIRIE KING
Made by Norwich Falls Pistol Co., c. 1880.

HANDGUN, REVOLVER
☐ **.22 Short R.F.**, 7 Shot, Spur Trigger, Solid Frame, Single Action, *Antique* 75.00 130.00

PREMIER
Tomas de Urizar y Cia., Eibar, Spain, c. 1920.

HANDGUN, SEMI-AUTOMATIC
☐ **.25 ACP**, Clip Fed, Blue, *Modern* 85.00 120.00

PREMIER
Brooklyn, N.Y.

SHOTGUN, DOUBLE BARREL, SIDE-BY-SIDE
☐ **Ambassador**, Various Calibers, Checkered Stock, Hammerless, Double Trigger, *Modern* 165.00 220.00
☐ **Brush King**, 12 and 20 Gauges, Checkered Stock, Hammerless, Double Trigger, *Modern* 125.00 165.00
☐ **Continental**, Various Calibers, Checkered Stock, Outside Hammers, Double Trigger, *Modern* 135.00 185.00
☐ **Magnum**, 10 Ga. 3½", Checkered Stock, Hammerless, Double Trigger, *Modern* 150.00 200.00
☐ **Magnum**, 12 Ga. Mag. 3", Checkered Stock, Hammerless, Double Trigger, *Modern* 135.00 180.00
☐ **Monarch**, Various Calibers, Hammerless, Double Trigger, Checkered Stock, Engraved, Adjustable Choke, *Modern* 250.00 350.00

340 / PREMIER

	V.G.	EXC.
☐ **Presentation**, Various Calibers, Hammerless, Double Trigger, Fancy Engraving, Fancy Checkering, Adjustable Choke, *Modern*	450.00	675.00
☐ **Presentation**, Various Calibers, Adjustable Choke, Double Trigger, Fancy Engraving, Fancy Checkering, Extra Shotgun Barrel, *Modern*	650.00	900.00
☐ **Regent**, Various Calibers, Checkered Stock, Hammerless, Double Trigger, *Modern*	110.00	155.00
☐ **Regent**, Various Calibers, Checkered Stock, Hammerless, Double Trigger, Extra Shotgun Barrel, *Modern*	200.00	300.00

PREMIER
Made by Stevens Arms.

RIFLE, BOLT ACTION

☐ **Model 52**, .22 L.R.R.F., Singleshot, Takedown, *Modern*	30.00	40.00
☐ **Model 53**, .22 L.R.R.F., Singleshot, Takedown, *Modern*	30.00	45.00
☐ **Model 66 Buckhorn**, .22 L.R.R.F., Tube Feed, Open Rear Sight, *Modern*	35.00	55.00

RIFLE, SLIDE ACTION

☐ **Model 75**, .22 L.R.R.F., Tube Feed, Hammerless, *Modern*	85.00	160.00

PREMIER
Made by Thomas E. Ryan, Norwich, Conn., c. 1870-1876.

HANDGUN, REVOLVER

☐ **.22 Short R.F.**, 7 Shot, Spur Trigger, Solid Frame, Single Action, *Antique*	90.00	160.00
☐ **.38 Long R.F.**, 6 Shot, Spur Trigger, Solid Frame, Single Action, *Antique*	90.00	160.00

PREMIER TRAIL BLAZER
Made by Stevens Arms.

RIFLE, SLIDE ACTION

☐ **Model 75**, .22 L.R.R.F., Tube Feed, Hammerless, *Modern*	85.00	160.00

PRESCOTT, E.A.
Worcester, Mass. 1860-1874.

HANDGUN, REVOLVER

☐ **.22 Short R.F.**, 7 Shot, Spur Trigger, Solid Frame, Single Action, *Antique*	90.00	150.00
☐ **.30 R.F.**, 6 Shot, Spur Trigger, Solid Frame, Single Action, *Antique*	95.00	155.00
☐ **.32 Short R.F.**, 6 Shot, Spur Trigger, Solid Frame, Single Action, *Antique*	95.00	155.00
☐ **"Navy" .32 Short R.F.**, 6 Shot, Single Action, Solid Frame, Finger-Rest Trigger Guard, *Antique*	220.00	300.00
☐ **"Navy" .38 Short R.F.**, 6 Shot, Single Action, Solid Frame, Finger-Rest Trigger Guard, *Antique*	250.00	325.00

PRICE, J.W.
Made by Stevens Arms.

SHOTGUN, SINGLESHOT

☐ **Model 90**, Various Gauges, Takedown, Automatic Ejector, Plain, Hammer, *Modern*	40.00	55.00

Prima

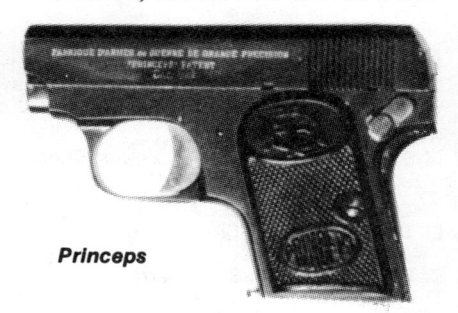

Princeps

PRIMA
Mre. d'Armes des Pyrenees, Hendaye, France.
HANDGUN, SEMI-AUTOMATIC
☐ **.25 ACP**, Clip Fed, *Modern* 95.00 135.00

V.G. EXC.

PRINCEPS
Tomas de Urizar, Eibar, Spain, c. 1920.
HANDGUN, SEMI-AUTOMATIC
☐ **.32 ACP**, Clip Fed, *Modern* 90.00 130.00

PRINCESS
Unknown maker, c. 1880.
HANDGUN, REVOLVER
☐ **.22 Short R.F.**, 7 Shot, Spur Trigger, Solid Frame, Single Action, *Antique* 90.00 160.00

PROTECTOR
Made by Norwich Falls Pistol Co., c. 1880.
HANDGUN, REVOLVER
☐ **.22 Short R.F.**, 7 Shot, Spur Trigger, Solid Frame, Single Action, *Antique* 90.00 160.00
☐ **.32 Short R.F.**, 5 Shot, Spur Trigger, Solid Frame, Single Action, *Antique* 95.00 170.00

PROTECTOR ARMS CO.
Spain, c. 1900.
HANDGUN, SEMI-AUTOMATIC
☐ **M 1918**, .25 ACP, Clip Fed, *Modern* 85.00 125.00

PURDEY, JAMES
RIFLE, DOUBLE BARREL, SIDE-BY-SIDE
☐ **.500 #2 Express**, Damascus Barrel, Outside Hammers, Under-Lever, Engraved, Ornate, *Antique* 2,500.00 3,500.00
RIFLE, PERCUSSION
☐ **.52**, Double Barrel, Side by Side, Damascus Barrel, Engraved, Fancy Wood, Gold Inlays, Cased with Accessories, *Antique* 5,000.00 6,000.00

PURDEY, JAS. & SONS
London, England, 1816 to Date.

342 / QUAIL

	V.G.	EXC.

RIFLE, DOUBLE BARREL, SIDE-BY-SIDE
☐ **Various Calibers**, Sidelock, Fancy Engraving, Fancy Checkering,
Fancy Wood, *Modern* 8,000.00 14,500.00

RIFLE, BOLT ACTION
☐ **Sporting Rifle**, Various Calibers, Fancy Wood, Checkered Stock,
Express Sights, *Modern* 1,450.00 2,250.00

SHOTGUN, DOUBLE BARREL, OVER-UNDER
☐ **12 Ga.**, Vent Rib, Single Selective Trigger, Pistol-Grip Stock,
Modern 9,000.00 16,000.00
☐ **Various Gauges**, Extra Barrels Only $3000.00-$5000.00
☐ **Purdy**, Various Gauges, Sidelock, Automatic Ejector, Double
Trigger, Fancy Engraving, Fancy Checkering, *Modern* 7,500.00 12,000.00
☐ **Purdy**, Various Gauges, Sidelock, Automatic Ejector, Single
Trigger, Fancy Engraving, Fancy Checkering, *Modern* 9,500.00 14,000.00
☐ **Woodward**, Various Gauges, Sidelock, Automatic Ejector, Double
Trigger, Fancy Engraving, Fancy Checkering, *Modern* 7,500.00 10,000.00
☐ **Woodward**, Various Gauges, Sidelock, Automatic Ejector, Single
Trigger, Fancy Engraving, Fancy Checkering, *Modern* 11,000.00 17,000.00

SHOTGUN, DOUBLE BARREL, SIDE-BY-SIDE
☐ **12 Ga.**, Extra Barrel, Vent Rib, Single Selective Trigger, Engraved,
Cased with Accessories, *Modern* 12,000.00 18,000.00
☐ **12 Ga.**, Extra Barrels, 10 Ga., Pistol-Grip Stock, Cased with
Accessories, *Modern* 12,000.00 18,000.00
☐ **Various Gauges**, Extra Barrels Only $2,500.00-$3,500.00
☐ **Featherweight**, Various Gauges, Sidelock, Automatic Ejector,
Double Trigger, Fancy Engraving, Fancy Checkering, *Modern* 8,500.00 12,000.00
☐ **Featherweight**, Various Gauges, Sidelock, Automatic Ejector,
Single Trigger, Fancy Engraving, Fancy Checkering, *Modern* 9,000.00 15,000.00
☐ **Game Gun**, Various Gauges, Sidelock, Automatic Ejector, Double
Trigger, Fancy Engraving, Fancy Checkering, *Modern* 8,000.00 13,000.00
☐ **Game Gun**, Various Gauges, Sidelock, Automatic Ejector, Single
Trigger, Fancy Engraving, Fancy Checkering, *Modern* 9,000.00 15,000.00
☐ **Pigeon Gun**, 12 Ga., Single Selective Trigger, Vent Rib, Cased
Straight Grip, *Modern* 9,000.00 15,000.00
☐ **Pigeon Gun**, Various Gauges, Sidelock, Automatic Ejector, Double
Trigger, Fancy Engraving, Fancy Checkering, *Modern* 7,000.00 12,000.00
☐ **Pigeon Gun**, Various Gauges, Sidelock, Automatic Ejector, Single
Trigger, Fancy Engraving, Fancy Checkering, *Modern* 8,000.00 13,000.00
☐ **Two-Inch**, 12 Ga. 2", Sidelock, Automatic Ejector, Double Trigger,
Fancy Engraving, Fancy Checkering, *Modern* 7,000.00 10,000.00
☐ **Two-Inch**, 12 Ga. 2", Sidelock, Automatic Ejector, Single Trigger,
Fancy Engraving, Fancy Checkering, *Modern* 8,500.00 12,500.00

SHOTGUN, SINGLESHOT
☐ **12 Ga.**, Vent Rib, Plain, Trap Grade, *Modern* 6,000.00 9,500.00

QUAIL
Made by Crescent, c. 1900.

SHOTGUN, DOUBLE BARREL, SIDE-BY-SIDE
☐ **Various Gauges**, Outside Hammers, Damascus Barrel, *Modern* 100.00 175.00
☐ **Various Gauges**, Hammerless, Steel Barrel, *Modern* 135.00 200.00
☐ **Various Gauges**, Hammerless, Damascus Barrel, *Modern* 100.00 175.00
☐ **Various Gauges**, Outside Hammers, Steel Barrel, *Modern* 125.00 190.00

SHOTGUN, SINGLESHOT
☐ **Various Gauges**, Hammer, Steel Barrel, *Modern* 55.00 85.00

	V.G.	EXC.

QUAIL'S FARGO
Tradename used by Dakin Gun Co. and Simmons Specialties.
SHOTGUN, DOUBLE BARREL, SIDE-BY-SIDE
- ☐ **12 Ga.**, Checkered Stock, Plain, *Modern* 120.00   165.00

QUEEN CITY
Made by Crescent for Elmira Arms Co., c. 1900.
SHOTGUN, DOUBLE BARREL, SIDE-BY-SIDE
- ☐ **Various Gauges**, Outside Hammers, Damascus Barrel, *Modern* 100.00   175.00
- ☐ **Various Gauges**, Hammerless, Steel Barrel, *Modern* 135.00   200.00
- ☐ **Various Gauges**, Hammerless, Damascus Barrel, *Modern* 100.00   175.00
- ☐ **Various Gauges**, Outside Hammers, Steel Barrel, *Modern* 125.00   190.00

SHOTGUN, SINGLESHOT
- ☐ **Various Gauges**, Hammer, Steel Barrel, *Modern* 55.00   85.00

RADIUM
Gabilondo y Urresti, Guernica, Spain, c. 1910
HANDGUN, SEMI-AUTOMATIC
- ☐ **.25 ACP**, Fixed Magazine, Side Loading, Blue, *Curio* 175.00   275.00

RADOM
Fabryka Broni w Radomu, Radom, Poland, c. 1930 through WWII.
HANDGUN, REVOLVER
- ☐ **Ng 30**, 7.62mm Nagant, Gas Seal, Double Action, *Curio* 135.00   185.00

HANDGUN, SEMI-AUTOMATIC
- ☐ **VIS 1935**, 9mm Luger, Clip Fed, Military, Nazi-Proofed, Early Type, *Modern* 150.00   225.00

Radom Ng 30

Radom VIS 1935 Polish

Radom VIS 1935 Early Nazi

Radom VIS 1935 Late Nazi

	V.G.	EXC.
☐ **VIS 1935**, 9mm Luger, Clip Fed, Military, Nazi-Proofed, Late Type, *Modern*	150.00	225.00
☐ **VIS 1935 Navy**, 9mm Luger, Clip Fed, Military, Nazi-Proofed, *Modern*	150.00	225.00
☐ **VIS 1935 Polish**, 9mm Luger, Clip Fed, Military, *Modern*	150.00	225.00

RANGER
Made by E.L. Dickinson, Springfield, Mass.

HANDGUN, REVOLVER
☐ **#2**, .32 Short R.F., 5 Shot, Spur Trigger, Solid Frame, Single Action, *Antique*	90.00	150.00

RANGER
Made by Stevens Arms.

RIFLE, SLIDE ACTION
☐ **Model 70**, .22 L.R.R.F., Solid Frame, Hammer, *Modern*	90.00	150.00
☐ **Model 75**, .22 L.R.R.F., Tube Feed, Hammerless, *Modern*	110.00	170.00

SHOTGUN, DOUBLE BARREL, SIDE-BY-SIDE
☐ **Model 315**, Various Gauges, Steel Barrels, Hammerless, *Modern*	95.00	165.00
☐ **Model 215**, 12 and 16 Gauges, Steel Barrels, Outside Hammers, *Modern*	95.00	165.00

SHOTGUN, SINGLESHOT
☐ **Model 89 Dreadnaught**, Varoius Gauges, Hammer, *Modern*	40.00	60.00

RANGER
Made by Hopkins & Allen, c. 1880.

HANDGUN, REVOLVER
☐ **.22 Short R.F.**, 7 Shot, Spur Trigger, Solid Frame, Single Action, *Antique*	90.00	150.00
☐ **.32 Short R.F.**, 6 Shot, Spur Trigger, Solid Frame, Single Action, *Antique*	95.00	160.00

RANGER ARMS, INC.
Gainesville, Tex., c. 1972.

RIFLE, BOLT ACTION
☐ **Bench Rest/Varminter**, Various Calibers, Singleshot, Target Rifle, Thumbhole Stock, Heavy Barrel, Recoil Pad, *Modern*	325.00	450.00
☐ **Governor Grade**, Various Calibers, Sporting Rifle, Fancy Checkering, Fancy Wood, Recoil Pad, Sling Swivels, *Modern*	300.00	400.00
☐ **Governor Grade Magnum**, Various Calibers, Sporting Rifle, Fancy Checkering, Fancy Wood, Recoil Pad, Sling Swivels, *Modern*	325.00	450.00
☐ **Senator Grade**, Various Calibers, Sporting Rifle, Fancy Checkering, Recoil Pad, Sling Swivels, *Modern*	250.00	350.00
☐ **Senator Grade Magnum**, Various Calibers, Sporting Rifle, Fancy Checkering, Recoil Pad, Sling Swivels, *Modern*	260.00	360.00
☐ **Statesman Grade**, Various Calibers, Sporting Rifle, Checkered Stock, Recoil Pad, Sling Swivels, *Modern*	175.00	250.00
☐ **Statesman Grade Magnum**, Various Calibers, Sporting Rifle, Checkered Stock, Recoil Pad, Sling Swivels, *Modern*	185.00	275.00

RASCH
Brunswick, Germany 1790-1810.

	V.G.	EXC.

RIFLE, FLINTLOCK
☐ **Yaeger**, Octagon Barrel, Brass Furniture, Engraved, Carved, Target Sights, *Antique* **2,500.00 3,450.00**

RATHFONG, GEORGE
Lancaster, Pa. 1774-1809. See U.S. Military, Kentucky Rifles.

RATHFONG, JACOB
Lancaster, Pa. 1810-1839. See Kentucky Rifles and Pistols.

RAVEN
HANDGUN, SEMI-AUTOMATIC
☐ **.25 ACP**, Clip Fed, Blue, *Modern* 30.00   50.00
☐ **.25 ACP**, Clip Fed, Nickel, *Modern* 30.00   50.00
☐ **.25 ACP**, Clip Fed, Chrome, *Modern* 30.00   50.00

REASOR, DAVID
Lancaster, Pa. 1749-1780. See Kentucky Rifles and Pistols.

RECK
Reck Sportwaffenfabrik, Arnsberg, West Germany.
HANDGUN, REVOLVER
☐ **.22 L.R.R.F.**, Double Action, Blue, *Modern* 20.00   30.00
HANDGUN, SEMI-AUTOMATIC
☐ **P-8**, .25 ACP, Clip Fed, Blue, *Modern* 40.00   60.00

RED CLOUD
HANDGUN, REVOLVER
☐ **.32 Long R.F.**, 5 Shot, Single Action, Solid Frame, Spur Trigger, *Antique* 90.00   160.00

RED JACKET
Made by Lee Arms, Wilkes-Barre, Pa., c. 1870.
HANDGUN, REVOLVER
☐ **.22 Long R.F.**, 7 Shot, Single Action, Solid Frame, Spur Trigger, *Antique* 90.00   160.00
☐ **.32 Short R.F.**, 5 Shot, Single Action, Solid Frame, Spur Trigger, *Antique* 95.00   165.00

RED MOUNTAIN ARSENAL
Parowen, Utah
AUTOMATIC WEAPON, SUBMACHINE GUN
☐ **Model 80C**, 9mm Luger and .45 ACP Combo, Clip Fed, With Conversion Kit, *Class 3* 250.00   350.00

REED, JAMES
Lancaster, Pa. 1778-1780. See Kentucky Rifles.

REFORM
August Schueler, Suhl, Germany, c. 1910.
HANDGUN, MANUAL REPEATER
☐ **.25 ACP**, 4 Barrels, Spur Trigger, Hammer, *Curio* 90.00   140.00

REFORM
Spain, unknown maker, c. 1920.
HANDGUN, SEMI-AUTOMATIC
☐ **.25 ACP**, Clip Fed, Blue, *Curio* 80.00 120.00

REGENT
Gregorio Bolumburu, Eibar, Spain, c. 1925.
HANDGUN, SEMI-AUTOMATIC
☐ **.25 ACP**, Clip Fed, Blue, *Modern* 80.00 125.00

REGENT
Karl Burgsmuller, Kreiensen, West Germany.
HANDGUN, REVOLVER
☐ **.22 L.R.R.F.**, Double Action, Blue *Modern* 25.00 40.00

REGINA
Gregorio Bolumburu, Eibar, Spain, c. 1920.
HANDGUN, SEMI-AUTOMATIC
☐ **Pocket**, .32 ACP, Clip Fed, Blue, *Modern* 85.00 125.00
☐ **Vest Pocket**, .25 ACP, Clip Fed, Blue, *Modern* 70.00 110.00

REGNUM
Tradename used by August Menz, Suhl, Germany.
HANDGUN, MANUAL REPEATER
☐ **.25 ACP**, 4 Barrels, Spur Trigger, Hammer, *Modern* 90.00 145.00

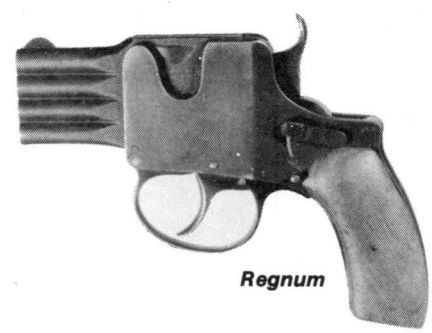

Regnum

Regina Vest Pocket

REID PATENT REVOLVERS
Made by W. Irving for James Reid, N.Y. 1862-1884.
HANDGUN, REVOLVER
☐ **.22 Short R.F.**, 7 Shot, Spur Trigger, Solid Frame, Single Action,
  Antique 140.00 265.00
☐ **.32 Short R.F.**, 7 Shot, Spur Trigger, Solid Frame, Single Action,
  Antique 185.00 340.00
☐ **.41 Short R.F.**, 5 Shot, Spur Trigger, Solid Frame, Single Action,
  Antique 385.00 550.00
☐ **My Friend**, .22 R.F., Knuckleduster, 7 Shot, *Antique* 225.00 375.00
☐ **My Friend**, .32 R.F., Knuckleduster, 7 Shot, *Antique* 285.00 450.00

REIMS
Azanza y Arrizabalaga, Eibar, Spain, c. 1914.

Reims 1914 .25

	V.G.	EXC.
HANDGUN, SEMI-AUTOMATIC		
☐ **1914 Model**, .25 ACP, Clip Fed, *Modern*	80.00	120.00
☐ **1914 Model**, .32 ACP, Clip Fed, *Modern*	90.00	135.00

REINA
Mre. d'Armes des Pyrenees, Hendaye, France, c. 1930.

HANDGUN, SEMI-AUTOMATIC
☐ **.32 ACP**, Clip Fed, Blue, *Modern* 90.00   135.00

REISING
Hartford, Conn. 1916-1924.

AUTOMATIC WEAPON, SUBMACHINE GUN
☐ **M50 Reising**, .45 ACP, Clip Fed, Wood Stock, Military, Cased with Accessories, *Class 3* 250.00   350.00
☐ **M50 Reising**, .45 ACP, Clip Fed, Wood Stock, Military, *Class 3* 175.00   275.00
☐ **M55 Reising**, .45 ACP, Clip Fed, Folding Stock, Military, *Class 3* ... 275.00   375.00

HANDGUN, SEMI-AUTOMATIC
☐ **Target (Hartford)**, .22 L.R.R.F., Clip Fed, Hammer, *Modern* 235.00   325.00
☐ **Target (N.Y.)**, .22 L.R.R.F., Clip Fed, Hammer, *Modern* 340.00   475.00

REMINGTON ARMS CO.
Eliphalet Remington, Herkimer County, N.Y. 1816-1831. Ilion, N.Y. 1831 to Date. 1856- E. Remington & Sons; 1888- Remington Arms Co.; 1910- Remington Arms U.M.C. Co.; 1925 to Date Remington Arms Co.

HANDGUN, DOUBLE BARREL, OVER-UNDER
☐ **Elliot Derringer**, 1st. Model, .41 Short R.F., Spur Trigger, Tip-Up, no Extractor, Markings on Sides of Barrel, E. Remington & Sons, *Antique* 375.00   650.00
☐ **Elliot Derringer**, 2nd. Model, .41 Short R.F., Spur Trigger, Tip-Up, with Extractor, Markings on Sides of Barrel, E. Remington & Sons, *Antique* 325.00   600.00
☐ **Elliot Derringer**, 3rd. Model, .41 Short R.F., Spur Trigger, Tip-Up, with Extractor, Markings on Top of Barrel, E. Remington & Sons, *Antique* 225.00   400.00
☐ **Elliot Derringer**, 4th Model, .41 Short R.F., Spur Trigger, Tip-Up, with Extractor, Markings on Top of Barrel, Remington Arms Co., *Curio* 200.00   350.00
☐ **Elliot Derringer**, 5th Model, .41 Short R.F., Spur Trigger, Tip-Up, with Extractor, Markings on Top of Barrel, *Modern* 200.00   340.00
☐ **Elliot Derringer**, 6th Model, .41 Short R.F., Spur Trigger, Tip-Up, with Extractor, Remington Arms Co. #'s L75925-L99941, *Modern* ... 175.00   300.00

348 / REMINGTON ARMS COMPANY

	V.G.	EXC.

HANDGUN, MANUAL REPEATER
- ☐ **Elliot Derringer**, .22 Short R.F., 5 Shot, Double Action, Ring Trigger, Rotating Firing Block, *Antique* 275.00   425.00
- ☐ **Elliot Derringer**, .32 Short R.F., 4 Shot, Double Action, Ring Trigger, Rotating Firing Block, *Antique* 270.00   400.00
- ☐ **Rider Magazine Pistol**, .32 Extra Short R.F., Tube Feed, Spur Trigger, 5 Shot, *Antique* 325.00   500.00

HANDGUN, PERCUSSION
- ☐ **.31, Beals #1**, Revolver, Pocket Pistol, 5 Shot, Octagon Barrel, 3" Barrel, *Antique* 275.00   425.00
- ☐ **.31, Beals #2**, Revolver, Pocket Pistol, 5 Shot, Octagon Barrel, 3" Barrel, Spur Trigger, *Antique* 975.00   1,800.00
- ☐ **.31, Beals #3**, Revolver, Octagon Barrel, 4" Barrel, Spur Trigger, with Loading Lever, *Antique* 600.00   1,100.00
- ☐ **.31, New Model Pocket**, Revolver, Safety Notches on Cylinder, Spur Trigger, 5 Shot, Octagon Barrel, *Antique* 275.00   525.00
- ☐ **.31, Rider Pocket**, Revolver, Double Action, 5 Shot, Octagon Barrel, 3" Barrel, *Antique* 225.00   450.00
- ☐ **.36, Beals Navy**, Revolver, Single Action, Octagon Barrel, 7½" Barrel *Antique* 375.00   650.00
- ☐ **.36, Belt Model**, Revolver, Safety Notches on Cylinder, Single Action, Octagon Barrel, 6½" Barrel, *Antique* 325.00   575.00
- ☐ **.36, Belt Model**, Revolver, Safety Notches on Cylinder, Double Action, Octagon Barrel, 6½" Barrel, *Antique* 450.00   900.00
- ☐ **.36, Model 1861 Navy**, Revolver, Channeled Loading Level, Single Action, Octagon Barrel, 7½" Barrel, *Antique* 375.00   650.00
- ☐ **.36, New Model Navy**, Revolver, Safety Notches on Cylinder, Single Action, Octagon Barrel, 7½" Barrel, *Antique* 425.00   700.00
- ☐ **.36 Police Model**, Revolver, Single Action, Octagon Barrel, Various Barrel Lengths, 5 Shot, *Antique* 300.00   525.00
- ☐ **.44, Beals Army**, Revolver, Single Action, Octagon Barrel, 8" Barrel, *Antique* 525.00   900.00
- ☐ **.44, Model 1861 Army**, Revolver, Channeled Loading Lever, Single Action, Octagon Barrel, 8" Barrel, *Antique* 400.00   650.00
- ☐ **.44, New Model Army**, Revolver, Safety Notches on Cylinder, Single Action, Octagon Barrel, 7½" Barrel, *Antique* 375.00   625.00

HANDGUN, REVOLVER
- ☐ **Iroquois**, .22 L.R.R.F., 7 Shot, Solid Frame, Spur Trigger, Single Action, Fluted Cylinder, *Antique* 190.00   295.00
- ☐ **Iroquois**, .22 L.R.R.F., 7 Shot, Solid Frame, Spur Trigger, Single Action, Unfluted Cylinder, *Antique* 270.00   395.00
- ☐ **Model 1875**, .44-40 WCF, Single Action, Western Style, Solid Frame, *Antique* 550.00   950.00
- ☐ **Model 1875**, .45 Colt, Single Action, Western Style, Solid Frame, *Antique* 500.00   900.00
- ☐ **Model 1890**, .44-40 WCF, Single Action, Western Style, Solid Frame, *Antique* 850.00   1,650.00
- ☐ **Smoot #1**, .30 Short R.F., 5 Shot, Solid Frame, Spur Trigger, Single Action, *Antique* 150.00   235.00
- ☐ **Smoot #2**, .32 Short R.F., 5 Shot, Solid Frame, Spur Trigger, Single Action, *Antique* 125.00   200.00
- ☐ **Smoot #3**, .38 Long R.F., 5 Shot, Solid Frame, Spur Trigger, Single Action, Birdhead Grip, *Antique* 160.00   280.00
- ☐ **Smoot #3**, .38 Long R.F., 5 Shot, Solid Frame, Spur Trigger, Single Action, Saw Handle Grip, *Antique* 170.00   320.00
- ☐ **Smoot #4**, .38 S & W, 5 Shot, Solid Frame, Spur Trigger, Single Action, no Ejector Housing, *Antique* 130.00   200.00

REMINGTON ARMS COMPANY / 349

	V.G.	EXC.
☐ **Smoot #4**, .41 Short R.F., 5 Shot, Solid Frame, Spur Trigger, Single Action, no Ejector Housing, *Antique*	115.00	175.00
☐ **Zig-Zag Derringer**, .22 Short R.F., Pepperbox, Double Action, 6 Shot, Ring Trigger, *Antique*	700.00	1,350.00

HANDGUN, SEMI-AUTOMATIC
☐ **Model 51**, .32 ACP, Clip Fed, Grip Safety, *Modern*	185.00	300.00
☐ **Model 51**, .380 ACP, Clip Fed, Grip Safety, *Modern*	225.00	350.00

HANDGUN, SINGLESHOT
☐ **#1 Vest Pocket**, .22 Short R.F., Iron Frame, no Breech Bolt, Spur Trigger, *Antique*	225.00	350.00
☐ **#2 Vest Pocket**, .30 Short R.F., Iron Frame, "Split Breech" Model, Spur Trigger, *Antique*	300.00	475.00
☐ **#2 Vest Pocket**, .41 Short R.F., Iron Frame, "Split Breech" Model, Spur Trigger, *Antique*	275.00	425.00
☐ **Elliot Derringer**, .41 Short R.F., Iron Frame, Birdhead Grip, no Breech Bolt, *Antique*	375.00	550.00
☐ **Mark III**, 10 Gauge, Signal Pistol, 9" Barrel, Spur Trigger, Brass Frame, *Curio*	85.00	145.00
☐ **Model 1865 Navy**, .50 Rem. Navy R.F., Rolling Block, Spur Trigger, 8½" Barrel, *Antique*	800.00	1,300.00
☐ **Model 1867 Navy**, .50 Rem., Rolling Block, 7" Barrel, *Antique*	425.00	700.00
☐ **Model 1871 Army**, .50 Rem., Rolling Block, 8" Barrel, *Antique*	325.00	500.00
☐ **Model 1891 Target**, Rolling Block, 12" Barrel, Add **15%-20%**		
☐ **Model 1891 Target**, Rolling Block, 10" Barrel, Add **15%-20%**		
☐ **Model 1891 Target**, .22 L.R.R.F., Rolling Block, 8" Barrel, Half-Octagon Barrel, Plain Barrel, *Antique*	675.00	1,100.00
☐ **Model 1891 Target**, .25 Short R.F., Rolling Block, 8" Barrel, Half-Octagon Barrel, Plain Barrel, *Antique*	450.00	675.00
☐ **Model 1891 Target**, .32 Long R.F., Rolling Block, 8" Barrel, Half-Octagon Barrel, Plain Barrel, *Antique*	525.00	800.00
☐ **Model 1891 Target**, .32 S & W, Rolling Block, 8" Barrel, Half-Octagon Barrel, Plain Barrel, *Antique*	625.00	1,000.00
☐ **Model 1891 Target**, .32-20 WCF, Rolling Block, 8" Barrel, Half-Octagon Barrel, Plain Barrel, *Antique*	700.00	1,200.00
☐ **Model 1901 Target**, .22 L.R.R.F., Rolling Block, 10" Barrel, Checkered Stock, Half-Octagon Barrel, *Modern*	600.00	975.00
☐ **Model 1901 Target**, .44 Russian, Rolling Block, 10" Barrel, Checkered Stock, Half-Octagon Barrel, *Modern*	650.00	1,175.00
☐ **XP-100**, .221 Rem. Fireball, Bolt Action, Target Nylon Stock, 10½" Barrel, Vent Rib, Open Sights, Cased, *Modern*	160.00	220.00
☐ **XP-100 Silhouette**, 7mm BR Rem., Bolt Action, Target Nylon Stock, 15" Barrel, Vent Rib, Open Sights, Cased, *Modern*	175.00	235.00

RIFLE, BOLT ACTION
☐ **Enfield 1914**, .303 British, Full-Stocked, Military, *Curio*	135.00	185.00
☐ **International (1961)**, Various Calibers, Singleshot, Target Stock, no Sights, with Accessories, *Modern*	250.00	375.00
☐ **Model 1907/15 French**, 8 x 50R Lebel, Military, *Curio*	95.00	160.00
☐ **Model 1907/15 French**, 8 x 50R Lebel, Carbine, Military, *Curio*	90.00	155.00
☐ **Model 1917 U.S.**, .30-06 Springfield, Full-Stocked, Military, *Curio*	145.00	225.00
☐ **Model 30A**, Various Calibers, Sporting Rifle, Plain, Open Rear Sight, *Modern*	160.00	230.00
☐ **Model 30F Premier**, Various Calibers, Sporting Rifle, Fancy Checkering, Fancy Engraving, Fancy Wood, *Modern*	475.00	625.00
☐ **Model 30R**, Various Calibers, Sporting Rifle, Plain, Carbine, Open Rear Sight, *Modern*	160.00	220.00

350 / REMINGTON ARMS COMPANY

	V.G.	EXC.
☐ **Model 30S**, Various Calibers, Sporting Rifle, Checkered Stock, Peep Sights, *Modern*	220.00	320.00
☐ **Model 33A**, .22 L.R.R.F., Plain, Singleshot, Open Rear Sight, *Modern*	35.00	55.00
☐ **Model 33A**, .22 L.R.R.F., Plain, Singleshot, Peep Sights, *Modern*	35.00	55.00
☐ **Model 33NRA**, .22 L.R.R.F., Plain, Singleshot, Peep Sights, Sling Swivels, *Modern*	40.00	65.00
☐ **Model 341A**, .22 L.R.R.F., Tube Feed, Takedown, Open Rear Sight, *Modern*	55.00	85.00
☐ **Model 341P**, .22 L.R.R.F., Tube Feed, Takedown, Peep Sights, *Modern*	60.00	95.00
☐ **Model 341SB**, .22 L.R.R.F., Tube Feed, Takedown, Smoothbore, *Modern*	50.00	70.00
☐ **Model 34A**, .22 L.R.R.F., Tube Feed, Takedown, Open Rear Sight, *Modern*	55.00	85.00
☐ **Model 34A**, .22 L.R.R.F., Tube Feed, Takedown, Lyman Sights, *Modern*	55.00	85.00
☐ **Model 34NRA**, .22 L.R.R.F., Tube Feed, Takedown, Lyman Sights, Target, *Modern*	65.00	95.00
☐ **Model 37A**, .22 L.R.R.F., 5 Shot Clip, Target Stock, Target Sights, Target Barrel, *Modern*	225.00	310.00
☐ **Model 37A**, .22 L.R.R.F., 5 Shot Clip, Target Stock, Target Sights, Target Barrel, Fancy Wood, *Modern*	250.00	335.00
☐ **Model 37AX**, .22 L.R.R.F., 5 Shot Clip, Target Stock, no Sights, Target Barrels, *Modern*	185.00	250.00
☐ **Model 40-XB CF-H2**, Various Calibers, Stainless Steel Barrel, Heavy Barrel, Target Stock, no Sights, *Modern*	275.00	450.00
☐ **Model 40-XB CF-S2**, Various Calibers, Stainless Steel Barrel, Target Stock, no Sights, *Modern*	300.00	475.00
☐ **Model 40-XB RF-H2**, .22 L.R.R.F., Heavy Barrel, Target Stock, no Sights, *Modern*	175.00	260.00
☐ **Model 40-XB RF-S2**, .22 L.R.R.F., Target Stock, no Sights, *Modern*	175.00	275.00
☐ **Model 40-XB-BR**, for 2 oz. Trigger, *Add* **$40.00-$65.00**		
☐ **Model 40-XB-BR**, Various Calibers, Stainless Steel Barrel, Heavy Barrel, Target Stock, no Sights, *Modern*	375.00	500.00
☐ **Model 40-XB-BR**, for Repeater, *Add* **$25.00**		
☐ **Model 40X-CFH2**, Various Calibers, Singleshot, Target Stock, no Sights, Heavy Barrel, *Modern*	175.00	260.00
☐ **Model 40X-CFS2**, Various Calibers, Singleshot, Target Stock, no Sights, *Modern*	165.00	240.00
☐ **Model 40X-H1**, .22 L.R.R.F., Singleshot, Target Stock, Target Sights, Heavy Barrel, *Modern*	165.00	225.00
☐ **Model 40X-H2**, .22 L.R.R.F., Singleshot, Target Stock, no Sights, Heavy Barrel, *Modern*	135.00	195.00
☐ **Model 40X-S1**, .22 L.R.R.F., Singleshot, Target Stock, Target Sights, *Modern*	155.00	200.00
☐ **Model 40X-S2**, .22 L.R.R.F., Singleshot, Target Stock, no Sights, *Modern*	135.00	175.00
☐ **Model 40XB Sporter**, .22 L.R.R.F., *Modern*	325.00	425.00
☐ **Model 40XC National Match**, .308 Winchester, Target Stock, Target Sights, *Modern*	375.00	525.00
☐ **Model 40XR Position**, .22 L.R.R.F., Target Stock, no Sights, *Modern*	235.00	325.00
☐ **Model 41A**, .22 L.R.R.F., Takedown, Singleshot, Plain, Open Rear Sight, *Modern*	35.00	55.00
☐ **Model 41AS**, .22 WRF, Takedown, Singleshot, Plain, Open Rear Sight, *Modern*	40.00	60.00

REMINGTON ARMS COMPANY / 351

Remington .44, Model 1861 Army

Remington Smoot #1

Remington Smoot #4

Remington Model 51

Remington Smoot #3

Remington Elliot Repeater

Remington Elliot Derringer

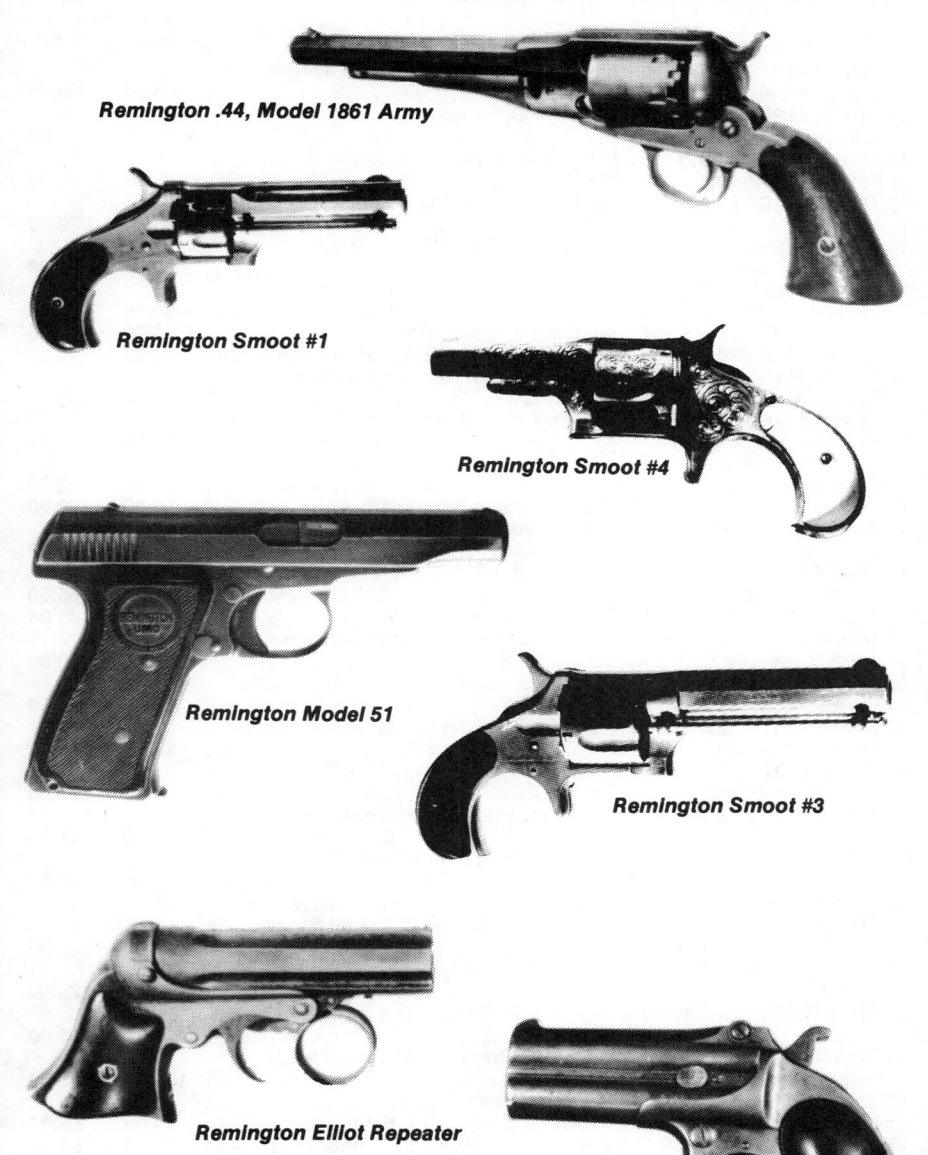

352 / REMINGTON ARMS COMPANY

	V.G.	EXC.
☐ **Model 41P**, .22 L.R.R.F., Takedown, Singleshot, Plain, Target Sights, *Modern*	40.00	60.00
☐ **Model 41SB**, .22 L.R.R.F., Takedown, Singleshot, Plain, Smoothbore, *Modern*	35.00	55.00
☐ **Model 510A**, .22 L.R.R.F., Singleshot, Open Rear Sight, Plain, Takedown, *Modern*	35.00	60.00
☐ **Model 510C**, .22 L.R.R.F., Singleshot, Carbine, Plain, Takedown, *Modern*	35.00	60.00
☐ **Model 51OP**, .22 L.R.R.F., Singleshot, Peep Sights, Plain, Takedown, *Modern*	35.00	60.00
☐ **Model 510SB**, .22 L.R.R.F., Singleshot, Smoothbore, Plain, Takedown, *Modern*	30.00	55.00
☐ **Model 510X**, .22 L.R.R.F., Singleshot, Plain, *Modern*	25.00	40.00
☐ **Model 510X**, .22 L.R.R.F., Singleshot, Plain, Smoothbore, *Modern*	25.00	40.00
☐ **Model 511A**, .22 L.R.R.F., Clip Fed, Open Rear Sight, Plain, Takedown, *Modern*	45.00	65.00
☐ **Model 511P**, .22 L.R.R.F., Clip Fed, Peep Sights, Plain, Takedown, *Modern*	45.00	70.00
☐ **Model 511SB**, .22 L.R.R.F., Clip Fed, Smoothbore, Plain, Takedown, *Modern*	35.00	60.00
☐ **Model 511X**, .22 L.R.R.F., Clip Fed, Plain, *Modern*	40.00	60.00
☐ **Model 512A**, .22 L.R.R.F., Tube Feed, Plain, Open Rear Sight, *Modern*	45.00	65.00
☐ **Model 512P**, .22 L.R.R.F., Tube Feed, Plain, Peep Sights, *Modern*	45.00	65.00
☐ **Model 512SB**, .22 L.R.R.F., Tube Feed, Plain, Smoothbore, *Modern*	40.00	65.00
☐ **Model 512X**, .22 L.R.R.F., Tube Feed, Plain, *Modern*	40.00	60.00
☐ **Model 513SA**, .22 L.R.R.F., Clip Fed, Sporting Rifle, Open Rear Sight, Takedown, Checkered Stock, *Modern*	70.00	120.00
☐ **Model 513SP**, .22 L.R.R.F., Clip Fed, Sporting Rifle, Peep Sights, Takedown, Checkered Stock, *Modern*	70.00	120.00
☐ **Model 513TR**, .22 L.R.R.F., Clip Fed, Target Stock, Target Sights, Takedown, *Modern*	90.00	140.00
☐ **Model 513TX**, .22 L.R.R.F., Clip Fed, Target Stock, no Sights, Takedown, *Modern*	70.00	120.00
☐ **Model 514**, .22 L.R.R.F., Singleshot, Plain, Open Rear Sight, *Modern*	25.00	40.00
☐ **Model 514BR (Youth)**, .22 L.R.R.F., Singleshot, Plain, Open Rear Sight, *Modern*	25.00	40.00
☐ **Model 514P**, .22 L.R.R.F., Singleshot, Plain, Peep Sights, *Modern*	30.00	45.00
☐ **Model 521TL**, .22 L.R.R.F., Takedown, Clip Fed, Target Stock, Lyman Sights, *Modern*	60.00	90.00
☐ **Model 540XR Position**, .22 L.R.R.F., Target Stock, no Sights, *Modern*	145.00	225.00
☐ **Model 540XRJR Position**, .22 L.R.R.F., Target Stock, no Sights, *Modern*	135.00	200.00
☐ **Model 541-S**, .22 L.R.R.F., Clip Fed, Checkered Stock, Fancy Wood, *Modern*	135.00	185.00
☐ **Model 580**, .22 L.R.R.F., Singleshot, Plain, *Modern*	40.00	60.00
☐ **Model 580 BR (Youth)**, .22 L.R.R.F., Singleshot, Plain, *Modern*	35.00	55.00
☐ **Model 580 SB**, .22 L.R.R.F., Singleshot, Plain, Smoothbore, *Modern*	35.00	55.00
☐ **Model 581**, .22 L.R.R.F., Clip Fed, Plain, *Modern*	55.00	80.00
☐ **Model 581**, .22 L.R.R.F., Clip Fed, Plain, Left-Hand, *Modern*	55.00	85.00
☐ **Model 582**, .22 L.R.R.F., Tube Feed, Plain, *Modern*	65.00	95.00
☐ **Model 591**, 5mm Rem. RFM, Clip Fed, Monte Carlo Stock, Plain, *Modern*	90.00	135.00
☐ **Model 592**, 5mm Rem. RFM, Tube Feed, Monte Carlo Stock, Plain, *Modern*	90.00	135.00

REMINGTON ARMS COMPANY / 353

	V.G.	EXC.
☐ **Model 600**, Various Calibers, Vent Rib, Carbine, Checkered Stock, *Modern*	145.00	200.00
☐ **Model 600**, Various Calibers, Vent Rib, Carbine, Magnum, Recoil Pad, Checkered Stock, *Modern*	175.00	240.00
☐ **Model 600 Montana Centennial**, Trap Grade, Carbine, Checkered Stock, Commemorative, *Curio*	200.00	275.00
☐ **Model 660**, Various Calibers, Carbine, Checkered Stock, *Modern*	145.00	200.00
☐ **Model 660**, Various Calibers, Carbine, Magnum, Recoil Pad, Checkered Stock, *Modern*	175.00	250.00
☐ **Model 700 Safari**, Various Calibers, Magnum, Checkered Stock, Fancy Wood, *Modern*	325.00	450.00
☐ **Model 700ADL**, Various Calibers, Checkered Stock, *Modern*	155.00	220.00
☐ **Model 700ADL**, Various Calibers, Magnum, Checkered Stock, *Modern*	175.00	235.00
☐ **Model 700BDL**, Various Calibers, Checkered Stock, Fancy Wood, *Modern*	195.00	265.00
☐ **Model 700BDL**, Various Calibers, Magnum, Checkered Stock, Fancy Wood, *Modern*	200.00	275.00
☐ **Model 700BDL**, Various Calibers, Heavy Barrel, Varmint, Checkered Stock, Fancy Wood, *Modern*	215.00	300.00
☐ **Model 700BDL**, Various Calibers, Checkered Stock, Fancy Wood, Magnum, Left-Hand, *Modern*	220.00	300.00
☐ **Model 700BDL**, Various Calibers, Checkered Stock, Fancy Wood, Left-Hand, *Modern*	200.00	280.00
☐ **Model 700C Custom**, Various Calibers, Checkered Stock, Fancy Wood, *Modern*	345.00	475.00
☐ **Model 700D Peerless**, Various Calibers, Fancy Checkering, Fancy Wood, Engraved, *Modern*	575.00	750.00
☐ **Model 700F Premier**, Various Calibers, Fancy Checkering, Fancy Wood, Fancy Engraving, *Modern*	975.00	1,450.00
☐ **Model 720A**, Various Calibers, Sporting Rifle, Open Rear Sight, *Modern*	160.00	210.00
☐ **Model 720A**, Various Calibers, Sporting Rifle, Target Sights, *Modern*	185.00	245.00
☐ **Model 720R**, Various Calibers, Sporting Rifle, Open Rear Sight, Carbine, *Modern*	165.00	235.00
☐ **Model 720R**, Various Calibers, Sporting Rifle, Target Sights, Carbine, *Modern*	190.00	250.00
☐ **Model 720S**, Various Calibers, Sporting Rifle, Target Sights, *Modern*	190.00	250.00
☐ **Model 721**, For .300 H & H Magnum, *Add* **$20.00-$35.00**		
☐ **Model 721 Peerless**, Various Calibers, Long Action, Sporting Rifle, Fancy Wood, Engraved, Fancy Checkering, *Modern*	500.00	675.00
☐ **Model 721 Premier**, Various Calibers, Long Action, Sporting Rifle, Fancy Wood, Fancy Engraving, Fancy Checkering, *Modern*	825.00	1,250.00
☐ **Model 721 Special**, Various Calibers, Long Action, Sporting Rifle, Checkered Stock, Fancy Wood, *Modern*	135.00	185.00
☐ **Model 721A**, Various Calibers, Long Action, Sporting Rifle, Plain, *Modern*	120.00	165.00
☐ **Model 721ADL**, Various Calibers, Long Action, Sporting Rifle, Checkered Stock, *Modern*	135.00	175.00
☐ **Model 721BDL**, Various Calibers, Long Action, Sporting Rifle, Monte Carlo Stock, Checkered Stock, Fancy Wood, *Modern*	145.00	185.00
☐ **Model 722**, For .222 Rem. *Add* **$25.00-$35.00**		
☐ **Model 722A**, , Various Calibers, Short Action, Sporting Rifle, Plain, *Modern*	115.00	155.00

354 / REMINGTON ARMS COMPANY

	V.G.	EXC.
☐ **Model 722ADL**, Various Calibers, Short Action, Sporting Rifle, Checkered Stock, *Modern*	135.00	175.00
☐ **Model 722BDL**, Various Calibers, Short Action, Sporting Rifle, Checkered Stock, Fancy Wood, *Modern*	145.00	195.00
☐ **Model 722D Peerless**, Various Calibers, Short Action, Sporting Rifle, Fancy Wood, Fancy Checkering, Engraved, *Modern*	475.00	650.00
☐ **Model 722F Premier**, Various Calibers, Short Action, Sporting Rifle, Fancy Wood, Fancy Engraving, Fancy Checkering, *Modern*	750.00	975.00
☐ **Model 725ADL**, Various Calibers, Long Action, Sporting Rifle, Checkered Stock, Fancy Wood, *Modern*	175.00	240.00
☐ **Model 725ADL**, Various Calibers, Long Action, Magnum, Sporting Rifle, Checkered Stock, Fancy Wood, *Modern*	350.00	465.00
☐ **Model 725D Peerless**, Various Calibers, Long Action, Sporting Rifle, Engraved, Fancy Checkering, Fancy Wood, *Modern*	500.00	675.00
☐ **Model 725F Premier**, Various Calibers, Long Action, Sporting Rifle, Fancy Engraving, Fancy Checkering, Fancy Wood, *Modern*	875.00	1,250.00
☐ **Model 788**, Various Calibers, Clip Fed, Plain, *Modern*	130.00	165.00
☐ **Model 788**, Various Calibers, Clip Fed, Left-Hand, Plain, *Modern*	140.00	175.00
☐ **Nylon 10**, .22 L.R.R.F., Singleshot, Plastic Stock, *Modern*	40.00	55.00
☐ **Nylon 10-SB**, .22 L.R.R.F., Singleshot, Plastic Stock, Smoothbore, *Modern*	30.00	45.00
☐ **Nylon 12**, .22 L.R.R.F., Tube Feed, Plastic, *Modern*	50.00	75.00
RIFLE, LEVER ACTION		
☐ **Nylon 76**, .22 L.R.R.F., Tube Feed, Plastic Stock, *Modern*	60.00	95.00

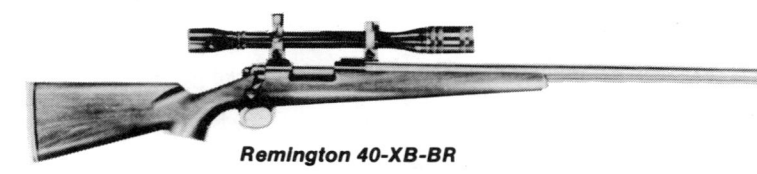

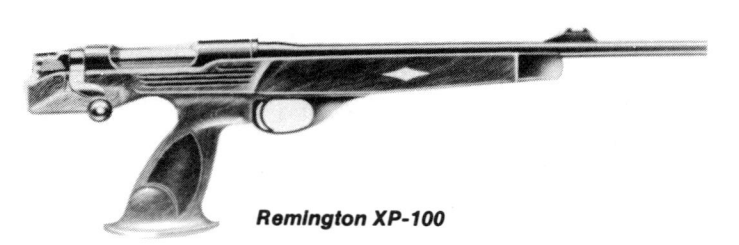

Remington 40-XB-BR

Remington XP-100

RIFLE, SEMI-AUTOMATIC

☐ **Model Four**, Various Calibers, Clip Fed, Sporting Rifle, Open Rear Sight, Checkered Stock, Fancy Wood, *Modern*	220.00	295.00
☐ **Model 10C Mohawk**, .22 L.R.R.F., Clip Fed, Plastic Stock, *Modern*	45.00	65.00
☐ **Model 16**, .22 Rem. Automatic R.F., Takedown, Tube Feed, *Modern*	135.00	200.00
☐ **Model 16D**, .22 Rem. Automatic R.F., Takedown, Tube Feed, Checkered Stock, Engraved, *Modern*	285.00	375.00
☐ **Model 16F**, .22 Rem. Automatic R.F., Takedown, Tube Feed, Fancy Checkering, Fancy Engraving, *Modern*	635.00	775.00
☐ **Model 241A**, .22 L.R.R.F., Tube Feed, Takedown, Open Rear Sight, *Modern*	170.00	240.00

REMINGTON ARMS COMPANY / 355

	V.G.	EXC.
☐ **Model 241A**, .22 Short R.F., Tube Feed, Takedown, Open Rear Sight, *Modern*	160.00	220.00
☐ **Model 241D**, .22 L.R.R.F., Takedown, Tube Feed, Fancy Checkering, Engraved, *Modern*	290.00	375.00
☐ **Model 241F**, .22 L.R.R.F., Takedown, Tube Feed, Fancy Checkering, Fancy Engraving, *Modern*	650.00	775.00
☐ **Model 24A**, .22 L.R.R.F., Takedown, Plain, *Modern*	115.00	160.00
☐ **Model 24A**, .22 Short R.F., Takedown, Plain, *Modern*	95.00	145.00
☐ **Model 24C**, .22 L.R.R.F., Takedown, Checkered Stock, *Modern*	120.00	165.00
☐ **Model 24D Peerless**, .22 L.R.R.F., Takedown, Fancy Checkering, Engraved, *Modern*	335.00	450.00
☐ **Model 24F Premier**, .22 L.R.R.F., Takedown, Fancy Checkering, Fancy Engraving, *Modern*	725.00	875.00
☐ **Model 550-2G**, .22 Short R.F., Takedown, Open Rear Sight, Plain, *Modern*	50.00	85.00
☐ **Model 550A**, .22 L.R.R.F., Takedown, Open Rear Sight, Plain, *Modern*	50.00	80.00
☐ **Model 550P**, .22 L.R.R.F., Takedown, Peep Sights, Plain, *Modern*	60.00	95.00
☐ **Model 552A**, .22 L.R.R.F., Tube Feed, Plain, *Modern*	65.00	95.00
☐ **Model 552BDL**, .22 L.R.R.F., Tube Feed, Checkered Stock, *Modern*	75.00	110.00
☐ **Model 552C**, .22 L.R.R.F., Tube Feed, Carbine, Plain, *Modern*	65.00	90.00
☐ **Model 552GS**, .22 Short R.F., Tube Feed, Plain, *Modern*	70.00	105.00
☐ **Model 740A**, Various Calibers, Clip Fed. Sporting Rifle, Open Rear Sight, Plain, *Modern*	145.00	215.00
☐ **Model 740ADL**, Various Calibers, Clip Fed, Sporting Rifle, Open Rear Sight, Checkered Stock, *Modern*	155.00	220.00
☐ **Model 740BDL**, Various Calibers, Clip Fed, Sporting Rifle, Open Rear Sight, Checkered Stock, Fancy Wood, *Modern*	175.00	235.00
☐ **Model 740D Peerless**, Various Calibers, Clip Fed, Sporting Rifle, Open Rear Sight, Fancy Checkering, Engraved, *Modern*	650.00	875.00
☐ **Model 740F Premier**, Various Calibers, Clip Fed, Sporting Rifle, Open Rear Sight, Fancy Checkering, Fancy Engraving, *Modern*	975.00	1,400.00
☐ **Model 7400**, Various Calibers, Clip Fed, Sporting Rifle, Open Rear Sight, Checkered Stock, *Modern*	200.00	270.00
☐ **Model 742**, .30-06 Springfield, Bicentennial, Clip Fed, *Modern*	200.00	285.00
☐ **Model 742**, Various Calibers, Clip Fed, Sporting Rifle, Open Rear Sight, Checkered Stock, *Modern*	185.00	255.00
☐ **Model 742 Canadian Centennial**, Clip Fed, Sporting Rifle, Open Rear Sight, Checkered Stock, Commemorative, *Curio*	200.00	300.00
☐ **Model 742ADL**, Various Calibers, Clip Fed, Sporting Rifle, Open Rear Sight, Checkered Stock, *Modern*	175.00	240.00
☐ **Model 742BDL**, Various Calibers, Clip Fed, Sporting Rifle, Open Rear Sight, Checkered Stock, Fancy Wood, *Modern*	185.00	275.00
☐ **Model 742C**, Various Calibers, Clip Fed, Sporting Rifle, Open Rear Sight, Carbine, Checkered Stock, *Modern*	180.00	265.00
☐ **Model 742CDL**, Various Calibers, Clip Fed, Sporting Rifle, Open Rear Sight, Carbine, Fancy Wood, *Modern*	190.00	280.00
☐ **Model 742D Peerless**, Various Calibers, Clip Fed, Sporting Rifle, Open Rear Sight, Fancy Checkering, Engraved, *Modern*	650.00	875.00
☐ **Model 742F Premier**, Various Calibers, Clip Fed, Sporting Rifle, Open Rear Sights, Fancy Checkering, Engraved, *Modern*	1,300.00	1,700.00
☐ **Model 81A**, Various Calibers, Plain, Takedown, *Modern*	200.00	300.00
☐ **Model 81D Peerless**, Various Calibers, Takedown, Fancy Checkering, Engraved, *Modern*	525.00	650.00
☐ **Model 81F Premier**, Various Calibers, Takedown, Fancy Checkering, Fancy Engraving, Fancy Wood, *Modern*	875.00	1,250.00
☐ **Model 8A Standard**, Various Calibers, Plain, *Modern*	195.00	270.00

356 / REMINGTON ARMS COMPANY

	V.G.	EXC.
☐ **Model 8C Special**, Various Calibers, Checkered Stock, *Modern* ...	220.00	320.00
☐ **Model 8D Peerless**, Various Calibers, Fancy Checkering, Light Engraving, *Modern*	450.00	600.00
☐ **Model 8E Expert**, Various Calibers, Fancy Checkering, Engraved, *Modern*	600.00	850.00
☐ **Model 8F Premier**, Various Calibers, Fancy Checkering, Fancy Engraving, Fancy Wood, *Modern*	875.00	1,150.00
☐ **Nylon 11**, .22 L.R.R.F., Clip Fed, Plastic Stock, *Modern*	45.00	60.00
☐ **Nylon 66**, .22 L.R.R.F., Tube Feed, Plastic Stock, *Modern*	55.00	75.00
☐ **Nylon 66**, .22 L.R.R.F., Tube Feed, Bicentennial, Plastic Stock, *Modern*	55.00	85.00
☐ **Nylon 66 GS**, .22 Short R.F., Tube Feed, Plastic Stock, *Modern* ...	55.00	80.00
☐ **Model 77**, .22 L.R.R.F., Clip Fed, Plastic Stock, *Modern*	50.00	75.00

RIFLE, SINGLESHOT

	V.G.	EXC.
☐ **Beals**, .32 R.F., Sliding Barrel, Plain, *Antique*	245.00	350.00
☐ **Hepburn #3**, Various Calibers, Sporting Rifle, Checkered Stock, Hammer, *Curio*	350.00	550.00
☐ **Model 1**, Various Calibers, Rolling Block, Sporting Rifle, Adjustable Sights, Plain Stock, *Curio*	175.00	325.00
☐ **Model 1**, Various Calibers, Rolling Block, Target, Adjustable Sights, Checkered Stock, *Curio*	475.00	625.00
☐ **Model 4**, .22 L.R.R.F., Rolling Block, Takedown, *Modern*	115.00	165.00
☐ **Model 4S Boy Scout**, .22 L.R.R.F., Rolling Block, Full-Stocked, *Curio*	225.00	400.00
☐ **Model 4S Boy Scout**, .22 L.R.R.F., Rolling Block, Full-Stocked, with Bayonet, *Curio*	340.00	500.00
☐ **Model 5**, Various Calibers, Rolling Block, Sporting Rifle, Adjustable Sights, Plain Stock, *Curio*	250.00	425.00
☐ **Model 6**, .22 L.R.R.F., Rolling Block, Takedown, *Modern*	85.00	135.00
☐ **Model 6**, .32 Long Rifle, Rolling Block, Takedown, *Modern*	85.00	130.00
☐ **Model 7**, Various Rimfires, Rolling Block, Target, Adjustable Sights, Checkered Stock, *Curio*	575.00	925.00
☐ **Model 7**, Various Rimfires, Rolling Block, Target, Swiss Buttplate, Checkered Stock, Adjustable Sights, *Curio*	750.00	1,250.00
☐ **Model 7**, Various Rimfires, Rolling Block, Target, Swiss Buttplate, Checkered Stock, Peep Sights, *Curio*	775.00	1,350.00
☐ **1867 Navy**, .50/70 C.F., Military, Carbine, *Antique*	400.00	600.00
☐ **1867 Cadet Navy**, .50/45 C.F., Military, *Antique*	500.00	700.00
☐ **Split Breech**, .46 R.F., Military, Carbine, *Antique*	375.00	550.00
☐ **Split Breech**, .50 R.F., Military, Carbine, *Antique*	475.00	750.00

RIFLE, SLIDE ACTION

	V.G.	EXC.
☐ **Model Six**, Various Calibers, Clip Fed, Sporting Rifle, Open Rear Sight, Monte Carlo Stock, Checkered Stock, *Modern*	200.00	275.00
☐ **Model 12A Standard**, .22 L.R.R.F., Plain Round Barrel, Tube Feed, *Modern*	115.00	160.00
☐ **Model 12B Gallery**, .22 Short R.F., Plain, Round Barrel, Tube Feed, *Modern*	110.00	150.00
☐ **Model 12C**, .22 L.R.R.F., Plain, Octagon Barrel, Tube Feed, Target, *Modern*	125.00	200.00
☐ **Model 12C-NRA**, .22 L.R.R.F., Plain, Octagon Barrel, Tube Feed, Peep Sights, *Modern*	170.00	250.00
☐ **Model 12CS Special**, .22 WRF, Plain, Octagon Barrel, Tube Feed, *Modern*	125.00	200.00
☐ **Model 12D Peerless**, .22 L.R.R.F., Checkered Stock, Octagon Barrel, Tube Feed, Light Engraving, *Modern*	325.00	425.00
☐ **Model 12E Expert**, .22 L.R.R.F., Fancy Checkering, Octagon Barrel, Tube Feed, Engraved, *Modern*	450.00	600.00

REMINGTON ARMS COMPANY / 357

	V.G.	EXC.
☐ **Model 12F Premier**, .22 L.R.R.F., Fancy Checkering, Octagon Barrel, Tube Feed, Fancy Engraving, Fancy Wood, *Modern*	700.00	850.00
☐ **Model 121A**, .22 L.R.R.F., Takedown, Tube Feed, Plain, *Modern*	150.00	225.00
☐ **Model 121A**, .22 Short R.F., Takedown, Tube Feed, Plain, *Modern*	125.00	180.00
☐ **Model 121D Peerless**, .22 L.R.R.F., Takedown, Tube Feed, Fancy Checkering, Engraved, *Modern*	450.00	600.00
☐ **Model 121F Premier**, .22 L.R.R.F., Takedown, Tube Feed, Fancy Checkering, Fancy Engraving, *Modern*	750.00	900.00
☐ **Model 121S**, .22 WRF, Takedown, Tube Feed, Plain, *Modern*	135.00	190.00
☐ **Model 121SB**, .22 L.R.R.F., Takedown, Tube Feed, Plain, Smoothbore, *Modern*	140.00	175.00
☐ **Model 14½ A**, Various Calibers, Tube Feed, Short Action, Plain, *Modern*	175.00	250.00
☐ **Model 14½ R**, Various Calibers, Tube Feed, Short Action, Carbine, Plain Barrel, *Modern*	235.00	310.00
☐ **Model 141A**, Various Calibers, Takedown, Tube Feed, Plain, *Modern*	175.00	250.00
☐ **Model 141D Peerless**, Various Calibers, Takedown, Tube Feed, Fancy Checkering, Engraved, *Modern*	450.00	600.00
☐ **Model 141F Premier**, Various Calibers, Takedown, Tube Feed, Fancy Checkering, Fancy Engraving, *Modern*	850.00	1,050.00
☐ **Model 141R**, Various Calibers, Takedown, Tube Feed, Plain, Carbine, *Modern*	175.00	250.00
☐ **Model 14A**, Various Calibers, Tube Feed, Plain, *Modern*	150.00	225.00
☐ **Model 14C Special**, Various Calibers, Tube Feed, Checkered Stock, *Modern*	180.00	250.00
☐ **Model 14D Peerless**, Various Calibers, Tube Feed, Fancy Checkering, Engraved, *Modern*	425.00	550.00
☐ **Model 14F Premier**, Various Calibers, Tube Feed, Fancy Checkering, Fancy Wood, Fancy Engraving, *Modern*	750.00	1,000.00
☐ **Model 14R**, Various Calibers, Tube Feed, Carbine, Plain, *Modern*	190.00	275.00
☐ **Model 25A**, Various Calibers, Takedown, Plain, *Modern*	150.00	225.00
☐ **Model 25D Peerless**, Various Calibers, Takedown, Checkered Stock, Engraved, *Modern*	450.00	600.00
☐ **Model 25F Premier**, Various Calibers, Takedown, Fancy Checkering, Fancy Engraving, *Modern*	800.00	1,050.00
☐ **Model 25R**, Various Calibers, Takedown, Plain, Carbine, *Modern*	175.00	250.00
☐ **Model 572**, .22 L.R.R.F., Tube Feed, Open Rear Sight, Lightweight, Fancy Checkering, Chrome, *Modern*	60.00	100.00
☐ **Model 572A**, .22 L.R.R.F., Tube Feed, Open Rear Sight, Plain, *Modern*	75.00	110.00
☐ **Model 572BDL**, .22 L.R.R.F., Tube Feed, Open Rear Sight, Checkered Stock, *Modern*	85.00	125.00
☐ **Model 572SB**, .22 L.R.R.F., Tube Feed, Plain, Smoothbore, *Modern*	70.00	110.00
☐ **Model 760**, .30-06 Springfield, Bicentennial, Clip Fed, *Modern*	175.00	240.00
☐ **Model 760A**, Various Calibers, Clip Fed, Sporting Rifle, Open Rear Sight, Plain, *Modern*	150.00	200.00
☐ **Model 760ADL**, Various Calibers, Clip Fed, Sporting Rifle, Open Rear Sight, Monte Carlo Stock, Checkered Stock, *Modern*	175.00	235.00
☐ **Model 760BDL**, Various Calibers, Clip Fed, Sporting Rifle, Open Rear Sight, Monte Carlo Stock, Checkered Stock, *Modern*	195.00	260.00
☐ **Model 760C**, Various Calibers, Clip Fed, Sporting Rifle, Open Rear Sight, Carbine, Plain, *Modern*	165.00	225.00
☐ **Model 760CDL**, Various Calibers, Clip Fed, Sporting Rifle, Open Rear Sight, Carbine, Checkered Stock, *Modern*	190.00	265.00
☐ **Model 760D Peerless**, Various Calibers, Clip Fed, Sporting Rifle, Open Rear Sight, Fancy Checkering, Engraved, *Modern*	575.00	850.00

358 / REMINGTON ARMS COMPANY

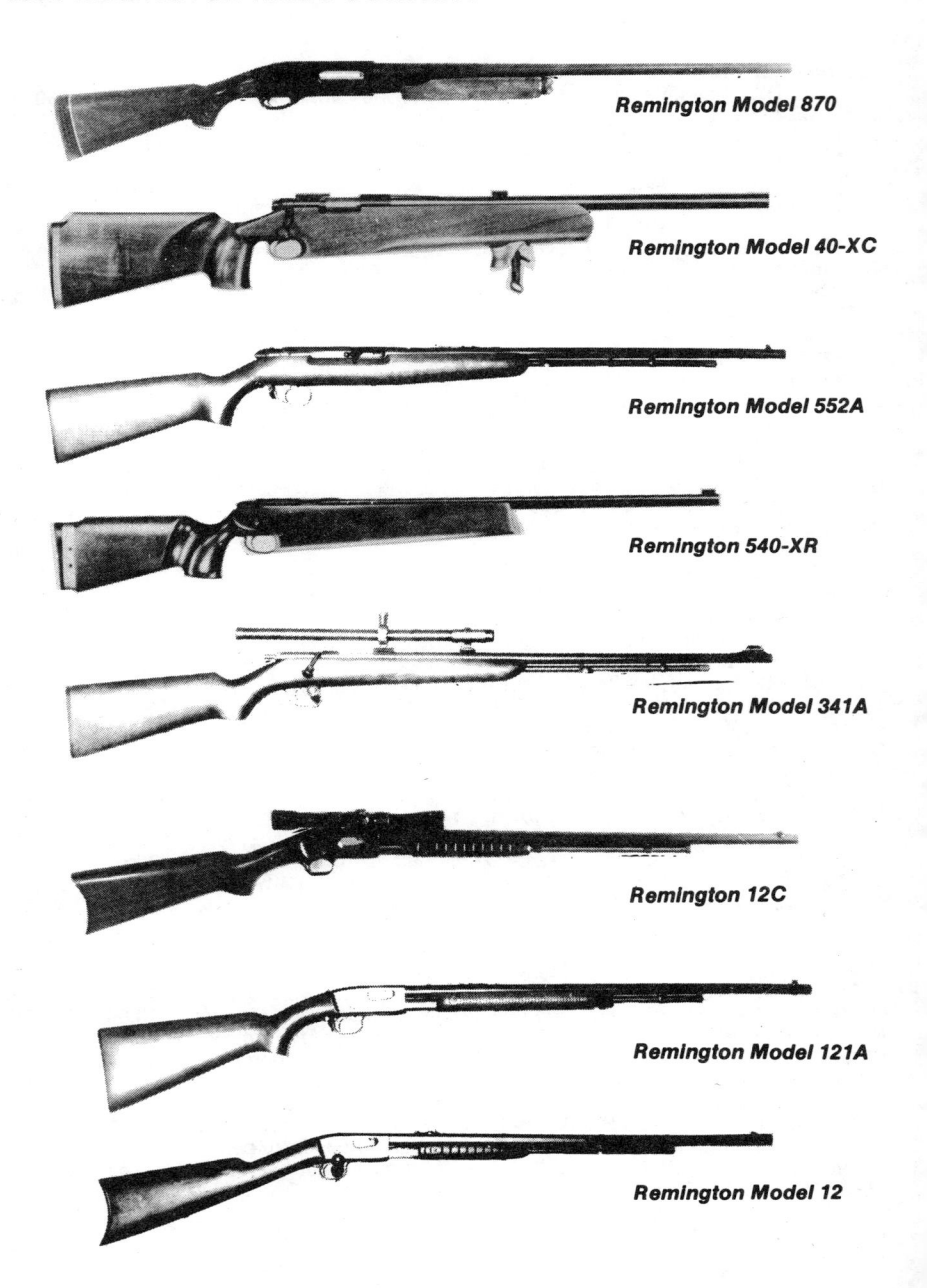

Remington Model 870

Remington Model 40-XC

Remington Model 552A

Remington 540-XR

Remington Model 341A

Remington 12C

Remington Model 121A

Remington Model 12

REMINGTON ARMS COMPANY / 359

	V.G.	EXC.

- ☐ **Model 760F Premier**, Various Calibers, Clip Fed, Sporting Rifle, Open Rear Sight, Fancy Checkering, Fancy Engraving, *Modern* ... **1,200.00 1,700.00**
- ☐ **Model 7600**, Various Calibers, Clip Fed, Sporting Rifle, Open Rear Sight, Monte Carlo Stock, Checkered Stock, *Modern* **175.00 235.00**

SHOTGUN, DOUBLE BARREL, OVER-UNDER
- ☐ **Model 32**, Raised Solid Rib, *Add* **$55.00-$75.00**
- ☐ **Model 32**, for Vent Rib, *Add* **$95.00-$125.00**
- ☐ **Model 32**, 12 Ga., Skeet Grade, Engraved, Fancy Checkering, *Modern* **850.00 1,150.00**
- ☐ **Model 32A**, 12 Ga., Double Trigger, Automatic Ejector, Plain Barrel, Engraved, Checkered Stock, *Modern* **450.00 600.00**
- ☐ **Model 32A**, 12 Ga., Single Selective Trigger, Automatic Ejector, Plain Barrel, Engraved, Checkered Stock, *Modern* **675.00 975.00**
- ☐ **Model 32D**, 12 Ga., Fancy Checkering, Fancy Wood, Fancy Engraving, *Modern* **1,550.00 2,250.00**
- ☐ **Model 32E**, 12 Ga., Fancy Checkering, Fancy Wood, Fancy Engraving, *Modern* **2,150.00 2,800.00**
- ☐ **Model 32F**, 12 Ga., Fancy Checkering, Fancy Wood, Fancy Checkering, *Modern* **3,000.00 4,250.00**
- ☐ **Model 32TC**, 12 Ga., Trap Grade, Single Selective Trigger, Engraved, Fancy Checkering, *Modern* **1,150.00 1,650.00**
- ☐ **Model 3200**, 12 Ga., Field Grade, Automatic Ejector, Single Selective Trigger, Vent Rib, Checkered Stock, *Modern* **675.00 875.00**
- ☐ **Model 3200**, 12 Ga., Skeet Grade, Automatic Ejector, Single Selective Trigger, Vent Rib, Checkered Stock, *Modern* **700.00 1,000.00**
- ☐ **Model 3200**, 12 Ga., Trap Grade, Automatic Ejector, Single Selective Trigger, Vent Rib, Checkered Stock, *Modern* **700.00 1,000.00**
- ☐ **Model 3200**, 12 Ga. Mag. 3", Field Grade, Automatic Ejector, Single Selective Trigger, Vent Rib, Checkered Stock, *Modern* **675.00 950.00**
- ☐ **Model 3200 Competition**, 12 Ga., Skeet Grade, Automatic Ejector, Single Selective Trigger, Vent Rib, Engraved, *Modern* **850.00 1,200.00**
- ☐ **Model 3200 Competition**, 12 Ga., Skeet Grade, Automatic Ejector, Single Selective Trigger, Vent Rib, Engraved, Extra Barrels, *Modern* **2,750.00 3,950.00**
- ☐ **Model 3200 Competition**, 12 Ga., Trap Grade, Automatic Ejector, Single Selective Trigger, Vent Rib, Engraved, *Modern* **850.00 1,200.00**

SHOTGUN, DOUBLE BARREL, SIDE-BY-SIDE
- ☐ **Model 1882**, Various Gauges, Hammer, Damascus Barrel, Checkered Stock, Double Trigger, *Antique* **240.00 395.00**
- ☐ **Model 1883**, Various Gauges, Hammer, Damascus Barrel, Checkered Stock, Double Trigger, *Antique* **240.00 395.00**
- ☐ **Model 1883**, Various Gauges, Hammer, Steel Barrel, Checkered Stock, Double Trigger, *Antique* **275.00 425.00**
- ☐ **Model 1894 A E**, Various Gauges, Hammerless, Damascus Barrel, Automatic Ejector, Checkered Stock, Double Trigger, *Curio* **175.00 300.00**
- ☐ **Model 1894 A E O**, Various Gauges, Hammerless, Steel Barrel, Automatic Ejector, Checkered Stock, Double Trigger, *Curio* **375.00 500.00**
- ☐ **Model 1894 A O**, Various Gauges, Hammerless, Steel Barrel, Plain, Checkered Stock, Double Trigger, *Curio* **325.00 450.00**
- ☐ **Model 1894 B**, Various Gauges, Hammerless, Damascus Barrel, Light Engraving, Checkered Stock, Double Trigger, *Curio* **150.00 225.00**
- ☐ **Model 1894 B E**, Various Gauges, Hammerless, Damascus Barrel, Automatic Ejector, Light Engraving, Checkered Stock, *Curio* **250.00 375.00**
- ☐ **Model 1894 B E O**, Various Gauges, Hammerless, Steel Barrel, Automatic Ejector, Light Engraving, Checkered Stock, *Curio* **475.00 700.00**
- ☐ **Model 1894 B O**, Various Gauges, Hammerless, Steel Barrel, Light Engraving, Checkered Stock, Double Trigger, *Curio* **375.00 500.00**

360 / REMINGTON ARMS COMPANY

	V.G.	EXC.
☐ **Model 1894 C**, Various Gauges, Hammerless, Damascus Barrel, Engraved, Checkered Stock, Double Trigger, *Curio*	275.00	400.00
☐ **Model 1894 C E**, Various Gauges, Hammerless, Damascus Barrel, Automatic Ejector, Engraved, Checkered Stock, *Curio*	350.00	475.00
☐ **Model 1894 C E O**, Various Gauges, Hammerless, Steel Barrel, Automatic Ejector, Engraved, Checkered Stock, *Curio*	675.00	950.00
☐ **Model 1894 C O**, Various Gauges, Hammerless, Steel Barrel, Engraved, Checkered Stock, Double Trigger, *Curio*	550.00	750.00
☐ **Model 1894 D**, Various Gauges, Hammerless, Damascus Barrel, Fancy Engraving, Fancy Checkering, Fancy Wood, *Curio*	475.00	650.00
☐ **Model 1894 D E**, Various Gauges, Hammerless, Damascus Barrel, Automatic Ejector, Fancy Engraving, Fancy Checkering, *Curio*	550.00	750.00
☐ **Model 1894 D E O**, Various Gauges, Hammerless, Steel Barrel, Automatic Ejector, Fancy Engraving, Fancy Checkering, *Curio*	850.00	1,400.00
☐ **Model 1894 D O**, Various Gauges, Hammerless, Steel Barrel, Fancy Engraving, Fancy Checkering, Fancy Wood, *Curio*	675.00	1,250.00
☐ **Model 1894 E**, Various Gauges, Hammerless, Damascus Barrel, Fancy Engraving, Fancy Checkering, Fancy Wood, *Curio*	700.00	950.00
☐ **Model 1894 E E**, Various Gauges, Hammerless, Damascus Barrel, Automatic Ejector, Fancy Engraving, Fancy Checkering, *Curio*	775.00	1,100.00
☐ **Model 1894 E E O**, Various Gauges, Hammerless, Steel Barrel, Automatic Ejector, Fancy Engraving, Fancy Checkering, *Curio*	1,800.00	2,500.00
☐ **Model 1894 E O**, Various Gauges, Hammerless, Steel Barrel, Fancy Engraving, Fancy Checkering, Fancy Wood, *Curio*	1,600.00	2,300.00
☐ **Model 1894 Special**, Various Gauges, Hammerless, Steel Barrel, Automatic Ejector, Fancy Engraving, Fancy Checkering, *Curio*	4,000.00	6,500.00
☐ **Model 1894-A**, Various Gauges, Hammerless, Damascus Barrel, Plain, Checkered Stock, Double Trigger, *Curio*	95.00	175.00
☐ **Model 1900 K**, 12 and 16 Gauges, Hammerless, Steel Barrel, Plain, Checkered Stock, *Curio*	175.00	300.00
☐ **Model 1900 K D**, 12 and 16 Gauges, Hammerless, Damascus Barrel, Plain, Checkered Stock, *Curio*	100.00	200.00
☐ **Model 1900 K E D**, 12 and 16 Gauges, Hammerless, Damascus Barrel, Automatic Ejector, Palm Rest, Checkered Stock, *Curio*	150.00	250.00
☐ **Model 1900 KE**, 12 and 16 Gauges, Hammerless, Steel Barrel, Automatic Ejector, Plain, Checkered Stock, *Curio*	250.00	375.00
☐ **Model Parker 920**, 12 Ga., Double Trigger, Checkered Stock, *Modern*	575.00	900.00

SHOTGUN, SEMI-AUTOMATIC

	V.G.	EXC.
☐ **Autoloading**, 12 Ga., for Solid Rib, *Add* **$25.00-$35.00**		
☐ **Autoloading-0**, 12 Ga., Takedown, Riot Gun, Plain, *Modern*	120.00	170.00
☐ **Autoloading-1**, 12 Ga., Takedown, Plain, *Modern*	125.00	175.00
☐ **Autoloading-2**, 12 Ga., Takedown, Checkered Stock, *Modern*	165.00	225.00
☐ **Autoloading-4**, 12 Ga., Takedown, Fancy Checkering, Fancy Wood, Engraved, *Modern*	435.00	575.00
☐ **Autoloading-6**, 12 Ga., Takedown, Fancy Checkering, Fancy Wood, Fancy Engraving, *Modern*	725.00	975.00
☐ **Model 11**, for Vent Rib, *Add* **$35.00-$45.00**		
☐ **Model 11**, Raised Solid Rib, *Add* **$15.00-$25.00**		
☐ **Model 11 Sportsman**, Various Gauges, Skeet Grade, Vent Rib, Light Engraving, Checkered Stock, *Modern*	200.00	300.00
☐ **Model 11-48 D Tournament**, Various Gauges, Vent Rib, Fancy Wood, Fancy Engraving, Fancy Checkering, *Modern*	400.00	525.00
☐ **Model 11-48 Duck**, Various Gauges, Vent Rib, Checkered Stock, *Modern*	130.00	185.00
☐ **Model 11-48 R**, 12 Ga., Riot Gun, Plain Barrel, *Modern*	90.00	135.00

REMINGTON ARMS COMPANY / 361

	V.G.	EXC.

- ☐ **Model 11-48 RSS**, 12 Ga., Open Rear Sight, Slug, Checkered Stock, *Modern* 135.00 190.00
- ☐ **Model 11-48 SA**, Various Gauges, Skeet Grade, Vent Rib, Checkered Stock, *Modern* 135.00 200.00
- ☐ **Model 11-48A**, Various Gauges, Plain Barrel, *Modern* 100.00 160.00
- ☐ **Model 11-48B**, Various Gauges, Vent Rib, Checkered Stock, Fancy Wood, *Modern* 115.00 165.00
- ☐ **Model 11-48F Premier**, Various Gauges, Vent Rib, Fancy Wood, Fancy Engraving, Fancy Checkering, *Modern* 800.00 1,100.00
- ☐ **Model 1100**, for Left Hand, *Add* $25.00-$35.00
- ☐ **Model 1100**, 12 Ga. Lightweight, *Add* $15.00-$20.00
- ☐ **Model 1100**, for .28 Ga. or .410 Ga., *Add* $15.00-$20.00
- ☐ **Model 1100**, 12 Ga., Bicentennial, Skeet Grade, Vent Rib, Checkered Stock, *Modern* 225.00 325.00
- ☐ **Model 1100**, Various Gauges, Plain Barrel, Checkered Stock, *Modern* 200.00 285.00
- ☐ **Model 1100**, Various Gauges, Vent Rib, Checkered Stock, *Modern* 225.00 315.00
- ☐ **Model 1100**, Various Gauges, Plain Barrel, Magnum, Checkered Stock, *Modern* 210.00 275.00
- ☐ **Model 1100**, Various Gauges, Vent Rib, Magnum, Checkered Stock, *Modern* 250.00 325.00
- ☐ **Model 1100**, Various Gauges, Skeet Grade, Vent Rib, Checkered Stock, *Modern* 240.00 325.00
- ☐ **Model 1100 Cutts**, Various Gauges, Skeet Grade, Vent Rib, Checkered Stock, *Modern* 260.00 340.00
- ☐ **Model 1100 D Tournament**, Various Gauges, Vent Rib, Fancy Checkering, Fancy Wood, Fancy Engraving, *Modern* 600.00 950.00
- ☐ **Model 1100 Deer Gun**, Various Gauges, Open Rear Sight, Checkered Stock, *Modern* 245.00 325.00
- ☐ **Model 1100 F Premier**, Various Gauges, Vent Rib, Fancy Checkering, Fancy Wood, Fancy Engraving, *Modern* 1,400.00 1,875.00
- ☐ **Model 1100 TA**, 12 Ga., Bicentennial, Trap Grade, Vent Rib, Checkered Stock, *Modern* 280.00 375.00
- ☐ **Model 1100 TA**, 12 Ga., Bicentennial, Trap Grade, Vent Rib, Monte Carlo Stock, Checkered Stock, *Modern* 295.00 390.00
- ☐ **Model 1100 TA**, 12 Ga., Trap Grade, Vent Rib, Checkered Stock, *Modern* 265.00 375.00
- ☐ **Model 1100 TA**, 12 Ga., Trap Grade, Vent Rib, Checkered Stock, Monte Carlo Stock, *Modern* 320.00 400.00
- ☐ **Model 11A**, 12 Ga., Plain Barrel, *Modern* 120.00 175.00
- ☐ **Model 11A Sportsman**, Various Gauges, Plain Barrel, Light Engraving, *Modern* 125.00 175.00
- ☐ **Model 11B**, 12 Ga., Plain Barrel, Fancy Wood, Checkered Stock, *Modern* 160.00 200.00
- ☐ **Model 11B Sportsman**, Various Gauges, Plain Barrel, Light Engraving, Checkered Stock, *Modern* 170.00 235.00
- ☐ **Model 11C**, 12 Ga., Plain Barrel, Trap Grade, Fancy Checkering, Fancy Wood, *Modern* 200.00 300.00
- ☐ **Model 11D**, 12 Ga., Plain Barrel, Fancy Checkering, Fancy Wood, Fancy Engraving, *Modern* 500.00 550.00
- ☐ **Model 11D Sportsman**, Various Gauges, Plain Barrel, Engraved, Fancy Checkering, *Modern* 400.00 550.00
- ☐ **Model 11E**, 12 Ga., Plain Barrel, Fancy Checkering, Fancy Wood, Fancy Engraving, *Modern* 575.00 700.00
- ☐ **Model 11E Sportsman**, Various Gauges, Plain Barrel, Fancy Checkering, Fancy Wood, Fancy Engraving, *Modern* 575.00 725.00

362 / REMINGTON ARMS COMPANY

	V.G.	EXC.
☐ **Model 11F**, 12 Ga., Plain Barrel, Fancy Checkering, Fancy Wood, Fancy Engraving, *Modern*	700.00	950.00
☐ **Model 11F Sportsman**, Various Gauges, Plain Barrel, Fancy Checkering, Fancy Wood, Fancy Engraving, *Modern*	700.00	950.00
☐ **Model 11R**, 12 Ga., Riot Gun, Military, *Modern*	110.00	160.00
☐ **Model 11R**, 12 Ga., Riot Gun, Commercial, *Modern*	100.00	150.00
☐ **Model 48-D Sportsman**, Various Gauges, Vent Rib, Fancy Checkering, Fancy Wood, Fancy Engraving, *Modern*	450.00	600.00
☐ **Model 48-F Sportsman**, Various Gauges, Vent Rib, Fancy Checkering, Fancy Wood, Fancy Engraving, *Modern*	825.00	1,100.00
☐ **Model 48-SA Sportsman**, Various Gauges, Skeet Grade, Vent Rib, Checkered Stock, *Modern*	140.00	190.00
☐ **Model 48A Sportsman**, Various Gauges, Plain Barrel, *Modern*	100.00	150.00
☐ **Model 48B Sportsman**, Various Gauges, Vent Rib, Checkered Stock, *Modern*	115.00	170.00
☐ **Model 58 ADL**, 12 and 20 Gauges, Vent Rib, Recoil Pad, Checkered Stock, Magnum, *Modern*	160.00	210.00
☐ **Model 58 ADL**, Various Gauges, Plain Barrel, Checkered Stock, *Modern*	130.00	175.00
☐ **Model 58 ADL**, Various Gauges, Vent Rib, Checkered Stock, *Modern*	150.00	215.00
☐ **Model 58 ADX**, Various Gauges, Vent Rib, Checkered Stock, Fancy Wood, *Modern*	150.00	210.00
☐ **Model 58 BDL**, Various Gauges, Plain Barrel, Checkered Stock, Fancy Wood, *Modern*	150.00	210.00
☐ **Model 58 BDL**, Various Gauges, Vent Rib, Checkered Stock, Fancy Wood, *Modern*	150.00	215.00
☐ **Model 58 D Tournament**, Various Gauges, Vent Rib, Fancy Checkering, Fancy Wood, Fancy Engraving, *Modern*	450.00	625.00
☐ **Model 58 F Premier**, Various Gauges, Vent Rib, Fancy Checkering, Fancy Wood, Fancy Engraving, *Modern*	950.00	1,250.00
☐ **Model 58 RSS**, 12 Ga. Slug, Open Rear Sight, Checkered Stock, *Modern*	145.00	195.00
☐ **Model 58 SA**, Various Gauges, Skeet Grade, Vent Rib, Checkered Stock, *Modern*	175.00	245.00
☐ **Model 58 TB**, 12 Ga., Trap Grade, Vent Rib, Checkered Stock, *Modern*	175.00	245.00
☐ **Model 878 A**, 12 Ga., Plain Barrel, *Modern*	100.00	145.00
☐ **Model 878 A**, 12 Ga., Vent Rib, *Modern*	110.00	155.00
☐ **Model 878 ADL**, 12 Ga., Plain Barrel, Checkered Stock, *Modern*	110.00	155.00
☐ **Model 878 ADL**, 12 Ga., Vent Rib, Checkered Stock, *Modern*	125.00	170.00
☐ **Model 878 D**, 12 Ga., Vent Rib, Fancy Checkering, Fancy Wood, Fancy Engraving, *Modern*	450.00	550.00
☐ **Model 878 F**, 12 Ga., Vent Rib, Fancy Checkering, Fancy Wood, Fancy Engraving, *Modern*	750.00	975.00
☐ **Model 878 SA**, 12 Ga., Skeet Grade, Vent Rib, Checkered Stock, *Modern*	145.00	200.00

SHOTGUN, SINGLESHOT

	V.G.	EXC.
☐ **Model 3 (M1893)**, 12 Ga., 24 Ga., 28 Ga., *Add $30.00*		
☐ **Model 3 (M1893)**, Various Gauges, Takedown, Plain, *Curio*	85.00	115.00
☐ **Model 9 (M1902)**, Various Gauges, Automatic Ejector, Plain, *Curio*	80.00	110.00
☐ **Model Parker 930**, 12 Ga., Trap Grade, Vent Rib, Automatic Ejector, Fancy Checkering, *Modern*	975.00	1,500.00
☐ **Model Parker 930**, 12 Ga., Trap Grade, Vent Rib, Automatic Ejector, Fancy Checkering, Fancy Engraving, *Modern*	1,800.00	2,650.00

	V.G.	EXC.
SHOTGUN, SLIDE ACTION		
☐ **Model 10A**, 12 Ga., Takedown, Plain, *Modern*	140.00	185.00
☐ **Model 10B**, 12 Ga., Takedown, Checkered Stock, Fancy Wood, *Modern*	165.00	225.00
☐ **Model 10C**, 12 Ga., Takedown, Fancy Wood, Checkered Stock, *Modern*	180.00	250.00
☐ **Model 10D**, 12 Ga., Takedown, Fancy Checkering, Fancy Wood, Engraved, *Modern*	425.00	575.00
☐ **Model 10E**, 12 Ga., Takedown, Fancy Checkering, Fancy Wood, Fancy Engraving, *Modern*	575.00	750.00
☐ **Model 10F**, 12 Ga., Takedown, Fancy Checkering, Fancy Engraving, Fancy Wood, *Modern*	725.00	975.00
☐ **Model 10R**, 12 Ga., Takedown, Riot Gun, Plain, *Modern*	95.00	150.00
☐ **Model 10S**, 12 Ga., Takedown, Trap Grade, Checkered Stock, *Modern*	160.00	225.00
☐ **Model 17**, 20 Ga., for Solid Rib, *Add* **$25.00-$40.00**		
☐ **Model 17A**, 20 Ga., Takedown, Plain, *Modern*	155.00	200.00
☐ **Model 17B**, 20 Ga., Takedown, Checkered Stock, *Modern*	180.00	250.00
☐ **Model 17C**, 20 Ga., Takedown, Fancy Wood, Checkered Stock, *Modern*	240.00	325.00
☐ **Model 17D**, 20 Ga., Takedown, Fancy Wood, Fancy Checkering, Engraved, *Modern*	400.00	550.00
☐ **Model 17E**, 20 Ga., Takedown, Fancy Wood, Fancy Checkering, Fancy Engraving, *Modern*	550.00	775.00
☐ **Model 17F**, 20 Ga., Takedown, Fancy Wood, Fancy Checkering, Fancy Engraving, *Modern*	800.00	975.00
☐ **Model 17R**, 20 Ga., Takedown, Riot Gun, Plain, *Modern*	125.00	190.00
☐ **Model 1908-0**, 12 Ga., Takedown, Riot Gun, Plain, *Modern*	125.00	190.00
☐ **Model 1908-1**, 12 Ga., Takedown, Plain, *Modern*	135.00	190.00
☐ **Model 1908-3**, 12 Ga., Takedown, Checkered Stock, Fancy Wood, *Modern*	165.00	225.00
☐ **Model 1908-4**, 12 Ga., Takedown, Fancy Checkering, Fancy Wood, Engraved, *Modern*	400.00	525.00
☐ **Model 1908-6**, 12 Ga., Takedown, Fancy Checkering, Fancy Wood, Fancy Engraving, *Modern*	650.00	975.00
☐ **Model 29**, for Solid Rib, *Add* **$25.00-$35.00**		
☐ **Model 29**, for Vent Rib, *Add* **$35.00-$55.00**		
☐ **Model 29A Sportsman**, 12 Ga., Plain Barrel, Takedown, *Modern*	140.00	220.00
☐ **Model 29B**, 12 Ga., Checkered Stock, Takedown, *Modern*	150.00	225.00
☐ **Model 29C**, 12 Ga., Trap Grade, Takedown, *Modern*	175.00	265.00
☐ **Model 29R**, 12 Ga., Riot Gun, Plain Barrel, *Modern*	100.00	160.00
☐ **Model 29S**, 12 Ga., Trap Grade, Plain Barrel, Checkered Stock, *Modern*	160.00	225.00
☐ **Model 29TA**, 12 Ga., Trap Grade, Vent Rib, Checkered Stock, *Modern*	175.00	275.00
☐ **Model 29TC**, 12 Ga., Trap Grade, Vent Rib, Checkered Stock, Fancy Wood, *Modern*	225.00	325.00
☐ **Model 29TD**, 12 Ga., Trap Grade, Vent Rib, Fancy Checkering, Fancy Wood, Engraved, *Modern*	375.00	525.00
☐ **Model 29TE**, 12 Ga., Trap Grade, Vent Rib, Fancy Checkering, Fancy Wood, Fancy Engraving, *Modern*	550.00	700.00
☐ **Model 29TF**, 12 Ga., Trap Grade, Vent Rib, Fancy Checkering, Fancy Wood, Fancy Engraving, *Modern*	700.00	950.00
☐ **Model 31**, for Vent Rib, *Add* **$45.00-$60.00**		
☐ **Model 31**, for Solid Rib, *Add* **$15.00-$30.00**		
☐ **Model 31**, Various Gauges, Skeet Grade, Vent Rib, Checkered Stock, Fancy Wood, *Modern*	325.00	450.00

	V.G.	EXC.
☐ **Model 31A**, Various Gauges, Plain Barrel, *Modern*	135.00	190.00
☐ **Model 31B**, Various Gauges, Plain Barrel, Checkered Stock, Fancy Wood, *Modern*	210.00	325.00
☐ **Model 31D Tournament**, Various Gauges, Plain Barrel, Checkered Stock, Fancy Wood, Engraved, *Modern*	500.00	675.00
☐ **Model 31E Expert**, Various Gauges, Plain Barrel, Fancy Checkering, Fancy Wood, Fancy Engraving, *Modern*	600.00	825.00
☐ **Model 31F Premier**, Various Gauges, Plain Barrel, Fancy Checkering, Fancy Wood, Fancy Engraving, *Modern*	850.00	1,300.00
☐ **Model 31H Hunter**, Various Gauges, Checkered Stock, Fancy Wood, Plain Barrel, *Modern*	250.00	335.00
☐ **Model 31R**, 12 Ga., Plain Barrel, Riot Gun, *Modern*	140.00	195.00
☐ **Model 31S**, 12 Ga., Raised Matted Rib, Checkered Stock, Fancy Wood, *Modern*	300.00	450.00
☐ **Model 31TC**, 12 Ga., Trap Grade, Vent Rib, Recoil Pad, *Modern*	325.00	450.00
☐ **Model 870**, for Lightweight 20, *Add* **$20.00-$25.00**		
☐ **Model 870**, for .28 Ga. or .410 Ga., *Add* **$15.00-$20.00**		
☐ **Model 870**, for Left-Hand, *Add* **$10.00-$15.00**		
☐ **Model 870**, Various Gauges, Plain Barrel, Checkered Stock, *Modern*	165.00	210.00
☐ **Model 870**, Various Gauges, Vent Rib, Checkered Stock, *Modern*	190.00	240.00
☐ **Model 870**, Various Gauges, Plain Barrel, Magnum, Checkered Stock, *Modern*	185.00	230.00
☐ **Model 870**, Various Gauges, Vent Rib, Magnum, Checkered Stock, *Modern*	200.00	260.00
☐ **Model 870 All American**, 12 Ga., Trap Grade, Vent Rib, Fancy Checkering, Engraved, *Modern*	450.00	585.00
☐ **Model 870 Brushmaster**, 12 and 20 Gauges, Open Rear Sight, Recoil Pad, Checkered Stock, *Modern*	170.00	230.00
☐ **Model 870 Competition**, 12 Ga., Trap Grade, Vent Rib, Checkered Stock, Singleshot, *Modern*	240.00	325.00
☐ **Model 870 D Tournament**, Various Gauges, Vent Rib, Fancy Checkering, Fancy Wood, Fancy Engraving, *Modern*	600.00	875.00
☐ **Model 870 Deergun**, 12 Ga., Open Rear Sight, Checkered Stock, *Modern*	165.00	225.00
☐ **Model 870 F Premier**, Various Gauges, Vent Rib, Fancy Checkering, Fancy Wood, Fancy Engraving, *Modern*	1,450.00	1,900.00
☐ **Model 870 Police**, 12 Ga., Open Rear Sight, *Modern*	165.00	220.00
☐ **Model 870 Police**, 12 Ga., Plain Barrel, *Modern*	150.00	200.00
☐ **Model 870 SA**, 12 Ga., Bicentennial, Skeet Grade, Vent Rib, Checkered Stock, *Modern*	185.00	265.00
☐ **Model 870SA**, Various Gauges, Skeet Grade, Vent Rib, Checkered Stock, *Modern*	195.00	265.00
☐ **Model 870SA Cutts**, Various Gauges, Skeet Grade, Vent Rib, Checkered Stock, *Modern*	190.00	260.00
☐ **Model 870SC**, Various Gauges, Skeet Grade, Vent Rib, Checkered Stock, *Modern*	195.00	265.00
☐ **Model 870TB**, 12 Ga., Trap Grade, Vent Rib, Checkered Stock, *Modern*	185.00	250.00
☐ **Model 870TB**, 12 Ga., Trap Grade, Vent Rib, Checkered Stock, Monte Carlo Stock, *Modern*	190.00	260.00
☐ **Model 870TB**, 12 Ga., Bicentennial, Trap Grade, Vent Rib, Checkered Stock, *Modern*	190.00	260.00
☐ **Model 870TB**, 12 Ga., Bicentennial, Trap Grade, Vent Rib, Checkered Stock, Monte Carlo Stock, *Modern*	190.00	260.00
☐ **Model 870TC**, 12 Ga., Trap Grade, Vent Rib, Checkered Stock, *Modern*	240.00	325.00

	V.G.	EXC.
☐ **Model 870TC**, 12 Ga., Trap Grade, Vent Rib, Checkered Stock, Monte Carlo Stock, *Modern*	245.00	330.00
SILENCED WEAPON, RIFLE		
☐ **Rem. 40XB Sniper**, .308 Win., Heavy Barrel, Scope Mounted, Silencer, *Class 3*	575.00	825.00

REPUBLIC
Spain, unknown maker.

HANDGUN, SEMI-AUTOMATIC
☐ **.32 ACP**, Clip Fed, Long Grip, *Modern* 95.00   140.00

RETRIEVER
Made by Thomas Ryan, Norwich, Conn. 1870-1876.

HANDGUN, REVOLVER
☐ **.32 Short R.F.**, 5 Shot, Spur Trigger, Solid Frame, Single Action, *Antique* 90.00   160.00

REVELATION
Trade Name for Western Auto.

RIFLE, BOLT ACTION
☐ **Model 107**, .22 WMR, Clip Fed, *Modern* 40.00   65.00
☐ **Model 210B**, 7mm Rem. Mag., Checkered Stock, Monte Carlo Stock, *Modern* 135.00   175.00
☐ **Model 220A**, .308 Win., Checkered Stock, Monte Carlo Stock, *Modern* 120.00   165.00
☐ **Model 220AD**, .308 Win., Checkered Stock, Monte Carlo Stock, Fancy Wood, *Modern* 145.00   195.00
☐ **Model 220B**, .243 Win., Checkered Stock, Monte Carlo Stock, *Modern* 120.00   160.00
☐ **Model 220BD**, .243 Win., Checkered Stock, Monte Carlo Stock, Fancy Wood, *Modern* 145.00   195.00
☐ **Model 220C**, .22-250, Checkered Stock, Monte Carlo Stock, *Modern* 120.00   160.00
☐ **Model 220CD**, .22-250, Checkered Stock, Monte Carlo Stock, Fancy Wood, *Modern* 145.00   195.00

RIFLE, LEVER ACTION
☐ **Model 117**, .22 L.R.R.F., Tube Feed, *Modern* 45.00   65.00

RIFLE, SEMI-AUTOMATIC
☐ **Model 125**, .22 L.R.R.F., Clip Fed, *Modern* 35.00   55.00

RIFLE, SINGLESHOT
☐ **Model 100**, .22 L.R.R.F., *Modern* 20.00   35.00

SHOTGUN, BOLT ACTION
☐ **Model 312B**, 12 Ga., Clip Fed, *Modern* 35.00   50.00
☐ **Model 312BK**, 12 Ga., Clip Fed, Adjustable Choke, *Modern* 40.00   60.00
☐ **Model 316B**, 16 Ga., Clip Fed, *Modern* 30.00   45.00
☐ **Model 316BK**, 16 Ga., Clip Fed, Adjustable Choke, *Modern* 30.00   50.00
☐ **Model 325B**, 20 Ga., Clip Fed, *Modern* 35.00   50.00
☐ **Model 325BK**, 20 Ga., Clip Fed, Adjustable Choke, *Modern* 40.00   55.00
☐ **Model 330**, .410 Ga., Clip Fed, *Modern* 30.00   45.00

SHOTGUN, SLIDE ACTION
☐ **Model 310**, Various Gauges, Plain Barrel, Takedown, *Modern* 85.00   130.00
☐ **Model 310R**, Various Gauges, Vent Rib, Takedown, *Modern* 90.00   135.00

REV-O-NOC
Made by Crescent for Hibbard-Spencer-Bartlett Co., Chicago.

	V.G.	EXC.

SHOTGUN, DOUBLE BARREL, SIDE-BY-SIDE
- ☐ **Various Gauges**, Outside Hammers, Damascus Barrel, *Modern* 100.00 175.00
- ☐ **Various Gauges**, Hammerless, Steel Barrel, *Modern* 135.00 200.00
- ☐ **Various Gauges**, Hammerless, Damascus Barrel, *Modern* 100.00 175.00
- ☐ **Various Gauges**, Outside Hammers, Steel Barrel, *Modern* 125.00 190.00

SHOTGUN, SINGLESHOT
- ☐ **Various Gauges**, Hammer, Steel Barrel, *Modern* 55.00 85.00.00

REYNOLDS, PLANT & HOTCHKISS
Also see Plant's Mfg. Co.

HANDGUN, REVOLVER
- ☐ **.25 Short R.F.**, 5 Shot, Single Action, Spur Trigger, 3" Barrel, Antique 125.00 175.00

R.G. INDUSTRIES
R.G. tradename belongs to Rohm GmbH, Sontheim/Brenz, W. Germany, and after 1968 also made in Miami, Fla. for American consumption.

HANDGUN, DOUBLE BARREL, OVER-UNDER
- ☐ **RG-16**, .22 WMR, 2 Shot, Derringer, *Modern* 25.00 35.00
- ☐ **RG-17**, .38 Special, 2 Shot, Derringer, *Modern* 25.00 35.00

HANDGUN, REVOLVER
- ☐ **Partner**, .38 Special, 6 Shot, Double Action, Swing-Out Cylinder, *Modern* 40.00 60.00
- ☐ **RG-14**, .22 L.R.R.F., 6 Shot, Double Action, *Modern* 20.00 30.00
- ☐ **RG-23**, .22 L.R.R.F., 6 Shot, Double Action, *Modern* 25.00 40.00
- ☐ **RG-30**, .22LR/.22 WMR Combo, 6 Shot, Double Action, Swing-Out Cylinder, *Modern* 35.00 50.00
- ☐ **RG-30**, .22 L.R.R.F., 6 Shot, Double Action, Swing-Out Cylinder, *Modern* 25.00 35.00
- ☐ **RG-30**, .22 WMR, 6 Shot, Double Action, Swing-Out Cylinder, *Modern* 25.00 40.00
- ☐ **RG-30**, .32 S & W Long, 6 Shot, Double Action, Swing-Out Cylinder, *Modern* 25.00 40.00
- ☐ **RG-31**, .32 S & W Long, 6 Shot, Double Action, *Modern* 25.00 40.00
- ☐ **RG-31**, .38 Special, 5 Shot, Double Action, *Modern* 25.00 40.00
- ☐ **RG-38S**, .38 Special, 6 Shot, Double Action, Blue, *Modern* 35.00 55.00
- ☐ **RG-38S**, .38 Special, 6 Shot, Double Action, Nickel Plated, *Modern* 35.00 55.00
- ☐ **RG-40**, .38 Special, 6 Shot, Double Action, Swing-Out Cylinder, *Modern* 35.00 55.00
- ☐ **RG-57**, .357 Magnum, 6 Shot, Double Action, Swing-Out Cylinder, *Modern* 50.00 80.00
- ☐ **RG-57**, .44 Magnum, 6 Shot, Double Action, Swing-Out Cylinder, *Modern* 65.00 100.00
- ☐ **RG-63**, .22 L.R.R.F., 6 Shot, Double Action, Western Style, *Modern* 25.00 35.00
- ☐ **RG-66**, .22LR/.22 WMR Combo, 6 Shot, Single Action, Western Style, *Modern* 25.00 40.00
- ☐ **RG-66T**, .22LR/.22 WMR Combo, 6 Shot, Single Action, Western Style, Adjustable Sights, *Modern* 30.00 45.00
- ☐ **RG-74**, .22 L.R.R.F., 6 Shot, Double Action, Swing-Out Cylinder, *Modern* 35.00 50.00
- ☐ **RG-88**, .357 Magnum, 6 Shot, Double Action, Swing-Out Cylinder, *Modern* 60.00 85.00

HANDGUN, SEMI-AUTOMATIC
- ☐ **RG-25**, .25 ACP, *Modern* 30.00 45.00

	V.G.	EXC.
☐ **RG-26**, .25 ACP, *Modern*	30.00	45.00

RHEINMETALL
Rheinsche Metallwaren u. Maschinenfabrik, Sommerda, Germany 1922-1927.
HANDGUN, SEMI-AUTOMATIC
	V.G.	EXC.
☐ **.32 ACP**, Clip Fed, Blue, *Curio*	195.00	300.00

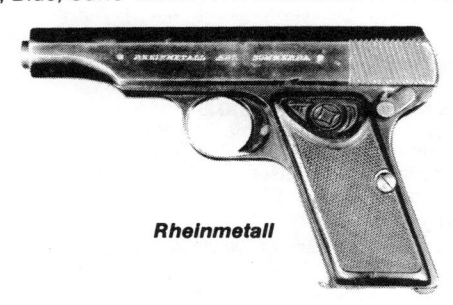

Rheinmetall

RICHARDS, W.
Belgium, c. 1900
SHOTGUN, DOUBLE BARREL, SIDE-BY-SIDE
	V.G.	EXC.
☐ **Various Gauges**, Outside Hammers, Damascus Barrel, *Modern*	100.00	175.00
☐ **Various Gauges**, Hammerless, Steel Barrel, *Modern*	135.00	200.00
☐ **Various Gauges**, Hammerless, Damascus Barrel, *Modern*	100.00	175.00
☐ **Various Gauges**, Outside Hammers, Steel Barrel, *Modern*	125.00	190.00

SHOTGUN, SINGLESHOT
	V.G.	EXC.
☐ **Various Gauges**, Hammer, Steel Barrel, *Modern*	55.00	85.00

RICHARDSON INDUSTRIES
New Haven, Conn.
SHOTGUN, SINGLESHOT
	V.G.	EXC.
☐ **Model R-5**, 12 Ga., 24" Barrel, *Modern*	20.00	35.00

RICHLAND ARMS CO.
Bussfield, Mich.
SHOTGUN, DOUBLE BARREL, OVER-UNDER
	V.G.	EXC.
☐ **Model 808**, 12 Ga., Single Trigger, Checkered Stock, Vent Rib, *Modern*	200.00	325.00
☐ **Model 810**, 10 Ga. 3½", Double Trigger, Checkered Stock, Vent Rib, *Modern*	320.00	425.00
☐ **Model 828**, 28 Ga., Single Trigger, Checkered Stock, *Modern*	225.00	290.00
☐ **Model 844**, 12 Ga., Single Trigger, Checkered Stock, *Modern*	160.00	220.00

SHOTGUN, DOUBLE BARREL, SIDE-BY-SIDE
	V.G.	EXC.
☐ **Model 200**, Various Gauges, Double Trigger, Checkered Stock, *Modern*	175.00	240.00
☐ **Model 202**, Various Gauges, Double Trigger, Extra Shotgun Barrel, *Modern*	250.00	325.00
☐ **Model 707 Deluxe**, 12 and 20 Gauges, Double Trigger, *Modern*	200.00	275.00

368 / RICKARD ARMS

	V.G.	EXC.
☐ **Model 707 Deluxe**, 12 and 20 Gauges, Double Trigger, Checkered Stock, Extra Shotgun Barrel, *Modern*	250.00	350.00
☐ **Model 711**, 10 Ga. 3½", Double Trigger, *Modern*	190.00	265.00
☐ **Model 711**, 12 Ga. Mag. 3", Double Trigger, *Modern*	180.00	225.00

RIFLE, PERCUSSION
☐ **Wesson Rifle**, .50, Set Triggers, Target Sights, Reproduction, *Antique* 140.00   200.00

RICKARD ARMS
Made by Crescent for J.A. Rickard Co. Schenectady, N.Y.

SHOTGUN, DOUBLE BARREL, SIDE-BY-SIDE
☐ **Various Gauges**, Outside Hammers, Damascus Barrel, *Modern* 100.00   175.00
☐ **Various Gauges**, Hammerless, Steel Barrel, *Modern* 135.00   200.00
☐ **Various Gauges**, Hammerless, Damascus Barrel, *Modern* 100.00   175.00
☐ **Various Gauges**, Outside Hammers, Steel Barrel, *Modern* 125.00   190.00

SHOTGUN, SINGLESHOT
☐ **Various Gauges**, Hammer, Steel Barrel, *Modern* 55.00   85.00

RIGBY, JOHN & CO.
Dublin, Ireland & London, England from 1867.

RIFLE, BOLT ACTION
☐ **.275 Rigby**, Sporting Rifle, Express Sights, Checkered Stock, *Modern* 1,400.00   2,250.00
☐ **.275 Rigby**, Sporting Rifle, Lightweight, Express Sights, Checkered Stock, *Modern* 1,400.00   2,250.00
☐ **.350 Rigby**, Sporting Rifle, Express Sights, Checkered Stock, *Modern* 1,400.00   2,250.00
☐ **Big Game**, .416 Rigby, Sporting Rifle, Express Sights, Checkered Stock, *Modern* 1,400.00   2,250.00

RIFLE, DOUBLE BARREL, SIDE-BY-SIDE
☐ **Best Grade**, Various Calibers, Sidelock, Double Trigger, Express Sights, Fancy Engraving, Fancy Checkering, *Modern* 7,500.00   13,000.00
☐ **Second Grade**, Various Calibers, Box Lock, Double Trigger, Express Sights, Fancy Engraving, Fancy Checkering, *Modern* 5,500.00   8,500.00
☐ **Third Grade**, Various Calibers, Box Lock, Double Trigger, Express Sights, Engraved, Checkered Stock, *Modern* 4,000.00   5,500.00

SHOTGUN, DOUBLE BARREL, SIDE-BY-SIDE
☐ **Chatsworth**, Various Gauges, Box Lock, Automatic Ejector, Double Trigger, Fancy Engraving, Fancy Checkering, *Modern* 1,750.00   2,500.00
☐ **Regal**, Various Gauges, Sidelock, Automatic Ejector, Double Trigger, Fancy Engraving, Fancy Checkering, *Modern* 5,500.00   9,000.00
☐ **Sackville**, Various Gauges, Box Lock, Automatic Ejector, Double Trigger, Fancy Engraving, Fancy Checkering, *Modern* 2,000.00   3,000.00
☐ **Sandringham**, Various Gauges, Sidelock, Automatic Ejector, Double Trigger, Fancy Engraving, Fancy Checkering, *Modern* 4,000.00   6,500.00

RIPOLI

HANDGUN, MIQUELOT-LOCK
☐ **Ball Butt**, Brass Inlay, Light Ornamentation, *Antique* 1,500.00   2,400.00
☐ **Pair**, Fluted Barrel, Pocket Pistol, Engraved, Silver Furniture, *Antique* 5,000.00   7,000.00

ROBBINS & LAWRENCE
Robbins, Kendall & Lawrence, Windsor, Vt. 1844-1857. Became Robbins & Lawrence about 1846. Also see Sharps, U.S. Military.

HANDGUN, PERCUSSION

	V.G.	EXC.
☐ **Pepperbox**, Various Calibers, Ring Trigger, *Antique*	375.00	550.00

ROBIN HOOD
Made by Hood Firearms Norwich, Conn., c. 1875.

HANDGUN, REVOLVER
	V.G.	EXC.
☐ **.22 Short R.F.**, 7 Shot, Spur Trigger, Solid Frame, Single Action, *Antique*	90.00	160.00
☐ **.32 Short R.F.**, 5 Shot, Spur Trigger, Solid Frame, Single Action, *Antique*	95.00	170.00

ROESSER, PETER
Lancaster, Pa. 1741-1782. See Kentucky Rifles and Pistols.

ROGERS & SPENCER
Willowvale, N.Y., c. 1862.

HANDGUN, PERCUSSION
	V.G.	EXC.
☐ **.44 Army**, Single Action, *Antique*	525.00	775.00

ROLAND
Francisco Arizmendi, Eibar, Spain, c. 1922.

HANDGUN, SEMI-AUTOMATIC
	V.G.	EXC.
☐ **.25 ACP**, Clip Fed, Blue, *Curio*	80.00	120.00
☐ **.32 ACP**, Clip Fed, Blue, *Curio*	90.00	130.00

ROME REVOLVER AND NOVELTY WORKS
Rome, N.Y., c. 1880.

HANDGUN, REVOLVER
	V.G.	EXC.
☐ **.32 Short R.F.**, 5 Shot, Spur Trigger, Solid Frame, Single Action, *Antique*	90.00	160.00

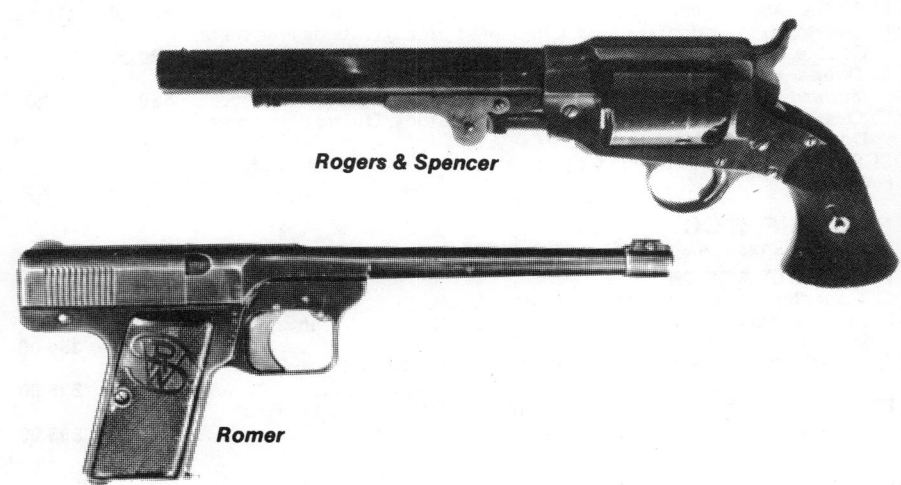

Rogers & Spencer

Romer

ROMER
Romerwerke AG, Suhl, Germany, c. 1925.

HANDGUN, SEMI-AUTOMATIC

	V.G.	EXC.
☐ **.22 L.R.R.F.**, Clip Fed, 2½" and 6½" Barrels, Blue, *Curio*	625.00	950.00
☐ **.22 L.R.R.F.**, Clip Fed, One Barrel, Blue, *Curio*	535.00	825.00

ROOP, JOHN
Allentown, Pa., c. 1775. See Kentucky Rifles.

ROSSI
Amadeo Rossi S.A., Sao Leopoldo, Brazil.

HANDGUN, REVOLVER

- ☐ **Model 31**, .38 Special, Solid Frame, Swing-Out Cylinder, 5 Shot, 4" Barrel, *Modern* ... 70.00 / 95.00
- ☐ **Model 51**, .22 L.R.R.F., Solid Frame, Swing-Out Cylinder, Adjustable Sights, 5 Shot, 6" Barrel, *Modern* ... 65.00 / 85.00
- ☐ **Model 68**, .38 Special, Solid Frame, Swing-Out Cylinder, Adjustable Sights, 5 Shot, 3" Barrel, *Modern* ... 70.00 / 95.00
- ☐ **Model 69**, .32 S & W Long, Solid Frame, Swing-Out Cylinder, Adjustable Sights, 5 Shot, 3" Barrel, *Modern* ... 60.00 / 80.00
- ☐ **Model 70**, .22 Short R.F., Solid Frame, Swing-Out Cylinder, Adjustable Sights, 5 Shot, 3" Barrel, *Modern* ... 60.00 / 80.00

HANDGUN, SINGLESHOT

- ☐ **.22 Short R.F.**, Derringer, *Modern* ... 35.00 / 50.00

RIFLE, SLIDE ACTION

- ☐ **Saddle Ring**, .357 Mag., Tube Feed, Hammer, Carbine, *Modern* ... 120.00 / 160.00
- ☐ **Saddle Ring**, .357 Mag., Tube Feed, Hammer, Carbine, Engraved, *Modern* ... 160.00 / 210.00
- ☐ **Gallery**, .22 L.R.R.F., Tube Feed, Takedown, Hammer, *Modern* ... 65.00 / 95.00
- ☐ **Gallery**, .22 L.R.R.F., Tube Feed, Takedown, Hammer, Carbine, *Modern* ... 65.00 / 95.00

SHOTGUN, DOUBLE BARREL, SIDE-BY-SIDE

- ☐ **12 Ga. Mag. 3"**, Checkered Stock, Hammerless, Double Trigger, *Modern* ... 125.00 / 180.00
- ☐ **12 Ga. Mag. 3"**, Hammerless, Double Trigger, *Modern* ... 120.00 / 175.00
- ☐ **Overland**, 12 and 20 Gauges, Checkered Stock, Outside Hammers, Double Trigger, *Modern* ... 130.00 / 165.00
- ☐ **Overland**, 12 and 20 Gauges, Outside Hammers, Double Trigger, *Modern* ... 130.00 / 165.00
- ☐ **Overland II**, Various Gauges, Checkered Stock, Outside Hammers, Double Trigger, *Modern* ... 145.00 / 195.00
- ☐ **Squire Model 14**, Various Gauges, Hammerless, Double Trigger, *Modern* ... 120.00 / 175.00

ROSS RIFLE CO.
Quebec, Canada. Also see Canadian Military.

RIFLE, BOLT ACTION

- ☐ **Canadian Issue**, .303 British, Military, *Modern* ... 155.00 / 220.00
- ☐ **Model 1903 MK I**, .303 British, Sporting Rifle, Open Rear Sight, *Modern* ... 265.00 / 350.00
- ☐ **Model 1905 MK II**, Various Calibers, Sporting Rifle, Open Rear Sight, *Modern* ... 220.00 / 325.00
- ☐ **Model 1910 MK III**, Various Calibers, Sporting Rifle, Open Rear Sight, Checkered Stock, *Modern* ... 190.00 / 295.00

ROTTWEIL
Germany, Imported by Eastern Sports Milford, N.H.

	V.G.	EXC.

RIFLE, DOUBLE BARREL, OVER-UNDER
☐ **Standard Grade**, Various Calibers, Engraved, Fancy Checkering, Open Rear Sight, *Modern* 1,550.00 2,200.00

SHOTGUN, DOUBLE BARREL, OVER-UNDER
☐ **Montreal**, 12 Ga., Trap Grade, Vent Rib, Single Selective Trigger, Checkered Stock, *Modern* 1,350.00 1,800.00
☐ **Olympia**, 12 Ga., Skeet Grade, Single Selective Trigger, Automatic Ejector, Vent Rib, Engraved, *Modern* 1,450.00 2,100.00
☐ **Olympia**, 12 Ga., Trap Grade, Single Selective Trigger, Automatic Ejector, Vent Rib, Engraved, *Modern* 1,450.00 2,100.00
☐ **Olympia 72**, 12 Ga., Skeet Grade, Trap Grade, Single Selective Trigger, Checkered Stock, *Modern* 1,250.00 1,800.00
☐ **Supreme**, 12 Ga., Vent Rib, Single Selective Trigger, Checkered Stock, *Modern* 1,150.00 1,700.00
☐ **Supreme**, 12 Ga., Field Grade, Single Selective Trigger, Automatic Ejector, Vent Rib, Engraved, *Modern* 1,450.00 2,100.00
☐ **American**, 12 Ga., Trap Grade, Single Selective Trigger, Automatic Ejector, Vent Rib, Engraved, *Modern* 1,450.00 2,100.00

ROVIRO, ANTONIO
Iqualada, Spain, c. 1790.

HANDGUN, MIQUELET-LOCK
☐ **Pair**, Belt Pistol, Belt Hook, Engraved, Light Ornamentation, *Antique* 3,500.00 5,000.00

ROYAL
Possibly Hopkins & Allen, c. 1880.

HANDGUN, REVOLVER
☐ **.22 Short R.F.**, 7 Shot, Spur Trigger, Solid Frame, Single Action, *Antique* 90.00 160.00
☐ **.32 Short R.F.**, 5 Shot, Spur Trigger, Solid Frame, Single Action, *Antique* 95.00 170.00

ROYAL
M. Zulaika y Cia., Eibar, Spain.

HANDGUN, SEMI-AUTOMATIC
☐ **Mauser M1896 Type**, 7.63mm, Blue, *Modern* 250.00 375.00
☐ **Novelty**, .25 ACP, Clip Fed, Blue, *Curio* 155.00 195.00
☐ **Novelty**, .32 ACP, Clip Fed, Blue, *Curio* 165.00 215.00
☐ **.32 ACP**, Clip Fed, Long Grip, *Modern* 120.00 170.00
☐ **12 Shot**, .32 ACP, Clip Fed, Long Grip, *Modern* 160.00 235.00

RUBY
Gabilondo y Cia., Vitoria, Spain.

HANDGUN, REVOLVER
☐ **Ruby Extra** For Engraving *Add* **$40.00-$55.00**
☐ **Ruby Extra** For Chrome Plating *Add* **$20.00-$30.00**
☐ **Ruby Extra Model 14**, .22 L.R.R.F., Double Action, Blue, Swing-Out Cylinder, *Modern* 45.00 70.00
☐ **Ruby Extra Model 14**, .32 S & W Long, Double Action, Blue, Swing-Out Cylinder, *Modern* 45.00 70.00

372 / RUGER

Royal 12 Shot

Royal Novelty .32

Ruby .45

Ruby .32

	V.G.	EXC.
☐ **Ruby Extra Model 12**, .38 Spec., Double Action, Blue, Swing-Out Cylinder, *Modern*	55.00	80.00
HANDGUN, SEMI-AUTOMATIC		
☐ .32 ACP, Clip Fed, Blue, *Curio*	110.00	150.00

RUGER
Sturm, Ruger & Co., Southport, Conn.
☐ **For Bicentennial Stamping**, *Add* **5%-10%**

AUTOMATIC WEAPON, SUBMACHINE GUN

	V.G.	EXC.
☐ **AC-556**, .223 Rem., Clip Fed, Wood Stock, with Compensator, *Class 3*	200.00	275.00
☐ **AC-556F**, .223 Rem., Clip Fed, Folding Stock, with Compensator, *Class 3*	200.00	325.00
☐ **K AC-556**, .223 Rem., Clip Fed, Stainless, Wood Stock, with Compensator, *Class 3*	290.00	365.00
☐ **K AC-556F**, .223 Rem., Clip Fed, Stainless, Folding Stock, with Compensator, *Class 3*	300.00	400.00

	V.G.	EXC.

HANDGUN, REVOLVER
- ☐ **Brass Gripframe**, *Add* $20.00-30.00
- ☐ **.22 L.R.R.F.**, Western Style, Single Action, Blue, Lightweight, Early Model, *Modern* 225.00 300.00
- ☐ **"Magna-port IV"**, .44 Magnum, Western Style, Single Action, Commemorative, *Modern* 950.00 1,400.00
- ☐ **Bearcat**, .22 L.R.R.F., Western Style, Single Action, Blue, Brass Grip Frame, *Modern* 150.00 225.00
- ☐ **Bearcat**, .22 L.R.R.F., Western Style, Single Action, Blue, Aluminum Gripframe, Early Model, *Modern* 175.00 265.00
- ☐ **Blackhawk**, .30 Carbine, Western Style, Single Action, Blue, New Model, *Modern* 130.00 160.00
- ☐ **Blackhawk**, .30 Carbine, Western Style, Single Action, Blue, *Modern* 150.00 200.00
- ☐ **Blackhawk**, .357 Magnum, Western Style, Single Action, Blue, New Model, *Modern* 130.00 160.00
- ☐ **Blackhawk**, .357 Magnum, Western Style, Single Action, Blue, *Modern* 150.00 200.00
- ☐ **Blackhawk**, .357 Magnum, Western Style, Single Action, Blue, Flat-Top Frame, Early Model, *Modern* 300.00 400.00
- ☐ **Blackhawk**, .357 Magnum, Western Style, Single Action, Blue, 10" Barrel, *Modern* 475.00 650.00
- ☐ **Blackhawk**, .357 Magnum, Western Style, Single Action, Stainless Steel, New Model, *Modern* 140.00 180.00
- ☐ **Blackhawk**, .357 Magnum/9mm Combo, Western Style, Single Action, Blue, New Model, *Modern* 150.00 200.00
- ☐ **Blackhawk**, .357 Magnum/9mm Combo, Western Style, Single Action, Blue, *Modern* 165.00 225.00
- ☐ **Blackhawk**, .41 Magnum, Western Style, Single Action, Blue, New Model, *Modern* 125.00 175.00
- ☐ **Blackhawk**, .41 Magnum, Western Style, Single Action, Blue, *Modern* 150.00 200.00
- ☐ **Blackhawk**, .45 Colt, Western Style, Single Action, Blue, *Modern* 155.00 210.00
- ☐ **Blackhawk**, .45 Colt, Western Style, Single Action, Blue, New Model, *Modern* 135.00 175.00
- ☐ **Blackhawk**, .45 Colt/.45 ACP Combo, Western Style, Single Action, Blue, *Modern* 155.00 200.00
- ☐ **Blackhawk**, .45 Colt/.45 ACP Combo, Western Style, Single Action, Blue, *Modern* 185.00 245.00
- ☐ **Security-Six**, .357 Magnum, Double Action, Swing-Out Cylinder, Stainless Steel, Adjustable Sights, *Modern* 165.00 225.00
- ☐ **Security-Six**, .357 Magnum, Double Action, Swing-Out Cylinder, Blue, Adjustable Sights, *Modern* 140.00 180.00
- ☐ **Service-Six**, .357 Magnum, Double Action, Swing-Out Cylinder, Blue, *Modern* 120.00 160.00
- ☐ **Service-Six**, .357 Magnum, Double Action, Swing-Out Cylinder, Stainless Steel, *Modern* 135.00 185.00
- ☐ **Service-Six**, 9mm Luger, Double Action, Swing-Out Cylinder, Blue, *Modern* 125.00 150.00
- ☐ **Service-Six**, 9mm Luger, Double Action, Swing-Out Cylinder, Stainless Steel, *Modern* 135.00 185.00
- ☐ **Service-Six**, .38 Special, Double Action, Swing-Out Cylinder, Blue, *Modern* 125.00 150.00
- ☐ **Service-Six**, .38 Special, Double Action, Swing-Out Cylinder, Stainless Steel, *Modern* 140.00 180.00
- ☐ **Single-Six**, .22 L.R.R.F., Western Style, Single Action, Blue, Engraved, Cased, *Modern* 575.00 775.00

374 / RUGER

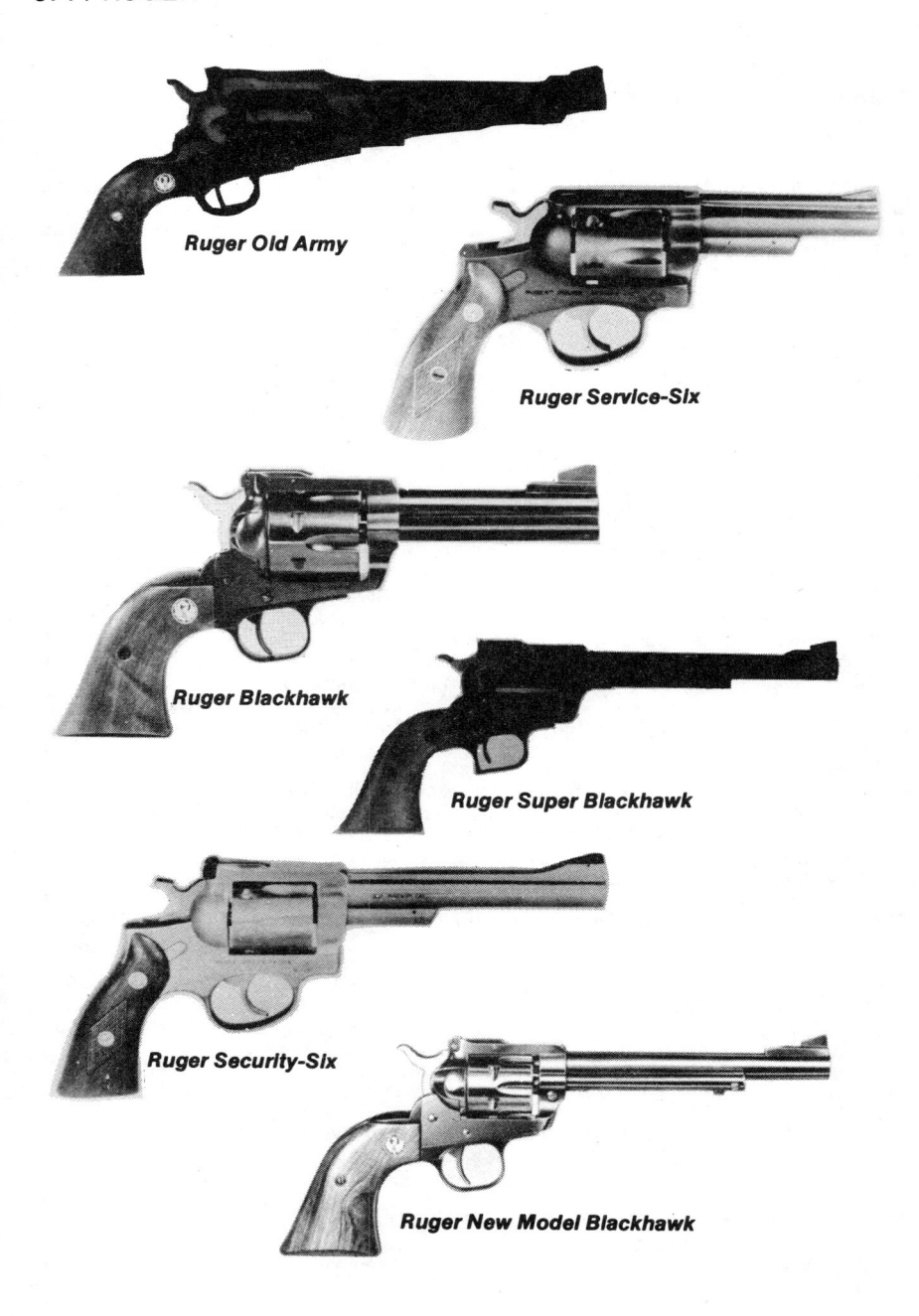

Ruger Old Army

Ruger Service-Six

Ruger Blackhawk

Ruger Super Blackhawk

Ruger Security-Six

Ruger New Model Blackhawk

RUGER / 375

	V.G.	EXC.
☐ **Single-Six**, .22 L.R.R.F., Western Style, Single Action, Blue, Flat Loading Gate, Early Model, *Modern*	200.00	275.00
☐ **Single-Six Colorado Centennial**, .22 L.R.R.F., Commemorative, Cased, *Curio*	175.00	275.00
☐ **Speed-Six**, .357 Magnum, Double Action, Swing-Out Cylinder, Blue, *Modern*	90.00	120.00
☐ **Speed-Six**, .357 Magnum, Double Action, Swing-Out Cylinder, Stainless Steel, *Modern*	135.00	180.00
☐ **Speed-Six**, .38 Special, Double Action, Swing-Out Cylinder, Blue, *Modern*	115.00	145.00
☐ **Speed-Six**, .38 Special, Double Action, Swing-Out Cylinder, Stainless Steel, *Modern*	135.00	180.00
☐ **Speed-Six**, 9mm Luger, Double Action, Swing-Out Cylinder, Blue, *Modern*	115.00	145.00
☐ **Super Blackhawk**, .44 Magnum, Western Style, Single Action, Blue, New Model, *Modern*	140.00	185.00
☐ **Super Blackhawk**, .44 Magnum, Western Style, Single Action, Blue, *Modern*	180.00	250.00
☐ **Super Blackhawk**, .44 Magnum, Western Style, Single Action, Blue, Flat-Top Frame, Early Model, *Modern*	475.00	650.00
☐ **Super Blackhawk**, .44 Magnum, Western Style, Single Action, Blue, 10" Barrel, *Modern*	500.00	675.00
☐ **Super Single Six**, .22LR/.22 WMR Combo, Western Style, Single Action, Blue, New Model, *Modern*	90.00	135.00
☐ **Super Single Six**, .22LR/.22 WMR Combo, Western Style, Single Action, Blue, New Model, 9½" Barrel, *Modern*	95.00	140.00
☐ **Super Single Six**, .22LR/.22 WMR Combo, Western Style, Single Action, Blue, *Modern*	130.00	165.00
☐ **Super Single Six**, .22LR/.22 WMR Combo, Western Style, Single Action, Blue, 9½" Barrel, *Modern*	140.00	175.00
☐ **Super Single Six**, .22LR/.22 WMR Combo, Western Style, Single Action, Stainless Steel, New Model, *Modern*	130.00	160.00
☐ **Redhawk**, .44 Magnum, Double Action, Stainless, Interchangeable Sights, Swingout Cylinder, *Modern*	180.00	275.00

HANDGUN, SEMI-AUTOMATIC

	V.G.	EXC.
☐ **MK I**, .22 L.R.R.F., Clip Fed, Adjustable Sights, Target Pistol, *Modern*	95.00	140.00
☐ **MK I**, .22 L.R.R.F., Clip Fed, Adjustable Sights, Target Pistol, Wood Grips, *Modern*	110.00	150.00
☐ **MK II**, .22 L.R.R.F., Clip Fed, Adjustable Sights, Target Pistol, *Modern*	95.00	140.00
☐ **MK II**, .22 L.R.R.F., Clip Fed, Adjustable Sights, Target Pistol, Bull Barrel, *Modern*	100.00	140.00
☐ **Standard**, .22 L.R.R.F., Clip Fed, *Modern*	80.00	115.00
☐ **Standard MK II**, .22 L.R.R.F., Clip Fed, *Modern*	80.00	115.00
☐ **Standard (Under #25600)**, .22 L.R.R.F., Clip Fed, Early Model, Blue, *Modern*	185.00	250.00

HANDGUN, SINGLESHOT

	V.G.	EXC.
☐ **Hawkeye**, .256 Win. Mag., Western Style, Single Action, Blue, *Modern*	425.00	600.00

HANDGUN, PERCUSSION

	V.G.	EXC.
☐ **Old Army**, .44, Single Action, Blue, Adjustable Sights, Reproduction, *Antique*	120.00	165.00
☐ **Old Army**, .44, Single Action, Stainless, Adjustable Sights, Reproduction, *Antique*	120.00	165.00

376 / RUGER

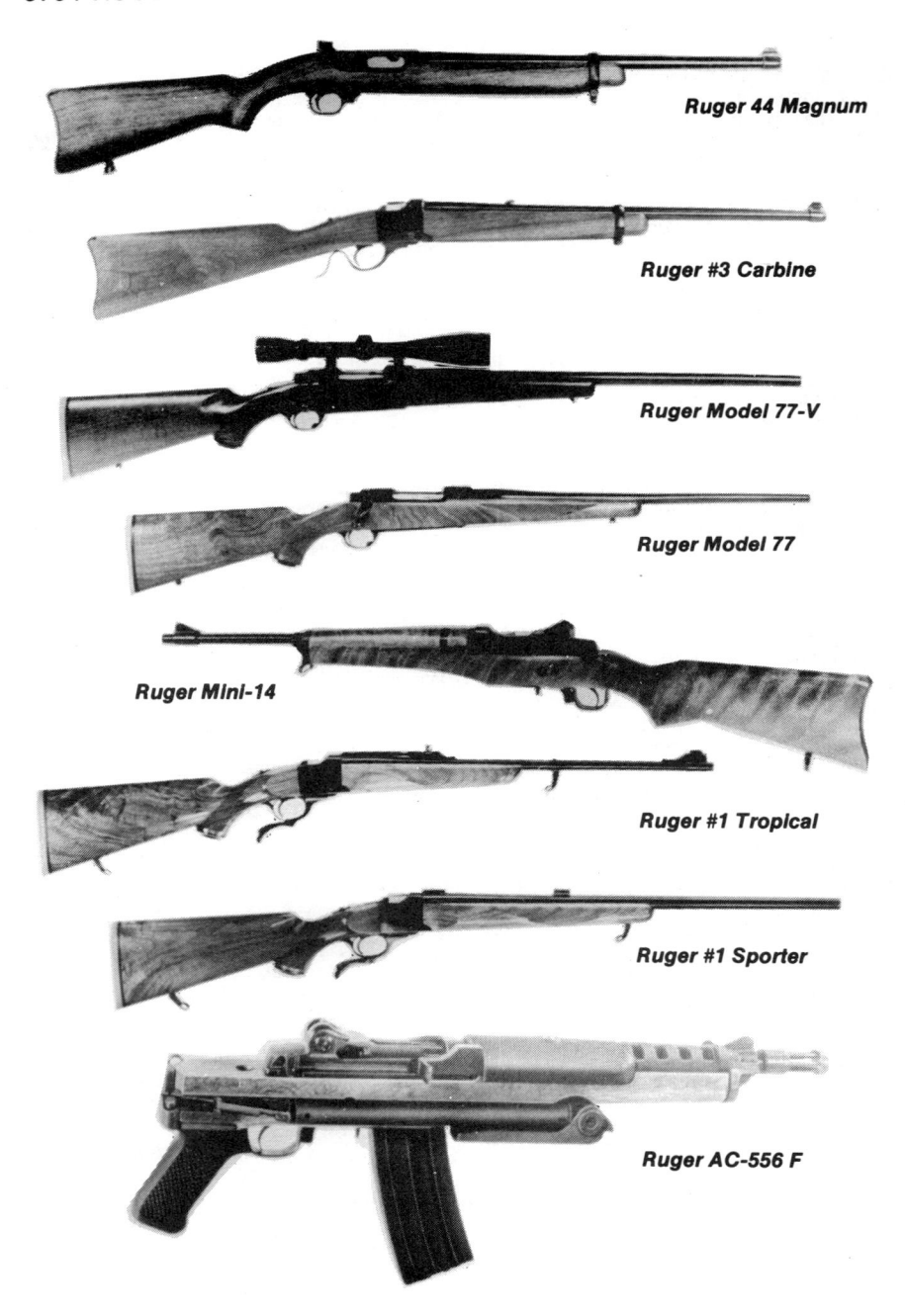

Ruger 44 Magnum

Ruger #3 Carbine

Ruger Model 77-V

Ruger Model 77

Ruger Mini-14

Ruger #1 Tropical

Ruger #1 Sporter

Ruger AC-556 F

	V.G.	EXC.
RIFLE, BOLT ACTION		
☐ **M-77**, for .338 Win. Mag., *Add* **$10.00-$15.00**		
☐ **M-77**, for .458 Win. Mag., *Add* **$40.00-$50.00**		
☐ **M-77R**, Various Calibers, Checkered Stock, Scope Mounts, no Sights, *Modern*	180.00	250.00
☐ **M-77RS**, Various Calibers, Checkered Stock, Open Rear Sight, Scope Mounts, *Modern*	190.00	265.00
☐ **M-77ST**, Various Calibers, Checkered Stock, Open Rear Sight, *Modern*	180.00	250.00
☐ **M-77V**, Various Calibers, Heavy Barrel, Varmint, no Sights, Scope Mounts, Checkered Stock, *Modern*	180.00	250.00
RIFLE, SEMI-AUTOMATIC		
☐ **10/22**, .22 L.R.R.F., Clip Fed, Plain, *Modern*	60.00	80.00
☐ **10/22 Canadian Centennial**, .22 L.R.R.F., Commemorative, *Curio*	60.00	120.00
☐ **10/22 International**, .22 L.R.R.F., Clip Fed, Full-Stocked, *Modern*	90.00	135.00
☐ **10/22 Sporter I**, .22 L.R.R.F., Clip Fed, Monte Carlo Stock, *Modern*	65.00	95.00
☐ **10/22 Sporter II**, .22 L.R.R.F., Clip Fed, Checkered Stock, *Modern*	70.00	115.00
☐ **10/22 Deluxe**, .22 L.R.R.F., Clip Fed, Checkered Stock, *Modern*	75.00	110.00
☐ **Mini-14**, .223 Rem., Clip Fed, Carbine, *Modern*	160.00	225.00
☐ **Mini-14**, .223 Rem., Clip Fed, Carbine, Stainless, *Modern*	185.00	260.00
☐ **Mini-14/20 GB**, .223 Rem., Clip Fed, Carbine, with Flash Hider and Bayonet Stud, *Modern*	160.00	225.00
☐ **Mini-14/20 GB-F**, .223 Rem., Clip Fed, Carbine, Stainless, with Flash Hider and Bayonet Stud, *Modern*	185.00	260.00
☐ **K Mini-14/20 GB**, .223 Rem., Clip Fed, Carbine, with Flash Hider and Bayonet Stud, Folding Stock, *Modern*	220.00	290.00
☐ **K Mini-14/20 GB-F**, .223 Rem., Clip Fed, Carbine, Stainless, with Flash Hider and Bayonet Stud, Folding Stock, *Modern*	245.00	320.00
☐ **Model 44 Deluxe**, .44 Magnum, Tube Feed, Plain, Peep Sights, Sling Swivels, *Modern*	170.00	225.00
☐ **Model 44 International**, .44 Magnum, Tube Feed, Full-Stocked, *Modern*	175.00	235.00
☐ **Model 44 Sporter**, .44 Magnum, Tube Feed, Monte Carlo Stock, *Modern*	175.00	235.00
☐ **Model 44 Standard**, .44 Magnum, Tube Feed, Plain, Open Rear Sight, *Modern*	160.00	225.00
RIFLE, SINGLESHOT		
☐ **#1 Canadian Centennial Deluxe**, Commemorative, *Curio*	500.00	800.00
☐ **#1 Light Sporter**, Various Calibers, Open Rear Sight, Checkered Stock, *Modern*	190.00	275.00
☐ **#1 Medium Sporter**, Various Calibers, Open Rear Sight, Checkered Stock, *Modern*	190.00	275.00
☐ **#1 Standard Sporter**, Various Calibers, no Sights, Scope Mounts, Checkered Stock, *Modern*	190.00	275.00
☐ **#1 Tropical**, Various Calibers, Open Rear Sight, Checkered Stock, *Modern*	190.00	275.00
☐ **#1 Varminter**, Various Calibers, Heavy Barrel, no Sights, Checkered Stock, *Modern*	190.00	275.00
☐ **#2 Canadian Centennial Set**, Commemorative, *Curio*	375.00	500.00
☐ **#3 Canadian Centennial Set**, Commemorative, *Curio*	265.00	375.00
☐ **#3 Carbine**, Various Calibers, Open Rear Sight, *Modern*	145.00	195.00
SILENCED WEAPON, PISTOL		
☐ **MK I (MAC)**, .22 L.R.R.F., Semi-Automatic, Adjustable Sights, Clip Fed, Target Pistol, *Class 3*	400.00	600.00

	V.G.	EXC.
SILENCED WEAPON, RIFLE		
☐ **10/22 (MAC)**, .22 L.R.R.F., Semi-Automatic, Clip Fed, Military, Class 3	600.00	800.00
SHOTGUN, DOUBLE BARREL, OVER-UNDER		
☐ **Red Label**, 12 or 20 Gauges, Checkered Stock, *Modern*	475.00	600.00

RUMMEL
Made by Crescent for A.J. Rummel Arms Co., Toledo, Ohio.

	V.G.	EXC.
SHOTGUN, DOUBLE BARREL, SIDE-BY-SIDE		
☐ **Various Gauges**, Outside Hammers, Damascus Barrel, *Modern*	100.00	175.00
☐ **Various Gauges**, Hammerless, Steel Barrel, *Modern*	135.00	200.00
☐ **Various Gauges**, Hammerless, Damascus Barrel, *Modern*	100.00	175.00
☐ **Various Gauges**, Outside Hammers, Steel Barrel, *Modern*	125.00	190.00
SHOTGUN, SINGLESHOT		
☐ **Various Gauges**, Hammer, Steel Barrel, *Modern*	55.00	85.00

RUPERTUS, JACOB
Philadelphia, Pa. 1858-1899.

	V.G.	EXC.
HANDGUN, DOUBLE BARREL, SIDE-BY-SIDE		
☐ **.22 Short R.F.**, Derringer, Side-Swing Barrel, Iron Frame, Spur Trigger, *Antique*	275.00	400.00
HANDGUN, REVOLVER		
☐ **.22 Short R.F.**, Pepperbox, 8 Shot, Iron Frame, Spur Trigger, *Antique*	250.00	375.00
☐ **.22 Short R.F.**, 7 Shot, Spur Trigger, Solid Frame, Single Action, *Antique*	120.00	165.00
☐ **.32 Short R.F.**, 5 Shot, Spur Trigger, Solid Frame, Single Action, *Antique*	125.00	180.00
☐ **.38 Short R.F.**, 5 Shot, Spur Trigger, Solid Frame, Single Action, *Antique*	125.00	190.00
☐ **.41 Short R.F.**, 5 Shot, Spur Trigger, Solid Frame, Single Action, *Antique*	145.00	210.00
HANDGUN, SINGLESHOT		
☐ **.22 Short R.F.**, Derringer, Side-Swing Barrel, Iron Frame, Spur Trigger, *Antique*	150.00	230.00
☐ **.32 Short R.F.**, Derringer, Side-Swing Barrel, Iron Frame, Spur Trigger, *Antique*	140.00	185.00
☐ **.38 Short R.F.**, Derringer, Side-Swing Barrel, Iron Frame, Spur Trigger, *Antique*	145.00	190.00

RUPP, HERMAN
Pa. 1784. See Kentucky Rifles.

RUPP, JOHN
Allentown, Pa. See U.S. Military, Kentucky Rifles and Pistols.

RUPPERT, WILLIAM
Lancaster, Pa., c. 1776. See U.S. Military, Kentucky Rifles and Pistols.

RUSH, JOHN
Philadelphia, Pa. 1740-1750. See Kentucky Rifles and Pistols.

RUSSIAN MILITARY / 379

Russian Military M1890 Communist

Russian Military Tokarev

Russian Military Handgun Percussion

RUSSIAN MILITARY

	V.G.	EXC.

AUTOMATIC WEAPON, ASSAULT RIFLE
- ☐ **AVS 36 Simonava**, 7.62 X 39 Russian, Clip Fed, Wood Stock, *Class 3* 725.00   975.00

AUTOMATIC WEAPON, HEAVY MACHINE GUN
- ☐ **Goryunov SG-43**, 7.62 X 39 Russian, Belt Fed, Heavy Barrel, *Class 3* 1,300.00   1,850.00

AUTOMATIC WEAPON, LIGHT MACHINE GUN
- ☐ **Degtyarov DP**, 7.62 X54R Russian, Drum Magazine, Bipod, *Class 3*   975.00   1,650.00

AUTOMATIC WEAPON, SUBMACHINE GUN
- ☐ **PPS-43**, 7.62mm Tokarev, Clip Fed, Folding Stock, *Class 3* 725.00   975.00
- ☐ **PPSH-41**, 7.62mm Tokarev, Clip Fed, Wood Stock, *Class 3* 525.00   775.00

HANDGUN, FLINTLOCK
- ☐ **Nicholas I**, Tula Arsenal, Military, *Antique* 650.00   875.00

HANDGUN, FREE PISTOL
- ☐ **MC**, .22 L.R.R.F., Clip Fed, *Modern* 175.00   235.00
- ☐ **MCU**, .22 Short, Clip Fed, *Modern* 200.00   285.00
- ☐ **Vostok M-T0Z-35**, .22 L.R.R.F., *Modern* 490.00   675.00
- ☐ **Vostok M-T0Z-35**, .22 L.R.R.F., Cased with Accessories, *Modern*... 675.00   900.00

HANDGUN, REVOLVER
- ☐ **M1890**, 7.62mm Nagent, Gas-Seal Cylinder, Imperial, *Curio* 150.00   195.00
- ☐ **M1890**, 7.62mm Nagent, Gas-Seal Cylinder, Communist, *Curio* ... 130.00   170.00

HANDGUN, SEMI-AUTOMATIC
- ☐ **Makarov**, 9mm Makarov, Clip Fed, Double Action, *Modern* 575.00   850.00
- ☐ **Tokarev**, 7.62mm Tokarev, Clip Fed, *Modern* 175.00   275.00

Russian Military M1890 Imperial

Russian Military Makarov

	V.G.	EXC.
RIFLE, BOLT ACTION		
☐ **KK M. CM 2**, .22 L.R.R.F., Match Rifle, Target Sights, *Modern*	225.00	325.00
☐ **M1891 Moisin-Nagent**, 7.62 X 54R Russian, Military, *Modern*	80.00	125.00
☐ **M1891 Remington**, 7.62 X 54R Russian, Military, *Modern*	95.00	145.00
☐ **M1910**, 7.62 X 54R Russian, Military, Carbine, *Modern*	85.00	130.00
RIFLE, PERCUSSION		
☐ **Berdan II**, .42, Military, *Antique*	320.00	425.00
RIFLE, SEMI-AUTOMATIC		
☐ **M1940 Tokarev**, 7.62 X 54R Russian, Clip Fed, Military, *Modern*	120.00	220.00
☐ **SKS**, 7.62 X 39 Russian, Carbine, Military, *Modern*	170.00	245.00

RWS
Rheinische-Westfalische Sprengstoff, since 1931. Now Dynamit Nobel AG, Troisdorf-Oberlar, West Germany.

RIFLE, BOLT ACTION
☐ **Repeater**, Various Calibers, Checkered Stock, Set Triggers, Open Sights, *Modern* 235.00 325.00

RYAN, THOMAS
Norwich, Conn., c. 1870.

HANDGUN, REVOLVER
☐ **.22 Short R.F.**, 7 Shot, Spur Trigger, Solid Frame, Single Action, *Antique* 90.00 160.00
☐ **.32 Short R.F.**, 5 Shot, Spur Trigger, Solid Frame, Single Action, *Antique* 95.00 170.00

SABLE
Belgium, unknown maker.

HANDGUN, REVOLVER
☐ **Baby Hammerless**, .22 Short R.F., Folding Trigger, *Modern* 70.00 100.00

SAKO
O.Y. Sako AB, Riihmaki, Finland.

	V.G.	EXC.

RIFLE, BOLT ACTION
- ☐ **Deluxe (Garcia)**, Various Calibers, Sporting Rifle, Monte Carlo Stock, Fancy Checkering, Long Action, *Modern* **320.00 425.00**
- ☐ **Deluxe (Garcia)**, Various Calibers, Sporting Rifle, Monte Carlo Stock, Fancy Checkering, Medium Action, *Modern* **325.00 425.00**
- ☐ **Deluxe (Garcia)**, Various Calibers, Sporting Rifle, Monte Carlo Stock, Fancy Checkering, Short Action, *Modern* **325.00 425.00**
- ☐ **Finnbear**, Various Calibers, Sporting Rifle, Monte Carlo Stock, Checkered Stock, Long Action, *Modern* **325.00 425.00**
- ☐ **Finnbear Carbine**, Various Calibers, Sporting Rifle, Monte Carlo Stock, Checkered Stock, Long Action, Full-Stocked, *Modern* **340.00 450.00**
- ☐ **Forester**, Various Calibers, Sporting Rifle, Monte Carlo Stock, Checkered Stock, Medium Action, *Modern* **300.00 400.00**
- ☐ **Forester**, Various Calibers, Sporting Rifle, Monte Carlo Stock, Checkered Stock, Medium Action, Heavy Barrel, *Modern* **300.00 400.00**
- ☐ **Forester Carbine**, Various Calibers, Sporting Rifle, Monte Carlo Stock, Checkered Stock, Medium Action, Full-Stocked, *Modern*.... **325.00 450.00**
- ☐ **Hi-Power Mauser (FN)**, Various Calibers, Sporting Rifle, Monte Carlo Stock, Checkered Stock, *Modern*........................... **275.00 375.00**
- ☐ **Magnum Mauser (FN)**, Various Calibers, Sporting Rifle, Monte Carlo Stock, Checkered Stock, *Modern*........................... **300.00 420.00**
- ☐ **Model 74 (Garcia)**, Various Calibers, Sporting Rifle, Monte Carlo Stock, Checkered Stock, Long Action, *Modern*.................... **250.00 350.00**
- ☐ **Model 74 (Garcia)**, Various Calibers, Sporting Rifle, Monte Carlo Stock, Checkered Stock, Medium Action, *Modern*.................. **250.00 350.00**
- ☐ **Model 74 (Garcia)**, Various Calibers, Sporting Rifle, Monte Carlo Stock, Checkered Stock, Short Action, *Modern* **250.00 350.00**
- ☐ **Model 74 (Garcia)**, Various Calibers, Sporting Rifle, Monte Carlo Stock, Checkered Stock, Heavy Barrel, Medium Action, *Modern* ... **270.00 365.00**
- ☐ **Model 74 (Garcia)**, Various Calibers, Sporting Rifle, Monte Carlo Stock, Checkered Stock, Heavy Barrel, Short Action, *Modern* **270.00 365.00**
- ☐ **Model 78 (Stoeger)**, .22 L.R.R.F., Sporting Rifle, Monte Carlo Stock, Checkered Stock, *Modern* **185.00 250.00**
- ☐ **Model 78 (Stoeger)**, .22 Hornet, Sporting Rifle, Monte Carlo Stock, Checkered Stock, *Modern* **220.00 300.00**
- ☐ **Model 78 (Stoeger)**, .22 W.M.R., Sporting Rifle, Monte Carlo Stock, Checkered Stock, *Modern* **200.00 280.00**
- ☐ **Model 78 (Stoeger)**, .22 L.R.R.F., Sporting Rifle, Monte Carlo Stock, Checkered Stock, Heavy Barrel, *Modern* **200.00 285.00**
- ☐ **Vixen**, Various Calibers, Sporting Rifle, Monte Carlo Stock, Checkered Stock, Short Action, *Modern* **240.00 335.00**
- ☐ **Vixen**, Various Calibers, Sporting Rifle, Monte Carlo Stock, Checkered Stock, Short Action, Heavy Barrel, *Modern* **250.00 360.00**
- ☐ **Vixen Carbine**, Various Calibers, Sporting Rifle, Monte Carlo Stock, Checkered Stock, Short Action, Full-Stocked, *Modern* **275.00 380.00**

RIFLE, LEVER ACTION
- ☐ **Finnwolf**, Various Calibers, Sporting Rifle, Monte Carlo Stock, Checkered Stock, *Modern* **250.00 375.00**

ST. LOUIS ARMS CO.
Belgium for Shapleigh Hardware Co., c. 1900.

SHOTGUN, DOUBLE BARREL, SIDE-BY-SIDE
- ☐ **Various Gauges**, Outside Hammers, Damascus Barrel, *Modern* **100.00 175.00**
- ☐ **Various Gauges**, Hammerless, Steel Barrel, *Modern* **135.00 200.00**
- ☐ **Various Gauges**, Hammerless, Damascus Barrel, *Modern* **100.00 175.00**
- ☐ **Various Gauges**, Outside Hammers, Steel Barrel, *Modern* **125.00 190.00**

	V.G.	EXC.
SHOTGUN, SINGLESHOT		
☐ **Various Gauges**, Hammer, Steel Barrel, *Modern*	55.00	85.00

SAMPLES, BETHUEL
Urbana, Ohio. See Kentucky Rifles and Pistols.

SANDERSON
Portage, Wisc.

SHOTGUN, DOUBLE BARREL, SIDE-BY-SIDE
	V.G.	EXC.
☐ **M200-S 1**, Various Gauges, Checkered Stock, Automatic Ejectors, Engraved, *Modern*	300.00	400.00
☐ **Neumann**, Various Gauges, Checkered Stock, Automatic Ejectors, Engraved, *Modern*	175.00	250.00
☐ **Neumann**, 10 Gauge Mag., Checkered Stock, Automatic Ejectors, Engraved, *Modern*	300.00	400.00

SARASQUETA, VICTOR
Victor Sarasqueta, Eibar, Spain from 1934.

RIFLE, DOUBLE BARREL, SIDE-BY-SIDE
	V.G.	EXC.
☐ **Various Calibers**, Sidelock, Automatic Ejector, Fancy Engraving, Fancy Checkering, *Modern*	1,750.00	2,500.00

SHOTGUN, DOUBLE BARREL, SIDE-BY-SIDE
	V.G.	EXC.
☐ **#10**, Various Gauges, Sidelock, Fancy Checkering, Fancy Engraving, *Modern*	675.00	975.00
☐ **#11**, Various Gauges, Sidelock, Fancy Checkering, Fancy Engraving, *Modern*	900.00	1,200.00
☐ **#12**, Various Gauges, Sidelock, Fancy Checkering, Fancy Engraving, *Modern*	1,200.00	1,450.00
☐ **#2**, Various Gauges, Double Trigger, Checkered Stock, Light Engraving, *Modern*	135.00	190.00
☐ **#3**, Various Gauges, Double Trigger, Checkered Stock, Light Engraving, *Modern*	190.00	295.00
☐ **#4**, Various Gauges, Sidelock, Checkered Stock, Light Engraving, *Modern*	240.00	345.00
☐ **#4E**, Various Gauges, Sidelock, Checkered Stock, Light Engraving, *Modern*	275.00	400.00
☐ **#5**, Various Gauges, Sidelock, Checkered Stock, Light Engraving, *Modern*	250.00	350.00
☐ **#5E**, Various Gauges, Sidelock, Checkered Stock, Light Engraving, *Modern*	300.00	435.00
☐ **#6**, Various Gauges, Sidelock, Fancy Checkering, Engraved, *Modern*	280.00	375.00
☐ **#6E**, Various Gauges, Sidelock, Fancy Checkering, Engraved, *Modern*	375.00	495.00
☐ **#7**, Various Gauges, Sidelock, Fancy Checkering, Engraved, *Modern*	375.00	495.00
☐ **#7E**, Various Gauges, Sidelock, Fancy Checkering, Engraved, *Modern*	450.00	585.00
☐ **#8**, Various Gauges, Sidelock, Fancy Checkering, Fancy Engraving, *Modern*	565.00	690.00
☐ **#9**, Various Gauges, Sidelock, Fancy Checkering, Fancy Engraving, *Modern*	675.00	820.00
☐ **Super Deluxe**, Various Gauges, Sidelock, Fancy Checkering, Fancy Engraving, *Modern*	1,800.00	2,400.00

SAUER, J.P. AND SOHN / 383

Sauer Model H 38

Sauer Bar Pistole

Sauer Roth-Sauer

Sauer Model 1913 .25

Sauer Model 1913 .32

SAUER, J.P. & SOHN
V.G.   EXC.

1855 to date, first in Suhl, Germany, now in Eckernforde, West Germany. Also see Hawes for listing of revolvers.

COMBINATION WEAPON, DOUBLE BARREL, OVER-UNDER
☐ **BBF**, Various Calibers, Double Trigger, Set Trigger, Engraved, Checkered Stock, *Modern* 900.00   1,450.00
☐ **BBF Deluxe**, Various Calibers, Double Trigger, Set Trigger, Fancy Engraving, Fancy Checkering, *Modern* 1,150.00   1,700.00

COMBINATION WEAPON, DRILLING
☐ **Model 3000E**, Various Calibers, Double Trigger, Engraved, Checkered Stock, *Modern* 1,300.00   1,750.00
☐ **Model 3000E Deluxe**, Various Calibers, Double Trigger, Fancy Engraving, Fancy Checkering, *Modern* 1,450.00   2,100.00

HANDGUN, MANUAL REPEATER
☐ **Bar Pistole**, 7mm, Double Barrel, 4 Shot, Folding Trigger, *Curio* ... 275.00   350.00

384 / SAUER, J.P. AND SOHN

	V.G.	EXC.

HANDGUN, SEMI-AUTOMATIC
- ☐ **Behorden**, .32 ACP, Clip Fed, *Modern* 175.00 275.00
- ☐ **Behorden**, .32 ACP, Clip Fed, Lightweight, *Modern* 325.00 425.00
- ☐ **Behorden 4mm**, .32 ACP, Clip Fed, Extra Barrel, *Modern* 575.00 800.00
- ☐ **Behorden Dutch Navy**, .32 ACP, Clip Fed, Military, *Modern*........ 300.00 400.00
- ☐ **Model 1913**, .25 ACP, Clip Fed, *Modern* 165.00 245.00
- ☐ **Model 1913**, .32 ACP, Clip Fed, *Modern* 175.00 250.00
- ☐ **Model 28**, .25 ACP, Clip Fed, *Modern* 190.00 275.00
- ☐ **Model H 38**, .25 ACP, Double Action, Clip Fed, Hammer, *Modern* 275.00 400.00
- ☐ **Model H 38**, .32 ACP, Double Action, Clip Fed, Hammer, Commercial, *Modern* 235.00 325.00
- ☐ **Model H 38**, .32 ACP, Double Action, Clip Fed, Hammer, Nazi-Proofed, Military, *Modern* 195.00 250.00
- ☐ **Model H 38**, .32 ACP, Double Action, Clip Fed, Hammer, Lightweight, *Modern* 475.00 600.00
- ☐ **Model H 38 Police**, .32 ACP, Double Action, Clip Fed, Hammer, Nazi-Proofed, *Curio*.. 375.00 500.00
- ☐ **W.T.M. 1922**, .25 ACP, Clip Fed, *Modern* 175.00 250.00
- ☐ **W.T.M. 1928**, .25 ACP, Clip Fed, *Modern* 190.00 275.00
- ☐ **W.T.M. 1928/2**, .25 ACP, Clip Fed, *Modern* 160.00 235.00
- ☐ **Roth-Sauer**, 8mm, Clip Fed, *Curio*............................... 600.00 900.00

RIFLE, BOLT ACTION
- ☐ **Mauser Custom**, Various Calibers, Set Trigger, Checkered Stock, Octagon Barrel, *Modern*.. 335.00 500.00

SHOTGUN, DOUBLE BARREL, OVER-UNDER
- ☐ **Model 66 GR I**, 12 Ga., Single Selective Trigger, Selective Ejector, Hammerless, Sidelock, Engraved, *Modern* 950.00 1,350.00
- ☐ **Model 66 GR I**, 12 Ga., Skeet Grade, Selective Ejector, Hammerless, Sidelock, Engraved, *Modern* 800.00 1,200.00
- ☐ **Model 66 GR II**, 12 Ga., Single Selective Trigger, Selective Ejector, Hammerless, Sidelock, Fancy Engraving, *Modern* 1,000.00 1,600.00
- ☐ **Model 66 GR II**, 12 Ga., Skeet Grade, Selective Ejector, Hammerless, Sidelock, Fancy Engraving, *Modern* 925.00 1,250.00
- ☐ **Model 66 GR II**, 12 Ga., Trap Grade, Selective Ejector, Hammerless, Sidelock, Fancy Engraving, *Modern* 950.00 1,300.00
- ☐ **Model 66 GR III**, 12 Ga., Single Selective Trigger, Selective Ejector, Hammerless, Sidelock, Fancy Engraving, *Modern* 1,650.00 2,350.00
- ☐ **Model 66 GR III**, 12 Ga., Skeet Grade, Selective Ejector, Hammerless, Sidelock, Fancy Engraving, *Modern* 1,150.00 1,800.00
- ☐ **Model 66 GR III**, 12 Ga., Trap Grade, Selective Ejector, Hammerless, Sidelock, Fancy Engraving, *Modern* 1,150.00 1,800.00
- ☐ **Model GR I**, 12 Ga., Trap Grade, Selective Ejector, Hammerless, Sidelock, Engraved, *Modern* 800.00 1,200.00

SHOTGUN, DOUBLE BARREL, SIDE-BY-SIDE
- ☐ **.410 Gauge**, Double Trigger, Light Engraving, *Modern* 425.00 600.00
- ☐ **Artemis I**, 12 Ga., Single Selective Trigger, Engraved, Checkered Stock, *Modern*...2,450.00 3,500.00
- ☐ **Artemis II**, 12 Ga., Single Selective Trigger, Fancy Engraving, Fancy Checkering, *Modern* 3,000.00 4,000.00
- ☐ **Royal**, 12 and 20 Gauges, Single Selective Trigger, Engraved, Checkered Stock, *Modern* 500.00 850.00
- ☐ **Model Kim**, Various Gauges, Double Triggers, Checkered Stock, Light Engraving, *Modern* 175.00 275.00
- ☐ **Model VIII**, Various Gauges, Double Triggers, Checkered Stock, Light Engraving, *Modern* 175.00 275.00

SAVAGE ARMS COMPANY / 385

	V.G.	EXC.
☐ **Model VIII DES**, Various Gauges, Single Selective Trigger, Selective Ejectors, Checkered Stock, Light Engraving, *Modern*	175.00	275.00
☐ **Model VIII DES-01**, Various Gauges, Single Selective Trigger, Selective Ejectors, Checkered Stock, Engraved, *Modern*	250.00	350.00
☐ **Model VIII DES-07**, Various Gauges, Single Selective Trigger, Selective Ejectors, Checkered Stock, Fancy Engraving, *Modern*	350.00	475.00
☐ **Model VIII DES-05**, Various Gauges, Single Selective Trigger, Selective Ejectors, Checkered Stock, Fancy Engraving, Sideplates, *Modern*	550.00	775.00

SATA
Sabotti & Tanfoglio Fabbrica d'Armi, Gardone Val Trompia, Italy.

HANDGUN, SEMI-AUTOMATIC

	V.G.	EXC.
☐ **.22 Short**, Clip Fed, Blue, *Modern*	90.00	145.00
☐ **.25 ACP**, Clip Fed, Blue, *Modern*	95.00	150.00

SAVAGE ARMS CO.
Utica, N.Y., 1893-1899, renamed Savage Arms Co. 1899. J. Stevens Arms Co. Springfield Arms Co. and A.H. Fox are all part of Savage. Also See U.S. Military.

AUTOMATIC WEAPON, HEAVY MACHINE GUN

	V.G.	EXC.
☐ **M2 Browning**, .50 BMG, Belt Fed, Tripod, *Class 3*	3,500.00	4,350.00

AUTOMATIC WEAPON, SUBMACHINE GUN

	V.G.	EXC.
☐ **Thompson M1928A1**, .45 ACP, Clip Fed, with Compensator, Lyman Sights, *Class 3*	1,200.00	1,650.00

COMBINATION WEAPON, DOUBLE BARREL, OVER-UNDER

	V.G.	EXC.
☐ **Model 24**, Various Calibers, Hammer, *Modern*	70.00	95.00
☐ **Model 24-C**, .22/20 Ga., Hammer, *Modern*	75.00	115.00
☐ **Model 24-D**, Various Calibers, Hammer, *Modern*	80.00	120.00
☐ **Model 24-V**, Various Calibers, Checkered Stock, Hammer, *Modern*	95.00	140.00
☐ **Model 2400**, Various Calibers, Checkered Stock, Hammer, *Modern*	375.00	475.00

HANDGUN, SEMI-AUTOMATIC

☐ **Model 1907**, Factory Nickel, *Add* **$35.00-$45.00**
☐ **Model 1907**, Grade A Engraving (Light), *Add* **$75.00-$95.00**
☐ **Model 1907**, Grade C Engraving (Fancy), *Add* **$225.00-$300.00**

	V.G.	EXC.
☐ **Model 1907 (1908)**, .32 ACP, Clip Fed, Burr Cocking Piece, (under #10,899), *Curio*	180.00	250.00
☐ **Model 1907 (1909)**, .32 ACP, Clip Fed, Burr Cocking Piece, (#'s-10,900-70,499), *Curio*	150.00	190.00
☐ **Model 1907 (1912)**, .32 ACP, Clip Fed, Burr Cocking Piece, (Higher # than 70500), *Curio*	135.00	175.00
☐ **Model 1907 (1913)**, .380 ACP, Clip Fed, Burr Cocking Piece, *Curio*	180.00	250.00
☐ **Model 1907 (1914)**, .32 ACP, Spur Cocking Piece, *Curio*	135.00	170.00
☐ **Model 1907 (1914)**, .380 ACP, Spur Cocking Piece, *Curio*	145.00	200.00
☐ **Model 1907 (1918)**, .32 ACP, Clip Fed, no Cartridge Indicator, Burr Cocking Piece, (After # 175,000), *Curio*	120.00	155.00
☐ **Model 1907 (1918)**, .32 ACP, Clip Fed, Spur Cocking Piece, (After # 195000), *Curio*	140.00	180.00
☐ **Model 1907 (1918)**, .380 ACP, Clip Fed, Burr Cocking Piece, (After # 10000B), *Curio*	200.00	275.00
☐ **Model 1907 Military**, .32 ACP, Clip Fed, Burr Cocking Piece, *Curio*	115.00	145.00
☐ **Model 1907 Military**, .32 ACP, Clip Fed, Burr Cocking Piece, (Portuguese Contract), *Curio*	265.00	350.00
☐ **Model 1915**, .32 ACP, Clip Fed, Hammerless, Grip Safety, *Curio*	175.00	240.00
☐ **Model 1915**, .380 ACP, Clip Fed, Hammerless, Grip Safety, *Curio*	250.00	325.00

386 / SAVAGE ARMS COMPANY

	V.G.	EXC.
☐ **Model 1917**, .32 ACP, Clip Fed, Spur Cocking Piece, Flared Grip, *Curio*	155.00	200.00
☐ **Model 1917**, .380 ACP, Clip Fed, Spur Cocking Piece, Flared Grip, *Curio*	185.00	235.00
☐ **Military Model**, .45 ACP, Clip Fed, Original, *Curio*	2,700.00	3,500.00
☐ **Military Model**, .45 ACP, Clip Fed, Surplus, Reblue, *Curio*	1,500.00	2,500.00
☐ **.25 ACP**, Clip Fed, Blue, *Curio*	3,450.00	4,500.00

HANDGUN, SINGLESHOT

☐ **Model 101**, .22 L.R.R.F., Western Style, Single Action, Swing-Out Cylinder, *Modern*	75.00	120.00

RIFLE, BOLT ACTION

☐ **Model 10**, .22 L.R.R.F., Target Sights, (Anschutz), *Modern*	85.00	130.00
☐ **Model 110**, Magnum Calibers, *Add* **$15.00**		
☐ **Model 110**, Various Calibers, Open Rear Sight, Checkered Stock, *Modern*	120.00	160.00
☐ **Model 110-B**, Various Calibers, Open Rear Sight, *Modern*	135.00	180.00
☐ **Model 110-BL**, Various Calibers, Open Rear Sight, Left-Hand, *Modern*	145.00	195.00
☐ **Model 110-C**, Various Calibers, Clip Fed, Open Rear Sight, *Modern*	145.00	190.00
☐ **Model 110-CL**, Various Calibers, Clip Fed, Open Rear Sight, Left-Hand, *Modern*	150.00	200.00
☐ **Model 110-E**, Various Calibers, Open Rear Sight, *Modern*	120.00	160.00
☐ **Model 110-EL**, Various Calibers, Open Rear Sight, Left-Hand, *Modern*	130.00	170.00
☐ **Model 110-M**, Various Calibers, Open Rear Sight, Monte Carlo Stock, Checkered Stock, Magnum Action, *Modern*	145.00	190.00
☐ **Model 110-MC**, Various Calibers, Open Rear Sight, Monte Carlo Stock, Checkered Stock, *Modern*	120.00	160.00
☐ **Model 110-MCL**, Various Calibers, Open Rear Sight, Monte Carlo Stock, Checkered Stock, Left-Hand, *Modern*	125.00	165.00
☐ **Model,110-ML**, Various Calibers, Open Rear Sight, Monte Carlo Stock, Checkered Stock, Magnum Action, Left-Hand, *Modern*	155.00	200.00
☐ **Model 110-P**, Various Calibers, Open Rear Sight, Fancy Wood, Monte Carlo Stock, Fancy Checkering, Sling Swivels, *Modern*	250.00	325.00
☐ **Model 110-PE**, Various Calibers, Engraved, Fancy Checkering, Fancy Wood, Sling Swivels, *Modern*	435.00	550.00
☐ **Model 110-PEL**, Various Calibers, Engraved, Fancy Checkering, Fancy Wood, Sling Swivels, Left-Hand, *Modern*	435.00	550.00
☐ **Model 110-PL**, Various Calibers, Fancy Wood, Monte Carlo Stock, Fancy Checkering, Sling Swivels, Left-Hand, *Modern*	275.00	350.00
☐ **Model 111**, Various Calibers, Clip Fed, Monte Carlo Stock, Checkered Stock, *Modern*	170.00	225.00
☐ **Model 112-V**, Various Calibers, Singleshot, no Sights, *Modern*	160.00	210.00
☐ **Model 1407**, Sights Only, *Add* **$55.00-$80.00**		
☐ **Model 1407 "I.S.U."**, .22 L.R.R.F., Heavy Barrel, no Sights, (Anschutz), *Modern*	320.00	425.00
☐ **Model 1407-L "I.S.U."**, .22 L.R.R.F., Heavy Barrel, no Sights, Left-Hand, (Anschutz), *Modern*	340.00	450.00
☐ **Model 1408**, .22 L.R.R.F., Heavy Barrel, no Sights, (Anschutz), *Modern*	250.00	350.00
☐ **Model 1408-ED**, .22 L.R.R.F., Heavy Barrel, no Sights, (Anschutz), *Modern*	365.00	450.00
☐ **Model 1408-L**, .22 L.R.R.F., Heavy Barrel, no Sights, Left-Hand, (Anschutz), *Modern*	250.00	350.00
☐ **Model 1411**, Sights Only, *Add* **$55.00-$80.00**		
☐ **Model 1411 "Prone"**, .22 L.R.R.F., Heavy Barrel, no Sights, (Anschutz), *Modern*	350.00	475.00

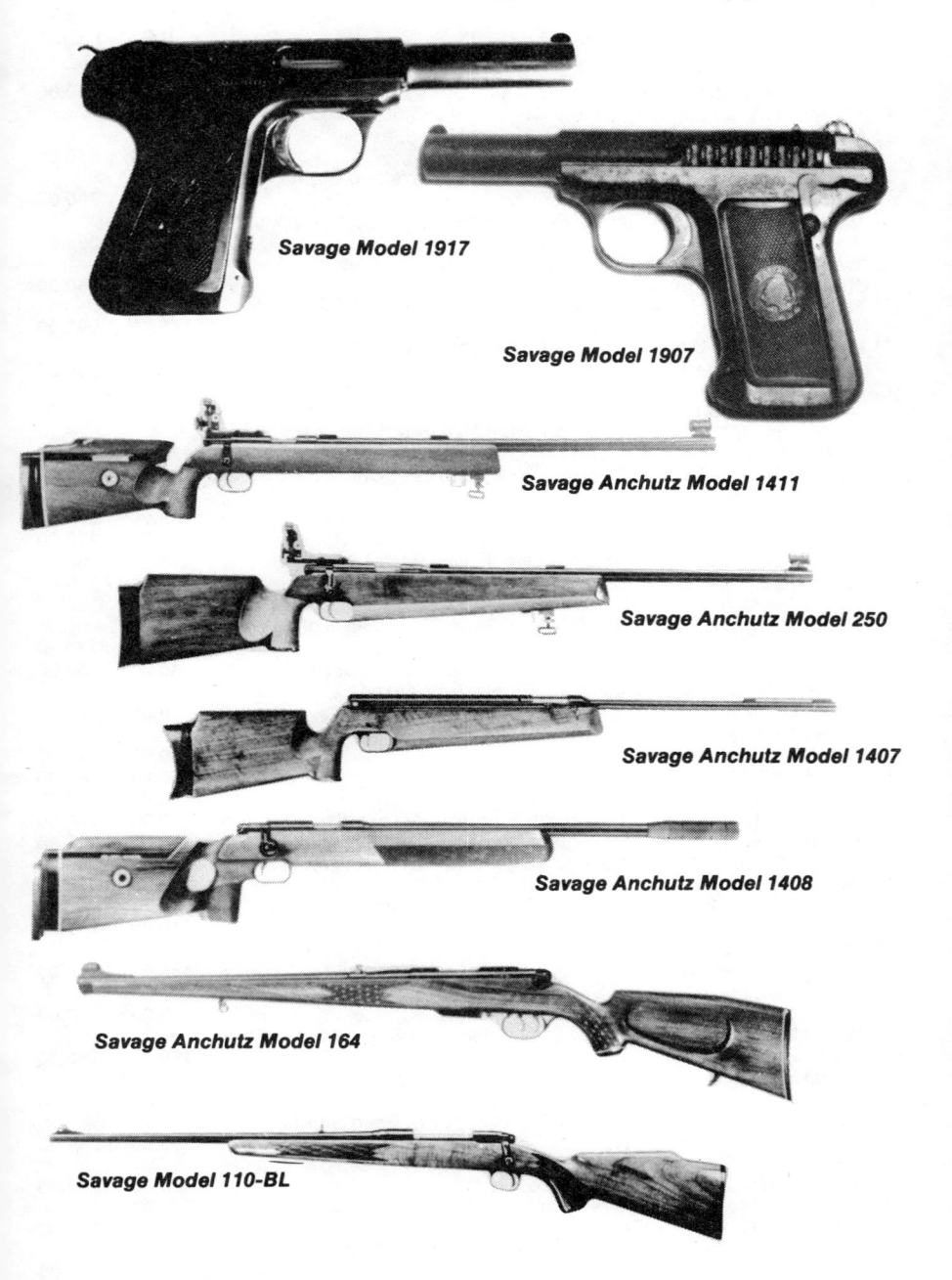

SAVAGE ARMS COMPANY / 387

Savage Model 1917

Savage Model 1907

Savage Anchutz Model 1411

Savage Anchutz Model 250

Savage Anchutz Model 1407

Savage Anchutz Model 1408

Savage Anchutz Model 164

Savage Model 110-BL

388 / SAVAGE ARMS COMPANY

	V.G.	EXC.
☐ **Model 1411-L "Prone"**, .22 L.R.R.F., Heavy Barrel, no Sights, Left-Hand, (Anschutz), *Modern*	375.00	500.00
☐ **Model 1413**, .22 L.R.R.F., Sights Only, *Add* **$55.00-$80.00**		
☐ **Model 1413 "Match"**, .22 L.R.R.F., Heavy Barrel, no Sights, (Anschutz), *Modern*	525.00	650.00
☐ **Model 1413-L "Match"**, .22 L.R.R.F., Heavy Barrel, no Sights, Left-Hand, (Anschutz), *Modern*	575.00	700.00
☐ **Model 1418**, .22 L.R.R.F., Clip Fed, Mannlicher, Fancy Checkering, (Anschutz), *Modern*	240.00	325.00
☐ **Model 1432**, .22 Hornet, Sporting Rifle, Clip Fed, Fancy Checkering, (Anschutz), *Modern*	350.00	450.00
☐ **Model 1433**, .22 Hornet, Mannlicher, Clip Fed, Fancy Checkering, (Anschutz), *Modern*	375.00	525.00
☐ **Model 1518**, .22 WMR, Clip Fed, Mannlicher, Fancy Checkering, (Anschutz), *Modern*	250.00	350.00
☐ **Model 1533**, .222 Rem., Mannlicher, Clip Fed, Fancy Checkering, (Anschutz), *Modern*	375.00	500.00
☐ **Model 164**, .22 L.R.R.F., Sporting Rifle, Clip Fed, Checkered Stock, (Anschutz), *Modern*	175.00	245.00
☐ **Model 164-M**, .22 WMR, Sporting Rifle, Clip Fed, Checkered Stock, (Anschutz), *Modern*	175.00	245.00
☐ **Model 19-H**, .22 Hornet, 5 Shot Clip, Peep Sights, *Modern*	195.00	275.00
☐ **Model 19-L**, .22 L.R.R.F., 5 Shot Clip, Lyman Sights, *Modern*	140.00	185.00
☐ **Model 19-M**, .22 L.R.R.F., 5 Shot Clip, Heavy Barrel, *Modern*	145.00	200.00
☐ **Model 19-N.R.A.**, .22 L.R.R.F., 5 Shot Clip, Full-Stocked, Peep Sights, *Modern*	125.00	160.00
☐ **Model 19-Speed Lock**, .22 L.R.R.F., 5 Shot Clip, Peep Sights, *Modern*	125.00	170.00
☐ **Model 1904**, .22 L.R.R.F., Singleshot, Takedown, *Modern*	40.00	60.00
☐ **Model 1904-Special**, .22 L.R.R.F., Singleshot, Takedown, Fancy Wood, *Modern*	65.00	90.00
☐ **Model 1905**, .22 L.R.R.F., Target, Singleshot, Takedown, Swiss Buttplate, *Modern*	50.00	75.00
☐ **Model 1905-B**, .22 L.R.R.F., *Modern*	40.00	60.00
☐ **Model 1905-Special**, .22 L.R.R.F., Fancy Wood, *Modern*	85.00	130.00
☐ **Model 1911**, .22 Short R.F., Target, Singleshot, Takedown, *Modern*	40.00	60.00
☐ **Model 20**, Various Calibers, Open Rear Sight, *Modern*	165.00	225.00
☐ **Model 20**, Various Calibers, Peep Sights, *Modern*	190.00	250.00
☐ **Model 23A**, .22 L.R.R.F., 5 Shot Clip, Open Rear Sight, *Modern*	110.00	140.00
☐ **Model 23AA**, .22 L.R.R.F., 5 Shot Clip, Open Rear Sight, Monte Carlo Stock, *Modern*	110.00	145.00
☐ **Model 23B**, .25-20 WCF, 5 Shot Clip, Open Rear Sight, Monte Carlo Stock, *Modern*	135.00	170.00
☐ **Model 23C**, .32-20 WCF, 5 Shot Clip, Open Rear Sight, Monte Carlo Stock, *Modern*	135.00	170.00
☐ **Model 23D**, .22 Hornet, 5 Shot Clip, Open Rear Sight, Monte Carlo Stock, *Modern*	190.00	245.00
☐ **Model 3**, .22 L.R.R.F., Singleshot, Takedown, Open Rear Sight, *Modern*	30.00	45.00
☐ **Model 3-S**, .22 L.R.R.F., Singleshot, Takedown, Peep Sights, *Modern*	30.00	45.00
☐ **Model 3-ST**, .22 L.R.R.F., Singleshot, Takedown, Peep Sights, Sling Swivels, *Modern*	35.00	50.00
☐ **Model 340**, Various Calibers, Clip Fed, *Modern*	85.00	130.00
☐ **Model 340-C**, Various Calibers, Clip Fed, Carbine, *Modern*	85.00	130.00
☐ **Model 340-S Deluxe**, Various Calibers, Clip Fed, Peep Sights, *Modern*	95.00	135.00

	V.G.	EXC.
☐ **Model 342**, .22 Hornet, Clip Fed, *Modern*	115.00	150.00
☐ **Model 342-S**, .22 Hornet, Clip Fed, Peep Sights, *Modern*	95.00	145.00
☐ **Model 4**, .22 L.R.R.F., 5 Shot Clip, Takedown, *Modern*	35.00	55.00
☐ **Model 4-M**, .22 WMR, 5 Shot Clip, Takedown, *Modern*	45.00	70.00
☐ **Model 4-S**, .22 L.R.R.F., 5 Shot Clip, Takedown, Peep Sights, *Modern*	45.00	60.00
☐ **Model 40**, Various Calibers, Open Rear Sight, *Modern*	160.00	220.00
☐ **Model 45 Super**, Various Calibers, Peep Sights, Checkered Stock, *Modern*	180.00	245.00
☐ **Model 5**, .22 L.R.R.F., Tube Feed, Takedown, Open Rear Sight, *Modern*	45.00	65.00
☐ **Model 5-S**, .22 L.R.R.F., Tube Feed, Takedown, Peep Sights, *Modern*	45.00	65.00
☐ **Model 54**, .22 L.R.R.F., Sporting Rifle, Clip Fed, Fancy Checkering, (Anschutz), *Modern*	275.00	370.00
☐ **Model 54-M**, .22 WMR, Sporting Rifle, Clip Fed, Fancy Checkering, (Anschutz), *Modern*	295.00	385.00
☐ **Model 63**, .22 L.R.R.F., Singleshot, Open Rear Sight, *Modern*	30.00	45.00
☐ **Model 63-K**, .22 L.R.R.F., Singleshot, Open Rear Sight, *Modern*	30.00	45.00
☐ **Model 63-M**, .22 WMR, Singleshot, Open Rear Sight, *Modern*	35.00	55.00
☐ **Model 64**, .22 L.R.R.F., Sights Only, *Add* **$30.00-$55.00**		
☐ **Model 64**, .22 L.R.R.F., Heavy Barrel, no Sights, (Anschutz), *Modern*	155.00	215.00
☐ **Model 64-CS**, .22 L.R.R.F., Heavy Barrel, no Sights, Lightweight, (Anschutz), *Modern*	175.00	250.00
☐ **Model 64-CSL**, .22 L.R.R.F., Heavy Barrel, no Sights, Left-Hand, Lightweight, (Anschutz), *Modern*	185.00	260.00
☐ **Model 64-L**, .22 L.R.R.F., Heavy Barrel, no Sights, Left-Hand, (Anschutz), *Modern*	165.00	220.00
☐ **Model 64-S**, .22 L.R.R.F., Heavy Barrel, no Sights, (Anschutz), *Modern*	190.00	260.00
☐ **Model 64-SL**, .22 L.R.R.F., Heavy Barrel, no Sights, Left-Hand, (Anschutz), *Modern*	215.00	270.00
☐ **Model 65-M**, .22 WMR, Clip Fed, Open Rear Sight, *Modern*	50.00	75.00
☐ **Model 73**, .22 L.R.R.F., Singleshot, *Modern*	25.00	40.00
☐ **Model 73-Y Boys**, .22 L.R.R.F., Singleshot, *Modern*	25.00	40.00

RIFLE, LEVER ACTION

	V.G.	EXC.
☐ **Model 1892**, .30-40 Krag, Hammerless, Rotary Magazine, Military, *Antique*	875.00	1,400.00
☐ **Model 1895**, .303 Savage, Hammerless, Rotary Magazine, Open Rear Sight, *Antique*	475.00	700.00
☐ **Model 1899**, .30-30 Win., Hammerless, Rotary Magazine, Full-Stocked, Military, *Modern*	700.00	1,250.00
☐ **Model 1899**, Various Calibers, Hammerless, Rotary Magazine, Open Rear Sight, *Modern*	175.00	250.00
☐ **Model 1899 A2**, Various Calibers, Hammerless, Rotary Magazine, Checkered Stock, *Modern*	175.00	265.00
☐ **Model 1899 AB**, Various Calibers, Light Engraving, Checkered Stock, Hammerless, Rotary Magazine, *Modern*	335.00	425.00
☐ **Model 1899 BC**, Various Calibers, Light Engraving, Checkered Stock, Hammerless, Rotary Magazine, *Modern*	300.00	385.00
☐ **Model 1899 Excelsior**, Various Calibers, Light Engraving, Checkered Stock, Featherweight, Hammerless, Rotary Magazine, *Modern*	475.00	675.00
☐ **Model 1899 Leader**, Various Calibers, Engraved, Checkered Stock, Hammerless, Rotary Magazine, *Modern*	450.00	650.00

390 / SAVAGE ARMS COMPANY

	V.G.	EXC.
☐ **Model 1899 Monarch**, Various Calibers, Fancy Engraving, Fancy Checkering, Ornate, Hammerless, Rotary Magazine, *Modern*	1,950.00	2,750.00
☐ **Model 1899 Premier**, Various Calibers, Fancy Engraving, Fancy Checkering, Takedown, Hammerless, Rotary Magazine, *Modern*	1,250.00	1,650.00
☐ **Model 1899 Rival**, Various Calibers, Fancy Engraving, Fancy Checkering, Hammerless, Rotary Magazine, *Modern*	975.00	1,500.00
☐ **Model 1899 Victor**, Various Calibers, Engraved, Fancy Checkering, Hammerless, Rotary Magazine, *Modern*	650.00	925.00
☐ **Model 89**, .22 L.R.R.F., Singleshot, Open Rear Sight, *Modern*	35.00	50.00
☐ **Model 99**, for Extra Barrel, Add **$75.00-$110.00**		
☐ **Model 99 E**, Various Calibers, Solid Frame, Carbine, Hammerless, Rotary Magazine, *Modern*	150.00	210.00
☐ **Model 99-1895 Anniversary**, .308 Win., Octagon Barrel, Hammerless, Rotary Magazine, *Modern*	200.00	265.00
☐ **Model 99-358**, .358 Win., Solid Frame, Hammerless, Rotary Magazine, *Modern*	160.00	230.00
☐ **Model 99-A**, Various Calibers, Solid Frame, Hammerless, Rotary Magazine, *Modern*	165.00	225.00
☐ **Model 99-B**, Various Calibers, Takedown, Hammerless, Rotary Magazine, *Modern*	185.00	275.00
☐ **Model 99-C**, Various Calibers, Clip Fed, Solid Frame, Featherweight, Hammerless, *Modern*	165.00	235.00
☐ **Model 99-CD**, Various Calibers, Hammerless, Clip Fed, Solid Frame, Monte Carlo Stock, *Modern*	190.00	250.00
☐ **Model 99-DE**, Various Calibers, Solid Frame, Monte Carlo Stock, Light Engraving, Hammerless, Rotary Magazine, *Modern*	250.00	325.00
☐ **Model 99-DL**, Various Calibers, Solid Frame, Monte Carlo Stock, Hammerless, Rotary Magazine, *Modern*	175.00	230.00
☐ **Model 99-E**, Various Calibers, Solid Frame, Hammerless, Rotary Magazine, *Modern*	165.00	210.00
☐ **Model 99-EG**, Various Calibers, Takedown, Checkered Stock, Hammerless, Rotary Magazine, *Modern*	170.00	225.00
☐ **Model 99-F**, Various Calibers, Featherweight, Takedown, Hammerless, Rotary Magazine, *Modern*	210.00	275.00
☐ **Model 99-F**, Various Calibers, Solid Frame, Featherweight, Hammerless, Rotary Magazine, *Modern*	165.00	225.00
☐ **Model 99-G**, Various Calibers, Takedown, Checkered Stock, Hammerless, Rotary Magazine, *Modern*	180.00	240.00
☐ **Model 99-H**, Various Calibers, Carbine, Solid Frame, Hammerless, Rotary Magazine, *Modern*	165.00	225.00
☐ **Model 99-K**, Various Calibers, Takedown, Light Engraving, Checkered Stock, Hammerless, Rotary Magazine, *Modern*	550.00	800.00
☐ **Model 99-PE**, Various Calibers, Solid Frame, Monte Carlo Stock, Engraved, Hammerless, Rotary Magazine, *Modern*	475.00	700.00
☐ **Model 99-R**, Various Calibers, Solid Frame, Checkered Stock, Pre-War, Hammerless, Rotary Magazine, *Modern*	300.00	425.00
☐ **Model 99-R**, Various Calibers, Solid Frame, Checkered Stock, Hammerless, Rotary Magazine, *Modern*	175.00	225.00
☐ **Model 99-RS**, Various Calibers, Solid Frame, Peep Sights, Pre-War, Hammerless, Rotary Magazine, *Modern*	245.00	350.00
☐ **Model 99-RS**, Various Calibers, Solid Frame, Peep Sights, Hammerless, Rotary Magazine, *Modern*	185.00	240.00
☐ **Model 99-T**, Various Calibers, Solid Frame, Featherweight, Hammerless, Rotary Magazine, *Modern*	220.00	300.00

RIFLE, SEMI-AUTOMATIC

☐ **Model 1912**, .22 L.R.R.F., Half-Octagon Barrel, Takedown, Clip Fed, *Curio*	125.00	195.00

	V.G.	EXC.
☐ **Model 6**, .22 L.R.R.F., Takedown, Tube Feed, Open Rear Sight, *Modern*	50.00	70.00
☐ **Model 6-S**, .22 L.R.R.F., Takedown, Tube Feed, Peep Sights, *Modern*	55.00	75.00
☐ **Model 60**, .22 L.R.R.F., Monte Carlo Stock, Checkered Stock, Tube Feed, *Modern*	55.00	80.00
☐ **Model 7**, .22 L.R.R.F., 5 Shot Clip, Takedown, Open Rear Sight, *Modern*	45.00	60.00
☐ **Model 7-S**, .22 L.R.R.F., 5 Shot Clip, Takedown, Open Rear Sight, *Modern*	50.00	70.00
☐ **Model 80**, .22 L.R.R.F., Tube Feed, *Modern*	40.00	55.00
☐ **Model 88**, .22 L.R.R.F., Tube Feed, *Modern*	45.00	65.00
☐ **Model 90**, .22 L.R.R.F., Carbine, Tube Feed, *Modern*	45.00	70.00

RIFLE, SINGLESHOT

	V.G.	EXC.
☐ **Model 219**, Various Calibers, Hammerless, Top Break, Open Rear Sight, *Modern*	50.00	70.00
☐ **Model 219L**, Various Calibers, Hammerless, Top Break, Open Rear Sight, Side Lever, *Modern*	50.00	70.00
☐ **Model 221**, .30-30 Win., Hammerless, Top Break, Extra Shotgun Barrel, *Modern*	55.00	85.00
☐ **Model 222**, .30-30 Win., Hammerless, Top Break, Extra Shotgun Barrel, *Modern*	60.00	90.00
☐ **Model 223**, .30-30 Win., Hammerless, Top Break, Extra Shotgun Barrel, *Modern*	60.00	90.00
☐ **Model 227**, .30-30 Win., Hammerless, Top Break, Extra Shotgun Barrel, *Modern*	60.00	90.00
☐ **Model 228**, .30-30 Win., Hammerless, Top Break, Extra Shotgun Barrel, *Modern*	60.00	90.00
☐ **Model 229**, .30-30 Win., Hammerless, Top Break, Extra Shotgun Barrel, *Modern*	60.00	90.00
☐ **Model 71 Stevens Favorite**, .22 L.R.R.F., Lever Action, Falling Block, Favorite, *Modern*	85.00	140.00
☐ **Model 72**, .22 L.R.R.F., Lever Action, Falling Block, *Modern*	55.00	80.00

RIFLE, SLIDE ACTION

	V.G.	EXC.
☐ **Model 170**, Various Calibers, Open Rear Sight, *Modern*	110.00	145.00
☐ **Model 170-C**, .30-30 Win., Carbine, Open Rear Sight, *Modern*	95.00	135.00
☐ **Model 1903**, .22 L.R.R.F., Hammerless, Clip Fed, Octagon Barrel, *Modern*	70.00	120.00
☐ **Model 1903-EF**, .22 L.R.R.F., Hammerless, Clip Fed, Octagon Barrel, Fancy Wood, Engraved, *Modern*	375.00	500.00
☐ **Model 1903-Expert**, .22 L.R.R.F., Hammerless, Clip Fed, Octagon Barrel, Checkered Stock, Light Engraving, *Modern*	175.00	250.00
☐ **Model 1909**, .22 L.R.R.F., Half-Octagon Barrel, Takedown, Clip Fed, *Modern*	75.00	125.00
☐ **Model 1914**, .22 L.R.R.F., Half-Octagon Barrel, Takedown, Tube Feed, *Modern*	115.00	150.00
☐ **Model 1914-E.F.**, .22 L.R.R.F., Half-Octagon Barrel, Takedown, Tube Feed, Fancy Engraving, *Modern*	475.00	600.00
☐ **Model 1914-Expert**, .22 L.R.R.F., Half-Octagon Barrel, Takedown, Tube Feed, Light Engraving, *Modern*	325.00	425.00
☐ **Model 1914-Gold Medal**, .22 L.R.R.F., Half-Octagon Barrel, Takedown, Tube Feed, Checkered Stock, Light Engraving, *Modern*	210.00	275.00
☐ **Model 25**, .22 L.R.R.F., Tube Feed, Octagon Barrel, Open Rear Sight, Monte Carlo Stock, *Modern*	85.00	125.00
☐ **Model 29**, .22 L.R.R.F., Tube Feed, Octagon Barrel, Open Rear Sight, Monte Carlo Stock, *Modern*	120.00	175.00

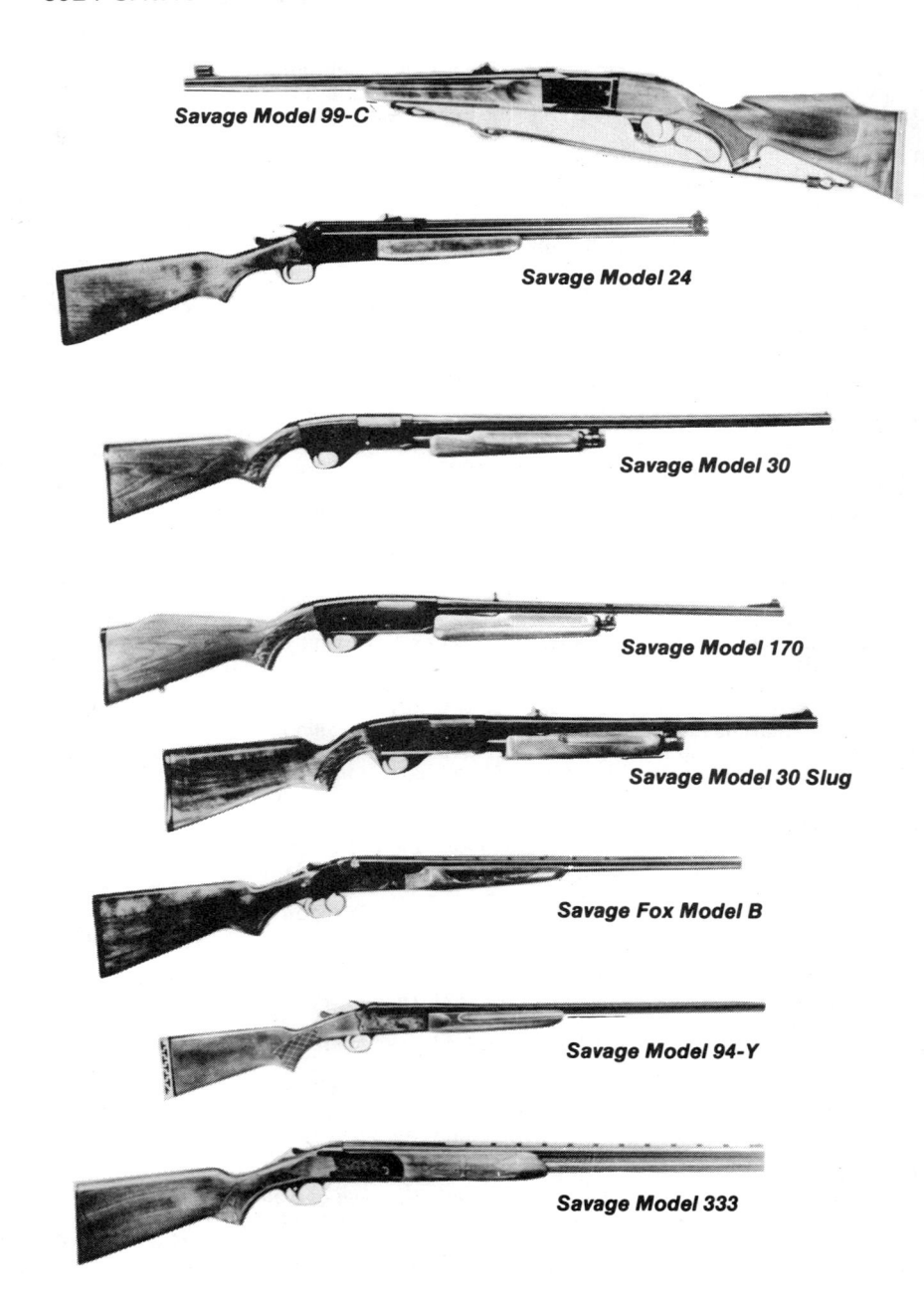

392 / SAVAGE ARMS COMPANY

Savage Model 99-C

Savage Model 24

Savage Model 30

Savage Model 170

Savage Model 30 Slug

Savage Fox Model B

Savage Model 94-Y

Savage Model 333

SAVAGE ARMS COMPANY / 393

	V.G.	EXC.
☐ **Model 29**, .22 L.R.R.F., Tube Feed, Round Barrel, Open Rear Sight, *Modern*	110.00	140.00
☐ **Model 29-G**, .22 Short R.F., Tube Feed, *Modern*	115.00	150.00

SHOTGUN, BOLT ACTION

	V.G.	EXC.
☐ **Model 58**, .410 Ga., Singleshot, *Modern*	40.00	60.00

SHOTGUN, DOUBLE BARREL, OVER-UNDER

	V.G.	EXC.
☐ **Model 242**, .410 Ga., Hammer, Single Trigger, *Modern*	85.00	125.00
☐ **Model 330**, 12 and 20 Gauges, Hammerless, Single Selective Trigger, *Modern*	275.00	360.00
☐ **Model 330**, 12 and 20 Gauges, Hammerless, Extra Shotgun Barrel, Cased, *Modern*	350.00	450.00
☐ **Model 333**, 12 and 20 Gauges, Hammerless, Vent Rib, Single Selective Trigger, *Modern*	350.00	450.00
☐ **Model 333-T**, 12 Ga., Hammerless, Vent Rib, Trap Grade, Single Selective Trigger, *Modern*	325.00	425.00
☐ **Model 420**, Various Gauges, Hammerless, Takedown, Double Trigger, *Modern*	190.00	250.00
☐ **Model 420**, Various Gauges, Hammerless, Takedown, Single Trigger, *Modern*	235.00	300.00
☐ **Model 430**, Various Gauges, Hammerless, Takedown, Checkered Stock, Recoil Pad, Double Trigger, *Modern*	220.00	280.00
☐ **Model 430**, Various Gauges, Hammerless, Takedown, Checkered Stock, Recoil Pad, Single Trigger, *Modern*	260.00	350.00
☐ **Model 440**, 12 Ga., Hammerless, Vent Rib, Single Selective Trigger, Checkered Stock, *Modern*	175.00	250.00
☐ **Model 440-B**, 20 Ga., Hammerless, Vent Rib, Checkered Stock, *Modern*	200.00	280.00
☐ **Model 444**, 12 Ga., Hammerless, Vent Rib, Single Selective Trigger, Checkered Stock, Selective Ejector, *Modern*	225.00	290.00
☐ **Model 444-T**, 12 Ga., Hammerless, Trap Grade, *Modern*	225.00	290.00

SHOTGUN, DOUBLE BARREL, SIDE-BY-SIDE

	V.G.	EXC.
☐ **Model B Fox**, Various Gauges, Hammerless, Vent Rib, Double Trigger, *Modern*	165.00	220.00
☐ **Model B-SE Fox**, Various Gauges, Hammerless, Vent Rib, Selective Ejector, Single Trigger, *Modern*	180.00	250.00

SHOTGUN, SEMI-AUTOMATIC

	V.G.	EXC.
☐ **Model 720**, 12 Ga., Tube Feed, Checkered Stock, Plain Barrel, *Modern*	110.00	145.00
☐ **Model 720-P**, 12 Ga., Checkered Stock, Adjustable Choke, *Modern*	120.00	155.00
☐ **Model 720-R**, 12 Ga., Riot Gun, *Modern*	100.00	145.00
☐ **Model 721**, 12 Ga., Tube Feed, Checkered Stock, Raised Matted Rib, *Modern*	140.00	175.00
☐ **Model 722**, 12 Ga., Tube Feed, Checkered Stock, Vent Rib, *Modern*	155.00	195.00
☐ **Model 723**, 16 Ga., Tube Feed, Checkered Stock, Plain Barrel, *Modern*	100.00	140.00
☐ **Model 724**, 16 Ga., Tube Feed, Checkered Stock, Raised Matted Rib, *Modern*	110.00	150.00
☐ **Model 725**, 16 Ga., Tube Feed, Checkered Stock, Vent Rib, *Modern*	110.00	150.00
☐ **Model 726**, 12 and 16 Gauges, 3 Shot, Checkered Stock, Plain Barrel, *Modern*	110.00	145.00
☐ **Model 727**, 12 and 16 Gauges, 3 Shot, Checkered Stock, Raised Matted Rib, *Modern*	120.00	155.00
☐ **Model 728**, 12 and 16 Gauges, 3 Shot, Checkered Stock, Vent Rib, *Modern*	125.00	165.00
☐ **Model 740-C**, 12 and 16 Gauges, Skeet Grade, *Modern*	155.00	195.00
☐ **Model 745**, 12 Ga., Lightweight, *Modern*	135.00	175.00

394 / SANTA BARBARA

	V.G.	EXC.
☐ **Model 750**, 12 Ga., *Modern*	155.00	195.00
☐ **Model 750-AC**, 12 Ga., Adjustable Choke, *Modern*	155.00	195.00
☐ **Model 750-SC**, 12 Ga., Adjustable Choke, *Modern*	160.00	200.00
☐ **Model 755**, 12 and 16 Gauges, *Modern*	130.00	160.00
☐ **Model 755-SC**, 12 and 16 Gauges, Adjustable Choke, *Modern*	135.00	175.00
☐ **Model 775**, 12 and 16 Gauges, Lightweight, *Modern*	140.00	185.00
☐ **Model 775-SC**, 12 and 16 Gauges, Adjustable Choke, Lightweight, *Modern*	145.00	185.00

SHOTGUN, SINGLESHOT
☐ **Model 220**, Various Gauges, Hammerless, Takedown, *Modern*	33.00	50.00
☐ **Model 220-AC**, Various Gauges, Hammerless, Takedown, Adjustable Choke, *Modern*	40.00	55.00
☐ **Model 220-P**, Various Gauges, Hammerless, Takedown, Adjustable Choke, *Modern*	45.00	65.00
☐ **Model 94-C**, Various Gauges, Hammer, Takedown, *Modern*	40.00	60.00
☐ **Model 94-Y Youth**, Various Gauges, Hammer, Takedown, *Modern*	40.00	55.00

SHOTGUN, SLIDE ACTION
☐ **Model 21-A**, 12 Ga., Hammerless, Takedown, *Modern*	110.00	140.00
☐ **Model 21-B**, 12 Ga., Hammerless, Takedown, Raised Matted Rib, *Modern*	120.00	150.00
☐ **Model 21-C**, 12 Ga., Hammerless, Takedown, Riot Gun, *Modern*	95.00	130.00
☐ **Model 21-D**, 12 Ga., Hammerless, Takedown, Trap Grade, *Modern*	165.00	225.00
☐ **Model 21-E**, 12 Ga., Hammerless, Takedown, Fancy Wood, Fancy Checkering, Vent Rib, *Modern*	200.00	275.00
☐ **Model 28-A**, 12 Ga., Hammerless, Takedown, *Modern*	115.00	145.00
☐ **Model 28-B**, 12 Ga., Hammerless, Takedown, Raised Matted Rib, *Modern*	120.00	150.00
☐ **Model 28-C**, 12 Ga., Hammerless, Takedown, Riot Gun, *Modern*	95.00	135.00
☐ **Model 28-D**, 12 Ga., Hammerless, Takedown, Trap Grade, *Modern*	165.00	225.00
☐ **Model 28-S**, 12 Ga., Hammerless, Takedown, Fancy Checkering, *Modern*	150.00	195.00
☐ **Model 30**, For Vent Rib, Add **$15.00-$20.00**		
☐ **Model 30**, Various Gauges, Hammerless, Solid Frame, *Modern*	85.00	120.00
☐ **Model 30-AC**, Various Gauges, Hammerless, Solid Frame, Adjustable Choke, *Modern*	85.00	120.00
☐ **Model 30-ACL**, Various Gauges, Hammerless, Solid Frame, Left-Hand, Adjustable Choke, *Modern*	95.00	130.00
☐ **Model 30-D**, Various Gauges, Hammerless, Solid Frame, Light Engraving, Recoil Pad, *Modern*	115.00	150.00
☐ **Model 30-L**, Various Gauges, Hammerless, Solid Frame, Left-Hand, *Modern*	95.00	125.00
☐ **Model 30-Slug**, 12 Ga., Hammerless, Solid Frame, *Modern*	95.00	135.00
☐ **Model 30-T**, 12 Ga., Hammerless, Solid Frame, Monte Carlo Stock, Recoil Pad, Vent Rib, *Modern*	115.00	155.00

SANTA BARBARA
Santa Barbara of America, Inc. of Irving, Tx. on Mauser actions made in La Caruna, Spain.

RIFLE, BOLT ACTION
☐ **Sporter**, Various Calibers, Custom Made, Medium Quality, *Modern*	90.00	130.00
☐ **Sporter**, Various Calibers, Custom Made, High Quality, *Modern*	130.00	180.00

SCHALL & NC
Hartford, Conn.

HANDGUN, MANUAL REPEATER
☐ **.22 L.R.R.F.**, Target Pistol, Clip Fed, *Curio*	275.00	365.00

Schall .22

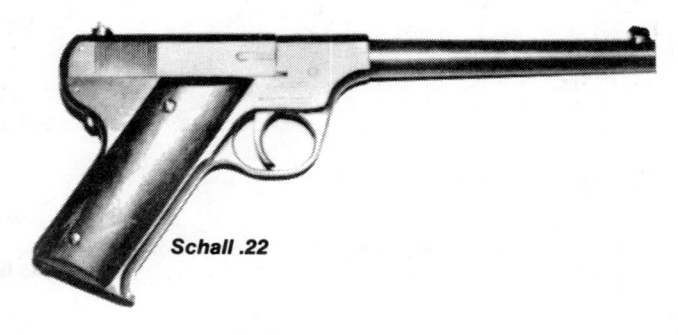

SCHUTZEN RIFLES, UNKNOWN MAKER

	V.G.	EXC.

RIFLE, SINGLESHOT
- **Aydt System**, Various Calibers, Dropping Block, Plain Tyrol Stock, Light Engraving, Target Sights, *Modern* 350.00 600.00
- **Aydt System**, Various Calibers, Dropping Block, Fancy Tyrol Stock, Fancy Engraving, Target Sights, *Modern* 575.00 900.00
- **Martini System**, Various Calibers, Dropping Block, Fancy Tyrol Stock, Fancy Engraving, Target Sights, *Modern* 525.00 825.00

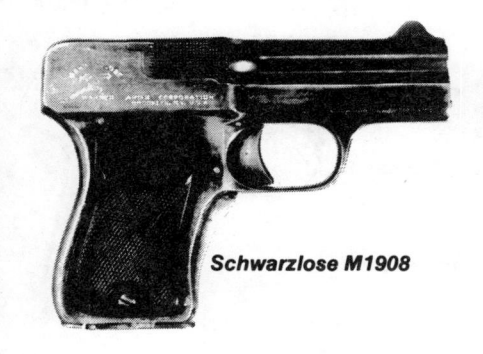

Schwarzlose M1908

Schwarzlose M1908 WAC

SCHWARZLOSE
Andreas W. Schwarzlose, Berlin, Germany 1911-1927.

HANDGUN, SEMI-AUTOMATIC
- **Standardt**, 7.63mm Mauser, Clip Fed, Blue, *Curio* 2,000.00 2,850.00
- **M 1908 Pocket**, .32 ACP, Blow-Forward, Clip Fed, Grip Safety, *Curio* 325.00 475.00
- **M 1908 W.A.C. Pocket**, .32 ACP, Blow-Forward, Clip Fed, Grip Safety, *Curio* 300.00 450.00

SCOTT ARMS CO.
Probably Norwich Fall Pistol Co., c. 1880.

HANDGUN, REVOLVER
- **.32 Short R.F.**, 5 Shot, Spur Trigger, Solid Frame, Single Action, *Antique* 90.00 160.00

SCOTT, D.
Edinburgh, Scotland 1727-1745.

	V.G.	EXC.

HANDGUN, FLINTLOCK
☐ **Queen Anne Type**, .59, Screw Barrel, Holster Pistol, Marked
"Edinboro," *Antique* **950.00 1,500.00**

SCOTT REVOLVER-RIFLE
Hopkins & Allen, c. 1880.

HANDGUN, REVOLVER
☐ **24½" Brass Barrel**, .38 Short R.F., 5 Shot, Spur Trigger, Solid
Frame, Single Action, *Antique* **145.00 250.00**

SCOUT
Made by Stevens.

SHOTGUN, DOUBLE BARREL, SIDE-BY-SIDE
☐ **Model 311**, Various Gauges, Hammerless, Steel Barrel, *Modern*.... **95.00 165.00**

SCOUT
Made by Hood Firearms for Frankfurt Hardware of Milwaukee, Wisc., c. 1870.

HANDGUN, REVOLVER
☐ **.32 Short R.F.**, 5 Shot, Spur Trigger, Solid Frame, Single Action,
Antique **90.00 160.00**

S.E.A.M. Eibar-13

Sears Youth

Sears 12 Ga. Bolt Action

S.E.A.M.
Fab. d'Armes de Soc. Espanola de Armas y Municiones, Eibar, Spain.

HANDGUN, SEMI-AUTOMATIC
☐ **Eibar Type**, .25 ACP, 13 Slide Grooves, Fair Quality, Clip Fed,
Blue, *Modern* **85.00 120.00**
☐ **Eibar Type**, .25 ACP, 11 Slide Grooves, Good Quality, Clip Fed,
Blue, *Modern* **100.00 145.00**
☐ **Walther Type**, .25 ACP, Clip Fed, Blue, *Modern* **140.00 195.00**

SEARS
Sears, Roebuck & Co., Chicago, Ill. Also see Ted Williams.

	V.G.	EXC.
RIFLE, BOLT ACTION		
☐ **Semi-Sporterized Mauser**, 8mm Mauser, Converted Military, *Modern*	75.00	115.00
☐ **Sporterized Mauser**, 8mm Mauser, Converted Military, Recoil Pad, *Modern*	85.00	125.00
SHOTGUN, BOLT ACTION		
☐ **.410 Gauge**, Singleshot, Plain, *Modern*	20.00	35.00
☐ **.410 Gauge**, Clip Fed, Blue, Plain, *Modern*	30.00	45.00
☐ **12 or 20 Gauges**, Clip Fed, Blue, Plain, *Modern*	35.00	50.00
☐ **12 or 20 Gauges**, Clip Fed, Adjustable Choke, Blue, Plain, *Modern*	35.00	55.00
SHOTGUN, SINGLESHOT		
☐ **Various Gauges**, Top Break, Plain, *Modern*	30.00	40.00
☐ **Youth**, 20 or .410 Gauges, Plain, *Modern*	30.00	40.00

SECRET SERVICE SPECIAL
Made for Fred Biffar, Chicago by Iver-Johnson and Meriden.

	V.G.	EXC.
HANDGUN, REVOLVER		
☐ **.32 S & W**, 5 Shot, Top Break, Hammerless, Double Action, *Modern*	80.00	125.00
☐ **.38 S & W**, 5 Shot, Top Break, Hammerless, Double Action, *Modern*	80.00	125.00

SECURITY INDUSTRIES OF AMERICA
Little Ferry, N.J.

	V.G.	EXC.
HANDGUN, REVOLVER		
☐ **Police Pocket**, .357 Magnum, Stainless Steel, 2" Barrel, Swing-Out Cylinder, Double Action, Spurless Hammer, *Modern*	120.00	165.00
☐ **Police Security Spec**, .38 Special, Stainless Steel, 2" Barrel, Swing-Out Cylinder, Double Action, *Modern*	95.00	135.00
☐ **Security Undercover**, .357 Magnum, Stainless Steel, 2½" Barrel, Swing-Out Cylinder, Double Action, *Modern*	115.00	160.00

SEDGLEY, R.F., INC.
Philadelphia, Pa. 1911-1938. Successor to Henry Kolb.

	V.G.	EXC.
HANDGUN, REVOLVER		
☐ **Baby Hammerless**, .22 L.R.R.F., Double Action, Folding Trigger, *Modern*	85.00	145.00
RIFLE, BOLT ACTION		
☐ **Springfield**, Various Calibers, Sporting Rifle, Lyman Sights, Checkered Stock, *Modern*	300.00	375.00
☐ **Springfield**, Various Calibers, Sporting Rifle, Lyman Sights, Checkered Stock, Left-Hand, *Modern*	340.00	425.00
☐ **Springfield**, Various Calibers, Sporting Rifle, Lyman Sights, Checkered Stock, Full-Stocked, *Modern*	375.00	500.00
☐ **Springfield**, Various Calibers, Sporting Rifle, Lyman Sights, Checkered Stock, Full-Stocked, Left-Hand, *Modern*	375.00	500.00

SELECTA
Echave y Arizmendi, Eibar, Spain.

	V.G.	EXC.
HANDGUN, SEMI-AUTOMATIC		
☐ **Model 1918**, .25 ACP, Double Safety, Clip Fed, *Modern*	110.00	150.00
☐ **Model 1918**, .25 ACP, Triple Safety, Clip Fed, *Modern*	130.00	170.00
☐ **Model 1919**, .32 ACP, Double Safety, Clip Fed, *Modern*	120.00	165.00
☐ **Model 1919**, .32 ACP, Triple Safety, Clip Fed, *Modern*	140.00	180.00

Sedgeley Baby Hammerless

Selecta Model 1919

SEMMERLING
Semmerling Corp., Newton, Mass.

	V.G.	EXC.

HANDGUN, MANUAL REPEATER
☐ **LM-4**, .45 ACP, Double Action, Clip Fed, *Modern* 400.00 565.00

SHAKANOOSA ARMS MFG. CO.
1862-1864. See Confederate Military

RIFLE, PERCUSSION
☐ **.58**, Military, Carbine, (C S A), *Antique* 1,250.00 1,750.00
☐ **.58**, Military, (C S A), *Antique* 950.00 1,300.00

SHARPE
English, 1670-1680.

HANDGUN, FLINTLOCK
☐ **Pair**, Pocket Pistol, Screw Barrel, Octagon, High Quality, *Antique* 1,850.00 3,200.00

SHARPS
Made by Shiloh Products, Farmingdale, N.Y.

RIFLE, PERCUSSION
☐ **Model 1859 New Model Cavalry Carbine**, .54, Reproduction, *Antique* 250.00 350.00
☐ **Model 1863 Cavalry Carbine**, .54, Reproduction, *Antique* 200.00 300.00
☐ **Model 1863 Sporting Rifle #3**, .54, Reproduction, *Antique* 235.00 350.00
☐ **Model 1863 Sporting Rifle #2**, .54, Reproduction, *Antique* 275.00 370.00
☐ **Model 1862 Robinson Confederate Cavalry Carbine**, .54, Reproduction, *Antique* 225.00 325.00
☐ **Model 1863 New Model Military Rifle**, .54, Reproduction, *Antique* 240.00 350.00

RIFLE, SINGLESHOT
☐ **Model 1874 Military Rifle**, Various Calibers, Reproduction, *Modern* 250.00 380.00
☐ **Model 1874 Military Carbine**, Various Calibers, Reproduction, *Modern* 225.00 325.00
☐ **Model 1874 Hunter's Rifle**, Various Calibers, Reproduction, *Modern* 245.00 350.00
☐ **Model 1874 Business Rifle**, Various Calibers, Reproduction, *Modern* 250.00 350.00
☐ **Model 1874 Sporting Rifle #2**, Various Calibers, Reproduction, *Modern* 325.00 450.00
☐ **Model 1874 Sporting Rifle #3**, Various Calibers, Reproduction, *Modern* 250.00 375.00

Sharps .30 R.F.

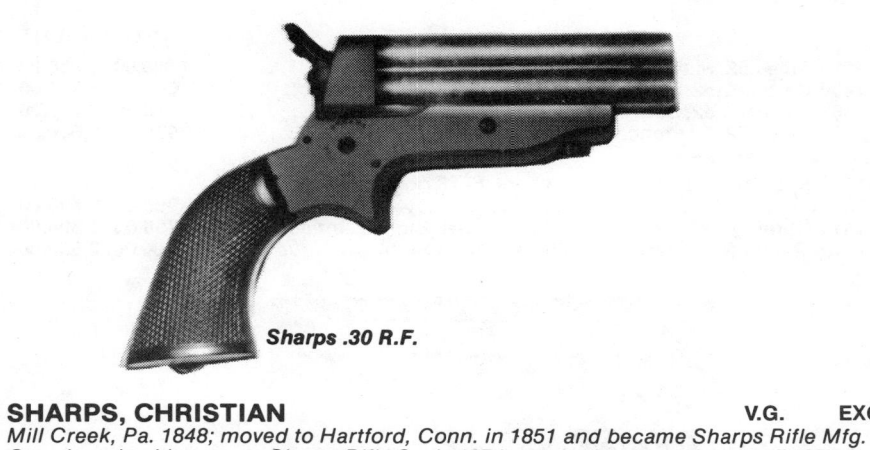

SHARPS, CHRISTIAN
V.G.   EXC.

Mill Creek, Pa. 1848; moved to Hartford, Conn. in 1851 and became Sharps Rifle Mfg. Co., changing it's name to Sharps Rifle Co. in 1874, continuing operations until 1881. In 1854 formed C. Sharps & Co. in Philadelphia, Pa., became Sharps & Hankins in 1862, C. Sharps & Co. again in 1866, and continued until 1874.

HANDGUN, MULTI-BARREL
- ☐ **.22 R.F.**, Model 1, 4 Barreled Pistol, Frame to Muzzle Distance ⅛", *Antique* 265.00   375.00
- ☐ **.22 R.F.**, Model 1, 4 Barreled Pistol, Frame to Muzzle Distance ½", *Antique* 195.00   275.00
- ☐ **.22 R.F.**, Model 1, 4 Barreled Pistol, Frame to Muzzle Distance ¼", *Antique* 235.00   345.00
- ☐ **.22 R.F.**, Model 1, 4 Barreled Pistol, Frame to Muzzle Distance ¼", Iron Frame, *Antique* 340.00   465.00
- ☐ **.30 R.F.**, Model 2, 4 Barreled Pistol, Frame to Muzzle Distance ⅝", *Antique* 220.00   325.00
- ☐ **.30 R.F.**, Model 2, 4 Barreled Pistol, Frame to Muzzle Distance ¾", *Antique* 290.00   430.00
- ☐ **.32 R.F.**, Model 3, 4 Barreled Pistol, Mechanism in Frame, *Antique*   290.00   450.00
- ☐ **.32 R.F.**, Model 3, 4 Barreled Pistol, Mechanism on Hammer, *Antique* 260.00   365.00
- ☐ **.32 R.F. Bulldog**, Model 4, 4 Barreled Pistol, Screw Under Frame, *Antique* 260.00   365.00
- ☐ **.32 R.F. Bulldog**, Model 4, 4 Barreled Pistol, Pin on Side of Frame, *Antique* 290.00   425.00

HANDGUN, PERCUSSION
- ☐ **Revolver**, .25, Tip-Up, 6 Shot, Blue, Spur Trigger, Single Action, *Antique* 525.00   875.00
- ☐ **Bryce Revolver**, .25, Tip-Up, 6 Shot, Blue, Spur Trigger, Single Action, *Antique* 575.00   950.00

HANDGUN, SINGLESHOT
- ☐ **Small Frame**, Various Calibers, Single Action, Dropping Block, Hammer, *Antique* 975.00 1,800.00
- ☐ **Medium Frame**, Various Calibers, Single Action, Dropping Block, Hammer, *Antique* 995.00 1,950.00

RIFLE, PERCUSSION
- ☐ **1851 Carbine**, .52, Maynard Primer, *Antique* 1,350.00 2,500.00
- ☐ **1852 Carbine**, .52, Pellet Primer, *Antique* 625.00   875.00
- ☐ **1853 Carbine**, .52, Pellet Primer, *Antique* 645.00   950.00
- ☐ **1855 Carbine**, .52, Maynard Primer, *Antique* 795.00 1,500.00

400 / SHARPSHOOTER

	V.G.	EXC.
☐ **1855 Rifle**, .52, Maynard Primer, *Antique*	1,300.00	1,950.00
☐ **1859 Carbine**, .52, Pellet Primer, *Antique*	640.00	995.00
☐ **1863 Carbine**, .52, Lawrence Cut-off, *Antique*	475.00	785.00
☐ **1863 Rifle**, .52, Lawrence Cut-off, *Antique*	975.00	1,500.00

RIFLE, SINGLESHOT
- ☐ **1874 Sporting Rifle**, Various Calibers, Set Trigger, Target Sights, *Antique* 995.00 1,800.00
- ☐ **1874 Hunting Rifle**, Various Calibers, Open Sights, *Antique* 750.00 1,300.00
- ☐ **Long Range Rifle**, Various Calibers, Target Sights, *Antique* 1,800.00 2,850.00

Sharp-Sooter .32

SHARPSHOOTER
Hijos de Calixto Arrizabalaga, Eibar, Spain, c. 1920.

HANDGUN, SEMI-AUTOMATIC
- ☐ "**Sharp-Sooter**", .25 ACP, Clip Fed, Hammer, Hinged Barrel, Blue, *Curio* 140.00 195.00
- ☐ "**Sharp-Sooter**", .32 ACP, Clip Fed, Hammer, Hinged Barrel, Blue, *Curio* 160.00 225.00
- ☐ "**Sharp-Sooter**", .380 ACP, Clip Fed, Hammer, Hinged Barrel, Blue, *Curio* 195.00 280.00

S.I.G.
Schweizerische Industrie Gesellschaft, Neuhausen, Switzerland since 1857.

AUTOMATIC WEAPON, ASSAULT RIFLE
- ☐ **SIG 510**, .308 Win., Clip Fed, Bipod, *Class 3* 950.00 1,400.00

HANDGUN, SEMI-AUTOMATIC
- ☐ **P210 Luxus**, Various Calibers, Clip Fed, Fancy Engraving, Gold Inlay, High-Polish Blue Finish, Carved Wood Grips, *Modern* 1,750.00 2,650.00
- ☐ **P210-1**, .22 L.R.R.F., Clip Fed, Blue, High-Polish Finish, Wood Grips, *Modern* 700.00 1,150.00
- ☐ **P210-1**, .30 Luger, Clip Fed, Blue, High-Polish Finish, Wood Grips, *Modern* 725.00 1,175.00
- ☐ **P210-1**, 9mm Luger, Clip Fed, Blue, High-Polish Finish, Wood Grips, *Modern* 725.00 1,175.00
- ☐ **P210-1**, .22 L.R.R.F., Conversion Unit Only, *Modern* 375.00 500.00
- ☐ **P210-1**, Various Calibers, Clip Fed, High-Polish Finish, with 3 Caliber Conv. Units, Wood Grips, *Modern* 1,275.00 1,850.00
- ☐ **P210-2**, .30 Luger, Clip Fed, Blue, Plastic Stock, *Modern* 675.00 950.00
- ☐ **P210-2**, 9mm Luger, Clip Fed, Blue, Plastic Stock, *Modern* 650.00 900.00
- ☐ **P210-5**, .30 Luger, Clip Fed, Blue, Plastic Stock, Target Pistol, 6" Barrel, *Modern* 750.00 1,200.00
- ☐ **P210-5**, 9mm Luger, Clip Fed, Blue, Plastic Stock, Target Pistol, 6" Barrel, *Modern* 700.00 1,150.00

S.I.G. P 210-6

Simplex

	V.G.	EXC.
☐ **P 225 SIG-Sauer**, 9mm Luger, Clip Fed, Double Action, Blue, *Modern*	260.00	375.00
☐ **P 230 SIG-Sauer**, 9mm Police, Clip Fed, Double Action, Blue, *Modern*	245.00	335.00
☐ **P 230 SIG-Sauer**, Various Calibers, Clip Fed, Double Action, Blue, *Modern*	200.00	300.00
☐ **SP 47/8**, 9mm Luger, Clip Fed, German Border Patrol, *Modern*	1,150.00	1,800.00
☐ **SP 47/8**, 9mm Luger, Clip Fed, Swiss Military, *Modern*	1,650.00	2,500.00

RIFLE, SEMI-AUTOMATIC

☐ **SIG AMT**, .308 Win., Clip Fed, Bipod, *Modern*	700.00	1,100.00
☐ **SIG STG-57**, 7.5 Swiss, Clip Fed, Bipod, *Modern*	775.00	1,200.00

SILE

HANDGUN, SEMI-AUTOMATIC

☐ **Seecamp**, .25 ACP, Double Action, Clip Fed, Stainless Steel, *Modern* ... 85.00 130.00

SIMPLEX

Made in Belgium. Also see Bergmann.

HANDGUN, SEMI-AUTOMATIC

☐ **Simplex**, 8mm Bergmann, Blue, *Curio* ... 400.00 650.00

SIMSON & CO.

Waffenfabrik Simson & Co., Suhl, Germany 1910-1939. Also see Luger.

HANDGUN, SEMI-AUTOMATIC

☐ **Vest Pocket**, .25 ACP, Clip Fed, Blue, *Modern* ... 300.00 450.00

RIFLE, BOLT ACTION

☐ **Precision Carbine**, 6mm Shot, Singleshot, Plain, *Modern*	35.00	50.00
☐ **Precision Carbine**, 9mm Shot, Singleshot, Plain, *Modern*	40.00	60.00
☐ **Model 1933**, .22 Extra Long, Singleshot, Checkered Stock, Target Sights, *Modern*	70.00	95.00
☐ **Sportrifle #7**, .22 Extra Long, Singleshot, Checkered Stock, Target Sights, *Modern*	55.00	80.00

SHOTGUN, DOUBLE BARREL, OVER-UNDER

☐ **Trap Grade**, 12 Ga., Automatic Ejectors, Checkered Stock, Engraved, Cocking Indicators, *Modern* ... 950.00 1,500.00

402 / SINGER

Simson Vest Pocket

Singer .25

	V.G.	EXC.

SHOTGUN, DOUBLE BARREL, SIDE-BY-SIDE
- ☐ **Astora**, Various Calibers, Checkered Stock, Plain, *Modern* 200.00 300.00
- ☐ **Magnum**, 12 Gauge 3", Checkered Stock, Engraved, *Modern* 500.00 700.00
- ☐ **Monte Carlo**, 12 Ga., Checkered Stock, Fancy Engraving, Automatic Ejectors, Sidelock, *Modern* 900.00 1,500.00

SINGER
Arizmendi y Goenaga, Eibar, Spain.
HANDGUN, SEMI-AUTOMATIC
- ☐ **.25 ACP**, Clip Fed, Blue, *Modern* 80.00 125.00
- ☐ **.32 ACP**, Clip Fed, Blue, *Modern* 90.00 135.00

SINGER
Frantisek Dusek, Opocno, Czechoslovakia.
HANDGUN, SEMI-AUTOMATIC
- ☐ **Duo**, .25 ACP, Clip Fed, Blue, *Modern* 80.00 115.00

SJOGREN
Sweden.
SHOTGUN, SEMI-AUTOMATIC
- ☐ **12 Ga.**, 5 Shot, Checkered Stock, Recoil Operated, *Curio* 300.00 400.00

SKB
Tokyo, Japan.
SHOTGUN, DOUBLE BARREL, OVER-UNDER
- ☐ **Model 500**, 12 and 20 Gauges, Field Grade, Selective Ejector, Vent Rib, *Modern* 250.00 350.00
- ☐ **Model 500**, 12 Ga. Mag. 3", Field Grade, Selective Ejector, Vent Rib, *Modern* 260.00 360.00
- ☐ **Model 600**, 12 Ga., Trap Grade, Selective Ejector, Vent Rib, *Modern* 360.00 460.00
- ☐ **Model 600**, 12 Ga., Trap Grade, Selective Ejector, Vent Rib, Monte Carlo Stock, *Modern* 360.00 460.00
- ☐ **Model 600**, 12 and 20 Gauges, Field Grade, Selective Ejector, Vent Rib, *Modern* 350.00 440.00
- ☐ **Model 600**, 12 and 20 Gauges, Skeet Grade, Selective Ejector, Vent Rib, *Modern* 360.00 460.00
- ☐ **Model 600**, 20 and .410 Gauges, Skeet Grade, Selective Ejector, Vent Rib, *Modern* 360.00 470.00
- ☐ **Model 600 Combo Set**, Various Gauges, Skeet Grade, Selective Ejector, Vent Rib, Cased, *Modern* 800.00 1,100.00

SMITH AND WESSON / 403

	V.G.	EXC.
☐ **Model 680 English**, 12 and 20 Gauges, Field Grade, Selective Ejector, Vent Rib, *Modern*	370.00	460.00
☐ **Model 700**, 12 Ga., Trap Grade, Selective Ejector, Vent Rib, *Modern*	400.00	550.00
☐ **Model 700**, 12 Ga., Trap Grade, Selective Ejector, Vent Rib, Monte Carlo Stock, *Modern*	400.00	550.00
☐ **Model 700**, 12 and 20 Gauges, Skeet Grade, Selective Ejector, Vent Rib, *Modern*	400.00	550.00
☐ **Model 700 Combo Set**, Various Gauges, Skeet Grade, Selective Ejector, Vent Rib, Cased, *Modern*	900.00	1,450.00

SHOTGUN, SEMI-AUTOMATIC

☐ **900 Deluxe**, 12 and 20 Gauges, Vent Rib, *Modern*	150.00	180.00
☐ **900 XL**, 12 Ga., Trap Grade, *Modern*	170.00	225.00
☐ **900 XL**, 12 Ga., Trap Grade, Monte Carlo Stock, *Modern*	170.00	230.00
☐ **900 XL**, 12 and 20 Gauges, Skeet Grade, *Modern*	160.00	215.00
☐ **900 XL Deluxe**, 12 and 20 Gauges, Vent Rib, *Modern*	160.00	200.00
☐ **900 XL Slug**, 12 and 20 Gauges, Open Rear Sight, *Modern*	150.00	200.00

SLOANS
Importers, N.Y.C. Also see Charles Daly.

SHOTGUN, DOUBLE BARREL, SIDE-BY-SIDE

☐ **POS**, .410 Ga., Checkered Stock, Hammerless, Double Trigger, *Modern*	115.00	155.00
☐ **POS**, 10 Ga., 3½", Checkered Stock, Hammerless, Double Trigger, *Modern*	135.00	185.00
☐ **POS**, 12 and 20 Gauges, Checkered Stock, Hammerless, Double Trigger, *Modern*	100.00	150.00
☐ **POS Coach Gun**, 12 and 20 Gauges, Checkered Stock, Outside Hammers, Double Trigger, *Modern*	115.00	155.00

S-M CORP.
Sydney Manson, Alexandria, Va., c. 1953.

HANDGUN, SEMI-AUTOMATIC

☐ **Sporter**, .22 L.R.R.F., Blowback, *Modern*	80.00	125.00

SMITH & WESSON
Started in Norwich, Conn. in 1855 as Volcanic Repeating Arms Co.. Reorganized at Springfield, Mass. as Smith & Wesson in 1857 (Volcanic Repeating Arms moved to New Haven, Conn. in 1856 and was purchased in 1857 by Winchester Repeating Arms Co.). Smith & Wesson at Springfield, Mass. to date. Also see U.S. Military.

AUTOMATIC WEAPON, SUBMACHINE GUN

☐ **Model 76**, 9mm Luger, Clip Fed, Commercial, *Class 3*	425.00	575.00

HANDGUN, REVOLVER

☐ **.32 Double Action**, .32 S & W, 1st Model, Top Break, 5 Shot, Straight-Cut Sideplate, Rocker Cylinder Stop, *Antique*	800.00	1,350.00
☐ **.32 Double Action**, .32 S & W, 2nd Model, Top Break, 5 Shot, Irregularly-Cut Sideplate, Rocker Cylinder Stop, *Antique*	120.00	190.00
☐ **.32 Double Action**, .32 S & W, 3rd Model, Top Break, 5 Shot, Irregularly-Cut Sideplate, *Antique*	110.00	175.00
☐ **.32 Double Action**, .32 S & W, 4th Model, Round-Back Trigger Guard, Top Break, 5 Shot, Irregularly-Cut Sideplate, *Modern*	95.00	160.00
☐ **.32 Double Action**, .32 S & W, 5th Model, Round-Back Trigger Guard, Top Break, 5 Shot, Irregularly-Cut Sideplate, Front Sight Forged on Barrel, *Modern*	95.00	165.00

404 / SMITH AND WESSON

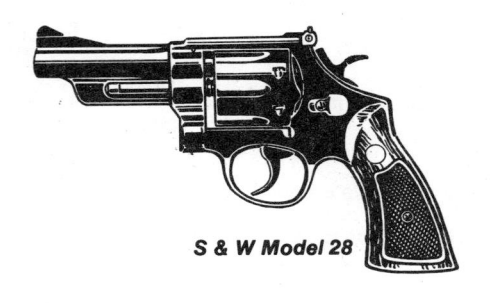

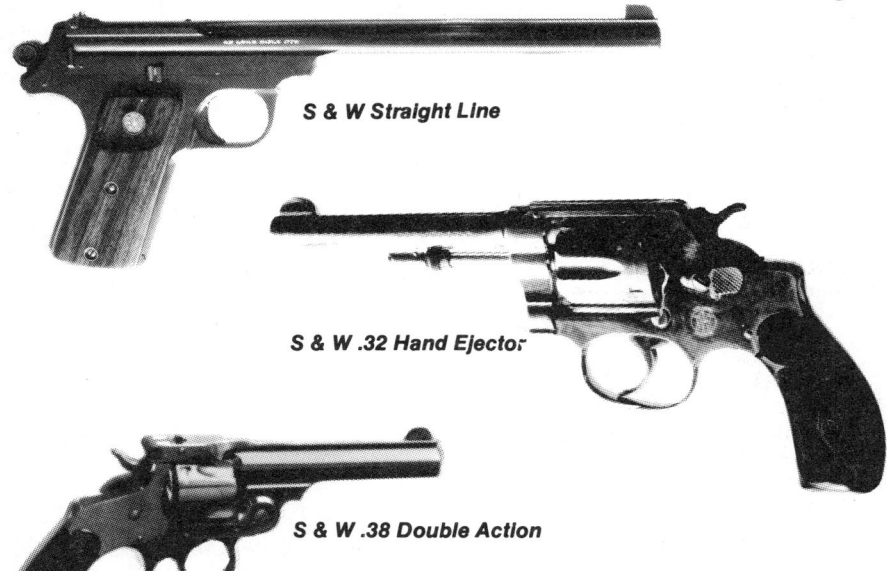

S & W Model 28

S & W Model 39

S & W Straight Line

S & W .32 Hand Ejector

S & W .38 Double Action

S & W .38 Hand Ejector 1st Model

SMITH AND WESSON / 405

	V.G.	EXC.
☐ **.32 Hand Ejector**, .32 S & W Long, 1st Model, Solid Frame, Swing-Out Cylinder, Hammer Actuated Cylinder Stop, 6 Shot, *Modern*	325.00	475.00
☐ **.32 Hand Ejector**, .32 S & W Long, Solid Frame, Swing-Out Cylinder, 6 Shot, Target Sights, Double Action, *Modern*	275.00	400.00
☐ **.32 Hand Ejector 1903**, .32 S & W Long, Solid Frame, Swing-Out Cylinder, 6 Shot, Double Action, *Modern*	100.00	185.00
☐ **.32 Regulation Police**, .32 S & W Long, Solid Frame, Swing-Out Cylinder, 6 Shot, Double Action, *Modern*	100.00	165.00
☐ **.32 Safety Hammerless**, .32 S & W, 1st Model, Double Action, Top Break, 5 Shot, Push-Button Latch, *Modern*	145.00	250.00
☐ **.32 Safety Hammerless**, .32 S & W, 2nd Model, Double Action, Top Break, 5 Shot, T Latch, *Modern*	95.00	160.00
☐ **.32 Safety Hammerless**, .32 S & W, 3rd Model, Double Action, Top Break, 5 Shot, Over #170,000, *Modern*	95.00	170.00
☐ **.32 Single Action**, .32 S & W, Top Break, Spur Trigger, 5 Shot, *Antique*	225.00	350.00
☐ **.32 Single Action**, .32 S & W, 6" or 8" Barrel, *Add 50%-75%*		
☐ **.32 Single Action**, .32 S & W, 10" Barrel, *Add 75%-100%*		
☐ **.38 D A Perfected**, .38 S & W, Solid Trigger Guard, Thumbpiece, Hand-Ejector Action, Top Break, Double Action, *Modern*	190.00	300.00
☐ **.38 D A Perfected**, .38 S & W, made without Thumbpiece, Hand-Ejector Action, Top Break, Double Action, *Modern*	350.00	465.00
☐ **.38 Double Action**, .38 S & W, 1st Model, Straight-Cut Sideplate, Rocker Cylinder Stop, Double Action, Top Break, 5 Shot, *Antique*	425.00	675.00
☐ **.38 Double Action**, .38 S & W, 2nd Model, Irregularly-Cut Sideplate, Rocker Cylinder Stop, Double Action, Top Break, 5 Shot, *Antique*	120.00	190.00
☐ **.38 Double Action**, .38 S & W, 3rd Model, Irregularly-Cut Sideplate, Double Action, Top Break, 5 Shot, *Antique*	110.00	185.00
☐ **.38 Double Action**, .38 S & W, 4th Model, #'s 322,701-539,000, Double Action, Top Break, 5 Shot, *Modern*	95.00	160.00
☐ **.38 Double Action**, .38 S & W, 5th Model, #'s 539,001-554,077, Double Action, Top Break, 5 Shot, *Modern*	90.00	155.00
☐ **.38 Double Action**, .38 S & W, 4th Model, #'s 322,701-539,000, Double Action, Top Break, 5 Shot, Adjustable Sights, *Modern*......	295.00	425.00
☐ **.38 Double Action**, .38 S & W, 5th Model, #'s 539,001-554,077, Double Action, Top Break, 5 Shot, Adjustable Sights, *Modern*......	280.00	375.00
☐ **.38 Hand Ejector**, .38 Long Colt, 1st. Model, Solid Frame, Swing-Out Cylinder, No Cylinder-Pin Front-Lock, U.S. Army Model, *Modern*	400.00	675.00
☐ **.38 Hand Ejector**, .38 Long Colt, 1st. Model, Solid Frame, Swing-Out Cylinder, No Cylinder-Pin Front-Lock, U.S. Navy Model, *Modern*	425.00	650.00
☐ **.38 Hand Ejector**, .38 Long Colt, 2nd Model, Solid Frame, Swing-Out Cylinder, U.S. Navy Model, *Modern*	400.00	625.00
☐ **.38 Hand Ejector**, .38 Special, 1st Model, Solid Frame, Swing-Out Cylinder, no Cylinder-Pin Front-Lock, *Modern*	200.00	335.00
☐ **.38 Hand Ejector**, .38 Special, 1st Model, Solid Frame, Swing-Out Cylinder, no Cylinder-Pin Front-Lock, Adjustable Sights, *Modern*	385.00	550.00
☐ **.38 Hand Ejector**, .38 Special, 2nd Model, Solid Frame, Swing-Out Cylinder, *Modern*	175.00	275.00
☐ **.38 Hand Ejector**, .38 Special, 2nd Model, Solid Frame,Swing-Out Cylinder, Adjustable Sights, *Modern*	375.00	525.00
☐ **.38 Hand Ejector 1902**, .38 Special, Military and Police, Solid Frame, Swing-Out Cylinder, Double Action, *Modern*	170.00	250.00
☐ **.38 Hand Ejector 1902**, .38 Special, Military and Police, Solid Frame, Swing-Out Cylinder, Double Action, Adjustable Sights, *Modern*	300.00	425.00

406 / SMITH AND WESSON

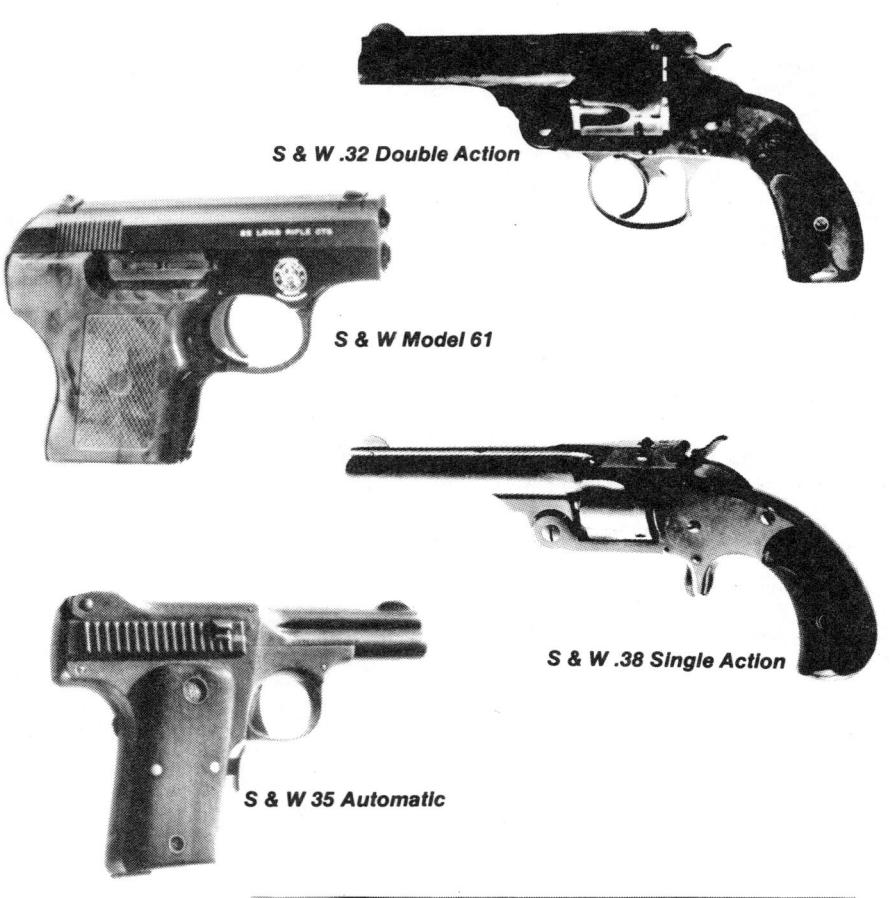

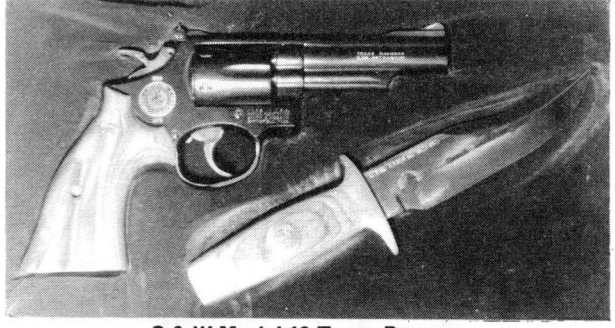

S & W .32 Double Action

S & W Model 61

S & W .38 Single Action

S & W 35 Automatic

S & W Model 19 Texas Ranger

SMITH AND WESSON / 407

	V.G.	EXC.
☐ **.38 Hand Ejector 1905**, .38 Special, Military and Police, Solid Frame, Swing-Out Cylinder, Double Action, *Modern*	145.00	240.00
☐ **.38 Hand Ejector 1905**, .38 Special, Military and Police, Solid Frame, Swing-Out Cylinder, Double Action, Adjustable Sights, *Modern*	300.00	435.00
☐ **.38 Safety Hammerless**, .38 S & W, 1st Model-Button Latch, Release on Left Topstrap, Top Break, Double Action, *Antique*	220.00	350.00
☐ **.38 Safety Hammerless**, .38 S & W, 2nd Model-Button Latch, Release on Top of Frame, Top Break, Double Action, *Antique*	170.00	265.00
☐ **.38 Safety Hammerless**, .38 S & W, 3rd Model-Button Latch, Release on Rear Topstrap, Top Break, Double Action, *Antique*	140.00	225.00
☐ **.38 Safety Hammerless**, .38 S & W, 4th Model T-Shaped Latch, Top Break, Double Action, *Modern*	115.00	210.00
☐ **.38 Safety Hammerless**, .38 S & W, 5th Model T-Shaped Latch, Top Break, Double Action, Front Sight Forged on Barrel, *Modern*	110.00	190.00
☐ **.38 Single Action**, .38 S & W, 1st Model, Baby Russian, Top Break, Spur Trigger, *Antique*	220.00	325.00
☐ **.38 Single Action**, .38 S & W, 2nd Model, Top Break, Spur Trigger, Short Ejector Housing, *Antique*	140.00	225.00
☐ **.38 Single Action**, .38 S & W, 3rd Model, Top Break, with Trigger Guard, *Modern*	375.00	550.00
☐ **.38 Single Action**, .38 S & W, 3rd Model, Top Break, with Trigger Guard, with Extra Single-Shot Barrel, *Modern*	600.00	850.00
☐ **.38 Single Action**, .38 S & W, Mexican Model, Top Break, Spur Trigger, 5 Shot, *Modern*	1,100.00	1,600.00
☐ **.38 Win. Double Action**, .38-40 WCF, Top Break, *Modern*	650.00	975.00
☐ **.44 Double Action**, for Target Sights, *Add 20%-30%*		
☐ **.44 Double Action**, .44 Russian, 1st Model, Top Break, 6 Shot, *Antique*	375.00	500.00
☐ **.44 Double Action**, .44 Russian, Wesson Favorite, 6 Shot, Lightweight, Top Break, *Antique*	975.00	1,600.00
☐ **.44 Double Action Frontier**, for Target Sights, *Add 20%-30%*		
☐ **.44 Double Action Frontier**, .44-40 WCF, Top Break, 6 Shot, *Antique*	450.00	650.00
☐ **.44 Hand Ejector**, Calibers other than .44 Spec., *Add 15%-25%*		
☐ **.44 Hand Ejector**, 1st Model, for Target Sights, *Add 20%-30%*		
☐ **.44 Hand Ejector**, Calibers other than .44 Spec., *Add 15%-25%*		
☐ **.44 Hand Ejector**, 2nd Model, for Target Sights, *Add 20%-30%*		
☐ **.44 Hand Ejector**, 3rd Model, for Target Sights, *Add 20%-30%*		
☐ **.44 Hand Ejector**, .44 Special, 1st Model, Triple-Lock, Solid Frame, Swing-Out Cylinder, New Century, *Modern*	450.00	675.00
☐ **.44 Hand Ejector**, .44 Special, 2nd Model, Un-Shrouded Ejector Rod, Solid Frame, Swing-Out Cylinder, *Modern*	325.00	450.00
☐ **.44 Hand Ejector**, .44 Special, 3rd Model, Shrouded Ejector Rod, Solid Frame, Swing-Out Cylinder, *Modern*	275.00	400.00
☐ **.455 MK II Hand Ejector**, Solid Frame, Swing-Out Cylinder, Double Action, Military, *Modern*	250.00	425.00
☐ **22/32 Bekeart Model**, .22 L.R.R.F., #'s 138,220-139,275, Target Pistol, Double Action, Adjustable Sights, 6" Barrel, *Modern*	375.00	525.00
☐ **22/32 Hand Ejector**, .22 L.R.R.F., Target Pistol, Double Action, Adjustable Sights, 6" Barrel, *Modern*	190.00	290.00
☐ **22/32 Kit Gun**, .22 L.R.R.F., Early Model, Double Action, Adjustable Sights, 4" Barrel, *Modern*	150.00	225.00
☐ **32/20 Hand Ejector**, .32-20 WCF, 1st Model, Solid Frame, Swing-Out Cylinder, 6 Shot, no Cylinder-Pin Front-Lock, *Modern*	250.00	365.00
☐ **32/20 Hand Ejector 1902**, .32-20 WCF, 2nd Model, Solid Frame, Swing-Out Cylinder, 6 Shot, *Modern*	200.00	300.00

408 / SMITH AND WESSON

	V.G.	EXC.
☐ **32/20 Hand Ejector 1902**, .32-20 WCF, 2nd Model, Solid Frame, Swing-Out Cylinder, 6 Shot, Adjustable Sights, *Modern*	325.00	450.00
☐ **32/20 Hand Ejector 1905**, .32-20 WCF, Solid Frame, Swing-Out Cylinder, 6 Shot, Adjustable Sights, *Modern*	275.00	400.00
☐ **32/20 Hand Ejector 1905**, .32-20 WCF, Solid Frame, Swing-Out Cylinder, 6 Shot, *Modern*	175.00	280.00
☐ **38/200 British**, .38 S & W, Military & Police, Solid Frame, Swing-Out Cylinder, Double Action, Military, *Modern*	95.00	175.00
☐ **First Model Schofield**, .45 S & W, Top Break, Single Action, Military, *Antique*	775.00	1,400.00
☐ **First Model Schofield**, .45 S & W, Top Break, Single Action, Commercial, *Antique*	1,450.00	2,200.00
☐ **First Model Schofield**, .45 S & W, Wells Fargo, Top Break, Single Action, *Antique*	850.00	1,200.00
☐ **K-22 Hand Ejector**, .22 L.R.R.F., 1st Model, Double Action, Adjustable Sights, 6" Barrel, *Modern*	170.00	245.00
☐ **K-22 Masterpiece**, .22 L.R.R.F., 2nd Model K-22 Hand Ejector, Speed Lock Action, Double Action, Adjustable Sights, 6" Barrel, *Modern*	275.00	400.00
☐ **K-32 Hand Ejector**, .32 S & W Long, 1st Model, Pre-War, 6 Shot, Adjustable Sights, Target Pistol, *Modern*	400.00	550.00
☐ **K-32 Hand Ejector**, .32 S & W Long, 2nd Model, Post-War, 6 Shot, Adjustable Sights, Target Pistol, *Modern*	160.00	240.00
☐ **Model #1**, .22 Short R.F., 1st Issue, Tip-Up, Spur Trigger, 7 Shot, *Antique*	1,700.00	2,650.00
☐ **Model #1**, .22 Short R.F., 2nd Issue, Tip-Up, Spur Trigger, 7 Shot, *Antique*	750.00	1,300.00
☐ **Model #1**, .22 Short R.F., 3rd Issue, Tip-Up, Spur Trigger, 7 Shot, *Antique*	450.00	825.00
☐ **Model #1½**, .32 Short R.F., 1st Issue, Tip-Up, Spur Trigger, 5 Shot, Non-Fluted Cylinder, *Antique*	190.00	345.00
☐ **Model #1½**, .32 Short R.F., 2nd Issue, Tip-Up, Spur Trigger, 5 Shot, Fluted Cylinder, *Antique*	185.00	335.00
☐ **Model #2 Old Army**, .32 Long R.F., Tip-Up, Spur Trigger, 6 Shot, *Antique*	300.00	450.00
☐ **Model #3 American**, .44 Henry, 1st Model, Single Action, Top Break, 6 Shot, *Antique*	900.00	1,650.00
☐ **Model #3 American**, .44 Henry, 2nd Model, #'s 8,000-32,800, Single Action, Top Break, 6 Shot, *Antique*	800.00	1,475.00
☐ **Model #3 American**, .44 S & W, 1st Model, Single Action, Top Break, 6 Shot, *Antique*	650.00	900.00
☐ **Model #3 American**, .44 S & W, 2nd Model #'s 8,000-32,800, Single Action, Top Break, 6 Shot, *Antique*	550.00	800.00
☐ **Model #3 Frontier**, .44-40 WCF, Single Action, Top Break, 6 Shot, *Antique*	750.00	1,150.00
☐ **Model #3 New Model**, Calibers other than .44 Russian, *Add* 40%-60%		
☐ **Model #3 New Model**, .44 Russian, Australian Police with Shoulder Stock, *Add* 200%-225%		
☐ **Model #3 New Model**, .44 Russian, Single Action, Top Break, 6 Shot, *Antique*	450.00	675.00
☐ **Model #3 New Model**, .44 Russian Japanese Navy Issue, *Add* 30%-45%		
☐ **Model #3 New Model**, .44 Russian, Australian Police with Shoulder Stock, *Add* 200%-225%		
☐ **Model #3 New Model**, .44 Russian, Argentine Model, *Add* **25%-35%**		
☐ **Model #3 New Model**, .44 S & W, Turkish Model, *Add* **15%-25%**		

S & W Model 27

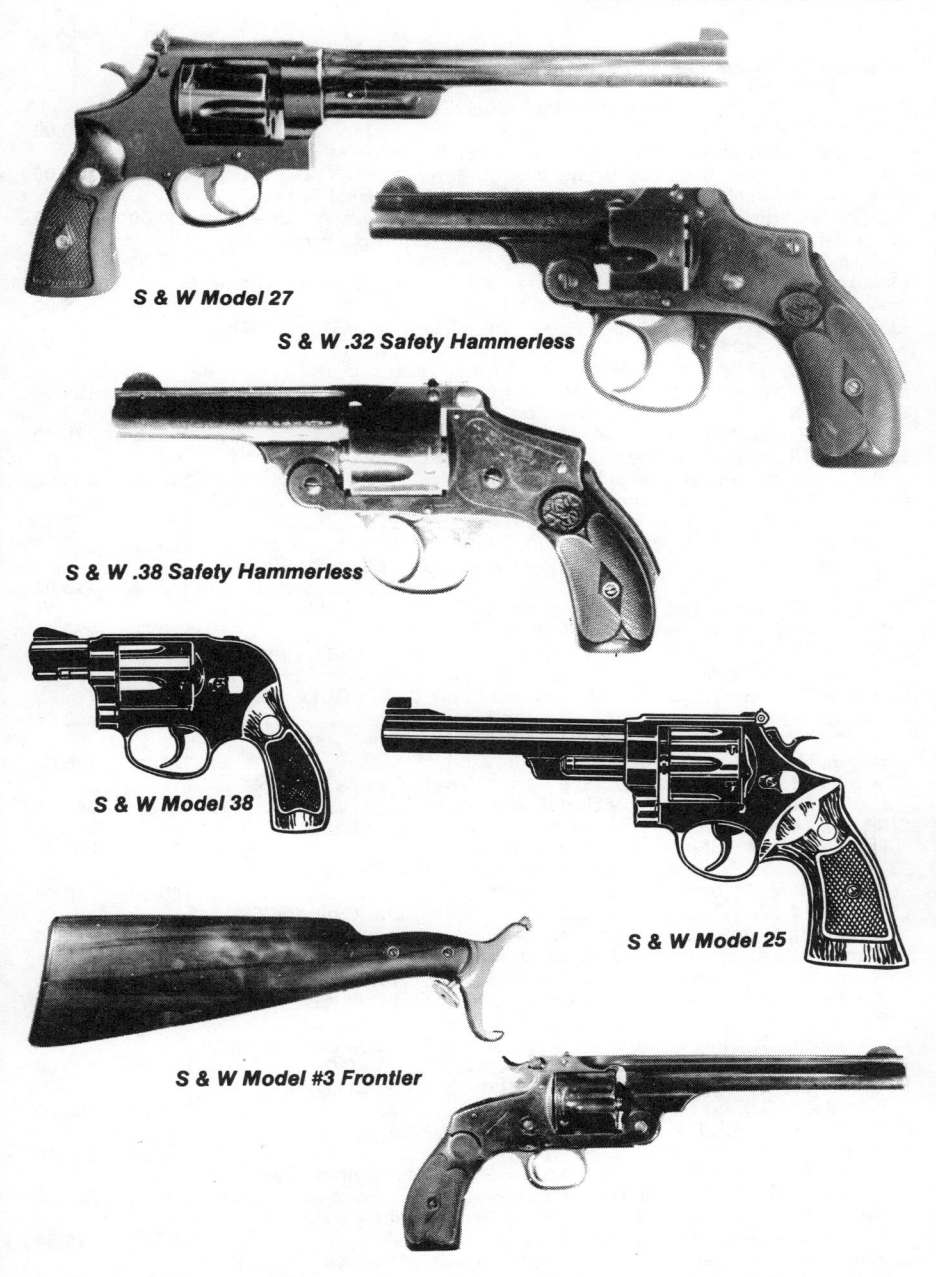

S & W .32 Safety Hammerless

S & W .38 Safety Hammerless

S & W Model 38

S & W Model 25

S & W Model #3 Frontier

410 / SMITH AND WESSON

	V.G.	EXC.
☐ **Model #3 New Model**, Various Calibers Other Than .44 Russian, Add **40%-60%**		
☐ **Model #3 Russian**, .44 Russian, 1st Model, Single Action, Top Break, 6 Shot, Military, *Antique*	575.00	800.00
☐ **Model #3 Russian**, .44 Russian, 2nd Model, Finger-Rest Trigger Guard, Single Action, Top Break, 6 Shot, *Antique*	450.00	750.00
☐ **Model #3 Russian**, .44 Russian, 2nd Model, Finger-Rest Trigger Guard, Single Action, Top Break, with Shoulder Stock, *Antique*	800.00	1,300.00
☐ **Model #3 Russian**, .44 Russian, 3rd Model, Front Sight Forged on Barrel, Single Action, Top Break, 6 Shot, *Antique*	625.00	850.00
☐ **Model #3 Target**, .32-44 S & W, .38-44 S & W, New Model #3, Single Action, Top Break, *Modern*	475.00	675.00
☐ **Target Models**, For Target Hammer, Target Trigger, Target Stocks, Add **$30.00-$40.00**		
☐ **Model 10**, .38 Special, Double Action, Blue, Various Barrel Lengths, Swing-Out Cylinder, *Modern*	125.00	165.00
☐ **Model 10**, .38 Special, Double Action, Swing-Out Cylinder, 4" Barrel, Heavy Barrel, Blue, *Modern*	135.00	175.00
☐ **Model 10**, .38 Special, Double Action, Swing-Out Cylinder, 4" Barrel, Heavy Barrel, Nickel Plated, *Modern*	140.00	185.00
☐ **Model 10**, .38 Special, Double Action, Swing-Out Cylinder, Various Barrel Lengths, Nickel Plated, *Modern*	135.00	175.00
☐ **Model 11**, .38 S & W, Double Action, Swing-Out Cylinder, *Modern*	220.00	300.00
☐ **Model 12**, .38 Special, Double Action, Swing-Out Cylinder, Various Barrel Lengths, Blue, *Modern*	150.00	210.00
☐ **Model 12**, .38 Special, Double Action, Swing-Out Cylinder, Various Barrel Lengths, Nickel Plated, *Modern*	170.00	230.00
☐ **Model 12 USAF**, .38 Special, Double Action, Swing-Out Cylinder, Lightweight, *Modern*	250.00	375.00
☐ **Model "13" Army**, .38 Special, Double Action, Swing-Out Cylinder, Lightweight, *Modern*	325.00	450.00
☐ **Model 13**, .357 Magnum, Double Action, Swing-Out Cylinder, 4" Barrel, Heavy Barrel, Blue, *Modern*	125.00	175.00
☐ **Model 13**, .357 Magnum, Double Action, Swing-Out Cylinder, 4" Barrel, Nickel Plated, Heavy Barrel, *Modern*	135.00	185.00
☐ **Model 14**, .38 Special, Double Action, Swing-Out Cylinder, 6" Barrel, Blue, Adjustable Sights, *Modern*	150.00	200.00
☐ **Model 14**, .38 Special, Double Action, Swing-Out Cylinder, 8⅜" Barrel, Blue, Adjustable Sights, *Modern*	160.00	210.00
☐ **Model 14 SA**, .38 Special, Single Action, Swing-Out Cylinder, 6" Barrel, Blue, Adjustable Sights, *Modern*	170.00	225.00
☐ **Model 14 SA**, .38 Special, Single Action, Swing-Out Cylinder, 8⅜" Barrel, Blue, Adjustable Sights, *Modern*	175.00	235.00
☐ **Model 15**, .38 Special, Double Action, Swing-Out Cylinder, Various Barrel Lengths, Blue, Adjustable Sights, *Modern*	145.00	180.00
☐ **Model 15**, .38 Special, Double Action, Swing-Out Cylinder, Various Barrel Lengths, Nickel Plated, Adjustable Sights, *Modern*	155.00	190.00
☐ **Model 16**, .32 S & W Long, Double Action, Swing-Out Cylinder, Adjustable Sights, Target Pistol, *Modern*	225.00	350.00
☐ **Model 17**, .22 L.R.R.F., Double Action, Swing-Out Cylinder, 6" Barrel, Adjustable Sights, Blue, *Modern*	160.00	215.00
☐ **Model 17**, .22 L.R.R.F., Double Action, Swing-Out Cylinder, 8⅜" Barrel, Adjustable Sights, Blue, *Modern*	170.00	225.00
☐ **Model 18**, .22 L.R.R.F., Double Action, Swing-Out Cylinder, 4" Barrel, Adjustable Sights, Blue, *Modern*	130.00	215.00
☐ **Model 19**, .357 Magnum, Double Action, Swing-Out Cylinder, Various Barrel Lengths, Adjustable Sights, Blue, *Modern*	175.00	250.00

SMITH AND WESSON / 411

	V.G.	EXC.
☐ **Model 19**, .357 Magnum, Double Action, Swing-Out Cylinder, Various Barrel Lengths, Adjustable Sights, Nickel Plated, *Modern*	150.00	260.00
☐ **Model 19 Texas Ranger**, .357 Magnum, Commemorative, Blue, Cased, with Knife, *Curio*	375.00	550.00
☐ **Model 1917**, .45 Auto-Rim, Double Action, Swing-Out Cylinder, *Modern*	300.00	425.00
☐ **Model 1917**, .45 Auto-Rim, Double Action, Swing-Out Cylinder, Military, *Modern*	200.00	300.00
☐ **Model 20**, .38 Special, Double Action, Swing-Out Cylinder, *Modern*	225.00	350.00
☐ **Model 21**, .44 Special, Double Action, Swing-Out Cylinder, Various Barrel Lengths, *Modern*	350.00	475.00
☐ **Model 22**, .45 Auto-Rim, Double Action, Swing-Out Cylinder, *Modern*	225.00	350.00
☐ **Model 23**, .38 Special, Double Action, Swing-Out Cylinder, Adjustable Sights, Target Pistol, *Modern*	325.00	450.00
☐ **Model 24**, .44 Special, Double Action, Swing-Out Cylinder, Various Barrel Lengths, Adjustable Sights, *Modern*	325.00	425.00
☐ **Model 25**, .45 Auto-Rim, Double Action, Swing-Out Cylinder, Target Pistol, Blue, Cased with Accessories, *Modern*	245.00	340.00
☐ **Model 25**, .45 Auto-Rim, Double Action, Swing-Out Cylinder, Target Pistol, Blue, *Modern*	220.00	300.00
☐ **Model 26**, .45 Auto-Rim, Double Action, Swing-Out Cylinder, *Modern*	350.00	500.00
☐ **Model 27**, .357 Magnum, Double Action, Swing-Out Cylinder, Pre-War, Adjustable Sights, *Modern*	375.00	550.00
☐ **Model 27**, .357 Magnum, Double Action, Swing-Out Cylinder, Various Barrel Lengths, Adjustable Sights, Blue, *Modern*	220.00	300.00
☐ **Model 27**, .357 Magnum, Double Action, Swing-Out Cylinder, Nickel Plated, *Modern*	225.00	310.00
☐ **Model 27**, .357 Magnum, Double Action, Swing-Out Cylinder, 8⅜" Barrel, Blue, *Modern*	235.00	320.00
☐ **Model 27**, .357 Magnum, Double Action, Swing-Out Cylinder, 8⅜" Barrel, Nickel Plated, *Modern*	235.00	320.00
☐ **Model 27**, .357 Magnum, Double Action, Various Barrel Lengths, Adjustable Sights, Cased with Accessories, Blue, *Modern*	250.00	350.00
☐ **Model 27**, .357 Magnum, Double Action, 8⅜" Barrel, Adjustable Sights, Cased with Accessories, Nickel Plated, *Modern*	260.00	360.00
☐ **Model 27**, .357 Magnum, Double Action, Various Barrel Lengths, Adjustable Sights, Cased with Accessories, Nickel Plated, *Modern*	250.00	350.00
☐ **Model 27**, .357 Magnum, Double Action, 8⅜" Barrel, Adjustable Sights, Cased with Accessories, Blue, *Modern*	260.00	360.00
☐ **Model 27 with Registration**, .357 Magnum, Double Action, Swing-Out Cylinder, Pre-War, Adjustable Sights, *Modern*	575.00	875.00
☐ **Model 28**, .357 Magnum, Double Action, Various Barrel Lengths, Adjustable Sights, Blue, *Modern*	165.00	215.00
☐ **Model 28**, .357 Magnum, Double Action, Various Barrel Lengths, Target Grips, Adjustable Sights, Blue, *Modern*	175.00	225.00
☐ **Model 29**, .44 Magnum, Double Action, Various Barrel Lengths, Adjustable Sights, Swing-Out Cylinder, Blue, *Modern*	270.00	365.00
☐ **Model 29**, .44 Magnum, Double Action, Various Barrel Lengths, Adjustable Sights, Swing-Out Cylinder, Nickel Plated, *Modern*	280.00	375.00
☐ **Model 29**, .44 Magnum, Double Action, 8⅜" Barrel, Adjustable Sights, Swing-Out Cylinder, Blue, *Modern*	300.00	400.00
☐ **Model 29**, .44 Magnum, Double Action, 8⅜" Barrel, Adjustable Sights, Swing-Out Cylinder, Nickel Plated, *Modern*	310.00	410.00
☐ **Model 29**, .44 Magnum, Double Action, Various Barrel Lengths, Adjustable Sights, Cased with Accessories, Blue, *Modern*	300.00	400.00

412 / SMITH AND WESSON

	V.G.	EXC.
☐ **Model 29**, .44 Magnum, Double Action, Various Barrel Lengths, Adjustable Sights, Cased with Accessories, Nickel Plated, *Modern*	310.00	410.00
☐ **Model 29**, .44 Magnum, Double Action, 8⅜" Barrel, Adjustable Sights, Cased with Accessories, Blue, *Modern*	320.00	420.00
☐ **Model 29**, .44 Magnum, Double Action, 8⅜" Barrel, Adjustable Sights, Cased with Accessories, Nickel Plated, *Modern*	330.00	430.00
☐ **Model 30**, .32 S & W Long, Double Action, Swing-Out Cylinder, *Modern*	175.00	275.00
☐ **Model 31**, .32 S & W Long, Double Action, Swing-Out Cylinder, Various Barrel Lengths, Nickel Plated, *Modern*	150.00	200.00
☐ **Model 31**, .32 S & W Long, Double Action, Swing-Out Cylinder, Various Barrel Lengths, Blue, *Modern*	140.00	185.00
☐ **Model 32**, .38 S & W, Double Action, Swing-Out Cylinder, 2" Barrel, *Modern*	160.00	235.00
☐ **Model 33**, .38 S & W, Double Action, Swing-Out Cylinder, *Modern*	180.00	250.00
☐ **Model 34**, .22 L.R.R.F., Double Action, Swing-Out Cylinder, Various Barrel Lengths, Adjustable Sights, Blue, *Modern*	165.00	210.00
☐ **Model 34**, .22 L.R.R.F., Double Action, Swing-Out Cylinder, Various Barrel Lengths, Adjustable Sights, Nickel Plated, *Modern*	175.00	220.00
☐ **Model 35**, .22 L.R.R.F., Double Action, Swing-Out Cylinder, Target Pistol, Adjustable Sights, *Modern*	220.00	300.00
☐ **Model 36**, .38 Special, Double Action, Swing-Out Cylinder, Various Barrel Lengths, Blue, *Modern*	145.00	195.00
☐ **Model 36**, .38 Special, Double Action, Swing-Out Cylinder, Various Barrel Lengths, Nickel Plated, *Modern*	160.00	210.00
☐ **Model 36**, .38 Special, Double Action, Swing-Out Cylinder, 3" Barrel, Heavy Barrel, Blue, *Modern*	140.00	190.00
☐ **Model 36**, .38 Special, Double Action, Swing-Out Cylinder, 3" Barrel, Heavy Barrel, Nickel Plated, *Modern*	150.00	200.00
☐ **Model 37**, .38 Special, Double Action, Swing-Out Cylinder, Various Barrel Lengths, Lightweight, Blue, *Modern*	150.00	200.00
☐ **Model 37**, .38 Special, Double Action, Swing-Out Cylinder, Various Barrel Lengths, Lightweight, Nickel Plated, *Modern*	160.00	210.00
☐ **Model 38**, .38 Special, Swing-Out Cylinder, 2" Barrel, Hammer Shroud, Nickel Plated, Double Action, *Modern*	175.00	235.00
☐ **Model 38**, .38 Special, Double Action, Swing-Out Cylinder, 2" Barrel, Hammer Shroud, Blue, *Modern*	165.00	220.00
☐ **Model 40**, .38 Special, Double Action, Swing-Out Cylinder, Hammerless, *Modern*	265.00	375.00
☐ **Model 42**, .38 Special, Double Action, Swing-Out Cylinder, Hammerless, Lightweight, *Modern*	325.00	475.00
☐ **Model 43**, .22 L.R.R.F., Double Action, Swing-Out Cylinder, Adjustable Sights, Lightweight, *Modern*	300.00	400.00
☐ **Model 45**, .22 L.R.R.F., Double Action, Swing-Out Cylinder, Commercial, *Modern*	475.00	750.00
☐ **Model 45 USPO**, .22 L.R.R.F., Double Action, Swing-Out Cylinder, *Modern*	425.00	550.00
☐ **Model 48**, .22 WMR, Double Action, Swing-Out Cylinder, Various Barrel Lengths, Blue, Adjustable Sights, *Modern*	165.00	225.00
☐ **Model 48**, .22 WMR, Double Action, Swing-Out Cylinder, 8⅜" Barrel, Blue, Adjustable Sights, *Modern*	175.00	235.00
☐ **Model 49**, .38 Special, Double Action, Swing-Out Cylinder, 2" Barrel, Hammer Shroud, Nickel Plated, *Modern*	170.00	230.00
☐ **Model 49**, .38 Special, Double Action, Swing-Out Cylinder, 2" Barrel, Hammer Shroud, Blue, *Modern*	155.00	210.00
☐ **Model 50**, .38 Special, Double Action, Swing-Out Cylinder, Adjustable Sights, *Modern*	475.00	750.00

	V.G.	EXC.
☐ **Model 51**, .22LR/.22 WMR Combo, Double Action, Swing-Out Cylinder, Adjustable Sights, *Modern*	375.00	500.00
☐ **Model 51**, .22 WMR, Double Action, Swing-Out Cylinder, Adjustable Sights, *Modern*	300.00	400.00
☐ **Model 53**, .22 Rem. Jet, Double Action, Swing-Out Cylinder, Adjustable Sights, *Modern*	425.00	575.00
☐ **Model 53**, .22 Rem. Jet, Double Action, Swing-Out Cylinder, Adjustable Sights, Extra Cylinder, *Modern*	475.00	650.00
☐ **Model 56**, .38 Special, Double Action, Swing-Out Cylinder, 2" Barrel, Adjustable Sights, *Modern*	575.00	850.00
☐ **Model 57**, .41 Magnum, Double Action, Swing-Out Cylinder, Various Barrel Lengths, Blue, Adjustable Sights, *Modern*	225.00	310.00
☐ **Model 57**, .41 Magnum, Double Action, Swing-Out Cylinder, Various Barrel Lengths, Nickel Plated, Adjustable Sights, *Modern*	225.00	310.00
☐ **Model 57**, .41 Magnum, Double Action, Swing-Out Cylinder, 8⅜" Barrel, Blue, Adjustable Sights, *Modern*	230.00	320.00
☐ **Model 57**, .41 Magnum, Double Action, Swing-Out Cylinder, 8⅜" Barrel, Nickel Plated, Adjustable Sights, *Modern*	230.00	320.00
☐ **Model 57**, .41 Magnum, Double Action, Swing-Out Cylinder, Various Barrel Lengths, Blue, Cased with Accessories, *Modern*	250.00	340.00
☐ **Model 57**, .41 Magnum, Double Action, Swing-Out Cylinder, Various Barrel Lengths, Nickel Plated, Cased with Accessories, *Modern*	260.00	350.00
☐ **Model 57**, .41 Magnum, Double Action, Swing-Out Cylinder, 8⅜" Barrel, Blue, Cased with Accessories, *Modern*	260.00	350.00
☐ **Model 57**, .41 Magnum, Double Action, Swing-Out Cylinder, 8⅜" Barrel, Blue, Cased with Accessories, *Modern*	260.00	350.00
☐ **Model 58**, .41 Magnum, Double Action, Swing-Out Cylinder, 4" Barrel, Blue, *Modern*	220.00	300.00
☐ **Model 58**, .41 Magnum, Double Action, Swing-Out Cylinder, 4" Barrel, Nickel Plated, *Modern*	230.00	320.00
☐ **Model 60**, .38 Special, Double Action, Swing-Out Cylinder, Stainless Steel, Adjustable Sights, *Modern*	650.00	900.00
☐ **Model 60**, .38 Special, Double Action, Swing-Out Cylinder, Stainless Steel, 2" Barrel, *Modern*	185.00	250.00
☐ **Model 60**, .38 Special, Double Action, Swing-Out Cylinder, Early High Polish Stainless Steel, 2" Barrel, *Modern*	235.00	350.00
☐ **Model 63**, .22 L.R.R.F., Double Action, Swing-Out Cylinder, Stainless Steel, 4" Barrel, Adjustable Sights, *Modern*	175.00	225.00
☐ **Model 64**, .38 Special, Double Action, Swing-Out Cylinder, Stainless Steel, Various Barrel Lengths, *Modern*	140.00	190.00
☐ **Model 65**, .357 Magnum, Double Action, Swing-Out Cylinder, Stainless Steel, 4" Barrel, Heavy Barrel, *Modern*	165.00	215.00
☐ **Model 66**, .357 Magnum, Double Action, Swing-Out Cylinder, Stainless Steel, 2½" Barrel, *Modern*	195.00	260.00
☐ **Model 66**, .357 Magnum, Double Action, Swing-Out Cylinder, Stainless Steel, Various Barrel Lengths, *Modern*	175.00	240.00
☐ **Model 67**, .38 Special, Double Action, Swing-Out Cylinder, Stainless Steel, 4" Barrel, *Modern*	165.00	225.00
☐ **Model 547**, 9mm Luger, Double Action, Swing-Out Cylinder, Blue, *Modern*	165.00	220.00
☐ **Model 581**, .357 Magnum, Double Action, Swing-Out Cylinder, Blue, *Modern*	165.00	220.00
☐ **Model 586**, .357 Magnum, Double Action, Swing-Out Cylinder, Blue, Adjustable Sights, *Modern*	190.00	250.00
☐ **Model 629**, .44 Magnum, Double Action, Swing-Out Cylinder, Stainless Steel, Adjustable Sights, *Modern*	330.00	450.00

414 / SMITH AND WESSON

	V.G.	EXC.
☐ **Model 681**, .357 Magnum, Double Action, Swing-Out Cylinder, Stainless Steel, *Modern*	175.00	220.00
☐ **Model 686**, .357 Magnum, Double Action, Swing-Out Cylinder, Stainless Steel, Adjustable Sights, *Modern*	185.00	250.00
☐ **Model M Hand Ejector**, .22 Long R.F., 1st Model Ladysmith, Solid Frame, Swing-Out Cylinder, Double Action, *Curio*	525.00	775.00
☐ **Model M Hand Ejector**, .22 Long R.F., 2nd Model Ladysmith, Solid Frame, Swing-Out Cylinder, Double Action, *Curio*	450.00	650.00
☐ **Model M Hand Ejector**, .22 Long R.F., 3rd Model Ladysmith, Solid Frame, Swing-Out Cylinder, Double Action, *Curio*	400.00	600.00
☐ **Model M Hand Ejector**, .22 Long R.F., 3rd. Model Ladysmith, Solid Frame, Swing-Out Cylinder, Double Action, Adjustable Sights, *Curio*	650.00	875.00
☐ **Second Model Schofield**, .45 S & W, Knurled Latch, Top Break, Single Action, Military, *Antique*	850.00	1,250.00
☐ **Second Model Schofield**, .45 S & W, Knurled Latch, Top Break, Single Action, Commercial, *Antique*	975.00	1,650.00
☐ **Second Model Schofield**, .45 S & W, Wells Fargo, Knurled Latch, Top Break, Single Action, *Antique*	850.00	1,200.00
☐ **Victory**, .38 Special, Military & Police, Solid Frame, Swing-Out Cylinder, Double Action, Military, *Modern*	95.00	150.00

HANDGUN, SEMI-AUTOMATIC

	V.G.	EXC.
☐ **.32 ACP**, Blue, *Curio*	650.00	1,150.00
☐ **.32 ACP**, Nickel Plated, *Curio*	800.00	1,350.00
☐ **.35 S & W Automatic**, Blue, *Curio*	450.00	525.00
☐ **.35 S & W Automatic**, Nickel Plated, *Curio*	475.00	625.00
☐ **Model 39**, 9mm Luger, Double Action, Steel Frame, *Curio*	850.00	1,400.00
☐ **Model 39**, 9mm Luger, Double Action, Blue, *Modern*	190.00	250.00
☐ **Model 39**, 9mm Luger, Double Action, Nickel Plated, *Modern*	200.00	280.00
☐ **Model 39-1**, .38 AMU, Double Action, *Curio*	850.00	1,300.00
☐ **Model 41**, .22 L.R.R.F., Various Barrel Lengths, *Modern*	195.00	275.00
☐ **Model 41-1**, .22 Short R.F., Various Barrel Lengths, *Modern*	265.00	350.00
☐ **Model 44**, 9mm Luger, Single Action, *Modern*	1,200.00	1,950.00
☐ **Model 46**, .22 L.R.R.F., Various Barrel Lengths, *Modern*	240.00	325.00
☐ **Model 52**, .38 Special, Blue, *Modern*	320.00	425.00
☐ **Model 59**, 9mm Luger, Double Action, Blue, *Modern*	200.00	280.00
☐ **Model 59**, 9mm Luger, Double Action, Nickel Plated, *Modern*	245.00	325.00
☐ **Model 61-1**, .22 L.R.R.F., Clip Fed, Nickel Plated, *Modern*	170.00	250.00
☐ **Model 61-1**, .22 L.R.R.F., Clip Fed, Blue, *Modern*	155.00	220.00
☐ **Model 61-2**, .22 L.R.R.F., Clip Fed, Nickel Plated, *Modern*	150.00	215.00
☐ **Model 61-2**, .22 L.R.R.F., Clip Fed, Blue, *Modern*	150.00	200.00
☐ **Model 61-3**, .22 L.R.R.F., Clip Fed, Nickel Plated, *Modern*	150.00	210.00
☐ **Model 61-3**, .22 L.R.R.F., Clip Fed, Blue, *Modern*	145.00	195.00
☐ **Model 439**, 9mm Luger, Double Action, Blue, *Modern*	220.00	300.00
☐ **Model 439**, 9mm Luger, Double Action, Nickel Plated, *Modern*	240.00	320.00
☐ **Model 459**, 9mm Luger, Double Action, Blue, *Modern*	250.00	350.00
☐ **Model 459**, 9mm Luger, Double Action, Nickel Plated, *Modern*	290.00	375.00
☐ **Model 539**, 9mm Luger, Double Action, Blue, *Modern*	220.00	300.00
☐ **Model 539**, 9mm Luger, Double Action, Nickel Plated, *Modern*	240.00	320.00
☐ **Model 559**, 9mm Luger, Double Action, Blue, *Modern*	250.00	350.00
☐ **Model 559**, 9mm Luger, Double Action, Nickel Plated, *Modern*	290.00	375.00

HANDGUN, SINGLESHOT

	V.G.	EXC.
☐ **Model 1891**, .22 L.R.R.F., Target Pistol, Single Action, 1st Model, Various Barrel Lengths, *Antique*	225.00	365.00
☐ **Model 1891**, .22 L.R.R.F., Target Pistol, Single Action, 2nd Model, no Hand or Cylinder Stop, *Modern*	200.00	325.00

SMITH AND WESSON / 415

S & W Model 586

S & W Model 66

S & W Model 547

S & W Model 586 Stainless

S & W Model 41

S & W Model #1

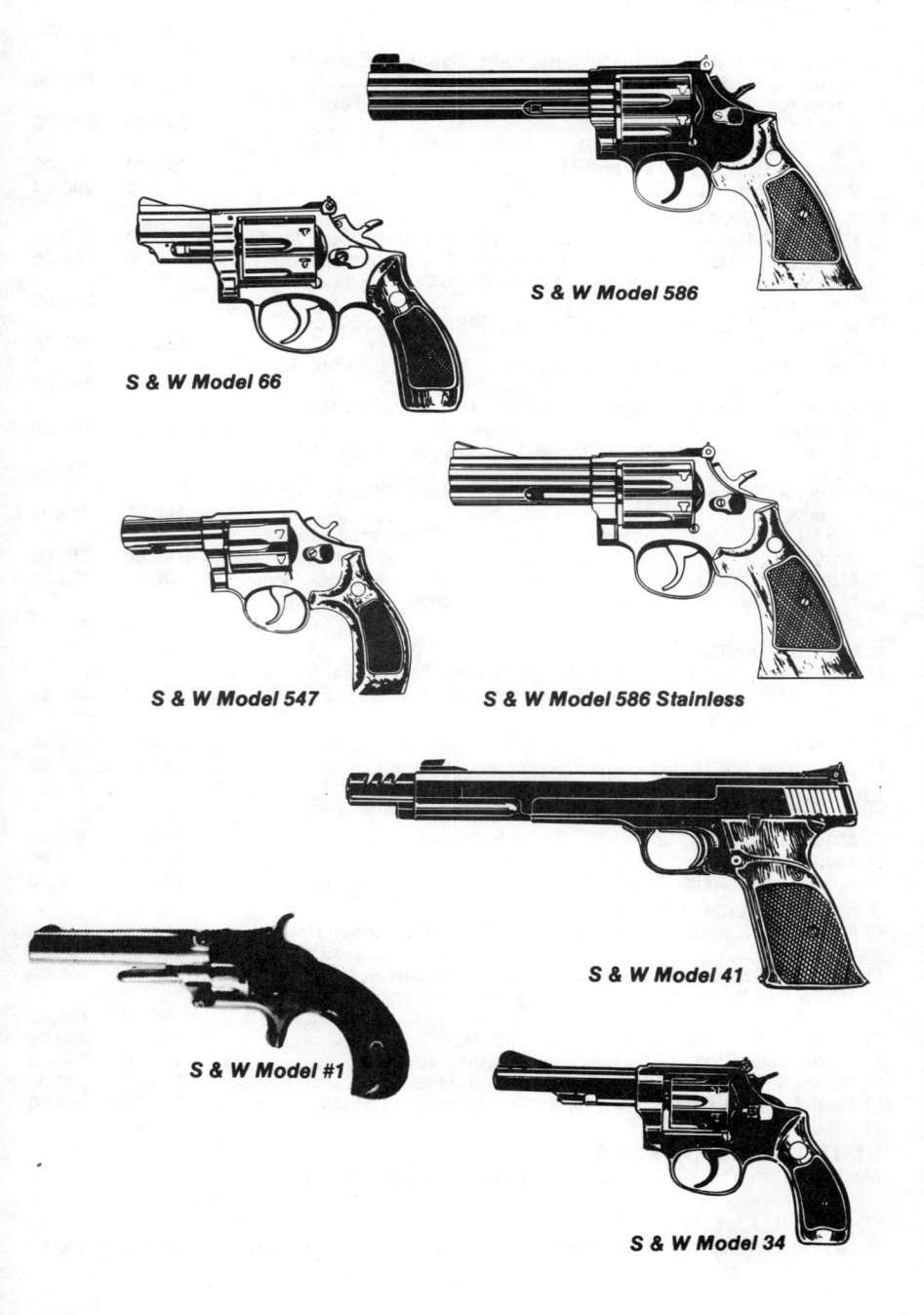

S & W Model 34

416 / SMITH, ANTHONY

	V.G.	EXC.
☐ **Model 1891 Set**, Various Calibers, Extra Cylinder, Extra Barrel, Target Pistol, Single Action, 1st Model, *Antique*	550.00	750.00
☐ **Perfected**, .22 L.R.R.F., Double Action, Top Break, Target Pistol, *Modern*	250.00	350.00
☐ **Perfected Olympic**, .22 L.R.R.F., Double Action, Top Break, Tight Bore and Chamber, Target Pistol, *Modern*	450.00	625.00
☐ **Straight Line**, .22 L.R.R.F., Cased, *Curio*	600.00	1,000.00

RIFLE, BOLT ACTION

☐ **Model 125 Deluxe**, Various Calibers, Monte Carlo Stock, *Modern*	145.00	190.00
☐ **Model 125 STD**, Various Calibers, Monte Carlo Stock, *Modern*	130.00	165.00
☐ **Model 1500**, Various Calibers, Monte Carlo Stock, Checkered Stock, *Modern*	175.00	250.00
☐ **Model 1500 Deluxe**, Various Calibers, Monte Carlo Stock, Checkered Stock, *Modern*	200.00	285.00
☐ **Model 1500 Magnum**, Various Calibers, Monte Carlo Stock, Checkered Stock, *Modern*	180.00	275.00
☐ **Model 1500 Varmint**, Various Calibers, Monte Carlo Stock, Checkered Stock, Heavy Barrel, *Modern*	220.00	300.00
☐ **Model A**, Various Calibers, Monte Carlo Stock, Checkered Stock, *Modern*	200.00	300.00
☐ **Model B**, Various Calibers, Monte Carlo Stock, Checkered Stock, *Modern*	180.00	275.00
☐ **Model C**, Various Calibers, Sporting Rifle, Checkered Stock, *Modern*	180.00	275.00
☐ **Model D**, Various Calibers, Mannicher, Checkered Stock, *Modern*	200.00	300.00
☐ **Model E**, Various Calibers, Monte Carlo Stock, Mannlicher, *Modern*	210.00	320.00

RIFLE, REVOLVER

☐ **Model 320**, .320 S & W Rifle, Single Action, Top Break, 6 Shot, Adjustable Sights, Cased with Accessories, *Antique*	2,250.00	3,500.00

RIFLE, SEMI-AUTOMATIC

☐ **Light Rifle**, MK I, 9mm Luger, Clip Fed, Carbine, *Curio*	1,300.00	1,950.00
☐ **Light Rifle MK II**, 9mm Luger, Clip Fed, Carbine, *Curio*	1,900.00	2,600.00

SHOTGUN, SEMI-AUTOMATIC

☐ **Model 1000 Field**, 12 Ga., Vent Rib, *Modern*	220.00	325.00
☐ **Model 1000 Field**, 12 Ga. 3", Vent Rib, *Modern*	230.00	350.00
☐ **Model 1000 Slug**, 12 Ga., Open Sights, *Modern*	225.00	350.00
☐ **Model 1000 Skeet**, 12 Ga., Vent Rib, *Modern*	250.00	375.00

SHOTGUN, SLIDE ACTION

☐ **Model 916 Eastfield**, Various Gauges, Vent Rib, Recoil Pad, *Modern*	90.00	135.00
☐ **Model 916 Eastfield**, Various Gauges, Plain Barrel, *Modern*	95.00	145.00
☐ **Model 916 Eastfield**, Various Gauges, Plain Barrel, Recoil Pad, *Modern*	90.00	130.00
☐ **Model 3000 Field**, 12 Ga. 3", Vent Rib, *Modern*	150.00	250.00
☐ **Model 3000 Slug**, 12 Ga. 3", Open Sights, *Modern*	150.00	250.00
☐ **Model 3000 Police**, 12 Ga., Open Sights, *Modern*	140.00	230.00
☐ **Model 3000 Police**, 12 Ga., Open Sights, Folding Stock, *Modern*	175.00	270.00

SMITH, ANTHONY
Northampton, Pa., 1770-1779. See Kentucky Rifles and Pistols.

SMITH, L.C. GUN CO.
Syracuse, N.Y., 1877-1890, in 1890 became Hunter Arms, and in 1948 became a division of Marlin.

L.C. Smith Field Grade

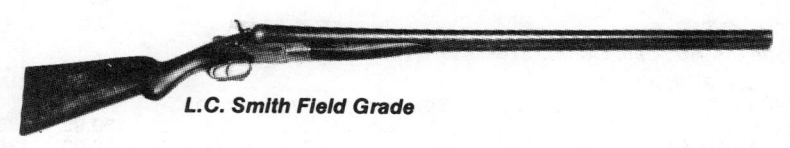

	V.G.	EXC.

SHOTGUN, DOUBLE BARREL, SIDE-BY-SIDE
- ☐ **Crown Grade**, Various Calibers, Sidelock, Single Selective Trigger, Automatic Ejector, Fancy Engraving, Fancy Checkering, *Modern*... **2,700.00 3,750.00**
- ☐ **Crown Grade**, Various Calibers, Sidelock, Double Trigger, Automatic Ejector, Fancy Engraving, Fancy Checkering, *Modern*... **2,450.00 3,400.00**
- ☐ **Field Grade**, Various Calibers, Sidelock, Double Trigger, Checkered Stock, Light Engraving, *Modern*... **500.00 725.00**
- ☐ **Field Grade**, Various Calibers, Sidelock, Double Trigger, Automatic Ejector, Checkered Stock, Light Engraving, *Modern*... **450.00 675.00**
- ☐ **Field Grade**, Various Calibers, Sidelock, Single Trigger, Checkered Stock, Light Engraving, *Modern*... **475.00 700.00**
- ☐ **Field Grade**, Various Calibers, Sidelock, Single Trigger, Automatic Ejector, Checkered Stock, Light Engraving, *Modern*... **475.00 675.00**
- ☐ **Ideal Grade**, Various Calibers, Sidelock, Double Trigger, Checkered Stock, Engraved, *Modern*... **475.00 675.00**
- ☐ **Ideal Grade**, Various Calibers, Sidelock, Double Trigger, Automatic Ejector, Checkered Stock, Engraved, *Modern*... **500.00 825.00**
- ☐ **Ideal Grade**, Various Calibers, Sidelock, Single Selective Trigger, Checkered Stock, Engraved, *Modern*... **700.00 1,150.00**
- ☐ **Ideal Grade**, Various Calibers, Sidelock, Single Selective Trigger, Automatic Ejector, Engraved, Checkered Stock, *Modern*... **775.00 1,200.00**
- ☐ **Marlin Deluxe**, 12 Ga., Double Trigger, Checkered Stock, Vent Rib, *Modern*... **400.00 525.00**
- ☐ **Marlin Field**, 12 Ga., Double Trigger, Checkered Stock, *Modern*... **275.00 425.00**
- ☐ **Monogram Grade**, Various Calibers, Sidelock, Single Selective Trigger, Automatic Ejector, Fancy Engraving, Fancy Checkering, *Modern*... **4,250.00 6,500.00**
- ☐ **Olympic Grade**, Various Calibers, Sidelock, Single Selective Trigger, Automatic Ejector, Engraved, Checkered Stock, *Modern*... **700.00 950.00**
- ☐ **Premier Grade**, Various Calibers, Sidelock, Single Selective Trigger, Automatic Ejector, Fancy Engraving, Fancy Checkering, *Modern*... **7,500.00 11,500.00**
- ☐ **Skeet Grade**, Various Calibers, Sidelock, Single Selective Trigger, Automatic Ejector, Engraved, Checkered Stock, *Modern*... **750.00 1,150.00**
- ☐ **Skeet Grade**, Various Calibers, Sidelock, Single Trigger, Automatic Ejector, Engraved, Checkered Stock, *Modern*... **675.00 975.00**
- ☐ **Specialty Grade**, Various Calibers, Sidelock, Double Trigger, Engraved, Checkered Stock, *Modern*... **775.00 1,200.00**
- ☐ **Specialty Grade**, Various Calibers, Sidelock, Single Selective Trigger, Automatic Ejector, Engraved, Checkered Stock, *Modern*... **850.00 1,225.00**
- ☐ **Trap Grade**, 12 Ga., Sidelock, Single Selective Trigger, Automatic Ejector, Engraved, Checkered Stock, *Modern*... **775.00 1,150.00**

SHOTGUN, SINGLESHOT
- ☐ **Crown Grade**, 12 Ga., Trap Grade, Vent Rib, Automatic Ejector, Fancy Engraving, Fancy Checkering, *Modern*... **2,000.00 2,750.00**
- ☐ **Olympic Grade**, 12 Ga., Trap Grade, Vent Rib, Automatic Ejector, Engraved, Fancy Checkering, *Modern*... **775.00 1,200.00**
- ☐ **Specialty Grade**, 12 Ga., Trap Grade, Vent Rib, Automatic Ejector, Engraved, Fancy Checkering, *Modern*... **1,200.00 1,650.00**

SMITH, OTIS A.
Middlefield & Rockfall, Conn. 1873-1890.

HANDGUN, REVOLVER

	V.G.	EXC.
☐ **.22 Short R.F.**, 7 Shot, Spur Trigger, Solid Frame, Single Action, *Antique*	90.00	160.00
☐ **.32 S & W**, 5 Shot, Single Action, Top Break, Spur Trigger, *Antique*	80.00	135.00
☐ **.32 Short R.F.**, 5 Shot, Spur Trigger, Solid Frame, Single Action, *Antique*	90.00	160.00
☐ **.38 Short R.F.**, 5 Shot, Spur Trigger, Solid Frame, Single Action, *Antique*	95.00	170.00
☐ **.41 Short R.F.**, 5 Shot, Spur Trigger, Solid Frame, Single Action, *Antique*	120.00	195.00

SMITH, STOEFFEL
Pa. 1790-1800. See Kentucky Rifles and Pistols.

SMITH, THOMAS
London, England, c. 1850.

RIFLE, PERCUSSION
☐ **16 Ga.**, Smoothbore, Anson-Deeley Lock, Octagon Barrel, Fancy Wood, Cased with Accessories, *Antique* 2,000.00 2,950.00

SMITH, WM.
England

HANDGUN, SEMI-AUTOMATIC
☐ **Pocket**, .25 ACP, Clip Fed, 1906 Browning Type, *Modern* 325.00 425.00

SMOKER
Made by Johnson Bye & Co. 1875-1884.

HANDGUN, REVOLVER
☐ **#1**, .22 Short R.F., 7 Shot, Spur Trigger, Solid Frame, Single Action, *Antique* 90.00 160.00
☐ **#2**, .32 Short R.F., 5 Shot, Spur Trigger, Solid Frame, Single Action, *Antique* 95.00 170.00
☐ **#3**, .38 Short R.F., 5 Shot, Spur Trigger, Solid Frame, Single Action, *Antique* 95.00 170.00
☐ **#4**, .41 Short R.F., 5 Shot, Spur Trigger, Solid Frame, Single Action, *Antique* 120.00 195.00

SNAPHAUNCE, UNKNOWN MAKER

HANDGUN, SNAPHAUNCE
☐ **.45 Italian Early 1700's**, Holster Pistol, Half-Octagon Barrel, Engraved, Carved, High Quality, Steel Furiture, *Antique* 2,000.00 2,500.00
☐ **Early 1800's Small**, Plain, *Antique* 600.00 1,000.00
☐ **English Late 1500's**, Ovoid Pommel, Engraved, Gold Damascened, High Quality, *Antique* 9,750.00 20,000.00
☐ **Italian Early 1700's**, Medium Quality, Brass Furniture, Plain, *Antique* 750.00 1,000.00
☐ **Italian 1700's**, High Quality, Belt Pistol, Light Ornamentation, *Antique* 1,800.00 2,800.00

RIFLE, SNAPHAUNCE
☐ **Arabian**, .59, Ornate, Inlaid with Silver, Ivory buttstock Inlays, *Antique* 400.00 600.00
☐ **Italian Mid-1600's**, Half-Octagon Barrel, Carved, Engraved, Silver Inlay, Steel Furniture, Ornate, *Antique* 6,000.00 10,000.00

SODIA, FRANZ
Ferlach, Austria

                          V.G.   EXC.

COMBINATION WEAPON, MULTI-BARREL
- **Bochdrilling**, Various Calibers, Fancy Wood, Fancy Checkering, Fancy Engraving, *Antique* 2,300.00 3,750.00
- **Doppelbuchse**, Various Calibers, Fancy Wood, Fancy Checkering, Fancy Engraving, *Antique* 1,700.00 2,750.00
- **Over-Under Rifle**, Various Calibers, Fancy Wood, Fancy Checkering, Fancy Engraving, *Antique* 1,600.00 2,400.00

SOLER
Ripoll, Spain, c. 1625.

HANDGUN, WHEEL-LOCK
- **Enclosed Mid-1600's**, Ball Pommel, Ornate, *Antique* 7,000.00 12,500.00

SOUTHERN ARMS CO.
Made by Crescent for H. & D. Folsom, N.Y.C.

SHOTGUN, DOUBLE BARREL, SIDE-BY-SIDE
- **Various Gauges**, Outside Hammers, Damascus Barrel, *Modern* 100.00 175.00
- **Various Gauges**, Hammerless, Steel Barrel, *Modern* 135.00 200.00
- **Various Gauges**, Hammerless, Damascus Barrel, *Modern* 100.00 175.00
- **Various Gauges**, Outside Hammers, Steel Barrel, *Modern* 125.00 190.00

SHOTGUN, SINGLESHOT
- **Various Gauges**, Hammer, Steel Barrel, *Modern* 55.00 85.00

SPAARMAN, ANDREAS
Berlin, Germany, c. 1680.

RIFLE, FLINTLOCK
- **.72**, Jaeger, Octagon Barrel, Swamped, Rifled, Iron Mounts, Ornate, Set Trigger, *Antique* 3,000.00 3,950.00

Spanish Military Model 400 M1913-16

Spanish Military Model 400

SPANISH MILITARY
Also see Astra, Star.

	V.G.	EXC.
AUTOMATIC WEAPON, SUBMACHINE GUN		
☐ **Star Z-63**, 9mm Luger, Clip Fed, *Class 3*	500.00	750.00
HANDGUN, SEMI-AUTOMATIC		
☐ **Jo-Lo-Ar**, 9mm Bergmann, Clip Fed, Military, Hammer, *Curio*	155.00	235.00
☐ **M1913-16 Campo-Giro**, 9mm Bergmann, Clip Fed, Military, *Curio*	165.00	250.00
RIFLE, BOLT ACTION		
☐ **Destroyer**, 9mm Bayard Long, Clip Fed, Carbine, *Modern*	80.00	140.00
☐ **M98 La Caruna**, 8mm Mauser, Military, *Curio*	80.00	125.00
RIFLE, SEMI-AUTOMATIC		
☐ **CETME Sport**, .308 Win., Clip Fed, *Modern*	295.00	425.00

Spencer Roper

SPENCER ARMS CO.
Windsor, Conn. 1886-1888.

	V.G.	EXC.
SHOTGUN, SLIDE ACTION		
☐ **Spencer-Roper**, 12 Ga., Tube Feed, *Antique*	245.00	375.00

SPENCER GUN CO.
Made by Crescent for Hibbard & Spencer Bartlett, c. 1900.

	V.G.	EXC.
SHOTGUN, DOUBLE BARREL, SIDE-BY-SIDE		
☐ **Various Gauges**, Outside Hammers, Damascus Barrel, *Modern*	100.00	175.00
☐ **Various Gauges**, Hammerless, Steel Barrel, *Modern*	135.00	200.00
☐ **Various Gauges**, Hammerless, Damascus Barrel, *Modern*	100.00	175.00
☐ **Various Gauges**, Outside Hammers, Steel Barrel, *Modern*	125.00	190.00
SHOTGUN, SINGLESHOT		
☐ **Various Gauges**, Hammer, Steel Barrel, *Modern*	55.00	85.00

SPENCER SAFETY HAMMERLESS
Made by Columbia Armory, Tenn., c. 1892.

	V.G.	EXC.
HANDGUN, REVOLVER		
☐ **.38 S & W**, 5 Shot, Top Break, Hammerless, Double Action, *Antique*	55.00	95.00

SPITFIRE
Arizona.

	V.G.	EXC.
AUTOMATIC WEAPON, SUBMACHINE GUN		
☐ **Spitfire**, .45 ACP, Clip Fed, Wood Stock, *Class 3*	150.00	215.00

SPORTSMAN
Made by Steven Arms.

	V.G.	EXC.
SHOTGUN, DOUBLE BARREL, SIDE-BY-SIDE		
☐ **M 315**, Various Gauges, Hammerless, Steel Barrel, *Antique*	95.00	165.00
SHOTGUN, SINGLESHOT		
☐ **Model 90**, Various Gauges, Takedown, Automatic Ejector, Plain, Hammer, *Antique*	35.00	55.00

SPORTSMAN
Made by Crescent for W. Bingham Co. Cleveland, Ohio, c. 1900.

	V.G.	EXC.

SHOTGUN, DOUBLE BARREL, SIDE-BY-SIDE
- ☐ **Various Gauges**, Outside Hammers, Damascus Barrel, *Modern* 100.00 175.00
- ☐ **Various Gauges**, Hammerless, Steel Barrel, *Modern* 135.00 200.00
- ☐ **Various Gauges**, Hammerless, Damascus Barrel, *Modern* 100.00 175.00
- ☐ **Various Gauges**, Outside Hammers, Steel Barrel, *Modern* 125.00 190.00

SHOTGUN, SINGLESHOT
- ☐ **Various Gauges**, Hammer, Steel Barrel, *Modern* 55.00 85.00

SPRINGFIELD ARMORY
Geneseo, Ill.

AUTOMATIC WEAPON, ASSAULT RIFLE
- ☐ **M1A**, .308 Win., Clip Fed, Silencer, *Class 3* 750.00 1,000.00
- ☐ **M1A (M-14)**, .308 Win., Clip Fed, Commercial, *Class 3* 525.00 650.00

RIFLE, SEMI-AUTOMATIC
- ☐ **M1A Super Match**, .308 Win., Clip Fed, Version of M-14, Heavy Barrel, *Modern* 475.00 675.00
- ☐ **M1A Match**, .308 Win., Clip Fed, Version of M-14, *Modern* 400.00 600.00
- ☐ **M1A Standard**, .308 Win., Clip Fed, Version of M-14, *Modern* 375.00 525.00
- ☐ **M1A Standard**, .308 Win., Clip Fed, Version of M-14, Folding Stock, *Modern* 425.00 575.00

SPRINGFIELD ARMS
Made by Crescent, c. 1900.

SHOTGUN, DOUBLE BARREL, SIDE-BY-SIDE
- ☐ **Various Gauges**, Outside Hammers, Damascus Barrel, *Modern* 100.00 175.00
- ☐ **Various Gauges**, Hammerless, Steel Barrel, *Modern* 135.00 200.00
- ☐ **Various Gauges**, Hammerless, Damascus Barrel, *Modern* 100.00 175.00
- ☐ **Various Gauges**, Outside Hammers, Steel Barrel, *Modern* 125.00 190.00

SHOTGUN, SINGLESHOT
- ☐ **Various Gauges**, Hammer, Steel Barrel, *Modern* 55.00 85.00

SPY
Made by Norwich Falls Pistol Co., c. 1880.

HANDGUN, REVOLVER
- ☐ **.22 Short R.F.**, 7 Shot, Spur Trigger, Solid Frame, Single Action, Antique 90.00 160.00

SQUARE DEAL
Made by Crescent for Stratton-Warren Hdw. Co., Memphis, Tenn.

SHOTGUN, DOUBLE BARREL, SIDE-BY-SIDE
- ☐ **Various Gauges**, Outside Hammers, Damascus Barrel, *Modern* 100.00 175.00
- ☐ **Various Gauges**, Hammerless, Steel Barrel, *Modern* 135.00 200.00
- ☐ **Various Gauges**, Hammerless, Damascus Barrel, *Modern* 100.00 175.00
- ☐ **Various Gauges**, Outside Hammers, Steel Barrel, *Modern* 125.00 190.00

SHOTGUN, SINGLESHOT
- ☐ **Various Gauges**, Hammer, Steel Barrel, *Modern* 55.00 85.00

SQUIBMAN
Made by Squires, Bingham, Makati, Phillipines.

422 / SQUIRES BINGHAM

	V.G.	EXC.
HANDGUN, REVOLVER		
☐ **Model 100 D**, .38 Spec., Double Action, Blue, Swing-Out Cylinder, Vent Rib, *Modern*	100.00	140.00
☐ **Model 100 DC**, .38 Spec., Double Action, Blue, Swing-Out Cylinder, *Modern*	80.00	125.00
☐ **Thunder Chief**, .38 Spec., Double Action, Blue, Swing-Out Cylinder, Vent Rib, Heavy Barrel, *Modern*	120.00	160.00
RIFLE, SEMI-AUTOMATIC		
☐ **Auto**, .22 L.R.R.F., Clip Fed, Shell Deflector, Flash Hider, *Modern*	35.00	55.00

SQUIRES BINGHAM
Makati, Phillipines.

	V.G.	EXC.
HANDGUN, REVOLVER		
☐ **M 100-D**, .22LR/.22 WMR Combo, Double Action, Solid Frame, Swing-Out Cylinder, Adjustable Sights, *Modern*	60.00	85.00
RIFLE, BOLT ACTION		
☐ **M 14D**, .22 L.R.R.F., Clip Fed, Checkered Stock, *Modern*	35.00	55.00
☐ **M 15**, .22 WMR, Clip Fed, Checkered Stock, *Modern*	55.00	75.00
RIFLE, SEMI-AUTOMATIC		
☐ **M-16**, .22 L.R.R.F., Clip Fed, Flash Hider, *Modern*	45.00	65.00
☐ **M20D**, .22 L.R.R.F., Clip Fed, Checkered Stock, *Modern*	45.00	65.00
SHOTGUN, SLIDE ACTION		
☐ **M 30/28**, 12 Ga., Plain, *Modern*	70.00	115.00

STAGGS-BILT
Staggs Enterprises, Phoenix, Ariz., c. 1970.

	V.G.	EXC.
COMBINATION WEAPON, OVER-UNDER		
☐ **20 Ga./.30-30**, Top Break, Hammerless, Double Triggers, Top Break, *Modern*	75.00	110.00

STANDARD ARMS CO.
Wilmington, Del., 1909-1911.

	V.G.	EXC.
RIFLE, SEMI-AUTOMATIC		
☐ **Model G**, Various Calibers, Takedown, Tube Feed, Hammerless, *Curio*	225.00	345.00
RIFLE, SLIDE ACTION		
☐ **Model M**, Various Calibers, Takedown, Tube Feed, Hammerless, *Curio*	185.00	265.00

STANLEY
Belgium, c. 1900.

	V.G.	EXC.
SHOTGUN, DOUBLE BARREL, SIDE-BY-SIDE		
☐ **Various Gauges**, Outside Hammers, Damascus Barrel, *Modern*	100.00	175.00
☐ **Various Gauges**, Hammerless, Steel Barrel, *Modern*	135.00	200.00
☐ **Various Gauges**, Hammerless, Damascus Barrel, *Modern*	100.00	175.00
☐ **Various Gauges**, Outside Hammers, Steel Barrel, *Modern*	125.00	190.00
SHOTGUN, SINGLESHOT		
☐ **Various Gauges**, Hammer, Steel Barrel, *Modern*	55.00	85.00

STAR / 423

STANTON
London, England, c. 1778.
HANDGUN, FLINTLOCK
	V.G.	EXC.
☐ **.55 Officers**, Belt Pistol, Screw Barrel, Box Lock, Brass, *Antique*	995.00	1,850.00

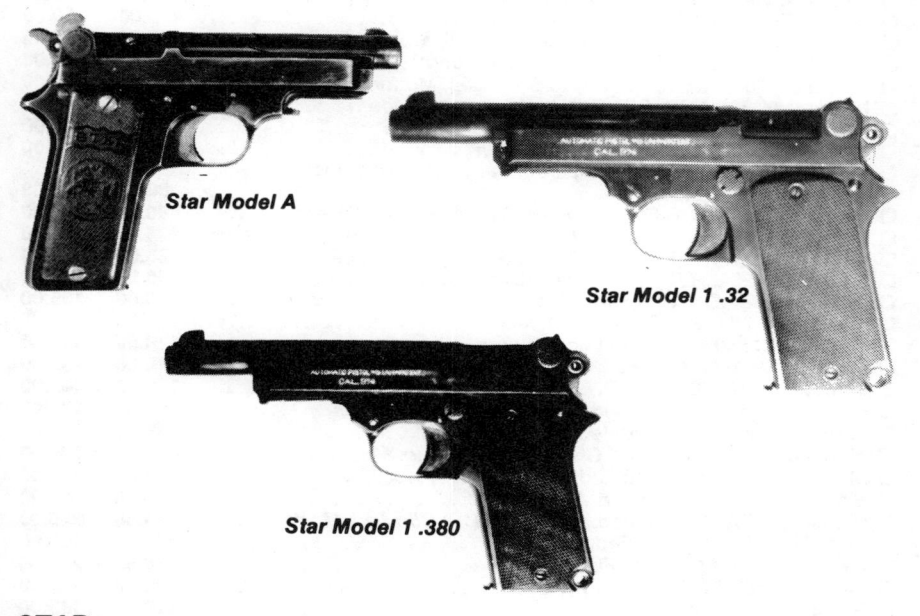

Star Model A

Star Model 1 .32

Star Model 1 .380

STAR
Made by Bonifacio Echeverria, Eibar, Spain 1911 to date.
AUTOMATIC WEAPON, MACHINE-PISTOL
	V.G.	EXC.
☐ **Model MD**, .45 ACP, Clip Fed, Holster Stock, *Class 3*	650.00	850.00
☐ **Model MD**, 7.63 Mauser, Clip Fed, Holster Stock, *Class 3*	550.00	750.00
☐ **Model MD**, 9mm Luger, Clip Fed, Holster Stock, *Class 3*	650.00	800.00

AUTOMATIC WEAPON, SUBMACHINE GUN
☐ **Model Z-45**, 9mm Luger, Clip Fed, Folding Stock, *Class 3*	400.00	525.00
☐ **Model Z-62**, 9mm Luger, Clip Fed, Folding Stock, *Class 3*	450.00	575.00
☐ **Model Z-63**, 9mm Luger, Clip Fed, Folding Stock, *Class 3*	525.00	675.00

HANDGUN, SEMI-AUTOMATIC
☐ **Model A**, .25 ACP, Clip Fed, *Modern*	140.00	190.00
☐ **Model A**, .38 ACP, Clip Fed, *Modern*	95.00	145.00
☐ **Model A**, .45 ACP, Clip Fed, Early Model, Adjustable Sights, Various Barrel Lengths, *Modern*	145.00	195.00
☐ **Model A**, 7.63 Mauser, Clip Fed, Early Model, Adjustable Sights, Various Barrel Lengths, Stock Lug, *Modern*	900.00	1,300.00
☐ **Model A**, 9mm Bergmann, Clip Fed, Early Model, Adjustable Sights, Various Barrel Lengths, *Modern*	125.00	165.00
☐ **Model A**, Various Calibers, Holster Stock, *Add $150.00-$250.00*		
☐ **Model AS**, .38 Super, Clip Fed, *Modern*	125.00	165.00
☐ **Model B**, 9mm Luger, Clip Fed, *Modern*	125.00	165.00
☐ **Model B**, 9mm Luger, Clip Fed, Early Model, Various Barrel Lengths, *Modern*	125.00	165.00

424 / STAR GAUGE

	V.G.	EXC.
☐ **Model BKM**, 9mm Luger, Clip Fed, Lightweight, *Modern*	150.00	200.00
☐ **Model BKS-Starlight**, 9mm Luger, Clip Fed, Lightweight, *Modern*	175.00	225.00
☐ **Model BM**, 9mm Luger, Clip Fed, Steel Frame, *Modern*	150.00	200.00
☐ **Model C**, 9mm Bayard Long, Clip Fed, 8 Shot, *Modern*	120.00	160.00
☐ **Model C O**, .25 ACP, Clip Fed, *Modern*	110.00	150.00
☐ **Model C U**, .25 ACP, Clip Fed, Lightweight, *Modern*	85.00	125.00
☐ **Model D**, .380 ACP, Clip Fed, 6 Shot, *Modern*	115.00	150.00
☐ **Model D**, .380 ACP, Clip Fed, 15 Shot Clip, *Modern*	130.00	170.00
☐ **Model DK**, .380 ACP, Clip Fed, Lightweight, *Modern*	110.00	145.00
☐ **Model E Vest Pocket**, .25 ACP, Clip Fed, *Modern*	110.00	140.00
☐ **Model F**, .22 L.R.R.F., Clip Fed, *Modern*	90.00	135.00
☐ **Model F R S**, .22 L.R.R.F., Clip Fed, Target Pistol, Adjustable Sights, *Modern*	80.00	130.00
☐ **Model F T B**, .22 L.R.R.F., Clip Fed, Target Pistol, *Modern*	80.00	115.00
☐ **Model F-Olympic**, .22 Short R.F., Clip Fed, Target Pistol, *Modern*	135.00	175.00
☐ **Model F-Sport**, .22 L.R.R.F., Clip Fed, 6" Barrel, *Modern*	80.00	120.00
☐ **Model FR**, .22 L.R.R.F., Clip Fed, *Modern*	95.00	135.00
☐ **Model H**, .32 ACP, Clip Fed, 7 Shot, *Modern*	100.00	135.00
☐ **Model HF**, .22 L.R.R.F., Clip Fed, *Modern*	135.00	180.00
☐ **Model HN**, .380 ACP, Clip Fed, *Modern*	110.00	145.00
☐ **Model I**, .32 ACP, Clip Fed, 9 Shot, *Modern*	110.00	135.00
☐ **Model Lancer**, .22 L.R.R.F., Clip Fed, Lightweight, *Modern*	100.00	145.00
☐ **Model M**, .38 ACP, Clip Fed, *Modern*	100.00	135.00
☐ **Model Militar**, 9mm, Clip Fed, *Modern*	135.00	170.00
☐ **Model MMS**, 7.63 Mauser, Clip Fed, Stock Lug, *Modern*	675.00	1,000.00
☐ **Model NZ**, .25 ACP, Clip Fed, *Modern*	325.00	425.00
☐ **Model 1**, .25 ACP, Clip Fed, *Modern*	185.00	250.00
☐ **Model 1**, .32 ACP, Clip Fed, *Mo, .380 ACP, Clip Fed, Modern*	185.00	250.00
☐ **Model P**, .45 ACP, Clip Fed, *Modern*	130.00	160.00
☐ **Model PD**, .45 ACP, Clip Fed, *Modern*	160.00	240.00
☐ **Model S**, .380 ACP, Clip Fed, *Modern*	95.00	135.00
☐ **Model S I**, *Modern*	110.00	145.00
☐ **Model Militar**, 9mm, Clip Fed, *Modern*	135.00	175.00
☐ **Model NZ**, .25 ACP, Clip Fed, *Modern*	325.00	425.00
☐ **Model 1**, .25 ACP, Clip Fed, *Modern*	180.00	240.00
☐ **Model 1**, .32 ACP, Clip Fed, *Mo .32 ACP, Clip Fed, Modern*	85.00	120.00
☐ **Model SM**, .380 ACP, Clip Fed, *Modern*	95.00	130.00
☐ **Model Starfire**, .380 ACP, Clip Fed, Lightweight, *Modern*	95.00	135.00
☐ **Model Starlet**, .25 ACP, Clip Fed, Lightweight, *Modern*	80.00	120.00
☐ **Model Super A**, .38 ACP, Clip Fed, *Modern*	120.00	165.00
☐ **Model Super B**, 9mm Luger, Clip Fed, *Modern*	115.00	160.00
☐ **Model Super M**, .38 Super, Clip Fed, *Modern*	115.00	160.00
☐ **Model Super P**, .45 ACP, Clip Fed, *Modern*	135.00	185.00
☐ **Model Super S**, .380 ACP, Clip Fed, *Modern*	110.00	145.00
☐ **Model Super S I**, .32 ACP, Clip Fed, *Modern*	90.00	135.00

RIFLE, SINGLESHOT
| ☐ **Rolling Block**, Various Calibers, Carbine, *Modern* | 110.00 | 150.00 |

STAR GAUGE
Spain, Imported by Interarms.

SHOTGUN, DOUBLE BARREL, SIDE-BY-SIDE
| ☐ **12 and 20 Gauges**, Checkered Stock, Adjustable Choke, Double Trigger, *Modern* | 150.00 | 225.00 |

STARR ARMS CO.
Yonkers and Binghamton, N.Y. 1860-1868

STERLING ARMS CORPORATION / 425

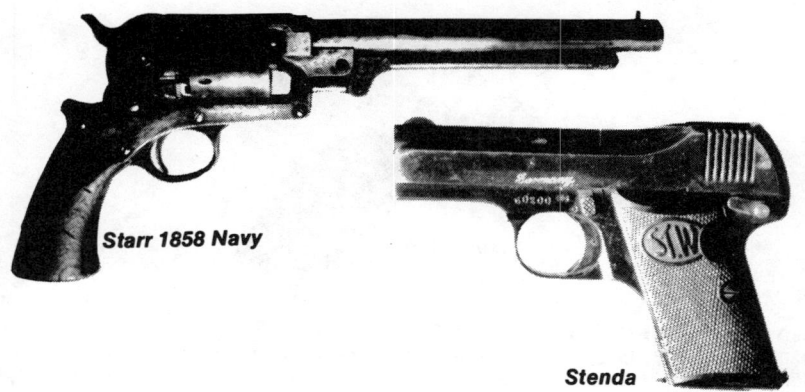

Starr 1858 Navy

Stenda

	V.G.	EXC.

HANDGUN, PERCUSSION
- **1858 Navy**, .36, Revolver, 6 Shot, 6" Barrel, Double Action, *Antique* 400.00 650.00
- **1858 Army**, .44, Revolver, 6 Shot, 6" Barrel, Double Action, *Antique* 300.00 485.00
- **1863 Army**, .44, Revolver, 6 Shot, 6" Barrel, Double Action, *Antique* 375.00 585.00

RIFLE, PERCUSSION
- **Carbine**, .54, Underlever, *Antique* 450.00 675.00

RIFLE, SINGLESHOT
- **Carbine**, .52 R.F., Underlever, *Antique* 500.00 800.00

STATE ARMS CO.
Made by Crescent for J.H. Lau & Co., c. 1900.

SHOTGUN, DOUBLE BARREL, SIDE-BY-SIDE
- **Various Gauges**, Outside Hammers, Damascus Barrel, *Modern* 100.00 175.00
- **Various Gauges**, Hammerless, Steel Barrel, *Modern* 135.00 200.00
- **Various Gauges**, Hammerless, Damascus Barrel, *Modern* 100.00 175.00
- **Various Gauges**, Outside Hammers, Steel Barrel, *Modern* 125.00 190.00

SHOTGUN, SINGLESHOT
- **Various Gauges**, Hammer, Steel Barrel, *Modern* 55.00 85.00

STEIGLEDER, ERNST
Suhl & Berlin, Germany 1921-1935.

RIFLE, DOUBLE BARREL, SIDE-BY-SIDE
- **Various Calibers**, Box Lock, Engraved, Checkered Stock, Color Case Hardened Frame, *Modern* 1,850.00 2,600.00

STENDA
Stenda Werke Waffenfabrik, Suhl, Germany, c. 1920.

HANDGUN, SEMI-AUTOMATIC
- **.32 ACP**, Blue, Clip Fed, *Modern* 135.00 195.00

STERLING ARMS CORP.
Gasport and Lockport, N.Y.

426 / STERLING ARMS CORPORATION

Sterling PPL

	V.G.	EXC.
HANDGUN, SEMI-AUTOMATIC		
☐ **#283 Target 300**, .22 L.R.R.F., Hammer, Adjustable Sights, Various Barrel Lengths, *Modern*	85.00	125.00
☐ **#284 Target 300 L**, .22 L.R.R.F., Hammer, Adjustable Sights, Tapered Barrel, *Modern*	85.00	125.00
☐ **#285 Huskey**, .22 L.R.R.F., Hammer, Heavy Barrel, *Modern*	75.00	115.00
☐ **#286 Trapper**, .22 L.R.R.F., Hammer, Tapered Barrel, *Modern*	75.00	115.00
☐ **Model 300B**, .25 ACP, Blue, *Modern*	55.00	80.00
☐ **Model 300N**, .25 ACP, Nickel Plated, *Modern*	60.00	85.00
☐ **Model 300S**, .25 ACP, Stainless Steel, *Modern*	60.00	95.00
☐ **Model 302B**, .22 L.R.R.F., Blue, *Modern*	55.00	80.00
☐ **Model 302N**, .22 L.R.R.F., Nickel Plated, *Modern*	60.00	85.00
☐ **Model 302S**, .22 L.R.R.F., Stainless Steel, *Modern*	65.00	95.00
☐ **Model 400B**, .380 ACP, Blue, Clip Fed, *Modern*	95.00	145.00
☐ **Model 400N**, .380 ACP, Nickel Plated, Clip Fed, *Modern*	100.00	150.00
☐ **Model 400S**, .380 ACP, Stainless Steel, Clip Fed, *Modern*	135.00	175.00
☐ **Model 402**, .22 L.R.R.F., Blue, Clip Fed, *Modern*	75.00	110.00
☐ **Model 402**, .22 L.R.R.F., Nickel Plated, Clip Fed, *Modern*	75.00	110.00
☐ **Model 402 MkII**, .32 ACP, Blue, Clip Fed, *Modern*	95.00	145.00
☐ **Model 402 MkIIS**, .32 ACP, Stainless Steel, Clip Fed, *Modern*	135.00	175.00
☐ **Model 450**, .45 ACP, Clip Fed, Double Action, Adjustable Sights, Blue, *Modern*	165.00	250.00
☐ **Model PPL**, .380 ACP, Short Barrel, Clip Fed, *Modern*	110.00	145.00
RIFLE, SINGLESHOT		
☐ **Backpacker**, .22 L.R.R.F., Takedown, *Modern*	25.00	35.00

STERLING ARMS CORP.
Made by Crescent for H. & D. Folsom, c. 1900.

	V.G.	EXC.
SHOTGUN, DOUBLE BARREL, SIDE-BY-SIDE		
☐ **Various Gauges**, Outside Hammers, Damascus Barrel, *Modern*	100.00	175.00
☐ **Various Gauges**, Hammerless, Steel Barrel, *Modern*	135.00	200.00
☐ **Various Gauges**, Hammerless, Damascus Barrel, *Modern*	100.00	175.00
☐ **Various Gauges**, Outside Hammers, Steel Barrel, *Modern*	125.00	190.00
SHOTGUN, SINGLESHOT		
☐ **Various Gauges**, Hammer, Steel Barrel, *Modern*	55.00	85.00

STERLING REVOLVERS
Maker unknown, c. 1880.

	V.G.	EXC.
HANDGUN, REVOLVER		
☐ **.22 Short R.F.**, 7 Shot, Spur Trigger, Solid Frame, Single Action, Antique	90.00	160.00
☐ **.32 Short R.F.**, 5 Shot, Spur Trigger, Solid Frame, Single Action, Antique	95.00	170.00

STEVENS, J. ARMS & TOOL CO.
Chicopee Falls, Mass. 1864-1886. Became J. Stevens Arms & Tools Co. in 1886, absorbed Page-Lewis Arms Co., Davis-Warner Arms Co., and Crescent Firearms Co. in 1926. Became a subsidiary of Savage in 1936.

	V.G.	EXC.

COMBINATION WEAPON, DOUBLE BARREL, OVER-UNDER
- ☐ **Model 22-410**, .22-.410 Ga., Hammer, Plastic Stock, *Modern* 55.00   80.00
- ☐ **Model 22-410**, .22-.410 Ga., Hammer, Wood Stock, *Modern* 65.00   95.00

HANDGUN, SINGLESHOT
- ☐ **1888 #1**, Various Calibers, Tip-Up, Octagon Barrel, Open Rear Sight, *Antique* 95.00   145.00
- ☐ **1888 #2 "Gallery"**, .22 L.R.R.F., Tip-Up, Octagon Barrel, Open Rear Sight, *Antique* 100.00   140.00
- ☐ **1888 #3 "Combined Sight"**, Various Calibers, Tip-Up, Octagon Barrel, *Antique* 115.00   155.00
- ☐ **1888 #4 "Combined Sight"**, .22 L.R.R.F., Tip-Up, Octagon Barrel, *Antique* 110.00   145.00
- ☐ **1888 #5 "Expert"**, Various Calibers, Tip-Up, Half Octagon Barrel, *Antique* 115.00   155.00
- ☐ **1894 "New Ideal"**, Various Calibers, Level Action, Falling Block, Vernier Sights, *Antique* 200.00   285.00
- ☐ **Model 23 "Sure-Shot"**, .22 L.R.R.F., Side-Swing Barrel, Hammer, *Antique* 75.00   110.00
- ☐ **Model 34 "Hunters Pet"**, Various Rimfires, Tip-Up, Octagon Barrel, with Shoulder Stock, *Curio* 280.00   375.00
- ☐ **Model 39 New Model Pocket Shotgun**, Various Calibers, Tip-Up, Smoothbore, with Shoulder Stock, *Class 3* 110.00   150.00
- ☐ **Model 40 New Model Pocket Rifle**, Various Calibers, Tip-Up, with Shoulder Stock, *Curio* 280.00   375.00
- ☐ **Model 42 Reliable Pocket Rifle**, .22 L.R.R.F., Tip-Up, with Shoulder Stock, *Curio* 175.00   250.00
- ☐ **Model "Offhand"**, .410 Ga., Tip-Up, *Class 3* 180.00   250.00
- ☐ **Model 10**, .22 L.R.R.F., Tip-Up, Target, Various Barrel Lengths, *Modern* 90.00   140.00
- ☐ **Model 34 "Hunters Pet"**, Various Rimfires, Tip-Up, Half-Octagon Barrel, with Shoulder Stock, Vernier Sights, *Curio* 325.00   400.00
- ☐ **Model 35 "Offhand"**, .22 L.R.R.F., Tip-Up, Target, Various Barrel Lengths, *Modern* 200.00   275.00
- ☐ **Model 35 "Offhand"**, .22 L.R.R.F., Tip-Up, Target, Ivory Grips, Various Barrel Lengths, *Modern* 230.00   325.00
- ☐ **Model 35 Autoshot**, .410 Ga., Tip-Up, Various Barrel Lengths, *Class 3* 175.00   235.00
- ☐ **Model 37 "Gould"**, Various Calibers, Tip-Up, *Modern* 195.00   265.00
- ☐ **Model 38 "Conlin"**, .22 L.R.R.F., Tip-Up, *Modern* 240.00   325.00
- ☐ **Model 41**, .22 L.R.R.F., Tip-Up, Pocket Pistol, *Modern* 110.00   145.00
- ☐ **Model 43 "Diamond"**, .22 L.R.R.F., Tip-Up, Spur Trigger, 6" Barrel, Octagon Barrel, *Modern* 120.00   165.00
- ☐ **Model 43 "Diamond"**, .22 L.R.R.F., Tip-Up, Spur Trigger, 10" Barrel, Octagon Barrel, *Modern* 135.00   180.00
- ☐ **Model 43 "Diamond"**, .22 L.R.R.F., Tip-Up, Spur Trigger, 6" Barrel, Globe Sights, *Modern* 140.00   185.00
- ☐ **Model 43 "Diamond"**, .22 L.R.R.F., Tip-Up, Spur Trigger, 10" Barrel, Globe Sights, *Modern* 175.00   225.00

RIFLE, BOLT ACTION
- ☐ **Model 053 Buckhorn**, Various Rimfires, Singleshot, Peep Sights, *Modern* 40.00   55.00
- ☐ **Model 056 Buckhorn**, .22 L.R.R.F., 5 Shot Clip, Peep Sights, *Modern* 45.00   70.00

428 / STEVENS, J. ARMS AND TOOL COMPANY

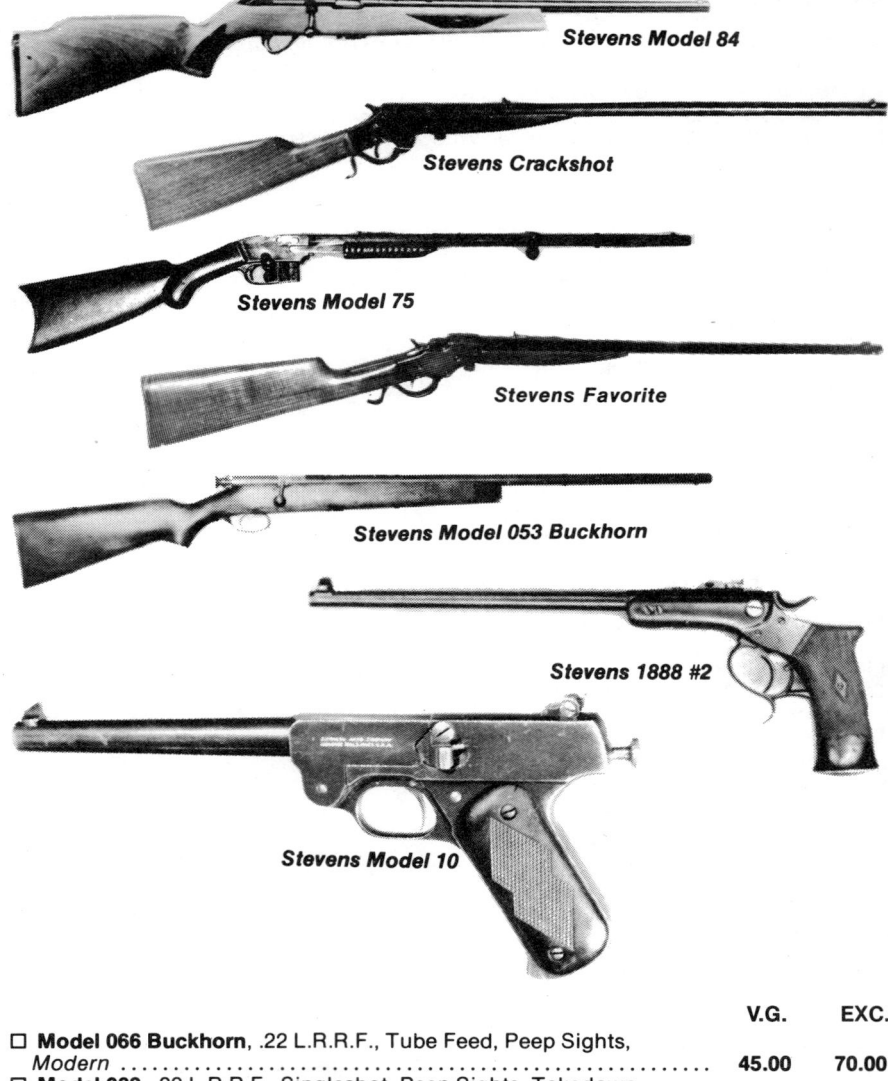

Stevens Model 84

Stevens Crackshot

Stevens Model 75

Stevens Favorite

Stevens Model 053 Buckhorn

Stevens 1888 #2

Stevens Model 10

	V.G.	EXC.
☐ **Model 066 Buckhorn**, .22 L.R.R.F., Tube Feed, Peep Sights, *Modern*	45.00	70.00
☐ **Model 083**, .22 L.R.R.F., Singleshot, Peep Sights, Takedown, *Modern*	30.00	50.00
☐ **Model 084**, .22 L.R.R.F., 5 Shot Clip, Peep Sights, Takedown, *Modern*	35.00	55.00
☐ **Model 086**, .22 L.R.R.F., Tube Feed, Takedown, Peep Sights, *Modern*	45.00	65.00
☐ **Model 15**, .22 L.R.R.F., Singleshot, (Springfield), *Modern*	25.00	40.00
☐ **Model 15Y**, .22 L.R.R.F., Singleshot, *Modern*	30.00	40.00

	V.G.	EXC.
☐ **Model 322**, .22 Hornet, Clip Fed, Carbine, Open Rear Sight, *Modern*	80.00	120.00
☐ **Model 322-S**, .22 Hornet, Clip Fed, Carbine, Peep Sights, *Modern*	85.00	125.00
☐ **Model 325**, .30-30 Win., Clip Fed, Carbine, Open Rear Sight, *Modern*	80.00	120.00
☐ **Model 325-S**, .30-30 Win., Clip Fed, Carbine, Peep Sights, *Modern*	85.00	125.00
☐ **Model 416**, .22 L.R.R.F., 5 Shot Clip, Peep Sights, Target Stock, *Modern*	110.00	175.00
☐ **Model 419**, .22 L.R.R.F., Singleshot, Peep Sights, *Modern*	45.00	75.00
☐ **Model 48**, .22 L.R.R.F., Singleshot, Takedown, *Modern*	30.00	40.00
☐ **Model 49**, .22 L.R.R.F., Singleshot, Takedown, *Modern*	30.00	40.00
☐ **Model 50**, .22 L.R.R.F., Singleshot, Takedown, *Modern*	30.00	40.00
☐ **Model 51**, .22 L.R.R.F., Singleshot, Takedown, *Modern*	30.00	40.00
☐ **Model 52**, .22 L.R.R.F., Singleshot, Takedown, *Modern*	35.00	45.00
☐ **Model 53**, .22 L.R.R.F., Singleshot, Takedown, *Modern*	35.00	45.00
☐ **Model 56 Buckhorn**, .22 L.R.R.F., 5 Shot Clip, Open Rear Sight, *Modern*	40.00	55.00
☐ **Model 65 "Little Krag"**, .22 L.R.R.F., Singleshot, Takedown, *Modern*	95.00	150.00
☐ **Model 66 Buckhorn**, .22 L.R.R.F., Tube Feed, Open Rear Sight, *Modern*	40.00	55.00
☐ **Model 82**, .22 L.R.R.F., Singleshot, Peep Sights, (Springfield), *Modern*	30.00	45.00
☐ **Model 83**, .22 L.R.R.F., Singleshot, Open Rear Sight, Takedown, *Modern*	25.00	40.00
☐ **Model 84**, .22 L.R.R.F., 5 Shot Clip, Open Rear Sight, Takedown, *Modern*	35.00	55.00
☐ **Model 86**, .22 L.R.R.F., Tube Feed, Takedown, Open Rear Sight, *Modern*	45.00	60.00

RIFLE, LEVER ACTION

☐ **Model 425**, Various Calibers, Hammer, *Curio*	150.00	225.00
☐ **Model 430**, Various Calibers, Hammer, Checkered Stock, *Curio*	175.00	265.00
☐ **Model 435**, Various Calibers, Hammer, Light Engraving, Fancy Checkering, *Curio*	250.00	375.00
☐ **Model 440**, Various Calibers, Hammer, Fancy Checkering, Fancy Engraving, Fancy Wood, *Curio*	575.00	875.00

RIFLE, SEMI-AUTOMATIC

☐ **Model 057 Buckhorn**, .22 L.R.R.F., 5 Shot Clip, Peep Sights, *Modern*	55.00	75.00
☐ **Model 076 Buckhorn**, .22 L.R.R.F., Peep Sights, Tube Feed, *Modern*	55.00	80.00
☐ **Model 085 Springfield**, .22 L.R.R.F., 5 Shot Clip, Peep Sights, *Modern*	55.00	80.00
☐ **Model 57 Buckhorn**, .22 L.R.R.F., 5 Shot Clip, Open Rear Sight, *Modern*	50.00	70.00
☐ **Model 76 Buckhorn**, .22 L.R.R.F., Open Rear Sight, Tube Feed, *Modern*	50.00	75.00
☐ **Model 85 Springfield**, .22 L.R.R.F., 5 Shot Clip, Open Rear Sight, *Modern*	50.00	75.00
☐ **Model 87**, .22 L.R.R.F., Tube Feed, Open Rear Sight, *Modern*	50.00	75.00
☐ **Model 87-S**, .22 L.R.R.F., Peep Sights, Tube Feed, *Modern*	55.00	80.00
☐ **Model 87K Scout**, .22 L.R.R.F., Tube Feed, Open Rear Sight, Carbine, *Modern*	55.00	80.00

RIFLE, SINGLESHOT

☐ **1888 #10 "Range"**, Various Calibers, Tip-Up, Half-Octagon Barrel, Fancy Wood, Vernier Sights, *Antique*	165.00	225.00

430 / STEVENS, J. ARMS AND TOOL COMPANY

	V.G.	EXC.
☐ 1888 #11 "Ladies", Various Calibers, Tip-Up, Half-Octagon Barrel, Open Rear Sight, *Antique*	130.00	160.00
☐ 1888 #12 "Ladies", Various Calibers, Tip-Up, Half-Octagon Barrel, Open Rear Sight, Fancy Wood, *Antique*	170.00	245.00
☐ 1888 #13 "Ladies", Various Calibers, Tip-Up, Half-Octagon Barrel, Vernier Sights, *Antique*	165.00	225.00
☐ 1888 #14 "Ladies", Various Calibers, Tip-Up, Half-Octagon Barrel, Vernier Sights, Fancy Wood, *Antique*	215.00	275.00
☐ 1888 #15 "Crack Shot", Various Calibers, Tip-Up, Half-Octagon Barrel, Peep Sights, *Antique*	165.00	210.00
☐ 1888 #16 "Crack Shot", Various Calibers, Tip-Up, Half-Octagon Barrel, Peep Sights, Fancy Wood, *Antique*	180.00	235.00
☐ 1888 #6 "Expert", Various Calibers, Tip-Up, Half-Octagon Barrel, Fancy Wood, *Antique*	135.00	185.00
☐ 1888 #7 "Premier", Various Calibers, Tip-Up, Half-Octagon Barrel, Globe Sights, *Antique*	130.00	175.00
☐ 1888 #8 "Premier", Various Calibers, Tip-Up, Half-Octagon Barrel, Fancy Wood, Globe Sights, *Antique*	160.00	210.00
☐ 1888 #9 "Range", Various Calibers, Tip-Up, Half-Octagon Barrel, Vernier Sights, *Antique*	145.00	185.00
☐ **Model 101 Featherweight**, .44-40 WCF, Lever Action, Tip-Up, Smoothbore, Takedown, Half-Octagon Barrel, *Modern*	115.00	150.00
☐ **Model 101**, with Extra 22 Barrel, .44-40 WCF, Lever Action, Tip-Up, Smoothbore, Takedown, Half-Octagon Barrel, *Modern*	165.00	220.00
☐ **Model 11 "Ladies"**, Various Rimfires, Tip-Up, Open Rear Sight, *Modern*	115.00	160.00
☐ **Model 12 "Marksman"**, Various Rimfires, Hammer, Lever Action, Tip-Up, *Modern*	85.00	125.00
☐ **Model 13 "Ladies"**, Various Rimfires, Tip-Up, Vernier Sights, *Modern*	130.00	170.00
☐ **Model 14 "Little Scout"**, .22 L.R.R.F., Hammer, Rolling Block, *Curio*	95.00	145.00
☐ **Model 14½ "Little Scout"**, .22 L.R.R.F., Hammer, Rolling Block, *Modern*	75.00	120.00
☐ **Model 15 "Maynard Jr."**, .22 L.R.R.F., Lever Action, Tip-Up, *Modern*	75.00	120.00
☐ **Model 15½ "Maynard Jr."**, .22 L.R.R.F., Lever Action, Tip-Up, *Modern*	75.00	125.00
☐ **Model 17**, Various Rimfires, Lever Action, Takedown, Favorite, Open Rear Sight, *Modern*	90.00	140.00
☐ **Model 18**, Various Rimfires, Lever Action, Takedown, Favorite, Vernier Sights, *Modern*	95.00	150.00
☐ **Model 19**, Various Rimfires, Lever Action, Takedown, Favorite, Lyman Sights, *Modern*	95.00	150.00
☐ **Model 2**, Various Rimfires, Tip-Up, Open Rear Sight, *Modern*	145.00	200.00
☐ **Model 20**, Various Rimfires, Lever Action, Takedown, Favorite, Smoothbore, *Curio*	80.00	120.00
☐ **Model 26**, Crack-Shot, Various Rimfires, Lever Action, Takedown, Open Rear Sight, *Curio*	80.00	130.00
☐ **Model 26½**, Various Rimfires, Lever Action, Takedown, Smoothbore, *Modern*	90.00	130.00
☐ **Model 27**, Various Rimfires, Lever Action, Takedown, Favorite, Octagon Barrel, Open Rear Sight, *Modern*	100.00	150.00
☐ **Model 28**, Various Rimfires, Lever Action, Takedown, Favorite, Octagon Barrel, Vernier Sights, *Modern*	115.00	160.00
☐ **Model 29**, Various Rimfires, Lever Action, Takedown, Favorite, Octagon Barrel, Lyman Sights, *Modern*	115.00	160.00

	V.G.	EXC.
☐ **Model 404**, .22 L.R.R.F., Hammer, Falling Block, Target Sights, Full Stocked, *Modern*	365.00	475.00
☐ **Model 414 "Armory"**, .22 L.R.R.F., Lever Action, Lyman Sights, *Modern*	220.00	325.00
☐ **Model 417½**, Various Calibers, Lever Action, Walnut Hill, *Modern*	320.00	425.00
☐ **Model 417-0**, Various Calibers, Lever Action, Walnut Hill, *Modern*	325.00	425.00
☐ **Model 417-1**, Various Calibers, Lever Action, Lyman Sights, Walnut Hill, *Modern*	320.00	425.00
☐ **Model 417-2**, Various Calibers, Lever Action, Vernier Sights, Walnut Hill, *Modern*	340.00	450.00
☐ **Model 417-3**, Various Calibers, Lever Action, no Sights, Walnut Hill, *Modern*	320.00	420.00
☐ **Model 418**, .22 L.R.R.F., Lever Action, Takedown, Walnut Hill, *Modern*	190.00	275.00
☐ **Model 418½**, Various Rimfires, Lever Action, Takedown, Walnut Hill, *Modern*	185.00	265.00
☐ **Model 44 "Ideal"**, Various Calibers, Lever Action, Rolling Block, *Modern*	225.00	320.00
☐ **Model 44½ "Ideal"**, Various Calibers, Lever Action, Falling Block, *Modern*	320.00	400.00
☐ **Model 49 "Ideal"**, Various Calibers, Walnut Hill, Lever Action, Falling Block, Engraved, Fancy Checkering, *Modern*	575.00	850.00
☐ **Model 5**, Various Rimfires, Tip-Up, Vernier Sights, *Modern*	160.00	225.00
☐ **Model 51 "Pope"**, Various Calibers, Schutzen Rifle, Lever Action, Falling Block, Engraved, Fancy Checkering, *Modern*	600.00	800.00
☐ **Model 52 "Pope, Jr."**, Various Calibers, Schutzen Rifle, Lever Action, Falling Block, Engraved, Fancy Checkering, *Modern*	550.00	775.00
☐ **Model 54 "Pope"**, Various Calibers, Schutzen Rifle, Lever Action, Falling Block, Fancy Engraving, Fancy Checkering, *Modern*	650.00	900.00
☐ **Model 56 "Pope Ladies"**, Various Calibers, Schutzen Rifle, Lever Action, Falling Block, Fancy Checkering, *Modern*	300.00	425.00
☐ **Model 7 "Swiss Butt."**, Various Rimfires, Tip-Up, Vernier Sights, *Modern*	165.00	240.00

RIFLE, SLIDE ACTION
☐ **Model 70**, .22 L.R.R.F., Hammer, Solid Frame, *Modern*	115.00	165.00
☐ **Model 71**, .22 L.R.R.F., Hammer, Solid Frame, *Modern*	120.00	180.00
☐ **Model 75**, .22 L.R.R.F., Tube Feed, Hammerless, *Modern*	125.00	200.00
☐ **Model 80**, Various Rimfires, Tube Feed, Takedown, *Modern*	110.00	150.00

SHOTGUN, BOLT ACTION
☐ **Model 237**, 20 Ga., Takedown, Singleshot, (Springfield), *Modern*	30.00	45.00
☐ **Model 258**, 20 Ga., Takedown, Clip Fed, *Modern*	45.00	60.00
☐ **Model 37**, .410 Ga., Takedown, Singleshot, (Springfield), *Modern*	30.00	45.00
☐ **Model 38**, .410 Ga., Takedown, Clip Fed, (Springfield), *Modern*	35.00	50.00
☐ **Model 39**, .410 Ga., Takedown, Tube Feed, (Springfield), *Modern*	40.00	55.00
☐ **Model 58**, .410 Ga., Takedown, Clip Fed, *Modern*	40.00	55.00
☐ **Model 59**, .410 Ga., Takedown, Tube Feed, *Modern*	45.00	60.00

SHOTGUN, DOUBLE BARREL, OVER-UNDER
☐ **Model 240**, .410 Ga., Hammer, Plastic Stock, *Modern*	115.00	165.00
☐ **Model 240**, .410 Ga., Hammer, Wood Stock, *Modern*	125.00	170.00

SHOTGUN, DOUBLE BARREL, SIDE-BY-SIDE
☐ **M 315**, Various Gauges, Hammerless, Steel Barrel, *Modern*	125.00	175.00
☐ **Model 215**, 12 and 16 Gauges, Outside Hammers, Steel Barrel, *Modern*	100.00	160.00
☐ **Model 235**, Various Gauges, Outside Hammers, Checkered Stock, Steel Barrel, *Modern*	100.00	160.00

432 / STEVENS, J. ARMS AND TOOL COMPANY

	V.G.	EXC.
☐ **Model 250**, Various Gauges, Outside Hammers, Checkered Stock, Steel Barrel, *Modern*	100.00	160.00
☐ **Model 255**, 12 and 16 Gauges, Outside Hammers, Checkered Stock, Steel Barrel, *Modern*	100.00	160.00
☐ **Model 260 "Twist"**, Various Gauges, Outside Hammers, Checkered Stock, Damascus Barrel, *Modern*	90.00	145.00
☐ **Model 265 "Krupp"**, 12 and 16 Gauges, Outside Hammers, Checkered Stock, Steel Barrel, *Modern*	100.00	160.00
☐ **Model 270 "Nitro"**, Various Gauges, Outside Hammers, Checkered Stock, Damascus Barrel, *Modern*	125.00	165.00
☐ **Model 311**, Various Gauges, Hammerless, Steel Barrel, *Modern*	135.00	190.00
☐ **Model 311 ST**, Various Gauges, Hammerless, Steel Barrel, Single Trigger, *Modern*	145.00	200.00
☐ **Model 3151**, Various Gauges, Hammerless, Recoil Pad, Front and Rear Bead Sights, *Modern*	125.00	185.00
☐ **Model 330**, Various Gauges, Hammerless, Checkered Stock, *Modern*	115.00	160.00
☐ **Model 335**, 12 and 16 Gauges, Hammerless, Steel Barrel, Checkered Stock, Double Trigger, *Modern*	125.00	165.00
☐ **Model 345**, 20 Ga., Hammerless, Checkered Stock, Steel Barrel, Double Trigger, *Modern*	125.00	165.00
☐ **Model 355**, 12 and 16 Gauges, Hammerless, Steel Barrel, Checkered Stock, Double Trigger, *Modern*	110.00	160.00
☐ **Model 365 "Krupp"**, 12 and 16 Gauges, Hammerless, Checkered Stock, Steel Barrel, Double Trigger, *Modern*	125.00	175.00
☐ **Model 375 "Krupp"**, 12 and 16 Gauges, Hammerless, Light Engraving, Fancy Checkering, Double Trigger, Steel Barrel, *Modern*	135.00	185.00
☐ **Model 385 "Krupp"**, 12 and 16 Gauges, Hammerless, Fancy Engraving, Fancy Checkering, Double Trigger, Steel Barrel, *Modern*	170.00	225.00
☐ **Model 515**, Various Gauges, Hammerless, *Modern*	100.00	145.00
☐ **Model 5151**, Various Gauges, Hammerless, Steel Barrel, *Modern*	125.00	160.00
☐ **Model 530**, Various Gauges, Hammerless, Steel Barrel, Double Trigger, *Modern*	100.00	155.00
☐ **Model 530 ST**, Various Gauges, Hammerless, Steel Barrel, Single Trigger, *Modern*	135.00	190.00
☐ **Model 530M**, Various Gauges, Hammerless, Plastic Stock, *Modern*	90.00	130.00

SHOTGUN, PUMP

	V.G.	EXC.
☐ **Model 520**, 12 Ga., Takedown, *Modern*	95.00	145.00
☐ **Model 620**, Various Gauges, Takedown, *Modern*	90.00	140.00

SHOTGUN, SEMI-AUTOMATIC

	V.G.	EXC.
☐ **Model 124**, 12 Ga., Plastic Stock, *Modern*	75.00	115.00

SHOTGUN, SINGLESHOT

	V.G.	EXC.
☐ **Various Gauges**, Hammer, Automatic Ejector, *Modern*	45.00	65.00
☐ **Various Gauges**, Hammer, Automatic Ejector, Raised Matted Rib, *Modern*	50.00	70.00
☐ **1888 "New Style"**, Various Gauges, Tip-Up, Hammer, Damascus Barrel, *Antique*	175.00	230.00
☐ **Model 100**, Various Gauges, Selective Ejector, Hammer, *Modern*	35.00	50.00
☐ **Model 102**, .410 Ga., Hammer, Featherweight, *Modern*	30.00	45.00
☐ **Model 102**, 24, 28, and 32 Gauges, Hammer, Featherweight, *Modern*	35.00	50.00
☐ **Model 104**, .410 Ga., Hammer, Featherweight, Automatic Ejector, *Modern*	40.00	50.00

STEVENS, J. ARMS AND TOOL COMPANY / 433

	V.G.	EXC.
☐ Model 104, 24, 28, and 32 Gauges, Hammer, Automatic Ejector, Featherweight, *Modern*	50.00	65.00
☐ Model 105, 20 Ga., Hammer, *Modern*	30.00	40.00
☐ Model 105, 28 Ga., Hammer, *Modern*	35.00	45.00
☐ Model 106, .410 Ga. 2½", Hammer, *Modern*	25.00	35.00
☐ Model 106, .44-40 WCF, Hammer, Smoothbore, *Modern*	35.00	45.00
☐ Model 106, 32 Ga., Hammer, *Modern*	30.00	40.00
☐ Model 107, Various Gauges, Hammer, Automatic Ejector, *Modern*	40.00	55.00
☐ Model 108, .410 Ga. 2½", Hammer, Automatic Ejector, *Modern*	30.00	40.00
☐ Model 108, .44-40 WCF, Hammer, Automatic Ejector, Smoothbore, *Modern*	40.00	50.00
☐ Model 108, 32 Ga., Hammer, Automatic Ejector, *Modern*	35.00	45.00
☐ Model 110, Various Gauges, Selective Ejector, Checkered Stock, Hammer, *Modern*	35.00	50.00
☐ Model 120, Various Gauges, Selective Ejector, Fancy Checkering, Hammer, *Modern*	40.00	55.00
☐ Model 125 Ladies, 20 Ga., Automatic Ejector, Hammer, *Modern*	40.00	55.00
☐ Model 125 Ladies, 28 Ga., Automatic Ejector, Hammer, *Modern*	45.00	65.00
☐ Model 140, Various Gauges, Selective Ejector, Hammerless, Checkered Stock, *Modern*	45.00	65.00
☐ Model 160, Various Gauges, Hammer, *Modern*	30.00	40.00
☐ Model 165, Various Gauges, Automatic Ejector, Hammer, *Modern*	30.00	45.00
☐ Model 170, Various Gauges, Automatic Ejector, Hammer, Checkered Stock, *Modern*	35.00	45.00
☐ Model 180, Various Gauges, Hammerless, Automatic Ejector, Checkered Stock, Round Barrel, *Modern*	55.00	80.00
☐ Model 182, 12 Ga., Hammerless, Automatic Ejector, Light Engraving, Checkered Stock, Trap Grade, *Modern*	75.00	115.00
☐ Model 185, For Damascus Barrel, *Deduct 25%*		
☐ Model 185, For 16 or 20 Gauge, *Add 20%*		
☐ Model 185, 12 Ga., Hammerless, Automatic Ejector, Checkered Stock, Half-Octagon Barrel, *Modern*	95.00	130.00
☐ Model 190, For Damascus Barrel, *Deduct 25%*		
☐ Model 190, For 16 or 20 Gauge, *Add 20%*		
☐ Model 190, 12 Ga., Hammerless, Automatic Ejector, Fancy Checkering, Light Engraving, Half-Octagon Barrel, *Modern*	120.00	160.00
☐ Model 195, For Damascus Barrel, *Deduct 25%*		
☐ Model 195, For 16 or 20 Gauge, *Add 20%*		
☐ Model 195, 12 Ga., Hammerless, Automatic Ejector, Fancy Checkering, Fancy Engraving, Half-Octagon Barrel, *Modern*	195.00	265.00
☐ Model 89 Dreadnaught, Various Gauges, Hammer, *Modern*	50.00	65.00
☐ Model 90, Various Gauges, Takedown, Automatic Ejector, Plain, Hammer, *Modern*	40.00	55.00
☐ Model 93, 12 and 16 Gauges, Hammer, *Modern*	35.00	50.00
☐ Model 94, Various Gauges, Takedown, Automatic Ejector, Plain, Hammer, *Modern*	35.00	50.00
☐ Model 944, .410 Ga., Hammer, Automatic Ejector, (Springfield), *Modern*	35.00	50.00
☐ Model 94A, Various Gauges, Hammer, Automatic Ejector, *Modern*	35.00	50.00
☐ Model 94C, Various Gauges, Hammer, Automatic Ejector, *Modern*	35.00	50.00
☐ Model 95, 12 and 16 Gauges, *Modern*	35.00	50.00
☐ Model 958, .410 Ga., Automatic Ejector, Hammer, *Modern*	35.00	50.00
☐ Model 958, 32 Ga., Automatic Ejector, Hammer, *Modern*	45.00	60.00
☐ Model 97, 12 and 16 Gauges, Hammer, Automatic Ejector, *Modern*	35.00	45.00
☐ Model 970, 12 Ga., Hammer, Automatic Ejector, Checkered Stock, Half-Octagon Barrel, *Modern*	45.00	55.00

434 / STEVENS, JAMES

	V.G.	EXC.
SHOTGUN, SLIDE ACTION		
☐ **Model 520**, 12 Ga., Takedown, *Modern*	110.00	145.00
☐ **Model 522**, 12 Ga., Trap Grade, Takedown, Raised Matted Rib, *Modern*	110.00	150.00
☐ **Model 621**, Various Gauges, Hammerless, Checkered Stock, Raised Matted Rib, Takedown, *Modern*	110.00	155.00
☐ **Model 620**, Various Gauges, Takedown, *Modern*	100.00	140.00
☐ **Model 67**, Various Gauges, Hammerless, Solid Frame, (Springfield), *Modern*	80.00	110.00
☐ **Model 67-VR**, Various Gauges, Hammerless, Solid Frame, Vent Rib, (Springfield), *Modern*	90.00	125.00
☐ **Model 77**, For Vent Rib, *Add* **$10.00-$15.00**		
☐ **Model 77**, 12 and 16 Gauges, Hammerless, Solid Frame, *Modern*	110.00	150.00
☐ **Model 77**, Various Gauges, Hammerless, Solid Frame, *Modern*	90.00	130.00
☐ **Model 77 S C**, 12 and 16 Gauges, Hammerless, Solid Frame, Recoil Pad, Adjustable Choke, *Modern*	120.00	160.00
☐ **Model 77-AC**, Various Gauges, Hammerless, Solid Frame, Adjustable Choke, *Modern*	85.00	120.00
☐ **Model 77-M**, 12 Ga., Hammerless, Solid Frame, Adjustable Choke, *Modern*	90.00	130.00
☐ **Model 820**, 12 Ga., Hammerless, Solid Frame, *Modern*	85.00	120.00

STEVENS, JAMES
SHOTGUN, PERCUSSION
☐ **14 Ga.**, Double Barrel, Side by Side, Engraved, Light Ornamentation, *Antique*	375.00	550.00

STEYR
Since 1963 in Steyr, Austria as Werndl Co.; in 1869 became Oesterreichische Waffenfabrik Gesellschaft; after WW I became Steyr Werke; in 1934 became Steyr-Daimler-Puch. Also see German Military, Austrian Military, Mannlicher-Schoenauer.

Steyr Solothurn

Steyr Model 1912

Steyr Model 1909

STOCKMAN, HANS / 435

	V.G.	EXC.

AUTOMATIC WEAPON, SUBMACHINE GUN
☐ **MP Solothurn 34**, 9mm Mauser, Clip Fed, *Class 3* 850.00 1,300.00

HANDGUN, SEMI-AUTOMATIC
☐ **Model 1901 Mannlicher**, 7.63mm Mannlicher, Commercial, *Curio*   400.00   650.00
☐ **Model 1905 Mannlicher**, 7.63mm Mannlicher, Military, *Curio* 250.00   375.00
☐ **Model 1908**, .32 ACP, Clip Fed, Tip-Up, *Modern* 125.00   175.00
☐ **Model 1909**, .25 ACP, Clip Fed, Tip-Up, *Modern* 100.00   155.00
☐ **Model 1909**, .32 ACP, Clip Fed, Tip-Up, *Modern* 115.00   165.00
☐ **Model 1911**, 9mm Steyr, Commercial, *Curio*......................   320.00   400.00
☐ **Model 1912**, 9mm Luger, Nazi-Proofed, Military, *Curio* 275.00   400.00
☐ **Model 1912**, 9mm Steyr, Military, *Curio* 165.00   250.00
☐ **Model 1912 Roumanian**, 9mm Steyr, Military, *Curio*................   200.00   300.00
☐ **Model GB**, 9mm Luger, Clip Fed, Double Action, *Modern* 265.00   350.00
☐ **Model SP**, .32 ACP, Clip Fed, Double Action, *Modern* 175.00   275.00
☐ **Solothurn**, .32 ACP, Clip Fed, *Modern* 130.00   185.00

Steyr Model 1908

Stery Model SP

Franz Stock .25

Franz Stock .22

STOCK, FRANZ
Franz Stock Maschinen u. Werkbaufabrik, Berlin, Germany 1920-1940.

HANDGUN, SEMI-AUTOMATIC
☐ **.22 L.R.R.F.**, Clip Fed, *Modern*.................................   160.00   225.00
☐ **.25 ACP**, Clip Fed, *Modern* 145.00   200.00
☐ **.32 ACP**, Clip Fed, *Modern* 155.00   220.00

STOCKMAN, HANS
Dresden, Germany 1590-1621.

HANDGUN, WHEEL-LOCK
☐ **Pair**, Holster Pistol, Pear Pommel, Horn Inlays, Light
 Ornamentation, *Antique* 9,000.00 15000.00

STOEGER, A.F.
Stoeger Arms Corp., N.Y.C., now in South Hackensack, N.J. Also see Luger.

V.G.   EXC.

COMBINATION WEAPON, OVER-UNDER
☐ **Model 290**, Various Calibers, Blitz System, Box Lock, Double Triggers, Engraved, Checkered Stock, *Modern* 800.00 1,200.00

COMBINATION WEAPON, DRILLING
☐ **Model 259**, 3 Calibers, Side Barrel, Box Lock, Double Triggers, Checkered Stock, *Modern* 950.00 1,500.00
☐ **Model 297**, Various Calibers, 2 Rifle Barrels, Box Lock, Double Triggers, Engraved, Checkered Stock, *Modern* 975.00 1,600.00
☐ **Model 300**, Vierling, 4 Barrels, Box Lock, Double Triggers, Checkered Stock, *Modern* 1,250.00 2,000.00

SHOTGUN, DOUBLE BARREL, SIDE-BY-SIDE
☐ **Victor Special**, 12 Ga., Checkered Stock, Double Triggers, *Modern*   120.00   175.00

SHOTGUN, SINGLESHOT
☐ **Model 27 Trap**, 12 Ga., Engraved, Vent Rib, Checkered Stock, Recoil Pad, *Modern* 500.00   750.00

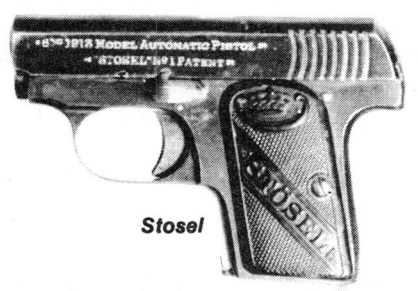

Stosel

STUART, JOHAN
Edinburgh, Scotland 1701-1750.

HANDGUN, SNAPHAUNCE
☐ **All Steel Highland**, Engraved, Scroll Butt, Ball Trigger, *Antique* 7,000.00 10,000.00

SULLIVAN ARMS CO.
Made by Crescent for Sullivan Hardware, Anderson, S.C., c. 1900.

SHOTGUN, DOUBLE BARREL, SIDE-BY-SIDE
☐ **Various Gauges**, Outside Hammers, Damascus Barrel, *Modern* 100.00   175.00
☐ **Various Gauges**, Hammerless, Steel Barrel, *Modern* 135.00   200.00
☐ **Various Gauges**, Hammerless, Damascus Barrel, *Modern* 100.00   175.00
☐ **Various Gauges**, Outside Hammers, Steel Barrel, *Modern* 125.00   190.00

SHOTGUN, SINGLESHOT
☐ **Various Gauges**, Hammer, Steel Barrel, *Modern* 55.00   85.00

SUTHERLAND, JAMES
Edinburgh, Scotland, c. 1790.

HANDGUN, FLINTLOCK
☐ **.50**, all Steel, Engraved, Ram's Horn Butt, *Antique* 1,750.00 2,500.00

T.A.C. / 437

Swiss Military Vetterli

Swiss Military Percussion Rifle

Swiss Military M1882

SWISS MILITARY

	V.G.	EXC.
AUTOMATIC WEAPON, SUBMACHINE GUN		
☐ **MP Solothurn 34**, 9mm Mauser, Clip Fed, *Class 3*	850.00	1,300.00
HANDGUN, REVOLVER		
☐ **M1872 Swiss Ordnance**, 10.4mm R.F., Double Action, Blue, Military, *Antique*	500.00	750.00
☐ **M1872/78 Swiss Ordnance**, 10.4mm C.F., Double Action, Blue, Military, *Antique*	275.00	400.00
☐ **M1882 Swiss Ordnance**, 7.5mm, Double Action, Blue, Military, *Antique*	125.00	165.00
☐ **M1882 Swiss Ordnance**, 7.5mm, Double Action, Blue, Military, With Holster Stock and All Leather, *Antique*	900.00	1,500.00
RIFLE, BOLT ACTION		
☐ **Vetterli**, Carbine, .41 Swiss R.F., Tube Feed, Military, *Antique*	285.00	400.00
☐ **Vetterli**, Bern 1878, .41 Swiss R.F., Tube Feed, Military, *Antique*	100.00	165.00
☐ **Vetterli**, Bern 1878/81, .41 Swiss R.F., Tube Feed, Military, *Antique*	100.00	170.00
☐ **M 1889**, 7.5 x 55 Swiss, Military, *Modern*	115.00	165.00
☐ **M 1889/1900**, 7.5 x 55 Swiss, Short Rifle, *Curio*	375.00	600.00
☐ **M 1893**, 7.5 x 55 Swiss, Military, *Curio*	375.00	600.00
☐ **M1911 Schmidt Rubin**, 7.5 x 55 Swiss, Clip Fed, Military, *Curio*	90.00	145.00
☐ **M1911 Schmidt Rubin**, 7.5 x 55 Swiss, Clip Fed, Carbine, Military, *Curio*	110.00	155.00
RIFLE, PERCUSSION		
☐ **Federal Rifle**, .41 Caliber, Full Stocked, *Antique*	475.00	775.00

T.A.C.
Trocaola, Aranzabal y Cia., Eibar, Spain.

438 / TALLARES

	V.G.	EXC.

HANDGUN, REVOLVER
- ☐ **Modelo Militar**, .44 Spec., S & W Triple Lock Copy, Double Action, Blue, *Modern* 155.00 225.00
- ☐ **OP No. 2 Mk.I**, .455 Eley, British Military, Double Action, Top Break, *Curio* 110.00 160.00
- ☐ **S & W Frontier Copy**, .44 American, Double Action, Break Top, Blue, *Modern* 90.00 135.00
- ☐ **S & W M&P Copy**, .38 Spec., Double Action, Blue, *Modern* 55.00 85.00

TALLARES
Tallares Armas Livianas Argentinas, Punta Alta, Argentina.

HANDGUN, SEMI-AUTOMATIC
- ☐ **T.A.L.A.**, .22 L.R.R.F., Clip Fed, *Modern* 80.00 125.00

TANARMI
Made in Italy, Imported by Excam.

HANDGUN, REVOLVER
- ☐ **E-15**, For Chrome, *Add* **$5.00**
- ☐ **E-15**, .22LR/.22 WMR Combo, Single Action, Western Style, *Modern* 25.00 40.00
- ☐ **E-15**, .22 L.R.R.F., Single Action, Western Style, *Modern* 20.00 30.00
- ☐ **TA-22**, For Chrome, *Add* **$5.00**
- ☐ **TA-22**, .22LR/.22 WMR Combo, Single Action, Western Style, Brass Grip Frame, *Modern*... 40.00 60.00
- ☐ **TA-22**, .22 L.R.R.F., Single Action, Western Style, Brass Grip Frame, *Modern* 30.00 45.00
- ☐ **TA-76**, For Chrome, *Add* **$5.00**
- ☐ **TA-76**, .22LR/.22 WMR Combo, Single Action, Western Style, *Modern* 30.00 45.00
- ☐ **TA-76**, .22 L.R.R.F., Single Action, Western Style, *Modern* 25.00 35.00

Tanke

TANKE
Maker unknown.

HANDGUN, SEMI-AUTOMATIC
- ☐ **.25 ACP**, Clip Fed, *Modern* 80.00 120.00

TANNER
Andrae Tanner, Werkstatte fur Praszisionswaffen, Fulenbach, Switzerland.

RIFLE, BOLT ACTION
- ☐ **Standard UIT**, .308 Win., Singleshot, Target Rifle, Monte Carlo Target Stock, *Modern* 875.00 1,300.00

	V.G.	EXC.
☐ **Standard UIT**, .308 Win., Repeater, Target Rifle, Monte Carlo Target Stock, *Modern*	900.00	1,350.00
☐ **300m Match**, .308 Win., Offhand Target Rifle, Target Stock, Palm Rest, *Modern*	900.00	1,500.00
☐ **50m Match**, .22 L.R.R.F., Offhand Target Rifle, Target Stock, Palm Rest, *Modern*	675.00	1,000.00
☐ **Hunting Match**, Various Calibers, Checkered Monte Carlo Stock, Singleshot, *Modern*	800.00	1,200.00

TANQUE
Ojanguran y Vidosa, Eibar, Spain, c. 1930.
HANDGUN, SEMI-AUTOMATIC

	V.G.	EXC.
☐ **.25 ACP**, Clip Fed, *Modern*	110.00	155.00

TARGA
Guiseppi Tanfoglio, Gardone Val Trompia, Italy, imported by Excam.
HANDGUN, SEMI-AUTOMATIC
☐ **Chrome Plating** For All Models *Add* $5.00

	V.G.	EXC.
☐ **GT22B**, .22 L.R.R.F., Clip Fed, Blue, *Modern*	65.00	90.00
☐ **GT32C**, .22 L.R.R.F., Clip Fed, Blue, *Modern*	65.00	95.00
☐ **GT27**, .25 ACP, Clip Fed, Blue, *Modern*	30.00	40.00
☐ **GT380B**, .380 ACP, Clip Fed, Blue, *Modern*	65.00	110.00
☐ **GT380BE**, .380 ACP, Clip Fed, Engraved, Blue, *Modern*	95.00	140.00
☐ **GT380XE**, .380 ACP, Clip Fed, *Modern*	95.00	140.00
☐ **GT32XEB**, .32 ACP, Clip Fed, *Modern*	85.00	125.00

T.A.R.N.
Swift Rifle Co., London, England, c. 1943.
HANDGUN, SEMI-AUTOMATIC

	V.G.	EXC.
☐ **Polish Air Force**, 9mm Luger, Clip Fed, Blue, *Curio*	2,500.00	3,750.00

TAURUS
Forjas Taurus S.A., Porto Alegre, Brazil.
HANDGUN, REVOLVER

	V.G.	EXC.
☐ **Model 65**, .38 Special, Solid Frame, Swing-Out Cylinder, Double Action, *Modern*	80.00	120.00
☐ **Model 66**, .38 Special, Solid Frame, Swing-Out Cylinder, Double Action, Adjustable Sights, *Modern*	90.00	135.00
☐ **Model 73**, .32 S & W Long, Solid Frame, Swing-Out Cylinder, Double Action, Fixed Sights, *Modern*	55.00	90.00
☐ **Model 74**, .32 S & W Long, Solid Frame, Swing-Out Cylinder, Double Action, Adjustable Sights, *Modern*	60.00	95.00
☐ **Model 80**, .38 Special, Solid Frame, Swing-Out Cylinder, Double Action, *Modern*	75.00	115.00
☐ **Model 82**, .38 Special, Solid Frame, Swing-Out Cylinder, Double Action, Heavy Barrel, *Modern*	70.00	110.00
☐ **Model 83**, .38 Special, Solid Frame, Swing-Out Cylinder, Double Action, Adjustable Sights, *Modern*	80.00	120.00
☐ **Model 84**, .38 Special, Solid Frame, Swing-Out Cylinder, Double Action, Adjustable Sights, *Modern*	80.00	120.00
☐ **Model 85**, .38 Special, Solid Frame, Swing-Out Cylinder, Double Action, 3" Barrel, *Modern*	70.00	110.00
☐ **Model 86**, .38 Special, Solid Frame, Swing-Out Cylinder, Double Action, Adjustable Sights, 6" Barrel, *Modern*	85.00	130.00

	V.G.	EXC.
☐ **Model 94**, .22 L.R.R.F., Solid Frame, Swing-Out Cylinder, Double Action, Adjustable Sights, *Modern*	90.00	135.00
☐ **Model 96**, .22 L.R.R.F., Solid Frame, Swing-Out Cylinder, Double Action, Adjustable Sights, 6" Barrel, *Modern*	85.00	125.00

HANDGUN, SEMI-AUTOMATIC
- ☐ **PT-92**, 9mm Luger, Clip Fed, Blue, Double Action, *Modern* 165.00 225.00
- ☐ **PT-99**, 9mm Luger, Clip Fed, Blue, Double Action, *Modern* 195.00 285.00

T.D.E.
El Monte, Calif. Also see Auto-Mag

HANDGUN, SEMI-AUTOMATIC
- ☐ **Backup**, .380 ACP, Stainless Steel, *Modern* 135.00 180.00

TED WILLIAMS
Trade name of Sears Roebuck, also see Sears.

RIFLE, BOLT ACTION
- ☐ **Model 52703**, .22 L.R.R.F., Singleshot, Plain, *Modern* 25.00 40.00
- ☐ **Model 52774**, .22 L.R.R.F., Clip Fed, Plain, *Modern* 35.00 55.00
- ☐ **Model 53**, Various Calibers, Checkered Stock, *Modern* 120.00 155.00

RIFLE, LEVER ACTION
- ☐ **Model 120**, .30-30 Win., Carbine, *Modern* 60.00 80.00

RIFLE, SEMI-AUTOMATIC
- ☐ **Model 34**, .22 L.R.R.F., *Modern* 35.00 55.00
- ☐ **Model 34**, .22 L.R.R.F., Carbine, *Modern* 35.00 55.00
- ☐ **Model 3T**, .22 L.R.R.F., Checkered Stock, *Modern* 65.00 85.00
- ☐ **Model 52811**, .22 L.R.R.F., Plain, Tube Feed, Takedown, *Modern*... 45.00 60.00
- ☐ **Model 52814**, .22 L.R.R.F., Checkered Stock, Clip Fed, Takedown, *Modern* 75.00 115.00

SHOTGUN, BOLT ACTION
- ☐ **Model 51106**, 12 or 20 Gauges, Clip Fed, Adjustable Choke, *Modern* 45.00 60.00
- ☐ **Model 51142**, .410 Gauge, Clip Fed, *Modern* 40.00 50.00

SHOTGUN, DOUBLE BARREL, OVER-UNDER
- ☐ **Model Laurona**, 12 Ga., Checkered Stock, Light Engraving, Double Trigger, Vent Rib, *Modern* 240.00 325.00
- ☐ **Model Zoli**, 12 Ga., Checkered Stock, Light Engraving, Double Trigger, Vent Rib, Automatic Ejector, *Modern* 150.00 275.00
- ☐ **Model Zoli**, 12 and 20 Gauges, Checkered Stock, Light Engraving, Double Trigger, Vent Rib, *Modern* 200.00 280.00

SHOTGUN, DOUBLE BARREL, SIDE-BY-SIDE
- ☐ **Model 51226**, 12 and 20 Gauges, Plain, Double Trigger, *Modern* ... 80.00 125.00
- ☐ **Model Laurona**, 12 and 20 Gauges, Checkered Stock, Light Engraving, Hammerless, *Modern* 115.00 155.00

SHOTGUN, SEMI-AUTOMATIC
- ☐ **Model 300**, 12 Ga., Plain, *Modern* 115.00 150.00
- ☐ **Model 300**, 12 and 20 Gauges, Checkered Stock, Vent Rib, Adjustable Choke, *Modern* 135.00 175.00
- ☐ **Model 300**, 12 and 20 Gauges, Checkered Stock, Vent Rib, *Modern* 125.00 165.00

SHOTGUN, SINGLESHOT
- ☐ **Model 5108**, Various Gauges, Plain, *Modern* 35.00 45.00

SHOTGUN, SLIDE ACTION
- ☐ **Model 200**, 12 and 20 Gauges, Checkered Stock, Vent Rib, Adjustable Choke, *Modern* 125.00 155.00

	V.G.	EXC.
☐ **Model 200**, 12 and 20 Gauges, Checkered Stock, Vent Rib, *Modern*	110.00	140.00
☐ **Model 200**, 12 and 20 Gauges, Plain, *Modern*	80.00	110.00
☐ **Model 200**, 12 and 20 Gauges, Checkered Stock, Plain Barrel, *Modern*	90.00	125.00
☐ **Model 51454**, .410 Ga., Plain, *Modern*	65.00	95.00

TEN STAR
Belgium, c. 1900.

SHOTGUN, DOUBLE BARREL, SIDE-BY-SIDE

	V.G.	EXC.
☐ **Various Gauges**, Outside Hammers, Damascus Barrel, *Modern*	100.00	175.00
☐ **Various Gauges**, Hammerless, Steel Barrel, *Modern*	135.00	200.00
☐ **Various Gauges**, Hammerless, Damascus Barrel, *Modern*	100.00	175.00
☐ **Various Gauges**, Outside Hammers, Steel Barrel, *Modern*	125.00	190.00

SHOTGUN, SINGLESHOT

☐ **Various Gauges**, Hammer, Steel Barrel, *Modern*	55.00	85.00

TERRIBLE
Hijos de Calixto Arrizabalaga, Eibar, Spain, c. 1930.

HANDGUN, SEMI-AUTOMATIC

☐ **.25 ACP**, Clip Fed, Blue *Modern*	85.00	125.00

TERRIER
Made by J. Rupertus, Philadelphia, Pa. Sold by Tryon Bros., c. 1880.

HANDGUN, REVOLVER

	V.G.	EXC.
☐ **.22 Short R.F.**, 7 Shot, Spur Trigger, Solid Frame, Single Action, *Antique*	90.00	160.00
☐ **.32 Short R.F.**, 5 Shot, Spur Trigger, Solid Frame, Single Action, *Antique*	95.00	170.00
☐ **.38 Short R.F.**, 5 Shot, Spur Trigger, Solid Frame, Single Action, *Antique*	95.00	170.00
☐ **.41 Short R.F.**, 5 Shot, Spur Trigger, Solid Frame, Single Action, *Antique*	120.00	195.00

TERROR
Made by Forehand & Wadsworth, c. 1870.

HANDGUN, REVOLVER

☐ **.32 Short R.F.**, 5 or 6 Shot, Spur Trigger, Solid Frame, Single Action, *Antique*	90.00	160.00

TEUF-TEUF
Arizmendi y Goenaga, Eibar, Spain, c. 1912.

HANDGUN, SEMI-AUTOMATIC

☐ **.25 ACP**, Clip Fed, Blue, *Curio*	85.00	125.00

TEUF-TEUF
Unknown Belgian maker, c. 1907.

HANDGUN, SEMI-AUTOMATIC

☐ **.25 ACP**, Clip Fed, Blue, *Curio*	115.00	155.00

TEXAS RANGER
Made by Stevens Arms.

442 / THAMES ARMS COMPANY

	V.G.	EXC.

SHOTGUN, SINGLESHOT
☐ **Model 95**, 12 and 16 Gauges, *Modern* 35.00   50.00

THAMES ARMS CO.
Norwich, Conn., c. 1907.

HANDGUN, REVOLVER
☐ **.22 L.R.R.F.**, 7 Shot, Double Action, Top Break, *Curio* 45.00   95.00
☐ **.32 S & W**, 5 Shot, Double Action, Top Break, *Curio* 45.00   95.00
☐ **.38 S & W**, 5 Shot, Double Action, Top Break, *Curio* 45.00   95.00

THAYER, ROBERTSON & CARY
Norwich, Conn., c. 1907.

HANDGUN, REVOLVER
☐ **.32 S & W**, 5 Shot, Double Action, Top Break, *Curio* 45.00   95.00
☐ **.38 S & W**, 5 Shot, Double Action, Top Break, *Curio* 45.00   95.00

Thompson M1928

Thompson Model 27A5

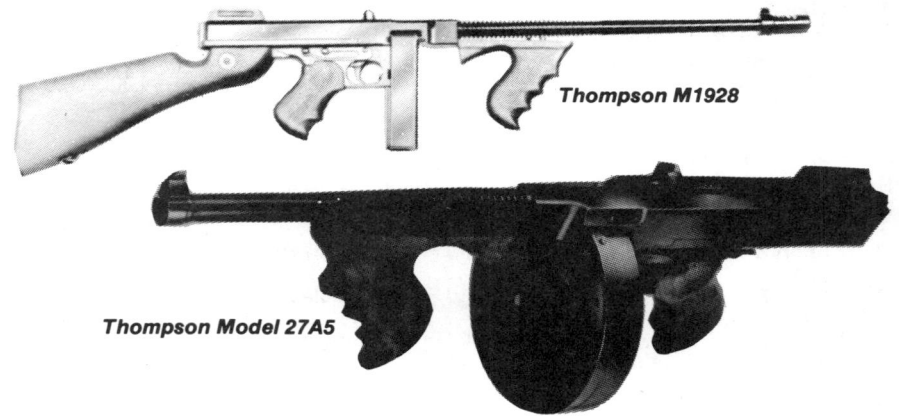

THOMPSON
Developed by Auto-Ordnance, invented by Gen. John T. Thompson, made by various companies. Also see Numrich Arms.

AUTOMATIC WEAPON, SUBMACHINE GUN
☐ **M1**, .45 ACP, Clip Fed, with Compensator, Military, Plain Barrel,
   Class 3 .... 600.00   900.00
☐ **M1921A**, .45 ACP, Early Model, Clip Fed, without Compensator,
   Lyman Sights, Curio, *Class 3* 2,000.00   2,500.00
☐ **M1921AC**, .45 ACP, Early Model, Clip Fed, with Compensator,
   Lyman Sights, Curio, *Class 3* 2,300.00   2,800.00
☐ **M1921AC**, .45 ACP, Early Model, Clip Fed, with Compensator,
   Cased with Accessories, Curio, *Class 3* 3,400.00   4,000.00
☐ **M1921AC**, .45 ACP, Early Model, Clip Fed, with Compensator,
   Metric Lyman Sights, Curio, *Class 3* 2,800.00   3,500.00
☐ **M1928 (Numrich)**, .45 ACP, Clip Fed, with Compensator, Lyman
   Sights, *Class 3* 400.00   500.00
☐ **M1928 Navy**, .45 ACP, Clip Fed, with Compensator, Lyman Sights,
   Finned Barrel, *Class 3* 1,900.00   2,400.00

THOMPSON/CENTER / 443

	V.G.	EXC.

- ☐ **M1928 Navy**, .45 ACP, Clip Fed, with Compensator, Lyman Sights, Finned Barrel, British Proofs, *Class 3* **2,300.00 2,750.00**
- ☐ **M1928 Navy**, .45 ACP, Clip Fed, with Compensator, Lyman Sights, Finned Barrel, Cased with Accessories, *Class 3* **2,500.00 3,000.00**
- ☐ **M1928A1 (AO)**, .45 ACP, Clip Fed, with Compensator, Adjustable Sights, Finned Barrel, Military, *Class 3* **1,200.00 1,600.00**
- ☐ **M1928A1 (AO)**, .45 ACP, Clip Fed, with Compensator, Military, Plain Barrel, *Class 3* **800.00 1,100.00**
- ☐ **M1928A1 (S)**, .45 ACP, Clip Fed, with Compensator, Lyman Sights, *Class 3* **1,000.00 1,400.00**
- ☐ **M1A1**, .45 ACP, Clip Fed, with Compensator, Military, Plain Barrel, *Class 3* **550.00 850.00**

HANDGUN, SEMI-AUTOMATIC
- ☐ **Model 27A5**, .45 ACP, Clip Fed, Finned Barrel, Adjustable Sights, with Compensator, (Numrich), *Modern* **175.00 265.00**

RIFLE, SEMI-AUTOMATIC
- ☐ **M1927**, .45 ACP, Clip Fed, with Compensator, Short Barreled Rifle, Lyman Sights, Curio, *Class 3* **4,000.00 5,000.00**
- ☐ **Model 27A1**, .45 ACP, Clip Fed, without Compensator, (Numrich), *Modern* **275.00 350.00**
- ☐ **Model 27A1**, .45 ACP, Clip Fed, without Compensator, Cased with Accessories, (Numrich), *Modern* **225.00 325.00**
- ☐ **Model 27A1 Deluxe**, .45 ACP, Clip Fed, Finned Barrel, Adjustable Sights, with Compensator, (Numrich), *Modern* **225.00 315.00**
- ☐ **Model 27A1 Deluxe**, .45 ACP, Clip Fed, Finned Barrel, Adjustable Sights, with Compensator, Cased with Accessories, *Modern* **320.00 375.00**
- ☐ **Model 27A3**, .22 L.R.R.F., Clip Fed, Finned Barrel, Adjustable Sights, with Compensator, (Numrich), *Modern* **275.00 350.00**

THOMPSON, SAMUEL
Columbus, Ohio 1820-1822. See Kentucky Rifles.

THOMPSON/CENTER
Rochester, N.H.

HANDGUN, SINGLESHOT
- ☐ **Contender**, Various Calibers, Adjustable Sights, Rifle Conversion Kit with Buttstock, Long Barrel, Not Factory, *Modern* **245.00 325.00**
- ☐ **Contender**, Various Calibers, Adjustable Sights, *Modern* **145.00 190.00**
- ☐ **Contender**, Various Calibers, Adjustable Sights, Vent Rib, *Modern* **150.00 200.00**
- ☐ **Contender**, Various Calibers, Adjustable Sights, Heavy Barrel, *Modern* **145.00 190.00**
- ☐ **Contender**, Various Calibers, Adjustable Sights, Super 14" Barrel, *Modern* **155.00 215.00**
- ☐ **Contender**, Various Calibers, Heavy Barrel, no Sights, *Modern* **145.00 195.00**

RIFLE, FLINTLOCK
- ☐ **.45 Hawken**, Set Trigger, Octagon Barrel, with Accessories, Reproduction, *Antique* **165.00 220.00**
- ☐ **.45 Hawken**, Set Trigger, Octagon Barrel, Reproduction, *Antique* **155.00 210.00**
- ☐ **.50 Hawken**, Set Trigger, Octagon Barrel, with Accessories, Reproduction, *Antique* **165.00 220.00**
- ☐ **.50 Hawken**, Set Trigger, Octagon Barrel, Reproduction, *Antique* **155.00 210.00**

HANDGUN, PERCUSSION
- ☐ **.45 Patriot**, Set Trigger, Octagon Barrel, Reproduction, *Antique* ... **85.00 130.00**
- ☐ **.45 Patriot**, Set Trigger, Octagon Barrel, with Accessories, Reproduction, *Antique* **90.00 145.00**

444 / THOMPSON/CENTER

Thompson/Center Renegade

Thompson/Center Hawken

Thompson/Center Seneca

Thompson/Center Patriot

Thompson/Center Contender H.B.

Thompson/Center Contender V.R.

	V.G.	EXC.
RIFLE, PERCUSSION		
☐ **.36 Seneca**, Set Trigger, Octagon Barrel, with Accessories, Reproduction, *Antique*	160.00	210.00
☐ **.36 Seneca**, Set Trigger, Octagon Barrel, Reproduction, *Antique*	150.00	200.00
☐ **.45 Hawken**, Set Trigger, Octagon Barrel, with Accessories, Reproduction, *Antique*	160.00	210.00
☐ **.45 Hawken**, Set Trigger, Octagon Barrel, Reproduction, *Antique*	150.00	200.00
☐ **.45 Seneca**, Set Trigger, Octagon Barrel, with Accessories, Reproduction, *Antique*	160.00	210.00
☐ **.45 Seneca**, Set Trigger, Octagon Barrel, Reproduction, *Antique*	150.00	200.00
☐ **.50 Hawken**, Set Trigger, Octagon Barrel, with Accessories, Reproduction, *Antique*	160.00	210.00
☐ **.50 Hawken**, Set Trigger, Octagon Barrel, Reproduction, *Antique*	150.00	200.00
☐ **.54 Renegade**, Set Trigger, Octagon Barrel, with Accessories, Reproduction, *Antique*	130.00	165.00
☐ **.54 Renegade**, Set Trigger, Octagon Barrel, Reproduction, *Antique*	120.00	150.00

THREE-BARREL GUN CO.
Moundsville, W. Va., 1906-1908, also at Wheeling, W. Va. as Royal Gun Co. and as Hollenbeck Gun Co.

V.G.   EXC.

COMBINATION WEAPON, DRILLING
☐ **Various Calibers**, Damascus Barrel, *Antique* 675.00   995.00

THUNDER
Martin Bascaran, Eibar, Spain, made for Alberdi, Teleria y Cia. 1912-1919.

HANDGUN, SEMI-AUTOMATIC
☐ **M 1919**, .25 ACP, Clip Fed, *Curio* 80.00   120.00

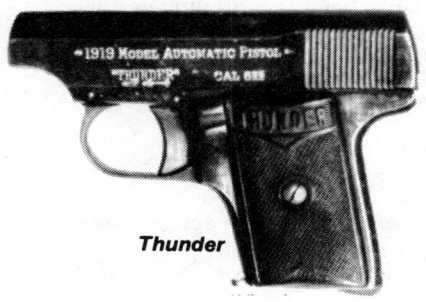

Thunder

TIGER
Maker Unknown, c. 1880.

HANDGUN, REVOLVER
☐ **#2**, .32 Short R.F., 5 Shot, Spur Trigger, Solid Frame, Single Action, *Antique* 90.00   160.00

TIGER
Made by Crescent for J.H. Hill Co. Nashville, Tenn., c. 1900.

SHOTGUN, DOUBLE BARREL, SIDE-BY-SIDE
☐ **Various Gauges**, Outside Hammers, Damascus Barrel, *Modern* 80.00   150.00
☐ **Various Gauges**, Outside Hammers, Steel Barrel, *Modern* 90.00   175.00

SHOTGUN, SINGLESHOT
☐ **Various Gauges**, Hammer, Steel Barrel, *Modern* 45.00   75.00

TIKKA
Oy Tikkakoski AB, Tikkakoski, Finland.

RIFLE, BOLT ACTION
☐ **Model 55 Standard**, Various Calibers, Clip Fed, Checkered Stock, *Modern* 185.00   275.00
☐ **Model 55 Sporter**, Various Calibers, Clip Fed, Checkered Stock, Heavy Barrel, *Modern* 220.00   295.00
☐ **Model 55 Deluxe**, Various Calibers, Clip Fed, Checkered Stock, *Modern* 220.00   295.00
☐ **Model 65 Standard**, Various Calibers, Clip Fed, Checkered Stock, *Modern* 185.00   275.00
☐ **Model 65 Sporter**, Various Calibers, Clip Fed, Checkered Stock, Target Rifle, Heavy Barrel, *Modern* 300.00   390.00
☐ **Model 65 Deluxe**, Various Calibers, Clip Fed, Checkered Stock, *Modern* 220.00   295.00

TINDALL & DUTTON
London, England 1790-1820.

V.G.   EXC.

HANDGUN, FLINTLOCK
☐ **Pocket Pistol**, Various Calibers, Boxlock, *Antique* 300.00   425.00

TINGLE MFG. CO.
Shelbyville, Ind.

HANDGUN, PERCUSSION
☐ **Model 1960 Target**, Octagon Barrel, Rifled, Reproduction, *Antique*   90.00   135.00

RIFLE, PERCUSSION
☐ **Model 1962 Target**, Octagon Barrel, Brass Furniture, Rifled, Reproduction, *Antique* 140.00   195.00

SHOTGUN, PERCUSSION
☐ **Model 1960**, 10 or 12 Gauges, Vent Rib, Double Barrel, Over-Under, Reproduction, *Antique* 150.00   210.00

TIPPING & LAWDEN
Birmingham, England, c. 1875.

HANDGUN, REVOLVER
☐ **Thomas Patent**, .450, Solid Frame, Double Action, *Antique* 300.00   425.00

HANDGUN, MANUAL REPEATER
☐ **Sharps Derringer**, Various Calibers, 4 Barrels, Spur Trigger, Cased with Accessories, *Antique* 425.00   675.00

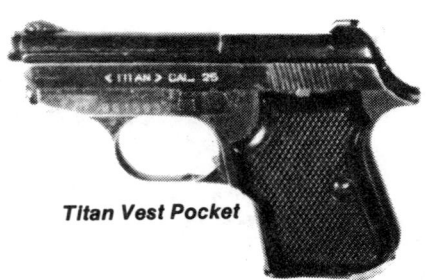

Titan Vest Pocket

TITAN
Guiseppi Tanfoglio, Gardone Val Trompia, Italy. Also see F.I.E.

HANDGUN, SEMI-AUTOMATIC
☐ **Vest Pocket**, .25 ACP, Clip Fed, Hammer, *Modern* 45.00   60.00

TOMPKINS
Varsity Mfg. Co., Springfield, Mass., c. 1947.

HANDGUN, SINGLESHOT
☐ **Target**, .22 L.R.R.F., Full Stock, *Modern* 135.00   210.00

TOWER'S POLICE SAFETY
Made by Hopkins & Allen, Norwich, Conn. c. 1875

HANDGUN, REVOLVER
☐ **.38 Short R.F.**, 5 Shot, Spur Trigger, Solid Frame, Single Action, *Antique* 95.00   170.00

TRADEWINDS, INC.
Tacoma, Wash., also see HVA.

　　　　　　　　　　　　　　　　　　　　　　　　　　V.G.　　　EXC.

RIFLE, BOLT ACTION
☐ **Husky (Early)**, Various Calibers, Checkered Stock, Monte Carlo Stock, *Modern* .... 225.00　325.00
☐ **Husky M-5000**, Various Calibers, Checkered Stock, Clip Fed, *Modern* .... 130.00　190.00
☐ **Husqvarna**, Various Calibers, Checkered Stock, Monte Carlo Stock, Lightweight, *Modern* .... 300.00　425.00
☐ **Husqvarna**, Various Calibers, Checkered Stock, Monte Carlo Stock, Lightweight, Full-Stocked, *Modern* .... 325.00　450.00
☐ **Husqvarna Crown Grade**, Various Calibers, Checkered Stock, Monte Carlo Stock, *Modern* .... 325.00　475.00
☐ **Husqvarna Imperial**, Various Calibers, Checkered Stock, Monte Carlo Stock, Lightweight, *Modern* .... 300.00　425.00
☐ **Husqvarna Imperial Custom**, Various Calibers, Checkered Stock, Monte Carlo Stock, *Modern* .... 300.00　425.00
☐ **Husqvarna Presentation**, Various Calibers, Checkered Stock, Monte Carlo Stock, *Modern* .... 425.00　600.00
☐ **Model 1998**, .222 Rem., no Sights, Heavy Barrel, Target Stock, *Modern* .... 265.00　375.00
☐ **Model 600K**, Various Calibers, Clip Fed, no Sights, Heavy Barrel, Set Trigger, *Modern* .... 170.00　250.00
☐ **Model 600S**, Various Calibers, Clip Fed, Heavy Barrel, Octagon Barrel, *Modern* .... 160.00　210.00

RIFLE, SEMI-AUTOMATIC
☐ **Model 260A**, .22 L.R.R.F., 5 Shot Clip, Checkered Stock, *Modern*　85.00　135.00

SHOTGUN, DOUBLE BARREL, OVER-UNDER
☐ **Gold Shadow Indy**, 12 Ga., Field Grade, Engraved, Fancy Checkering, Automatic Ejector, Vent Rib, *Modern* .... 1,000.00　1,400.00
☐ **Gold Shadow Indy**, 12 Ga., Skeet Grade, Engraved, Fancy Checkering, Automatic Ejector, Vent Rib, *Modern* .... 1,000.00　1,400.00
☐ **Gold Shadow Indy**, 12 Ga., Trap Grade, Engraved, Fancy Checkering, Automatic Ejector, Vent Rib, *Modern* .... 1,000.00　1,400.00
☐ **Shadow Indy**, 12 Ga., Field Grade, Automatic Ejector, Vent Rib, Checkered Stock, *Modern* .... 325.00　425.00
☐ **Shadow Indy**, 12 Ga., Skeet Grade, Automatic Ejector, Vent Rib, Checkered Stock, *Modern* .... 325.00　425.00
☐ **Shadow Indy**, 12 Ga., Trap Grade, Automatic Ejector, Vent Rib, Checkered Stock, *Modern* .... 325.00　425.00
☐ **Shadow-7**, 12 Ga., Field Grade, Automatic Ejector, Vent Rib, *Modern* .... 200.00　300.00
☐ **Shadow-7**, 12 Ga., Skeet Grade, Automatic Ejector, Vent Rib, *Modern* .... 200.00　300.00
☐ **Shadow-7**, 12 Ga., Trap Grade, Automatic Ejector, Vent Rib, *Modern* .... 200.00　300.00

SHOTGUN, DOUBLE BARREL, SIDE-BY-SIDE
☐ **Model G-1032**, 10 Ga. 3½", Checkered Stock, *Modern* .... 140.00　160.00
☐ **Model G-1228**, 12 Ga. Mag. 3", Checkered Stock, *Modern* .... 130.00　165.00
☐ **Model G-2028**, 20 Ga. Mag., Checkered Stock, *Modern* .... 130.00　165.00

SHOTGUN, SEMI-AUTOMATIC
☐ **Model D-200**, 12 Ga., Field Grade, Vent Rib, Engraved, *Modern* .... 155.00　200.00
☐ **Model H-150**, 12 Ga., Field Grade, *Modern* .... 125.00　160.00
☐ **Model H-170**, 12 Ga., Field Grade, Vent Rib, *Modern* .... 140.00　180.00
☐ **Model T-220**, 12 Ga., Trap Grade, Vent Rib, Engraved, *Modern* .... 155.00　200.00

TRUST SUPRA
Fab. d'Armes de Guerre de Grande Precision, Eibar, Spain.

HANDGUN, SEMI-AUTOMATIC
☐ **.25 ACP**, Clip Fed, Blue, *Modern* .... V.G. 85.00 EXC. 120.00

TUE-TUE
C.F. Galand, Liege, Belgium and Paris, France.

HANDGUN, REVOLVER
☐ **Velo Dog**, Various Calibers, Double Action, Hammerless, *Curio* ... 85.00 135.00

TURBIAUX
J.E. Turbiaux, Paris, France, c. 1885.

HANDGUN, MANUAL REPEATER
☐ **Le Protector**, Various Calibers, Palm Pistol, *Antique* 350.00 500.00

TURNER
Dublin, c. 1820.

HANDGUN, FLINTLOCK
☐ **.62**, Double Barrel, Pocket Pistol, Platinum Furniture, Plain, *Antique* 875.00 1,500.00

TURNER & ROSS
Made by Hood Firearms, Norwich, Conn., c. 1875.

HANDGUN, REVOLVER
☐ **.22 Short R.F.**, 7 Shot, Spur Trigger, Solid Frame, Single Action, *Antique* 90.00 160.00

TWIGG
London, England 1760-1813.

HANDGUN, FLINTLOCK
☐ **.58**, Pair, Belt Pistol, Flared, Octagon Barrel, Cased with Accessories, Plain, *Antique* 2,500.00 3,350.00

TYCOON
Made by Johnson-Bye, Worcester, Mass. 1873-1887.

HANDGUN, REVOLVER
☐ **#1**, .22 Short R.F., 7 Shot, Spur Trigger, Solid Frame, Single Action, *Antique* 90.00 160.00
☐ **#2**, .32 Short R.F., 5 Shot, Spur Trigger, Solid Frame, Single Action, *Antique* 145.00 190.00
☐ **#3**, .38 Short R.F., 5 Shot, Spur Trigger, Solid Frame, Single Action, *Antique* 95.00 160.00
☐ **#4**, .41 Short R.F., 5 Shot, Spur Trigger, Solid Frame, Single Action, *Antique* 105.00 140.00
☐ **#5**, .44 Short R.F., 5 Shot, Spur Trigger, Solid Frame, Single Action, *Antique* 150.00 225.00

TYROL
Made in Belgium for Tyrol Sport Arms, Englewood, Colo., c. 1963.

RIFLE, BOLT ACTION
☐ **Model DCM**, Various Calibers, Mannlicher Style, Checkered Stock, Recoil Pad, *Modern* 165.00 225.00

	V.G.	EXC.
☐ **Model DC**, Various Calibers, Mannlicher Style, Checkered Stock, *Modern*	150.00	200.00
☐ **Model DM**, Various Calibers, Checkered Stock, *Modern*	135.00	175.00

UHLINGER, W.L. & CO.
Philadelphia, Pa., c. 1880.

HANDGUN, REVOLVER
☐ .22 R.F., 7 Shot, Spur Trigger, Solid Frame, Single Action, Antique	145.00	225.00
☐ .32 Short R.F., 6 Shot, Spur Trigger, Solid Frame, Single Action, Antique	165.00	275.00

U.M.C. ARMS CO.
Probably Norwich Arms Co., c. 1880.

HANDGUN, REVOLVER
☐ .32 Short R.F., 5 Shot, Spur Trigger, Solid Frame, Single Action, Antique	90.00	160.00

UNION
Fab. Francaise.

HANDGUN, SEMI-AUTOMATIC
☐ .32 ACP, Ruby Style, Clip Fed, *Modern*	130.00	185.00
☐ .32 ACP, Ruby Style, with Horseshoe Magazine, *Modern*	600.00	850.00

UNION
France, M. Seytres.

HANDGUN, SEMI-AUTOMATIC
☐ .25 ACP, Clip Fed, Long Grip, *Modern*	75.00	120.00
☐ .32 ACP, Clip Fed, Long Grip, *Modern*	75.00	120.00

UNION
Unceta y Cia., Guernica, Spain 1924-1931.

HANDGUN, SEMI-AUTOMATIC
☐ **Model I**, .25 ACP, Clip Fed, *Modern*	95.00	140.00
☐ **Model II**, .25 ACP, Clip Fed, *Modern*	90.00	135.00
☐ **Model III**, .32 ACP, Clip Fed, *Modern*	110.00	155.00
☐ **Model IV**, .32 ACP, Clip Fed, *Modern*	110.00	155.00

UNION FIREARMS CO.
Toledo, Ohio, c. 1910.

HANDGUN, SEMI-AUTOMATIC, REVOLVER
☐ **Lefever Patent**, .32 S & W, 5 Shot, Top Break, *Curio*	525.00	875.00
☐ **Reifgraber Patent**, .32 S & W, 8 Shot, *Curio*	600.00	950.00

UNION JACK
Made by Hood Firearms Norwich, Conn., c. 1880.

HANDGUN, REVOLVER
☐ **.22 Short** R.F., 7 Shot, Spur Trigger, Solid Frame, Single Action, Antique	90.00	160.00
☐ **.32 Short** R.F., 5 Shot, Spur Trigger, Solid Frame, Single Action, Antique	95.00	170.00

450 / UNION JACK

Uhlinger .32

Union (Fab. Francaise) .32

Union (Fab. Francaise) with Horseshoe

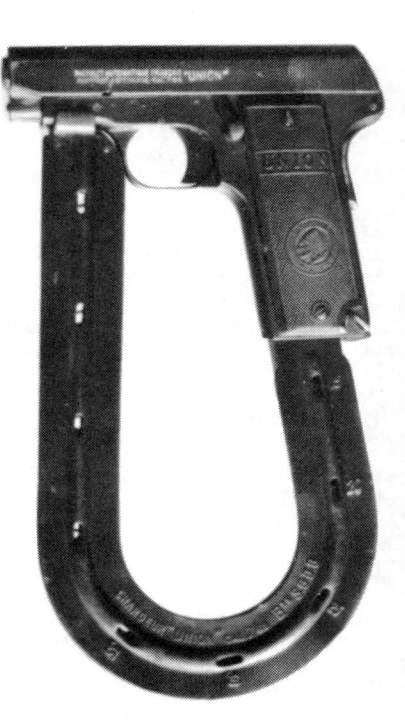

Union Model I .25

	V.G.	EXC.

UNION REVOLVER
Maker unknown, c. 1880.
HANDGUN, REVOLVER
- ☐ **.22 Short R.F.**, 7 Shot, Spur Trigger, Solid Frame, Single Action, Antique ..... 90.00 — 160.00
- ☐ **.32 Short R.F.**, 5 Shot, Spur Trigger, Solid Frame, Single Action, Antique ..... 95.00 — 170.00

UNIQUE
Made by C.S. Shattuck, c. 1880.
HANDGUN, REVOLVER
- ☐ **.32 Short R.F.**, 5 Shot, Spur Trigger, Solid Frame, Single Action, Antique ..... 95.00 — 190.00
- ☐ **.38 Short R.F.**, 5 Shot, Spur Trigger, Solid Frame, Single Action, Antique ..... 95.00 — 190.00

HANDGUN, REPEATER
- ☐ **Shattuck Palm Pistol**, Various Calibers, 4 Shot, *Curio* ..... 375.00 — 600.00

UNIQUE
Mre. d'Armes de Pyrenees, Hendaye, France, 1923 to date.
HANDGUN, SEMI-AUTOMATIC
- ☐ **Kriegsmodell**, .32 ACP, Clip Fed, Magazine Disconnect, 9 Shot, Nazi-Proofed, Hammer, *Curio* ..... 165.00 — 245.00
- ☐ **Model 10**, .25 ACP, Clip Fed, Magazine Disconnect, *Modern* ..... 80.00 — 125.00
- ☐ **Model 11**, .25 ACP, Clip Fed, Magazine Disconnect, Grip Safety, Cartridge Indicator, *Modern* ..... 110.00 — 150.00
- ☐ **Model 12**, .25 ACP, Clip Fed, Magazine Disconnect, Grip Safety, *Modern* ..... 90.00 — 130.00
- ☐ **Model 13**, .25 ACP, Clip Fed, Magazine Disconnect, Grip Safety, 7 Shot, *Modern* ..... 85.00 — 125.00
- ☐ **Model 14**, .25 ACP, Clip Fed, Magazine Disconnect, Grip Safety, 9 Shot, *Modern* ..... 90.00 — 130.00
- ☐ **Model 15**, .32 ACP, Clip Fed, Magazine Disconnect, 6 Shot, *Modern* ..... 80.00 — 120.00
- ☐ **Model 16**, .32 ACP, Clip Fed, Magazine Disconnect, 7 Shot, *Modern* ..... 80.00 — 120.00
- ☐ **Model 17**, .32 ACP, Clip Fed, Magazine Disconnect, 9 Shot, Nazi-Proofed, *Curio* ..... 145.00 — 200.00
- ☐ **Model 17**, .32 ACP, Clip Fed, Magazine Disconnect, 9 Shot, *Modern* ..... 90.00 — 130.00
- ☐ **Model 18**, .32 ACP, Clip Fed, Magazine Disconnect, 6 Shot, *Modern* ..... 90.00 — 130.00
- ☐ **Model 19**, .32 ACP, Clip Fed, Magazine Disconnect, 7 Shot, *Modern* ..... 85.00 — 125.00
- ☐ **Model 20**, .32 ACP, Clip Fed, Magazine Disconnect, 9 Shot, *Modern* ..... 110.00 — 145.00
- ☐ **Model 21**, .380 ACP, Clip Fed, Magazine Disconnect, 6 Shot, *Modern* ..... 110.00 — 145.00
- ☐ **Model 51**, .32 ACP, Clip Fed, Magazine Disconnect, 9 Shot, *Modern* ..... 70.00 — 125.00
- ☐ **Model 51**, .380 ACP, Clip Fed, Magazine Disconnect, 6 Shot, *Modern* ..... 70.00 — 125.00
- ☐ **Model 52**, .22 L.R.R.F., Clip Fed, Hammer, Various Barrel Lengths, *Modern* ..... 75.00 — 115.00
- ☐ **Model 540**, .32 ACP, Clip Fed, Magazine Disconnect, 9 Shot, *Modern* ..... 70.00 — 125.00

452 / UNIQUE

Unique Model L

	V.G.	EXC.
☐ **Model 550**, .380 ACP, Clip Fed, Magazine Disconnect, 6 Shot, *Modern*	70.00	125.00
☐ **Model C**, .32 ACP, Clip Fed, 9 Shot, Hammer, *Modern*	75.00	110.00
☐ **Model D-1**, .22 L.R.R.F., Clip Fed, Hammer, 3" Barrel, *Modern*	70.00	100.00
☐ **Model D-2**, .22 L.R.R.F., Clip Fed, Hammer, Adjustable Sights, 4" Barrel, *Modern*	85.00	120.00
☐ **Model D-3**, .22 L.R.R.F., Clip Fed, Hammer, Adjustable Sights, 8" Barrel, *Modern*	85.00	130.00
☐ **Model D-4**, .22 L.R.R.F., Clip Fed, Hammer, Muzzle Brake, Adjustable Sights, 9½" Barrel, *Modern*	95.00	155.00
☐ **Model D-6**, .22 L.R.R.F., Clip Fed, Hammer, Adjustable Sights, 6" Barrel, *Modern*	85.00	120.00
☐ **Model E-1**, .22 Short R.F., Clip Fed, Hammer, 3" Barrel, *Modern*	60.00	85.00
☐ **Model E-2**, .22 Short R.F., Clip Fed, Hammer, Adjustable Sights, 4" Barrel, *Modern*	85.00	120.00
☐ **Model E-3**, .22 Short R.F., Clip Fed, Hammer, Adjustable Sights, 8" Barrel, *Modern*	85.00	120.00
☐ **Model E-4**, .22 Short R.F., Clip Fed, Hammer, Muzzle Brake, Adjustable Sights, 9½" Barrel, *Modern*	95.00	150.00
☐ **Model F**, .380 ACP, Clip Fed, 8 Shot, Hammer, *Modern*	80.00	125.00
☐ **Model L (Corsair)**, .22 L.R.R.F., Clip Fed, Hammer, Lightweight, *Modern*	75.00	120.00
☐ **Model L (Corsair)**, .22 L.R.R.F., Clip Fed, Hammer, *Modern*	80.00	120.00
☐ **Model L (Corsair)**, .32 ACP, Clip Fed, Hammer, Lightweight, *Modern*	70.00	110.00
☐ **Model L (Corsair)**, .32 ACP, Clip Fed, Hammer, *Modern*	70.00	110.00
☐ **Model L (Corsair)**, .380 ACP, Clip Fed, Hammer, Lightweight, *Modern*	80.00	125.00
☐ **Model L (Corsair)**, .380 ACP, Clip Fed, Hammer, *Modern*	90.00	130.00
☐ **Model Mikros**, .25 ACP, Clip Fed, Magazine Disconnect, 6 Shot, *Modern*	80.00	120.00
☐ **Model RD (Ranger)**, .22 L.R.R.F., Clip Fed, Hammer, *Modern*	50.00	70.00
☐ **Model RD (Ranger)**, .22 L.R.R.F., Clip Fed, Muzzle Brake, Hammer, *Modern*	60.00	85.00
☐ **Model DES/69**, .22 L.R.R.F., Clip Fed, Target Pistol, *Modern*	225.00	325.00
☐ **Model DES/VO**, .22 L.R.R.F., Clip Fed, Rapid Fire Target Pistol, *Modern*	250.00	350.00
☐ **Model DES/VO 79**, .22 L.R.R.F., Clip Fed, Rapid Fire Target Pistol, Gas Ports, *Modern*	300.00	400.00

RIFLE, BOLT ACTION

☐ **Dioptra 4131**, .22 W.M.R., Checkered Stock, Open Sights, *Modern*	200.00	300.00
☐ **Dioptra 3121**, .22 L.R.R.F., Checkered Stock, Open Sights, *Modern*	175.00	225.00

UNIVERSAL / 453

	V.G.	EXC.
☐ **Dioptra 3121**, .22 L.R.R.F., Checkered Stock, Target Sights, Modern	200.00	300.00
☐ **Model T-66**, .22 L.R.R.F., Target Stock, Target Sights, Singleshot, Modern	300.00	400.00
☐ **Audax**, .22 L.R.R.F., Checkered Stock, Open Sights, Modern	100.00	150.00

UNITED STATES ARMS
Riverhead, N.Y., distributed by Mossberg.

HANDGUN, REVOLVER
☐ **Abilene**, .44 Magnum, Single Action, Western Style, Adjustable Sights, *Modern* 125.00 185.00
☐ **Abilene**, .44 Magnum, Stainless Steel, Single Action, Western Style, Adjustable Sights, *Modern* 145.00 200.00
☐ **Abilene**, .44 Magnum, Stainless Steel, Single Action, Western Style, 10" Barrel, Adjustable Sights, *Modern* 165.00 225.00
☐ **Abilene**, Various Calibers, Single Action, Western Style, Adjustable Sights, *Modern* 125.00 175.00
☐ **Abilene**, Various Calibers, Single Action, Western Style, Adjustable Sights, Stainless Steel, *Modern* 145.00 200.00

UNIVERSAL
Made by Hopkins & Allen, Norwich, Conn., c. 1890.

HANDGUN, REVOLVER
☐ **.32 S & W**, 5 Shot, Double Action, Solid Frame, *Curio* 45.00 75.00

UNIVERSAL
Hialeah, Fla.

HANDGUN, SEMI-AUTOMATIC
☐ **Model 3000 Enforcer**, .30 Carbine, Clip Fed, *Modern* 130.00 175.00
☐ **Model 3005 Enforcer**, .30 Carbine, Clip Fed, Nickel Plated, *Modern* 145.00 185.00
☐ **Model 3010 Enforcer**, .30 Carbine, Clip Fed, Gold Plated, *Modern* 150.00 190.00

RIFLE, SEMI-AUTOMATIC
☐ **Model 1001**, .30 Carbine, Carbine, Clip Fed, *Modern* 85.00 125.00
☐ **Model 1002**, .30 Carbine, Carbine, Clip Fed, Bayonet Lug, *Modern* 90.00 130.00
☐ **Model 1003**, .30 Carbine, Carbine, Clip Fed, Walnut Stock, *Modern* 85.00 120.00
☐ **Model 1004**, .30 Carbine, Carbine, Clip Fed, Scope Mounted, *Modern* 95.00 130.00
☐ **Model 1010**, .30 Carbine, Carbine, Clip Fed, Nickel Plated, *Modern* 120.00 160.00
☐ **Model 1011 Deluxe**, .30 Carbine, Carbine, Clip Fed, Nickel Plated, Monte Carlo Stock, *Modern* 125.00 170.00
☐ **Model 1015**, .30 Carbine, Carbine, Clip Fed, Gold Plated, *Modern* 125.00 170.00
☐ **Model 1016 Deluxe**, .30 Carbine, Carbine, Clip Fed, Gold Plated, Monte Carlo Stock, *Modern* 140.00 180.00
☐ **Model 1025 Ferret**, .256 Win. Mag., Carbine, Clip Fed, Sporting Rifle, *Modern* 115.00 150.00
☐ **Model 1025 Ferret**, .30 Carbine, Carbine, Clip Fed, Sporting Rifle, *Modern* 110.00 145.00
☐ **Model 1941 Field Commander**, .30 Carbine, Carbine, Clip Fed, Fancy Wood, *Modern* 110.00 150.00

RIFLE, SLIDE ACTION
☐ **Vulcan 440**, .44 Magnum, Clip Fed, Sporting Rifle, Open Rear Sight, *Modern* 125.00 160.00

454 / UNIVERSAL

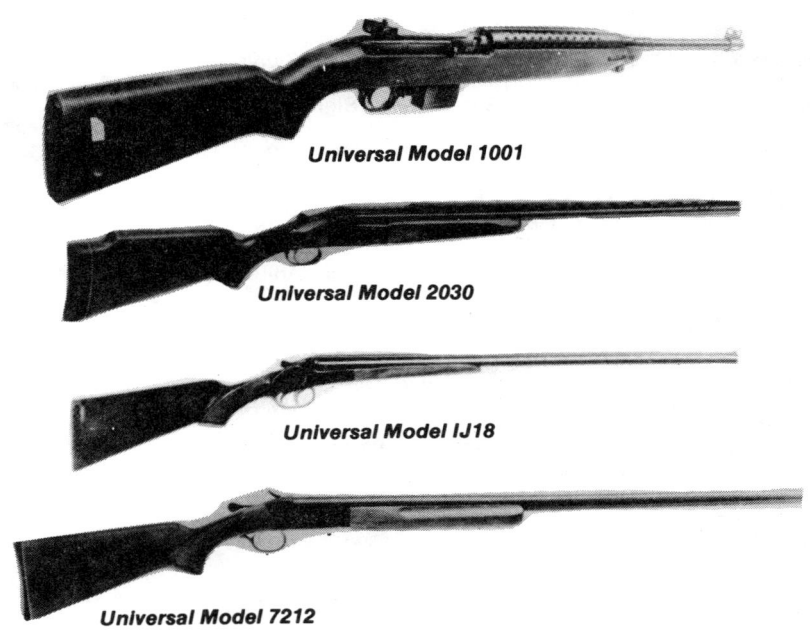

Universal Model 1001

Universal Model 2030

Universal Model IJ18

Universal Model 7212

	V.G.	EXC.

SHOTGUN, DOUBLE BARREL, OVER-UNDER
- ☐ **Baikal 1J-27**, 12 Ga., Double Trigger, Vent Rib, Engraved, Checkered Stock, *Modern* 150.00   200.00
- ☐ **Baikal 1J-27**, 12 Ga., Double Trigger, Vent Rib, Engraved, Checkered Stock, Automatic Ejector, *Modern* 160.00   220.00
- ☐ **Baikal MC-5**, 20 Ga., Double Trigger, Engraved, Checkered Stock, Solid Rib, *Modern* 300.00   400.00
- ☐ **Baikal MC-6**, 20 Ga., Skeet Grade, Extra Shotgun Barrel, Single Trigger, Engraved, Checkered Stock, *Modern* 450.00   650.00
- ☐ **Baikal MC-7**, 12 and 20 Gauges, Single Selective Trigger, Solid Rib, Fancy Engraving, Fancy Checkering, Selective Ejector, *Modern* 900.00   1,300.00
- ☐ **Baikal MC-8**, 12 Ga., Double Trigger, Monte Carlo Stock, Checkered Stock, *Modern* 400.00   600.00
- ☐ **Model 7312**, 12 Ga., Trap Grade, Vent Rib, Engraved, Checkered Stock, Monte Carlo Stock, *Modern* 700.00   900.00
- ☐ **Model 7312**, 12 Ga., Skeet Grade, Vent Rib, Engraved, Checkered Stock, Monte Carlo Stock, *Modern* 700.00   900.00
- ☐ **Model 7412**, 12 Ga., Trap Grade, Vent Rib, Fancy Engraving, Checkered Stock, Single Selective Trigger, *Modern* 600.00   800.00
- ☐ **Model 7412**, 12 Ga., Skeet Grade, Vent Rib, Fancy Engraving, Checkered Stock, Single Selective Trigger, *Modern* 600.00   800.00
- ☐ **Model 7712**, 12 Ga. Mag. 3", Recoil Pad, Checkered Stock, Single Trigger, Vent Rib, *Modern* 175.00   225.00
- ☐ **Model 7812**, 12 Ga. Mag. 3", Automatic Ejector, Recoil Pad, Checkered Stock, Single Trigger, Vent Rib, *Modern* 275.00   350.00
- ☐ **Model 7912**, 12 Ga. Mag. 3", Automatic Ejector, Engraved, Checkered Stock, Single Trigger, Vent Rib, *Modern* 500.00   650.00

U.S. ARMS COMPANY / 455

	V.G.	EXC.
☐ **Over-Wing**, 12 and 20 Gauges, Field Grade, Vent Rib, Double Trigger, Checkered Stock, Magnum, *Modern*	135.00	185.00

SHOTGUN, DOUBLE BARREL, SIDE-BY-SIDE

	V.G.	EXC.
☐ **Model 2030**, 10 Ga., 3½", Field Grade, Hammerless, Light Engraving, Checkered Stock, *Modern*	140.00	175.00
☐ **Model 7112**, 12 Ga., Field Grade, Hammerless, Light Engraving, Checkered Stock, *Modern*	115.00	150.00
☐ **Model IJ58M**, 12 Ga., Hammerless, Recoil Pad, Checkered Stock, *Modern*	95.00	130.00
☐ **Model TOZ 66/54**, 12 Ga., Outside Hammers, Checkered Stock, *Modern*	85.00	120.00
☐ **Model TOZ67**, 12 Ga., Outside Hammers, Riot Gun, Nickel Plated, Gold Plated, *Modern*	135.00	175.00

SHOTGUN, SEMI-AUTOMATIC

	V.G.	EXC.
☐ **Model 7512**, 12 Ga., Checkered Stock, Vent Rib, *Modern*	155.00	200.00
☐ **Model 7512**, 12 Ga. Mag. 3", Checkered Stock, Vent Rib, *Modern*	165.00	210.00
☐ **Model 7512**, 12 Ga. Mag. 3", Checkered Stock, Monte Carlo Stock, Vent Rib, *Modern*	165.00	210.00

SHOTGUN, SINGLESHOT

	V.G.	EXC.
☐ **Model 7212**, 12 Ga., Trap Grade, Vent Rib, Engraved, Checkered Stock, Monte Carlo Stock, *Modern*	475.00	600.00
☐ **Model IJ18**, 12 Ga., Hammerless, *Modern*	30.00	40.00

UNWIN & ROGERS
Yorkshire, England, c. 1850.

HANDGUN, PERCUSSION

	V.G.	EXC.
☐ **Knife Pistol** with Ramrod and Mould, Cased with Accessories, *Antique*	750.00	1,100.00

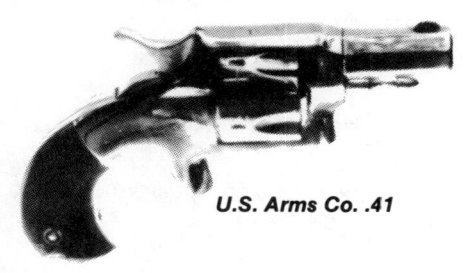

U.S. Arms Co. .41

U.S. ARMS CO.
Brooklyn, N.Y. 1874-1878.

HANDGUN, REVOLVER

	V.G.	EXC.
☐ **.22 Short R.F.**, 7 Shot, Spur Trigger, Solid Frame, Single Action, *Antique*	90.00	160.00
☐ **.32 Short R.F.**, 5 Shot, Spur Trigger, Solid Frame, Single Action, *Antique*	95.00	170.00
☐ **.38 Short R.F.**, 5 Shot, Spur Trigger, Solid Frame, Single Action, *Antique*	95.00	170.00
☐ **.41 Short R.F.**, 5 Shot, Spur Trigger, Solid Frame, Single Action, *Antique*	120.00	195.00

U.S. ARMS CO.
Made by Crescent for H & D Folsom, c. 1900.

456 / U.S. MILITARY

	V.G.	EXC.

SHOTGUN, DOUBLE BARREL, SIDE-BY-SIDE
- ☐ **Various Gauges**, Outside Hammers, Damascus Barrel, *Modern* 100.00   175.00
- ☐ **Various Gauges**, Hammerless, Steel Barrel, *Modern* 135.00   200.00
- ☐ **Various Gauges**, Hammerless, Damascus Barrel, *Modern* 100.00   175.00
- ☐ **Various Gauges**, Outside Hammers, Steel Barrel, *Modern* 125.00   190.00

SHOTGUN, SINGLESHOT
- ☐ **Various Gauges**, Hammer, Steel Barrel, *Modern* 55.00   85.00

U.S. MILITARY

AUTOMATIC WEAPON, ASSAULT RIFLE
- ☐ **AR-15**, .223 Rem., Clip Fed, Early Model, *Class 3* 600.00   950.00
- ☐ **M-1 Garand (Win)**, .30-06 Springfield, Clip Fed, Experimental, *Class 3* 4,000.00 6,000.00
- ☐ **M14**, .308 Win., Clip Fed, Reproduction, Wood Stock, *Class 3* 1,000.00 1,400.00
- ☐ **M14 H&R**, .308 Win., Clip Fed, Wood Stock, *Class 3* 3,000.00 4,500.00
- ☐ **M16**, .223 Rem., Clip Fed, Military, *Class 3* 600.00   850.00
- ☐ **M16-M A C**, .22 L.R.R.F., Clip Fed, Conversion Unit Only, *Class 3* 65.00   110.00
- ☐ **M16A1**, .223 Rem., Clip Fed, Military, *Class 3* 650.00   875.00
- ☐ **M1918 Bar (Winchester)**, .30-06 Springfield, Clip Fed, Bipod, Modern, *Class 3* 1,400.00 2,000.00
- ☐ **M63 Stoner**, .308 Win., Clip Fed, Military, *Class 3* 3,500.00 5,000.00
- ☐ **T-48**, .308 Win., Clip Fed, Military, *Class 3* 3,000.00 3,750.00

AUTOMATIC WEAPON, HEAVY MACHINE GUN
- ☐ **M1906 Colt**, .30-06 Springfield, Belt Fed, Tripod, Potato Digger, Military, *Class 3* 1,500.00 2,250.00
- ☐ **M1906 Marlin**, .30-06 Springfield, Belt Fed, Tripod, Potato Digger, Military, *Class 3* 1,600.00 2,250.00
- ☐ **M1906 Marlin**, .308 Win., Belt Fed, Tripod, Potato Digger, Military, *Class 3* 1,400.00 2,000.00
- ☐ **M1917**, .30-06 Springfield, Belt Fed, Tripod, *Class 3* 5,750.00 7,000.00
- ☐ **M1917 Marlin**, .30-06 Springfield, Belt Fed, Tripod, Potato Digger, Military, *Class 3* 1,400.00 2,000.00
- ☐ **M1917A1**, .30-06 Springfield, Belt Fed, Tripod, *Class 3* 3,650.00 4,750.00
- ☐ **M2 Browning**, .50 Bmg, Belt Fed, Heavy Barrel, Military, *Class 3* ... 2,000.00 3,000.00
- ☐ **M2 Browning (Colt)**, .50 Bmg, Belt Fed, Heavy Barrel, Military, Tripod, *Class 3* 3,000.00 4,000.00
- ☐ **M2 Browning (Savage)**, .50 Bmg, Belt Fed, Tripod, *Class 3* 3,250.00 4,500.00

AUTOMATIC WEAPON, LIGHT MACHINE GUN
- ☐ **Benet-Mercie U.S.N. 1912**, .30-06 Springfield, Clip Fed, Dewat, *Class 3* 2,000.00 2,750.00
- ☐ **M1919A6**, .30-06 Springfield, Belt Fed, Wood Stock, Bipod, *Class 3* 975.00 1,750.00
- ☐ **M1941 Johnson**, .30-06 Springfield, Clip Fed, Military, Bipod, *Class 3* 1,400.00 2,000.00
- ☐ **M1944 Johnson**, .30-06 Springfield, Belt Fed, Monopod, *Class 3* ... 2,600.00 3,400.00
- ☐ **M1946 Johnson**, .30-06 Springfield, Belt Fed, *Class 3* 2,400.00 3,500.00
- ☐ **M60**, .308 Win., Belt Fed, Bipod, *Class 3* 1,800.00 2,500.00
- ☐ **M60**, .308 Win., Belt Fed, *Class 3* 2,500.00 3,500.00

AUTOMATIC WEAPON, SUBMACHINE GUN
- ☐ **M-180**, .22 L.R.R.F., 177 Round Drum Magazine, *Class 3* 275.00   350.00
- ☐ **M-2 (Win)**, .30 Carbine, Clip Fed, Military, *Class 3* 375.00   550.00
- ☐ **M-3**, .45 ACP, Clip Fed, Military, *Class 3* 375.00   550.00
- ☐ **M1 Thompson**, .45 ACP, Clip Fed, with Compensator, Military, Plain Barrel, *Class 3* 800.00 1,400.00
- ☐ **M1A1 Thompson**, .45 ACP, Clip Fed, with Compensator, Military, Plain Barrel, *Class 3* 650.00   950.00

U.S. MILITARY / 457

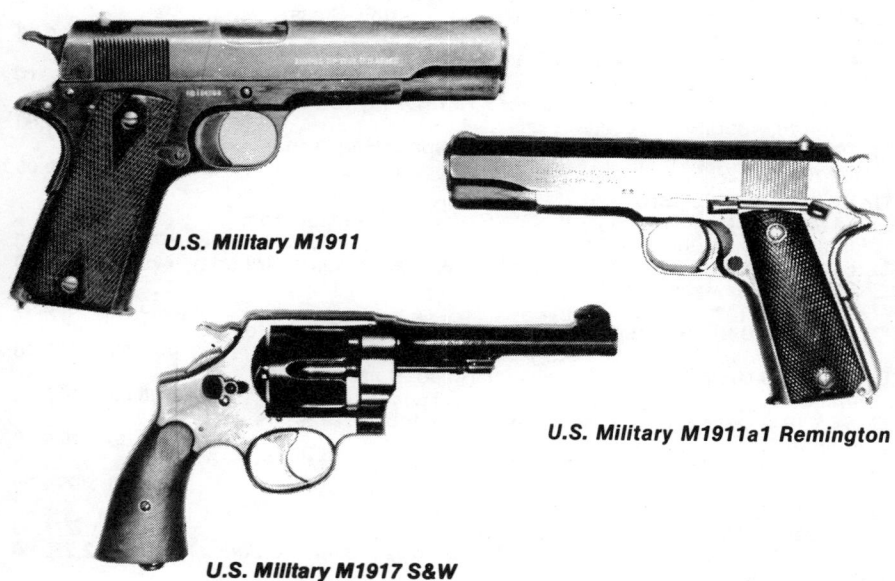

U.S. Military M1911a1

U.S. Military M1909 Army

U.S. Military M1911

U.S. Military M1911a1 Remington

U.S. Military M1917 S&W

	V.G.	EXC.
☐ **M2**, .30 Carbine, Clip Fed, Military, Carbine, *Class 3*	300.00	425.00
☐ **M3**, 9mm Luger, Clip Fed, Military, *Class 3*	450.00	675.00
☐ **M3 Grease Gun**, .45 ACP, Clip Fed, Military, Silencer, *Class 3*	700.00	975.00
☐ **M3A1 Grease Gun**, .45 ACP, Clip Fed, Military, Flash Hider, *Class 3*	550.00	800.00
☐ **M50 Reising**, .45 ACP, Clip Fed, Wood Stock, Military, *Class 3*	160.00	225.00
☐ **M50 Reising**, .45 ACP, Clip Fed, Wood Stock, Military, Cased with Accessories, *Class 3*	225.00	325.00
☐ **M55 Reising**, .45 ACP, Clip Fed, Folding Stock, Military, *Class 3*	225.00	325.00
☐ **XM177E2**, .223 Rem., Clip Fed, Folding Stock, Silencer, Short Rifle, Military, *Class 3*	1,200.00	1,850.00

458 / U.S. MILITARY

	V.G.	EXC.

HANDGUN, FLINTLOCK
- ☐ **.54 M1805 (06)**, Singleshot, Smoothbore, Brass Mounts, Dated 1806, *Antique* 2,200.00 3,350.00
- ☐ **.54 M1805 (06)**, Singleshot, Smoothbore, Brass Mounts, Dated 1807, *Antique* 1,300.00 2,100.00
- ☐ **.54 M1805 (06)**, Singleshot, Smoothbore, Brass Mounts, Dated 1808, *Antique* 1,350.00 1,950.00
- ☐ **.54 M1807-8**, Singleshot, Smoothbore, Brass Mounts, Various Contractors, *Antique* 2,500.00 3,500.00
- ☐ **.54 M1816**, Singleshot, Smoothbore, S North Army, Brass Furniture, *Antique* 450.00 725.00
- ☐ **.54 M1819**, Singleshot, Smoothbore, S North Army, Iron Mounts, *Antique* 650.00 950.00
- ☐ **.54 M1826**, Singleshot, Smoothbore, S North Army, Iron Mounts, *Antique* 750.00 1,200.00
- ☐ **.54 M1836**, Singleshot, Smoothbore, R Johnson Army, Iron Mounts, *Antique* 575.00 825.00
- ☐ **.64 M1808**, Singleshot, Smoothbore, S North Army, Brass Furniture, *Antique* 1,350.00 1,800.00
- ☐ **.69 M1799**, Singleshot, North & Cheney, Brass Furniture, Brass Frame, *Antique* 10,000.00 18,000.00
- ☐ **.69 M1811**, Singleshot, Smoothbore, S North Army, Brass Furniture, *Antique* 1,375.00 2,150.00
- ☐ **.69 M1817 (18)**, Singleshot, Smoothbore, Springfield, Iron Mounts, *Antique* 1,700.00 2,500.00

HANDGUN, PERCUSSION
- ☐ **.54 M1836**, Singleshot, Smoothbore, Gedney Conversion from Flintlock, Iron Mounts, *Antique* 675.00 975.00
- ☐ **.54 M1842 Aston**, Singleshot, Smoothbore, Brass Mounts, *Antique* 425.00 550.00
- ☐ **.54 M1842 Johnson**, Singleshot, Smoothbore, Brass Mounts, *Antique* 425.00 550.00
- ☐ **.54 M1843 Deringer Army**, Singleshot, Smoothbore, Brass Mounts, *Antique* 425.00 725.00
- ☐ **.54 M1843 Deringer Army**, Singleshot, Rifled, Brass Mounts, *Antique* 700.00 975.00
- ☐ **.54 M1843 Deringer Navy**, Singleshot, Smoothbore, Brass Mounts, *Antique* 650.00 875.00
- ☐ **.54 M1843 N P Ames**, Singleshot, Smoothbore, Brass Mounts, *Antique* 600.00 775.00
- ☐ **.58 M1855 Springfield**, Singleshot, Rifled, Brass Mounts, with Shoulder Stock, *Antique* 600.00 775.00
- ☐ **.58 M1855 Springfield**, Singleshot, Rifled, Brass Mounts, *Antique* 1,450.00 2,250.00

HANDGUN, REVOLVER
- ☐ **M1889 Navy Colt**, .38 Long Colt, 6 Shot, 6" Barrel, Double Action, Swing-Out Cylinder, *Antique* 200.00 400.00
- ☐ **M1892 New Army Colt**, .38 Long Colt, 6 Shot, 6" Barrel, Double Action, Swing-Out Cylinder, *Antique* 175.00 300.00
- ☐ **M1892 New Navy Colt**, .38 Long Colt, 6 Shot, 6" Barrel, Double Action, Swing-Out Cylinder, *Antique* 175.00 275.00
- ☐ **M1896 New Army Colt**, .38 Long Colt, 6 Shot, 6" Barrel, Double Action, Swing-Out Cylinder, *Antique* 150.00 250.00
- ☐ **M1902 Army Colt**, .45 Colt, 6 Shot, 6" Barrel, Double Action, *Curio* 350.00 575.00
- ☐ **M1905 U.S.M.C. Colt**, .38 Long Colt, 6 Shot, 6" Barrel, Double Action, Swing-Out Cylinder, *Curio* 675.00 975.00
- ☐ **M1905 U.S.M.C. Colt**, .38 Special, 6 Shot, 6" Barrel, Double Action, Swing-Out Cylinder, *Curio* 650.00 975.00

U.S. MILITARY / 459

	V.G.	EXC.
☐ **M1909 Army Colt**, .45 Colt, 6 Shot, 5½" Barrel, Double Action, *Curio*	275.00	450.00
☐ **M1909 U.S.M.C. Colt**, .45 Colt, 6 Shot, 5½" Barrel, Double Action, *Curio*	450.00	675.00
☐ **M1909 U.S.N. Colt**, .45 Colt, 6 Shot, 5½" Barrel, Double Action, *Curio*	350.00	525.00
☐ **M1917 Army Colt**, .45 Auto-Rim, 6 Shot, 5½" Barrel, Double Action, *Curio*	250.00	375.00
☐ **M1917 S & W**, .45 Auto-Rim, Double Action, Swing-Out Cylinder, *Curio*	250.00	375.00

HANDGUN, SEMI-AUTOMATIC

	V.G.	EXC.
☐ **Hi Standard H-D M/O.S.S.**, .22 L.R.R.F., Clip Fed, Silencer, Hammer, *Class 3*	550.00	750.00
☐ **M1900 Colt**, .38 ACP, Clip Fed, 6" Barrel, Military, *Curio*	625.00	950.00
☐ **M1902 Colt**, .38 ACP, Clip Fed, 6" Barrel, Military, *Curio*	450.00	625.00
☐ **M1903 Colt**, .32 ACP, Clip Fed, Modern, *Curio*	375.00	500.00
☐ **M1903 Colt**, .380 ACP, Clip Fed, Modern, *Curio*	375.00	500.00
☐ **M1905/07 Colt**, .45 Colt, Clip Fed, Blue, Military, *Curio*	1,500.00	2,250.00
☐ **M1908 Colt**, .32 ACP, Clip Fed, Military, *Curio*	300.00	450.00
☐ **M1908 Colt**, .32 ACP, Clip Fed, Military, Magazine Disconnect, *Curio*	275.00	400.00
☐ **M1908 Colt**, .380 ACP, Clip Fed, Military, *Curio*	300.00	450.00
☐ **M1908 Colt**, .380 ACP, Clip Fed, Military, Magazine Disconnect, *Curio*	275.00	400.00
☐ **M1911**, .45 ACP, Clip Fed, *Curio*	375.00	575.00
☐ **M1911 Springfield**, .45 ACP, Clip Fed, *Curio*	450.00	700.00
☐ **M1911A1**, .45 ACP, Clip Fed, *Curio*	275.00	425.00
☐ **M1911A1 Ithaca**, .45 ACP, Clip Fed, *Curio*	325.00	475.00
☐ **M1911A Remington**, .45 ACP, Clip Fed, *Curio*	325.00	475.00
☐ **M1911A1 Singer**, .45 ACP, Clip Fed, *Curio*	2,150.00	3,500.00
☐ **M1911A1 U.S. & S.**, .45 ACP, Clip Fed, *Curio*	400.00	575.00

HANDGUN, SINGLESHOT

	V.G.	EXC.
☐ **Liberator**, .45 ACP, Military, *Curio*	150.00	225.00
☐ **Liberator**, .45 ACP, Silencer, Militaary, *Class 3*	300.00	375.00

RIFLE, BOLT ACTION

	V.G.	EXC.
☐ **M1871 Ward-Burton**, .50 C.F., Iron Mountings, Rifle, *Antique*	500.00	800.00
☐ **M1871 Ward-Burton**, .50 C.F., Iron Mountings, Carbine, *Antique*	600.00	950.00
☐ **M1882 Chaffee-Reese**, 45-70, Rifle, *Antique*	500.00	800.00
☐ **M1892/6 Krag**, .30-40 Krag, Rifle, *Antique*	240.00	375.00
☐ **M1895 Lee Straight Pull**, 6mm Lee Navy, Musket, *Antique*	550.00	800.00
☐ **M1896 Krag**, .30-40 Krag, Rifle, *Antique*	275.00	400.00
☐ **M1896 Krag**, .30-40 Krag, Cadet, *Antique*	1,375.00	2,000.00
☐ **M1896 Krag**, .30-40 Krag, Carbine, *Antique*	375.00	550.00
☐ **M1898 Krag**, .30-40 Krag, Carbine, *Curio*	475.00	775.00
☐ **M1898 Krag**, .30-40 Krag, Rifle, *Curio*	200.00	350.00
☐ **M1899 Krag**, .30-40 Krag, Carbine, *Curio*	250.00	400.00
☐ **M1903**, .30-06 Springfield, Machined Parts, *Modern*	200.00	325.00
☐ **M1903/5**, 30-03 Springfield, *Curio*	650.00	1,100.00
☐ **M1903/5**, 30-06 Springfield, *Curio*	200.00	350.00
☐ **M1903/7**, 30-06 Springfield, Early Receivers, *Curio*	350.00	600.00
☐ **M1903/WWI**, 30-06 Springfield, *Curio*	300.00	450.00
☐ **M1903/Postwar**, 30-06 Springfield, *Curio*	250.00	375.00
☐ **M1903 National Match**, .30-06 Springfield, Target Rifle, *Curio*	500.00	700.00
☐ **M1903A1**, .30-06 Springfield, Parkerized, Checkered Butt, Machined Parts, *Curio*	170.00	250.00
☐ **M1903A1 National Match**, .30-06 Springfield, Target Rifle, *Curio*	450.00	650.00

U.S. MILITARY

	V.G.	EXC.
☐ **M1903A3**, .30-06 Springfield, Stamped Parts, *Curio*	150.00	225.00
☐ **M1903A4 Sniper**, .30-06 Springfield, Scope Mounts, *Curio*	650.00	975.00
☐ **M1917 Eddystone**, .30-06 Springfield, *Curio*	145.00	200.00
☐ **M1917 Remington**, .30-06 Springfield, *Curio*	155.00	220.00
☐ **M1917 Winchester**, .30-06 Springfield, *Curio*	160.00	235.00
☐ **M1922 Trainer**, .22 L.R.R.F., Target Rifle, *Curio*	600.00	950.00
☐ **M1922M2 Trainer**, .22 L.R.R.F., Target Rifle, *Curio*	400.00	575.00
☐ **M40-XB Sniper (Rem.)**, .308 Win., Heavy Barrel, Scope Mounted, Silencer, *Class 3*	600.00	875.00

RIFLE, FLINTLOCK

	V.G.	EXC.
☐ .52, M1819 Hall, Rifled, Breech Loader, 32½" Barrel, 3 Bands, *Antique*	1,650.00	2,600.00
☐ .52, M1819 Hall Whitney, Rifled, Breech Loader, 32½" Barrel, 3 Bands, *Antique*	1,450.00	2,500.00
☐ .54, M1803 Harper's Ferry, Rifled, 32½" Barrel, *Antique*	1,400.00	2,250.00
☐ .54, M1807 Springfield, Indian, Carbine, 27¾" Barrel, *Antique*	1,400.00	2,300.00
☐ .54, M1814 Ghriskey, Rifled, 36" Barrel, *Antique*	1,400.00	2,500.00
☐ .54, M1814 Harper's Ferry, Rifled, 36" Barrel, *Antique*	775.00	1,500.00
☐ .54, M1817 (Common Rifle), Rifled, 36" Barrel, 3 Bands, *Antique*	1,150.00	2,100.00
☐ .54, M1839 Springfield, Cadet Musket, 40½" or 36" Barrel, 3 Bands, *Antique*	1,100.00	2,100.00
☐ .64, M1837 Hall, Carbine, 23" Barrel, 2 Bands, *Antique*	975.00	1,700.00
☐ .64, M1837 Jenks, Musketoon, 25⅝" or 19½" Barrel, 2 Bands, *Antique*	975.00	1,700.00
☐ .69, M1795 Penn. Contract, Musket, 3 Bands, 44½" Barrel, *Antique*	900.00	1,700.00
☐ .69, M1795 Springfield, Musket, 3 Bands, 44½" Barrel, *Antique*	900.00	1,700.00
☐ .69, M1795 U.S. Contract, Musket, 3 Bands, 44½" Barrel, *Antique*	900.00	1,700.00
☐ .69, M1795 Va. Contract, Musket, 3 Bands, 44½" Barrel, *Antique*	900.00	1,700.00
☐ .69, M1795/98 Whitney, Musket, 3 Bands, 43" Barrel, *Antique*	1,100.00	1,800.00
☐ .69, M1808 Harper's Ferry, Musket, 3 Bands, 44½" Barrel, *Antique*	700.00	1,150.00
☐ .69, M1808 N.Y. Contract, Musket, 40" Barrel, 3 Bands, *Antique*	700.00	1,400.00
☐ .69, M1808 Springfield, Musket, 3 Bands, 44½" Barrel, *Antique*	700.00	1,200.00
☐ .69, M1808 U.S. Contract, Musket, 42" Barrel, 3 Bands, *Antique*	650.00	1,100.00
☐ .69, M1812 Contract, Musket, 40" Barrel, 3 Bands, *Antique*	675.00	1,300.00
☐ .69, M1812 Springfield, Musket, 42" Barrel, 3 Bands, *Antique*	750.00	1,400.00
☐ .69, M1813 (Conversion), Short Musket, 32½" Barrel, 2 Bands, *Antique*	650.00	1,200.00
☐ .69, M1816 Contract, Musket, 42" Barrel, 3 Bands, *Antique*	600.00	1,200.00
☐ .69, M1816 State Militia, Musket, 42" Barrel, 3 Bands, *Antique*	500.00	1,100.00
☐ .69, M1816 U.S. Musket, 42" Barrel, 3 Bands, *Antique*	450.00	975.00
☐ .69, M1817 U.S., Cadet Musket, 36" Barrel, 3 Bands, *Antique*	600.00	1,200.00
☐ .69, M1835 Contract, Adjustable, 42" Barrel, 3 Bands, *Antique*	900.00	1,850.00
☐ .69, M1835 U.S., Musket, 42" Barrel, 3 Bands, *Antique*	975.00	1,900.00
☐ .69, M1840 U.S., Musketoon, 26" Barrel, 2 Bands, *Antique*	1,150.00	2,000.00
☐ **M1808 Harper's Ferry**, Blunderbuss, 27¾" Barrel, *Antique*	5,000.00	8,750.00

RIFLE, LEVER ACTION

	V.G.	EXC.
☐ **Ball Repeating Carbine**, .56-56 Spencer R.F., Tube Feed, *Antique*	650.00	900.00
☐ **Gallager**, 56-62 Spencer, Singleshot, Carbine, *Antique*	450.00	650.00
☐ **Spencer**, .56-50 Spencer R.F., Repeater, Carbine, 7 Shot, Falling Block, *Antique*	400.00	625.00
☐ **Peabody**, Various Calibers, Rifle, *Antique*	225.00	350.00
☐ **Peabody**, Various Calibers, Carbine, *Antique*	375.00	500.00
☐ **Spencer**, .56-52 Spencer R.F., Repeater, Carbine, 7 Shot, Falling Block, *Antique*	475.00	650.00
☐ **Spencer**, .56-56 Spencer R.F., Repeater, 7 Shot, Falling Block, Rifle, *Antique*	675.00	900.00

U.S. MILITARY / 461

U.S. Military M1840 Hall-North

U.S. Military Spencer

U.S. Military Triplett & Scott

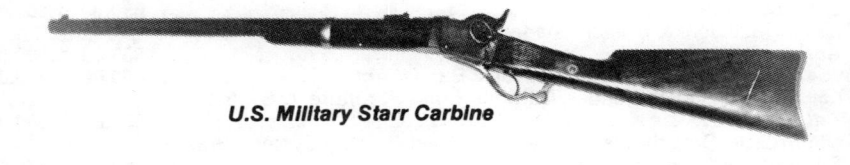

U.S. Military Starr Carbine

U.S. Military M1819 Hall

462 / U.S. MILITARY

	V.G.	EXC.

- ☐ **Spencer**, .56-56 Spencer R.F., Repeater, Carbine, 7 Shot, Falling Block, *Antique* 525.00   750.00
- ☐ **Starr**, .52 R.F., Singleshot, Carbine, *Antique* 450.00   700.00

RIFLE, PERCUSSION
- ☐ **.44**, M1841 Colt, Revolver, Carbine, 8 Shot, *Antique* 6,000.00   9,500.00
- ☐ **.50 Gallagher**, Breech Loader, Carbine, Military, *Antique* 400.00   575.00
- ☐ **.50 Gwyn & Cambell**, Breech Loader, Carbine, Cosmopolitan, *Antique* 450.00   650.00
- ☐ **.50 Joslyn**, Breech Loader, Carbine, *Antique* 850.00   1,400.00
- ☐ **.50 Maynard**, Breech Loader, Carbine, without Tape Priming System, *Antique* 475.00   650.00
- ☐ **.50 Maynard**, Breech Loader, Carbine, *Antique* 575.00   850.00
- ☐ **.52 Smith**, Breech Loader, Carbine, *Antique* 475.00   750.00
- ☐ **.52**, M1838 Hall-North, Carbine, 21" Barrel, 2 Bands, *Antique* 850.00   1,650.00
- ☐ **.52**, M1840 Hall-North, Breech Loader, Carbine, 21" Barrel, 2 Bands, *Antique* 750.00   1,400.00
- ☐ **.52**, M1843 Hall-North, Breech Loader, 21" Barrel, 2 Bands, *Antique* 650.00   1,350.00
- ☐ **.53 Greene**, Breech Loader, Carbine, *Antique* 575.00   900.00
- ☐ **.54 Cal. Burnside**, Breech Loader, Carbine, 1st Model, Singleshot, *Antique* 850.00   1,750.00
- ☐ **.54 Cal. Burnside**, Breech Loader, Carbine, 2nd Model, Singleshot, *Antique* 550.00   950.00
- ☐ **.54 Cal. Burnside**, Breech Loader, Carbine, 3rd Model, Singleshot, *Antique* 475.00   675.00
- ☐ **.54 Cal. Burnside**, Breech Loader, Carbine, 4th Model, Singleshot, *Antique* 475.00   650.00
- ☐ **.54 Gibbs**, Breech Loader, Carbine, Marked William F. Brooks Mfg. Co., *Antique* 650.00   950.00
- ☐ **.54 Greene**, Breech Loader, Under-Hammer, Bolt Action, *Antique* 575.00   850.00
- ☐ **.54 Merrill**, Breech Loader, Carbine, *Antique* 475.00   700.00
- ☐ **.54 Merrill Navy**, Breech Loader, Brass Furniture, *Antique* 575.00   850.00
- ☐ **.54 Starr**, Breech Loader, Carbine, *Antique* 475.00   675.00
- ☐ **.54**, M1836 Hall-North, Rifled, Breech Loader, Carbine, 21" Barrel, 2 Bands, *Antique* 850.00   1,400.00
- ☐ **.54**, M1839 Jenks, Breech Loader, Rifled, 35⅝" Barrel, 3 Bands, *Antique* 800.00   1,500.00
- ☐ **.54**, M1841 U.S., Rifled, 33" Barrel, 2 Bands, *Antique* 600.00   950.00
- ☐ **.56 Sharps**, Breech Loader, Carbine, Brass Furniture, U.S. 1852, *Antique* 650.00   900.00
- ☐ **.56 Sharps**, Breech Loader, Carbine, Pellet Priming System, Brass Furniture, Adjustable Sights, *Antique* 550.00   875.00
- ☐ **.56 Sharps**, Breech Loader, Carbine, with Tape Priming System, Brass Furniture, *Antique* 625.00   900.00
- ☐ **.57**, M1841 U.S., Cadet Musket, 40" Barrel, 2 Bands, *Antique* 700.00   1,150.00
- ☐ **.57**, M1851 U.S., Cadet Musket, Rifled, 40" Barrel, 2 Bands, *Antique* 700.00   1,200.00
- ☐ **.57**, M1851 U.S., Cadet Musket, Smoothbore, 40" Barrel, 2 Bands, *Antique* 650.00   1,100.00
- ☐ **.58 Lindner**, Breech Loader, Carbine, Rising Block, *Antique* 675.00   1,150.00
- ☐ **.58**, M1841 Contract, Rifled, 33" Barrel, 2 Bands, (Mississippi Rifle), *Antique* 600.00   950.00
- ☐ **.58**, M1855 U.S., Rifled, 40" Barrel, 3 Bands, with Tape Priming System, *Antique* 900.00   1,550.00
- ☐ **.58**, M1855 U.S., Carbine, Rifled, 22" Barrel, 1 Band, with Tape Priming System, *Antique* 950.00   1,700.00

	V.G.	EXC.
☐ .64, M1833 Hall-North, Rifled, Breech Loader, Carbine, 26⅛" Barrel, 2 Bands, *Antique*	800.00	1,450.00
☐ .69, M1842 U.S., Musket, 42" Barrel, 3 Bands, *Antique*	525.00	750.00
☐ .69, M1842 U.S., Musket, 42" Barrel, 3 Bands, *Antique*	550.00	800.00
☐ .69, M1847 Artillery, Musketoon, 26" Barrel, 2 Bands, Steel Furniture, *Antique*	600.00	950.00
☐ .69, M1847 Cavalry, Musketoon, 26" Barrel, 2 Bands, Brass Furniture, *Antique*	550.00	800.00
☐ .69, M1847 Sappers, Musketoon, 26" Barrel, 2 Bands, Bayonet Stud on Right Side, *Antique*	850.00	1,400.00
☐ **M 1864 Training Rifle**, Military, Wood Barrel, *Antique*	65.00	125.00

RIFLE, SEMI-AUTOMATIC

	V.G.	EXC.
☐ **M1941 Johnson**, 30-06 Springfield, Military, *Curio*	325.00	475.00
☐ **M-1 Carbine**, .30 Carbine, Clip Fed, *Curio*	175.00	275.00
☐ **M-1 Carbine Irwin-Pedersen**, .30 Carbine, Clip Fed, *Curio*	475.00	700.00
☐ **M-1 Carbine Quality Hdw.**, .30 Carbine, Clip Fed, *Curio*	525.00	800.00
☐ **M-1 Carbine Winchester**, .30 Carbine, Clip Fed, *Curio*	250.00	365.00
☐ **M-1 Garand**, .30-06 Springfield, Military, *Curio*	525.00	800.00
☐ **M-1 Garand National Match**, .30-06 Springfield, Military, Target Sights, Target Trigger, Target Barrel, *Curio*	700.00	975.00
☐ **M-1 Garand Winchester**, .30-06 Springfield, *Curio*	675.00	925.00
☐ **M-180**, .22 L.R.R.F., Carbine, 177 Round Drum Magazine, *Modern*	255.00	325.00
☐ **M-1A1 Carbine**, .30 Carbine, Clip Fed, Folding Stock, *Modern*	350.00	475.00
☐ **M-4 Survival Rifle**, .22 Hornet, Short Barrel, *Class 3*	475.00	650.00

RIFLE, SINGLESHOT

	V.G.	EXC.
☐ **Ballard Military Carbine**, .44 Long R.F., Falling Block, *Antique*	325.00	475.00
☐ **Ballard Military Carbine**, .54 Ballard R.F., Falling Block, *Antique*	375.00	500.00
☐ **Ballard Military Rifle**, .54 Ballard R.F., Falling Block, *Antique*	425.00	550.00
☐ **Gallagher**, .56-50 Spencer R.F., Carbine, Military, *Antique*	375.00	550.00
☐ **Joslyn**, .50-70 Government. R.F., Army Rifle, Converted to Centerfire, *Antique*	500.00	800.00
☐ **Joslyn**, .56-56 Spencer R.F., Carbine, *Antique*	450.00	600.00
☐ **1873 Springfield**, .45-70 Government, Trap Door Action, 32⅜" Barrel, *Antique*	350.00	475.00
☐ **M1873 Springfield**, .45-70 Government, Trap Door Action, Carbine, 21¾" Barrel, *Antique*	475.00	675.00
☐ **M1873 Springfield**, .45-70 Government, Trap Door Action, Cadet Rifle, 29½" Barrel, *Antique*	400.00	625.00
☐ **M1875 Officer's Model**, .45-70 Government, Trap Door Action, 26" Barrel, *Antique*	2,500.00	3,750.00
☐ **M1884 Springfield**, .45-70 Government, Trap Door Action, Buffington Sights, *Antique*	325.00	450.00
☐ **1884 Springfield**, .45-70 Government, Trap Door Action, Carbine, Buffington Sights, *Antique*	400.00	550.00
☐ **M1884 Springfield**, .45-70 Government, Trap Door Action, Cadet Rifle, Buffington Sights, *Antique*	375.00	550.00
☐ **Palmer**, .56-50 Spencer R.F., Carbine, Military, E.G. Lamson & Co., *Antique*	475.00	775.00
☐ **Sharps & Hankins Navy**, .52-70 Sharps R.F., Breech Loader, *Antique*	500.00	725.00
☐ **Sharps & Hankins Navy**, .52-70 Sharps R.F., Breech Loader, Carbine, *Antique*	425.00	750.00
☐ **Starr**, .56-56 Spencer R.F., Breech Loader, Carbine, *Antique*	450.00	675.00
☐ **Triplett & Scott**, .50 R.F., Breech Loader, *Antique*	425.00	600.00
☐ **Warner**, .56-50 Spencer R.F., Brass Frame, Carbine, *Antique*	650.00	975.00
☐ **Wesson**, .44 Long R.F., Breech Loader, Carbine, *Antique*	450.00	650.00

464 / U.S. REVOLVER COMPANY

	V.G.	EXC.
SHOTGUN, SINGLESHOT		
☐ **Model 1881**, 20 Gauge, "Forager" Trapdoor, *Antique*	500.00	950.00
☐ **Model 107-Hawaii**, 12 Ga., Hammer, Automatic Ejector, (Stevens), *Modern*	65.00	90.00
SHOTGUN, SLIDE ACTION		
☐ **M 520 Savage**, 12 Ga., Riot Gun, Military, *Modern*	95.00	150.00
☐ **Model 520 Riot**, 12 Ga., Takedown, (Stevens), *Modern*	80.00	145.00
☐ **Model 620 Riot**, 12 Ga., Takedown, (Stevens), *Modern*	80.00	145.00

U.S. REVOLVER CO.
Made by Iver Johnson.

	V.G.	EXC.
HANDGUN, REVOLVER		
☐ **.22 L.R.R.F.**, 7 Shot, Top Break, Double Action, *Modern*	55.00	90.00
☐ **.22 Short R.F.**, 7 Shot, Spur Trigger, Solid Frame, Single Action, *Antique*	90.00	150.00
☐ **.32 S & W**, 5 Shot, Double Action, Solid Frame, *Modern*	45.00	80.00
☐ **.32 S & W**, 5 Shot, Top Break, Hammerless, Double Action, *Modern*	55.00	95.00
☐ **.32 S & W**, 5 Shot, Double Action, Top Break, *Modern*	45.00	95.00
☐ **.32 Short R.F.**, 5 Shot, Spur Trigger, Solid Frame, Single Action, *Antique*	90.00	160.00
☐ **.38 S & W**, 5 Shot, Double Action, Solid Frame, *Modern*	45.00	70.00
☐ **.38 S & W**, 5 Shot, Top Break, Hammerless, Double Action, *Modern*	55.00	95.00
☐ **.38 S & W**, 5 Shot, Double Action, Top Break, *Modern*	45.00	95.00

VALIANT
Made by Stevens Arms for Spear & Co., Pittsburgh, Pa.

	V.G.	EXC.
RIFLE, BOLT ACTION		
☐ **Model 51**, .22 L.R.R.F., Singleshot, Takedown, *Modern*	30.00	40.00

VALMET
Valmet Oy, Tourula Works, Jyvaskyla, Finland.

	V.G.	EXC.
AUTOMATIC WEAPON, ASSAULT RIFLE		
☐ **M78 LMG**, .308 Win., Clip Fed, Bipod, *Class 3*	700.00	1,100.00
☐ **Model 718S**, .223 Rem., Clip Fed, Commercial, *Class 3*	450.00	650.00
RIFLE, SEMI-AUTOMATIC		
☐ **M78 HV**, .223 Rem., Clip Fed, Bipod, *Modern*	700.00	1,100.00
☐ **M78 Standard**, .308 Win., Clip Fed, Bipod, *Modern*	700.00	1,100.00
☐ **M-62S**, 7.62 x 39 Russian, Clip Fed, AK-47 Type, Sporting Version of Military Rifle, *Modern*	550.00	775.00
☐ **M-72S**, .223 Rem., Clip Fed, AK-47 Type, Sporting Version of Military Rifle, *Modern*	475.00	700.00

VALOR ARMS
Importers Miami, Fla.

	V.G.	EXC.
HANDGUN, REVOLVER		
☐ **.22 L.R.R.F.**, Double Action, Lightweight, *Modern*	15.00	25.00
☐ **.32 S & W**, Double Action, Lightweight, *Modern*	15.00	25.00

VANDERFRIFT, ISAAC AND JEREMIAH
Philadelphia, Pa. 1809-1815. See Kentucky Rifles and Pistols.

VEGA
Sacramento, Calif.

	V.G.	EXC.

HANDGUN, SEMI-AUTOMATIC
- ☐ **Vega 1911a1**, .45 ACP, Stainless Steel, Clip Fed, *Modern* 200.00 295.00
- ☐ **Vega 1911a1**, .45 ACP, Adjustable Sights, Stainless Steel, Clip Fed, *Modern* 220.00 325.00

VELO DOG
Various makers, c. 1900.

HANDGUN, REVOLVER
- ☐ **5mm Velo Dog**, Hammerless, Folding Trigger, *Curio* 70.00 100.00
- ☐ **5mm Velo Dog**, Hammer, Folding Trigger, *Curio* 60.00 90.00
- ☐ **5mm Velo Dog**, Hammerless, Trigger Guard, *Curio* 60.00 90.00
- ☐ **.25 ACP**, Hammerless, Folding Trigger, *Curio* 70.00 100.00
- ☐ **.25 ACP**, Hammer, Folding Trigger, *Curio* 70.00 100.00

VENCEDOR
San Martin y Cia., Eibar, Spain.

HANDGUN, SEMI-AUTOMATIC
- ☐ **.25 ACP**, Clip Fed, Blue, *Modern* 80.00 120.00
- ☐ **.35 ACP**, Clip Fed, Blue, *Modern* 90.00 135.00

VENTURA IMPORTS (CONTENTO)
Seal Beach, Calif. Also see Bertuzzi and Piotti.

SHOTGUN, DOUBLE BARREL, OVER-UNDER
- ☐ **MK-1 Contento**, 12 Ga., Field Grade, Automatic Ejector, Single Selective Trigger, Engraved, Checkered Stock, *Modern* 325.00 450.00
- ☐ **MK-2 Contento**, 12 Ga., Field Grade, Automatic Ejector, Single Selective Trigger, Engraved, Checkered Stock, *Modern* 450.00 650.00
- ☐ **MK-2 Contento**, 12 Ga., Trap Grade, with Extra Single Trap Barrel, Engraved, Checkered Stock, *Modern* 750.00 1,100.00
- ☐ **MK-2 Luxe Contento**, 12 Ga., Field Grade, Automatic Ejector, Single Selective Trigger, Engraved, Checkered Stock, *Modern* 625.00 800.00
- ☐ **MK-2 Luxe Contento**, 12 Ga., Trap Grade, with Extra Single Trap Barrel, Engraved, Checkered Stock, *Modern* 950.00 1,300.00
- ☐ **MK-3 Contento**, 12 Ga., Field Grade, Automatic Ejector, Single Selective Trigger, Engraved, Checkered Stock, *Modern* 750.00 1,000.00
- ☐ **MK-3 Contento**, 12 Ga., Trap Grade, with Extra Single Trap Barrel, Engraved, Checkered Stock, *Modern* 1,200.00 1,700.00
- ☐ **MK-3 Luxe Contento**, 12 Ga., Field Grade, Automatic Ejector, Single Selective Trigger, Engraved, Checkered Stock, *Modern* 950.00 1,300.00
- ☐ **MK-3 Luxe Contento**, 12 Ga., Trap Grade, with Extra Single Trap Barrel, Engraved, Checkered Stock, *Modern* 1,450.00 2,000.00
- ☐ **Nettuno Contento**, 12 Ga., Field Grade, Automatic Ejector, Single Selective Trigger, Engraved, Checkered Stock, *Modern* 250.00 375.00

SHOTGUN, DOUBLE BARREL, SIDE-BY-SIDE
- ☐ **Ventura Model 51**, 12 and 20 Gauges, Boxlock, Checkered Stock, *Modern* 250.00 375.00
- ☐ **Ventura Model 62 Standard**, 12 and 20 Gauges, Sidelock, Checkered Stock, Engraved, *Modern* 475.00 700.00
- ☐ **Ventura Model 64 Standard**, 12 and 20 Gauges, Sidelock, Checkered Stock, Engraved, *Modern* 475.00 700.00

VENUS
Tomas de Urizar y Cia., Eibar, Spain.

	V.G.	EXC.

HANDGUN, SEMI-AUTOMATIC
☐ **.32 ACP**, Clip Fed, *Modern* 85.00   125.00

VENUS
Venus Waffenwerk Oskar Will, Zella Mehlis, Germany, c. 1912.
HANDGUN, SEMI-AUTOMATIC
☐ **.32 ACP**, Target Pistol, Hammerless, Blue, *Curio* 325.00   540.00

VERNEY-CARRON
St. Etienne, France
HANDGUN, SEMI-AUTOMATIC
☐ **.25 ACP**, Clip Fed, Blue, *Modern* 125.00   165.00
SHOTGUN, DOUBLE BARREL, OVER-UNDER
☐ **Field Grade**, 12 Ga., Automatic Ejectors, Checkered Stock,
  Engraved, *Modern* 450.00   675.00

Vesta

Vici

VESTA
Hijos de A. Echeverra, Eibar, Spain.
HANDGUN, SEMI-AUTOMATIC
☐ **Pocket**, .32 ACP, Clip Fed, Long Grip, *Modern* 80.00   125.00
☐ **Vest Pocket**, .25 ACP, Clip Fed, *Modern*.......................... 80.00   120.00

VETERAN
Made by Norwich Falls Pistol Co., c. 1880.
HANDGUN, REVOLVER
☐ **.32 Short R.F.**, 5 Shot, Spur Trigger, Solid Frame, Single Action,
  Antique 90.00   160.00

VETO
Unknown maker, c. 1880.
HANDGUN, REVOLVER
☐ **.32 Short R.F.**, 5 Shot, Spur Trigger, Solid Frame, Single Action,
  Antique 90.00   160.00

VICI
Unknown Belgian maker.
HANDGUN, SEMI-AUTOMATIC
☐ **.25 ACP**, Clip Fed, *Modern* 85.00   125.00

VICTOR
Made by Crescent, c. 1900.

	V.G.	EXC.

SHOTGUN, DOUBLE BARREL, SIDE-BY-SIDE
- ☐ **Various Gauges**, Outside Hammers, Damascus Barrel, *Modern* 100.00   175.00
- ☐ **Various Gauges**, Hammerless, Steel Barrel, *Modern* 135.00   200.00
- ☐ **Various Gauges**, Hammerless, Damascus Barrel, *Modern* 100.00   175.00
- ☐ **Various Gauges**, Outside Hammers, Steel Barrel, *Modern* 125.00   190.00

SHOTGUN, SINGLESHOT
- ☐ **Various Gauges**, Hammer, Steel Barrel, *Modern* 55.00   85.00

VICTOR
Francisco Arizmendi, Eibar, Spain, c. 1916.

HANDGUN, SEMI-AUTOMATIC
- ☐ **.25 ACP**, Clip Fed, Blue, *Curio* 85.00   120.00
- ☐ **.32 ACP**, Clip Fed, Blue, *Curio* 95.00   135.00

VICTOR #1
Made by Harrington & Richardson, c. 1876.

HANDGUN, REVOLVER
- ☐ **.32 S & W**, 5 Shot, Single Action, Solid Frame, *Antique* 55.00   95.00
- ☐ **#1**, .22 Short R.F., 7 Shot, Spur Trigger, Solid Frame, Single Action, *Antique* 90.00   160.00
- ☐ **#2**, .32 Short R.F., 5 Shot, Spur Trigger, Solid Frame, Single Action, *Antique* 90.00   160.00

VICTOR SPECIAL
Made by Crescent for Hibbard-Spencer-Bartlett Co., c. 1900.

SHOTGUN, DOUBLE BARREL, SIDE-BY-SIDE
- ☐ **Various Gauges**, Outside Hammers, Damascus Barrel, *Modern* 100.00   175.00
- ☐ **Various Gauges**, Hammerless, Steel Barrel, *Modern* 135.00   200.00
- ☐ **Various Gauges**, Hammerless, Damascus Barrel, *Modern* 100.00   175.00
- ☐ **Various Gauges**, Outside Hammers, Steel Barrel, *Modern* 125.00   190.00

SHOTGUN, SINGLESHOT
- ☐ **Various Gauges**, Hammer, Steel Barrel, *Modern* 55.00   85.00

VICTORIA
Made by Hood Firearms, c. 1875.

HANDGUN, REVOLVER
- ☐ **.32 Short R.F.**, 5 Shot, Spur Trigger, Solid Frame, Single Action, *Antique* 90.00   160.00

Victoria .25

VICTORIA
Spain, Esperanza y Unceta, c. 1900.

                                                                             V.G.   EXC.

HANDGUN, SEMI-AUTOMATIC
- **M1911**, .32 ACP, Clip Fed, *Modern* 90.00   130.00
- **.25 ACP**, Clip Fed, *Modern* 85.00   120.00

VICTORY
M. Zulaica y Cia., Eibar, Spain.

HANDGUN, SEMI-AUTOMATIC
- **.25 ACP**, Clip Fed, *Modern* 110.00   140.00

VILAR
Spain, unknown maker 1920-1938.

HANDGUN, SEMI-AUTOMATIC
- **Pocket**, .32 ACP, Clip Fed, Long Grip, *Modern* 80.00   120.00

VINCITOR
M. Zulaica y Cia., Eibar, Spain.

HANDGUN, SEMI-AUTOMATIC
- **Model 1914**, .25 ACP, Clip Fed, Blue, *Curio* 95.00   140.00
- **Model 14 No. 2**, .32 ACP, Clip Fed, Blue, *Curio* 110.00   150.00

VINDEX
Mre. d'Armes des Pyrenees, Hendaye, France.

HANDGUN, SEMI-AUTOMATIC
- **.32 ACP**, Clip Fed, Blue, *Modern* 70.00   110.00

VIRGINIA ARMS CO.
Made by Crescent for Virginia-Caroline Co., c. 1900.

SHOTGUN, DOUBLE BARREL, SIDE-BY-SIDE
- **Various Gauges**, Outside Hammers, Damascus Barrel, *Modern* 100.00   175.00
- **Various Gauges**, Hammerless, Steel Barrel, *Modern* 135.00   200.00
- **Various Gauges**, Hammerless, Damascus Barrel, *Modern* 100.00   175.00
- **Various Gauges**, Outside Hammers, Steel Barrel, *Modern* 125.00   190.00

SHOTGUN, SINGLESHOT
- **Various Gauges**, Hammer, Steel Barrel, *Modern* 55.00   85.00

VIRGINIAN
Made by Interarms, Alexandria, Va.

HANDGUN, REVOLVER
- **Dragoon, Buntline**, Various Calibers, Single Action, Western Style, Target Sights, Blue, *Modern* 140.00   185.00
- **Dragoon, Deputy**, Various Calibers, Single Action, Western Style, Fixed Sights, Blue, *Modern* 140.00   175.00
- **Dragoon, Deputy**, Various Calibers, Single Action, Western Style, Fixed Sights, Stainless Steel, *Modern* 140.00   175.00
- **Dragoon, Silhouette**, .44 Magnum, Single Action, Western Style, Target Sights, Stainless Steel, *Modern* 160.00   225.00
- **Dragoon, Standard**, Various Calibers, Single Action, Western Style, Target Sights, Blue, *Modern* 140.00   185.00
- **Dragoon, Standard**, Various Calibers, Single Action, Western Style, Target Sights, Stainless Steel, *Modern* 145.00   195.00

WAFFENFABRIK BERN / 469

	V.G.	EXC.
☐ **Dragoon, Engraved**, Various Calibers, Single Action, Western Style, Target Sights, Blue, *Modern*	225.00	350.00
☐ **Dragoon, Engraved**, Various Calibers, Single Action, Western Style, Target Sights, Stainless Steel, *Modern*	250.00	375.00

VITE
Echave y Arizmendi, Eibar, Spain, c. 1913.

HANDGUN, SEMI-AUTOMATIC
☐ **Model 1912**, .25 ACP, Clip Fed, Blue, *Curio*	80.00	120.00
☐ **Model 1915**, .32 ACP, Clip Fed, Blue, *Curio*	85.00	125.00

VOERE
Voere GmbH, Vohrenbach, West Germany.

RIFLE, BOLT ACTION
☐ **Model 3145 DJV**, .223 Rem., Match Rifle, Target Stock, *Modern*	300.00	450.00
☐ **Model 2145**, .308 Win., Match Rifle, Target Stock, *Modern*	450.00	650.00
☐ **Premier Mauser**, Various Calibers, Sporting Rifle, Checkered Stock, Recoil Pad, Open Rear Sight, *Modern*	145.00	195.00
☐ **Shikar**, Various Calibers, Sporting Rifle, Fancy Checkering, Fancy Wood, Recoil Pad, no Sights, *Modern*	275.00	375.00
☐ **Titan-Menor**, Various Calibers, Sporting Rifle, Checkered Stock, Recoil Pad, Open Rear Sight, *Modern*	200.00	275.00

VOERE
Voere Tiroler Jagd u. Sportwaffenfabrik, Kufstein, Austria.

RIFLE, BOLT ACTION
☐ **Model 2155**, Various Calibers, Sporting Rifle, Checkered Stock, Open Rear Sight, *Modern*	175.00	225.00
☐ **Model 2165/1**, Various Calibers, Sporting Rifle, Checkered Stock, Recoil Pad, Open Rear Sight, *Modern*	300.00	400.00

VOLUNTEER
Made by Stevens Arms for Belknap Hardware Co., Louisville, Ky.

SHOTGUN, SINGLESHOT
☐ **Model 94**, Various Gauges, Takedown, Automatic Ejector, Plain, Hammer, *Modern*	40.00	60.00

VULCAN ARMS CO.
Made by Crescent, c. 1900.

SHOTGUN, DOUBLE BARREL, SIDE-BY-SIDE
☐ **Various Gauges**, Outside Hammers, Damascus Barrel, *Modern*	100.00	175.00
☐ **Various Gauges**, Hammerless, Steel Barrel, *Modern*	135.00	200.00
☐ **Various Gauges**, Hammerless, Damascus Barrel, *Modern*	100.00	175.00
☐ **Various Gauges**, Outside Hammers, Steel Barrel, *Modern*	125.00	190.00

SHOTGUN, SINGLESHOT
☐ **Various Gauges**, Hammer, Steel Barrel, *Modern*	55.00	85.00

WAFFENFABRIK BERN
Eidgenosssische Waffenfabrik, Bern, Switzerland. Also see Swiss Military.

RIFLE, BOLT ACTION
☐ **Model 31**, 7.5mm Swiss, Military Style, *Modern*	425.00	600.00
☐ **Model 31 Target**, 7.5mm Swiss, Military Style, Match Rifle, Target Sights, *Modern*	525.00	775.00

WALDMAN
Arizmendi Y Goenaga, Eibar, Spain.

	V.G.	EXC.
HANDGUN, SEMI-AUTOMATIC		
☐ **.25 ACP**, Clip Fed, *Curio*	85.00	125.00
☐ **.32 ACP**, Clip Fed, *Curio*	95.00	140.00

WALMAN
F. Arizmendi Y Goenaga, Eibar, Spain.

HANDGUN, SEMI-AUTOMATIC
- ☐ **.25 ACP**, Clip Fed, *Curio* 85.00 125.00
- ☐ **.32 ACP**, Clip Fed, *Curio* 95.00 140.00
- ☐ **.380 ACP**, Clip Fed, *Curio* 150.00 200.00

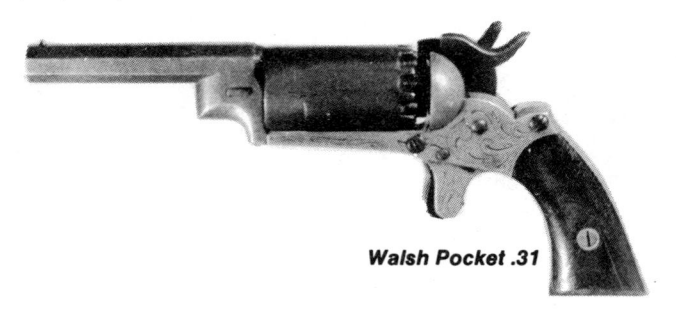

Walsh Pocket .31

WALSH FIREARMS CO.
N.Y.C., c. 1860.

HANDGUN, PERCUSSION
- ☐ **Navy**, .36, Revolver, 12 Shot, Double-Charge Cylinder, *Antique* ... 1,250.00 2,000.00
- ☐ **Pocket**, .31, Revolver, 12 Shot, Double-Charge Cylinder, *Antique* 450.00 650.00

WALSH, JAMES
Philadelphia, Pa. 1775-1779. See Kentucky Rifles and Pistols and U.S. Military.

WALTHER
First started in 1886 by Carl Walther in Zella Mehlis, Germany. After his death in 1915 the firm was operated by his sons Fritz, George, and Erich, and after WWII moved to Ulm/Donau, West Germany. Also see German Military, Manurhin.

HANDGUN, SEMI-AUTOMATIC
- ☐ **Model 1**, .25 ACP, Blue, *Curio* 185.00 295.00
- ☐ **Model 2**, .25 ACP, Pop-Up Rear Sight, Blue, *Curio* 400.00 750.00
- ☐ **Model 3**, .32 ACP, Blue, *Curio* 450.00 700.00
- ☐ **Model 3/4**, .32 ACP, Takedown Lever, Blue, *Curio* 185.00 295.00
- ☐ **Model 4**, .32 ACP, Blue, *Curio* 160.00 240.00
- ☐ **Model 5/2**, .25 ACP, no Sights, Blue, *Curio* 160.00 235.00
- ☐ **Model 5**, .25 ACP, Solid Rib, Blue, *Curio* 160.00 235.00
- ☐ **Model 6**, 9mm Luger, Blue, *Curio* 825.00 1,350.00
- ☐ **Model 7**, .25 ACP, Blue, *Curio* 200.00 320.00
- ☐ **Model 8**, .25 ACP, Blue, *Modern* 170.00 265.00
- ☐ **Model 8**, .25 ACP, Blue, Lightweight, *Modern* 250.00 375.00
- ☐ **Model 9**, .25 ACP, Blue, *Modern* 195.00 285.00
- ☐ **Model GSP**, .22 L.R.R.F., 5 Shot Clip, Target Pistol, *Modern* 475.00 700.00
- ☐ **Model GSP C**, .22 Short, 5 Shot Clip, Target Pistol, *Modern* 550.00 775.00

WALTHER / 471

	V.G.	EXC.
☐ **Model GSP C**, .22 Short, 5 Shot Clip, Target Pistol, with .22 L.R. Conversion Kit, *Modern*	800.00	1,300.00
☐ **Model HP**, .30 Luger, Single Action, *Modern*	3,650.00	5,000.00
☐ **Model HP**, .30 Luger, Single Action, Wood Grips, *Modern*	3,800.00	5,500.00
☐ **Model HP**, Commercial Finish, 9mm Luger, Double Action, Lightweight, *Modern*	2,500.00	3,500.00
☐ **Model HP Croation**, 9mm Luger, Double Action, Military, *Curio*	2,950.00	4,000.00
☐ **Model HP Exposed Extractor**, 9mm Luger, Double Action, Military, *Curio*	975.00	1,650.00
☐ **Model HP Late Military**, 9mm Luger, Double Action, Military, *Curio*	675.00	900.00
☐ **Model HP Late Serial # Placement**, 9mm Luger, Action, Military, *Curio*	675.00	900.00
☐ **Model HP Round Pin Early**, 9mm Luger, Double Action, Military, *Curio*	850.00	1,200.00
☐ **Model HP Swedish**, 9mm Luger, Double Action, Military, *Curio*	975.00	1,400.00
☐ **Model HP Waffenamt**, 9mm Luger, Double Action, Military, *Curio*	575.00	775.00
☐ **Model AP Armee Pistole**, 9mm Luger, Double Action, Hammerless, Blue, *Modern*	4,000.00	6,500.00
☐ **Model OSP**, .22 Short R.F., 5 Shot Clip, Target Pistol, *Modern*	550.00	725.00
☐ **Model PP Sport**, .22 L.R.R.F., Target Pistol, Clip Fed, *Modern*	250.00	395.00
☐ **Olympia Funkamph**, .22 L.R.R.F., Target Pistol, *Modern*	675.00	975.00
☐ **Olympia Hunting**, .22 L.R.R.F., Target Pistol, *Modern*	445.00	595.00
☐ **Olympia Rapid Fire**, .22 L.R.R.F., Target Pistol, *Modern*	495.00	725.00
☐ **Olympia Sport**, .22 L.R.R.F., Target Pistol, *Modern*	395.00	575.00
☐ **P.38**, 9mm Luger, Double Action, Military, *Modern*	325.00	475.00
☐ **P.38 (Current)**, .22 L.R.R.F., Double Action, *Modern*	375.00	500.00
☐ **P.38 (Current)**, .30 Luger, Double Action, Blue, *Modern*	325.00	450.00
☐ **P.38 (Current)**, 9mm Luger, Double Action, *Modern*	300.00	425.00
☐ **P.38 "480"**, 9mm Luger, Double Action, Military, *Curio*	595.00	850.00
☐ **P.38 1st. Model Zero Series**, 9mm Luger, Double Action, *Modern*	775.00	1,200.00
☐ **P.38 2nd. Model Zero Series**, 9mm Luger, Double Action, Military, *Curio*	625.00	950.00
☐ **P.38 3rd. Model Zero Series**, 9mm Luger, Double Action, Military, *Curio*	525.00	850.00
☐ **P.38 ac No Date**, 9mm Luger, Double Action, Military, *Curio*	695.00	975.00
☐ **P.38 ac-45 Zero Series**, 9mm Luger, Double Action, Military, *Curio*	395.00	550.00
☐ **P.38 ac-40**, 9mm Luger, Double Action, Military, *Curio*	445.00	550.00
☐ **P.38 ac-41**, 9mm Luger, Double Action, Military, *Curio*	425.00	550.00
☐ **P.38 ac-41 Military Finish**, 9mm Luger, Double Action, Military, *Curio*	345.00	450.00
☐ **P.38 ac-42**, 9mm Luger, Double Action, Military, *Curio*	285.00	395.00
☐ **P.38 ac-43 Double Line**, 9mm Luger, Double Action, Military, *Modern*	285.00	395.00
☐ **P.38 ac-43 Police**, 9mm Luger, Double Action, Military, *Modern*	725.00	995.00
☐ **P.38 ac-43 Single Line**, 9mm Luger, Double Action, Military, *Curio*	295.00	445.00
☐ **P.38 ac-43 WaA135**, 9mm Luger, Double Action, Military, *Curio*	325.00	450.00
☐ **P.38 ac-44**, 9mm Luger, Double Action, Military, *Curio*	295.00	400.00
☐ **P.38 ac-44 Police**, 9mm Luger, Double Action, Military, *Curio*	725.00	995.00
☐ **P.38 ac-44 WaA140**, 9mm Luger, Double Action, Military, *Curio*	375.00	450.00
☐ **P.38 ac-45**, 9mm Luger, Double Action, Military, *Curio*	295.00	395.00
☐ **P.38 ac-45 Mismatch**, 9mm Luger, Double Action, Military, *Curio*	295.00	395.00
☐ **P.38 byf-42**, 9mm Luger, Double Action, Military, *Curio*	395.00	550.00
☐ **P.38 byf-43**, 9mm Luger, Double Action, Military, *Curio*	295.00	395.00
☐ **P.38 byf-43 Police**, 9mm Luger, Double Action, Military, *Modern*	625.00	950.00
☐ **P.38 byf-44**, 9mm Luger, Double Action, Military, *Curio*	295.00	395.00
☐ **P.38 byf-44 Police F Dual T**, 9mm Luger, Double Action, Military, *Modern*	550.00	795.00

472 / WALTHER

Walther PP Super

Walther Olympia

Walther PP .32

Walther Model 3/4

Walther Model 5

Walther Model 2/5

Walther Model 2

	V.G.	EXC.
☐ **P.38 byf-44 Police L Dual T**, 9mm Luger, Double Action, Military, *Modern*	950.00	1,400.00
☐ **P.38 byf-44 Police L**, 9mm Luger, Double Action, Military, *Modern*	650.00	900.00
☐ **P.38 cyq**, 9mm Luger, Double Action, Military, *Curio*	295.00	395.00
☐ **P.38 cyq 1945**, 9mm Luger, Double Action, Military, *Curio*	350.00	450.00
☐ **P.38 cyq Zero Series**, 9mm Luger, Double Action, Military, *Curio*	325.00	450.00
☐ **P.38 svw-45**, 9mm Luger, Double Action, Military, *Curio*	375.00	500.00
☐ **P.38 svw-45 French**, 9mm Luger, Double Action, Military, *Modern*	450.00	575.00
☐ **P.38 svw-45 Police**, 9mm Luger, Double Action, Military, *Modern*	875.00	1,200.00
☐ **P.38 svw-46**, 9mm Luger, Double Action, Military, *Modern*	495.00	695.00
☐ **P.38k**, 9mm Luger, Double Action, Short Barrel, *Modern*	350.00	450.00
☐ **P.38-IV (P.4)**, 9mm Luger, Double Action, *Modern*	350.00	450.00
☐ **P.5**, 9mm Luger, Interarms, Double Action, Blue, *Modern*	450.00	650.00
☐ **PP**, .22 L.R.R.F., Double Action, Pre-War, Commercial, Nickel Plated, *Curio*	350.00	525.00
☐ **PP**, .22 L.R.R.F., Double Action, Pre-War, Commercial, Nickel Plated, Nazi-Proofed, *Curio*	350.00	525.00
☐ **PP**, .22 L.R.R.F., Double Action, Pre-War, Commercial, High-Polish Finish, *Modern*	295.00	450.00
☐ **PP**, .22 L.R.R.F., Double Action, Pre-War, Commercial, High-Polish Finish, Nazi-Proofed, *Modern*	345.00	475.00
☐ **PP**, .22 L.R.R.F., Double Action, Lightweight, *Modern*	345.00	475.00
☐ **PP**, .25 ACP, Double Action, Pre-War, Commercial, High-Polish Finish, *Curio*	975.00	1,550.00
☐ **PP**, .32 ACP, Double Action, Pre-War, Commercial, Lightweight, High-Polish Finish, *Curio*	425.00	575.00
☐ **PP**, .32 ACP, Double Action, Pre-War, Nazi-Proofed, Lightweight, High-Polish Finish, *Curio*	425.00	575.00
☐ **PP**, .32 ACP, Double Action, Pre-War, Nazi-Proofed, Lightweight, *Curio*	375.00	500.00
☐ **PP**, .32 ACP, Double Action, Pre-War, Commercial, Nickel Plated, *Curio*	375.00	500.00
☐ **PP**, .32 ACP, Double Action, Pre-War, Commercial, Nickel Plated, Nazi-Proofed, *Curio*	375.00	500.00
☐ **PP**, .32 ACP, Double Action, Pre-War, Commercial, High-Polish Finish, *Modern*	265.00	375.00
☐ **PP**, .32 ACP, Double Action, Pre-War, Commercial, High-Polish Finish, Nazi-Proofed, *Modern*	295.00	395.00
☐ **PP**, .32 ACP, Double Action, Pre-War, Commercial, Nazi-Proofed, *Modern*	265.00	375.00
☐ **PP**, .32 ACP, Double Action, Lightweight, *Curio*	350.00	475.00
☐ **PP**, .380 ACP, Double Action, Pre-War, Commercial, High-Polish Finish, *Modern*	345.00	475.00
☐ **PP**, .38 ACP, Double Action, Pre-War, Commercial, High-Polish Finish, Nazi-Proofed, *Modern*	395.00	495.00
☐ **PP**, .380 ACP, Double Action, Pre-War, Commercial, Nickel Plated, *Curio*	750.00	950.00
☐ **PP**, .380 ACP, Double Action, Pre-War, Commercial, Nickel Plated, Nazi-Proofed, *Curio*	700.00	900.00
☐ **PP**, .380 ACP, Double Action, Lightweight, *Modern*	345.00	495.00
☐ **PP "Nairobi"**, .32 ACP, Double Action, Pre-War, High-Polish Finish, *Curio*	625.00	840.00
☐ **PP (Current)**, .22 L.R.R.F., Double Action, *Modern*	300.00	400.00
☐ **PP (Current)**, .32 ACP, Double Action, Blue, *Modern*	275.00	375.00
☐ **PP (Current)**, .380 ACP, Double Action, Blue, *Modern*	290.00	400.00

474 / WALTHER

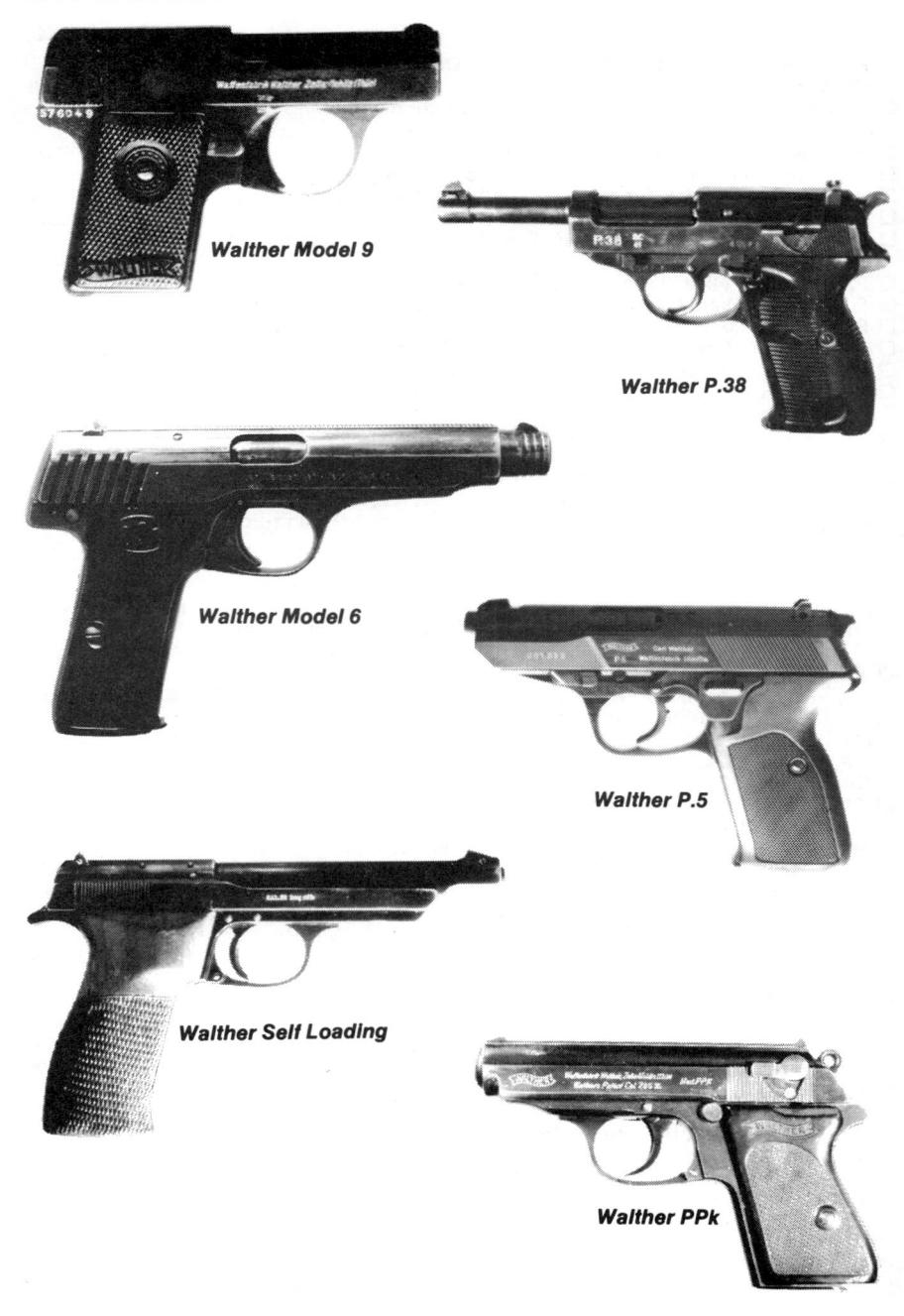

Walther Model 9

Walther P.38

Walther Model 6

Walther P.5

Walther Self Loading

Walther PPk

WALTHER / 475

	V.G.	EXC.
☐ **PP (Early) 90 Degree Safety**, .32 ACP, Double Action, Pre-War, Commercial, High-Polish Finish, *Modern*	350.00	475.00
☐ **PP (Early) Bottom Magazine Release**, .380 ACP, Double Action, Pre-War, Commercial, High-Polish Finish, *Curio*	875.00	1,450.00
☐ **PP AC**, .380 ACP, Double Action, Pre-War, Nazi-Proofed, *Modern*	550.00	775.00
☐ **PP AC Police F**, .32 ACP, Double Action, Pre-War, Nazi-Proofed, *Curio*	350.00	425.00
☐ **PP AC Waffenamt**, .32 ACP, Double Action, Pre-War, Nazi-Proofed, *Curio*	350.00	450.00
☐ **PP Bottom Magazine Release**, .32 ACP, Double Action, Pre-War, Commercial, High-Polish Finish, *Curio*	450.00	550.00
☐ **PP Bottom Magazine Release**, .32 ACP, Double Action, Pre-War, Commercial, High-Polish Finish, Lightweight, *Curio*	450.00	550.00
☐ **PP Czech**, .32 ACP, Double Action, Pre-War, Commercial, High-Polish Finish, *Curio*	675.00	875.00
☐ **PP Mark II "Manurhin"**, .22 L.R.R.F., Double Action, High-Polish Finish, Blue, *Curio*	395.00	525.00
☐ **PP Mark II "Manurhin"**, .32 ACP, Double Action, High-Polish Finish, Blue, *Curio*	375.00	475.00
☐ **PP Mark II "Manurhin"**, .380 ACP, Double Action, High-Polish Finish, Blue, *Curio*	395.00	500.00
☐ **PP NSKK**, .32 ACP, Double Action, Pre-War, High-Polish Finish, Nazi-Proofed, *Curio*	795.00	1,200.00
☐ **PP PDM**, .32 ACP, Double Action, Pre-War, High-Polish Finish, *Curio*	495.00	625.00
☐ **PP Persian**, .380 ACP, Double Action, Pre-War, Commercial, High-Polish Finish, *Curio*	1,500.0	2,200.00
☐ **PP Police C**, .32 ACP, Double Action, Pre-War, High-Polish Finish, Nazi-Proofed, *Curio*	395.00	500.00
☐ **PP Police C**, .32 ACP, Double Action, Pre-War, Nazi-Proofed, *Curio*	375.00	475.00
☐ **PP Police F**, .32 ACP, Double Action, Pre-War, Nazi-Proofed, *Curio*	350.00	425.00
☐ **PP Presentation**, Double Action, Lightweight, *Modern*	575.00	800.00
☐ **PP RFV**, .32 ACP, Double Action, Pre-War, High Polish, *Curio*	475.00	600.00
☐ **PP RFV**, .32 ACP, Double Action, Pre-War, Nazi-Proofed, *Curio*	425.00	550.00
☐ **PP RJ**, .32 ACP, Double Action, Pre-War, High-Polish Finish, *Curio*	450.00	550.00
☐ **PP SS**, .22 L.R.R.F., Double Action, Pre-War, High-Polish Finish, *Curio*	725.00	900.00
☐ **PP SA**, .32 ACP, Double Action, Pre-War, High-Polish Finish, *Curio*	600.00	800.00
☐ **PP Stoeger**, .32 ACP, Double Action, Pre-War, High-Polish Finish, *Curio*	500.00	675.00
☐ **PP Super**, 9 x 18mm, Clip Fed, Blue, *Modern*	365.00	500.00
☐ **PP Verchromt**, .32 ACP, Double Action, Pre-War, Commercial, *Curio*	625.00	825.00
☐ **PP Verchromt**, .380 ACP, Double Action, Pre-War, Commercial, *Curio*	750.00	1,100.00
☐ **PP with Lanyard Loop**, .32 ACP, Double Action, Pre-War, Commercial, High-Polish Finish, Nazi-Proofed, *Modern*	425.00	550.00
☐ **PP Waffenamt**, .32 ACP, Double Action, Pre-War, High-Polish Finish, Nazi-Proofed, *Curio*	350.00	475.00
☐ **PP Waffenamt**, .32 ACP, Double Action, Pre-War, Nazi-Proofed, *Curio*	325.00	450.00
☐ **PP Waffenamt**, .380 ACP, Double Action, Pre-War, High-Polish Finish, Nazi-Proofed, *Curio*	500.00	645.00
☐ **PPK**, .22 L.R.R.F., Double Action, Pre-War, Commercial, Nickel Plated, *Curio*	500.00	625.00

476 / WALTHER

	V.G.	EXC.
☐ **PPK**, .22 L.R.R.F., Double Action, Pre-War, Commercial, Nickel Plated, Nazi-Proofed, *Curio*	450.00	575.00
☐ **PPK**, .22 L.R.R.F., Double Action, Pre-War, Commercial, High-Polish Finish, *Modern*	395.00	500.00
☐ **PPK**, .22 L.R.R.F., Double Action, Pre-War, Commercial, High-Polish Finish, Nazi-Proofed, *Modern*	425.00	575.00
☐ **PPK**, .22 L.R.R.F., Double Action, Post-War, *Modern*	275.00	375.00
☐ **PPK**, .22 L.R.R.F., Double Action, Lightweight, Post-War, *Modern*	395.00	525.00
☐ **PPK**, .25 ACP, Double Action, Pre-War, Commercial, High-Polish Finish, *Curio*	1,150.00	1,700.00
☐ **PPK**, .32 ACP, Double Action, Pre-War, Commercial, Nickel Plated, *Curio*	425.00	575.00
☐ **PPK**, .32 ACP, Double Action, Pre-War, Commercial, Nazi-Proofed, Nickel Plated, *Curio*	425.00	575.00
☐ **PPK**, .32 ACP, Double Action, Pre-War, Commercial, Lightweight, High-Polish Finish, *Curio*	475.00	600.00
☐ **PPK**, .32 ACP, Double Action, Pre-War, Nazi-Proofed, Lightweight, High-Polish Finish, *Curio*	475.00	600.00
☐ **PPK**, .32 ACP, Double Action, Pre-War, Nazi-Proofed, Lightweight, *Curio*	395.00	525.00
☐ **PPK**, .32 ACP, Double Action, Pre-War, Commercial, High-Polish Finish, *Modern*	325.00	475.00
☐ **PPK**, .32 ACP, Double Action, Pre-War, Commercial, High-Polish Finish, Nazi-Proofed, *Modern*	345.00	500.00
☐ **PPK**, .32 ACP, Double Action, Pre-War, Commercial, Nazi-Proofed, *Modern*	325.00	475.00
☐ **PPK**, .32 ACP, Double Action, Post-War, *Modern*	225.00	300.00
☐ **PPK**, .32 ACP, Double Action, Lightweight, Post-War, *Modern*	395.00	550.00
☐ **PPK**, .380 ACP, Double Action, Pre-War, Commercial, Nickel Plated, *Curio*	900.00	1,200.00
☐ **PPK**, .380 ACP, Double Action, Pre-War, Commercial, Nickel Plated, Nazi-Proofed, *Curio*	950.00	1,475.00
☐ **PPK**, .380 ACP, Double Action, Pre-War, Commercial, High-Polish Finish, *Modern*	625.00	900.00
☐ **PPK**, .380 ACP, Double Action, Pre-War, Commercial, High-Polish Finish, Nazi-Proofed, *Modern*	775.00	1,100.00
☐ **PPK**, .380 ACP, Double Action, Post-War, *Modern*	350.00	475.00
☐ **PPK**, .380 ACP, Double Action, Lightweight, Post-War, *Modern*	395.00	575.00
☐ **PPK "Nairobi"**, .32 ACP, Double Action, Pre-War, High-Polish Finish, *Curio*	700.00	1,050.00
☐ **PPK (Early) 90 Degree Safety**, .32 ACP, Double Action, Pre-War, Commercial, High-Polish Finish, *Modern*	375.00	500.00
☐ **PPK (Early) Bottom Magazine Release**, .380 ACP, Double Action, Pre-War, Commercial, High-Polish Finish, *Curio*	900.00	1,400.00
☐ **PPK Czech**, .32 ACP, Double Action, Pre-War, Commercial, High-Polish Finish, *Curio*	750.00	975.00
☐ **PPK DRP**, .32 ACP, Double Action, Pre-War, High-Polish Finish, *Curio*	500.00	675.00
☐ **PPK DRP**, .32 ACP, Double Action, Pre-War, High-Polish Finish, Nickel Plated, *Curio*	635.00	885.00
☐ **PPK Mark II "Manurhin"**, .22 L.R.R.F., Double Action, High-Polish Finish, Blue, *Curio*	525.00	700.00
☐ **PPK Mark II "Manurhin"**, .22 L.R.R.F., Double Action, High-Polish Finish, Blue, Lightweight, *Curio*	625.00	835.00
☐ **PPK Mark II "Manurhin"**, .32 ACP, Double Action, High-Polish Finish, Blue, *Curio*	475.00	625.00

	V.G.	EXC.
☐ **PPK Mark II "Manurhin"**, .32 ACP, Double Action, High-Polish Finish, Blue, Lightweight, *Curio*	525.00	735.00
☐ **PPK Mark II "Manurhin"**, .380 ACP, Double Action, High-Polish Finish, Blue, *Curio*	500.00	665.00
☐ **PPK Mark II "Manhurin"**, .380 ACP, Double Action, High-Polish Finish, Blue, Lightweight, *Curio*	575.00	725.00
☐ **PPK Model PP**, .32 ACP, Double Action, Pre-War, Commercial, High-Polish Finish, *Curio*	1,200.00	1,650.00
☐ **PPK Party Leader**, .32 ACP, Double Action, Pre-War, High-Polish Finish, *Curio*	995.00	1,450.00
☐ **PPK PDM**, .32 ACP, Double Action, Pre-War, High-Polish Finish, Lightweight, *Curio*	875.00	1,200.00
☐ **PPK Police C**, .32 ACP, Double Action, Pre-War, High-Polish Finish, Nazi-Proofed, *Curio*	425.00	550.00
☐ **PPK Police C**, .32 ACP, Double Action, Pre-War, Nazi-Proofed, *Curio*	395.00	525.00
☐ **PPK Police F**, .32 ACP, Double Action, Pre-War, Nazi-Proofed, *Curio*	375.00	500.00
☐ **PPK RFV**, .32 ACP, Double Action, Pre-War, High-Polish Finish, *Curio*	600.00	885.00
☐ **PPK RZM**, .32 ACP, Double Action, Pre-War, High-Polish Finish, *Curio*	475.00	645.00
☐ **PPK RZM**, .32 ACP, Double Action, Pre-War, High-Polish Finish, Nickel Plated, *Curio*	685.00	950.00
☐ **PPK Stoeger**, .32 ACP, Double Action, Pre-War, High-Polish Finish, *Curio*	575.00	825.00
☐ **PPK Verchromt**, .32 ACP, Double Action, Pre-War, Commercial, *Curio*	700.00	925.00
☐ **PPK Verchromt**, .32 ACP, Double Action, Pre-War, Commercial, Lightweight, *Curio*	1,250.00	1,750.00
☐ **PPK Verchromt**, .380 ACP, Double Action, Pre-War, Commercial, *Curio*	900.00	1,300.00
☐ **PPK Waffenamt**, .32 ACP, Double Action, Pre-War, High-Polish Finish, Nazi-Proofed, *Curio*	500.00	650.00
☐ **PPK Waffenamt**, .32 ACP, Double Action, Pre-War, Nazi-Proofed, *Curio*	400.00	525.00
☐ **PPK Waffenamt**, .380 ACP, Double Action, Pre-War, High-Polish Finish, Nazi-Proofed, *Curio*	875.00	1,350.00
☐ **PPKS (Current)**, .22 L.R.R.F., Double Action, *Modern*	245.00	350.00
☐ **PPKS (Current)**, .32 ACP, Double Action, Blue, *Modern*	300.00	400.00
☐ **PPKS (Current)**, .380 ACP, Double Action, Blue, *Modern*	300.00	400.00
☐ **Self-Loading**, .22 L.R.R.F., Target Pistol, *Modern*	365.00	475.00
☐ **TPH**, .22 L.R.R.F., Double Action, Clip Fed, *Modern*	300.00	450.00

RIFLE, BOLT ACTION

	V.G.	EXC.
☐ **Model B**, Various Calibers, Checkered Stock, Mauser Action, Set Triggers, *Modern*	225.00	350.00
☐ **GX-1 Match**, .22 L.R.R.F., Singleshot, Target Stock, with Accessories, *Modern*	675.00	875.00
☐ **KKJ**, .22 Hornet, 5 Shot Clip, Open Rear Sight, Checkered Stock, *Modern*	340.00	425.00
☐ **KKJ**, .22 Hornet, 5 Shot Clip, Open Rear Sight, Checkered Stock, Set Trigger, *Modern*	360.00	450.00
☐ **KKJ**, .22 L.R.R.F., 5 Shot Clip, Open Rear Sight, Checkered Stock, *Modern*	275.00	375.00
☐ **KKJ**, .22 L.R.R.F., 5 Shot Clip, Open Rear Sight, Checkered Stock, Set Trigger, *Modern*	310.00	485.00

	V.G.	EXC.
☐ **KKJ**, .22 WMR, 5 Shot Clip, Open Rear Sight, Checkered Stock, *Modern*	295.00	370.00
☐ **KKJ**, .22 WMR, 5 Shot Clip, Open Rear Sight, Checkered Stock, Set Trigger, *Modern*	320.00	400.00
☐ **KKJ International Match**, .22 L.R.R.F., Singleshot, Target Stock, with Accessories, *Modern*	500.00	675.00
☐ **Model KKW**, .22 L.R.R.F., Pre-WW2, Singleshot, Tangent Sights, Military Style Stock, *Modern*	400.00	525.00
☐ **Model V**, Singleshot, Sporting Rifle, Open Rear Sight, *Modern*	275.00	350.00
☐ **Model V "Meisterbushse"**, Singleshot, Pistol-Grip Stock, Target Sights, *Modern*	290.00	375.00
☐ **Moving Target**, .22 L.R.R.F., Singleshot, Target Stock, with Accessories, *Modern*	525.00	675.00
☐ **Olympic**, .22 L.R.R.F., Singleshot, Target Stock, with Accessories, *Modern*	400.00	550.00
☐ **Prone "400"**, .22 L.R.R.F., Singleshot, Target Stock, with Accessories, *Modern*	375.00	475.00
☐ **UIT Match**, .22 L.R.R.F., Singleshot, Target Stock, with Accessories, *Modern*	550.00	725.00
☐ **UIT Super**, .22 L.R.R.F., Singleshot, Target Stock, with Accessories, *Modern*	500.00	650.00

RIFLE, SEMI-AUTOMATIC
☐ **Model 1**, Clip Fed, Carbine, *Modern*	175.00	275.00
☐ **Model 2**, .22 L.R.R.F., Clip Fed, *Modern*	175.00	275.00

SHOTGUN, DOUBLE BARREL, SIDE-BY-SIDE
☐ **Model S.F.**, 12 or 16 Gauges, Checkered Stock, Cheekpiece, Double Triggers, Sling Swivels, *Modern*	275.00	400.00
☐ **Model S.F.D.**, 12 or 16 Gauges, Checkered Stock, Cheekpiece, Double Triggers, Sling Swivels, *Modern*	325.00	500.00

WAMO
Wamo Mfg. Co., San Gabriel, Calif.

HANDGUN, SINGLESHOT
☐ **Powermaster**, .22 L.R.R.F., Target Pistol, *Modern*	75.00	115.00

WARNANT
L. & J. Warnant Freres, Hognee, Belgium.

HANDGUN, SEMI-AUTOMATIC
☐ **.25 ACP**, Clip Fed, Blue, *Curio*	140.00	200.00

HANDGUN, REVOLVER
☐ **.32 S & W**, Double Action, Folding Trigger, Break Top, *Curio*	50.00	80.00
☐ **.38 S & W**, Double Action, Folding Trigger, Break Top, *Curio*	50.00	80.00

HANDGUN, SINGLESHOT
☐ **Traff**, 6mm R.F., Spur Trigger, Parlor Pistol, *Curio*	30.00	55.00
☐ **Traff**, 9mm R.F., Spur Trigger, Parlor Pistol, *Curio*	35.00	60.00

RIFLE, SINGLESHOT
☐ **Amelung**, Various Rimfires, Plain, Parlor Rifle, *Curio*	35.00	50.00
☐ **Amelung**, Various Rimfires, Checkered Stock, Set Triggers, , Parlor Rifle, *Curio*	65.00	85.00

SHOTGUN, SINGLESHOT
☐ **12 Ga.**, Checkered Stock, Cheekpiece, *Curio*	35.00	50.00

WARNER
Warner Arms Corp., Brooklyn, N.Y., formed about 1912, moved to Norwich, Mass. in 1913, and in 1917 merged and became Davis-Warner Arms Corp., Assonet, Mass., out of business about 1919. Also see Schwarzlose.

	V.G.	EXC.
SEMI-AUTOMATIC		
☐ **Infallable**, .32 ACP, Clip Fed, *Modern*	135.00	195.00
☐ **The Infallable**, .32 ACP, Clip Fed, *Modern*	155.00	220.00

WARREN ARMS CORP.
Belgium, c. 1900.

SHOTGUN, DOUBLE BARREL, SIDE-BY-SIDE
☐ **Various Gauges**, Outside Hammers, Damascus Barrel, *Modern* 100.00   175.00
☐ **Various Gauges**, Hammerless, Steel Barrel, *Modern* 135.00   200.00
☐ **Various Gauges**, Hammerless, Damascus Barrel, *Modern* 100.00   175.00
☐ **Various Gauges**, Outside Hammers, Steel Barrel, *Modern* 125.00   190.00

SHOTGUN, SINGLESHOT
☐ **Various Gauges**, Hammer, Steel Barrel, *Modern* 55.00   85.00

WATSON BROS.
London, England 1885-1931.

RIFLE, BOLT ACTION
☐ **.303 British**, Express Sights, Sporting Rifle, Checkered Stock, *Modern* 425.00   650.00

RIFLE, DOUBLE BARREL, SIDE-BY-SIDE
☐ **.450/.400 N.E. 3"**, Double Trigger, Recoil Pad, Plain, Cased, *Modern* 2,750.00   3,750.00

WATTERS, JOHN
Carlisle, Pa. 1778-1785. See Kentucky Rifles.

WEATHERBY'S, INC.
South Gate, Calif.

HANDGUN, SINGLESHOT
☐ **Mk. V Silhouette**, Various Calibers, Thumbhole Target Stock, Target Sights, *Modern* 400.00   600.00

RIFLE, BOLT ACTION
☐ **For German Manufacture** Add 30%-50%
☐ **Deluxe**, .378 Wby. Mag., Magnum, Checkered Stock, *Modern* 300.00   400.00
☐ **Deluxe**, Various Calibers, Checkered Stock, *Modern* 200.00   275.00
☐ **Deluxe**, Various Calibers, Magnum, Checkered Stock, *Modern* 225.00   350.00
☐ **Mark V**, .378 Wby. Mag., Checkered Stock, *Modern* 395.00   475.00
☐ **Mark V**, .460 Wby. Mag., Checkered Stock, *Modern* 475.00   575.00
☐ **Mark V**, Various Calibers, Varmint, Checkered Stock, *Modern* 300.00   400.00
☐ **Mark V**, Various Calibers, Checkered Stock, *Modern* 300.00   400.00
☐ **Vanguard**, Various Calibers, Checkered Stock, *Modern* 225.00   300.00

RIFLE, SEMI-AUTOMATIC
☐ **Mark XXII**, .22 L.R.R.F., Clip Fed, Checkered Stock, *Modern* 150.00   200.00
☐ **Mark XXII**, .22 L.R.R.F., Tube Feed, Checkered Stock, *Modern* 175.00   235.00

SHOTGUN, DOUBLE BARREL, OVER-UNDER
☐ **Regency**, 12 Ga., Trap Grade, Vent Rib, Checkered Stock, Engraved, Single Selective Trigger, *Modern* 575.00   700.00
☐ **Regency**, Field Grade, 12 and 20 Gauges, Vent Rib, Checkered Stock, Engraved, Single Selective Trigger, *Modern* 550.00   675.00

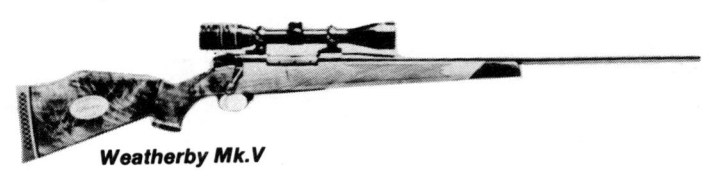

Weatherby Mk.V

SHOTGUN, SEMI-AUTOMATIC
- ☐ **Centurion**, 12 Ga., Field Grade, Vent Rib, Checkered Stock, *Modern* 150.00 220.00
- ☐ **Centurion**, 12 Ga., Trap Grade, Checkered Stock, Vent Rib, *Modern* 185.00 245.00
- ☐ **Centurion Deluxe**, 12 Ga., Checkered Stock, Vent Rib, Light Engraving, Fancy Wood, *Modern* 210.00 265.00

SHOTGUN, SLIDE ACTION
- ☐ **Patrician**, 12 Ga., Field Grade, Checkered Stock, Vent Rib, *Modern* 125.00 190.00
- ☐ **Patrician**, 12 Ga., Trap Grade, Checkered Stock, Vent Rib, *Modern* 150.00 220.00
- ☐ **Patrician**, Deluxe, 12 Ga., Checkered Stock, Light Engraving, Fancy Wood, Vent Rib, *Modern* 180.00 230.00

WEAVER, CRYPRET
Pa., c. 1818. See Kentucky Rifles

WEBLEY & SCOTT
Located in Birmingham, England operating as P. Webley & Son, 1860-1897; Webley & Scott Revolver & Arms Co.. 1898-1906; Webley & Scott since 1906.

HANDGUN, REVOLVER
- ☐ **#1**, .577 Eley, Solid Frame, Double Action, Blue, *Curio* 100.00 160.00
- ☐ **British Bulldog**, Various Calibers, Solid Frame, Double Action, *Curio* 80.00 135.00
- ☐ **Tower Bulldog**, Various Calibers, Solid Frame, Double Action, *Curio* 80.00 120.00
- ☐ **Webley Kaufmann**, .45 Colt, Top Break, Square-Butt, Commercial, *Antique* 350.00 450.00
- ☐ **Webley Mk 1**, .455 Revolver Mk 1, Top Break, Round Butt, Military, *Antique* 150.00 225.00
- ☐ **Webley Mk 1***, .455 Revolver Mk 1, Top Break, Round Butt, Military, *Antique* 160.00 200.00
- ☐ **Webley Mk 1** Navy**, .455 Revolver Mk 1, Top Break, Round Butt, Military, *Modern* 140.00 190.00
- ☐ **Webley Mk 2**, .455 Revolver Mk 1, Top Break, Round Butt, Military, *Antique* 160.00 220.00
- ☐ **Webley Mk 2***, .455 Revolver Mk 1, Top Break, Round Butt, Military, *Curio* 160.00 220.00
- ☐ **Webley Mk 2****, .455 Revolver Mk 1, Top Break, Round Butt, Military, *Curio* 160.00 220.00
- ☐ **Webley Mk 3**, .455 Revolver Mk 1, Top Break, Round Butt, Military, *Curio* 170.00 245.00
- ☐ **Webley Mk 4**, .455 Revolver Mk 1, Top Break, Round Butt, Military, *Curio* 160.00 220.00
- ☐ **Webley Mk 5**, .455 Revolver Mk 1, Top Break, Round Butt, Military, *Curio* 170.00 245.00
- ☐ **Webley Mk 6**, .455 Revolver Mk 1, Top Break, Square-Butt, Military, *Curio* 140.00 200.00
- ☐ **Webley Mk 6**, Detachable Buttstock Only 150.00 250.00
- ☐ **Webley Mk III M & P**, .38 S & W, Top Break, Square-Butt, Commercial, *Modern* 95.00 165.00

WEBLEY AND SCOTT / 481

Webley #1

Webley Model 1906

Webley Fosbury

Webley Model 1909 M&P

Webley Model 1909 .32

Webley Model 1909 .25

482 / WEBLEY AND SCOTT

Webley Model 1913

Webley Model 1913 Mk 1 #2

Webley Tower Bulldog

Webley Model 1913 Mk 1

Webley-Green

	V.G.	EXC.
☐ **Webley Mk IV**, .22 L.R.R.F., Top Break, Square-Butt, Commercial, Modern	160.00	225.00
☐ **Webley Mk IV**, .38 S & W, Top Break, Square-Butt, Military, *Curio*	125.00	175.00
☐ **Webley R I C**, .455 Revolver Mk 1, Solid Frame, Square-Butt, Commercial, *Antique*	95.00	145.00
☐ **Webley-Green**, .455 Revolver Mk 1, Top Break, Square-Butt, Commercial, Target Pistol, *Antique*	250.00	375.00
☐ **Webley-Green**, .476 Enfield Mk 3, Top Break, Square-Butt, Commercial, Target Pistol, *Antique*	300.00	450.00

HANDGUN, SEMI-AUTOMATIC

	V.G.	EXC.
☐ **Model 1904**, .455 Webley Auto., Clip Fed, Grip Safety, Hammer, *Curio*	565.00	775.00
☐ **Model 1906**, .25 ACP, Clip Fed, Hammer, *Modern*	135.00	195.00
☐ **Model 1909**, .32 ACP, Clip Fed, Hammerless, *Modern*	190.00	295.00
☐ **Model 1909**, .25 ACP, Clip Fed, Hammerless, *Modern*	165.00	250.00
☐ **Model 1909 M & P**, 9mm Browning Long, Clip Fed, Hammer, *Curio*	325.00	425.00
☐ **Model 1909 M & P**, 9mm Browning Long, South African Police, Clip Fed, Hammer, *Curio*	425.00	625.00
☐ **Model 1910**, .38 ACP, Clip Fed, Hammerless, *Curio*	265.00	395.00
☐ **Model 1911 Metro Police**, .32 ACP, Clip Fed, Hammer, *Modern*	165.00	245.00
☐ **Model 1911 Metro Police**, .380 ACP, Clip Fed, Hammer, *Modern*	200.00	310.00
☐ **Model 1913**, .38 ACP, Clip Fed, Hammerless, *Curio*	265.00	395.00
☐ **Model 1913 Mk 1**, .455 Webley Auto., Clip Fed, Grip Safety, Military, Hammer, *Curio*	295.00	425.00
☐ **Model 1913 Mk 1 #2**, .455 Webley Auto., Clip Fed, Grip Safety, Adjustable Sights, Hammer, *Curio*	575.00	850.00

HANDGUN, SEMI-AUTOMATIC REVOLVER

	V.G.	EXC.
☐ **Webley-Fosbery**, .455 Revolver Mk 1, Top Break, Military, *Curio*	700.00	1,200.00
☐ **Webley-Fosbery (Union Arms)**, .32 S & W, Top Break, Military, *Curio*	675.00	1,150.00
☐ **Webley-Fosbery .38 Cal.**, Top Break, Military, *Curio*	775.00	1,275.00

HANDGUN, SINGLESHOT

	V.G.	EXC.
☐ **Model 1911**, .22 L.R.R.F., Automatic Style, *Modern*	200.00	300.00
☐ **Target**, .22 L.R.R.F., Tip-Up Barrel, Target Sights, Target Grips, *Modern*	150.00	220.00

SHOTGUN, DOUBLE BARREL, SIDE-BY-SIDE

	V.G.	EXC.
☐ **Model 700**, 12 and 20 Gauges, Box Lock, Hammerless, Checkered Stock, Light Engraving, Double Trigger, *Modern*	300.00	450.00
☐ **Model 700**, 12 and 20 Gauges, Box Lock, Hammerless, Checkered Stock, Light Engraving, Single Trigger, *Modern*	350.00	500.00
☐ **Model 701**, 12 and 20 Gauges, Box Lock, Hammerless, Checkered Stock, Fancy Engraving, Double Trigger, *Modern*	600.00	800.00
☐ **Model 701**, 12 and 20 Gauges, Box Lock, Hammerless, Checkered Stock, Fancy Engraving, Single Trigger, *Modern*	650.00	850.00
☐ **Model 702**, 12 and 20 Gauges, Box Lock, Hammerless, Checkered Stock, Engraved, Double Trigger *Modern*	425.00	600.00
☐ **Model 702**, 12 and 20 Gauges, Box Lock, Hammerless, Checkered Stock, Engraved, Single Trigger, *Modern*	475.00	650.00

WELSHANTZ, DAVID
York, Pa. 1780-1783. See Kentucky Rifles, U.S. Military.

WELSHANTZ, JACOB
York, Pa. 1777-1792. See Kentucky Rifles, U.S. Military.

WELSHANTZ, JOSEPH
York, Pa. 1779-1783. See Kentucky Rifles, U.S. Military.

                                                                                        V.G.   EXC.

WESSON & HARRINGTON
Worcester, Mass. 1871-1874. Succeeded by Harrington and Richardson

HANDGUN, REVOLVER
- [ ] **.22 Short R.F.**, 7 Shot, Spur Trigger, Solid Frame, Single Action, *Antique* 90.00   160.00
- [ ] **.32 Short R.F.**, 5 Shot, Spur Trigger, Solid Frame, Single Action, *Antique* 90.00   160.00
- [ ] **.38 Short R.F.**, 5 Shot, Spur Trigger, Solid Frame, Single Action, *Antique* 95.00   180.00

WESSON, FRANK
Worcester, Mass. 1854 to 1865. 1865-1875 at Springfield, Mass. Also see U.S. Military, Wesson & Harrington, Harrington & Richardson.

HANDGUN, SINGLESHOT
- [ ] **Model 1859**, .22 Short, Tip-Up Barrel, Spur Trigger, *Antique* 140.00   200.00
- [ ] **Model 1862**, .22 Short, Tip-Up Barrel, Spur Trigger, *Antique* 120.00   170.00
- [ ] **Model 1859**, .30 R.F., Tip-Up Barrel, Spur Trigger, *Antique* 140.00   200.00
- [ ] **Model 1862**, .30 R.F., Tip-Up Barrel, Spur Trigger, *Antique* 140.00   200.00
- [ ] **Model 1859**, .32 R.F., Tip-Up Barrel, Spur Trigger, *Antique* 140.00   200.00
- [ ] **Model 1862**, .32 R.F., Tip-Up Barrel, Spur Trigger, *Antique* 140.00   200.00
- [ ] **Model 1862 Pocket Rifle**, .22 Short, Small Frame, Spur Trigger, Target Sights, Detachable Stock, *Antique* 200.00   350.00
- [ ] **Model 1862 Pocket Rifle**, Various Calibers, Medium Frame, Spur Trigger, Target Sights, Detachable Stock, *Antique* 175.00   300.00
- [ ] **Model 1870 Pocket Rifle**, .22 Short, Small Frame, Spur Trigger, Target Sights, Detachable Stock, *Antique* 200.00   350.00
- [ ] **Model 1870 Pocket Rifle**, Various Calibers, Medium Frame, Spur Trigger, Target Sights, Detachable Stock, *Antique* 175.00   300.00
- [ ] **Model 1870 Pocket Rifle**, Various Calibers, Large Frame, Spur Trigger, Target Sights, Detachable Stock, *Antique* 400.00   550.00

HANDGUN, DOUBLE BARREL, OVER-UNDER
- [ ] **Vest Pocket**, .22 Short, Twist Barrel, Spur Trigger, *Antique* 300.00   500.00
- [ ] **Vest Pocket**, .32 Short, Twist Barrel, Spur Trigger, *Antique* 200.00   350.00
- [ ] **Vest Pocket**, .41 Short, Twist Barrel, Spur Trigger, with Knife, *Antique* 400.00   650.00

RIFLE, SINGLESHOT
- [ ] **.32 Long R.F.**, Double Trigger, Tip-Up, *Antique* 350.00   475.00

WESTERN ARMS CO.
HANDGUN, REVOLVER
- [ ] **.32 Long R.F.**, 5 Shot, Folding Trigger, Double Action, *Antique* 55.00   95.00

WESTERN FIELD
Trade name for Montgomery Ward.

RIFLE, BOLT ACTION
- [ ] **Model 56 Buckhorn**, .22 L.R.R.F., 5 Shot Clip, Open Rear Sight, *Modern* 35.00   55.00
- [ ] **Model 724**, .30-06 Springfield, Checkered Stock, Full-Stocked, *Modern* 125.00   170.00
- [ ] **Model 732**, .30-06 Springfield, Checkered Stock, Recoil Pad, *Modern* 135.00   175.00
- [ ] **Model 734**, 7mm Rem. Mag., Checkered Stock, Recoil Pad, *Modern* 140.00   190.00

WESTERN FIELD / 485

	V.G.	EXC.
☐ **Model 765**, .30-06 Springfield, Checkered Stock, *Modern*	115.00	150.00
☐ **Model 770**, Various Calibers, Checkered Stock, Sling Swivels, *Modern*	135.00	175.00
☐ **Model 78**, Various Calibers, Checkered Stock, Sling Swivels, *Modern*	135.00	175.00
☐ **Model 780**, Various Calibers, Checkered Stock, Sling Swivels, *Modern*	125.00	160.00
☐ **Model 815**, .22 L.R.R.F., Singleshot, *Modern*	15.00	25.00
☐ **Model 822**, .22 WMR, Clip Fed, *Modern*	35.00	55.00
☐ **Model 83**, .22 L.R.R.F., Singleshot, Open Rear Sight, Takedown, *Modern*	20.00	40.00
☐ **Model 830**, .22 L.R.R.F., Clip Fed, *Modern*	30.00	45.00
☐ **Model 832**, .22 L.R.R.F., Clip Fed, Checkered Stock, *Modern*	30.00	45.00
☐ **Model 84**, .22 L.R.R.F., 5 Shot Clip, Open Rear Sight, Takedown, *Modern*	30.00	45.00
☐ **Model 840**, .22 W.M.R., Clip Fed, *Modern*	40.00	55.00
☐ **Model 842**, .22 L.R.R.F., Tube Feed, *Modern*	35.00	45.00
☐ **Model 852**, .22 L.R.R.F., Clip Fed, *Modern*	35.00	45.00
☐ **Model 86**, .22 L.R.R.F., Tube Feed, Takedown, Open Rear Sight, *Modern*	35.00	55.00

RIFLE, LEVER ACTION

	V.G.	EXC.
☐ **Model 72**, .30-30 Win., Pistol-Grip Stock, Plain, Tube Feed, *Modern*	75.00	115.00
☐ **Model 72C**, .30-30 Win., Straight Grip, Plain, Tube Feed, *Modern*	75.00	115.00
☐ **Model 79**, .30-30 Win., Pistol-Grip Stock, Plain, Tube Feed, *Modern*	75.00	120.00
☐ **Model 865**, .22 L.R.R.F., Tube Feed, Sling Swivels, *Modern*	40.00	65.00
☐ **Model 895**, .22 L.R.R.F., Tube Feed, Carbine, *Modern*	35.00	65.00

RIFLE, SEMI-AUTOMATIC

	V.G.	EXC.
☐ **Model 808**, .22 L.R.R.F., Tube Feed, *Modern*	35.00	50.00
☐ **Model 828**, .22 L.R.R.F., Clip Fed, Checkered Stock, *Modern*	40.00	55.00
☐ **Model 836**, .22 L.R.R.F., Tube Feed, *Modern*	40.00	55.00
☐ **Model 846**, .22 L.R.R.F., Tube Feed, *Modern*	40.00	55.00
☐ **Model 850**, .22 L.R.R.F., Clip Fed, *Modern*	40.00	55.00
☐ **Model 880**, .22 L.R.R.F., Tube Feed, *Modern*	35.00	50.00
☐ **Model M-1**, .30 Carbine, Clip Fed, *Modern*	85.00	135.00

SHOTGUN, BOLT ACTION

	V.G.	EXC.
☐ **Model 150**, .410 Ga., Clip Fed, *Modern*	35.00	55.00
☐ **Model 172-5**, 12 and 20 Gauges, Magnum, Clip Fed, Adjustable Choke, *Modern*	45.00	60.00

SHOTGUN, DOUBLE BARREL, SIDE-BY-SIDE

	V.G.	EXC.
☐ **12 and 20 Gauges**, Single Trigger, Hammerless, Checkered Stock, *Modern*	110.00	150.00
☐ **Various Gauges**, Hammerless, Plain, *Modern*	80.00	125.00
☐ **Long-Range**, Various Gauges, Double Trigger, Hammerless, *Modern*	120.00	165.00
☐ **Long-Range**, Various Gauges, Single Trigger, Hammerless, *Modern*	140.00	195.00
☐ **Model 330**, Various Gauges, Hammerless, Checkered Stock, *Modern*	95.00	155.00
☐ **Model 5151**, Various Gauges, Hammerless, Steel Barrel, *Modern*	95.00	155.00

SHOTGUN, SEMI-AUTOMATIC

	V.G.	EXC.
☐ **Model 600**, 12 Ga., Takedown, Plain Barrel, Checkered Stock, *Modern*	95.00	135.00
☐ **Model 600**, 12 Ga., Takedown, Vent Rib, Checkered Stock, *Modern*	110.00	150.00

486 / WESTLEY RICHARDS

	V.G.	EXC.

SHOTGUN, SINGLESHOT
- **Model 100**, Various Gauges, Hammerless, Adjustable Choke, Modern ... 35.00 / 50.00
- **Trap**, 12 Ga., Hammer, Solid Rib, Checkered Stock, Modern ... 55.00 / 85.00

SHOTGUN, SLIDE ACTION
- **Model 500**, .410 Ga., Plain, Takedown, Modern ... 85.00 / 125.00
- **Model 502**, .410 Ga., Checkered Stock, Light Engraving, Takedown, Vent Rib, Modern ... 95.00 / 130.00
- **Model 520**, 12 Ga., Takedown, Modern ... 90.00 / 135.00
- **Model 550**, 12 and 20 Gauges, Checkered Stock, Light Engraving, Vent Rib, Takedown, Modern ... 100.00 / 135.00
- **Model 550**, 12 and 20 Gauges, Checkered Stock, Light Engraving, Vent Rib, Takedown, Adjustable Choke, Modern ... 115.00 / 150.00
- **Model 550**, 12 and 20 Gauges, Plain, Takedown, Modern ... 95.00 / 125.00
- **Model 620**, Various Gauges, Takedown, Modern ... 95.00 / 145.00

WESTLEY RICHARDS
London, England, Since 1812.

RIFLE, BOLT ACTION
- **Best Quality**, Various Calibers, Express Sights, Fancy Wood, Fancy Checkering, Repeater, Modern ... 1,500.00 / 2,300.00

RIFLE, DOUBLE BARREL, OVER-UNDER
- **Ovundo**, 12 Ga., Ventilated Barrels, Vent Rib, Single Selective Trigger, Extra Barrel, Detachable Side Lock, Modern ... 10,000.00 / 15,500.00

RIFLE, DOUBLE BARREL, SIDE-BY-SIDE
- **Best Quality**, Various Calibers, Box Lock, Double Trigger, Fancy Engraving, Fancy Checkering, Express Sights, Modern ... 3,750.00 / 6,000.00
- **Best Quality**, Various Calibers, Sidelock, Double Trigger, Fancy Engraving, Fancy Checkering, Express Sights, Modern ... 9,500.00 / 13,500.00

SHOTGUN, DOUBLE BARREL, OVER-UNDER
- **Ovundo**, 12 Ga., Sidelock, Single Selective Trigger, Selective Ejector, Fancy Engraving, Fancy Checkering, Modern ... 9,750.00 / 17,500.00

SHOTGUN, DOUBLE BARREL, SIDE-BY-SIDE
- 10 Ga. Pinfire, Engraved, Carbine, Antique ... 450.00 / 700.00
- **Best Quality**, Various Gauges, Sidelock, Hammerless, Fancy Engraving, Fancy Checkering, Double Trigger, Modern ... 7,500.00 / 11,000.00
- **Best Quality**, Various Gauges, Sidelock, Hammerless, Fancy Engraving, Fancy Checkering, Single Selective Trigger, Modern ... 8,000.00 / 13,000.00
- **Best Quality**, Various Gauges, Box Lock, Hammerless, Fancy Engraving, Fancy Checkering, Double Trigger, Modern ... 5,500.00 / 8,500.00
- **Best Quality**, Various Gauges, Box Lock, Hammerless, Fancy Engraving, Fancy Checkering, Single Selective Trigger, Modern ... 6,000.00 / 9,500.00
- **Best**, Pigeon, 12 Ga. Mag. 3", Sidelock, Hammerless, Fancy Engraving, Fancy Checkering, Double Trigger, Modern ... 11,500.00 / 18,000.00
- **Best**, Pigeon, 12 Ga. Mag. 3", Sidelock, Hammerless, Fancy Engraving, Fancy Checkering, Single Selective Trigger, Modern ... 13,500.00 / 19,000.00
- **Deluxe Quality**, Various Gauges, Sidelock, Hammerless, Fancy Engraving, Fancy Checkering, Double Trigger, Modern ... 8,500.00 / 12,000.00
- **Deluxe Quality**, Various Gauges, Sidelock, Hammerless, Fancy Engraving, Fancy Checkering, Single Selective Trigger, Modern ... 9,000.00 / 13,000.00
- **Deluxe Quality**, Various Gauges, Box Lock, Hammerless, Fancy Engraving, Fancy Checkering, Double Trigger, Modern ... 5,500.00 / 7,750.00
- **Deluxe Quality**, Various Gauges, Box Lock, Hammerless, Fancy Engraving, Fancy Checkering, Single Selective Trigger, Modern ... 6,500.00 / 8,500.00

WHEEL-LOCK, UNKNOWN MAKER / 487

	V.G.	EXC.

- ☐ **Model E**, Various Gauges, Box Lock, Hammerless, Engraved, Double Trigger, Selective Ejector, *Modern* 3,500.00 5,000.00
- ☐ **Model E**, Various Gauges, Box Lock, Hammerless, Engraved, Double Trigger, *Modern* 2,800.00 3,750.00
- ☐ **Model E Pigeon**, 12 Ga. Mag. 3", Box Lock, Hammerless, Engraved, Double Trigger, Selective Ejector, *Modern* 4,000.00 5,500.00
- ☐ **Model E Pigeon**, 12 Ga. Mag 3", Box Lock, Hammerless, Engraved, Double Trigger, *Modern* 3,300.00 4,250.00

SHOTGUN, SINGLESHOT
- ☐ **12 Ga.**, Trap Grade, Vent Rib, Fancy Engraving, Fancy Checkering, Hammerless, *Modern* 5,500.00 8,000.00
- ☐ **12 Ga.**, Vent Rib, Plain, Monte Carlo Stock, Trap Grade, *Modern* ... 1,800.00 2,600.00

WESTON, EDWARD
Sussex, England 1800-1835.
HANDGUN, FLINTLOCK
- ☐ **.67**, Pair, Duelling Pistols, Octagon Barrel, Silver Furniture, Plain, *Antique* 1,600.00 2,575.00

WHEEL-LOCK, UNKNOWN MAKER
COMBINATION WEAPON, PISTOL
- ☐ **German**, 1500's War-Hammer, All Metal, *Antique* 9,000.00 15,000.00

HANDGUN, WHEEL-LOCK
- ☐ **Augsburg**, Late 1500's, Ball Pommel, Engraved, Ornate, *Antique* 14,000.00 20,000.00
- ☐ **Brescian**, Mid-1600's, Military, Fish-Tail Butt, Plain, *Antique* 1,500.00 2,500.00
- ☐ **Embellished Original**, Ornate, *Antique* 2,500.00 3,500.00
- ☐ **Enclosed Lock German**, Mid-1600's, Engraved, Holster Pistol, *Antique* 3,000.00 3,750.00
- ☐ **Enclosed Lock**, Late 1600's, Military, Plain, *Antique* 1,500.0 2,500.00
- ☐ **English**, Mid-1600's, Ornate, *Antique* 14,000.00 20,000.00
- ☐ **English**, Mid-1600's, Military, Holster Pistol, Plain, *Antique* 1,500.00 2,500.00
- ☐ **French**, Early 1600's, Military, Silver Inlay, *Antique* 2,500.00 3,500.00
- ☐ **German**, 1600, Dagger-Handle Butt, Military, Plain, *Antique* 2,000.00 2,750.00
- ☐ **German**, Late 1500's, Carved, Horn Inlays, Ball Pommel, Flattened, *Antique* 12,500.00 18,000.00
- ☐ **German**, Mid-1500's, Horn Inlays, Dagger-Handle Butt, Gold and Silver Damascened, Ornate *Antique* 35,000.00 25,000.00
- ☐ **German**, Mid-1600's, Military, Fish-Tail Butt, Plain, *Antique* 1,2500.00 2,000.00
- ☐ **German Puffer**, Late 1500's, Horn Inlays, Ball Pommel, *Antique* ... 6,000.00 10,000.00
- ☐ **German Style**, Reproduction, Engraved, Inlays, High Quality, *Antique* 1,400.00 1,950.00
- ☐ **Italian**, 1500's, Dagger-Handle, External Mechanism, *Antique* 9,000.00 16,500.00
- ☐ **Late 1500's Odd Butt**, all Metal, Engraved, Ornate, *Antique* 7,000.00 10,000.00
- ☐ **Old Reproduction**, High Quality, *Antique* 1,200.00 1,800.00
- ☐ **Pair Brescian**, Mid-1600's, Inlays, Engraved, Ornate, Fish-Tail Butt, *Antique* 18,000.00 25,000.00
- ☐ **Pair Dutch**, Mid-1600's, Holster Pistol, Gold Damascened, Inlays, Ornate, *Antique* 18,000.00 25,000.00
- ☐ **Pair Saxon**, Late 1500's, Ball Pommel, Medium Ornamentation, *Antique* 14,000.00 20,000.00
- ☐ **Pair Saxon**, Late 1500's, Ball Pommel, Light Ornamentation, *Antique* 9,000.00 15,000.00
- ☐ **Pair Saxon**, Late 1500's, Ball Pommel, Inlays, Engraved, *Antique* 24,000.00 30,000.00

488 / WHITNEY ARMS COMPANY

	V.G.	EXC.

- ☐ **Saxon**, Double Barrel, Over-Under, Inlays, Ornate, Ball Pommel, *Antique* 24,000.00 30,000.00
- ☐ **Saxon**, Dated 1579, Horn Inlays, Engraved, Ball Pommel, *Antique* 6,000.00 10,000.00
- ☐ **Saxon**, Late 1500's, Ball Pommel, Checkered Stock, Military, Plain, *Antique* 4,000.00 6,000.00

RIFLE, WHEEL-LOCK
- ☐ **Brandenburg 1620**, Cavalry Rifle, Military, *Antique* 5,500.00 8,000.00

WHITNEY ARMS CO.
New Haven, Conn. 1866-1776, also see U.S. Military.

HANDGUN, PERCUSSION
- ☐ **Hooded Cylinder**, .28, 6 Shot, Hammer, *Antique* 750.00 1,400.00
- ☐ **Whitney-Beals**, .31, Ring Trigger, 7 Shot, *Antique* 275.00 400.00
- ☐ **Navy**, .36, 6 Shot, Colt 1851 Type, *Antique* 400.00 800.00

HANDGUN, REVOLVER
- ☐ **.22 Short R.F.**, 7 Shot, Spur Trigger, Solid Frame, Single Action, *Antique* 90.00 160.00
- ☐ **.38 Short R.F.**, 5 Shot, Spur Trigger, Solid Frame, Single Action, *Antique* 90.00 160.00
- ☐ **.32 Short R.F.**, 5 or 6 Shots, Spur Trigger, Solid Frame, Single Action, *Antique* 95.00 170.00

RIFLE, SINGLESHOT
- ☐ **Whitney-Howard**, .44 R.F., Carbine, Lever Action, *Antique* 200.00 375.00
- ☐ **Whitney-Howard**, .44 R.F., Rifle, Lever Action, *Antique* 300.00 450.00
- ☐ **Phoenix**, Various Calibers, Carbine, Hammer, *Antique* 400.00 700.00
- ☐ **Phoenix**, Various Calibers, Rifle, Hammer, *Antique* 200.00 350.00
- ☐ **Rolling Block**, Various Calibers, Carbine, *Antique* 350.00 500.00
- ☐ **Rolling Block**, Various Calibers, Rifle, *Antique* 225.00 350.00

RIFLE, LEVER ACTION
- ☐ **Kennedy**, Various Calibers, Tube Feed, Plain, *Antique* 300.00 550.00
- ☐ **Model 1886**, Various Calibers, Tube Feed, Plain, *Antique* 500.00 850.00

SHOTGUN, DOUBLE BARREL, SIDE-BY-SIDE
- ☐ **12 Ga.**, Damascus Barrel, Outside Hammers, *Antique* 175.00 300.00

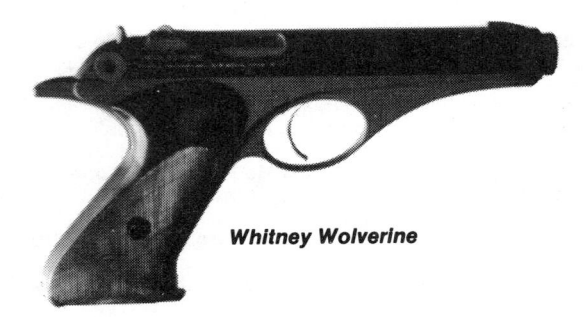

Whitney Wolverine

WHITNEY FIREARMS CO.
Hartford, Conn. 1955-1962

HANDGUN, SINGLESHOT
- ☐ **Wolverine**, .22 L.R.R.F., Blue, *Modern* 90.00 130.00

WILKINSON ARMS
South El Monte, Calif., c. 1976.

V.G. **EXC.**

HANDGUN, SEMI-AUTOMATIC
☐ **Diane**, .25 ACP, Clip Fed, Blue, *Modern* 95.00 150.00

WILKINSON ARMS
Parma, Ind.

HANDGUN, SEMI-AUTOMATIC
☐ **Linda**, 9mm Luger, Clip Fed, Blue, *Modern* 200.00 300.00

WILKINSON ARMS CO.
Made in Belgium for Richmond Hardware Co. Richmond, Va., c. 1900.

SHOTGUN, DOUBLE BARREL, SIDE-BY-SIDE
☐ **Various Gauges**, Outside Hammers, Damascus Barrel, *Modern* 100.00 175.00
☐ **Various Gauges**, Hammerless, Steel Barrel, *Modern* 135.00 200.00
☐ **Various Gauges**, Hammerless, Damascus Barrel, *Modern* 100.00 175.00
☐ **Various Gauges**, Outside Hammers, Steel Barrel, *Modern* 125.00 190.00

SHOTGUN, SINGLESHOT
☐ **Various Gauges**, Hammer, Steel Barrel, *Modern* 55.00 85.00

WILLIAMS, FREDERICK
Birmingham, England 1893-1929.

SHOTGUN, DOUBLE BARREL, SIDE-BY-SIDE
☐ **12 Ga.**, Damascus Barrel, Outside Hammers, Checkered Stock, Engraved, *Antique* 300.00 450.00

WILLIAMSON, DAVID
Brooklyn, N.Y. and Greenville, N.J. 1864-1874. Also see Moore's Patent Firearms Co.

HANDGUN, SINGLESHOT
☐ **.41 Short R.F.**, Derringer, Nickel Plated, *Antique* 195.00 300.00

WINCHESTER REPEATING ARMS CO.
New Haven, Conn. 1866 to date. In 1857 Oliver Winchester reorganized the Volcanic Repeating Arms Co. into the New Haven Arms Co., and it became Winchester Repeating Arms Co. in 1866. In 1869 Winchester absorbed Fogerty Repeating Rifle Co., and the American Rifle Co. The Spencer Repeating Arms Co. in 1870 and Adironack Arms Co. in 1874. In 1981 was purchased by U.S. Repeating Arms Co. Also see U.S. Military

☐ **For Custom Features**, Add 50%-100%
☐ **For Special Sights**, Add 25%-50%

AUTOMATIC WEAPON, ASSAULT RIFLE
☐ **M-1 Garand (Win)**, .30-06 Springfield, Clip Fed, Experimental, Class 3 .... 6,000.00 9,000.00
☐ **M1918 BAR**, .30-06 Springfield, Clip Fed, Bipod, *Modern*, Class 3 1,750.00 2,650.00

AUTOMATIC WEAPON, SUBMACHINE GUN
☐ **M-2**, .30 Carbine, Clip Fed, Military, Class 3 .... 475.00 750.00

RIFLE, BOLT ACTION
☐ **Hotchkiss**, .40-65 Win., Sporting Rifle, *Antique* 750.00 1,000.00
☐ **Hotchkiss 1st Model Fancy**, .45-70 Government, Sporting Rifle, *Antique* 500.00 850.00
☐ **Hotchkiss 1st Model**, .45-70 Government, Military, Rifle, *Antique* .. 300.00 600.00
☐ **Hotchkiss 1st Model**, .45-70 Government, Military, Carbine, *Antique* 350.00 650.00
☐ **Hotchkiss 1st Model**, .45-70 Government, Sporting Rifle, *Antique* 400.00 700.00

490 / WINCHESTER REPEATING ARMS COMPANY

	V.G.	EXC.
☐ **Hotchkiss 2nd Model**, .45-70 Government, Military, Rifle, *Antique*	400.00	700.00
☐ **Hotchkiss 2nd Model**, .45-70 Government, Military, Carbine, *Antique*	450.00	750.00
☐ **Hotchkiss 2nd Model**, .45-70 Government, Sporting Rifle, *Antique*	500.00	800.00
☐ **Hotchkiss 3rd Model**, .45-70 Government, Military, Rifle, *Antique*	350.00	700.00
☐ **Hotchkiss 3rd Model**, .45-70 Government, Military, Carbine, *Antique*	450.00	800.00
☐ **Hotchkiss 3rd Model**, .45-70 Government, Sporting Rifle, *Antique*	550.00	900.00
☐ **Lee Straight-Pull**, 6mm Lee Navy, Musket, *Antique*	450.00	600.00
☐ **Lee Straight-Pull**, 6mm Lee Navy, Sporting Rifle, *Antique*	500.00	750.00
☐ **M121**, .22 L.R.R.F., Singleshot, *Modern*	35.00	50.00
☐ **M121-Y**, .22 L.R.R.F., Singleshot, *Modern*	35.00	50.00
☐ **M121 Deluxe**, .22 L.R.R.F., Singleshot, *Modern*	45.00	60.00
☐ **M131**, .22 L.R.R.F., Clip Fed, Open Rear Sight, *Modern*	55.00	75.00
☐ **M135**, .22 WMR, Clip Fed, *Modern*	60.00	85.00
☐ **M141**, .22 WMR, Tube Feed, *Modern*	50.00	70.00
☐ **M145**, .22 WMR, Tube Feed, *Modern*	60.00	80.00
☐ **M1900**, .22 Long R.F., Singleshot, *Modern*	60.00	110.00
☐ **M1902**, Various Rimfires, Singleshot, *Curio*	75.00	150.00
☐ **M1904**, Various Rimfires, Singleshot, *Curio*	75.00	150.00
☐ **Thumb Trigger**, .22 L.R.R.F., Singleshot, *Curio*	150.00	225.00
☐ **M43**, Various Calibers, Sporting Rifle, *Modern*	150.00	250.00
☐ **M43 Special Grade**, Various Calibers, *Modern*	175.00	300.00
☐ **M47**, .22 L.R.R.F., Singleshot, *Modern*	50.00	85.00
☐ **M52**, .22 L.R.R.F., Heavy Barrel, *Modern*	225.00	375.00
☐ **M52 Slow-Lock**, .22 L.R.R.F., *Modern*	175.00	250.00
☐ **M52 Speed-Lock**, .22 L.R.R.F., *Modern*	220.00	300.00
☐ **M52 Sporting**, .22 L.R.R.F., Rifle, *Modern*	550.00	800.00
☐ **M52-B**, .22 L.R.R.F., *Modern*	225.00	325.00
☐ **M52-B**, .22 L.R.R.F., Heavy Barrel, *Modern*	250.00	375.00
☐ **M52-B**, .22 L.R.R.F., Bull Gun, *Modern*	275.00	425.00
☐ **M52-B**, .22 L.R.R.F., Sporting Rifle, *Modern*	525.00	775.00
☐ **M52-C**, .22 L.R.R.F., *Modern*	220.00	300.00
☐ **M52-C**, .22 L.R.R.F., Standard Barrel, *Modern*	225.00	325.00
☐ **M52-C**, .22 L.R.R.F., Bull Gun, *Modern*	300.00	425.00
☐ **M52-D**, .22 L.R.R.F., *Modern*	275.00	425.00
☐ **M52 International**, .22 L.R.R.F., *Modern*	475.00	700.00
☐ **M52 International Prone**, .22 L.R.R.F., *Modern*	375.00	525.00
☐ **M54**, .270 Win., Carbine, *Curio*	450.00	700.00
☐ **M54**, .30-06 Springfield, Sniper Rifle, *Modern*	375.00	550.00
☐ **M54**, Various Calibers, Carbine, *Modern*	300.00	500.00
☐ **M54**, Various Calibers, Sporting Rifle, *Modern*	325.00	500.00
☐ **M54 Match**, Various Calibers, Sniper Rifle, *Modern*	425.00	650.00
☐ **M54 National Match**, Various Calibers, *Modern*	375.00	500.00
☐ **M54 Super Grade**, Various Calibers, *Modern*	375.00	550.00
☐ **M54 Target**, Various Calibers, *Modern*	350.00	525.00
☐ **M56**, .22 L.R.R.F., Sporting Rifle, Clip Fed, *Modern*	75.00	150.00
☐ **M57**, Various Rimfires, Target, *Modern*	300.00	400.00
☐ **M58**, .22 L.R.R.F., Singleshot, *Modern*	70.00	120.00
☐ **M59**, .22 L.R.R.F., Singleshot, *Modern*	85.00	145.00
☐ **M60**, .22 L.R.R.F., Singleshot, *Modern*	70.00	120.00
☐ **M60-A**, .22 L.R.R.F., Target, Singleshot, *Modern*	115.00	150.00
☐ **M67**, Various Rimfires, Singleshot, *Modern*	60.00	90.00
☐ **M67 Boy's Rifle**, Various Rimfires, Singleshot, *Modern*	60.00	90.00
☐ **M68**, Various Rimfires, Singleshot, *Modern*	75.00	110.00
☐ **M69**, .22 L.R.R.F., Clip Fed, *Modern*	90.00	140.00
☐ **M69 Match**, .22 L.R.R.F., Clip Fed, *Modern*	110.00	165.00

WINCHESTER REPEATING ARMS COMPANY / 491

	V.G.	EXC.
☐ **M69 Target**, .22 L.R.R.F., Clip Fed, *Modern*	95.00	140.00
☐ **M70 Action Only**, Various Calibers, Pre'64, *Modern*	180.00	250.00
☐ **M70**, For Pre-War, *Add 25%-50%*		
☐ **M70**, For Mint Unfired Pre'64 *Add 50%-100%*		
☐ **M70 African**, .458 Win. Mag., Pre'64, *Modern*	650.00	900.00
☐ **M70 Alaskan**, Various Calibers, Pre'64, Checkered Stock, *Modern*	475.00	650.00
☐ **M70 Barreled Action Only**, Various Calibers, Pre'64, Checkered Stock, *Modern*	275.00	400.00
☐ **M70 Bull Gun**, Various Calibers, Pre'64, Checkered Stock, *Modern*	575.00	775.00
☐ **M70 Carbine**, Various Calibers, Pre'64, Checkered Stock, *Modern*	550.00	750.00
☐ **M70 Featherweight Sporter Grade**, Various Calibers, Pre'64, Checkered Stock, *Modern*	550.00	750.00
☐ **M70 Featherweight**, Various Calibers, Pre'64, Checkered Stock, *Modern*	450.00	650.00
☐ **M70 National Match**, .30-06 Springfield, Pre'64, *Modern*	550.00	775.00
☐ **M70 Standard**, Various Calibers, Pre'64, Checkered Stock, *Modern*	450.00	675.00
☐ **M70 Target**, Various Calibers, Pre'64, Checkered Stock, *Modern*	575.00	850.00
☐ **M70 Varmint**, Various Calibers, Pre'64, Checkered Stock, *Modern*	475.00	675.00
☐ **M70 Westerner**, Various Calibers, Pre'64, Checkered Stock, *Modern*	450.00	650.00
☐ **Model 70**, Various Calibers, Post '64, Checkered Stock, Open Rear Sight, Magnum Action, *Modern*	150.00	225.00
☐ **Model 70 African**, .458 Win. Mag., Post '64, Checkered Stock, Open Rear Sight, Magnum Action, *Modern*	250.00	350.00
☐ **Model 70 International Match**, .308 Win., Post '64, Checkered Stock, Target Stock, *Modern*	300.00	450.00
☐ **Model 70 Standard**, Various Calibers, Post '64, Checkered Stock, Open Rear Sight, *Modern*	140.00	200.00
☐ **Model 70 Target**, Various Calibers, Post '64, Checkered Stock, Target Stock, *Modern*	225.00	335.00
☐ **Model 70 Varmint**, Various Calibers, Post '64, Checkered Stock, Heavy Barrel, *Modern*	165.00	215.00
☐ **Model 70A**, Various Calibers, Post '64, Magnum Action, *Modern*	145.00	235.00
☐ **Model 70A Police**, Various Calibers, Post '64, *Modern*	140.00	190.00
☐ **Model 70A Standard**, Various Calibers, Post '64, *Modern*	130.00	180.00
☐ **M70 Super Grade**, Various Calibers, Pre'64, *Modern*	550.00	800.00
☐ **Model 70XTR Featherweight**, Various Calibers, No Sights, *Modern*	270.00	350.00
☐ **Model 70XTR Featherweight**, Various Calibers, with Sights, *Modern*	290.00	375.00
☐ **Model 70XTR Sporter**, Various Calibers, *Modern*	220.00	300.00
☐ **Model 70XTR Super Express Magnum**, .375 H&H, *Modern*	350.00	475.00
☐ **Model 70XTR Super Express Magnum**, .458 Win., *Modern*	375.00	500.00
☐ **Model 70XTR Varmint**, Various Calibers, *Modern*	220.00	300.00
☐ **Model 70XTR Westerner**, Various Calibers, No Scope, *Modern*	175.00	250.00
☐ **M72**, .22 L.R.R.F., Tube Feed, *Modern*	90.00	130.00
☐ **M75**, .22 L.R.R.F., Sporting Rifle, Clip Fed, *Modern*	195.00	275.00
☐ **M75 Target**, .22 L.R.R.F., Clip Fed, *Modern*	165.00	240.00
☐ **M99 Thumb Trigger**, Various Rimfires, Singleshot, *Modern*	175.00	325.00
☐ **Model 52 I.M.**, .22 L.R.R.F., Post '64, Heavy Barrel, Target Stock, *Modern*	390.00	550.00
☐ **Model 52 I.M.I.S.U.**, .22 L.R.R.F., Post '64, Heavy Barrel, Target Stock, *Modern*	425.00	600.00
☐ **Model 52 I.M. Kenyon**, .22 L.R.R.F., Post '64, Heavy Barrel, Target Stock, *Modern*	425.00	550.00
☐ **Model 52 International Prone**, .22 L.R.R.F., Post '64, Heavy Barrel, Target Stock, *Modern*	300.00	425.00

492 / WINCHESTER REPEATING ARMS COMPANY

	V.G.	EXC.
☐ **Model 52D**, .22 L.R.R.F., Post '64, Heavy Barrel, Target Stock, *Modern*	175.00	275.00
☐ **Model 670**, Various Calibers, Post '64, Scope Mounted, *Modern*	120.00	170.00

RIFLE, DOUBLE BARREL, SIDE-BY-SIDE

☐ **Model 21**, .405 Win., Checkered Stock, Fancy Wood, *Modern*	7,500.00	12,500.00

RIFLE, LEVER ACTION

☐ **Henry**, .44 Henry, Brass Frame, Rifle, *Antique*	3,500.00	6,000.00
☐ **Henry**, .44 Henry, Brass Frame, Military, Rifle, *Antique*	4,000.00	6,750.00
☐ **Henry**, .44 Henry, Iron Frame, Rifle, *Antique*	5,000.00	8,000.00
☐ **M 88**, Various Calibers, Clip Fed, Checkered Stock, Open Rear Sight, *Modern*	175.00	275.00
☐ **M1866**, .44 Henry, Musket, *Antique*	900.00	1,750.00
☐ **M1866**, .44 Henry, Rifle, *Antique*	950.00	1,950.00
☐ **M1866**, .44 Henry, Carbine, *Antique*	850.00	1,600.00
☐ **M1866 Improved Henry**, .44 Henry, Carbine, *Antique*	850.00	1,750.00
☐ **M1866 Improved Henry**, .44 Henry, Rifle, *Antique*	1,100.00	2,000.00
☐ **M1873**, Various Calibers, Rifle, *Modern*	650.00	1,250.00
☐ **M1873**, Various Calibers, Musket, *Modern*	750.00	1,450.00
☐ **M1873**, Various Calibers, Carbine, *Modern*	600.00	1,100.00
☐ **M1873 1 of 1,000**, Various Calibers, Rifle, *Antique*	6,000.00	12,000.00
☐ **M1873**, For Deluxe, *Add* **$350.00-$500.00**		
☐ **M1873**, For Extra Fancy Deluxe, *Add* **$2,000.00-$5,000.00**		
☐ **M1873 Special**, under #525,299, Various Calibers, Sporting Rifle, *Antique*	900.00	1,750.00
☐ **M1973 Special**, Various Calibers, Sporting Rifle, *Modern*	750.00	1,600.00
☐ **M1873**, under #525,299, Various Calibers, Musket, *Antique*	800.00	1,400.00
☐ **M1873**, under #525,299, Various Calibers, Carbine, *Antique*	650.00	1,200.00
☐ **M1873**, under #525,299, Various Calibers, Rifle, *Antique*	850.00	1,400.00
☐ **M1876**, Various Calibers, Carbine, *Antique*	800.00	1,500.00
☐ **M1876**, Various Calibers, Octagon Barrel, Rifle, *Antique*	650.00	1,300.00
☐ **M1876**, Various Calibers, Round Barrel, Rifle, *Antique*	600.00	1,150.00
☐ **M1876**, Various Calibers, Musket, *Antique*	1,400.00	2,200.00
☐ **M1876**, For Deluxe, *Add* **$400.00-$550.00**		
☐ **M1876**, For Extra Fancy Deluxe, *Add* **$2,000.00-$5,000.00**		
☐ **M1876 RCMP**, Various Calibers, Carbine, *Antique*	950.00	1,500.00
☐ **M1886**, Various Calibers, Rifle, *Modern*	400.00	650.00
☐ **M1886**, Various Calibers, Carbine, *Modern*	600.00	875.00
☐ **M1886**, Various Calibers, Musket, *Modern*	650.00	950.00
☐ **M1886**, For Deluxe, *Add* **$200.00—$400.00**		
☐ **M1886**, For Extra Fancy Deluxe, *Add* **$1,500.00-$3,500.00**		
☐ **M1886**, under #118,443, Various Calibers, Musket, *Antique*	600.00	1,150.00
☐ **M1886**, under #118,443, Various Calibers, Rifle, *Antique*	475.00	775.00
☐ **M1886**, under #118,443, Various Calibers, Carbine, *Antique*	600.00	1,100.00
☐ **M150**, .22 L.R.R.F., Tube Feed, *Modern*	60.00	85.00
☐ **M250**, .22 L.R.R.F., Tube Feed, *Modern*	65.00	95.00
☐ **M250 Deluxe**, .22 L.R.R.F., Tube Feed, *Modern*	70.00	110.00
☐ **M255**, .22 WMR, Tube Feed, *Modern*	70.00	100.00
☐ **M255 Deluxe**, .22 WMR, Tube Feed, *Modern*	85.00	125.00
☐ **M53**, Various Calibers, *Modern*	400.00	675.00
☐ **M55**, Various Calibers, *Modern*	375.00	650.00
☐ **M64**, .219 Zipper, Pre'64, *Modern*	400.00	550.00
☐ **M64**, .30-30 Win., Late Model, *Modern*	125.00	200.00
☐ **M64**, Various Calibers, Pre'64, *Modern*	325.00	425.00
☐ **M64 Deer Rifle**, Various Calibers, Pre'64, *Modern*	350.00	475.00
☐ **M65**, .218 Bee, *Modern*	600.00	850.00
☐ **M65**, Various Calibers, *Modern*	375.00	550.00

WINCHESTER REPEATING ARMS COMPANY / 493

	V.G.	EXC.
☐ M71, .348 Win., Tube Feed, *Modern*	350.00	500.00
☐ M71 Special, .348 Win., Tube Feed, *Modern*	475.00	650.00
☐ M92, Various Calibers, Rifle, *Modern*	375.00	475.00
☐ M92, Various Calibers, Carbine, *Modern*	450.00	575.00
☐ M92, Various Calibers, Musket, *Modern*	500.00	700.00
☐ M92, For Takedown, Add **$150.00-$275.00**		
☐ M92, under #103316, Various Calibers, Rifle, *Antique*	375.00	550.00
☐ M92, under #103316, Various Calibers, Carbine, *Antique*	450.00	650.00
☐ M92, under #103316, Various Calibers, Musket, *Antique*	500.00	800.00
☐ M94, .30-30 Win., Carbine, Late Model, *Modern*	95.00	140.00
☐ M94, .44 Magnum, Carbine, *Modern*	170.00	285.00
☐ M94, Various Calibers, Carbine, Pre'64, *Modern*	275.00	425.00
☐ M94, Various Calibers, Carbine, Pre-War, *Modern*	325.00	500.00
☐ M94, Various Calibers, Rifle, Pre-War, *Modern*	350.00	550.00
☐ M94, Various Calibers, Rifle, Takedown, Pre-War, *Modern*	425.00	650.00
☐ M94 Alaska Centennial, .30-30 Win., Commemorative, Carbine, *Curio*	850.00	1,450.00
☐ M94 Antique, .30-30 Win., Carbine, *Modern*	65.00	100.00
☐ Antlered Game, .30-30 Win., Commemorative, *Modern*	300.00	425.00
☐ M94 Bicentennial, .30-30 Win., Commemorative, *Curio*	450.00	695.00
☐ M94 Buffalo Bill 1 of 300, .30-30 Win., Commemorative, Rifle, *Curio*	850.00	1,450.00
☐ M94 Buffalo Bill, .30-30 Win., Commemorative, Rifle, *Curio*	195.00	290.00
☐ M94 Buffalo Bill, .30-30 Win., Commemorative, Carbine, *Curio*	195.00	290.00
☐ M94 Buffalo Bill Set, .30-30 Win., Commemorative, *Curio*	475.00	625.00
☐ M94 Canadian Centennial, .30-30 Win., Commemorative, Rifle, *Curio*	195.00	290.00
☐ M94 Canadian Centennial, .30-30 Win., Commemorative, Carbine, *Curio*	195.00	290.00
☐ M94 Canadian Centennial Set, .30-30 Win., Commemorative, *Curio*	450.00	625.00
☐ M94 Centennial 66, .30-30 Win., Commemorative, Rifle, *Curio*	225.00	350.00
☐ M94 Centennial 66, .30-30 Win., Commemorative, Carbine, *Curio*	225.00	350.00
☐ M94 Centennial 66 Set, .30-30 Win., Commemorative, *Curio*	525.00	750.00
☐ M94 Classic, .30-30 Win., Carbine, *Modern*	125.00	200.00
☐ M94 Classic, .30-30 Win., Rifle, *Modern*	125.00	200.00
☐ M94 Cowboy 1 of 300, .30-30 Win., Commemorative, Carbine, *Curio*	950.00	1,725.00
☐ M94 Cowboy, .30-30 Win., Commemorative, Carbine, *Curio*	300.00	425.00
☐ M94 Deluxe, Various Calibers, Pre-War, *Modern*	750.00	1,000.00
☐ Duke, .32-40 Win., Commemorative, *Modern*	1,500.00	2,250.00
☐ M94 Golden Spike, .30-30 Win., Commemorative, Carbine, *Curio*	225.00	325.00
☐ M94 Illinois, .30-30 Win., Commemorative, Carbine, *Curio*	195.00	290.00
☐ John Wayne, .32-40 Win., Commemorative, *Modern*	450.00	600.00
☐ M94 Klondike, .30-30 Win., Commemorative, *Curio*	300.00	425.00
☐ Legendary Frontiersman, .38-55 Win., Commemorative, *Modern*	300.00	425.00
☐ Legendary Lawman, .30-30 Win., Commemorative, *Modern*	300.00	425.00
☐ Limited Edition I, .30-30 Win., Commemorative, *Modern*	975.00	1,750.00
☐ Limited Edition II, .30-30 Win., Commemorative, *Modern*	975.00	1,750.00
☐ M94 Lone Star, .30-30 Win., Commemorative, Rifle, *Curio*	240.00	350.00
☐ M94 Lone Star, .30-30 Win., Commemorative, Carbine, *Curio*	240.00	350.00
☐ M94 Lone Star Set, .30-30 Win., Commemorative, *Curio*	550.00	750.00
☐ Matched Set of 1,000, M94 .30-30 Win. and M9422M .22 WMR, Commemorative, *Modern*	2,350.00	3,000.00
☐ M94 Nebraska Centennial, .30-30 Win., Commemorative, Carbine, *Curio*	750.00	1,250.00
☐ M94 NRA, .30-30 Win., Commemorative, Musket, *Curio*	195.00	290.00
☐ M94 NRA, .30-30 Win., Commemorative, Rifle, *Curio*	195.00	295.00
☐ M94 NRA Set, .30-30 Win., Commemorative, *Curio*	475.00	625.00

494 / WINCHESTER REPEATING ARMS COMPANY

	V.G.	EXC.
☐ **Oliver Winchester**, .38-55 Win., Commemorative, *Modern*	400.00	520.00
☐ **M94 RCMP**, .30-30 Win., Commemorative, *Curio*	400.00	650.00
☐ **M94 Texas Ranger**, .30-30 Win., Commemorative, *Curio*	400.00	525.00
☐ **M94 Theodore Roosevelt**, .30-30 Win., Commemorative, Rifle, *Curio*	225.00	325.00
☐ **M94 Theodore Roosevelt**, .30-30 Win., Commemorative, Carbine, *Curio*	225.00	325.00
☐ **M94 Theodore Roosevelt Set**, .30-30 Win., Commemorative, *Curio*	525.00	700.00
☐ **U.S. Border Patrol**, .30-30 Win., Commemorative, *Modern*	675.00	950.00
☐ **Wells Fargo**, .30-30 Win., Commemorative, *Modern*	450.00	595.00
☐ **M94 Wyoming Diamond Jubilee**, .30-30 Win., Commemorative, Carbine, *Curio*	850.00	1,450.00
☐ **M94**, under #50,000, Various Calibers, Carbine, *Antique*	425.00	575.00
☐ **M94**, under #50,000, Various Calibers, Rifle, *Antique*	450.00	650.00
☐ **M94XTR**, .30-30 Win., *Modern*	130.00	175.00
☐ **M94 Standard**, .30-30 Win., *Modern*	120.00	165.00
☐ **M94 Antique**, .30-30 Win., *Modern*	130.00	175.00
☐ **M94 Trapper**, .30-30 Win., *Modern*	120.00	160.00
☐ **M94XTR Big Bore**, .375 Win., *Modern*	145.00	200.00
☐ **M95**, Various Calibers, Rifle, *Modern*	450.00	650.00
☐ **M95**, Various Calibers, Carbine, *Modern*	550.00	775.00
☐ **M95**, Various Calibers, Musket, *Modern*	575.00	850.00
☐ **M95**, For Takedown, Add $100.00-$200.00		
☐ **M95**, under #19,477, Various Calibers, Rifle, *Antique*	525.00	850.00
☐ **M95**, under #19,477, Various Calibers, Carbine, *Antique*	650.00	950.00
☐ **Model 9422**, .22 L.R.R.F., Tube Feed, *Modern*	115.00	160.00
☐ **Model 9422M**, .22 WMR, Tube Feed, *Modern*	125.00	175.00
☐ **Model 9422XTR**, .22 L.R.R.F., Tube Feed, *Modern*	135.00	200.00
☐ **Model 9422MXTR**, .22 WMR, Tube Feed, *Modern*	165.00	215.00

RIFLE, SEMI-AUTOMATIC

	V.G.	EXC.
☐ **M100**, Various Calibers, Clip Fed, *Modern*	225.00	375.00
☐ **M100**, Various Calibers, Clip Fed, Carbine, *Modern*	200.00	350.00
☐ **M1903**, .22 Win. Auto. R.F., Tube Feed, *Modern*	175.00	300.00
☐ **M1905**, Various Calibers, Clip Fed, *Modern*	325.00	500.00
☐ **M1907**, .351 Win. Self-Loading, Clip Fed, *Modern*	275.00	425.00
☐ **M1907 Police**, .351 Win. Self-Loading, Clip Fed, *Modern*	300.00	475.00
☐ **M1910**, .401 Win. Self-Loading, Clip Fed, *Modern*	275.00	425.00
☐ **M190**, .22 L.R.R.F., Tube Feed, *Modern*	45.00	65.00
☐ **M190 Deluxe**, .22 L.R.R.F., Tube Feed, *Modern*	50.00	75.00
☐ **M290**, .22 L.R.R.F., Tube Feed, *Modern*	55.00	85.00
☐ **M290**, .22 L.R.R.F., Tube Feed, Checkered Stock, *Modern*	60.00	90.00
☐ **M290 Deluxe**, .22 L.R.R.F., Tube Feed, Monte Carlo Stock, *Modern*	65.00	95.00
☐ **M490 Deluxe**, .22 L.R.R.F., Clip Fed, Monte Carlo Stock, *Modern*	165.00	250.00
☐ **M55 Automatic**, .22 L.R.R.F., *Modern*	90.00	140.00
☐ **M63**, .22 L.R.R.F., Tube Feed, *Modern*	300.00	425.00
☐ **M74**, .22 L.R.R.F., Clip Fed, *Modern*	115.00	175.00
☐ **M77**, .22 L.R.R.F., Clip Fed, *Modern*	75.00	115.00
☐ **M77**, .22 L.R.R.F., Tube Feed, *Modern*	75.00	115.00

RIFLE, SINGLESHOT

	V.G.	EXC.
☐ **Model 310**, .22 L.R.R.F., Bolt Action, *Modern*	50.00	70.00
☐ **High-Wall**, Various Calibers, Sporting Rifle, *Curio*	325.00	500.00
☐ **High-Wall**, Various Calibers, Sporting Rifle, Takedown, *Curio*	450.00	650.00
☐ **High-Wall**, Various Calibers, Schutzen Rifle, Takedown, *Curio*	975.00	1,600.00
☐ **High-Wall**, Various Calibers, Schutzen Rifle, *Curio*	850.00	1,200.00
☐ **Low-Wall**, .22 Long R.F., Musket, *Curio*	225.00	350.00
☐ **Low-Wall**, Various Calibers, Sporting Rifle, *Curio*	235.00	350.00

WINCHESTER REPEATING ARMS COMPANY / 495

Winchester Model 94 Carbine

Winchester Model 1873 Carbine

Winchester Model 73 Musket

Winchester Model 1895

Winchester Model 67

Winchester Model 94 Trapper

Winchester Model 1886

Winchester Model 1886 Custom

	V.G.	EXC.
☐ **Winder**, .22 Long R.F., Musket, Takedown, *Curio*	325.00	475.00
☐ **Winder**, .22 Long R.F., Musket, *Curio*	275.00	400.00

RIFLE, SLIDE ACTION

	V.G.	EXC.
☐ **M1890**, Various Rimfires, *Modern*	220.00	325.00
☐ **M1890**, Various Rimfires, Solid Frame, *Curio*	250.00	350.00
☐ **M1890**, under #64,521, Various Rimfires, *Antique*	275.00	400.00
☐ **M1906**, .22 L.R.R.F., Tube Feed, Hammer, *Modern*	250.00	375.00
☐ **M270**, .22 L.R.R.F., Tube Feed, *Modern*	60.00	85.00
☐ **M270 Deluxe**, .22 L.R.R.F., Tube Feed, *Modern*	75.00	110.00
☐ **M275**, .22 WMR, Tube Feed, *Modern*	70.00	100.00
☐ **M275 Deluxe**, .22 WMR, Tube Feed, *Modern*	85.00	125.00
☐ **M61**, .22 L.R.R.F., Tube Feed, *Modern*	250.00	375.00
☐ **M61**, Various Rimfires, Tube Feed, Octagon Barrel, *Modern*	300.00	425.00
☐ **M61 Magnum**, .22 WMR, Tube Feed, *Modern*	300.00	450.00
☐ **M62**, .22 L.R.R.F., Tube Feed, Hammer, *Modern*	250.00	375.00
☐ **M62 Gallery**, .22 Short R.F., Tube Feed, Hammer, *Modern*	275.00	400.00

SHOTGUN, BOLT ACTION

	V.G.	EXC.
☐ **Model 36**, 9mm Shotshell, Takedown, Singleshot, *Curio*	125.00	200.00
☐ **Model 41**, .410 Ga., Takedown, Singleshot, *Modern*	125.00	200.00
☐ **Model 41**, .410 Ga., Takedown, Singleshot, Checkered Stock, *Modern*	150.00	245.00

SHOTGUN, DOUBLE BARREL, OVER-UNDER

	V.G.	EXC.
☐ **Model 101**, 12 Ga., Trap Grade, Monte Carlo Stock, Single Trigger, Automatic Ejector, Engraved, *Modern*	575.00	750.00
☐ **Model 101**, 12 Ga., Trap Grade, Single Trigger, Automatic Ejector, Checkered Stock, Engraved, *Modern*	575.00	750.00
☐ **Model 101**, 12 Ga. Mag. 3", Vent Rib, Single Trigger, Automatic Ejector, Checkered Stock, Engraved, *Modern*	550.00	725.00
☐ **Model 101**, Various Gauges, Skeet Grade, Single Trigger, Automatic Ejector, Checkered Stock, Engraved, *Modern*	575.00	750.00
☐ **Model 101**, Various Gauges, Featherweight, Single Trigger, Automatic Ejector, Checkered Stock, Engraved, *Modern*	575.00	750.00
☐ **Model 101 3 Ga. Set**, Various Gauges, Skeet Grade, Single Trigger, Automatic Ejector, Checkered Stock, Engraved, *Modern*	1,100.00	1,650.00
☐ **Model 101 Field**, Various Gauges, Vent Rib, Single Trigger, Automatic Ejector, Checkered Stock, Engraved, *Modern*	500.00	725.00
☐ **Model 101 Pigeon**, 12 Ga., Trap Grade, Single Trigger, Automatic Ejector, Checkered Stock, Engraved, *Modern*	500.00	725.00
☐ **Model 101 Pigeon**, 12 Ga., Trap Grade, Monte Carlo Stock, Single Trigger, Automatic Ejector, Engraved, *Modern*	500.00	725.00
☐ **Model 101 Pigeon**, 12 and 20 Gauges, Skeet Grade, Single Trigger, Automatic Ejector, Checkered Stock, Engraved, *Modern*	575.00	800.00
☐ **Model 101 Magnum**, 12 Ga. 3", Single Trigger, Automatic Ejector, Checkered Stock, Engraved, *Modern*	575.00	750.00
☐ **Model 101 Pigeon**, Various Gauges, Field Grade, Single Trigger, Automatic Ejector, Checkered Stock, Engraved, *Modern*	575.00	800.00
☐ **Model 96**, 12 Ga., Trap Grade, Vent Rib, Checkered Stock, *Modern*	395.00	575.00
☐ **Model 92**, 12 Ga., Trap Grade, Vent Rib, Monte Carlo Stock, *Modern*	395.00	575.00
☐ **Model 96**, 12 and 20 Gauges, Field Grade, Vent Rib, Checkered Stock, *Modern*	380.00	560.00
☐ **Model 96**, 12 and 20 Gauges, Skeet Grade, Vent Rib, Checkered Stock, *Modern*	390.00	570.00
☐ **Xpert**, 12 Ga., Trap Grade, Vent Rib, Checkered Stock, *Modern*	395.00	575.00
☐ **Xpert**, 12 Ga., Trap Grade, Vent Rib, Monte Carlo Stock, *Modern*	395.00	575.00

WINCHESTER REPEATING ARMS COMPANY / 497

	V.G.	EXC.

- ☐ **Xpert**, 12 and 20 Gauges, Field Grade, Vent Rib, Checkered Stock, *Modern* 380.00 560.00
- ☐ **Xpert**, 12 and 20 Gauges, Skeet Grade, Vent Rib, Checkered Stock, *Modern* 390.00 570.00

SHOTGUN, DOUBLE BARREL, SIDE-BY-SIDE
- ☐ **Model 21**, For Extra Barrels, *Add* 25%-30%
- ☐ **Model 21**, For Vent Rib, *Add* **$350.00**
- ☐ **Model 21**, .410 Ga., Checkered Stock, Fancy Wood, *Modern* 4,500.00 7,500.00
- ☐ **Model 21**, 12 Ga., Trap Grade, Hammerless, Single Selective Trigger, Selective Ejector, Vent Rib, *Modern* 2,900.00 4,250.00
- ☐ **Model 21**, 12 Ga., Trap Grade, Hammerless, Single Selective Trigger, Selective Ejector, Raised Matted Rib, *Modern* 2,700.00 4,000.00
- ☐ **Model 21**, 12 and 16 Gauges, Skeet Grade, Hammerless, Single Selective Trigger, Selective Ejector, Vent Rib, *Modern* 2,800.00 4,000.00
- ☐ **Model 21**, 12 and 16 Gauges, Skeet Grade, Hammerless, Single Selective Trigger, Selective Ejector, Raised Matted Rib, *Modern* 2,900.00 4,250.00
- ☐ **Model 21**, 12 and 16 Gauges, Field Grade, Double Trigger, Automatic Ejector, Hammerless, *Modern* 2,250.00 3,400.00
- ☐ **Model 21**, 12 and 16 Gauges, Field Grade, Double Trigger, Selective Ejector, Hammerless, *Modern* 2,450.00 3,550.00
- ☐ **Model 21**, 12 and 16 Gauges, Field Grade, Single Selective Trigger, Automatic Ejector, Hammerless, *Modern* 2,450.00 3,700.00
- ☐ **Model 21**, 12 and 16 Gauges, Field Grade, Single Selective Trigger, Selective Ejector, Hammerless, *Modern* 2,500.00 3,750.00
- ☐ **Model 21**, 20 Ga., Skeet Grade, Hammerless, Single Selective Trigger, Selective Ejector, Vent Rib, *Modern* 2,950.00 4,550.00
- ☐ **Model 21**, 20 Ga., Skeet Grade, Hammerless, Single Selective Trigger, Selective Ejector, Raised Matted Rib, *Modern* 2,800.00 4,300.00
- ☐ **Model 21**, 20 Ga., Field Grade, Double Trigger, Automatic Ejector, Hammerless, *Modern* 2,500.00 3,700.00
- ☐ **Model 21**, 20 Ga., Field Grade, Double Trigger, Selective Ejector, Hammerless, *Modern* 2,650.00 3,900.00
- ☐ **Model 21**, 20 Ga., Field Grade, Single Selective Trigger, Automatic Ejector, Hammerless, *Modern* 2,700.00 4,000.00
- ☐ **Model 21**, 20 Ga., Field Grade, Single Selective Trigger, Selective Ejector, Hammerless, *Modern* 2,900.00 4,100.00
- ☐ **Model 21 Custom**, 12 Ga., Hammerless, Single Selective Trigger, Selective Ejector, Fancy Engraving, Fancy Checkering, *Modern* 4,500.00 6,000.00
- ☐ **Model 21 Custom**, 20 Ga., Hammerless, Single Selective Trigger, Selective Ejector, Fancy Engraving, Fancy Checkering, *Modern* 4,750.00 6,750.00
- ☐ **Model 21 Duck**, 12 Ga. Mag. 3", Hammerless, Single Selective Trigger, Selective Ejector, Raised Matted Rib, *Modern* 2,000.00 3,900.00
- ☐ **Model 21 Duck**, 12 Ga. Mag. 3", Hammerless, Single Selective Trigger, Selective Ejector, Vent Rib, *Modern* 2,500.00 3,950.00
- ☐ **Model 21 Grand American**, 12 Ga., Hammerless, Single Selective Trigger, Selective Ejector, Fancy Engraving, Fancy Checkering, *Modern* 6,500.00 9,500.00
- ☐ **Model 21 Grand American**, 20 Ga., Hammerless, Single Selective Trigger, Selective Ejector, Fancy Engraving, Fancy Checkering, *Modern* 7,000.00 10,500.00
- ☐ **Model 21 Pigeon**, 12 Ga., Hammerless, Single Selective Trigger, Selective Ejector, Fancy Engraving, Fancy Checkering, *Modern* 4,500.00 6,250.00
- ☐ **Model 21 Pigeon**, 12 Ga., Hammerless, Single Selective Trigger, Selective Ejector, Fancy Engraving, Fancy Checkering, *Modern* 4,800.00 7,000.00
- ☐ **Model 23 English**, 12 or 20 Gauges, Hammerless, Single Trigger, Selective Ejector, Engraved, Fancy Checkering, *Modern* 600.00   850.00

498 / WINCHESTER REPEATING ARMS COMPANY

Winchester Model 1911

Winchester Model 1906

Winchester Model 1905

Winchester Model 101

Winchester Model 190

Winchester Model 1400

Winchester Model 1200

Winchester Model 1887 Deluxe

WINCHESTER REPEATING ARMS COMPANY / 499

	V.G.	EXC.
☐ **Model 23 Pigeon**, 12 or 20 Gauges, Hammerless, Single Trigger, Selective Ejector, Engraved, Fancy Checkering, *Modern*	550.00	800.00
☐ **Model 23 Grand European**, 12 Ga., Hammerless, Single Selective Trigger, Selective Ejector, Fancy Engraving, Fancy Checkering, *Modern*	775.00	1,200.00
☐ **Model 24**, Various Gauges, Double Trigger, Automatic Ejector, *Modern*	250.00	325.00

SHOTGUN, LEVER ACTION

	V.G.	EXC.
☐ **M1887**, Various Gauges, *Antique*	325.00	450.00
☐ **M1887 Deluxe Grade**, Various Gauges, *Antique*	375.00	550.00
☐ **M1901**, 10 Ga. 2⅞", Tube Feed, Damascus Barrel, *Curio*	325.00	450.00
☐ **Model 1887**, 10 Ga. 2⅞", Tube Feed, Checkered Stock, Damascus Barrel, *Curio*	350.00	475.00
☐ **Model 1887**, 10 Ga. 2⅞", Tube Feed, Plain, *Curio*	300.00	400.00
☐ **Model 1887**, 12 Ga., Damascus Barrel, Checkered Stock, Tube Feed, *Curio*	375.00	500.00
☐ **Model 1887**, 12 Ga., Tube Feed, Plain, *Curio*	325.00	425.00
☐ **Model 1887**, under #64842, 10 Ga. 2⅞", Damascus Barrel, Checkered Stock, Tube Feed, *Antique*	400.00	525.00
☐ **Model 1887**, under #64842, 10 Ga. 2⅞", Tube Feed, Plain, *Antique*	325.00	450.00
☐ **Model 1887**, under #64842, 12 Ga., Tube Feed, Plain, *Antique*	350.00	475.00
☐ **Model 1887**, under #64842, 12 Ga., Tube Feed, Checkered Stock, Damascus Barrel, *Antique*	425.00	550.00
☐ **Model 1901**, 10 Ga. 2⅞", Tube Feed, Plain, *Curio*	325.00	500.00

SHOTGUN, SEMI-AUTOMATIC

	V.G.	EXC.
☐ **Model 1400 Trap**, 12 Ga., Vent Rib, *Modern*	180.00	250.00
☐ **Model 1400 Trap**, 12 Ga., Monte Carlo Stock, Vent Rib, *Modern*	200.00	275.00
☐ **Model 1400 Trap**, 12 Ga., Vent Rib, Recoil Reducer, *Modern*	220.00	300.00
☐ **Model 1400 Skeet**, 12 and 20 Gauges, Vent Rib, *Modern*	180.00	250.00
☐ **Model 1400 Deer**, 12 Ga., Open Sights, Slug Gun, *Modern*	165.00	225.00
☐ **Model 1400 Field**, 12 and 20 Gauges, Winchoke, *Modern*	150.00	200.00
☐ **Model 1400 Field**, 12 and 20 Gauges, Winchoke, Vent Rib, *Modern*	165.00	225.00
☐ **Model 1400 Mk.II Trap**, 12 Ga., Vent Rib, *Modern*	180.00	250.00
☐ **Model 1400 Mk.II Trap**, 12 Ga., Monte Carlo Stock, Vent Rib, *Modern*	200.00	275.00
☐ **Model 1400 Mk.II Trap**, 12 Ga., Vent Rib, Recoil Reducer, *Modern*	220.00	300.00
☐ **Model 1400 Mk.II Skeet**, 12 and 20 Gauges, Vent Rib, *Modern*	180.00	250.00
☐ **Model 1400 Mk.II Deer**, 12 Ga., Open Sights, Slug Gun, *Modern*	165.00	225.00
☐ **Model 1400 Mk.II Field**, 12 and 20 Gauges, Winchoke, *Modern*	150.00	200.00
☐ **Model 1400 Mk.II Field**, 12 and 20 Gauges, Winchoke, Vent Rib, *Modern*	165.00	225.00
☐ **Model 1500**, 12 or 20 Gauges, Field Grade, Plain, *Modern*	200.00	275.00
☐ **Model 1500**, 12 or 20 Gauges, Field Grade, Vent Rib, *Modern*	220.00	300.00
☐ **Model 1911**, 12 Ga., Takedown, Plain, *Modern*	220.00	300.00
☐ **Model 1911**, 12 Ga., Takedown, Checkered Stock, *Modern*	250.00	375.00
☐ **Model 40**, 12 Ga., Takedown, Field Grade, *Modern*	225.00	325.00
☐ **Model 40**, 12 Ga., Takedown, Skeet Grade, Adjustable Choke, *Modern*	275.00	375.00
☐ **Model 50**, 12 Ga., Trap Grade, Vent Rib, Monte Carlo Stock, *Modern*	325.00	450.00
☐ **Model 50**, 12 and 20 Gauges, Field Grade, Plain Barrel, Checkered Stock, *Modern*	200.00	275.00
☐ **Model 50**, 12 and 20 Gauges, Field Grade, Vent Rib, Checkered Stock, *Modern*	220.00	300.00
☐ **Model 50**, 12 and 20 Gauges, Skeet Grade, Vent Rib, Checkered Stock, *Modern*	290.00	420.00

500 / WINCHESTER REPEATING ARMS COMPANY

	V.G.	EXC.
SHOTGUN, SINGLESHOT		
☐ **Model 101**, 12 Ga., Trap Grade, Vent Rib, *Modern*	350.00	450.00
☐ **Model 20**, .410 Ga. 2½", Takedown, Hammer, Checkered Stock, *Modern*	165.00	250.00
☐ **Model 37**, For Red Letter **Add 25%-40%**		
☐ **Model 37**, .410 Ga., Takedown, Automatic Ejector, Plain Barrel, *Modern*	85.00	125.00
☐ **Model 37**, 12 Ga., Takedown, Automatic Ejector, Plain Barrel, *Modern*	75.00	115.00
☐ **Model 37**, 16 Ga., Takedown, Automatic Ejector, Plain Barrel, *Modern*	65.00	100.00
☐ **Model 37**, 20 Ga., Takedown, Automatic Ejector, Plain Barrel, *Modern*	75.00	120.00
☐ **Model 37**, 28 Ga., Takedown, Automatic Ejector, Plain Barrel, *Modern*	95.00	145.00
☐ **Model 37A**, Various Gauges, *Modern*	50.00	65.00
☐ **Model 37A Youth**, Various Gauges, *Modern*	50.00	65.00
☐ **Model 37**, 12 Ga., Takedown, Automatic Ejector, Plain Barrel, *Modern*	35.00	50.00
☐ **Model 37 Youth**, 12 Ga., Takedown, Automatic Ejector, Plain Barrel, *Modern*	35.00	50.00
☐ **High Wall**, 20 Ga., Falling Block, Plain, *Curio*	400.00	650.00
SHOTGUN, SLIDE ACTION		
☐ **Model 12**, 12 Ga., Pre'64, Takedown, Trap Grade, Raised Matted Rib, *Modern*	475.00	700.00
☐ **Model 12**, 12 Ga., Pre'64, Takedown, Trap Grade, Vent Rib, *Modern*	525.00	775.00
☐ **Model 12**, 12 Ga., Pre'64, Takedown, Trap Grade, Vent Rib, Monte Carlo Stock, *Modern*	575.00	825.00
☐ **Model 12**, 12 Ga., Pre-War, Takedown, Vent Rib, *Modern*	475.00	525.00
☐ **Model 12**, 12 Ga., Pre-War, Takedown, Riot Gun, *Modern*	250.00	375.00
☐ **Model 12**, 12 Ga., Post '64, Trap Grade, Checkered Stock, *Modern*	425.00	525.00
☐ **Model 12**, 12 Ga., Post '64, Trap Grade, Monte Carlo Stock, *Modern*	425.00	525.00
☐ **Model 12**, Various Gauges, Pre'64, Takedown, Skeet Grade, Raised Matted Rib, *Modern*	425.00	650.00
☐ **Model 12**, Various Gauges, Pre'64, Takedown, Skeet Grade, Vent Rib, *Modern*	475.00	700.00
☐ **Model 12**, Various Gauges, Pre'64, Takedown, Skeet Grade, Plain Barrel, *Modern*	400.00	625.00
☐ **Model 12**, Various Gauges, Pre'64, Takedown, Skeet Grade, Plain Barrel, Adjustable Choke, *Modern*	425.00	650.00
☐ **Model 12**, Various Gauges, Pre'64, Takedown, Raised Matted Rib, *Modern*	425.00	600.00
☐ **Model 12**, Featherweight, Various Gauges, Pre'64, Takedown, *Modern*	400.00	575.00
☐ **Model 12**, Heavy Duck, 12 Ga. Mag. 3", Pre'64, Takedown, Vent Rib, *Modern*	400.00	625.00
☐ **Model 12**, Heavy Duck, 12 Ga. Mag. 3", Pre'64, Takedown, *Modern*	375.00	550.00
☐ **Model 12**, Heavy Duck, 12 Ga. Mag. 3", Pre'64, Takedown, Raised Matted Rib, *Modern*	425.00	600.00
☐ **Model 12**, Pigeon Grade, 12 Ga., Pre'64, Takedown, Trap Grade, Vent Rib, *Modern*	800.00	1,250.00
☐ **Model 12**, Pigeon Grade, 12 Ga., Pre'64, Takedown, Trap Grade, Raised Matted Rib, *Modern*	750.00	1,100.00
☐ **Model 12**, Pigeon Grade, Various Gauges, Pre'64, Takedown, Skeet Grade, Raised Matted Rib, *Modern*	650.00	975.00

WINFIELD ARMS COMPANY / 501

	V.G.	EXC.
☐ **Model 12**, Pigeon Grade, Various Gauges, Pre'64, Takedown, Skeet Grade, Vent Rib, *Modern*	750.00	1,100.00
☐ **Model 12**, Pigeon Grade, Various Gauges, Pre'64, Takedown, Skeet Grade, Plain Barrel, Adjustable Choke, *Modern*	600.00	900.00
☐ **Model 12**, Pigeon Grade, Various Gauges, Pre'64, Takedown, Field Grade, Plain Barrel, *Modern*	600.00	875.00
☐ **Model 12**, Pigeon Grade, Various Gauges, Pre'64, Takedown, Field Grade, Vent Rib, *Modern*	650.00	925.00
☐ **Model 12**, Standard, Various Gauges, Pre'64, Takedown, *Modern*	375.00	500.00
☐ **Model 12**, Super Pigeon, 12 Ga., Post '64, Takedown, Vent Rib, Engraved, Checkered Stock, *Modern*	1,250.00	1,950.00
☐ **Model 1200**, For Recoil Reducer *Add* $35.00-$50.00		
☐ **Model 1200 Field**, 12 and 20 Gauges, Adjustable Choke, *Modern*	125.00	160.00
☐ **Model 1200 Field**, 12 and 20 Gauges, Adjustable Choke, Vent Rib, *Modern*	130.00	165.00
☐ **Model 1200 Field**, 12 and 20 Gauges, *Modern*	110.00	140.00
☐ **Model 1200 Field**, 12 and 20 Gauges, Vent Rib, *Modern*	120.00	150.00
☐ **Model 1200 Field**, 12 Ga. Mag. 3", *Modern*	125.00	160.00
☐ **Model 1200 Field**, 12 Ga. Mag. 3", Vent Rib, *Modern*	135.00	170.00
☐ **Model 1200 Deer**, 12 Ga., Open Sights, *Modern*	125.00	165.00
☐ **Model 1200 Riot**, 12 Ga., *Modern*	110.00	150.00
☐ **Model 1200 Defender**, 12 Ga., *Modern*	120.00	160.00
☐ **Model 1200 Police**, 12 Ga., *Modern*	170.00	250.00
☐ **Model 1200 Stainless**, 12 Ga., *Modern*	170.00	250.00
☐ **Model 1300**, 12 or 20 Gauges, Plain Barrel, *Modern*	140.00	190.00
☐ **Model 1300**, 12 or 20 Gauges, Vent Rib, *Modern*	155.00	210.00
☐ **Model 1300**, 12 or 20 Gauges, Plain Barrel, Winchoke, *Modern*	160.00	225.00
☐ **Model 1300**, 12 or 20 Gauges, Vent Rib, Winchoke, *Modern*	175.00	250.00
☐ **Model 1300 Deer**, 12 Ga., Open Sights, *Modern*	170.00	235.00
☐ **Model 25**, 12 Ga., Solid Frame, Plain Barrel, *Modern*	175.00	245.00
☐ **Model 25**, 12 Ga., Solid Frame, Riot Gun, *Modern*	160.00	220.00
☐ **Model 42**, .410 Ga., Field Grade, Takedown, *Modern*	475.00	650.00
☐ **Model 42**, .410 Ga., Field Grade, Takedown, Raised Matted Rib, *Modern*	525.00	700.00
☐ **Model 42**, .410 Ga., Skeet Grade, Takedown, Raised Matted Rib, *Modern*	625.00	825.00
☐ **Model 42 Deluxe**, .410 Ga., Takedown, Vent Rib, Fancy Checkering, Fancy Wood, *Modern*	675.00	900.00
☐ **Model 97**, 12 Ga., Solid Frame, Plain, *Modern*	185.00	250.00
☐ **Model 97**, 12 Ga., Takedown, Plain, *Modern*	225.00	300.00
☐ **Model 97**, 12 Ga., Takedown, Riot Gun, *Modern*	250.00	350.00
☐ **Model 97**, 12 Ga., Solid Frame, Riot Gun, *Modern*	225.00	300.00
☐ **Model 97**, 16 Ga., Solid Frame, Plain, *Modern*	160.00	225.00
☐ **Model 97**, 16 Ga., Takedown, Plain, *Modern*	180.00	250.00
☐ **Model 97 Pigeon**, 12 Ga., Takedown, Checkered Stock, *Modern*	725.00	1,100.00
☐ **Model 97 Tournament**, 12 Ga., Takedown, Checkered Stock, *Modern*	475.00	700.00
☐ **Model 97 Trap**, 12 Ga., Takedown, Checkered Stock, *Modern*	400.00	550.00
☐ **Model 97 Trench**, 12 Ga., Solid Frame, Riot Gun, Military, *Curio*	325.00	450.00
☐ **Model 97 Trench**, 12 Ga., Solid Frame, Riot Gun, Military, with Bayonet, *Curio*	375.00	500.00

WINFIELD ARMS CO.
Made by Norwich Falls Pistol Co., c. 1880.

HANDGUN, REVOLVER

	V.G.	EXC.
☐ **.32 Short R.F.**, 5 Shot, Spur Trigger, Solid Frame, Single Action, *Antique*	90.00	160.00

WINFIELD ARMS CO.
Made by Crescent, c. 1900.

	V.G.	EXC.

SHOTGUN, DOUBLE BARREL, SIDE-BY-SIDE
- ☐ **Various Gauges**, Outside Hammers, Damascus Barrel, *Modern* 100.00 175.00
- ☐ **Various Gauges**, Hammerless, Steel Barrel, *Modern* 135.00 200.00
- ☐ **Various Gauges**, Hammerless, Damascus Barrel, *Modern* 100.00 175.00
- ☐ **Various Gauges**, Outside Hammers, Steel Barrel, *Modern* 125.00 190.00

SHOTGUN, SINGLESHOT
- ☐ **Various Gauges**, Hammer, Steel Barrel, *Modern* 55.00 85.00

WINGERT, RICHARD
Lancaster, Pa. 1775-1777. See Kentucky Rifles, U.S. Military.

WINOCA ARMS CO.
Made by Crescent for Jacobi Hardware Co., Philadelphia, Pa.

SHOTGUN, DOUBLE BARREL, SIDE-BY-SIDE
- ☐ **Various Gauges**, Outside Hammers, Damascus Barrel, *Modern* 100.00 175.00
- ☐ **Various Gauges**, Hammerless, Steel Barrel, *Modern* 135.00 200.00
- ☐ **Various Gauges**, Hammerless, Damascus Barrel, *Modern* 100.00 175.00
- ☐ **Various Gauges**, Outside Hammers, Steel Barrel, *Modern* 125.00 190.00

SHOTGUN, SINGLESHOT
- ☐ **Various Gauges**, Hammer, Steel Barrel, *Modern* 55.00 85.00

WINSLOW ARMS CO.
Established in Venice, Fla. about 1962, moved to Osprey, Fla. about 1976, and is now in Camden, S.C.

RIFLE, BOLT ACTION
- ☐ **For Left hand Action**, Add $45.00-$65.00
- ☐ **Crown**, Various Calibers, Carved, Fancy Wood, Inlays, *Modern* 735.00 1,100.00
- ☐ **Emperor**, Various Calibers, Carved, Fancy Engraving, Ornate, Fancy Wood, Inlays, *Modern* 3,850.00 5,000.00
- ☐ **Imperial**, Various Calibers, Carved, Engraved, Fancy Wood, Inlays, *Modern* 2,100.00 2,800.00
- ☐ **Regal**, Various Calibers, Fancy Checkering, Inlays, *Modern* 390.00 525.00
- ☐ **Regent**, Various Calibers, Inlays, Carved, Fancy Wood, *Modern* ... 475.00 650.00
- ☐ **Regimental**, Various Calibers, Carved, Inlays, *Modern* 550.00 825.00
- ☐ **Royal**, Various Calibers, Carved, Fancy Wood, Inlays, *Modern* 950.00 1,400.00
- ☐ **Varmint**, Various Calibers, Fancy Checkering, Inlays, *Modern* 475.00 675.00

SHOTGUN, DOUBLE BARREL, OVER-UNDER
- ☐ **Hammerless**, 12 and 20 Gauges, Single Trigger, Checkered Stock, Inlays, *Modern* 600.00 925.00

SHOTGUN, DOUBLE BARREL, SIDE-BY-SIDE
- ☐ **Hammerless**, 12 Ga., Single Trigger, Checkered Stock, Inlays, *Modern* 500.00 725.00

WITHERS, MICHAEL
Lancaster, Pa. 1774-1805. See Kentucky Rifles, U.S. Military.

WITTES HDW. CO.
Made by Stevens Arms.

SHOTGUN, DOUBLE BARREL, SIDE-BY-SIDE
- ☐ **Model 311**, Various Gauges, Hammerless, Steel Barrel, *Modern*.... 95.00 165.00

	V.G.	EXC.

SHOTGUN, SINGLESHOT
- ☐ **Model 90**, Various Gauges, Takedown, Automatic Ejector, Plain, Hammer, *Modern* 35.00 55.00
- ☐ **Model 94**, Various Gauges, Takedown, Automatic Ejector, Plain, Hammer, *Modern* 35.00 55.00

WOGDON
London, England & Dublin, Ireland 1760-1797.

HANDGUN, FLINTLOCK
- ☐ **.56**, Officers, Holster Pistol, Flared, Octagon Barrel, Steel Furniture, Engraved, High Quality, *Antique* 1,650.00 2,750.00

WOLF
Spain, c. 1900.

HANDGUN, SEMI-AUTOMATIC
- ☐ **.25 ACP**, Clip Fed, *Modern* 90.00 125.00

WOLF, A.W.
Suhl, Germany, c. 1930.

SHOTGUN, DOUBLE BARREL, SIDE-BY-SIDE
- ☐ **12 Ga.**, Engraved, Platinium Inlays, Ivory Inlays, Ornate, Cased, *Modern* 5,000.00 6,750.00

WOLFHEIMER, PHILIP
Lancaster, Pa., c. 1774. See Kentucky Rifles.

WOLVERINE ARMS CO.
Made by Crescent for Fletcher Hardware Co., c. 1900.

SHOTGUN, DOUBLE BARREL, SIDE-BY-SIDE
- ☐ **Various Gauges**, Outside Hammers, Damascus Barrel, *Modern* 100.00 175.00
- ☐ **Various Gauges**, Hammerless, Steel Barrel, *Modern* 135.00 200.00
- ☐ **Various Gauges**, Hammerless, Damascus Barrel, *Modern* 100.00 175.00
- ☐ **Various Gauges**, Outside Hammers, Steel Barrel, *Modern* 125.00 190.00

SHOTGUN, SINGLESHOT
- ☐ **Various Gauges**, Hammer, Steel Barrel, *Modern* 55.00 85.00

WOODWARD, JAMES & SONS
London, England.

SHOTGUN, DOUBLE BARREL, OVER-UNDER
- ☐ **Best Quality**, Various Gauges, Sidelock, Automatic Ejector, Double Trigger, Fancy Engraving, Fancy Checkering, *Modern* 10,000.00 15,000.00
- ☐ **Best Quality**, Various Gauges, Sidelock, Automatic Ejector, Single Trigger, Fancy Engraving, Fancy Checkering, *Modern* 11,000.00 17,000.00

SHOTGUN, DOUBLE BARREL, SIDE-BY-SIDE
- ☐ **Best Quality**, Various Gauges, Sidelock, Automatic Ejector, Double Trigger, Fancy Engraving, Fancy Checkering, *Modern* 8,500.00 12,000.00
- ☐ **Best Quality**, Various Gauges, Sidelock, Automatic Ejector, Single Trigger, Fancy Engraving, Fancy Checkering, *Modern* 9,000.00 13,500.00

SHOTGUN, SINGLESHOT
- ☐ **12 Ga.**, Trap Grade, Vent Rib, Hammerless, Fancy Engraving, Fancy Checkering, *Modern* 8,000.00 14,000.00

WORTHINGTON ARMS
Made by Stevens Arms.
SHOTGUN, DOUBLE BARREL, SIDE-BY-SIDE

	V.G.	EXC.
☐ **M 315**, Various Gauges, Hammerless, Steel Barrel, *Modern*	95.00	165.00
☐ **Model 215**, 12 and 16 Gauges, Outside Hammers, Steel Barrel, *Modern*	95.00	160.00

WORTHINGTON ARMS CO.
Made by Crescent for Geo. Worthington Co., Cleveland, Ohio.
SHOTGUN, DOUBLE BARREL, SIDE-BY-SIDE

	V.G.	EXC.
☐ **Various Gauges**, Outside Hammers, Damascus Barrel, *Modern*	100.00	175.00
☐ **Various Gauges**, Hammerless, Steel Barrel, *Modern*	135.00	200.00
☐ **Various Gauges**, Hammerless, Damascus Barrel, *Modern*	100.00	175.00
☐ **Various Gauges**, Outside Hammers, Steel Barrel, *Modern*	125.00	190.00

SHOTGUN, SINGLESHOT

	V.G.	EXC.
☐ **Various Gauges**, Hammer, Steel Barrel, *Modern*	55.00	85.00

WORTHINGTON, GEORGE
Made by Stevens Arms.
SHOTGUN, DOUBLE BARREL, SIDE-BY-SIDE

	V.G.	EXC.
☐ **M 315**, Various Gauges, Hammerless, Steel Barrel, *Modern*	90.00	160.00
☐ **Model 215**, 12 and 16 Gauges, Outside Hammers, Steel Barrel, *Modern*	85.00	155.00
☐ **Model 311**, Various Gauges, Hammerless, Steel Barrel, *Modern*	95.00	165.00

WUETHRICH
W. Wuthrich, Werkzeugbau, Lutzelfluh, Switzerland.
RIFLE, SINGLESHOT

	V.G.	EXC.
☐ **Falling Block**, Various Calibers, Engraved, Fancy Wood, Scope Mounted, *Modern*	875.00	1,250.00

YATO
Hamada Arsenal, Japan.
HANDGUN, SEMI-AUTOMATIC

	V.G.	EXC.
☐ **Yato**, .32 ACP, Clip Fed, Pre-War, *Curio*	1,850.00	2,950.00
☐ **Yato**, .32 ACP, Clip Fed, Military, *Curio*	1,300.00	2,150.00

YDEAL
Made by Francisco Arizmendi, Eibar, Spain.
HANDGUN, SEMI-AUTOMATIC

	V.G.	EXC.
☐ **.25 ACP**, Clip Fed, Blue, *Modern*	90.00	125.00
☐ **.32 ACP**, Clip Fed, Blue, *Modern*	100.00	140.00

YOU BET
Made by Hopkins & Allen, c. 1880.

	V.G.	EXC.
HANDGUN, REVOLVER		
☐ **.22 Short R.F.**, 7 Shot, Spur Trigger, Solid Frame, Single Action, Antique	90.00	160.00

YOUNG AMERICA
See Harrington & Richardson Arms Co.

YOUNG, HENRY
Easton, Pa. 1774-1780. See Kentucky Rifles.

YOUNG, JOHN
Easton, Pa. 1775-1788. See Kentucky Rifles, U.S. Military.

Z
Ceska Zbrojovka, Prague, Czechoslovakia.

HANDGUN, SEMI-AUTOMATIC
☐ **Vest Pocket**, .25 ACP, Clip Fed, *Modern* 80.00   120.00

Z-B
AUTOMATIC WEAPON, LIGHT MACHINE GUN
☐ **VZ-26**, 8mm Mauser, Finned Barrel, Clip Fed, Bipod, *Class 3* 2,150.00   2,950.00

ZABALA
Spain.

SHOTGUN, DOUBLE BARREL, SIDE-BY-SIDE
☐ **12 Ga.**, Boxlock, Chackered Stock, Double Triggers, *Modern* 110.00   165.00

ZANOTTI
Ravenna, Italy.

HANDGUN, FLINTLOCK
☐ **Brescia Style**, .50, Carved Stock, Engraved, Reproduction, *Antique*   70.00   125.00

ZARAGOZA
Zaragoza, Mexico.

HANDGUN, SEMI-AUTOMATIC
☐ **Corla**, .22 L.R.R.F., Clip Fed, Blue, *Modern* 325.00   450.00

ZASTAVA
Zavodi Crvena Zastava, Kragujevac, Yugoslavia. Also see Mark X.

HANDGUN, SEMI-AUTOMATIC
☐ **Model 65**, 9mm Luger, Clip Fed, Blue, *Modern* 175.00   240.00
☐ **Model 67**, .32 ACP, Clip Fed, Blue, *Modern* 85.00   135.00

ZEHNA
Made by E. Zehner Waffenfabrik, Suhl, Germany 1919-1928.

HANDGUN, SEMI-AUTOMATIC
☐ **Vest Pocket**, .25 ACP, Under #5,000, Clip Fed, Blue, *Curio* 165.00   250.00
☐ **Vest Pocket**, .25 ACP, Clip Fed, Blue, *Curio* 195.00   285.00

ZEPHYR
Tradename of A.F. Stoeger.

506 / ZOLI, ANGELO

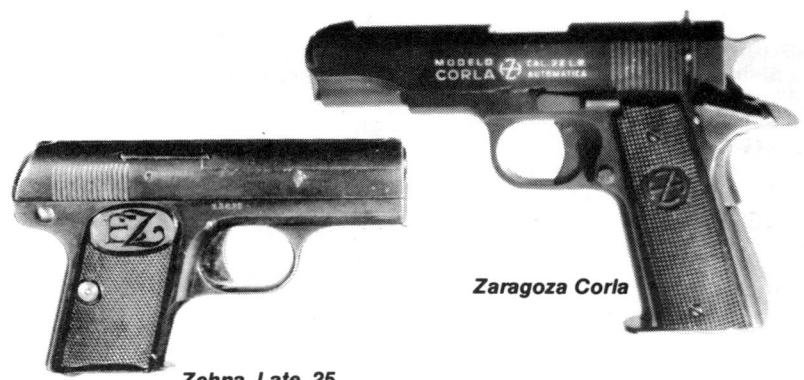

Zaragoza Corla

Zehna, Late .25

	V.G.	EXC.
SHOTGUN, DOUBLE BARREL, SIDE-BY-SIDE		
☐ **Woodlander II**, Various Gauges, Checkered Stock, Boxlock, Double Triggers, Light Engraving, *Modern*	150.00	200.00
☐ **Sterlingworth II**, Various Gauges, Checkered Stock, Sidelock, Double Triggers, Light Engraving, *Modern*	220.00	300.00

ZOLI, ANGELO
Brescia, Italy.

RIFLE, PERCUSSION
☐ **.50 Hawkin**, Brass Furniture, Reproduction, *Antique* 100.00   150.00

SHOTGUN, DOUBLE BARREL, OVER-UNDER
☐ **Angel**, 12 Ga., Trap Grade, Single Selective Trigger, Engraved, Checkered Stock, *Modern* 350.00   450.00
☐ **Angel**, 12 and 20 Gauges, Field Grade, Single Selective Trigger, Engraved, Checkered Stock, *Modern* 325.00   400.00
☐ **Condor**, 12 Ga., Trap Grade, Single Selective Trigger, Engraved, Checkered Stock, *Modern* 300.00   375.00
☐ **Condor**, 12 and 20 Gauges, Single Selective Trigger, Field Grade, Checkered Stock, Engraved, *Modern* 275.00   350.00
☐ **Monte Carlo**, 12 Ga., Trap Grade, Single Selective Trigger, Engraved, Checkered Stock, *Modern* 425.00   525.00
☐ **Monte Carlo**, 12 and 20 Gauges, Field Grade, Single Selective Trigger, Engraved, Checkered Stock, *Modern* 400.00   500.00

ZOLI, ANTONIO
Gardone, V.T., Italy.

SHOTGUN, DOUBLE BARREL, OVER-UNDER
☐ **Golden Snipe**, 12 Ga., Trap Grade, Single Trigger, Automatic Ejector, Engraved, Checkered Stock, *Modern* 325.00   425.00
☐ **Golden Snipe**, 12 and 20 Gauges, Vent Rib, Single Trigger, Automatic Ejector, Engraved, Checkered Stock, *Modern* 290.00   370.00
☐ **Golden Snipe**, 12 and 20 Gauges, Skeet Grade, Single Trigger, Automatic Ejector, Engraved, Checkered Stock, *Modern* 325.00   425.00
☐ **Silver Snipe**, 12 Ga., Trap Grade, Single Trigger, Vent Rib, Engraved, Checkered Stock, *Modern* 270.00   350.00
☐ **Silver Snipe**, 12 and 20 Gauges, Vent Rib, Single Trigger, Engraved, Checkered Stock, *Modern* 240.00   320.00

| | V.G. | EXC. |

☐ **Silver Snipe**, 12 and 20 Gauges, Skeet Grade, Single Trigger, Vent Rib, Engraved, Checkered Stock, *Modern* 270.00 350.00
SHOTGUN, DOUBLE BARREL, SIDE-BY-SIDE
☐ **Silver Hawk**, 12 and 20 Gauges, Double Trigger, Engraved, Checkered Stock, *Modern* 250.00 325.00

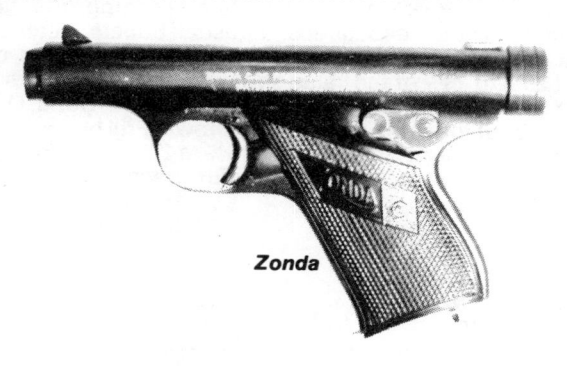

Zonda

ZONDA
Hispano Argentina Fab. de Automiviles, Buenos Aires, Argentina.
HANDGUN, SINGLESHOT
☐ **.22 L.R.R.F.**, Blue, *Modern* 195.00 275.00

Zulaica .32

ZULAICA
M. Zulaica y Cia., Eibar, Spain.
HANDGUN, SEMI-AUTOMATIC
☐ **.32 ACP**, Clip Fed, Blue, Military, *Curio* 95.00 135.00
AUTOMATIC REVOLVER
☐ **.22 L.R.R.F.**, Zig-Zag Cylinder, Blue, *Curio* 525.00 875.00

CARTRIDGE PRICES

The newcomers joining the swelling ranks of cartridge collectors have made prices in this specialized field quite volatile because of increased demand. This trend will continue for the foreseeable future.

The prices shown are based on the average value of a single cartridge with (unless otherwise noted) a common headstamp ranging from very good to excellent condition. Rare headstamps, unusual bullets, scarce case construction, will add to the value of the item. On common cartridges, empty cases are worth about **20%** to **25%** of the value shown; with rare calibers the empties should bring about **75%** to **80%** of the price of the loaded round. Dummies and blanks are worth about the same as the value shown. Full boxes of ammunition of common type should earn a discount of **15%** to **20%** per cartridge, whereas full boxes of rare ammo will command a premium because of the collectability of the box itself.

	V.G.	EXC.
☐ .145 **Alton Jones**, *Modern*	2.00	3.00
☐ .17 **Alton Jones**, *Modern*	1.00	1.75
☐ .17 **Rem.**, Jacketed Bullet, *Modern*	.50	.65
☐ .218 **Bee**, Various Makers, *Modern*	.50	.65
☐ .219 **Zipper**, Various Makers, *Modern*	.75	1.00
☐ .22 **BB Cap R.F.**, Lead Bullet *Antique*	.15	.20
☐ .22 **CB Cap R.F.**, Lead Bullet *Antique*	.15	.20
☐ .22 **CB Cap R.F.**, Two Piece Case, *Antique*	.20	.30
☐ .22 **Extra Long R.F.**, Various Makers, *Curio*	.80	1.10
☐ .22 **Hi-Power**, Various Makers, *Modern*	.70	1.00
☐ .22 **Hornet**, Various Makers, *Modern*	.45	.60
☐ .22 **L.R.R.F.**, Various Makers, *Modern*	.05	.10
☐ .22 **L.R.R.F.**, Shotshell, Various Makers, *Modern*	.10	.15
☐ .22 **L.R.R.F.**, Brass Case Russian, *Antique*	.35	.45
☐ .22 **L.R.R.F.**, Brass Case Austrian, *Antique*	.25	.40
☐ .22 **L.R.R.F.**, British Raised K, *Antique*	2.40	3.00
☐ .22 **L.R.R.F.**, Wadcutter, *Modern*	.35	.45
☐ .22 **L.R.R.F.**, Tracer, U.M.C., *Modern*	.50	.70
☐ .22 **L.R.R.F.**, Tracer, Gevelot, *Modern*	.15	.25
☐ .22 **L.R.R.F.**, Devastator, *Modern*	.15	.25
☐ .22 **L.R.R.F.**, U.M.C., "S & W Long", *Modern*	3.25	4.50
☐ .22 **Long R.F.**, Various Makers, *Modern*	.04	.08
☐ .22 **Long R.F.**, Lead Bullet *Antique*	.15	.25
☐ .22 **Maynard Extra Long**, Various Makers, *Curio*	.90	1.50
☐ .22 **Newton**, Soft Point Bullet, *Modern*	9.00	14.00
☐ .22 **Rem. Auto. R.F.**, Various Makers, *Modern*	.30	.45
☐ .22 **Rem. Jet**, Jacketed Bullet, *Modern*	.35	.50
☐ .22 **Short R.F.**, Various Makers, *Modern*	.03	.05
☐ .22 **Short R.F.**, Blank Cartridge, Various Makers, *Modern*	.05	.10
☐ .22 **Short R.F.**, Copper Case Raised "U", *Antique*	2.65	3.25
☐ .22 **Short R.F.**, Copper Case Raised "H", *Antique*	2.25	2.75
☐ .22 **Short R.F.**, Lead Bullet *Antique*	.15	.25
☐ .22 **WCF**, Various Makers, *Modern*	.55	.75
☐ .22 **Win. Auto. R.F.**, Various Makers, *Modern*	.25	.35
☐ .22 **WMR**, Various Makers, *Modern*	.10	.15
☐ .22 **WMR**, Shotshell, Various Makers, *Modern*	.15	.20
☐ .22 **WRF**, Various Makers, *Modern*	.10	.15
☐ .22-15-60 **Stevens**, Lead Bullet *Curio*	2.75	3.50

CARTRIDGE PRICES / 509

	V.G.	EXC.
☐ .22-3000 G & H, Soft Point Bullet, *Modern*	1.45	2.00
☐ .220 Swift, Various Makers, *Modern*	.70	.95
☐ .221 Rem. Fireball, Various Makers, *Modern*	.40	.55
☐ .222 Rem., Various Makers, *Modern*	.45	.55
☐ .222 Rem. Mag., Various Makers, *Modern*	.40	.50
☐ .22-250, Various Makers, *Modern*	.45	.60
☐ .223 Rem., Various Makers, *Modern*	.40	.50
☐ .223 Rem., Military, Various Makers, *Modern*	.30	.40
☐ .223 Armalite, Experemental, *Modern*	3.75	4.75
☐ .224 Wby., Varmintmaster, *Modern*	.75	1.00
☐ .224 Win., Experemental, *Modern*	3.00	4.00
☐ .224 Win., E2 Ball WCC 58, *Modern*	4.25	6.00
☐ .225 Win., Various Makers, *Modern*	.40	.55
☐ .230 Long, Various Makers, *Modern*	1.20	1.50
☐ .230 Short, Various Makers, *Modern*	.70	.90
☐ .236 U.S. Navy Rimless, *Modern*	5.00	7.00
☐ .236 U.S. Navy Rimmed, *Modern*	3.25	5.00
☐ .240 Belted N.E., Jacketed Bullet, *Modern*	.80	1.25
☐ .240 Flanged N.E., Various Makers, *Modern*	2.25	2.75
☐ .240 Wby. Mag., *Modern*	.80	1.20
☐ .242 Rimless N.E., Various Makers, *Modern*	3.25	4.75
☐ .243 Win., Various Makers, *Modern*	.45	.65
☐ .244 H & H Mag., Jacketed Bullet, *Modern*	3.00	4.50
☐ .244 Halger Mag., Various Makers, *Modern*	20.00	25.00
☐ .244 Rem., Various Makers, *Modern*	.60	.95
☐ .246 Purdey, Soft Point Bullet, *Modern*	2.80	3.75
☐ .247 Wby. Mag., *Modern*	.85	1.30
☐ .25 ACP, Various Makers, *Modern*	.20	.30
☐ .25 L.F., Various Makers, #50 Allen, *Curio*	3.50	4.50
☐ .25 Rem., Various Makers, *Modern*	.85	1.15
☐ .25 Short R.F., Lead Bullet *Antique*	.30	.40
☐ .25 Stevens, Wood Shotshell Bullet, *Modern*	.70	1.00
☐ .25 Stevens Short R.F., Various Makers, *Modern*	.25	.40
☐ .25 Stevens Long R.F., Various Makers, *Modern*	.25	.35
☐ .25-06 Rem., Various Makers, *Modern*	.50	.65
☐ .25-20 WCF, Lead Bullet, Various Makers, *Modern*	.30	.40
☐ .25-20 WCF, Jacketed Bullet, Various Makers, *Modern*	.35	.45
☐ .25-21, Jacketed Bullet, *Curio*	3.25	4.00
☐ .25-25, Various Makers, *Modern*	3.00	3.75
☐ .25-35 WCF, Various Makers, *Modern*	.55	.75
☐ .25-36, Jacketed Bullet, *Curio*	1.75	2.25
☐ .250 Savage, Various Makers, *Modern*	.50	.70
☐ .255 Rook, Various Makers, *Curio*	.75	1.20
☐ .256 Gibbs Mag., Various Makers, *Modern*	3.50	4.75
☐ .256 Newton, Soft Point Bullet, *Modern*	1.65	2.00
☐ .256 Win. Mag., Various Makers, *Modern*	.40	.55
☐ .257 Roberts, Various Makers, *Modern*	.45	.65
☐ .257 Wby. Mag., *Modern*	.90	1.30
☐ .26 BSA, Soft Point Bullet, *Modern*	3.25	4.00
☐ .264 Win. Mag., Various Makers, *Modern*	.55	.70
☐ .267 Rem. R.F., Experimental, *Curio*	7.75	9.75
☐ .270 Wby. Mag., *Modern*	.85	1.20
☐ .270 Win., Various Makers, *Modern*	.55	.70
☐ .270 Win., Flare Cartridge, Various Makers, *Modern*	1.60	2.25
☐ .275 Flanged Mag., Various Makers, *Modern*	1.50	2.00
☐ .275 H & H Mag., Various Makers, *Modern*	3.25	4.00
☐ .275 Rigby, Various Makers, *Modern*	2.65	3.50

510 / CARTRIDGE PRICES

	V.G.	EXC.
☐ .276 **Pederson**, Various Makers, Miliary, *Curio*	2.20	3.00
☐ .276 **Garand**, Military, Experimental, *Curio*	2.25	3.00
☐ .276 **Enfield**, Various Makers, Miliary, *Modern*	5.75	8.00
☐ .28 **Cup Primed Cartridge**, Various Makers, *Curio*	8.25	9.75
☐ .28-30-120 **Stevens**, Lead Bullet, *Curio*	3.30	4.25
☐ .280 **Flanged N.E.**, Various Makers, *Modern*	3.20	4.00
☐ .280 **Halgar Mag.**, Various Makers, *Modern*	3.65	4.50
☐ .280 **Jeffery**, Various Makers, *Modern*	4.50	5.75
☐ .280 **Rem.**, Various Makers, *Modern*	.50	.65
☐ .280 **Ross**, Various Makers, *Modern*	2.25	3.50
☐ .280/30 **Experimental**, Various Makers, Miliary, *Modern*	6.75	9.00
☐ .284 **Win.**, Various Makers, *Modern*	.50	.65
☐ .295 **Rook**, Various Makers, *Modern*	.70	.95
☐ .297/.230 **Morris**, Various Makers, *Modern*	.70	.95
☐ .297/.230 **Morris Short**, Various Makers, *Modern*	.60	.90
☐ .297/.250 **Rook**, Various Makers, *Modern*	.60	.95
☐ .297 **R. F. Revolver**, Various Makers, *Modern*	3.00	4.00
☐ .30 **Carbine**, Various Makers, *Modern*	.35	.45
☐ .30 **Carbine**, Various Makers, Military, *Modern*	.25	.35
☐ .30 **Cup Primed Cartridge**, Various Makers, *Curio*	6.25	7.50
☐ .30 **H & H Super Mag. Flanged**, Various Makers, *Modern*	2.50	3.50
☐ .30 **Long R.F.**, Merwin Cone Base, *Antique*	23.00	27.50
☐ .30 **Long R.F.**, Various Makers, *Antique*	1.50	2.00
☐ .30 **Luger**, Various Makers, *Modern*	.35	.45
☐ .30 **Newton**, Soft Point Bullet, *Modern*	2.00	2.75
☐ .30 **Pederson**, Various Makers, Military, *Modern*	2.25	3.00
☐ .30 **Rem.**, Various Makers, *Modern*	.50	.65
☐ .30 **Short R.F.**, Various Makers, *Curio*	3.00	3.90
☐ .30-03 **Springfield**, Various Makers, *Curio*	1.50	2.00
☐ .30-06 **Springfield**, Various Makers, *Modern*	.50	.65
☐ .30-06 **Springfield**, Various Makers, Military, *Modern*	.25	.35
☐ .30-06 **Springfield**, Accelerator, *Modern*	.55	.75
☐ .30-06 **Springfield**, Flare Cartridge, Various Makers, *Modern*	1.70	2.25
☐ .30-30 **Wesson**, Lead Bullet, *Curio*	19.00	26.00
☐ .30-30 **Win.**, Various Makers, *Modern*	.40	.50
☐ .30-30 **Win.**, Bicentennial, Various Makers, *Modern*	.50	.65
☐ .30-30 **Win.**, Flare Cartridge, Various Makers, *Modern*	1.60	2.25
☐ .30-40 **Krag**, Various Makers, *Modern*	.50	.65
☐ .300 **AMU Mag.**, Various Makers, Military, *Modern*	2.00	2.75
☐ .300 **Hoffman Mag.**, Soft Point Bullet, *Modern*	2.50	3.50
☐ .300 **H & H Mag.**, Various Makers, *Modern*	.75	.95
☐ .300 **Rook**, Various Makers, *Modern*	.80	1.20
☐ .300 **Savage**, Various Makers, *Modern*	.50	.65
☐ .300 **Sherwood**, Various Makers, *Modern*	1.75	2.75
☐ .300 **Wby. Mag.**, *Modern*	.85	1.20
☐ .300 **Win. Mag.**, Various Makers, *Modern*	.65	.90
☐ .303/.22, Soft Point Bullet, *Modern*	6.75	8.50
☐ .303 **British**, Various Makers, *Modern*	.50	.65
☐ .303 **Lewis Rimless**, Various Makers, Military, *Modern*	3.50	4.50
☐ .303 **Mag.**, Various Makers, *Modern*	3.00	4.00
☐ .303 **Savage**, Various Makers, *Modern*	.50	.65
☐ .305 **Rook**, Various Makers, *Modern*	1.25	1.75
☐ .308 **Norma Mag.**, Various Makers, *Modern*	1.00	1.40
☐ .308 **Win.**, Various Makers, *Modern*	.50	.65
☐ .308 **Win.**, Various Makers, Military, *Modern*	.30	.40
☐ .308 **Win.**, Flare Cartridge, Various Makers, *Modern*	1.70	2.25
☐ .31 **Eley R.F.**, Lead Bullet, Dished Base, *Modern*	9.50	14.00

CARTRIDGE PRICES / 511

	V.G.	EXC.
☐ .31 **Crispin**, Patent Ignition, *Antique*	120.00	150.00
☐ .31 **Milbank**, Patent Ignition, *Antique*	40.00	55.00
☐ .31 **Theur**, Patent Ignition, *Antique*	9.00	13.00
☐ .31 **Volcanic**, Patent Ignition, *Antique*	11.00	15.00
☐ .310 **Cadet**, Various Makers, *Modern*	.95	1.50
☐ .318 **Rimless N.E.**, Various Makers, *Modern*	1.30	1.75
☐ .32 **ACP**, Various Makers, *Modern*	.25	.35
☐ .32 **Ballard Extra Long**, Lead Bullet, *Curio*	.90	1.35
☐ .32 **Colt New Police**, Various Makers, *Modern*	.25	.35
☐ .32 **Extra Long R.F.**, Various Makers, *Curio*	5.00	6.50
☐ .32 **Extra Short R.F.**, Lead Bullet, *Antique*	.65	.95
☐ .32 **Ideal**, Lead Bullet, *Curio*	.80	1.25
☐ .32 **Teat-Fire Cartridge**, Various Makers, *Curio*	2.75	3.50
☐ .32 **L.F.**, Various Makers, #52 Allen, *Curio*	5.75	7.50
☐ .32 **Long Colt**, Various Makers, *Modern*	.20	.30
☐ .32 **Long R.F.**, Various Makers, *Modern*	6.00	7.50
☐ .32 **Long R.F.**, Shotshell, *Curio*	.30	.45
☐ .32 **Long Rifle**, Lead Bullet, *Antique*	3.50	4.50
☐ .32 **Rem.**, Various Makers, *Modern*	.50	.65
☐ .32 **Rem. Rimless**, Various Makers, *Modern*	.60	.75
☐ .32 **S & W**, Various Makers, *Modern*	.20	.30
☐ .32 **S & W**, Shotshell, Various Makers, *Modern*	.15	.25
☐ .32 **S & W**, Blank Cartridge, Various Makers, *Modern*	.15	.25
☐ .32 **S & W Long**, Various Makers, *Modern*	.20	.30
☐ .32 **Short Colt**, Various Makers, *Modern*	.20	.30
☐ .32 **Short R.F.**, Various Makers, *Modern*	.25	.35
☐ .32 **Win. Self-Loading**, Various Makers, *Modern*	.50	.65
☐ .32 **Win. Special**, Various Makers, *Modern*	.50	.65
☐ .32-20 **WCF**, Lead Bullet, Various Makers, *Modern*	.55	.70
☐ .32-20 **WCF**, Jacketed Bullet, Various Makers, *Modern*	.80	1.10
☐ .32-30 **Rem.**, Lead Bullet, *Curio*	3.70	4.30
☐ .32-35 **Stevens & Maynard**, Lead Bullet, *Curio*	3.60	4.25
☐ .32-40 **Bullard**, Lead Bullet, *Curio*	2.10	2.75
☐ .32-40 **Rem.**, Lead Bullet, *Curio*	1.80	2.65
☐ .32-40 **WCF**, Various Makers, *Modern*	.40	.55
☐ .320 **Rook**, Various Makers, *Modern*	.60	.95
☐ .320 **Extra Long Rifle**, Various Makers, *Modern*	1.85	2.50
☐ .322 **Swift**, Various Makers, *Modern*	4.50	5.50
☐ .33 **BSA**, Soft Point Bullet, *Modern*	3.00	3.75
☐ .33 **Win.**, Soft Point Bullet, *Modern*	.95	1.55
☐ .333 **Flanged N.E.**, Various Makers, *Modern*	3.25	4.50
☐ .333 **Rimless N.E.**, Various Makers, *Modern*	3.25	4.50
☐ .338 **Win. Mag.**, Various Makers, *Modern*	.70	1.00
☐ .340 **Wby. Mag.**, *Modern*	.85	1.30
☐ .340 **R.F. Revolver**, Various Makers, *Modern*	1.75	2.50
☐ .348 **Win.**, Various Makers, *Modern*	.85	1.20
☐ .35 **Allen R.F.**, Lead Bullet, *Curio*	10.00	14.00
☐ .35 **Newton**, Soft Point Bullet, *Modern*	3.25	4.00
☐ .35 **Rem.**, Various Makers, *Modern*	.50	.65
☐ .35 **S & W Auto.**, Jacketed Bullet, *Curio*	.70	1.00
☐ .35 **Win.**, Various Makers, *Modern*	2.25	3.00
☐ .35 **Win. Self-Loading**, Various Makers, *Modern*	.50	.65
☐ .35-30 **Maynard**, Lead Bullet, with Riveted Head, *Curio*	8.00	12.00
☐ .35-30 **Maynard**, Lead Bullet, without Riveted Head, *Curio*	5.00	6.50
☐ .35-40 **Maynard**, Various Makers, *Curio*	8.50	12.00
☐ .350 **Rem. Mag.**, Various Makers, *Modern*	.85	1.10
☐ .350 **Rigby**, Various Makers, *Modern*	3.00	3.75

512 / CARTRIDGE PRICES

	V.G.	EXC.
☐ .351 Win. Self-Loading, Various Makers, *Modern*	1.25	1.80
☐ .357 **Magnum**, Lead Bullet, Various Makers, *Modern*	.30	.40
☐ .357 **Magnum**, Jacketed Bullet, Various Makers, *Modern*	.30	.40
☐ .358 **Norma Mag.**, Various Makers, *Modern*	.95	1.25
☐ .358 **Win.**, Various Makers, *Modern*	.65	.90
☐ .36 **L. F.**, #56 Allen, Various Makers, *Curio*	5.50	7.00
☐ .36 **Crispin**, Patent Ignition, *Antique*	145.00	195.00
☐ .36 **Theur Navy**, Patent Ignition, *Antique*	9.00	14.00
☐ .360 **#5 Rook**, Various Makers, *Modern*	8.00	12.00
☐ .360 **N.E.**, Various Makers, *Modern*	1.20	1.75
☐ .360 **N.E. #2**, Various Makers, *Curio*	2.00	2.75
☐ .369 **Purdey**, Soft Point Bullet, *Curio*	5.25	6.50
☐ .370 **Flanged**, Various Makers, *Modern*	1.25	1.85
☐ .375 **Flanged Mag. N.E.**, Various Makers, *Modern*	2.10	2.75
☐ .375 **Flanged N.E.**, Various Makers, *Modern*	2.45	3.25
☐ .375 **H & H Mag.**, Various Makers, *Modern*	1.00	1.40
☐ .375 **Rimless N.E. 2¼"**, Various Makers, *Curio*	.90	1.30
☐ .375/.303 **Axite**, Various Makers, *Curio*	1.75	2.50
☐ .378 **Wby. Mag.**, *Modern*	2.00	3.00
☐ .38 **ACP**, Various Makers, *Modern*	.25	.35
☐ .38 **AMU**, Various Makers, Military, *Modern*	.40	.55
☐ .38 **Ballard Extra Long**, Lead Bullet, *Curio*	1.25	1.75
☐ .38 **Extra Long R.F.**, Lead Bullet, *Curio*	4.00	5.00
☐ .38 **Long CF**, Lead Bullet, *Curio*	.50	.65
☐ .38 **Long Colt**, Various Makers, *Modern*	.30	.40
☐ .38 **Long R.F.**, Various Makers, *Curio*	2.75	3.75
☐ .38 **S & W**, Various Makers, *Modern*	.25	.35
☐ .38 **S & W**, Blank Cartridge, Various Makers, *Modern*	.15	.25
☐ .38 **Short R.F.**, Various Makers, *Modern*	2.50	3.50
☐ .38 **Short R.F.**, Shotshell, *Curio*	.35	.50
☐ .38 **Short Colt**, Various Makers, *Modern*	.20	.25
☐ .38 **Special**, Lead Bullet, Various Makers, *Modern*	.25	.35
☐ .38 **Special**, Flare Cartridge, Various Makers, *Modern*	1.50	2.00
☐ .38 **Special**, Sub-Velocity Ammo, Various Makers, *Modern*	.15	.20
☐ .38 **Special**, Shotshell, Various Makers, *Modern*	.25	.35
☐ .38 **Special**, Blank Cartridge, Various Makers, *Modern*	.15	.25
☐ .38 **Special**, Tracer, Military, *Modern*	.30	.45
☐ .38 **Super**, Various Makers, *Modern*	.25	.35
☐ .38-40 **Rem. Hepburn**, Various Makers, *Curio*	2.50	3.50
☐ .38-40 **WCF**, Various Makers, *Modern*	.45	.60
☐ .38-44, Various Makers, *Modern*	.25	.35
☐ .38-45 **Bullard**, Lead Bullet, *Curio*	4.25	5.25
☐ .38-50 **Ballard**, Lead Bullet, *Curio*	4.75	5.50
☐ .38-50 **Maynard**, Various Makers, *Curio*	8.50	12.00
☐ .38-50 **Rem. Hepburn**, Lead Bullet, *Curio*	2.60	3.25
☐ .38-55 **Win. & Ballard**, Various Makers, *Modern*	.95	1.40
☐ .38-56 **Win.**, Lead Bullet, *Curio*	2.00	2.75
☐ .38-72 **Win.**, Lead Bullet, *Curio*	3.10	3.75
☐ .38-90 **Win. Express**, Lead Bullet, *Curio*	5.50	6.75
☐ .380 **ACP**, Various Makers, *Modern*	.25	.35
☐ .380 **Revolver**, Various Makers, Military, *Modern*	.40	.50
☐ .380 **Revolver**, Shotshell, *Modern*	.70	.95
☐ .40-40 **Maynard**, Lead Bullet, *Curio*	9.00	11.50
☐ .40-50 **Sharps (Necked)**, Lead Bullet, *Curio*	4.25	5.00
☐ .40-50 **Sharps (Straight)**, Lead Bullet, *Curio*	3.50	4.25
☐ .40-60 **Marlin**, Various Makers, *Curio*	6.00	12.00
☐ .40-60 **Maynard**, Lead Bullet, *Curio*	12.00	17.00

CARTRIDGE PRICES / 513

	V.G.	EXC.
☐ .40-60 Win., Various Makers, *Modern*	2.75	3.50
☐ .40-63 Ballard, Lead Bullet, *Antique*	6.25	7.25
☐ .40-65 Win., Lead Bullet, *Curio*	1.85	2.50
☐ .40-70 Ballard, Lead Bullet, *Curio*	3.25	4.25
☐ .40-70 Maynard, Lead Bullet, *Curio*	13.00	18.00
☐ .40-70 Peabody "What Cheer", Lead Bullet, *Curio*	22.00	29.00
☐ .40-70 Rem., Lead Bullet, *Curio*	3.65	4.50
☐ .40-70 Sharps (Necked), Various Makers, *Curio*	4.50	5.50
☐ .40-70 Sharps (Straight), Various Makers, *Curio*	4.00	5.00
☐ .40-70 Win., Lead Bullet, *Antique*	3.50	4.00
☐ .40-72 Win., Various Makers, *Modern*	1.75	2.50
☐ .40-75 Bullard, Lead Bullet, *Curio*	5.30	6.50
☐ .40-82 Win., Various Makers, *Modern*	2.00	2.75
☐ .40-82 Win., Shotshell, Various Makers, *Modern*	3.75	4.50
☐ .40-85 Ballard, Lead Bullet, *Curio*	4.75	6.00
☐ .40-90 Ballard, Lead Bullet, *Curio*	5.75	7.00
☐ .40-90 Peabody "What Cheer", Lead Bullet, *Curio*	45.00	58.00
☐ .40-90 Sharps (Necked), Various Makers, *Curio*	4.50	6.75
☐ .40-90 Sharps (Straight), Lead Bullet, *Curio*	8.75	11.50
☐ .40-110 Win., Lead Bullet, *Curio*	16.00	21.50
☐ .400 Nitro 3", Various Makers, *Modern*	5.50	6.75
☐ .400/.350 Rigby Flanged, Various Makers, *Modern*	2.75	3.75
☐ .400/.360 Purdey Flanged, Various Makers, *Curio*	2.85	3.75
☐ .400/.375 H & H, Various Makers, *Modern*	3.00	3.75
☐ .401 Herter Mag., Various Makers, *Modern*	.70	1.10
☐ .401 Win. Self-Loading, Various Makers, *Modern*	.95	1.30
☐ .404 N.E., Various Makers, *Modern*	2.80	3.50
☐ .405 Win., Jacketed Bullet, *Modern*	1.20	1.50
☐ .41 Long Colt, Wood Shotshell Bullet, *Modern*	1.20	1.55
☐ .41 Long Colt, Various Makers, *Modern*	.45	.60
☐ .41 Long R.F., Various Makers, *Curio*	3.50	4.50
☐ .41 Short C. F., Lead Bullet, *Modern*	.30	.40
☐ .41 Magnum, Jacketed Bullet, Various Makers, *Modern*	.35	.45
☐ .41 Magnum, Lead Bullet, Various Makers, *Modern*	.30	.40
☐ .41 Short R.F., Various Makers, *Modern*	2.00	2.80
☐ .41 Swiss R.F., Various Makers, *Modern*	1.50	2.25
☐ .41 Swiss R.F., Kynoch with Raised "C", *Antique*	3.75	4.50
☐ .41 Volcanic, Patent Ignition, *Antique*	13.00	19.00
☐ 416 Rigby, Soft Point Bullet, *Modern*	3.75	4.75
☐ .42 Allen R.F., Lead Bullet, *Antique*	3.00	3.75
☐ .42 Cup Primed Cartridge, Various Makers, *Curio*	6.75	8.50
☐ .425 Westley Richards Mag., Various Makers, *Modern*	3.50	4.25
☐ .44 AMP, Various Makers, *Modern*	.75	1.00
☐ .44 Bulldog, Lead Bullet, *Antique*	.45	.60
☐ .44 Colt, Various Makers, *Modern*	.60	.85
☐ .44 Crispin, Patent Ignition, *Antique*	145.00	175.00
☐ .44 Evans Short, Various Makers, *Curio*	4.50	6.00
☐ .44 Extra Long Ballard, Lead Bullet, *Curio*	7.50	9.50
☐ .44 Henry R.F., Blank Cartridge, *Curio*	3.50	4.50
☐ .44 Henry R.F., Lead Bullet, *Curio*	2.00	2.75
☐ .44 L.F., #58 Allen, Various Makers, *Curio*	14.00	18.00
☐ .44 Long R.F., Various Makers, *Curio*	4.00	5.50
☐ .44 Russian, Lead Bullet, *Modern*	.60	.85
☐ .44 S & W, Various Makers, *Modern*	.25	.35
☐ .44 S & W, Sub-Velocity Ammo, Various Makers, *Modern*	.15	.25
☐ .44 Magnum, Various Makers, *Modern*	.40	.55
☐ .44 Magnum, Shotshell, Various Makers, *Modern*	.40	.55

514 / CARTRIDGE PRICES

	V.G.	EXC.
☐ **.44 Short R.F.**, Lead Bullet, *Curio*	.85	1.25
☐ **.44 Short R.F.**, Blank Cartridge, *Antique*	.30	.40
☐ **.44 Theur**, Patent Ignition, *Antique*	17.00	22.00
☐ **.44 Webley**, Blank Cartridge, *Curio*	.35	.50
☐ **.44-100 Ballard**, Lead Bullet, *Curio*	9.50	14.00
☐ **.44-100 Wesson**, Lead Bullet, *Curio*	2.50	3.50
☐ **.44-40 WCF**, Various Makers, *Modern*	.45	.65
☐ **.44-40 WCF**, Shotshell, Various Makers, *Modern*	.70	.95
☐ **.44-60 Sharps**, Lead Bullet, *Curio*	4.00	4.75
☐ **.44-60 Win.**, Lead Bullet, *Curio*	2.50	3.25
☐ **.44-70 Maynard**, Lead Bullet, *Curio*	33.00	45.00
☐ **.44-75 Ballard Everlasting**, Lead Bullet, *Curio*	2.50	3.50
☐ **.44-77 Sharps & Rem.**, Lead Bullet, *Curio*	4.75	5.75
☐ **.44-90 Rem.**, Lead Bullet, *Curio*	7.75	9.50
☐ **.44-90 Rem. Special**, Various Makers, *Curio*	15.00	20.00
☐ **.44-90 Sharps**, Various Makers, *Curio*	7.50	9.00
☐ **.44-95 Peabody "What Cheer"**, Lead Bullet, *Curio*	27.00	34.00
☐ **.440 Eley R.F.**, Lead Bullet, no Headstamp, *Modern*	.55	.75
☐ **.442 Eley R.F.**, Lead Bullet, no Headstamp, *Modern*	.65	.90
☐ **.444 Marlin**, Various Makers, *Modern*	.55	.70
☐ **.45 ACP**, Various Makers, *Modern*	.30	.40
☐ **.45 ACP**, Military, Tracer, *Modern*	.55	.70
☐ **.45 Auto-Rim**, Various Makers, *Modern*	.30	.40
☐ **.45 Colt**, Various Makers, *Modern*	.30	.40
☐ **.45 Colt**, Wood Shotshell Bullet, *Modern*	1.45	2.00
☐ **.45 Danish R.F.**, Lead Bullet, no Headstamp, *Modern*	14.00	19.00
☐ **.45 S & W**, Various Makers, *Modern*	2.00	2.75
☐ **.45 Teat-Fire Cartridge**, Various Makers, *Curio*	45.00	55.00
☐ **.45 Webley**, Lead Bullet, *Modern*	.70	.95
☐ **.45-100 Ballard**, Various Makers, *Curio*	7.50	11.00
☐ **.45-100 Sharps**, Lead Bullet, *Curio*	12.00	17.00
☐ **.45-125 Win.**, Lead Bullet, *Curio*	18.00	24.00
☐ **.45-50 Peabody**, Lead Bullet, *Curio*	13.00	17.00
☐ **.45-60 Win.**, Lead Bullet, *Curio*	1.70	2.25
☐ **.45-70 Marlin**, Various Makers, *Modern*	4.25	5.00
☐ **.45-70 Government**, Various Makers, *Modern*	.50	.65
☐ **.45-70 Van Choate**, Lead Bullet, *Curio*	27.00	35.00
☐ **.45-75 Sharps**, Lead Bullet, (Rigby), *Curio*	8.00	12.00
☐ **.45-75 Sharps**, Lead Bullet, *Curio*	7.00	9.00
☐ **.45-75 Win.**, Various Makers, *Modern*	1.50	2.50
☐ **.45-80 Sharpshooter**, Various Makers, *Curio*	1.70	2.50
☐ **.45-85 Marlin**, Various Makers, *Modern*	4.75	5.50
☐ **.45-85 Win.**, Lead Bullet, *Curio*	4.00	5.00
☐ **.45-90 Win.**, Lead Bullet, *Curio*	2.40	3.25
☐ **.45-90 Win.**, Jacketed Bullet, *Curio*	3.00	3.80
☐ **.450 Gatling**, Various Makers, *Modern*	4.50	5.50
☐ **.450 #2 N.E. 3½"**, Various Makers, *Modern*	7.00	9.50
☐ **.450 Long Revolver**, Various Makers, *Curio*	1.30	1.75
☐ **.450 N.E. 3¼"**, Various Makers, New Make, *Modern*	3.75	4.50
☐ **.450 N.E. 3¼"**, Various Makers, *Curio*	4.75	6.00
☐ **.450 Revolver**, Various Makers, *Curio*	.70	.95
☐ **.450 #1 Carbine**, Various Makers, *Modern*	4.00	5.25
☐ **.450 Rigby Match 2.4"**, Soft Point Bullet, *Modern*	3.00	4.00
☐ **.450/.400 BPE**, Various Makers, *Modern*	2.95	3.75
☐ **.450/.400 Mag. N.E. 3¼"**, Various Makers, *Modern*	4.00	5.50
☐ **.450/.400 N.E. 3"**, Various Makers, *Modern*	3.75	4.50
☐ **.454 Casull Mag.**, Various Makers, *Modern*	.45	.65

CARTRIDGE PRICES / 515

	V.G.	EXC.
☐ .455 Revolver Mk 1, Jacketed Bullet, Military, *Modern*	.50	.65
☐ .455 Webley Mk 2, Various Makers, *Modern*	.60	.85
☐ .458 Win. Mag., Various Makers, Full Jacketed Bullet, *Modern*	1.60	2.00
☐ .458 Win. Mag., Soft Point Bullet, Various Makers, *Modern*	.95	1.35
☐ .46 Extra Long R.F., Various Makers, *Curio*	16.00	20.00
☐ .46 Extra Short R.F., Lead Bullet, *Curio*	20.00	25.00
☐ .46 Long R.F., Lead Bullet, *Antique*	2.50	3.50
☐ .46 Remington & Ballard, Lead Bullet, *Curio*	5.00	6.75
☐ .46 Short R.F., Various Makers, *Curio*	5.00	6.50
☐ .460 Wby. Mag., *Modern*	1.60	2.20
☐ .470 N.E., Various Makers, *Modern*	4.00	5.00
☐ .475 #2 N.E., Various Makers, *Modern*	6.25	7.50
☐ .475 N.E., Various Makers, *Modern*	5.75	7.00
☐ .476 N.E., Soft Point Bullet, *Modern*	5.75	7.00
☐ 5-in-One, Blank Cartridge, Various Makers, *Modern*	.50	.60
☐ .50 BMG, Various Makers, Military, *Modern*	.95	1.55
☐ .50 Rem., Various Makers, *Curio*	2.50	3.50
☐ .50 Rem. Navy R.F., Various Makers, *Curio*	20.00	25.00
☐ .50 U.S. Carbine, Various Makers, *Curio*	3.75	5.00
☐ .50-100 Win., Various Makers, *Curio*	5.00	7.00
☐ .50-110 Win., Lead Bullet, *Curio*	3.75	5.00
☐ .50-115 Bullard, Lead Bullet, *Curio*	5.50	7.00
☐ .50-140 Sharps, Lead Bullet, *Curio*	33.00	45.00
☐ .50-140 Win. Express, Lead Bullet, *Curio*	85.00	120.00
☐ .50-50 Maynard, Lead Bullet, *Curio*	5.50	6.75
☐ .50-70 Government R.F., Various Makers, *Curio*	30.00	35.00
☐ .50-70 Musket, New Make, Various Makers, *Modern*	1.40	1.75
☐ .50-70 Musket, Various Makers, *Curio*	9.00	13.00
☐ .50-70 Musket, Shotshell, Various Makers, *Modern*	5.00	7.00
☐ .50-90 Sharps, Lead Bullet, *Curio*	14.00	20.00
☐ .50-90 Win., Various Makers, *Curio*	2.50	3.50
☐ .500 #2 Express, Soft Point Bullet, *Modern*	4.00	5.50
☐ .500 Jeffery, Various Maker, *Modern*	12.00	18.00
☐ .500 Irish Constabulary Revolver, Various Makers, *Modern*	17.00	22.00
☐ .500 N.E. 3", Various Makers, *Modern*	3.75	4.75
☐ .500 Nitro BPE, Various Makers, *Curio*	6.75	8.50
☐ .500/.450 #1 Express, Various Makers, *Modern*	3.75	5.00
☐ .500/.450 #2 Musket, Various Makers, *Modern*	3.00	4.00
☐ .500/.450 Mag. N.E. 3¼", Various Makers, *Modern*	7.00	8.75
☐ .500/.465 N.E., Various Makers, *Modern*	4.50	5.50
☐ .505 Gibbs, Lead Bullet, *Modern*	6.50	8.00
☐ .52-70 Sharps R.F., Lead Bullet, *Curio*	30.00	38.00
☐ .54 Ballard R.F., Lead Bullet, *Curio*	35.00	45.00
☐ .55-100 Maynard, Lead Bullet, *Curio*	32.50	42.00
☐ .56-46 Spencer R.F., Various Makers, *Curio*	20.00	27.50
☐ .56-50 Spencer R.F., WRA, Commercial, *Antique*	1.75	2.50
☐ .56-52 Spencer R.F., Various Makers, *Curio*	3.00	4.00
☐ .56-52 Spencer R.F., Shotshell, Various Makers, *Curio*	17.50	22.50
☐ .56-56 Spencer R.F., Various Makers, *Antique*	5.50	6.75
☐ .577 N.E. 2¾", Various Makers, *Modern*	6.00	8.75
☐ .577 N.E. 3", Various Makers, *Modern*	7.00	9.75
☐ .577 Snyder, Various Makers, *Modern*	4.00	5.75
☐ .577 Snyder, Shotshell, Various Makers, *Modern*	5.00	6.75
☐ .577/.450 Martini-Henry, Various Makers, *Modern*	4.25	5.50
☐ .577/.500 3⅛", Various Makers, *Modern*	5.50	7.00
☐ .58 Berdan, Various Makers, *Curio*	4.50	6.50
☐ .58 Gatling R.F., Lead Bullet, *Curio*	22.00	28.50

516 / CARTRIDGE PRICES

	V.G.	EXC.
☐ .58 Joslyn Carbine R.F., Various Makers, *Curio*	27.00	35.00
☐ .58 Mont Storm R.F., Various Makers, *Curio*	33.00	42.00
☐ .58 U.S. Musket, Lead Bullet, *Curio*	10.00	18.00
☐ .600 N.E., Lead Bullet, *Curio*	20.00	28.00
☐ .70-150 Win., Cartridge Board Dummy, *Curio*	100.00	140.00
☐ 2mm Rimfire, Blank Cartridge, *Modern*	.10	.15
☐ 2mm Rimfire, Lead Bullet, *Modern*	.30	.40
☐ 2.7mm Kolibri, Jacketed Bullet, *Curio*	11.00	15.00
☐ 3mm Kolibri, Various Makers, *Curio*	12.00	16.00
☐ 4mm R.F., Lead Bullet, *Antique*	.15	.20
☐ 4.25mm Liliput, Jacketed Bullet, *Curio*	4.75	6.50
☐ 5.5mm Soemmerda, Various Makers, *Modern*	2.75	3.50
☐ 5.5mm Velo Dog, Lead Bullet, *Curio*	.45	.65
☐ 5.6 x 33 Rook, Various Makers, *Modern*	1.20	1.60
☐ 5.6 x 35R Vierling, Various Makers, *Modern*	.50	.80
☐ 5.6 x 50R Mag., Various Makers, *Modern*	.90	1.30
☐ 5.6 x 50 Mag., Various Makers, *Modern*	.90	1.30
☐ 5.6 x 52R, Various Makers, *Modern*	.75	.95
☐ 5.6 x 57, Various Makers, *Modern*	.95	1.30
☐ 5.6 x 61 Vom Hofe Express, Soft Point Bullet, *Modern*	3.75	4.75
☐ 5.6 x 57R, Various Makers, *Modern*	.95	1.40
☐ 5.6 x 61R Vom Hofe Express, Various Makers, *Modern*	3.50	4.50
☐ 5.7mm Target Pistol, Various Makers, *Modern*	3.50	4.25
☐ 5.75mm Velo-Dog, Various Makers, *Modern*	.90	1.25
☐ 5.75mm Velo-Dog Short, Various Makers, *Modern*	1.75	2.50
☐ 5mm Bergmann, Various Makers, *Curio*	6.50	9.00
☐ 5mm Bergmann, Grooved, Various Makers, *Curio*	4.75	6.50
☐ 5mm Brun, Various Makers, *Modern*	10.00	15.00
☐ 5mm Clement, Soft Point Bullet, *Curio*	3.50	4.50
☐ 5mm French Revolver, Various Makers, *Modern*	.60	.80
☐ 5mm Pickert, Various Makers, *Modern*	12.00	17.50
☐ 5mm Rem. RFM, Jacketed Bullet, *Modern*	.15	.25
☐ 6 x 58 Forster, Various Makers, *Curio*	6.50	8.75
☐ 6 x 58R Forster, Various Makers, *Curio*	3.35	4.20
☐ 6.35mm Pickert, Various Makers, *Modern*	4.25	5.50
☐ 6.5 x 48R Sauer, Various Makers, *Curio*	2.20	2.75
☐ 6.5 x 52 Mannlicher-Carcano, Various Makers, *Modern*	.65	.80
☐ 6.5 x 54 M.S., Various Makers, *Modern*	1.15	1.40
☐ 6.5 x 54 Mauser, Soft Point Bullet, *Modern*	2.20	2.75
☐ 6.5 x 55 Swedish, Various Makers, *Modern*	.65	.80
☐ 6.5 x 57, Various Makers, *Modern*	.95	1.35
☐ 6.5 x 57R, Various Makers, *Modern*	.95	1.35
☐ 6.5 x 58 Vergueiro, Various Makers, Military, *Modern*	4.50	5.50
☐ 6.5mm Dutch, Various Makers, Military, *Modern*	.15	.20
☐ 6.5 x 58R Sauer, Jacketed Bullet, *Modern*	1.90	2.75
☐ 6.5mm Jap, Various Makers, *Modern*	.65	.80
☐ 6.5 x 68 Schuler, Various Makers, *Modern*	1.25	1.70
☐ 6.5 x 68R, Various Makers, *Modern*	1.60	2.25
☐ 6.5mm Bergmann, Various Makers, *Curio*	8.00	11.00
☐ 6.5mm Bergmann Grooved, Various Makers, *Curio*	5.75	7.00
☐ 6.50mm Mannlicher, Various Makers, *Modern*	4.75	6.50
☐ 6.8mm Gasser, Various Makers, *Modern*	4.50	5.75
☐ 6.8mm Schulhof, Various Makers, *Modern*	2.80	3.75
☐ 6mm Lee Navy, Various Makers, Military, *Modern*	2.00	3.00
☐ 6mm Loron, Patent Ignition, *Antique*	3.50	4.25
☐ 6mm Flobert, 2 Piece Case, *Antique*	.40	.55
☐ 6mm Merveilleux, Various Makers, *Modern*	1.75	2.50

CARTRIDGE PRICES / 517

	V.G.	EXC.
☐ **6mm Protector**, Various Makers, *Modern*	1.20	1.80
☐ **6mm Rem.**, Various Makers, *Modern*	.50	.65
☐ **6.5mm Reg. Mag.**, Various Makers, *Modern*	.75	1.00
☐ **7 x 57R**, Various Makers, *Modern*	.85	1.20
☐ **7 x 61 Norma**, Various Makers, *Modern*	.85	1.25
☐ **7 x 64 Brenneke**, Various Makers, *Modern*	.95	1.45
☐ **7 x 64**, Various Makers, *Modern*	.95	1.40
☐ **7 x 65R**, Various Makers, *Modern*	.95	1.45
☐ **7 x 72R**, Various Makers, *Modern*	2.50	3.50
☐ **7 x 72R**, Dummy Cartridge, *Curio*	2.50	3.25
☐ **7 x 73 Vom Hofe**, Soft Point Bullet, *Modern*	7.75	9.50
☐ **7.25mm Adler**, Various Makers, *Modern*	65.00	90.00
☐ **7.35mm Carcano**, Various Makers, Military, *Modern*	.15	.20
☐ **7.5 x 54 MAS**, Various Makers, Military, *Modern*	.15	.25
☐ **7.5 x 55 Swiss**, Military, *Modern*	.70	.90
☐ **7.5mm Swedish Nagent**, Various Makers, *Modern*	.65	.85
☐ **7.5mm Swiss Nagent**, *Modern*	.75	.95
☐ **7.6mm Mauser Revolver**, Various Makers, *Modern*	5.75	8.50
☐ **7.62 x 39 Russian**, Various Makers, Military, *Modern*	.30	.45
☐ **7.62 x 39 Russian**, Various Makers, *Modern*	.45	.65
☐ **7.62 x 54R Russian**, Various Makers, *Modern*	.65	.80
☐ **7.62mm Nagent**, Various Makers, Military, *Modern*	1.45	1.95
☐ **7.62mm Tokarev**, Various Makers, Military, *Modern*	.40	.60
☐ **7.63 Mannlicher**, Various Makers, Military, *Modern*	.15	.25
☐ **7.63 Mauser**, Various Makers, *Modern*	.20	.30
☐ **7.65 Borchardt**, Various Makers, *Modern*	2.50	3.25
☐ **7.65mm Francotte**, Various Makers, *Modern*	18.00	25.00
☐ **7.65mm Glisenti**, Various Makers, *Modern*	75.00	95.00
☐ **7.65mm Pickert**, Various Makers, *Modern*	3.50	4.50
☐ **7.65 Roth-Sauer**, Various Makers, *Curio*	2.50	3.75
☐ **7.65 x 53 Mauser**, Military, *Modern*	.55	.75
☐ **7.65 Argentine**, Various Makers, *Modern*	.65	.80
☐ **7.65 Argentine Navy Match**, Military, *Curio*	25.00	35.00
☐ **7.7mm Jap**, Various Makers, *Modern*	.60	.80
☐ **7.7mm Bittner**, Various Makers, *Modern*	25.00	32.50
☐ **7.8mm Bergmann #5**, Various Makers, *Modern*	5.00	7.50
☐ **7.92 x 33 Kurz**, Various Makers, Military, *Modern*	.80	1.25
☐ **7mm Baer**, Various Makers, *Modern*	1.80	2.50
☐ **7mm Charola**, Various Makers, *Modern*	5.50	6.50
☐ **7mm Flobert**, Lead Bullet, *Antique*	.40	.50
☐ **7mm French Revolver**, Various Makers, *Modern*	.95	1.55
☐ **7mm H & H**, Soft Point Bullet, *Modern*	1.70	2.50
☐ **7mm Mauser**, Various Makers, *Modern*	.50	.65
☐ **7mm Mauser**, Various Makers, Military, *Modern*	.25	.35
☐ **7mm Nambu**, Various Makers, *Curio*	6.00	8.50
☐ **7mm Rem. Mag.**, Various Makers, *Modern*	.65	.90
☐ **7mm Rem. Mag.**, Various Makers, Flare Cartridge, *Modern*	1.70	2.25
☐ **7mm Rigby Mag.**, Soft Point Bullet, *Modern*	2.25	3.00
☐ **7mm Target Pistol**, Various Makers, *Modern*	1.90	2.50
☐ **7mm Vom Hofe S.E.**, Various Makers, *Modern*	7.00	8.50
☐ **7mm Wby. Mag.**, *Modern*	.85	1.20
☐ **8 x 48R Sauer**, Various Makers, *Curio*	3.50	4.50
☐ **8 x 50R Lebel**, Various Makers, Military, *Modern*	.25	.35
☐ **8 x 50R Mannlicher**, Various Makers, *Modern*	1.75	2.50
☐ **8 x 51 Mauser**, Various Makers, *Curio*	.95	1.35
☐ **8 x 51R Mauser**, Various Makers, *Curio*	4.75	6.50
☐ **8 x 56R Mannlicher**, Various Makers, Military, *Modern*	4.75	6.00

518 / CARTRIDGE PRICES

	V.G.	EXC.
☐ 8 x 56R Kropatschek, Various Makers, Military, *Curio*	.30	.40
☐ 8 x 57 Jrs, Various Makers, *Modern*	.90	1.25
☐ 8 x 575, Various Makers, *Modern*	.65	.85
☐ 8 x 58R Krag, Jacketed Bullet, Military, *Modern*	2.50	3.25
☐ 8 x 58R Saver, Various Makers, *Curio*	3.25	4.00
☐ 8 x 60 Mauser, Various Makers, *Modern*	1.80	2.50
☐ 8 x 60S, Various Makers, *Modern*	1.30	1.70
☐ 8 x 64 Brenneke, Various Makers, *Modern*	1.50	2.00
☐ 8 x 68S, Various Makers, *Modern*	1.20	1.55
☐ 8 x 75, Various Makers, *Curio*	3.50	4.25
☐ 8 x 75R, Various Makers, *Curio*	2.75	3.75
☐ 8.1 x 72R, Lead Bullet, *Modern*	2.75	3.45
☐ 8.15 x 46R, Lead Bullet, *Modern*	.90	1.20
☐ 8.15 x 46R, Soft Point Bullet, *Modern*	1.50	2.00
☐ 8mm Bergmann #4, Various Makers, *Modern*	9.50	14.00
☐ 8mm Bergmann-Simplex, Various Makers, *Modern*	1.80	2.50
☐ 8mm Dormus, Various Makers, *Modern*	9.75	16.00
☐ 8mm Gaulois, Various Makers, *Curio*	.95	1.30
☐ 8mm Lebel Revolver, Various Makers, Military, *Modern*	.50	.65
☐ 8mm Lebel Revolver, Various Makers, *Modern*	.95	1.50
☐ 8mm Kromar, Various Makers, *Modern*	32.00	45.00
☐ 8mm Mauser, Various Makers, *Modern*	.50	.65
☐ 8mm Mitrailleuse, Various Makers, *Modern*	.95	1.35
☐ 8mm Nambu, Various Makers, Military, *Modern*	1.25	3.50
☐ 8mm Pieper Revolver, Lead Bullet, *Modern*	1.10	1.50
☐ 8mm Protector, Various Makers, *Modern*	.90	1.25
☐ 8mm Rast-Gasser, Various Makers, *Modern*	1.20	1.50
☐ 8mm Schulhof, Various Makers, *Modern*	4.50	6.50
☐ 8mm Steyr Revolver, Various Makers, *Modern*	45.00	65.00
☐ 8mm Roth-Steyr, Various Makers, *Modern*	.95	1.50
☐ 9 x 56 M.S., Soft Point Bullet, *Modern*	.85	1.20
☐ 9 x 63, Various Makers, *Modern*	2.75	3.50
☐ 9.3 x 53R Swiss, Lead Bullet, *Curio*	.90	1.25
☐ 9.3 x 57, Various Makers, *Modern*	.95	1.30
☐ 9.3 x 57R, Various Makers, *Modern*	3.50	4.50
☐ 9.3 x 62 Mauser, Various Makers, *Modern*	1.25	1.65
☐ 9.3 x 64 Brenneke, Various Makers, *Modern*	1.50	2.00
☐ 9.3 x 72R, Various Makers, *Modern*	1.50	2.00
☐ 9.3 x 74R, Various Makers, *Modern*	1.60	2.10
☐ 9.3 x 82R, Lead Bullet, *Modern*	2.00	2.75
☐ 9.3 x 82R, Soft Point Bullet, *Modern*	2.50	3.25
☐ 9.4mm Dutch Rev., Various Makers, *Modern*	2.50	3.50
☐ 9.5 x 57 M.S., Various Makers, *Modern*	1.25	1.90
☐ 9.5 x 60R Turkish, Lead Bullet, *Modern*	20.00	28.00
☐ 9mm Bayard Long, Various Makers, Military, *Modern*	.30	.40
☐ 9mm Borchardt, Various Makers, *Modern*	60.00	75.00
☐ 9mm Browning Long, Various Makers, *Modern*	.90	1.50
☐ 9mm Devisme, Patent Ignition, *Antique*	7.00	12.00
☐ 9mm Devisme, *Modern*	1.45	1.95
☐ 9mm Danish Ronge, Lead Bullet, *Modern*	.45	.75
☐ 9mm Flobert, Lead Bullet, *Antique*	.35	.55
☐ 9mm Campo Giro, Various Makers, *Modern*	12.00	17.00
☐ 9mm Gasser-Kropatschek Rev., Various Makers, *Modern*	3.50	4.50
☐ 9mm Glisenti, Various Makers, *Modern*	.95	1.50
☐ 9mm Bergmann, Jacketed Bullet, Military, *Modern*	.30	.40
☐ 9mm Luger, Various Makers, *Modern*	.30	.40
☐ 9mm Luger, Various Makers, Military, *Modern*	.25	.35

CARTRIDGE PRICES / 519

	V.G.	EXC.
☐ **9mm**, Lead Bullet, *Modern*	4.75	5.50
☐ **9mm Makarov**, Jacketed Bullet, Military, *Modern*	10.00	15.00
☐ **9mm Mauser**, Various Makers, *Modern*	.80	1.20
☐ **9mm Nagent**, Various Makers, *Modern*	1.50	2.20
☐ **9mm Salvo Squeeze Bore**, Various Makers, *Curio*	15.00	23.00
☐ **9mm Steyr**, Various Makers, Military, *Modern*	.55	.85
☐ **10mm Hirst Auto Pistol**, Various Makers, *Modern*	16.00	23.00
☐ **10mm Soerabaja**, Lead Bullet, *Antique*	3.00	4.00
☐ **10,15 x 61R Jarmann**, Paper-Patched, Lead Bullet, *Curio*	4.00	5.50
☐ **10.3 x 65R Baenziger**, Soft Point Bullet, *Modern*	3.25	4.75
☐ **10.4 Italian Revolver**, Military, *Modern*	1.00	1.70
☐ **10.4mm Swiss Ordnance Rev.**, Various Makers, *Modern*	2.75	3.75
☐ **10.4 x 47R Italian Vetterli**, Jacketed Bullet, *Modern*	.75	1.10
☐ **10.6mm Schulhof**, Various Makers, *Modern*	1.65	2.25
☐ **10.6mm Spanish Ordnance Rev.**, Various Makers, *Modern*	1.20	1.75
☐ **10.75 x 58R Berdan**, Military, Various Makers, *Curio*	1.25	1.75
☐ **10.75 x 68 Mauser**, Various Makers, *Modern*	1.50	2.00
☐ **10.75 x 73**, Various Makers, *Modern*	1.70	2.25
☐ **19.8mm Montenegrin Rev.**, Various Makers, *Modern*	10.00	16.00
☐ **11 x 59R Gras**, Jacketed Bullet, *Curio*	.95	1.50
☐ **11 x 59R Gras**, Lead Bullet, *Curio*	1.30	1.80
☐ **11.15 x 58R Werndl**, Lead Bullet, *Modern*	4.50	5.75
☐ **11.15 x 60R Mauser**, Lead Bullet, *Modern*	4.00	5.00
☐ **11.15 x 65R**, Lead Bullet, *Modern*	2.75	3.50
☐ **11.2mm Gasser**, Various Makers, *Modern*	7.00	8.50
☐ **11.43 x 50R Egyptian**, Various Makers, *Modern*	1.75	2.75
☐ **11.43 x 50R Egyptian**, Wood Shotshell Bullet, *Modern*	3.00	3.75
☐ **11.5 x 57R Spanish**, Various Makers, *Modern*	2.75	3.75
☐ **11.5mm Montenegrin-Gasser**, Various Makers, *Modern*	6.50	8.75
☐ **11.5mm Werder**, Various Makers, *Modern*	5.75	8.00
☐ **11mm Danish Ordnance Rev.**, Various Makers, *Modern*	24.00	30.00
☐ **11mm Chassepot**, Patent Ignition, *Antique*	4.75	6.00
☐ **11mm Devisme**, Patent Ignition, *Antique*	8.50	12.00
☐ **11mm French Ordnance**, Various Makers, *Curio*	.70	1.10
☐ **11mm German Service**, Various Makers, *Curio*	.95	1.65
☐ **11mm Loran**, Patent Ignition, *Antique*	2.75	3.50
☐ **11mm Mannlicher**, Military, Paper-Patched Lead Bullet, *Curio*	.35	.45
☐ **11mm Rapnael**, Patent Ignition, Outside Primed, *Antique*	16.00	25.00
☐ **11mm Rapnael**, Patent Ignition, Inside Primed, *Antique*	24.00	35.00
☐ **12.7 Russian M.G.**, Various Makers, Military, *Modern*	.55	.75
☐ **15mm French Rev.**, Various Makers, *Modern*	11.00	16.00
☐ **4 Ga.**, Various Makers, Paper Case, Shotshell, *Modern*	3.00	4.00
☐ **8 Ga.**, Various Makers, Paper Case, Shotshell, *Modern*	2.75	3.75
☐ **10 Ga. 2⅞"**, Shotshell, Various Makers, *Modern*	.60	.75
☐ **10 Ga. 2⅞"**, Brass Case, Various Makers, *Modern*	2.65	3.50
☐ **10 Ga. 2⅞"**, Paper Case, Shotshell, Various Makers, *Modern*	2.00	2.85
☐ **10 Gauge 3½"**, Shotshell, Various Makers, *Modern*	.75	1.00
☐ **12 Ga.**, Flare Cartridge, Various Makers, *Modern*	1.75	2.50
☐ **12 Ga.**, Buckshot, Various Makers, *Modern*	.70	.90
☐ **12 Ga.**, Shotshell, Various Makers, *Modern*	.40	.55
☐ **12 Ga.**, Slug, Various Makers, *Modern*	.45	.60
☐ **12 Ga.**, Blank Cartridge, Various Makers, *Modern*	.25	.35
☐ **12 Ga.**, Twin-Shot Blank Cartridge, Various Makers, *Modern*	1.40	1.85
☐ **12 Ga.**, Black Powder Loads, Shotshell, Various Makers, *Modern*	.80	1.20
☐ **12 Ga.**, Brass Case, Various Makers, *Modern*	2.50	3.50
☐ **12 Ga. Mag. 3"**, Shotshell, Various Makers, *Modern*	.55	.70
☐ **12 Ga. Mag. 3"**, Slug, Various Makers, *Modern*	.55	.75

CARTRIDGE PRICES

	V.G.	EXC.
☐ **14 Ga.**, Brass Case, Various Makers, *Modern*	6.00	11.00
☐ **16 Ga. 2⁹/₁₆"**, Brass Case, *Modern*	2.00	2.75
☐ **16 Ga. 2¾"**, Slug, Various Makers, *Modern*	.50	.65
☐ **16 Ga. 3¾"**, Shotshell, Various Makers, *Modern*	.35	.50
☐ **16 Ga. 2¾"**, Buckshot, Various Makers, *Modern*	.40	.50
☐ **20 Ga.**, Shotshell, Various Makers, *Modern*	.35	.50
☐ **20 Ga.**, Buckshot, Various Makers, *Modern*	.40	.55
☐ **20 Ga.**, Slug, Various Makers, *Modern*	.45	.60
☐ **20 Ga. Mag.**, Shotshell, Various Makers, *Modern*	.35	.55
☐ **24 Ga.**, Paper Case, *Modern*	3.50	4.50
☐ **28 Ga.**, Shotshell, Various Makers, *Modern*	.35	.50
☐ **28 Ga.**, Brass Case, Various Makers, *Modern*	1.50	2.00
☐ **32 Ga.**, Paper Case, *Modern*	3.50	4.50
☐ **.410 Ga. 2½"**, Shotshell, Various Makers, *Modern*	.35	.45
☐ **.410 Ga. 3"**, Shotshell, Various Makers, *Modern*	.40	.55
☐ **2mm Pinfire**, Blank Cartridge, *Antique*	.30	.40
☐ **5mm Pinfire**, Various Makers, *Antique*	.55	.75
☐ **7mm Pinfire**, Various Makers, *Antique*	.60	.85
☐ **9mm Pinfire**, Lead Bullet, *Antique*	.75	.95
☐ **12mm Pinfire**, Lead Bullet, *Antique*	.75	.90
☐ **15mm Pinfire**, Lead Bullet, *Antique*	4.00	5.50
☐ **12 Ga. Pinfire**, Shotshell, *Antique*	.70	.90
☐ **20 Ga. Pinfire**, Shotshell, *Antique*	.75	.95

INDEX

AUTOMATIC WEAPON, ASSAULT RIFLE
Argentine Military 38
Armalite 39
Australian Military 47
Austrian Military 47
Beretta 59
British Military 72
Colt 105
F.N. 169
German Military 186
Harrington & Richardson 198
Heckler & Koch 207
Italian Military 232
M.A.C. 274
Russian Military 379
S.I.G. 400
Springfield Armory 329
U.S. Military 456
Valmet 464
Winchester 489

AUTOMATIC WEAPON, HEAVY MACHINE GUN
British Military 72
Chinese Military 100
Colt 105
German Military 186
India Military 229
Marlin Firearms Co. 279
Russian Military 379
Savage Arms Co. 385
U.S. Military 456

AUTOMATIC WEAPON, LIGHT MACHINE GUN
British Military 72
BSA 86
Colt 1065
Czechoslavakian Military 138
F.N. 170
French Military 178
German Military 186
Japanese Military 244
Russian Military 379
U.S. Military 456
Z-B 505

AUTOMATIC WEAPON, MACHINE PISTOL
Astra 42
Azul 49
Bushmaster 90
Mauser 290
Star 423

AUTOMATIC WEAPON, SUBMACHINE GUN
American Arms International 34
Argentine Military 38
Austrian Military 47
Auto Ordnance (Thompson) 48
Beretta 59
British Military 72
Chinese Nationalist Military 100
Colt 105
Danish Military 139
Erma 158
French Military 178
German Military 186
Harrington & Richardson 198
Heckler & Koch 207
Hungarian Military 226
Ingram 230
Israeli Military 231
Italian Military 232
Japanese Military 245

M.A.C. 274
North Vietnam Military 322
PJK 337
Plainfield Machine Co. 340
Red Mountain Arsenal 345
Reising 347
Ruger 372
Russian Military 379
Savage Arms Co. 385
Smith & Wesson 403
Spanish Military 420
Spitfire 420
Star 423
Steyr 435
Swiss Military 437

Thompson 442
U.S. Military 456
Winchester 489

AUTOMATIC WEAPON, MACHINE PISTOL
Bushmaster 90
Mauser 290
Star 423

CARTRIDGE PRICES 508-520

COMBINATION WEAPON, DRILLING
Baker, W.H. & Co. 53
Bone 53
Cartridge Firearms, Unkown Maker ...94
Charles Daly 96
Colt 105
Greifeld 192
Heym 211
Kettner, Ed 249
Krieghoff 254
Merkel 298
Sauer, J.P. & Sohn 383
Stoeger, A.F. 436
Three-Barrel Gun Co. 445

COMBINATION WEAPON, DOUBLE BARREL OVER-UNDER
Armsport 41
Bauer 55
Bronco 75
Ferlach 164
Fie 166
Greifeld & Co. 192
Hege 208
Heym 211
Italguns International 231
Ithaca Gun Co. 233
Krieghoff 254
Merkel 297
Pieper 335
Pieper, Henri 336
Sauer, J.P. & Sohn 383
Savage Arms Co. 385
Staggs-Bilt 422
Stevens, J. Arms & Tool Co. 427
Stoeger, A.F. 436
Valmet 464

COMBINATION WEAPON, PERCUSSION
Allen & Thurber 30
Amsden, B.W. 36
Chase, William 98
Heym 211

HANDGUN, AUTOMATIC REVOLVER
Zulaica 507

HANDGUN, COMBINATION, MULTI-BARREL
Sharps, Christian 399
Sodia, Franz 419

HANDGUN, DOUBLE BARREL, OVER-UNDER
American Arms Co. 33
Atlas Arms 45
Buddy Arms 87
Buffalo Arms 88
Excam 160
Fie 164
Great Western 191
High Standard 212
Hy Hunter 228
Kimel Industries 250
Mitchell Arms 304
Panzer 327
Remington 347
R.G. Industries 366
Rupertus 378
Wesson, Frank 484

HANDGUN, DOUBLE BARREL, SIDE-BY-SIDE
Garrucha 185

HANDGUN, FLINTOCK
Aerts, Jan......................27
Annely, L. 37
Armsport 44
Austrian Military 47
Bache 51
Banister, T. 55
Blake, Ann 67
Bleiberg 68
Bond, Edward 69
Bond, Wm. 69
Booles 70
British Military 72
Bumford 89
Clarkson, J. 101
Comminazzo, or Cominazzi 130
Cornforth 134
C.V.A. (Connecticut Valley Arms) ..136
Cosens, James 134
Dalby, David 139
Dixie Gun Works 147
Dobson, T. 149
Dumares, B. 150
Edgeson 153
Egg, Durs 154
Esteva, Pedro 159
Fie 164
Unkown Makers 169
French Military 178
German Military 186
Gill, Thomas 188
Goff, Daniel 189
Groom, Richard 193
Hollis, Richard 220
Jones, J.N. & Co. 247
Ketland & Co. 249
Ketland, William & Co. 249
Lesconne, A. 264
Macloed 274
Maiche, A. 275
Manton, Joseph 278
Mortimore, H W. & Co. 306
Navy Arms 313
Nichols, John 319
Noys, R. 323
Page, T. 326
Pickfatt, Humphrey 334

522 / INDEX

Russian Military 378	Houiller, Blanchard 225	Bloodhound 68
Scott, D. 396	Iver Johnson 238	Blue Jacket 68
Sharpe 398	Jones, J.N. & Co. 247	Blue Whistler 68
Stanton 423	Lang, Joseph 258	Bonanza 69
Sutherland, James 436	Lyman Gun Sight Corp. 272	Boston Bulldog 70
Sutherland, Ramsey 436	Manhattan Firearms Mfg. Co. 275	Boy's Choice 70
Tindall & Dutton 446	Manton, Joseph 278	British Bulldog (Forehand &
Turner 448	Markwell Arms Co. 279	Wadsworth) 71
Twigg 448	Marstan, Stanhope 288	British Bulldog (Johnson, Bye &
U.S. Military 458	Marstan, William 288	Co.) 71
Weston, Edward 487	Massachusetts Arms Co. 289	British Military 72
Wogdon 503	Navy Arms 313	Bronco 76
Zanotti 505	Remington 348	Brooklyn Arms Co. 76
	Robbins & Lawrence 369	Brutus 87
HANDGUN, REPEATER	Rogers & Spencer 369	Buffalo Bill 88
Alfa 29	Ruger 375	Bull Dozer 88
Bittner, Gustav 67	Russian Military 379	Bulldog 89
Chicago Firearms Co. 99	Sharp, Christian 399	Bulls Eye 89
C.O.P. 134	Starr Arms Co. 425	Cadet 90
Fiala 164	Thompson/Center 443	Capt. Jack 91
Gaulois 185	Tingle Mfg. Co. 446	Cartridge Firearms, Unkown
Hartford Arms & Equipment Co. ... 204	Unknown Maker 233	Makers 91
Marveilleux 301	Unwin & Rogers 455	Centennial 94
Minneapolis Firearms Co. 303	U.S. Military 458	Challenge 95
Mitrailleuse 304	Walsh Firearms Co. 470	Champion 95
Mossberg, O.F. & Sons 306	Whitney Arms. Co. 488	Charter Arms 98
Reform 345		Chicago Arms 99
Regnum 346	HANDGUN, REVOLVER	Chicago Arms Co. 99
Remington 348	Acme 25	Chicnester 99
Sauer, J.P. & Sohn 383	Acme Arms 25	Chieftain 99
Schall & Co. 394	Acme Hammerless 25	Clerke 102
Semmerling 398	Aetna 27	Clipper 103
Tipping & Lawden 446	Aetna Arms 27	Cody Manufacturing Co. 103
Turbiaux 448	Ajax Army 27	Cogswell & Harrison 103
Unique 151	Alamo 28	Colon 104
	Alaska 28	Colt 109
HANDGUN, ROCKET PISTOL	Alert 28	Columbian 130
M.B. Associates 295	Alexia 28	Comet 130
	Alexis 29	Commander 130
HANDGUN, PERCUSSION	Alfa 29	Cone, D.D. 131
Adams 26	Allen 30	Connecticut Arms Co. 132
Afferbach, William 27	Allen & Wheelock 31	Conquerer 132
Allen & Thurber 30	Allen, Ethan 32	Continental 133
Allen & Wheelock 31	All-Right Firearms Co. 33	Continental Arms Co. 133
Allen, Ethan 32	America 33	Copeland, F. 134
Alsop, C.R. 33	American Boy 34	Crescent 135
American Standard Tool Co. 35	American Bulldog 34	Creedmore 135
Andrus & Osborne 36	American Eagle 35	Crown Jewel 135
Armsport 41	American Gun Co. 35	C.Z. 137
Austrian Military 47	American Arms Co. 33	Czar 138
Bacon Arms Co. 50	American Standard Tool Co. 35	Daisy 138
Baker, Ezekiel 52	Americus 35	Daly Arms Co. 139
Bannister 55	Anschutz 37	Danish Military 139
Beattie, James 57	Apache 37	Dan Wesson Arms 140
Beerstecher, Frederick 57	Apalozo, Hermanos 38	Dardick 142
Billinghurst, William 67	Argentine Military 38	Dead Shot 143
Bitterlich 67	Aristocrat 39	Decker, Wilhelm 144
Blanch, John A. 68	Armi Jager 40	Defender 144
Blunt, Orison & Syms 69	Arminius (Pickert) 40	Defiance 144
Clark, F.H. 101	Arriola Hermanos 42	Dek-Du 144
Classic Arms 101	Astra 44	Deringer Rifle & Pistol Works ... 145
Colt 105	Aubrey 46	Despatch 145
Confederate Military 131	Austrian Military 47	Dictator 148
C.V.A. (Connecticut Valley Arms) . 136	Automatic 48	Dreadnaught 149
Constable, Richard 132	Automatic Hammerless 48	Dutch Military 151
Cooper Firearms Mfg. Co. 133	Avenger 49	Eagle 151
Deringer, Henry 145	Babcock 50	Eagle Arms Co. 152
Dixie Gun Works 147	Baby Bulldog 50	Earlhood 152
Egg, Charles 154	Baby Russian 50	Earthquake 152
Egg, Durs 154	Bacon Arms Co. 50	Eastern Arms 153
FIE 165	Bang Up 55	Elector 154
Firearms, Customs Made 167	Bayard 56	Electric 155
French Military 178	Bernadelli 65	E.M.F. 155
German Military 187	Bicycle 66	Em-Ge 155
High Standard 213	Big Bonanza 66	Empire 156
Hilliard 218	Bison 67	Empire Arms 157
Hopkins & Allen 220		

INDEX / 523

Empire State 157	Leader. 260	Rossi 370
Empress 157	Lee Arms Co. 260	Royal. 371
Encore. 157	Lefacheux 262	Ruby 371
Enterprise. 158	Liberty (Hood) 264	Ruger 373
Erma 158	Liberty (Montrose, Calif.) 264	Rupertus, Jacob 378
Excam 160	Liberty Chief 264	Russian Military 379
Excelsior 161	Lion 265	Ryan, Thomas 380
Express. 161	Little Giant 266	Sable 380
Favorite 163	Little John 266	Schmidt, Herbert. 394
Favorite Navy 163	Little Joker 266	Scott Arms Co. 395
Federal Arms 163	Llama 267	Scott Revolver-Rifle 396
FIE 165	Lowell Arms Co. 269	Scout 397
Fiehl & Weeks Firearms Co. . . . 167	Lower, J.P. 269	Secret Service Special 397
Firearms, Custom Made 167	Maltby-Curtis 275	Security Industries of America . . 397
Firearms International 168	Maltby-Henley & Co. 275	Sedgley 397
Firearms Specialties 169	Manhurin 275	Smith & Wesson 403
Forehand Arms Co. 171	Marlin Firearms Co. 279	Smoker 418
Forehand & Wadsworth. 171	Marquis of Lorne 288	Spencer Safety Hammerless 420
Francotte, August 175	Mauser 290	Spy 421
Freedom Arms 178	Mayer & Soehne 295	Squibman 421
French Military 178	Meriden 297	Squires Bingham 422
Frontier 180	Merrimac 300	Sterling Revolvers 426
Fryberg, Andrew 181	Merwin & Bray 301	Swamp Angel 436
Galand, Charles Francois 181	Merwin, Hulbert & Co. 301	Swedish Military 436
Galef 182	Metropolitan Police 302	Swift 436
Garate, Anitua 184	Miroku 303	Swiss Military 437
Garrison 184	Mitchell Arms 304	T.A.C. 438
Gasser 185	Monarch 305	Tanarmi 438
Gatling Arms & Ammunition 185	Moore Patent Fire Arms Co. 306	Taurus 439
Geco 186	Mossberg 306	Terrier 441
Gem 186	Mountain Eagle 311	Terror 441
German Military 187	Napoleon 312	Thames Arms Co. 442
Gibralter 188	National 312	Thayer, Robertson & Cary 442
Glisenti 189	Navy Arms 314	Tiger 445
Governor (Bacon) 190	Nero (Rupertus) 317	Tipping & Lawden. 446
Governor (Various Makers) 190	New Nambu 318	Tower's Police Safety 446
Grant 191	New York Pistol Co. 318	Tramps Terror 446
Great Western 191	Nonpareil 321	True Blue 447
Gross Arms Co. 193	North American Arms Co. 321	Tue-Tue. 448
Guardian 194	Norwich Arms Co. 322	Uhlinger 449
Half-Breed 195	O.M. 324	U.M.C. Arms Co. 449
Hammerli 196	Orbea Hermanos 324	Union Jack 449
Hard Pan 197	Osgood Gun Works 325	Union Revolver 451
Harrington & Richardson 198	Our Jake 324	Unique 451
Hartford Arms Co. 204	Paragon 327	United States Arms 453
Hawes Firearms 205	Parker-Hale 330	Universal 453
H.D.H. 207	Parker Safety Co. 330	U.S. Arms 445
Hero 210	Parole 331	U.S. Military 458
Herters 210	Patriot 331	U.S. Revolver Co. 464
Higgens, J.C. 212	Penetrator 332	Valor Arms 464
High Standard 213	Perfect 333	Velo Dog 465
Hood Fire Arms Co. 220	Perfection Automatic Revolver 333	Veteran 466
Hopkins & Allen 220	PIC 334	Veto 466
Hopkins, C.W. 224	Pinafore 365	Victor 467
Howard Arms 224	Pioneer 336	Victoria 467
Husqvarna 226	Plants Mfg. Co. 338	Warnant 478
Hy Hunter 228	Prairie King 339	Webley & Scott 480
Hy Score 228	Premier 340	Wesson & Harrington. 484
Imperial 229	Prescott, E.A. 340	Western Arms 484
Imperial Arms 229	Princess 341	White, Rollin Arms Co. 487
I.N.A. 229	Protector 342	White Star 487
Indian Sales 230	Radom 343	Whitney Arms 488
International 231	Ranger (Stevens) 344	Wide Awake. 489
Israeli Military 231	Ranger (H & R) 344	Winfield Arms Co. 503
Italiaguns 231	Reck 345	You Bet 504
Italian Military 232	Red Cloud 345	
Iver Johnson 238	Red Jacket 345	**HANDGUN SEMI-AUTOMATIC**
Izarra 243	Regent 346	A & R Sales 25
Jager 244	Reid Patent Revolvers 346	Acha 25
Japanese Military 245	Remington 349	Action 2
Jewel 245	Retriever 365	Adler 26
Kittemaug 251	Reynolds, Plant & Hotchkiss 366	Alfa 29
Kleinguenther's 251	R.G. Industries 366	Alkartasuna 29
Kolb 253	Rob Roy 369	Allies 33
Korth 254	Robin Hood 369	American Arms & Ammunition
Kynoch Gun Factory 256	Rome Revolver & Novelty Works . . . 369	Co. 34

524 / INDEX

American Firearms Co. 35
AMT......................36
Apache....................37
Argentine Military 38
Arizaga, Gaspar 39
Arrizabalaga, Hijos De Calixto......42
Ascaso, Francisco 42
Astra.....................42
Atlas.....................45
Audax....................46
Austrian Military 47
AutoMag...................47
Automatic Pistol 48
Avion 49
Azanza Y Arrizabalga 49
Back Up (AMT) 36
Bauer 55
Bayard....................56
Beholla 57
Benelli....................58
Beretta 59
Bergmann..................63
Bernardelli 64
Bernardon-Martin 66
Bersa 66
BRF 71
Britarms 71
British Military 73
Bronco 74
Browning 77
Budischowsky................87
Buffalo 87
Buhag 88
Bulwark 89
Bushmaster 90
C.A.C. 90
Canadian Military 90
Cartridge Firearms, Unknown
    Makers 93
Cebra 94
Celta 94
Charola Y Anitua 97
Charter Arms................98
Chinese Nationalists Military 100
Chlewski, Witold..............101
Clement, Charles..............102
Colon....................104
Colonial 104
Colt 124
Connecticut Arms & Mfg. Co. 130
Continental (Bertrand)...........132
Continental (Rheinische Waffen) ...133
C.O.Q. 134
Criolla 135
C.Z. 137
Danish Military 139
Danton 140
Day Arms Co. 143
Debatir 144
Delu 145
Destroyer 145
Destructor 146
Detonics 146
Diane (Wilkinson Arms)..........148
Dickson..................148
Domino..................149
Dreyse 149
Duo 150
DWM 151
E.A. (Eschava)...............151
E.A. (Eulogio)...............151
Echasa 153
Egyptian Military 154
Erika 158
Erma 158
Essex 159

Excam...................160
Express..................161
Fabrique D'Armes De Guerre.......161
Fabrique D'Armes De Guerre De Grand
    Precision 161
Falcon...................162
Fast....................162
Femaru..................163
FIE.....................164
Fiel.....................165
Firearms, Custom Made 167
Francotte, August.............176
French Military 180
Frommer..................180
FTL....................181
Galef 182
Galesi 183
Gallus 183
Garate, Anitua 184
Gavage 185
Gecado 185
Glisenti 189
Grant, Hammond.............193
Gustaf, Carl (Husqvarna) 194
Gustloff Werke 194
Haenal, C.G................195
Hammerli.................196
Harrington & Richardson 200
Hartford Arms & Equipment Co. ...204
Hawes Firearms 205
H & D...................206
Heckler & Koch 207
Hege 208
Heinzelmann 208
Helfricht 208
Helvice 209
Hermetic 209
Higgins, J.C. 212
High Standard 214
Hungarian Military 226
Husqvarna 226
H.V.A. (Husqvarna) 226
Hy Hunter 228
Indian Arms 230
Interdynamic 230
Italian Military 232
Iver Johnson 241
Jaga 244
Jager 244
Japanese Military 245
Jennings.................245
Jieffco (Liege, Belgium) 246
Jieffco (Davis-Warner) 246
Jo-Lo-Ar 247
Joffre 246
Jupiter 247
Kaba Spezial (Suhl) 247
Kaba Spezial (Eibar) 247
Kart 247
Kimball 249
Kirikkale.................251
Kohout 253
Kommer, Theodor 253
Lahti 256
Lancelot 257
Langenhan 258
Le Basque 259
Le Francaise 259
Le Martiny 259
Le Mono Bloc............259
Le Sans Pariel............260
Le Toutacier.............260
Leonhardt...............263
Lepage.................263
Lepco..................263
L.E.S. 263

Liberty 264
Libia 264
Liegeoise D'Armes A Feu 265
Lightning 265
Lignose..................265
Liliput 265
Little Tom (Czechoslovakia).......266
Little Tom (Austria) 266
Llama 267
Longines.................268
Looking Glass 268
Luger...................269
Lur-Panzer................272
MAB 274
M.A.C...................274
Mamba..................275
Mann 267, 275
ManuFrance...............278
Mars (Spain) 288
Mars (Czechoslovakia) 288
Mars Automatic Pistol Syndicate ..288
Marte 289
Martian.................289
Martian Commercial 289
Mauser..................290
Mayor, Francois 295
Meloir 295
Menta 295
Menz, August 295
Mercury.................297
Mexican Military............302
Mikros 302
Military 303
Mondial 305
M.S. 311
New Nambu 318
Niva 320
Norton (Budischowsky) 86, 314
Numrich Arms Co. 315
Omega 324
Ortgies 325
Owa 325
P.A.F. 326
Pantax 327
Paramount 327
Perla 334
Phoenix 334
Pic 334
Pieper 334
Pinkerton 336
Plainfield Machine Co. 337
Plus Ultra 338
Praga 339
Premier.................339
Prima 341
Princeps 341
Protector Arms Co...........341
PZK 341
Radium 343
Reck 345
Reform 346
Regent..................346
Regina 346
Reims 347
Reina 347
Remington 349
Republic 365
R.G. Industries 366
Reinmetall...............367
Rigarmi 369
Rino Galesi 369
Romer 370
Royal..................372
Ruby 372
Ruger 375
Russian Military 379

INDEX / 525

Sata...384	HANDGUN, SINGLESHOT	Stockman, Hans...435
Sauer, J.P. & Co...383	Allen & Wheelock...31	Unknown Makers...487
Savage Arms Co...385	Allen, Ethan...32	HANDGUN, MATCHLOCK
Schouboe...390	Anschutz, Udo...37	Unknown Makers...290
Schwarzlose...396	Arminius (Pickert)...40	
S.E.A.M...396	Austrian Military...47	RIFLE, BOLT ACTION
Selecta...397	Autostand...49	Acra...26
Sharpshooter...400	Bacon Arms Co...50	Alaskan...28
S.I.G...400	Bicycle...66	Apex Rifle Co...38
Sile...401	Big Horn...66	Armi Jager...39
Simplex...401	British Military...73	Armsport...41
Simson & Co...401	Brown Mfg. Co...76	Austrian Military...47
Singer (Spain)...402	Buchel, Ernst Frederick...87	Belgian Military...58
Singer (Czechoslovokia)...402	Buffalo Stand...88	British Military...73
S-M Corp...403	Cartridge Firearms, Unknown	BRNO...75
Smith & Wesson...414	Makers...93	Brown Mfg. Co...76
Smith, Wm...420	Colt...127	Brown Precision Co...76
Spanish Military...420	Crescent Fire Arms Co...135	Browning...79
Star...423	C.Z....137	BSA...86
Stenda...425	Dickinson, J.& L...148	Canadian Military...90
Sterling Arms Co...426	Driscoll, J.B...150	Cartridge Firearms, Unknown
Steyr...435	Eclipse...153	Makers...93
Franz Stock...435	E.M.F...156	Champlin Firearms...95
Stosel...435	Firearms, Custom Made...167	Charles Daly...96
Tallares...438	Forehand & Wadsworth...172	Chilean Military...100
Tanke...438	Gem...180	Chinese Military...100
Tanque...439	Glaser Waffen...188	Chinese Nationalist Military...100
Targa...439	Hafdasa...195	Churchill, E.J. & Robert...100
T.A.R.N...439	Hammerli...196	Cogswell & Harrison...103
Taurus...440	Harrington & Richardson...200	Colt...128
T.D.E...440	Hartford Arms & Equipment Co...204	Continental...133
Terrible...441	Hawes Firearms...206	Cruso...136
Teuf-Teuf (Spain)...441	Hopkins & Allen...222	C.Z....138
Teuf-Teuf (Belgium)...441	Hy Hunter...228	Czechoslavakian Military...138
Thompson...443	Mendoza...296	Danish Military...139
Thunder...445	Merril Co...299	Dubiel Arms Co...150
Titan (Italy)...446	Merrimac Arms & Mfg. Co...300	Dumoulin Freres Et Cie...150
Titan (Spain)...446	Merwin & Bray...300	Dutch Military...150
Titanic...446	Moore Patent Fire Arms Co...306	84 Gun Co...154
Triomph...446	National...312	Erma...159
Trust...448	Navy Arms...315	Essex...159
Trust Supra...448	Remington...349	Finnish Lion...168
Union...449	Rossi...370	Firearms, Custom Made...168
Union Firearms Co...449	Ruger...375	F.N....170
Unique...451	Rupertus, Jacob...378	Frankonia...177
Universal...453	Savage Arms Co...386	French Military...180
U.S. Military...449	Schultz & Larsen...399	Galef...182
Vega...465	Sharps, Christian...399	German Military...187
Vencedor...465	Sheriden...402	Glaser Waffen...189
Venus...466	Smith & Wesson...420	Golden Eagle...189
Verney—Carron...466	Stevens, J. Arms & Tool Co...427	Greek Military...191
Vesta...466	Thompson/Center...443	Greifelt & Co...192
Vici...466	U.S. Military...459	Griffen & Howe...193
Victor...467	Warnant...478	Gruenel...193
Victory...467	Weatherby's Inc...479	Gustloff Werke...194
Vilar...468	Webley & Scott...483	Haenel, C.G....195
Vincitor...468	Wesson, Frank...484	Hammerli...197
Vindex...469	Williamson, David...489	Harrington & Richardson...200
Vite...469	Zonda...507	Herold...210
Waldman...470		Herters...210
Walther...470	HANDGUN, MIQUELET-LOCK	Heym...211
Wamo...478	Busoms...89	Higgins, J.C....212
Warnant...478	Bustindui, Juan Esteban...89	High Standard...217
Warner...479	Echaberria, Artura...150	Holland & Holland...219
Webley & Scott...483	Pous, Eudal...331	Hopkins & Allen...222
Wichita Engineering & Supply...489	Ripoli,...362	Hungarian Military...226
Wilkinson Arms (California)...489	Roviro, Antonio...365	Husqvarna...226
Wilkinson Arms (Indiana)...489	Unknown Makers...300	H.V.A. (Husqvarna)...226
Wolf...503		Hy Hunter...228
Yato...504	HANDGUN, WHEEL-LOCK	India Military...229
Ydeal...504	Cominazzo, or Cominazzi...130	International Distributers...231
Z...505	Franci, Piero Inzi...175	Italian Military...232
Zaragoza...505	Gesscer, Georg...188	Ithaca Gun Co...233
Zastava...505	Horolt, Lorenz...224	Iver Johnson...243
Zehna...505	Lignitz, I.H....265	Jackson Hole Rifle Co...243
Zulaica...507	Mann, Michel...276	
	Solar...419	

526 / INDEX

Japanese Military 245
Johnson Automatics 246
Kassner Imports 247
Kimber 249
King Nitro 251
Kleinguenther's 251
Kodiak Mfg. Co. 252
Krico 254
Kruschitz 256
Lancaster, Charles 257
M.A.C. 274
Mannlicher-Schoenauer 276
ManuFrance 278
Mark X 279
Martin, Alexander 280
Mauser 292
Mendoza 296
Meteor 301
Mexican Military 302
Midland 302
Mossberg 307
Musgrave 311
Musketeer 312
National Ordnance 312
Navy Arms 315
Newton Arms Co. 319
Nikko Sporting Firearms 319
Noble 320
Northwesterner 322
Omega 324
Parker-Hale 330
Peerless 331
Pieper 335
Portuguese Military 338
Premier 340
Purdey, Jas. & Sons 342
Ranger Arms 344
Remington 349
Revelation 365
Rigby, John & Co. 368
Ross Rifle Co. 370
Ruger 377
Russian Military 380
RWS 380
Sako 381
Santa Barbara 381
Saturn 382
Sauer, J.P. & Sohn 384
Savage Arms Co. 386
Schilling, V. Charles 395
Schultz & Larsen 396
Sedgely 397
Shilen 400
Smith & Wesson 418
Spanish Military 420
Squires Bingham 422
Stevens, J. Arms & Tool Co. 427
Swedish Military 436
Swiss Military 437
Tanner 438
Ted Williams 440
Tikka 445
Tradewinds, Inc. 446
Unique 452
U.S. Military 459
Valiant 464
Voere (W. Germany) 469
Voere (Austria) 469
Waffenfabrik Bern 469
Walther 477
Watson Bros. 479
Weatherby's, Inc 479
Western Field 484
Westley Richards 486
Whitworth 489
Wichita Engineering 489
Winchester 489

Winslow Arms Co. 502

RIFLE, DOUBLE BARREL OVER-UNDER
Armsport 41
BRNO 75
Browning 81
Heym 210
Kleinguenther's 253
Krieghoff Gun Co. 255
Mannlichter-Schoenauer 275
Mauser 294
Merkel 298
Rottweil 371
Valmet 468
Westley Richards 486

RIFLE, DOUBLE BARREL SIDE-BY-SIDE
Armsport 41
Bernadelli 64
Dumoulin Freres et Cie 150
Fraser, D. & J. 177
Henry, Alexander 210
Holland & Holland 219
Merrimac Arms & Mfg. Co 300
Purdey, James 341
Purdey, Jas. & Sons 342
Rigby, John & Co. 368
Sarasqueta, Victor 382
Steigleder, Ernst 425
Watson Bros. 481
Westley Richards 486
Winchester 492

RIFLE, FLINTLOCK
Adams, Joseph 26
Akrill, E. 27
Armsport 40
Barnett & Son 55
British Military 74
C.V.A. (Connecticut Valley Arms) . . 136
Dixie Gun Works 151
Dutch Military 151
Ellis, Rubin 155
Fecht, G. Van Der 163
FIE 166
French Military 180
Harpers Ferry Arms Co. 197
Hopkins & Allen 222
Ketland, T. 249
Le Baron 258
Lobinger, Johann 268
Lyman Gun Sight Corp. 272
Navy Arms 317
Nock, Henry 321
Parr, J. 330
Rasch 345
Spaarman, Andreas 419
Sutherland, Ramsey 440
Thompson/Center 443
U.S. Military 459

KENTUCKY RIFLES & PISTOLS
Albrecht, Andrew 28, 248
Allbrecht, Henry 28, 248
Aldenderfer, M. 28, 248
Allegheny Works 29, 248
Allen, Silas 32, 248
Anggstadt, A. & J. 36, 248
Angstadt, Peter 36, 248
Angush, James 36, 248
Anstadt, Jacob 37, 248
Armstrong, John 42, 248
Backhouse, Richard 49, 248
Baker, John 52, 248
Barlow, J. 54, 248
Bauer, George 55, 248
Beck, Gideon 56, 248
Beck, John 56, 248

Bell, John 56, 248
Berlin, Abraham 63, 248
Boniwitz, James 69, 248
Bosworth 69, 248
Calderwood, William 89, 248
Carpenter, John 90, 248
Carroll, Lawrence 90, 248
Deberiere, Henry 141, 248
Dehuff, Abraham 142, 248
Deringer, Henry, Sr. 142, 248
Derr, John 142, 248
Drippard, F. 147, 248
Early, Amos 149, 248
Edmonds, J. 150, 248
Evans, Stephan 157, 248
Farnot, Frank 158, 248
Farnot, Frederick 159, 248
Fenno 160, 248
Ferree, Jacob 161, 248
Fesig, Conrad 161, 248
Figthorn, Andrew 163, 248
Folger, William H. 166, 248
Fondersmith, John 167, 248
Foulkes, Adam 168, 248
Gautec 179, 248
Glassbrenner, David 183, 248
Glazier, John 183, 248
Golcher, John 184, 248
Golcher, Joseph 184, 248
Gonter, Peter 184, 248
Graeff, William 185, 248
Grave, John 185, 248
Gregory 186, 248
Gumph, Christopher 188, 248
Hadden, James 189, 248
Gaeffer, John 189, 248
Hampton, John 191, 248
Harris, Henry 197, 248
Hawkins, Henry 200, 248
Heckert, Philip 200, 248
Hennch, Peter 202, 248
Hess, Jacob 204, 248
Hess, Samuel 204, 248
Hillegas, J. 211, 248
Hockley, James 211, 248
Humberger, Peter Jr 218, 248
Humberger, Peter Sr 218, 248
Hutz, Benjamin 220, 248
Jones, Charles 239, 248
Keim, John 240
Kraft 246, 246, 248
Lefever, Philip 254, 248
Lefever, Samuel 254, 248
Leitner, Adam 255, 248
Lennard 255, 248
Lescher 256, 248
Lord, J. 261, 248
Meyesch 286, 248
McCoy, Alexander 287, 248
McCoy, Kester 287, 248
McCullough, George 287, 248
Messersmith, Jacob 293, 248
Metzger, J. 294, 248
Meuhirter, S. 294, 248
Muller, Mathias 295, 248
Mills, Benjamin 295, 248
Moll, David 297, 248
Moll, John 297, 248
Moll, John, III 297, 248
Moll, John Jr. 297, 248
Moster, Geo. 302, 248
Newcomer, John 310, 248
Nunnemacher, Abraham 315.240
Palmer, Thomas 318, 248
Pannabecker, Jefferson 318, 248
Parkhill, Andrew 323, 248
Parsons, Hiram 323, 248

INDEX / 527

Peck, Abijah 323, 248
Pence, Jacob 324, 248
Pennypacker, Daniel 324, 248
Pennypacker, Wm. 324, 248
Raffsnyder, John 337, 248
Rathfang, Geo. 338, 248
Rathfong, Jacob 338, 248
Reasor, David 338, 248
Reed, James 338, 248
Ritter, Jacob 362, 248
Roesser, Peter 363, 248
Roop, John 364.240
Rupp, Herman 372.240
Rupp, John 372, 248
Ruppert, William 373, 248
Rush, John 373, 248
Samples, Bethuel 376, 248
Scheaner, Wm. 389, 248
Shell, John 396, 248
Shorer, Andrew 396, 248
Smith, Stoeffel 414, 248
Sweitzer, Daniel & Co. 434, 248
Vanderfrift, Isaac &
  Jeremiah 464, 248
Walsh, James 469, 248
Watters, John 478, 248
Weaver, Crypret 479, 248
Welshantz, David 483
Walshantz, Jacob 483, 248
Walshantz, Joseph 483, 248
Willis, Richard 490, 248
Wingert, Richard 503, 248
Withers, Michael 504, 248
Wolfheimer, Philip 504, 248
Young, Henry 506, 248
Young, John 506, 248

RIFLE, LEVER ACTION
Adirondack Arms. Co. 26
Armsport 40
Browning 80
Bullard Repeating Co 88
Burgess, Andrew 89
Dixie Gun Works 147
El Tigre 155
E.M.F. 156
Erma 159
Evans 160
Higgins, J.C. 212
Ithaca Gun Co. 233
Marlin Firearms. Co. 281
Miroku 302
Mossberg, O.F. & Sons 309
Navy Arms 315
Noble 320
Remington 354
Sako 381
Stevens, J. Arms & Tool Co. 429
Ted Williams 440
U.S. Military 461
Western Field 485
Whitney Arms Co. 489
Winchester 492

RIFLE, PERCUSSION
Abbey, J.F. & Co 25
Adams 26
Alfa 29
Allen & Wheelock 31
Allen, C.B. 32
Amsden, B.W. 36
Anschutz, E. 37
Armsport 40
Ashville Armory 42
Baker, W.H. & Co. 53
Barnett, J. & Sons 55
Beck, Isaac 57

Billingshurst, William 67
Bisbee, D.H. 67
Blickensdoerfer & Schilling 68
Blumenfeld 69
Boyington, John 70
British Military 74
Brockway, Norman S. 75
Brown, John & Sons 76
Colt 128
Confederate Military 131
C.V.A. (Connecticut Valley Arms) .. 136
Constable, Richard 132
Cosmopolitan Arms 134
Daniels, Henry & Charles 139
Davis, N.R. & Co. 143
Deane, Adams & Deane (Adams) 26
Dixie Gun Works 147
Dutton, John S. 150
Fay, Henry C. 163
FIE 166
Frazier, Clark K. 178
French Military 180
German Military 188
Great Western Gun Works 191
Harpers Ferry Arms Co. 197
Harrington & Richardson 201
Hawkin, J. & S. 206
Hopkins & Allen 222
Lyman Gun Sight Corp. 273
Markwell Arms Co. 279
Meier, Aldolphus 294
Navy Arms 316
Parker-Hale 330
Purdey, James 341
Richland Arms Co. 368
Russian Military 380
Shakanoosa Arms Mfg. Co. 398
Sharps 398
Sharps, Christian 398
Smith, Thomas 418
Starr Arms Co 425
Swiss Military 437
Thompson/Center 443
Tingle Mfg. Co 446
Unkown Makers 330
U.S Military 460
Zoli, Angelo 506

RIFLE PILLOCK
Billingshurst, William 66
Cherrington, Thomas P 102

RIFLE, REVOLVER
Allen & Wheelock 31
Navy Arms 318
Smith & Wesson 415

RIFLE, SEMI-AUTOMATIC
A & R Sales 25
Alpine Industries 33
American Arms Co. 34
Apache 37
Armalite 39
Armi Jager 39
Astra 44
Belgian Military 58
Beretta 60
Bergmann 63
BRNO 74
Browning 80
Bushmaster 90
Charter Arms 98
Colt 128
Commando 130
Demro 145
Dreyse 149
Eagle Gun Co. 155

Egyptian 155
E.M.F. 156
Erma 159
F.N. 170
Franchi 174
German Military 188
Gevarm 188
Harrington & Richardson 201
Heckler & Koch 207
Higgins, J.C. 212
Israeli Military 231
Ithaca Gun Co. 233
Iver Johnson 242
J. & R. 243
J.G.L. 246
Johnson Automatics 246
Kassnar Imports 248
Kodiak Mfg. Co. 253
ManuFrance 278
Marlin Firearms 285
Mauser 294
Mexican Military 302
Miroku 304
Mossberg. O.F. & Sons 310
National Ordnance 313
Navy Arms 316
Noble 323
Pioneer 336
PJK 337
Plainfield Machine Co. 337
Remington 354
Ruger 377
Russian Military 380
Savage Arms Co. 390
S.I.G. 401
Smith & Wesson 416
Spanish Military 420
Springfield Armory 420
Squibman 422
Squires Bingham 422
Stevens, J. Arm & Tool Co. 429
Super Range Goose 436
Ted Williams 440
Thompson 443
Tradewinds, Inc. 447
Universal 453
U.S. Military 463
Valmet 465
Walther 478
Weatherby's, Inc. 479
Western Field 485
Winchester 494

RIFLE, SINGLE SHOT
Agawam Arms 27
Allen & Wheelock 32
Armi Jager 39
Australian Military 47
Baker Gun & Forging Co. 50
Ball & Williams 53
Ballard Rifle 53
Ballard & Co. 54
Bay State Arms Co. 56
Bayard 57
British Military 74
Bronco 76
Browning 81
BSA 86
Bullard Repeating Arms Co. 89
Cartridge Firearms, Unknown
  Makers 93
Cherokee Arms Co. 99
Clerke 103
Colt 129
Confederate Military 132

528 / INDEX

Danish Military 139
Farrow Arms Co. 162
Firearms, Custom Made 168
Folk's Gun Works 170
Frankonia.....................177
Frazier, Jay 178
German Military 188
Grayhawk Arms Corp............193
Hauck, Wilber 205
Hopkins & Allen 223
Howard Brothers 225
Hyper 228
Jack Rabbit 243
Lowell Arms Co. 266
Lyman Sight Corp. 269
Miroku 304
Mossberg, O.F. & Sons 310
Mt. Vernon Arms................314
Navy Arms.....................317
Orbea 324
Quackenbush..................341
Remington 355
Savage Arms Co. 391
Schmidt, Ernst.................394
Sharp's 398
Sharps, Christian 400
Star 424
Starr Arms Co. 425
Sterling Arms Co. 425
Stevens, J. Arms & Tool Co 429
Swedish Military 435
U.S. Military 463
Warrant 478
Wesson, Frank 484
Whitney Arms Co...............488
Whitney Firearms Co. 488
Wickliffe 489
Winchester 494
Wuethrich.....................504

RIFLE, SLIDE ACTION
Browning 81
BSA 87
Burgess, Andrew 89
Colt 129
Harrington & Richardson 202
Higgins, J.C. 212
High Standard 217
Mossberg, O.F. & Sons 310
Noble........................320
Premier 340
Premier Trail Blazer 340
Ranger 341
Remington 356
Rossi 370
Savage Arms Co. 391
Stevens, J. Arms & Tool Co......431
Universal 453
Winchester 496

RIFLE, WHEELOCK
Blangle, Joseph................68
I.P..........................231
Klett, Simon 252

SHOTGUN, BOLT ACTION
F.N. 270
Harrington & Richardson 202
Higgins, J.C. 212
Marlin Firearms Co. 287
Mauser 294
Mossberg, O.F.& Sons 310
Savage Arms Co. 393
Sears........................397
Stevens, J. Arms & Tool Co.....434
Ted Williams 440
Western Field 485

SHOTGUN, DOUBLE BARREL OVER-UNDER
Adamy Gerbruder 26
Allen 30
Armsport 41
Astra 44
Atlas Arms 45
AyA..........................49
Baikal 51
Beretta 60
Bertuzzi 66
Boito 69
Bonehill, C.G. 70
Boss & Co. Ltd. 70
Breda 70
Breton 75
BRNO........................75
Browning 81
Champlin 95
Churchill, E.J. & Robert 101
Contento (Ventura Imports) ...465
Dakin Gun Co. 138
FIE 166
Firearms, Custom Made 168
Forever Yours 172
Franchi 174
Galef 182
Golden Eagle 190
Greifelt 192
Harrington & Richardson 203
Holland & Holland 219
I A B 229
Italguns International 232
Kassnar Imports 248
Kleinguenther's 251
Krieghoff 255
Lames 253
Laurona 258
Mannlicher-Schoenauer 276
ManuFrance..................278
Marlin Firearms Co. 287
Mauser 294
Merkel 298
Miida 302
Miroku 304
Morrone 306
Nikko Sporting Firearms 319
Parker Brothers..............330
Purdey, Jas. & Sons 342
Remington 359
Richards, W. 367
Richland Arms Co. 368
Rottweil 371
Ruger 378
Sauer, J.P. & Sohn 384
Savage Arms Co. 401
SKB 402
Stevens, J. Arms & Tool Co.....431
Ted Williams 440
Tradewinds, Inc. 447
Universal 454
Valmet 464
Ventura Imports (Contendo) ..465
Weatherby's, Inc. 479
Westley Richards 486
Winchester 496
Woodward, James & Sons 503
Zoli, Angelo 506
Zoli, Antonio 506

SHOTGUN, DOUBLE BARREL SIDE-BY-SIDE
Acme Arms 25
Alfa 29
Allen & Wheelock 32
American Arms Co. 33
American Barlock Wonder 34
American Gun Co. 35

Aristocrat....................39
Armsport 41
Astra 44
Atlas Arms..................45
Aya 49
Baikal 51
Baker Gun & Forging Co......51
Baker, W.H. & Co. 52
Bayard 57
Bellmore Gun Co. 58
Bernadelli..................65
Bland, T. & Sons 68
Blumenfeld.................69
Boito 69
Boss & Co. Ltd. 70
BRNO......................75
Caroline Arms 91
Cartrige Firearms, Unknown
   Makers 93
Central 94
Central Arms Co. 94
Chapius 95
Charles Daly 96
Cherokee Arms Co. 98
Chesapeake Gun Co. 98
Churchill, E.J. & Robert 101
Clement, Charles...........102
Clement, J.B. 102
Cogswell & Harrison 103
Colt 129
Compeer 131
Contendo (Ventura Imports).466
Continental 133
Crescent Firearms Co. 135
Crucelegui 136
Cumberland Arms Co. 136
Dakin Gun Co. 138
Darne 142
Davenport, W.H. 142
Davidson 142
Davis, N.R & Co. 143
Eastern 152
El Faisan 154
Elgin Arms Co. 155
Empire Arms Co. 157
Enders Oakleaf............157
Enders Royal Service 157
Erbi 158
Essex 159
Evans, Wlliam 159
Excelsior 161
Famars 162
Faultless 162
Faultless Goose Gun.......163
Ferlach 165
FIE 166
Firearms International 169
Forbes, F.F. 169
Franchi 174
Francotte, August 176
Franklin, A.W. 177
Galand, Charles Francois ..182
Galef 182
Gamba 184
Greener, W.W. 191
Gustloff Werke 194
Hackett, Edwin & George..194
Harrington & Richardson ..203
Harrison Arms Co. 204
Hartford Arms 204
Harvard 204
Henry Gun Co.............209
Hercules 209
Hermitage Arms Co........210
Higgins, J.C. 212
Holland & Holland 219
Hollis, Charles & Sons 220

INDEX / 529

Hopkins & Allen 224	Sanderson 382	Harrington & Richardson 202
Howard Arms 225	Sarasqueta, Victor 382	Hollis, Richard................220
Hummer 225	Sauer, J.P. & Sohn 384	Lane & Read 257
Hunting World 226	Scout 396	Manton, Joseph 278
Ingram, Charles 230	Sickel's Arms Co. 402	Navy Arms...................317
Interchangeable 230	SKB 415	Nook, Henry..................321
Interstate Arms...............230	L.C. Smith 417	Parker, William................330
Ithaca Gun Co................234	Southern Arms 419	Stevens, James................434
Iver Johnson 242	Spencer Gun Co...............420	Tingle Mfg. Co. 446
Jackson Arms Co..............243	Sportsman (Stevens) 420	Unkown Makers 333
Kassnar Imports 248	Sportsman (Crescent) 421	
King Nitro...................250	Springfield Arms...............421	SHOTGUNS, SEMI-AUTOMATIC
Kingland Special 251	Square Deal 421	Armalite 39
Kingland 10-Star 251	Stanley 422	Atis 45
Kleinguenther's 251	Star Gauge 424	Auto-Pointer 49
Knickerbocker (Crescent) 252	State Arms Co. 425	Benelli 58
Knickerbocker (Stevens) 252	Sterling Arms 426	Beretta 62
Knockabout 252	Stevens, J. Arms & Tool Co. 431	Blumenfeld 68
Knoxall 252	Stoeger, A.F. 431	Breda 71
Lakeside 257	Sullivan Arms 436	Browning 85
Leader Gun Co................260	Ted Williams 440	Charles Daly 97
Lee Special 260	Ten Star 441	Colt 129
Lee's Munner Special 261	Tiger 445	Cosmi 134
Lefaucheux 261	Tradewinds 447	Franchi 175
LeFever Sons & Co. 261	Triumph 447	Galef 183
Leigh, Henry 262	Universal 455	Harrington & Richardson 204
Mannlicher-Schoenauer 277	U.S. Arms Co. 456	Herters 204
Manton, J. 277	Ventura imports (Contendo) 565	Higgins, J.C. 217
ManuFrance..................278	Victor 467	High Standard 217
Marshwood 288	Victor Special 467	Ithaca Gun Co.................236
Massachusetts Arms 289	Virginia Arms 468	Kleinguenther's 252
Matador 290	Vulcan Arms 469	La Salle 257
Mauser 294	Walther.....................478	Ljutic Industries 266
Mercury 297	Warren Arms 479	ManuFrance..................278
Merkel......................299	Webley & Scott 483	Noble.......................320
Metropolitan 301	Western Field 485	Parker—Hale 330
Mississippi Valley Arms 304	Westley Richards 486	Remington 360
Mohawk 305	Whitney Arms Co..............488	Savage Arms Co. 393
Monitor.....................305	Wilkinson Arms 489	Sjogren.....................402
Mt. Vernon Arms..............311	Williams, Frederick 489	SKB 403
National Arms Co. 312	Wilmont Arms 490	Smith & Wesson 420
New Rival 318	Wiltshire Arms 490	Squires Bingham 422
New York Arms Co. 318	Winchester..................497	Standard Arms 423
Newport 319	Winfield Arms Co..............502	Stevens, J. Arms & Tool Co......432
Noble.......................320	Winoca Arms 502	Ted Williams 439
Norwich Arms Co. 322	Winslow Arms 502	Tradewinds, Inc...............444
Not-Nac Mfg. Co 323	Wittes Hdw. Co. 502	Universal 452
Occidental 323	Wolf, A.W. 503	Weatherby's, Inc. 479
Olympic 324	Wolverine Arms 503	Western Field 484
Oxford Arms 325	Woodward, James & Sons 503	Winchester..................500
Oxford Arms Co. 325	Worthington Arms 504	
Paragon 327	Worthington Arms Co..........504	SHOTGUN, SINGLE SHOT
Parker Brothers...............327	Worthington, Geo..............504	Alfa 29
Peerless 331	Zabola......................505	American Arms................33
Perfection 333	Zephyr 505	American Champion 34
Piedmont 335	Zoli, Antonio 505	American Gun Co..............35
Pieper 335		Armsport 41
Pioneer Arms Co. 337	SHOTGUN, FLINTLOCK	Astra 45
Piotti 337	Dixie Gun Works 149	Atlas Arms 45
Premier 339	Parker, William 330	Baikal 50
Purdey, Jas. & Sons 342	Richards, John 365	Baker Gun & Forging Co. 51
Quail 342	Unkown Makers 169	Baker Gun Co.................52
Quail's Fargo 343	Wilson, R....................490	Barker, T.....................54
Queen City 343		Bay State Arms 55
Ranger 344	SHOTGUN, LEVER ACTION	Bellmore Gun Co. 57
Remington 359	Marlin Firearms Co. 286	Beretta 62
Rev-O-Noc 366	Winchester..................499	Big Horn 66
Richards, W..................367		Boito 68
Richland Arms Co. 367	SHOTGUN, PERCUSSION	Bronco 75
Richter, Charles 367	Abbey, J.F. & Co. 25	Browning 84
Rickard Arms 368	Alfa 29	Caroline Arms 90
Rigby, John & Co..............368	Allen & Wheelock 32	Cartridge Firearms, Unknown
Riverside Arms 369	Armsport 41	Maker 92
Rossi 370	Briggs, William 71	Central 93
Rummel 378	Davis, N.R. & Co..............143	Central Arms Co. 93
St. Louis Arms 381	Dixie Gun Works 149	Champlin 94
	Galand, Charles Francois........182	Chesapeake Gun Co. 97

530 / INDEX

Climas..........................102	Old Timer......................316	Galef............................176
Compeer.......................129	Olympic........................316	Harrington & Richardson.........197
Continental....................131	Oxford Arms Co................318	Higgins, J.C....................206
Crescent Firearms.............134	Palmetto.......................318	High Standard..................206
Cruso..........................134	Parker Bros....................322	Ithaca Gun Co..................225
Cumberland Arms Co...........134	Peerless.......................323	La Salle........................250
Davenport, W.H................140	Perfection.....................325	ManuFrance....................270
Davis, N.R. & Co...............140	Phillipine Military..............326	Marlin Firearms................277
Delphian.......................142	Piedmont......................327	Mossberg, O.F..................302
Diamond.......................144	Pioneer Arms..................327	Noble..........................312
Eastern........................150	Price, J.W.....................333	Remington.....................356
Elgin...........................152	Purdey, Jas. & Sons............334	Revelation.....................358
Empire Arms Co................154	Quail..........................335	Savage Arms...................388
Enders Oakleaf.................154	Queen City....................336	Smith & Wesson................413
Enders Royal Service...........155	Ranger........................337	Spencer Arms Co...............417
Essex..........................156	Remington....................356	Squires Bingham...............418
Faultless.......................159	Rev-O-Noc....................359	Standard Arms.................419
Faultless Goose Gun............159	Richards, W...................360	Stevens, J. Arms & Tool Co.....430
F.I.E...........................163	Richter, Charles...............361	Ted Williams...................438
Forbes, F.F....................167	Rickard Arms..................361	U.S. Military...................463
Franchi........................170	Rummel.......................372	Weatherby's, Inc................479
Gibralter......................182	St. Louis Arms Co..............375	Western Field..................484
Goose Gun....................184	Sears..........................392	Winchester....................501
Greener, W.W.................186	Sickel's Arms Co...............396	
Harrison Arms Co..............197	L.C. Smith....................413	SNAPHAUNCE, HANDGUNS & RIFLES
Harrington & Richardson.......195	Southern Arms................416	Beretta, Giovanni................62
Hartford Arms..................198	Spencer Gun Co...............417	Glenn, Robert..................183
Harvard........................198	Sportsman (Stevens)...........417	I G.............................221
Henry Gun Co.................203	Sportsman (Crescent)..........417	Mutti, Gerolimo................304
Hercules.......................203	Springfield Arms...............418	Mutti, Giesu...................304
Hermitage.....................203	Square Deal...................418	Stuart, Johan..................433
Hermitage Arms Co............203	Stanley........................419	Unkown Makers................433
Hermitage Gun Co.............203	State Arms Co.................422	
Herters........................204	Sterling Arms Co...............423	**PHOTOGRAPHS**
Higgins, J.C....................206	Stevens, J. Arms & Tool Co.....429	
Holland & Holland..............211	Stoeger, A.F...................432	AMT............................ 36
Holmes, Bill....................213	Sullivan Arms Co...............433	Anschutz....................... 37
Howard Arms..................217	Super Dreadnaught............433	Argintine Military.............. 39
Hummer.......................217	Ted Williams...................438	Astra........................... 43
Hunter Arms (L.C.Smith).......413	Ten Star.......................438	Auto Mag....................... 48
I.A.B............................221	Texas Ranger..................439	Bayard......................... 56
Interstate Arms C0..............223	Tiger...........................443	Beretta......................... 60
Iver Johnson...................230	Tradewinds, Inc................444	Bernadelli...................... 64
Jack Rabbit....................235	Universal......................452	Big Horn........................ 67
Jackson Arms..................235	U.S. Arms Co..................452	BRF............................ 71
Kingland Special................242	U.S. Military...................463	British Military................. 73
Kingland 10—Star..............242	Victor..........................466	Brooklyn Arms.................. 76
Knickerbocker..................244	Victor Special..................466	Browning....................... 77
Knoxall........................244	Virginia Arms Co...............468	Budischowsky.................. 87
Lakeside.......................248	Volunteer......................468	Cartridge Firearms, Unknown
Lang, Joseph..................250	Vulcan Arms...................468	Maker....................... 92
Leader Gun Co.................252	Warnant.......................478	Charola Anitua................. 97
Lee Special....................252	Warren Arms..................478	Chicago Palm Pistol............ 99
Lee's Munner Special..........253	Western Field..................484	Chinese Military Tokarev.......100
LeFever Sons & Co.............253	Westley Richards...............485	Chysewski.....................101
Little Pet......................258	Whippet.......................487	Clement.......................102
Ljutic Industries................259	White Powder Wonder..........487	Cogswell & Harrison...........104
Long Range Wonder...........260	Wilkinson Arms Co.............487	Colt.........106, 110, 115, 120, 125
Long Tom.....................260	Wilmont Arms Co..............490	Continental Arms...............133
ManuFrance...................170	Wiltshire Arms Co..............490	C.O.P..........................133
Massachusetts Arms...........281	Winchester....................501	C.Z............................137
Mauser........................286	Winfield Arms Co...............503	Danton........................139
Merrimac Arms & Mfg. Co......292	Winoca Arms Co...............503	Debatir........................143
Metropolitan...................293	Winslow Arms Co..............504	Destroyer......................146
Mississippi Valley Arms........296	Wittes Hdw. Co................504	Dreyse........................150
Mohawk.......................297	Wolverine Arms Co............504	Dutch Military.................151
Monitor.......................298	Woodward, James & Sons.....505	Eagle Arms....................152
National Arms Co..............304	Worthington Arms Co..........505	Echasa........................153
New Chieftain..................310		E.M.F..........................156
New Rival......................310	**SHOTGUN, SLIDE ACTION**	Fabrique De Guerre............161
New York Arms Co.............310	Beretta..........................62	Femaru........................164
Nitro Proof....................312	Browning.......................84	Forehand Arms Co..............171
Northwesterner................314	Burgess, Andrew................88	Francotte......................176
Norwich Arms..................314	Colt............................128	French Military............179, 180
Not-Nac Mfg. Co...............315	Eastfield (Smith & Wesson)....413	
Oak Leaf......................315	Firearms, Custom Made........164	

INDEX / 531

Frommer 181	Merwin, Hulbert 301	Simplex 401
Galesi 184	Miroku 304	Simson 402
Gaulois 185	Mondial 306	Singer 402
Gavage 185	Mossberg 307	Smith & Wesson 404, 406, 409, 415
German Military 187	Nikko 319	L.C. Smith 417
Glaser Waffen 189	Norwegian Military 322	Spanish Military 419
Gustloff Werke 194	Obea Hermanos 324	Spencer 420
Haenel Schmelsser 195	Ortgies 325	Star 423
Hafdasa 195	P.A.F. Junior 326	Starr 425
Harrington & Richardson 199	Paramount 327	Stenda 425
H.D.H. 206	Percussion, Unknown Makers 332	Sterling 426
Hege 208	Phoenix Arms Co. 334	Stevens 428
High Standard 214, 216	PIC 334	Steyr 434, 435
Hopkins & Allen 221	Pieper 335	Franz Stock 435
Hungarian Military 225	Pinafore 336	Stoesel 436
Husqvarna 227	Plants 338	Swiss Military 437
India Military 229	Portuguese Military 339	Tanke 438
Italian Military 232	Praga 339	Thompson 442
Iver Johnson 242	Premier 341	Thompson/Center 444
Jager 244	Princeps 341	Thunder 445
Japanese Military 245	Radom 343	Titan 446
Jo-Lo-Ar 246	Regina 346	Uhlinger 450
Kimball 250	Regnum 346	Union 450
Kommer 253	Reims 347	Unique 452
Kynoch 256	Remington Arms Co. 351, 354, 358	Universal 454
Lancelot 257	Rheinmetall 367	U.S. Arms Co. 455
Langenhan 258	Rogers & Spencer 369	U.S. Military 457, 461
Le Basque 259	Romer 369	Vesta 466
Le Francaise 259	Royal 372	Vici 466
Leonhardt Gering 263	Ruby 372	Victoria 467
Lepage 263	Ruger 374, 376	Walsh 470
Lepco 263	Russian Military 379, 380	Walther 472, 474
Liberty 264	Sauer, J.P. & Sohn 383	Weatherby's, Inc. 480
Lignose 265	Savage Arms Co. 387, 392	Webley & Scott 481, 482
Longines 268	Schall 395	Whitney 448
Luger 270	Schwarzlose 395	Winchester 495, 498
Mab 273	S.E.A.M. 396	Worthington Arms 504
Mann 276	Sears 396	Zaragoza 506
Marlin Firearms Co. .. 280, 282, 284	Sedgely 398	Zehna 506
Martian 289	Selecta 398	Zonda 507
Mauser 291	Sharps 399	Zulaica 507
Menta 296	Sharpshooter 400	
Menz 296	S.I.G. 401	

DESCRIPTION	DATE PURCHASED	COST	DATE SOLD	PRICE	CONDITION

Does your gun have broken, missing, or poor quality grips?
If so, you should know about us!

We manufacture the finest reprodutcion grips and buttplates available. Both front and back have been cast as the originals were, and they are guaranteed to fit your gun!

We have the world's largest selection, with grips and buttplates for over 500 different guns now available.

For our free list please send a S.A.S.E. to:

Byron's
P.O. Box 796
Casselberry, Fla. 32707

Members report
SAVINGS of $1,000.00 and more
as a result of **American Collector Club** membership

American Collector Club
Membership Number: 01110MSM0110
Expiration Date: 10/87

MARY M MCSMITH
0110 EAST ANYWHERE
TIMBUCKTOO US 01110

is an Associate in good standing and entitled to all Associate benefits and opportunities through the expiration date shown above.

James K. Barker
Associate Director

Watch for this emblem

10
in shops offering automatic discounts to members.

This card can save you money too!

Members receive **American Collector** each month

Featuring collectables of the last 100 years, special American Collector editions spotlight
* Roseville   * Americana   * Paper
* Modern Dolls   * Porcelain   * Glass
* Clocks & Watches * Political   * Pottery
* Antique Dolls   * Patriotic   * Toys
* Limited Editions * Advertising   * Jewelry

There are regular columns for collectors of:
* Books   * Bottles   * Photographica   * Dolls
* Records   * Nippon   * Barberiana   * Jars
* Stoneware   * Glass   * Stocks & Bonds * Paper

Questions are answered in "Readers Ask," "What Is It?" challenges. It's helpful, fun and informative!
American Collector is just one of many ACC member Benefits!

Your member-only newsletter brings you news, reference info, book discounts up to 70%, other special money-savers, FREE member bonuses several times a year.

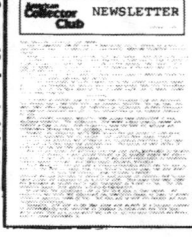

* Book Discounts
* Barter through ACE
* Discounts on Collectables
* FREE bonus gifts
* Publication Discounts
* A sample of Member Benefits

Members often save more than annual dues in the first month of membership.

For buyers of this Official Guide, 5-month trial membership, $9.95; 12 months, $20.

Send your application to:

American Collector Club
P.O. Drawer C (HC), Kermit, TX 79745

How did your plates do?

Reco's "Little Boy Blue" by John McClelland
UP 214% in 1 Year

Some limited edition plates gained more in the same year, some less, and some not at all ... But Plate Collector readers were able to follow the price changes, step by step, in Plate Price Trends, a copyrighted feature appearing in each issue of the magazine.

Because The Plate Collector is your best source guide ... has more on limited editions than all other publications combined ... and gives you insight into every facet of your collecting ... you too will rate it

Your No. 1. Investment
In Limited Editions.

In 1972, Plate Collector was the first to feature limited editions only. It's expanded, adding figurines, bells and prints, earning reader raves like you see below.

To bring you the latest, most valuable information, our editors crisscross the continent. Sometimes stories lead them to the smaller Hawaiian Islands, or to the porcelain manufacturers of Europe.

Their personal contact with artisans, hobby leaders, collectors, artists and dealers lets you share an intimate view of limited editions.

Each fat, colorful issue brings you new insight, helps you enjoy collecting more.

You'll find Plate Collector a complete source guide. Consider new issue information and new issue announcements, often in full color. Use the ratings of new releases and wide array of dealer ads to help you pick and choose the best.

Read regular columns, including one on Hummels, and check current market values in Plate Price Trends to add to your storehouse of knowledge.

You'll profit from tips on insurance, decorating, taxes ... just a sample of recurring feature subjects.

Read Plate Collector magazine to become a true limited edition art insider. Order now. See new and old plates in sparkling color. Enjoy 2 issues every month, delivered to your home at savings up to 37% from newsstand price.

12 issues (6 months) $17.50
24 issues (year) $30
The PLATE COLLECTOR
P.O. Box 1041-HC   Kermit, TX 79745

To use VISA and MasterCard, include all raised information on your card.

Here is Plate Collector, as viewed by our readers in unsolicited quotes ...

"Objective and Impartial," has "great research," yet is warm and personal ... "I am delighted in 'our' magazine." A New York couple says flatly, "It is the best collector magazine on the market."

"Quality printing is valuable to me because there are no stores near me where I can view and decide," says an Arizona reader. It is "a major guide to the plates I buy," says a Massachusetts reader, while "It is the best investment in a magazine I ever made," comes from Illinois.

"I enjoy your articles on artists," "The full-color pictures are great," "Your staff was most helpful," "I depend on Plate Collector," and "I look forward to receiving it twice a month," are other reader reactions.

A California reader said simply, "I am glad there is a Plate Collector."

There is only one...
THE OFFICIAL
PRICE GUIDE

THE MULTI-PURPOSE REFERENCE GUIDE!!

THE OFFICIAL PRICE GUIDES SERIES has gained the reputation as the standard barometer of values on collectors' items. When you need to check the market price of a collectible, turn first to the OFFICIAL PRICE GUIDES . . . for impartial, unbiased, current information that is presented in an easy-to-follow format.

- **CURRENT VALUES FOR BUYING AND SELLING.** ACTUAL SALES that have occurred in all parts of the country are CAREFULLY EVALUATED and COMPUTERIZED to arrive at the most ACCURATE PRICES AVAILABLE.

- **CONCISE REFERENCES.** Each OFFICIAL PRICE GUIDE is designed primarily as a *guide to current market values.* They also include a useful summary of the information most readers are seeking: a history of the item; how it's manufactured; how to begin and maintain a collection; how and where to sell; addresses of periodicals and clubs.

- **INDEXED FORMAT.** The novice as well as the seasoned collector will appreciate the unique alphabetically *indexed format* that provides *fast retrieval* of information and prices.

- **FULLY ILLUSTRATED.** All the OFFICIAL PRICE GUIDES are richly illustrated. Many feature COLOR SECTIONS as well as black-and-white photos.

Over 20 years of experience has made
THE HOUSE OF COLLECTIBLES
the most respected price guide authority!

PRICE GUIDE SERIES

American Silver & Silver Plate
Today's silver market offers excellent opportunities *to gain big profits* — if you are well informed. *Over 15,000 current market values* are listed for 19th and 20th century American made Sterling, Coin and Silverplated flatware and holloware. Special souvenir spoon section. *ILLUSTRATED.*
$9.95-2nd Edition, 544 pgs., 5⅜" x 8", paperback, Order #: 184-5

Antique & Modern Firearms
This unique book is an encyclopedia of gun lore featuring over *21,000 listings with histories* of American and foreign manufacturers *plus a special section on collector cartridges values. ILLUSTRATED.*
$9.95-3rd Edition, 544 pgs., 5⅜" x 8", paperback, Order #: 363-5

Antiques & Other Collectibles
Introduces TODAY'S world of antiques with *over 62,000 current market values* for the most complete listing of antiques and collectibles IN PRINT! In this *new — 768 PAGE edition, many new categories have been added to keep fully up-to-date with the latest collecting trends. ILLUSTRATED.*
$9.95-3rd Edition, 768 pgs., 5⅜" x 8", paperback, Order #: 172-1

Antique Jewelry
Over *10,000 current collector values* for the most extensive listing of antique jewelry ever published, Georgian, Victorian, Art Nouveau, Art Deco. *Plus a special full color gem identification guide. ILLUSTRATED.*
$9.95-2nd Edition, 640 pgs., 5⅜" x 8", paperback, Order #: 354-6

Bottles Old & New
Over *22,000 current buying and selling prices* of both common and rare collectible bottles . . . ale, soda, bitters, flasks, medicine, perfume, poison, milk and more. *Plus expanded sections on Avon and Jim Beam. ILLUSTRATED.*
$9.95-6th Edition, 640 pgs., 5⅜" x 8", paperback, Order #: 350-3

Collector Cars
Over *36,000 actual current prices* for 4000 models of antique and classic automobiles — U.S. and foreign. Complete with engine specifications. *Special sections on auto memorabilia values and restoration techniques. ILLUSTRATED.*
$9.95-3rd Edition, 544 pgs., 5⅜" x 8", paperback, Order #: 181-0

Collector Knives
Over *14,000 buying and selling prices* on U.S. and foreign pocket and sheath knives. *Special sections on bicentennial, commemorative, limited edition, and handmade knives.* By J. Parker & B. Voyles. *ILLUSTRATED.*
$9.95-5th Edition, 640 pgs., 5⅜" x 8", paperback, Order #: 324-4

Collector Plates
Destined to become the "PLATE COLLECTORS' BIBLE." This unique price guide offers the most comprehensive listing of collector plate values — *in Print! Special information includes: company histories; artist backgrounds; and helpful tips on buying, selling and storing a collection. ILLUSTRATED.*
$9.95-1st Edition, 640 pgs., 5⅜" x 8", paperback, Order #: 349-X

Collector Prints
Over *14,750 detailed listings* representing over 400 of the most famous collector print artists from Audubon and Currier & Ives, to modern day artists. *Special feature includes gallery/artist reference chart. ILLUSTRATED.*
$9.95-4th Edition, 544 pgs., 5⅜" x 8", paperback, Order #: 189-6

PUBLISHED BY: *THE HOUSE OF COLLECTIBLES, INC.*
1900 PREMIER ROW, ORLANDO, FL 32809   PHONE: (305) 857-9095

PRICE GUIDE SERIES

Comic & Science Fiction Books
Over **31,000 listings with current values** for comic and science fiction publications **from 1903-to-date**. Special sections on Tarzan, Big Little Books, Science Fiction publications and paperbacks. *ILLUSTRATED.*
$9.95-6th Edition, 544 pgs., 5⅜" x 8", paperback, Order #: 353-8

Hummel Figurines & Plates
The most complete guide ever published on every type of Hummel — including the most recent trademarks and size variations, with **4,500 up-to-date prices. Plus tips on buying, selling and investing.** *ILLUSTRATED.*
$9.95-3rd Edition, 448 pgs., 5⅜" x 8", paperback, Order #: 325-X

Military Collectibles
This detailed historical reference price guide covers the largest accumulation of military objects — 15th century-to-date — listing over **12,000 accurate prices. Special expanded Samuri sword and headdress sections.** *ILLUSTRATED.*
$9.95-2nd Edition, 544 pgs., 5⅜" x 8", paperback, Order #: 191-8

Music Machines
Virtually every music related collectible is included in this guide — over **11,000 current prices. 78 recordings, mechanical musical machines, and instruments.** *ILLUSTRATED.*
$9.95-2nd Edition, 544 pgs., 5⅜" x 8", paperback, Order #: 187-X

Old Books & Autographs
Descriptions of the finest literary collectibles available, with over **11,000 prices for all types of books:** Americana, bibles, medicine, cookbooks and more. **Plus an updated autograph section.** *ILLUSTRATED.*
$9.95-4th Edition, 510 pgs., 5⅜" x 8", paperback, Order #: 351-1

Paper Collectibles
Old Checks, Invoices, Books, Magazines, Newspapers, Ticket Stubs and even Matchbooks — any paper items that reflects America's past — are gaining collector value. This book contains **over 25,000 current values** and descriptions for all types of paper collectibles. *ILLUSTRATED.*
$9.95-2nd Edition, 608 pgs., 5⅜" x 8", paperback, Order #: 186-1

Pottery & Porcelain
Over **10,000 current prices and listings** of fine pottery and porcelain, plus an extensive Lenox china section. **Special sections on identifying china trademarks and company histories.** *ILLUSTRATED.*
$9.95-2nd Edition, 544 pgs., 5⅜" x 8", paperback, Order #: 188-8

Records
Over **31,000 current prices** of collectible singles, EPs, albums, plus 20,000 memorable song titles recorded by over 1100 artists. **Rare biographies and photos are provided for many well known artists.** *ILLUSTRATED.*
$9.95-4th Edition, 544 pgs., 5⅜" x 8", paperback, Order #: 356-2

Royal Doulton
This authoritative guide to Royal Doulton porcelains contains over **3,500 detailed listings** on figurines, plates and Toby jugs. Includes tips on buying, selling and displaying. **Plus an exclusive numerical reference index.** *ILLUSTRATED.*
$9.95-2nd Edition, 544 pgs., 5⅜" x 8", paperback, Order #: 355-4

Wicker
You could be sitting on a **fortune!** Decorators and collectors are driving wicker values to unbelievable highs! This pictorial price guide **positively identifies all types** of Victorian, Turn of the century and Art Deco wicker furniture. **A special illustrated section on wicker repair is included.** *ILLUSTRATED.*
$9.95-1st Edition, 416 pgs., 5⅜" x 8", paperback, Order #: 348-1

PUBLISHED BY: *THE HOUSE OF COLLECTIBLES, INC.*
1900 PREMIER ROW, ORLANDO, FL 32809 PHONE: (305) 857-9095

MINI PRICE GUIDE SERIES

Antiques & Flea Markets
Discover the fun and profit of collecting antiques with this handy pocket reference to *over 15,000 types of collectibles*. Avoid counterfeits and learn the secrets to successful buying and selling. *ILLUSTRATED*.
$2.50-1st Edition, 240 pgs., 4" x 5½", paperback, Order #: 308-2

Pete Rose Baseball Cards
This guide lists *over 44,000 current market values* for baseball cards – Bowman, Burger King, Donruss, Fleer, O-Pee-Chee and Topps. *Includes a full color PETE ROSE limited edition collector card. ILLUSTRATED*.
$2.50-2nd Edition, 288 pgs., 4" x 5½", paperback, Order #: 322-8

Comic Books
Young and Old are collecting old comic books for fun *and Profit!* This handy ''pocket-sized'' price guide lists current market values and detailed descriptions for the most sought-after ''collectible'' comic books. *Buying, selling and storing tips are provided for the beginning collector. ILLUSTRATED.*
$2.50-1st Edition, 240 pgs., 4" x 5½", paperback, Order #: 345-7

Dolls
Doll collecting is one of America's favorite hobbies and this guide lists *over 3,000 actual market values* for all the manufacturers! Kewpies, Howdy Doody, Shirley Temple, GI Joe plus comprehensive listings of Barbies. *ILLUSTRATED*.
$2.95-1st Edition, 240 pgs., 4" x 5½", paperback, Order #: 316-3

O.J. Simpson Football Cards
The world famous O.J. Simpson highlights this comprehensive guide to football card values. *Over 21,000 current collector prices* are listed for: Topps, Bowman, Fleer, Philadelphia and O-Pee-Chee. *Includes a full color O.J. SIMPSON limited edition collector card. ILLUSTRATED*.
$2.50-2nd Edition, 256 pgs., 4" x 5½", paperback, Order #: 323-6

Hummels
How much are your Hummels worth? You can become an expert on these lovely figurines with this complete guide, *FULLY ILLUSTRATED*, with a handy numerical index that puts descriptions and market prices at your fingertips. Learn why the slightest variation could mean hundreds in value.
$2.95-1st Edition, 240 pgs., 4" x 5½", paperback, Order #:318-X

Paperbacks & Magazines
Old discarded paperbacks and magazines could be worth 50-100 times their original cover price. Learn how to identify them. *Thousands* of descriptions and prices show which issues are rare. *ILLUSTRATED*.
$2.50-1st Edition, 240 pgs., 4" x 5½", paperback, Order #: 315-5

Scouting Collectibles
Discover the colorful history behind scouting, relive childhood memories and profit from those old family heirlooms. *Thousands of prices* are listed for all types of Boy and Girl Scout memorabilia. *ILLUSTRATED*.
$2.50-1st Edition, 240 pgs., 4" x 5½", paperback, Order #: 314-7

Toys
Kids from eight to eighty enjoy collecting toys and this comprehensive guide has them all! Trains, trucks, comic and movie character, space toys, boats and **MORE**. *Over 5,000 current market values* of toys, old and new, plus investment tips and histories. *ILLUSTRATED*.
$2.95-1st Edition, 240 pgs., 4" x 5½", paperback, Order #: 317-1

PUBLISHED BY: *THE HOUSE OF COLLECTIBLES, INC.*
1900 PREMIER ROW, ORLANDO, FL 32809   PHONE: (305) 857-9095

NUMISMATIC SERIES

THE BLACKBOOKS are more than just informative books, they are the most highly regarded authority on the nation's most popular hobbies.

1983 Blackbook Price Guide of United States Coins

A coin collector's guide to current market values for all U.S. coins from 1616 to date—over *16,000 prices*. THE OFFICIAL BLACKBOOK OF COINS has gained the reputation as the most reliable, up-to-date guide to U.S. Coin values. This new special 1983 edition features, an exclusive gold and silver identification guide. Learn how to test, weigh and calculate the value of any item made of gold or silver. Proven professional techniques revealed for the first time. Take advantage of the current "BUYERS' MARKET" in gold and silver. *ILLUSTRATED.*
$2.95-21st Edition, 288 pgs., 4" x 5½", paperback, Order #: 342-2

1983 Blackbook Price Guide of United States Paper Money

Over *8,200 buying and selling prices* covering U.S. currency from 1861 to date. Every note issued by the U.S. government is listed and priced, including many Confederate States notes. Error Notes are described and priced, and there are detailed articles on many phases of the hobby for beginners and advanced collectors alike. *ILLUSTRATED.*
$2.95-15th Edition, 240 pgs., 4" x 5½", paperback, Order #: 343-0

1983 Blackbook Price Guide of United States Postage Stamps

Featuring all U.S. stamps from 1847 to date pictured in full color. Over *18,750 current selling prices*. You will find new listings for the most current commemorative and regular issue stamps, a feature not offered in any other price guide, at any price! There were numerous important developments in the fast moving stamp market during the past year and they are all included in this *NEW REVISED EDITION*. *ILLUSTRATED.*
$2.95-5th Edition, 240 pgs., 4" x 5½", paperback, Order #: 344-9

INVESTORS SERIES

The Official Investor's Guide Series shows you, *step by step*, how to select the right items for your investment program, how to avoid the many pitfalls that can foil new investors, with full instructions on when to sell and *How And Where To Sell* in order to realize the *Highest Possible Profit.*

Investors Guide to Gold, Silver, Diamonds

All you need to know about making money trading in the precious metals and diamond markets. This practical, easy-to-read investment guide is for everyone in all income brackets. *ILLUSTRATED.*
$6.95-1st Edition, 208 pgs., 5⅜" x 8", paperback, Order #: 171-3

Investors Guide to Gold Coins

The first complete book on investing in gold coins. Exclusive price performance charts trace all U.S. gold coin values from *1955 to date*. *ILLUSTRATED.*
$6.95-1st Edition, 288 pgs., 5⅜" x 8", paperback, Order #: 300-7

Investors Guide to Silver Coins

The most extensive listing of all U.S. silver coins. Detailed price performance charts trace actual sales figures from *1955 to date*. *ILLUSTRATED.*
$6.95-1st Edition, 288 pgs., 5⅜" x 8", paperback, Order #: 301-5

Investors Guide to Silver Dollars

Regardless of your income, you can *become a successful silver dollar investor*. Actual sales figures for every U.S. silver dollar *1955 to date*. *ILLUSTRATED.*
$6.95-1st Edition, 192 pgs., 5⅜" x 8", paperback, Order #: 302-3

PUBLISHED BY: *THE HOUSE OF COLLECTIBLES, INC.*
1900 PREMIER ROW, ORLANDO, FL 32809   PHONE: (305) 857-9295